A NEW MAP of the TERRAQUEOUS GLOBE according to the latest Discoveries and most general Divisions of it into CONTINENTS and OCEANS.

Louie Graff
Box 21535
Emory University
Atlanta, Georgia 30322

CIVILIZATION PAST AND PRESENT

A survey of the history of man—his political, economic, social, religious, intellectual, and artistic activities—from the earliest times to the present, in Europe, in Asia, in Africa, and in the Americas.

SINGLE-VOLUME EDITION

CIVILIZATION

Past and Present

SINGLE-VOLUME EDITION

T. WALTER WALLBANK, Professor of History, University of Southern California

ALASTAIR M. TAYLOR, Visiting Professor, Queen's University

NELS M. BAILKEY, Professor of History, Tulane University

SCOTT, FORESMAN AND COMPANY   Chicago, Atlanta, Dallas, Palo Alto, Fair Lawn, N. J.

PREFACE

When the original planning of the two-volume *Civilization Past and Present* was begun, well before World War II, the majority of the American people had not yet fully adjusted to participation in world affairs, nor, in some respects, had the college curriculums. Today, however, in our age of global interdependence and atomic anxiety, the study of world history has come to be viewed as essential, for only by understanding the past can one assess both the perils and the opportunities of the present. Moreover, the two-volume *Civilization Past and Present*, first published in 1942, was the first text that dealt not merely with political history but with all facets—economic, artistic, intellectual, social, religious, and political—of world culture, and that treated the history of man not as a European experience nor as a western experience, but as a global experience through which all the great cultural systems have interacted to produce the present-day world.

Originally published in 1956, the single-volume edition of *Civilization Past and Present* has been rewritten and reorganized in order to present a balanced coverage of all periods of history. Extensive reorganization has been undertaken in the treatment of the following periods: the civilizations of antiquity, the Middle Ages in Europe and the Near East, the Renaissance and the Reformation, and the early modern period. In addition, the narrative of nineteenth-century European history has been substantially modified; the important political events are presented within a nation-by-nation framework.

To continue the standards of scholarship aimed at in the two-volume edition, the authors once again employed the ideas and suggestions of the same distinguished group of historical specialists: Professor James E. Gillespie, formerly of Pennsylvania State University; Professor L. Carrington Goodrich, Columbia University; Professor Harold J. Grimm, Ohio State University; Professor Alfred Guillaume, Princeton University; Professor H. W. Janson, New York University; Professor Hans Kohn, City College of New York; Professor Franklin C. Palm, University of California; Professor Stuart Piggott, University of Edinburgh; Sir Maurice Powicke, Oxford University; and Professor C. A. Robinson, Jr., Brown University. The authors have also profited greatly by the numerous thought-provoking comments from users of the 1956 edition. A special word of thanks goes to Professor Charles J. Miller of Calvin College, who assisted in the preparation of Chapters 31 and 32.

This volume attempts first of all to achieve flexibility. While basically designed for courses in world history or world civilization, the text is also appropriate for western civilization survey courses. Nonwestern material—contained in Chapters 4, 15, 26, and 29—may be assigned as outside reading or eliminated entirely without impairing the narrative of western history. In addition, the division of the book into eight units (a total of thirty-two chapters) makes the text convenient for use in schools employing either the semester or the quarter system.

In keeping also with the spirit of this major revision, new black-and-white illustrations have been selected and the format of the text has been completely redesigned. The black-and-white maps, too, have been redesigned for clarity and appropriateness to the new organization of the text. Four-color plates display subjects chosen for their historical significance as well as for their intrinsic value as great works of art, while the sixteen-page historical atlas consists of a selection of full-page and double-page six-color reference maps. Additional features —such as the two-page interchapters appearing with each unit and serving as introductions for the material in the unit, a prologue explaining the authors' approach to the study of history and the value of the discipline, chapter bibliographies, a general bibiliography, chronological charts, and an index with a pronunciation key—are indicative of the authors' attempt to produce a comprehensive, well-balanced text.

T. Walter Wallbank, Professor of History,
University of Southern California

Alastair M. Taylor, Visiting Professor of International Relations,
Queen's University

Nels M. Bailkey, Professor of History,
Tulane University

NOTE TO THE STUDENT

This book has been developed with the dual purpose of helping you acquire a solid knowledge of past events and, equally important, of helping you think more constructively about the significance of those events for the difficult times in which we live. In the Prologue, you will learn more about studying the meaning of history. This note is intended to acquaint you with the principal features of the text.

THE INTERCHAPTERS

Aid in the organization and review of your reading will be provided by the interchapters, brief introductions outlining the material to be covered in each unit.

THE COLOR PLATES

The full-color art reproductions comprise one of the most striking features of this edition. The works of art have been carefully selected and faithfully reproduced to illustrate, in every case, some facet of a culture pattern discussed in the text. They are, moreover, very much worth your attention purely as works of art.

SUGGESTIONS FOR READING

In addition to a special list of readings (entitled "The Historian's Workshop") at the end of the book, you will find in each chapter an annotated bibliography, pertaining especially to that chapter and listing special historical studies, biographies, and reputable historical fiction, as well as collections of source materials. As indicated in the listings, many of these works can be purchased in inexpensive paperbound editions. These bibliographies will provide you with ample readings from which to develop special reports or with which to improve your understanding of a given subject.

THE CHRONOLOGICAL CHARTS

For each unit, the editors have prepared a chronological chart showing the sequence of events within that unit. By studying these charts, you can fix in your mind the relationship of events in the various parts of the world that you have been studying.

THE MAPS

Liberally distributed throughout this volume are spot maps designed to make clear the nature of a single distinctive event or idea discussed in the text. You will also find black-and-white maps in the text which illustrate larger areas. Located at the end of the book are sixteen pages of full-color reference maps, showing most of the major areas of the world and virtually every town, political subdivision, and geographic feature mentioned in the text.

THE PRONUNCIATION KEY

In the index, the correct pronunciation is given for most proper names. Thus you will find it easy, as well as extremely helpful, to look up the correct pronunciation of the names of persons and places referred to in the text.

Contents

COLOR PLATES

Following page 84: 1 Sumerian offering stand; 2 Wooden boat from Egyptian tomb; 3 Greek vase; 4 Pottery vase from Minos; 5 Etruscan tomb painting; 6 Mosaic from Pompeii; 7 Painting at Dura-Europos

Following page 196: 8 Italian Romanesque architecture; 9 The Alhambra at Granada; 10 Stained-glass window from Cathedral of Le Mans

Following page 340: 11 Bronze statue of Shiva; 12 Japanese statue; 13 Painted silk scroll (detail)

Following page 404: 24 "The Surrender of Breda"; 15 "Cardinal Richelieu"; 16 "The Anatomy Lesson"; 17 "Adoration of the Magi"

Following page 580: 18 "The Fighting *Temeraire* Towed to Her Last Berth"; 19 "Peasant of the Camargue"; 20 "Thomas Carlyle"; 21 "The Execution of Maximilian"; 22 "Le Moulin de la Galette"

Following page 788: 23 "Three Musicians"; 24 "Temptation of St. Anthony"; 25 "25 "Zapatistas"; 26 "Red Petals"

Credits for the color plates listed above can be found on page 805.

Note: Drawings on cover from photos furnished by Encyclopedia of Modern Art and the American Museum of Natural History.

A Prologue:
Perspective on Man

If the time span of our planet—now estimated as some five billion years—were telescoped into a single year, the first eight months would be devoid of any life. The next two months would be taken up with very primitive animal forms, and not until well into December would any mammals appear. In this "year," man—or rather *Pithecanthropus erectus*, our ape-man ancestor—would not mount the global stage until between 10 and 11 P.M. on December 31. And how has man spent that brief allotment? He has given over almost half it—the equivalent of some 500,000 years—to making tools and weapons out of stone. His revolutionary changeover from a food-hunting nomad to a farmer who raised grain and domesticated animals would occur in the last sixty seconds. And into that final minute would also be crowded all of his other discoveries: how to use metals; how to create civilizations along the banks of rivers and around the perimeters of seas; how to master the oceans; how to harness steam, then gas, electricity, oil, and, finally, in our own lifetime, atomic energy. Thus, among man's greatest achievements on earth has been his de-

velopment of tools, machines, and controlled power—in short, technology. Yet even this planet earth—this speck of cosmic dust in an immense universe—no longer satisfies man's technological ambitions. Man has at last succeeded in escaping the age-old bondage to the earth and is about to propel himself into the interplanetary age.

At present, man's technology is moving ahead at supersonic speed, and each day sees it further accelerated. Meanwhile, however, there has been no corresponding increase in man's own mental or physical capacity. He probably has no more native intelligence than his Stone Age ancestors —and undoubtedly less muscle! So we come to a fundamental question. How is twentieth-century man to cope with the ever widening disparity between what he *is* and what he *has*? How can he control and utilize his tremendous technological powers for the happiness of himself and others and not for nuclear self-annihilation? Today he seeks to conquer other planets before he has learned to govern his own.

Surely an indispensable step toward solving contemporary man's dilemma—technology without the requisite control, and power without adequate wisdom—must be a better understanding of how man and all his works became what they are today. Only by understanding the past can mankind assess both the perils and the opportunities of the present. This accumulated experience, the memory of the race, is available for study. We call it *history*.

THE "USE" OF HISTORY

Definition of history. Let us first see what we mean by the term *history*. History is the record of the past actions of mankind, based upon surviving evidence. The historian uses this evidence to compose accurate accounts and to reach conclusions which he believes are valid. In this way, he becomes an interpreter of the development of mankind.

History shows that all patterns and problems in human affairs are the products of a complex process of growth. By throwing light on that process, history provides a means for profiting from human experience. There would be no landmarks, no points of reference, no foundations on which to build if the individual were bereft of the knowledge of his past. The system of government under which he lives, the frontiers of his country and its economy—such factors of direct concern to a person's existence are meaningful because of history. In our age of global interdependence and atomic propulsion, the neglect of history would be more than folly—it could prove suicidal.

THE "HOW" OF HISTORY

Is history a science? There is more than one way of treating the past. In dealing with the American Revolution, for example, the historian may describe its events in narrative form. Or he may prefer to concentrate on an analysis of its general causes or perhaps compare its stages of evolution with the patterns of revolution in other countries.

Because of this analytical function, historical writing has sometimes been regarded as a science. But the historian does not seek to attain the same kind of results as the scientist. In his laboratory, the latter can verify his conclusions by repeating his experiment under controlled conditions. He also attempts to classify the phenomenon in a general group or category. The historian, on the other hand, is more likely to consider events in terms of their uniqueness. This is because each

event takes place at a particular time and in a particular place. And because that time is now past, he cannot verify his conclusions by duplicating the circumstances in which the event occurred. Moreover, history is concerned fundamentally with the lives and actions of men, and therefore the historian's search for causes is bound to be relatively subjective as compared with that of the physical scientist.

Nevertheless, historians insist that history should be written as scientifically as possible and that evidence should be analyzed with the same objective attitude employed by the scientist when he examines natural phenomena. This scientific spirit requires the historian to handle his evidence according to established rules of historical analysis, to recognize his own biases and attempt to eliminate their effects from his work, and to draw only such conclusions as the evidence warrants.

Historical method. Employing the "historical method," the historian first searches for *sources*. Without them there can be no history. They may consist of material remains such as bones, tools, weapons, and pottery; oral traditions such as myths, legends, and songs; pictorial data such as drawings and maps; and, of course, written records ranging from ancient manuscripts to treaties, diaries, books, and yesterday's newspaper.

Next, the historian analyzes his sources to infer the facts. This process has two parts. *External criticism* tests the genuineness of the source. The importance of external criticism was demonstrated dramatically in recent years by the unmasking of a hoax—Piltdown Man—which had long duped scientists. Generally, however, the historian has to deal with less spectacular problems, such as checking ancient documents for errors that have crept into the text through faulty copying or translating.

The second part of the analytical process is called *internal criticism*. In evaluating written materials, the historian seeks to ascertain the author's meaning and the accuracy of his work. To do so may require study of the language of the era, or the circumstances in which the author's statement was made. A politician's memoirs may be highly suspect because of an almost universal tendency to present oneself in print in the most favorable light. Official documents must also be examined for what they may conceal as well as reveal.

The final step in historical method is *synthesis*. Here the historian must determine which factors in a given situation are most relevant to his purpose. This delicate process of selection underscores the role that subjectivity plays in the writing of history. "The more complex the events dealt with, the wider their spread in time and space, the greater are the calls made upon the historian's judgment."[1]

THE "WHY" OF HISTORY

Historical analysis. The historian seeks to describe not only *what* has happened in the past but also *why* society changes. Any search of this kind raises a number of fundamental questions: the roles of Providence, the individual, and the group in history; the extent to which historical events are unique or fit into patterns; and the problem of whether there is "progress" in human affairs. The answers vary with the different philosophical views of mankind.

Providence and the individual. Those who hold the teleological view see in history the guidance of a Divine Will, directing human destinies according to a cosmic purpose. Prevalent in medieval thought, this theory lost ground with the spread of rationalistic doctrines and scientific triumphs. But in our own day there has been a reaction against the nineteenth century's comfortable assumption that human betterment is inevitable. To one distinguished historian, for example, "a religious interpretation of the whole drama of human life is the only one that is tenable for a moment. . . ."[2]

Other historians have minimized the role of Providence while exalting the role of the individual in the historical process. Among them was Thomas Carlyle, who maintained that the Alexanders, Muhammads, and Cromwells were the "Great Men" whose leadership ultimately determined the course of human events. Later historians discounted this generalization by emphasizing the impact of economic and other "impersonal" forces. But in an age which tends toward centralized control, especially in dictatorships, we underestimate at our peril the power that can be wielded by a Hitler or a Stalin.

"Laws" and "forces" in history. The opponents of Carlyle's approach often contend that history is determined by "forces" and "laws" and by the actions of entire societies. One geographer, for example, even argued that a people's genius and progress were decided principally by climate. We can reject such an extreme claim but—as we shall see when we take up the earliest, or fluvial, civilizations—physical environment does play a significant part in the development of human societies.

Sociologists approach history primarily by analyzing the origins, institutions, and functions of groups. Some attach special importance to population factors as criteria for judging the evolution of a given society, while others analyze societies in terms of the division of labor within them, or in terms of the relationships between various major forces—such as the spirit of Protestantism and the ethics of early modern capitalism.

Karl Marx's theory of history. The most explosive interpretation of history in modern times was made by Karl Marx. To him, irresistible economic forces governed men and determined trends in history. Thus the feudal system was displaced as a result of new methods of production, the growth of a moneyed economy, and the gradual emancipation of serfs. Marx also contended that the shift from one economic stage to another—such as from feudalism to capitalism—is attained by sporadic upheavals, or revolutions. This is because the class controlling the methods of production eventually resists further progress in order to maintain its vested interests. As a result, society consists of the "exploiters" and the "exploited." Marx predicted, however, that the proletariat would overthrow the exploiting capitalists, once the conflicts inherent in the free enterprise system provided it with the necessary strength. The end result would be a classless society, followed by a gradual withering away of the state itself.

Despite the spread of Marx's doctrine in the contemporary world, many of his basic assumptions have been conclusively disproved by natural events. Thus, Marx assumed that the spectacular poverty of industrial workers of his own day would spread and deepen. Instead, social legislation and higher productivity have enabled the living standards of the "exploited" masses in capitalist countries to become higher than ever before. And what of Marx's "classless" society? In Soviet Russia and its Marxist satellites, the state controls all aspects of a stratified society in which there exists a wage and privilege differential (far greater than that existing in western societies) between the administrative bureaucracy, the army officers, and the professional elite on the one hand and the masses of workers and peasants on the other.

Theories of civilization. Other attempts have been made to explain the rise and fall of civilizations according to a set of principles. Early in this century, a disillusioned German, Oswald Spengler, maintained that civilizations were like organisms; each grew with the "superb aimlessness" of a flower and passed through a cycle of spring, summer, autumn, and winter. He declared that western civilization was in its winter period and had already entered a state of rapid decline.

Spengler influenced the English historian Arnold J. Toynbee, whose works became best sellers after World War II. To Toynbee, "challenge and response" explain the rise and fall of civilizations. Man achieves civilization "as a response to a challenge in a situation of special difficulty which rouses him to make a hitherto unprecedented effort."[3] Thus the ancient Egyptians built their civilization by learning to control the Nile River. It is Toynbee's view that a civilization continues to grow so long as it is motivated by creative individuals; when they can no longer inspire the majority, social disunity brings about decline and disintegration. While rejecting Spengler's view that all civilizations are fated to die after traversing some predetermined life curve, Toynbee warns that the West is in peril because of a weakening of its spiritual fiber.

Role of the unforeseen. We should also point out that many eminent historians profess to find no recurring pattern in past events. Thus H. A. L. Fisher of Oxford wrote: "I can see only one emergency following upon another as wave follows wave, only one great fact with respect to which, since it is unique, there can be no generalizations, only one safe rule for the historian: that he should recognize in the development of human destinies the play of the contingent and the unforeseen."[4]

Is the course of history inevitable? All this leads to the question: Are men really free to make alternative choices, or does history obey impersonal laws and forces—in short, is the course of history inevitable? To pose the question only invites others in turn. Can anyone say what would have happened to our contemporary world had Hitler, as a corporal in the First World War, been killed? Would Nazism still have come into existence in the 1920's, and would German history still have taken a similar course?

We seem to have to choose between either "inevitable" laws—which appear to leave no room for significant freedom of action—or the equally extreme alternative view that makes every event a unique act, so that history becomes merely the record of unrelated episodes. Can we not avoid this dilemma? Even though all events are in various respects unique, they also contain elements which permit comparison—as in the case of the origin and course of revolutions in different countries. The comparative approach permits us to seek relationships between historical phenomena and to group them into movements, or patterns, or civilizations.

The authors of this book eschew any single "theory" of history. They have tried to be eclectic in their approach because there is merit in a number of basic concepts. These include the important effects of physical environment on social organization and institutions; the powerful roles played not only by economic but also by political and religious factors; and the impact exerted upon events by various outstanding personalities occupying key positions in history.

The question of progress. Somewhere along the line, the student is likely to ask: "Are we making any progress? Are problems being solved? Is mankind getting better?" The spokesmen of the optimistic nineteenth century confidently answered "Yes!" but those of our crisis-ridden century are by no means so sure. Such questions in any case are difficult to assess because of the problem of defining terms such as *progress* or *better*. Those who equate progress with material advancement might do well to remember that the Athens of Socrates and Aristotle produced an unsurpassed galaxy of thinkers and artists without the benefit of electricity, deep-freezes, TV, or ICBM's. Conversely, the advanced literacy and technology boasted by Nazi Germany did not prevent that nation from wallowing in the moral depravity which created concentration camps and gas chambers.

Nevertheless, our lawmakers, educators, and scientists do proceed on the assumption that progress can be both defined and defended on rational grounds. Here is a list of factors which might be applied in any test of man's progress in history. It should include *material advancement:* improved living and health standards, increased agricultural and industrial efficiency, and a distribution of goods so as to benefit the greatest number of people. *Intellectual and spiritual progress* calls for educational opportunities for all and is measured in terms of creative achievements in science, the humanities, and the arts. For example, Einstein's theory constitutes an advance over Newton's theory of gravitation because it points to the solution of the same problems as the earlier theory and hitherto inexplicable problems as well. *Social progress* covers the "pursuit of happiness" and includes such essentials as equal status for women, abolition of conditions of servitude, just laws, and enlightened treatment of prisoners and the insane.

Improvement of political organization is yet another area to consider. In a democracy, progress can be tested by the opportunities for the individual to assume public responsibilities, and by the protection of his right to hold views at variance with those held by others, especially in the case of minorities. In today's world, the growth of *international cooperation* becomes basic in any discussion of progress. This calls for the maintenance of peace and security, the peaceful settlement of international disputes, and improved world-wide economic and social standards.

THE CULTURAL APPROACH
TO HISTORY

The universal culture pattern. History represents the interplay of man with his environment and of man with his fellow man. In coping with this interaction of physical and human factors, men have always expressed themselves in terms of certain fundamental needs. These form the basis of a "universal culture pattern" and deserve to be enumerated.

1. *The need to make a living.* Man must have food, shelter, clothing, and the means to provide for his children's survival.

2. *The need for law and order.* From the earliest times, communities have had to keep peace among their members, protect property, and defend themselves against external attack.

3. *The need for social organization.* To enable people to make a living, raise families, and maintain law and order, a social structure is necessary. But this creates in turn certain problems. For example, the proponents of Anglo-American democracy and of Soviet Marxism differ fundamentally in their concepts of the relative importance of the individual and the social organization of which he forms a part.

4. *The need for knowledge and learning.* Languages and writing systems enable man to transmit the knowledge painfully acquired from experience. As societies grow more complex, there is an increasing need to preserve knowledge and to make it available through education to as many people as possible.

5. *The need for self-expression.* Man has responded creatively to his environment from the days when he decorated the walls of caves with paintings of the animals he hunted. Likewise, music, poetry, and the dance are of ancient lineage, while architecture has known many periods as creative as our own.

6. *The need for religious expression.* As ancient as man himself is his attempt to answer the "why" of his existence. Primitive peoples responded to their environment by attempting to propitiate what they feared. Later, much that was once deemed supernatural could be explained by science in terms of natural phenomena. Yet today, no less than before, we continue to search for answers to the ultimate questions of existence.

The concept of "culture." These six briefly described needs have been common to men at all times and in all places, and together they form the basis of a culture pattern universal in scope. To carry this concept one step further: when a group of people behave similarly and share the same institutions and ways of life, they can be said to possess a common culture. Each person born into that group will in turn derive from it his basic way of life. All peoples, then, possess cultures. It follows that the basic differences between the farmers of ancient China and those of present-day Nebraska are due mainly to the fact that their culture traits are at different stages of development or that they have worked out different methods of solving the same problems of existence.

Civilization defined. Certain cultures are designated as *civilizations*. What is meant by this term? When men no longer have to submit to brute necessity but begin instead to dominate their environment, they are at last in a position to remold their patterns of living and to transmit a common social heritage. When this process continues to the point where men exert a wide control over nature and have developed a highly complex culture pattern—including an urban structure superimposed upon an agricultural base—they can be said to possess a civilization. (The emergence of the first civilizations is treated in Chapter 1.)

Diffusion as a factor in culture change. Cultures are never static or wholly isolated. A particular culture may have an individuality which sets it off sharply from other cultures, but invariably it has been influenced by external contacts. Such contacts may be either peaceful or warlike, and they meet with varying degrees of resistance. The early American colonists took from the Indians the use of corn, while the latter obtained the horse from the newcomers. On the other hand, the Second World War saw the Nazis and Japanese force their cultures upon subjugated peoples with no permanent results.

Environment and invention in culture change. While geography has profoundly influenced cultures, we need not exaggerate its importance. While riverine civilizations evolved along the Nile and the Tigris-Euphrates, for example, none emerged in the physically comparable valleys of the Jordan and the Rio Grande.[5] Moreover, environmental influences become less marked as man gains increasing mastery over nature, as shown by the transformation of deserts in southwestern United States into rich citrus belts and truck-farming regions through the use of irrigation.

Invention is therefore another important source of culture change. The automobile has revolutionized transportation, the growth of cities, and even home life. The automobile itself was made possible only by a host of earlier inventions beginning with that most ancient and indispensable aid to transportation, the wheel.

Is race a factor in culture change? Just as there is no pure culture developed in isolation by one group, so there is no pure race of people. Ethnic types have intermingled along with the diffusion of cultures. *Race*, a much misused term, has value only in denoting the major human divisions, each with its own distinctive physical characteristics: Caucasian (white), Mongoloid (yellow), and Negroid (black). No race has ever possessed a monopoly of culture, though for a specific period one race may produce an impressive record of cultural creativity.

Culture lag. Some parts of a culture pattern change more rapidly than others, so that one institution sometimes becomes outmoded in relation to others in a society. When different parts of a society fail to mesh harmoniously, the condition is often called "culture lag." The status of women has been a flagrant example of culture lag, for despite the progressive democratization of political institutions, women were enfranchised only in this century. Again, the 1930's witnessed the tragedy of hunger in the midst of plenty because economic institutions failed to cope adequately with the fruits of a swiftly advancing technology. In international affairs, we find at the present time a dangerous culture lag. The attempts of the United Nations to limit atomic energy to peaceful use have been repeatedly frustrated by insistence upon the rights of national sovereignty, though obviously the effects of any nuclear war cannot be contained within national boundaries. Failure to rectify this culture lag could well prove fatal to life on this planet. As we follow the story of man through the ages, we shall see how the drag of tradition and inertia on the part of well-meaning persons can at times be as dangerous as the overt acts of tyrants and dictators.

THE CHALLENGE

A century of conflict. The twentieth century has been phenomenally fruitful in raising economic, social, and health standards. But ours is also a century of conflict. It has been said that contemporary man is involved in three kinds of conflict: with nature, with his fellow man, and with himself. In some ways, the first can be richly rewarding. Thus the harnessing of atomic energy holds out hope for almost unlimited human advancement. But, meanwhile, we are depleting the earth's natural resources at an unprecedented rate, and vast areas of the globe are ravaged by erosion.

These unresolved conflicts with nature in turn increase human tensions. Hundreds of millions in underdeveloped regions are hungry, a situation that breeds social unrest and political conflict. Today, all Asia and Africa demand political freedom; but if chaos or new forms of aggression are not to follow the granting of independence, the new nations must be offered support in raising the living standards of the masses. However, this aid must come from the industrial powers, who themselves are dangerously split into ideologically warring camps, East and West. Tensions abound among both the strong and the weak.

Today's tensions find repercussions within man himself, as is shown by the increasing incidence of nervous and mental disorders and by the feelings of general insecurity among average people everywhere.

No time for defeatism. To many, it seems almost hopeless to try to rectify a world which, in Hamlet's phrase, seems so "out of joint." The authors disagree heartily with these prophets of doom. A study of history should prove that the "good old days" were actually not that good and that every age has had to bear its full burden of dire forebodings. In any case, this is no time for defeatism. History teaches us that man has never yet given up his struggle for survival and the betterment of life. The authors agree with the scholar who wrote: "Others claim man will destroy himself, which is of course a political prediction. This seems to me a fate as unlikely as committing suicide by holding your breath. Man, for all his frailties, is now one of the toughest, most tenacious, most adaptable animals in the kingdom . . . and I am sure that he is here to stay."[6]

How old the universe is and how the planet earth came into being may never be known precisely, but modern scientists believe that our world has been circling the sun for 4,500,000,000 to 5,000,000,000 years. During that incredibly long time, the earth changed from a gaseous to a liquid state and finally solidified; waters formed in craters of the earth's shell, and in their depths the first life took form. As one geological epoch succeeded another, single-celled and then multicelled organisms evolved, and some of them learned to live on land. Eventually this ceaseless process of adaptation to environment brought forth the mammal class, of which man is a member.

Remains of the earliest human beings, unearthed in Java, China, and elsewhere, are at least half a million years old. The time span from those remote days to about 5000 B.C. is usually referred to as prehistoric, or preliterate, times. By far the greatest part of that time span was taken up by man's relentless struggle for survival—a struggle during which he learned to make fire, shape crude weapons and tools from stone, and domesticate some few plants and animals. The latter achievement was of revolutionary consequence, for a measure of control over plants and animals meant that man could settle in one place and become a farmer and herdsman, a food producer rather than a forager.

Thus the stage was set for a progressively rapid extension of man's control over his environment. A new era of existence was heralded with the invention of writing, the discovery of metallurgy, progress in arts and crafts, and the organization of larger social and political units. These momentous advances were concentrated in several great river valleys where the well-watered, fertile soil produced abundant harvests. Villages and cities sprang up, inhabited by men with diverse talents and trades: priests, potters, basket weavers, toolmakers, and merchants.

Along the banks of rivers, then, we must look for the first civilizations. We shall find them widely scattered: Mesopotamia straddled the Tigris and the Euphrates; Egypt stretched along the Nile; India arose along the Indus and the Ganges; and China expanded eastward from the region of the Wei and the Hwang Ho. Prolific in their gifts to mankind, these civilizations possessed similarities at least as arresting as their differences. In all four, political systems were developed, crafts flourished and commerce expanded, calendars and systems of writing were invented, art and literature of extraordinary beauty were created, and religions and philosophies came into being to satisfy men's inner yearnings.

Indebted to the Egyptians and Mesopotamians, the inhabitants of Crete, Troy, and Mycenae fashioned a wealthy, sophisticated, commercial culture. Much of their civilization was lost in the turmoil of the second millennium B.C., but enough remained to serve as the foundation for the structure about to be built by the Indo-European tribes which migrated into the area—the Greeks. Possessed of an insatiable curiosity about man and man's world, the Greeks enjoyed a freedom of thought and expression unknown in earlier societies. Their fierce passion to remain untrammeled, however, was too often unrestrained. Thus, in the promising democracy of Athens, the citizens proved unable to achieve long-term stability along with liberty, while in the larger sphere the failure of the Greek city-states to find a workable basis for cooperation doomed them all to political disaster. Although the conquest of the city-states by King Philip of Macedonia ended the Hellenic Age, the influence of the Greeks was destined to increase. The establishment of a vast empire in the Near East by Philip's talented son, Alexander the Great, ushered in the Hellenistic Age—a period of commercial expansion and the widespread diffusion of Greek culture.

Meanwhile, a new power—Rome—had been evolving on the Italian peninsula. After five centuries of modest growth, this city-state embarked upon a career of unprecedented expansion. The splendor of Roman arms was matched by skill in administration, wisdom in law, and ingenuity in the practical arts of engineering and communication. These talents and abilities enabled the Romans to erect a Mediterranean empire which survived until the fifth century A.D. Probably the greatest achievement of the Roman empire was the skillful maintenance of a diversity of cultures and religions within a political unity. To the Romans we owe a debt for preserving and disseminating classical culture, for it is the legacy of Graeco-Roman culture which is the foundation of western civilization.

CHAPTER 1

Along the Banks of Rivers

THE CIVILIZATIONS OF THE ANCIENT NEAR EAST

Introduction. More than a million years ago, human creatures first appeared on earth, naked in a world of enemies. The story of man's journey out of the darkness of ignorance and fear covers a period of hundreds of thousands of years during which he mastered the skills necessary for survival. Early man's most important achievements concern agriculture and the ways of life it engendered. Wild beasts were tamed as work animals or kept for their meat and hides. The first farmers scattered kernels of grain on the earth and waited patiently for harvest time. Because their fields and flocks could supply most of their wants, a settled existence became possible and men were no longer compelled to move on endlessly in search of food, as their food-gathering ancestors had done for countless generations. Where the land was good, these

ancient farmers were able to acquire more food than they needed for survival—surpluses to tide them over seasons of cold and drought. Thus, in green oases, along the banks of rivers, and on fertile plateaus, farming villages sprang up.

In early Egyptian picture writing, a town is shown as a cross within a circle—the intersection of two pathways enclosed by a wall. The symbol is an appropriate one, for in the history of mankind ⊗ —the town—marks the spot where civilization as we know it began.

Within the towns the business of living took new turns. Communal effort remained essential —all the men in a village might help in erecting a wall of brick or wood to protect the inhabitants against marauding nomads—but it was no longer necessary for each man to concentrate solely on farming or hunting. True, the majority farmed, but there were now craftsmen turning out specialized wares, merchants trading with friendly neighbors, and priests conducting religious ceremonies. While contributing to the well-being of the community, each performed a distinct function. As life became more stable, time could be found for intellectual and artistic pursuits which enriched the lives of the participants and developed a cultural heritage.

A culture can endure only if the knowledge necessary for its survival is passed on from generation to generation. Early peoples relied on information transmitted by word of mouth—an undependable means of communication. But as towns and cities grew up and cultures became increasingly complex, methods for keeping records were devised and systems of writing were created. To many authorities, the development of writing is a prerequisite to civilization.

The rise of the four earliest civilizations— the Sumerian, the Egyptian, the Indian, and the Chinese—took place, in each case, within the valley of a great river system. The Greek historian Herodotus called Egypt "the gift of the Nile," and the other three civilizations were no less indebted to their locations in rich river valleys. In this chapter we shall trace the progress of civilization in the Near East. In Chapter 4 we shall see the stirrings of civilization far to the east, in India and in China.

TOOLS AND ART OF

EARLY MAN

Pithecanthropus and the dawn of Paleolithic culture. In 1891 there were found the fossil fragments of *Pithecanthropus erectus* (erect ape-man), or Java Man. Excavations in 1927-1929 near Peking uncovered skeletal remains of another early member of the *Pithecanthropus* group, labeled *Pithecanthropus pekinensis (Sinanthropus)*, or Peking Man. Classed as slightly younger than Java Man, Peking Man was also considered more advanced because he possessed a larger brain.

Pithecanthropus fossils date back more than half a million years. Ape-man was about five feet tall, had heavy brows and a receding forehead, and by modern standards had relatively low intelligence. Fossil remains now disclose that this group inhabited extensive areas of the earth and lived in temperate as well as tropical climates.

Artifacts found near Peking show that Peking Man fashioned his tools by converting broken bones into implements and by striking pieces of rock with other stones. Since this chipping method of making implements was the most distinct feature of man's earliest culture, the first stage in man's cultural development is known as the Paleolithic, or Old Stone, Age. Strictly speaking, Paleolithic is a cultural and not a chronological term, and Paleolithic methods and customs survived among backward peoples into modern times. However, the term is generally used to refer to the prehistoric period when the Paleolithic was mankind's highest cultural level.

For hundreds of thousands of years the hand-ax—used for killing prey and cutting and scraping hides—was the dominant tool for early Paleolithic men. But different types of tools and various techniques for making them existed during early Paleolithic times. Some were core tools—that is, they were made by trimming a block of stone to a required shape. Others were flake tools, fashioned from large flakes which had been broken off from a block of stone.

Neanderthal Man and *Homo sapiens*. The next early man to whom we should give attention is *Homo neanderthalensis*, or Neanderthal Man. The skeletal remains of Neanderthal Man were first found near Düsseldorf, Germany, in 1856. These remains reveal that he had a long skull, deep-sunk eyes, a low forehead, large brow ridges, and a long, flat-cheeked face. About five feet tall, he possessed a thick-set body, short forearms, and a slouching posture. A powerful hunter, he killed his quarry with wooden spears and, like Peking Man, used animal bones and stones as tools. He adapted himself to cold weather by using fire and living in caves whenever possible.

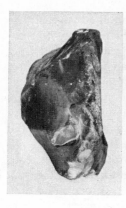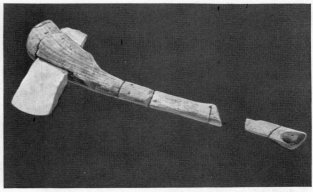

At the left is a Paleolithic hand-ax; in the center, an improved Paleolithic hand-ax with more flaking; at the right, a Neolithic ax.

Late Paleolithic times saw the displacement of Neanderthal Man by *Homo sapiens*, described as a "modern European type." The reason for the extinction of Neanderthal is conjectural. He may have died out or been absorbed by *Homo sapiens*. Perhaps Neanderthal Man constituted a specialized line of development in the evolution of mankind and did not represent, as was formerly supposed, an intermediate stage between *Pithecanthropus* and *Homo sapiens*.

Late Paleolithic cultures. By 15,000 B.C., *Homo sapiens* inhabited Africa, Australia, and southwest Asia as well as Europe. The tools made by these men were blade tools—narrow parallel-sided flakes characteristic of late Paleolithic times. A tool shaped like a chisel, the burin, was used for working bone, antlers, ivory, and wood into implements for specialized purposes. Handles were attached to many tools and weapons, and spears were launched more effectively with spear throwers—shafts with hooklike projections fitting into the butt end of the spear. The bow was invented late in this period, probably in North Africa.

To withstand the cold weather, late Paleolithic peoples fashioned garments from sewn skins. The groups who followed reindeer herds lived in tents and huts made of hides or brush. In present-day Czechoslovakia and southern Russia, where mammoths were hunted, early men constructed underground communal houses with mammoth ribs for roof supports. Shallow caves were used for shelter in the limestone hills of western Europe.

The first artists. One of the highest achievements of the men of late Paleolithic times was their art. Man was an artist endeavoring to give expression to his creative imagination long before he could write or fashion a metal knife.

In 1879 Sautuola, a Spanish nobleman, was exploring a cave on his Altamira estate in northern Spain, when his small daughter, who had accompanied him, suddenly cried, "Toros! toros!" ("Bulls! bulls!") The father turned around and saw the little girl pointing to the ceiling. He perceived a thrilling sight, a long procession of magnificently drawn bison. Later, other caves in Spain and France yielded many other examples of prehistoric art.

In the Altamira murals the outline of the animals was usually traced in black and then shaded with a mixture of red, black, and yellow colors. These paintings of animals, with their actions, attitudes, and skillfully drawn anatomy, show that man was observing keenly the world around him. By drawing pictures of food animals, man believed that he could wield some sort of magical power over his prey. Occasionally, he drew arrows piercing the animals he hoped to kill. In addition, Paleolithic man chiseled pictures on rock and bone, modeled in clay, and made bas-relief friezes on cave walls.

Animals like this reindeer were carved on stone by early man.

From food gathering to food producing. Paleolithic men could not control their food supply. So long as they relied on foraging, hunting, fishing, and trapping, they were dependent on the natural food supply in a given area to keep from starving. But while Paleolithic men continued their food-gathering pattern of existence in Europe, Africa, and Australia, groups of people in the Near East began to cultivate edible plants and to breed animals. Often described as the "first economic revolution" in the history of man, this momentous change from a food-gathering to a food-producing economy initiated the Neolithic Age. Paleolithic man was a hunter; Neolithic man became a farmer and herdsman.

Neolithic cultures and the beginning of agriculture. Neolithic cultures are usually characterized by cultivation of grains, domestication of animals, pottery making, and the use of polished stone tools (hence, the use of Neolithic, or New Stone, as a term to describe these cultures). Actually, all four characteristics are not always present in a Neolithic culture. We must also keep in mind that the Neolithic Age is a cultural and not a chronological period. While Neolithic settlements in Palestine date back perhaps 8000 years, the cultivation of edible plants and the domestication of animals did not appear in Britain until some 4500 years ago.

Neolithic farmers combined agriculture with hunting to furnish themselves with sufficient food. They also kept animals to supply food, clothing, and transportation. After wild dogs were tamed, goats, sheep, pigs, cattle, and horses were domesticated.

Pottery was made in quantity—the fragility of the materials used no longer being the handicap it had been to food-gathering nomads. Clothing and baskets had been fashioned in pre-Neolithic cultures, but the pattern of Neolithic life gave women more time to develop skills in the domestic arts. Despite the thousands of years of man's progress, the process of weaving today is essentially the same as that employed in early primitive societies.

In Neolithic Europe, where wood was abundant, rectangular timber houses were constructed; some had two rooms, a gabled roof, and walls of split saplings. Remains found near lakes in Switzerland show that even on soft, swampy earth the builders were able to erect houses by placing them on wooden foundations or on piles going down into the ground.

Neolithic artisans ground and polished stones to produce axes, adzes, and chisels with strong and sharp cutting edges. Methods were devised for drilling holes in stone; boulders were used for grinding grain, and stone bowls for storage.

PRIMITIVE THOUGHT AND CUSTOM

Analysis of primitive societies. Perhaps it is natural for most of us, living as we do in a highly complex machine-age society, to assume that primitive men, prehistoric or modern, would possess few laws, little education, and only the simplest codes of conduct. But this is far from true. The organization of a primitive society may be as complex as our own. Rules regarding the role of parents, the treatment of children, the punishment of the evildoer, the conduct of business, the worship of the gods, and the conventions of eating and recreation have existed for thousands of years, along with methods to compel the individual to do "the correct thing."

How can we know about those features of the culture of early man which are not apparent from the remains of tools and other objects? We can glean much from the earliest myths and epics, which originated in prehistoric times before the invention of writing and which reflect early man's ideas and customs. We can also apply conclusions anthropologists have drawn from studies of the cultures of present-day primitive societies. But here a word of caution is necessary. Because the general level of technological development in a modern-day primitive society appears to be similar to the level of achievement reached in a prehistoric society, it does not follow that all aspects of the two cultures are comparable. Furthermore, it is often difficult to measure in what degree modern primitive societies have been affected by the impact of advanced civilizations like our own.

The elementary and extended family. Among all peoples, past and present, the basic social unit appears to be the elementary family group—parents and their offspring. Anthropologists do not know what marriage customs were prevalent in the earliest societies, but monogamy—one husband and one wife—was probably most common.

The extended family—an individual family together with a circle of related persons who usually trace their descent through their mothers and are bound together by mutual loyalty—is often found in primitive social groupings. The extended family strengthens the elementary unit both in obtaining food and in protecting its members against other groups. Because of its social and economic advantages, this form of organization may have existed in ancient times.

The clan and the tribe. A third primitive social unit is the clan—a group of individuals within a community who believe that they have a common ancestor and therefore are "of one blood, or of one soul." A clan is patrilineal if its members trace their relationship through the male line, and matrilineal if through the female.

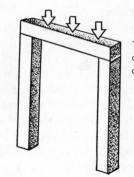

The weight of the material above the opening pushes down on the lintel.

POST AND LINTEL CONSTRUCTION

First used by Neolithic men, post and lintel construction is a simple solution to the problem of supporting weight above an opening. Because the one-piece lintel carries the weight, the strength of the material determines the width of the aperture.

Many primitive peoples identify their clans by a totem—an animal or some natural object—which is revered and is made the subject for amulets of various sorts. Forms of totemism in modern-day society include military insignia, the emblems of such organizations as the Elks and Moose, and animal mascots used by college football teams.

A fourth grouping which some primitive peoples form is the tribe. This term lacks a precise definition, but it may be thought of as applying to a community characterized by a common speech or distinctive dialect, a common cultural heritage, and a specific inhabited territory. Group loyalty is a strong trait among members of a tribe and is often accompanied by a contempt for the peoples and customs of other communities. For example, some Eskimos were found to speak of neighboring Indians as "children of a louse's egg."

Collective responsibility in law and government. In primitive societies, ethical behavior consists in not violating custom. The close relationships that exist in extended families and clans encourage conformity.

The concept of justice among the individuals of a primitive group is synonymous with maintaining equilibrium. Thus, if one man steals another's property, the economic equilibrium has been unjustly disturbed. Such a theft constitutes a wrong against the individual; and, where modern legal procedure calls for punishment of the thief, in primitive societies justice is achieved by a settlement between the injured man and the thief. If the thief restores what has been stolen or its equivalent, the victim is satisfied and the thief is not punished. On the other hand, certain acts are considered dangerous to the whole group and require punishment by the entire community. Treason, witchcraft, and incest are typical offenses in this category. Such acts are not settled by the payment of compensation; the punishment meted out is usually death. If a member of a clan gets into trouble too often, his fellows will regard him as a social nuisance and an economic liability; thus they may outlaw him from the group or execute him.

Scholars theorize that in food-gathering societies and the earliest food-producing societies, as in primitive societies of today, the governing political body was small and of a democratic character. The adults participated in the decisions of the group, with special deference being paid to the views of the older tribal members because of their greater experience and knowledge of the group's traditions and ceremonies. In the more advanced food-producing communities, however, government tended to fall increasingly under the control of the richest members, who formed a council of elders. In time there emerged a hereditary chief of the tribe or community, who pledged to rule according to the unwritten custom of his tribe and in consultation with his council. In the event of serious decisions, such as going to war, it was necessary for him to obtain the consent of a general assembly of all the adult men. The presence of this strong representative element has led a modern scholar to call this earliest form of government "primitive democracy."[1]

Religion and magic. Perhaps the strongest single force in the life of primitive people is religion. It colors every aspect of their existence: birth, initiation into the tribe, marriage, hunting, farming, war, and death. Religious beliefs among primitive peoples have taken different forms, such as animism, the belief that all things, from men to stones, are inhabited by souls; and animatism, the belief in a nonmaterial, impersonal force or essence which animates everything in nature. Attributing to the supernatural all the natural phenomena he cannot otherwise explain, primitive man turns to witches and wizards, diviners, rainmakers, and medicine men to ward off droughts, famines, floods, and plagues through magical powers of communication with the spirits. For him, magic and religion are closely associated.

As people grew more civilized and learned more of the secrets of nature, they became less concerned with propitiating forces which they had previously been unable to understand. Rather, they became increasingly concerned with revering what they held to be the ultimate moral and spiritual authority in the universe. Civilized peoples developed the great monotheistic faiths, based on belief in one God with whom every individual can communicate freely.

THE DAWN OF CIVILIZATION

Great advances in technology. During the fourth millennium B.C. some of the most significant discoveries and inventions in human history were achieved. A revolution as far-reaching as that which occurred in agriculture was brought about by Neolithic man's discovery of how to use metals to make tools and weapons. By 3000 B.C. metallurgy, the plow, the wheeled vehicle, the potter's wheel, and new forms of propulsion—including the harnessing of animals for land transportation and the use of sails for seagoing ships—had laid the foundations for a type of economy and social order markedly different from anything previously known. Already some aspects of this new order had manifested themselves. For example, metalworking in copper and bronze required the services of metalsmiths, who devoted their full time and increasing knowledge to their particular craft. Because full-time specialists did not raise their own food, a surplus had to be produced by the rest of the community. Around the settlements like those in the

Syrian steppes and the Iranian plateaus, there was too little arable land for the people to raise large amounts of grain and thus accumulate surpluses. In such circumstances few full-time specialists could be employed, the full potential of the new discoveries and inventions could not be realized, and therefore the means to create a new type of society were lacking. A more congenial physical environment was necessary. It was found in the alluvial valleys of certain great rivers.

The Fertile Crescent, cradle of civilization. These river valleys (except for those in China) lie in a broad steppe and mountain region stretching from North Africa across the Arabian peninsula and the Iranian plateau to the northwest section of the Indian subcontinent. Within this region is found the Fertile Crescent, a narrow band of fertile land connecting the Persian Gulf with the eastern Mediterranean coast. Domination of the Fertile Crescent was contested by tribes which represented two of the great language families of mankind—the Indo-European-speaking peoples (Aryans), and the Semitic-speaking peoples (Semites). Emigrants from the region of the Black and Caspian seas brought Indo-European tongues to the Fertile Crescent, while Semitic languages were spoken by natives of southwestern Asia. A third, much smaller, language family was the Hamitic, to which the tongues of the Egyptians and other peoples of northeastern Africa belonged. Let us now trace the course of civilization among these language groups.

Authorities do not all agree about the definition of "civilization." Many scholars believe, however, that one of its prerequisites must be the use of writing. Another prerequisite, in their view, is the development of a culture to the point where its communities deserve the term "cities"—that is, are capable of sustaining a considerable number of specialists to cope with the religious, political, and economic needs of a society. If we accept the view that both the invention of writing and the advent of the city distinguish the emergence of civilization, the people of Sumer deserve the credit for having created the first civilization in world history.

MESOPOTAMIA: THE FIRST CIVILIZATION

Emergence of the first civilization in Sumer. The lower reaches of the land enclosed by the Tigris and Euphrates rivers—in what is now Iraq—were known in ancient days both as Babylonia and Mesopotamia (from the Greek, meaning "between rivers"). The delta of this river system was in turn called Sumer. Its rich soil was admirably suited for raising dates, as well as both summer and winter crops of grain. Broken by river channels teeming with fish and refertilized every year by alluvial silt, the delta had a splendid agricultural potential—but one which could be developed only by large-scale cooperative efforts. "Arable land had literally to be created out of a chaos of swamps and sandbanks by a 'separation' of land from water; the swamps . . . drained; the floods controlled; and lifegiving waters led to the rainless desert by artificial canals."[2] Provided these steps were taken, the fertile soil could produce more than a hundred times the amount of grain sown. In this way, food surpluses could be accumulated, making possible a diversified economy that would include tradesmen and potters and other craftsmen who did not farm. On the other hand, the plain had no stone for building or for making tools and no timber except that available from its palm trees.

The early inhabitants of Sumer, who may have migrated from highlands east of the Tigris, brought with them the knowledge of how to use copper for tools and weapons. During the fourth millennium, unprecedented advances in Sumer influenced the development of other riverine cultures. Evidence indicates that certain technical inventions eventually made their way to both the Nile and the Indus valleys. Chief among these were the wheeled vehicle and the potter's wheel. The discovery in Egypt of cylinder seals similar in shape to those used in Sumer attests to contact between the two areas toward the end of the fourth millennium B.C. Sumer appears also to have exerted considerable in-

The weight of the material above the opening pushes down on the arch.

THE ARCH

Because the large stones necessary for one-piece lintels were not available in Sumer as they were in Egypt, the Sumerians used mud bricks to form arches. Instead of supporting the direct down-thrust of weight as in post and lintel construction, the wedge-shaped bricks pressing against each other transferred the weight outward and down to the ground.

fluence on Egyptian architecture and writing. The monumental brick temples that were erected in Sumer influenced the construction of houses and palaces in early Egypt. For their temples and tombs the Egyptians used stone.

There is a strong possibility that the Mesopotamian and Egyptian systems of writing are related, although more probably the Egyptians were merely stimulated by example to develop a script of their own. Whereas the script of the people of Sumer evolved in the direction of abstract symbols, the Egyptian script retained its pictorial images. Here is an example of how cultures during their most formative stages may influence one another and yet continue to develop unique features which stamp them as distinctive civilizations.

Life in Sumerian city-states. Around 3000 B.C. a number of independent city-states evolved in Sumer. These resembled the city-states of later times in Greece and Renaissance Italy in that they were independent and would not recognize outside authority. The most prosperous period of the Sumerian city-states lasted from about 2900 to 2400 B.C. The history of this period in Sumer,

however, is chiefly a chronicle of continual rivalry and fighting among the city-states. In the long run the inability of the Sumerians to unite proved their undoing.

The Sumerian city-state was a theocracy, for the local god was believed to be the real sovereign. His earthly representative was the *ensi*, the high priest and city governor, who acted as the god's steward in both religious and secular functions. Though endowed with divine rights by virtue of being the human agents of the gods, the *ensis* were not considered divine themselves.

Like life on a medieval manor, early Sumerian society was highly collectivized, with the temples of the city god and subordinate deities assuming the central role. "Each temple owned lands which formed the estate of its divine owners. Each citizen belonged to one of the temples, and the whole of a temple community—the officials and priests, herdsmen and fishermen, gardeners, craftsmen, stonecutters, merchants, and even slaves—was referred to as 'the people of the god X.' "[3] That part of the temple land called "common" was worked by all members of the community, while the remaining land was divided among the citizens for their support at a rental of from one third to one sixth of the crop.

How would the ancient Sumerian city of Erech have looked to an approaching visitor? Dominating the flat countryside would be the great ziggurat, or temple, a lofty, terraced tower, built in the shape of a pyramid and crowned by a sanctuary, or "high place." For the people of Erech, this was the "holy of holies," sacred to the local god. Leaving the farmers in the fields and the river fishermen who resided with them in nearby towns, the visitor would see, upon entering the city, the merchants, potters and basketmakers, and local officials engaged in their specialized tasks. At the temple, the traveler would find great storerooms for grain, and priests allotting fields for cultivation, supplying seeds, draft animals, and tools, and arranging for trade with other cities or foreign lands. Scribes would be at work inscribing thin tablets of clay with picture signs. Some tablets might bear the impressions of cylinder seals, small stone cylinders engraved with a design (see picture, p. 19). The scribes would be using a system of counting based on the unit 60, still used over five thousand years later in our modern world in computing divisions of time and angles. Examining the clay tablets, the visitor would find that they were memoranda used in administering the temple, which was at once the warehouse and workshop of the entire community. Some of the scribes might be making an inventory of the goats and sheep received that day to be sacrificed as part of the temple's ritual; others might be drawing up wage lists.

Sumerian writing. Writing in Sumeria originated through the use of picturelike signs to designate objects (pictographs); the second step was the representation of ideas (ideographs). The third advance was the use of signs to represent the sounds of syllables—the stage called syllabic, or phonetic, writing. By giving the signs a phonetic value, the Sumerians could spell out names and compound words instead of inventing new signs. The use of syllabic signs reduced the total number of signs from two thousand to some six hundred by 2900 B.C.

In writing, a scribe used a square-tipped reed to make impressions in soft clay tablets. The impressions took on a wedge shape, hence the term "cuneiform" (from the Latin *cuneus*, meaning "wedge"). The cuneiform system of writing was adopted by many other peoples of the Near East, including the Hittites, Babylonians, and Persians, and it stayed in use until the Phoenician alphabet superseded it shortly before Christ's birth.

Akkadian dominance. North of Sumer lay the narrow region of Akkad, inhabited by a Semitic-speaking people, who had absorbed Sumerian culture. In the twenty-fourth century B.C., Sargon, a strong ruler of Akkad, conquered Sumer and established the first empire in history. In addition to Sumer and Akkad, his empire extended "from the lower sea to the upper sea" (the Persian Gulf to the Mediterranean Sea), according to Sargon's inscriptions.

Like some of the later Sumerian rulers of the previous period, Sargon was a *lugal* (great man), a purely secular ruler in contrast to the priestly *ensis* he removed from power. This development in ancient Mesopotamia represents an early step in the secularization of society, a recurrent theme in the history of civilization. The Sumerian *lugals* had seized power during crises brought on by wars and the breakdown of the collectivistic temple economy. Like the later Greek tyrant, the *lugal* was a usurper who rode to power on a wave of popular discontent. For example, we are told that at Lagash a generation before Sargon's time, "when Urukagina had received the lugalship . . . he removed from the inhabitants of Lagash usury, forestalling, famine, robbery, attacks; he established their freedom . . . [and] protected the widow and the orphan from the powerful man."[4]

Very proud of his lower-class origins, Sargon boasted that his humble, unwed mother had been forced to abandon him: "She set me in a basket of rushes . . . [and] cast me into the river."[5] Rescued and brought up by a gardener, Sargon rose to power through the army. As *lugal*, Sargon looked after the welfare of the lower classes, distributing part of the temple lands among them. In addition, he aided the rising class of private merchants. At their request he once sent his army to far-off Asia Minor to protect a colony of merchants from interference by a local ruler. We are told that Sargon "did not sleep" in his efforts to promote prosperity; trade moved as freely "as the Tigris where it flows into the sea," with the result that "on the quay where the ships are moored there is brisk activity; all lands lie in peace, their inhabitants prosperous and contented."[6]

Despite these innovations the successors of Sargon were unable either to withstand the attacks of foreign invaders or to overcome the deep-rooted isolationism of the Sumerian cities. As a result, the house of Sargon collapsed about 2180 B.C.

Sumerian revival. Order and prosperity were restored half a century later by the *lugals* of the Third Dynasty of Ur (*c.* 2125-

This life-sized head of Hammurabi, the Babylonian king and lawgiver, was carved during his reign. The stylization of beard and eyebrows and the regularity of features of the face are part of the artistic conventions of the time.

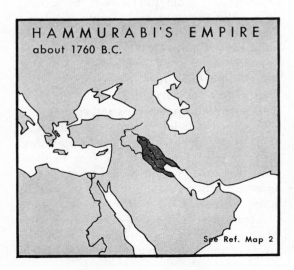

HAMMURABI'S EMPIRE
about 1760 B.C.

See Ref. Map 2

2025 B.C.). By creating a unified Sumerian state, these rulers solved the problem of internal rebellion. The temple-cities became provinces administered by governors who were watched closely by a corps of "messengers." The "church" became an arm of the state; the high priests were state appointees, and although temple property was secularized, the temple economic organization was retained and used as the state's agent in rigidly controlling the economy.

At the head of this bureaucratic state stood the now-deified ruler, celebrated in hymns as a heaven-sent messiah who "brings splendor to the land . . . savior of orphans whose misery he relieves . . . the vigilant shepherd who conducts the people unto cooling shade."[7] Much of what we now call social legislation was passed by these "vigilant shepherds." Such laws were called "rightings" (Sumerian *nig-si-sa*, usually translated "equity"), since their object was the righting of existing wrongs. The prologue to the law code of Ur-Nammu, founder of the dynasty, declared that it was the king's purpose to see that "the orphan did not fall a prey to the powerful" and that "the man of one shekel did not fall a prey to the man of one mina (sixty shekels)."[8]

Disaster struck Ur about 2025 B.C. when wandering barbarian hordes destroyed the city. For more than two centuries, disunity and frequent warfare again characterized Mesopotamian history. Political instability was accompanied by depression, inflated prices, and acute hardship for the lower classes. Merchants, however, utilized the absence of state controls to emerge as fullfledged capitalists who amassed great wealth and invested their capital in banking operations and in land. (The Akkadian word for capital, *qaqqadum*, meaning "head," influenced later peoples; our word *capital* is derived from the Latin form, *caput*.[9]) The stronger local rulers of the period freed the poor from debt slavery and issued a variety of social laws which are best illustrated by the similar legislation of Hammurabi, who finally brought an end to this troubled period.

To the right is a Babylonian cylinder seal and to the left an impression taken from it. Some authorities believe that the seal shows King Gilgamesh and his friend Enkidu (a creature half bull and half man) fighting a water buffalo and a lion.

Hammurabi and the Babylonian empire. Semitic-speaking Amorites from Syria, under the rule of their capable king, Hammurabi, finally brought all of lower Mesopotamia under one rule by 1760 B.C. Hammurabi's empire had its capital in Babylon, previously an obscure village on the Euphrates. From this time on, the Sumerians never again figured politically in history, but their culture persisted as the foundation for all subsequent civilizations in the Tigris-Euphrates valley.

Hammurabi is best known for his law code, which contained nearly three hundred laws touching on economic, social, and moral life. As stated in the prologue, Hammurabi's objective was "to cause justice to prevail in the land, to destroy the wicked and the evil, to prevent the strong from oppressing the weak . . . and to further the welfare of the people."[10]

Hammurabi's legislation reëstablished a state-controlled economy in which merchants were required to obtain a "royal permit," interest was limited to 20 per cent, and prices were set for basic commodities and fees charged by physicians, veterinarians, and builders. Minimum wages were also set and debt slavery was limited to three years.

In family life various provisions protected wives and children, although a wife who has "set her face to go out and play the part of a fool, neglect her house, belittle her husband"[11] could be divorced without alimony. Or the husband could take another wife and compel the first to remain as a servant. Punishments were graded in their severity; the higher the culprit in the social scale, the more severe the penalty.

In the epilogue to the code, Hammurabi eloquently summed up his efforts to provide social justice for his people:

Let any oppressed man, who has a cause, come before my image as king of righteousness! Let him read the inscription on my monument! Let him give heed to my weighty words! And may my monument enlighten him as to his cause and may he understand his case! May he set his heart at ease! (and he will exclaim): "Hammurabi indeed is a ruler who is like a real father to his people. . . ."[12]

Mathematics and astronomy. Like the Sumerians before them, the Babylonians used a system of counting based on a unit of 60. The tablets recovered from Babylonia contain tables for multiplication and division and for square and cube roots. In addition to solving linear and quadratic equations, the Babylonian mathematicians worked geometry problems to determine the areas of circles and polygons. They were also the

In this wall painting from an Egyptian tomb, a laborer bends over a plow which is drawn by two yoked cows. Above, a man breaks up the soil, and another cuts down a tree with an ax.

first to employ a sign for zero and to give numbers a definite value according to their position. In writing 505, for example, the first 5 represented hundreds, the last 5 units, and for the zero they used a sign that meant "not." "That 'not' corresponds approximately to our 'naught,' which in itself is the same as the zero."[13]

The necessity in an agricultural society of charting and recording the seasons explains in large part the early development of calendars in both the Tigris-Euphrates and Nile basins. A lunar calendar of twelve months was adopted, each month beginning when a new moon appeared. The resulting discrepancy between the cycles of the moon and the agricultural seasons of the solar year was met by the addition of an extra month to the Mesopotamian year when the necessity arose.

Babylonian literature. The Babylonians borrowed many stories and legends from Sumerian literature. The longest and the most famous narrative in Babylonian literature was *Gilgamesh*. The hero of the epic, Gilgamesh, was supposedly a king of ancient Erech who sought to gain the secret of immortality. In the account of his travels, a famous tale borrowed from the Sumerians

appears—the story of the flood. The remarkable resemblances between the Babylonian version and the Old Testament account can be seen in these lines from *Gilgamesh*:

Whatever I [had] of gold I loaded aboard her;
Whatever I had of the seed of all living creatures [I loaded] aboard her.
After I had caused all my family and relations to go up into the ship,
I caused the game of the field, the beasts of the field, [and] all the craftsmen to go [into it] . . .
I entered the ship and closed my door . . .
I sent forth a dove and let [her] go.
The dove went away and came back to me;
There was no resting-place, and so she returned . . .
[Then] I sent forth a raven and let [her] go.
The raven went away, and when she saw that the waters had abated,
She ate, she flew about, she cawed, [and] did not return.[14]

Fall of the Babylonian empire. The pattern of disunity and struggle, all too familiar in Mesopotamia, reasserted itself following Hammurabi's death. Also, mountaineers from the east and north raided the Babylonian cities. Among these invaders were the Hittites, an Indo-European people from Asia Minor. Shortly after 1600 B.C. the Hittites pushed down the Euphrates and attacked Babylon. The capital fell, carrying with it the empire founded by Hammurabi's dynasty. But the Hittite intruders did not entirely erase the rich cultural legacy created by the Sumerians and the Babylonians, and a later empire arose with Babylon as its capital (see p. 32). Meanwhile, in a neighboring river valley, another civilization had emerged.

EGYPT: GIFT OF THE NILE

Neolithic developments along the Nile. In Paleolithic times most of North Africa was covered with vegetation. A decrease in rainfall forced men to search for food in the Nile valley, which up to the second millennium was covered with marshes. There, papyrus and rushes grew to heights taller than a man, and animal life abounded.

The valley was dominated by the Nile River, which rises and falls with unusual precision. The rise begins early in July and continues until the banks are overrun, reaching its crest in September. By the end of October the river is once more contained within its banks. Vegetation thrives in the moist, fertile soil, and crops are harvested in April or early May.

By the fifth millennium, Neolithic peoples were cultivating wheat and barley on the Nile's flood plain. Proficient in carving and in working flint, these people also made small tools and pins out of copper, although they did not know how to cast it or how to make bronze. (Egypt did not acquire a bronze metallurgy until about 2000 B.C.) The copper ore was imported as were lead, lapis lazuli,

and silver—evidence of substantial trade with western Asia.

The entire period up to the unification of Egypt under one ruler in 3100 B.C. is known as the Predynastic period. The political units in existence were nomes, each of which was a small independent principality.

The Old Kingdom (3100-2270 B.C.). About 3100 B.C., Menes, a dynamic leader, united Egypt and established a single capital city. This event marks the beginning of the Dynastic period.

The first six dynasties constitute the period known as the Old Kingdom. It was at the beginning of the First Dynasty that the Egyptians began to develop a system of writing. Cities were neither as large nor as important in Egypt as in Mesopotamia, but in

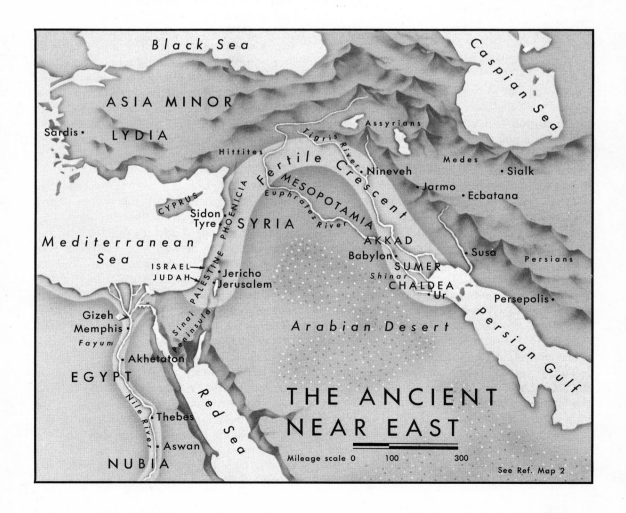

THE ANCIENT NEAR EAST

Mileage scale 0   100   300

See Ref. Map 2

Shown above is the great Sphinx at Gizeh and Pharaoh Khafre's pyramid, second largest of all the pyramids (originally 471 feet high). To build these structures, stone blocks were excavated from quarries across the Nile, floated on rafts when the valley was flooded, and then dragged up brick ramps. The Sphinx, now marred by vandalism and flying sand, once had a pharaoh's face, perhaps Khafre's; the body is that of a lion.

the transition to civilization in Egypt, most other economic and social developments were roughly comparable to those occurring in Sumer during the fourth millennium. During the Old Kingdom a number of capable pharaohs encouraged economic growth and the expansion of trade. Boats were dispatched to Lebanon for timber, and mining expeditions obtained copper from the nearby Sinai peninsula.

Egyptian government was theocratic—that is, the pharaoh combined religious and political functions. He was both an earthly king and a god, the chief priest of the land and the spiritual representative of the nation in all its important religious rites.

The Egyptian belief that the pharaoh was the son of the sun god and would return to the heavens after death led to the practice of mummification and to the building of large tombs for the rulers. The Egyptians further believed that the pharaoh could not live after death unless two conditions were met: his soul had to be nourished by offerings of food

and his body preserved from disturbance and natural decay. The art of mummification was carried on by skilled craftsmen, headed by a chief embalmer holding priestly rank. During the Old Kingdom the nobles and pharaohs sought to protect their remains by providing permanent tombs, the most spectacular of which were the royal pyramids. These were located near Memphis, a city at the head of the Nile delta which was the capital during most of the Old Kingdom period.

Toward the end of the Sixth Dynasty the authority of the pharaohs was undermined by the growing power and wealth of the nobility and the priesthood. The nomes became virtually autonomous, and for some two centuries, known as the First Intermediate Period (2270-2060 B.C.), dynasties rose and fell quickly, leaving chaos behind.

The Middle Kingdom (2060-1785 B.C.). Egypt was rescued from its political anarchy by a prince from the south, who reunited the country and established his capital at Thebes. The nobility remained powerful and paid only nominal tribute to the pharaoh. With the accession of the Twelfth Dynasty, however, vigorous rulers regained the power and splendor enjoyed by the pharaohs in the Old Kingdom.

Deriving their main support from the lower classes, the pharaohs of this dynasty promoted the welfare of the downtrodden. One of them claimed: "I gave to the destitute and brought up the orphan. I caused him who was nothing to reach (his goal), like him who was (somebody)."[15] No longer was the nation's wealth expended on pyramids, but on public works. The largest of these, an irrigation project, resulted in the reclamation of 27,000 acres of arable land. Finally, a concession that has been called "the democratization of the hereafter" gave the members of the lower classes the right to have their bodies mummified after death. Now all men, not just the pharaoh and the nobles, could achieve immortality for their souls.

The prosperous Twelfth Dynasty was succeeded by a less competent one, which lost control of the country. Once more Egypt was racked by civil war as provincial governors fought for the pharaoh's throne. During the last century of this Second Intermediate Period (1785-1580 B.C.), the Hyksos, a mixed but preponderantly Semitic people, easily conquered the weakened Egyptians. It is thought that soon thereafter Joseph and his brothers entered Egypt, since it is "probable that the Hebrews would find a friendly reception in Egypt at a time when the country was under rulers who themselves were of Semitic descent."[16]

The Empire or New Kingdom (1580-1085 B.C.). During the period of Hyksos control, some native Egyptian princes had retained southern Egypt. Eventually these rulers expelled the Hyksos and reunited the country to establish the New Kingdom, or Empire. This last great era in dynastic Egypt centers around the exploits of the pharaohs of the Eighteenth Dynasty.

The pharaohs of the Empire enforced their absolute rule with standing armies equipped with horses and war chariots, both of which had been introduced into Egypt by the Hyksos. The threat of the provincial governors was removed by replacing them with royal appointees. Thutmose III (*c.* 1501-1447 B.C.), the "Napoleon of Egypt," conquered Syria, Phoenicia, and Palestine. Nubia and northern Sudan were also brought under his sway. In order to ensure closer ties and more uniform administration within the Empire, Thutmose III educated Near Eastern princes in Egypt. Obelisks, tall and pointed stone columns, were erected to commemorate his memorable reign; the four remaining ones have been transported out of Egypt to adorn the cities of Istanbul, Rome, London, and New York.

Under Amenhotep III (*c.* 1411-1375 B.C.) the Empire reached a dazzling height. Tribute flowed in from conquered lands; and Thebes, the imperial capital, became the most magnificent city in the world. Many statues of Amenhotep III and a number of monuments survive, including the temple of Luxor, on the walls of which is depicted the account of this pharaoh's divine birth as the son of the supreme god Amon-Re.

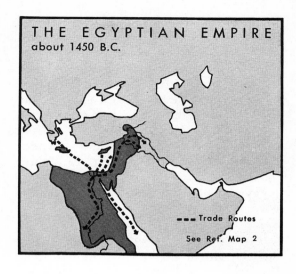

THE EGYPTIAN EMPIRE about 1450 B.C.

--- Trade Routes

See Ref. Map 2

During the reign of the succeeding pharaoh, Amenhotep IV (*c.* 1375-1358 B.C.), however, the Empire began to decline. Early in his reign he adopted as his religion the worship of Aton (whose symbol was the sun's disk) in the place of Amon-Re. The pharaoh changed his name to Akhenaton ("He who is devoted to Aton"), left Amon-Re's city to found a new capital (Akhetaton), and passed the rest of his life in worshiping Aton and in composing hymns and prayers (see p. 27). Akhenaton neglected his kingdom, and Egypt's Asiatic provinces gradually collapsed, despite urgent appeals for assistance from his harassed officials. At home the wealthy priests of Amon-Re encouraged dissension. Upon his death his new capital city was deserted, and the priests of Amon-Re regained their former dominance.

The Egyptians soon sought to regain their power in Palestine and Syria, where they came in conflict with the Hittites (see p. 28). Ramses II (1292-1225 B.C.) of the Nineteenth Dynasty, pharaoh of the Hebrew oppression and Exodus, was partially successful in restoring the glory of the Empire, but it was Egypt's last display of national vigor. Thereafter, the royal authority gradually declined as the power of the priests of Amon-Re rose.

Period of Decadence (1085-332 B.C.). During the Period of Decadence, the priesthood at Thebes became so strong that the high priest was able to found his own dynasty. Egypt ceased to be a factor in international affairs, except as the object of foreign conquest. Ethiopian domination was followed by Assyrian (671-651 B.C.). Egypt passed under Persian rule in 525 B.C.; and two hundred years later this ancient land came within the domain of Alexander the Great. Greek rule marked the end of the thirty Egyptian dynasties which had existed for nearly three thousand years.

Egyptian economy and society. While the governmental system in Egypt was an extreme absolutism, the economy has been called "theocratic socialism." In theory, the pharaoh owned all the land, decided when the fields should be sown, controlled the irrigation system, and received the surplus from the crops produced by the laborers who toiled on the huge royal estates. A complex but efficient administrative system supported the centralized absolutism of the pharaoh.

In Egyptian society, three main social divisions existed: (1) the upper class, including the priests, the court nobility, and the landed aristocracy; (2) the middle class, composed of merchants and craftsmen; and (3) the lower class, made up of laborers. The stratification was not rigid, and people of merit could elevate themselves into a higher social rank.

In the days of the Empire, Egypt proper, not including the subject peoples, had a population of about seven million. The great bulk of the people were semislaves, who were subject to forced labor—working on the roads, tilling the royal fields, or hauling huge stones for temples, pyramids, and obelisks. The laborers lived in squalid villages made up of small mud and thatch houses with only a few crude jars, boxes, and stools as furnishings. The merchants and skilled craftsmen of the middle class had more comfortable and pretentious dwellings, and the homes of the nobility were palatial, with luxurious furnishings and beautiful gardens.

Largely because all landed property descended from mother to daughter, the status of Egyptian women was exceptionally favorable. Upon the death of his wife a husband lost the use of the property, which was then inherited by the daughter and her husband. Brother and sister marriages often took place within Egyptian ruling families to ensure the right of succession to the throne, which was always through the female line.

Although agriculture remained the basic economic activity, industry and trade developed rapidly after the early days of the Old Kingdom. Because of the Nile and the proximity to the Mediterranean and Red seas, most of Egypt's trade was carried on by ships. International trade reached its height at the time of the Empire, when Egypt controlled the trade routes of the Near East. Imperial commerce traveled along four main routes: the Nile River; the Red Sea, which was connected by a canal to the Nile delta; a caravan route to Mesopotamia and southern Syria; and the Mediterranean Sea, connecting northern Syria, Greece, and Crete and other islands with the delta of the Nile. Egyptian products such as wheat, linens, gold wares, and scarabs used as charms were exchanged for ostrich feathers, metal weapons, spices, tapestries, woods, gold, and silver.

Mathematics and science. The Egyptians, who could cope only with very simple algebra problems, were much less skilled in mathematical theory than the Mesopotamians. On the other hand, the Egyptians had a considerable knowledge of practical geometry. The obliteration of field boundaries by the annual flooding of the Nile made land measurement a necessity. Similarly, a knowledge of geometry was essential in computing the dimensions of ramps for raising stones during the construction of pyramids. In these and other engineering projects—the building of dams and irrigation systems, the erection of heavy obelisks, the construction of walls and ceilings of temples—the Egyptians were superior to their Mesopotamian contemporaries, and the practical bent of their learning is evident. They also had considerable knowledge of chemistry, of the healing properties of herbs, and of anatomy.

Like the Mesopotamians, the Predynastic Egyptians devised a lunar calendar of twelve months with thirty days in each month; this

Osiris sits in judgment as the dog-headed god, Anubis, weighs the heart of a lady temple musician against a feather. Isis stands behind the musician. The scene was inscribed on papyrus and buried with the mummy of the woman.

calendar, of course, fell short of a year's actual length. Around the beginning of the Old Kingdom a more accurate calendar was invented, based on a different principle and directly attributable to the Nile's importance in the agricultural economy. Egyptians observed that the reappearance of the bright star Sirius at the dawn of the summer solstice closely corresponded with the Nile's annual flooding. Having worked out the average interval between the appearances of the star, they retained the twelve thirty-day months of the old lunar calendar but added five extra days to bring the total number of days in the year to 365. (This calendar year was six hours short of the solar year; the error was corrected in Roman times when Julius Caesar added an extra day every four years.)

Egyptian religion. As in most other ancient societies, religion saturated Egyptian life and influenced every aspect of its culture. "The kings of Egypt were gods; its pyramids were an 'act of faith'; its art was rooted in religious symbolism; its literature began as religious decoration of tombs, temples, and pyramids; its science centered in the temple; its gods were conceived to be in intimate touch with men and alive as men; a vast part of its wealth and energy was spent in the effort to secure the continuance of the physical life after death."[17]

Early Egyptian religion had no strong ethical character, but gradually the idea was developed that eternal life was a reward for those who had been good and just while alive. During the Middle Kingdom the cult of Osiris combined the new emphasis on moral conduct with a way to escape death and became very popular. According to an ancient myth, Osiris was the god of the Nile, and the rise and fall of the river symbolized his death and resurrection. The myth recounted that Osiris had been murdered by Seth, his evil brother, who cut the victim's body into many pieces. Isis, the bereaved widow, collected all the pieces and put them together. In this way Osiris was resurrected and became immortal. Osiris was thus the first mummy, and every mummified Egyptian was a second Osiris.

But only a soul free of sin would be permitted to live forever in the Happy Field of Food. At the time of soul testing, Osiris weighed the candidate's heart against the feather of truth. If the ordeal was not passed, a horrible creature devoured the rejected heart. During the Empire the priesthood of Osiris became corrupt and claimed that it alone knew clever methods of surviving the soul testing. Charms and magical prayers and formulas were sold to the living as insurance policies guaranteeing them a happy

This bust of Akhenaton reveals the freedom given to the artists of his reign to stress the individuality of their ruler, even to the point of exaggerating his physical characteristics. The symbol on the front of the headdress represents the Sacred Serpent (the cobra), symbol of royalty.

immortality after death. They constitute collectively what is known as the Book of the Dead, which was placed in the tomb.

Akhenaton's religious reformation was directed against both the venal priesthood of Osiris and the wealthy and powerful priesthood of the supreme god Amon-Re. As we have seen (p. 23), Akhenaton failed to replace Amon-Re and the multiplicity of lesser gods with a single cosmic force (Aton, symbolized by the sun's disk); his monotheism was too cold and intellectual to attract the masses with their yearning for a blessed hereafter. He succeeded only in arousing factionalism among his subjects, and his successors returned to the worship of the many traditional deities.

Monumentalism in architecture. The most impressive and enduring types of Egyptian architecture were the tombs and the temples. From the beginning of the Old Kingdom, which was the heyday of pyramid building, the pharaohs sought to protect their bodies by erecting enormous stone tombs. It was the pharaoh Khufu who built a great pyramid covering a base of thirteen acres, rising 481 feet into the air, and requiring more than two million limestone blocks, each weighing about two and a half tons. This stupendous monument was built without mortar, yet some of the stones were so perfectly fitted that a knife cannot be inserted in the joint. The pyramids are a striking expression of Egyptian civilization. In their dignity, massiveness, and repose, they reflect the religion-motivated character of Egyptian society.

As the achievement of the Old Kingdom can be seen in its pyramids, the glory of the Empire survives in the temples at Thebes. On the east side of the Nile stand the ruins of the magnificent temples of Karnak and Luxor. The temple of Karnak contained a huge colonnaded hall, divided into three aisles with a much higher roof above the center aisle. This technique, which permitted the walls supporting the high center roof to be pierced with windows, was later used in the Roman basilica and the Gothic cathedral.

Sculpture and painting. Like its architecture, Egypt's sculpture was simple and formal. Imposing figures banked the entrances to tombs and temples, and low reliefs decorated the walls. The sculptors of the Old Kingdom simplified and standardized the bodies, individualizing only the face. The human figure is always shown looking directly ahead (see illustration, p. 27), with a rigidity very much in keeping with the austere architectural settings of the statues. So that they would not be dwarfed by their massive backdrops, many of the statues were made colossal in size. The Egyptians customarily represented the gods in statuary by placing an animal's head on a human body. The Sphinx (see illustration, p. 22) is an exception to this rule; its purpose apparently was to symbolize the power of a king, whose likeness was imposed on the body of an animal.

During the rule of the "heretic" pharaoh Akhenaton, an unprecedented naturalism was introduced. Akhenaton and his beautiful queen, Nefertiti, were portrayed realistically by sculptors, who depicted even the ungainly paunch of the pharaoh and showed the couple in happy but far from godlike family scenes. By and large, Akhenaton's death inaugurated a return to traditional religious and esthetic conventions.

Painting in Egypt was used to decorate the walls of tombs and palaces. No attempt was made to show objects in perspective, and the scenes give an appearance of flatness. The effect of distance was conveyed by making objects overlap in a series or by putting one object above another. Another convention employed was to depict everything from its most characteristic angle. Often the head, arms, and legs were shown in side view and the eye, shoulders, and chest in front view. To emphasize his importance, the ruler or god was shown larger than the other figures. Certain colors—rich reds and yellows with black and blue-green for contrast—were generally used in all paintings.

Writing and literature. In Egypt, as in Sumer, writing began with pictures. But unlike the Mesopotamian signs, the Egyptian hieroglyphs ("sacred signs") remained primarily pictorial throughout the span of this great civilization. One reason lay in the fact that it was much easier for Egyptian scribes to draw on papyrus than it had been for the Sumerians to incise their clay tablets. At first the hieroglyphs represented only objects, but later they came to stand for ideas and sounds. About 3000 B.C. the Egyptians were using specific characters for certain vowels and consonants, although they never developed a purely alphabetical system of writing.

The oldest literature in Egypt consists of the Pyramid Texts, a group of religious hymns and prayers sculptured on the walls of the burial chambers in the pyramids of the Fifth and Sixth Dynasties of the Old Kingdom. During the Middle Kingdom, literature became more secular and varied; this is shown especially in the collections of folk tales and proverbs.

The temple of Luxor, built by Amenhotep III, was altered by later pharaohs, especially Ramses II (1292-1225 B.C.). In the court of Ramses II (above), notice the reliefs on the columns and the stylized rigidity of the colossal statues of the ruler.

The most beautiful surviving piece of Egyptian literature is Akhenaton's *Hymn to the Sun*. A few lines indicate its poetic beauty and its conception of one all-powerful and beneficent Creator.

Thy dawning is beautiful in the horizon of the sky,
O living Aton, beginning of life!
When thou risest in the eastern horizon,
Thou fillest every land with thy beauty.
Thou art beautiful, great, glittering, high above every land,
Thy rays, they encompass the lands, even all that thou hast made.
How manifold are thy works!
They are hidden from before us,
O sole god, whose powers no other possesseth.
Thou didst create the earth according to thy heart
While thou wast alone.[18]

The Rosetta Stone, discovered in Egypt in 1799 by an officer in Napoleon's army, supplied the means by which Jean Champollion was able in 1822 to decipher Egyptian writing. On the stone a decree is inscribed in three different languages, as is shown by the section reproduced here. The bottom layer of writing is Greek, which Champollion could read. Working from the Greek he was able to figure out the other inscriptions. The middle layer is Egyptian demotic, a simplification of the more formal system of hieroglyphic writing above it.

THE HITTITE EMPIRE
about 1300 B.C.

See Ref. Map 2

THE HITTITES

The Hittite empire. About the time of the Hyksos' rule over Egypt, an Indo-European people, the Hittites, began forging a powerful empire in central Asia Minor. Arriving by an unknown route and at an unknown time, the Hittites conquered the indigenous peoples and, in the centuries following 2000 B.C., rapidly extended their influence.

Late in the seventeenth century B.C. the Hittite armies began to drive to the east and south. One of the kings, Mursilish I (c. 1620-1590 B.C.) conquered north Syria and then pushed down the Euphrates valley, destroying the Babylonian empire (see p. 20). Internal troubles, however, reduced the Hittite kingdom to virtual anarchy, and during this time the pharaoh Thutmose III captured Syria. A new era began in the thirteenth century, when energetic Hittite kings created an empire which again included Syria, lost by the Egyptian pharaoh Akhenaton. Pharaoh Ramses II moved north from Palestine in a heroic but vain attempt to reconquer Syria. Ambushed and forced back to Palestine after a bloody battle, Ramses in 1269 B.C agreed to a treaty of peace. Much like a modern agreement this treaty guaranteed nonaggression, mutual aid against outside attack, and extradition of political fugitives.

The Hittite empire was destined to crumble quickly, however. By 1200 B.C. various other Indo-European peoples settled in Asia Minor and conquered the Hittites.

Hittite civilization. The Hittite state was militaristic in character. At the head of the state was the king, supreme in military and religious affairs, while the principal state offices were occupied by his relatives. As his vassals, the nobles held large estates from the king and in return provided weapons and men for war. The masses worked the land as peasants, and the towns were populated by numerous craftsmen, including potters, weavers, smiths, and leatherworkers. The Hittites are credited with being the first people to work iron.

The Hittites adopted the Babylonian cuneiform script; and their literature, art, and religion were clearly under Mesopotamian influence. While their law code shows some similarity to the code of Hammurabi, it differs in prescribing more humane punishments. Instead of retaliation ("an eye for an eye"), the Hittite code makes greater use of restitution and compensation.

The chief importance of Hittite culture lies in the legacy it left to the peoples of Asia Minor, including the Greeks who later settled along its western coast. In this way some aspects of Mesopotamian culture were transmitted to the West (see Chapter 2).

While the Hittite empire was at its height, droves of Semitic-speaking nomads, including the Phoenicians and the Hebrews, filtered west toward Syria and Palestine. Following the Hittite collapse in 1200 B.C., no one nation was powerful enough to enforce its domination on the peoples of the Fertile Crescent. A number of small states flourished independently for nearly five hundred years.

THE ERA OF SMALL STATES

The Phoenicians. Taking advantage of their location on the seacoast (see map, p. 21), the Phoenicians concentrated on trade and colonization. Sailing all over the Mediterranean and even venturing through the Strait of Gibraltar and down the west coast of Africa, these intrepid sailors marketed their wares with great success. Trade was fostered by industries in the home ports of Tyre and Sidon. The Phoenicians were skilled manufacturers, and their textiles, glassware, and metal goods were widely distributed. Their purple dye was famous throughout the Mediterranean.

The Phoenicians founded a host of colonies around the shores of the Mediterranean, the greatest of which was Carthage, a city destined to be destroyed centuries later by the Romans in the Punic Wars. Unlike other contemporary nations, the Phoenicians did not attempt to unite their cities politically or to extend their holdings by conquest.

The inhabitants of Phoenicia made their most important contribution to learning by the perfection of the alphabet. The origin of the alphabet is still a moot question. Perhaps between 1800 and 1600 B.C. certain western Semitic peoples, influenced by Egypt's semi-alphabetical writing, started to evolve a simplified method of writing. Carrying on the experiment, the Phoenicians developed a system made up of individual consonants. Their alphabet consisted of twenty-two consonant symbols, the vowel signs being introduced later by the Greeks. The first two symbols of the Phoenician alphabet were *aleph* and *beth*, which mean "ox" and "house," respectively. Phoenician merchants carried the alphabet to peoples around the Mediterranean, and Syrian traders transported it inland throughout the Near East, where it helped to displace cuneiform.

The Hebrew kingdoms. In war, diplomacy, inventions, and art, the Hebrews made little splash in the stream of history. In ethics and religion, however, their contribution to world civilization was tremendous, even though they were few in number and weak in political power. From this people we have received Judaism, Christianity—the faith that after two thousand years remains dominant in the western world—and the great Judaic-Christian tradition of ethics and morality.

The Hebrews appear to have come originally from the lower Euphrates valley, but for centuries they wandered in search of a homeland. Eventually, they filtered into the land of Canaan, later to be called Palestine. Tucked between the desert and the sea, this small region was only 150 miles long and very narrow, about the size of the state of Vermont. According to tradition, some of the Hebrews were enslaved by the Egyptians, but they were led out of bondage by Moses, who gave his people the Ten Commandments and a new conception of a single tribal deity, Yahweh.

The Hebrews had to contend for Palestine against the Canaanites (a mixed Semitic and Hittite people), who were defeated, and later the Philistines, a warlike people from whom we get the word *Palestine*. Under King David (1000-960 B.C.) the Hebrews subjugated the Philistines and established a promising kingdom. Palestine reached the height of its influence during the reign of David's son, Solomon. In the words of the Old Testament:

And God gave Solomon wisdom and understanding exceeding much, and largeness of heart, even as the sand that *is* on the sea shore. And Solomon's wisdom excelled the wisdom of all the children of the east country, and all the wisdom of Egypt. For he was wiser than all men . . . and his fame was in all nations round about. And he spoke three thousand proverbs; and his songs were a thousand and five. . . . And there came of all people to hear the wisdom of Solomon, from all kings of the earth, which had heard of his wisdom.[19]

Despite his proverbial wisdom, however, Solomon levied such heavy taxes that in time popular discontent split the realm into two kingdoms—Israel in the north and Judah in the south. Thus weakened, the Hebrews were more vulnerable to attack and invasion. In 722 B.C. the Assyrians conquered Israel; and in 586 B.C. Judah fell to Nebuchadnezzar, a Chaldean king, who captured Jerusalem and carried all but the poorest inhabitants into exile. After the Chaldeans had been defeated by the Persians later in the fifth century, the Hebrews were permitted to return to Jerusalem and to restore the temple destroyed by Nebuchadnezzar.

Persian rule was followed by that of the Greeks and the Romans. In the first century A.D. the Jews rebelled against the rule of the Roman emperors. Jerusalem was totally destroyed in the savage fighting that ensued, and much of the population of Palestine was massacred or dispersed. The Jews were driven to all parts of the earth, and *Diaspora,* the "scattering," burdened the Jews for many centuries to come.

The years since the scattering have been filled with sorrow and tragedy for the Jewish people. To the miseries of the medieval ghetto (the city quarter to which Jews were restricted) was added the horror of the pogrom (organized massacre) in early modern times. Recent years witnessed brutal persecution in many lands, especially in Nazi Germany. It is against this background that we should assess the passionate struggle of the Zionists to reëstablish a Jewish homeland in Palestine and the pride of present-day Israel.

Monotheism among the Hebrews. Originally the Hebrew religion was a primitive polytheism, the worship of many gods. Gradually the concept of one tribal god, Yahweh (Jehovah), a stern, warlike deity, developed. After their entrance into Palestine, however, many of the Hebrews adopted not only the more sophisticated and luxurious manner of living of the Canaanites but also their religious customs. This was especially true of the northern Hebrews.

About 750 B.C. a succession of great spiritual leaders, the Prophets, purged Hebrew thought and religion of all corrupting influence. In doing so, they elevated and dignified the concept of Yahweh to the exclusion of other gods, thus establishing a monotheistic religion. Such Prophets as Amos, Isaiah, and Ezekiel taught that God was a loving Father, that He alone was the true God of the universe. In the words of Micah, often cited as containing the essence of higher religion:

He hath showed thee, O man, what *is* good; and what doth the LORD require of thee, but to do justly, and to love mercy, and to walk humbly with thy God?[20]

When the Hebrews returned to Jerusalem to rebuild the temple, the writings of the Law, the Prophets, and the Psalms were collected. Not until Christian times, however, were these and other writings put into one book, the Old Testament. All of us are familiar with the power and beauty of some, at least, of its great passages. As a work of literature it remains unsurpassed; but it is more than that. "It is Israel's life story—a story that cannot be told adequately apart from the conviction that God had called this people in his grace, separated them from the nations for a special responsibility, and commissioned them with the task of being his servant in the accomplishment of his purpose."[21]

LATER EMPIRES OF

WESTERN ASIA

Assyrian expansion. By 700 B.C. the era of small states was practically at an end. For two hundred years the Assyrians had been bidding for control of the Near East. In 910 B.C. they had seized Babylon, a generation later they marched to the Mediterranean, in 722 B.C. they conquered Israel, and by 671 B.C. they were the masters of Egypt.

Racially the Assyrians were a mixed stock, predominantly Semitic. Reared in the invigorating climate of a mountainous region and schooled for a thousand years by constant war, the Assyrians, mostly peasants, became formidable soldiers. The secret of Assyria's creation of an empire was threefold: a matchless, well-equipped army, the terrorization of all people who resisted Assyrian rule, and the most advanced system of political administration developed up to that time.

The Assyrian empire existed by and for its army, which was the most highly trained and efficient of its day. Assyrian soldiers were the first to be outfitted with iron weapons. The bow, with vicious iron-tipped arrows, was their principal weapon. After a stream of well-directed arrows had weakened the enemy, the Assyrian heavy cavalry and chariots smashed the ranks of their foes with relentless fury. All the ancient world dreaded these fighters who, in Byron's well-known words, "came down like a wolf on the fold."

The second factor in the success of the Assyrians was their use of systematic terrorization: the burning of cities together with the massacre of some captives and the deportation of others. In the long run the transplanting of conquered peoples served to make early civilizations more cosmopolitan and to bring the inventions and customs of one people more quickly to the attention of others.

The well-coordinated system of political administration developed by Assyrian rulers was the third factor in the success of the empire. Theoretically, the Assyrian king himself drew up the laws, made all the decisions con-

THE ASSYRIAN EMPIRE about 700 B.C.

See Ref. Map 2

cerning war and peace, and fixed tax rates. In practice, however, much of the work was performed by court officials, assisted by scribes. The officials formed a kind of council which advised the king, but he alone usually bore the responsibility for the most important state decisions and policies. Communication between the ruler and his provincial governors required roads, and thus the earliest system of nation-wide highways, as well as a postal system, was inaugurated.

The Assyrian rulers "thus laid secure administrative foundations for central rule of the entire Near East from Mesopotamia to Egypt. It was these secure foundations . . . which made first the Persian, later Alexander's empire possible and which are therefore a—perhaps the—major conditioning factor behind all of the following Hellenistic and Roman history. . . ."[22]

Assyrian art and architecture. In order to glorify themselves and enhance their prestige, Assyrian rulers built imposing and luxurious palaces. The royal palace at Khorsabad, built into the wall of the city on a high platform, had thick and heavy walls like those of a fortress. The palace contained not only the king's living quarters and the royal stables but also a temple and a ziggurat.

The arch, borrowed from Babylonia, became an impressive feature in Assyrian palace gates. To guard the gateways the Assyrians installed huge, human-headed, winged

Probably intended as supernatural guardians, man-headed bulls weighing forty tons and standing sixteen feet high flanked the palace gateways at Khorsabad. These winged creatures were carved with five legs. The fifth leg was placed opposite the one shown farthest to the right in this side view, so that when looked at from the front both legs could be seen.

lions and bulls (see illustration) carved from imported stone.

The lower portions of the interior palace walls were masked with stone reliefs, and the upper portions were painted in bright colors. Assyrian cruelty and ferocity are reflected in the vigorous reliefs of battles and hunting scenes. Although the beards and hair of men and the muscles, manes, and claws of beasts are all stylized, the figures in the reliefs are remarkably real. They contrast sharply with the static and monumental winged bulls.

Assyrian kings were interested in preserving records of the past, and the royal annals were kept with great care. At immense cost and effort the knowledge of the Near East was gathered for King Ashurbanipal's library, which contained over 22,000 clay tablets. These tablets provided modern scholars with their first knowledge of Sumero-Babylonian literature.

Downfall of the Assyrian empire. By the middle of the seventh century B.C. the sturdy Assyrian stock had been decimated by wars,

the task of ruling such a huge empire was proving extremely difficult, and the cruelties of the Assyrians had created implacable foes, intent on their downfall. To the north and northeast the Indo-European Medes* and Persians were on the march. A group of Semites, the Chaldeans, revolted against Assyrian rule, captured Babylonia, and in 612 B.C. joined the Medes in demolishing Nineveh, the Assyrian capital. In the whole city not one building was left standing.

With the exception of their animal sculpture, their innovations in military science, and their ability as imperial administrators, the Assyrians made few original contributions to civilization. Their role was rather one of borrowing from the cultures of other peoples, unifying the best elements into a new product, and assisting in its dissemination over the Fertile Crescent.

The Lydian kingdom. The final destruction of the Assyrian empire in 612 B.C. left the following powers to struggle over the crumbs of empire: the Medes and Persians, the Chaldeans, the Egyptians, and the Lydians.

The Lydians (see map, p. 21) were the first to coin money; as early as the ninth century B.C., they were using this method of exchange. The wealth of Lydia, one of the most prosperous nations of ancient times, was based on a flourishing commerce, an advantageous geographical position near busy trade routes, and the possession of valuable gold-bearing streams. The most famous king of this wealthy state was Croesus, and the phrase "rich as Croesus" is a reminder of Lydian opulence. With the defeat of Croesus by the Persians, Lydia ceased to exist.

The Chaldean empire. While the Median kingdom controlled the highland region, the Chaldeans, with their capital at Babylon, were masters of the Fertile Crescent. Nebuchadnezzar, becoming king of the Chaldeans in 604 B.C., raised Babylonia to another epoch

*The Medes were an Indo-European people who by 1000 B.C. had established themselves just east of Assyria. They extended their overlordship to the Persians, who were of the same racial ancestry as the Medes and for a time were content to be their vassals.

THE CHALDEAN EMPIRE
about 600 B.C.

See Ref. Map 2

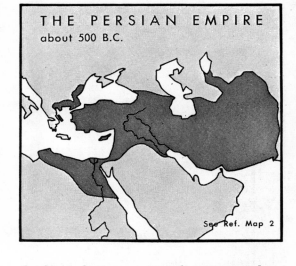

THE PERSIAN EMPIRE
about 500 B.C.

See Ref. Map 2

of brilliance after more than a thousand years of eclipse. By defeating the Egyptians in Syria, Nebuchadnezzar ended their hopes of re-creating their empire. In 586 B.C. the Chaldean king destroyed Jerusalem and carried several thousand Hebrew captives to Babylon.

Babylon was rebuilt and became one of the greatest cities of its day. The tremendous city walls were wide enough at the top to have rows of small houses on either side with a space between them large enough for the passage of a chariot. The immense palace of Nebuchadnezzar towered terrace upon terrace, each resplendent with masses of ferns, flowers, and trees. These roof gardens, the famous Hanging Gardens of Babylon, were so beautiful that they were selected by the Greeks as one of the seven wonders of the ancient world.

Continuing the work of the Mesopotamians in mathematics and astronomy, the Chaldeans observed the heavens and, without any telescopes or accurate time-recording instruments, worked out detailed tables of the movements of the sun, moon, and planets, using mathematics to figure the velocity, acceleration, and positions of these bodies. They were able to predict eclipses, and one astronomer computed the length of the year to within twenty-six minutes.

The Chaldeans also observed the movements of celestial bodies in order to foretell the future by interpreting their supposed influence on human affairs. These early astrologers identified groups of stars with the twelve signs of the zodiac, an imaginary belt in the heavens in which each sign covered 30 degrees of a full circle.

Persian imperialism. During the long reign of Nebuchadnezzar, the Chaldean empire flourished; but after his death Chaldean power quickly crumbled. Meanwhile the Persians suddenly rose to prominence and soon eclipsed all the great states of the ancient world. Within twenty years Cyrus the Great, the vigorous Persian leader, created a great empire. In 550 B.C. he threw off the Median yoke and, after defeating King Croesus four years later, he gained control of the Lydian kingdom and of those Greek cities in Asia Minor which were under the nominal control of Lydia. Then he turned east, establishing his power as far as the frontier of India. Babylon was next on his list; with little resistance the city capitulated to the Persians in 539 B.C. Following the death of Cyrus, his son Cambyses conquered Egypt. At the beginning of the fifth century B.C. the next ruler, Darius I, began a series of campaigns against the Greek mainland. The struggle between the Greeks and the Persians ended about 150 years later with the resounding defeat of the Persians by the youthful Alexander the Great of Macedonia (see Chapter 2).

A double staircase, decorated with reliefs, led to the magnificent audience hall where the Persian emperors received foreign envoys and visiting dignitaries. Persepolis was constructed during the reigns of Darius and his successor Xerxes.

Persian government. The governmental structure of Persia was built upon the Assyrian model but was far more efficient than its predecessor. The imperial system, first designed by Cyrus the Great to administer his extensive dominions, was carried to completion by Darius. Four capitals—Susa, Ecbatana, Babylon, and Persepolis—were established in various parts of the empire; and the total empire was divided into twenty-one provinces, or satrapies, each governed by a provincial governor called a satrap. To check the satraps, a secretary and a military official representing the king were installed in every province. Also, special inspectors, "the Eyes and Ears of the King," traveled throughout the realm.

Realizing the need for good communications, the Persians built great imperial post roads, which in the thoroughness of their construction rivaled the later Roman roads. The main highways connected the important cities of the empire. Along the Royal Road between Sardis and Susa there was a post station every fourteen miles, where the king's messengers could obtain fresh horses. By means of this ancient pony express, royal messengers could cover a distance of 1500 miles in a little more than seven days; ordinary travelers took three months.

The Persian empire was the first to attempt governing many different racial groups on the principle of equal responsibilities and rights for all peoples. In the Persians' treatment of subject peoples there was a humaneness and consideration that had been absent completely in the Assyrian government. For example, the Persians respected the gods of all conquered peoples. The king concerned himself with the prosperity of every section of his empire, so that all provinces would be able to pay the tribute levied against them; the tax burden, however, was not excessive. The introduction of a uniform system of coinage did much to weld the empire together.

Persian religion and art. The religion of the Persians was founded by a prophet named Zoroaster (or Zarathustra). Although the date of his birth is a matter of dispute, recent scholarship puts it at 660 B.C. Zoroaster taught that there was a continuous struggle in the world between two cosmic forces—Ahura Mazda, who symbolized righteousness, and Ahriman, who was the summation of everything evil. Ultimately, the sayings and legends concerning Zoroaster were collected into the sacred book, the *Zend-Avesta*. The *Zend-Avesta* conceived the end of the world as a mighty battle between Mazda and Ahriman in which the forces of good would prevail. Then would come a last judgment involving a heaven for some and a hell for others. The word *paradise* is Persian in its origin. The wise toleration of the Persian rulers was perhaps a result of their religion.

In art the Persians borrowed largely from their predecessors in the Fertile Crescent, especially the Assyrians. Their most important work was in palace architecture, the best remains of which are at Persepolis.

SUMMARY

In this chapter the evolution of human affairs from primitive culture to civilization has been recounted. The first great period of cultural evolution is called the Paleolithic, or Old Stone, Age. The chief all-purpose tool of this cultural stage was the hand-ax, in wide use for hundreds of thousands of years. Late Paleolithic cultures included features such as the making of blade tools and the lifelike depiction of animals, painted on the walls of caves. Perhaps eight thousand years ago, the Neolithic stage was initiated with the appearance of food-producing communities in western Asia. Neolithic cultures are usually characterized by the cultivation of grains, the domestication of animals, pottery making, and the fashioning of polished stone tools. The revolutionary change from a food-gathering to a food-producing economy made possible the rise of civilizations.

Civilization rose in Mesopotamia during the course of the fourth millennium B.C. and in Egypt nearer the end of the same millennium. These two civilizations were river-made, one by the Nile, the other by the Tigris and Euphrates rivers. In each case their respective inhabitants succeeded in making the transition from a food-gathering to a food-producing economy; they began to use metals and in this way acquired increasing technological mastery over their environment; they constructed dams and irrigation ditches and thus achieved a still more sedentary way of life in which towns developed, along with new forms of economic, political, and social organization.

While the age of most nations is no more than a few centuries, the time span of Egyptian civilization must be reckoned in thousands of years. The words *monumental* and *timeless* best describe Egyptian culture. The Egyptians built colossal statues and huge tombs; their burial customs were designed to outwit time itself. The state centered upon the absolute rule of the pharaohs; economic life was patterned on the seasonal ebb and flow of the Nile.

The story of ancient Mesopotamia is primarily concerned with the achievements of the Sumerians and the later adoption of their civilization by various invaders. The most important of these new states was Babylon, created by Hammurabi. Following an era of brilliant Babylonian civilization, the Hittites conquered Syria and Babylon. In Syria the duel between the Egyptians and the Hittites, which weakened both contestants, gave small nations—for example, Phoenicia and the Hebrew kingdoms—a chance to enjoy a brief period of independence. Political diversity was ended by the rise of the Assyrian empire, which lasted about three hundred years (900-600 B.C.). After the fall of Assyria, Chaldea under Nebuchadnezzar became a powerful civilization, but the expansion of Persia terminated its independence. Persia, in its turn, became one of the greatest empires the world had seen.

We have examined a large and complex canvas of human history. At a glance, it may seem that, like the Sphinx and the Hanging Gardens of Babylon, the peoples and events depicted there belong to the long-dead past. Yet features of our own civilization can be traced back to cultural elements of those bygone days, and the political strife which racks the region now has some of its roots in the period we have studied.

SUGGESTIONS FOR READING

A. Montagu, *Man: His First Million Years,** Mentor. A compact and well-written summary covering both archaeology and cultural anthropology.

K. P. Oakley, *Man the Tool-Maker,** Phoenix. A brief but basic work about the evolution of Paleolithic cultures.

R. J. Braidwood, *Prehistoric Men,** Phoenix. An excellent introductory work by a noted anthropologist.

*Indicates an inexpensive paperbound edition.

A. Laming, *Lascaux: Paintings and Engravings,** Penguin. A lavishly illustrated study of prehistoric art.

V. G. Childe, *What Happened in History,** Penguin. Man's development traced from Paleolithic through Roman times, with an emphasis on socio economic and technological factors. A more detailed and technical study by the same author is *New Light on the Most Ancient East,** Evergreen.

C. W. Ceram, *Gods, Graves and Scholars,* Knopf, 1951. A best-selling survey of archaeological discoveries in the whole area of the ancient Orient. *The Secret of the Hittites*, Knopf, 1956, by the same author, is a fascinating account of the rediscovery of this civilization by archaeologists.

Seton Lloyd, *Foundations in the Dust*,* Penguin. A most interesting history of archaeological discoveries in Mesopotamia.

H. Frankfort, *The Birth of Civilization in the Near East*,* Anchor. The best short yet scholarly account of the transition from primitive to civilized life in Sumer and Egypt. Especially valuable for its clear description of early political, economic, and social institutions.

Jack Finegan, *Light from the Ancient Past*, 2nd ed., Princeton, 1959. Contains a useful and up-to-date account of Mesopotamian and Egyptian history, viewed as background for the Old and New Testaments.

H. Frankfort et al., *Before Philosophy*,* Penguin. A scholarly interpretation of Egyptian and Mesopotamian thought; somewhat hard going but worth the effort. See also H. Frankfort, *Ancient Egyptian Religion*,* Torchbooks, which stresses the unchanging character of Egyptian religion.

S. Moscati, *The Face of the Ancient Orient*, Quadrangle Books, 1960. Perhaps the best survey of the literary, religious, and artistic achievements of the peoples of the ancient Orient from the Sumerians through the Persians. Includes valuable bibliographical references, numerous quotations from source materials.

S. N. Kramer, *History Begins at Sumer*,* Anchor. Records twenty-five "firsts" in the history of civilization, from "apple polishing" to moral ideals. Recommended especially to the student who questions the value of studying ancient history.

E. Chiera, *They Wrote on Clay*,* Phoenix. "No mystery story can be as exciting," wrote one reviewer of this brief and richly illustrated account of cuneiform writing and the variety of information to be found in the clay tablets of Mesopotamia.

G. Contenau, *Everyday Life in Babylon and Assyria*, St. Martin's, 1954. Contains a wealth of information about life in Mesopotamia between 700 and 530 B.C.

O. Neugebauer, *The Exact Sciences in Antiquity*, Princeton, 1952. Incorporates the most recent research on Mesopotamian contributions to science. A storehouse of information is C. J. Singer et al., eds., *From Early Times to Fall of Ancient Empires*, Vol. I of *A History of Technology*, Oxford, 1957.

C. H. Gordon, *Hammurapi's Code: Quaint or Forward-Looking?*,* Rinehart. A short commentary on the major laws, indicating that they are, for the most part, forward-looking.

H. Frankfort, *The Art and Architecture of the Ancient Orient*, Penguin, 1954. The best general work on the art of ancient Mesopotamia, Iran, Asia Minor, Syria, and Palestine. The companion volume for Egypt is W. S. Smith, *The Art and Architecture of Ancient Egypt*, Penguin, 1958.

I. E. S. Edwards, *The Pyramids of Egypt*,* Penguin. A fascinating account of how and why the pharaohs built their pyramids.

J. H. Breasted, *A History of Egypt*, Scribner's, 1924. A standard work, somewhat out-of-date in part, by America's most distinguished Egyptologist. See also his pioneer study, *Development of Religion and Thought in Ancient Egypt*,* Torchbooks.

G. Steindorff and K. C. Seele, *When Egypt Ruled the East*, Univ. of Chicago, 1957. Outstanding for its coverage of the period of the Egyptian Empire, with excellent chapters on art, literature, and religion.

J. A. Wilson, *The Culture of Ancient Egypt*,* Phoenix. Highly recommended as the most informative account of the development of all aspects of Egyptian civilization, including politics.

O. R. Gurney, *The Hittites*,* Penguin. An excellent authoritative account of Hittite politics, art, and social life.

B. W. Anderson, *Understanding the Old Testament*, Prentice-Hall, 1957. Readable and up-to-date. Traces the literary and theological development of the Old Testament within the framework of Hebrew history.

H. M. Orlinsky, *Ancient Israel*,* Cornell, 1954. A compact and valuable introduction by a noted scholar.

W. O. E. Oesterley and T. H. Robinson, *A History of Israel*, 2 vols., 2nd ed., Oxford, 1937. Widely acclaimed as the best general work on the subject. See also, by the same authors, *An Introduction to the Books of the Old Testament*,* Meridian.

A. T. Olmstead, *History of Assyria*, Scribner's, 1923. The standard and the only complete work on the subject, written with a pro-Assyrian slant.

A. T. Olmstead, *History of the Persian Empire*,* Phoenix. An excellent, admirably written survey of early Persian imperial development. Contains a detailed but controversial chapter on Zoroaster.

J. B. Pritchard, ed., *Ancient Near Eastern Texts Relating to the Old Testament*, 2nd ed., Princeton, 1955. The best collection of Sumerian, Semitic, Egyptian, and Hittite texts of all types, translated by leading scholars. An inexpensive edition of texts selected from the above work has been edited by I. Mendelsohn, *Religions of the Ancient Near East*,* Liberal Arts Press, 1955. T. H. Gaster, *The Oldest Stories in the World*,* Beacon, is a collection of Babylonian, Assyrian, and Hebrew tales, accompanied by helpful editorial notes.

H. J. Carroll, Jr., et. al., *The Development of Civilization*, I,* Scott, Foresman, 1961. A well-balanced collection of source materials, together with selected interpretations of various facets of history by modern scholars. See Part One, "Ancient Civilizations of the Near East."

Recommended historical fiction: H. Treece, *The Golden Strangers*, Random House, 1957 (Stone-Age Britain); M. Waltari, *The Egyptian*,* Pocket Books (Egypt at the time of Akhenaton); D. C. Wilson, *Prince of Egypt*,* Pocket Books (Moses in Egypt); Thomas Mann, *Joseph and His Brothers*, Knopf, 1948; I. Fineman, *Ruth*, Harper, 1949.

CHAPTER 2

The Glory That Was Greece

THE AEGEAN CULTURE, THE HELLENIC AND HELLENISTIC AGES

Introduction. Scarred by time and weather, the ruins of the Athenian Acropolis stand against a vivid blue sky and overlook the trees and buildings of a modern city sprawled beneath. These ruins are striking symbols of a departed civilization—the democracy of Athens at its height.

In the fifth century B.C., the temples and statuary of the Acropolis were gleaming and new, fresh from the hands of builders and sculptors. Five hundred years later, Plutarch wrote: "The works are . . . wonderful: because they were perfectly made in so short a time, and have continued so long a season. . . . [The Acropolis looks] at this day as if it were but newly done and finished, there is such a certain kind of flourishing freshness in it . . . that the injury of time cannot impair the sight thereof. As if every one of those . . . works had some living spirit in it, to make it seem young and fresh: and a soul that lived ever, which kept them in their good continuing state."[1]

Today the Acropolis bears the heavy "injury of time"; yet for us no less than for Plutarch ancient Athens has retained a "flourishing freshness." This quality of newness, together with a refined sense of symmetry and proportion, is characteristic of the Greek spirit and the dazzling achievements of Greek civilization. The ancient Greeks repeatedly demonstrated an ability to regard the world about them from a "young and fresh" perspective and to inject a love of proportion not only into their architecture but into almost everything they attempted. Yet in the crucial sphere of politics, their sense of proportion failed them. Instead of compromising their differences, the city-states quarreled continually, and that fervid individualism which moved them to brilliant creative efforts blinded them to the necessity of cooperation. Thus the political and economic life of the Greeks was marked by conflicts between the city-states until they were at last subjugated by King Philip of Macedonia, the father of Alexander the Great.

Yet as we shall see in this and later chapters, the Macedonian conquerors of Greece, in genuine admiration of the Greek cultural achievement, strove to perpetuate the learning of the city-states as they set forth to forge a world-state. Greece's accomplishment was indeed to prove so enduring that its magnificent legacy of knowledge and art would provide much of the cultural heritage of the West and, to a lesser extent, of the East. Thus the English poet Shelley could say with justification that "We are all Greeks." Probably no other people has made so lasting an impression upon man's intellectual history.

BACKGROUND FOR

GREEK CULTURE

Aegean maritime civilizations. Greek civilization was unique in so many ways that a student of history might infer that Greek culture developed in a vacuum or sprang full-blown from the rocky hills of this small land, free from any outside influences. Dazzling as it is for its intellectual and esthetic achievements, however, the civilization of Greece was preceded by flourishing cultures located on the lands surrounding the Aegean Sea. The three early centers of Aegean culture were Knossos on the island of Crete, Troy in Asia Minor, and Mycenae on the Greek mainland. A brief review of these cultures is essential in order to gain a proper historical perspective of the classical world.

Crete. The narrow island of Crete, which is only 160 miles long, was a stepping stone between Europe, Asia, and Africa. Cretan prosperity was built upon sea-borne trade and was maintained because the island's isolation protected it from invasion. By the fourth millennium B.C., Crete had commercial contacts with the Nile valley, and the islanders adopted and later modified Egyptian religious customs and social habits. Cultural indebtedness was not confined to Egypt, however, for excavated bronze articles testify to the influence of Mesopotamian technology.

By about 3000 B.C. the inhabitants of Crete had learned how to work bronze into tools and weapons. About a thousand years later, Cretan culture had developed to the point where settlements built around great palaces were being constructed at various sites on the island. However, the term "palace" is somewhat misleading. "These magnificent, many-storied stone buildings were not mere royal dwellings—they were a combination of royal residence, religious shrine, factory, and administrative center."[2]

The people were governed by a priest-king, who directed the profitable Mediterranean trade. The Cretans exported olive oil, wine, honey, and pottery in exchange for gold, precious stones, grain, and linen.

Our knowledge of Knossos, the ancient capital of Crete, is derived primarily from the twentieth-century researches carried on by Sir Arthur Evans and, after his death, by the British School of Archaeology at Athens. Evans unearthed the ruins of the great pal-

AEGEAN WORLD

Hellespont
Troy

Aegean Sea

Mycenae

Knossos

An inventory of jars in the palace of Nestor at Pylos is recorded on this clay tablet, inscribed with Linear Script B.

ace at Knossos. Rising several stories high along a hillside and sprawling over nearly six acres, this extraordinary building of un-burnt brick and limestone had numerous courtyards, corridors, and broad stairways. Walls were of painted plaster, many of them decorated with elaborate frescoes. Furnished with running water, the palace had a sanitation system surpassing anything constructed in western Europe until Roman times, and, after that, until the nineteenth century in England. Located in the center of the island, the palace was linked to other parts of Crete by well-made roads lined with luxurious dwellings.

The mystery of Cretan script. Early in the twentieth century, Evans discovered clay tablets bearing inscriptions of two kinds. The older group, dating back to 1800 B.C., he designated as Linear Script A, while the second group he called Linear Script B. Tablets bearing Linear A were found only on Crete, while Linear B was discovered first on Crete and later at Pylos and Mycenae on the Greek mainland. For decades scholars were unable to decipher the tablets. Finally, in 1952, the mystery was solved by an English scholar, Michael Ventris. Linear B proved to be an early Greek dialect identical with the Mycenaean language. In 1957 an American scholar, Professor Cyrus Gordon, announced that he believed Linear A probably consti-tuted Akkadian, a Semitic language which by the second millennium B.C. had been used widely in commerce and diplomacy through-out the eastern Mediterranean.[3]

The evidence from the tablets of Linear B script suggests that the Mycenaeans captured Knossos in 1500 B.C.; during their brief period of conquest they may have developed the Linear B script from the older script, Linear A, bringing it back with them later to the Greek mainland. Although scholars formerly believed that the great palace at Knossos was destroyed by a Mycenaean raiding party, it now seems more likely that the Cretans rose against their Mycenaean conquerors in 1400 B.C. and drove them from the island. Urban civilization continued to flourish in Crete for another two centuries after the conflict, but political leadership in the Aegean had by that time passed from Crete to Mycenae.

Troy, site of the Homeric epics. In the northwest extremity of Asia Minor, the city of Troy occupied a strategic position on the Hellespont (the straits between the Black and Aegean seas now known as the Dardanelles). From there, Troy could command both the sea traffic through the straits and the land caravans between Asia and Europe. For many years scholars thought that this city existed only in the epic poems of Homer. Heinrich Schliemann, a nineteenth-century amateur archaeologist, believed otherwise; and in 1870, after accumulating a fortune in various business enterprises, he put his theory to the test by beginning excavations at the legendary site of Troy. Within four years he had unearthed nine cities, built one on top of the other. He discovered a treasure of golden earrings, hairpins, and bracelets in the second city, which led him to believe that this was the city of Homer's epics. Later excavations carried out in the 1930's showed, however, that the seventh city was the one made famous by Homer.

Historians now believe that Homer's account of the Trojan War (dated by legend in the eleventh century B.C.) may have had a basis in fact. Because of their strategic location, the Trojans could exact tolls from European and Asiatic traders. The inhabitants of the Greek mainland may have decided to take drastic action to protect their commercial interests. Some scholars contend, however, that the archaeological evidence fits the view that the siege and destruction of Troy was carried on by Greek pirates in quest of booty. Neither of these theories, of course, corresponds—except in poetic imagination—to Homer's *Iliad*, in which Paris, a Trojan prince, abducted the beauteous Helen, the queen of Sparta, and brought the wrath of the Greeks and eventual destruction to Troy.

Mycenae. The third principal center of Aegean civilization arose on the Greek mainland at Mycenae. Roving tribes of Indo-European peoples, speaking an early form of Greek, may have entered Peloponnesus about 1900 B.C. and absorbed the earlier settlers, of whom little is known. These newcomers are called the Mycenaeans in order to differentiate them from the Greeks of a later period—the Hellenic Greeks of the eighth to the fourth centuries B.C.

Mycenae reached its apex between 1400 and 1200 B.C., later than either Crete or Troy. The Mycenaeans became masters of the Aegean Sea and enjoyed a culture that was, like those of Crete and Troy, urban, commercial, and prosperous. Moreover, from their contacts with other Aegean peoples, the Mycenaeans acquired much of the free and esthetic spirit which was the heritage of the later Greeks. On the mainland, numerous towns—the forerunners of the later Greek city-states—emerged, and Mycenaean colonies were established on the coasts of Asia Minor and Syria.

To Schliemann's unswerving faith in the existence of Homeric cities we are indebted again for the discovery of a store of wealth, including gold ornaments and a splendid regal crown, in the ancient *acropolis*, or citadel, of Mycenae. The luxuriously equipped royal palace had well-proportioned audience rooms and apartments, fresco-lined walls, floors of painted stucco, and large storerooms.

The Dorians. The incursion of the next wave of Indo-European peoples, the Dorians, was abrupt and violent. Entering the Greek mainland around 1200 B.C., they brought with them the ability to work iron into tools and weapons. A warlike people, they quickly occupied most of the Peloponnesus and destroyed the city of Mycenae. The interim period of about four hundred years between the heyday of the Mycenaean civilization and the beginning of classical times was marked by violence and conflict. But, as in the Middle Ages in Europe, to which this period of Greek history is often compared, relatively peaceful cultural intermingling also took place. The descendants of the Dorians included the Spartans and the Corinthians.

The Ionians. The sack of Mycenae had prompted many Mycenaeans to flee eastward into Attica, where some of them settled in Athens. Others went still farther east, sailing to a strip of seacoast in Asia Minor which became known as Ionia. In the Ionian towns, and chiefly at Miletus, the inhabitants retained the rich legacy of Mycenaean civilization and added to it elements of Near Eastern culture derived from the neighboring Lydians. The civilization that was to culminate among the Athenians—the kinsmen of the Ionians who had remained in Attica—was born in Ionia. Pioneers in exploration and trade, in science and philosophy, the Ionians "first kindled the torch of Hellenism." The word *Hellenism* is derived from *Hellas*, the Greek word for Greece.

When we speak of the Hellenic—or classical—phase of Greek civilization, we shall be referring to the period from the eighth to the fourth centuries B.C. when Greek civilization flourished in Ionia and on the Greek peninsula and when the principal center of Greek culture was Athens.

THE RISE OF HELLENIC CIVILIZATION

The influence of geography. The Greek peninsula is a jagged piece of land comprising some 45,000 square miles of mountain ranges and narrow plains. Geographical factors not only determined the maritime character of Greek civilization but also played an important part in shaping the events of Greek history. The numerous islands and indented coastlines of the Greek peninsula and of Asia Minor stimulated seagoing trade. Furthermore, the rocky soil and limited natural resources of the peninsula led the Greeks to seek their fortune on the sea and to establish colonies abroad. The numerous mountain ranges which crisscross the peninsula made internal communications extremely difficult and encouraged the development of a number of fiercely independent political units—the city-states.

The Homeric Age. Most of our information about the period following the Dorian invasions (about 1100 to 750 B.C.) is derived from the epics attributed to the blind poet Homer. A scholarly controversy surrounds the problem of Homer's existence and whether the *Iliad* and the *Odyssey* were composed by one person or by a number of poets. The period, nevertheless, can be conveniently labeled the Homeric Age because these poetic works offer vivid pictures of life in those times.

The men of the Homeric Age strove for heroic ideals, seeking imperishable fame at the expense of hardship, struggle, and even death. The greatest of human tragedies was thought to be the denial of the honor due to a preëminent warrior, and the wrath of Achilles —the theme of the *Iliad*—was the result of such a denial. To the Greeks, the gods were plainly "human"; Zeus, the king of the gods, was often the undignified victim of the plots of his wife, Hera, and other deities, and he asserted his authority through threats of violence. Hades, the abode of the dead, was a subterranean land of dust and darkness; and Achilles, as Homer tells us in the *Odyssey*, would have preferred to be a slave of the lowest man on earth than to be king in Hades. Society was clearly aristocratic, and the common man was reviled and beaten when he dared to question his betters. Yet the common man had certain political rights

as a member of the assembly that was summoned whenever a crisis, such as war, required his participation. Two other instruments of government described by Homer were the tribal king and his council. The king was hardly more than a chief among his peers, his fellow nobles, who sat in his council to advise him and to check any attempt he might make to exercise arbitrary power. Economic conditions were those of a simple, self-sufficient agricultural system much like that of the early Middle Ages.

The city-state: origin and political evolution. At first, the *polis*, or city-state, was only the elevated, fortified site—the *acropolis*—where the people could take refuge from attack or could worship in the local temple. With the growth of commerce and colonization during the seventh century B.C., another center developed below the *polis*, called the *asty*, where people lived and traded. In time, the two parts combined, and the territory surrounding the *acropolis* and the *asty* was brought under the jurisdiction of one unit—the *polis*. Thus, the city-state was formed. Our present word *politics* is derived from *polis*.

The political development of the Greek city-state was so rich and varied that it is difficult to think of a form of government not experienced—and given a lasting name—by the Greeks. Four major types of government evolved in most of the city-states: (1) monarchy of a limited sort, like that described in the Homeric epics; (2) oligarchy (rule of the few), arising when the aristocratic council ousted the king and abolished or restricted the popular assembly; (3) tyranny, imposed by one man who rode to power on the discontent of the lower classes; (4) democracy (rule of the people), occurring after the tyrant was deposed and the popular assembly was revived and made the chief organ of government. Democracy did not represent the final stage, however. After dissatisfaction with democratic government became widespread, many of the city-states turned again to one-man rule. The political evolution of the Greek city-states is best illustrated in the history of Athens (p. 43).

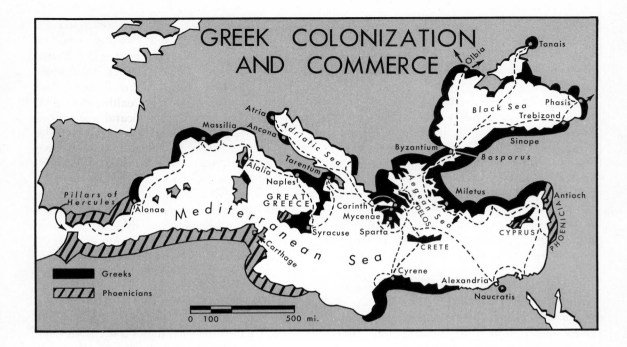

The Age of Nobles. By the middle of the eighth century B.C., the nobles, who had been the advisers to the tribal kings, took over the reins of government in most of the city-states. This transfer of power from hereditary rulers to aristocratic families initiated the Age of Nobles. Henceforth, politics was governed by class interests; and the land, formerly owned by the tribe, was transferred to private control. Although a popular assembly probably existed at this time, the common people had little or no voice in government.

Political developments were accompanied by unprecedented economic changes and growth. From 750 to 500 B.C. the Greeks embarked on large-scale colonization schemes. Their land was poor and, as the population grew, the problem of an adequate food supply became increasingly acute. Because of the ruthless policies of the powerful, land-rich nobles, many peasants were ready to follow any aspiring tyrant who promised land reform. As Plato later noted, colonization was promoted by the wealthy as a safety valve to ward off a threatened political and economic explosion:

When men who have nothing, and are in want of food, show a disposition to follow their leaders in an attack on the property of the rich—these, who are the natural plague of the state, are sent away by the legislator in a friendly spirit as far as he is able; and this dismissal of them is euphemistically termed a colony.[4]

Settlements sprang up on the islands of the Aegean and on the shores of the Black Sea. While not outstanding in Hellenic times, Byzantium on the Bosporus eventually became the eastern capital of the Roman empire; it is better known today by its later names, Constantinople and Istanbul. Eastern Sicily and southern Italy were colonized so extensively that the latter region became known as Great Greece. Colonies were planted as far west as present-day France—at Massilia, the forerunner of Marseilles—and Spain and on parts of the North African coast.

Colonial activity stimulated and was in turn affected by an expanding economy. In time the home states solved the problem of overpopulation by producing specialized wares—vases, metal goods, textiles, olive oil, and wine—for export in exchange for foodstuffs and raw materials from the colonies. But before this economic revolution was completed, the continuing land hunger of the peasants contributed to the replacement of oligarchy by tyranny in most of the Greek states. These tyrants distributed land to the peasants; by promoting further colonization, trade, and industry, they also accelerated the rise of a middle class and completed the "industrialization" of Greece.

Athens to 500 B.C. An examination of the political development of two of the Greek city-states—Athens in Attica and Sparta in the Peloponnesus—is vital to an understanding of classical Greece. In their individual histories these two city-states, less than a hundred miles apart and yet vastly different in character, mirror the strengths and weaknesses of Hellenic civilization.

By 700 B.C. the king in Athens was merely a high priest, and the assembly of the people was a powerless body. Control was concentrated in a council of nobles with the most important public office held by the archon, elected annually from the aristocracy. The good land on the plains also became concentrated in the hands of the nobility, while the peasants either became sharecroppers, who were reduced to debt slavery, or were forced to withdraw to the hills.

The cry of the common people for reform was answered in 594 B.C. by the election of Solon as archon. Because Solon's reforms were a compromise between the ultraconservative opposition of the nobles to any change and the radical demands of the commoners for immediate change, his name has became a byword for wise statesmanship. As he later wrote, "Before them both I held my shield of might,/And let not either touch the other's right."[5]

To ease economic unrest, Solon ended the debt slavery of the peasants, limited the amount of land which one man might own, and encouraged exports and industry by insisting that fathers teach their sons a trade. Among his political reforms, he revived the powers of the popular assembly, established a Council of Four Hundred to supervise the business of this body, and made property, not birth, the qualification for high office among the archons or in the Council. A law court was set up in which any citizen could be elected as judge to hear appeals from de-

cisions made by the archons or to try the magistrates for misdeeds.

It was not Solon's intention to establish a democracy; the popular assembly still could discuss only those matters which the Council put before it. But since wealth rather than birth was now the qualification for office, Solon had broadened the franchise, and in an expanding economy increasing numbers could afford to hold office. In this way Solon prepared the Athenians for democracy.

Solon's moderate economic and political reforms satisfied neither party, however. The peasants had obtained neither redivision of the land nor full political equality, while the nobles thought Solon had gone too far and regarded him as a traitor to his class. Solon's complaint describes what is too often the lot of moderate reformers:

Formerly they boasted of me vainly; with averted
  eyes
Now they look askance upon me; friends no
  more, but enemies.[6]

Solon had warned the Athenians to accept his moderate reforms lest "the people in its ignorance comes into the power of a tyrant." His prediction was soon fulfilled. In 560 B.C., after a period of civil strife, Pisistratus, a military leader and champion of the commoners, rose to power as tyrant. He solved the economic problem by banishing many nobles and distributing their estates among the poor and by promoting commerce and industry. Together with extensive public works and the patronage of culture, these reforms gave rise to a popular saying that "life under Pisistratus was paradise on earth."

Pisistratus was succeeded by his two sons, one of whom was assassinated and the other exiled. When the nobles, aided by Sparta, took this opportunity to restore oligarchy, Cleisthenes temporarily seized power in the year 508 B.C. and introduced a new system for classifying citizens which destroyed the remaining power of the noble families. For the old tribal units he substituted a new system of ten territorial units, or demes, each one embracing a cross section of citizens of all classes in the *polis*. The discussion and passage of laws remained the prerogative of the popular assembly, while the Council, raised by Cleisthenes to five hundred members selected by lot from the ten demes, was concerned with such policy matters as finance, foreign relations, and war. Thus a workable governmental system based on the political equality and participation of citizens was established; Athens was now a democracy.

A final reform of Cleisthenes was the peculiar institution of ostracism, an annual referendum in which a quorum of six thousand citizens could vote to banish for ten years any individual thought to be dangerous to the state.

Sparta to 500 B.C. In sharp contrast to Athens was the rival city-state Sparta. Sparta had not joined the other Greek cities in trade and colonization but had expanded instead by conquering and enslaving its neighbors. To guard against revolts by the state slaves (helots), who worked the land for their conquerors, Sparta was forced to deviate from the normal course of Greek political development and transform itself into a militaristic totalitarian state. Aristotle called the government of Sparta a "mixed constitution"; for the small minority of ruling Spartans it was a democracy, but for the great mass of subjected people it was an oligarchy.

The government included two kings, a small Council of Elders, and a popular assembly. True power resided in five overseers, the ephors, who were elected by the assembly and often wielded more influence than the dual monarchs.

The state enforced absolute subordination of the individual to its will. Throughout his life every Spartan was first of all a soldier. Sickly infants were left to die on lonely mountain tops; boys were taken from their families when they were seven years old to live under rigorous military discipline for the rest of their lives; girls were trained to become healthy mothers of warrior sons. As their men marched off to war, Spartan women cried out this warning: "Come back with your shield or on it."

While Sparta developed the physical fitness of its citizens and possessed the finest military machine in Greece, it remained backward culturally and politically. Travel was prohibited because the city fathers feared that alien ideas might disturb the status quo. Sparta's self-imposed isolation forbade those cultural contacts without which no balanced civilization can develop. Individual expression and creative thinking were effectively suppressed. Sparta is a classic example of how intellectual stagnation accompanies rigid social conformity and military regimentation.

To provide additional assurance that its helots remain uncontaminated by democratic ideas, Sparta allied itself with oligarchic parties in other Peloponnesian states and aided them in suppressing their local democrats. The resulting Spartan League of oligarchic states, in operation by the end of the sixth century B.C., was shortly to be faced by an Athenian-led union of democratic states.

UNITY AND STRIFE IN THE
HELLENIC WORLD

The Persian invasions. We will recall from Chapter 1 that after the Persians had overthrown the Medes in 550 B.C., their ruler, Cyrus the Great, founded a far-flung empire which included the Ionian city-states in Asia Minor. After Darius I ascended the throne, the Ionians revolted and, from 499 to 494 B.C., held out against their enemies. To their Ionian kinsmen the Athenians contributed twenty ships, concerning which the Greek historian Herodotus wrote:

These ships were the beginning of mischief both to the Greeks and to the barbarians.[7]

The odds against the Ionians were too great, and the Persians suppressed the revolt, burning Miletus in revenge.

The Athenians were stunned—for centuries Miletus had been the most brilliant of Hellenic cities. They were also fearful for their own safety. For his part Darius knew that the situation would remain unstable as long

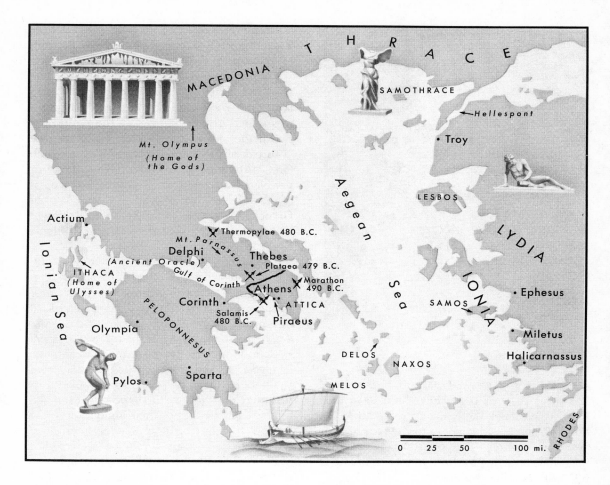

as the Athenians remained free to incite their kinsmen to revolt, and so he decided to punish Athens for aiding the Ionians. In 492 B.C. he sent an expedition through Thrace to conquer the Greek upstarts; but a storm partially destroyed the accompanying fleet, and the Persians returned home.

The battle of Marathon. In 490 B.C. another Persian expedition set forth from Asia Minor and sailed across the Aegean to the Bay of Marathon. With their cohorts, the Medes, the invaders numbered about twenty thousand men; the Athenians had only half that number. But the Greeks won an overwhelming victory, killing perhaps six thousand of their foe, with a loss of only 192 of their own forces.

The battle of Marathon was one of the most decisive in history. "The moral effect of the victory was stupendous . . . it was now demonstrated that the Greek warrior was superior to the Persian. The westward advance of the Asiatic empire was halted, and the Greeks were inspired with a fair hope of maintaining their freedom. To the Athenians, who almost single-handed had beaten a power thought to be irresistible, this victory served as an incentive to heroism. The glory of the Marathonian warriors never faded."[8]

End of the Persian Wars. When a new Persian army under Xerxes, Darius' successor, set sail for Greece ten years later, the Greeks were well prepared. The Athenians had feverishly built up their naval forces, and the Spartans agreed to command the land forces.

The Spartans guarded the mountain passes, finally encountering the huge Persian host at the narrow pass of Thermopylae. Numbering only 300, the Spartans were accompanied by a few thousand soldiers recruited from other Greek city-states. The enemy was reck-

Pericles

oned by Herodotus at 1,700,000, but a more likely figure is 250,000. For three days the Greeks held back the Persians; then a treacherous Greek led the enemy to the rear of the Spartan position. The Spartans put up a magnificent struggle but were annihilated by overwhelming numbers. Here is Herodotus' description of the final struggle:

Here they [the Greeks] defended themselves to the last, such as still had swords using them, and the others resisting with their hands and teeth; till the barbarians . . . encircled them upon every side, overwhelmed and buried the remnant which was left beneath showers of missile weapons.[9]

The Persians then advanced and burned Athens, whose inhabitants had fled, for they placed their faith in "wooden walls"—the Greek fleet. Their faith was not misplaced; the Greek fleet destroyed Xerxes' ships in the Bay of Salamis, and the tide of victory was turned. With his lines of communication cut off, the Persian king had no alternative but to retreat to Asia, although he left a strong force in Greece. One year later the Greeks roundly and decisively defeated this Persian

army at the battle of Plataea, located near Thebes, and Greece was henceforth safe from invasion from the East.

Culmination of Athenian democracy. The wise and judicious statesman Pericles was in large part responsible for the political progress which Athens enjoyed in the period between the end of the Persian Wars and the outbreak of the Peloponnesian War, in which Greeks fought fellow Greeks. The period of Pericles' leadership, from 460 to 429 B.C., is often referred to as the Golden Age of Greece. Athens was at the height of its power and was the undisputed capital of Hellenic civilization.

The office of archon which Solon had dignified by his wise statesmanship was no longer of great consequence. In Pericles' time the actual executive power resided in a board of ten, whose members were known as "generals." In some ways the board was comparable to a modern-day governmental cabinet. The generals had great political influence over the popular assembly; they often spoke at its meetings and helped to shape governmental policies. At the end of their annual term, the success or failure of their policies determined whether or not they would be reëlected.

Pericles had in mind the contrast between the Athenian and the Spartan constitutions when he expressed the idea that all citizens could participate fruitfully in the public life of the city-state:

Our constitution is named a democracy, because it is in the hands not of the few but of the many. But our laws secure equal justice for all in their private disputes, and our public opinion welcomes and honours talent in every branch of achievement, not for any sectional reason but on grounds of excellence alone. . . . We are lovers of beauty without extravagance, and lovers of wisdom without unmanliness. Wealth to us is not mere material for vainglory but an opportunity for achievement; and poverty we think it no disgrace to acknowledge but a real degradation to make no effort to overcome.[10]

The governments of Athens and of some other Greek city-states have been considered examples of pure democracy, where the entire citizen body gathered to participate in government, in contrast to the representative democracy of the United States. The Athenians did possess a representative apparatus—the Council of Five Hundred—but the representative form of government never evolved. Instead, the Greek citizenry relied on mass judgment.

The majority of the inhabitants of a city-state, however, were not recognized as citizens. Women, slaves, and foreigners were denied citizenship and had no voice in the government. Nor did they have any standing in the law courts. If a woman desired the protection of the law, she had to seek out a citizen to plead for her in court. Thus, Athenian democracy was very different from democracy as we think of it today.

Without doubt the Athenian form of government created the climate of political freedom which encouraged the intellectual and artistic outpourings of the Age of Pericles. Yet this system also bred fierce patriotic attachments to the *polis* which, as we shall later see, set limitations on the ability of the Athenians to federate with other Greek cities for the sake of common survival.

Economic and social life in Athens. Political developments were matched by economic growth and change. The prosperity that the Athenians enjoyed stemmed from the possession of large mercantile fleets and a virtual monopoly of trade throughout the eastern Mediterranean and Black Sea areas. Their chief rivals were the Phoenicians, from whom the Greeks adapted their own alphabet.

It has been estimated that Athens and the surrounding district had a slave population of 100,000 out of a total population of about 250,000. Those slaves in the wealthy homes were often treated like members of the family, and it was not uncommon for the masters to give them their freedom. But slaves on the galleys and in the mines were chained in gangs and subjected to wretched conditions. The use of slaves tended to increase class divisions, to concentrate wealth in the hands of slaveholders, and to prevent a search for new power sources. Instead, Greek society continued to rely on the overworked muscle power of its slaves.

Believing firmly in the words of Homer that "a sound mind in a manly body" was one of the greatest blessings in life, the Greeks gave sports a key role in their culture. They frequented the numerous gymnasiums and wrestling schools for exercise and recreation. Every four years the finest athletes from the city-states gathered at Olympia for the Olympic games held in honor of Zeus. Foot racing, leaping, wrestling, boxing, throwing the discus, and casting the javelin were the chief events.

Athenian culture was predominantly masculine. Aristotle wrote that "the male is by nature superior and the female inferior, the male ruler and the female subject."[11] In Periclean Athens, women did not participate in public life: their sphere of influence was restricted to the kitchen and the nursery.

Athenian imperialism. Athenian democracy at home was accompanied, ironically enough, by imperialistic policies abroad. The victory over Persia had been made possible by the unity of Hellenic arms. But with victory assured, unity quickly dissolved. Fearful of rebellion at home, Sparta recalled its troops and resumed its policy of isolation. Because they still feared a future Persian invasion from the east, Athens and some of the city-states located on the coast of the Aegean nearest to Asia Minor formed in 478 B.C. a defensive alliance known as the Delian League. This maritime confederacy was supported by contributions of ships, men, and money, and the League treasury was kept on the island of Delos.

As the most powerful member, Athens had the dominant vote in the League's affairs; it was made permanent head, given charge of the fleet, and empowered to collect money from the League members. Through the activities of the League, the Aegean was cleared of the Persians; and other Greek city-states and colonies joined the alliance. As the Persian threat decreased, however, various members of the League grew restive and felt it unnecessary to continue the confederacy.

The decision to continue the League rested with the Athenians, who were motivated by the fear that the Persian danger was still not

Although the original "Discus Thrower" by the Greek sculptor Myron no longer exists, Roman copies such as this one show us what it looked like.

the ground that it brought "freedom" from fear and want to the Greek world:

We secure our friends not by accepting favours but by doing them. . . . We are alone among mankind in doing men benefits, not on calculations of self-interest, but in the fearless confidence of freedom. In a word I claim that our city as a whole is an education to Greece. . . .[12]

The Peloponnesian War: the first phase. In 431 B.C. the Peloponnesian War broke out between the Spartan League and the Athenian empire. The conflict is a classic example of how fear can generate a war unwanted by either side. According to Thucydides:

The real but unavowed cause I consider to have been the growth of the power of Athens, and the alarm which it inspired in Lacedaemon [Sparta]; this made war inevitable.[13]

Several incidents served to ignite the underlying tension, and Sparta declared war on "the aggressors."

At the beginning of the war, Athens possessed a large empire, an unrivaled navy, and a rich treasury. Against this power Sparta raised a strong army, invaded Attica, and besieged Athens. Pericles depended on the navy's ability to maintain a food supply for Athens and to harass its enemies' coasts. Fate took a hand in this game, however. In the second year of the war, a plague carried off a third of the Athenian population. The death of Pericles, who was a victim of the plague, was a great blow to the Athenians, for leadership of the government passed to demagogues vastly inferior to Pericles in moral fiber and intelligence. In the words of Thucydides:

Pericles, by his rank, ability, and known integrity, was able to exercise an independent control over the masses—to lead them instead of being led by them. . . . With his successors it was different. More on a level with one another, and each grasping at supremacy, they ended by committing even the conduct of state affairs to the whims of the multitude. This, as might have been expected in a great imperial state, produced a host of blunders. . . .[14]

at an end and by the need to prevent the lucrative Mediterranean markets from falling into the hands of such commercial rivals as the Phoenicians. The Athenians used force to prevent withdrawal from the League; in effect, they created an Athenian empire. By aiding in the suppression of local aristocratic factions within its nearly three hundred subject states, Athens both eased the task of controlling its empire and emerged as the leader of a union of democratic states.

To many Greeks—above all to the members of the Spartan League and the suppressed aristocratic factions within the Athenian empire—Athens was a "tyrant city" and an "enslaver of Greek liberties." Pericles, on the other hand, justified Athenian imperialism on

After eight more years of warfare, a peace was arranged in 421 B.C. to end the first phase of this bitter conflict. During the succeeding breathing space, Athenian imperialism manifested itself in its worst form through the actions of Pericles' unworthy successors. In 416 B.C. an Athenian expedition embarked for Melos, a small Aegean island from which Athens had unjustly demanded tribute, to force the islanders to capitulate. An excerpt from Thucydides displays the tragic transformation of Athenian democracy into naked imperialism and the specious logic employed by the Athenians to justify it:

We believe that Heaven, and we know that men, by a natural law, always rule where they are stronger. We did not make that law nor were we the first to act on it; we found it existing, and it will exist for ever, after we are gone; and we know that you and anyone else as strong as we are would do as we do.[15]

The Athenians put all Melians of military age to death and sold the women and children into slavery.

The Peloponnesian War: the second phase. The second phase of the Peloponnesian War began in 415 B.C. with an Athenian expedition against Syracuse which was destined to spell disaster for Athens. The Athenians hoped to conquer Sicily and expand their commerce in the west. After two years of fighting, two great Athenian fleets and a large army were destroyed by the Syracusans and other rivals of Athens; many of the Athenian survivors were sold into slavery. The Peloponnesian War dragged on until the last Athenian fleet was defeated near the Hellespont in 405 B.C. One year later the Athenians capitulated. The old walls connecting Athens and its port city of Piraeus were torn down, all but twelve ships were destroyed, every foreign possession was stripped away, and Athens came under Sparta's control.

Aftermath of the war. The Peloponnesian War ruined the power of Athens and brought about the decline of all the Greek cities. Even the main victor, Sparta, was little better off than the vanquished, for wealth and power hastened the destruction of the old Spartan

virtues of frugality and simplicity. Many of the Greek city-states became seriously depopulated, a symptom of their overall deterioration. Unemployment was widespread, and some citizens were compelled to become soldiers of fortune. In public life intrigue and venality were rampant. The democratic ideal was degraded as the affairs of state were taken over by politicians, soldiers, and bankers. Although Athens continued as the business center of the Aegean, Hellas was in dissolution—the city-states had lost their vitality, and their citizenry, while remaining clever, had, with few exceptions, ceased to be creative.

These years witnessed constant clashes between various city-states, ending finally in the conquest of the Greek city-states by an Indo-European people from north of Greece —the Macedonians. With the triumphant conquest by Macedonia in 338 B.C., the Hellenic phase came to an inglorious end.

Various scholars believe that the failure of the Greek city-states to unite or to cooperate for their mutual benefit was responsible for the breakdown of Hellenic civilization. But the tantalizing question remains: would unity among the city-states have assured political survival? Large political entities such as Egypt, Assyria, and Persia ultimately succumbed to fragmentation and foreign rule. Nor does history offer any assurance that the incorporation of small units into a large one would have constituted an improvement in statehood.

What then should the Greek city-states have done? Should they have settled for a highly centralized form of government which would have been capable of keeping the peace—but which might also have robbed the inhabitants of individual city-states of the independence of mind and action that achieved such priceless cultural gains? Or could they have compromised by creating some intergovernmental organization—a Hellenic United Nations—with machinery for settling disputes peacefully?

As we shall see in the next section, the leaders of the Hellenistic Age tried to solve this problem by establishing absolutist dynasties based upon the theory of the divine right of kings. In Chapter 3, we shall examine the way in which the Romans handled the problems of freedom and imperial rule. These questions are no less important to us today.

THE GREEK GENIUS

The Greek character. The Greeks were the first to formulate many of the western world's fundamental concepts in philosophy, science, and art. How was it that a relative handful of people could bequeath such a legacy to civilization? The definitive answer may always elude the historian, but a good part of the explanation lies in environmental and social factors.

Unlike the Near Eastern monarchies, the *polis* was not governed by a "divine" ruler nor were the activities of its citizens circumscribed by elaborate taboos. In the more enlightened city-states, an alert, informed electorate was required to perform various civic duties and to take an active part in the discussions of the assembly. The Greeks relished debate and argument, and one of their most striking characteristics was their fondness for good talk. The nature of the universe and of man, man's duty to the state and to his fellow citizens, law and freedom, the purpose of art and poetry, the standards of a good life—these problems they discussed brilliantly and with pertinence for our times as much as theirs.

The Greek character was one of energy and bold experimentation tempered by the exercise of reason and clear judgment. Their curiosity about the natural world led them to an appreciation of the simplicity and balance in nature. They believed that an ideal life based on a harmony of interests and abilities should include a healthy balance of action and thought. The life of Sophocles offers an excellent example: an Athenian general and chief treasurer of the city, he also wrote such deeply moving tragedies as *Antigone* and *Oedipus Rex*.

To obtain harmony and balance, it was essential to avoid *hubris*. Meaning "pride" or "insolence," this term is a key to fathoming the Greek character. Resulting from human excesses and lying at the root of personal misfortune and social injustice, *hubris* invariably provoked *nemesis*, or retribution. According to the Greeks, an inexorable moral law would cause the downfall or disgrace of anyone guilty of *hubris*. Greek mythology offers many stories of *hubris* resulting in *nemesis*, and Athenian dramatists often employed this theme in poetic tragedies. Herodotus attributed the Persian defeat by the Greeks to Xerxes' unseemly desire to expand his empire by conquest, by which he called down upon himself the retribution of a jealous providence. Similarly, Thucydides contended that Athens' lust for power was responsible for the outbreak of the Peloponnesian War. The Athenians lost the war because they did not follow Pericles' advice to avoid party strife and new conquests.

The Greeks exhibited human frailties and failings—they could be suspicious, vindictive, and cruel. But at their best they were guided by the ideals that permeate their intellectual and artistic legacy. Their philosophy was profound; their art sublime. The philosopher Protagoras is credited with having said that "Man is the measure of all things"—a saying which sums up the Greek attitude toward themselves and the world of men. In short, the Greeks were humanists.

Greek religion. Early Greek religion abounded in a number of gods and goddesses who personified physical elements. Thus Demeter was the earth and giver of grain, Apollo, the sun and giver of light, and Poseidon, who dwelled in the sea, was the giver of waters. Other deities had special functions, such as Aphrodite, the goddess of love, Dionysus, the god of fertility and wine, and Athena Polias, the goddess of wisdom and the guardian of Athens. The Greeks of Homeric times believed in deities much like themselves, differing from ordinary men only in their immortality and their possession of supernatural powers. Zeus, the king of sky, earth, and men, was the chief god; he supposedly ruled the world from Mount Olympus with the aid of lesser deities.

Eventually some Greeks came to believe that the gods could not logically lead the malicious, jealous, ambitious, and intemperate lives that the myths recounted. The belief arose that there must be a reckoning after death for all mortals. The residence of the dead could be either Hades, a joyless region of shadows, or the Elysian Fields, the blissful abode of heroes and philosophers.

The desire to ascertain the divine will in this life explains the prominence of oracles, omens, and divination in Greek religion. The most famous oracle was at Delphi, where the wishes of Apollo (the god of prophecy as well as the sun god) were reputedly made known.

The nature of the universe. Philosophy arose from the insatiable curiosity of the Greeks in searching for the facts and laws of nature.

"The father of philosophy" is the title given to the statesman Thales of Miletus (c. 636-546 B.C.). Having learned from the Babylonians the secret of calculating eclipses, Thales concluded that such phenomena did not result from the whims of gods but from natural, fixed laws. Looking for the basic substance from which all else in the universe is composed, Thales finally concluded that it was water, which exists in different states or forms and is indispensable to the maintenance and growth of organisms. Although his views about a single basic substance are no longer tenable, it is important to realize that Thales was the first western philosopher to offer an explanation of life in terms of natural causes.

Many of the world's greatest philosophers have also been outstanding mathematicians. The Greek philosopher from Samos, Pythagoras (c. 582-500 B.C.), whose theorem in geometry is presumably known by every schoolboy, believed that the universe was founded on mathematical principles. He went so far as to maintain that everything had a numerical value and that, to obtain the principal characteristics of an object, one must "get its number." By experimenting with a vibrating cord, Pythagoras discovered that musical harmony is based on arithmetical proportions.

By the beginning of the fifth century B.C., some Greeks were criticizing the views of Thales. Water, they reasoned, could not change into a multitude of things absolutely unlike water. The problem of change thus became of paramount importance. Existence alone was real, they argued, and it was impossible for it to be other than eternal, immovable, and indivisible. Therefore, movement and change were logically impossible and only illusions of the mind. The contrary view held by Heraclitus (c. 540-475 B.C.) of Ephesus was that life was change and change alone. "Everything changes except change," declared Heraclitus. The entire universe is in flux; human bodies and minds are always changing.

Some thinkers concluded that the universe was composed of earth, water, fire, and air rather than a single substance, water, as Thales believed. Democritus (c. 460-370 B.C.) developed a theory that the universe was composed of indivisible atoms, which differed in shape, size, position, and arrangement but not in quality. Moving about continuously, atoms combined to create objects. To Democritus, reality was the mechanical motion of atoms. Scientists have used this theory to the present day, although we are now aware that the atom is neither indivisible nor indestructible.

As ideas developed about the make-up of the physical universe, questions arose as to the place of man in the scheme of things. A number of Greek philosophers interested themselves in problems of ethics, logic, and political theory. Three Hellenic philosophers during the later part of the fifth century B.C. and the early part of the succeeding century attacked these questions and laid down the most important lines of Greek thought.

Socrates, a martyr to truth. The most famous teachers of argument and debate were the Sophists, "men of wisdom," who prepared men for public speaking and hence for public life. While the Sophists claimed to teach all knowledge essential to the statesman, they insisted that truth was relative and denied the existence of any universal standards to guide human actions.

The outstanding opponent of the Sophists was the Athenian-born Socrates (*c.* 470-399 B.C.), a snub-nosed and ugly man but a fascinating conversationalist. In the words of the Roman statesman Cicero, Socrates was "the first to call philosophy down from the heavens and to set her in the cities of men, bringing her into their homes and compelling her to ask questions about life and morality and things good and evil."[16] He believed that by asking questions and by subjecting the answers to logical analysis, it was possible to come to agreement about ethical standards and rules of conduct. And so he would question passers-by in his function of midwife assisting in the birth of correct ideas (to use his own figure of speech). He might ask them, "What is piety and what impiety? what is the beautiful and what the ugly? what is the noble and what the base?"[17]

Socrates, who took as his motto the famous inscription on the temple of Apollo at Delphi, "Know thyself," linked virtue and knowledge. In time his quest for truth led to his undoing, for the Athenians, disillusioned by the Peloponnesian War, arrested him on the trumped-up charge of corrupting youth and engaging in political intrigue. Socrates was condemned to die, a fate which he accepted calmly and without rancor.

Wherefore, O judges, be of good cheer about death, and know of a certainty that no evil can happen to a good man, either in life or after death. . . . I am not angry with my condemners, or with my accusers; they have done me no harm, although they did not mean to do me any good; and for this I may gently blame them.

Still I have a favour to ask of them. When my sons are grown up, I would ask you, my friends, to punish them, and I would have you trouble them, as I have troubled you, if they seem to care about riches, or anything, more than about virtue; or if they pretend to be something when they are really nothing, then reprove them, as I have reproved you, for not caring about that for which they ought to care, and thinking that they are something when they are really nothing. And if you do this, both I and my sons will have received justice at your hands.

The hour of departure has arrived, and we go our ways—I to die, and you to live. Which is better God only knows.[18]

Plato and his Theory of Ideas. The greatest of Socrates' disciples was Plato (427?-347 B.C.), a member of the Athenian aristocracy. At the death of Socrates, Plato found Athens hostile to him, and so he traveled abroad for ten years. Upon his return he established the Academy, a famous school which existed for almost nine centuries.

Plato's philosophy centers on his Theory of Ideas. Like Socrates, Plato believed that truth exists and, furthermore, that it is eternal and fixed. Yet Plato saw that nothing experienced by the senses is permanent. Permanence can be found only in the realm of thought, the spiritual world of ideas or forms. To Plato an idea has a real existence apart from the intellect. In the world of ideas, certain universals such as Beauty, Truth, Justice, and the greatest of all—Good—exist. The concepts of justice, beauty, or truth in the world of the senses are only imperfect reflections of the eternal and changeless ideas. Because man's soul is linked with the idea world, the human soul is spiritual and immortal.

Plato expounded his concepts of an ideal state in the *Republic*, the first systematic treatise on political science. The state's basic function, founded on the Idea of Justice, was the satisfaction of the common good. In the ideal state, Plato contended, there should be three classes of people: workers to produce the necessities of life; warriors to guard the state; and philosophers to rule in the best interests of all the people. The society Plato favored would be a "spiritualized Sparta," in which the state vigorously regulated every aspect of a person's life. The family and private property were abolished on the grounds that both institutions bred selfishness, and marriage was controlled so that children would be produced eugenically. The *Republic* represents man's first attempt to devise a planned human society.

Aristotle, the encyclopedic philosopher. Plato's greatest pupil was Aristotle (384-322 B.C.), who set up his own school, the Lyceum, at Athens. In all history there has probably never been another man whose interests were so widespread or whose knowledge was so encyclopedic as Aristotle's. He investigated and wrote brilliantly in such diverse fields as art, biology, mathematics, astronomy, physics, psychology, rhetoric, logic, politics, ethics, and metaphysics.

Aristotle differed from Plato on the question of the existence of Ideas. For Aristotle, Real Being was found not in universal Ideas but in the particular fact, the individual thing, and the concrete object. Furthermore, he believed every concrete object to be composed of Form and Matter. In a marble statue, the marble is the Matter, while the shape conferred by the sculptor is the Form. In opposition to Plato, who separated Form and Matter, Aristotle claimed that neither Form nor Matter had any existence apart from the other.

In his treatment of ethics, Aristotle argued that happiness comes from an unobstructed pursuit of a rational life. Only by acting reasonably could one avoid the excesses of passion or oddities of the intellect. Elaborating upon the Greek ideal of moderation, he proposed his Doctrine of the Mean—namely, that all virtues lie between two extremes, each of which is a vice. Thus, to him, courage is the mean between cowardice and rashness.

In the study of formal logic, Aristotle devised the syllogism to point out fallacies in human reasoning. This deductive method of reasoning requires a trio of propositions. The first two propositions (the major and minor premises) must be plainly valid and logically related so that the third proposition, the conclusion, inevitably follows. For example, (1) all Greeks are human; (2) Aristotle is a Greek; (3) therefore Aristotle is human.

Differing with many of Plato's political theories, Aristotle contended that property and family are valuable incentives for the achievement of a good life. Because democracy had degenerated in Greece during his lifetime, Aristotle favored the rule of a single strong man. He formulated no concept of a planned mythical state such as Plato's *Republic,* but wrote only about the small *polis* of his own age.

Plato had condemned poetry, but Aristotle recognized the value of the poet in refining human passions. Aristotle defined tragedy as an imitation of a painful action or event (usually resulting in the death of the hero) which, by arousing pity and fear in the audience, effects a cleansing of those emotions. Drama critics today often use his esthetic theories when evaluating plays.

Hellenic scientific developments. The Greeks became adept at deductive reasoning (from general principles to particular facts) and made notable advances during Hellenic times in mathematics, logic, and the classification of physical forms and types. In such fields as medicine, physics, and zoology, however, theoretical conclusions were often drawn without sufficient proof. Unfortunately, the resultant errors—often ridiculous to modern minds—remained unquestioned for centuries because they had been accepted by such authorities as Aristotle.

A logical approach which is the reverse of the deductive method was also employed by the Hellenic Greeks. Reasoning inductively from particular facts to general principles, Aristotle made many advances in biology. From keen personal observation, the use of dissection, and a wealth of data gathered by fishermen, travelers, and scholars, he concluded that over a period of time an organism evolves from a simple to a more complex form. Furthermore, as the organism grows more complex, a corresponding increase in intelligence takes place.

Preconceived and false ideas about the human body blocked the development of medical science until 420 B.C., when Hippocrates, "the father of medicine," founded a school in which he emphasized the value of observation and the careful interpretation of symptoms. After conducting practical experiments, the members of this school were firmly convinced that disease resulted from natural and not supernatural causes. Writing of epilepsy, considered at the time a "sacred" or supernaturally inspired malady, one Hippocratic writer observed:

It seems to me that this disease is no more divine than any other. It has a natural cause just as other diseases have. Men think it supernatural because they do not understand it. But if they called everything supernatural which

In a scene from the film *Oedipus Rex* (1957), the regal figure of Oedipus confronts the humble shepherd who tells the king the secret of his birth. To his horror, Oedipus discovers that he has unwittingly murdered his own father and married his mother.

they do not understand, why, there would be no end of such things![19]

Hippocrates set forth a high code of professional ethics still sworn to by doctors today. In abridged form this oath is administered to graduates in medicine:

I will look upon him who shall have taught me this Art even as one of my parents. I will share my substance with him, and I will supply his necessities, if he be in need. I will regard his offspring even as my own brethren, and I will teach them this Art, if they would learn it, without fee or covenant. I will impart this Art by precept, by lecture and by every mode of teaching, not only to my own sons but to the sons of him who has taught me, and to disciples bound by covenant and oath, according to the Law of Medicine.

The regimen I adopt shall be for the benefit of my patients according to my ability and judg-ment, and not for their hurt or for any wrong. . . . Whatsoever things I see or hear concerning the life of men, in my attendance on the sick or even apart therefrom, which ought not to be noised abroad, I will keep silence thereon, counting such things to be as sacred secrets.[20]

The writing of history. History for the Hellenic Greeks was not an account of legendary events and mythical figures, nor were the forces of history attributable simply to the whims of the gods. The Greeks viewed history as a humanistic study by which historians sought to learn about the actions and characters of men. As such, history could be subjected to rational standards and critical judgment.

In his history of the Persian Wars, Herodotus of Halicarnassus (484?-425? B.C.) discerned the clash of two distinct civilizations, the Hellenic and the Near Eastern. His portrayal of both the Greeks and the Persians was eminently impartial, but his fondness for a good story often led him to include tall tales in his works.

Although Herodotus emphasized the effects of climate and geography upon social customs, the first truly scientific historian was Thucydides (*c.* 460-400 B.C.), who wrote a notably objective chronicle of the Peloponnesian War. To appreciate the extent of his objectivity, we must keep in mind that he was a contemporary of the events and, moreover, a loyal Athenian himself. Yet a reader can scarcely detect whether the historian favored Athens or Sparta. Thucydides describes his approach to his subject matter in this way:

With reference to the narrative of events, far from permitting myself to derive it from the first source that came to hand, I did not even trust my own impressions, but it rests partly on what I saw myself, partly on what others saw for me, the accuracy of the report being always tried by the most severe and detailed tests possible. My conclusions have cost me some labour from the want of coincidence between accounts of the same occurrences by different eyewitnesses, arising sometimes from imperfect memory, sometimes from undue partiality for one side or the other. The absence of romance in my history will, I fear, detract somewhat from its interest; but I shall be content if it is judged useful by those inquirers who desire an exact knowledge of the past as an aid to the interpretation of the future, which in the course of human things must resemble if it does not reflect it. My history has been composed to be an everlasting possession, not the show-piece of an hour.[21]

Greek poetry and drama. Literary periods can be classified according to dominant poetic forms which reflected particular stages of social evolution in Greece. First came the time of great epics, followed by periods in which lyric poetry and drama flourished.

In the ninth century B.C. the *Iliad* and the *Odyssey*, the two great epics attributed to Homer, were set down in their present form. The *Iliad*, describing the clash of arms between the Greeks and the Trojans "on the ringing plains of windy Troy," reflects the view prevailing among Greeks in those days that man's acts and fate are controlled by the gods. The *Odyssey*, relating the adventure-filled wanderings of Odysseus in his return to Greece after Troy's destruction, underscores the Greeks' romantic attachment to the sea at the time when they were engaged in their first wave of maritime exploration and colonization. These stirring epics provided inspiration and source material for generations of poets in the western world.

As Greek society became more sophisticated, a new type of poetry, written to be sung to the accompaniment of the lyre, arose in the Aegean islands. Its authors sang not of legendary events but of present delights and sorrows. This new note, personal and passionate, is found in the songs of the poetess Sappho, who lived in the sixth century B.C.

Without warning

As a whirlwind
swoops on an oak
Love shakes my heart[22]

Drama developed from the religious rites of the ancient Greeks, and the theater filled a civic-religious function in Greek society. In Athens, by the fifth century B.C., two forms—tragedy and comedy—had evolved. By depicting man in conflict with destiny, the tragedies expressed the Greek concern for achieving harmony and avoiding the excesses of passion or the intellect. Borrowing the familiar legends of gods and Homeric heroes for their plots, playwrights followed rigorous canons of form to arouse in the audience the pity and fear which Aristotle taught were essential to the purification of these emotions.

Most of the Greek plays have been lost; but of the writers of tragedies whose works survive, all were giants of their art. The plays of Aeschylus (525-456 B.C.) were imbued with his deeply religious spirit. In his trilogy, the *Oresteia,* for example, he concerns himself with *hubris,* as applied to the murder of the hero Agamemnon by his false queen, and then proceeds to work out its ramifications—of retribution and the duty of punishment—with inexorable logic. Aeschylus' successor

In the Parthenon (below), great care was taken to design a perfect building, both structurally and visually. The tops of the Doric columns lean toward the center of each colonnade; the steps curve upward at the center; and the columns are more widely spaced in the middle of each row than at the ends—all these refinements create an illusion of perfect regularity which would be lacking if the parts were actually regular. Sculpture adorned the triangular gables and parts of the frieze just below the gables; another sculptured frieze ran around the walls inside the colonnade. The whole building was once painted in bright colors. In the Erechtheum (center), a more slender order of column, the Ionic, was used. Shown at the top is an ornate capital of the third Greek order, the Corinthian, which was less popular with the Hellenic Greeks than with the Romans.

Sophocles (*c.* 496-406 B.C.) advanced the techniques of characterization, suspense, climax, and dialogue. His *Oedipus Rex*, a psychological study of a man pitted against fate, is considered a masterpiece. The works of the playwright Euripides (480?-406? B.C.) reveal the growing unorthodoxy of the times. In his most famous play, *Medea* (431 B.C.), Euripides rationalized about the gods and left many questions of fate open to doubt.

Comedies were bawdy and spirited. There were no libel laws in Athens, and Aristophanes (*c.* 445-385 B.C.), the famous comic dramatist, used the customs, institutions, and famous people of Athens as targets of his brilliant satires. His plays, containing barbed political commentary, criticized society much as the political cartoons in our daily newspapers do.

The Greeks as builders. In the sixth century B.C., architecture flourished in Ionia and Greece with the construction of large temples of stone, the form having developed from earlier wooden structures. The Persian invasion made Athens a heap of ruins, but the withdrawal of the invaders left the Athenians free to reconstruct the Acropolis into a treasury of temples and statues. Architecture reached its zenith in the Athens of the fifth century B.C.

The Parthenon, the Erechtheum, and the other temples on the Acropolis exhibit the highly developed features characteristic of Greek architecture (see photo, p. 56). Here the post and lintel construction, gable roof, marble colonnade, statues, and carved reliefs were subtly and precisely combined to attain the harmony that makes Greek structure so pleasing. The three orders, or styles, identified by the characteristics of the columns, were the Doric, which was used in the Parthenon; the Ionic, seen in the Erechtheum; and the later and more ornate Corinthian.

Other types of buildings, notably the stadiums, theaters, and gymnasiums, also express the Greek spirit and way of life. In the open-air theaters the circular shape of the spectators' sections and the plan of the orchestra section set a style which has survived in principle to the present day.

Greek sculpture and pottery. Early Greek sculptors, influenced by Egyptian models, adopted rigidly specified forms. Their statues followed the traditional Egyptian stance—one foot advanced and the arms hanging with clenched fists. It was during the fifth century B.C. that a group of excellent sculptors, concentrating on greater realism and movement, advanced far beyond the conventional patterns. Myron (about 500 B.C.) in his "Discus Thrower" created an athlete in motion (see photo, p. 48). This statue displays the idealization of the human form typical of Greek art in the Age of Pericles.

The making of pottery was a highly developed art in Greece. Abstract geometric designs or scenes from mythology or the life of the times were painted on the vases. (See Color Plate 3 for a picture of a red-figured vase.) From the Greek pottery which has survived, we can get an inkling of what Greek painting—most of which has been destroyed or lost—was like.

THE HELLENISTIC ACHIEVEMENT

The Macedonian conquest of Greece. To the north of Greece lay Macedonia, inhabited by hardy peasants and mountaineers who spoke an Indo-European dialect but who were culturally inferior to the Greeks. Under Philip II, who ascended the throne in 359 B.C., the Macedonians advanced rapidly. A man of great native ability and spirit, Philip had been a hostage at Thebes in his youth, and there had received a Greek education that had stirred his admiration and kindled in him a desire to win a place in the Hellenic world.

A master military strategist and a shrewd politician, Philip united Macedonia and then turned to the Greek city-states, which had been weakened by the Peloponnesian War. In 338 B.C. he defeated the Athenians and the Thebans, thus ending that period of Greek supremacy termed the Hellenic Age.

The following year, Philip formed a league of Greek city-states, allowing the members

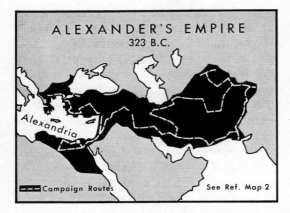

ALEXANDER'S EMPIRE
323 B.C.

Alexandria

Campaign Routes   See Ref. Map 2

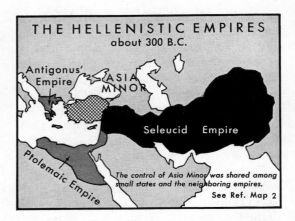

THE HELLENISTIC EMPIRES
about 300 B.C.

Antigonus'
Empire   ASIA
                MINOR

                                Seleucid   Empire

Ptolemaic Empire

The control of Asia Minor was shared among
small states and the neighboring empires.
                                See Ref. Map 2

to retain a large measure of self-government. As head of the league, Philip intended to prepare the forces of Greece and Macedonia for a war against Persia. In 336 B.C., however, he was assassinated, and his crown fell to his gifted twenty-year-old son, Alexander, who crushed unrest and rebellion in the league and proved himself a resolute, ambitious king from the beginning of his reign.

Alexander the Great. Like his father, the youthful Alexander (see Color Plate 6) was alive to the glories of Hellenic culture, having as a youth been tutored by Aristotle. Reveling in the heroic deeds of the *Iliad*, Alexander resolved to spread Greek culture throughout the world. Two years after Philip's death, Alexander set out to conquer the East with an army of 35,000 soldiers recruited from Macedonia and the league. In quick succession he subdued Asia Minor, Syria, Palestine, and Egypt. Then he marched to the Fertile Crescent and, in 331 B.C., defeated the powerful forces of Darius III, the Persian monarch. Alexander was now master of Persia, the proud empire that had controlled the Near East. He ventured as far east as the rich river valleys of India (see Chapter 4); but at last his weary soldiers forced him to turn back. In 323 B.C., while planning the conquest of the western Mediterranean, the youthful king died, the victim of fever. Although his many military successes were due largely to the superb army his father had created and to the disorganization within the Persian empire, Alexander in his own right was a skillful general and a gallant leader.

Alexander's legacy to political thought was the theory of divine kingship. His motive in claiming divine origin was not a religious one, however. To unify the lands he conquered and to keep the Greeks in line, he needed an effective instrument of administration. He solved the problem by deifying himself, thereby adopting a procedure which his contemporaries, as well as the earliest Greeks, practiced when honoring heroes. Alexander realized, as did the ambitious rulers who followed him, that royal policies and commands would be "sanctified" (and consequently strengthened) if they originated from a source—the monarch—who was considered divine.

The division of Alexander's empire. Alexander's death destroyed his plans for the "marriage of Europe and Asia." Since he left no heirs of suitable age or sufficient ability to carry on his mission, a struggle for power among his generals ensued. Within a few decades the empire was roughly divided among the African, Asian, and European elements: Egypt was ruled by the Ptolemy family; Alexander's conquered lands in Asia were governed by Seleucus and his descendants; and Macedonia and Greece constituted a separate power under Antigonus Gonatas. This three-part division of Alexander's empire constituted the Hellenistic world and lasted for three centuries—a period historians call the Hellenistic Age, dating from Alexander's death in 323 B.C. to the battle of Actium in 31 B.C. (see Chapter 3, p. 74). Some of the city-states in Greece continued to exist as independent political entities, however, and much of Asia Minor did not fall under the sway of the Seleucids. One important kingdom was Pergamum in Asia Minor (see Reference Map 2), which became an independent state in 282 B.C. This small but wealthy state boasted luxurious palaces and baths, a theater, and a library, second only to Alexandria's in size. Its scholars enjoyed a high reputation; Pergamum's fame has been perpetuated in the word *parchment*, derived from its name.

How did Alexander's successors try to resolve the crucial problem of creating workable political organizations in their sizable empires? The rulers adopted monarchical systems which were, particularly in the Seleucid and Ptolemaic domains, undisguised absolutisms, founded upon the theory of the divine right of kings. Political administration was centralized in a bureaucracy staffed by Greeks and Macedonians, an arrangement which created a vast gulf between a ruler and his subjects. A fairly large measure of self-government was conceded to the cities, however, and absolutism was tempered in the empire ruled by Antigonus and his successors. This pattern of semiautonomy influenced the Romans when they organized their rule over a far-flung empire.

Plagued by dynastic troubles and civil wars, the Hellenistic kingdoms soon began to crumble. The eastern reaches of Alexander's empire—India, Bactria, and Parthia—gradually drifted out of the Seleucid sphere of influence (see p. 61). By the end of the third century B.C., the new power of Rome had entered upon the scene, and in 30 B.C. the Romans swallowed up the last morsel, Egypt.

Economic growth and expansion. The Hellenistic Age was a time of great economic growth. In the wake of Alexander's conquests, a network of Greek cities was founded in the East, and thus new markets were created. An economic union between East and West hitherto unknown in the ancient world came into existence. This development was aided greatly by the introduction of a uniform coinage.

By the third century B.C., the center of trade had shifted from Greece to Egypt, Rhodes, and the coast of Asia Minor. Far larger than any of the Hellenic cities were Antioch in northern Syria, Seleucia-on-the-Tigris, and Alexandria on the Nile. Caravans from India poured overland into Damascus and Antioch; the riches of Arabia and the Fertile Crescent were brought by land and by sea to Alexandria.

Many industries were royal monopolies, and the state exercised close control over economic life. Industrial development was accompanied by greater specialization of workers and the organization of the apprentice system. In industry and agriculture, slaves were frequently employed, and chain gangs of criminals and prisoners of war toiled in the mines and quarries.

Despite the wealth of such cities as Alexandria and Antioch, discontent was rife. Harsh social and economic differences separated the rich from the poor; the development of industry did little to improve the material condition of the exploited workers. Political power, land, money, and trading privileges increasingly fell to royal favorites, and the majority of the population had neither political rights nor economic security.

Epicureanism, Stoicism, and Skepticism. Developments in philosophy reflected the political and psychological changes which took place as a result of Alexander's conquests. With the growing loss of freedom and the prevalence of internal disorder, philosophers ceased to formulate plans for ideal societies and shifted to the consideration of individual ethics and salvation. This emphasis on introspection in a world of political chaos led to the rise of three principal schools of thought—Epicureanism, Stoicism, and Skepticism.

Epicurus (342?-270 B.C.) of Samos did not believe in an afterlife; he taught that the highest good was to obtain pleasure for the body and the mind during one's lifetime. He maintained that the finest pleasures were intellectual, but many of his followers later distorted his teachings so that Epicureanism appeared to be concerned only with the gratification of sensual desires. In opposition to Epicureanism, Zeno of Cyprus (*c.* 336-*c.* 264 B.C.) argued that there should be but one aim in the world—freedom from the desires of life. His followers were the Stoics, and to them the ideal state was to be tranquil of soul and indifferent to pain and pleasure, joy and sorrow. These two philosophies were to have a marked effect upon the Romans.

The group known as the Skeptics reflected most clearly the doubts and misgivings of the times. According to this school, not only is it impossible to know anything outside the physical senses, but no two people can agree as to what is pleasurable or painful; pleasure for one is pain for another; one person feels cold when another feels warm. If no one can state what is true, the wise man, so the Skeptics argued, does not pretend to hold any opinions of his own but follows the customs of the region where he happens to live.

Discoveries in science and mathematics. In accord with the commercial and cosmopolitan character of the Hellenistic Age, the intellectual activities became more "down-to-earth." Hellenistic scientists were essentially "practical" in their aims, and their methodology emphasized specialization and experimentation. Although the Greek element remained predominant in Hellenistic learning, it was fused with such influences as Babylonian astronomy and Egyptian geometry. The results of this cultural melding were brilliant; not until early modern times did men make such important advances in scientific exploration.

The expansion of geographical knowledge incited scientists to make accurate maps and to plot the size of the earth, which had been identified as a globe through observation of its shadow in a lunar eclipse. Eratosthenes of Alexandria (276?-195? B.C.) calculated the circumference of the globe by measuring the difference in the angles of the noonday sun at Aswan and Alexandria during the summer solstice and estimating the distance between the two cities. According to some authorities he computed the earth's circumference at 24,662 miles, or less than 200 miles short of the actual figure by modern calculations.

In this period, astronomy also made rapid advances, so that one Alexandrian astronomer was able to compute the solar year correctly to within five minutes and the lunar month to within one second. In the third century B.C., Aristarchus put forward the radical theory that the earth rotates on its axis and moves in an orbit around the sun. Most of his contemporaries adhered, however, to the prevailing geocentric theory, which stated that the earth was stationary and that the sun revolved around it. Not until the sixteenth century A.D. were scientists again to espouse the views of Aristarchus.

Euclid, the most famous mathematician of Alexandria (*c.* 300 B.C.), developed the forms and theorems of plane geometry which are still taught today. Archimedes of Syracuse (287?-212 B.C.) contributed to higher mathematics by calculating the value of π. He also invented a terminology for expressing numbers up to any magnitude and laid the foundations of calculus. But it was in the field of physics that he excelled. Archimedes invented a compound pulley, the windlass, and an endless screw for pumping out ships and draining flooded fields, and he improved such military weapons as catapults.

The Hellenistic Greeks extended the advances in medicine made earlier by Hippocrates and his school. By dissecting bodies of dead criminals, they were able to trace the outlines of the nervous system, to master the principles of the circulation of the blood, and to ascertain that the brain, not the heart, was the true center of consciousness.

Architecture, sculpture, and literature. The host of new cities which sprang up in Hellenistic times served as a tremendous impetus to architecture. The new cities benefited from town planning: the streets were laid out according to a rectangular plan. The great public edifices were elaborate and highly ornamented; this was an age which preferred the more ornate Corinthian to the simpler Doric and Ionic orders.

In sculpture the artists' mastery over the technical aspects of their medium enticed them to display their skill in depicting violent scenes and dramatic poses. Stone was carved

A famous Hellenistic work is the marble altar of Zeus from Pergamum. The almost free-standing sculpture pictured here represents a struggle between the gods and the Titans. Notice how the legs of the defeated Titan have changed into serpents. In contrast to the harmony and restraint of earlier Greek sculpture, this work is full of agitation and violence.

into writhing forms. While displaying a realism which could make stone simulate flesh, Hellenistic sculpture lacks the balance and restraint which characterized Hellenic sculpture.

The quality of literature from the Hellenistic Age was generally inferior to that of the Hellenic Age. Yet, paradoxically enough, these sophisticated, urban times witnessed the production of superb pastoral poetry; perhaps, for jaded urbanites, it served as a means of "getting away from it all." Books were produced on a scale hitherto unknown, and great libraries were collected.

The Hellenistic contribution: the East. The greatest contribution of the Hellenistic Age was the diffusion of Greek culture throughout the ancient East and the newly rising West. In the East, the cities which Alexander and his successors built were the agents for spreading Hellenistic culture from the Aegean Sea to India and from the Caspian Sea to the cataracts of the Nile. Literate Asians learned Greek to facilitate trade, to become members of the ruling circles of the Hellenistic states, and to read Hellenic classics.

For a time the Seleucid empire provided' the peace and economic stability necessary to ensure the partial Hellenization of a vast area. But with an insufficient number of Greeks to colonize so large an area as the

Near East, the Greek city-states remained only islands in an Asian ocean. As time elapsed, this ocean encroached more and more upon the Hellenized areas.

The gradual weakening of the loosely knit Seleucid empire resulted eventually in the creation of independent kingdoms on the edge of the Hellenistic world. The Seleucid province of Bactria achieved independence in the middle of the third century B.C. Under its third king—a Greek who had married into the Seleucid royal family—Bactria became a strong state. For over a century the Bactrian kingdom shielded the Greek and Iranian peoples to the west from fierce nomads (see p. 100).

Also in the middle of the third century the kingdom of Parthia, situated between the Seleucid and Bactrian kingdoms, was founded by nomads who had thrust south from beyond the Caspian. After a century the Parthian rulers wrested Babylonia and Media from the Seleucids; Persia and parts of Bactria were added to these conquests to form the Parthian empire, destined to endure for almost five centuries. Although the empire was essentially a native Iranian state, it included a number of Greek cities, and the inhabitants absorbed some Hellenistic culture. Because of their strategic position between East and West, the Parthians dominated the rich trans-Asian caravan trade (see Chapter 4).

The Hellenistic contribution: the West. Although the Greeks and Macedonians of the Hellenistic Age created no empires in Europe, the diffusion of Hellenistic culture was none the less of the greatest significance to the West. Moreover, through the people of the Hellenistic world, the contemporary Romans became further acquainted with the great body of Greek culture from the classical, or Hellenic, period. The process by which Rome assimilated this legacy, which it later passed on to the peoples of western Europe, will be described in Chapters 3 and 5.

Rome's indebtedness to the past was acknowledged admirably by the Roman educator Quintilian (c. 35-95 A.D.):

With so many teachers and with so many examples has antiquity furnished us that no age can be thought more fortunate in the chance of its birth than our own age, for whose instruction men of earlier generations have earnestly laboured.[23]

SUMMARY

The two most important centers of the Aegean maritime civilization were Knossos on the island of Crete and Mycenae on the Greek mainland. Aegean civilization reached its zenith first in Crete (1750-1500 B.C.), where the island dwellers fashioned a sophisticated urban culture, synthesizing cultural elements from the Near East and Egypt. By the fifteenth century B.C., the center of Aegean culture had shifted to Mycenae on the Greek mainland, where another zenith was attained. The Mycenaean civilization endured until the warlike Dorians invaded the Peloponnesus and forced the Mycenaeans to flee eastward to Athens in Attica and Ionia in Asia Minor. There, by the eighth century B.C., fiercely independent city-states evolved a distinctly Hellenic culture which was to come to fruition in the classical period or Hellenic Age (the eighth to fourth centuries B.C.).

The Greek city-states of the Hellenic period exhibited one fatal defect—an inability to submerge individual differences for the sake of common survival. The city-states failed to adapt themselves to the political realities of the fifth century B.C., which had resulted from the colonial expansion and economic revolutions of previous centuries and which linked the destinies of Athens and other Greek cities with those of a larger Mediterranean community. This failure led to the disastrous Peloponnesian War.

Fortunately for the Greeks, Philip II, the Macedonian ruler who conquered the city-states sixty years after the Peloponnesian War, sincerely admired Hellenic culture—an admiration which was shared by his son, Alexander the Great. It was the ambitious and gallant Alexander who conquered the Near East and laid the boundaries for three large empires carved from his conquered lands. The Hellenistic Age, which began after Alexander's death, was primarily a period of economic expansion, but it was also an age of growing cosmopolitanism, of striking intellectual and artistic achievements, and of the wide diffusion of Greek culture.

Perhaps the greatest Greek contribution to western political thought was a body of theory which included the concepts of a democratic government responsible to the governed, of trial by jury, and of civil liberties.

In the nonpolitical fields, our debt to the Greeks is almost unlimited. They were the first to search after a rational explanation of the universe, and many of the philosophical and scientific problems they posed are still questions for which we are seeking answers. We can still find delight and food for thought in their epic poems, lyrics, tragedies, comedies, and historical writings. In architecture, sculpture, and minor arts, the work of the Greeks is a fresh and constant source of inspiration to both artists and laymen.

What is it about Greece that leads us to speak so admiringly? The secret lies in the originality with which the Greeks met every situation. Free of Near Eastern superstitions and traditions, they examined each problem in a spirit of critical inquiry and sought for an explanation that accorded with the natural world rather than supernatural law. Thus their view of life, something entirely new in the world's history, tended to be secular rather than religious, rational instead of credulous. This clear-cut, straightforward approach to life may have been the most lasting contribution of the Greeks to human history.

SUGGESTIONS FOR READING

A. J. B. Wace, *Mycenae*, Princeton, 1949. The history of Mycenae and its exploration as summarized by a British archaeologist. A more recent account, by an American archaeologist, is G. E. Mylonas, *Ancient Mycenae*, Princeton, 1957. An absorbing novel set in Mycenaean times is M. Renault, *The King Must Die*, Pantheon, 1958.

C. E. Robinson, *Hellas: A Short History of Ancient Greece,* Beacon, 1955. A concise, lucid survey. Among the more valuable and readable special studies on Greek politics, economics, and society are G. Glotz, *The Greek City and Its Institutions*, Knopf, 1929; A. Zimmern, *The Greek Commonwealth: Politics and Economics in Fifth Century Athens,* Oxford Paperbacks; H. Michell, *Sparta*, Cambridge Univ., 1952; and A. Andrewes, *The Greek Tyrants*, Hutchinson Univ. Library, 1956.

C. Lavell, *A Biography of the Greek People*, Houghton Mifflin, 1934. One of the best introductions to Greek civilization. A more advanced study is W. Jaeger, *Paideia: The Ideals of Greek Culture*, 3 vols., Oxford, 1939-1944. The ignoring of change and development as a factor in Greek culture mars the otherwise excellent introduction by G. L. Dickinson, *The Greek View of Life,* Univ. of Mich. H. D. F. Kitto, *The Greeks,* Penguin, is a stimulating interpretation which presupposes some prior knowledge of Greek history.

Edith Hamilton, *The Greek Way to Western Civilization,* Mentor. A very popular work displaying enthusiastic appreciation of the beauty and value of Hellenic literature. Other valuable books dealing with Greek literature include C. M. Bowra, *Ancient Greek Literature,* Galaxy; H. D. F. Kitto, *Greek Tragedy,* Anchor; E. Fuller, ed., *Plutarch: Lives of the Noble Greeks,* Dell; C. A. Robinson, Jr., ed., *Selections from the Greek and Roman Historians,* Rinehart; and R. Livingstone, ed., *Thucydides: The History of the Peloponnesian War,* Galaxy. Livingstone's translation is recommended for its useful notes, many of which point up the idea that "ancient Greece is twentieth-century Europe, incapable of union, tearing itself to pieces in wars it did not desire but could not avoid."

Greek mythology is surveyed in Edith Hamilton, *Mythology,* Mentor; a much fuller but highly opinionated treatment is R. Graves, *The Greek Myths,* 2 vols., Penguin. B. Farrington, *Greek Science,* Penguin, 1953, is a clear and valuable survey of scientific and technological development. The following standard and authoritative books on Greek philosophy have been reprinted by Meridian: E. Zeller, *Outlines of the History of Greek Philosophy;* J. Burnet, *Early Greek Philosophy;* A. E. Taylor, *Plato;* W. D. Ross, *Aristotle.* A good survey of Greek religion by an eminent authority is H. J. Rose, *Religion in Greece and Rome,* Torchbooks.

W. W. Tarn, *Hellenistic Civilization,* Meridian. The best account, arranged topically, of all aspects of Hellenistic civilization. Excellent studies of the career and motives of Alexander the Great, by the foremost British and American authorities on the subject, are W. W. Tarn, *Alexander the Great,* Beacon; and C. A. Robinson, Jr., *Alexander the Great: The Meeting of East and West in World Government and Brotherhood*, Dutton, 1947.

Recommended for the fine-arts student are G. M. A. Richter, *The Sculpture and Sculptors of the Greeks*, Yale, 1950, which contains over 700 photos; A. W. Lawrence, *Greek Architecture*, Penguin, 1957; G. Rodenwaldt, *The Acropolis*, Univ. of Okla., 1953; and E. Buschor, *Greek Vase-Painting*, Dutton, 1922.

*Indicates an inexpensive paperbound edition.

CHAPTER 3

The Grandeur That Was Rome

Introduction. As the Athenian saw the symbol of his city-state's democracy and culture in the rock-jutting Acropolis, so the Roman viewed the Forum as the symbol of imperial grandeur. Temples were to be found there, but in contrast to the Acropolis, the Forum was dominated by secular buildings—basilicas, the nearby Colosseum, and the great palace of the emperors rising on the neighboring Palatine Hill. Long vistas contributed to the effect of massiveness and opulence. While the Acropolis was crowned with statues to Athena, the Forum gloried in triumphal arches and columns commemorating military conquests. Rome was the capital of a world-state, extending from the Rhine to the Euphrates, and its citizens were proud of their imperial mission.

Although the buildings in the Forum appear fundamentally Greek in style, they are more monumental and sumptuous. The Hellenic architect most often employed the simple Doric order in his columns, but the Roman preferred the ornate Corinthian. Here, then, are two clues to an understanding of the Romans: they borrowed profusely from the Greeks, and they modified what they took. Adoption and adaptation are key words in the study of Roman civilization.

Rome was the great intermediary—the bridge over which passed the rich contributions of the Fertile Crescent, Egypt, and especially of Greece to form the basis of modern western civilization. The Romans replaced the anarchy of the Hellenistic Age with law and order and embraced the intellectual and artistic legacy of the conquered Greeks. As the Roman empire expanded, Hellenistic civilization was spread westward throughout Europe.

Yet Rome was more than an intermediary. It had greatness in its own right and made many important and original contributions to our western culture. Throughout a history which led from a simple farming community in the plain of Latium to a strong state which became the master of the Mediterranean and finally of the entire known western world, the Romans met one challenge after another with practicality and efficiency. In the shadows of the Roman legions went engineers and architects, so that today, scattered throughout the lands which once were part of the Roman empire, the remains of roads, walls, baths, basilicas, amphitheaters, and aqueducts offer convincing evidence of the Romans' technical prowess. Most lasting and far-reaching of all, their administrative institutions—the legal codes and governmental systems which they developed and modified to meet changing needs—have served as the framework of western political life.

EARLY ROME TO 509 B.C.

Early settlers of Italy. The Greeks and Romans were offshoots of a common Indo-European stock, and settlement of the Greek and Italian peninsulas followed stages that were broadly parallel. Between 2000 and 1000 B.C., when Indo-European peoples invaded the Aegean world, a western wing of this nomadic migration filtered into the Italian peninsula, then inhabited by indigenous Neolithic tribes. The first invaders, skilled in the use of copper and bronze, settled in the Po valley. There followed another wave of Indo-European tribes called the Italic people, who were equipped with iron weapons and tools; in time, the newer and older settlers intermingled and spread throughout the peninsula. The most important Italic tribe, the Latins, settled in the lower valley of the Tiber River, a region which became known as the plain of Latium.

For ages history had by-passed the western Mediterranean, but it was henceforth to become an increasingly significant area. By the ninth century B.C., the Etruscans, immigrants from Asia Minor, settled on the west coast of the Italian peninsula. Subjugating most of northern Italy, they turned southward and threatened the Latin settlements in Latium. After the eighth century, Greek colonists established city-states in southern Italy, known as Great Greece, and in Sicily. The Greeks disseminated the achievements of Hellenic culture; Sicily and Great Greece also served as a protective buffer against powerful and prosperous Carthage, the Phoenician colony established in North Africa around 800 B.C. No one at the time would have believed that the future of the entire Mediterranean belonged to an insignificant Latin village on the Tiber River, then in the shadow of Etruscan expansion. Here was Rome, destined to be ruler of the ancient world.

Rome's origins. According to ancient legend, Rome was founded by the twin brothers Romulus and Remus, who were saved from death in their infancy by a she-wolf who sheltered and suckled them; and in Virgil's *Aeneid* the founder was the Trojan warrior Aeneas. Turning from fable to fact, modern scholars believe that early in the eighth century B.C. the occupants of some small Latin settlements on hills in the Tiber

See Ref. Map 2

valley united and established a common meeting place, the Forum, around which the city of Rome grew up. Situated at a convenient place for fording the river and protected by the hills and marshes from invaders, Rome occupied a strategic location. Nevertheless, the Etruscans conquered Rome and during the sixth century ruled the city and the surrounding plain of Latium.

Some aspects of Etruscan culture had been borrowed from the inhabitants of Great Greece, and it seems certain that in this period much of the culture acquired in Etruscan contacts with Great Greece was passed on to the conquered Romans. From their Etruscan overlords, the Romans probably acquired some of their gods and goddesses and the practice of prophesying by examining animal entrails. From the conquerors, too, the conquered learned to build arches and vaults. Even the name *Roma* appears to be derived from the Etruscan word *ruma*. Although they were culturally indebted to the Etruscans, the Romans retained their own language and kept some of their Latin tribal customs intact.

The Roman monarchy. Rome's political growth followed a line of development similar to that of the Greek city-states: monarchy, oligarchy, and, finally, a limited democracy.

According to tradition, early Rome was ruled by kings elected by the people. After the Etruscan conquest, this elective system continued, although the kings chosen were, naturally enough, of Etruscan origin. The king's leadership of the state was based on the *imperium*—that is, the power of life and death over the people—which was symbolized by an eagle-headed scepter and an ax bound in a bundle of rods (*fasces*). The *fasces* symbol is found on the United States dime. This device from Roman times also provided both the symbol and the name for Mussolini's political creed of Fascism, which glorified the authority of the state.

Although the *imperium* was conferred by a popular assembly made up of all citizens, the king turned for advice to a council called the Senate. Each senator had a lifelong tenure, and the members of this group and their families constituted the patrician class. The other class of Romans, the plebeians, were mostly small farmers and artisans, who exercised little influence in government at this time.

THE EARLY REPUBLIC, 509-133 B.C. — DOMESTIC AFFAIRS

Establishment of the republic. In 509 B.C. the nobles led a revolt against a despotic Etruscan king and set up Rome as a republic in which they held the reins of power. The *imperium* was now transferred to two new officials, called consuls. Elected annually from the patrician class, the consuls invariably exercised their power in its interest. When the consular offices were first established, their powers were very broad: the consuls commanded the army and acted as high priests and supreme magistrates in Rome. In the event of a war or a serious domestic emergency, a dictator could be substituted for the two consuls, but he was given absolute power for six months only.

Demand for political equality. For two centuries following the establishment of the republic, the plebeians struggled for political and social equality. Although violence often accompanied their bitter conflict with the patricians, outright civil war was averted. Nor was it necessary for the plebeians to have recourse to tyrants to assist them in gaining their goals, as happened in the Greek city-states. Much of the success of the plebeians in this struggle was due to their tactics of collective action and to their having organized a corporate group within the state. This unofficial group was known as the Concilium Plebis, presided over by officials called tribunes, who had the job of safeguarding the interests of the plebeians and of negotiating with the consuls. Furthermore, the wars of conquest in which Rome presently found itself engaged gave the plebeians, indispensable in filling the ranks of the Roman army, greater bargaining power.

The advancement of the plebeians from the founding of the republic to about 300 B.C.

took two main lines: the safeguarding of their fundamental rights, and the progressive enlargement of their share of political power. Feeling that the laws of Rome were often interpreted to suit patrician interests, the plebeians demanded that the laws be written down and made available for all to see. As a result, the Laws of the Twelve Tables were drafted, inscribed on tablets of brass or wood, and set up publicly in the Forum.

The plebeians also acquired fundamental safeguards in the following ways: they secured the right to appeal a severe judicial sentence imposed by a consul and to be retried before the popular assembly; the tribunes eventually gained a veto power over any legislation or executive act that threatened the rights of the plebeians; and the latter acquired a new social status by the passage of a law permitting their marriage with patricians.

Little by little the plebeian class acquired more power in the functioning of the government. In 367 B.C. one consulship was opened to them, and by the end of that century, plebeians were admitted to important offices dealing with financial and social functions, formerly reserved for patricians. The right to hold high political offices proved to be a stepping stone to the Senate, and plebeians were finally allowed to enter that august body.

The long struggle for equality ended in 287 B.C. when the Concilium Plebis, having become a constitutional body known as the Tribal Assembly, gained the right to pass laws that were binding on all citizens. The Roman republic was now a democracy, yet in actual fact the senatorial aristocracy of patricians and rich plebeians continued to control the state. Having gained political and social equality, the plebeians were willing to allow the more experienced Senate to run the government during the remainder of this period of almost constant warfare down to 133 B.C.

The Roman citizen. The fundamental unit of early Roman society was the family, where the father's power was absolute, and strict discipline was imposed to instill in children those virtues to which the Romans attached particular importance—loyalty, courage, self-control, and respect for laws and ancestral customs.

The strength and simplicity of the Romans in the days of the early republic have been overromanticized by latter-day writers. But it is generally accepted that the Romans were stern, hard-working, and practical. The large issues of man's relationship to the universe and the possibilities of immortal life did not concern them unduly. Religious practices were confined to placating supernatural powers and enlisting divine support for the family and the state. The most important gods were Jupiter, who controlled the universe; Mars, the god of war; Janus, the guardian of the gateway to Rome; Juno, the patron saint of women; and Minerva, the goddess of war, skill, and wisdom.

THE EARLY REPUBLIC, 509-133 B.C.—FOREIGN AFFAIRS

Roman conquest of Italy. The growth of Rome from a settlement of modest size to the dominant power in the Mediterranean world in less than four hundred years (509-133 B.C.) is a remarkable story. By 270 B.C. Rome had conquered both the Etruscans and the Greeks of Great Greece and was master of all Italy south of the Po valley.

Rome's position was favored by geography. While the Italian peninsula has a great mountainous backbone, the Apennines, running down most of its length, the country is not so rugged as in Greece. Consequently the mountains did not constitute a barrier to political unification. Also, the Alps in the north kept all but the most intrepid barbarian tribes from entering the Italian peninsula. In addition, the Romans occupied a central position on the peninsula which made it difficult for their enemies to unite successfully against them.

In 493 B.C. Rome and the Latin League, composed of Latin peoples in the vicinity of Rome, entered into a league of defense against the Etruscans. This new combina-

The Roman legion—composed of 3000 heavily armed men, 1200 light-armed soldiers, and 300 cavalry—was like a pack of lions, incredibly swift and mobile. To achieve maximum maneuverability, the legions were divided into companies of 120 men, each company capable of independent action. In this relief, Roman troops are shown crossing a pontoon bridge.

tion was so successful that by the beginning of the fourth century B.C. it had become the chief power in central Italy. But the members of the Latin League grew alarmed at Rome's increasing strength, and war broke out between the former allies. With the victory of Rome in 338 B.C., the League was dissolved, and the member cities were forced to become Rome's allies. Thus the same year which saw the rise of Macedonia over Greece (see p. 57) also saw the rise of a new power in Italy.

The tempo of Roman conquests was stepped up. After defeating the Samnites, a strong Italic tribe of the Apennine Mountains in central Italy, Rome moved southward against the Greeks in Great Greece. At one point the Romans were defeated by the soldiers and war elephants of Pyrrhus, a king who had brought aid from Greece itself. But his triumph was bought at such

a price that ever since a dearly bought gain has been termed a "Pyrrhic victory." Pyrrhus was at length defeated, and by 270 B.C. all of the peninsula up to the valley of the Po had passed into Roman hands.

Treatment of conquered peoples. Instead of slaughtering or enslaving their defeated foes, the Romans usually treated them with justice and tact, in time creating a strong loyalty to Rome throughout the peninsula. Allies of Latin origin were granted a large share of self-government; and the other Italian allies, comprising the bulk of the conquered people, were required to adhere to Rome's foreign policy and to supply troops for Rome but were otherwise lightly ruled. Roman citizenship was a prized possession and was not extended to all peoples on the peninsula until the first century B.C.

In time, the term *Italia* came to be applied to the whole peninsula, indicating its military unity under the protection of Rome and anticipating the growth of national unity. Actual political and cultural unity, however, was still a long way off; the language and customs of Rome were not widely adopted in other parts of Italy for another two centuries.

The First Punic War. With the elimination in the third century B.C. of Great Greece (except for Sicily) as a threat to Roman supremacy in the West, only Carthage remained as Rome's rival. Much more wealthy and populous than Rome, with a magnificent navy that controlled the western Mediterranean and with a domain that included the northern coast of Africa, all of Sardinia, and parts of Spain, Corsica, and Sicily, Carthage seemed powerful enough to halt Roman expansion. But Carthage was governed by a selfish, wealthy commercial aristocracy, who hired mercenaries to fight for them. In the long run, the lack of a loyal body of free citizens, such as Rome had for its army, proved to be Carthage's fatal weakness.

In 264 B.C., war broke out between Rome and Carthage because both powers wished to dominate Sicily. Later termed the First Punic War (the Latin word for Phoenician was *punicus*), this conflict cost the Romans 200,000 men in disastrous naval engagements. Although they were not a seafaring people like the Carthaginians, the Romans nevertheless persisted in the conflict, raised money for new ships, trained their crews on land, and finally defeated their foes. In 241 B.C. the Carthaginians sued for peace; Rome annexed Sicily, Sardinia, and Corsica and gained naval supremacy in the western Mediterranean.

The contest with Hannibal. Thwarted by this defeat, Carthage concentrated upon enlarging its empire in Spain. But the Romans were determined to restrict the Carthaginian sphere of influence. While both powers jockeyed for position, a young Carthaginian general, Hannibal, precipitated the Second Punic War by attacking a Spanish town allied to Rome. Then, seizing the initiative again, Hannibal in 218 B.C. led an army of about 40,000 men, 9000 cavalry troops, and a detachment of elephants across the Alps and entered Italy. Although subjected to terrible privations in crossing the mountains, Hannibal's army proved its mettle and defeated the Romans three times within three years.

Hannibal's forces never matched those of the Romans in numbers. At the battle of Cannae, for example, some 70,000 Romans were wiped out by barely 50,000 Carthaginians. On the whole, Rome's allies remained loyal, and because the Romans controlled the seas, Hannibal received little aid from Carthage. Thus, although never decisively defeated in Italy, Hannibal was unable to inflict a knockout blow upon the Romans, who tenaciously kept up the struggle. The Second Punic War has been described as a "colossal contest between the nation Rome and the man Hannibal."[1]

The Romans finally obtained a general, Scipio, who was Hannibal's match in military strategy and who was bold enough to invade Africa. Forced to return home after fifteen years spent on Italian soil, Hannibal clashed with Scipio's legions at Zama, where the Carthaginians suffered a complete defeat (see map, p. 71). In a harsh treaty of 201 B.C., Carthage was forced to pay an indemnity, disarm its forces, and turn Spain over to the Romans. Hannibal sought asylum in Asia Minor but, pursued by the Romans, he committed suicide in 182 B.C. to prevent capture. His last words were reputed to have been:

Let us relieve the Romans of their anxiety; they are too impatient to wait for an old man to die.[2]

Roman intervention in the East. The defeat of Carthage left Rome free to turn eastward and settle a score with Philip V of Macedonia, who had assisted Hannibal during the Second Punic War. Fearful also that Philip might create a hostile coalition in the eastern Mediterranean, the Romans attacked Macedonia in 200 B.C. The heavy Macedonian phalanxes were no match for the mobile Roman legions, and three years later the Macedonians were roundly defeated.

During the Punic Wars, the heirs of Alexander's empire—the Antigonid dynasty in Macedonia, the Ptolemaic rulers in Egypt, and the Seleucids in Asia—had carried on seemingly endless wars among themselves. Early in the second century B.C., a Seleucid king appeared to be on the verge of dominating the Hellenistic world, but he was humbled by Roman legions in a quarrel over Greece and Asia Minor. Although the Romans annexed no territory from the Seleucids, they enhanced Roman prestige by this war and made it clear that the Seleucid ruler was to stay out of the Roman sphere of influence. In 168 B.C. Egypt allied itself with Rome, and most of the Mediterranean came under Roman sway.

Following the Macedonian defeat of 197 B.C., Rome permitted the Greek city-states in Hellas, formerly controlled by Macedonia, to rule themselves, subject only to Roman protection. But the Greeks continually quarreled among themselves and plotted against their protector. An end to this state of affairs came in 146 B.C., when the exasperated Romans burned Corinth. The city-states then came under a watchful and less liberal Roman rule.

Destruction of Carthage. In the meantime, Carthage had become no more than a protectorate of Rome, and there was little need to wage further war against the Carthaginians. Some Romans, however, genuinely feared a resurgence of Carthage's power, and the majority of citizens, spurred on by the victories in the East and sensing that Rome was destined to rule the world, lusted for conquest. Acting as the spokesman of the majority, Cato, an influential official, ended all his speeches with *"Carthago delenda est"*—"Carthage must be destroyed."

Treacherously provoking a war, the Romans besieged Carthage, and in spite of heroic resistance, the defenders of the city were overpowered and sold into slavery. In 146 B.C., the same year in which they destroyed Corinth, the Romans burned Carthage, plowed the ruins under, and flung salt into the furrows to destroy the fertility of the soil. Thus ended the Third Punic War, the final phase in the long struggle between Rome and Carthage. About a century later, however, the Romans rebuilt both Carthage and Corinth.

Rome, the ruler of the ancient world. In 133 B.C., another important extension of Roman power occurred when the king of Pergamum in Asia Minor, having no heir and realizing perhaps that Roman conquest was inevitable, willed his realm to Rome. Using this bequest as a start, Rome eventually took over Asia Minor and lands in the Near East.

By the end of the second century, then, the power of Rome extended all around the Mediterranean. Sicily, Sardinia, Corsica, Spain, Illyria, Macedonia, North Africa, and Asia Minor were spoils of war and were organized as provinces of the Roman republic. (See Reference Map 2.) Except for the advances northward into Europe, the later wars of Rome were to be waged not so much to enlarge as to consolidate its dominions.

THE LATE REPUBLIC,

133-30 B.C.

Economic and social conditions in the republic. The political history of Rome thus far consists of two dominant themes: the gradual liberalization of the government and the expansion of the Roman dominion over the Mediterranean world. Now let us examine some of the most important social and economic problems which Rome faced by the middle of the second century B.C. The historian Appian described the times thus:

. . . the powerful ones became enormously rich and the race of slaves multiplied throughout the country, while the Italian people dwindled in numbers and strength, being oppressed by penury, taxes, and military service.[3]

One of the most pressing problems facing the state was the growing tendency of the wealthy classes to control the land at the expense of the small farmers. Improved farming methods imported from Sicily encouraged rich aristocrats to buy up tracts of land and introduce large-scale farming. This trend was especially profitable because thousands of slaves from the conquered areas were available to work on the estates. The large slave plantations, called *latifundia,* had become common in Italy by about 200 B.C., while small farms were the exception.

When Sicily was conquered, its inhabitants were forced to pay a huge tribute in wheat. In addition cheap cereals were imported into Italy from Africa. Finding it impossible to compete with imported produce and large-scale farming methods, the small farmers flocked to Rome and created a city mob of unemployed malcontents. The disappearance of the small landowner was one of the basic causes of the degeneration of the Roman republic.

The land problem was further complicated by the government's earlier practice of leasing the territory acquired in the conquest of the Italian peninsula (known as public land) to anyone willing to pay a percentage of the crops or animals raised on it. Of course, only the wealthy plebeians or patricians could afford large tracts of land, and they leased, sold, and bequeathed it as if it were their own property.

Corruption in the government was another mark of the growing degeneracy of the Roman republic. Provincial officials seized opportunities for lucrative graft, and the upper classes in Rome scrambled selfishly for the profitable war contracts which supplied the army with wheat, meat, clothing, and weapons. The opulent living of the wealthy hastened the decay of the old Roman traits of discipline, simplicity, and respect for authority. Although in theory the government remained a democracy, in practice it was an oligarchy, as we have seen (p. 67). The tribunes, guardians of the people's rights, became mere yes men of the Senate.

Thus by the middle of the second century B.C., the government was in the hands of the wealthy, self-seeking Senate, which was unable to cope with the problems of governing a world-state; the bulk of the population in Italy was impoverished and landless; and Rome swarmed with fortune hunters, imported slaves, unemployed farmers, and discontented war veterans, who were convinced that the state owed them a living.

The next century (133-31 B.C.) was to see Rome convulsed by civil war, even while engaged in occasional foreign wars. The inefficiency of the Senate in carrying on foreign conflicts was noticeable, but most serious was its inability to solve the economic and social problems following in the wake of Rome's conquests. This weakness was to lead finally to the establishment of a dictatorship and the extinction of the republic.

Reform movements of the Gracchi. While a majority of the senators opposed any basic reforms, some citizens saw the need for drastic action, especially in regard to the land problem. Such a reformer was Tiberius Gracchus, who was elected as a tribune in 133 B.C. A scion of one of Rome's finest families, he was also a grandson of Scipio, the man who had defeated Hannibal.

Tiberius proposed to the Tribal Assembly an act limiting the holding of public land to three hundred acres per person. Much of the public land would in the future be held by the present occupants and their descendants, but the surplus was to be confiscated and allotted to landless Roman citizens. Although the Tribal Assembly adopted this

proposal by a wide majority, one of the tribunes, who sided with the senators, vetoed the measure. Tiberius took a fateful—and unconstitutional—step by having the Assembly depose the tribune in question, after which the agrarian bill was passed.

Tiberius again violated custom by standing for reëlection after completing his one-year term. His departures from custom at the expense of privileged and wealthy citizens were not allowed to proceed unchallenged. During the election, partisans of the Senate murdered Tiberius and three hundred of his followers and threw their bodies into the Tiber. The republic's failure at this point to solve its problems without bloodshed stands in striking contrast to its previous success in the advancement of constitutional development by peaceful means.

Tiberius' work was taken up by his younger brother, Gaius Gracchus, who was elected tribune in 123 B.C. Gaius' program included an extension of the policy of reallocating public land. He also wanted to establish colonies in southern Italy and northern Africa as outlets for Rome's surplus population, and to extend the Roman franchise to the Latin cities and to the Italian allies. To protect the poor against speculation in the grain market (especially in times of famine), Gaius committed the government to the purchase of wheat at a fair price and to its subsequent distribution to the urban masses at half the market price. Unfortunately, what was intended as a relief measure later became a dole, whereby free food was distributed—all too often for the advancement of astute politicians—to the entire proletariat.

In order to carry out his program, Gaius, like Tiberius, did not hesitate to weaken the power of the corrupt Senate. The senators' hired thugs again retaliated. In 121 B.C. three thousand of Gaius' followers were killed and Gaius committed suicide.

The Gracchi were inspired by idealistic motives, but it is doubtful whether their policies, even if fully implemented, could have solved Rome's dilemma. Rome had now developed into a world-wide power, and new forms of government were required to cope with its far-flung political commitments and the drastic changes that had taken place in its economic life. The Senate had shown that it had no intention of initiating the necessary legislation, and the Gracchi's deaths were ominous portents of the manner in which the Romans were to decide their internal disputes.

Civil war—first stage: Marius and Sulla. The Roman army had always been made up of farmers who owned their own land and who thought of themselves as loyal citizens of the republic. But this class of citizens had been victimized by adverse economic conditions. To save Rome from invasion by barbarians beyond the Alps, an able and popular general, Gaius Marius (155-86 B.C.), recruited landless farmers for long terms of service, trained them rigorously, and welded them into skillful military units. These professional soldiers swore allegiance to their commanders and were ready to follow them in every undertaking. Thus, about 100 B.C., the character of the army changed from a militia to a career service. Marius was loyal to the republic, but later generals were to use their military power to overthrow the government.

In 88 B.C. the ambitious king of Pontus in Asia Minor declared war on Rome. This declaration of war raised the question of the choice of a general to oppose him. It was customary to select one of the consuls then in office, and the Senate ordered Cornelius Sulla (138-78 B.C.), an able general and a stanch supporter of the Senate's preroga-

tives, to go east. However, those who opposed the Senate contended that important decisions in foreign affairs rested with the Tribal Assembly. As a countermove, this group chose Marius for the eastern command.

Thus the rivalry between Sulla and Marius exposed a fundamental weakness in the existing governmental machinery. In effect both the Senate and the Tribal Assembly claimed to be the ultimate authority in the state. The result of this conflict was disastrous: civil war broke out between the rival generals, each of whom in turn captured Rome with his personal army, and thousands of people on either side were slain in the attending reigns of terror. The first stage of civil war ended in a complete victory for Sulla, who assumed the office of dictator.

Sulla could have abolished the republic had he so desired. Instead, he set out to restore the preëminence of the Senate in order to protect the state from demagogues, ambitious generals, and civil disturbances. To this end, he increased the powers of the Senate and drastically curtailed those of the tribunes and the Tribal Assembly, giving the Senate the complete power over legislation which it had enjoyed two hundred years before. With the conviction that his work would be permanent, Sulla voluntarily resigned his dictatorship in 79 B.C. His changes, which had set the clock back two centuries, were not to last.

Civil war—second stage: Pompey and Caesar. The years of civil war had increased factionalism and discontent and had nursed the ambitions of individuals eager for personal power. Even with its increased powers, the Senate proved unable to cope with the foreign entanglements and domestic disturbances facing the state, and the people looked for new strong men to lead them. The first to come forward was a rich, proud general, Pompey (106-48 B.C.), who had won fame for his successful campaigns in Italy, Africa, and Spain. In 70 B.C. Pompey was elected a consul and, though he was a former partisan of Sulla, found it opportune to obtain the repeal of Sulla's laws against the Tribal Assembly. Pompey then embellished his reputation by widespread conquests in the East: he put an end to the protracted ambitions of the king of Pontus and later carried Roman influence and power to the Euphrates and beyond.

Still another strong man made his appearance in 59 B.C., when Julius Caesar (102?-44 B.C.) allied himself politically with Pompey and was elected consul. Caesar secured for himself an army with which he conquered Gaul, extended Roman frontiers to the Rhine, and even crossed the English Channel into Britain, though the Roman conquest of Britain was not effected until one hundred years later. When absent from Rome, Caesar cannily kept his name before the citizens of the capital by reporting his experiences in the lucidly written account of his military conquests, *Commentaries on the Gallic War*.

Jealous of Caesar's achievements in Gaul and fearful of his ultimate aims, Pompey turned against his former colleague and combined with the Senate to ruin him. When the Senate demanded in 49 B.C. that Caesar disband his army, the latter crossed the Rubicon—the river which formed the boundary between Italy and Cisalpine Gaul, therefore marking the limit of Caesar's province. By crossing the Rubicon—a phrase which we employ today for any step which commits a person to a given course of action—Caesar in effect declared war on Pompey and the Senate. He marched with his forces to Rome, while Pompey and most of the Senate fled eastward. Within a short time the senatorial opposition had been crushed, Pompey was dead, and Caesar was absolute master of Rome.

Caesar created a dictatorship, and during his brief period of rule (49-44 B.C.), he initiated far-reaching reforms. He weakened the power of the Senate and added provincial representatives to its membership, thus making it a more truly representative body. He regulated municipal constitutions, improved the administration of the provinces, inaugurated a public works program, reduced debts, and pared down the number of people receiving free grain. One of his major

Above is shown part of the Pont du Gard, a Roman aqueduct which for centuries brought water to Nîmes, France, then part of Roman Gaul.

acts was to reform the solar calendar in the light of Egyptian knowledge; with minor changes, this calendar is still in use today. Perhaps Caesar's most constructive act was the extension of Roman citizenship to Cisalpine Gaul and to the provinces outside Italy, "the starting-point of a process that transformed the Roman Empire from a military dominion into a commonwealth of equal partners."[4]

Caesar was one of the few leaders of his day who realized that the old republic was, in fact, dead. He believed that benevolent despotism alone could save Rome from continued civil war and the collapse of the state. Regarding his power as hereditary, he made it clear in his will that his grandnephew Octavian (63 B.C.-14 A.D.) was to be the heir to his position. But Caesar incurred the enmity of two very different groups of people: those who sought wealth for their own ends at the expense of the state, and those who still believed that the republic should be retained and who saw Caesar only as a dangerous tyrant. On the Ides (the fifteenth) of

March, 44 B.C., a group of conspirators stabbed Caesar to death in the Senate, and Rome was once more plunged into conflict.

Caesar's assassins had been offended by his trappings of monarchy—his purple robe, the statues erected in his honor, and the coins bearing his portrait—and they may have assumed that with his death the republic would be restored to its traditional status. But the majority of the Roman people were prepared to accept a successor to Caesar in power and in a position that stopped just short of a royal title. The real question was: Who was to be Caesar's successor?

Civil war—third stage: Antony and Octavian. After Caesar's death, his eighteen-year-old heir, Octavian, allied himself with one of Caesar's colleagues, Mark Antony (83?-30 B.C.), against the conspirators and other political opponents. Although he was not a conspirator, Cicero, the renowned orator and champion of the Senate, was put to death, and the conspirators' armies were routed. Then for more than a decade, Octavian and Antony exercised complete autocracy, thanks to their control over the army.

But the ambitions of each man proved too great for the alliance to endure. Antony became infatuated with the queen of Egypt, Cleopatra, whom he married. He even went so far as to transfer Roman territories to her dominions. Octavian took advantage of this high-handedness to arouse Rome and Italy against him. When Octavian's fleet met Antony's at Actium in Greece, Antony and Cleopatra deserted the battle and fled to Egypt. There Antony committed suicide, as did Cleopatra soon afterwards when Alexandria was captured in 30 B.C. At the end of a century of civil violence, Rome was at last united under one ruler, and the republic gave way to the empire. Two centuries of imperial greatness followed: this period, known as the *Pax Romana* (the Roman peace), lasted from 30 B.C. to about 235 A.D.

THE *PAX ROMANA*

Augustus initiates the *Pax Romana*. Following his triumphal return to Rome in 29 B.C., Octavian announced that he would "restore the republic." But he neither took this step nor established an outright monarchy. Instead he provided the Senate with considerable authority, consulted it on important issues, allowed it to retain control over about half of the provinces, and gave it the legislative functions of the nearly defunct Tribal Assembly. The Senate in return bestowed upon Octavian the title *Augustus*, by which he was known thereafter.

After 23 B.C., Augustus held the consulship only twice, and then for only a short part of the year. Where, then, did his strength lie? Throughout his career he kept the power of a tribune (which gave him control of legislation) and the power over the frontier provinces where the imperial armies were stationed. The chief source of Augustus' strength lay in the fact that the army, whose soldiers paid allegiance to him personally, was under his direction. As supreme leader of the army he held the title *imperator,* from which the modern term *emperor* is derived. Thus Augustus effected a compromise "between the need for a monarchical head of the empire and the sentiment which enshrined Rome's republican constitution in the minds of his contemporaries."[5] He summed up his position as that of *princeps,* or first among equals, and his form of government is therefore known as the principate. At the beginning of the empire, then, political power was divided between the Senate and the *princeps* (Augustus). For over two hundred years, this form of government endured, although during this time the Senate slowly faded into the background. After 235 A.D. (as we shall see in Chapter 5), there emerged an absolute monarchy which had no constitutional basis but was backed by the power of the legions.

At the outset of his reign as *princeps*, Augustus faced the problems of curing a sick society and removing the scars resulting from a century of civil strife. The aristocracy was too decadent to be patriotic, and in the cities an unemployed mob favored with free bread and circuses had long since lost interest in hard work.

Wisely, Augustus concentrated on internal problems. Although he extended Roman control as far as the Danube as a defense against barbarian invasions and also made a vain attempt to penetrate beyond the Rhine, expansion of the empire was not one of his major concerns. During his long reign, he improved administration in the provinces and trained a loyal body of civil servants. In addition, taxation was made more efficient and just, and the finances of the empire were placed on a sound basis.

The Julio-Claudian and the Flavian emperors. Augustus was followed by four descendants of his family, the line of the Julio-Claudians, who ruled from 14 to 68 A.D. Tiberius and Claudius were fairly efficient and devoted rulers; in Claudius' reign the Roman occupation of Britain began in 43 A.D. with an invasion which crushed the resistance of the Celtic inhabitants. The other two rulers of this imperial line were of a different stripe. Caligula acted like a madman; on one occasion he made his favorite horse a consul. Nero was infamous for his immorality, the murder of his wife and his mother, and his persecution of Christians in Rome.

During Nero's reign, in 64 A.D., a great fire devastated the capital. The Roman historian Tacitus has left us a vivid description of this catastrophe:

Whether the disaster was accidental or the wicked doing of the emperor is uncertain . . . but the fire was the most violent and destructive that had ever befallen the city. It began in the part of the circus adjacent to the Palatine and Caelian hills. It started in shops stacked with combustibles, was sped by the wind, and at once seized the whole length of the circus. There was no masonry of houses or walls of temples to retard it. First the blaze ran through the level areas, then rose to the hills and devastated the hollows. Its velocity outstripped preventive measures, for old Rome with its winding streets and irregular plan was vulnerable. Aggravating the evil were terrified and shrieking women, the feeble old and inexperienced young, people saving themselves or others, dragging the infirm or waiting for them, hurrying or delaying.[6]

The Julio-Claudian line ended with Nero's suicide in 68 A.D. After a struggle which saw

Augustus

four emperors assume power in the course of the following year, Flavius Vespasianus (Vespasian) gained ascendancy, restored orderly government to Rome, and founded the Flavian dynasty.

For thirty years (69-96 A.D.), the Flavian emperors provided the empire with good rule. By the time of the reign of the last Flavian emperor, all Romans recognized that their rule, good or bad, was provided by the emperor, not by an administration of equals: emperor and Senate. The fiction of republican institutions was giving way to a scarcely veiled monarchy.

The Antonines: "five good emperors." Under the "five good emperors" (96-180 A.D.) —known as the Antonine line—the Roman empire reached the height of its prosperity and power. Two of these emperors are especially worthy of notice.

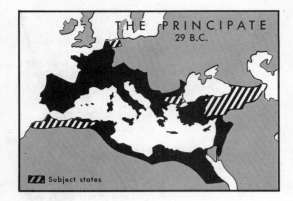

THE PRINCIPATE
29 B.C.

Subject states

Hadrian reigned from 117 to 138 A.D. His first important act was to consolidate the boundaries of the empire. In Germany he erected protective walls, and in Britain he raised Hadrian's Wall, a stone structure running across the narrowest part of the island. Hadrian traveled extensively throughout the empire and devoted his talents to its interests. New towns were founded, old ones restored, and public works were built.

The last of the "good emperors" was Marcus Aurelius, who ruled from 161 to 180 A.D. He approached Plato's ideal of the "philosopher king" and preferred the quiet contemplation of his books to the blood and brutality of the battlefield. Yet, ironically enough, he was repeatedly troubled during his reign by the attempted invasions of Germanic tribes along the northern frontier. While engaged in his Germanic campaigns, he wrote his *Meditations*, a philosophical work notable for its lofty idealism and love of humanity. No other emperor was more devoted to the service of the state.

The "immense majesty of the Roman peace." In the finest period of the empire, a vast area stretching from Britain to the Euphrates and from the North Sea to the Sahara was welded together into what a Roman author, Pliny the Elder, termed "the immense majesty of the Roman peace." Others were equally conscious of the rich benefits derived from Roman rule. To a writer of the late second century, it was:

. . . a world every day better known, better cultivated, and more civilized than before. Every-

where roads are traced, every district is known, every country opened to commerce. Smiling fields have invaded the forests; flocks and herds have routed the wild beasts; the very sands are sown; the rocks are planted; the marshes drained. There are now as many cities as there were once solitary cottages. Reefs and shoals have lost their terrors. Wherever there is a trace of life there are houses and human habitations, well-ordered governments and civilized life.[7]

This quotation throws significant light upon the period known as the *Pax Romana*. First of all, the *Pax Romana* applied to a vast area and population; by the reign of Hadrian, the empire comprised more than one and a quarter million square miles containing upwards of one hundred million people—Italians, Greeks, Egyptians, Germans, Celts, and others.

Secondly, this period witnessed the rapid increase of cities, particularly in frontier provinces; for example, some 160 towns were to be found in the frontier zone across the Rhine and another 120 north of the Danube in what is now Rumania. While the economy remained predominantly agricultural, the empire became progressively more urban in character, with towns and cities forming vital nerve centers linked together by a vast network of highways and waterways. A rich and varied commerce, the lifeblood of the empire, passed over the Roman roads. The empire lay secure behind natural frontiers guarded by well-trained armies, while within the empire the roads had been cleared of brigands, and the seas of pirates.

Thirdly, the *Pax Romana* saw the creation of a cosmopolitan world-state where races and cultures intermingled freely. What were the ties that held this vast empire together?

The Graeco-Roman cultural synthesis. Writing during the rule of Augustus, the Roman poet Virgil was the spokesman for what enlightened Romans felt to be the "mission" of the empire:

Others shall beat out the breathing bronze to softer lines . . . shall draw living lineaments from the marble; the cause shall be more eloquent on their lips; their pencils shall portray the pathways of heaven, and tell the stars in their arising: be thy charge, O Roman, to rule the nations in thine empire; this shall be thine art, to ordain the law of peace, to be merciful to the conquered and beat the haughty down.[8]

By "others," Virgil was referring to the Greeks, to whom the Romans willingly acknowledged a cultural debt. The Roman world-state, while enriched by many cultural strains, such as the Semitic, was predominantly a synthesis of Greek and Latin cultures. Thus the Romans learned the Greek language, copied Greek architecture, employed Greek sculptors, and identified their gods with Greek deities. Although Greek ways of life introduced sophisticated habits which were often corrupting to the Roman virtues of self-reliance, personal integrity, family cohesion, and discipline, Greek influences made the Romans on the whole less harsh and insensitive.

Largely because of their admiration for Greek culture and their belief in maintaining a diversity of cultures within a political unity, the Romans succeeded in establishing a world-state instead of a narrow national empire. While Latin was used in official circles and always in the law, Greek and other native tongues were permitted for everyday conversation in the provinces which had been the Hellenistic states. The Romans spread Greek knowledge, in addition to their own, throughout the world-state, and a synthesis of cultures took place among the diverse peoples. By assimilating and spreading Hellenic elements and preserving Hellenistic culture in the eastern provinces, the Romans helped to perpetuate the Greek legacy. The *Pax Romana* was the acme of Graeco-Roman civilization.

Governing the diverse state. At the head of this huge and diverse world-state stood the emperor, at once the chief defender and the symbol of unity, and an object of veneration. Yet a strong feature of the early period of imperial administration was the large measure of local self-government enjoyed by both provinces and cities. Hundreds of cities even issued their own coins. It was generally believed that such local autonomy contributed to imperial unity.

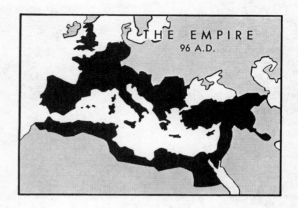

The Roman empire, however, lacked organic unity because it failed to work out means for direct participation by the ordinary citizens in political affairs. True, Roman citizenship had been granted to provinces beyond the Italian peninsula, but no machinery based on representative government had been devised. When one considers that most people of this time did not have the basic education or the current information necessary to form intelligent opinions about imperial affairs, it is doubtful that an adequate public policy could have been established through representative government.

Prosperity in trade and industry. The Roman empire was the economic as well as the political successor to the old Hellenistic monarchies. Rome's unification of the eastern and western segments of the empire had far-reaching economic consequences. The *Pax Romana* was responsible for the creation of new tastes in the West, the elimination of tolls and other artificial barriers, the suppression of piracy and brigandage, and the establishment of relatively good communications and a reliable coinage. All of these factors, in addition to improved methods of banking and credit, explain in large measure the vast economic expansion that occurred in the first and second centuries A.D., probably reaching its height during the reign of Hadrian.

Although the city was the dominant influence in Roman life, agriculture remained the basic economic activity in the empire. Huge

Many homes of the wealthy contained an open court planted with trees and flowers and surrounded by rooms opening onto a roofed veranda supported by columns; shown above is one end of such a court.

estates, often belonging to absentee owners, prospered. On these tracts large numbers of *coloni,* free tenants, tilled the soil. The *coloni* were gradually replacing slave labor, which was becoming increasingly hard to secure with the disappearance of the flow of captives from major wars.

The most important commercial center of the empire was Alexandria, hub of the rich trade with the East. Rome itself exported comparatively little. However, so much revenue poured into the capital from the provinces that its citizens had the necessary purchasing power to buy immense quantities of goods from other parts of the empire and even from regions far to the east of the imperial frontiers. Grain was one of the most important Roman imports, which also included textiles, papyrus, and a variety of luxury goods.

As with commerce, the advances made by industry were due to such general factors as the expansion of markets and demand rather than to any fundamental improvements in organization or technology. Machinery never supplanted handicrafts, and little large-scale production developed. Industry in the Roman empire was organized on a small shop basis and the producers were widely scattered, partly because of the difficulty and cost of distributing goods across such a wide empire, even with the comparatively good Roman transportation system.

Despite the general prosperity during the *Pax Romana,* by the time of the rule of the Antonines the Roman empire had in fact entered upon what has been described as its "Indian summer." Once the empire had ceased to expand geographically, its economy in turn became progressively more static. The army, which in the era of conquests had provided valuable plunder and slaves, proved to be a heavy expense to the state as defensive and immobile garrison forces. Another problem was that of the labor supply; as the number of slaves decreased, no development of machine power arose to take the place of man power. Other factors included the problems of soil exhaustion on old farms and the loss of money into the Oriental luxury trade (see p. 113). Such older areas as Italy tended to show more signs of decline than areas such as Gaul.

The effects of decline were not felt for many decades, however, because the "immense majesty of the Roman peace" served to conceal them. (The economic causes are analyzed further in Chapter 5.)

Rome, imperial capital. At the hub of the sprawling empire was Rome, a kaleidoscopic cross section of society during the *Pax Romana*. About a million inhabitants crowded into an area of a relatively few square miles around the Forum, the center of public and private life.

Augustus boasted that he had found a city of brick and had left one of marble. Nonetheless Rome presented a striking contrast of magnificence and tawdriness, of splendid public buildings and squalid tenements. The crowded narrow streets, lined with apartment houses and swarming with all manner of people, are described by the satirist Juvenal:

. . . Hurry as I may, I am blocked
By a surging crowd in front, while a vast mass
Of people crushes onto me from behind.
One with his elbow punches me, another
With a hard litter-pole: one bangs a beam
Against my head, a wine-cask someone else.
With mud my legs are plastered; from all sides
Huge feet trample upon me, and a soldier's
Hobnails are firmly planted on my toes.[9]

Roman social classes. The living conditions of slaves throughout the capital and the empire varied greatly. Those in domestic service were often treated humanely, and their years of efficient service perhaps rewarded by emancipation. Nor was it uncommon for freed slaves to rise to places of eminence in business and letters. On the other hand, conditions among slaves on the large estates could be indescribably harsh.

While a large proportion of the capital's populace was dependent upon state support in whole or in part, others made a fairly good living as artisans. These workers usually belonged to *collegia*, or guilds, of which there were about eighty, each comprising the workers of one trade. The *collegia* provided a hall for their members, cared for the sick, and arranged for feasts and celebrations. As in Hellenistic times, artisans in guilds could often bargain successfully for higher wages. Where working conditions were harsh, unorganized labor might be driven to strike or even riot before its demands for improvement were met.

With the coming of the empire, the aristocracy had tended to lose its power and influence to the wealthy business class. This class was often composed of newly rich families who spent much of their time and money in showing that they "had arrived." In contrast to the tenements of the poor, the homes of the rich were palatial, containing courts and gardens with elaborate fountains, rooms furnished with marble walls, mosaics on the floors, and numerous frescoes and other works of art. An interesting feature of Roman furniture was the abundance of couches and the scarcity of chairs. People usually reclined, even at meals—a custom which may have had its value during the mammoth dinners served by the wealthy gourmands, who even indulged in the practice of administering emetics to their guests so that they could disgorge their food and start afresh on more food.

Public entertainment. Recreation and sports played a key role in Roman social life. Romans, both rich and poor, were exceedingly fond of their public baths, which in the capital alone numbered eight hundred during the early days of the empire. The baths served the same purpose as our modern-day athletic clubs. In Rome the famous baths of Diocletian and Caracalla contained enclosed gardens, promenades, gymnasiums, libraries, and famous works of art as well as a wide variety of types of baths. An old Roman inscription expresses an interesting philosophy: "The bath, wine, and love ruin one's health but make life worth living."

Foot races, boxing, and wrestling were minor sports; chariot racing and gladiatorial contests were the chief amusements. The cry for "bread and circuses" reached such proportions that by the first century A.D. the Roman calendar had 159 days set aside as holidays, 93 of which were given over to games furnished at public expense. The most spectacular sport was chariot racing. The largest of six race courses at Rome was the Circus Maximus, a huge marble-faced structure measuring some 600 by 200 yards and seating at least 150,000 spectators. The games, which included upwards of 24 races each day, were presided over by the emperor or his representative. The crowds bet furiously on their favorite charioteers, whose fame equaled that of the all-American football heroes of our own day.

Scarcely less popular, but infinitely less civilized, the gladiatorial contests were also organized by the emperors as a regular feature on the amusement calendar. These cruel spectacles, which have no exact counterpart in any other civilization, were held in arenas, the largest and most famous of which was the Colosseum. The contests took various forms. Ferocious animals were pitted against armed combatants or occasionally even against unarmed men and women who had been condemned to death. Another type of contest was the fight to the death between gladiators, generally equipped with different types of weapons but matched on equal terms. It was not uncommon for the life of a defeated gladiator who had fought courageously to be spared at the request of the spectators. Although many Romans decried these bloodletting contests, there persisted a streak of cruelty in Roman public amusements which can scarcely be comprehended, far less condoned, today.

THE ROMAN CONTRIBUTION

Contributions in government. Roman political thinkers such as Cicero contributed the germinal ideas for many governmental theories destined to be influential in later centuries. Some of these deserve mention: the social-contract theory (that government originated as a voluntary agreement among citizens); the idea of popular sovereignty (that all power ultimately resides with the people); the principle of the separation of powers (that the legislative, executive, and judicial branches of the government should be kept separate); and the concept that law must be the paramount rule in government. The despotism of the Roman emperors in the last phases of the empire corroded many of these theories and in their place substituted the theory of the divine right of kings, which had originated with the divine honors

paid to Alexander. Yet these concepts were never lost sight of; they were transmitted to early modern times to form the theoretical basis of contemporary constitutional governments in the West. All important was the Roman tradition of unity and order within a great imperial structure. As we will see in later chapters, this concept was to play an important role in the politics of medieval Europe.

In still other ways did the Romans lay the political framework of modern Europe. Many current administrative divisions, such as the county and province, are derived from Roman practice. In some instances European boundaries are little altered from those existing under the Caesars. The medieval Church also modeled its organization, administrative units, and much of its law after that of the empire. In addition, both the eastern Roman emperors who ruled at Constantinople until 1453 and the German kings of western Europe retained Roman imperial titles and symbols of authority, a Roman system of public finances, and Roman law. The lasting influence of the Romans in government is further illustrated by such political terms in present-day use as *fiscal, senate, consul, plebiscite, citizens, municipal,* and *census.*

Evolution of Roman law. Of the contributions made by the Romans in government and politics, Roman law is preëminent. Abundant evidence of the fact exists today. Two great legal systems, Roman law and English common law, are the foundation of jurisprudence in most modern nations in the West. Roman law is the basis for the law codes of Italy, France, Spain, Scotland, and the Latin-American countries. Where English common law is used, as in the United States, there is also a basic heritage of great legal principles originated by ancient Roman jurists. In addition, Roman legal principles have strongly affected the development of Muslim law and the canon law of the Catholic Church; and international law has borrowed principles inherent in the Roman system.

Roman law evolved slowly during a period of a thousand years. In 449 B.C. the earliest

Above is the Colosseum, which covers nearly six acres in the center of the city of Rome and once provided seats for 45,000 people. Part of the floor of the arena has been removed to show the subterranean chambers which were used by the gladiators and for the dens of wild beasts. The chambers also housed water and drainage pipes which could quickly flood and drain the arena when it was used for mock naval battles. Dedicated to all the gods, the Pantheon (below) was built in 25 B.C. by Agrippa, Augustus' lieutenant, and later rebuilt by Hadrian.

provisions were written down in the Laws of the Twelve Tables. As Rome acquired vast territories, the old civil code (*jus civile*) did not prove sufficiently elastic and comprehensive to meet situations involving non-Romans. And so a new kind of law, the *jus gentium* (law of nations), developed. By the early centuries of the empire, a great mass of law had accumulated which had to be codified—that is, systematized and reduced to fundamental principles. The jurists who began this great work humanized and rationalized existing laws to meet the needs of a world-state. Yet a need remained for complete codification. Between 528 and 534 A.D., in the reign of Justinian, a complete codification of Roman law from all sources was accomplished (see p. 169), thus enabling it to be condensed in a few volumes and preserved easily for posterity.

Roman engineering and architecture. The empire's administrative needs required the building of a communication system of paved roads and bridges and the erection of huge public buildings and aqueducts for the cities. Pride in the empire led also to the erection of ostentatious monuments symbolizing Rome's dignity and might.

As road builders, the Romans surpassed all previous peoples. Constructed of layers of stone according to sound engineering principles, their roads were planned for the use of armies and messengers and were kept in constant repair. One of the earliest main Roman highways was the Appian Way, a heavily traveled route to the southeastern Italian ports, from which the Romans took ship for Greece and the eastern Mediterranean. Later the Flaminian Way, running northeast from Rome to the Adriatic Sea and connected with other roads to the northern provinces, was built. It has been said that the speed of travel possible on Roman highways was not surpassed until the early nineteenth century.

In designing their bridges, the Romans placed a series of arches next to one another to provide mutual support. The aqueducts consisted of several tiers of arches, one above the other, which provided a tall base for a water channel (see photo, p. 73). Fourteen aqueducts, stretching a total of 265 miles, supplied some fifty gallons of water daily for each inhabitant of Rome.

At first the Romans copied Greek architectural models, but later they combined basic Greek elements with developments that were distinctly Roman. The structural simplicity of Hellenic buildings was too restrained for the Romans, who developed new concepts for enclosing space. The static post and lintel system of the Greeks was replaced with the more dynamic structural system of the arch and vault (see diagram).

Another important advance in architectural engineering was the Romans' success in constructing concrete domes large enough to roof a substantial span. The weight of the dome was transferred directly to the walls, and since there was no sidewise thrust, no other support was necessary. The largest of the domed structures was a Roman temple, the Pantheon, which is still standing (see illustration, p. 81).

The basilica, an important Roman civic building, was a colonnaded building. It had a central nave with side aisles. To permit clerestory windows like those found in such Egyptian temples as Karnak, the central roof was elevated above the side walls. The influence of the Roman basilica on later architecture was very marked; in plan it contained the germ of the Gothic cathedral (see p. 240 for diagram).

Perhaps the most famous Roman edifice is the Colosseum (see photo, p. 81), a huge structure about one quarter of a mile around on the outside and with a seating capacity estimated to have been at least 45,000. The Colosseum utilized three stories of arches; for ornamental effect, columns were inserted between the arches. The columns were "engaged," which means that they were applied flat to the wall with only about a half of their diameter protruding.

Two basic characteristics of Roman construction were solidity and magnificence of conception. Roman buildings were built to last, and their vastness, grandeur, and decorative richness aptly symbolized the proud imperial spirit of Rome. Whereas the Greeks evolved the temple, theater, and stadium, the Romans contributed the triumphal arch, bath, basilica, amphitheater, and multistoried apartment house. Many of our modern public buildings show the influence of Roman models.

Realism in sculpture and painting. Although they were deeply influenced by Greek models, the Romans developed a distinctive sculpture of their own which tended to be realistic, secular, and individualistic. Perhaps the earlier Etruscan art had exerted a strong influence in this regard (for an example, see Color Plate 5). Whereas the Greeks idealized their subject matter and portrayed types rather than individuals, the Romans were at their best when producing lifelike busts of administrators, soldiers, and emperors. Roman coins with relief portraits of emperors served to glorify the Roman empire and were also effective propaganda for particular emperors. Equestrian statues, sculptured coffins, or sarcophagi, and the reliefs found on Roman imperial monuments were also exceptionally fine works of art. The Romans developed a great fund of decorative motifs such as cupids, garlands of flowers, and scrolls of various patterns; and these have continued in use to the present.

In painting, the Romans were technically far advanced; they relied to some extent on Greek models, adapting and embellishing Greek style according to their own tastes. The Romans were particularly skilled in painting frescoes; those still to be seen in Pompeii and elsewhere show that the artist drew the human figure accurately and showed objects in correct perspective.

Literary Rome. In literature as in art, the Romans turned to the Greeks for their models. Roman epic, dramatic, and lyric poetry forms were usually written in conscious imitation of Greek masterpieces. Compared with Greek literature, however, Latin writing was more moralistic and less speculative and imaginative. But it remains one of the world's great literatures largely because the Romans made original contributions in such fields as didactic poetry, historical writing, and satire.

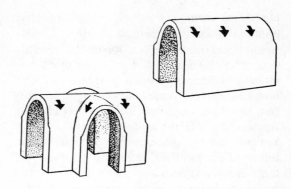

From the Etruscans, the Romans learned how to build the BARREL VAULT—a continuous series of arches forming a tunnel-like structure. The walls of the vault had to be thick and strong to support the sideways and downward pressure of the material above. An advance in technique was made when Roman engineers joined two barrel vaults at right angles to form an INTERSECTING VAULT. Because the weight of the material was then spread over a larger area, the walls did not need to be as thick as those of a barrel vault. Also, openings in the supporting walls furnished window space.

The most important development in early Latin literature was the drama. Tragic drama was not popular in Rome; but the people delighted in comedies, many of which were adapted from Greek originals. One of the Laws of the Twelve Tables punished political satire with death. Therefore, to avoid censure, Latin playwrights retained Greek characters and names even in the plays about Roman life.

The Golden Age of Latin literature. Although Latin literature had its beginnings before the Punic Wars, it was in the first century B.C. that it entered its first great period of creative activity. An outpouring of splendid intellectual effort coincided with the last stages of the republic. This period marks the first half of the Golden Age of Latin literature, known as the Ciceronian period because of the stature of Marcus Tullius Cicero (106-43 B.C.), the greatest master of Latin prose and perhaps the outstanding intellectual influence in Roman history. The Ciceronian period was also marked by the excellent historical narrative of Julius Caesar, *Commentaries on the Gallic War*.

Acclaimed as the greatest orator of his day, Cicero found time during his busy public life to write extensively on philosophy, political theory, rhetoric, and literary criticism. Some nine hundred of his letters still exist and these, together with his other numerous writings, give us unrivaled insight into Cicero as a personality, as well as into the problems and manners of republican Rome. Much of the value of Cicero's letters lies precisely in the fact that they were not intended for publication and so he spoke his mind freely. Cicero also made a rich contribution to knowledge by passing on to later ages much of Greek thought—especially that of Plato and the Stoics—and at the same time interpreting it from the standpoint of a Roman intellectual and practical man of affairs. He did more than any other Roman to make Latin a great literary language.

The Ciceronian period also witnessed the writing of exuberant lyrical poetry, the best of which was composed by Catullus (*c.* 87-54 B.C.), a young man-about-town who wrote intensely of his loves and hates. At the other end of the personality spectrum was Catullus' contemporary, Lucretius (99-55 B.C.), a poet immersed in Greek philosophy. His epic poem *On the Nature of Things* will be discussed on page 85.

To the new empire, Augustus brought political stability and a social and intellectual climate conducive to a further outpouring of poetry and prose. The second period of the Golden Age of Latin literature, the Augustan period, was notable particularly for its excellent poetry. Virgil (70-19 B.C.) was probably the greatest of all Roman poets. His masterpiece, a great national epic called the *Aeneid,* glorifies the family of Augustus and eloquently asserts Rome's destiny to conquer and rule the world. Using Homer's *Iliad* and *Odyssey* as his models, Virgil recounted the fortunes of Aeneas, the legendary founder of the Latin people, who came from his home in Troy to Italy. The *Aeneid* breathes Virgil's deep and enthusiastic patriotism and is as much a piece of imperial symbolism as Rome's triumphal arches.

Horace (65-8 B.C.) was famous for both lyrical odes and satirical verse. Succeeding generations of educated people have turned to Horace for enjoyment and quotable phrases because of his urbane viewpoint and polished style. Modeled on Aristotle's Doctrine of the Mean, Horace's philosophy stipulated a constant equanimity, even to the point of being indifferent to death.

Quite a different sort was Ovid (43 B.C.-17 A.D.), a poet akin to Catullus in spirit and personal life, who combined a predilection for themes on love with first-rate storytelling. In fact, it is largely through his *Metamorphoses* that classical mythology was transmitted to the modern world.

The Silver Age. The Silver Age of Latin Literature, a period of time which comprised the century and a quarter from the death of Augustus to the death of Hadrian (14-138 A.D.), was marked by a more critical and negative spirit than that of its predecessor. Whereas the Augustan period had evoked lyrical odes and a majestic epic, the Silver Age was memorable for its brilliant satirical poetry.

With Juvenal (55?-130 A.D.), satire in Latin poetry reached its peak. This master of poetic invective flayed the shortcomings of contemporary Roman society. His brilliant epigrammatic phrases were destined to influence the writings of the famous Neoclassical English satirists Jonathan Swift and Alexander Pope.

The writing of history. Historians, three of whom deserve mention, produced notable works during the Golden and Silver Ages. The first, Livy (59 B.C.-17 A.D.), was a contemporary of Virgil; his immense *History of Rome*, like the latter's *Aeneid*, is of epic proportions and glorifies Rome's conquests and achievements. Livy assembled the traditions of early Roman history and welded them into a single continuous narrative—a new procedure for historians and a valuable contribution to the writing of history.

Tacitus (55-117 A.D.), like the satirist Juvenal, was concerned with improving contemporary society, but he used history rather than poetry to serve his ends. In his *Germania*, Tacitus contrasted the life of the idealized, simple German tribes with the corrupt and immoral existence of the Roman

1 (left) **Sumerian offering stand of wood, inlay, and gold foil** (3000-2340 B.C.). The goat, symbol of male fertility, represents the god Tammuz. According to ancient legends, Tammuz was the lover of Ishtar, the earth goddess, who killed him and then later restored him to life. The Sumerians celebrated the yearly death and rebirth of vegetation by making offerings and sacrifices to these two deities.

2 (below) **Wooden scale model of a fishing and fowling boat** (2000 B.C.). Because they believed that the dead could partake of life's pleasures in the afterlife, the Egyptians furnished the tombs of their pharaohs and nobles with representations of life on earth—paintings, sculpture, and models like this one.

3 (far left) **Greek vase** (c. 400 B.C.). Decorated with scenes of a sculptor's workshop, the vase shows a sculptor painting a statue. Because so few Greek statues have retained their color, we tend to think of them as typically white or "stone-colored." Actually, Greek sculpture (and architecture as well) blazed with vivid color.

4 (upper left) **Vase from Minos** (c. 1700 B.C.). Ancient Cretan ceramics are notable for their fine craftsmanship and their designs based on natural forms; the flowers on this vase are lilies.

5 (left) **Etruscan tomb painting** (c. 480 B.C.). The Etruscans, like the Egyptians, surrounded their dead with wall paintings depicting both earthly pleasures and religious subjects. This player of the double pipes is taking part in a ritual dance.

6 (above) **Mosaic from Pompeii** (c. 100 B.C.). The mosaic, based on a fourth-century B.C. Greek painting, pictures the battle of Alexander and Darius III at Issus. Alexander, the figure in the detail shown here, is portrayed with the realistic excitement and movement characteristic of Greek art after the fifth century B.C.

7 Fresco from the synagogue at Dura-Europos (245-256 A.D.). Located on the Euphrates at the border between Mesopotamia and Roman territory, Dura-Europos flourished as a Graeco-Semitic trading center during the early centuries B.C. and A.D. The city was founded by Macedonians and settled by various Near Eastern peoples, and its culture emerged from this meeting of East and West. The Jews who embellished their synagogue with this depiction of the story of Mordecai's triumph over Haman, from the Book of Esther, were sufficiently Hellenized to ignore the traditional Hebrew prohibition of representational art. Significantly, the artist's style combines the realism of Roman frescoes with the "flat" forms typical of oriental art.

upper classes. In the *Annals,* a history of Rome from the death of Augustus to that of Nero, he used his vivid prose to depict the shortcomings of the emperors and their courts. Some of his brief, trenchant statements have been quoted for centuries; for example, "Tyranny is never secure" and (in his description of Roman conquest) "They make a solitude and call it peace." Critical in his use of source materials, Tacitus nevertheless suffered from the bias of his own senatorial class, so that he looked upon the emperors as tyrants. Consequently, he could not do justice in his writings to the positive contributions of imperial government.

The most famous Greek author in the Roman empire was Plutarch (46?-120? A.D.). Holding a governmental office under the Roman authority in his local city, he used his leisure time to carry out research on the outstanding figures in Roman and Greek history in order to discover what qualities make men great or ignoble. His most famous work, *The Parallel Lives,* contains forty-six biographies of famous Greeks and Romans, arranged in pairs for the purpose of comparison. Plutarch's *Lives* is a mine of invaluable information for the classical historian. Shakespeare used this work to obtain facts and historical background for such tragic dramas as *Julius Caesar* and *Antony and Cleopatra.*

Latin, the standard language for Rome's successors. Latin literature was the dominant influence in the development of vernacular languages and literature in much of Europe. Out of the Latin spoken by the common people in the Roman empire there gradually evolved during the Middle Ages the Romance languages, of which Italian, Spanish, Portuguese, French, and Rumanian are the major tongues. It is estimated, moreover, that more than half of our English words are of Latin origin. By early modern times, the vernacular languages had largely displaced Latin as a literary medium. But even today Ciceronian Latin remains a regular part of many educational curriculums, while the style of Latin used by Christian writers of the late empire is still employed by the Roman Catholic Church.

Stoicism and Epicureanism. Neither in science nor in philosophy did the Romans approach the Greeks. They contributed no original philosophical theories but preferred to adapt existing Greek systems of thought to suit their needs. As men of action with grave governmental responsibilities, the Romans paid scant attention to such abstract problems as the nature of the universe and of human knowledge. Instead, they concentrated on Hellenistic Greek ethics, which had an obvious bearing on questions of politics and personal behavior. As a consequence, the two main Hellenistic Greek ethical systems, Epicureanism and Stoicism, attracted far more interest in Rome than the speculations of Plato and Aristotle.

Epicureanism made its greatest impact during the last days of the republic, since men found its tenets comforting in a period of political upheaval when no one knew what the morrow would bring. As young men, Virgil and Horace embraced Epicureanism, but the poet-philosopher Lucretius was perhaps the most important Roman interpreter of this philosophy. In his work *On the Nature of Things,* Lucretius based his explanation of the "nature of things" on materialism and atomism. He called on men to free themselves from superstition and to rely instead upon their own resources, since the gods had nothing to do with the fate of human beings. Interpreting the views of Epicurus, Lucretius exhorted his readers to "make the most of today," to seek pleasure not in sensuous gratification but in philosophical serenity, and to have no fear of death.

More enduring, especially in the days of the empire, was the appeal of Stoicism as modified to suit the Roman temperament. It has been said that the Romans gave Stoicism "a dose of common sense," for they aimed at controlling rather than stifling their emotions. The goal of the Roman Stoic was right conduct—that is, to remain poised in a world full of uncertainty, pain, and sorrow. The solution advanced by Stoic thought was resignation and self-sufficiency. Man must not question the operation of natural law but, if wise, will accept whatever fate nature has in store for him, remaining in full control of his emotions and impervious to pleasure and pain alike.

One of the most outstanding Stoics was Seneca (4 B.C.-65 A.D.), Nero's tutor, a major writer of tragic dramas, and a significant essayist. He was regarded with high favor by the leaders of the early Christian Church for he came nearer to the concept of monotheism and the doctrine of immortality than most Romans. In addition, he emphasized the virtue of service to mankind and the concept of human brotherhood.

Science in the Roman empire. The Romans had little scientific curiosity, and they preferred to borrow the findings of Hellenistic science for their own practical uses. They became masters in applied medicine, public health, engineering, and map making.

The Romans instituted the first real hospitals and medical schools and developed the extensive practice of hydrotherapy—the use of mineral baths for healing. One of the first systems of public medical service was started in the early empire, and a large number of public doctors were employed in infirmaries where the poor could obtain free medical care. The Roman concern for public health was evident in the great aqueducts that supplied millions of gallons of water to Rome daily and in the admirable drainage systems.

Characteristic of their utilitarian approach to science was the Romans' predilection for amassing immense encyclopedias. The most important of these was the *Natural History* compiled by Pliny the Elder (23-79 A.D.), an enthusiastic collector of all kinds of scientific odds and ends. In writing his massive work, Pliny is reputed to have read more than two thousand books. The result is an intriguing mixture of fact and fable thrown together with scarcely any method of classification. It was the most widely read book on science during the empire and much of the Middle Ages. Pliny himself was suffocated by a rain of hot ashes while he was studiously observing the eruption of Mount Vesuvius at Pompeii.

If the Romans themselves were seldom preoccupied with scientific investigation, there were others in the empire who were engaged in serious research. During the *Pax Romana*, the Greeks at Alexandria continued their mathematical and geographical studies. Roman legions in Europe and Greek traders traveling to distant Asian lands provided geographers with important data for new maps of the world. The most famous geographer and astronomer was an Alexandrian scholar named Ptolemy, who lived in the middle of the second century A.D. His map work shows a comparatively accurate knowledge of a broad section of the Old World, and he used an excellent projection system for his maps (see illustration).

Unfortunately for his reputation in centuries to come, Ptolemy is often remembered for some of his serious errors. He exaggerated the length and width of the known world, an error which influenced Columbus' decision to set sail from Spain in search of Asia. Later explorers were also eager to find the *terra australis incognita*—a strip of land extending from Africa to Asia which Ptolemy had drawn on his maps. By chance they stumbled upon the continent which we know today as Australia. In the field of astronomy, Ptolemy's work includes the usual Hellenistic proofs that the world is round but accepts a theory already discarded by the Greek Aristarchus—that the world is at rest in the middle of the universe. As a result of Ptolemy's views, the geocentric theory was generally accepted in western Europe until the sixteenth century.

Still another Greek in the Roman empire advanced the scope of scientific knowledge. Born in Pergamum in Asia Minor, Galen (139?-200?) was a physician for a school of gladiators. His fame spread and he was called to Rome, where he became physician to Marcus Aurelius.

Galen was responsible for notable advances in physiology and anatomy; for example, he was the first to explain the mechanism of respiration. Forbidden by the Roman government to dissect human bodies, Galen experimented with animals and demonstrated that an excised heart can continue to beat outside the body and that injuries to one side of the

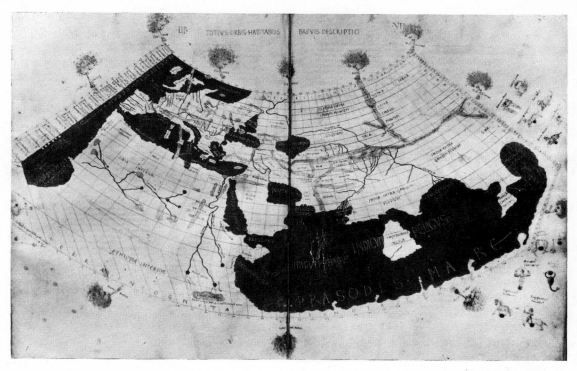

This map, designed by Ptolemy in the second century, represents the first attempt to project the curved surface of the earth on a flat surface. The outline of the European continent is easily recognizable at the upper left.

brain produce disorders in the opposite side of the body. The most experimental-minded of ancient physicians, he once wrote:

I confess the disease from which I have suffered all my life—to trust . . . no statements until, so far as possible, I have tested them for myself.[10]

His medical encyclopedia, in which he summarized the medical knowledge of his time, remained the standard authority for medical men until well into the Renaissance.

SUMMARY

The story of how Rome rose from the insignificant status of a muddy village along the banks of the river Tiber to the mighty position of ruler of the Mediterranean world will always remain one of the most fascinating epics in world history. Emerging from obscurity about the middle of the eighth century before Christ, the Latin people who clustered about Rome and its seven hills suc-

ceeded in 509 B.C. in ousting their Etruscan overlords and establishing a republic. Two themes are dominant in the next four hundred years of Roman history: the gradual democratization of the government and the conquest of the Mediterranean.

During the first two centuries, the plebeians succeeded in breaking down the privileged position of the patricians by obtaining recognition of their fundamental rights as citizens and by acquiring a more important share of political power. The influence of the democratic tradition is seen in the development of Roman law and political theory. Roman law was a basic influence upon subsequent legal thought in the West. The Romans left us the concepts of the supremacy of the law, of social contract, the sovereignty of the people, and the separation of governmental powers.

The other theme in the early history of Rome was the conquest of the Mediterranean. Between the years 509 and 270 B.C., the Romans crushed all resistance to their rule in Italy. They then turned their attention to Carthage, and after a herculean struggle Carthage surrendered in 201 B.C. Having conquered the West, the Romans turned toward the East and in short order defeated the successors of Alexander the Great. But as the Mediterranean world succumbed to the Roman legions, Rome itself faced civil war and degeneration.

Several patriotic reformers, such as the Gracchi brothers, tried to persuade the Senate to enact necessary reforms, but to no avail. Marius, Sulla, Pompey, and Julius Caesar mark the appearance of one-man rule and the end of the republic. Augustus, the heir of Caesar, ruled Rome wisely and well. On the surface the old republican characteristics of government, such as the Senate, were preserved, but Augustus wielded the real power in the new government, which is called the principate. For two hundred years, during the *Pax Romana,* many millions of people in Italy and the empire's provinces enjoyed peace and prosperity.

Through the Roman achievement of a single empire and a cosmopolitan culture, the Greek legacy was preserved, synthesized, and disseminated—and the Romans were able in their own right to make important contributions. Although they lacked the brilliance of the Greeks, they excelled in political theory, governmental administration, and jurisprudence. Their essentially conservative and judicious attitude of mind compensated for their lack of creativity. Primarily synthesists rather than innovators, the Romans willingly admitted their cultural indebtedness and by doing so exhibited a magnanimity characteristic of the Roman spirit at its best. The *Pax Romana* could have been fashioned and maintained only by a people grave in nature, mature in judgment, and aware of responsibilities.

SUGGESTIONS FOR READING

D. R. Dudley, *The Civilization of Rome,** Mentor. A concise, well-illustrated history, with close attention paid to literature and art. Other useful and readable surveys are R. Geer, *Classical Civilization: Rome,* 2nd ed., Prentice-Hall, 1950, which stresses culture; R. Barrow, *The Romans,** Penguin, which emphasizes the Roman mind and character; and M. Rostovtzeff, *Rome,** Galaxy, which is mainly political.

D. H. Lawrence, *Etruscan Places,** Compass. A fascinating appraisal of Etruscan culture by a novelist who sees the extinction of the Etruscan way of life by the "puritanical" Romans as a catastrophe for western civilization. The best scholarly study is H. Pallottino, *The Etruscans,** Penguin.

T. Mommsen, *The History of Rome,** Meridian. A compact edition of what is by common consent the most important history of the republic. Mommsen attributes the republic's fall largely to the Roman nobility, who are pictured as being like the reactionary German nobles of his own time—the 1840's. In R. E. Smith, *The Failure of the Roman Republic,* Cambridge Univ., 1955, the blame is placed upon the Gracchi. An objective attempt "to look back to the time when things went well and try to see what subsequently went wrong" is made in F. Cowell, *Cicero and the Roman Republic,** Penguin.

R. Syme, *The Roman Revolution,** Oxford. Provocatively argues that the principate of Augustus "was the work of fraud and bloodshed, based upon the seizure of power and redistribu-

tion of property by a revolutionary leader." Should be compared with the more balanced but less exciting study by F. B. Marsh, *The Founding of the Roman Empire,* Oxford, 1927.

M. P. Charlesworth, *The Roman Empire,* Oxford, 1951. A brief interpretative study. H. Mattingly, *Roman Imperial Civilisation,* Arnold, 1957, treats topically all aspects of civilization from Augustus to 476 A.D.

M. Johnson, *Roman Life,* Scott, Foresman, 1957. Contains a wealth of information about everyday life, lavishly illustrated. Imperial Rome during the second century A.D. is brought to life in J. Carcopino, *Daily Life in Ancient Rome,** Yale. S. Dill, *Roman Society from Nero to Marcus Aurelius,** Meridian, is a classic of social history; while a nontechnical work on the Roman economy is T. Frank, *An Economic History of Rome,* 2nd ed., Johns Hopkins, 1927.

M. Grant, *Roman Literature,** Penguin. A good introduction, illustrated by passages from the more important writers. Two well-known books by J. W. Duff, *A Literary History of Rome from the Origins to the Close of the Golden Age,* 3rd ed., E. Benn, Ltd., 1953, and *A Literary History of Rome in the Silver Age,* Scribner's, 1927, are unsurpassed for both attractiveness of style and the ability to relate literature and life. With its enlightening commentaries, the most useful collection of Roman sources is N. Lewis and M. Reinhold, *Roman Civilization,* 2 vols., Columbia Univ., 1951-1953.

The development of Roman major and minor arts is traced in H. B. Walters, *The Art of the Romans,* Macmillan, 1934.

*Indicates an inexpensive paperbound edition.

CHAPTER 4

The Asian Way of Life

ANCIENT INDIA AND CHINA TO 220 A.D.

Introduction. Throughout Asia today there is an enormous restlessness, as if a giant were waking from a long sleep and flexing his muscles. The peoples of Asia, stimulated by the spirit of nationalism, are conscious of their strength—of their tremendous man power, of their long-neglected natural resources, which twentieth-century science and technology are now developing, and of their significance in the world political picture. Their leaders are demanding a strong voice in the council of nations, and as that voice swells in volume, the giant is being heard.

This chapter will trace the genesis and development of the two oldest continuous civilizations now in existence—the Indian and the Chinese—in order to learn how their ancient institutions and attitudes continue to affect the life of Asia and, indirectly, our own lives. In addition, this chapter will examine the penetration of western culture into Asia and the resulting cultural countermovement. These exchanges provide us with our first view of historical development on a global scale.

An Indian scholar has written: "All that India can offer to the world proceeds from her philosophy."[1] Indian philosophers have consistently held a fundamental belief in the unity of life—a unity within which has been assimilated and synthesized a variety of beliefs and customs from both native and foreign cultures. Thus, a basic concept dominates the life and thought of both ancient and modern India—unity in diversity. India's intricate religious philosophy developed in ancient times, along with a unique social pattern, the caste system. Since ancient times, the focal point of Indian thought has been religion, and the focus of Indian society has been caste.

Where religion has dominated the customs and attitudes of India's people, the Chinese have been more humanistic and worldly. Their attitude toward life has led to a concern for natural science, the art of government, the keeping of historical records, and the formulation of down-to-earth ethical standards. But despite the very great differences in their cultures, these two nations of Asia have much in common. Weighed down by poverty, both can look back to days of ancient glory; striving to direct their own affairs, both can remember foreign conquerors; hemmed in by age-old tradition and custom, both find themselves in a world of nuclear power and space science. The course that these countries follow in the future will inevitably be conditioned by all that they have experienced in the long centuries since their birth.

INDIA*: UNITY IN DIVERSITY

Geography of India. We can think of India as a gigantic triangle, bounded on two sides by ocean and on the third by the mountain wall of the Himalayas. Through the passes to the northwest came the armed conquerors, restless tribes, and merchants and travelers who did much to shape the turbulent history of this land.

For purposes of discussion, the land can be divided into four parts: the westernmost portion is now known as Baluchistan; next to Baluchistan and north of the Narbada River is Hindustan; the area between the Narbada and Kistna rivers is called the Deccan; and the territory south of the Kistna River is called Tamil Land. Our interest lies principally in Hindustan, where India's earliest civilization developed.

In recent years some eminent scholars of ancient history have come to the conclusion that the ancient Near East should not be considered as isolated from the Asian lands to the east. Rather, we should conceive of a "Greater Near East" which extended beyond the Fertile Crescent through Iran and Baluchistan to the Indus valley. By taking this larger western Asian setting as the subject for investigations, archaeologists are discovering significant cultural relationships between Mesopotamia, Iran, and India.

The Indus civilization. How old is the Indus valley culture, which was the first Indian culture to reach a level of achievement which can be described as civilization? Some scholars have placed the beginnings of the Indus valley civilization in the millennium commencing about 2500 B.C., but a more recent estimate has revised this figure so that the time span is from 2200 to 1300 B.C.[2]

The Indus civilization eventually extended some 950 miles along the valley from the Himalayan foothills in the north to the coast, embracing an area estimated to have been twice the size of the Old Kingdom in Egypt and some four times the size of Sumer and Akkad. Harappa and Mohenjo-Daro, the two largest cities which have been excavated, were the political capitals and commercial centers of this region.

The Indus civilization comprised numerous cities and small towns, and although Harappa and Mohenjo-Daro were 350 miles apart, the Indus River made possible the maintenance of a strictly organized and uniform administration and economy over the large area. "From end to end of this territory, from some forty settlement sites, come pottery vessels of identical mass-produced types; houses are built of baked bricks of standard dimensions; stamp-seals are used engraved with similar scenes and a uniform script, as yet unread; a standard system of weights is recognizable."[3] Grains were cultivated, cattle and sheep domesticated, metals worked, textiles made, and trade carried on. There is evidence that considerable trade existed between the Indus cities and those of Sumer. While revealing characteristics typically Indian, the Indus valley civilization was based upon techniques and crafts similar to earlier Sumerian and

*Until the text deals with the creation of the separate states of India and Pakistan in 1947, the word *India* will refer to the *entire* subcontinent.

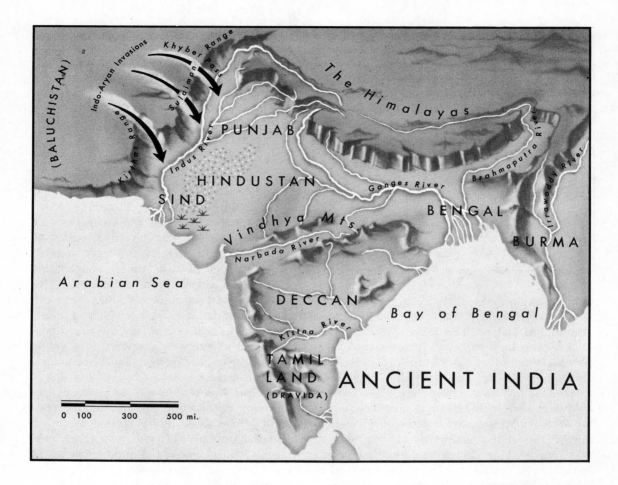

Egyptian methods, indicating some possible borrowing of culture.

For centuries the peoples of the Indus valley pursued a meticulously regulated, efficient, but relatively static way of life. At Mohenjo-Daro, however, excavations show clearly the decline of the city in its latter days. Street frontages were no longer strictly observed, the brickwork was becoming shoddy, and residential areas were degenerating into slums. Finally, groups of skeletons huddled together in their dwellings suggest that this city and perhaps the entire civilization came to a sudden end around 1300 B.C. We can only speculate on what great common disaster—plague, flood, or outside attack —may have overtaken these unfortunate people.

Indo-Aryan invasions of India. Sometime around 1500 B.C., there began an invasion of

India by a group of Aryans migrating from the shores of the Black and Caspian seas (see p. 15). In a few hundred years, they conquered and settled the upper Indus valley and began penetrating the Ganges region. A tall people with fair skins and long heads, the Aryans ate and drank heartily, fought readily, and lived a simple life. The number of cattle a man owned was the measure of his wealth, and the word for war meant "a desire for more cows." Each tribe was headed by a rajah, women had a high social status, and marriage was monogamous and confined to the group.

As time passed, the Indo-Aryan invaders contemptuously referred to the people they conquered as *Dasyu*, or slaves. Who were the *Dasyu*? They may have been members of the Indus valley civilization or descendants of them, physically resembling a clearly

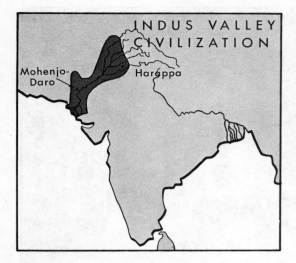

defined group, the Dravidians, who are known to have been the early inhabitants of southern India. (The residents encountered by the Indo-Aryans were described as people with an advanced culture and as dark-skinned, like the partially Negroid Dravidians.) Whoever they were, the *Dasyu* were overcome by the storm of invasion from the north. Indo-Aryan poetry tells of the wars the Aryans waged against the *Dasyu*, who were enslaved or driven southward, much as the North American Indians were pushed back by the pioneers. The *Dasyu*, however, possessed a civilization superior to that which the Indo-Aryans brought from the northwest; and the invaders borrowed many customs and ideas from the conquered people, including their system of land tenure and taxation and their village community. The native people of India also influenced the development of the Indo-Aryan tongue, Sanskrit.

The Vedic Age (c. 1500-900 B.C.). Prior to the invasion of India, the Indo-Aryan tribal structure included only two classes, the nobility and the common tribesmen. In the process of subjugating and settling among the dark-skinned natives, the Indo-Aryans realized that they would be absorbed racially unless they took steps to prohibit intermarriage. Class division now took on a new purpose—that of preserving purity of race. This concept is intrinsic in the Sanskrit

word for class, *varna*, which means "color." (It was translated later by Portuguese travelers as *casta*, from the Latin *castus*, meaning "pure"; hence, the term *caste*.)

The Indo-Aryan collections of religious hymns, the *Vedas*, are the oldest examples of Sanskrit literature. They provide us with a picture of the times in which they were composed, and they show that after the Indo-Aryan invaders had conquered the land, they settled down to village life, tilling and irrigating the soil and raising grains. In many ways village life was similar to that of modern India, although complexities of later Indian life such as the restriction of women's rights and the prohibition against eating cattle did not exist at this time. The most important figure of the village was the headman, sometimes elected and at other times holding his position by hereditary right. The village was composed of a group of families, and the villagers worked as farmers or artisans or both.

The Epic Age (c. 900-500 B.C.). About the beginning of the ninth century B.C., the center of power and culture shifted eastward from the upper Indus valley to the upper Ganges valley. There the Indo-Aryans created small, isolated city-states, each sovereign unto itself. The great epic poems which describe the life of these times tell of constant warfare and shifting military alliances among these city-states.

The cities of the Epic Age were surrounded by moats and walls, and their streets were well planned. Usually occupying a palace located at the center of a city, the rajah possessed powers greater than those of the village headman of the Vedic Age. He had his own retinue of followers and was advised by a royal council composed of his relatives and nobles. He received taxes and was probably, in theory at least, the owner of all land. In cities a tradesman class existed, and unskilled, menial tasks were performed by slaves.

The village community. In Vedic and Epic times the three pillars of traditional Indian society—the autonomous village, caste, and the joint-family—were erected. India has always been primarily agricultural, and its countryside is still a patchwork of thousands of villages. As we mentioned, the village in early times was made up of family groups, who possessed certain rights and duties and were governed by the headman. An elected council of villagers distributed the land and collected taxes. Women were allowed to serve on the council. Villages within a city-state enjoyed considerable autonomy, with the rajah's government hardly interfering at all as long as it received its quota of taxes. This system of self-governing villages continued until government became more centralized under British rule.

Growth of the caste system. The earliest caste division had been inaugurated to separate the Indo-Aryans from the *Dasyu*. In the Epic Age, however, caste became more sharply defined and complex as the Indo-Aryans themselves split into castes. The four castes recognized at this time were, in order of their rank: (1) the Brahmans, or priests; (2) the Kshatriyas, or warriors; (3) the Vaisyas, or traders, merchants, and bankers; and (4) the Sudras, or farm workers and serfs. In addition there was a group of outcastes, or Pariahs, called "untouchables" because their touch was considered defiling to the upper castes. The non-Aryan population remained at the bottom of the social scale, as Sudras and outcastes.

At first, the Kshatriyas had a higher social rank than the Brahmans; but as time went on, warfare declined while religion increased in importance. As educators of youth, historians, and intermediaries between the gods and men, the priests assumed the dominant position which they have successfully maintained into the twentieth century. Eventually, the four castes were subdivided into thousands of groups with special social, economic, and religious significance. The definition and order of importance of the four castes have remained much the same, however, throughout India's history.

The joint-family. The third pillar of Indian tradition was the joint-family. "Joint in food, worship, and estate," the family was made up of descendants of a common ancestor.

Scenes like this one show how little Indian village life has changed since the Vedic Age. Through the centuries, villagers have lived in houses with mud walls and thatched roofs. This picture shows cobblers at work.

The joint-family was governed by the patriarch during his lifetime; after his death, authority was transferred to the eldest son. All males of the group had to be consulted on serious matters since the property belonged to the family as a whole. Everything earned by individuals in the group went into a common fund, from which was drawn what was needed to supply each member. It was possible for a man to acquire property and to live in his own residence, but he had to show that his holdings had been obtained without use of the family patrimony.

The emphasis placed on the interests and security of the group rather than on the individual is a common denominator of the three pillars of Indian society—the autonomous village, the caste system, and the joint-family. Thus Indian society has always been concerned with stability rather than with progress in the western sense, and the individual Indian has tended to acquire a more passive outlook toward life than his western counterpart. This traditional emphasis upon the group also helps explain the socialistic approach of Nehru and his colleagues toward contemporary economic and social issues.

Language and literature. The Indo-Aryans were part of the huge Indo-European linguistic group and, therefore, bequeathed to India a language related to Persian, Greek, Latin, and most modern European languages, including English. The first wave of Indo-Aryans spoke a tongue which in its general features was closely related to the earliest Greek. The various dialects of the invading bands, mixed with the speech of the natives, gradually developed into Sanskrit. By the fourth century B.C., Sanskrit had evolved in such a fashion that the vernacular differed from the traditional Sanskrit of the priests and bards. The modern Indian language Hindi is derived from the speech of this period.

The oldest Sanskrit literature, the *Vedas* (meaning "knowledge"), consisted of thoughts concerning religion, philosophy, and magic. The earliest was the *Rig-Veda*, a peculiar collection of childlike questions (such as why white milk should come from red cows) and religious concepts of deep insight. The *Vedas* were passed orally from generation to generation by the Brahmans even long after writing was in common use.

After the *Vedas* had been composed, a series of prose commentaries on them began to be produced, including the famous *Upanishads* (from the term which means "a session," at which a teacher gives instruction in philosophical doctrine). Written between 800 and 600 B.C., the *Upanishads* extend and replace the old Vedic concepts with profound speculations about the ultimate truths of creation and life.

Around the end of the Epic Age, Indian poets composed two great epic masterpieces which were enriched by the profound thought of *Upanishad* philosophy. The *Mahabharata*, similar to the Greek *Iliad*, glorifies the Kshatriyan, or warrior, caste, as it recounts the struggle between two Indo-Aryan tribes. The most famous section of the *Mahabharata* is a philosophical poem called the *Bhagavad-Gita* (*The Lord's Song*).

The other magnificent epic, the *Ramayana*, has been likened to the Greek *Odyssey* because it tells of a hero's wanderings and his faithful wife's long vigil. Where the *Mahabharata* is a vigorous glorification of war and adventure, the *Ramayana* shows the growth of chivalric ideals among the Indo-Aryans. Both epics have provided all subsequent Indian literature with a vast supply of stories.

The *Upanishads*, core of Indian theology. The *Vedas* display the evolution of Indian religion from a simple belief in many gods toward a complete pantheism, a conception of the universe and everything in it as God. The pantheistic conception was subsequently developed with great subtlety in the *Upanishads*, which form the core of all subsequent Indian religious thought and are the foundation on which Hinduism was built.

The main tenets of the *Upanishads* may be briefly summarized:

(1) *Brahman*, the impersonal, immaterial force permeating the universe, and *Atman*, the Universal Soul to which all individual souls belong, are in turn one and indivisible.

(2) Therefore we, as individual souls, are one with *Brahman*—or, to use another term, God. The unity of life is the only reality.

(3) As individual souls living in a world of the senses, we think that we exist apart from the one Soul—but this is *maya*, or illusion. The illusion of separateness must be abandoned before we can perceive the truth.

(4) While living in this state of illusion, we place our faith in things which are transitory and unsatisfying, and hence we are afflicted with pain and sorrow. We can only win deliverance—*moksha*—by awareness of the One Reality.

(5) This awareness can be learned only through long experience in the world of the senses, requiring the incarnation of the soul into many physical bodies. Thus the doctrine of reincarnation is an integral feature of the *Upanishad* philosophy.

(6) The actions of all aspects of life are governed by an immutable, eternal moral law called *karma*. Stipulating that every action secures its own equal reaction, *karma* is akin to the Christian concept—"for whatsoever a man soweth, that shall he also reap." The workings of this cosmic law determine

the environment into which a person is born and the circumstances with which he must contend during his life.

(7) The purpose of human existence is spiritual. Life operates according to law and never by chance, nor can any individual soul be "lost," irrespective of its earthly limitations. It is always part of *Atman*, and eventually it will be consciously reabsorbed into *Brahman*. Then, and then only, will the soul be free.

Hinduism: a religious synthesis. The philosophy of the *Upanishads* permeates Hinduism. Although the main tenets of Hinduism can be summarized, as in the preceding section, it has been said that Hinduism is less a religion than a way of life, because it possesses no canon or precise doctrine of belief. Hinduism is a synthesis of varying concepts acquired over hundreds of years.

In time Hinduism acquired a trinity consisting of Brahma, the creator; Vishnu, the preserver; and Shiva, the destroyer. These names and others have often been used interchangeably for the Absolute Reality—that is, *Brahman*. Vishnu was a benevolent deity, working continually for the welfare of the world; his followers believe that he has appeared in some ten incarnations to save the world from disaster. The other great god is Shiva, who personifies the Life Force. As such, Shiva is worshiped by his devotees as embodying power, in both its constructive and destructive aspects. Some representations of Shiva portray him in terrifying guise, garlanded with skulls, while others show him as the Lord of Dancers, whose activities are the source of all cosmic movement. (See Color Plate 11.)

Main features of Hinduism. Hinduism achieved its more or less permanent structure about a thousand years after the *Upanishads*, in the early centuries of our Christian era. To provide an adequate explanation of Hinduism, we can best describe the main features of its later, completed form, which were rooted in the Hinduism of the Vedic and Epic ages.

(1) Hinduism gave the caste system a religious significance by linking it with the

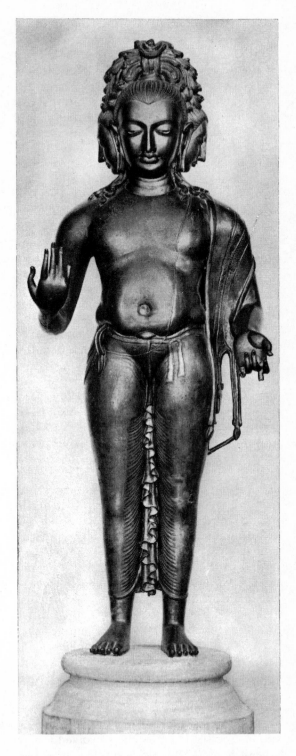

Found in Sind and dated at about 600 A.D., this gilt bronze statue of the Hindu god Brahma has four faces, three of which are visible here.

theory of reincarnation. The Hindus maintain that each of the four major castes was created so that an individual soul could learn of the experiences unique to each caste. On this basis, the Sudra is much nearer the beginning of the cycle of human incarnations than the Brahman, who presumably should be approaching the attainment of *moksha*.

(2) Early in the Christian era, Hindu thought developed into some six orthodox philosophical systems. Probably the most important of the six systems is *Vedanta*, on which modern intellectual Hinduism is largely based. To *Vedanta*—"there is only one single Absolute Reality, the *Brahman*, and outside the *Brahman*, there is nothing which actually and genuinely exists. The entire world which we behold is a cosmic illusion. . . . It is not until we attain to true knowledge that we find salvation and deliverance from the deception in which we are entangled."[4]

(3) Throughout the history of Hinduism there has persisted the ideal of asceticism, a practice already widespread when the *Upanishads* were being written. Some ascetics dwelt in the forest, others wandered through the countryside begging for alms, and still others engaged in bizarre forms of self-torture. The purpose of asceticism was not only to escape the snares resulting from attachment to the world of the senses but also, by rigorous self-discipline, to achieve mystical experiences and thus acquire greater spiritual insight. Yoga, known in the West principally because of the unusual physical powers and control attributed to its followers, is an orthodox Hindu system whose adherents maintain that through rigid discipline it is possible to acquire exalted states of consciousness and thereby attain *moksha*.

(4) In addition to its philosophical content, Hinduism has a strong emotional aspect. The value of *bhakti*, or devotion, had been accepted in early times as the *Bhagavad-Gita* reveals, but the worship of God was one of awe rather than love. Later, however, various south Indian teachers evolved a new type of *bhakti*. They declared that the surest way to salvation was by a fervid emotional surrender to God, who was depicted as full of love for mankind. This theistic approach has resulted in the creation of numerous devotional sects in Hinduism.

The simplicity of Gautama Buddha. During the time of the later *Vedas* and the *Upanishads* (900-600 B.C.), religious rites were supervised by the Brahmans. They kept a strict control over the people and stressed religious ceremonies, costly sacrifices, and the passive acceptance of Brahman dogmas. India stood in need of religious reform—and at this juncture Gautama Buddha (563?-483 B.C.) appeared. The Buddha (the "Enlightened One") stands out in history as one of the most profound influences in the life of mankind. This influence is due to two principal factors: the beauty and simplicity of his own life and the philosophical depth and ethical purity of his teaching.

Gautama was the son of a monarch who ruled a kingdom located at the foot of the Himalayas. As a privileged youth, he led a happy life and married his beautiful cousin, who bore him a son. One day, according to traditional Indian literature, Gautama was deeply shocked by the misery, disease, and sorrow that he saw was the lot of other men as he walked through the streets of his native city. The happiness which his wife and son offered him only made the world's suffering appear more unbearable by contrast. He determined to abandon palace life and seek in the outside world an answer to his questions about life and death. For seven years he dwelt in a forest, practicing the self-mortification rites of the ascetics he found there. Gautama almost died from fastings and self-tortures and at last concluded that these practices did not lead to wisdom.

One day, while sitting beneath a large tree meditating on the problem of human suffering, he received "enlightenment." From this insight, he constructed a religious philosophy that has affected the lives of millions of people for 2500 years. He soon attracted disciples, the most devoted being the faithful Ananda, who occupies the same position in Buddhist stories as the disciple John in the New Testament. Dressed always in a simple yellow robe, with begging bowl in hand, the Buddha wandered through the plains of the Ganges, preaching to the villagers who flocked to hear him. He spoke with everyone, regardless of caste, and, like Jesus, who congregated with sinners and publicans instead of the "respectable" Pharisees, he would decline the sumptuous banquets of nobles to partake of the simple hospitality of peasants and social outcasts.

When eighty years old and enfeebled by his constant travels, the Buddha one day was invited by a poor blacksmith to a meal. According to legend, the food was tainted, but Gautama ate it rather than offend his host, although he forbade his disciples to follow his example. Later in the day the Buddha was taken with severe pains, and he knew death was near. Calling his disciples together, he bade them farewell. Ananda burst into tears, and the master gently reproved him, saying, "Enough, Ananda! Do not let yourself be troubled; do not weep!"

Buddhist teachings. The fundamental teachings of the Buddha, briefly stated, consist of the Four Noble Truths, which were revealed to the Buddha in the Great Enlightenment:

"1. 'the truth of pain,' as manifest in 'birth, old age, sickness, death, sorrow, lamentation, dejection, and despair';

2. 'the truth of the cause of pain,' viz., craving for existence, passion, pleasure, leading to rebirth;

3. 'the truth of cessation of pain,' by ceasing of craving, by renunciation; and

4. 'the truth of the way that leads to the cessation of pain,' viz., the Middle Path, which is the Eight-fold Path consisting of 'right views, intention, speech, action, livelihood, effort, mindfulness, and concentration.' "[5]

In addition to these teachings, the Buddha set forth certain moral injunctions: not to kill, not to steal, not to speak falsely, not to be unchaste, and not to drink intoxicating liquors. The Buddha sought to strip the *Upanishad* teachings of the encumbrances and superstitions which, with the passage of time, had enveloped them. Gautama taught that a man's caste, whether Brahman or Sudra,

Dated about 185 B.C., this stone relief from a monument at Bharhut in the Ganges valley pictures a dream of Queen Maya, the mother of Gautama Buddha. As she slept, surrounded by servants, she dreamed that a white elephant walked three times around her couch and entered her body. When the Brahman priests learned of the dream, they prophesied that she would give birth to a child who would become a universal monarch if he followed a worldly life, an "Enlightened One" if he abandoned the world.

had no bearing on his spiritual stature. Only by living the true philosophy could one win deliverance from illusion (*maya*). Nor was the Buddha interested in rituals or ceremonies or priestly mediation between gods and man. As a consequence, Buddhism (unlike Hinduism) has no trinity, nor does it even postulate the existence of a God or First Cause.

According to the Buddha, the individual cannot hope to attain an ideal state so long as he remains attached by transitory desires to the wheel of birth and rebirth. Reincarnation is a necessary doctrine in Buddhism, for only by repeated lives can the individual come to realize that the world of the senses is but a spiritual illusion. Once this is learned, the path by which sorrow is removed opens to the seeker. The strict rules of the Eight-fold Path will free him from the bondage of rebirth and make possible a reabsorption into the Universal Life, the "slipping of the dewdrip into the Silent Sea"—the entry into *nirvana*.

What is *nirvana*? Does it constitute the total annihilation of the individual or rather the end of the illusion of separateness from the One Life? According to one Indian scholar, "*nirvana* is incommunicable, for the Infinite cannot be described by finite words. The utmost that we can do is to throw some light on it by recourse to negative terms. *Nirvana* is the final result of the extinction of the desire or thirst for rebirth . . . it is the incomparable and highest goal. . . . [The] Buddha purposely discouraged questions about the reabsorption of the individual soul, as being of no practical value in the quest for salvation."[6]

The Buddha and later Buddhism. The Buddha reformed Indian religion. He censured the rites and dogmas of the Brahmans, broke with the rules of caste, taught that all men are equal, and gave the world a code of morals whose purity is universally recognized. He founded orders of monks, and the monasteries gradually developed into important academic centers. During his lifetime, his teachings were disseminated through central India.

Though the Buddha was a reformer, after his death many of the evils which he had attacked crept, ironically enough, into Buddhism itself. In spite of the Buddha's ban against the worship of deities, in time men prayed to him as a god who could assure their salvation. Subsequently his teachings were elaborated into metaphysical beliefs, and Buddhism in its new form spread throughout eastern Asia.

INDIA UNDER THE MAURYAS
AND THE KUSHANS

Alexander the Great in India. In the sixth century B.C., there were about sixteen states or tribal territories in northern India, of which the most important was Magadha along the lower Ganges in northeastern India. In 326 B.C. Alexander the Great crossed the Indus, defeated an Indian army, and pushed on, hoping to subjugate Magadha. But before he could accomplish his purpose, he was forced to retrace his steps at the insistence of his weary, homesick soldiers. Although the immediate consequences of his visit were negligible, India and the West had met face to face for the first time.

Chandragupta Maurya. In 321 B.C. a new era was at hand for India. Chandragupta Maurya seized the Magadha state and in the next twenty-four years conquered all of northern India and founded the Maurya dynasty, which endured until about 185 B.C.

Chandragupta may be considered the first emperor of India, though his power did not extend to the southern regions of the subcontinent. He was a brilliant general and administrator, an alert thinker, and a colorful figure. Whether or not there is truth to a Greek historian's report that Chandragupta had once visited Alexander's camp in the Punjab, the Magadhan did maintain contacts with the Greeks after he became emperor and fostered a friendly exchange of information between the Seleucid empire and his own. He lived in great splendor; his court included Greek courtiers and was run according to Persian ceremonial, factors which scarcely endeared him to his Indian subjects.

The empire of Chandragupta was divided into three provinces, each of which was governed by a viceroy who had a staff of commissioners and officials to aid him. Justice was dispensed sternly but with fairness in both civil and criminal cases. Under the supervision of a well-organized war office was a large army. Excellent roads, marked by milestones, connected the many villages and towns; and a postal service was maintained by royal couriers, who could rest at inns placed along the highways.

All land belonged to the state, and agriculture was the chief source of wealth. Irrigation and crop rotation were practiced, and famines were almost unknown. Trade was cosmopolitan; in the bazaars were displayed goods from southern India, China, Mesopotamia, and Asia Minor. Indian ships sailed the Indian Ocean to the head of the Persian Gulf and to Arabia, and from these points

Indian goods were carried overland toward markets as distant as the cities of Greece. Also important in the Mauryan empire was manufacturing. Greek accounts refer to the making of arms and agricultural implements and the building of ships; northwestern India was famous for cotton cloth and silk yarn.

About 297 B.C., Chandragupta was succeeded by his son Bindusara. A charming story about Bindusara indicates the close cultural relations which existed at this time between the Mauryan and Seleucid rulers. Writing to Seleucus, Bindusara asked for a sample of Greek wine, some raisins, and a Sophist. In his reply Seleucus stated that he was sending the wine with pleasure, but that "it isn't good form among the Greeks to trade in philosophers."[7]

Asoka, propagator of Buddhism. Asoka, a son of Bindusara, reigned from 273 B.C. to 232 B.C. He was one of the few early kings who pursued the arts of peace more diligently than the arts of war; his first military campaign was also his last.

In 262 B.C. Asoka attacked the ancient state of Kalinga to the south, whose inhabitants resisted his invasion. In the war of extermination which followed, victory fell to Asoka, and hundreds of thousands of Kalingans were killed or captured. Thus Asoka extended his empire so that it included nearly all of India to the edge of Tamil Land. But the cruelty of the campaign horrified him, and he resolved never again to permit such acts of butchery. Soon after this war, Asoka was converted to Buddhism, whose gentle teachings increased his aversion to warfare.

As the years passed, Asoka became even more deeply religious. Everywhere throughout his empire he had his imperial edicts carved upon stone pillars, some of which still stand today. Stressing compassion, kindness to all living things, truth, purity, and liberality, the edicts were a practical application of the teachings of Buddha.

Termed "the first great royal patron of Buddhism," Asoka was also to Buddhism what Paul was to Christianity—a successful propagator of his faith. Asoka sent Buddhist missionaries to many lands—the Himalayan

regions, the Tamil kingdoms, Ceylon, Burma, and even as far away as Syria, Egypt, and Macedonia—to teach the gospel of salvation and equality. Thus transformed from a small Indian sect to a powerful religion, Buddhism began to make its influence felt beyond its homeland. Asoka's missionary efforts had enduring success in neighboring Asiatic lands, particularly in the land of Ceylon, where Buddhism is found today in its near original form.

Fall of the Mauryan empire. Almost immediately after Asoka's death in 232 B.C., his empire began to disintegrate. The last Mauryan emperor was assassinated in 185 B.C., and the state was then invaded by a ruler from southern India and also by Demetrius, the fourth Bactrian king, who swept into northwest India and overran the Punjab.

Although the Mauryan state had once been powerful, it crumbled almost overnight. So dramatic was the collapse and so grave the consequences that, like the decline and fall of the Roman empire, it has provoked much scholarly speculation. Whatever the reasons for the fall of the Mauryan empire, its contribution to world civilization survived, for "the moral ascendancy of Indian culture over a large part of the civilized world, which Asoka was mainly instrumental in bringing about, remained for centuries as a monument to . . . [India's] glory. . . ."[8]

Asoka's dome-shaped *stupas* were used to enshrine the relics of Buddhist saints or to mark a holy spot. Originally of earth, the mounds were later faced with brick and surrounded by a platform and four carved stone gateways. The umbrella rising from the boxlike structure on the dome is the Indian emblem of sovereignty which symbolizes the Buddha's princely birth. Over the centuries, the low dome was heightened into a tall, tower-like structure. As Buddhism spread to other countries, the *stupa* inspired magnificent temple architecture. Shown here is a *stupa* at Sanchi, India.

The Graeco-Bactrian kingdom. When Demetrius invaded northern India, he occupied Gandhara—an area whose inhabitants had been converted to Buddhism by Asoka. The Bactrians organized the chief Gandharan town as a Hellenistic city and even fashioned an acropolis there. Demetrius also acquired Taxila (an administrative center of the Mauryan empire) and Pataliputra, the Mauryan capital. Thus he ruled an area stretching from the Persian desert to the middle of the Ganges valley.

Demetrius organized his domain much as a Seleucid kingdom. In keeping with Alexander's ideal of bringing East and West together on a basis of equality, Demetrius issued a bilingual coinage bearing Greek inscriptions on one side and Indian on the other. "His realm was to be a partnership of Greek and Indian; he was not to be a Greek king of Indian subjects, but an Indian king no less than a Greek one, head of both races."[9]

His general, Menander, who subsequently ascended the throne, continued the concept of partnership. Whereas in the West, the Seleucid rulers had endeavored to create a basically Greek empire filled with Greek settlements, it was not possible to found Greek cities on any such scale in India. Thus Menander's kingdom was essentially Indian with a small Greek ruling class. The kingdom of Bactria attained a high state of culture before being crushed by the nomadic tribes which swept out of central Asia about the close of the second century B.C.

The Kushan empire. A turbulent period followed the fall of the Bactrian kingdom. But, by the first century A.D., the most important of the invading clans, the Kushans, had established themselves as masters of a large part of northwestern India and had founded another of the great empires in Indian history.

Kanishka, the most outstanding of the Kushan rulers, became king sometime between 78 and 128 A.D. (probably closer to the former date). All of northwest India, perhaps as far south as the Narbada River, and much of present Afghanistan to the north were under his sway. This enlightened monarch took over the civilization of the people he conquered. During his reign the arts and sciences flourished, imposing buildings were constructed, and advances were made in the field of medicine.

Mahayana and Hinayana Buddhism. Whereas Gautama Buddha had concerned himself primarily with the removal of individual suffering through a life of purity and self-denial, later Buddhists added to this central doctrine more emotional and metaphysical concepts, together with myths and rituals. To some Buddhists, this development was a corruption of the original Buddhism, but the more mystical approach had great appeal and in Kanishka's reign showed its strength.

An important systematization of Buddhist doctrine took place when Kanishka convened a great council of five hundred monks; from their work arose the *Mahayana*, or "Great Vehicle," school of Buddhism. The Mahayanists conceived of the Buddha as a Bodhisattva, an exalted being who renounced *nirvana* to save mankind. They claimed that their belief was the great vehicle for carrying men to salvation and that the earlier form of Buddhism represented the *Hinayana*, or "Lesser Vehicle." These terms were invented by the Mahayanists; the members of the rival school called themselves *Theravidins*—that is, followers of the Doctrine of the Elders. While the *Hinayana* remained primarily a moral philosophy, austere and rational, the more emotional *Mahayana* approach offered faith as a road to salvation.

Rapidly becoming popular in much of India, *Mahayana* Buddhism spread along the trade routes to the northeast as its believers converted the people of Nepal, Tibet, China, Korea, and Japan to the Buddhist faith. But *Mahayana* Buddhism did not obliterate the simpler *Hinayana* Buddhism of the *Theravidins*. Geographically speaking, the *Hinayana* may be considered the southern branch of Buddhism, for it was that form of Buddhism which spread from India and Ceylon to Burma, Thailand, Cambodia, the Malay peninsula, and Indonesia.

Like Asoka, Kanishka was a Buddhist convert who was instrumental in helping to make Buddhism a world religion. Hinduism, however, still had a strong hold on the Indian people. While the Buddhists had disregarded caste and accepted both the Greeks and the Kushans, the Hindus rejected the foreign invaders as outcastes. Gradually, the Indians came to consider Hinduism a more characteristically Indian movement than Buddhism. Therefore, although Kanishka helped to spread Buddhism to other countries, in the long run his support probably lessened its popularity within India.

Trade with the West. At the tip of the Indian peninsula lay the Tamil country, peopled by Dravidians who had long been absorbing elements of Hindu culture from the lands to the north of them. These states enjoyed commercial ties with the Hellenistic Greeks, particularly those in Egypt, and the vigor of the commercial contact is shown by some interesting examples of linguistic in-

Dating from the fifth century A.D., this sculpture of the Buddha is a handsome example of the Graeco-Buddhist art originating in the Indian province of Gandhara. Because of the Buddha's prohibitions against idolatry, artists had refrained for centuries from portraying the Buddha in human form. With the growth of the *Mahayana* school and the mystical approach, artists began to create figures of the Buddha. Scholars believed for many years that the blending of Greek and Indian techniques in Gandharan sculpture originated during the period of Bactrian rule over northern India. According to a more recent interpretation, Indian art was influenced by Roman sculpture as a result of Roman-Kushan communication late in the first century A.D. In either case, the influence on Gandharan art was clearly Greek, for both Roman and Bactrian art derived from Greek examples. The modeling of the features and hair of this sculpture show Greek influence; the elongated ear lobes, heavy-lidded eyes, mark on the forehead, knot of hair, and expression of deep repose are Indian.

fluences: the Hebrew term for peacock and the Greek words for ginger, cinnamon, and rice come from the Tamil language.

In Roman times the trade with the Tamil kingdoms was expanded still further. At the time when Augustus became head of the Roman world, the Tamil kingdoms sent him a congratulatory embassy, an honor never before paid a western prince. The ambassadors took about four years en route and bore such gifts as "a gigantic python, huge tortoises, and an armless boy who could shoot arrows and throw darts with his feet!"[10] In the period from Augustus' rule to the reign of the first Constantine, at least nine other embassies from India visited the Roman emperors to arrange for the protection and well-being of Indian ships and traders at Roman ports.

Roman merchants, meanwhile, dwelt in Tamil seaports, and through them precious metals, coins, wine, pottery, glassware, silverware, and even craftsmen and masons were brought to India. Tamil poets described Roman ships which carried a guard of archers to ward off pirates, while the Tamil kings themselves employed bodyguards of Roman soldiers, whose habit of wearing long coats aroused much comment in a land where comparative nudity was the rule.

For its part, India was exporting drugs, pearls, silks, muslins, and spices. In view of the magnitude of the Roman-Tamil trade, we can understand why Ptolemy showed considerable knowledge of the geography of India.

After the fall of the Kushans in 220 A.D., India entered into a chaotic period, to emerge later with a splendid Hindu civilization under the Guptas. This story goes beyond the limits of the present chapter, so let us now follow the direction of the missionaries of *Mahayana* Buddhism and the silk merchants who plodded eastward through central Asia toward China, the third great civilization of classical times.

CHINA: THE FORMATIVE CENTURIES

A land of many rivers. In a land of varied resources and vast extent, over four million square miles in area, the civilization of China arose and developed, for centuries almost completely isolated from outsiders by the ocean, deserts, and mountains. This isolation helps to explain the great measure of originality in China's culture pattern.

The river valleys of China mark out three major regions: the valley of the Hwang Ho, or Yellow River, in the north; the Yangtze valley in the central area; and, in the south, the shorter river valleys converging on the present-day city of Canton. These rivers were of crucial importance in the development of Chinese civilization. The rivers provided water for the irrigation of farm lands and served as a cheap and efficient transportation system. As in Egypt, the beginning of political organization was linked with geography: governing bodies were needed to construct and control irrigation systems. China has long been more homogeneous politically, racially, and culturally than other areas of comparable size, perhaps in part because mountains and deserts provided isolation from other countries, while its rivers provided natural means of communication throughout much of the area.

The Shang dynasty, China's first civilization. The early historic period in China, from about 1500 to 1100 B.C., is only vaguely known, but the existence of the Shang dynasty and culture is not a matter of doubt. Archaeological findings in the Hwang Ho valley indicate a fairly advanced level of culture and an organized state, covering a relatively small area in northern China. In the Shang period, some of the basic elements of later Chinese civilization were established; these included agrarian life, the raising of silkworms for raw silk, the development of writing upon which subsequent Chinese script was built, and the creation of splendid bronze vessels and art objects.

The most famous artistic expression of the Shang period is its magnificent bronzes. Bronzes unearthed in recent years display architectural massiveness and equilibrium, elegance of form, and decorative splendor. Inscriptions found on bronze pieces, ceremonial daggers, jade, and pottery indicate that writing was well advanced in this period. Shang writing was partly pictorial, partly

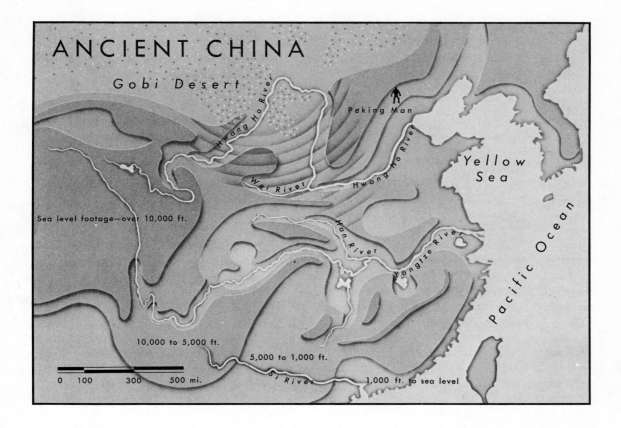

ideographic; the Shang Chinese possessed sufficient written words to express themselves with considerable facility.

Although the ruler of the state commanded the armies in battle, his political power evidently was not extensive; the more distant parts of the kingdom were under the control of strong nobles. The ruler's most important function seems to have been that of high priest. Homage was paid to ancestors in order not to offend the spiritual world, and the advice of these illustrious dead was sought by means of divination.

Archaeological discoveries prove that the Shang civilization was remarkably advanced, and urban people made their livelihood in specialized occupations and trade. The major part of the population, however, was composed of peasants who grew wheat, millet, and rice and raised cattle, sheep, pigs, and horses. Farming methods were primitive; for a plow, farmers used a sort of hoe that was held by one laborer and dragged through the soil by another man, who had bound himself to it with a rope.

Chou, longest of the dynasties. In the eleventh century B.C. the Shang ruling house was overthrown by a new, warlike power which had developed in the northwest—the Chou (1027-256 B.C.). To reward their supporters, the victorious Chou rulers distributed different regions as fiefs to their relatives and to the chieftains of those tribes that had helped make victory possible. The creation of numerous feudal states was to have long-range repercussions for Chinese civilization. In time the nobles became so determined to strengthen their own positions that the Chou rulers found it increasingly difficult to cope with them.

The final centuries of the Chou era are often referred to as the Era of Contending States. Warfare was incessant and was made more destructive by the introduction of new military techniques, such as the use of mounted companies of archers and catapults

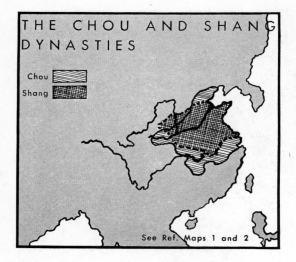

THE CHOU AND SHANG
DYNASTIES

Chou

Shang

See Ref. Maps 1 and 2

for sieges. The struggle for power eventually lay between two states. In 256 B.C. the Chou ruler was overthrown by the ruler of Ch'in, the most aggressive of the contending states, and the Chou dynasty came to an end.

Now let us focus upon the evolution, during these formative centuries of the Shang and Chou, of the attitudes and institutions which were to make Chinese culture unique and, in many cases, were to endure into the twentieth century.

Imperial rule and the Decree of Heaven. The Shang rulers believed that they occupied their throne by divine sanction. When they were conquered by the Chou, the latter felt it necessary to explain how they in turn had acquired a divine right to rule. In a proclamation to the conquered Shang people, the Chou leaders declared that heaven had once been satisfied with the Shang dynasty.

But your ruler . . . was extremely dissolute, and despised the commands of Heaven . . . he was lazy and slothful, slighted the labors of government, and did not make pure sacrifices, so that Heaven sent down this ruin on him.[11]

The Chou leaders stated that the Chou king, on the other hand,

. . . treated the multitudes well and was virtuous, and presided carefully over the sacrifices to the spirits and to Heaven. Heaven therefore instructed us to avail ourselves of its favor; it chose

us and gave us the decree of Shang, to rule over your many regions.[12]

In this way was born that novel political theory—the Decree of Heaven.

Typically Chinese in its conception and practicality, the Decree of Heaven not only provided for dynastic change and sanctioned the efforts of the successful competitors for the throne; it also set forth the doctrine that the interests of the people took precedence over those of the ruler, who held his powers only in trust (see p. 106). All Chinese rulers did not apply this estimable doctrine and make themselves the sincere servants of their subjects. But the doctrine endured and often served to justify action redressing the balance between the interests of the rulers and those of the people.

As a corollary of the Decree of Heaven, a Chou ruler called himself the Son of Heaven, a title retained by later monarchs. Regardless of his actual power at any time, the wang, or ruler, was considered to be indispensable to Chinese society in his dual capacity as ultimate juridical authority and priestly mediator.

The aristocracy. The wang and the aristocracy were sharply separated from the mass of the people on the basis of land ownership and family descent. Until the later stages of Chou rule, the nobility held the chief posts in the army and occupied the important administrative posts. The fact that the inherited privileges of the aristocrats depended on proof of their noble ancestry was at least part of the reason for the great emphasis which the Chinese placed upon ancestor worship and the elaborate rituals connected with it.

The customs of the Chinese nobility can be compared in a general way to the customs of the nobility of medieval Europe. Underlying the feudal structure was the code of chivalry, which was practiced in both war and peace. The code became so important to the nobility as a symbol of gentle breeding and so complex in its ramifications that the nobles devoted years to its mastery. Arrayed in breastplate and helmet, the Chinese noble waged war from his chariot and, to display his martial skill and social grace, "would come to the court of his seigneur to take part in tournaments of the noble sport of archery which was accompanied by musical airs and interspersed with elegant salutations, the whole regulated like a ballet."[13]

Village life in an agricultural economy. Although peasant proprietorship may have begun toward the end of the Chou period, throughout this long feudal era the masses in general had no political rights and possessed little or no land. The lower classes cultivated the fields for their lords, paid them taxes, and served as common soldiers in their armies. Families lived together in villages, which derived their names from the group that had founded them. Frequently situated on heights overlooking the fields and out of the reach of floods, these hamlets clustered about the residence of a local noble or, after feudal times, an official.

Chou innovations in cultivation increased productivity and modified the traditional feudal land system, stimulating a gradual changeover to private land ownership. But the farm population apparently still had difficulty eking out an existence. A central problem in Chinese economics has been that the majority of farmers worked on fields so small that they could not produce a crop surplus to tide them over during periods of scarcity.

Characteristics of Chinese philosophy. In the three hundred years beginning with the sixth century B.C., the outstanding philosophical teachings of China were formulated. In India, philosophers emphasized metaphysics: speculation concerning the nature of the Absolute and its cosmic and human manifestations. Many Chinese philosophers, on the other hand, have been preoccupied with man rather than with the cosmos. These philosophers have considered man basically from the standpoint not of his spiritual origins and attributes but of his moral qualities as an individual and his ethical obligations as a member of society.

The rise of Chinese philosophy in the latter part of the Chou period can be explained largely by the chaotic political situation during the Era of Contending States. It was not so much the form of political organization which troubled the Chinese philosophers: they accepted monarchy as natural. The problem to them was the creation of moral principles which should instill in ruler and subject alike the highest expressions of virtue and benevolence.

Confucius: his moral and social codes. The most famous and influential of all Chinese philosophers was Confucius. Born in 551 B.C. Confucius received a scholarly education and became an official in one of the feudal states. Kindly, urbane, and courteous, this learned gentleman resigned because he opposed certain actions of his ruler. He then established a school for young men, whom he instructed in ethics and politics. Described as "a punctilious gentleman of the old school" because of the statement in the *Analects* that "if his mat were not straight he would not sit [on] it,"[14] Confucius spent the last years of his life wandering with his pupils and died in 479 B.C.

Confucius postulated moral and social codes to govern the relationships of individuals with one another and with society as a whole. He went back to the feudal principle of *li*, which can be translated as "propriety" and which characterized proper conduct for those in a ruler's court. If the ruler and his officials treated one another with consideration, why should they not accord similar treatment to the common people? Confucius advocated a paternal form of government in which the ruler made himself responsible for the welfare of his people.

In the universe, heaven is the directing force; and in the family, father is the directing authority. In the State the position of the sovereign corresponds to that of heaven in the universe, and of father in the family.[15]

Confucius looked upon ancestor worship and obedience to the head of the family as a foundation for both family and political life.

Confucius taught that proper education would bring out the natural sympathy and good will latent in all men and so help develop the "superior man." Inherent in his philosophy was his insistence on the pursuit

Bronze ceremonial vessels, such as this one from the Chou dynasty, were used in rituals of ancestor worship.

of a lofty, ethical code of conduct. This included such basic virtues as faithfulness to oneself and others, devotion to the welfare of others, righteousness, wisdom, and sincerity. It has been maintained that Confucius' "real greatness lies in his transforming the feudal code of rites and etiquette into a universal system of ethics"[16] and in making it the ethical creed of the Chinese people.

Strengths and weaknesses of Confucianism. Like his Indian contemporary, the Buddha, Confucius looked upon himself as a reformer of existing abuses rather than as a prophet. Yet just as Gautama was later glorified as a godlike figure, so Confucius was elevated to an exalted position as a religious master. In 195 B.C. an emperor paid a visit to the tomb of Confucius and offered a sacrifice to his spirit, an event which gave rise to a national cult of the worship and veneration of this great philosopher.

This development is not too surprising in view of the enormous influence which the teachings of Confucius had on China's subsequent history. For centuries his texts were the subject matter in the official schools, and thus his conservatism and reverence for the past were inculcated into the national character. Unfortunately, Confucianism often sterilized Chinese thinking; scholars rehashed ancient Confucian texts instead of embarking upon original ideas. Likewise, Confucianism proved a useful tool in the hands of rulers who took advantage of its emphasis upon organized, traditional authority to safeguard their own interests at the expense of the people's.

Chinese thought was subsequently influenced by other philosophical schools, but there can be no denying the close agreement of outlook between Confucianism and the character of Chinese society. Both are empirical: they are concerned with workable, down-to-earth codes of conduct that can be understood by all classes of people. Both have emphasized the value of moral discipline and have tended to divorce ethics from metaphysics and the supernatural—an attitude at variance with the Indian. Finally, both Confucianism and Chinese society are humanistic: they insist upon the supremacy of human values and advocate the cultivation of our earthly existence as a fine art, indeed as the supreme good. "If we look for the secret of . . . [Confucius'] appeal, it seems probable that it lies in his insistence upon the supremacy of human values. Wisdom, he said, is to know men; virtue is to love men."[17]

Mencius, an outspoken democrat. A brilliant commentator on Confucianism and an outstanding thinker in his own right was Mencius (372?-289? B.C.). He was particularly concerned with the role of the people in government and with the question of when a ruler could be replaced. Whereas Confucius had emphasized the authority of the ruler, Mencius was a bold democrat who maintained:

The people are the most important element *in a nation*; the spirits of the land and grain are the next; the sovereign is the lightest.[18]

In his view, all political and economic institutions were created on behalf of the people. The ruler himself was placed in office only that he might serve the interests of his subjects. It followed logically that the right to govern required the consent of the governed and—like Thomas Jefferson two thousand years afterwards—Mencius bravely contended that the people had the right to rebel and depose their rulers if their welfare was not safeguarded. In other words, he linked the theory of the Decree of Heaven to the democratic concept of the will of the people.

Taoism: intuitive mysticism. Not all Chinese philosophers placed their chief emphasis on man and reason, however. While Confucius and his successors concentrated upon developing humanistic theories, other philosophers sought an intuitive, mystical approach to life. Of Lao-tzu, the most famous person associated with this school, we know very little. Traditionally, he is supposed to have been an older contemporary of Confucius, but a number of modern scholars believe that Lao-tzu properly belongs to the fourth century B.C. or even later. His views are found in the *Tao Te Ching*, which has been variously translated as "The Canon of the Way and of Virtue" and "Book of the World Law and Its Power." The primary meaning of the word *tao* is "road" or "way," but Lao-tzu used it in a metaphysical sense to represent the Absolute, the sum total of existence:

There is a thing, formless yet complete. Before Heaven and Earth it existed. Without sound, without substance, it stands alone without changing. It is all pervading and unfailing. One may think of it as the mother of all beneath Heaven. We do not know its name, but we term it *Tao*.[19]

Whereas the goal of Confucianism was the fully developed life in society, that of Taoism was to bring men into harmony with the basic laws of nature. Men can best achieve this harmony by retiring from the chaos and decadence which Lao-tzu saw in contemporary feudal society. They should then adhere to the doctrine of *wu wei*, which has been defined as "passive achievement" or refraining from any activity which is contrary to, or out of harmony with, nature. Lao-tzu pointed out that in nature all things work silently;

Confucius' great accomplishment was the formulation of an ethical code which governed the relationships between individuals and between the ruler and his subjects. Running counter to Confucianism, Lao-tzu's mystical philosophy of Taoism called upon men to seek salvation in nature rather than in society; thus Taoism broadened Chinese philosophical thought beyond the purely social boundaries set by Confucius. The Sung incense burner below shows Lao-tzu sitting placidly on a water buffalo. The portrait of Confucius above is a rubbing taken from a stone carving in the Temple of Confucius in Sian.

they fulfill their function and then return to their origin.

Because the Taoists believed that the secrets of the universe were to be gained not by reason but by an intuitive contemplation of the silent, ceaseless flow of nature in every atom of life, Taoism has much in common with Indian philosophy. Both were metaphysical, both emphasized the unity of all things, and both taught the return to the Absolute as the supreme goal. Taoism, however, did not evolve the intricate metaphysical system found in the *Upanishads*.

Chinese artistic expression. In general the Chinese arts are marked by restraint, a quality probably derived from Chinese conservatism and serenity. For example, a poem seldom employs a great deal of highly ornate language nor is it effusive in its effect.

During the Shang and Chou periods the Chinese were already skillful craftsmen and sensitive artists. Jade ornaments have been found in the earliest Chinese graves. From Shang times the Chinese cut jade into forms of fishes to use as "sound stones" which, when struck, emitted a clear tone for a considerable length of time. The ancient Chinese considered jade so sacred that it alone was used in fashioning ritualistic objects. Strikingly beautiful ceremonial bronzes were produced during the Shang period and for the next 1500 years. The bronzes served as sacrificial jars or libation cups in family ancestor worship.

Unquestionably the Chinese take first place among all peoples in the art of ceramics. Beautiful red and black pieces were created at least four thousand years ago. In the early Chou dynasty the art of pottery showed a marked decline, probably because bronze vessels had supplanted pottery on the tables of the rich. The production of pottery revived in the Era of Contending States, when vessels were made with a lustrous black surface, in shapes like bronze pieces. Much of this china was painted with geometric patterns in red and white after the pottery had been fired—a technique which differed from that of earlier times, when the pottery was painted before firing.

Taoism made a profound impression upon Chinese art. The Taoist and the Chinese artist alike are deeply introspective and intuitive in approach, seeking to understand the processes of nature that create the landscape. Painting to express his reaction to a scene is more important to the Chinese artist than depicting the landscape realistically. Unfortunately almost no examples survive of the earliest Chinese painting, but literary references indicate that it was an established art centuries before the birth of Christ.

Complex language: vehicle for sensitive poetry. In the Chinese spoken language, differences in meaning are achieved through the use of tones, of which there are from four to nine for each word sound. Thus the spoken language has some resemblance to singing or chanting. Unfortunately the spoken language has split into dialects so varied that a Cantonese usually cannot understand a man from the north. The written language, on the other hand, has remained comparatively unchanged. Under the Chou dynasty it assumed the form which, with some modifications, it possesses today. The historic continuity of the written language has advantages, for a literate Chinese today can read works written twenty centuries ago. The difficulty, however, is to become a literate Chinese; the language never developed beyond a primitive form expressing each idea with a different character, so that today it includes forty thousand separate characters, rather than the small alphabet of letters used in other languages.

During China's formative centuries, literature flourished. Although unfortunately most poetry written prior to the age of Confucius has been lost, 305 poems have been preserved in the *Shih Ching*, or *Book of Odes*. These poems were supposedly selected by Confucius from the poetry that was in existence in his time. From the *Shih Ching* we see that human nature has changed little and that the age-old problems of living affected the ancient Chinese much as they affect us. In our own age we can sympathize deeply with soldiers engaged in a conflict which they did not create:

How free are the wild geese on their wings,
And the rest they find on the bushy Yu trees!
But we, ceaseless toilers in the king's services,
Cannot even plant our millet and rice.

What will our parents have to rely on?
O thou distant and azure Heaven!
When shall all this end? . . .
What leaves have not turned purple?
What man is not torn from his wife?
Mercy be on us soldiers—
Are we not also men?[20]

CHINA: THE FIRST EMPIRES

Shih Huang Ti, the First Emperor. By 221 B.C. China was once more ruled by a single monarch, and the king of Ch'in assumed the august title Shih Huang Ti, or "First Emperor." Through his creation of the Chinese empire, he established a form of government which was to endure under various dynasties until 1912—that is, for over two thousand years.

To bolster his imperial government, Shih Huang Ti abolished the system of semi-independent states ruled by princes and organized the country into thirty-six military provinces, each governed by an appointed official who was both civil and military governor. The code of Ch'in was substituted for the conflicting law systems of the feudal states, weights and measures were standardized, and an imperial network of broad tree-lined highways was built.

To break the hold of the past, Shih Huang Ti took drastic measures against Confucian literature and scholars. He put into effect a proposal that:

. . . all historical records, save those of Ch'in, be burned; that all libraries of poetry, history, and philosophy, except those under the custody of the Eruditi [a group of scholars of great learning], be sent to the officials to be destroyed; . . . that all those who raise their voice against the present government in the name of antiquity be beheaded together with their families . . .[21]

Such Confucian classics as the *History* and the *Odes* were singled out for special attack, and on one occasion 460 Confucian scholars were said to have been executed for violating the imperial decree. No complete collection

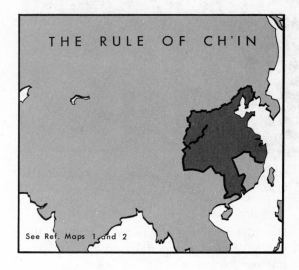

THE RULE OF CH'IN

See Ref. Maps 1 and 2

of ancient Chinese literature survived this violence, but after the fall of the Ch'in dynasty, it proved possible to piece together most of the classics.

Conquests of the "Chinese Caesar." Sometimes called the "Chinese Caesar," the First Emperor was an extraordinary man with the desire and ability to do things on a vast scale. To protect the empire from incursions by nomadic Hunnish marauders of interior Asia, Shih Huang Ti ordered the sectional walls that had previously been erected on the northern marches joined into one Great Wall which extended some fourteen hundred miles. Built of stone, the huge fortification was about twenty-five feet high and fifteen feet thick at the base. Because the wall was erected by forced labor at great effort, it was said that "every stone cost a human life." In addition to this defensive measure, the First Emperor enlarged the empire's territory by conquests which for the first time extended Chinese rule down to the south coast.

When Shih Huang Ti died in 210 B.C., he was succeeded by his inept son, who committed suicide within three years. The empire quickly fell prey to anarchy and violence. In 202 B.C., the same year in which the Romans defeated the Carthaginians at the battle of Zama, a general won control of China and, establishing his new capital of Changan, founded an illustrious line—the

The picture above shows a portion of the Great Wall of China.

Han dynasty. This dynasty continued the policy of strong imperial rule and endured for four centuries.

The Han dynasty: expansion under Wu Ti, the "Warrior Emperor." The early Han emperors had to contend with the fierce Huns, who kept hammering at the Great Wall. Finally, Wu Ti, the "Warrior Emperor" and greatest of the Han rulers (ruling from 140 to 87 B.C.), set out to bring the Huns under control.

Under brilliant generalship, the Chinese defeated the Huns decisively. By the end of the second century B.C., Wu Ti's military conquests had resulted in contact with western Asia—a contact which would lead to cultural and commercial exchange between China and India, and China and Europe. The expansionist policy of Wu Ti helped lay the foun-

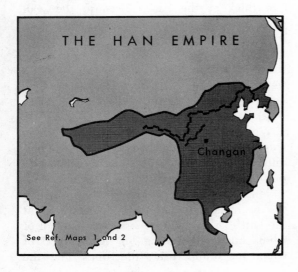

THE HAN EMPIRE

Changan

See Ref. Maps 1 and 2

dation for the development of trade across the entire Eurasian land mass.

The emperor also expanded his domain to include part of Korea and much of southern China, centering on the trading port of Canton. At the same time that the armies of the Roman republic were extending the Roman sphere of influence in the Mediterranean, Wu Ti was setting up a *Pax Sinica*, the Far Eastern counterpart of the *Pax Romana*. Because the Han period was marked by the growth of Chinese power and influence, as well as by a splendid flowering of thought and the arts, the Chinese even today refer to themselves as the "Sons of Han."

Domination of Confucianism. During the early years of the Han dynasty, the Confucian scholars once more became prominent. Now that strong imperial government was the accepted political institution, the conservative attachment of Confucian scholars to traditional institutions was a help rather than a hindrance to the imperial system. More important, the Han rulers saw the usefulness of learned men in government and established a civil service examination system based on the Confucian classics. This system endured with only a few changes until 1904. Whether or not learning the literary classics provided the best training for government, the creation of a highly educated civil service in China was a great forward step in government.

Important also for the growth of Confucianism was an imperial decree of 59 A.D. which ordered that sacrifices be made to the philosopher in government schools. During the Han period, the worship of Confucius became established as a great national cult, although it never became a religious faith appealing to the spiritual needs of the masses.

Han scholarship. The peace brought to China by the Han dynasty encouraged literature and science. The invention of paper in the first century A.D. proved of tremendous aid to literature. The Han performed a valuable service with the publication in 100 A.D. of the *Shuo Wên*, probably the oldest dictionary in the world. This period also witnessed the production of the first great

Chinese history, written by a contemporary of Wu Ti named Ssu-ma Ch'ien. His voluminous work has been highly praised, in part for its inclusion of a vast amount of information about ancient China, but even more for its freedom from superstition and its careful weighing of evidence.

Notable advances were made in the sciences during the Han period. For example, one scholar quite accurately reckoned the year at 365 and a fraction solar days. Although popular belief held that eclipses and such catastrophies as earthquakes were manifestations of heaven's displeasure, an outstanding scholar, Wang Ch'ung (27-100 A.D.), pointed out that:

On the average, there is one moon eclipse in about 180 days, and a solar eclipse in about every 41 or 42 months. Eclipses are regular occurrences and are not caused by political action. All anomalies and catastrophes are of the same class and are never dependent upon political events.[22]

Buddhism and Buddhist art enter China. In central Asia, where the Han had recently extended the *Pax Sinica*, the Chinese were in close contact with the Kushan empire in northwest India. This contact facilitated the spread of Buddhism from northwest India into China during the later Han dynasty, for Buddhist missionaries made their way through the heart of Asia along the same protected routes as the silk caravans.

A first-century Han emperor gave Buddhism official recognition and so initiated its spread within China, although its impact was not felt strongly throughout the land until after the Han period. At first, progress was hindered by the suspicions of the Chinese that Buddhist monasticism did not fit into the country's family tradition. But much of Buddhist mysticism was like that of Taoism, and the resemblance facilitated its eventual approval by many of the Chinese. Both *Hinayana* and *Mahayana* Buddhism were imported into China, but the latter, with its acceptance of Bodhisattvas and even local Chinese gods, gained the ascendancy. Today there are about ten separate Buddhist

Shown above is a Chinese sundial from the Han period. Constructed with remarkable precision, Chinese sundials were superior to any devised in the West until the thirteenth century A.D. The base and the vertical shaft have been reconstructed for this photograph.

sects in China, and in general their teachings have diverged widely from the doctrines taught by the Buddha.

The influence of Buddhism upon China proved to be extensive and enduring. Buddhism brought to the Chinese a new spiritual outlook in which salvation was held out to all classes, rich or poor, in contrast to the more aristocratic Confucianism. Moreover, Buddhist philosophy was sufficiently complex to engage the mind of the cleverest philosopher, while the Buddhist monasteries were havens for those who sought a life of contemplation.

Transported to China along with the Buddhist faith were the Gandharan Graeco-Indian artistic techniques and the *stupa* architecture (see caption, p. 100), from which the style of the Chinese pagoda is derived. In China, builders eventually created pagodas like tall spires, with multiple roofs or cornices and many ornamental projections (see illustration, p. 112).

The decline of the Han dynasty. The *Pax Sinica* of the Han period had brought to

This modern pagoda is based on a design 1300 years old.

China new lands, a new religion, and new developments in the arts, sciences, and scholarship. But in time this happy state of affairs came to an end as the Han dynasty lapsed into decadence. In 220 A.D. the last of the Han rulers was deposed, and while Chinese civilization was again to rise to an advanced state, China had first to endure a long period of transition and strife.

THE MEETING OF EAST

AND WEST

Beyond the Roman frontiers. During its period of greatest prosperity, the Graeco-Roman world-state, centered in the Mediterranean basin, maintained trade contacts extending far beyond the imperial boundaries. In the market quarter of imperial Rome, Chinese silk was sold, and Indian merchants frequented the streets of Alexandria. Strabo, the Greek geographer, stated that 120 ships sailed to India every year from Egyptian ports. During the four centuries which began

after 334 B.C. (the year when Alexander the Great entered Asia), the frontiers of civilization were progressively enlarged until finally a great chain of intercommunicating states stretched across Eurasia from the Atlantic to the Pacific.

The eastward drive of Hellenism was accompanied by a marked increase in economic activity throughout western Asia and in the exchange of goods between East and West. The trade between India and the West took several routes. From northern India, caravans proceeded across Parthia, while ships from southern Indian ports sailed to meet overland routes across Mesopotamia, Arabia, and Egypt.

Monsoons encourage sea traffic. After Egypt and other Hellenistic areas had succumbed to Roman conquest, the Romans took over the rich trade with the East. From the Roman standpoint, the routes from India that centered on Seleucia had serious disadvantages: they led through Parthian territory, and the caravans were subject to heavy tolls by the Parthian government. The high profits which caravan merchants made as middlemen also boosted costs. Therefore Augustus and his successors encouraged the use of the southern sea route to India.

Meanwhile, a most important discovery in navigation was made when mariners found how to use the monsoon winds which blow from the southwest across the Arabian Sea from May to October. Eliminating the tedious journey along the coasts, sailors could now voyage from Aden to the west coast of India across the open sea. Furthermore, ships could return from India by using the counter-monsoon blowing from the northeast between November and March. Thus round-trip voyages could be made in less than a year. This improvement in the sailing route encouraged western merchants to strike still farther east by ship, and they subsequently rounded the southern points of India and Ceylon.

The silk trade. The first move to pierce the land barrier separating China from the West was made by the Chinese rather than the Europeans. In 138 B.C. the Chinese emperor Wu Ti dispatched an ambassador into west central Asia to seek allies. Although the ambassador was unable to secure diplomatic alliances, he aroused Wu Ti's curiosity by describing the lands beyond the Pamirs and by showing his ruler the alfalfa and grape seeds he had carried back with him to China. Wu Ti resolved to open up trade relations with the peoples to the west. Thus, as a result of Chinese initiative, the use of silk spread to the Mediterranean during the early part of the first century B.C.

For their part, the Romans explored the silk route extending eastward from Syria. Roman merchants traveled past Bactria and over the Pamir Mountains as far as a place called the "Stone Tower," apparently in Chinese Turkestan. "Here was the meeting place of two worlds; a lonely rock among the mountains, towering above the waters of the Yarkand river. To this . . . came caravans from China and the countries of the farthest East. No word was spoken, but the merchants from east and west set down their wares in silence, and added or took away from the heap until the bargain was struck, after which the caravans made their way back across the mountains, rivers, and deserts."[23]

The silk caravans from northwest China which passed through Turkestan and Parthia before reaching the Roman dominions were also subject to heavy tolls. By diverting the caravans around Parthia to Indian ports and by transporting goods in Roman ships from there to the Red Sea and Egypt, the price of silk was reduced. As a result of this seaborne competition, the silk trade became highly developed; the reduction of prices made this commodity available for more than just the wealthiest people in the West.

Severance of East-West contacts. Unfortunately for the cause of international relations, commercial and cultural interchange among the three great civilizations of classical times was interrupted more and more frequently after the beginning of the third century A.D. With the overthrow of the Han dynasty in 220 A.D., China's power and prestige dwindled in central Asia. By coincidence, in the same year, the Kushan empire in northeast

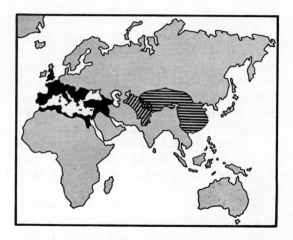

The Roman empire (black), the Kushan dominions in India (diagonal stripe), and the Han empire in China (horizontal stripe) are shown here about the year 100 A.D.

India succumbed, and Indian civilization also underwent a process of change and transition. About the same time, and probably most significant in the disruption of Eurasian relations, came the political and economic decline of the Graeco-Roman world (see Chapter 5).

An economic consequence of East-West trade. The volume of the Graeco-Roman world's Oriental trade had been surprisingly large. Because Roman exports to the East did not match in quantity or value the empire's imports of silk, spices, perfumes, gems, and other luxuries, the West had suffered seriously from an adverse balance of trade. Thus precious metals were continually being exported to Asia. Pliny declared that India, China, and Arabia drained away annually at least 100,000,000 sesterces (around $5,000,000 at a time when dollars had more purchasing value than today)—"that is the sum which our luxuries and our women cost us."[24] The discovery of vast hoards of Roman coins in India supports Pliny's statement.

One competent scholar has estimated that between the years 31 B.C. and 192 A.D. alone, Rome's trade with the Orient cost Rome a net money loss of about $500,000,000. This serious drain took place at a time when the known sources of gold and silver within the empire were being exhausted, and it must be reckoned as a prime cause of the deterioration of the imperial coinage and as one of the factors in the general economic decline of the Roman world.

The influence of West upon East. Roman contact with the East was made largely through trade with India and China and did at least increase substantially the knowledge of both sections of the world about each other. But Greek influence was even more consequential.

There is little doubt that the strongest Greek influence on Indian civilization was in the field of sculpture, as demonstrated by the results of the Graeco-Buddhist school at Gandhara, which in turn affected art forms in China and even in Japan. For a time, Indian coinage also bore the strong imprint of Hellenistic influence. Indian astronomy, which made many significant advances in its own right, also benefited from Greek learning.

The influence of East upon West. The trade with both India and China made a powerful impact on the economy of the Graeco-Roman world, as we have pointed out, and the conditions of life among those Romans and Greeks who could afford luxuries were made more comfortable by the importation of a variety of spices, muslins, and silks, as well as other objects of trade.

Whatever the immediate impact upon the West may have been, the long-range consequences of its meeting with the East were quite significant. With the contact once established, cultural exchange was going to continue, even though sometimes at a slow pace and by indirect means. Medieval Europe was to benefit from the success of the classical civilizations in establishing contact with each other. For example, "Chinese technological inventions poured into Europe in a continuous stream during the first thirteen centuries of the Christian era, just as later on the technological current flowed the other way."[25] No longer can an educated westerner assume the attitude that the meeting of East and West has always demonstrated the superiority of the West.

SUMMARY

From about 2200 to 1300 B.C., the Indian counterpart of the Nile and Tigris-Euphrates cultures existed in the Indus valley. Then, around 1500 B.C., Indo-Aryan nomads began to invade India, and as a result a new culture developed. The Indian language of Sanskrit evolved, and the oldest examples of Sanskrit literature, the *Vedas*, were composed. The *Upanishads*, commentaries on the *Vedas*, form the core of Hinduism, the pantheistic religion which has had an extraordinarily strong influence on Indian life. During Vedic and Epic times, the three pillars of Indian society—the autonomous village, the joint-family, and the caste system—evolved.

A lasting spiritual influence in Indian history and a significant influence the world over was Gautama Buddha. His ethical and moral teachings spread when Asoka sent missionaries into southern and southeastern Asia. Later, another monarch, Kanishka, called a council of theologians, from whose deliberations arose the *Mahayana* form of Buddhism. This form was adopted in central and eastern Asia.

In China, the Shang civilization began around 1500 B.C. in the Hwang Ho valley. During this period, the writing evolved which formed the basis for later Chinese script. The next dynasty—the Chou—had the longest existence of any dynasty in China's history. Chou times are considered China's classical period, for social customs, economic organization, philosophy, literature, and art which endured to modern times originated during that dynasty. Another of China's greatest dynasties, the Han, enlarged the bounds of the empire and established the *Pax Sinica*, in which the arts and scholarship flourished on a scale never before known in Far Eastern history.

Perhaps the greatest glory of ancient Chinese civilization was its contribution to philosophy. Such great thinkers as Confucius and Mencius sought to show men how to live rational, ethical lives. The ideas of these philosophers and of Lao-tzu, who developed an intuitive, mystical approach to life (Taoism), have exerted an incalculable influence upon Chinese culture for more than two thousand years.

During the centuries immediately preceding and following the birth of Christ, the great areas of civilization—Graeco-Roman, Indian, and Chinese—were connected by tenuous routes of commercial and cultural exchange. Although contact between East and West was eventually cut off, it continued long enough to establish a durable tradition in both the Orient and the Occident that beyond the mountains and deserts to the east or to the west lay other great civilizations. This tradition incited adventurous spirits many centuries later to bring the great "halves" of world civilization together once again.

SUGGESTIONS FOR READING

S. Piggott, *Prehistoric India,* * Penguin. Describes the Indus valley civilization and points out the relationship of western India to the whole of western Asia.

A. L. Basham, *The Wonder That Was India,* * Evergreen. A comprehensive, well-organized study of Indian culture prior to the coming of the Muslims in the eleventh century.

Excellent translations of Hindu religious texts are S. Prabhavananda and F. Manchester, trans., *The Upanishads: Breath of the Eternal,* * Mentor; and S. Prabhavananda and C. Isherwood, trans., *The Song of God—The Bhagavad-Gita,* * Mentor.

S. Radhakrishnan, *The Hindu View of Life,* Macmillan, 1927. Today's foremost Indian philosopher compares Hinduism with western philosophy. Recommended for an account of the origins and tenets of Hinduism is A. C. Bouquet, *Hinduism,* Longmans, 1950.

E. A. Burtt, ed., *The Teachings of the Compassionate Buddha,* * Mentor. Book I: selections from the early scriptures of Buddhism; Book II: excerpts from Chinese and Japanese Buddhist works. C. Humphreys, *Buddhism,* * Penguin, describes the life of the Buddha and the rise of the major branches of Buddhism.

A. Foucher, *The Beginnings of Buddhist Art,* Oxford, 1918. A classic in its field, this book concerns the relationship of Indian and Greek art. For other opinions on this controversial subject, see the works of A. Coomaraswamy: *The Dance of Shiva,* * Noonday; and *Christian and Oriental Philosophy of Art,* * Dover.

H. Hesse, *Siddhartha,* * New Directions. A young Indian meets the Buddha, a courtesan, and many temptations in this wise and charming novel of a quest for self-knowledge.

J. G. Andersson, *Children of the Yellow Earth,* Macmillan, 1934. Considered the standard work on the Neolithic Age in China. For information about pre-Shang and Shang periods, see H. G. Creel, *The Birth of China,* Ungar, 1954; and Chi Li, *The Beginnings of Chinese Civilization,* Univ. of Wash., 1957.

Yu-lan Fêng, ed., *History of Chinese Philosophy,* 2 vols., Princeton, 1952-1953. Probably the most authoritative work on this subject. Vol. I follows developments to 100 B.C.

Wu-Chi Liu, *A Short History of Confucian Philosophy* * Penguin. Written in nontechnical language, this systematic presentation of Confucianism correlates the major philosophical systems and defines the place of Confucianism in present-day China. Of special value is the discussion of the key term *tao.* Leonard

*Indicates an inexpensive paperbound edition.

Shih-lien Hsü, *The Political Philosophy of Confucianism,* Dutton, 1932, deals with the political thought of Confucius and Mencius. See also J. R. Ware, trans., *The Sayings of Confucius,* * Mentor.

Lao-tzu, *The Way of Life: Tao Te Ching* * (trans. by R. B. Blakney), Mentor. The complete text of this famous work. Arthur Waley, ed. and trans., *The Way and Its Power; A Study of the Tao Tê Ching and Its Place in Chinese Thought,* * Grove, is an interpretation of Lao-tzu's classic by a gifted scholar.

J. Needham and Wang Ling, *Science and Civilisation in China,* 3 vols., Cambridge Univ. Vol. I: *Introductory Orientation,* 1954; Vol. II: *History of Scientific Thought,* 1956; Vol. III: *Mathematics and the Science of the Heavens and the Earth,* 1960. Students interested in correcting misconceptions prevalent in the West regarding Chinese civilization should consult these volumes, first of a projected seven-volume study. In Vol. I, Needham examines the structure of the Chinese language, reviews the geography of China, and discusses scientific contacts between East and West. In Vol. II, he discusses the relationship of the major philosophical systems to Chinese science.

Lin Yutang, ed., *The Wisdom of China and India,* Modern Lib., 1955. An invaluable anthology of source materials, including hymns from the *Rig-Veda,* selections from the *Upanishads,* the *Ramayana,* and Buddhist scriptures, the aphorisms of Confucius, and selections from Mencius. Contains useful editorial comments.

Chapters 1-5 of D. Carter, *Four Thousand Years of Chinese Art,* Ronald, 1951, treat the art of the Shang and Chou periods. See also B. Gray, *Early Chinese Pottery and Porcelain,* Pitman, 1952.

M. Wheeler, *Rome Beyond the Imperial Frontiers,* * Penguin. A well-illustrated study of Rome's foreign trade practices under the empire and East-West cultural interchange. See also H. G. Rawlinson, *Intercourse Between India and the Western World from the Earliest Times to the Fall of Rome,* Cambridge Univ., 1928; E. H. Warmington, *The Commerce Between the Roman Empire and India,* Macmillan, 1928; and G. F. Hudson, *Europe and China; A Survey of Their Relations from the Earliest Times to 1800,* Longmans, 1931.

A stimulating study of Indian-Chinese cultural relations is E. C. Bagchi, *India and China; A Thousand Years of Cultural Relations,* Philosophical Lib., 1951.

For surveys of Chinese and Indian history with chapters pertinent to Chapter 4 text material, see List of Readings, p. 802.

NEAR EAST AND EGYPT

INDIA AND CHINA

B.C. 3000

Old Kingdom in Egypt 3100-2270—pyramids, hieroglyphics
Independent city-states in Sumer 2900-2400

Indus valley civilization 2200-1300—capitals at Mohenjo-Daro and Harappa; well-organized government and economy; excellent city planning; trade relations with Sumer

2000

Middle Kingdom in Egypt 2060-1785—public works and irrigation projects; canal from Nile River to Red Sea

Hammurabi rules lower Mesopotamia 1760; capital Babylon
Hittites capture Babylonia c. 1600
New Kingdom or Empire in Egypt 1580-1085

1500

Thutmose III c. 1501-1447—the "Napoleon of Egypt"

Invasion of India by Aryans from Black and Caspian seas c. 1500
Vedic Age c. 1500-900—beginning of three pillars of Indian society: autonomous village, caste system, joint-family

Vedas—oldest Sanskrit literature; religious hymns
Shang dynasty 1500-1100—China's first civilization—ruler functions as military commander and high priest; religious practices (ancestor worship, divination); agrarian economy and raising of silkworms; writing (partly pictorial, partly ideographic); magnificent bronzes

Amenhotep III c. 1411-1375—Egyptian empire at its height

Akhenaton c. 1375-1358—monotheism; naturalism in art
Era of small states in Near East 1200-700
Period of exploration and colonization by Phoenicians 1200; Carthage founded; Phoenicians develop alphabet

1000

Period of Decadence in Egypt 1085-332

The Hebrews—Palestine established; rules of David and Solomon; concept of monotheism gains acceptance

Chou dynasty 1027-256—China's "classical age"—feudal states; writing (ideograms); Decree of Heaven promulgated
Epic Age in India c. 900-500—caste system becomes more complex: priest, warrior, merchant, serf, "untouchable"
Upanishads 800-600—foundation of Hinduism

750

Assyria is master of Fertile Crescent 700; of Egypt 671
Zoroaster, born in 660, founds Persian religion
Destruction of Jerusalem by Nebuchadnezzar 586
Persian empire—Cyrus the Great conquers Near East; efficient imperial system established; great highways built

500

Persians conquer Egypt 525

Gautama Buddha 563?-483—founder of Buddhism
Confucius 551-479—most famous and influential of Chinese philosophers; ethical code of conduct becomes creed of Chinese

Chinese poetry collected in *Shih Ching*, or *Book of Odes*—
Two greatest Sanskrit epics composed: the *Mahabharata* (including the *Bhagavad-Gita*) and the *Ramayana*

400

300

Lao-tzu and Taoism—aim: to bring men into harmony with basic laws of nature; intuitive approach to life; *Tao Te Ching*
Mencius c. 372-289 links theory of Decree of Heaven to democratic concept of the will of the people in government
Alexander the Great crosses Indus valley 326
Chandragupta Maurya seizes the Magadha state in India, founds Maurya dynasty 321-c. 185
Asoka 273-232—"the first great royal patron of Buddhism"
Era of Contending States in China—Ch'in defeat Chou 256

200

Ch'in ruler Shih Huang Ti, or "First Emperor" 221-210
Han dynasty of China 202 B.C.-220 A.D.—strong imperial rule
Tamil kingdoms—Hindu states, chief trading area with the West
Mauryan empire falls 185; under Demetrius, Bactrian rule extends to India and Punjab; Graeco-Bactrian kingdom created
Han emperor Wu Ti 140-87—Huns defeated, domain expanded, literature, science advanced; silk trade with West 138

100

Kushan empire in India (first century-220 A.D.)
Kanishka, Kushan ruler c. 78-128—sponsors *Mahayana* ("Great Vehicle") school of Buddhism, which spreads north and east; *Hinayana* ("Lesser Vehicle") Buddhism spreads south, east

A.D. 100

GREECE

ROME

| | | 3000 B.C. |

Zenith of Cretan culture c. 2000
Indo-European tribes invade Peloponnesus 1900

Indo-Europeans invade Italian peninsula 2000-1000—first settlers in Po valley; Latins settle in lower Tiber valley — 2000

Mycenaeans capture Knossos 1500

1500

Cretans rebel against Mycenaeans 1400
Mycenae—master of the Aegean world 1400-1200

Dorians invade Greek mainland c. 1100; destroy Mycenae
Homeric Age 1100-750—tribal government; animistic religion; heroic ideals; aristocratic society; simple farming system

1000

Hellenic Age or "classical Greece" (eighth-fourth centuries)—rise of independent city-states
Age of Nobles 750-500—nobility gains political power; extensive Greek colonization, notably in Great Greece
Growth of Athenian democracy: Solon establishes Council of Four Hundred and court of appeals 594, broadens franchise; Pisistratus banishes nobles 560; Cleisthenes reclassifies citizens, introduces ostracism 508
Sparta—militaristic totalitarian state; cultural stagnation

Etruscans settle on Italy's west coast, dominate northern Italy
Rome founded—elective monarchy; *imperium* conferred by popular assembly; king's council (Senate); class divisions (patrician, plebeian) — 750
Greek colonists establish city-states in Great Greece, Sicily

Etruscans conquer Rome (sixth century); continue elective system
Nobles revolt against Etruscan king, establish Roman republic headed by two patrician consuls 509
Plebeians rise 509-300—Concilium Plebis formed; powers of patricians decreased — 500
Latin League allied with Rome against Etruscans 493

Spartan League (sixth century)—oligarchic states
Persian Wars: Persians suppress Ionians, destroy Miletus 494; Athenians defeat Persians at Marathon 490; Persians defeat Spartans at Thermopylae 480; Persian navy crushed at Salamis 480; Persian army defeated at Plataea 479
Delian League (478) becomes agency for Athenian imperialism
Golden Age of Greece (460-429) under rule of Pericles
Greek geniuses in Hellenic period: Thales, Pythagoras, Heraclitus, Democritus, Hippocrates, Socrates, Plato, Aristotle, Herodotus, Thucydides, Sappho, Aeschylus, Sophocles, Euripides, Aristophanes, Myron
Peloponnesian War 431-404—Athens vs. Spartan League

Laws of the Twelve Tables drafted 449

400

Philip II of Macedonia conquers Greece 338
Alexander the Great defeats Persia 331; founds divine kingship
Hellenistic Age 323-31—tripartite division of Alexander's empire under Ptolemy, Seleucus, and Antigonus Gonatas
Greek geniuses in Hellenistic period: Epicurus, Zeno, Euclid, Archimedes, Aristarchus, Eratosthenes

Rebellion of Latin League quelled by Rome; League dissolved 338

Samnites and Great Greece conquered by Rome (third century) — 300
First Punic War 264-241—Carthage beaten; Rome gains naval supremacy in western Mediterranean
Second Punic War c. 218-201—"colossal contest between the nation Rome and the man Hannibal"; Romans finally victorious at battle of Zama — 200
Rome defeats Macedonia 197; Rome defeats Seleucids; Egypt forms alliance with Rome 168; Rome destroys Corinth
Third Punic War—Rome destroys Carthage 146
The Gracchi unsuccessfully attempt reforms 133-121
Civil War—Sulla vs. Marius, Sulla and Senate victorious 88-79; — 100
Pompey vs. Caesar, Caesar becomes dictator 49-44; Octavian vs. Antony, Octavian defeats Antony and Cleopatra at battle of Actium 31
Golden Age of literature: Cicero, Caesar, Catullus, Lucretius, Virgil, Horace, Ovid, Livy
Octavian becomes Augustus, establishes principate; initiates **Pax Romana** (30 B.C.-235 A.D.)
Julio-Claudian line 14-68—Tiberius, Claudius, Caligula, Nero
Flavian emperors 69-96
Silver Age of literature: Juvenal, Tacitus, Plutarch, Seneca; scientists—Pliny the Elder, Ptolemy, Galen
Antonines, "five good emperors" 96-180 — 100 A.D.

PART 2 The Middle Ages

When we speak of the "fall" of Rome, perhaps we forget that the great classical tradition was carried on for another thousand years without interruption in Constantinople, or "New Rome." Until it fell in 1453, the Byzantine empire acted as a buffer for western Europe, staving off attack after attack from the east. The culminating series of attacks, resulting in the collapse of the empire, was launched by the adherents of Islam—a dynamic way of life developed by the followers of Muhammad, an eloquent prophet who instilled in his people a vital sense of their destiny to rule in the name of Allah. With unbelievable swiftness, the followers of the Prophet became rulers of the Near East, swept across North Africa and surged into Spain, and expanded eastward to the frontiers of China. The Muslims, the great middlemen of medieval times, shuttled back and forth across vast expanses, trading the wares of East and West and acting as the conveyors of culture. Throughout most of the Middle Ages, the East outshone the West even as Constantinople and Bagdad outdazzled in material magnificence and intellectual and artistic triumphs any capital in western Europe.

In Europe, after the inundation of the Roman empire by Germanic tribes in the fifth century brought lawlessness and fragmentation, a painful search for stability began. Centuries of disorder followed until Charlemagne established a new empire modeled on that of Rome. But Charlemagne's empire failed and, in the latter part of the ninth century, anarchy threatened again. The challenge was met by the rise of a new kind of political system—feudalism. Under feudalism, the landed nobility acted as police force, judiciary, and army. Buttressing this new political order was the manorial system—an economic order which provided food and life's necessities and divided men into two great classes: the fighters or nobles and the workers or serfs. Feudalism helped to restore a degree of strength and progress to western Europe, and by the eleventh century, decline had been halted. Yet feudalism and the manorial system were inherently rural and rigid, and already in existence were new forces destined to displace them. Shadowy outlines of new kingdoms—later to become Germany, France, England, and Spain—began to emerge under the direction of vigorous monarchs. Europe went on the offensive, ejecting the Muslims from the Iberian peninsula, breaking Muslim control of the Mediterranean, and launching crusades to capture Jerusalem from the infidel. The agrarian economy of feudal times gave way before the revival of trade and communications, the growth of towns, the increased use of money as a medium of exchange, and the rise of a new class in society—the bourgeoisie.

The greatest stabilizing force in Europe during the medieval period was the Church. Spreading its message of hope and salvation throughout Europe, it restrained and Christianized the crude Germanic tribes. Without the use of arms, the Church upheld a code of humane conduct and attempted—often successfully—to curb injustice. In short, the Church provided the nearest approach to effective and centralized supervision of European life during the Middle Ages. By the thirteenth century, when popes such as Innocent III bent proud monarchs to their will, the Church had reached the zenith of its influence as a kind of international government.

The Church was also the focus of medieval intellectual life. By sheltering precious manuscripts in its monasteries, it endeavored to preserve the best of classical culture. The Church was the chief patron of poets and artists, and it fostered a new institution of learning—the university. Roman law was rediscovered and newly systematized, and students began to study natural science. Scholars pondered the basic questions of existence, and such impressive works as Thomas Aquinas' *Summa Theologica* were produced. (Outside the universities, the artistry of Chaucer and of Dante heralded a rich future for literature in the vernacular tongues.)

Perhaps the true measure of the spirit and achievement of the Middle Ages is shown by its cathedrals. These soaring edifices illustrate the engineering and architectural mastery achieved by their builders, and the beauty of their sculpture and stained-glass windows attests to medieval artistic genius. And as the most imposing structures of the age, the cathedrals were the symbol of both the unqualified faith and the religious unity of Christendom. The Middle Ages was indeed the Age of Faith, when few people in the West, no matter what their manners or morals, lived without frequent and meaningful contact with the Church. Men were born, lived, and died under its protection.

CHAPTER 5

The City of God

THE RISE OF CHRISTIANITY AND
THE FALL OF ROME; UPHEAVAL
AND SURVIVAL IN THE WEST

Introduction. To the inhabitants of the Graeco-Roman world, Rome was "the Eternal City"—a proud designation which is still used today. When, therefore, in 410 A.D. the barbarian Visigoths responded to its magnetic lure by entering Italy and sacking the city, a cry of anguish reverberated throughout the crumbling empire. In distant Bethlehem, St. Jerome cried, "The lamp of the world is extinguished, and it is the whole world which has perished in the ruins of this one city."[1]

This chapter tells the story of the fall of the City of the Caesars and of the emergence, like the phoenix arising from the ashes, of "the City of God." It was St. Augustine who, in the wake of the Visigoths' capture of Rome, devised that phrase to represent the rise of a new Christian society on the ruins of paganism and a once

invincible empire—and to assure Christians that the community of the Most High would endure, although the greatest city on earth had fallen.

This period in history has many facets. One concerns the national history of the Jewish people, the coming of Jesus in the midst of their turbulent relations with the Romans, and the eventual triumph of His teachings. Another is the story of the progressive decline of the Roman empire during the time when Christianity was born and began to grow. A third element is the migration of barbarian peoples and their settlement in Europe—a movement which eventually broke down the imperial boundaries. A final aspect (to be discussed in Chapter 7) is the shift in civilization's center of gravity—from the West, overrun by barbarians, to the eastern shores of the Mediterranean and beyond.

The period of devastation and decline in the West was one of great historical significance. Graeco-Roman civilization, which had inherited much from the older civilizations of the Near East, was slowly blended with Germanic institutions to produce a new historical compound. In this process, the catalytic agent was the Christian Church. It is a fascinating story—how elements from the ancient Near East, Greece, Rome, and the Germanic tribes were fashioned into a new culture, which in time produced outstanding intellectual, literary, and artistic achievements for the enrichment of civilization throughout the world.

THE TRIUMPH OF
CHRISTIANITY

Rise of Jewish nationalism. At the very time when the principate of Augustus was laying the foundations of Rome's imperial greatness, events were taking place in a distant Roman province that would one day alter the course of western history. In order to see these events in the proper perspective, let us begin the story in Hellenistic Palestine.

Following the conquests of Alexander the Great in the Near East, Palestine was ruled at different times by the Ptolemies and the Seleucids. With their fervid adherence to monotheism, the Jewish people had already created a theocratic community, based upon the Pentateuch—the five books said to have been revealed by Jehovah to Moses—and supplemented by the teachings of the Prophets and the writings of scholars. Religious life centered on the great temple at Jerusalem. The most powerful figure was the high priest, assisted by two Sanhedrins, or councils: one civil and political, the other religious. The Hebrews, "the People of God," were a tightly knit clan; even the Jewish groups outside Palestine were linked by spiritual bonds to the temple and to a Law which they believed to be divinely inspired.

At the same time Hellenic influences were constantly at work among the Jews. Many learned to speak Greek, and the translation of the Hebrew Scriptures into Greek not only stimulated the use of that language among Jewish intellectuals but also broadened Jewish thought.

Greek influence might have become stronger had it not stirred up factionalism within the Jewish community in Jerusalem. Eventually, one puritanical group came to blows with a pro-Hellenic group favored by the Hellenistic Seleucid kings who ruled Palestine from Syria. The internal conflict gave the Seleucid king an opportunity to intervene, and in 168 B.C. he ordered the temple dedicated to the worship of Zeus. Viewing this decree as a blasphemous defilement, the Jews rebelled. Under their leader, Judas Maccabaeus, the Jews won military success, secured religious freedom, and rededicated the temple to Jehovah. In 142 B.C. the Syrian king was forced to recognize Jewish independence.

A Maccabean dynasty was created which reigned over most of Palestine. In time these rulers became worldly and corrupt, and factionalism again flared up. It was in the midst of a civil war that the Roman legions appeared on the scene.

Roman occupation of Palestine. Certain Jewish elements had appealed for help to Pompey, who was then completing Rome's conquest of Asia Minor and Syria. Seizing his opportunity, Pompey annexed Palestine in 64 B.C.

Eventually, Herod, a leader from a tribe that had long been enemies of the Jews, rose to power as a tool of the Romans. Appointed by the Roman Senate, he served as king of Judea from 37 to 4 B.C. Of exceptional ability, Herod fortified Jerusalem with great walls and towers and rebuilt the temple on a lavish scale. To the Jews, however, he remained a usurper who professed Judaism as a matter of expediency. Soon after Herod's death, Judea was made into a minor Roman province, which was ruled directly by a Roman governor.

The Jews themselves were unhappy and divided. During centuries of tribulation, the Prophets had taught that God would one day create a new Israel when righteousness prevailed under a divinely appointed leader, a Messiah. The Pharisees, the orthodox custodians of the religious tradition, believed that the age of righteousness could only appear when the Jewish people adhered strictly to God's commandments. But groups concerned less with a spiritual kingdom than with an independent political state called for rebellion.

Destruction of Jerusalem. In 66 A.D. violence erupted. The Roman garrison at Jerusalem was massacred, and the revolt spread beyond the walls of the city. The wholesale destruction of Jerusalem in 70 A.D. by Titus, son of Vespasian (see p. 75), spelled the end of the Hebrew state. The Jewish dream of an independent political state was to remain unrealized for almost nineteen centuries, until, as a result of United Nations action, the republic of Israel was proclaimed in 1948.

Development of Jewish religious thought. The destruction of Jerusalem did not destroy the most important single aspect of Jewish culture—its religion. Through centuries of suffering, captivity, and subjugation, the Jews had been taught by a succession of Prophets to cleave to their covenant with Jehovah and to safeguard their religious inheritance.

In the centuries just preceding and following the birth of Christ, Judaism exhibited vigor and strength. Advocating unswerving fidelity to the traditional beliefs, the Pharisees made up the strongest and most learned of the religious factions. From their ranks came the rabbis, scholars who expounded the Law and applied it to existing conditions. In the Gospels many Pharisees are severely criticized for their arrogance and for concerning themselves with the letter rather than the spirit of the Law. But from the second century B.C. to the second century A.D., it was the Pharisaic sect which provided Judaism with its greatest intellectual leaders. Moreover, by reëstablishing rabbinical schools following the fall of Jerusalem, the Pharisees did much to ensure that Judaism would endure as a religion.

The Dead Sea Scrolls. Contemporary with the Pharisees was another sect, the Essenes. In recent years the discovery of the Dead Sea Scrolls has added greatly to our knowledge of the Essenes and most certainly has enhanced their importance. We do not know what became of this ascetic group after the destruction of Jerusalem, but prior to their

Shown here is the partially unrolled Thanksgiving Scroll, one of the Dead Sea Scrolls possessed by the Hebrew University in Jerusalem. In 1947, while exploring caves above the desolate western shore of the Dead Sea, two Bedouin boys discovered some of the scrolls wrapped in linen and preserved in clay jars. Later, all the caves of the area were examined by scholars, and more scrolls came to light. Nearby were found the ruins of an ancient building believed to have been an Essene monastery, apparently destroyed by the Romans in 68 A.D. during the great revolt of the Jews.

death or dispersal they managed to hide their manuscripts.

Some scrolls are portions of the Old Testament, centuries older than the earliest text previously known. The analysis of the script used on the scrolls and radioactive carbon dating of fragments would place their composition in the first century B.C. Jewish and Christian scholars alike have been thrilled to read the Book of Isaiah in such ancient manuscript and to discover that the version we have been using, although based on much later sources, has been accurate except in some details.

As for the history of Christianity itself, the Dead Sea Scrolls have been described as constituting "a whole missing chapter of the history of the growth of religious ideas between Judaism and Christianity."[2] This interpretation of their importance results from analysis of those scrolls which describe the Essene sect in the first century B.C.—that is, just prior to the appearance of Christianity. Some scholars have attached much significance to the possible influence of Essene belief on the founding of Christianity. They also suggest that the Christian monastic tradition may owe its origin to the Essenes and that the ritual of the Last Supper bears striking resemblances to procedures found in the Essenes' Manual of Discipline. Other scholars have seen far less significance in the parallels between Essene and Christian belief. "It has even been said that the discoveries will revolutionize New Testament scholarship. This may perhaps cause some alarm. There is no danger, however, that our understanding of the New Testament will be so revolutionized by the Dead Sea Scrolls as to require a revision of any basic article of Christian faith."[3]

The life of Jesus. Whatever its possible debt to the Essenes, Christianity bears the unmistakable imprint of the personality of its founder, Jesus Christ. According to the Biblical account, He was born in Bethlehem in the reign of Herod; therefore He may have been born by the time of Herod's death (4 B.C.) rather than in the year which traditionally begins the Christian era. After spending the first thirty years of His life in the village of Nazareth as a carpenter, Jesus began His brief mission, preaching a gospel of love for one's fellow man, urging service to others, and condemning violence and selfishness.

The fame of Jesus' teaching and holiness spread among the Jews as He and His twelve devoted disciples traveled from village to village in Palestine. When He came to Jerusalem to attend the feast of the Passover, He was welcomed triumphantly by huge crowds which regarded Him as the promised Messiah. But Jesus was concerned with a spiritual, not an earthly, kingdom, and when the people saw that He had no intention of leading a nationalistic movement against the Romans, they turned against Him. His enemies then came forward—the moneylenders whom He had denounced, the Pharisees who feared that His movement might deprive them of their privileged position, the people who considered Him a disturber of the status quo, and those who saw Him as a blasphemer of Jehovah. Betrayed by Judas, one of His disciples, Jesus was condemned by Jewish authorities, turned over to the Roman officials for execution, and crucified.

With His death it seemed as though His cause had been exterminated. No written message had been left behind, and His few loyal followers were disheartened. Yet in the wake of His martyrdom, the Christian cause took on new impetus. Reports soon spread that Jesus had been seen after His Crucifixion and had spoken to His disciples, instructing them to spread His teachings. At first there were few converts within Palestine itself, because of the strongly traditional and exclusive character of Judaism during this period of national trouble. But the Hellenized Jews living in foreign lands, in contact with new ideas and modes of living, were less firmly committed to traditional Jewish doctrines. The new religion first made real headway among the Jewish communities in such cities as Athens, Antioch, Corinth, and Rome.

Paul's missionary work. As long as the followers of Jesus regarded Him exclusively

This early Christian fresco of St. Paul is from a wall of the Church of Santa Maria in Via Lata, Rome.

as a Messiah in the traditional Jewish sense, with no message for the salvation of non-Jews, the new religion could have no universal appeal. Largely through the missionary efforts of Paul, this obstacle was removed.

Born Saul, of strict Jewish origin, and raised in a Hellenistic city in Asia Minor, this great Christian saint possessed a wide knowledge of Greek ideas and Hellenistic literature. Saul was also a strict Pharisee, who held it his first duty to uphold the Law of his people. He considered Jesus and His followers to be blasphemers against the Law and took an active part in the persecution of Christians. One day, on the road to Damascus—in Saul's own words:

And it came to pass, that, as I made my journey, and was come nigh unto Damascus about noon, suddenly there shone from heaven a great light round about me.

And I fell unto the ground, and heard a voice saying unto me, Saul, Saul, why persecutest thou me?

And I answered, Who art thou, Lord? And he said unto me, I am Jesus of Nazareth, whom thou persecutest.

And they that were with me saw indeed the light, and were afraid; but they heard not the voice of him that spake to me.

And I said, What shall I do, Lord? And the Lord said unto me, Arise, and go into Damascus; and there it shall be told thee of all things which are appointed for thee to do.[4]

Saul, henceforth known as Paul, turned from being a persecutor into perhaps the greatest of Christian missionaries.

Paul also exercised great influence upon the shaping of Christian doctrine. He taught that Jesus was Christ, the Son of God, and that He had died to atone for the sins of mankind. Acceptance of this belief guaranteed life after death to Jews and gentiles alike if they observed His commandments and followed all of His teachings. After spending several years in Rome teaching and preaching, Paul was beheaded about 65 A.D. during the reign of the bestial emperor Nero. By this time, Christian communities had already been established in the major cities of the empire.

Government persecution of Christians. The Roman government tolerated any religion which did not threaten the safety or tranquillity of the state. While the worship of the emperor was considered an essential patriotic rite uniting all Roman subjects in common loyalty to the imperial government, Roman officials had no quarrel with a person's religious preference as long as he was willing to take part in the ceremonies of the state cult. But the Christians refused to participate in the ceremonies. To them there was only one God; no other could share their loyalty to Him. In the eyes of the Roman officials this attitude branded the Christians as traitors. In addition, the Christians would not serve in the army or hold political office. Intolerant of other religious sects, they would not associate with pagans or take part in social functions which they considered sinful or degrading.

The emperors began to persecute the Christians not because of intolerance of belief but because it seemed to them that the Christians threatened the very existence of the state. Also, the Christians could be used as convenient scapegoats for the increasing troubles of the time. In the third century a series of severe persecutions was undertaken; the first widespread campaign against the Christians was instigated by the emperor Decius in 250, and the last by Diocletian in 302. But there was to be no stamping out of the new religion by force. In fact, the Christians seemed to welcome martyrdom, so that a second-century Roman writer stated: "the Blood of the martyrs is the seed of the Church."[5]

Official recognition and acceptance. In 311 the emperor Galerius saw the failure of the efforts at suppression and issued an Edict of Toleration making Christianity a legal religion in the East. Later, the emperor Constantine was swayed toward Christianity during a desperate battle with the army of a rival for the throne. At the height of the conflict, tradition has it that the emperor saw emblazoned across the sky a cross with the words *In hoc signo vinces* ("By this sign thou shalt conquer"). He won the battle and henceforth favored Christianity. In 313 he issued the Edict of Milan, which legalized Christianity throughout the empire and put it on a par with all the pagan cults. Constantine's successors (with the exception of Julian) also carried out a pro-Christian policy.

To the sincere pagan, however, the depressing cultural, economic, and political conditions of the times made it seem that Rome was suffering from the renunciation of its protecting deities. In his brief reign (361-363), the emperor Julian sought in vain to revive paganism; as a result, he was branded Julian the Apostate.

In the latter part of the fourth century, the government withdrew its support of the pagan temples and transferred state support to the Christian Church. By 395, the end of the reign of Emperor Theodosius, Christianity was the sole and official religion of the state. Within less than four hundred years, in spite of all obstacles, Christianity had become the official religion of a world empire.

Reasons for the spread of Christianity. In its rise to preëminence, Christianity had had to compete with established classical philosophies and with numerous other new religions. Many of the educated classes had turned from belief in the old Roman gods to Stoicism and Epicureanism. Still other intellectuals had been attracted to Neo-Platonism, which taught that the only reality is spirit and that the soul's principal objective is to escape from the material world and get back to its spiritual home. There were also popular religions such as the worship of the Egyptian Isis and Osiris, the Greek Dionysus, and the Persian Mithras, god of light and of armies (a cult that was especially popular among the soldiers). These cults presented the idea of a divine protector and the promise of everlasting life. They offered new hope to their followers and stirred their emotions with ritual pomp and ceremony. Yet the need for a sounder hope and a truer emotion persisted.

The depressed and oppressed alike found the consolation and comradeship for which they hungered in Christianity. This faith upheld the equality of all men, taught that a loving Father had sent His only Son to atone for men's sins, and offered a vision of immortality and an opportunity to be "born again" and be cleansed of sin. Christian doctrines met the growing spiritual longing during a period when traditional standards were losing their value.

The cultural and administrative unity of the Roman empire made possible the rapid growth of Christianity into a world religion and its eventual acceptance as the official religion of the Graeco-Roman world. Moreover, Christianity was a dynamic, aggressive religion in its own right. Its teachings were definite, its converts displayed enthusiasm and zeal, and the courage with which the Christians faced death and persecution impressed even their bitterest enemies. In time also, a Church organization was created that was far more united and efficient than any possessed by its competitors.

Early Church organization. A strong and well-organized Christian movement did not arise immediately following the death of Christ, however. In fact, the early Christians at first drew little or no distinction between laity and clergy. Traveling teachers visited Christian communities, preaching and giving advice where it was needed. But this system soon proved inadequate. The steady growth in the number of Christians made necessary special Church officials who could devote all their time to religious work, clarify the body of Christian dogma, conduct Church services and rituals, and take care of funds. At first the officials were called elders, or presbyters, or were referred to as bishops or overseers. By the second century the offices of bishop and presbyter had become distinct. Village churches were administered by presbyters, who were responsible to the bishop controlling the mother church, usually located in a city. Thus the diocese evolved, a territorial administrative division under the jurisdiction of a bishop. The bishop had charge of all Church property in his diocese, had authority over the clergy, and was the official interpreter of Christian dogma.

A number of dioceses made up a province; the bishop of the most important city in each province enjoyed more prestige than his fellows and was known as an archbishop.

The provinces were grouped into a larger administrative division called a patriarchate. The title of patriarch was applied to the bishop of such great cities as Rome, Constantinople, and Alexandria. Thus, in the evolution of an organized hierarchy, the Church adapted the administrative divisions of the Roman empire and borrowed much of its law. The title of bishop, for example, came from an important office of the Roman municipality.

Foundations of Christian doctrine and worship. While the administrative structure of the Church was being erected, Christian beliefs were being spelled out and systematized. However, grave differences of opinions over doctrinal matters caused frequent clashes. One of the most important controversies was over Arianism. The basic issue in the Arian controversy was the relative position of the three persons of the Trinity. In the doctrine of the Trinity, Christ was regarded as one of three persons—God the Father, God the Son, and God the Holy Ghost. The common view of the equality of God and the Son was vigorously espoused by Athanasius (296?-373), the bishop of Alexandria and a notable champion of orthodoxy. On the other hand, Arius (256-336), a presbyter of Alexandria, believed that Christ was not God because He was not of a substance identical with God and was not coeternal with Him. So serious was the controversy that the emperor Constantine convened the Council of Nicaea in 325 to discuss the problem. The Arian belief was branded as heresy—an opinion or doctrine contrary to the official teachings of the Church—and Christ was declared to be cosubstantial with God the Father and coeternal. Thus the creed of Christianity became more subtle and complex, and the beliefs sustained at the Council of Nicaea were soon formulated into what is called the Nicene Creed. Some churches, notably the Roman Catholic Church, follow this creed today.

Another task for the early Church was the selection of an official body of Christian literature. To be accepted into this official body—the Christian canon—a piece of writing must be ascribed to divine inspiration. Early churchmen used this criterion in reducing the contents of the New Testament to twenty-seven books, from the much larger number which were originally included. All major Christian churches today use essentially the same New Testament, though in varying translations.

The service of worship in the early churches was plain and simple, consisting of prayer, Scripture reading, hymns, and preaching. Gradually the service was transformed into an elaborately beautiful ceremonial. In the early period of Christianity, the believer worshiped God and sought salvation largely through his own efforts. Following the growth of Church organization and ritual and the crystallization of its dogma, the Church was believed to be the indispensable intermediary between God and man.

Both the development of the Church's administrative hierarchy and the creation of a body of authoritative dogma owed much to the Church Fathers of the fourth and fifth centuries. In the East two noteworthy Church Fathers were Athanasius, whose views were accepted at the Council of Nicaea, and St. Basil (330-379), who founded many monasteries (see Chapter 10). In the West the two greatest Church Fathers were St. Jerome (340-420), famous for his Latin translation of the Bible, called the Vulgate, which in a revised form is still the official translation of the Catholic Church; and St. Augustine (354-430), possibly the most important of all the Fathers. St. Augustine's book *The City of God* had a marked influence upon the thought of the Middle Ages, and the views expounded in it became the foundation of much of the Church's theology.

The bishop of Rome becomes leader of the Church. A development of outstanding importance in the Christian movement was the rise of the bishop of Rome to a position of preëminence in the hierarchy of the Church. At first Rome was only one of several patriarchates, no more important than Alexandria, Jerusalem, Antioch, or Constantinople. But gradually the bishop at Rome became recognized as the leader of the Church and as-

Although none of the early Christian basilicas has escaped alterations, we can still obtain a general idea of how these buildings originally appeared. Above is shown part of the interior of the Basilica of Santa Sabina at Rome, built in 425.

sumed the title of pope—from the Greek word meaning "father."

Perhaps the most important factor in the rise of the papacy was the Petrine doctrine, which taught that the Roman Church had been founded by Peter, the leader of Christ's disciples. This doctrine stated that the Savior had appointed Peter as His successor and that Peter came to Rome and established his headquarters there as bishop of Rome. As successors of St. Peter, the subsequent bishops of Rome would govern all other dioceses.

There were many other factors explaining the development of the papacy at Rome. As the largest city in the West and the capital of the political world, Rome had a proud tradition. Rome had been the center of Christian persecution, and its Church was sanctified with an aura of martyrdom. Rome was also the hub of a strong Christian missionary movement. The churches founded by missionaries from Rome turned naturally to the mother Church and its bishop for help and guidance. Finally, the higher offices of the Church in the West were in the main filled by a series of outstanding administrators and theologians, whose efforts increased the power of the bishop of Rome.

The weakening of political power in the West and the transfer of the imperial authority from Rome to Constantinople in the fourth century resulted in the bishops there being overshadowed by the emperors, while in Rome the Church had almost no political competition. By the beginning of the seventh century, the bishop of Rome had become the spiritual leader of the western world.

DECLINE AND DIVISION IN

THE ROMAN WORLD

A century of civil war. Thus far in this chapter, the rise and eventual triumph of Christianity in the Graeco-Roman world has been traced. Now it will be shown that, for the greater part, this ascendancy took place at the very time when the empire was in a process of progressive deterioration. True, Rome reached its peak of prosperity and good government during the second century A.D. But from then on, unhappily, intellectual vigor and creative activity began to flag, and the appearance of still more obvious distress signals—political unrest and economic hardship—quickly followed.

Upon the death of Marcus Aurelius in 180 A.D., his son, Commodus, succeeded him. Unlike his father, Commodus was a cruel tyrant. After he had reigned twelve years, a group of conspirators bribed Commodus' athletic trainer to strangle his royal master.

Following the murder of Commodus, civil war broke out briefly among the army leaders, who fought for the privilege of placing a successor on the imperial throne. After much bloodshed, Septimius Severus was made emperor in 193. His accession marks the approaching end of the principate. The Senate lost all authority and began to lose its position as advisor to the emperor. From this time on, the emperors made no attempt to hide the fact that they were "army made" and would not tolerate interference from the Senate. By the third century, the emperor had become *dominus*, or "lord," and the principate had been replaced by absolute rule known as the dominate.

The line of Septimius Severus held the imperial office until 235, but after its extinction a period of anarchy ensued. In the next fifty years there were twenty-six emperors; only one died a natural death. During this unhappy period, Rome was lashed from without by foreign invaders and rent from within by bloody civil wars. The imperial scepter was dragged in the gutter by generals who murdered emperors and put themselves or their puppets on the throne. Meanwhile, the territory held by Rome north of the Danube was abandoned to the Goths, and in Asia a powerful new menace appeared—a reinvigorated Persia under the rule of the Sassanid dynasty.

Economic decline. As deadly to the well-being of the empire as governmental weakness and foreign invasions was the prolonged economic decline. The trend toward the concentration of land ownership in a few hands, which we noted in the discussion of the Gracchi, had continued. And, by the third century, land monopoly was so widespread that nearly all land in the empire was controlled by the emperor and a small aristocratic clique.

The small farmer could not, of course, compete with the large slave plantations. Forced to give up his little parcel of land, he became a *colonus*—that is, he obtained a plot of land from a large landholder. By arrangement with the landholder, the *colonus* was free to cultivate his patch of land, but in return he agreed to render many manual services in his landlord's fields. As time went on, the *colonus* became a semislave, technically a freeman but bound to the soil and going with the land if it changed owners. The adoption of this system was the first step toward serfdom, which was to play an important role in the social pattern of the Middle Ages.

To make matters worse, the monetary system became extremely confused. The currency was debased by reducing the content of precious metal in the Roman coins and thus making them less valuable. Therefore more coins were needed than before to buy the same quantity of goods, and the prices of commodities rose out of all reason. Civil war also decreased purchasing power, disturbed trade, and thus helped to undermine the prosperity of the cities.

Diocletian. A much-needed respite from the long decline took place during the reign of Diocletian (285-305). Civil war ended when he ascended the throne. A strong and capable administrator, Diocletian immediately made drastic attempts to restore governmental efficiency, defend the frontiers, and stop economic deterioration.

To increase the strength of the government, Diocletian completed the trend toward despotism initiated by Septimius Severus. The Senate was relegated to the status of a mere city council. Adorned in robes laden with jewels, the emperor surrounded himself with all the splendor of an oriental despot.

The administration of the empire was modified drastically. First of all, Diocletian introduced what he hoped would be a better method of succession to the throne. Realizing that the empire had become too large for one man to govern, he divided it. The eastern half he retained for his own administration, while in the West he created a coemperor who, like himself, was entitled to be an Augustus. Each Augustus in turn was assigned an assistant, termed *Caesar*. Since the Caesar would succeed the Augustus, the problem of succession was supposedly solved.

Next, Diocletian established a uniform system of administration throughout the empire. The provinces (including Italy) were grouped into thirteen dioceses, each under a vicar. The dioceses themselves were grouped into four prefectures, each under a prefect.

In addition, Diocletian strictly divided the civil and military administrations and insisted that the chain of command for each flow directly from the emperor. To keep watch over this vast bureaucracy, a large secret service was created. The once sturdy individualism of the Romans had been conquered at last by a rigid despotism.

Diocletian also made strenuous attempts to arrest economic decline in the empire. To improve the fiscal situation and check inflation, Diocletian sought to impose uniform taxation and fix maximum prices for goods and services. And so he issued a famous edict on prices, from whose preamble the following is taken:

Is anyone so dull and unfeeling as not to know, not to have seen, that the high prices in our markets, on which the daily life of our cities depends, are not checked by abundance or bumper crops? So abandoned is the passion for gain that men in the business . . . wickedly abhor the rains which make fields fertile, for the abundance which favorable weather brings they calculate as a loss. . . . Men with enough wealth to satisfy whole nations try to capture smaller fortunes and strive after ruinous percentages; concern for humanity in general persuades us to set a limit to the avarice of such men.[6]

Diocletian's edict defined prices for food, timber, textiles, and cosmetics; fixed the rates for silk and wool workers, painters, and schoolmasters; and determined freight rates. The edict proved impractical and unenforceable, however, so that in the end more drastic measures had to be attempted in an effort to stop the drift to economic ruin.

Constantine. After Diocletian and his fellow Augustus retired in 305, his grandiose system collapsed, and civil war broke out once again. A few years later, Constantine, one of the contestants for the throne, forged to the front. After sharing his rule for a few years with another emperor, he became sole ruler in 324.

In 332 Constantine decreed that henceforth no *colonus* could leave the soil and that the children of a *colonus* had to accept the same status as that of their father. In the cities a similar decree was applied to members of

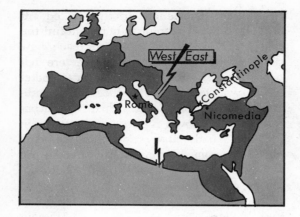

those guilds whose activities were essential to the state, such as baking and transportation. Born into and bound to their occupations, members had to marry within the guild and see their sons carry on the same line of work. Thus, to serve the economic interests of the state, a veritable caste system was established.

Division of the empire. The Roman world's center of gravity had been shifting progressively eastward for a considerable length of time. The change in administration of the government was so sweeping that Italy lost all of its former primacy, while Rome ceased even in name to be the seat of imperial authority. To govern the eastern half of the empire, Diocletian had set up his court at Nicomedia on the eastern coast of the Sea of Marmora. His was a logical choice, for the greatest dangers to the empire came from beyond the Danube River and from imperial Persia. But even more strategic than Nicomedia was the ancient site of Byzantium, across the water, selected by Constantine for a new capital city. This site could be reached only through a long, narrow channel which could be made practically impregnable and which possessed a splendid harbor at the crossroads of Europe and Asia.

Constantine had another motive for establishing a new capital. Rome was associated with a pagan past, and its Senate was a bastion of paganism. Favoring Christianity, Constantine believed that the Roman world should have a new—and from its outset, a Christian—capital. He dubbed his capital

New Rome, but it soon became known as Constantinople.

The erection of an eastern capital foreshadowed the impending division of the empire into two completely separate states, the East and the West. For about fifty years following the death of Constantine in 337, the unity of the empire was preserved by the rule of two joint emperors, one in the East and the other in the West. But after Theodosius divided it between his two sons in 395, the empire was never afterwards governed as a single unit. From this time on, a definite separation between the two halves was acknowledged, even though the fiction of imperial unity continued long afterward. Henceforth we can speak of a western Roman empire, which soon fell, and of the eastern Roman empire, which in time achieved a splendid Byzantine culture (see Chapter 7).

UPHEAVAL AND SURVIVAL

IN THE WEST

The Germanic tribes. Weakened by economic, social, and political decline, Rome had turned to the most extreme forms of absolutism in an effort to ride out the storm that threatened to engulf it. But its internal crisis was compounded by mounting external pressures that threatened to stave in its far-flung frontiers. The greatest danger lay to the north, the home of restless bands of fierce barbarians—the Germanic tribes. They covered Europe from the Rhine to southern Russia and from the Baltic to the Danube. From the Franks on the Rhine to the Goths on the Black Sea, they were grouped into tribes (whose names will appear in the text as each makes its bid for the spoils of a tottering empire). Seminomads, the Germans were at a cultural stage midway between a pastoral and an agricultural economy. They engaged in so little commerce that cattle, rather than money, were sufficient as a measure of value.

Each warrior leader had a retinue of followers, or *comites*, who were linked to him by personal loyalty. According to Tacitus:

When they go into battle, it is a disgrace for the chief to be surpassed in valour, a disgrace for his followers not to equal the valour of the chief. And it is an infamy and a reproach for life to have survived the chief, and returned from the field. To defend, to protect him, to ascribe one's own brave deeds to his renown, is the height of loyalty. The chief fights for victory; his vassals fight for their chief.[7]

In return for their fighting services the chief gave his warrior band, called the *comitatus*, food, weapons, and shelter. This institution had an important bearing on the origin of feudalism, the characteristic political system of the Middle Ages, which was based on the personal bond between knights and their feudal lords.

The German system of justice was based on the principle of compensation. For the infliction of specific injuries a stipulated payment termed a *bot* was required. The amount of compensation varied according to the severity of the crime and the social position of the victim. For example, it cost forty times as much to kill a man of rank as a common man. Some crimes were *botless*—that is, so grave in character that compensation could not be paid. A person charged with such a crime had to stand trial and produce oath-helpers who would swear to his innocence. If unable to obtain oath-helpers, he was subjected to trial by ordeal.

German political and legal practices influenced the institutions of later western civilization. This influence is particularly noticeable in medieval England. Parliamentary government owes something to the German tribal assembly, which was composed of all the freemen; the assembly elected the ruler and decided the basic policies of government. Possessing no written law, the Germans meted out justice according to tribal custom—a practice similar to the workings of English common law, which is based not so much on enacted law as upon a developing body of custom.

Roman-German contacts. From early in the first century A.D., the imperial frontier had been maintained by force of arms at the Rhine-Danube line. By erecting and policing walls along the frontier and by employing the policy of "divide and rule"—playing off one tribe against another—Rome kept the barbarians under control.

All contacts with these tribes were not warlike, however. Roman trade extended into Germany, and many Germans joined the Roman legions. While the use of barbarians in the army represented a short-term gain in men for the Romans, hard-pressed as they were on many fronts, in the long run the gradual change in the nature of the Roman armed forces paved the way for the rise to power of generals who were barbarian rather than Roman in origin.

In the last decades of the fourth century, a series of Germanic invasions of the empire began. A basic factor behind German restlessness seems to have been land hunger. Their numbers were increasing, much of their land was forest and swamp, and their methods of tillage were inefficient.

Wholesale barbarian invasions. Meanwhile, another restless people were on the move—the Huns. Mongolian nomads from central Asia who had for centuries plundered and slain their Asian neighbors, the Huns were superb horsemen and fighters.

In 372 A.D. the Huns crossed the Volga and conquered the easternmost German tribe, the Ostrogoths. Terrified at the prospect of being conquered in turn by the advancing Huns, the Visigoths petitioned the Romans to allow them to seek safety within the empire. Permission was granted, and in 376, bands of these Germans crossed the Danube into Roman territory. But the food and lands promised to the Visigoths by the Romans were not distributed to them in sufficient quantities; furthermore, the Roman officials irritated the newcomers by treating them harshly. In desperation the Visigoths turned upon the officials and pillaged the countryside. Planning to retaliate, the Roman emperor led an army to crush the Visigoths. But in the ensuing battle at Adrianople in 378, the legions were totally defeated and the emperor slain.

Adrianople has been described as one of history's decisive battles: it destroyed the legend of the invincibility of the Roman le-

Among the early Germans, trial by ordeal took three forms. In the first, the defendant had to lift a small stone out of a vessel of boiling water; unless his scalded arm had healed within a prescribed number of days, he was judged guilty. In the second, he had to walk blindfolded and barefoot across a floor strewn with pieces of red-hot metal; success in avoiding the metal was a sign of innocence. In the third, the bound defendant was thrown into a pool of water which had been blessed; if the water rejected him and he floated, he was believed guilty, but if he sank, he was believed innocent. A person was forced to endure one of these ordeals only when a strong presumption of guilt existed. Trial by ordeal still survived in medieval Europe. Here, a medieval queen, led by two bishops, walks over a red-hot grate to prove her marital fidelity.

gions and ushered in a century and a half of chaos. Soon barbarian tribes moved almost at will within the empire and began to destroy the governmental structure in the West. For a few years, the capable emperor Theodosius held them off, but after his death in 395 the Visigoths began to migrate and pillage under their leader, Alaric. He invaded Italy and in 410 his followers sacked Rome. Peace was made with the Roman officials, who ceded to the Visigoths a large tract of territory in southern Gaul. Here the Visigoths created an extensive kingdom, which at its zenith covered most of Spain as well.

Alaric's march had triggered wholesale invasion by the Germans along the northern frontier. In 406 the Roman defenses on the Rhine collapsed, and a flood of German tribes streamed into Gaul. The Vandals, another Germanic people, pushed their way through Gaul to Spain and, after pressure from the Visigoths, moved on to Africa, where they established a kingdom. In 455 the apex of Vandal power was reached when a raiding force sailed over from Africa and sacked Rome. Meanwhile, the Burgundians settled in the Rhone valley, and the Franks gradually spread across northern Gaul.

As the great German invasions penetrated the most important provinces of the empire, Roman authorities began withdrawing the legions from their outposts. After the last Roman troops left England in 407, the island was defenseless, and within a generation, swarms of Angles, Saxons, and Jutes from the base of the Danish peninsula and the German lowlands invaded Britain and took possession of most of the country.

While the Germanic peoples were relentlessly moving through the western part of the empire, a new danger arose. The Huns pushed farther into Europe to menace both Germans and Romans. Under their leader, Attila, the mounted nomads swept through Germany and in 451 crossed the Rhine. The Germans and Romans, fighting for common survival, joined forces to repel the Huns at the battle of Châlons and forced Attila to withdraw from Gaul. He threatened Italy for a brief time and planned to take Rome itself, but was persuaded not to—either by the appeal of Pope Leo I or by military problems of supply and the disease which ravaged his army. When he died in 453, the leaderless nomad bands lost their power and gradually ceased to threaten the empire.

The fall of Rome. What was happening to the imperial throne in the West during this turbulent period? As we have mentioned, after the death of the capable Theodosius in 395, the empire was divided between his two sons. Although Roman civilization did not perish with the sacking of the capital in 410 by the Visigoths and again in 455 by the Vandals, Roman rule in the West grew increasingly impotent and Roman emperors incompetent and decadent. The emperor was little more than a puppet. Leaders of the mercenary soldiers, whose ranks were by now mainly German, wielded the real power.

In 475 Orestes, a German commander of the troops, forced the Senate to elect his young son Romulus Augustus (satirically nicknamed *Augustulus,* meaning "Little Augustus") as emperor in the West. In the following year, another German commander, Odovacar, slew Orestes and, seeing no reason for continuing the sham of an imperial line, deposed Romulus Augustus and proclaimed himself head of the government. The deposition of the boy, who by a strange irony bore the names of the legendary founder of Rome and the founder of the empire, marks the traditional "fall" of the Roman empire.

Actually, no single date is accurate, for the fall of Rome was a long and complicated process. Yet 476 at least symbolizes the end of the Roman empire in the West, for in this year the long line of emperors inaugurated by Augustus ended and the outright control of Italy by Germanic leaders began. In the-

ory, Odovacar accepted the overlordship of the eastern emperor in Constantinople, who, now that the emperors in Rome were no more, considered Italy as one of his administrative divisions. But in reality the western part of the empire was in the hands of the Germans, and the emperors at Constantinople had little or no power there.

Theodoric's kingdom in Italy. Following the death of Attila, the Ostrogoths were free to migrate as other tribes were doing. Under their energetic king, Theodoric (*c.* 454-526), who had been educated at Constantinople, the Ostrogoths were galvanized into action.

Theodoric accepted a commission from the emperor in the East to reimpose the imperial authority over Italy, now in Odovacar's hands. In 488 he led his men into the Italian peninsula, where, after hard fighting, Odovacar sued for peace and was treacherously murdered. Theodoric then established a strong Ostrogothic kingdom in Italy with its capital at Ravenna. Because he appreciated the culture he had seen at Constantinople, Theo-

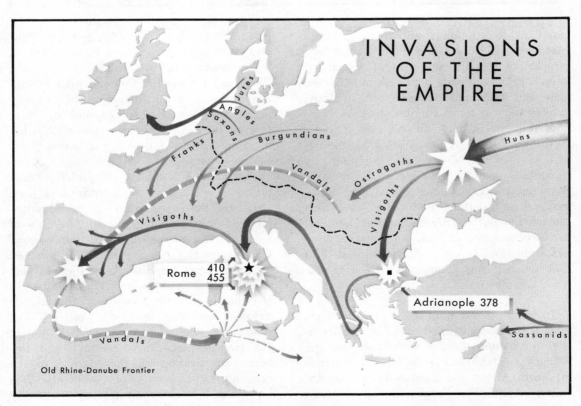

INVASIONS OF THE EMPIRE

Huns

Jutes

Angles

Saxons

Burgundians

Franks

Vandals

Ostrogoths

Visigoths

Visigoths

Rome 410 455

Adrianople 378

Sassanids

Vandals

Old Rhine-Danube Frontier

Jutes
Angles
Saxons

Germanic Peoples

Franks

Slavic Peoples

Germanic

Burgundians

Lombards

Huns

Visigoths

Ostrogoths

Goths

KINGDOM OF ODOVACAR

Rome

Constantinople

EAST ROMAN

Vandals

EMPIRE

BARBARIAN EUROPE
486 A. D.

doric made strenuous efforts to preserve classical civilization by retaining Roman law, supporting schools, and using Latin at his own court. Following his death in 526, civil war and factionalism broke out in Italy, paving the way for its conquest by the Byzantine emperor Justinian in 554 (see p. 160).

The Lombards. A few years after the destruction of the Ostrogothic kingdom by Justinian's army, a new wave of Germanic invaders, the Lombards, poured into northern and central Italy. Reputed to have been the most brutal and fierce of all the Germans, by 568 these people had established a powerful kingdom in Italy which endured until 774, when it was conquered by the Franks (see Chapter 6).

In less than one hundred years after German tribes had swarmed over the frontier in 406, the western Roman world had seen the Visigoths established in Spain, the Vandals in North Africa, the Burgundians in southeastern Gaul, the Franks in the northern

half of that country, the Ostrogoths in Italy, and the Angles, Saxons, and Jutes in Britain.

The problem of the fall of Rome. The shock and dismay felt by contemporary citizens throughout the Roman world on learning of Alaric's sack of the Eternal City were to echo down the centuries, leaving the impression that the fall of Rome was a major calamity, perhaps the greatest in history.

The sack of Rome in 410 and the other disasters overtaking the empire had been attributed by pagan writers to the abandonment of the ancient gods. In *The City of God*, St. Augustine disputed the pagans' charges, justified the new faith, and directed attention from conditions in the classical world to the new goals of Christianity. In so doing, he advanced the theory that history unfolds according to God's design. Thus Rome's fall was seen as an essential act in His overall plan—"the necessary and fortunate preparation for the triumph of the heavenly city where man's destiny was to be attained."[8] This view was challenged by historians of the eighteenth century. In particular, Edward Gibbon, author of the famous *Decline and Fall of the Roman Empire*, saw in Rome's fall a great tragedy, "the triumph of barbarism and religion." Because he argued that Christianity had played an important role in undermining the imperial structure, he has often been accused of maintaining an anti-Christian bias.

In our time some explanations of Rome's fall have been rooted in psychological theories. For example, the basic cause has been attributed to a weakening of morale in the face of difficulties, to a "loss of nerve." Or it has been argued that the ultimate failure of Rome came from its too complete success, which led to "a changed attitude of men's minds" and indolence and self-gratification among the ruling classes. Such subjective theories can scarcely be proven, however.

Historians tend increasingly to account for Rome's decline in terms of a variety of interacting forces. On the political side, the failure of civil power to control the army in the crucial period following the death of Marcus Aurelius resulted in military anarchy, the disintegration of central authority, and the weakening of Rome's ability to withstand external pressures. In the area of economic causes, the small farmer class disappeared and unemployment grew as more and more land was consolidated into huge *latifundia;* civil war and barbarian excursions disturbed trade relations; a debased currency and a crushing tax burden undermined the confidence of the people. Eventually the rigid economic and social decrees of Diocletian and Constantine created a vast bureaucracy which only aggravated existing ills.

By the fifth century, vast tracts of formerly cultivated land were left untilled. Meanwhile, the failure of communications and transportation, coupled with a drying up of the labor force in the cities, brought on progressive decentralization of the economy. Gradually, industry was transferred from cities to large country estates, and scores of once flourishing cities throughout the empire shrank into ghost towns. "Roman civilization had been essentially urban; medieval civiliza-

Reproduced above is a Renaissance painting of St. Augustine.

tion was to be essentially rural. With the decline of the towns the general level of civilization was lowered and western Europe began to assume its medieval aspect."[9]

The fusion of cultures. Now that we have discussed the movement of the barbarians into the empire and have examined the problem of the fall of Rome, the significance of the impact between barbarians and Romans should be pointed out. Before the terrible chaos of the fifth century, a gradual process of culture fusion, or blending, was taking place. The menace of the Huns accelerated the movement of the German tribes into the empire, and what had formerly been a process of peaceful infiltration became a pell-mell attack on the frontier provinces.

The barbarian invasions must not, however, be regarded as cataclysmic. True, ruthless pillaging by the invaders took place, and in certain sections of the empire, especially in Britain, Roman civilization was entirely wiped out. The Germans also seized a great deal of Roman land; perhaps as much as two thirds exchanged ownership. In the main, however, the blending and fusing of the cultures and the blood of the two peoples continued without interruption.

In most areas of the empire, the invaders still represented a minority of the population. Although the Germans viewed the Roman government as an enemy, they admired Roman civilization and continued to assimilate it. Thus the barbarian soon began to lose his Germanic speech, customs, and religion. Furthermore, most German leaders kept Roman administrative agencies largely intact and employed members of the old civil service. In governmental affairs the use of Latin was perpetuated; that is why hardly a trace of the Germanic languages remains in Italy, France, and Spain.

The role of the Church. The eagerness of most of the barbarian invaders to imitate Roman civilization helps explain the preservation of much classical culture. But in addition there was at work a powerful and positive force—the Christian Church—which assisted the fusion between conqueror and conquered and cushioned the shock of the impact between German and Roman. By the time of the collapse of the Roman empire, the Church had already become sufficiently powerful to fill the gap left by the vanished Caesars.

The Church had at its service the outstanding minds of the time. Furthermore, it had developed a self-governing organization with its own hierarchy and land-holdings, which provided both administrative and economic strength. It was therefore in a unique position to assume many secular responsibilities in the West when the Roman empire collapsed.

Missionary activity of the Church. The missionary activity of the Church was not only a Christianizing movement but one which disseminated civilization among the barbarians and aided in the fusion of Germanic and classical cultures.

One of the earliest Christian missionaries to the Germans was Ulfilas (c. 311-383), who spent forty years among the Visigoths and translated the Bible into Gothic. Ulfilas and other early missionaries were followers of Arius, and thus the heretical creed of Arianism came to be adopted by all the Germanic tribes in the empire except the Franks. The adoption by this powerful tribe of official Roman Catholic doctrines as espoused by the pope was to have momentous consequences for European statecraft (see Chapter 6).

Another great missionary was St. Patrick, who was born in Britain about 389 and later went to Ireland as a missionary. As a result of his activities, monasteries were set up there, and Christianity obtained a strong foothold. From the monasteries went a stream of monks to Scotland, northern England, the kingdom of the Franks, and even to Italy in the late sixth and seventh centuries. The Irish monks eagerly pursued scholarship, and their monasteries became centers of learning and repositories for priceless manuscripts.

The Church at Rome was also very active in the missionary movement. One significant mission was that of St. Augustine, who in 596 was sent by Pope Gregory the Great to the small kingdom of Kent in England. St. Augustine converted its king, the first Anglo-Saxon ruler officially to accept Christianity. Roman Christianity eventually spread all over England, and finally the Celtic Church founded by St. Patrick acknowledged the primacy of Rome. The English Church in turn took an important part in the expansion of Christianity on the Continent. The greatest missionary from England in the eighth century was St. Boniface, who spent thirty-five years among the German tribes. Known as "the Apostle of Germany," he established many abbeys and bishoprics before he was killed in 755 by pagan pirates. Roman Catholic missionaries were also active in Scandinavia and among the Slavic peoples of eastern Europe.

From the time of the fall of Rome, then, the three elements which, interwoven, were to create the pattern of western civilization in the Middle Ages were already coexisting: Graeco-Roman culture, the Christian Church, and German tribal organization. Here, in a sense, were the mind, spirit, and muscle which were to work together in western man during the next thousand years.

SUMMARY

Christianity's roots extend back into Jewish history long before the birth of Christ, and it is there that we find the concept of the Messiah, the divinely appointed leader who would create a new Israel. Under the rule of the Hellenistic Seleucid empire and later of Rome, the Jews hoped for such a Messiah to lead them to political independence; and when Jesus refused to head a political revolt against the Romans, His enemies brought about His condemnation and execution. But His teachings did not die with His Crucifixion. Interpreted largely through the efforts of St. Paul, they spread rapidly through the Roman empire. Despite persecution, converts flocked to the new faith, and finally, with the Edict of Milan in 313, Emperor Constantine made Christianity a legal religion. Thereafter the Church grew and flourished, with an organization based on the imperial Roman pattern, and a hierarchy of officials culminating in the pope at Rome.

From the end of the reign of Marcus Aurelius in 180 A.D., the Roman empire declined as its rulers became pawns of the army. Only Diocletian and Constantine were able to check the downward trend, and in the long run their system of despotism accentuated the major weaknesses of the failing state. When the Visigoths, pushed by the Huns, defeated Roman forces at the battle of Adrianople in 378, the gates of the empire burst open before the barbarian tribes. The date for the final collapse of Rome may be set at 476, when the last Roman emperor in the West was deposed and barbarian rulers assumed control.

The fall of Rome—one of the great dramatic developments in history—has been explained in a variety of ways by later historians. No single cause can be given: the collapse appears to have been the result of various interacting factors such as military anarchy, severe economic decline, political absolutism, and loss of intellectual vigor. Following the devastating invasions which overwhelmed the western half of the empire, a powerful new agency moved into the gap left by the Caesars; during the centuries which followed the waning of the classical world, it was the Christian Church which played the dominant role in the affairs of Europe.

As the Roman empire crumbled in the West, a new center of imperial strength arose in the East at Constantinople. As we shall see in Chapter 7, a unique civilization developed in the Roman empire of the East—the Byzantine—which persisted for a thousand years.

SUGGESTIONS FOR READING

E. Bevan, *Jerusalem Under the High Priests*, E. Arnold, 1904. The definitive work on the history of the Jews during the last two centuries B.C. An excellent, concise study of the complex nature of Judaism in the first century A.D. is C. Guignebert, *The Jewish World in the Time of Jesus*, Routledge and Kegan Paul, 1939. T. H. Robinson *et al.*, *A History of Israel*, 2 vols., Oxford (Clarendon Press), 1932, is a scholarly introduction to Jewish culture.

E. Wilson, *The Scrolls from the Dead Sea*, Oxford, 1955. Published originally in the *New Yorker* magazine (May 14, 1955), this is the most readable introduction to a fascinating subject. More scholarly treatments are M. Burrows, *The Dead Sea Scrolls*, Viking, 1955, which includes extensive translations; R. K. Harrison, *The Dead Sea Scrolls: An Introduction,** Torchbooks; A. P. Davies, *The Meaning of the Dead Sea Scrolls,** Mentor; and T. H. Gaster, *The Dead Sea Scriptures in English Translation,** Anchor.

*Indicates an inexpensive paperbound edition.

A vast number of books have been written about the origins and development of Christianity, and the works mentioned below represent only a few of the more important interpretations. The student should bear in mind that the author's viewpoint is bound to be affected by his own beliefs, whether positive or negative, Christian or non-Christian. Both T. R. Glover, *The Jesus of History*, Harper, 1916; and A. Edersheim, *The Life and Times of Jesus the Messiah*, 2 vols., Longmans, 1957, treat the life of Jesus and its implications from a conservative and devotional point of view. In *The Quest of the Historical Jesus*, Macmillan, 1948, Albert Schweitzer describes various interpretations of Jesus' life and states his own eschatological point of view, in which Jesus is viewed as a fallible human being. A classic on the form and method of Jesus' teaching is M. Goguel, *The Life of Jesus*, Macmillan, 1944. See also E. J. Goodspeed, *A Life of Jesus,** Torchbooks.

R. Heard, *An Introduction to the New Testament*, Black, 1950. The best nontechnical survey of the history and the results of New Testament scholarship. See also E. C. Hoskyns *et al.*,

The Riddle of the New Testament, Allenson, 1952, which accepts most of the results of Biblical criticism but rejects what is known as the modernist point of view.

A. Deissmann, *Paul: A Study in Social and Religious History*,* Torchbooks. A scholarly work on St. Paul's life and influence. A good fictionalized biography of St. Paul is S. Asch, *The Apostle*,* Pocket Books.

T. R. Glover, *The Conflict of Religions in the Early Roman Empire*,* Beacon. Describes the struggle for supremacy in the early centuries A.D. of various eastern religions (especially Mithraism and Christianity) and the political consequences of the conflict. Detailed descriptions of the Graeco-Roman religious environment out of which Christianity emerged are H. Willoughby, *Pagan Regeneration*, Univ. of Chicago, 1929; and F. Cumont, *The Oriental Religions in Roman Paganism*,* Dover.

L. M. O. Duchesne, *Early History of the Christian Church*, 3 vols., Longmans, 1909-1924. An excellent work by a liberal Roman Catholic historian. The conservative Protestant view of the development of Christianity is represented by K. S. Latourette, *A History of Christianity*, Harper, 1953.

E. R. Goodenough, *The Church in the Roman Empire*,* Holt (Berkshire Studies). A brief but excellent introduction. A well-known standard work is A. Harnack, *The Mission and Expansion of Christianity in the First Three Centuries*, Putnam, 1908. Outstanding among more recent detailed histories of Christianity during its first two centuries are W. M. Ramsay, *The Church in the Roman Empire Before A.D. 170*, Baker Book House, 1954; R. Bultmann, *Primitive Christianity in Its Contemporary Setting*,* Meridian; H. Leitzmann, *A History of Early Christianity*,* 2 vols., Meridian; and J. Weiss, *Earliest Christianity*,* 2 vols., Torchbooks.

E. Hatch, *The Influence of Greek Ideas on Christianity*,* Torchbooks. A scholarly account of early Christianity and its inheritance from the culture of ancient Greece. See also C. N. Cochrane, *Christianity and Classical Culture: A Study of Thought and Action from Augustus to Augustine*,* Galaxy, which describes "the revolution in thought and action which came about through the impact of Christianity upon the Graeco-Roman world."

H. S. Bettenson, ed., *Documents of the Christian Church*, Oxford (The World's Classics), 1947. Contains an excellent selection of early Christian documents accompanied by valuable editorial notes.

F. Lot, *The End of the Ancient World and the Beginning of the Middle Ages*,* Torchbooks. An indispensable classic on the transition from ancient to medieval civilization; attributes Rome's decline largely to economic causes. F. W. Walbank, *The Decline of the Roman Empire in the West*,* Abelard-Schuman, is a brief survey which emphasizes economic interpretations and "lessons for today." For brief, clear accounts of this very confused period, see R. F. Arragon, *The Transition from the Ancient to the Medieval World*,* Holt (Berkshire Studies); and S. Katz, *The Decline of Rome and the Rise of Medieval Europe*,* Cornell. The detailed study by M. Rostovtzeff, *The Social and Economic History of the Roman Empire*, 2 vols., 2nd ed., Oxford (Clarendon Press), 1957, attributes Rome's fall to "the gradual absorption of the educated classes by the masses." A brief survey of scholarly opinion on this subject is contained in R. M. Haywood, *The Myth of Rome's Fall*, Crowell, 1959.

E. Gibbon, *The History of the Decline and Fall of the Roman Empire*, 7 vols. (ed. by J. B. Bury), Methuen, 1901-1938. Probably the most famous work on the ancient world. Professor A. H. M. Jones' words about Gibbon are, however, worth quoting: "The reader . . . should be forewarned against Gibbons' great weakness, which is not so much anti-Christian bias as a temperamental incapacity to understand religion: to Gibbons' eighteenth-century rationalism a religious man was either a fool or a knave." Useful one-volume editions are D. A. Saunders, ed., *The Portable Gibbon: The Decline and Fall of the Roman Empire*,* Viking; and *The Triumph of Christendom in the Roman Empire** (Chs. XV-XX of the J. B. Bury edition), Torchbooks.

P. de Labriolle, *History and Literature of Christianity from Tertullian to Boethius*, Knopf, 1924; E. K. Rand, *Founders of the Middle Ages*,* Dover. Two important studies dealing with the intellectual side of the transition from ancient to medieval times. The social side, together with the intellectual, is treated in the well-known work by S. Dill, *Roman Society in the Last Century of the Roman Empire*,* Meridian.

J. B. Bury, *The Invasion of Europe by the Barbarians*, Macmillan, 1928. The best general work on the nature and effect of the Germanic invasions. See also H. S. B. Moss, *The Birth of the Middle Ages*, Oxford (G. Cumberlege), 1947. Also recommended are E. A. Thompson, *A History of Attila and the Huns*, Oxford (Clarendon Press), 1948, the best work on the subject; and T. Hodgkin, *Theodoric the Goth: The Barbarian Champion of Civilization*, Putnam, 1891, attractively written in the flowing style of nineteenth-century historians.

The Age of Diocletian: A Symposium,* Metropolitan Museum of Art, 1953. Six excellent short papers, presented by outstanding scholars, on the various aspects of an age which presents "so many striking parallels with our own times." An interesting but controversial book with a similar theme is H. J. Haskell, *The New Deal in Old Rome*, Knopf, 1939, by an American journalist with an anti-New Deal bias.

J. C. Burckhardt, *The Age of Constantine the Great*,* Anchor. A critical inquiry into the early fourth century, with Constantine's conversion viewed as an act of political expediency. For a concise biography, see A. H. M. Jones, *Constantine and the Conversion of Europe*, Macmillan, 1949, which stresses a religious motivation for Constantine's conversion.

W. Bryher, *The Roman Wall*, Pantheon, 1954. A novel which gives a vivid picture of the last days of the Roman empire in the West.

CHAPTER 6

Europe's Search for Stability

RISE AND FALL OF THE CAROLINGIAN EMPIRE;
FEUDALISM AND THE MANORIAL SYSTEM (500-1050)

Introduction. With the collapse in Europe of the old order and the triumph of the barbarians, unity and stability gave way to fragmentation and disorder. The only hope for the survival of western civilization lay with the rapidly growing Christian Church, which, by providing a spiritual authority to which a diversity of peoples could give loyalty and obedience, assumed something of the unifying role once performed by the Roman Caesars.

The first indication of the new forms which life and politics would take in the West came from the Germanic Franks in alliance with the Church. In the single century from 714 to 814, covering the reigns of the Frankish rulers from Charles Martel to Charlemagne, the Carolingian branch of the Franks gave Europe an interim of stability and progress. A great empire was fashioned, civilization and Christianity were extended to many of the barbarian tribes, and law and order were maintained.

This accomplishment of the Carolingians was premature, however. Charlemagne's empire could not endure, partly because it lacked the economic basis that had supported the Romans. By the ninth century, Muslim conquests had cut off European trade in the Mediterranean; inland trade shriveled up and urban life almost disappeared. In addition, the empire had no strong administrative machinery to compensate for the weakling Carolingian rulers who followed the dominating figure of Charlemagne on the throne; the empire disintegrated amid invasions and civil wars.

Out of the ruins of the Carolingian empire emerged a new technique of government known as feudalism and a new economic system, the manorial system. Based on local authority, feudalism was a poor and primitive substitute for a powerful, comprehensive central government; but it was better than no authority at all, and it survived for several hundred years. The manorial system of economy, rural and self-sufficient, was another stopgap institution, appropriate to its time and place but completely inadequate in terms of human progress.

The mixed heritage of western man was clearly evident in many medieval institutions. The savagery and brutality inherited from his barbarian ancestors made his practice under the code of chivalry far different from the chivalric ideal, but the existence of that code proved that he had inherited as well the idealism of classical times and the spiritual strivings of Christianity. In spite of its low ebb, civilization survived and retained within itself elements which were to germinate a new blossoming of city life, commerce, and culture by the end of the eleventh century.

NEW EMPIRE IN THE WEST

The Franks under the Merovingians. In the blending of the Roman and Germanic peoples and cultures, the part played by the Franks was especially significant. The Franks lived in the valley of the Rhine, along the right bank of the river close to the North Sea. In the fifth century the Franks began to move south and west into France (see map, p. 133).

Clovis I of the Merovingian House ruled the Franks from 481 to 511. Under his direction, the Franks conducted a notable series of conquests that made them the most powerful people in the West and the most useful to the Church. Clovis knew what he wanted—power and territory—and from his arsenal of weapons he used marriage alliances, treachery, assassination, and religious conversion to achieve his goal. As a first step Clovis and his allies disposed of Syagrius, a Roman general in central Gaul, who represented the last foothold of Roman authority anywhere in that land. The victor then turned against his friends and subdued them.

Clovis became converted to Christianity in 496. The sixth-century historian Gregory of Tours mentions that the conversion came about as a result of a battle, on the eve of which Clovis looked up to heaven and declared:

If thou wilt give me victory over my enemies and I prove that power which thy followers say they have proved concerning this, I will believe in this and will be baptized in thy name.[1]

The victory was won, and Clovis was baptized together with his warriors. He became the only orthodox Christian ruler in the West, for the other Germanic tribes were either pagan or embraced some heretical form of Christianity, such as Arianism (see p. 126).

The conversion of the Franks must be considered a decisive event in European history. Ultimately it led to an alliance of the Franks and the papacy, and immediately it brought local support to Clovis. Clovis had little interest in dogma or religion; what was important to him was the political significance of his faith. Clovis' conversion to orthodox Catholicism assured him the loyalty of the orthodox Catholic population, who still greatly outnumbered all the German conquerors in old Roman Gaul. Reasoning that the orthodox native population in the rest of Gaul would welcome deliverance from their Arian rulers, Clovis expanded his political and military realm in the name of Christian orthodoxy. He undermined the power of the Arian Germans in Burgundy as well as the pagan Germans along the Rhine.

Clovis' southern neighbors were the Visigoths, who ruled France south of the Loire River and all of Spain. In 507 Clovis attacked this kingdom; the Visigothic king was killed, and his people had to abandon most of their Gallic territory and retreat to Spain. Content with his conquests, Clovis spent the last years of his reign at Paris, the Frankish capital.

Decline of the Merovingians. For the space of two hundred years the history of western Europe is largely the narrative of the rise, expansion, and decline of the Frankish empire. After Clovis' death in 511, his sons and grandsons overthrew the Burgundian king and extended the Frankish domain to include all modern France, Belgium, and much of Germany. Papal missionaries followed sharp on the heels of the Frankish invaders.

At the .same time, however, the Merovingian House began to decay from inner weaknesses. The pernicious practice of dividing the realm among all the sons of the king resulted in constant civil war. Various members of the royal house plotted murders and became adept at intrigue and treachery. Gregory of Tours gives a vivid picture of the later Merovingians:

The court of the Merovingians was a brothel. . . . Drunkenness seems to have been the usual condition of all. Women got their lovers to murder their husbands. Everybody could be purchased for gold.[2]

These crimes and excesses had their effect; the Merovingian kings became weaklings, and many of them died after only a few years on the throne. Although in theory the Frankish state still retained its unity, for all practical purposes it had broken up into three separate kingdoms. In each of these areas the chief official in the royal household, the Mayor of the Palace, became the powerful figure. Their royal masters were mere puppets, the *rois fainéants* (do-nothing kings).

Muslim and Slavic invasions. At the time of Merovingian decay, a great, new wave of invasions threatened to engulf Europe. In the late seventh century the Muslim Arabs, made confident by their easy triumphs in Syria and Egypt, swept across North Africa and prepared to invade Spain. A great movement of Slavic people from the area that is now Russia also got under way. The origins of the restless Slavs are only vaguely suggested in ancient legend, but it seems that their original home was in the Pripet Marshes of western Russia (see map, p. 203). From this nucleus the Slavs fanned out in all directions, especially in the centuries between 500 and 900 A.D.

The western Slavs were the most dangerous threat to the Frankish kingdom. Filling the vacuum left by the Germanic tribes when they pushed into the Roman empire, the

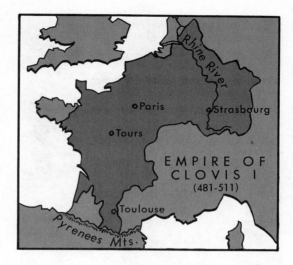

Slavs by 600 established the Elbe River as their frontier. The incessant fighting between the Slavs and the Germanic peoples is one of the significant themes of the Middle Ages.

Charles Martel and the rise of the Carolingians. During these perilous times of decaying Merovingian rule, those Mayors of the Palace who belonged to the Carolingian family defeated their rival Frankish Mayors and seized control. A new period of history began with the accession to power of Charles Martel, who became Mayor in 714. When he took over, the Frankish realm was in a critical condition. Charles beat down the rebellious nobles, restored unity among the often-divided Franks, strengthened the eastern frontier against the inroads of the Slavs, and virtually ruled the kingdom. For the time being, however, the Merovingian kings were kept as harmless figureheads at the court.

Charles Martel's greatest achievement was his victory over the Muslim invaders of Europe. In 711 an army of Moors from North Africa had invaded Spain, and by 718 the weak kingdom of the Visigoths had completely crumbled. Only a few isolated Christian communities survived the conquest. With the peninsula under control, the Muslims looked across the Pyrenees for new lands to conquer. After a number of sorties in which various Frankish cities were raided, the Muslim host hurled itself full force deep into the Frankish kingdom. In 732 Charles Martel

An idealized study of Charlemagne by Albrecht Dürer shows him with the imperial crown and other symbols of authority.

cavalry, and he began to build up such a force of professional mounted soldiers. A large amount of land was distributed for this purpose. Each warrior obtained enough land to maintain himself, his equipment, and a designated number of war horses. It is said of Charles that he "put the medieval knight on horseback," and this reform, as we shall see, was also to have important implications in the growth of feudalism.

Pepin the Short. Pepin the Short, son of Charles Martel, was a worthy successor to his great father. Ruling from 741 to 768, he continued to strengthen the Frankish state. To legalize the regal power which the Mayors of the Palace already exercised, he requested and received from the pope a ruling which stipulated that he who had the actual power should be the legal ruler. In this maneuvering, St. Boniface (p. 136) was the intermediator, and in the winter of 751-752 Pepin was elected king by the Franks and crowned by St. Boniface. The last Merovingian was quietly shelved in a secluded monastery. A few years later (in 754), Pope Stephen reaffirmed the earlier coronation by anointing Pepin as king.

Behind the pope's action lay his need for a powerful ally. In 751 the Lombards, a warlike Germanic people, had conquered the exarchate of Ravenna (the seat of Byzantine government in Italy) and demanded tribute from the pope. After the coronation of Pepin, the Frankish ruler promised to intervene in Italy and pledged to the pope the exarchate of Ravenna, once it was conquered. In 756 a Frankish army forced the Lombard king to relinquish his conquests and pay an indemnity, and Pepin officially conferred the territory of the exarchate of Ravenna upon the pope. Known as the Donation of Pepin, the gift made the pope a temporal ruler over the Papal States, a strip of territory that extended from coast to coast, cutting the peninsula in two.

The alliance between the Franks and the papacy, foreshadowed by the conversion of Clovis in 496 and thoroughly sealed by Pepin, not only influenced the direction of medieval history but also affected the course of politics

encountered the Muslims at Tours. Muslim losses were heavy, and during the night the invaders retreated toward Spain.

A major military reform was advanced by the battle of Tours. For some time before this conflict, the effectiveness of mounted soldiers had been growing, aided by the perfection of the stirrup and better iron weapons. At Tours the Frankish leader had observed the effectiveness of the quick-striking Muslim and of religion for centuries to come. This alliance between pope and king paved the way for the creation of the Holy Roman Empire; it contained the germs of the bitter struggle waged between the temporal and spiritual powers of western Europe; and, for better or worse, it created the Papal States, whose existence complicated the political unification of Italy down to 1871.

Charlemagne: the man and his conquests. In 768 Pepin's son, Charlemagne (Charles the Great), inherited the Frankish kingdom. Under this ruler, the Frankish state and the Carolingian House reached the summit of their power. Einhard, a biographer of Charlemagne and a member of his court, pictured his king as a natural leader of men. He was tall, physically strong, a great horseman, and always in the van of the hunt. A successful statesman and administrator, he had great respect for learning. In extending his territory by conquest and spreading Christian civilization by force when necessary, Charlemagne carried on the policies of the Merovingian king Clovis, but on a much grander scale.

Taking advantage of feuds among the Muslims in Spain, Charlemagne attempted to set up a buffer state between the Frankish kingdom and the Muslim territories south of the Pyrenees. In 778 Charlemagne and his army crossed the Pyrenees with indifferent success. As the Frankish army moved back to the north, its rear guard was set upon by wild mountaineers. In the melee, the Frankish leader, a gallant knight named Roland, was killed. The memory of his heroism was later enshrined in the great medieval epic, the *Chanson de Roland* (the *Song of Roland*). On later expeditions the Franks drove the Muslims back to the Ebro River and set up a buffer state known as the Spanish Mark, or March, with Barcelona as its capital (see map, p. 144).

Charlemagne's greatest conquest was against the Saxon tribes between the Rhine and the Elbe rivers. To destroy paganism, Charlemagne proclaimed harsh laws against any Saxon who refused to be baptized. Eating meat during Lent, cremating the dead

(an old pagan practice), and pretending to be baptized were offenses punishable by death. The Church and its priests were the main agents for pressing Charlemagne's rigorous program forward.

Like his father before him, Charlemagne intervened in Italian politics. Expansionist ambition drove the Lombard king to invade again the territories of the papacy. At the behest of the pope, Charlemagne defeated the Lombards in 774 and proclaimed himself their king. While in Italy, he cemented his father's alliance with the Church by celebrating Easter in Rome and by confirming the Donation of Pepin.

Saxony and north Italy had been conquered, but the empire's eastern frontier was continually threatened by fierce tribes. The Avars, Asiatic nomads, had settled in the valley of the Danube, and from this locale they continuously raided their neighbors. In a series of six campaigns, Charlemagne completely exterminated the Avars and then set up his own military province in the valley of the Danube to guard against any possible future plundering by eastern nomads. Called the East Mark, this territory later became Austria.

Charlemagne's coronation in Rome. The most important single event in the momentous reign of Charlemagne took place on Christmas Day in the year 800. At the Christmas service Charlemagne knelt before the altar at St. Peter's while the pope placed a crown on his head amid the cries of the assembled congregation:

To Charles Augustus crowned of God, great and pacific Emperor of the Romans, long life and victory![3]

This ceremony demonstrated that the memory of the Roman empire still survived as a vital tradition in Europe and that there was a strong desire to reëstablish the political unity that had existed in the Roman world before the invasions of the fifth century. Implicit also in this coronation was another great theme of medieval history, the struggle between the empire and the papacy. Charlemagne was crowned not only by, but

CHARLEMAGNE'S
"ROMAN EMPIRE"
about 814

presumably with the consent of, the pope. He was emperor by the grace of God, with heaven and its earthly agency, the Church, on his side. But it was not all gain for the ruler; the Church could claim its superiority over Charlemagne and other kings as well. "From this time on papal and imperial power stood side by side, each claiming supreme authority over all human affairs and relationships. The future was inevitably to witness a direct collision."[4]

His empire and government. The extent of Charlemagne's empire was impressive. His territories included all of the western area of the old Roman empire except Africa, Britain, southern Italy, and most of Spain. In the east the frontier stretched from the Baltic south to the Adriatic Sea, while in the west the line followed the coast from Denmark south to northern Spain (see map, above).

Five defensive provinces, or marks, protected the empire against hostile neighbors. These included the East Mark in the Avar country and the Spanish Mark.

All of the Carolingian territories were divided into administrative divisions, each under a count. By the law of 802, Charlemagne created the *missi dominici*, the king's envoys, who checked on local officials—the counts in particular. These itinerant officials were sent throughout the country to see that justice was done, to check the roads, to administer the oath of allegiance, to listen to grievances, and to send accused officials back to the king's court for trial. In order to prevent collusion between the *missi dominici* and the local officials, no envoy was allowed to work in the area where he lived, and no two justices could be teamed for more than one year.

By and large, Charlemagne's subjects enjoyed a high degree of law, order, and good government—a remarkable achievement when one considers the huge area involved.

The Carolingian Renaissance. It is to the credit of Charlemagne that he not only created a large and efficiently administered empire but also fostered learning. His efforts to advance education and scholarship prompted later historians to speak of this period as the Carolingian Renaissance. In 789 a royal ordinance decreed:

Let every monastery and every abbey have its school, where boys may be taught the psalms . . . singing, arithmetic, and grammar; and let the books that are given them be free from faults, and let care be taken that the boys do not spoil them either when reading or writing.[5]

The preservation of classical manuscripts and the reform of handwriting were significant achievements of the Carolingian revival. To correct the old texts and compose new ones, Charlemagne imported Anglo-Saxon and Irish copyists. They replaced the old Merovingian cursive script with a more legible style of writing known as Carolingian minuscule—the foundation for the roman type face, which is still widely used.

At Aix-la-Chapelle, his capital, the Carolingian ruler strove to recapture something of the grandeur of Rome, importing marbles and statuary from Italy. But the splendor of Aix-la-Chapelle was artificial. During a good part of his reign, Charlemagne's court, like those of many medieval rulers, was itinerant; with his retinue he moved about the land, remaining in one place only as long as the accumulated supplies of the particular district would support his followers.

Accomplishments of the Carolingians. In 814 Charlemagne died at Aix-la-Chapelle. This ruler, so remote in time from our own day, must be considered one of the great constructive statesmen of world history. He extended Christian civilization in Europe, set up barriers against incursions of the Slav and Avar, and gave western Europe a breathing space in which law and order were again

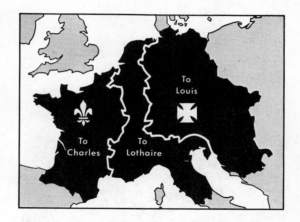

In 843, the Carolingian empire was divided among the grandsons of Charlemagne by the Treaty of Verdun.

enforced, permitting the process of fusion to go on between Germanic, Roman, and Christian elements.

Charlemagne's empire afforded no more than a breathing space, however, for its territories were too vast and its peoples too diverse to be held together under existing conditions after the dominating character of its creator had passed from the scene. Charlemagne had no standing army, no fleet, and no bureaucratic administrative machine comparable to that of Roman times. The Frankish economy was agricultural and localized, and the fiscal system was inadequate to maintain an effective and permanent administration.

The greatness of the Carolingian House was the achievement of three strong rulers—Charles Martel, Pepin the Short, and Charlemagne—during a single century from 714 to 814. To undo the achievements of this great trio took only one ruler and scarcely more than twenty-five years. The once mighty empire disintegrated amid the confusion of weak rulers, civil wars, and bloody feuds.

The division of the empire. Before Charlemagne's death he presided at the coronation of Louis the Pious, his surviving son. Louis the Pious subsequently partitioned his realm among his sons, and bitter rivalry broke out among the brothers and their father. In 840 Louis the Pious died, a tragic and brokenhearted figure.

Above is a restored sailing ship of the type used in Viking invasions of the ninth and tenth centuries. These long, narrow vessels were powered by long oars or by sails when the wind was favorable, and their high prows were often carved in the form of a fearsome animal, sometimes a dragon. The Viking fleets were composed of as many as 350 ships, each capable of carrying a hundred men.

After the father's death, strife continued among the three surviving sons. Lothair, the elder, was opposed by the two younger— Louis the German and Charles the Bald. In 842 the younger brothers joined forces in the famous Strasbourg Oaths. The text of these oaths is significant in that one part was in early French, the other in early German. The first could be understood by Charles' followers, who lived mainly west of the Rhine; the other by the followers of Louis the German, who lived east of the Rhine. These oaths are evidence that the Carolingian empire was splitting into two linguistic parts— East Frankland, the forerunner of Germany, and West Frankland, which became France.

In 843 the warring brothers called a halt to their fighting, came painfully to an agreement at Verdun, and split the Carolingian lands three ways. Charles the Bald obtained the western part and Louis the German the eastern; Lothair, who retained the title of emperor, obtained an illogical middle kingdom comprising both Italy and a narrow corridor, not more than 150 miles wide, running from central Italy to the North Sea.

The importance of the Treaty of Verdun is that it began the shaping of the modern European nations France and Germany and gave political recognition to the cultural and linguistic division shown in the Strasbourg Oaths. Unfortunately, Lothair's middle area north of the Alps, called Lotharingia or Lorraine, encompassed both Latin and Teutonic cultures and, although it was divided in 870 between Charles and Louis, the area was disputed for centuries. Lorraine remained one of the cockpits of Europe, a land drenched with the blood of countless French and German peoples.

After the empire had been split up by the Treaty of Verdun, the Carolingian rulers continued to go downhill. The last of the East Frankish rulers died in 911. In West Frankland the nobles, ignoring the eighteen-year-old Carolingian prince, chose Odo, Count of Paris, as king in 887.

Invaders on all sides. The Carolingian empire not only decayed from internal feuds but also was battered by new waves of invaders. Slavic tribes raided eastern Germany, and to these were added the dreaded Magyars, a ruthless, nomadic people who had migrated from central Asia.

In addition, new Muslim invasions threatened Europe. By the ninth century, the Muslims held Sicily and had swept all non-Muslim trade from the Mediterranean, breaking the commercial ties that had linked Europe with other areas since classical times. But by far the most widespread and destructive raiders came from Scandinavia.

Invasions by the Vikings. During the ninth and tenth centuries, Swedes, Danes, and Norwegians—collectively known as Vikings—stormed out of their remote forests and fiords. The reason for this expansion is not clear. Some historians stress overpopulation and a surplus of young men. There are scholars who believe that Norse expansion was a countermovement of northern paganism against the stern Christian missionary expansion of Charlemagne. Others see a clue in the fact that the Vikings had devised expert sailing techniques, which enabled them to traverse the seas far from land.

The range of Viking expansion was amazing. The Vikings went as far as North America to the west and the Caspian Sea to the east. Their marauding filled civilized Europeans with a fear that is reflected in an old litany of the Church: "From the fury of the Northmen, O Lord deliver us."

Three main routes of Viking expansion can be identified (see map below). The outer path, followed mainly by the Norwegians, swung westward to Ireland and the coast of Scotland. Between 800 and 850, Ireland was ravaged severely. Monasteries, the centers of the flourishing culture attained by the Irish Celts, were destroyed. Another route, the eastern line, was followed chiefly by the Swedes, who went down the rivers of Russia as merchants and soldiers of fortune (see Chapter 7). The Danes took the middle passage, raiding the east coast of England and the shores of Germany, France, and Spain. By the end of the eighth century, Viking raids had begun against England; in the middle of the next century their full fury broke upon all Europe. On the Continent the dragon boats sailed up such navigable rivers as the Rhine, Scheldt, Seine, and Loire, and in particular the Vikings devastated northwest France, destroying dozens of abbeys and towns.

In 911 a treaty was arranged between Rollo, the Viking leader, and the king of France. This agreement recognized the Viking occupation of what became Normandy and acknowledged their leader as a duke and vassal of the French king. The Vikings, or Normans, quickly adopted Christian civilization, and Rouen, their capital, become known as the town of a hundred churches.

Europe in 900. During its heyday (714-814) the Carolingian empire had ruled most of western Europe, but by the middle of the ninth century the protection that its once well-organized and efficient government had offered no longer existed. In large areas of the empire, population declined, lands went out of production, and there was a shortage of food. It was obvious that the central govern-

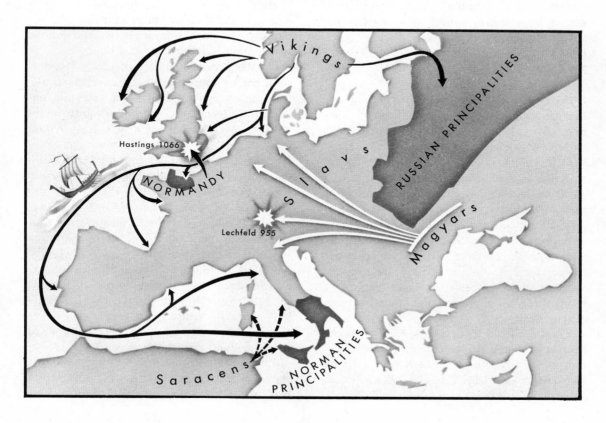

ment was no longer able to ward off foreign attacks. The ninth-century invasions of the Vikings and other raiders confirmed this.

Muslim expansion in the Mediterranean had by the ninth century brought an end to European trade. The great inland sea, once the basis for the prosperity and civilization of the classical world, was at the mercy of Muslim pirates. When the Mediterranean was closed to European ships, the inland trade also vanished. Oriental products, such as papyrus, spices, and silks, were no longer traded in Europe; ports, such as Marseilles, shriveled up; urban life almost disappeared; and the middle class, which had been supported by trade, sank into insignificance.

To replace centralized rule and a culture based on trade, a new form of government and a new economy had to be devised. Feudalism and the manorial system now rose to fill the gap. Feudalism was really a transitional political stage, for it was seldom more than a poor substitute for a closely knit and centralized government; but following the collapse of a unified political system, it served as a stopgap until a more effective government could be developed.

FEUDALISM

The origins of feudalism. European feudalism grew out of Roman and German practices. These early customs can be divided into two general types—those connected with landholding and those with a man-to-man agreement of mutual protection.

In the late Roman empire, the owners of the *latifundia* were steadily adding land to their already extensive holdings. Unable to manage their tracts, the nobles granted portions to other people in exchange for particular services, a practice called *beneficium*. Military service was the usual exchange. From these origins arose the feudal system of land tenure.

By the fifth century the ability of the Roman emperor to protect his subjects had disappeared, and citizens had to depend on the patronage system, by which a Roman noble organized a group of less fortunate

citizens as a personal bodyguard and in return looked after their wants and interests. A similar arrangement existed among the German tribes in the institution of *comitatus*. The German chiefs chose outstanding warriors as a personal retinue; the warriors swore to serve their chief loyally, and in return they were provided with food and military equipment. The personal bonds of feudalism arose from the combination of patronage and *comitatus*. When the retainer was reimbursed by a grant of land, the feudal institution of vassalage had arrived.

Feudalism defined. Through Merovingian times the gradual rise of feudal institutions continued, and it came to a climax in the confusion attending the collapse of the Carolingian empire. As the Carolingian kings lost their power, they were forced to recognize the *beneficium* as a hereditary possession, or fief, and to exempt the fief from royal interference. Thus the lords won the right to govern their holdings without being responsible to the monarch. At about this time changes were also taking place in the organization of the army; Charles Martel's plan for mounted knights, supported by land grants, was gaining wider support.

On the economic side, when the Muslims destroyed western Europe's overseas trade, this region retrogressed to a self-sufficient agricultural economy with very little commercial, urban activity. The land was divided up into manors, whose inhabitants grew or made almost everything they needed. Without trade, money almost ceased to circulate.

Out of all these elements—the Roman and Germanic customs of land tenure and personal protection, the virtual disappearance of small landowners, the rise of the independent landed aristocracy, the creation of the mounted knight, and the end of Mediterranean commerce—new patterns of society, feudalism and the manorial system, rapidly took shape in western Europe.

Feudalism can be said to have emerged as a well-defined governmental system throughout most of western Europe by the year 900. It was a system in which political authority was wielded by the landed nobility, who,

FEUDAL RELATIONSHIPS

German Emperor

King of France

Archbishop of Rheims

Archbishop of Sens

Bishop of Langres

Bishop of Autun

Duke of Burgundy

Bishop of Auxerre

Abbot of St. Denis

Subvassal

Subvassal

Subvassal

Subvassal

COUNT OF CHAMPAGNE

Subvassal

Subvassal

Subvassal

Arrows indicate the lord to whom homage is done and from whom one or more fiefs are held. Adapted from Samuel Harding, *New Medieval and Modern History,* American Book, 1925, p. 59.

though theoretically subordinate to the king, actually took the law into their own hands in many instances. As a form of government, feudalism was able to maintain some semblance of law and order on the local level, but it could not perform the functions of a strong, centralized administration. The feudal system existed throughout western Europe, but our description of it applies particularly to the form it took in France.

The feudal hierarchy. At the top stood the emperor or king, and all the land in his dominions belonged to him. He kept large areas for his personal use (royal or crown lands) and invested the highest nobles—such as dukes and counts (in England, earls)— with the remainder. Those nobles holding lands directly from the king were called tenants-in-chief. They in turn parceled out portions of their fiefs to lesser nobles. The lowest in the scale of vassals was the knight, whose fief was just sufficient to support one mounted warrior.

Except for the king, at the top of feudal society, and the knight with his single fief, the usual situation of a nobleman was to be both a vassal and a lord. For example, if Count A received a fief from the king, he might subinfeudate part of it to Baron B, who in turn might subinfeudate part of it to Baronet C, and so on down to the simplest knight, Sir D. In practice, a king might even hold land from and be the vassal of another king, as in the case of John of England. This ruler was the vassal of King Philip of France for certain French lands, yet he in no way thought himself the inferior of Philip.

Subinfeudation became a problem when a conflict of loyalties arose (see chart). For example, in order to add to his land, B might also have received a fief from and sworn fealty to X, a noble as powerful as A. If A and X should go to war against one another, on which side does B, the vassal of both A and X, fight? This dilemma was partially solved by the custom of liege homage. When a vassal received his first fief, he pledged liege homage to that lord. This meant that this obligation was to have top priority over services that he might later pledge to other lords.

The Church's role in feudalism. Another complicating factor in feudalism was the inclusion of the Church in the system. The Church held land in essentially three ways: a donor sometimes gave the Church a piece of land in return for prayers for himself or his family; some lands came freely to the Church; and other property was held in the same manner that any lay fief was held. In the latter case the Church official who obtained the fief was obligated to the lord for certain services. Military service, involving the bloodshed which a clergyman was supposed to refrain from personally, was provided through his secular representative, the *advocatus*.

As the Church's holdings grew, a fundamental conflict arose in that its officials owed their loyalty as churchmen to the pope but, as vassals holding land, had obligations to their feudal lords. There was a serious clash of loyalties here, which was partially responsible for the bitter struggle between the heads of the feudal system, the kings, and the head of the Church, the pope (see p. 227).

Class structure. Medieval society conventionally consisted of three distinct classes: the nobles, the peasants, and the clergy. Each of these groups had its own task to perform. Since the vassals usually gave military service to their lord in return for their fiefs, the nobles were primarily fighters, belonging to an honored society quite distinct from the peasant people—freemen, villeins, and serfs; in an age of physical violence, society obviously would accord first place to the man with the sword rather than to the man with the hoe. The peasants were the workers; attached to the manors, they produced the crops and did all the menial labor. The Church drew on both the noble and the peasant classes for the clergy. Although the higher churchmen held land as vassals under the feudal system, the clergy formed a class largely separate from nobility and peasantry.

Relation of lord and vassal. One of the principal elements of feudalism was a personal bond that was forged between a lord and a vassal. In the ceremony known as the act of homage, the vassal knelt before his lord, or suzerain, and promised to be his "man." In the oath of fealty which followed, the vassal swore on the Bible or some other sacred object that he would remain true to his lord. Next, in the ritual of investiture, a lance, glove, or even a bit of straw was handed the vassal to signify his jurisdiction (not ownership) over the fief.

The feudal contract thus entered into by lord and vassal was considered sacred and binding upon both parties. Breaking this tie of mutual obligations was considered a felony, because it was the basic agreement of feudalism and hence of medieval society. The lord for his part was obliged to give his vassal protection and justice and to respect the honor and persons of his wife and children. The vassal's primary duty was military service. He and his knights were expected to devote forty days' service each year to the lord without payment. In addition, the vassal was obliged to assist the lord in rendering justice in the lord's court. At certain times, such as when he had to ransom a son captured in war, the lord also had the right to demand money payments, called "aids."

Medieval warfare. The final authority in the Middle Ages was force, and the general atmosphere of the era was one of violence. Although much of the fighting was done for the king, private wars of feud or fortune and even warfare for its own sake were common. Recalcitrant vassals, particularly in France, frequently made war upon their suzerains.

War was considered a normal occupation by the ambitious nobles of the time, for success offered glory and rich rewards. First of all, land was the only real source of wealth, and its supply was limited. Holdings could be increased by taking on another fief or, if the land was not available, by marriage or war. If marriage was not feasible, war was always an alternative. If successful, warfare enlarged a noble's territory; and, if they produced nothing else, forays and raids kept a man in good mettle. To die in battle was the only honorable end for a spirited gentleman; to die in bed was a "cow's death."

The constant wars became so destructive that the Church felt compelled to limit the fighting. About the year 990 the Church inaugurated the Peace of God, by which all persons who pillaged sacred places or refused to spare noncombatants were cursed and banned from the sacraments. A far more effective check of knightly pugnacity—the Truce of God—appeared in the south of France early in the next century. This restraint inaugurated certain "closed seasons" by limiting the times when the nobles could fight. Originally the period covered by the truce included only Friday, Saturday, and Sunday of each week. Later the period was lengthened from sunset on Wednesday to sunrise on Monday and included certain long seasons, such as the one from the beginning of Lent through Whitsuntide.

An evaluation of feudalism. What shall be our general estimate of feudalism? Feudalism was crude and makeshift, but it brought some order out of the chaos into which Europe had fallen. It stabilized society and created a system of law and order. It even contributed to democracy, for its principle that feudal law was above the king (as witnessed in the Magna Carta—see p. 208) was later used by the middle class to curb royal absolutism.

One historian states that feudalism "concealed in its bosom the weapons with which it would be itself one day smitten."[6] By maintaining a king at the head of the hierarchy, feudalism was keeping intact the vestiges of monarchy, which would gradually reassert itself and restore centralized government.

THE MANORIAL SYSTEM

The manor in relation to feudalism. We have discussed feudalism, the political system of medieval times. Now we turn to the economic organization, the manorial system. The feudal system was the means whereby protection was obtained for society; the manor was the agency which provided the necessary food for the members of both feudal and manorial groups. Feudalism and the manorial system evolved independently, but they were intimately connected.

The term *manorial system* refers to the type of economic and social system which centered around the manor. The manorial system governed the methods of agriculture, the lives of the serfs, and their relationships with each other and with the lord of the manor.

German and Roman origins of the manor. Like feudalism, the manor seems to have had its origins in both Roman and German institutions. In the late Roman empire, taxes were so high that the small landholder was often unable to pay them. To counter this problem, the practice of *precarium* arose, whereby the small farmer gave his land to the owner of the local *latifundium*, who assumed the tax burden. The nobleman allowed the original owner, now a *colonus*, to cultivate the land as a sharecropper. This arrangement was cemented by the imperial decree that bound all Roman citizens, including the *coloni*, to their occupations. By the end of the Roman empire, *precarium* was widespread, and the system carried over into medieval times.

The German contribution is not so easily traced. Some scholars maintain that many of the German villagers who settled in Roman territory had a status comparable to slavery or serfdom. At any rate, it can be argued that in the medieval manor Roman and Germanic elements were blended.

Agriculture, the chief function of the manor. The manor varied in size from one locality to another. A small one might contain only about a dozen households. Since the allotment to each family averaged about 30 acres, the small manors probably included about 350 acres of tillable land, not counting the meadows, woods, waste land, and the lord's demesne. A large manor might contain fifty families and a total area of 5000 acres.

The center of the manor was the village, with the thatched cottages of the peasants grouped together along one street. Around

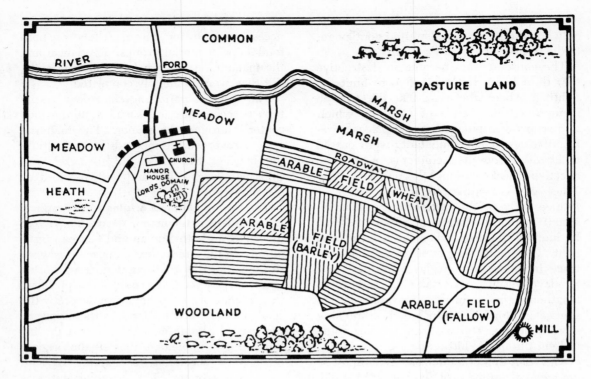

A manor usually contained all or most of the following: (1) the lord's demesne, or domain—the best land on the manor, cultivated for him by his serfs; (2) the lord's close, a part of the demesne rented out to a tenant cultivator; (3) the tenures of the villagers, divided according to the open-field system into strips separated by narrow paths of uncultivated turf; (4) the meadow land, used in common by the peasantry and the lord; (5) the woods, also held in common; (6) the waste land; (7) the domain of the village priest, or "God's domain," cultivated for the priest by the villagers. The serf's holdings were scattered among various fields, so that each villager would receive land of equal quality; the lord's demesne, from one third to two fifths of the manor, might be set off from the villagers' tenures or distributed among them. This chart is reproduced from Dorothy Mills, *The Middle Ages*, Putnam, 1935, p. 135.

each cottage was a space large enough for a vegetable patch, chicken yard, haystack, and stable. An important feature of the landscape was the village church, together with the priest's house and the burial ground. If the manor was large, the lord's dwelling might be a castle, with the village built up to its walls; if small, a manor house surmounted a knoll on the demesne. The fields stretched out from the village, and along the roads the villagers trudged to work.

Crop cultivation. It is dangerous to generalize too sweepingly about agricultural methods, because differences in locality, fertility of soil, crop production, and other factors resulted in a variety of farming methods. But if we study farming as practiced in northwestern Europe, we can discover some common factors. The implements which the peasants used were extremely crude; the plow was a cumbersome affair with heavy wheels, often requiring as many as eight draft animals to pull it. There were also crude harrows, sickles, beetles for breaking up clods, and flails for threshing. Inadequate methods of farming resulted in soil that was soon worn out. It has been estimated that the average yield per acre was only six to eight bushels of wheat, a fourth of the modern yield.

Medieval farmers learned that wheat or rye could be planted in the autumn as well as in the spring. As a result they divided the land into three fields, with one planted in the fall, another in the spring, and the third left lying fallow. Furthermore, it was discovered that while a continuation of the same crop soon exhausts the soil, the alternation of crops does not bleed the land so quickly.

Pasture and woods. Each tenant was really a shareholder in the village community, not only in the open fields, but also in the meadow, pasture, wood, and waste lands. His rights in these common lands were determined by the number of acres he held in the open fields.

The wooded land was valuable as a place to graze pigs, the most common animal on the manor. Again the tenant was limited in the number of pigs which he might turn loose there. The tenant could also gather dead wood in the forest, but cutting down green wood was prohibited unless authorized by the lord.

Administration of the manor. Though the lord might live on one of his manors, each manor was administered by such officials as the steward, the bailiff, and the reeve.

The steward, the highest ranking official, was general overseer for all his lord's manors, supervised the business of the manors, acted as the lord's legal adviser, and presided over the manorial court. It was the bailiff's duty to supervise the cultivation of the demesne, to collect rents, dues, and fines, to keep the manor's financial accounts, and to inspect the work done by the peasants. The reeve was the "foreman" of the villagers, chosen by them and representing their interests.

It is difficult to distinguish the various social classes which made up the manor community. Furthermore, in status and function these classes differed not only from locality to locality but from period to period. However, they can be roughly divided into three major categories: the lord and his officials, the free element, and the semifree group. All classes except the first belonged to the peasantry, for whether free or semifree they were not members of the feudal hierarchy.

There often were freemen on the manor, however small a proportion of its population they may have represented. They possessed personal freedom and were not subject to the same demands as the semifree people.

The freeman did not have to work in the lord's fields himself but could send substitutes. He paid cash rent for his holding and, if he wanted to leave, could locate a new tenant for the land, provided the transfer took place in open court in the lord's presence and the new man was acceptable to the lord. Aside from these privileges, however, the freeman was little different from the semifree man.

The semifree persons, the serfs, were bound to the manor, which they could not leave without the lord's consent. Serfdom was a hereditary status, the children of a serf being attached to the soil as their parents were. Among the semifree class was a group possessing special privileges—the villeins. By paying a fee, the villein could usually obtain the lord's permission to leave the manor, or send his son to learn a handicraft or enter the Church.

The lord of the manor was bound by the force of custom to respect certain rights of his serfs. So long as they paid their dues and services, serfs could not be evicted from their holdings. Although a serf could not appear in court against his lord or a freeman, he could appeal to the manor court against any of his fellows.

Whereas the peasants found in the manor their economic, political, legal, and social life, to the lord the manor was essentially a source of income. The earnings came from three obligations imposed on the peasantry: (1) services in the form of labor, (2) dues levied on the peasant, and (3) manorial monopolies.

The most important service was "week-work." The peasant had to donate two or three days' work each week to the lord. The week-work included such jobs as repairing roads or bridges or carting manure to the fields. Because the lord's demesne "had always to be plowed first, sowed first, and reaped first," the peasant had to perform extra work, "boon-work," at these times.

Various dues or payments—usually in produce, in money if it was available—were made to the lord. The *taille* (or tallage) was the most common manorial levy. Freeman,

Into this medieval print the artist has crowded the whole life of a manorial village. A hunting party is shown in the foreground, the ladies riding behind the knights. The castle, with its moat and drawbridge, dominates the countryside. In the midst of the village houses, which are surrounded by a fence, stands the church. Note also the mill and the millrace at the left and what appears to be a wine or cider press to the right of the mill. In the upper right corner, a serf is using the heavy plow common in northwestern Europe (the artist has shown only two draft animals). The nets were apparently set to catch hares, and below them stands a wayside shrine. Visible on the horizon is a gibbet with buzzards wheeling over it.

villein, and serf were taxed one or more times a year by the *taille*.

In addition to receiving income from services and dues, the lord grew richer from certain monopolies. On the manor the lord operated the grain mill, the oven for baking bread, and the wine and cider press. Since the peasant was prohibited from taking his grain, flour, and fruit elsewhere, the lord collected a toll each time these services were needed.

Self-sufficiency of the manor. Economically the manor was almost self-sufficient. The food essential to sustain the local population was raised on the manor. Where rainfall was sufficient, flax for making linen was cultivated. Leather for boots was tanned on the manor, and yarn for clothing was spun at home. Specialized jobs were performed by the village miller, butcher, carpenter, and blacksmith. A few commodities, such as salt, iron, and millstones, had to be imported and were generally procured from one of the country fairs.

Because of bad roads and other dangers of travel, communication with the outside world was extremely limited. A rare journey beyond the manor, the arrival of a pilgrim who had visited faraway shrines or of a recent bride from another manor gave the inhabitants their only glimpses of the outside world. The manor remained the center of the peasants' lives; many of them never left its confines.

THE AGE OF CHIVALRY

Chivalry in feudal society. One of the most interesting and significant legacies of the Middle Ages is its concept of chivalry, a code which governed the deeds of all truly perfect and gentle knights. Such paragons are found in the accounts of Sir Lancelot and Sir Galahad in Sir Thomas Malory's *Morte d'Arthur*. We find them also in the *Song of Roland*, where the hero, surrounded by his foes, cries: "Death rather than dishonor."

The word *chivalry*, derived from the French *chevalier* (horseman), denotes a code of etiquette and honor only for the aristocracy. By the chivalric code the knight was required to be faithful to his lord and his vows, to champion the Church against its enemies, and to protect women, children, and the infirm. Furthermore, the chivalric ideal stipulated personal traits such as generosity, courtesy, and reverence toward womanhood. Chivalry reached its zenith in the twelfth and thirteenth centuries.

Unfortunately, the practice of chivalry was quite different from the theory. While he might cloak his motives under high-sounding words, the average knight continued to fight, plunder, and abuse women, especially those of the lower class.

Women in general shared the characteristics of the menfolk. They lived in a crude and often brutal age devoid of many of our modern refinements. Like their husbands, medieval women were heavy drinkers and eaters. It is said that a common compliment to a member of the fair sex was that she was "the fairest woman who ever drained a bottle."[7]

Training for knighthood. From the time they were boys, men of the nobility underwent a rigid training for knighthood. A boy was kept in the care of his mother until the age of seven. Then his father sent him to the household of a relative, a friend, or the father's suzerain. There he became a page, attending the ladies, running their errands,

In this medieval picture of the knighting ceremony, the knight is being armed. The men behind him hold his helmet and shield; two others fasten his sword and spurs.

and learning the rudiments of religion, manners, hawking, and hunting. During this segment of his training, he was imbued with the virtue of obedience. When about fifteen or sixteen, he became a squire and prepared himself seriously for the art of war. He learned to keep a knight's equipment in good order, to ride a war horse with dexterity, and to handle the sword, the shield, and the lance correctly. The squire also waited on his lord and lady at the table and learned music and poetry and the popular medieval games of chess and backgammon.

If not already knighted on the battlefield for valor, the squire was usually considered eligible for knighthood at twenty-one. By the twelfth century the Church claimed a role in the ceremony on the grounds that the knight was privileged to serve God in the secular world. The knighting ceremony was invested with impressive symbolism. The candidate took a bath to symbolize purity and watched his weapons before the altar in an all-night vigil, confessing and making resolutions to be a worthy knight. During the solemn Mass which followed, his sword was blessed on the altar by the priest or bishop. The climax of the ceremony came when the candidate, kneeling before his lord, received a light blow on the neck or shoulder (the accolade), as the lord pronounced these words: "In the name of God, Saint Michael, and Saint George I dub thee knight. Be valiant." The ceremony was designed to impress upon the knight that he must be virtuous and valiant, loyal to his suzerain and to God.

Heraldry. With its unique decorative designs, worn by each noble family on its armor and helmets, heraldry was one of the more colorful aspects of chivalry. Noble families took great pride in displaying on their armor an honored heraldic device, the symbol of the family dignity. Two hundred and eighty-five variations of the cross were devised by ingenious feudal artists, while such real and fictitious animals as the lion, leopard, griffin, dragon, unicorn, and a host of others could be found in fanciful postures on the shields of noble families. A man's social position was evident in his coat of arms, for its quarterings, or divisions, showed to which noble families its owner was related.

Castles as fortresses and homes. The life of the nobles centered about the castle. The earliest of these structures, mere wooden blockhouses, were built in the ninth century. Stone was not used until the late eleventh century; and even then only the central tower, the donjon, was built of stone. Not until the twelfth and thirteenth centuries, when chivalry was in full bloom, were massive castles constructed all in stone.

The donjon was the focal point of the castle; it was surrounded by an open space which contained storerooms, workshops, and a chapel. The outside walls of the castle were surmounted by turrets from which arrows, boiling oil, and various missiles might be showered upon the attackers. Beyond the wall was the moat, a steep-sided ditch filled with water to deter the enemy. The only entrance to the castle lay across the drawbridge. The portcullis, a heavy iron grating which could be lowered rapidly to protect the gate, was a further barrier against unwanted intrusion.

Life in the castle was anything but comfortable or romantic. The lord at first dwelt in the donjon, but by the thirteenth century he had built more spacious quarters. Because the castle was designed for defense, it possessed no large windows, and the rooms were dark and gloomy. The stone walls were bare except for occasional tapestries to allay the draft and dampness, and huge fireplaces provided the only warmth in the drafty rooms.

Amusements of the nobles. The average noble derived his pleasures primarily from outdoor sports. Because the knight had been trained from birth in military matters, he considered warfare fine entertainment. In peacetime the joust and tournament substituted for actual battle. The joust was a conflict between two armed knights, each equipped with a blunted lance with which he attempted to unseat the other. The tournament was a general melee in which groups of knights attacked each other. Often fierce fighting ensued, with frequent casualties.

The nobles were very fond of hunting, and the constant demand for fresh meat afforded a legitimate excuse for galloping over the countryside. Most hunting was done in the nearby forests, but at times an unlucky peasant's crops might be ruined during the chase. Some great nobles had scores of horses and hounds trained in hunting the stag and wild boar.

A similar outdoor pastime, which lords, ladies, and even high Church dignitaries delighted in, was falconry, a method of hunting with predatory birds. The hawks were reared with the utmost care, and large companies of lords and ladies spent many afternoons eagerly wagering with one another as to whose falcon would bring down the first victim. The interest was so great that nobles often attended Mass with hooded falcons on their wrists.

SUMMARY

The political history in this chapter includes certain key events and institutions from the time of Clovis through the reign of Charlemagne to the invasions of the intrepid Vikings in the ninth century. The conversion of Clovis to Christianity and the subsequent Frankish alliance with the papacy meant that the most energetic of the German tribes had united with the greatest existing force for civilization and refinement in western Europe. This was the Christian Church, which incorporated both the new religion and some of the best of the old Roman tradition.

As Charlemagne amassed a sizable empire in Europe, he spread the Roman-Christian tradition. Although his empire was unique in early medieval Europe for its well-organized government, it depended too heavily on the forceful personality of its founder and did not survive his inferior successors. After the Carolingian collapse, new political and economic patterns evolved to meet the turbulent conditions of the time.

Feudalism was a bridge between the all-embracing imperial governments of the Romans and Carolingians and the diversity of national states so characteristic of modern Europe. Like so many things in medieval civilization, feudalism was a blend of German and Roman customs, enriched and humanized by the ideals of Christianity. The people who held land under feudal tenure were a privileged caste of landed aristocrats whose main function was military service. Set apart from the feudal nobles but forming the backbone of economic life was the vast majority of the people—the serfs. On the manors, the economic units of medieval life, the serfs were the human machines which grew the food for all medieval people and which performed the heavy labor needed. They were politically inarticulate, tied to the soil, and seldom masters of their destinies.

SUGGESTIONS FOR READING

The Cambridge Medieval History, 8 vols., 2nd ed., Cambridge Univ., 1924-1936. Best used for reference, these volumes— a first-rank achievement of historical scholarship—include valuable bibliographies. Recommended for student use is the two-volume abridgment by C. W. Previté-Orton, The Shorter Cambridge Medieval History, Cambridge Univ., 1952. An eye-opening summary of the principal scholarly interpretations and debates on selected topics in medieval history is contained in B. Lyon, The Middle Ages in Recent Historical Thought,* American Historical Assoc. (Service Center for Teachers of History), 1959. For other works which survey the history of the Middle Ages, see the List of Readings, p. 801.

J. M. Wallace-Hadrill, The Barbarian West, 400-1000, Hutchinson Univ. Library, 1952. A short survey built around the theme that "awareness of the classical heritage and anxiety to preserve it characterized the Western barbarians." A well-written introduction to this period, with chapters on Byzantium and Islam, is R. E. Sullivan, Heirs of the Roman Empire,* Cornell. C. Dawson, The Making of Europe,* Meridian, is a fuller account which stresses the role of the Church in making this period perhaps "the most creative age" in European history. See also W. C. Bark, Origins of the Medieval World, Stanford, 1958, which inverts Gibbon and holds that "the regression of civilization in the West from the Roman level was a fortunate occurrence." H. Pirenne, Mohammed and Charlemagne,* Meridian, presents the famous thesis that Roman civilization was uprooted more by the Muslim conquest of the Mediterranean in the seventh century than by the earlier Germanic invasions. For an excellent description of the barbarized society governed by the early Frankish kings, see Sir Samuel Dill, Roman Society in Gaul in the Merovingian Age, Macmillan, 1926.

*Indicates an inexpensive paperbound edition.

J. Bronsted, The Vikings,* Penguin. The best and most recent popular introduction to a fascinating subject. G. Turville-Petre, The Heroic Age of Scandinavia, Hutchinson Univ. Library, 1951, describes the Norse way of life as reflected in their heroic legends.

C. Stephenson, Medieval Feudalism,* Great Seal Books; F. L. Ganshof, Feudalism, Longmans, 1952. Two good, clear introductions to a subject which often baffles students.

Valuable for an understanding of the manorial system are J. H. Clapham et al., eds., The Agrarian Life of the Middle Ages, Cambridge Univ., 1941, Vol. I of The Cambridge Economic History of Europe from the Decline of the Roman Empire; and H. S. Bennett, Life on the English Manor, Cambridge Univ., 1938. Good short surveys include S. Painter, Medieval Society,* Cornell; and N. Neilson, Medieval Agrarian Economy,* Holt (Berkshire Studies). Beautifully written is E. Power, Medieval People,* Anchor, which contains fictionalized sketches of people of various social positions and occupations.

S. Painter, French Chivalry: Chivalric Ideas and Practices in Medieval France,* Great Seal Books. A delightful essay on the feudal, religious, and courtly aspects of chivalry.

R. Winston, Charlemagne: From the Hammer to the Cross, Bobbs-Merrill, 1954. Probably the best biography of Charlemagne in English. The career of the foremost scholar at Charlemagne's court is well presented in E. S. Duckett, Alcuin, Friend of Charlemagne: His World and His Work, Macmillan, 1951. The Carolingian Renaissance is covered in detail in the last half of M. L. W. Laistner, Thought and Letters in Western Europe, A.D. 500 to 900, Cornell, 1957. See also Vol. I of H. O. Taylor, The Medieval Mind: A History of the Development of Thought and Emotion in the Middle Ages, 2 vols., Harvard, 1949, which is unsurpassed for the history of ideas.

CHAPTER 7

Citadel and Conqueror

THE BYZANTINE EMPIRE, EARLY RUSSIA,
AND MUSLIM EXPANSION

Introduction. When we speak of the fall of the Roman empire, we sometimes forget that in fact only the western portion of that empire succumbed to the German invaders and entered into what has been described as its "Dark Ages." In the East, despite many vicissitudes, the east Roman or Byzantine empire stood for a thousand years as a citadel protecting an unappreciative West slowly emerging from semibarbarism.

Furthermore, the Byzantine empire made great contributions to civilization: Greek language and learning were preserved for posterity; the Roman imperial system was continued and Roman law codified; the Greek Orthodox Church converted the Slavic peoples and fostered the development of a splendid new Graeco-Oriental art which was dedicated to the glorification of the Christian religion. Situated at the crossroads of East and West, Constantinople acted as the disseminator of culture for all peoples who came in contact with the empire. Called with justification "The City," this rich and turbulent metropolis was to the early Middle Ages what Athens and Rome had been to classical times. By the time the empire collapsed in 1453, its religious mission and political conceptions had borne fruit among the Slavic peoples of eastern Europe and especially among the Russians. The latter were to lay claim to the Byzantine tradition and to dub Moscow the "Third Rome."

The only rival of Byzantine civilization close at hand was the culture developed by followers of the Prophet Muhammad, who united the Arabian peninsula under the banner of his new religion, Islam, with its fundamental teachings of monotheism. The dynamic faith of Muhammad spread so rapidly that within a hundred years after the

Prophet's death his followers had established a vast empire stretching from the Pyrenees to the Indus. This breath-taking religious and political expansion was followed by a flowering of Islamic culture which rivaled the achievements of the Byzantine empire and far surpassed those of contemporary western Europe. It is becoming increasingly apparent that no people contributed more to the preservation and dissemination of learning in the early Middle Ages than did the Muslims.

BYZANTINE HISTORY:

A PANORAMA OF

TRIUMPHS AND DEFEATS

From the founding of Constantinople to Justinian, 330-527. At the southern extremity of the Bosporus stands a promontory that juts out from Europe toward Asia, with the Sea of Marmora to the south and a long harbor known as the Golden Horn to the north. On this peninsula stood the ancient Greek city of Byzantium, which Constantine enlarged considerably and formally christened "New Rome" in 330 A.D. This new capital soon became known throughout the world as Constantinople, the city of Constantine.

Constantine had chosen his site carefully. The city commanded the waterway connecting the Mediterranean and the Black seas and separating Europe and Asia. Both commercially and politically, Constantinople was in a position to influence a rich region extending from the Adriatic to the Persian Gulf and as far north as the territory surrounding the Dnieper River. Moreover, the site lent itself easily to defense; it enabled Constantinople not only to become the great warehouse for East-West commerce but above all to be a buffer protecting Europe from attack.

In Chapter 5 we saw how both the eastern and western provinces of the Roman empire were beset with dangers from beyond the northern frontier during the fourth and fifth centuries. Storming into the empire, Visigoths, Huns, and Ostrogoths pillaged the Balkans and threatened Constantinople. But the greater strength of the eastern provinces saved them from the fate which befell Rome.

As the western half of the Roman empire crumbled, Constantinople turned eastward for its livelihood and culture, becoming gradually less Roman and western and more Greek and Oriental. A panorama of triumphs and defeats, Byzantine history for the next one thousand years can be divided into four main periods—expansion, peril, recovery, and disintegration.

Justinian's reconquests. The history of the empire in the sixth century focuses upon the reign of Justinian (527-565), a ruler whose ambition was to restore the Roman empire to its ancient scope and grandeur. Much of his success he owed to his wife, Theodora, who had been a dancer and was said to be the daughter of a circus animal trainer. But Theodora proved to be a brave empress and a wise counselor. In 532, early in Justinian's reign, occurred the Nike rebellion (named after the victory cry of the rioters), the most famous of many popular revolts which have led historians to characterize Byzantine history as a despotism tempered by revolution. Theodora's coolness and bravery inspired her hard-pressed husband to remain in the capital and crush the rebellion:

May I never be separated from this purple, and may I not live that day on which those who meet me shall not address me as mistress. If, now, it is your wish to save yourself, O Emperor, there is no difficulty. For we have much money, and there is the sea, here the boats . . . as for myself, I approve a certain ancient saying that royalty is a good burial-shroud.[1]

To carry out his plan for recovering the lost half of the Roman empire from the semi-barbarians of the West, Justinian first bought off a revived Persian empire which threatened his possessions in the Near East. Then in 533 he seized North Africa and the islands of the western Mediterranean from the Vandals. After many years of exhausting warfare, his generals wrested the southeastern portion of

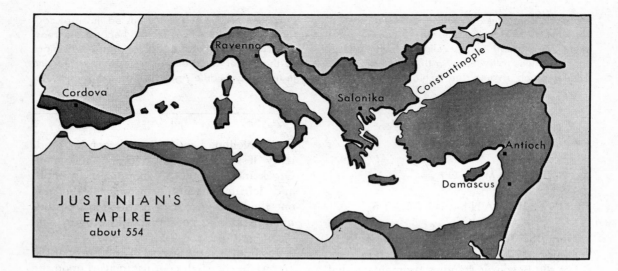

JUSTINIAN'S
EMPIRE
about 554

Spain from the Visigoths and took Italy from the Ostrogoths, driving the remnant back across the Alps. But Justinian's empire was still much smaller than the Roman empire at its height. Only a small part of Spain was his; nor had he recovered Gaul, Britain, or southern Germany. Moreover, the empire was now seriously weakened, both militarily and financially.

In domestic affairs, as in warfare, Justinian sought to restore the dignity and splendor of the Roman empire. In this area are found his greatest accomplishments, the codification of Roman law and the erection of the great Church of Hagia Sophia, both to be described later in this chapter.

Three centuries of peril, 565-867. With Justinian's death, the first and perhaps the greatest period of Byzantine history ended. Now followed an era of peril lasting from the middle of the sixth to the middle of the ninth century. Justinian's successors concentrated increasingly upon saving the provinces in the East rather than fighting on both eastern and western fronts. In 568 the Lombards established a new kingdom in Italy, leaving the empire in control only of Sicily, southern Italy, and some territory around Ravenna. Fierce Slavic and Asiatic tribes invaded the Balkans and menaced Constantinople.

When Heraclius (610-641) ascended the throne, the empire was in a perilous position.

The Slavs threatened from the north, and the Persians had conquered Syria and Jerusalem. While one Persian army conquered Egypt, other forces advanced to a point in Asia Minor opposite Constantinople. In three brilliant campaigns against the Persians (622-628), Heraclius defeated them so decisively that he regained Syria, Palestine, and Egypt.

Although the centuries-old menace of the Persians had now been removed, the eastern empire was confronted with a new danger. The early part of the seventh century saw in Arabia the birth of a new faith—Islam. With fanatical zeal the Muslims began a wholesale conquest of the eastern and southern provinces of the empire. By the end of the century their armies had subjugated Palestine, Syria, Egypt, North Africa, and part of Asia Minor, while their navies seized Cyprus and Rhodes and harassed Byzantine shipping in the Aegean. An Arabian fleet and army even besieged Constantinople annually for several years, and the distracted empire was also losing its grip on the Balkans to a new Hunnish menace, the Bulgars, who in 680 settled in what is now Bulgaria.

By 700 the eastern empire stood on the brink of disintegration. The power of the emperor sometimes extended little farther than the environs of the capital and a fringe of ports in the eastern Mediterranean. In Asia Minor the emperor's hold was precarious, and in the western Mediterranean, his power was disappearing altogether.

Then came the rule of Leo III (717-741), who restored order for a time to the hard-pressed Byzantine empire. Defeating the Muslims on the sea in several engagements, Leo also successfully repulsed their siege of Constantinople in 717 and 718. His extensive internal reforms included a new law code and an increased centralization of government. Leo's religious policies, however, caused widespread dissension and started a quarrel known as the iconoclastic controversy (see p. 164).

Last period of grandeur, 867-1057. The decline of the empire, brought to a halt by Leo III, began again after his death. Then in the ninth century, under the strong Macedonian dynasty (867-1057), the third period of Byzantine history was initiated as the empire rode out a new storm of external attack by sea and by land. While the Muslims were defeated in the Aegean, Byzantine armies held back the powerful Bulgarians, who sought to possess all of the Balkans.

It was under the dynamic leadership of Basil II (976-1025) that the empire in its third period reached a high level of power and prosperity. Byzantine military forces finally crushed their Bulgarian foes severely. On one occasion fifteen thousand Bulgars were blinded and only a handful left with a single eye each to guide the rest home. (The Bulgarian king is said to have died of shock when this sightless multitude returned.) Basil the "Bulgar-slayer," as he was called, incorporated the Bulgarian kingdom into the empire, but was unable to recover the lost provinces in Palestine, Egypt, and the West.

Basil II was friendly with Vladimir, the prince of Kiev in southern Russia, and was instrumental in bringing about that ruler's conversion to Christianity. Other Russians also began to adopt Christian beliefs and gradually accepted various Byzantine customs and much of Byzantine learning. Trade augmented these friendly relations.

Four centuries of decline: Part I, 1057-1204. At the end of the Macedonian dynasty in 1057, the Byzantine empire embarked on its last tempestuous journey of decline. At times obvious and rapid, then again imperceptible and gradual, imperial decline was due chiefly to the rise of commercial rivals and to invasions by Muslims and Christians alike.

Within the orbit of Byzantine commerce a dangerous rival was emerging—the city of Venice, founded in the fifth and sixth centuries by refugees who fled the barbarian invasions of northern Italy and found safety on a cluster of small islands off the northern Adriatic coast. The island city of Venice was relatively safe from the barbarian hordes and

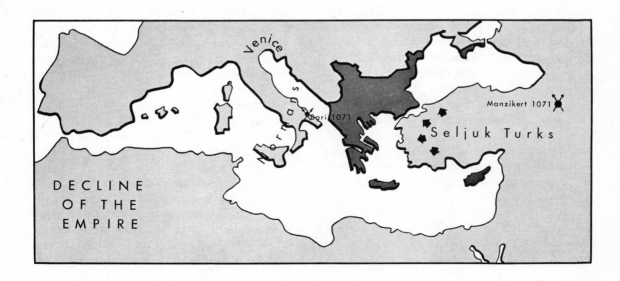

DECLINE OF THE EMPIRE

so remained under Byzantine sovereignty when most of the Italian peninsula was over-run. As subjects of the Byzantine empire, the Venetians enjoyed access to the eastern Mediterranean trade but were far enough away from Constantinople to run their own affairs. By the eleventh century, Venice had acquired economic supremacy in the Adriatic, and ambitious Venetian merchants were dreaming of supplanting Byzantine commercial supremacy over all the eastern Mediterranean.

In the eleventh century also, the Byzantine emperors were confronted with two new foes. The formidable Seljuk Turks (see p. 179) threatened Asia Minor; and the adventurous Normans, led by Robert Guiscard (see p. 186), began to carve out possessions for themselves in southern Italy. The Byzantine army was defeated by the Turks at the critical battle of Manzikert in 1071, and all of Asia Minor was soon lost. By an unfortunate coincidence, Bari, the empire's last stronghold in southern Italy, was captured by the Normans in the same year that the battle of Manzikert took place.

In 1081, with the empire deprived of rich possessions and sapped by growing commercial rivalry, an able general, Alexius Comnenus, became emperor by a coup d'état. Soon afterwards, in 1096, the first crusaders from the West appeared on the scene. Hoping to obtain some European mercenary forces to help defeat the Turks, Alexius had appealed to Pope Urban II for assistance, but he was thrown into consternation to find a host of crusaders, including the dreaded Normans, approaching the capital. The western response to Urban's appeal to save the eastern empire and the Holy Land from the Seljuks was met with suspicion by the Byzantines, who viewed the pope as heretical and the crusaders as potentially dangerous to the eastern empire. Adroitly, Alexius encouraged the crusaders to leave his hospitality as quickly as possible and attack his Seljuk enemies. The successful weakening of Muslim power by the First Crusade enabled Alexius to recover valuable portions of the lost territory in Asia Minor.

With the Fourth Crusade (1202-1204), the envy and enmity which had been building up for decades in the West against the Byzantine empire were converted into violence. The Venetians, upon whom the crusading army was dependent for ships and money, persuaded the crusaders to attack Constantinople. The crusaders could not withstand the lure of a campaign which would make their fortunes and at the same time would appear to be justified by the reunification of the Roman and Orthodox churches. When the crusaders arrived at the environs of Constantinople, the Byzantine ruler refused to pay the heavy tribute they demanded. In April 1204, Constantinople was attacked by land and sea.

A French noble, who accompanied the Fourth Crusade, described the downfall of the city:

[I saw] . . . the great churches and the rich palaces melting and falling in, and the great streets filled with merchandise burning in the flames. . . . The booty gained was so great that none could tell you the end of it: gold and silver, and vessels and precious stones, and samite, and cloth of silk, and robes vair [squirrel] and grey, and ermine, and every choicest thing found upon the earth . . . never, since the world was created, had so much booty been won in any city.[2]

The booty was divided according to prior agreement: three eighths went to the crusaders, and three eighths to the Venetians, while a quarter was reserved for an emperor who was to be selected from among the leading crusaders. Included among the loot were many Byzantine art treasures which subsequently adorned churches in the West; however, many priceless works of art were destroyed.

In truth, the Fourth Crusade dealt the empire a blow from which it never fully recovered.

Four centuries of decline: Part II, 1204-1453. Following the sack of Constantinople in 1204, a Latin empire was established which endured until 1261. In that year Michael Palaeologus, ruler of an unconquered remnant of the empire in Asia Minor, allied himself with Genoa (which was jealous of Venetian commercial supremacy in the eastern Mediterranean) and reconquered Constantinople from the Latin emperor. The rule of the Palaeologi lasted until the demise of the Byzantine empire—a span of two centuries of further decline in imperial power.

Internally, the empire was disturbed by civil wars, revolts by the lower classes, and bitter religious disputes between the eastern clergy and the emperors who sought western aid by attempting to heal the rupture between the Orthodox and Roman churches. Taxes and customs duties diminished, coinage was debased, and the military and naval forces grew fatally weak.

Externally, the situation was critical. Holding only a small portion of its former territory, the empire was surrounded by ambitious rivals and foes: the Latins still retained southern Greece, the Venetians and Genoese each possessed coastal cities and island territories of the empire, and in the thirteenth and fourteenth centuries powerful Slavic kingdoms developed in the Balkans. While the Slavs weakened the empire by prolonged warfare, the Venetians and Genoese exploited Constantinople's troubles in order to strengthen their commercial positions at Byzantine expense.

During the fourteenth century, too, a new and ultimately fatal menace arose in Asia Minor. The Ottoman Turks, former subjects of the Seljuk sultans, became independent. In the struggle with the Slavs, the Byzantines called the Ottomans to their support, but these allies, sensing their opportunity, quickly changed from rescuers to conquerors. Seizing Gallipoli, the Turks by-passed Constantinople and pushed into the Balkans.

The end came in 1453. After a magnificent defense of Constantinople, in which Constantine XI confronted the Turkish army of nearly 160,000 soldiers with only 9000 fighting men (half of whom were foreign mercenaries), the great eastern bulwark of Christian civilization collapsed before the might of Islam. As the Turks stormed the walls of the city, the emperor rushed to meet them, crying out as he was cut down:

God forbid that I should live an Emperor without an Empire! As my city falls, I will fall with it.[3]

The fall of Constantinople reverberated throughout the contemporary world. The last direct link with the classical era was shattered. First Rome had perished, now New Rome; and an epoch that had seemed eternal had passed into history.

Reasons for the endurance of the Byzantine empire. As the preceding résumé of Byzantine history has shown, the empire's political life had always been stormy. During its thousand years of existence, it experienced some sixty-five revolutions and the abdications or murders of more than sixty emperors. How did the empire manage to survive for such a long period?

One reason lay in its continuous use of a money economy, in contrast to the primitive barter economy then prevailing in the West. The money economy facilitated trade and the payment of taxes and enabled the empire to maintain standing military and naval forces. Until the latter days of the empire, Byzantine military science was relatively advanced and the armed forces effective. Also, the Byzantines had a secret weapon called "Greek fire," an inflammable chemical mixture whose contents were jealously guarded and are still not definitely known to us. As from a modern flame thrower, Greek fire was catapulted out of tubes onto the decks of enemy ships.

Of great significance for the endurance, as well as the character, of the empire was the wholesale loss of African, Italian, and eastern territory by the year 700. The lands still under the emperor's control were now more homogeneous; most of the population was Greek. Thus historians speak of the seventh century as the period when the eastern Roman empire was transformed into the "Byzantine" empire—that is, transformed into a Hellenized civilization taking its name appropriately from the original Greek settlement on which Constantinople had been built.

Another basic reason for the empire's endurance was its centralized system of administration. While the West was broken up into numerous feudal principalities, the Byzantines were governed by a strong monarchy, aided by a well-trained bureaucracy. By providing continuity of administration, this bureaucracy helped the empire to ride out its political storms. The emperor was consecrated with holy oil by the patriarch and thus claimed to rule by divine right. He regulated church, state, business, and military affairs with an iron hand; the individual had little voice in the government. So absolute was the control of the emperor that the early title *autokrator* has been carried over into the English word *autocracy*, meaning "absolute supremacy." Only a successful revolution could depose him.

Another factor in the endurance of the empire was the Orthodox Church. Linked as it was to the state, the Church automatically claimed the loyalty of the people. Although the Church has been accused of becoming progressively intolerant and rigid during the lifetime of the Byzantine empire, its orthodoxy and apparent imperviousness to change had its compensations. In later years, when the empire was beset by troubles from without and within, the Church, as the stanchest ally of the throne, stood granitelike in its resistance against political disintegration.

THE ORTHODOX CHURCH

Collaboration between Church and state. The Byzantine, or Orthodox, Church not only dominated religious and cultural life in the empire but was also interwoven with the political fabric. Whereas the Roman Church did not identify itself with the Roman empire or any other state in the West but became an international body, the Orthodox Church was a state church closely allied with the policies and the administration of the Byzantine empire. In essence, the Church was a department of the state, and the emperor exercised wide control over all spiritual affairs. In many respects, the patriarch of Constantinople had a position analogous to that of the pope in Rome—but with a significant difference. The patriarch was appointed by the emperor, who selected him from a list of candidates drawn up by a council of bishops.

Such blending of authority over Church and state in the office of emperor has been termed "Caesaropapism" (combining the functions of Caesar and pope). We shall see that this political philosophy was later adopted by the Russian tsars.

The iconoclastic controversy. Relations between the eastern and western branches of the Church, continually undermined by what Constantinople viewed as Rome's excessive claims of primacy, declined sharply in the eighth century as a result of the religious policies of Leo III. Although Leo had no use for Islam as a religion, he agreed with its contention that the employment of images and pictures in worship led eventually to idolatry. Therefore, he issued his famous edict of 725 forbidding image worship as superstitious and irreverent. It was decreed that religious statues be removed and that all church walls be whitewashed to cover pictures of the saints.

In Constantinople, rioting in protest against his iconoclasm, or image breaking, broke out immediately. The demonstration was put down by troops, who killed some of the rioters. When the patriarch of Constantinople objected to the imperial decree, he was replaced by another man more agreeable to the emperor's will. Riots continued to break out in Greece and Italy, and the pope at Rome called a council of bishops who read out of the Church all those who had accepted the program of iconoclasm. Relations between the Church of Rome and the Byzantine Church were strained for a hundred years.

Final separation of the churches. In 843 the controversy over iconoclasm was settled by the restoration of images in the eastern Church, but other sources of friction made permanent reunion impossible. Exactly when the final breaking point was reached is difficult for scholars to determine. The traditional date of 1054, when a papal legate quarreled violently with the patriarch of Constantinople, has been challenged in favor of the later date of 1204, when crusaders completely alienated the Orthodox people and clergy. One modern scholar has written: "[The Byzantines] . . . could not forget the

Fourth Crusade . . . and henceforward . . . in the hearts of the East Christians the schism was complete, irremediable and final."[4]

The important fact is that for centuries the papacy in the West and the Orthodox Church in the East steadily grew apart until they came to maintain distinctly separate existences, each viewing the other with suspicion and intolerance. This hostility was the main reason why in the fifteenth century the West stood idly by and saw the Byzantine empire—long the buffer for western Europe against the Turk—smashed by the forces of Islam.

Missionary activity of the Church. To the Orthodox Church goes the credit for converting many Slavic tribes to Christianity. About 863, two missionaries, Cyril and Methodius, set out from Constantinople to bring the gospel to the pagan Slavs. They took with them translations of the Bible and the divine service written in an alphabet of modified Greek characters adapted to the Slavic languages. (The Cyrillic alphabet, used even now in many Slavic countries, is named after Cyril, though he may not have invented it.)

The work begun by the two brothers triumphed among Slavs to the east and south, so that ultimately the Orthodox Church extended throughout eastern Europe. From the Orthodox Church sprang the Russian Church and an accompanying extension of Byzantine culture into Russia. Today, five hundred years after the final collapse of the Byzantine empire, the Orthodox Church still retains a great deal of importance and vitality in eastern Europe.

BYZANTINE SOCIETY

AND CULTURE

Byzantine prosperity. During the early Middle Ages, Constantinople was called "The City" with good reason. Visitors were fascinated by the vitality of the citizens of this metropolis, the pomp and pageantry of the court and Church, the scholarly and artistic endeavors, and the wealth which far surpassed anything to be found in the West.

A gold bezant

The complex urban civilization of the Byzantine world rested upon a foundation of strong and well-diversified economic activities. For centuries a stable agricultural system provided city and country folk with adequate food—at prices fixed by the state; and a varied industrial and commercial economy successfully supported large urban populations. The decline of population which had contributed to the collapse of the Roman empire in the West did not occur in the East.

Geography was another major factor responsible for Byzantine prosperity. Constantinople stood at the crossroads of Europe and Asia, and its site ensured its being a port of transit for a great marine trading basin extending from the Adriatic to southern Russia. This greater center of trade exported two main types of goods: the products manufactured within the empire itself and the products which came from the East and were reëxported from the empire's trading centers.

Prosperous trade supported and was in turn stimulated by the existence of a sound gold currency. In the West, a decline in commerce had been attended by a shrinkage in the supply and use of money. The Byzantine empire, on the other hand, retained a currency of such excellence that its gold bezant was a medium of international exchange.

Besides being the greatest trading center of the early Middle Ages, Constantinople had industries which supplied Christendom with many products. The city specialized in luxury goods and was famous for its textiles. Until the time of Justinian, all of the raw silk necessary for manufacturing fabrics had been imported from China; but after silkworms had been smuggled out of China about 550

A.D., silk production began to flourish within the empire. Silken fabrics embroidered with gold and silver thread and fashioned into costly vestments for church services or court attire were eagerly sought all over Europe. The silk industry was a profitable state monopoly.

At Constantinople, tradesmen and members of the professions were organized into a system of guilds. Although the guilds were given monopolistic rights, governmental regulations controlled such matters as wages, prices, and working conditions. Employers were not allowed to exploit their laborers ruthlessly, but the craftsmen in turn were bound to their guilds. The state designated when and where goods manufactured by the guilds were to be sold, and official decrees also fixed prices for purchasing raw materials. Thus the government kept a close watch over industry and working conditions.

Constantinople, city of contrasts. Centering, of course, in Constantinople, social life in the empire was colorful. The city itself had three centers: the imperial palace, the Church of Hagia Sophia, and the giant Hippodrome.

Court ceremonial—borrowed largely from the glittering Persian rituals—was arranged to impress foreigners and Byzantines alike with the emperor's exalted nature and his remoteness from mundane matters. An envoy to the palace was escorted through great lines of uniformed guards and dignitaries into a resplendent hall. At the appointed time a curtain was raised, disclosing the emperor clad in his imperial robes and seated on his throne. Golden lions flanked the throne and golden birds perched in pomegranate trees. While the envoy prostrated himself, the throne was raised aloft, symbolizing the unapproachability of the heir of the Caesars. During the audience, the emperor remained motionless, silent, and aloof, while a court official spoke in his name.

Seating eighty thousand spectators, the Hippodrome was the scene of hotly disputed chariot races. Like the chariot drivers of ancient Rome, each charioteer wore one of four colors; rival factions were named after the colors, the most prominent of these groups being the Greens and the Blues. These antagonistic factions differed on religious and political as well as sporting grounds and were the source of the dangerous Nike rebellion which nearly overthrew Justinian in 532.

Byzantine art: a unique synthesis. While Byzantine art was basically Roman in character during the period of the first Constantine and his immediate successors, the new capital's eastern location could not fail to bring additional artistic forces into play. The Hellenistic tradition had persisted in Alexandria and Antioch, and Constantinople was exposed also to influences from Persia. By the sixth century these elements were fused with the strong Christian spirit that had motivated New Rome since its inception; the result of this fusion was a new style of a uniquely Byzantine character.

Byzantine painting, for example, displays a synthesis of different—and even conflicting—cultural influences. The Greek tradition provided a graceful and idealistic approach; however, art historians point out that while classical elements remained in Byzantine art, Oriental influences, with their emphasis upon a formalized style, vivid coloring, and ornamentation, eventually predominated.

Church architecture. The first great age of Byzantine art was associated with Justinian, who commissioned the magnificent Church of Hagia Sophia (Holy Wisdom), as well as many other churches and secular buildings. When Hagia Sophia—henceforth to be the spiritual capital of Orthodox Christendom—was dedicated in 537, Justinian is said to have exclaimed:

Glory be to God, who hath deemed me worthy to complete so great a work. I have outdone thee, O Solomon![5]

No other Byzantine church equaled Hagia Sophia in size or magnificence. The crowning glory of Hagia Sophia is its dome. With forty windows piercing its base, it seems to the viewer far below to float in the air. The dome also represents a major advance in architecture. The Romans had been able to construct a huge dome in the Pantheon, but

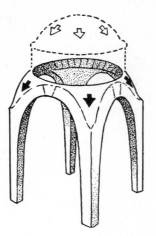

Among the notable art forms and techniques developed by the Byzantines is that of mosaics. At the right above is a mosaic of the Virgin and Child from a Byzantine church. Panel paintings, such as the one at the right of Christ, done in the fourteenth century, were also used to decorate places of worship. An outstanding Byzantine architectural achievement is shown above (top). Although the Romans had attempted to construct a square building topped with a dome, the Byzantines were the first to succeed. They used PENDENTIVES—triangular, curved segments placed at each corner of the substructure and joined to form a continuous circle. The diameter of the circle determined the diameter of the dome. Moreover, the weight of the dome was received by the pendentives, which distributed the thrust to the corners of the four supporting piers. Pendentives were used in constructing the huge dome of the magnificent Hagia Sophia in Constantinople (above). The slender minarets were added by the Turks when they captured the city and converted the church into a mosque.

it had been erected upon massive circular walls which limited the shape of the building. The method used to support the dome of Hagia Sophia utilized pendentives and permitted flexibility in the design of domed structures (see diagram, p. 167.)

Over the centuries many other splendid structures employed the pendentive principle. A favorite design, with symbolic appeal, was a church in the shape of a cross, surmounted by a dome. A still further development was a five-domed church, which was cross-shaped, with a central dome at the crossing and a smaller dome on each of the four arms. The most famous existing example of this design is St. Mark's in Venice.

Vivid mosaics and decorative arts. The second outstanding period of Byzantine art followed the iconoclastic controversy and lasted from the middle of the ninth century to the sack of Constantinople in 1204. This age was notable for producing the finest examples of Byzantine decorative art.

In the decoration of churches, Byzantine artists made extensive use of mosaics—brilliant decorations formed by cementing small pieces of multicolored glass or stone into patterns. The rich colors of the mosaics increased the splendor of the church interiors and heightened the emotional appeal of the rituals. They also served as useful teaching devices by presenting the viewer with scenes from the Bible and with images of Christ, the Virgin, and the saints.

With their penchant for vivid colors and elaborate detail, Byzantine artists excelled in a number of decorative arts, such as carving in ivory, the illumination of manuscripts, and the decoration of book covers, chests, thrones, and altars. Constantinople was renowned for its cloisonné technique, by which enamel was inlaid between thin gold bands which formed the design.

Wall and panel painting. The third important period of Byzantine artistic activity took place during the fourteenth and fifteenth centuries, when Byzantium was no longer wealthy. This revival expressed itself in brilliant paintings on walls and panels, a form of art necessitated in some measure by the need to find cheaper substitutes for expensive mosaics and enamels.

Like mosaics, wall paintings were employed to decorate churches. Icons—panel paintings of sacred personages—were used in daily worship. As in mosaics, the subject matter of Byzantine painting was treated symbolically rather than realistically; ". . . like much of the art of today, which is not easy to understand at first glance, its significance lies below the surface; it is an art of the spirit rather than of the flesh, and must be approached from that point of view."[6]

Byzantine painting during this period wielded an influence far beyond the confines of the now diminutive empire. In contemporary Italy, such a master as Giotto was directly affected by Byzantine iconography. Similarly, Russian painting at this time reflected many Byzantine developments.

The preservation of classical learning. The official adoption of the Greek language in the formative centuries of the empire proved a stimulus to the preservation of classical works in philosophy, literature, and science. The scholars who perpetuated the Greek tradition were not clerics, as in the West, but members of the civil service.

Scholarship in the empire flourished, particularly between the ninth and twelfth centuries. Most of the scholars were concerned with recovering and classifying Hellenic and Hellenistic learning. An impressive amount of the Greek contributions to mathematics, biology, medicine, and the physical sciences was recovered by Byzantine scholars, and from them in turn the Muslim scientists derived much of their knowledge. The preservation of Greek philosophy and literature kept alive the interest in classical culture which was to make possible the flowering of scholarship centuries later in Italy—a movement known as humanism. Byzantine scholarship suffered, however, from being imitative rather than creative. Although scholars performed useful work in compiling the Greek classics, their own contributions tended to be only a rehash of classical works.

Another great achievement of Byzantine scholarship was the codification of Roman civil law. In 528 Justinian convoked a commission of scholars to gather and classify the vast, disorganized, and often contradictory mass of law which had accumulated during centuries of Roman government. The result was a great legal work popularly known as the Justinian Code and formally titled the *Corpus Juris Civilis*. It organized the imperial law of the last four centuries into the *Codex* and included as well the *Digest* of the writings of republican and imperial jurists, and the *Institutes*, a commentary on the principles underlying the laws. Appended to the main text were the *Novels*, the laws promulgated by Justinian and written in Greek, now the dominant language of the empire. By this codification, Rome's priceless legal heritage was preserved and passed on to posterity.

EARLY RUSSIA

The Slavs. While the fortunes of the Byzantine empire had been ebbing and flowing, its culture had exercised a continuous and substantial influence upon the development of Russia in its formative centuries. Let us now take up the account of the origin and rise of the Russian state.

The ancestors of the Russians were the Slavic tribes, whose original home was the wooded marshland along the modern border of Poland and Russia. In the period of German migration, the Slavs had an opportunity to expand until they filled much of eastern and central Europe. Three main groups existed at this time. The Western Slavs lived in an area extending from the Vistula River valley west to the Elbe, where they had contacts with the Germans. The Southern Slavs had infiltrated the eastern empire and constituted a large part of the Balkan population. The Eastern Slavs, from whom the Russians are descended, held land from the Carpathian Mountains to the Don River.

Founding of a Russian state. About the time when their Viking brethren from Denmark and Norway were plundering and conquering western Europe (see p. 146), Swedish Norsemen, the Varangians, began to

RUSSIA 1000

venture down the waterways from the eastern Baltic to the Black and Caspian seas. The Slavic settlements along the rivers often hired the fierce Varangians as protectors. According to the earliest of the *Russian Chronicles*, written by a monk in Kiev around the beginning of the twelfth century, one such warrior, the half-legendary Rurik, was employed by the people of Novgorod. In about 862 he became the prince of the city, and his brothers and companions established themselves in other cities, one being Kiev. On Rurik's death he was succeeded in Novgorod by a Varangian relative named Oleg, who seized Kiev in about 882 and thus extended his authority into southern Russia.

The founding of the first Russian state dates back to the joining of these key centers along the river route. The Norsemen soon merged with the Slavs but the name *Rus* (meaning "seafarers"), by which the Slavs knew the Norse, persisted and came to be identified with the state which the Norse had founded and which was centered upon Kiev.

Kievan Russia was less a political entity than a commercial entity, a coordinated group of princely states with a common interest in maintaining trade along the river routes. Russian histories tell of military expeditions against Constantinople itself soon after 900, partly as typical Viking raids for plunder and partly to extort treaties which opened up a profitable Russian-Byzantine trade.

Christianity in Kievan Russia. The official conversion of the Russians to Christianity took place about 989 under Prince Vladimir of Kiev. According to the *Russian Chronicles,* Vladimir shopped around before making his choice of religions. He rejected Islam because of its injunctions against the use of strong drink; Judaism, because the God of

St. Basil's Cathedral in Moscow displays the Russian onion dome.

the Jews could not be considered very powerful since He had allowed them to be ejected from their Holy Land; and Roman Christianity, because the pope entertained dangerous ideas about his superiority to all secular rulers. There remained the Orthodox Church of the Byzantines, which was presented to Vladimir's subjects as his choice.

From the outset the Kievan princes followed the Byzantine example and kept the Church dependent on them, even for its revenues, so that the Russian Church and state were always closely linked. The Russians also copied the Byzantines in Church ritual, theology, and such practices as monasticism.

Yaroslav the Wise, a scholarly monarch. Kiev reached its greatest splendor in the reign of Yaroslav the Wise (1019-1054 A.D.). This scholarly monarch translated Greek works, beautified Kiev, and built churches, one of which was the cathedral he called Hagia Sophia. By defeating the barbaric Asiatic horsemen who were constantly threatening his southeastern borders, he ensured the security of his provinces. By negotiating marriage alliances for his children with the royal families of Poland, Norway, Hungary, and France, he managed to secure a place in the politics of Europe.

Following the death of Yaroslav, however, the princes of the various cities fought among themselves for possession of the Kievan state; and to these disruptions was added the devastation of the nomads who roamed uncomfortably close to the capital. Thus it was that long before Kiev had lost its apparent primacy among the Russian city-states, it had lost much of its power, wealth, and population.

When the Mongols destroyed Kiev in 1240 (see p. 262), there was no longer any doubt that the supremacy of Kievan Russia was ended. In Chapter 11, we shall trace the rise of the new center of Russian power—the grand duchy of Moscow.

Byzantine aspects of Kievan culture. During the Kievan period, the importance of commercial contacts between Constantinople and Kiev and the growth of the power of the Orthodox Church were the chief factors responsible for the strength of Byzantine influences in Russia. Architecture, for example, came within the province of the Church. The cathedral which was built in Kiev by order of Prince Vladimir in the tenth century was designed by architects from Constantinople and was Byzantine in plan and style. In time architects developed a distinctly Russian style, including the characteristic "onion dome," which is merely a fanciful "helmet" covering the dome (see illustration). The decoration of churches also followed Byzantine models. In fact, the earliest mosaics, as well as mural and icon paintings, appear to have been the work of Byzantine artists who were brought to Russia.

The adaptation of the Greek alphabet to the Slavic tongue and the translation of Church liturgy into Slavic stimulated the growth of Russian literature. Although at first Kievan literature consisted for the most part of translations of Byzantine works or of original material based on Byzantine models, in time a literature of the Russian people emerged, as epics of their fierce struggles to resist barbaric nomads from the steppes appeared. But the use of Slavic in the Church also had less beneficial effects for Russian cultural development. Many churchmen remained ignorant of Latin and sometimes lacked even a good knowledge of Greek; hence the majority of the learned had no direct contact with the literature in those two languages. Much of the cultural isolationism of the Russians in the past has been ascribed to this factor.

Broadly speaking, by the eleventh century and particularly during the reign of Yaroslav the Wise, Kievan Russia could boast of a culture which was probably not inferior to its contemporary cultures in western Europe. For this achievement Kiev was primarily obligated to the Byzantine empire, which at the time enjoyed the highest cultural level in Christendom. In the wake of the fall of Constantinople in 1453, the Russians would appropriate even more of the Byzantine tradition, dubbing the new Russian center of Moscow the "Third Rome."

MUHAMMAD AND HIS FAITH

Pre-Islamic Arabia. In our examination of the history of the Byzantine empire, we had occasion to mark the swift rise of a rival religious culture, Islam, imbued with expansionist aims. In 1453, adherents of that faith succeeded in conquering the eastern citadel of Christianity. We shall now trace the genesis and meteoric expansion of Islam, together with the splendid civilization which it fostered.

The term *Islam*, meaning "submission to God," is derived from the Muslim holy book, the Koran. The followers of Muhammad, the founder of the faith, are known as Muslims. (This faith is often referred to as Muhammadanism, but Muslims frown on this term, which implies the worship and deification of Muhammad.)

The story begins in Arabia, a quadrangular peninsula with an area of about 1,200,000 square miles. Much of it is desert, and rainfall is scarce in the remainder of the peninsula. Thus, vegetation is scant and very little land is suitable for agriculture.

Although the racial origin of the Arabs is obscure, it is known that they belong to the Semitic language group. During the first millennium B.C., some Arab kingdoms developed a high state of civilization, but the fourth to sixth centuries A.D. witnessed a decline of settled life in Arabia and an increase in nomadism. Throughout much of Arabia, and particularly of the interior, nomadism was the only way of life. Driven from place to place by the barren environment in their search for pastures to sustain their flocks, the nomads, or Bedouins, led a precarious existence. The Bedouins lived according to a tribal pattern; at the head of the tribe was the sheik, elected and advised by the heads of the related families comprising the tribe. Aside from their flocks, the Bedouins relied for survival on booty from raids on settlements and on passing caravans.

The Bedouins worshiped a large number of gods and spirits, many of whom were believed to inhabit trees, wells, and stones. Each tribe had its own god, symbolized gen-

Still living in many ways like their nomad ancestors, present-day Bedouins of the Arabian Desert have pitched their tent in the ruins of an abandoned town.

erally by a sacred stone which served as an altar where communal sacrifices were offered.

Although the Bedouins led a primitive and largely isolated existence, they were influenced by contacts with other groups. By the latter half of the sixth century, Christian and Jewish groups were found throughout the Arabian peninsula. Their religious convictions and moral principles had a strong effect on the natives, and their monotheistic beliefs were later incorporated into Islamic doctrine.

Mecca. Many of the more advanced Arab cities were in Hejaz, among them Mecca, destined to be the key city in the Islamic religion. Fifty miles inland from the port of Jiddah, Mecca was favorably located for trade. Its merchants carried on business with southern Arabia, with Ethiopia across the Red Sea, and with the Byzantine and Persian empires. Mecca was controlled by the Quraysh, an Arabian tribe whose members formed trading companies that cooperated in dispatching large caravans north and south. The government of the city was in the hands of a syndicate of Quraysh merchants.

These same businessmen were also concerned with protecting a source of income derived from the annual pilgrimage of tribes to a famous religious sanctuary at Mecca. Known as the Kaaba (cube), this square temple contained the sacred Black Stone, by legend brought to Abraham and his son Ishmael by Gabriel. According to tradition, the stone was originally white but had been blackened by the sins of those touching it. The Kaaba housed the images of some 360 local deities and fetishes.

Muhammad, founder of Islam. Into this environment at Mecca was born a man destined to transform completely the religious, political, and social organization of his people. Muhammad (570-632) came from a family belonging to the Quraysh tribe. Left an orphan in early life, he was brought up by an uncle and later engaged in the caravan trade. Little is known of Muhammad's early years, but his first biographer relates that he was influenced by a monotheist named Zayd, who may have been either a Jewish or a Christian convert.

When he was about twenty years old, Muhammad entered the service of a wealthy widow, Khadija, whose caravans traded with Syria. In his twenty-fifth year he married his employer, who was some fifteen years his senior. Despite the difference in their ages, the marriage was a happy one; and they had four daughters who survived to maturity.

Muhammad was apparently in the habit of retiring to a small cave in the nearby foothills to meditate and pray. On one occasion he is supposed to have heard a dreadful voice saying: "O Muhammad! Thou art Allah's messenger." This was the first of a series of revelations and visions.

Muhammad did not arrive at his conclusions overnight, nor did he regard himself from the outset as a prophet. On the contrary, he was at first afraid that he had been possessed by a spirit and even contemplated suicide. During his periods of doubt and anguish, Muhammad was comforted by Khadija, and finally he became certain that he was a divinely appointed prophet of Allah, "*The* God." He became convinced that this deity was the only God and that Allah had commanded him to preach of men's duty to their Creator and repentance of their sins, for the judgment of God was at hand. These doctrines obviously resemble the Christian and Jewish monotheistic concepts which were becoming increasingly prevalent in the peninsula.

At first Muhammad had little success in attracting followers. His first converts were his wife, his cousin Ali, and Abu Bakr, a leading merchant of the Quraysh tribe who was highly respected for his integrity. Abu Bakr remained the constant companion of the Prophet during his persecution and exile and, as we shall see, was to become the first caliph of Islam. Most of the other early converts were slaves and members of oppressed groups. Opposition came from the leading citizens, who either ridiculed Muhammad's doctrine of resurrection (pre-Islamic Arabs had only the vaguest notions on the subject of existence after death) or feared that his monotheistic teaching might harm the city's lucrative pilgrimage trade to the Kaaba.

The Hegira and triumphal return to Mecca. The first encouraging development occurred when a group of pilgrims from Medina, a prosperous town supported by agriculture and handicrafts, accepted the Prophet's teachings. Meanwhile, the increased persecution of the Muslims in Mecca encouraged the Prophet to migrate with his band to Medina.

Carried out in secrecy, this migration took place in 622 and is known as the Hegira (from the word *hijra*, which means "the breaking of former ties"). The Hegira was such a turning point in Muhammad's career that the year in which it occurred is counted as the first in the Muslim calendar. In Mecca, Muhammad's own kinsmen had persecuted him, but in Medina he was acknowledged as a leader with divine authority in spiritual and temporal matters. He commanded the Muslims to turn toward Mecca when praying. This practice served to recognize the city as the spiritual capital of Islam and at the same time emphasized the need for its conquest from the pagan trading oligarchy that governed it.

It was in the year 630 that Muhammad marched on Mecca with an army. His

In this Muslim miniature, a Christian monk bows before the young Muhammad, in whom he recognizes the signs of a prophet. An angel anoints the head of the child.

old enemies were forced to surrender to the Prophet, who acted with magnanimity toward them. His first act was to cast out of the Kaaba its multitude of idols and fetishes; but the temple itself, together with the Black Stone, was preserved as the supreme center of Islam, the "Mecca" to which each devout Muslim should make a pilgrimage during his lifetime.

With Mecca and Medina both under his control, Muhammad became the undisputed master of the Hejaz. Tribe after tribe of Bedouins throughout Arabia offered him their loyalty. In the two remaining years of his life, he consolidated Islam's position. Upon his death in 632, the Prophet left behind a faith which had united Arabia and which was to astound the world with its militant expansion.

The Koran, the Muslim bible. Muslims believe that the Koran contains the actual word of God as revealed to Muhammad. The Prophet's revelations occurred over a period of more than twenty years, and before his death many of the messages had been written down. Abu Bakr, Muhammad's successor, ordered the compilation of all these materials, including the passages which had only been committed to memory by his followers. Twenty years after the death of the Prophet, an authorized version was prepared, which has remained the official text to the present day.

Because the Koran must never be used in translation for worship, the spread of Islam created a great deal of linguistic unity, which still remains today. Arabic supplanted many local languages as the language of daily use, and that part of the Muslim world which stretches from Morocco to Iraq is still Arabic-speaking. Furthermore, this book of the seventh century remains the last word on Muslim theology, law, and social institutions and is therefore still the most important textbook in Muslim universities. As a result of all the uses of the Koran, the followers of Islam have little difficulty reading Arabic even though their speech may differ widely.

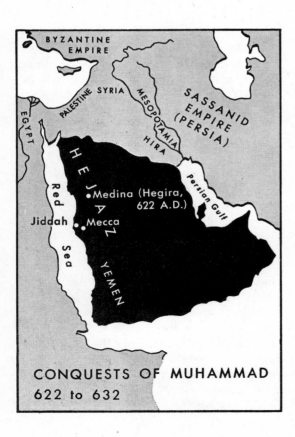

CONQUESTS OF MUHAMMAD 622 to 632

Theology of the Islamic faith. Within the Koran one may find the central tenet of Islam—monotheism. There is only one God, Allah; this is proclaimed five times daily from the minaret of the mosque as the faithful are called to prayer:

God is most great. I testify that there is no God but Allah. I testify that Muhammad is God's Apostle. Come to prayer, come to security. God is most great.[7]

While Allah is the only God, many other supernatural figures are acknowledged, as in Christianity. Islamic angels, for example, are similar to those described in the Bible. In addition, there exist jinn, who are spirits midway between angels and men. Some jinn are good, while others are evil; the most powerful of the latter group is Satan. Islam recognizes the existence of prophets who preceded Muhammad. The Koran mentions twenty-eight, of whom four are Arabian, eighteen are found in the Old Testament, three in the New Testament (including Jesus), and one of the remainder has been identified as Alexander the Great. But to Muslims the greatest prophet is, of course, Muhammad. No superhuman status or miraculous power is ascribed to him, but he was chosen to proclaim God's message of salvation.

Geography played an important role in the Prophet's concepts of heaven and hell, even as it did in Hebrew literature. Both heaven and hell are described in terms that incite an immediate reaction in people who live in the desert. Those who have submitted to Allah's rule—the charitable, humble, and forgiving, and those who have fought for His faith—shall dwell in a Garden of Paradise, reposing in the cool shade, eating delectable foods, attended by "fair ones with wide, lovely eyes like unto hidden pearls," and hearing no vain speech or recrimination, but only "Peace! Peace!" This veritable oasis is far different from the agonies of a desert hell, which awaits the unbelievers, the covetous, and the erring. Cast into hell with its "scorching wind and shadow of black smoke," they will drink of boiling water.

Above is shown a page from a Koran of about the ninth century.

Islam imposes on all Muslims four obligations, known as the "Pillars of Faith"—prayer, almsgiving, fasting, and a pilgrimage to Mecca. Prayers are said five times a day, and each occasion involves a number of recitations. They are to be repeated either alone or, preferably, in a mosque. The Muslim is required to give alms, a practice regarded as expressing piety and contributing to one's salvation. During the month of Ramadan, the ninth month of the lunar year, Muslims fast. Since food and drink are prohibited between sunrise and sunset, this is a very strenuous observance, although sick persons and travelers are exempted providing they fast for an equal length of time later. The second chapter of the Koran commands Muslims to make a pilgrimage to Mecca, where they go through traditional ceremonies, such as kissing the Black Stone in the Kaaba. Each Muslim should make the pilgrimage to Mecca at least once during his lifetime if he has the means.

The Koran also provides the Muslims with a body of ethical teachings. Idolatry, infanticide, usury, gambling, the drinking of wine, and the eating of pork are all prohibited. Similarly, Islam encouraged the humane treatment of slaves and regulated such matters as the guardianship of orphans and divorce. Muslim men were allowed four wives (and an unspecified number of concubines), but if he could not treat them all with equal kindness and impartiality, a husband should retain but one.

Pervading Islam was the principle of equality. There was no priesthood. There were leaders of worship in the mosques and there were the ulema, who interpreted the sacred law. But they were all laymen. Muhammad stressed the essential unity of all true believers and thus prevented dangerous class distinctions and ensured equality of all Muslims before the law. In this way Islam was spared the priestly tyranny which arose in India, where the Brahmans considered themselves superior to all other classes in the rigid caste system.

Islamic law. In addition to being a religion, Islam offered a system of government, law, and society. The Islamic community was an excellent example of a theocratic state, one in which religious rulers hold all power, political and religious.

Especially in the period of expansion after the Prophet's death, the Islamic state required detailed rules covering a variety of new situations. The code that was developed was based partly on pre-Islamic legal customs. Before Muhammad's time, each tribe had its own Sunna, or body of custom, which served as a law code. By compiling the recollections of the Prophet's companions, his followers prepared a Sunna based on his life and teachings.

Using the Koran and the Sunna as their sources, Islamic jurists developed a body of canon law which regulated all aspects of Muslim life. The law was held to be as divinely inspired as the sources on which it was based. Its development and interpretation were in the hands of doctors of law, the ulema. Agreement among the ulema set the seal of orthodoxy on questions of text and doctrine, with the result that Islamic law became progressively authoritarian and static.

THE SPREAD OF ISLAM

Expansion under the first four caliphs. Muhammad left no son to succeed him; and, even if he had, neither his unique position as the Prophet nor Arab custom permitted any such automatic succession. Acting swiftly, Muhammad's associates selected the Prophet's most trusted friend and adviser, Abu Bakr, as his official successor, the caliph. The title of caliph (from *khalīfa*, meaning "deputy") carried with it the controlling power in both religious and political affairs.

During the reigns of the first four caliphs (632-661), Islam spread rapidly. It was one of the beliefs of the Prophet that any Muslim dying in battle for the faith was assured entrance into paradise. This sanctification of warfare bred into the Arabs, already a fierce fighting people, a fanatical courage that proved well-nigh irresistible. Moreover, the prospect of rich and fertile territory, and plunder in addition, proved a strong incen-

tive to a people who had been eking out a bare existence from the desert.

The Islamic cause was also aided by political upheavals occurring outside of Arabia. The Muslim triumphs in the Near East can be partly accounted for by the long series of wars between the Byzantine and Persian empires. The Byzantine victory in 628 had left both sides exhausted and open to conquest. In the year 636, Arab forces conquered Syria. The Muslims then wrested Iraq from the Persians and, within ten years after Muhammad's death, they conquered Persia itself. The greater part of Egypt, where Byzantine rule was harsh and corrupt, fell with little resistance in 640 and the rest shortly afterwards. Thus, by the end of the reigns of the first four caliphs, Islam had vastly increased its territory (see map).

The imposition of a poll tax on all non-Muslims fostered a great number of conversions to Islam. Contrary to exaggerated accounts in the West of the forceful infliction of Islam upon conquered peoples, the Jews and Christians outside of Arabia enjoyed Muslim protection. This was because they belonged to tolerated religions.

Islam is among the most tolerant religions in minimizing and demolishing the obstacles of race and nationality. The new religion converted and embraced peoples of many colors and cultures. In Africa, for example, ". . . Islam recognized no race discrimination. The converted Negro was readily admitted into Islamic society, and to him the Moslem was a brother not only in name but throughout the sphere of social life."[8] This equalitarian feature of Islam certainly aided its expansion.

Arab domination under the Umayyads. The reigns of the first four caliphs were followed by the Umayyad dynasty (661-750) which established its capital at Damascus in Syria. Henceforth, the caliphate was to be a hereditary office, not, as previously, a position filled by election.

Pushing through Asia Minor, the Umayyad armies attacked Constantinople in 670, but the Byzantine capital withstood all Muslim sieges until 1453. In the West, the Muslims

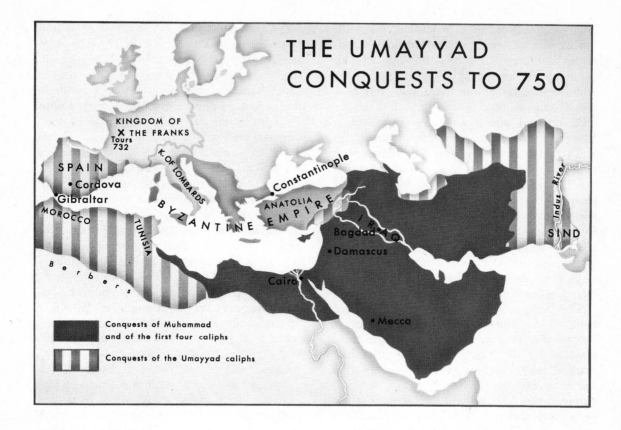

THE UMAYYAD CONQUESTS TO 750

KINGDOM OF THE FRANKS
X Tours 732
SPAIN
• Cordova
Gibraltar
MOROCCO
TUNISIA
Berbers
K. OF LOMBARDS
B Y Z A N T I N E   E M P I R E
Constantinople
ANATOLIA
Cairo •
Bagdad
• Damascus
• Mecca
Indus River
SIND

Conquests of Muhammad and of the first four caliphs

Conquests of the Umayyad caliphs

enjoyed greater success. They subdued the whole of North Africa, even though the Berbers, a desert tribal people, resisted stubbornly. The next logical jump was across the Strait of Gibraltar into the weak kingdom of the Visigoths in Spain. The governor of Muslim North Africa sent his general, Tarik, and an army across the strait into Spain in 711. Seven years later the weak kingdom of the Visigoths had completely crumbled. The Muslims swept across what is now south and central France and were only turned back by Charles Martel in the decisive battle of Tours in 732 (see p. 142), exactly a century after Muhammad's death. Meanwhile, the Muslims had been expanding eastward into central Asia. By the eighth century, they could claim for the caliph lands as far off as Turkestan and the Indus valley.

The source of Umayyad power was the Arabs, who formed a privileged ruling aristocracy greatly outnumbered by the non-Arab converts to Islam—Egyptians, Syrians,

Persians, Berbers, and many others. Many of these possessed cultures much more advanced than that of the Arabs themselves, and the economic and cultural life of the Arab empire depended on these people. But not being Arab by birth, they were treated as second-class Muslims. Though they fought in Islamic armies, they received less pay and booty than the Arabs and at the same time were subjected to high taxation. Resentment grew among the non-Arabic Muslims and eventually helped bring about the downfall of the Arab kingdom of the Umayyads.

The Abbasids, high tide of Islam. In 750 the Umayyad dynasty was crushed by rebels, and a new dynasty, the Abbasid, ruled Islam from 750 to 1258. The city of Bagdad was built in 762 as the capital of the new dynasty.

The fall of the Umayyad dynasty marked the end of Arab predominance; henceforth, Persians and other non-Arabs were to create a new political order. The Arab aristocracy had led the forces of conquest during the great period of Islamic expansion, but with the advent of more stable political conditions, the important status thus far held by the Arab soldier was given to the merchant and administrator. In the social and economic spheres, too, the change of dynasties reflected and also encouraged new forces. The traditional Arabic patterns of nomadism and tribal war were giving way before economic prosperity and the growth of town life. The Abbasid caliph who built Bagdad forecast that it would become the "most flourishing city in the world"; and indeed it rivaled Constantinople for that honor, situated as it was on the trade routes linking West and East. At the same time, such peacetime pursuits as the arts and scholarship were encouraged.

The location of a new capital at Bagdad resulted in a shift of Islam's center of gravity to the province of Iraq, whose soil, watered by the Tigris and Euphrates, had cradled man's earliest civilizations. In this ancient center of many brilliant and despotic empires, the Abbasid caliphs set themselves up as Oriental potentates, surrounded by a lavish court life that would have distressed the simple-living Prophet. Bagdad was sufficiently removed from Mediterranean contacts to evolve a Near Eastern culture in which Persian influence predominated.

The Abbasid dynasty marked the high tide of Islamic power and civilization. In the early years of the caliphate, the empire was greater in size than the domain of the Roman Caesars; it was the product of an expansion during which the Muslims had "assimilated to their creed, speech, and even physical type, more aliens than any stock before or since, not excepting the Hellenic, the Roman, the Anglo-Saxon or the Russian."[9] The assimilation process was not limited to peoples; this Islamic state drew on the entire known world for customs, culture, and inventions.

Trade, industry, and agriculture. From the eighth to the twelfth centuries, the Muslim world enjoyed a prosperity such as post-Roman Europe did not experience until early modern times. In contact with three continents, the Muslims could shuttle goods back and forth from China to western Europe and from Russia to central Africa. Another reason for Islam's economic well-being lay in the tolerance of its rulers, who allowed non-Muslim merchants and craftsmen to reside in their territories and carry on commerce with their home countries. The presence of such important urban centers as Bagdad, Cairo, and Cordova stimulated trade and industry throughout the Muslim world.

The cosmopolitan nature of Bagdad was evident in its bazaars, which contained goods from all over the known world. There were spices, minerals, and dyes from India; gems and fabrics from central Asia; honey and wax from Scandinavia and Russia; and ivory and gold dust from Africa. One bazaar in the city specialized in goods from China, including silks, musk, and porcelain.

The textile industries of the Muslims, which were particularly prosperous, produced silk, cotton, muslin, and linen goods. Metal, leather, enamel, pottery, and luxury goods similar to Byzantine manufactures were also produced in abundance. As in the Byzantine empire, the workers in the large Islamic cities were organized into guilds and crafts supervised by the government.

Under the rule of the Abbasids, agriculture was both extensive and profitable. Vast irrigation projects in Iraq resulted in an increase of cultivable land which yielded large crops of fruits and cereals. Wheat came from the Nile valley, cotton from North Africa, olives and wine from Spain, wool from eastern Asia Minor, and horses from Persia. As in medieval Europe, the land was worked by serfs and by free peasants, whose lot was for the most part miserable. Large landowners used slaves on their estates.

The opulent reign of Harun-al-Rashid. Just as the Abbasid was the most brilliant of Muslim dynasties, so the rule of Harun-al-Rashid (786-809) was the most spectacular of the Abbasid reigns. He was the contemporary of the great Charlemagne, and there can be no doubt that Harun was the more powerful ruler of the two and the symbol of the more highly advanced culture. The two monarchs were on most friendly terms, even though their friendship arose out of self-interest. Charlemagne wanted Harun as a possible ally against the Byzantine emperors. Harun, on the other hand, saw Charlemagne as an ally against the Umayyad rulers of the Spanish caliphate, who had broken away from Abbasid rule. Numerous embassies and presents were exchanged between Charlemagne and Harun. The Muslim sent the Christian rich fabrics, aromatics, and even an elephant. An intricate clock from Bagdad seems to have been looked upon as a miracle in the primitive West.

Relations between the Abbasid caliphate and the Byzantine empire were never very cordial, and conflicts often broke out along the constantly shifting border that separated Christian and Muslim territories. Harun-al-Rashid once replied to a communiqué from the Byzantine emperor in the following terms:

In the name of God, the Merciful, the Compassionate. From Haroun, Commander of the Faithful, to Nicephorus, the dog of the Greeks. I have read your letter, you son of a she-infidel, and you shall see the answer before you hear it.[10]

Whereupon the irate caliph sent forth expeditions to ravage Asia Minor.

In the days of Harun-al-Rashid, Bagdad's wealth and splendor equaled that of Constantinople, and its chief glory was the royal palace. With its annexes for eunuchs, officials, and a harem, the caliph's residence occupied a third of Bagdad. Gorgeously furnished with the richest rugs, cushions, and curtains which the Orient could create, the caliph's audience chamber must have been breath-taking in its effect.

Disintegration of the Abbasid empire. Despite the unprecedented prosperity of the far-flung Islamic world, the political unity of Islam began to disappear almost immediately after the Arab empire reached its full extent. With the accession of the Abbasid dynasty, the caliphs in the Near East, at the center of Islam, began to lose their hold on the Muslims in the West. The first sign of political disintegration appeared as early as 756 when a member of the deposed Umayyad

According to tradition, this little ivory elephant is a piece from a chess set given to Charlemagne by Harun-al-Rashid.

family set up his own dynasty at Cordova in Spain. In the tenth century its ruler assumed the title of caliph, as did also the governor of Egypt.

In the latter part of the tenth century, Turkish nomads, called Seljuks, migrated from Asia into the Abbasid lands, where they accepted Islam. The Seljuks then began to seize land from the Abbasids and, after annexing most of Persia, gained control of Bagdad in 1055 and absorbed Iraq. Later, the Seljuks conquered Syria and Palestine, and then proceeded to annex part of Asia Minor from the Byzantines (see map, p. 161). It was the great advance by the Seljuks that prompted the First Crusade in 1095. The Seljuks permitted the Abbasids to retain nominal rule, but a new and terrible enemy was to change everything.

Early in the thirteenth century, the redoubtable Genghis Khan succeeded in uniting the nomads of Mongolia; he and his successors conquered eastern and central Asia (see Chapters 11 and 15) and swept into Persia and Iraq. In 1258, a grandson of Genghis Khan captured Bagdad and slew the caliph.

Not only had the Abbasid dynasty come to an end, but so did much of the vast irrigation system that had supported the land since ancient times. Iraq fell into a state of collapse from which it did not recover until our own century. The Mongol ruling class was eventually absorbed into the Muslim culture of Persia and Iraq, and the dynasty established by the Mongols survived for only a short time.

The Ottoman Turks. Following the Mongol destruction of the Seljuk sultanate in Asia Minor, this region had attracted other Turks from central Asia, among them the Ottomans. The newcomers adopted Islam fanatically and began to gain control of the former Abbasid dominions. The Ottomans also pitted themselves against the Byzantines, and in 1453 Constantinople fell to them. The formidable Turks pressed on into southeastern Europe, driving as far as Vienna, where they were turned back with difficulty in 1529 and again in 1683. Meanwhile, they had conquered Iraq, much of Arabia, and all of North Africa as far west as Morocco. This Turkish empire lived on into the twentieth century, though with progressive weakness.

We have now reviewed the evolution of Islam in western Asia and in the lands around the Mediterranean. We shall see that Islam expanded later into other parts of the world. In Chapter 15 we shall trace its expansion as a great missionary faith and as a civilization into south and southeast Asia.

ISLAMIC CULTURE

Borrowing the best from other cultures. The high attainment of the Muslims in the intellectual and artistic fields cannot be attributed to the Arabs, who as a group remained unprogressive, but rather to those peoples within the far-flung empire who had embraced Islam. Although the Muslims made some important contributions in science, the brilliance of Muslim learning was due not to native genius but to Islam's ability to synthesize the best in other cultures. Under Harun-al-Rashid and his successors, Indian and Persian works were preserved and the works of Aristotle, Euclid, Ptolemy, and Archimedes were translated into Arabic. This knowledge formed the basis of Muslim learning, which in turn was later transmitted to scholars in western Europe.

Advances in medicine. The two hundred years between 900 and 1100 can be called the golden age of Muslim learning. This period was particularly significant for advances made in medicine.

The first and perhaps greatest Muslim physician was Al-Razi (*c.* 860-925), better known to the West as Rhazes. One of the great doctors of all time, Rhazes wrote more than two hundred works, of which one of the most famous is *On Smallpox and Measles*, the first clear description of the symptoms and treatment of these diseases. His most monumental writing was the *Comprehensive Book*, a huge medical encyclopedia. In it he cites for each disease all Greek, Syrian, Arabian, Persian, and Indian authorities and includes his own personal experiences and opinions as well. Translations of the encyclopedia were later used by many European physicians.

The most familiar name in Muslim medicine is that of Avicenna (980-1037), great physicist, philosopher, and physician. Into his vast *Canon of Medicine* he packed all the legacy of Greek knowledge together with Arabic medical learning. In the twelfth century the *Canon* was translated into Latin and was so much in demand that it was issued sixteen times in the last half of the fifteenth century and more than twenty times in the sixteenth. It is still read and used in the Orient today.

Medical theory was augmented by practical application. Hospitals operating throughout the empire were divided into sections for men and women. The qualifications of physicians and druggists were subject to inspection. In spite of a ban against the study of anatomy and a few other limitations imposed on the Muslims by their religious scruples, their medical men were in many ways superior to their European contemporaries.

Progress in other sciences. Although other branches of science did not keep pace with medicine, they did make progress. Physics continued along the paths of inquiry laid down by Hellenistic thinkers, but, meanwhile, Muslim scientists arose who were no mere copyists. Alhazen (965-1039?) developed optics to a remarkable degree and challenged the view of Ptolemy and Euclid that the eye sends out visual rays to its object. The chief source of all medieval western writers on optics, he interested himself in optic reflections and illusions and examined the refraction of light rays through air and water.

Significant advances were made in the field of mathematics. In this field the Muslims were particularly indebted to the Greeks and Hindus, from whom they learned most of their arithmetic, geometry, and algebra. From the Greeks came the geometry of Euclid and the fundamentals of trigonometry which Ptolemy had worked out. From the Hindus came the nine signs now known as the Arabic numerals. It may be that the Muslims invented the all-important zero, although some scholars would assign this honor to the Indians. Two names deserve special mention when we speak of Muslim algebra: Al-Khwarizmi (d. about 840) wrote treatises on astronomy, the Hindu method of calculation, algebra, and arithmetic, while the poet Omar Khayyám (d. 1123?) advanced even beyond Al-Khwarizmi in equations. Where Al-Khwarizmi dealt only with quadratics, Omar Khayyám devoted much of his treatise on algebra to cubic equations.

The flourishing trade and widespread administration of the Muslim lands stimulated the science of geography. Greek treatises were translated, and tables of latitudes and longitudes were set up. Although the first world maps made by the Muslims showed Mecca in the center (medieval Christians honored Jerusalem similarly), all in all, during the Middle Ages, the geographical knowledge of the Muslims was far superior to that of any people in Christendom.

Islamic literature and scholarship. In the western world, a knowledge of Islamic literature tends to be limited to *A Thousand and*

The experiments of Muslim chemists produced many new drugs and chemicals. Here a Muslim druggist, having set up his laboratory outdoors, distills medicinal wine for use as cough medicine.

One Nights and to the hedonistic poetry of Omar Khayyám. The former is a collection of tales, often erotic and told with a wealth of local color. The fame of the latter is partly due to the musical (though not overaccurate) translation of the *Rubáiyát* by Edward FitzGerald. Here are some stanzas from the poem which will indicate its beautiful imagery and gentle pessimism:

We are no other than a moving row
Of Magic Shadow-shapes that come and go
   Round with the Sun-illumined Lantern held
In Midnight by the Master of the Show;

But helpless Pieces of the Game He plays
Upon this Checker-board of Nights and Days;
   Hither and thither moves, and checks, and slays,
And one by one back in the Closet lays. . . .

The Moving Finger writes; and, having writ,
Moves on: nor all your Piety nor Wit
   Shall lure it back to cancel half a Line,
Nor all your Tears wash out a Word of it.

And that inverted Bowl they call the Sky,
Whereunder crawling coop'd we live and die,
   Lift not your hands to *It* for help—for It
As impotently moves as you or I.[11]

The lavish use of imagery and rhythmical phrasing characterizes much of Islamic prose.

As the first important prose work in Islamic literature, the Koran set the stylistic pattern for Muslim writers even down to modern times. The holy book was designed particularly to be recited aloud; anyone who has listened to the chanting of the Koran can testify to its cadence, melody, and power.

Philosophy, a favorite Muslim subject, developed as a result of contacts with other cultures. Thus Muslim philosophy is essentially Greek in origin and structure, though it also contains some Indian elements. Avicenna, the physician with many talents, wrote commentaries on Aristotle as well as some on Muslim philosophers. These studies were translated into Latin and had a far-reaching effect on European thought. Like the medieval Christian philosophers (see Chapter 10), Muslim thinkers were largely concerned with applying Aristotelian principles to religious problems as a means of bolstering orthodox creeds, and we find many prominent philosophers attempting to reconcile reason with faith. For example, Averroës (c. 1126-1198) attempted to harmonize faith and reason for Islam, a project which St. Thomas Aquinas undertook for Christianity in the next century.

Islamic historiography found its finest expression in the work of ibn-Khaldun (1332-1406), who has been judged "the first writer to treat history as the proper object of a special science."[12] Despite his busy life in public affairs among rulers and statesmen, he found time to write a large general history, dealing particularly with the history of the Arabs in Spain and Africa. The book maintains that history should analyze man's social development, which ibn-Khaldun held to be the result of the interaction of society and physical environment. He defined the historian's function as follows:

Know that the true purpose of history is to make us acquainted with human society, *i.e.*, with the civilization of the world, and with its natural phenomena, such as savage life, the softening of manners, attachment to the family and the tribe, the various kinds of superiority which one people gains over another, the kingdoms and diverse dynasties which arise in this way, the different trades and occupations to which men devote themselves in order to earn their livelihood, the sciences and arts; in fine, all the manifold conditions which naturally occur in the development of civilization.[13]

Whereas Christian historians of the Middle Ages believed in a static concept of events, ibn-Khaldun conceived of history as an evolutionary process, in which societies and institutions change continually.

Art and architecture. As might be expected, religious attitudes played an important part in Muslim art. Because the Prophet inveighed strongly against idols and their worship, there was a prejudice against pictorial representation of human and animal figures. In general, the effect of this prejudice was to encourage the development of stylized and geometrical design.

Like Muslim learning, Muslim art borrowed from many sources. Islamic artists and craftsmen copied Byzantine, Persian, and Chinese models and eventually integrated what they had learned into a distinctive and original style.

The Muslims excelled in two fields—architecture and the decorative arts. That Islamic architecture can boast of many large and imposing structures is not surprising, because it drew much of its inspiration from the Byzantines and Persians, who were monumental builders. In time an original style of building evolved; the great mosques embody such typical features as domes, arcades, and minarets, the slender towers from which the faithful are summoned to prayer. The horseshoe arch is another graceful and familiar feature of Muslim architecture.

On the walls and ceilings of their buildings, the Muslims gave full reign to their love of ornamentation and beauty of detail. This quality is shown to advantage in the Alhambra palace at Granada (see Color Plate 9), the walls of which are carved into intricate and beautiful patterns. The Spanish interpretation of the Muslim tradition was particularly delicate and elegant. Other outstanding examples of Islamic architecture are to be found in India; one such building is the Taj Mahal, which is based largely on Persian motifs.

Being restricted in their subject matter, Muslim craftsmen conceived beautiful patterns from flowers and geometric figures. Even the graceful script made a delicate ornamentation on walls and the sides of urns. Tiles and mosaics were employed effectively to produce the lavish and conventionalized patterns. Muslim decorative skill also found expression in such fields as carpet and rug weaving, brass work, and the making of steel products inlaid with precious metals.

SUMMARY

We have examined two rival but equally fascinating civilizations: the first, a citadel of classical and Christian culture; the second, a dynamic Islam, conqueror alike of kingdoms and of the spiritual allegiance of populations stretching from Gibraltar to Java. With the conquest of Constantinople in 1453, this second civilization overwhelmed its rival.

When Constantine chose the site for New Rome, he picked a location that was geographically excellent from the point of view of protection and also of trade. Constantinople's tradition as the eastern capital of the Roman empire encouraged Justinian to attempt to recover the western territory which had been under Roman rule; but these efforts failed, and in the long run Byzantium had to fight continually against invasions that diminished its empire on all sides. In 1453 the Ottoman Turks conquered "The City," and the empire of a thousand years was destroyed.

For a millennium the empire had acted as a buffer state, repulsing attacks while the weak, divided West grew in strength. And, while learning was all but lost in medieval western Europe, the Byzantine world remained the custodian of classical knowledge and ideals until a resurgent West was able to assimilate its classical heritage.

Constantinople did much more than all this. Roman, Greek, and Oriental elements were fused into a distinct and original culture; Slavic peoples were converted to Christianity; and the benefits of civilization were brought to Russia and neighboring lands.

The Norsemen who founded a Russian state by joining Kiev and Novgorod also set up trade with Constantinople which continued for centuries. Through this medium, culture and religion were imported into Russia from the eastern empire. While Constantinople itself fell, its heritage was in many ways maintained in the new Slavic state spreading across the vast Russian plain.

Into a desert area populated by nomadic Bedouins and a few scattered groups of townsmen, was born Muhammad (570-632), the founder of the Islamic religion. Soon after Muhammad's death, his monotheistic teachings were compiled in the Koran, the Muslim bible.

During the reigns of the first four caliphs and the century of the Umayyad dynasty (661-750), great strides were made in annexing new territories and peoples. But the Umayyad dynasty was based on a ruling hierarchy of Arabs, and the resentment of the non-Arabs produced a revolution which set the Abbasid dynasty (750-1258) on a new throne in Bagdad.

During the early Abbasid period, Islam reached the high point of its geographical expansion and cultural achievements, and a ribbon of Muslim peoples extended from Spain across three continents to the Far East. Unparalleled prosperity evolved from a combination of successful trade, industry, and agriculture. But the Muslims were not able to maintain an integrated empire; and despite a religious unity, which still exists, politically the empire broke up into smaller Muslim states.

The Muslims were especially gifted in science, literature, and philosophy. But we should not forget that Muslim intellectual life was in good part the product of a genius for synthesizing varying cultures rather than creating original contributions. The Muslim's great diffusion of Greek and Arabic knowledge was a tremendous factor in the revival of classical learning and the coming of the Renaissance in Europe.

Why, one may ask, has Islamic civilization in modern times failed to retain its cultural supremacy? One reason was the influx of semibarbarous peoples into Islamic lands during the Middle Ages. Another was the stagnation resulting from a too rigid interpretation of the Koran. Still another was the corrupt and despotic rule of such Muslim dynasties as the Ottomans in Turkey, who destroyed all progressive movements.

But a new day is at hand for modern Islam. The Muslims have amply proved that they have the intellectual and administrative gifts to make themselves a great people, and the rejuvenation of Turkey after the First World War under the able guidance of the late Mustafa Kemal Atatürk has indicated a possible road for the modern followers of Muhammad the Prophet. In addition to the Turks, other Muslim people have been on the march in recent times. The Arab peoples of North Africa and the Near East—Tunisians, Moroccans, Egyptians, Iraqis, and Syrians—not to mention other Muslim peoples such as the Iranians, Pakistanis, and Indonesians, have experienced a remarkable and dynamic awakening. This Muslim revival constitutes one of the major themes of the twentieth-century world.

SUGGESTIONS FOR READING

N. H. Baynes, *The Byzantine Empire,* Oxford, 1949; C. Diehl, *History of the Byzantine Empire,* Hafner, 1945. Two excellent short accounts of Byzantine history. The most readable of the detailed histories of Byzantium is A. A. Vasiliev, *History of the Byzantine Empire, 324-1453,* Univ. of Wis., 1952; the most up-to-date interpretive study is G. Ostrogorsky, *History of the Byzantine State,* Rutgers, 1957. See also Vols. II and IV of *The Cambridge Medieval History.* J. B. Bury, *The History of the Later Roman Empire, From the Death of Theodosius I to the Death of Justinian,** 2 vols., Dover, is a major work of historical scholarship, unequaled for the period covered.

S. Runciman, *Byzantine Civilization,** Meridian. Recommended as the best-written and most interesting survey of all aspects of Byzantine civilization. Also valuable but more detailed is the collection of essays edited by N. H. Baynes and H. S. B. Moss, *Byzantium, An Introduction to East Roman Civilization,** Oxford. There is an excellent chapter on Byzantine civilization, with a valuable bibliography, in F. B. Artz, *The Mind of the Middle Ages, A.D. 200-1500: An Historical Survey,* 3rd ed., Knopf, 1958.

C. Diehl, *Byzantine Portraits,* Knopf, 1927. Biographical sketches of exceptional literary merit by a distinguished scholar; particularly vivid is the account of the empress Theodora. P. N. Ure, *Justinian and His Age,** Penguin, describes in detail Justinian's work in reviving the glories of Rome.

R. M. French, *The Eastern Orthodox Church,* Hutchinson Univ. Library, 1951. Recommended as a short, lucid introduction. Another useful introduction to the Orthodox Church, its evolution and ideology, is B. J. Kidd, *The Churches of Eastern Christendom, From A.D. 451 to the Present Time,* Morehouse, 1927. More specialized and detailed is J. M. Hussey, *Church and Learning in the Byzantine Empire, 867-1185,* Oxford, 1937. S. Runciman, *The Eastern Schism,* Oxford (Clarendon Press), 1955, disentangles the history of the schism between eastern and western Christianity from the legends that have surrounded it.

D. Talbot Rice, *Byzantine Art,* Oxford (Clarendon Press), 1935. A good brief treatment of all aspects of Byzantine art. For

*Indicates an inexpensive paperbound edition.

superb reproductions of Byzantine mosaics in color, without which they cannot be fully appreciated, see A. Grabar, *Byzantine Painting,* Skira, 1953. T. G. Jackson, *Byzantine and Romanesque Architecture,* 2 vols., Macmillan, 1933, is the standard authority on the architecture of the early Middle Ages.

F. Nowak, *Medieval Slavdom and the Rise of Russia,* Holt (Berkshire Studies), 1930. A short, lucid introduction. Early Russia is treated authoritatively and in detail by G. Vernadsky and M. Karpovich in the first two volumes of the multivolumed history of Russia being published by the Yale Univ. Press: *Ancient Russia,* 1943, and *Kievan Russia,* 1948.

P. K. Hitti, *The Arabs: A Short History,** Gateway. An abridgment of the leading scholarly general history of the Arabs. Another highly recommended introduction is B. Lewis, *The Arabs in History,** Torchbooks.

T. Andrae, *Mohammed: The Man and His Faith,* Barnes and Noble, 1956; and D. S. Margoliouth, *Mohammed and the Rise of Islam,* Putnam, 1927. Two good studies of the Prophet and his work. For an interpretation and translation of the Koran, see M. M. Pickthall, *The Meaning of the Glorious Koran,** Mentor. H. A. R. Gibb, *Mohammedanism: An Historical Survey,** Mentor, traces the rise of Islamic teachings and clarifies the various sects of Islam. See also A. Guillaume, *Islam,** Penguin.

S. Lane-Pool, *The Story of the Moors in Spain,* Unwin, 1896; and R. P. Dozy, *Spanish Islam,* Chatto and Windus, 1913. Interesting popular accounts.

D. L. E. O'Leary, *Arabic Thought and Its Place in History,* Dutton, 1939; and, by the same author, *How Greek Science Passed to the Arabs,* Humanities Press, 1957. Two good popular books on the subject. There is an excellent chapter on Islamic civilization, with a full bibliography, in F. B. Artz, *The Mind of the Middle Ages,* cited above. R. A. Nicholson, *A Literary History of the Arabs,* Cambridge Univ., 1930, traces the growth of Arab thought and culture through its literature.

P. Wittek, *The Rise of the Ottoman Empire,* The Royal Asiatic Society, 1938. A good introduction; originally presented as a lecture. H. A. Gibbons, *The Foundation of the Ottoman Empire,* Century, 1916, covers the period from 1300 to 1403.

CHAPTER 8

The West Takes the Offensive

THE CRUSADES AND THE RISE OF TRADE, TOWNS, AND A NEW SOCIETY: 1050-1300

Introduction. Some periods in history seem haunted by disaster and decline. In the centuries following the collapse of Charlemagne's empire, most Europeans undoubtedly felt that the future held little promise and that good times belonged to the past. And they had sound reasons for their pessimism, for the Continent had become a crazy quilt of antagonistic feudal states. No longer was there an effective central government to maintain peace and enforce laws over large territories, and with political fragmentation had come economic relapse. Trade was at a low ebb; industry was stagnant; and the economy was predominantly rural. It was a time when hopes were dim.

In this chapter, we shall trace the emergence of a new Europe—a Europe which in the eleventh century burst the shackles of the "Dark Ages."

With the ejection of the Muslims from Sicily and the successful challenge to Muslim control of the Mediterranean, Christian Europe went on the offensive. In northern Spain, a few bands of Christians sparked a long, heroic struggle against the Muslims in a movement known as the *Reconquista*, meaning "reconquest"; but the most dramatic manifestation of Europe's new dynamism was the crusades. Spurred on by religious fervor, love of adventure, and, in some cases, selfish hopes of personal gain, the crusaders set out to drive the Muslims from the Holy Land and free Jerusalem from the infidel. These expansive movements led in turn to the recovery of international trade and the rise of flourishing new towns. New markets stimulated the growth of industry and crafts; and everyday business transactions were made more efficient by the development of banking and the use of money, which superseded the old exchange by barter. All these factors sounded the death knell for the manorial system.

Above all, the forces transforming the western world led to the growth of a new class in society—townsmen, the bourgeoisie or middle class. The status of a member of the middle class was based not on ancestry or the ownership of large estates, as was the case with the feudal aristocrat, but on possession of goods and money. At first the bourgeoisie were barely tolerated by the ruling nobility, but gradually the townsmen gained influence as well as wealth. Hereafter, the middle class exerted a powerful influence on history.

EUROPE AGAINST

THE MUSLIMS

Norman conquests in Italy and Sicily. About the year 1000, southern Italy was a battleground for rival Lombard dukes, the Byzantine empire, and the Muslims. The Lombards ruled several duchies; the eastern empire controlled the "heel and toe" of the peninsula; and across the Strait of Messina the Muslims were secure in Sicily.

Into this cockpit of warfare the Normans came in 1016. One famous house, that of Tancred of Hauteville, had twelve husky sons whose exploits were extraordinary. One blond giant of this family, Robert Guiscard, established his authority over his fellow Normans and by 1071 extinguished the last Byzantine port in southern Italy. Meanwhile, Robert had allied himself with the pope and, in return, the papacy recognized him as ruler of southern Italy and of Sicily, still in Muslim hands. Under the leadership of Robert and his brother Roger, the Normans crossed the Strait of Messina in the face of a large Muslim fleet and gained a footing on Sicily just a few years before William the Conqueror crossed the Channel to invade England. In 1072 Palermo was captured, and twenty years later the entire island of Sicily had fallen to the Normans.

Venice, Genoa, and Pisa battle the Muslims. While the Normans had been ejecting the Muslims from Sicily, similar offensives had been going on elsewhere in the Mediterranean. The rapidly advancing city of Venice had cleared the Adriatic Sea and in 1002 had won a great naval victory over a Muslim fleet. This enhanced Venetian trade in the eastern Mediterranean. Genoa and Pisa also began to fight the Muslims, capturing Corsica and Sardinia. Finally, by about 1100, the Mediterranean was again open to Christian commerce.

Muslim civilization in Spain. Although the offensive of the West had cleared the Muslims from the waters of the Mediterranean, Muslim power remained in Spain. We will recall that with the fall of Rome in the fifth century, Visigothic tribes had settled in Spain; but they in turn had fallen to the Muslim invasion (see p. 141). Muslim Spain was ruled from Damascus until 756, when it became an independent Muslim state under the Umayyads.

From their capital in Cordova, the Umayyad rulers (756-1031) inaugurated a brilliant era. The Caliphate of Cordova, as Muslim Spain was then called, made many economic and cultural advances. Water power was harnessed to drive mills, new crops such as rice and sugar were introduced, and grain cultivation flourished. Important products included wine, olive oil, leather goods, weapons, glass, and tapestries.

Cordova itself far outshone contemporary European cities and attained a pinnacle of luxury and beauty. In a sense the capital was the intellectual center of the western world. Scholars from Christian Europe came to Muslim Spain to study, and through them much of the learning of the Arabs passed to France and Italy.

Despite its accomplishments in the economic and intellectual fields, Muslim Spain was politically weak and disunited. Spain had been conquered by a medley of Arabs, Syrians, Berbers, and Egyptians. The invaders themselves were outnumbered by the native population. The Caliphate reached the height of its power in the tenth century (912-1002), but thereafter began to decline. The caliphs after about 1000 were a mediocre lot, unable to withstand the pressures of their chief officials. In 1031 the Umayyads were overthrown, and the Caliphate of Cordova was replaced by twenty-three separate Muslim kingdoms.

Early Christian victories in the *Reconquista*. During the period of Muslim dominance, the following Christian states survived in the north of Spain: the province of Barcelona in the east, peopled mainly by the Catalans; in the west, Leon; and in between, Navarre, inhabited mainly by the Basques. These Christian states slowly gathered strength and expanded south through the hills, Leon leading the way. Within this newly conquered territory, many castles were built, and thus it gained its name: Castile. In the mid-tenth century, Castile became strong enough to throw off the rule of the king of Leon and to develop into an independent Christian kingdom.

The disintegration of the Caliphate of Cordova into small Muslim states after 1031 opened the way for further Christian advances: Castile captured a large part of what was to become Portugal; the southern border of Castile was pushed from the Douro to the Tagus River; and the kings of Toledo and Seville accepted the overlordship of the ruler of Castile. For nearly five hundred years more, this reconquest, the *Reconquista,* was to continue (see Chapter 9). Militant expansion in the name of Christianity was to color the formative years of the two modern nations—Spain and Portugal—in the Iberian peninsula.

THE CRUSADES:

"GOD WILLS IT!"

The call to a crusade. The most dramatic expression of Europe on the offensive was the crusades. For hundreds of years, peaceful pilgrims had been traveling from Europe to the Holy Land. Until the eleventh century,

Above is shown the interior of the Great Mosque at Cordova, built during the Muslim occupation of Spain.

Christian pilgrims had met little trouble in the Holy Land; the Muslim governors had been enlightened rulers who were willing to permit the Christians to visit their shrines.

In the early eleventh century, however, Christian pilgrims began to be persecuted, and when the Seljuk Turks, new and fanatical converts to Islam, came sweeping and plundering into the Near East, the situation became especially aggravated. The Seljuks seized Jerusalem from their fellow Muslims and then swept north into Asia Minor. Byzantine forces desperately tried to bar the invader, but at the battle of Manzikert (1071) the eastern emperor was killed

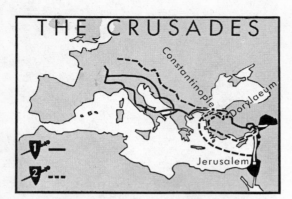

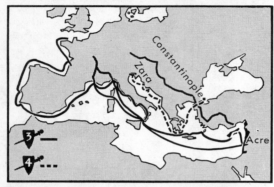

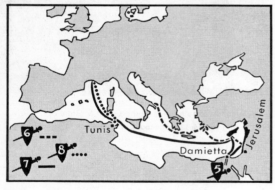

First Crusade to rescue both the Byzantine empire and the Holy Land. Preaching at the Council of Clermont in that year, he exhorted Christians to take up the cross and strive for a cause that promised not merely spiritual rewards but material gain as well, when Christians should possess the Holy Land that "flowed with milk and honey." At the end of his impassioned oration the crowd shouted, "God wills it"—the expression which the crusaders later used in battle.

The primary impetus behind the crusades was undoubtedly religious; they constituted in effect a holy war, and following Pope Urban's appeal, there was a real and spontaneous outpouring of religious enthusiasm. The word *crusade* itself is derived from "taking the cross," after the example of Christ. On the way to the Holy Land, the crusader wore the cross on his breast. The devout Christian believed that if he took the cross and fulfilled his vow, he would enjoy indulgence from purgatorial sufferings for his past sins. The papacy, moreover, hoped that the religious enthusiasm following in the wake of the crusades would strengthen its own position. Furthermore, the Church was eagerly promoting the Peace and Truce of God (see p. 151) in an effort to mitigate the evils of feudal warfare; and the pope saw in the crusades an outlet for the restless, pugnacious nobles. Their warring energies could be channeled for the glory of God.

Some crusaders were motivated by worldly considerations. When a crusader put the red cross on his tunic, he became a privileged person. Through the influence of the Church, he was exempt from taxes, and his debts were temporarily canceled; the Church assumed responsibility for his property and dependents while he was away from home. Also, some nobles saw a chance to seize valuable land in Syria, and merchants in the Italian city-states recognized a demand for Italian ships to carry the crusaders and their supplies to the Holy Land. Thus, the crusades did clearly offer an opportunity for material as well as spiritual profit.

First Crusade gains a foothold in Jerusalem. From the end of the eleventh century

and his army scattered. Constantinople itself was threatened, and frantic appeals were sent to Europe and to the pope in particular for aid. Tales of alleged Turkish mistreatment of Christian pilgrims were circulated throughout Europe, and though there is much evidence that these atrocity stories were propaganda, men's minds became inflamed.

In 1095 Pope Urban II answered the pleas of the Byzantine emperor, Alexius Comnenus, and of the eastern Christians by calling the to the end of the thirteenth, there were eight distinct crusades, as well as various small expeditions which from time to time attempted to wrest the Holy Land from the infidel Saracens.

The First Crusade, led principally by princes and nobles from Normandy, Toulouse, parts of Germany, and southern Italy, proceeded overland to Constantinople. Having expected the help of European mercenaries against the Seljuks, Alexius Comnenus was taken aback when the crusaders arrived in Constantinople. He hastily directed the crusading zeal against the Turks, who were forced back in Asia Minor. The First Crusade was the most successful of the eight; with not more than 3000 knights and 12,000 infantry, it broke the back of Turkish resistance. Against terrible odds it won great victories at Dorylaeum and Antioch, and its crusaders fought with incredible valor. Above all, it captured the Holy City—Jerusalem. Unfortunately, with this religious exaltation went fanaticism and intolerance, as this contemporary account of the Christian entrance into Jerusalem shows:

But now that our men had possession of the walls and towers, wonderful sights were to be seen. Some of our men . . . cut off the heads of their enemies; others shot them with arrows, so that they fell from the towers; others tortured them longer by casting them into the flames. Piles of heads, hands, and feet were to be seen in the streets of the city. It was necessary to pick one's way over the bodies of men and horses. But these were small matters compared to what happened at the Temple of Solomon [where] . . . men rode in blood up to their knees and bridle reins. Indeed it was a just and splendid judgment of God that this place should be filled with the blood of the unbelievers, since it had suffered so long from their blasphemies.[1]

The First Crusade conquered lands in Syria and Asia Minor and created the feudal Latin kingdom of Jerusalem, which lasted from 1099 to 1187.

When the kingdom of Jerusalem found itself in danger, St. Bernard of Clairvaux organized the Second Crusade in 1147. But this crusade ended after the failure to capture Damascus.

The "Crusade of Kings." The fall of Jerusalem to the Muslims in 1187 and Saladin's efforts to end Christian rule in Syria served to provoke the Third Crusade (1189). The three leading monarchs of Europe—Frederick Barbarossa of Germany, Richard I (the Lion-Hearted) of England, and Philip Augustus of France—set forth on their holy mission. Frederick was drowned; and, after a quarrel with Richard, Philip went home before the hostilities were over. Saladin and Richard remained as the chief protagonists.

This crusade was distinguished by the valor and dignity of Saladin and Richard. Saladin, "the merciful, chivalrous, and upright zealot," exhibited qualities of character duplicated by few of his Christian opponents. His common-sense approach to a settlement was evidenced when he proposed that Richard I should marry his sister and be given Palestine as a wedding present, a proposal which shocked the Europeans.

Richard and Saladin agreed to a three-year truce by which Christians were given control of a small strip of eastern Mediterranean coast, and pilgrims were allowed to visit Jerusalem. The truce scarcely compensated for the cost of such an expensive crusade.

Religious ideal missing from Fourth Crusade. The Fourth Crusade is an example of the degradation of a religious ideal. The few knights who answered Innocent III's call were unable to meet the outrageous shipping charges demanded by the Venetians (see p. 162). The Venetians persuaded them to pay off the sum by capturing the Christian town of Zara on the Adriatic coast, which had long proved troublesome to Venetian trading interests. After Zara had been captured, the merchants of Venice next pressured the crusaders into attacking Constantinople. After conquering and sacking the capital of the eastern empire, the crusaders set up the Latin empire (1204-1261) to rule the area.

Later crusades fail. The thirteenth century saw other crusades. In the ill-fated Children's Crusade in 1212, thousands of youngsters were sold into slavery by Marseilles merchants. The Fifth Crusade captured Damietta in Egypt in 1219, only to lose it

An illustration from a medieval manuscript shows Saladin wresting the cross from King Richard during the Third Crusade.

The dissentious Christian participants in this "Crusade of Kings" proved to be no match for the firmly united, zealous infidels.

and fail altogether. The Sixth Crusade in 1228, organized by Frederick II, differed from previous attempts in that it involved no slaughter, pillage, or robbery. Through Frederick's negotiating skill and tolerance, it gained privileges for Christian pilgrims far superior to any gained previously. The Christians were granted Jerusalem and other shrines in the Holy Land, but this arrangement ended in 1244 with the Muslim conquest of the Holy City. As a result of this loss, Louis IX of France organized the Seventh Crusade, but despite the zeal and devotion of the leader it proved a fiasco from beginning to end. In 1270 Louis attempted another crusade to Tunis but died at Carthage. Then, in swift succession, the feudal states created by the crusaders in the Near East were captured by the Turks, and in 1291, Acre, the last stronghold of the Christians, fell into the hands of the Muslims.

The crusader states. Altogether in the Holy Land, four crusader principalities had been established. Throughout the two centuries of their existence, these states formed a narrow ribbon along the eastern Mediterranean surrounded by a vast Muslim hinterland of hostile Seljuk Turks. (A modern parallel is Israel with its Muslim neighbors.) Into the crusader states the conquerors introduced a complex system of feudalism. The political structure was based upon the "Assizes of Jerusalem," which constituted the most perfect example of feudal law in the Middle Ages.

For two centuries the crusader states constituted a fertile point of cultural contact between the West and East, with little or no effect upon the latter but with important influences upon the European West. In the Holy Land the European nobles who sought a permanent home became Orientalized. Their houses were like Moorish villas, decorated and furnished with divans of brocade, Persian rugs, mosaic floors, and silk hangings. These transplanted men of France or south

Germany became tolerant and easygoing, trading and even hunting with Muslims. Frequently there was bad blood between these domiciled crusaders and the visiting nobles who had merely come for a short stay and a dash against the infidel.

The states were protected by the semi-monastic military orders—the Templars (Knights of the Temple, so called because their first headquarters was on the site of the old temple of Jerusalem) and the Hospitalers (Knights of St. John of Jerusalem, called the Hospitalers because they had originally been formed as a hospital order). Combining monasticism and militarism, these orders had as their aims the protection of all pilgrims and perpetual war against the Muslims. These men of the cross could put five hundred armed knights into the field; and their great castles guarded the roads and passes against Muslim attack.

The crusades evaluated. Even though the crusades failed to achieve permanently their specific objective, they should not be written off as mere adventures. On the contrary, their influence extended over a much wider geographical field than just the Holy Land. Politically the crusades weakened the Byzantine empire and accelerated its fall. Furthermore, by depleting the ranks of the nobles, they strengthened the rising power of the kings and national monarchies in western Europe. Much of the crusading fervor carried over to the fight against the Muslims in Spain and the pagan Slavs in eastern Europe.

The contact with the East widened the scope of the Europeans, ended their isolation, and exposed them to a vastly superior civilization. Although it is easy to exaggerate the economic and social effects of the crusades, they undoubtedly lessened the obstacles to commerce; they also indirectly assisted the growth of great ports and the rise of cities, the emergence of a money economy, and the increased contact between Europe and the unknown interior of Asia. The crusades as a movement were a manifestation of the dynamic vitality and expansive spirit of Europe, evident in many fields by the end of the eleventh century.

THE RISE OF TRADE AND TOWNS

Revitalized trade routes. The new spirit in Europe was manifested not only by the crusades but also by new activity in the field of trade. As we have seen (p. 186), the first area to be opened up was the Mediterranean, which proved to be only a starting point in the reëmergence of trade; soon goods were being carried to the Far East and throughout Europe. Exports from India and China were brought to Italy in ever expanding quantities by the merchants of Venice, Genoa, and Pisa. From there the goods were transported over inland trade routes to the important markets of Europe. The easiest route from the Mediterranean to Flanders was via Marseilles, up the Rhone valley, then north to the Flemish cities.

The second great trade system was that which tied together eastern and northern with western Europe. The raw materials of the Baltic region—tar, fur, hides, and timber—were exchanged for English wool, Flemish cloth, or Oriental luxuries which had come by way of Italy. Closely related to this northern trade system was the Varangian route from the eastern Baltic down the rivers of Russia to Constantinople and the Black Sea.

In the fourteenth century, two more major trade lanes developed within Europe. An all-sea route connected the central Mediterranean with England and northern Europe via the Strait of Gibraltar. The old overland route from northern Italy through the Alpine passes to central Europe was also developed. From Venice and other north Italian cities, trade flowed through such passes as the Brenner to Augsburg, Nuremberg, Leipzig, and Lübeck, sharply reducing the business of the Rhone valley route.

Fairs, centers of European trade. Along the main European trade routes, fairs became meeting places for merchants from Italy and northern Europe. For two centuries these fairs were the most important European market places. The most famous fairs were held in Champagne in northeastern France.

The fair was an important and elaborate event, held either seasonally or annually in specified areas of each European country. Regular laws governing the region were set aside when the fair was held and in their place was substituted a commercial code called the "law merchant." Special courts settled all disputes which arose. In England they were called "pie-powder courts," from the French *pied-poudré,* meaning "dusty foot."

The fair was of great value in that it was a clearing house for both goods and ideas. From all over Europe, men congregated and exchanged information about new methods in industry, agriculture, and transportation. The fairs were largely responsible for the growing use cf bills of exchange, letters of credit, and a money economy. They helped break down the provincialism of the manor and the isolation of the town.

Factors in the rise of towns. The resurgence of trade in Europe was the prime cause of the revitalization of towns. To understand the importance of the revival of town life, we must remember that the urban civilization of the Romans had practically disappeared with the empire. During the early Middle Ages, manufacturing languished, and city life became almost extinct, but from 1000 to 1200 the town became the invaluable agency in the growth of trade, the development of manufacturing, and the nurturing of art and thought. Trade and towns had an interacting effect on each other; the towns arose because of trade, but they also stimulated trade by providing greater markets and by producing goods for the merchants to sell.

In the revival of both commerce and cities, geography played an important role. It determined the location of certain strategic towns and conditioned the type of commercial activities in which the towns engaged. Rivers, which were important in the evolution of ancient civilizations, played an equally important role in the development of medieval towns. They were natural highways on which articles of commerce could be easily transported, and many communities arose to take advantage of a site at the confluence of two important streams. Again, some towns arose where a river might be easily crossed by a ford or bridge, "Ox-ford" or "Cambridge," for example. Locations near a mountain pass or on a good coastal harbor were also desirable. Italian coastal towns were open to rich trade with the Near East and Africa.

Often at a strategic geographic location, a feudal noble had already erected a fortification—a castle, or "burg." Such a stronghold offered the merchants a good stopping place; buildings were erected, and a permanent merchant colony, which was known as the "faubourg," grew up. The population was made up largely of merchants and artisans, who were free of the feudal bonds which still bound the serfs within the burg. The old burg remained the abode of the noble or bishop with his retinue of soldiers and officials. As time went on, the old stronghold failed to grow, but the faubourg rapidly expanded and broke away from restrictions imposed by the burg.

Other factors besides trade and geography contributed to the rise of towns. Perhaps the most striking of the social factors was the growth of population. The number of people in Europe after the fall of Rome is estimated at 30,000,000; by 1300 it had doubled. This rapid increase in population has not been satisfactorily explained. The stabilization of feudal society with its furtherance of public safety and the ending of bloody foreign invasions may have been contributing factors.

Another factor interacting with the growth of towns was the decline of serfdom. Many serfs escaped from the manors and made their way to the towns. After living a year and a day in the town, a serf was considered a freeman. A former serf could completely alter his old position and become a wealthy and influential craftsman or merchant in the town.

Merchant guilds and craft guilds. When the merchants and artisans settled in the towns, they organized themselves into guilds, which were useful not only for business but also for social and political purposes. There were two distinct kinds of guilds: merchant and craft.

The basic purpose of the merchant guild was to ensure monopoly of trade within a given locality. Membership usually included all merchants of a particular town, although merchants from other places were occasionally permitted to join. With a monopoly of the town's import and export trade, the guild could enforce its standards as it willed. All alien merchants were supervised closely and made to pay tolls. Disputes among merchants were settled at the guild court according to its own legal code. The guilds tried to make sure that the customers were not cheated: weights and measures were checked, and a standard quality for goods was insisted upon. To allow only a legitimate profit, a just price was fixed which was considered fair to both the producer and consumer.

When guilds first appeared, there was no adequate central government to protect merchants as they carried on their trading activities throughout the land. As a result the guilds assumed some functions which would otherwise have been governmental. If a merchant was imprisoned in another town, the guild tried to secure his release at its own expense. If a merchant of a London guild refused to pay a debt owed to a merchant of a guild in Bristol, the merchant guild in the latter town would seize the goods of any London merchant coming to Bristol.

The guild functions stretched beyond business and politics into charitable and social activities. If a guildsman fell into poverty, he was aided. Members attended social meetings in the guildhall, and each member was expected to attend the feast and "drink the guild" or be fined.

Increased commerce brought a quickening of industrial life in the towns so that, in the eleventh century especially, the artisans began to organize. Craftsmen in each of the medieval trades—weaving, cobbling, tanning, and so on—joined forces. The result was the craft guild, which differed from the merchant guild in that membership was limited to artisans in one particular craft.

The general aims of the craft guilds were the same as those of the merchant guilds—

A guild master judges the work of a mason and a carpenter

the creation of a monopoly and the enforcement of a set of trade rules. Each guild had a monopoly of a certain article in a particular town, and regulations were enforced to protect the consumer from bad workmanship and inferior materials.

The craft guild also differed from the merchant guild in its recognition of three distinct classes of workers—apprentices, journeymen, and master craftsmen. The relationship between the master and his workmen was very personal. The apprentice was a youth who lived at the master's house and was taught the trade thoroughly. Although he received no wages, all his physical needs were supplied. His apprenticeship lasted from three to twelve years, depending upon individual circumstances and the type of craft. When his schooling was finished, the youth became a journeyman (from the French journée, meaning "day's work"). He was then eligible to receive wages and to be hired by a master for varying periods of service. When about twenty-three, the journeyman sought admission into the guild as a master. To be accepted he had to prove his ability and integrity. In the later Middle Ages, some crafts demanded the making of a "master piece"— for example, a pair of shoes that the master shoemakers would find acceptable in every way.

Unfortunately the master craftsmen in the closing years of the Middle Ages sought to make their rule monopolistic and placed unnecessary restrictions upon the journeymen. Furthermore, it was expensive to set up a shop, and many journeymen could not afford it. Hence the guilds suffered from lack of young blood, and rejected journeymen set up their own organizations outside the jurisdiction of the older guilds. In the fifteenth and sixteenth centuries, the guilds were in the hands of a few wealthy masters who elected the guild officials from their own clique.

Acquiring urban freedom. The guilds played an important role in local government. Both artisans and merchants, even though freemen, were subject to the lord upon whose domain the city stood. The citizens of the towns were not bound to the manor, and they resented the fact that the lord collected taxes as though they were serfs. In particular the tolls and dues imposed on the market rankled with the merchants. Friction arose as the faubourg tried to declare its independence of the old burg. The townsmen demanded the privileges of governing themselves—of making their own laws, administering their own justice, levying their own taxes, and issuing their own coinage. Naturally the lord resented the impertinent upstarts who asked for their own government. But the towns won their independence in various ways.

One way was to become a commune, a self-governing town. The merchant guilds, in particular, forced the lord to agree to a charter which specifically granted the town certain rights to self-government. Often a charter had to be won by a revolt; in other circumstances it had to be purchased, for the feudal lord was always in need of money. By 1200 the Lombard towns, as well as many French and Flemish towns, could boast of communal privileges.

Since the guilds had played such a large part in winning the concessions, they proceeded to run the commune, even though only a small portion of the town's inhabitants belonged to the guilds. Thus the guilds and the local government became closely allied, and a "businessman's government" often excluded from citizenship those who had not helped to procure the charter.

Where the royal authority was strong, we find "privileged" towns. In a charter granted to the town by the monarch, the inhabitants

While earlier harnesses had choked an animal pulling a heavy load, the collars worn by the horses in this illustration place weight on the shoulders rather than on the neck; this invention of the early tenth century gave horses four times the pulling power of the draft animals of former times. Two other inventions of the same century were: the tandem harness, which utilized the strength of several horses; and the horseshoe, which provided better traction and protection for the hoofs. Of these inventions it has been said that they did for the eleventh and twelfth centuries what the steam engine did for the nineteenth.

won extensive financial and legal powers. The town was given management of its own finances and paid its taxes in a lump sum to the king. It was also generally given the right to elect its own officials and organize its own guilds. The king was glad to grant such a charter, for it weakened the power of his nobles and at the same time won him the support of the townsmen.

Founding new towns was still another way in which feudal restrictions were broken down. Shrewd lords and ecclesiastics, who recognized the increasing importance of cities and the impossibility of checking their development, founded carefully planned centers with well-laid-out streets and open squares. As a means of obtaining inhabitants, many inducements were offered in the form of personal privileges and tax limitations. Berlin was such a town.

Technological and industrial advances. The increase in population and the growing urban demand for food stimulated advances in technology. For example, the water-driven mill, which had been invented before the time of Christ, did not become common until the tenth and eleventh centuries; and the windmill, developed in the twelfth century, was a common feature of the European landscape by 1300.

As trading, the towns, and the craft guilds grew, so did industry. It was carried on by artisans working in their own shops rather than in factories. The great product of western Europe was woolen cloth. It was first made in Flanders, where the presence of a special clay, called "fuller's earth," aided in the production of exceptionally fine cloth. England also developed an important cloth industry from the fleece of its native sheep. Other industries that made substantial strides were those producing iron, coal, cotton and linen textiles, and silk.

The use of money, banking, and credit. All the aspects of Europe's expansion—the crusades, the rapid revival of trade, the rise of cities, and the expansion of industry—had far-reaching effects on the financial structure. The first big change came with the reappearance of money as a medium of exchange. The large amount of coin which began to circulate showed that money had been hoarded in the uncertain centuries following the fall of Rome. In the thirteenth century, silver coins were superseded in international trade by gold, especially the florin from Florence and the ducat from Venice.

As the clink of the new coins in the pockets of merchants became a common feature of business life, primitive forms of banking and credit began to appear. The Lombards and Florentines in Italy became the first bankers. The all-important technique of "symbolic transfer" was invented. By this system a man deposited his money in a bank and received in return a receipt, which could later be cashed in any of the offices of the same bank. This method was very useful during the crusades, when the Templars arranged a system whereby crusaders could deposit money in the Paris office and withdraw it from the office in the Holy Land. Thus the crusaders avoided the dangerous practice of carrying large amounts of cash on the long journey from Europe to the Near East. The Templars practically monopolized foreign exchange in the twelfth century.

The banks expanded their services to include lending money and found ways of circumventing the Church's disapproval of usury. If a sum was not repaid promptly, a kind of service charge could be levied. If the money was lent at great risk, it became permissible to charge interest.

The Hanseatic League. Sometimes a group of towns followed the model of the merchant guilds and joined forces to establish their rights and to win special privileges in foreign towns. Probably the most important agent in the development of European commercial and urban life outside Italy and Flanders was a great trade association comprising the northern German cities. In the thirteenth century this Hanseatic League originated among such cities as Cologne, Lübeck, Danzig, and Hamburg; as it grew, other large river towns were included. The League built up a lucrative monopoly on Baltic and North Sea trade. Its wealth came primarily from its control of the Baltic herring fisheries, its corner on Russian trade, and its rich business with England and the Low Countries. Therefore, it established permanent trading stations in such leading European centers as London and Bruges and in strategic locations like Novgorod, key town in the Russian trade. Until the fifteenth century, the Hanseatic League remained the great distributor of goods to northern Europe.

In lieu of strong political power in Germany, the Hanseatic League formed its own organization to cope with political problems. A representative council dealt with trading problems common to all member cities, and a navy safeguarded its commerce from pirates and even waged an occasional war.

THE EMERGENCE OF A NEW SOCIETY

The typical town. The medieval city was not large by modern standards. It has been estimated that Paris by 1450 had grown to a population of 300,000, which made it the largest city in Christian Europe. In 1400, London had merely 40,000 inhabitants. In spite of the relatively small populations, the towns were crowded. The inhabitants of the early towns had built walls around the faubourg, but the city usually outgrew these in a short time.

Since the area within the walls was at a premium, medieval towns were more crowded than the average modern city. Shops were even built on bridges (as on the Ponte Vecchio, which still stands in Florence), and buildings were erected to a height of seven or more stories. The houses projected over the street with each additional story so that it was often possible for persons at the tops of houses opposite one another to touch hands.

The streets below were dark and narrow and almost invariably crooked, although they were often designed to be wide enough "to give passage to a horseman with his lance across his saddle-bows." The streets were full of discordant sounds—drivers yelled at pedestrians to get out of the way of the

horses and oxen; dogs, pigs, and geese added their alarms; merchants bawled out their wares; people of every description jostled past one another; and unoiled signs above inns and shops creaked ominously in the wind, constantly threatening to crash down on the skull of some innocent passer-by.

The bourgeoisie. The triumph of the townsmen in their struggle for greater self-government was significant. It meant that a new class had evolved in Europe, a powerful, independent, and self-assured group, whose interest in trade instead of warfare was to revolutionize all social and economic history. The members of this class were referred to as the burghers or the bourgeoisie.

The bourgeoisie emerged in the twelfth century to challenge the primacy of the landholding nobility. Initially, the haughty lords looked down on the bourgeoisie and sought in every way to block their influence. What the aristocracy failed to realize was that these self-made men would be the controlling group in future years. With the rise of towns and the bourgeoisie went the fall of feudalism, the waning of the Middle Ages, and the advent of modern society.

In the new towns, the old feudal classifications of noble, clergy, and peasant did not apply. A medieval townsman's rank was based on money and goods, rather than birth and land. At the top of the social scale were the great merchant and banking families, the princes of trade, bearing such names as Medici, Fugger, and Coeur. Then came the moderately wealthy merchants and below them the artisans and small shopkeepers. In the lowest slot was the unskilled laborer. His lot was miserable, and his poverty and discontent were destined to influence modern history.

The decline of serfdom. Attracted by the freedom of town life, many serfs simply ran away from their manors and established themselves in a town. As a result the serfs on the manors became unreliable. Often the serfs secured enough money to buy their freedom by selling food surpluses in the towns. Gradually, the lords accepted a money payment from the serfs as a substitute

8 (left) **Italian Romanesque architecture of the eleventh and twelfth centuries.** In the center we see the Cathedral of Pisa; in the foreground, the baptistery; and in the background, the famous "leaning tower." Contrary to legend, the bell tower was not built in this manner but began to lean later as it settled—a process that has now been arrested.

9 (below) **The Alhambra at Granada, Spain** (c. 1380) —the finest surviving example of a Muslim palace. Famous for the lacelike delicacy of its ornamental carvings and the graceful proportions of its architectural elements, the Alhambra remains one of the glories of Islamic architecture. Shown here is the Court of Lions.

10 Stained-glass window from the Cathedral of Le Mans, France (c. 1150). With the development of the Gothic architecture and the pointed arch, solid masonry walls were no longer necessary for structural support. In northern European churches, wall paintings were replaced by stained-glass windows such as this one, which pictures the Virgin Mary and the apostles.

for their old obligations of labor and produce. The final step was for the lord to rent out his lands to free tenants, who cultivated his demesne. Former serfs became satisfied tenants or, on occasion, members of the yeoman class who owned their small farms.

As the manorial services were commuted to money, serfdom progressively decayed in Europe. As early as the eleventh century it had disappeared in Normandy. It had largely died out as an institution in England and France by 1500, although in the latter country, particularly, many of the old and vexatious services were retained. In eastern Europe, feudalism and serfdom persisted until the nineteenth century.

Peasant revolts. The improvement in the status of the serfs did not necessarily mean that life was pleasant and untroubled. The twelfth and thirteenth centuries were almost a boom period; but economic depression, unrest, and tension followed in the period from 1350 to 1450. The Black Death, a terrible plague, struck western Europe in 1347, decimating and demoralizing society. In the towns the mortality rate reached 30 to 40 per cent. The overall figure may have averaged about 20 per cent. Coupled with this blow was the destruction and death caused by the Hundred Years' War between France and England (1337-1453).

One of the symptoms of economic setback was the outbreak of peasant revolts—in England and France in the fourteenth century, in Germany in the sixteenth. One of the best-known peasant rebellions was the Wat Tyler uprising in England in 1381. The decimation of the peasant population after the Black Death caused a rise in the wages of the day laborers. Parliament tried to legislate against this pay raise but succeeded only in incurring the anger of the peasants. This resentment was fanned by the sermons of a priest, John Ball, known as the first English socialist. He railed against the riches of the lords and declared that things would never go well in England until there were no more masters and until all distinctions were leveled. Near London, Ball preached his most famous sermon to a vast mass of rebellious peasants led by Wat Tyler. In his message the priest used as his text the famous lines:

When Adam delved and Eve span,
Who was then the gentleman?[2]

As in the case of other revolts, this uprising was crushed amid a welter of blood and broken promises.

Depression and economic stagnation began to be eased by the end of the fifteenth century. The period for the appearance of strong and efficient monarchies was at hand; and Europe was on the verge of discovering another frontier, the Americas.

SUMMARY

Constructive forces fashioning a new Europe became apparent in the period between 1050 and 1300. The great achievement of the eleventh century was offensive action by the forces of western Europe. The Muslims were ejected from Sicily, Corsica, and Sardinia. They lost naval supremacy in the Mediterranean, and a Christian reconquest was initiated in Spain. Above all, in 1095 a great movement, the crusades, was initiated. While the objective was to push the Muslims out of the Holy Land, the crusades opened new doors for the narrow, ingrown Europeans.

In the twelfth and thirteenth centuries, new forces were generated, creating a transformed Europe. These currents were a revitalized trade, new towns, expansion of industry, and a money economy. A new society began to take shape; the bourgeoisie emerged and serfdom declined. The medieval economic way of life was passing, giving way to new institutions. In the political realm, in spite of feudalism with its many local sovereignties, the tradition of kingship persisted. Ultimately, aided substantially by these new economic forces, the kings were to impose their will on the nobles and become masters of new nations. The beginnings of this movement, which are contemporary with the developments described in this chapter, will be set forth in Chapter 9.

SUGGESTIONS FOR READING

C. H. Haskins, *The Normans in European History*, Houghton Mifflin, 1915. A popular work of absorbing interest; concentrates on the achievements of the Normans in southern Italy and Sicily as well as in France and England, up to the beginning of the thirteenth century.

S. Runciman, *A History of the Crusades*, 3 vols., Cambridge Univ., 1951-1954. The latest complete account; highly recommended for both its literary and historical merit. R. A. Newhall, *The Crusades,** Holt (Berkshire Series), is a brief, lucid introduction to the subject. Authoritative essays by leading scholars are contained in K. M. Setton and M. W. Baldwin, eds., *The First Hundred Years*, Univ. of Penn., 1955, Vol. I of *A History of the Crusades*. D. C. Munro, *The Kingdom of the Crusaders*, Appleton-Century, 1935, is an absorbing account of the crusades as well as of the kingdom of Jerusalem. The character of the early crusading spirit is clearly revealed in the selected source materials edited by A. C. Krey, *The First Crusade: The Accounts of Eye-Witnesses and Participants*, Princeton, 1921.

Harold Lamb, *The Crusades: Iron Men and Saints; The Flame of Islam*, 2 vols. in one, Doubleday, 1945. Combines sufficient historical accuracy with vivid imaginative writing to provide a stirring account of the First Crusade and the struggle thereafter to hold the Holy Land. A historically sound novel touching on the crusades, written by a master of historical fiction, is Zoe Oldenbourg, *The Cornerstone*, Pantheon, 1955.

R. M. Smail, *Crusading Warfare (1097-1193)*, Cambridge Univ., 1956. A well-written study of "feudal society organized for war"; describes the weapons, organization, and tactics of both the Latin and Muslim armies together with the nature and function of the crusaders' castles. English castle architecture is interestingly described and superbly illustrated in W. D. Simpson, *Castles from the Air*, Scribner's, 1949. C. W. C. Oman, *The Art of War in the Middle Ages: A.D. 378-1515,** Cornell, is the standard work on the subject.

H. Pirenne, *Economic and Social History of Medieval Europe,** Harvest. A highly recommended little book; includes facts and interpretations which do much to clarify all aspects of the medieval economic and social revival. Other useful surveys are S. Baldwin, *Business in the Middle Ages,** Holt (Berkshire Series); P. Boissonade, *Life and Work in Medieval Europe*, Knopf, 1927, which also treats Byzantine industry and commerce; and J. W. Thompson, *Economic and Social History of the Middle Ages*, Century, 1928. H. Heaton, *Economic History of Europe*, Harper, 1948, contains an excellent survey of the economy of the Middle Ages.

*Indicates an inexpensive paperbound edition.

J. H. Clapham et al., eds., *Trade and Industry in the Middle Ages*, Cambridge Univ., 1954, Vol. II of *The Cambridge Economic History of Europe from the Decline of the Roman Empire*. The most recent scholarly survey. For discussion of English trade and industry, see the two studies by L. F. Salzman, *English Industries in the Middle Ages*, Oxford, 1923; and *English Trade in the Middle Ages*, Oxford, 1931. Good reading on the careers of early capitalists includes I. Origo, *The Merchant of Prato, Francesco di Marco Datini, 1335-1410*, Knopf, 1957; T. B. Costain, *The Moneyman*, Doubleday, 1951, a popular historical novel on the spectacular rise and fall of the fifteenth-century French capitalist Jacques Coeur; and the last two chapters in E. Power, *Medieval People,** Anchor. See also M. Beard, *The History of the Business Man*, Macmillan, 1938.

D. M. Stenton, *English Society in the Early Middle Ages (1066-1307),** Penguin, Vol. III of *The Pelican History of England*. A brief, comprehensive, and readable account of the life of the rich and the poor, the economy, church affairs, and government. Equally readable and informative is the preceding volume in the same series, D. Whitelock, *The Beginnings of English Society.** A well-illustrated popular account is M. and C. H. B. Quennell, *Everyday Life in Anglo-Saxon, Viking, and Norman Times*, Batsford, 1952. G. G. Coulton, *Medieval Panorama,** Meridian, contains numerous short essays of uneven interest on life in England from the eleventh to the sixteenth centuries.

A. Luchaire, *Social France at the Time of Philip Augustus*, Ungar, 1957. A determined effort by a brilliant French historian to prove that the age of chivalry was also an age of violence, anarchy, and cruelty; one of the great books on medieval history. J. Evans, *Life in Medieval France*, Phaidon, 1957; and A. Tilley, ed., *Medieval France: A Companion to French Studies*, Cambridge Univ., 1922, are comprehensive surveys arranged topically.

C. W. C. Oman, *The Great Revolt of 1381*, Oxford, 1906. A good small book on the peasant uprising in England. See also the pertinent chapters in G. M Trevelyan, *England in the Age of Wyclif*, Longmans, 1906; and B. Jarrett, *Social Theories of the Middle Ages, 1200-1500*, Little, Brown, 1926.

H. Pirenne, *Medieval Cities,** Anchor. A masterful study which relates the growth of towns to the revival of trade. A more technical work on town origins, with particular attention given to England, is C. Stephenson, *Borough and Town*, Mediaeval Academy, 1933. For the Italian communes see the excellent chapter in Vol. V of *The Cambridge Medieval History*. Vol. VII of the same work contains a good chapter on the Hanseatic League.

CHAPTER 9

Nations in the Making

EUROPEAN POLITICAL HISTORY: 1050-1300

Introduction. At the end of the twelfth century a new spirit was manifest in Europe. Trade revived, cities grew, and national kingdoms developed their power at the expense of their feudal competitors. Inadequate to meet the demands of a new and progressive society in the making, feudalism was on the wane.

Perhaps the greatest weakness of feudalism was its inability to guarantee law and order. Whenever the law was defied, an agency was needed to see that the forces of justice would triumph over the lawbreakers; and, except in local affairs, feudalism provided no such agency. The welter of feudal principalities, each with its own law courts for dispensing justice, made uniformity in legal codes and judicial procedure impossible. As a result, confusion, inefficiency, and injustice were common.

The inefficiency inherent in the feudal system also acted as a stumbling block to progress and prosperity. Trade and commerce depended, then as now, on good transportation; it was vital that there be decent roads and that these roads be kept in repair. But under feudalism a poverty-stricken or merely indolent noble might refuse to look after the stretch of main highway passing through his domain, and even if the road became impassable, there would be no single, overriding authority to force him to repair it.

In any well-governed country, it is essential that there be a body of skilled administrators to map out foreign policy and to plan measures pertaining to domestic affairs. Under the feudal system, however, the units of government were too small and the opportunities for administrative accomplishment too limited to support capable staffs of civil servants. Only by welding the confusing multiplicity of fiefs and principalities into a unified scheme of government could the lack of a uniform currency be remedied, the many irritating toll and tariff barriers imposed by local barons be removed, trade advanced, and justice established. The ills of feudalism could be cured only by the creation of sovereign national states.

We shall see in this chapter how monarchs in France and England expanded their power, improved the machinery of government, and rallied their people around them, thus laying the foundations for such states. In Germany and Italy, however, efforts to create a national state ended in failure, and in Spain unification was retarded by the formidable task of ousting the Muslims.

THE GENESIS OF

MODERN ENGLAND

Aftermath of the Romans. When the Roman legions returned to Italy in the fifth century, they left the Celtic natives of Britain at the mercy of the Germanic invaders—Angles, Saxons, Jutes, and Frisians. These savage tribes laid waste to Britain, destroying the old villas and massacring the population. Proof of the force with which the invader struck is the fact that almost no traces of the Celtic language remain in Modern English. Not only did the invaders wage war against the Celts, but the various Anglo-Saxon tribes fought among themselves. At one time there were seven distinct little tribal kingdoms, all jealous and hostile, on the island of Britain.

The Anglo-Saxon monarchy. Gradually, peace and order came to the distracted island as rivalries among the kingdoms began to diminish. In the ninth century, the kingdom of Wessex held the dominant position. Its first task was to turn back a new wave of invaders, the Danes. This accomplishment was largely the work of the Wessex king, Alfred the Great (871-899), one of England's finest monarchs. Alfred defeated the Danes in battle and then arranged a treaty with them, whereby the Danes settled in the central part of England. Danes and Saxons soon intermarried, and all differences between the two groups disappeared.

Not only a successful warrior, Alfred the Great made notable contributions in government. He reorganized the army, improved the system of local government, and issued a set of laws, which reflect his desire to see the average man protected from wrongdoing and violence.

Alfred also advanced the intellectual life of England. He founded a palace school and encouraged the writing of the *Anglo-Saxon Chronicle* (the earliest existing vernacular history of any nation) and the translation into Anglo-Saxon of such classics as Boethius' *Consolation of Philosophy*.

In the tenth century the power of the central government lagged and with it the ability to keep order at home and repel outside attacks. The impotence of the kingdom is well illustrated in the unhappy reign of Ethelred the Unready (978-1016), who was unable to keep a firm hand on the great nobles or to cope with a new attack by the Danes.

In its political structure, the major defect of Anglo-Saxon England was the weakness of its central government: the inability of the king to control his great nobles. But as a positive contribution to political history, the Anglo-Saxons developed local, representative government to a strong degree. They left us a valuable legacy—the tradition of the people's participation in their government. In the local political divisions—the vill, hundred, and shire—numerous assemblies and courts (moots) were utilized in which any freeman had the right to participate if he were chosen to do so by his fellows. Here was one of the seeds that later flowered into democratic government. It is an interesting carry-over that American law students call their trial cases "moot court cases," and that our modern title of sheriff is derived from the name of the shire's most important official, the reeve of the shire.

Dating probably from the twelfth century, the Bayeux tapestry depicts the Norman Conquest. From this embroidered strip of linen, 231 feet long and 20 inches wide, two sections are reproduced. At the left, William's soldiers cross the Channel in their Viking dragon boats. At the right, English yeomen defend a hill against the Normans during the battle of Hastings.

Following the reign of Ethelred, the Anglo-Saxons were overrun by the Vikings, and King Canute ruled England as well as Denmark and Norway. Canute proved to be a wise and Christian king, respecting the rights and customs of his Anglo-Saxon subjects. After his death, chaos again prevailed until some semblance of order was achieved by the return to the throne in 1042 of descendants of the Anglo-Saxon rulers. The central government was not closely knit, however, and the king had little control over the powerful earls. This decline in government was reversed when the Normans conquered England.

The Norman Conquest. The Norman Conquest of England really began in the reign of Edward the Confessor (1042-1066). Although he was English, he had spent most of his youth in Normandy; and as king of England he showed a pro-Norman bias. On his death in 1066 the Witan—the council of the kingdom—selected Harold, a powerful English earl, as the new ruler. Immediately William, Duke of Normandy, claimed the English throne, basing his demand on a flimsy hereditary right and on the assertion that Edward had promised him the crown.

One of the most outstanding statesmen and soldiers of his time, William had subdued the rebellious nobles and from then on was the absolute master of Normandy. The central authority of the duke of Normandy contrasted sharply with the situation in England, where the powerful earls were continually embarrassing the king.

By the clever use of propaganda, apparently an effective weapon as far back as the eleventh century, William secured the sanction of the pope, which gave his invasion the flavor of a crusade. He secured a well-equipped army of hard-fighting adventurers, mostly Norman knights, who looked upon the conquest of England as an investment which would pay them rich dividends in the form of lands and serfs.

The cross-channel maneuver was hazardous; five thousand men and many horses had to be transported in open boats. After disembarking, William and his men faced King Harold and his army. On October 14, 1066, at Hastings, the clash of Norman and Saxon occurred:

. . . the battle commenced on both sides. They fought with ardour, neither giving ground, for great part of the day. Finding this, William gave a signal to his party, that, by a feigned flight, they should retreat. Through this device, the close body of the English, opening for the purpose of cutting down the straggling enemy, brought upon itself swift destruction; for the Normans, facing about, attacked them thus disordered, and compelled them to fly. In this manner, deceived by a stratagem, they met an honourable death in avenging their country; nor indeed were they at all wanting to their own revenge, as, by frequently making a stand, they slaughtered their pursuers in heaps: for, getting possession of an eminence, they drove down the Normans, when roused with indignation and anxiously striving to gain the higher ground, into the valley beneath, where, easily hurling their javelins and rolling down stones on them as they stood below, they destroyed them to a

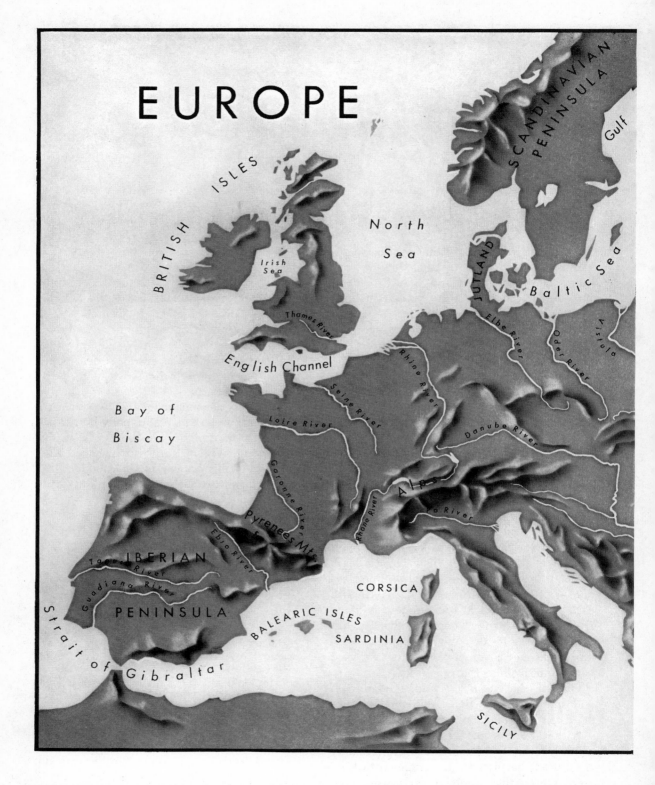

EUROPE

SCANDINAVIAN PENINSULA

Gulf

BRITISH ISLES

North Sea

Irish Sea

JUTLAND

Baltic Sea

Elbe River

Oder River

Vistula

Thames River

English Channel

Rhine River

Seine River

Danube River

Bay of Biscay

Loire River

Garonne River

Alps

Pyrenees Mts.

Po River

Rhone River

Ebro River

IBERIAN

Tagus River

Guadiana River

PENINSULA

CORSICA

BALEARIC ISLES

SARDINIA

Strait of Gibraltar

SICILY

Natural boundaries such as mountains, rivers, and seas have played an important role in shaping the history of Europe. As you study this map, you can probably pick out some of the boundaries which were to divide nations in later times. Compare this map

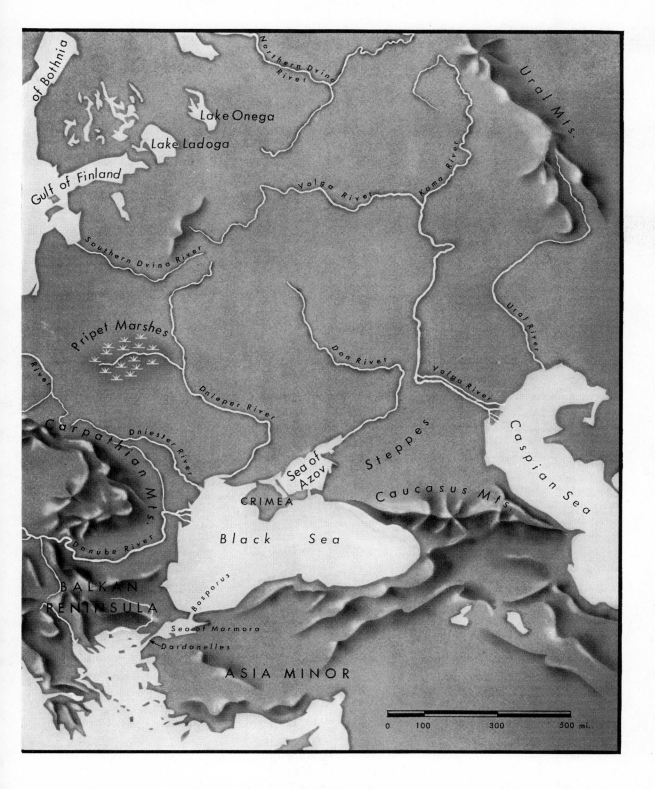

with Reference Map 6, which shows later political boundaries. In reading succeeding chapters, notice that some of the trouble spots have been those where no natural boundaries exist; for example, Germany and France have been archenemies for centuries.

man. . . . This vicissitude of first one party conquering, and then the other, prevailed as long as the life of Harold continued; but when he fell, from having his brain pierced with an arrow, the flight of the English ceased not until night.[1]

The defeat spelled the end of Anglo-Saxon rule and the beginning of a new pattern of events in England.

William the Conqueror centralizes the government. With victory achieved at Hastings, William had made himself king of England. Now he faced the task of strengthening his new realm. From the outset, all of his policies were pointed toward a single goal—the organization of a centralized government. And, sensibly, he utilized some of the institutions with which the English were familiar. This policy was apparent particularly in the field of local government: such administrative divisions as the Saxon shire and the hundred were retained, along with the system of local courts. But the long arm of royal power reached the local level through the king's commissioners, who toured the shires, and the sheriffs, who became the effective local agents of the king.

William the Conqueror's determination to make his power supreme is also demonstrated by the way in which he introduced feudalism into England. In Anglo-Saxon England, a full-grown feudal system had not developed, even though there were tendencies in that direction. In his homeland, William had learned that powerful nobles, ruling over extensive domains, were a constant source of trouble. Therefore, he broke up the great Saxon earldoms, leaving small provinces which served as efficient administrative units without posing a serious military threat.

First of all, William rewarded a number of Normans with fiefs in England, providing himself with a backlog of support for his rule in an alien country. Then, from all the landholders in England, regardless of whether or not they were his immediate vassals, William exacted homage and an oath "that they would be faithful to him against all other men."[2] Because every man owed his first allegiance to the crown, a disgruntled noble would be hard put to call out his own vassals against the king. In addition, William demanded that all his vassals and their vassals in turn provide him with armed knights when the necessity arose. Thus William advanced political feudalism, retained the manorial system, and fused the two into a fully developed feudal structure.

William did not depend solely upon feudal levies for his military forces; he retained the old Anglo-Saxon militia in which every man was required to have arms commensurate with his means, whether he was a fully equipped knight or a peasant with his bow and arrows. Thus the king had in readiness a powerful fighting force of common people to crush a rebellious baron.

The Domesday Survey is another excellent example of the methodical manner by which William took over full control of England. He wanted an accurate census of the economic resources of his country as a basis for an equitable tax. In 1085 and 1086, royal commissioners collected testimony from special sworn juries. The complaints and even riots which the inventory caused are evident in the grumblings of a Saxon chronicler:

So very narrowly did he cause the survey to be made that there was not a single hide nor a rood of land, nor—it is shameful to relate that which he thought no shame to do—was there an ox or a cow or a pig passed by that was not set down in the accounts. . . .[3]

In line with his policy of controlling all aspects of the government, William revamped the old Anglo-Saxon Witan, which had elected and advised the kings. The new Norman ruler changed its title to the Great Council and converted it into a feudal body composed of his tenants-in-chief. The Council acted as a court of trial and as an advisory body in making laws. He also established a permanent council of royal advisers, the Curia Regis. From these institutions eventually emerged Parliament, whose powers were in time to supersede the monarch's.

King William's determination to be master in his own house is also seen in his attitude toward the Church. Although he permitted the Church to retain its courts, in which canon law was administered, he denied them the right to appeal cases to the high courts of Rome without royal consent.

Thus William, who has been called England's drillmaster, started the conquered island on the path to nationhood. In his efforts to abolish civil strife and competing authorities, he ruthlessly oppressed any opposition to his will. Although his policies may appear to us extremely harsh, they were essential for the unification and prosperity of England.

William's successors. William II, who followed his father, was a disappointing namesake. His reign was darkened by cruelty and capricious rule. Succeeding him was his brother, Henry I, an able monarch who carried on William the Conqueror's objective of developing a strong centralized government. Soon after becoming king, Henry taunted the strongest noble in the land into rebellion and then promptly overthrew him and seized his lands. No further revolts took place during his rule.

The Great Council, made up of the chief nobles, met occasionally to advise the king on matters of state, and the Curia Regis grew in importance. In addition, a staff of professional civil servants introduced a new efficiency to the government. Itinerant justices had been used by William the Conqueror, but Henry had them travel more regularly throughout the kingdom to bring the king's law and justice to all citizens.

Henry's achievements in strengthening the monarchy were almost undone by the nineteen years of chaos which followed his death in 1135. Stephen, a weak king, permitted the nobles to pillage, rob, and fight among themselves.

Henry II's judicial reforms. Anarchy ceased with the accession of Henry II (1154-1189), the founder of the Plantagenet House in England. As a result of his inheritance and his marriage to Eleanor of Aquitaine, Henry II found himself sovereign of a great empire stretching from Scotland to the Pyrenees. The English holdings in France exceeded the land directly ruled by the French kings, who eyed their vassal rival with jealousy and

Above is shown part of the Tower of London, long used as a prison for those accused of crimes against the English monarchs. The oldest part of the fortress, the White Tower, was erected during the reign of William the Conqueror.

fear. The year of Henry's accession to the throne, 1154, marks the beginning of the strife between England and France which runs like a red thread through the tapestry of medieval history.

Stephen, Henry's ineffectual predecessor, had left him a sorry heritage. Confusion and corruption existed in the judicial system. The royal courts administered by the king's justices and the old Saxon tribunals of the shire and the hundred faced strong competition from both the baronial courts, run independently by feudal lords, and the Church courts, which threatened to extend their supremacy over the whole realm.

In a series of decrees, called assizes, Henry II thoroughly reorganized the judicial system. The Assize of Clarendon (1166), which laid down the basic features of Henry's new court system, was a landmark in English legal history. It was the first attempt to weaken the feudal courts of the nobility. Stressing the old Germanic principle of the right and duty of all free men to take part in their government, the Assize of Clarendon indirectly prepared the way for self-government for the English people.

The Assize of Clarendon dealt specifically with two very important aspects of the English judicial system: itinerant justices and the jury system. Royal judges had been sent on circuit to dispense justice in the reign of Henry I, but it was Henry II who made justice regularly available on the local level.

More important, the Assize of Clarendon made the jury system an integral part of British justice. Until Henry's time, the king had the right to summon a body of men to bear witness under oath about the truth of any question concerning the royal interest. For example, William the Conqueror had used this system in the Domesday Survey. By the Assize of Clarendon, the king's sheriffs were to select a certain number of men who, when summoned before the itinerant justices, would report all local crimes that had occurred since the judges had last been in the locality. Thus the jury functioned much as a modern-day grand jury does in that the juries of the shires provided the information for an indictment. From the provisions in the Assize of Clarendon, trial by jury* eventually

*What are some of the important points in the working of trial by jury as we know it today? A person accused of a clearly defined civil or criminal offense is brought to trial before a judge. Witnesses must swear an oath to tell the truth and are questioned in the presence of the accused by the litigants or their lawyers, not by the judge. The validity of the witnesses' testimony is weighed by the jury, and only after the jury has pronounced its verdict in the case is the judge allowed to impose sentence, punishment, or penalty according to law.

The workings of Roman law offer an interesting contrast. "Under Roman law, and systems derived from it, a trial in those turbulent centuries, and in some countries even today, is often an inquisition. The judge makes his own investigation into the civil wrong or the public crime, and such investigation is largely uncontrolled. The suspect can be interrogated in private. He must answer all questions put to him. His right to be represented by a legal adviser is restricted. The witnesses against him can testify in secret and in his absence. And only when these processes have been accomplished is the accusation or charge against him formulated and published. Thus often arise secret intimidation, enforced confessions, torture, and blackmailed pleas of guilty."[4]

evolved and became the most characteristic feature of the judicial system in all English-speaking nations. Later, trial by jury was to be carried to the far corners of the earth as a hallmark of justice.

Henry's judicial reforms implemented the growth of the common law—one of the most important factors in welding the English people into a nation. Unlike Roman law, English common law is not codified; it is the result of custom, not legislation. Beginning with the reign of Edward I, the most important decisions of the royal justices were collected into the Year Books. These legal opinions became the basis for future decisions made in the king's courts, superseded the many diverse systems of local justice in the shires, and became the law common to all Englishmen.

Thomas à Becket, victim of Church-state rivalry. While Henry skillfully diminished the activities of the baronial courts by making the royal courts more powerful, against his other legal rival—the Church courts—he was not so successful. When he appointed Thomas à Becket as archbishop of Canterbury, the king assumed that his worldly friend would easily be persuaded to cooperate, but Becket proved to be stubbornly independent, stoutly contesting any move to reduce the authority of the Church.

In 1164 Henry issued the Constitutions of Clarendon, which stipulated that all members of the clergy accused of any crime should first be taken before a royal court, not an ecclesiastic court. Henry's idea was to prevent the abuses resulting from "benefit of clergy"—the principle that the Church had the sole right to punish its clergy. If the king's court thought that a crime had been committed, the culprit was to be tried in a Church court. If pronounced guilty, he would then be turned over to the civil authorities for punishment. This arrangement seemed a fair remedy for abuses of benefit of clergy, but Becket would have none of it.

Years of bitter controversy followed. Once, in a fit of passion, Henry upbraided his courtiers for failing to avenge him of the "turbulent priest." Taking the king at his word, a group of knights rode to Canterbury and seized Becket. An eyewitness wrote:

At the third blow he [Thomas] fell on his knees and elbows, offering himself a living victim, and saying in a low voice, 'For the name of Jesus and the protection of the church I am ready to embrace death.' Then the third knight inflicted a terrible wound as he lay, by which the sword was broken against the pavement . . . the blood white with the brain, and the brain red with blood, dyed the surface of the virgin mother church . . . in the colors of the lily and the rose.[5]

The uproar that the murder caused destroyed all chance of reforming the Church courts. For the remainder of the Middle Ages, Church and state in England continued to differ on the matter of the court system. Benefit of clergy remained an obstacle to the royal ambitions for equal justice for all Englishmen.

Henry's successors. Historians have rightly regarded Henry as an outstanding statesman and one of England's greatest kings. His accomplishments include the creation of a truly national judiciary, development of the common law, and the introduction of the jury system.

But, as after William the Conqueror's reign, the good beginning made by Henry II was marred by the foolish mistakes of his successors. Having no taste for the prosaic tasks of government, Richard the Lion-Hearted wasted his country's wealth on forays in Europe and military expeditions to the Holy Land. As we saw in Chapter 8, Richard earned fame in the Third Crusade as a peerless knight in his struggle against Saladin, the leader of the Saracens.

John's powers limited by the Magna Carta. Richard's successor, his brother John, was no improvement as a ruler. In fact, in a contest to determine the worst king ever to wear the English crown, John would most likely be the winner, or certainly the runner-up. Yet history on occasion seems to turn personal defects into public progress. Winston Churchill has written: ". . . when the long tally is added it will be seen that the British nation and the English-speaking world owe

A detail from a medieval illumination depicts the murder of Thomas à Becket.

far more to the vices of John than to the labours of virtuous sovereigns."[6]

After losing most of the land on the Continent which he held as fiefs of the king of France, King John alienated his own barons by attempting to collect illegal feudal dues and permitting infractions of the feudal law. His tyranny brought on civil war in which the nobles were victorious. In 1215, John unwillingly affixed his seal to the Magna Carta, one of the most important documents in the history of human freedom.

To Englishmen of the time, this document did not appear to introduce any new constitutional principles. It was merely an agreement between the barons and the king, the aristocracy and the monarchy. But the seeds of political liberty were inherent in the Magna Carta. Certain provisions contained in the document proved to be of vital importance in the development of representative government:

Perhaps the earliest authentic view of Parliament in session, this picture shows a meeting called by Edward I. The dignitaries occupying the outer benches are Church officials and secular lords. In the center are members of the judiciary seated on woolsacks to remind them that wool was vital to the English economy. Just below them are the representatives from the towns and shires.

Clause XII. [Taxation or feudal aid except those sanctioned by custom] . . . shall be levied in our kingdom only by the common consent of our kingdom [i.e., by the king's Great Council.]

Clause XXXIX. No free man shall be taken or imprisoned or dispossessed, or outlawed, or banished, or in any way destroyed . . . except by the legal judgment of his peers or by the law of the land.

Clause XL. To no one will we sell, to no one will we deny, or delay right or justice.[7]

The limitations upon the king's power applied in 1215 only to freemen—that is, to the clergy, the barons, and a relatively small number of rural freeholders and burghers. Little or nothing was said in the charter about the rights of the majority of the population—the serfs living on the manors. As the feudal system gradually disappeared, however, the term *freeman* came to include every Englishman.

The importance of the Magna Carta does not lie in its original purpose but rather in the subsequent use made of it. Two great principles were potential in the charter: (1) the law is above the king; and (2) the king can be compelled by force to obey the law of the land. This principle of the limited power of the crown was to play an important role in the seventeenth-century struggle against the despotism of the Stuart kings. Clause XII was interpreted to guarantee the principle of no taxation without representation and Clause XXXIX to guarantee trial by jury.

First meeting of the English Parliament. As we recall, William the Conqueror converted the Witan into a feudal body, the Great Council; and under Henry I the Curia Regis became an important permanent advisory group. Several times a year the Great Council met with the Curia Regis. Here, then, were the ancestors of Parliament.

During the reign of Henry III, the son of King John, the first meeting of Parliament was called—in the midst of a rebellion. In order to gain the widest possible popular support, Simon de Montfort, the leader of the rebellion, convened the Great Council in 1265; and to it he summoned two knights from every shire and two from every city and borough. This meeting, which broadened the membership and radically changed the character of the Great Council, was the first Parliament in English history.

The first meetings of the English Parliament coincided with a general trend throughout Europe. In the thirteenth and fourteenth centuries, there appeared assemblies such as the Estates-General in France, the Cortes in Spain, and the Diet in Germany. Except for the English Parliament, none of these assemblies fulfilled their early promise. They either ceased to exist or remained completely under the monarch's thumb.

Parliament gains stature. During the reign of the next king, Edward I (1272-1307), Parliament first became important. Following the pattern set by Simon de Montfort, Edward continued the practice of summoning representatives of counties and towns to meetings of the Great Council. In 1295, he called the "model Parliament," the most representative group yet convened. Two years later the king agreed that certain taxes could not be levied without the assent of Parliament, a principle that assured that body of being summoned from time to time.

From Edward's reign on, Parliament became more and more essential to English government. In calling Parliaments, the English kings had no idea of making any concession to popular government. Their main objective was revenue. As recognition of the growing wealth and influence of the bourgeoisie and as a means of ·obtaining another source of revenue, the English kings along with other European monarchs began the practice of including representatives of the bourgeoisie in the feudal councils. By the fourteenth century it became mandatory to consult Parliament, and the kings realized, too late, the threat that this new agency represented to their royal prerogatives.

Early in the fourteenth century, Parliament divided into two houses—the House of Lords, representing the barons, and the House of Commons, composed of the knights and the middle classes. The Commons soon discovered its power as the main source of money for the king. Using this "power of the purse" as a weapon, Parliament forced the king to agree that no tax could be levied without its consent.

Further important gains were made by Parliament in lawmaking, which had originally been solely a royal function. The House of Commons presented petitions to the king with the request that they be enacted into law. Gradually the right to initiate legislation through petition was obtained. Again, Parliament's "power of the purse" turned the trick.

Widening the boundaries of the realm. Edward I initiated the policy directed toward uniting the people in Britain—English, Scots, and Welsh—under the English crown. In 1284 Wales was conquered; later, Edward gave his oldest son the title of Prince of Wales. A dispute over succession to the Scottish throne in the 1290's gave Edward his opportunity to intervene in the land to the north. After calling upon him to settle the dispute,

the Scots accepted him as their overlord. Then Edward unwisely demanded that the Scots furnish him with troops to fight in English wars. Under the courageous William Wallace, rebellion quickly flared up, but Wallace was defeated and hanged as a traitor. The fires of Scottish nationalism continued to burn on despite numerous attempts to put out the flames.

Edward II, the next English monarch, attempted to humble the Scots, but at the battle of Bannockburn (1314) the Scots were victorious and won their independence. Thus permanent union between England and Scotland was forestalled until 1603, and Bannockburn remained for centuries a symbol of Scottish pride and patriotism.

During the two and a half centuries preceding the death of Edward I in 1307, England was experiencing a formative period in political institutions. Two extraordinarily important concepts were slowly being incorporated into England's government: (1) the idea expressed in the Magna Carta that consent of the barons was necessary to royal authority was being broadened to include the consent of all elements of English society, and (2) Parliament was becoming the agency which both formulated and voiced the opinions of the citizens.

THE BEGINNINGS OF THE
FRENCH NATIONAL STATE

Political decentralization. In the France from which William the Conqueror set sail, the monarchy barely existed. As we saw in Chapter 6, the later Carolingian rulers were weaklings. During the decline of this royal house, the nobility set up small independent states (see map, p. 215) and largely ignored the monarchs. Nevertheless, except for a ten-year interval during the reign of Odo (see p. 146), the Carolingian kings maintained their precarious grasp on the throne.

Political decentralization was heightened by the bitter rivalry of contenders for the throne—a rivalry which lasted until the last Carolingian king died in 987. As his successor, the nobles selected Hugh Capet, Count of Paris, a descendant of King Odo.

The "kingdom" which Hugh Capet theoretically ruled was roughly comparable to, but smaller than, modern France. The territory which Hugh actually controlled was a small feudal duchy, a region twenty-five miles long and a little more wide, surrounding Paris. It was almost encircled by rivers—hence, perhaps, its name: the Ile de France. The royal domain was surrounded by the great feudal holdings which made up more than three quarters of the country. These large independent dukedoms, such as Flanders, Normandy, Anjou, and Poitou, were a law unto themselves. Their rulers paid little attention to the king and only tolerated him as a figurehead.

Early Capetians; groundwork for future greatness. The Capetian line of kings, founded by Hugh Capet in 987, ruled France until 1328. Starting with little power and a limited amount of territory under their direct rule, these monarchs patiently but inexorably extended their control over the great dukedoms. France literally was made by its kings, for ultimately the royal domain, in which the king's word was law, came to coincide with the boundaries of the entire country.

The powerful nobles who elected Hugh Capet to the kingship had no thought of giving the Capetian family a monopoly on the royal office. But the Capetian kings with the support of the Church cleverly arranged for the election and coronation of their heirs. Before the king died, the young prince was crowned by the Church and became "associated" with his father in his rule; after the king's death, his son was crowned again. For three hundred years the House of Capet never lacked a male heir, and by the end of the twelfth century the hereditary principle had become so ingrained that French kings no longer took the precaution of crowning their sons during their own lifetime.

In the late tenth and throughout the eleventh centuries, there was little tangible evidence that the Capetian kings were going to fulfill their destiny. These kings of France had no hand in the stirring events of their time. While they remained historical non-entities, one of their vassals, the duke of Normandy, seized the throne of England; another became the founder of the kingdom of Portugal; and a neighboring Flemish noble became head of the kingdom of Jerusalem.

The first four Capetians did not antagonize the mighty vassals but were content to bide their time. Amid the feuds of the vassals, the kings maintained a precarious existence, nimbly hopping from one side to the other as the fortunes of war changed. In 1108 the fourth Capetian was succeeded by his son Louis VI, also known as Louis the Fat. This event heralded the end of Capetian weakness and the beginning of progress toward royal primacy in France. At the outset of his reign, Louis, with the encouragement of his chief adviser, Abbot Suger, determined to crush the lawless barons who were defying royal authority. In the words of the abbot:

A king, when he takes the royal power, vows to put down with his strong right arm insolent tyrants whensoever he sees them vex the state with endless wars, rejoice in rapine, oppress the poor, destroy the churches, give themselves over to lawlessness which, and it be not checked, would flame out into ever greater madness . . .[8]

The "war of the brigands," as the king's expeditions against the nobles were called, was a long, slow process, but in the end the castles of the defiant vassals were captured and in many cases torn down. By asserting his authority, Louis made his word law in the Ile de France, established a center from which royal power could be extended, substantially increased royal revenues, and built up the prestige of the French monarchy.

Philip Augustus extends royal rule. The great expansion of royal control in France took place between 1180 (the year of the accession of Philip II) and 1314 (the date of Philip IV's death). By the end of this period, the French monarchy had become the strongest in Europe. The three most outstanding rulers during this period of unification were Philip II (known also as Philip Augustus), who increased his domain into a substantial kingdom; Louis IX, who ennobled and dignified the French crown; and Philip IV, who made the government a centralized, efficient despotism.

Philip Augustus' greatest struggle was his effort to wrest from the English Plantagenets the territory they held in France. Ruling these vast holdings was Henry II, and while the redoubtable Henry lived, Philip made little headway. He did, however, make Henry's life wretched by fomenting plots and by encouraging Henry's faithless sons to revolt. During the reigns of the next two English kings, Richard the Lion-Hearted and John, Philip gained control of half the Plantagenet possessions in France by trickery and warfare.

Philip not only increased his domain threefold but also strengthened the royal administrative system by devising new agencies for centralized government and tapping many new sources of revenue. New officials, called bailiffs and seneschals, performed duties similar to those carried out in England by itinerant justices and sheriffs. A corps of loyal officials, recruited not from the feudal nobility but from the ranks of the bourgeoisie, was collected around the king. These professional civil servants—many of them lawyers acquainted with the workings of Roman law—soon developed into expert governmental advisers and administrators. As in England, special administrative departments were created: the *parlement*, a supreme court of justice (not to be confused with the English Parliament, which became primarily a legislative body); the Chamber of Accounts, a financial body; and the Royal or Privy Council, a group of advisers who assisted the king in the conduct of the daily business of the state. The Capetian rulers, like the English monarchs, were creating an efficient central government that was gradually to eliminate competition from the feudal barons and other powerful nobles.

In this early phase of consolidation of royal power, the Church usually allied itself with the monarchy. In France as in England, however, the kings sometimes collided with the Church. For example, Philip II flouted Church authority in annulling his marriage; Innocent III was determined that

A detail from the Duke of Berry's *Book of Hours* shows the Louvre as it looked during the time of Philip II. The French king built this fortress as a storage place for his records and money.

no secular monarch should defy the Church on such a matter. The upshot was that the pope imposed an interdict on France, Philip backed down, and his wife again became his queen. The first round between Church and state went to the Church.

Inadvertently, the Church helped to expand the royal domain. In southern France, particularly in Toulouse, the heretical Albigensian sect flourished. Determined to stamp out this sect, Innocent III in 1208 called the Albigensian crusade (see p. 230). Although Philip was not enthusiastic, he allowed his vassals to participate. After his death in 1223, his successor, Louis VIII, led a new crusade to crush the remnants of Albigensian resistance. By the time he died, royal power had been established in much of southern France. The French king's realm now stretched from the coast of the English Channel to the shores of the Mediterranean.

Louis IX dignifies the throne. After the brief reign of Louis VIII, France passed under the rule of Louis IX (1226-1270), better known as St. Louis because of his nobility of character. In the rough-and-tumble melee of European rivalries, St. Louis' policies of government were exceptional. His ideal was peace, and he made substantial sacrifices to attain it.

Despite the fact that little territory was added to the royal domain during his reign, Louis IX imbued the monarchy with a quality perhaps more precious—moral dignity. Just, sympathetic, and peace-loving, St. Louis convinced his subjects that the monarchy was the most important agency for assuring their happiness and well-being.

Louis' passion for justice and good government was reflected in significant developments in the machinery of government. Special officials, similar to the *missi dominici* of Charlemagne, were created to check on the bailiffs and seneschals and to hold them to a strict account of the activities which transpired in their terms of office. Certain matters, such as treason and crimes on the highways, were declared to be the exclusive jurisdiction of the royal courts. Furthermore, cases from feudal courts could now be appealed to the royal bench in Paris. The growth and improvement of the judicial *parlement* was also encouraged.

Louis endeavored to hear his subjects' problems and complaints personally. A courtier of the time has left us this sketch:

Many a time it happened that in summer time he would go and sit down in the wood at Vincennes, with his back to an oak, and make us take our seats around him. And all those who had complaints to make came to him without hindrance from ushers or other folk. Then he asked them with his own lips: "Is there any one here who has a cause?" Those who had a cause stood up when he would say to them; "Silence all, and you shall be dispatched [judged] one after another."[9]

Climax of Capetian rule under Philip IV.

The reign of Philip IV, the Fair (1285-1314), climaxed three centuries of Capetian rule. The antithesis of his saintly grandfather, Philip was a man of craft, violence, and deceit. One of Philip's harshest acts was the suppression of the wealthy order of the Knights Templars. After their efforts during the crusades, the Knights had turned to banking as their main business. Heavily in debt to them, Philip trumped up charges against the order and had many members tortured and burned at the stake.

In the area of Church-state rivalry, the most dramatic event in this period was the conflict between Philip and Pope Boniface VIII. As we shall see in Chapter 11, Boniface made sweeping claims to supremacy over secular powers. He was speaking in the tones of Innocent III, but the national state had reached the point where such leaders as Philip IV would not brook interference with their authority no matter what the source. The result of this controversy was the humiliation of Boniface, a blow from which the medieval papacy never recovered.

In domestic affairs the real importance of Philip's reign lies in the increasing power and improved organization of the government, with its heart in Paris and its fingers extended over much of France. Philip's astute civil servants, recruited mainly from the middle class, concentrated their efforts on exalting the power of their monarch. On several occasions the king convened the Estates-General, in which the Church, the

These maps show the growth of royal power in France. The royal domain, directly subject to the king, is shown in black; the broken-line boundary indicates the extent of his feudal suzerainty to the east and the south. English holdings are diagonally striped. Strife between England and France runs like a red thread through the tapestry of medieval history.

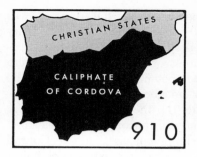

The gradual unification of Spain is shown by the three maps above. The Muslims (black) were slowly driven south until, in 1492, they were ousted from Granada. United Spain (striped) took over Navarre in 1515 and Portugal in 1580.

nobility, and the townsmen were represented. Although there was a hint that this body might develop the "power of the purse" as in England, the opportunity was missed. The Estates-General never became as powerful as Parliament.

Several themes are evident in this period of French consolidation—expansion of the area under royal control, attempts to expel the English from France, the growth of the machinery of centralized government, and the exaltation of the throne. Each theme marks a particular aspect of France's growth from a confused medley of feudal states to a powerful nation. By the end of the fifteenth century this process was to be completed (see Chapter 11).

CHRISTIAN RECONQUESTS

IN SPAIN

The Reconquista. The unification of Spain was a more complex process than that of either France or England. The customary rivalry between the feudal aristocracy and the royal authority was complicated by another significant element—a religious crusade. Unification required the ejection from Spain of the Muslims, with their alien religion and civilization. Unity also called for the integration of several diminutive nations, each possessing its own way of life.

As we saw in Chapter 8, the Christian groups which had survived the Muslim con-

quest slowly gathered strength and expanded southward. In the ninth century, northern Spain became suffused with a religious zeal centering around Santiago de Compostela, reputed to be the site where the body of the apostle St. James was found. The bones of the saint were enshrined in a great cathedral and thousands of pilgrims came to the shrine. Banners were consecrated there, and the battle cry of the Christian soldiers became "Santiago" (a contraction of "Sante Iago," St. James' name in Spanish). The collapse of the Caliphate of Cordova in 1031 gave the Christians the opportunity for a full-scale offensive, and about fifty years later the Muslim stronghold of Toledo was captured. Knights from France and other parts of Europe flocked to northern Spain—some to seek adventure, some to serve God.

El Cid, symbol of Spanish nationalism. During the struggle with the Moors, a mounting patriotism blended with a fanatical religious spirit. The symbol of national reawakening was an eleventh-century soldier of fortune, El Cid Campeador. His exploits against the Muslims thrilled Europe, and he soon became the greatest hero in Spanish literature. Here is a portion of the most famous poem about him, *Poema del Cid*:

Before their breasts, the war-shields there have they buckled strong,
The lances with the pennons they laid them low along,
And they have bowed their faces over the saddlebow,
And thereaway to strike them with brave hearts did they go.

He who in happy hour was born with great did
    call:
"For the love of the Creator, smite them, my
    gallants all.
I am Roy Diaz of Bivar, the Cid, the Campe-
    ador."
At the rank where was Per Vermudoz the mighty
    strokes they bore.
They are three hundred lances that each a
    pennon bear.
At one blow every man of them his Moor has
    slaughtered there,
And when they wheeled to charge anew as many
    more were slain.
You might see great clumps of lances lowered
    and raised again . . .
Cried the Moors "Mahound!" The Christians
    shouted on Saint James of Grace.
On the field Moors thirteen hundred were slain
    in little space.[10]

In the poem, El Cid is characterized as the
perfect Christian knight, although in reality
he fought for gain and was not adverse to
fighting under the Muslim standard.

In 1212 on the field of Las Navas de Tolosa, the Christians achieved a great victory.
A few years later they captured Cordova
and Seville, and by the end of the thirteenth
century, Moorish influence was confined to
Granada (see Reference Map 3). The reconquest then halted until the latter part of
the fifteenth century (see Chapter 11).

FAILURES OF THE NATIONAL

STATE: GERMANY AND ITALY

Saxon foundations for future greatness.
After the collapse of Charlemagne's empire,
the political unit ultimately to be known as
Germany began to crystallize east of the
Rhine. Germany in the ninth and tenth
centuries was a loose political union of
five duchies—Bavaria, Franconia, Saxony,
Swabia, and Lorraine. Each was ruled by a
duke, who possessed his own army and
governmental assembly and was in effect a
sovereign ruler. The loyalty of the German
peoples to their duchies rather than to a
central government has colored the history
of Germany from the days of Charlemagne
to those of Hitler.

The independence of the duchies was
somewhat tempered by the tradition of kingship, which, despite the fact that the Carolingian monarchs of the ninth century were
weak and incompetent, carried over from the
days of Charlemagne. When the last Carolingian died in 911, the rulers of the duchies
elected Conrad of Franconia to be their king.
Although incompetent as a ruler, Conrad
recommended a capable man to succeed him:
Henry the Fowler, Duke of Saxony. It was
Henry who founded the illustrious line of
Saxon kings which ruled Germany from 919
to 1024.

**Henry the Fowler, founder of Saxon
strength.** Henry I (919-936) was strong enough
to obtain recognition of his kingship from
the other dukes. While the rulers of the
duchies retained a large amount of autonomy,
they were no longer completely independent.
By this means, Germany achieved a strong
and orderly government while Spain was
still under Muslim rule and France and England had just barely moved in the direction
of strong statehood.

Against the border enemies, Henry was
equally successful. He pushed back the
Danes, occupied the narrow neck of their
peninsula, and established the Dane Mark
as a protective buffer. This occupation initiated the long rivalry between Danes and
Germans over Schleswig-Holstein. Inroads
were also made against the Northern Slavs
across the Elbe, where in 928 Brandenburg
was set up as another defensive mark. Farther to the east, in Bohemia, the Saxon ruler
forced the Slavic Czechs to recognize his
overlordship. And on the southeastern frontier of Germany, Henry defeated the Magyar raiders in 933.

Otto the Great. Otto I, the Great (936-973),
continued the policies of his father. Reso-
lutely intent upon exalting the status of
German kingship and recalling the glory of
Charlemagne, he went to Aix-la-Chapelle
(Aachen) to be crowned.

Realizing that the great hindrance to German unity was the truculence of the nobles,
Otto initiated a policy of getting control of
the unruly duchies and setting up his own rela-

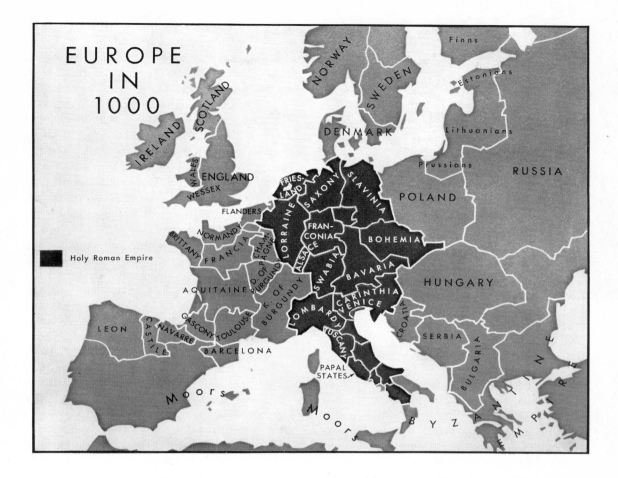

tives and favorites as their rulers. As an extra precaution he appointed, as supervising officials, counts who were directly responsible to the king. These officials were similar in function to the *missi* of Charlemagne.

Otto also sought to strengthen the power of the monarchy by allying it to the Church. He distributed vast lands to the bishops, and in return the ecclesiastical fiefs were expected to furnish contributions to the king's treasury and men for the royal army. These episcopal warriors often made up three quarters of the king's forces. The relationship between the bishops and the sovereign was mainly a feudal one. The bishops were appointed by the king, and their first obedience was to his royal person.

One of Otto's greatest triumphs was his defeat of the Magyars, who in 955 launched an invasion which threatened to engulf all of Germany. In the battle of Lechfeld (see map, p. 147), Otto crushed his foes. The people of the time compared Lechfeld to the battle of Tours; and Otto the Great, like Charles Martel, was hailed as the savior of Europe. The remaining Magyars gave up invading Germany and settled quietly in Hungary.

The eastward movement. In addition to frustrating the invasions of the dreaded Magyars, Otto continued German expansion eastward against the Slavs. Along the Elbe and Saale rivers, which constituted the Slavic line, five new defensive marks were created.

For hundreds of years the Germans continued this eastward movement, pushing from the Elbe to the Oder and eventually to the Vistula River. Impelled by a desire for land and adventure, the colonists brought with them Christianity. In power and scope,

This magnificent imperial crown was made for Otto I. The small portrait (center) represents King Solomon.

this eastward surge of the German people can be compared to the American westward movement from the Alleghenies to the Pacific. "What the New West meant to young America . . . the new East meant to medieval Germany. Each region beckoned the pioneer, the young and lusty of every generation, who sought for cheap lands and new freedom in the wilderness."[11]

This expansion was perhaps the greatest achievement of the medieval Germans. Had it not been for this move eastward, modern Germany would have been a narrow strip of land wedged in between the Rhine and the Elbe; it has been estimated that 60 per cent of German territory before the First World War had been taken from the Slavs.

On the other hand, the duel between the Slavs and the Germans continued to bring many serious problems to eastern Europe. Because the borders between the German colonists and the Slav natives were never clearly defined, pockets of Slavs and Germans intermingled. This mixed-up ethnic situation has caused serious disputes and conflicts in modern times. For example, it gave Hitler the excuse to claim Czechoslovakia (Bohemia)

because of the substantial German minority in the Czech population.

Otto's search for empire. Like so many men of the Middle Ages, Otto the Great tended to look back over his shoulder into the past. A devout believer in the imperial tradition, he regarded the Roman and Carolingian empires as the golden ages of man. As an American historian succinctly put it: "His objective was Empire, and his model was Charlemagne."[12] This pursuit of an empire became a characteristic pattern in the reigns of subsequent Saxon kings; and with each new attempt in Italy, Germany suffered.

Italy in the tenth century was a tempting field for an invader. Lacking an outstanding noble family or a commanding leader to unify the peninsula after the decline of the Carolingian empire, Italy had broken up into warring fragments. In the north the old Lombard crown was frequently the object of various rival contenders. In central Italy were the Papal States, where the pope presided not only as head of the Christian Church, but also as political ruler. The pope's authority was often flouted by the restless and uncouth nobility. Farther south were two Lombard duchies; and, finally, at the extreme tip of the peninsula, the Byzantine empire retained a shaky foothold on the Italian mainland. Here and there were rising, dynamic cities, such as Venice, which eventually became strong and healthy miniature nations with citizens who were avid patrons of the arts.

Romance as well as politics lured Otto to Italy. Queen Adelaide, the widow of the former king of Lombardy, had been imprisoned by a usurper. Her plight stirred Otto's chivalric notions—and his political ambitions also. Therefore, in 951, he crossed the Alps, met Adelaide, who had escaped, and married her. He then dethroned her captor and proclaimed himself ruler of the kingdom of Italy.

On his second expedition to Italy in 962, he was crowned emperor by the pope. No doubt Otto thought of himself as the successor of the imperial Caesars and Charlemagne; and, in fact, his empire later became known as the Holy Roman Empire. Otto's coronation was a momentous event that was to tie Italy and Germany, pope and emperor, into a forced and unnatural union.

Saxon policies evaluated. The distracting, even malevolent, effect of the Saxon pursuit of an Italian empire is shown by the reign of Otto III (983-1002). Contemptuous of Germany and eager to reëstablish the imperial glories of times past, the young ruler made Rome his capital, built a palace there, and styled himself *imperator Romanorum*, meaning "emperor of the Romans." During his reign, Germany was largely ignored. But notwithstanding Otto's love for Italy and his good intentions, the fickle Roman populace revolted; Otto fled for his life and died heartbroken at the age of twenty-one.

Despite the distractions in Italy, the Saxon rulers were the most powerful in Europe at that time. The early kings in particular had achieved notable successes within Germany. They had curbed the divisive tendencies of the duchies, they had utilized the Church as an ally, and they had permanently halted Magyar pillaging in German provinces. In comparison with other European monarchs of the same period, the Saxon rulers stood out as giants among a crowd of dwarfs.

On the other hand, the Saxon kings pursued policies which led eventually to the loss of Germany's position of preëminence among the nations of Europe. Germany was to become the prime example of political localism and royal impotence. Serious mistakes were made by the kings in domestic policy: (1) In the long run the ducal policy of Otto the Great was a failure, for his appointees—relatives and favorites—made their holdings hereditary and attached themselves to local traditions in defiance of the crown. (2) A system of royal courts was never established which would have given the king not only a source of revenue but also the loyalty of his subjects. (3) Ultimately the Saxon alliance with the Church miscarried; it led to a bitter struggle between the popes and the emperors. By bringing the German Church into their political system and by assuming emperorship, German monarchs had exercised their overlordship, not only at home but also in Rome. They appointed the great bishops in their realm and also controlled the election of the popes. For a century this secular mastery functioned smoothly, but beneath the surface lingered a deep and implacable rivalry between pope and emperor. A bitter conflict was to ensue, centering around the king's rights in appointing Church officials who were at the same time the king's feudal vassals. This conflict was known as the Investiture Struggle (see pp. 227-228).

All these factors impeded national unification in Germany, but most decisive was the king's dream of empire. It is the view of many historians that the union of Germany and Italy in the form of an empire was in the long run deeply inimical to the best interests of both countries.

The Saxon rulers in a sense repeated the error of the Carolingians. They tried to do too much; they scattered their energies. They raised their sights too high and failed to hit any target, even the immediate one of German unity. The royal policies would better have been devoted to building up the German kingdom.

The Salian emperors vs. the Church. In 1024 the Saxon kings were succeeded by a new royal line, the Salian House, whose members set about with vigor to create a centralized monarchy. In the next fifty years a trained and loyal body of officials was recruited, the Church lands were brought under the king's management, and better sources of revenue were tapped. Under Henry IV (1056-1106), the monarchy reached the height of its power and there appeared to be hope for a strong, united Germany.

Yet it was during Henry's reign also that the first major reversal to unification occurred. The conflict between Henry IV and Pope Gregory VII, culminating in Gregory's humiliation of Henry at Canossa, resulted from the Investiture Struggle. In 1122, by the Concordat of Worms, a compromise on the subject of lay investiture was finally achieved. This quarrel was only a side issue, however. At stake was the foundation of a strong monarchy in Germany. As long as popes could dictate the actions of German kings and encourage their vassals to defy royal authority, a strong monarchy could not develop.

The real victors in the Investiture Struggle were the German nobles, who allied themselves with the papacy and continued to wage war against the monarchy long after the reign of Henry IV. From the time of Henry's death in 1106 until the accession of Frederick Barbarossa in 1152, the Welfs of Bavaria and the Hohenstaufens of Swabia, along with other noble factions, fought each other without being restrained by any supreme authority. The outcome was that the structure of a strong national state was wrecked. Despite some recovery of royal power later on, the evil effects of this period were never eradicated; the heritage of these decades hindered the development of a unified Germany until modern times.

Prosperity in divided Italy. Italy was even less unified than Germany. Jealous of one another and of their independence, the prosperous city-states in northern Italy joined the struggle between the German emperors and the papacy. The Welf-Hohenstaufen rivalry in Germany was reflected in Italy in the clash between the Guelphs and the Ghibellines. The former were usually propapal; the latter strongly favored the German monarchy's imperial claims in Rome. Amidst the turmoil, the vitality, wealth, and culture of the northern Italian cities increased.

A brilliant civilization also flourished on the island of Sicily. By 1127 the Norman conquests resulted in the establishment of the kingdom of Naples and Sicily. Under the able rule of Roger II (1130-1154), this kingdom became one of the strongest and wealthiest states in Europe. During his reign, busy merchant fleets nurtured the Mediterranean towns; the income of Palermo was said to exceed that of the English government. Scholars from all over the East and Europe traveled to Roger's court, which ranked next to Spain's in the translation of Arabic documents. Life and culture in the Sicilian kingdom was diverse and colorful, including as it did Norman, Byzantine, Italian, and Arabic elements.

From the middle of the twelfth century to roughly the midpoint of the thirteenth, the history of Naples and Sicily and also the developments over the whole Italian peninsula were fatally entwined with the history of Germany and hinged on the rise and fall of a powerful German royal house: the Hohenstaufen.

Frederick Barbarossa. From 1152 to 1190 the German throne was occupied by Frederick I of the House of Hohenstaufen. (He was known as Frederick Barbarossa because of his red beard.) Seeking to rectify the damage done by the Investiture Struggle and to reëstablish his imperial power in Italy, he constantly stressed two points: that the emperor did not obtain his authority from the pope and that his empire was entirely secular, above and separate from the Church. To Frederick Barbarossa is credited the phrase "Holy Roman Empire" as the official title of the lands he claimed in Germany and Italy.

Frederick spent about twenty-five years fighting intermittently in Italy, but the final result was failure. The opposition from the popes and the liberty-loving north Italian cities was too strong. But Frederick did score a diplomatic triumph by marrying his son to the heiress of the throne of Naples and Sicily. The new threat of Hohenstaufen encirclement of northern and central Italy made it vital to the papacy that this royal house be destroyed.

Frederick II, a brilliant failure. It fell to the lot of Frederick Barbarossa's grandson, Frederick II (1194-1250), to meet the pope's challenge. Left an orphan at an early age, Frederick was brought up as the ward of the most powerful of medieval popes, Innocent III. During the minority of Frederick, the empire fell on evil days; and rebellious groups fought continually. In 1215, Frederick gained effective control of the empire and, until his death in 1250, gave it some degree of order.

The papacy and the empire fought for supremacy in Italy throughout Frederick's reign. In this struggle the emperor faced the same implacable opposition his grandfather had and experienced the same failure.

Frederick also clashed with the papacy in another sphere. Embarking on a crusade at the pope's insistence, he turned back because of illness. Later, however, although excommunicated by the pope, he negotiated with the Muslims and obtained important concessions, including the Holy City, Jerusalem. Ignoring this success, the pope excommunicated Frederick again, tried to dethrone him, called him "this scorpion spewing poison from the sting of his tail,"[13] and wound up a papal condemnation with the charge that "Frederick maintains that no man should believe aught but what may be proved by the power and reason of nature."[14] This latter charge was an attack upon the young emperor's philosophy of life, which was antireligious and—for his time—even revolutionary (see p. 235).

Frederick had little or no interest in Germany. During his reign, he stayed away from German soil and made it his policy to surrender whatever the princes demanded just so long as they were quiet. Absorbed in the tangled affairs of Italy, Frederick permitted the German nobles to consolidate their power and to destroy the framework of any central authority. At heart he was a Mediterranean monarch; he shaped Sicily into a modern state, politically and economically. As long as he lived, this brilliant but erratic Hohenstaufen held his empire against adversaries. After he died, however, the empire quickly disintegrated. In less than twenty years after his death, the allies of the pope defeated Frederick's descendants in battle, and the Hohenstaufen house was annihilated.

Significance of the fall of the Hohenstaufens. How important was the fall of the House of Hohenstaufen? In Italy the victory of the papacy was more apparent than real, for its struggle against the emperors lost it much of its integrity and prestige. Men had seen popes using spiritual means to achieve earthly ambitions. More and more, popes acted like the Italian princes, playing the game of diplomacy amid the shifting rivalries on the peninsula. This involvement in worldly concerns and the accompanying decay in ideals help to explain the revolt against papal authority—one of the themes of Chapter 13.

The Holy Roman Empire never again achieved the brilliance it had enjoyed in the reign of Frederick Barbarossa. The emperors usually did not try to interfere in Italian affairs, and the practice of going to Rome to receive the imperial crown from the pope ceased. In German affairs the emperors no longer even attempted to assert their authority over the increasingly powerful noble families. After the fall of the Hohenstaufens, Germany lapsed more and more into political disunity.

SUMMARY

During the period from the middle of the eleventh century to the end of the thirteenth, England and France arose as pioneers in national unification. The first country to achieve an organized nationhood was England. Its development was notable also for its legal and constitutional achievements: the common law, the jury system, itinerant or circuit judges, early recognition of the need for popular consent to royal authority, and the creation of representative government through Parliament.

The essential pattern of historical development was similar in each nation, although each had its distinctive problems. (1) At first, the kings were faced with serious competitors to their royal authority, usually the Church and the feudal nobility; (2) the kings overthrew the competitors by building an efficient system of royal government that, above all, gave the people a more efficient standard of justice than they could obtain in the Church or feudal courts; and (3) the kings made alliances with the rising middle class in the cities against their common enemy, the landed gentry. Above all, the kings had at their disposal a professional civil service, a standing army, and a well-organized treasury department.

In England, the Normans secured a single kingdom in 1066 as a result of the Conquest, and the task of successive English kings was that of building up the machinery of royal administration and keeping their competitors under control. English medieval history is the story of the gradual, sometimes interrupted, approach toward this objective. But in France, the movement toward the consolidation of royal power started from a small area—from the minuscule Ile de France. Each noble had to be subordinated and brought within the framework of royal authority. It was a tedious task, but it was largely accomplished by the Capetians by the end of the thirteenth century.

Nation-making in Spain was unique, suffused as it was with the idea of a crusade and with religious fervor. In the mid-eleventh century, the Christian Spanish states began the *Reconquista* in earnest, but not until the end of the fifteenth century would the task be completed.

Instead of creating a strong national state at home, German kings for hundreds of years sought the prize of empire over the Alps. But, in the face of resistance from the Italian cities, the treachery of the German nobles, and the opposition of the papacy, Frederick Barbarossa and Frederick II failed to achieve their goal.

During the period from 1300 to 1650, the budding nation-states of England and France reached full maturity, Spanish unification was completed, and the nucleus of a national state in Russia was created. It is this story which will be taken up in Chapters 11 and 14.

SUGGESTIONS FOR READING

H. Pirenne, *A History of Europe*,* 2 vols., Anchor. Unsurpassed as a synthesis of the main strands of European history from the fall of Rome through the Reformation; a "best buy" for anyone's history shelf. Vol. I covers the period up to the beginning of the thirteenth century. A vivid picture of twelfth-century French and English politics and personalities is contained in the beautifully written biography by Amy Kelly, *Eleanor of Aquitaine and the Four Kings*,* Vintage. R. W. Southern, *The Making of the Middle Ages*,* Yale, is a stimulating book of essays for those who have mastered the basic factual material; it deals with the main themes of medieval civilization, including government.

S. Painter, *The Rise of the Feudal Monarchies*,* Cornell. A brief, clear picture of political developments in England, France, and Germany from the beginning of the tenth to the end of the thirteenth century. Z. N. Brooke, *A History of Europe from 911 to 1198*, Unwin, 1951, is a useful general history of the major part of the period dealt with in this chapter. Unsurpassed as a detailed comparative study of the emergence of monarchy is C. Petit-Dutaillis, *The Feudal Monarchy in France and England from the Tenth to the Thirteenth Century*, Kegan Paul, 1936.

F. M. Powicke, *Medieval England, 1066-1485*, Home Univ. Library, 1948. An excellent short summary by a leading English medievalist. Another recommended summary is H. M. Cam, *England Before Elizabeth*,* Torchbooks. Vol. I of G. M. Trevelyan's classic *History of England*,* 3 vol., Anchor, covers English history from Anglo-Saxon times through the thirteenth century. Good detailed treatments of English history during the period covered by this chapter include H. W. C. Davis, *England Under the Normans and Angevins, 1066-1272*, Methuen, 1949; F. Barlow, *The Feudal Kingdom of England, 1042-1216*, Longmans, 1955; and G. O. Sayles, *The Medieval Foundations of England*,

Methuen, 1952, which is strong on constitutional development.

F. M. Stenton, *Anglo-Saxon England*, Oxford (Clarendon Press), 1947. This scholary study has largely superseded previous histories of this period. Other outstanding works of historical scholarship on phases of English history to the end of the thirteenth century include F. M. Stenton, *The First Century of English Feudalism*, Oxford (Clarendon Press), 1932, covering the century following 1066; A. L. Poole, *From Domesday Book to Magna Carta, 1087-1216*, Oxford (Clarendon Press), 1951; and F. M. Powicke, *The Thirteenth Century, 1216-1307*, Oxford (Clarendon Press), 1953.

Two first-rate historical novels dealing with the Norman Conquest of England are H. Muntz, *The Golden Warrior*, Scribner's, 1949; and W. Bryher, *The Fourteenth of October*, Pantheon, 1952.

W. A. Morris, *Constitutional History of England to 1216*, Macmillan, 1930; G. B. Adams, *Constitutional History of England*, Holt, 1949; and A. B. White, *Making of the English Constitution, 449-1485*, Putnam, 1925, are good brief accounts of this complicated subject. More detailed and difficult, but indispensable for the serious student of law, are J. E. A. Jolliffe, *Constitutional History of Medieval England*, Van Nostrand, 1937; and F. Pollock and F. W. Maitland, *The History of English Law Before the Time of Edward I*, Cambridge Univ., 1903.

G. L. Haskins, *Growth of English Representative Government*, Univ. of Penn., 1948. An excellent introduction to the history of Parliament. Among other important works on this subject are A. F. Pollard, *The Evolution of Parliament*, Longmans, 1926; and D. Pasquet, *Essay on the Origins of the House of Commons*, Cambridge Univ., 1925.

E. S. Duckett, *Alfred the Great: The King and His England*,* Phoenix. A sound, well-documented study of Alfred as warrior, political innovator, and promoter of learning. F. M.

*Indicates an inexpensive paperbound edition.

Stenton, *William the Conqueror and the Rule of the Normans*, Putnam, 1908, is probably the best biography of the Conqueror. The age of Henry II, Richard I, and John is brought to life in the enjoyable medieval success story by S. Painter, *William Marshall: Knight-Errant, Baron, and Regent of England*, Johns Hopkins, 1933. Also recommended are Kate Norgate, *Richard Lion Heart*, Macmillan, 1924; S. Painter, *The Reign of King John*, Johns Hopkins, 1949; and F. M. Powicke, *King Henry III and the Lord Edward*, Oxford (Clarendon Press), 1947. The twelfth-century conflict between Church and state is mirrored in the sympathetic biography of Thomas à Becket by A. Duggan, *My Life for a Sheep*,* Image.

F. Funck-Brentano, *The Middle Ages*, Putnam, 1923. A brief and highly readable survey of medieval France. R. Fawtier, *The Capetian Kings of France*, St. Martin's, 1960, is excellent for a discussion of the growth of royal power. See also the works by Luchaire, Evans, and Tilley listed on p. 198.

F. Perry, *St. Louis, the Most Christian King*, Putnam, 1901. An interesting but narrowly conceived biography. A work much broader in scope and presenting a clear picture of French feudal politics in the early thirteenth century is S. Painter, *The Scourge of the Clergy, Peter of Dreux, Duke of Brittany*, Johns Hopkins, 1937.

R. B. Merriman, *The Rise of the Spanish Empire in the Old World and the New*, 3 vols., Macmillan, 1918. Vol. I of this classic work contains the best general account in English of the rise of the medieval kingdoms of Castile and Aragon. More recent specialized studies are H. J. Chaytor, *A History of Aragon and Catalonia*, Methuen, 1933; and R. M. Pidal, *The Cid and His Spain*, Murray, 1934.

J. Bryce, *The Holy Roman Empire*,* Schocken Books. A masterpiece which presents a clear outline of both the history and the political theory of the empire. A convenient general history, loaded with facts but weak on interpretation, is T. F. Tout, *The Empire and the Papacy, 918-1273*, Macmillan, 1921. The latest and best work on medieval Germany, G. Barraclough, *The Origins of Modern Germany*, Blackwell, 1949, shows that the roots of many modern German problems go back to the Middle Ages. J. W. Thompson, *Feudal Germany*, Univ. of Chicago, 1928, contains a good account of the eastward expansion of the Germans.

P. Villari, *Medieval Italy from Charlemagne to Henry VII*, Unwin, 1910. Designed for the general reader and still highly regarded. Recommended as a good general survey of Italian history is L. Salvatorelli, *A Concise History of Italy*, Oxford, 1939.

E. Kantorowicz, *Frederick the Second, 1194-1250*, Ungar, 1957. A scholarly and provocative biography of one of the most interesting medieval personalities. See also G. Slaughter, *The Amazing Frederick*, Macmillan, 1947.

CHAPTER 10

To the Glory of God

FAITH, THOUGHT, AND ART IN MEDIEVAL EUROPE

Introduction. With justification the Middle Ages have been called the Age of Faith. To the medieval Christian, the basic purpose of life was salvation of the soul, not the search for scientific fact or the control of nature or other goals which have preoccupied the lives of people in other eras. Whether or not he lived fully on this earth was of secondary concern to a medieval man so long as he achieved salvation in the next life. With rare exceptions, Europeans were born, lived, and died under the protection of the Church; this institution gave meaning and direction to their lives. Just as its monasteries dotted the countryside and its towering cathedrals dominated the towns, so the Church and its influence permeated the social fabric of western Christendom.

In an age abounding in physical affliction and social injustice, the Church provided consolation and brought warmth and color to monotonous lives. To our medieval ancestors, Christianity was as vivid and rich as the stained-glass windows in the churches where they worshiped. Sermons abounded in lurid descriptions of hell and depicted heaven as "a splendor that is sevenfold brighter and clearer than the sun." Above all else, the people received the sacraments to obtain the graces they needed to achieve their salvation, the goal of all Christians.

The Church also molded the intellectual, the artistic, and, for several centuries, the political life of the West. The greatest thinkers of the age were enlisted by the Church to translate classical and Arabic treatises, to develop philosophical theories, and to make those educational advances that culminated in the establishment of the universities. Poets and troubadours and such literary titans as Dante and Chaucer interwove spiritual and human themes in their works. Architects, sculptors, and other craftsmen pooled their talents to fashion Romanesque and Gothic buildings. Church administration, with authority stemming from the pope and passing through a hierarchy of archbishops and bishops to the parish priest, provided the nearest approach to a universal government during the Middle Ages.

The underlying difference between our medieval ancestors and ourselves would appear to be one of perspective. To them theology was the "science of sciences," whereas today there are those who say that we have made science our theology. Yet this difference is not due exclusively to the extension of knowledge during the intervening centuries. It lies also in the fundamental premise governing the lives of our medieval forefathers. They believed in a world order, divinely created and maintained. For

them, the universe possessed an inner coherence and harmony, which it was the function of the theologian and the scientist alike to discover. Revelation and knowledge, faith and reason, Church and state, spirit and matter—these dualities could be reconciled in a great spiritual and social synthesis.

The purpose of this chapter is largely to examine the methods by which our ancestors sought to realize this synthesis and the measure of their success. As a first step, we shall trace the institutional growth of the one universal organization of medieval Europe, the Church. Next we shall watch its progressive assumption of secular powers, culminating in the triumphs of Innocent III. Finally, we shall see how, under the sponsorship of the Church, scholars and philosophers, scientists and inventors, and artists and artisans labored for the glory of God and the salvation of man.

THE SPIRIT AND STRUCTURE

OF THE MEDIEVAL CHURCH

The Church in the "Dark Ages." In Chapter 5 we saw how powerful and extensive was the influence of the Church in the preservation of classical civilization and in the conversion of the barbarous Germans to Christianity. As the Church developed an autonomous organization with its own hierarchy and landholdings, its secular power grew. During the reign of Gregory the Great (590-604), the power of the papacy in Italy increased sharply. Gregory "ordered the police, regulated markets, coined money, maintained civil and criminal courts, repaired the walls and aqueducts, supported schools and hospitals, commanded the militia, and defended the city in the case of attack."[1]

In still other practical ways the Church made its influence more extensive and enduring. This was a vital period of missionary activity, when the Christian message was carried throughout Europe. Monasteries were constructed which served as havens for those who sought a contemplative life, as repositories of learning for scholars, and often as progressive farming centers.

The theological position of the Church. The nature and process of salvation were set forth in theology—the field of study which deals with the nature of God and His relations to the universe and man. According to the theology of the Church, Adam had bequeathed the taint of original sin to his descendants, so that all the human race was displeasing in the sight of God. But He did not leave man without hope. Jesus, the Son of God, had sacrificed Himself upon the cross to atone for mankind's sins, and through His sacrifice God gave man an opportunity to earn salvation. This opportunity was bestowed only on those who believed in redemption through Christ's atonement and who followed His precepts. But salvation itself was won only with the grace of God. Since man could perform no act worthy of salvation without divine grace, how was this to be earned? The theologians taught that God bestowed His grace on man by means of sacraments through the Church and its officials.

The problems of theology attracted the attention primarily of the intellectuals. The majority of the people then, as today, accepted the current beliefs without very much questioning. To the unlettered, the following points constituted the essentials of the Christian faith: (1) the creation and fall of Adam, (2) the Birth and Crucifixion of Christ, (3) the Last Judgment, (4) the horrors of hell, (5) the eternal bliss of heaven, and (6) the usefulness of the sacraments in helping them win salvation.

The sacraments. The sacraments have been defined as outward or visible signs instituted by Christ to signify and to give grace. By the twelfth century seven sacraments had been recognized: Baptism, Confirmation, Holy Eucharist, Penance, Extreme Unction, Holy Orders, and Matrimony.

In Baptism the taint of original sin was washed away and the person given a Christian name, hence "christening." Confirmation strengthened the character of the recipient, especially in his formative years. The sacrament of Matrimony was instituted to give the married couple spiritual help—although celibacy was prescribed for those who entered the Church as a career. Holy Orders, or ordination into the priesthood, was administered by the bishop. This sacrament conferred the power and grace to perform the sacred duties of the clergy; the ordained priest was capable of administering all sacraments except Confirmation and Holy Orders. Penance enabled sins committed after Baptism to be forgiven through the absolution of the priest. Extreme Unction was administered when death appeared imminent; it forgave remaining sins and bestowed grace and spiritual strength on the dying Christian.

Perhaps the most important sacrament was the Holy Eucharist, defined as "both a sacrament and a sacrifice; in it Our Savior, Jesus Christ, body and blood, soul and divinity, under the appearance of bread and wine, is contained, offered, and received." The significance of this sacrament can be fully appreciated only when the doctrine of transubstantiation is understood. According to this doctrine, when the priest performing the Mass pronounces over the bread and wine the words Christ used at the Last Supper, "This is My Body. . . . This is the chalice of My Blood . . . ," a miracle then takes place. To all outward appearances, the bread and wine remain unchanged, but in "substance" they have been transformed into the very body and blood of the Savior.

Enforcing belief. The Church possessed a legal system of its own and very effective methods of enforcing its teachings and commands. Canon law was compiled from the Scriptures, the writings of the Church Fathers, the disciplinary and doctrinal rules made by Church councils, and the decrees of the popes. In time the Church issued its official body of canon law, the ecclesiastical counterpart of the Justinian Code (see p. 169). Canon law guided the Church courts in judging perjury, blasphemy, sorcery, usury (for the medieval Church denounced moneylending), and heresy. Heresy was the most horrible of all crimes in medieval eyes. A murder was a crime against a fellow man, but the heretic's disbelief in the teachings of Christ or His Church was considered a crime against God Himself.

Although comparatively late in its history the medieval Church sometimes resorted to outright physical punishment, the chief weapons to support clerical authority were spiritual penalties. The most powerful of these was excommunication, which meant exclusion from the Church. The seriousness of this penalty lay in the denial of the sacraments, thereby endangering salvation.

Interdict, which has been termed "an ecclesiastical lockout," was likewise a powerful instrument. Whereas excommunication was directed against individuals, interdict punished whole groups of people, such as the inhabitants of an entire area. In the area thus penalized, Church services were withheld, along with all sacraments other than Baptism, Penance, Confirmation, and Extreme Unction.

The papacy. The influence of the medieval Church was felt by every inhabitant of every hamlet throughout western Europe. The universality and power of the Church rested not only upon a systematized, uniform creed but also upon the most highly organized administrative system in the West.

At the head was the pope, or bishop of Rome (see Chapter 5). The geographical extent and the vast membership of the Church required that the pope have administrative assistance. This was provided by the Curia, originally the papal court, which in the course of time developed an intricate administrative system. Judicial and secretarial problems were handled by the papal Chancery, financial matters by the Camera, and disciplinary questions by the Penitentiary. From 1059 on, the leading ecclesiastics of the Curia formed the College of Cardinals, which elected the new pope; this method has continued to the present day.

The higher clergy. Europe was divided into a number of ecclesiastical provinces, each administered by an archbishop. A province comprised in turn several dioceses.

While the archbishop was responsible for a diocese of his own, called an archdiocese, the other dioceses in each province were managed by bishops. A diocese was made up of many parishes and numerous religious houses. The bishop's court held a wide jurisdiction over both clergy and laity. Because the claims of lay courts challenged the bishop's domain, especially on such matters as wills and dowries, which had both a spiritual and a secular character, the scope of his administrative and disciplinary powers was a very controversial issue.

The priest in his parish. The real foundation on which the medieval Church rested was the ordinary people in the parishes. In the last analysis the Church's strength depended upon the ability of the parish priest to administer the sacraments, attend the sick, hear confessions, supervise the morals of the parish, and hold the respect of his parishioners. Although the priest was very likely of humble birth and little education, he was father confessor, social worker, policeman, and recreation director, all rolled into one. In most cases he was a credit to his Church.

Although religion was indispensable to our ancestors, a glance at a medieval parish church would reveal a scene that would strike the modern mind as exceedingly informal: "the knight sauntered about with hawk on wrist, his dogs following, and perhaps fighting, behind; the women gathered to-gether and talked (as women do) and laughed and took mental notes of each other's dresses for future imitation or disparagement."[2] Despite the apparent lack of reverence, the congregation regarded with awe the altar where the solemn mystery of transubstantiation took place.

The regular clergy. So far we have discussed the secular clergy, who administered the Church's services and communicated its teachings to the laity. But another great branch of churchmen also existed—the regular clergy, so called because they lived by a rule (*regula*) within monasteries. These monks were the men who desired to lead lives of contemplation, simplicity, and seclusion from the world.

The monastic way of life actually originated before Christianity, having existed in Judaism, for example, among the Essenes, who sought to isolate themselves from worldly preoccupations (see p. 123). As early as the third century A.D. in the East, Christian ascetics, who had abandoned the worldly life and become hermits, could be found. Some ascetics went so far as to denounce even beauty as evil and, in pursuit of spiritual perfection by subordinating their flesh, tortured themselves and fasted to an unusual degree. In Syria, for example, St. Simeon Stylites lived for thirty years on top of a pillar sixty feet high, braving pain and harsh weather.

In time, however, such extreme asceticism brought a reaction. As a more moderate expression of asceticism, Christians in Egypt developed the monastic life, wherein men seeking a common spiritual goal lived together under a common set of regulations. St. Basil (330-379), a Greek from Asia Minor pioneered in the monastic life by substituting hard labor, works of charity, and a communal life for the asceticism of the hermit. The Rule of St. Basil still remains the standard guide for monasteries of the eastern Church.

In western monasticism the work of St. Benedict (*c.* 480-543) paralleled St. Basil's efforts in the East. About 520, St. Benedict led a band of followers to a hill in Italy

In the sixth and seventh centuries, when the Continent was suffering from the shock of barbarian invasions, monasteries in Ireland provided a safe haven for learning. There men studied Greek and Latin, copied and preserved manuscripts, and in illuminating them produced masterpieces of art. The beauty of their work can be seen in this page from *The Book of Kells,* a manuscript which was probably the product of an entire scriptorium working for a number of years.

named Monte Cassino, where they erected a monastery. There he composed a set of important monastic rules. Under the Benedictine Rule, the monks took vows of poverty and obedience to the abbot, the head of the monastery. Divine worship was the chief duty of a monk; the brothers participated in eight services every day. The Rule also stressed the value of manual work, and six or seven hours of labor were required daily.

The monks as custodians of knowledge. Perhaps the most significant contribution of the monasteries was toward the preservation of learning. For many years after the fall of the Roman empire, classical learning had declined in the West, although it did not die out completely. In the sixth century,

a Roman scholar, Boethius, who had entered the service of the Ostrogothic king Theodoric, translated Greek works into Latin. These translations were the only source of Greek learning available to medieval scholars until six hundred years later, when more complete accounts were obtained through Arabic sources. Unjustly accused of treachery by Theodoric, Boethius was thrown into prison, where he wrote *The Consolation of Philosophy* while awaiting his execution. This work later became a popular philosophical treatise.

Cassiodorus, a contemporary of Boethius who had also served Theodoric, devoted most of his life to the collection and preservation of classical knowledge. By encouraging the monks to copy valuable manuscripts, he was instrumental in making the monasteries centers of learning. Following his example, many monasteries established scriptoria, departments concerned exclusively with copying manuscripts.

During the early Middle Ages in Europe, most education took place in the monasteries, which sheltered the few teachers and scholars of the time. Thus, in a monastery in northern England, the Venerable Bede (*c.* 673-735) wrote his *Ecclesiastical History of the English Nation,* the best account we have of almost two hundred years of English history.

Church revenues. The Church received its revenues from various sources. The tithe, which took one tenth of every man's income, and fees for performing religious services provided sources of money for the parishes. A large source of revenue for the Church was the income from its lands. The tracts of land contributed to bishoprics and monasteries by kings and nobles were not held free of obligations, as we have seen in the discussion of feudalism in Chapter 6. Nevertheless, the Church eventually became the largest landholder in medieval Europe.

The wealth of this huge organization was a source of both strength and weakness. Its great riches enabled it to perform functions and support charities which the states neglected. But this wealth also encouraged abuses and worldliness among the clergy, conditions which disillusioned the common people.

THE CHURCH MILITANT

The Church-state rivalry. Medieval political theory begins with the concept of a universal community divided into two spheres —the spiritual and the temporal. As Pope Gelasius I declared in the fifth century, God had entrusted spiritual and temporal powers to two authorities—the Church and the state—each supreme in its own sphere.

When Pepin and later Charlemagne were crowned by the pope, the temporal prestige and authority of the head of the Church rose. From the ecclesiastical point of view these coronations could be interpreted to signify the supremacy of the pope over secular rulers. On the other hand, Charlemagne's imperial authority threatened the popes.

The Holy Roman Empire was created in 962 when the German king, Otto the Great, was crowned in Rome (see p. 216). This act reëmphasized the concept of the dual leadership of pope and emperor. The empire, it was said, was the legitimate successor of the old Roman empire. Universal authority was claimed for it, though its actual power was confined to Germany and Italy. At first the papacy looked to the German king for protection against feudal abuses and the unruly Italian nobles and Roman mobs. From the Church's viewpoint, however, this arrangement soon had its drawbacks, for the German kings continued to interfere in ecclesiastical affairs—even in the election of popes— to serve royal purposes.

Another aspect of the controversy between Church and state centered around the problem of lay investiture. Theoretically, a bishop or abbot on assuming his office was subject to two investitures. His spiritual authority was bestowed by an ecclesiastical official and his feudal or civil authority by the king or a noble. In Germany, the monarch came to control both the appointment and the installation of bishops.

The king and nobles had granted many of the Church lands to the higher clergy, who became their vassals. The new bishop had to do them homage for his fief and received from them his ring and pastoral staff, the symbols of his spiritual office. Furthermore, the nobility were given control over Church property during the vacancy between the death of one incumbent and the selection of his successor, which meant that powerful laymen had an important stake in the election to Church offices. Thus "to all intents and purposes the German Church was a state Church."[3]

For his part, the king was anxious to have a faithful vassal on each bishop's throne for a number of reasons. The most important need was to have the vast Church lands furnish loyal feudal troops for the royal armies. Many German bishops proved to be valiant warriors. Faithful bishops were also the most reliable and best-educated men to counsel a king and administer the royal government and finances.

The pope, therefore, had reason to complain about his bishops on spiritual and temporal grounds alike. The papacy was rescued from its plight, however, by a great religious revival and the advent of Pope Gregory VII and his powerful successors.

The Cluniac reform. Beginning in the tenth century and reaching full force in the next, the religious revival affected all classes. Plagues, famines, and chaos had turned the common people increasingly toward religion at the same time that Church officials recognized the deplorable conditions within the feudalized Church.

The most far-reaching force of the revival was the new monastic order of Cluny, founded in 910. From the original monastery in Burgundy and its many daughter houses all over western Europe, there radiated a tremendous impulse for reform. The Cluniac program called for enforcement of clerical celibacy and the abolition of simony, whereby an ecclesiastical office was sold to the highest bidder or was acquired by bribery. (The term comes from Simon the magician, who tried to buy the gift of the Holy

Spirit from the apostles.) The success of reform depended on freeing the Church from secular control and establishing absolute papal authority over all clerics. These became the further goals of the Cluniac reformers. In 1059 they achieved a major success with the establishment of the College of Cardinals to elect the pope, thereby freeing the papacy from secular influence.

Gregory VII. The most ambitious proponent of the Cluniac reform was Gregory VII (1073-1085), who raised the papacy to unprecedented heights. Gregory held as his ideal the creation of an international government under papal control. Instead of conceding equality between the ecclesiastical and secular powers, Gregory VII maintained that the Church was supreme. Until his death in 1085, he devoted his extraordinary energy to breaking all resistance to the Church. Outstanding among Gregory's attempts at reforms—and certainly the most difficult to enforce—were his efforts to suppress simony and lay investiture.

The quarrel with Henry IV. In 1075 Gregory VII formally prohibited lay investiture and threatened to excommunicate any layman who performed it and any ecclesiastic who submitted to it. This drastic act was the same as declaring war against Europe's rulers, since almost all of them practiced lay investiture. The climax to the struggle occurred in Gregory's clash with the emperor Henry IV. The latter was accused of simony in appointing his own choice to the archbishopric of Milan and was summoned to Rome to explain his conduct. Henry's answer was to convene a synod of German clergy in 1076 and to depose the pope. In retaliation, Gregory excommunicated Henry and deposed him in turn, absolving his subjects from their oaths of allegiance.

At last, driven by a revolt among his barons to make peace with the pontiff, Henry appeared in January 1077 before Gregory at Canossa, a castle in the Apennines. Here, garbed as a penitent, the emperor stood barefoot in the snow of the courtyard and begged forgiveness for three days until, in Gregory's words:

We loosed the chain of the anathema and at length received him into the favor of communion and into the lap of the Holy Mother Church.[4]

This dramatic humiliation of the emperor did not in fact put an end to the quarrel, nor do contemporary accounts attach much significance to the incident—public penance in those days was not uncommon even for kings. Yet the pope had made progress toward freeing the Church from interference by laymen and toward increasing the power and prestige of the papacy. The problem of lay investiture was settled in 1122 by the compromise known as the Concordat of Worms. The Church maintained the right to approve, if not to choose, the holder of a clerical office. The candidate, such as a bishop, was invested by the king as a feudal official and was then consecrated by the archbishop, who invested him with his spiritual functions, as symbolized by the ring and pastoral staff. Henceforth the problem of lay investiture never again became so acute.

THE CHURCH TRIUMPHANT

The papacy's zenith: Innocent III. For hundreds of years the Church had been strengthening its own position and the preëminence of the pope. Through the efforts of Gregory VII and the success of the early crusades, the papacy emerged as potentially the most powerful office in Europe. In the hands of a strong leader, the papacy could reign supreme even among the monarchies of Europe. Such a leader was Innocent III, a scholarly and brilliant pontiff who occupied the papal throne from 1198 to 1216. Like Gregory VII, he held an exalted view of his office. He once wrote:

The successor of Peter is the Vicar of Christ: he has been established as a mediator between God and man, below God but beyond man; less than God but more than man; who shall judge all and be judged by no one.[5]

Innocent III told the princes of Europe that the papacy was as the sun, whereas the kings were as the moon. As the moon derives its light from the sun, so the kings derived their powers from the pope.

Innocent III was also sufficiently powerful to impose his will on all the major rulers, including the monarchs of England, France, and Germany. In the case of King John of England, a struggle developed over the election of the archbishop of Canterbury, and Innocent placed England under interdict and excommunicated John. Under pressure from his subjects, John capitulated to Innocent by becoming his vassal, receiving England back as a fief, and paying him an annual monetary tribute. Next, the pope forced Philip Augustus of France to comply with the Church's moral code by taking back as his queen the woman he had divorced with the consent of the French bishops. As for the Holy Roman Empire, Innocent lent his full moral weight to the enemies of the existing emperor. After the secular ruler was defeated in battle, the pope promptly deposed him at the Lateran Council in 1215 and confirmed his own protégé, Frederick II.

The papacy had attained the zenith of its temporal power. Innocent's ideal of a papal theocracy seemed realized, for the nations of Europe acknowledged the power of Christ's vicar. Innocent III's goal to "judge all and be judged by no one" was achieved.

From the reign of Innocent III until the end of the thirteenth century, the Church radiated power and splendor. Yet weaknesses were evident in the lessening of religious zeal in the later crusades, in the need for renewed internal reform, and in the growth of heresy. Whereas the first three crusades had enhanced the papacy's prestige, the remainder exposed not only the mercenary motives of many of the participants but also the attempts by some popes to further their own temporal interests.

New monastic reforms. We will recall that the monastic order of Cluny had come into being to reform the increasing laxity of the older orders. Unfortunately, the Cluniac order itself gradually relaxed its early strictness; and a new order, the Cistercian, was founded in 1098 at Cîteaux as the second movement of monastic reform.

Above is a mosaic of the brilliant and powerful Pope Innocent III from the Villa Cantina of Poli, Italy.

The Cistercian movement received its greatest impetus from the zealous efforts of St. Bernard of Clairvaux in the twelfth century. The abbeys were situated in solitary places, and the monastic discipline emphasized austerity and manual labor. So ascetic was the order that in none of the Cistercian abbeys were sculptured figures permitted, and Bernard inveighed against the beautification of churches in general:

Oh! vanity of vanities! but not more vain than foolish. . . . What has all this imagery to do with monks, with professors of poverty, with men of spiritual minds? . . . In fact, such an endless variety of forms appears everywhere that it is more pleasant to read in the stonework than in books, and to spend the day in admiring these oddities than in meditating on the Law of God.[6]

Spurred on by this militant denouncer of wealth and luxury in any form, the Cistercian order had founded 343 abbeys in France and elsewhere in western Europe by the time of Bernard's death in 1153, and more than double that number by the end of the century. Yet even the Cistercians found it difficult to revive the old sense of purpose. The economic basis of monasticism was almost exclusively agricultural, so that the Cistercians living at a distance from the townspeople were not able to cope adequately with the growth of secularism and the rise of heresy in the towns.

Heresy: growth and suppression. Heresy has been defined by the Church as "obstinate adherence to opinions arbitrarily chosen in defiance of accepted ecclesiastical teaching and interpretation."[7] The two major heretical sects at this time were the Albigensians in southern France and the Waldensians in southern France and northern Italy.

Harking back to old Christian heresies, the Albigensians—so called because their center was at Albi in southern France—thought of the world as the battleground of the opposing forces of good and evil. The world of matter was inherently evil, and the Church with its great organization and material wealth was likewise evil. The Albigensians condemned many activities of the state and the individual, even condemning marriage for perpetuating the human species in this sinful world.

The Waldensians derived their name from Peter Waldo, a merchant of Lyons who gave up his possessions in 1176 to found a lay order called the Poor Men of Lyons. While the principal complaint of the Waldensians was the wealth and worldliness of the Church, their actual heresy came from denying the efficacy of the sacraments unless administered by worthy priests. Because of some of their views, the Waldensians have sometimes been considered as forerunners of the Protestant Revolt.

For ten years Innocent III tried to reconvert these heretical groups. Failing, in 1208 he instigated a crusade against the prosperous and cultured French region of Toulouse, where the Albigensian heresy was widespread. The crusade began with horrible slaughter to the cry of "Kill them all, God will know His own!" Soon the original religious motive was lost in a selfish rush to seize the wealth of the accused. In time the heresy was almost completely destroyed, along with the flourishing culture of southern France. The time was to come, however, when the popes could not suppress heresy as successfully as they had destroyed the Albigensians. Meanwhile, the Waldensians fled into northern Spain and also into Lombardy, the Rhineland, and Bohemia. There they merged with local groups which were also discontented with the Church.

The Inquisition. In the thirteenth century, the Church devised the Inquisition to cope with the rising tide of heresy and to bring about religious conformity. The Inquisition was an elaborate system of inquiry into the beliefs of persons suspected of heresy. The accused were tried in the Inquisition's court without the aid of legal counsel. If the accused person confessed and renounced his heresy he was "reconciled" with the Church on performance of penance. If he did not voluntarily confess, he could be subjected to torture. If this failed to extort a confession, the prisoner could be declared a heretic and turned over to the secular authorities, perhaps to be burned at the stake.

In any evaluation of the Inquisition, it should be remembered that the soul was considered incomparably more important than the body—therefore to torture a suspected heretic was justifiable if by confession his soul could be saved from the greater tortures of hell. Furthermore, the use of torture and the denial of legal counsel prevailed in civil as well as in ecclesiastical courts.

The Franciscans and Dominicans. The quickening tempo of European life in the thirteenth century was reflected in the rise of national states, the growth of cities and commerce, and the creation of universities. In response to the challenge of these changing conditions, the Dominican and Franciscan orders were inaugurated to bring about an inspiring reform in the Church. Instead of living a sequestered existence in a monastery, the members of these orders began itinerant preaching throughout the countryside and towns.

The Franciscans were founded by St. Francis of Assisi (1182?-1226), who, like Waldo of Lyons, rejected riches and spread the gospel of poverty and Christian simplicity. St. Francis stipulated that the friars could use but not own property. Simplicity of life and humanitarianism were fundamentals in the Rule of St. Francis, who exemplified the best of medieval idealism:

I counsel . . . and exhort my brethren in our Lord Jesus Christ that they brawl not . . . but that they be meek, peaceable, soft, gentle, and courteous and lowly, honestly speaking and answering to every man as unto them accordeth and belongeth.[8]

The second order of friars was founded by St. Dominic (1170?-1221), a well-educated Spaniard whose early career had been spent fighting the Albigensian heresy in southern France. There he decided that to combat the strength and zeal of its opponents, the Church should have champions who could preach the gospel with apostolic fervor. Dominic's order of friar-preachers dedicated themselves to preaching and teaching as a means of maintaining and spreading the doctrines of the Church and of converting nonbelievers.

The Franciscans and Dominicans fought heresy with vigor. While never formally vested in the friars, the Inquisition came to be placed chiefly in their hands, with the Dominicans playing a prominent role. As they became investigators of heresy and active in papal affairs, the preaching orders increased in importance but lost much of their original simplicity and freshness. Yet their message and zeal had done much to reform the Church and to provide it with moral and intellectual leadership at a time when such leadership was badly needed. In later centuries they also made outstanding contributions to the Church by their missionary efforts around the world.

A medieval illumination illustrates one of the legends about St. Francis of Assisi; so great was his love for all God's creatures that he once preached a sermon to the birds.

Veneration of saints and relics. Thus far in this chapter, we have considered the Church largely as a universal religious and political body. Its appeal to ordinary men, however, did not lie in its theology or its claims to universal authority, but in the extraordinary degree to which the Church entered their lives. They were born into it, and they died in its embrace; it was their moral guide and their spiritual sustenance; and it brought them solace on this earth and assured them the means of salvation in the next life.

The veneration of the Virgin Mary was one of the most potent forces in medieval religion. In an age when even the most educated persons believed that thunderstorms, plagues, and famines were the evil designs of the devil and that hell loomed perilously close, it seemed natural to pray to the Mother of Christ for protection and comfort.

As an earthly mother supplicates for mercy on behalf of her erring child, so the Virgin Mary could be counted on to supplicate her Son in heaven for her children on earth, particularly in answer to their prayers. Many magnificent Gothic cathedrals, such as Notre Dame (Our Lady) in Paris, were dedicated to Mary as symbols of the people's devotion.

Medieval people believed that relics of saints had miraculous powers. Such a relic as the bone of a saint supposedly would halt disease or create abundant harvests. The manner in which unscrupulous venders of fake relics sometimes duped illiterate persons has been vividly recounted by Chaucer in his description of the Pardoner in *The Canterbury Tales*:

No pardoner could beat him in the race,
For in his wallet he had a pillow case
Which he represented as Our Lady's veil;
He said he had a piece of the very sail
St. Peter, when he fished in Galilee
Before Christ caught him, used upon the sea.
He had a latten cross embossed with stones
And in a glass he carried some pig's bones,
And with these holy relics, when he found
Some village parson grubbing his poor ground,
He would get more money in a single day
Than in two months would come the parson's
    way.
Thus with his flattery and his trumped-up stock
He made dupes of the parson and his flock.[9]

Nevertheless, many relics were genuine. Furthermore, this reverence of relics stimulated artists to design elaborate caskets and reliquaries decorated with gold, silver, or enamel to hold the bones.

THE INTELLECTUAL

SYNTHESIS

The Church as the center of intellectual activity. While Europe gradually recovered from the shock of the Roman empire's demise, the Church was the mainstay of European civilization. The medieval schools were nearly always run by the Church, manuscripts were preserved and copied in the monasteries, and the original thinking of scholars and philosophers centered on theological problems.

During the Middle Ages, men were just as eager as the Greeks had been to explain the problems of life, but the approaches differed. The Greeks emphasized reason; medieval men emphasized faith more than reason. Furthermore, the latter labored under handicaps from which classical thinkers were spared. Where the Greek philosopher possessed freedom, the medieval philosopher was bound by authority. Based on sources considered infallible, the Church's dogmas were not to be questioned.

The term *Scholasticism* covers the whole range of attempts to reconcile faith and reason. Nearly all the intellectual activity of the period was concerned in one way or another with this problem. The controversy between Realists and Nominalists was one of the most important aspects of Scholasticism.

Realism versus Nominalism. Both Realists and Nominalists claimed complete allegiance to the Church and included within their ranks eminent ecclesiastics, although the Church as a whole tended to favor the Realists.

Their battleground was the problem of universal Ideas. On this point Plato had argued that Ideas have reality apart from their existence in men's minds. A specific object was *real* only in so far as it represented the nature of its Idea (see p. 52). Thus Plato himself, for example, was real inasmuch as he partook of the Idea of Man. Aristotle, taking an opposite view, maintained that individuals exist as individuals—a person such as Plato was himself real. To Aristotle a human being was a real entity, not just a reflection of the universal Idea of Man. To the Realists in the Middle Ages, only universal Ideas could be real and exist independently. To the Nominalists, abstract concepts such as universal Ideas were only names (*nomina*) and had no real existence.

Both Realism and Nominalism—if carried to their logical extremes—resulted in principles equally abhorrent to the Church. Realism became pantheism (the universe as a whole is God), and Nominalism became materialism (the universe is composed solely of matter). In 1092 the Council of Soissons condemned Nominalism as heretical.

Abélard and Conceptualism. A compromise between Realism and Nominalism was offered by the scholarly Pierre Abélard (1079-1142) in his theory of Conceptualism. He said that universal terms exist only as thoughts or concepts in men's minds. Thus, he distinguished between a thing itself and its name. How do we get the mental concept "chair"? By seeing many chairs and sitting in them, we note certain similarities common to all. From these similarities, our observation and experience build up a concept "chair." Therefore, Abélard argued, there exists in particular things a similarity of qualities, which in the abstract form a concept. To that extent, therefore, terms which identify a class of things are objectively valid.

Perhaps Abélard's greatest significance lies in the challenge he issued against the mental habits of his age. Man must learn to doubt, he said, for doubting leads one to inquire, and inquiry leads to truth. While he himself never transcended superimposed authority, he stimulated intellectual curiosity by compiling a list of contradictory statements taken from the most authoritative writings of the Church in a work entitled *Sic et Non* (Yes and No). By doing so he helped establish the method employed by later Scholastic thinkers in their attempts to reconcile conflicting authorities.

Abélard's promising career as a dialectician at the University of Paris was cut short by an ill-starred romance with his pupil, the learned and beautiful Héloïse, niece of the canon of Notre Dame. The two lovers were married in secret, but the uncle, falsely believing that Abélard planned to abandon Héloïse, hired thugs who attacked and emasculated the scholar. Both Abélard and Héloïse then sought refuge in the Church—Pierre as a monk and Héloïse as the abbess of a nunnery.

Attempts to reconcile classical learning and Church dogma. In the twelfth century, a study of Greek learning with its Muslim additions was undertaken by western scholars who translated Muslim editions of ancient writings. Prior to this time, Byzantine and Muslim scholarship had been far superior to western scholarship. The result of this

Shown here is a painting of St. Thomas Aquinas by Fra Angelico.

translating activity was that a host of new ideas, particularly in science and philosophy, were introduced to western scholars. The horizons of knowledge in the West were expanded to include not only Arabic learning but also such important classical works as Euclid's *Geometry*, Ptolemy's *Almagest*, Hippocrates' and Galen's treatises in medicine, and all of Aristotle's writings.

As his works became known, Aristotle's authority was generally accepted as second only to that of the Scriptures. But because the Church's teachings were considered infallible, his ideas, as well as those of other great thinkers from antiquity, had to be reconciled with existing dogmas. By applying Aristotelian logic to the new sciences and philosophy and attempting to harmonize them with the Scriptures and Church dogmas, theologians hoped that the purpose of God's plan would then stand revealed. Toward this end they wrote compendiums of knowledge called *summae* (sum totals).

Scholasticism reached its zenith with St. Thomas Aquinas (1225?-1274). In his *Summa*

Theologica this brilliant Italian Dominican set out to reconcile Aristotle and the Church's dogma—in other words, reason and faith. Aquinas maintained that the divine plan could be understood either by reason or by faith. In case of a contradiction, faith won out, because of the possibility of human error in reasoning. So convincing was St. Thomas in settling this conflict that his works continue to be used as basic texts in Catholic schools.

This reconciliation of reason and faith was attacked in the works of two Franciscans, Duns Scotus (d. 1308) and William of Occam (d. *c.* 1349), who elaborated on Aquinas' belief that certain doctrines are beyond discovery by the use of reason. They argued that if the human intellect could not understand divinely revealed truth it could hope to comprehend only the natural world and should not intrude upon the sphere of divine truth. Such a position tended to separate science and philosophy from theology and to free science for further inquiry into the natural world. As a result the unifying authority of the Church over all branches of knowledge was weakened.

Significance of Scholasticism. Having attained its zenith in the thirteenth century, Scholasticism declined rapidly. What was the total significance of this movement and what meaning does it hold for us today?

Scholasticism has often been used as a term of reproach, for its adherents concentrated on theological subtleties, discouraged independent thought, and neglected the opportunities of the natural world while concentrating on the hereafter. It is this last criticism that finds most favor in our own century, which is so taken with delving into the mysteries of science. But it should be remembered that the Scholastics sought to unify all aspects of life and to work out an all-embracing system of faith, logic, and science. Though their efforts may not have succeeded, the task should not be looked upon askance by people of our own age, especially when we consider its magnitude. Increasingly today we recognize the importance of reconciling science and faith in an age that has so much of the former (which Scholasticism lacked) and so little of the latter (which Schoolmen had in abundance).

Medieval science. Because of the emphasis upon authority and the all-pervasive influence of the Church, the early medieval atmosphere was not conducive to free scientific investigation. Those who studied science were churchmen, and their findings were supposed to illuminate rather than contradict the dogmas of the theologians. Perhaps the greatest obstacle facing science in the early Middle Ages was ignorance of Greek learning. Knowledge was limited to such compilations as the *Etymologies* of St. Isidore, bishop of Seville. Written in the seventh century, this fascinating encyclopedia included a jumble of odds and ends whose accuracy can be judged from a sample excerpt:

XI, 3, 23. The race of the Sciopodes is said to live in Ethiopia. They have one leg apiece, and are of a marvellous swiftness, and the Greeks call them Sciopodes from this, that in summertime they lie on the ground on their backs and are shaded by the greatness of their feet.[10]

The *Etymologies* remained a standard work of reference in the western world for three hundred years.

When Greek and Arabic works were translated in the twelfth century, the West came into possession of a magnificent legacy of scientific knowledge. Arabic numerals and the symbol *zero* made possible the decimal system of computation. Algebra came from the Arabs and trigonometry from the Muslims. Euclid's *Geometry* was also made available. Leonard of Pisa made a great original contribution to mathematics in the thirteenth century when he worked out a method to extract square roots and to solve quadratic and cubic equations. On the other hand, Ptolemy's belief that the earth was the center of the universe, a fallacious theory destined to handicap astronomy for centuries, was accepted by most people. It should be emphasized, however, that educated men in the Middle Ages believed the earth to be round, not flat.

Physics was based on Aristotle's theory of four elements (water, earth, air, and fire) and on his theories of dynamics—doctrines which it took centuries to disprove completely. The science of chemistry was dominated largely by Aristotelian concepts, mixed in with magic and alchemy. Like the Muslim alchemist, his European counterpart tried in vain to transmute base metals into gold and silver and to obtain a magic elixir, but in both cases the attempts did much to advance experimental science.

Frederick II and Roger Bacon. Two notable exceptions to the medieval rule of subservience to authority were the emperor Frederick II and the Franciscan monk Roger Bacon. Frederick gathered about him in his Sicilian court many distinguished scholars (irrespective of their religious beliefs) and corresponded with others in distant lands. His treatise *On the Art of Hunting with Falcons* is still considered largely accurate. He indulged in many experiments, one of which was a test to determine which language children would speak if they were raised in conditions of absolute silence. The experiment was a failure because all the children died.

Endowed with a bold and lively mind, Roger Bacon (1214-1292) favored the inductive method and criticized the other techniques of his day. In his *Opus Maius* this Franciscan states:

There are four principal stumbling blocks to comprehending truth, which hinder well-nigh every scholar: the example of frail and unworthy authority, long-established custom, the sense of the ignorant crowd, and the hiding of one's ignorance under the show of wisdom.[11]

Bacon himself made important contributions to optics, mechanics, geography, and astronomy.

Inventions in the late Middle Ages. That the later Middle Ages were not lacking in ingenuity is shown in this partial list of inventions. In the twelfth century the mariner's compass was invented; this was followed about 1300 by the invention of the rudder, and in the fourteenth and fifteenth centuries by changes in the design of ships. The West's acquaintance in the thirteenth century with gunpowder, which was invented by the Chinese (discussed in Chapter 15), was followed in the fourteenth and fifteenth centuries by further developments in armor and fortifications and by the invention of firearms and artillery. The fourteenth century also witnessed the introduction of the blast furnace and progress in ironworking.

Medieval medicine. By the thirteenth century, learned Muslim commentaries on Galen and Hippocrates and on Aristotle's biology were available in the West. Greek and Arab theories dominated until the Renaissance and even later in northern Europe. This knowledge, coupled with their own discoveries and improved techniques, made medieval doctors more than just barbers who engaged in bloodletting. Yet the state of medical knowledge and practice was, by our standards at least, still primitive. This can be seen in the prevalence of superstitious beliefs and the resort to magical practices, the general lack of concern for public sanitation, the periodic decimation of entire populations by epidemics such as the Black Death, and that significant indicator of the state of public health—the infant mortality rates, which were staggeringly high.

Origin of universities. The old rhetoric schools of Rome had a curriculum of seven liberal arts, separated into two divisions: a *trivium* consisting of grammar, rhetoric, and dialectic; and a *quadrivium* of arithmetic, music, geometry, and astronomy. When the Roman empire in the West fell, the task of education went to the Church; and the classical liberal arts were adapted to prepare youths for the ministry. Schools were maintained in most of the monasteries. Thus, in the seventh and eighth centuries, the Benedictine abbeys became important education centers. A number of schools were founded in connection with important cathedrals—Paris, Chartres, Canterbury, and Toledo.

The renaissance of the twelfth century brought back classical learning to the West, and with it unprecedented numbers of students came to the schools. The revival of learning and the development of professional studies in law, medicine, and theology led to

Medieval students are pictured in a fifteenth-century manuscript. At the left, they oppose one another in "disputation," the class debates which went on for hours. The students at the right are gambling in university rooms, a practice strictly forbidden by school authorities. As a rule the student attended only one or two classes a day, but each might be three hours long. The first met at daybreak in an unheated, often windowless hall; the professor lectured from a platform while the students sat on low benches. The texts were costly hand-copied manuscripts, which were rented out to those students with sufficient funds; the less fortunate copied the lectures on wax tablets. Many students did not study at night because they could not afford candles. The more exuberant sometimes spent their evenings roistering or fighting the townsmen; often they were forced to scale the college walls to get back to their rooms after the doors were barred.

the rise of organized centers of learning—the universities, which soon eclipsed the less dynamic monastic and cathedral schools.

Originally, the word *university* meant a group of persons possessing a common purpose. In this case it referred to a guild of learners, both teachers and students, analogous to the craft guilds with their masters and apprentices (see p. 193). In the thirteenth century the universities had no campuses and little property or money, and the masters taught in hired rooms or religious houses. If the university was dissatisfied with its treatment by the townspeople, it could migrate elsewhere. The earliest universities—Bologna, Paris, and Oxford—were not officially founded or created, but in time the popes and kings granted charters to establish new centers of learning. The charters gave legal status to the universities and rights to the students, such as freedom from military service and from the jurisdiction of town officials.

Two systems: Bologna and Paris. Two of the most famous medieval universities were at Bologna in northern Italy and at Paris. The students who flocked to Bologna organized themselves into guilds, largely to pro-tect themselves against the rapacious townspeople, who raised the cost of food and lodging at the expense of the students. Because the student guilds also controlled the administration of the university, Bologna was an undergraduate paradise. In the earliest statutes (1317), we read that a professor requiring leave of absence even for one day had first to obtain permission from his own students. Failure to secure an audience of at least five students resulted in a fine which was the same as that for being absent from his class.

At the university in Paris, conditions developed differently. This university, which had grown out of the cathedral school of Notre Dame, specialized in theology and became the most influential intellectual center in medieval Europe. Its administration was far different from Bologna's. The chancellor of Notre Dame, who had long been accustomed to exercising authority over the cathedral school, never allowed the students to obtain control of the burgeoning university. In turn, the power of the chancellor was restricted by a papal bull in 1231, which recognized the rights of the masters and protected the scholars in various ways.

The collegiate system. Universities owned no dormitories, and students lived in rented rooms or pooled their resources to obtain housing on a cooperative basis. With masters' fees and living expenses to pay, the impoverished student labored under decided handicaps. A philanthropic patron, however, sometimes provided quarters where poor scholars could board free of charge. One such patron was Robert de Sorbon, the royal chaplain to the saintly Louis IX. About 1257 Robert endowed a hall for sixteen needy students working for their doctorates in theology. Thus was founded the Collège de Sorbonne; and the University of Paris is still popularly known by the name of its great benefactor.

As more colleges were established, the large universities became collections of colleges in which the students lived and studied. Although organization by colleges finally disappeared in the University of Paris where the system originated, at both Oxford and Cambridge the collegiate system has remained from medieval times as an integral part of the university.

Curriculum and degrees. The degrees available at medieval universities were similar to those offered today. The bachelor's degree, which could be obtained after studying from three to five years, was not considered very important. For a master's degree, particular emphasis was placed on the study of the works of Aristotle. Scholars studied for a doctorate in one of the three great professions—theology, law, and medicine—by reading texts relevant to their chosen field. It was no easy matter to get a doctorate from a medieval university; many years of preparation were required, and at the final examination the candidate had to defend his thesis publicly for hours against the learned attacks of the dean and the masters. If successful in his defense, the candidate then stood the cost of a banquet for his examiners.

The modern university resembles its medieval alma mater in its primary purpose for existence: the organization of an institution for the advancement of human knowledge and the training of each new generation of students. In details, too, the similarities remain. Colleges still offer a stated curriculum, formal instruction, examinations, and degrees. The gowns and hoods seen at every commencement are the same kind of attire that the medieval students wore. The voluminous sleeves originally functioned as carriers for books or food.

Latin language and literature. While localized languages were generally spoken, among the educated people Latin served as an international means of communication. In this common tongue lay much of the cohesion of the Middle Ages, for virtually all the crucial communications of the Church, governments, and schools were in Latin. Religious and political documents, treatises on law and medicine, and essays on theology were all written in this language.

Latin poetry experienced periods of revival, the greatest of which came in the eleventh and twelfth centuries. After the twelfth century, however, literary expression in Latin could not compete successfully against the rising tide of literature in the vernacular tongues.

Any misconception that the Middle Ages were simply otherworldly and long-faced will be rudely shattered by glancing at the madcap literature of the students, who unhesitatingly proclaimed the pleasures of wine, women, and song. Known as goliardic poetry, this form of verse was written by wandering students. An example is the *Confession of Golias*, in which the poet asks a prelate to grant him absolution for his misdeeds:

'Tis most arduous to make
  Nature's self-surrender;
Seeing girls, to blush and be
  Purity's defender!
We young men our longings ne'er
  Shall to stern law render,
Or preserve our fancies from
  Bodies smooth and tender. . . .

In the public house to die
  Is my resolution;
Let wine to my lips be nigh
  At life's dissolution:

That will make the angels cry,
  With glad elocution,
"Grant this toper, God on high,
  Grace and absolution!"[12]

Vernacular epic and lyric poetry. The types
of medieval vernacular literature were varied.
Down to the thirteenth century, the com-
monest manner of expression was poetry, of
which the epic was the earliest form. The
Anglo-Saxon *Beowulf*, the German *Hilde-
brandslied*, and the Norse sagas were composed as early as the seventh and eighth
centuries. Later, around the beginning of
the thirteenth century, the German saga was
recast into the *Nibelungenlied* (*Song of the
Nibelungs*), which tells the stirring legends
of Siegfried, Brünhild, and the wars against
the Huns. These same stories were used in
Richard Wagner's music dramas *Der Ring
des Nibelungen* in the nineteenth century.

From the eleventh to the thirteenth centuries, French vernacular literature developed the *chansons de geste*, songs of heroic
deeds, centering on Charlemagne and ascrib-
ing to him and his knights the chivalric

Bologna and Paris influenced other European universities.
Bologna left its mark on Italy, southern France, and Spain.
Paris became the model of universities founded in northern
France, England, Germany, the Low Countries, and the rest
of northern Europe. By the end of the fifteenth century,
there were about eighty universities in Europe.

code and religious fervor of the crusades.
The most famous of these *chansons*, the *Song
of Roland*, tells of the deeds and death of
Roland in the Pyrenees while defending the
rear of the Frankish army. To dramatize the
legendary splendor of King Arthur and his
Round Table, the Arthurian cycle was created in England in the twelfth century,
largely from Welsh and other Celtic sources.

In the twelfth and thirteenth centuries,
while the poets of northern France were
creating the *chansons de geste*, the troubadours of southern France were singing their
poems of chivalry and courtly love. The
troubadour spirit spread to other countries;
in Germany, for example, minnesingers
entertained the nobility with love lyrics.

Tales of counting house and kitchen. All
of the foregoing types of poetry were designed primarily for the chivalric aristocracy.
The self-made burgher preferred more practical and shrewd tales. His taste was grati-
fied by the bawdy *fabliaux* and the animal
stories about Reynard the Fox, a clever, unscrupulous creature. Still another class of
literature, which circulated for centuries by
word of mouth before being written down,
developed for the illiterate common people.
The Robin Hood ballads of the fourteenth
century were built around the theme of
robbing the rich to give to the poor. In the
same century the *Vision of Piers Plowman*,
condemning the injustices of a social system
that had brought on the peasant revolts,
was composed.

Dante Alighieri. The vernacular was also
used by two of the greatest writers of the
period—Dante and Chaucer. "The medieval
synthesis, something of the old and something
of the new" describes Dante Alighieri (1265-
1321). While this Florentine stressed the importance of the outmoded Holy Roman Empire, at the same time he defended the new
use of the vernacular tongue as a literary medium and also as the language needed for a
united Italy. Dante brooded over ideas born
of his knowledge of Latin classics, his profound religious sense, and his understanding
of the Scholastics; and the eventual result was
a masterpiece, the *Divine Comedy*. Dante is

led through hell and purgatory by his teacher Virgil, symbol of pagan learning, but it is Beatrice, symbol of divine love, who guides him through paradise. Thus Dante shows his allegiance both to medieval ideology and to the rising appreciation of classical civilization.

The wit of Chaucer. Geoffrey Chaucer (1340?-1400) is one of the greatest figures in medieval literature. In the *Canterbury Tales*, Chaucer reveals a cross section of contemporary English life, customs, and thought. The twenty-nine pilgrims, who assembled in April 1387 at an inn before journeying to the shrine of St. Thomas à Becket at Canterbury, were a motley group. The "truly perfect, gentle knight," just returned from warring against the "heathen in Turkey," was accompanied by his son, a young squire who loved so much by night that "he slept no more than does a nightingale." The clergy was represented by the coy prioress who "would weep if she but saw a mouse caught in a trap,"[13] the rotund monk who loved to eat fat swan and ride good horses, the friar who knew the best taverns and all the barmaids in town, and the poor parish priest who was a credit to his faith. There were also the merchant who could talk only of business, the threadbare Oxford student, the miller with a wart on his nose, and the worthy wife of Bath, who had married five times and was now visiting Christian shrines in search of a sixth husband.

Chaucer's fame rests securely upon his skill as a storyteller. The Midland dialect he used was the linguistic base for the language of future English literature, just as Dante's use of the Tuscan dialect fixed the Italian tongue.

THE ESTHETIC SYNTHESIS

Artistic correlation. The *Summa Theologica* of St. Thomas Aquinas and the *Divine Comedy* of Dante represent the best intellectual expressions of the medieval spirit. Similarly, the Gothic cathedral is the ultimate artistic expression of the age. Each of these masterpieces represents a different aspect of the attempt to organize everything into an overall pattern which would glorify God.

The order and form of Scholastic thought find their counterparts in the structure and style of the Gothic edifices. A Scholastic treatise was systematically arranged in logical parts; the cathedral was similarly articulated in space. The main sections, such as the nave, transept, and apse, were individually distinctive yet were integrated into a coherent structure.

Early Christian churches. In design, early Christian churches imitated the plan of the Roman basilicas. In this design a rectangle is divided into three aisles: a central aisle, or nave, ending in a semicircular apse, and a lower-ceilinged aisle on each side. The side aisles were separated from the nave by a row of semicircular arches. In the fourth century, the basilica plan was modified by the addition of a transept across the aisles between the apse and the nave. Later, by the elongation of the apse and the extension of the transept beyond the side aisles, the essentially "T" shape of the basilica was modified to form a cross. In this way Christian symbolism was added to the basic plan of the building.

Romanesque architecture. A tremendous architectural revival occurred in the eleventh century. In the years between 1000 and 1150, the characteristic features of Romanesque architecture were established. (The Cathedral of Pisa, an example of Italian Romanesque architecture, is pictured in Color Plate 8.) While ornamentation differed with locality, the round arch was a standard Romanesque feature. Both barrel and ribbed-groin vaults were used; for example, the barrel vault supported the roof over the nave, and the ribbed vault, that of the aisles and transept. Thick outside walls were necessary to support the heavy stone vaults and roofs. Because the walls would be weakened by large window apertures, the interiors were dark and gloomy. From the practical standpoint, the stone vaults were desirable to make the churches more fireproof; on the esthetic plane, they made the churches look more massive and

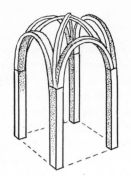

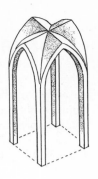

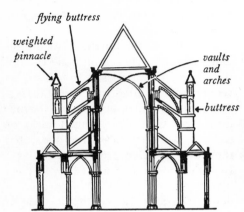

flying buttress

weighted
pinnacle

vaults
and
arches

buttress

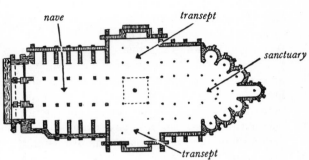

nave

transept

sanctuary

transept

Derived from the intersecting vaults used by the Romans, the RIBBED-GROIN VAULT (drawing at upper left) was made up of arches which span the sides of a square, with groin arches crossing diagonally from corner to corner. Vaults of this type were an important feature of the eleventh- and twelfth-century architecture known as Romanesque. The use of RIBBED-GROIN VAULTS WITH POINTED ARCHES (upper left) enabled structures of the Gothic period to reach greater heights than had been attainable with the semicircular arch. One of the finest examples of this type of architecture is the thirteenth-century, French-Gothic Amiens Cathedral (opposite page, lower left). Typically Gothic—in addition to its pointed arches—are Amiens' triple doors, sculptural decoration (lower right), rose window dedicated to the Virgin, and cruciform plan. The cross section and floor plan of Amiens (opposite page, center position) show some of the more important Gothic structural elements—the vault, arch, weighted pinnacle, buttress, and flying buttress. The photo below shows the interior of Gloucester Cathedral, in England. English Gothic cathedrals were generally lower and longer than the French structures, and, toward the end of the fourteenth century, they utilized multiple vaulting ribs, which appear here as branching column tops near the ceiling. Gloucester Cathedral is an early example of the late Gothic Perpendicular style, in which the emphasis is on the vertical, as evidenced by the rectangular sections in its great east window.

monumental. The name *Romanesque* came to be applied at a much later date to this style of architecture, because it was thought to resemble that used by the Romans.

Gothic architecture. Actually, no clear-cut cleavage exists between Romanesque and Gothic. There was a gradual evolutionary process, which reached its culmination in the thirteenth and fourteenth centuries. The architects of the Gothic-style cathedral developed ribbed-groin vaults with pointed arches, which allowed more window space. These architectural elements resulted in a vault whose thrust could be concentrated on a few strong structural supports. Part of the weight was carried down to the ground by columns within the building and part by flying buttresses at points along the walls. With such vaulting and buttresses, the weight of the roof was largely shifted off the walls (see diagram of cross section and floor plan).

The important principles of the concentration of thrusts and counterthrusts were worked out, so that the Gothic structure was supported by its essential frame. Between the buttresses, exquisite stained-glass windows were set into the walls. The dark, somber interior of the Romanesque churches gave way to the jeweled light of the Gothic interiors (see Color Plate 10).

Toward the end of the Middle Ages, the wealth accruing from the economic revival encouraged the development of secular Gothic architecture. Town halls and guildhalls, the residences of the rich, and the chateaux of the nobles all borrowed the delicate Gothic style from the cathedrals.

Sculpture and stained glass. Thirteenth-century Gothic sculpture was carved to fit into the total composition of the cathedral. To use sculpture to the best architectural advantage, the subject was often distorted to achieve a particular effect. As long as sculpture remained strongly bound to its architectural setting, the individuality of the separate statues was suppressed. This was done to emphasize the "serial" character of the entire band of statues across the façade.

The making of stained-glass windows in medieval times was a fine art whose excellence has not since been duplicated. A stained-glass window is composed of small pieces of colored glass held together in a pattern by metal strips which both braced the glass and emphasized the design. By adding various minerals to molten glass, thirteenth-century craftsmen achieved brilliant hues. Details were painted on the glass.

SUMMARY

The traditional division of history into "ancient," "medieval," and "modern" is fundamentally arbitrary and artificial in that history is a continuous process. Applying the same common denominator—"medieval" —to the thousand turbulent years between the fifth and fifteenth centuries obscures the wide variations that existed during the period. For five centuries after the fall of Rome, western civilization was on the defensive against invading barbarians from the east and north. The Church took the lead in fusing classical, barbarian, and Christian elements and nurtured such intellectual activity as existed. By the eleventh century, Europe had shifted to the offensive, and its resurgence of strength was reflected in the Church's militant drive to political triumph in the thirteenth century.

Maintaining its power through centuries of political upheaval, the Church possessed the only unified system of law and administration in Europe and intimately affected the life of every person in Europe. It gave man a sense of security against the dangers on earth and those beyond. To perform its historical mission, the Church required a hierarchy of clergy and an elaborate doctrine, accompanied by methods for enforcing its will. We have followed the areas of reform, watched the Church's power reach its apex in the age of Innocent III, and noted signs of its eventual decline.

Within the Church, thinkers wrestled with philosophical issues, such as the Realist-Nominalist controversy and the compromise offered in Conceptualism. In the thirteenth century, such famous Scholastics as St. Thomas Aquinas made herculean attempts to reconcile faith and reason, Church authority and classical thought.

Stimulated by the acquisition of Greek and Arabic knowledge, science and education established new frontiers. The earliest universities grew from unorganized groups of scholars and students to important centers of learning. Bologna and Paris, in particular, directly affected other universities. In literature, Latin, the international language of the educated, slowly gave way to the vernacular tongues. Chaucer and Dante, giants in the literary field, both wrote in their native languages and did much to develop modern English and Italian respectively.

Evolving from Romanesque patterns, the splendid Gothic cathedrals were the greatest artistic achievement of the medieval period. The rounded arches and massive walls of Romanesque architecture were replaced by the ribbed-groin vaults with pointed arches and the flying buttresses of the soaring Gothic cathedrals. This style carried over from churches to town halls and urban dwellings.

SUGGESTIONS FOR READING

M. W. Baldwin, *The Mediaeval Church,** Cornell. A clear, erudite essay on all aspects of the Church's development through the pontificate of Innocent III. See also S. Baldwin, *The Organization of Medieval Christianity,* Holt (Berkshire Studies), 1929. A more detailed general account is A. C. Flick, *The Rise of the Medieval Church and Its Influence on the Civilisation of Western Europe from the First to the Thirteenth Century,* Putnam, 1909.

S. R. Packard, *Europe and the Church Under Innocent III,* Holt (Berkshire Studies), 1927. An admirable introduction to the medieval papacy at the height of its power. A longer scholarly study is W. Ullman, *Growth of Papal Power in the Middle Ages,* Barnes and Noble, 1956. The rival political theories supporting the Church-state conflict are judiciously set forth in C. H. McIlwain, *The Growth of Political Thought in the West,* Macmillan, 1932; and G. H. Sabine, *A History of Political Theory,* Holt, 1954.

H. Waddell, *The Desert Fathers,** Ann Arbor. A classic discussion of the asceticism which preceded the rise of monasticism. Important works on western monastic orders are E. C. Butler, *Benedictine Monachism,* Longmans, 1919; and A. Jessopp, *The Coming of the Friars,* Allan and Unwin, 1903. On the founders of the friars, see J. Jorgensen, *St. Francis of Assisi,** Image; and B. Jarrett, *Life of Saint Dominic,* Burns, Oates, and Washbourne, 1934.

H. C. Lea, *A History of the Inquisition of the Middle Ages,* 3 vols., S. A. Russell, 1955. A detailed discussion of medieval heresies and the methods employed by the Church in dealing with heretics. A more moderate and balanced treatment is J. Guiraud, *The Medieval Inquisition,* Benziger, 1930. Excellent on Peter Waldo and other early medieval heretics is E. Davidson, *Forerunners of St. Francis,* Houghton Mifflin, 1927. The best account of the Albigensian heresy is S. Runciman, *The Medieval Manichee,** Compass.

H. O. Taylor, *The Emergence of Christian Culture in the West: The Classical Heritage of the Middle Ages,** Torchbooks; and, by the same author, *The Medieval Mind,* 2 vols., Harvard, 1949, are unsurpassed for the history of medieval intellectual and emotional development. See also F. B. Artz, *The Mind of the Middle Ages, A.D. 200-1500,* Knopf, 1958. C. H. Haskins has written two important and attractive books on aspects of medieval thought: *The Renaissance of the Twelfth Century,** Meridian; and *The Rise of Universities,** Cornell.

Source readings recommended as supplements to this chapter: see Part Four, pp. 303-319, 337-347 of H. J. Carroll, Jr., *et al.,* *The Development of Civilization,** I, Scott, Foresman, 1961.

P. Vignaux, *Philosophy in the Middle Ages,** Meridian; F. Copleston, *Medieval Philosophy,** Torchbooks. Two fine introductions. See also the authoritative studies by E. Gilson: *Reason and Revelation in the Middle Ages,** Scribner's; and *The Spirit of Medieval Philosophy,* Scribner's, 1940. For science see A. C. Crombie, *Medieval and Early Modern Science,** 2 vols., Anchor. Also recommended is F. Copleston, *Aquinas,** Penguin. A fine historical novel is H. Waddell, *Peter Abelard,** Compass.

Medieval vernacular literature is surveyed in two works by W. Ker: *The Dark Ages,** Mentor; and *Epic and Romance,** Dover. For Latin poetry see H. Waddell, *Mediaeval Latin Lyrics,** Penguin; and *The Wandering Scholars,** Anchor. Convenient introductions to Dante and Chaucer are C. Grandgent, *Discourses on Dante,* Harvard, 1924; and M. Chute, *Geoffrey Chaucer of England,** Dutton.

C. R. Morey, *Christian Art,** Norton; and, by the same author, *Mediaeval Art,* Norton, 1942, are two valuable introductory works. Medieval architecture is described concisely in N. Pevsner, *An Outline of European Architecture,** Penguin. For greater detail see J. Evans, *Art in Mediaeval France,* Oxford, 1948; K. J. Conant, *Early Medieval Church Architecture,* Johns Hopkins, 1942; and O. Von Simpson, *The Gothic Cathedral,* Pantheon, 1956.

Stimulating interpretations of the interrelationship of medieval art, thought, and spirit are H. Adams, *Mont-Saint-Michel and Chartres,** Anchor; E. Mâle, *The Gothic Image: Religious Art in France of the Thirteenth Century,** Torchbooks; and E. Panofsky, *Gothic Architecture and Scholasticism,** Meridian. A. Temko, *Notre-Dame of Paris,** Compass, is an absorbing "biography" of a great cathedral.

*Indicates an inexpensive paperbound edition.

EUROPE

100 Century of decline in Rome 180-285—civil wars, "army-made" emperors, economic hardship, invasions by foreign powers
Diocletian (285-305) strengthens government by despotism; modifies empire administration; attempts to arrest economic decline

300 Ulfilas c. 311-383—Christian missionary to Visigoths; St. Augustine of Hippo 354-430, author of *The City of God*
Christianity legalized throughout Roman empire by Edict of Milan 313
Constantine sole emperor of Rome 324-337; establishes economic caste system
Battle of Adrianople 378—"invincible" Roman legions defeated by Visigoths
Theodosius divides Roman empire into eastern and western states 395; Christianity becomes sole and official state religion 395

400 German invasions begin 406; Rome sacked by Visigoths 410; by Vandals 455
Battle of Châlons 451—German-Roman alliance repels Huns led by Attila
Odovacar deposes Romulus Augustus 476—symbolizes end of Roman empire in the West; German control of Italy begins
Clovis I, Merovingian ruler of the Franks (481-511), becomes Christian 496; expands realm to Gaul, Burgundy, Rhineland, France
Theodoric defeats Odovacar 488; establishes Ostrogothic kingdom in Italy; attempts to preserve classical civilization

500 Slavs invade Europe 500-900; establish Elbe River as western frontier c. 600
Merovingian decline 511—Frankish state divided among Clovis' sons, who become puppet rulers; civil wars, crimes decay kingdoms

600 Pope Gregory the Great 590-604—increase in power of papacy in Italy; period of missionary activity and monastery construction
St. Augustine of Canterbury (596) converts Anglo-Saxon king of Kent to Christianity

700 St. Boniface (eighth century)—"the Apostle of Germany"
Muslims from North Africa conquer Spanish Visigoths 711-718
Charles Martel, Carolingian Mayor of the Palace, rules Franks 714-741; restores Frankish unity; legalizes Carolingian power
Pepin the Short (741-768) ends rule of Merovingian kings; crowned king of Franks by St. Boniface 751; reaffirmed by Pope Stephen 754; conquers Ravenna and makes it "Donation of Pepin" to pope (creation of Papal States) 756
Charlemagne (768-814) extends empire in Germany, Danube valley, north Italy, and Spain; crowned Emperor of the Romans by pope 800; establishes *missi dominici* system 802; fosters Carolingian Renaissance

800 Slavic, Magyar, Muslim, and Viking invasions terrorize Europe (ninth-tenth centuries); Muslim sea control diminishes trade
Treaty of Verdun divides Carolingian empire into West Frankland, East Frankland, and Lorraine 843
Alfred the Great (871-899) establishes strong Anglo-Saxon kingdom in England; improves army, local government, schooling
Novgorod and Kiev merge c. 882—first Russian state; Byzantine-Russian trade begins c. 900

900 Feudalism well established in western Europe c. 900
Treaty between Viking leader Rollo and king of France awards Normandy to Vikings 911; Vikings (Normans) adopt Christianity
Henry I, the Fowler (919-936), founds Saxon strength in Germany; successfully defends domain against Danes, Slavs, Magyars
Otto I, the Great (936-973), centralizes German government; routs Magyars at battle of Lechfeld 955; crowned emperor by pope 962
Ethelred the Unready 978-1016—power of English government lags; invasion by Canute, Viking king; Anglo-Saxon rule restored 1042
Hugh Capet (987) founds Capetian dynasty which ruled France until 1328

1000 Truce of God inaugurates "closed seasons" to curb warfare (eleventh century)
Normans arrive in Italy 1016
Reign of Yaroslav the Wise 1019-1054—peak of Kievan Russia; Byzantine influences in art and literature
Salian House succeeds Saxon kings, begins rule of Germany 1024; attempts to create centralized monarchy
Pope Gregory VII (1025-1085) supports Cluniac religious reform; attempts to suppress simony and lay investiture
Umayyads overthrown in Caliphate of Cordova, replaced by separate Muslim kingdoms; *Reconquista* gains strength 1031
Henry IV 1056-1106—peak of German monarchy's power; Pope Gregory VII humiliates Henry in Investiture Struggle
College of Cardinals formed to elect pope 1059
Norman rule of England begins with defeat of King Harold by William, Duke of Normandy, at battle of Hastings 1066; William centralizes government; initiates well-knit feudal system; establishes Great Council and Curia Regis; supervises Domesday Survey
Fall of Bari to Normans 1071—last Byzantine stronghold in Italy
First Crusade—Jerusalem captured; Latin kingdom of Jerusalem established 1099-1187

1100 Renaissance of the twelfth century—classical learning revived in the West; rise of universities; development of professional studies; revival of Latin poetry; development of vernacular literature; Romanesque and Gothic styles in architecture
Welf-Hohenstaufen rivalry (1106-1152) wrecks structure for a strong German state
Louis the Fat 1108—first strong Capetian ruler in France; builds prestige of French monarchy
Concordat of Worms (1122) mitigates problem of lay investiture; Church maintains right to approve clerical offices
Kingdom of Naples and Sicily formed 1127; becomes strong state under Roger II 1130-1154
Second Crusade 1147—Christians under St. Bernard of Clairvaux fail to capture Damascus
Frederick Barbarossa (1152-1190) claims German and Italian lands as "Holy Roman Empire"; seeks to restore rule in Italy
Henry II (1154-1189) attempts to limit "benefit of clergy"; reforms English judicial system by Assize of Clarendon 1166
St. Dominic (1170-1221) founds Dominican order; St. Francis of Assisi (1182?-1226) founds Franciscan order
Philip II (Augustus) 1180-1223—French monarchy becomes strongest in Europe; expands domain
Third Crusade 1189—the "Crusade of Kings" (Frederick Barbarossa, Richard the Lion-Hearted, Philip Augustus)
Frederick II 1194-1250—brilliant but erratic Hohenstaufen ruler; continues power struggle with papacy; neglects Germany

1200 Pope Innocent III 1198-1216—zenith of temporal power of papacy; Inquisition begins (thirteenth century)
Fourth Crusade 1202-1204—crusaders sack Constantinople
Reconquista—Christians defeat Muslims at Las Navas de Tolosa 1212
King John of England signs Magna Carta 1215—limits power of English monarch
St. Thomas Aquinas (1225?-1274) reconciles faith and reason in *Summa Theologica*; represents zenith of Scholasticism
Louis IX (1226-1270) brings dignity to the French crown
First Parliament in English history convenes 1265
Under Edward I (1272-1307), Parliament becomes important
Philip IV, the Fair (1285-1314), centralizes French government; humiliates Pope Boniface VII
Acre, last Christian stronghold in Holy Land, conquered by Muslims 1291

1300 Scotland wins independence from England in battle of Bannockburn 1314
1400 Hundred Years' War between France and England 1337-1453

NEAR EAST AND BYZANTINE EMPIRE

Jesus Christ c. 4 B.C.-c. 30 A.D.
Paul d. c. 65—greatest of early Christian missionaries
Jewish rebellion (66-70) climaxed by destruction of Jerusalem; end of Hebrew state

100

300

Council of Nicaea 325—Arianism branded heretical; Christ declared cosubstantial with God the Father; formulation of Nicene Creed
Constantine establishes eastern capital, New Rome (Constantinople) 330
St. Basil (330-379) establishes Rule of St. Basil

400

500

Justinian (527-565) crushes Nike rebellion 532; extends Byzantine domain into Italy, Spain, North Africa; codifies Roman law

600

Muhammad 570-632—the Hegira, migration of Muhammad from Mecca to Medina 622; triumphal return to Mecca 630
Heraclius, Byzantine emperor (610-641), defeats Persians in three campaigns 622-628; regains Syria, Palestine, Egypt
Reigns of first four caliphs 632-661—elective office established; Islamic conquest of Syria, Iraq, most of Egypt, and Persia (c. 642);
official version of Koran completed 652

700

Umayyad dynasty 661-750—hereditary office; expands in North Africa, Turkestan, Indus valley, Spain; defeated by Franks at Tours 732

Leo III (717-741) repulses Muslims 717, 718; initiates new law code; centralizes Byzantine government; starts iconoclastic controversy
between eastern and western churches 725-843
Abbaside dynasty 750-1258—end of Arab predominance; peak of Islamic power, civilization, and prosperity
Independent Muslim dynasty set up in Spain under Umayyads 756—early sign of political disintegration of Abbasid empire
Harun-al-Rashid 786-809—most spectacular reign of the Abbaside empire; establishes friendly terms with Charlemagne

800

900

Golden age of Muslim learning 900-1100—advances in medicine, mathematics, literature, philosophy, architecture, decorative
arts; geniuses of this period and later: Al-Razi, Avicenna, Alhazen, Al-Khwarizmi, Omar Khayyám, Averroës, ibn-Khaldun

Basil II, Byzantine emperor 976-1025—empire reaches high level of power and prosperity; Basil defeats Bulgars

1000

Seljuks seize Persia and Iraq, conquer Bagdad (1055); later conquer Syria, Palestine, part of Asia Minor

Battle of Manzikert 1071—Byzantine army defeated by Seljuks
Alexius Comnenus becomes Byzantine emperor by coup d'état 1081; induces First Crusade to turn against his Seljuk enemies 1095   1100

1200

Fourth Crusade 1202-1204—Constantinople attacked by Crusaders; Latin empire rules 1204-1261; schism between eastern and western
churches final

Fall of Abbasid dynasty; Bagdad conquered by Mongols 1258

Rule of Palaeologi 1261-1453—decline in the imperial power of Byzantine empire

1300
1400

Constantinople falls to Ottoman Turks 1453—final collapse of eastern bulwark of Christian civilization

PART 3 The Transition to Modern Times

So far in our study of history, we have encountered a number of societies which emphasized the group at the expense of the individual —societies such as that of ancient Egypt, for example, or of medieval Europe. In other societies, such as that of classical Greece, individualism counted for more than collectivism. During the period which historians speak of as early modern times, the interests and rights of the individual were again in the ascendant. In the political sphere, this emphasis upon individualism was manifested by the creation of nation-states; in the realm of thought and art, it produced the Renaissance; in the area of religion, it split Christendom through the Reformation; and in the field of exploration, it resulted in the discovery and colonization of the Americas and the reopening of the East to western trade.

By the end of the fifteenth century, the medieval ideal of universal political unity had been shattered as national monarchies gained supremacy in England, France, and Spain. Despite opposition from popes and nobles alike, vigorous monarchs in these countries succeeded in their attempts at nation-making—a process that fostered and was in turn supported by a growing national consciousness among the common people. In Germany and Italy, however, unification was hampered by many obstacles, and in eastern Europe nation-making proceeded slowly, though Russia emerged as a powerful state after throwing off the Mongol yoke.

In the realm of thought, Italian scholars known as humanists discovered in the manuscripts of ancient Greece and Rome the same emphasis on individual freedom which was rapidly gaining momentum in their own day, and with this spirit of individualism sprang up an unashamed delight in the beauties and joys of life. Heeding Protagoras' ancient maxim that "Man is the measure of all things" and revolting against medieval authority and asceticism, Renaissance man was impelled by a new spirit of independence, a new hunger for experience. The creative vigor of the Italian Renaissance in literature, thought, and the fine arts surged throughout Europe, resulting in one of the most fruitful epochs in the cultural history of mankind.

The religious diversity of the modern western world can also be attributed to the reaffirmation of the interests and claims of the individual. Substituting the authority of the Scriptures for that of the Roman Church and interposing no priestly mediator between the individual and his God, dynamic leaders such as Luther, Calvin, and Zwingli won followers to their banners. No longer the supreme arbiter of religious life, the Roman Church nevertheless continued as a potent force, launching a strong reform movement of its own.

Finally, the economic structure of western Europe was transformed radically in early modern times. The quickening of town life abetted the rise of a new and forceful middle class, whose members were the chief supporters and benefactors of the system of economic individualism known as capitalism. Furthermore, overseas expansion stimulated trade, increased wealth, and introduced to European markets an abundance of products previously scarce or unknown. So important was the new trade and its many influences on European life and manners that it is referred to as the Commercial Revolution. The barter economy of the Middle Ages was superseded by one of money, banks, and stock exchanges; and Europe rapidly became the economic center of the world.

Up to the fifteenth century, Asia had been equal or superior to Europe in military power and cultural attainments. But as the West advanced, China and India declined in power and creativity. The European scramble for empire had serious consequences. In Asia, important trading concessions were wrung from the natives; in the New World, indigenous peoples were decimated and their cultures all but erased; in tropical Africa, the Europeans established a lucrative slave trade and reaped rich profits from this callous exploitation of human lives. From the mid-point of the seventeenth century to our own day, European civilization—the most creative, expansive, and aggressive on earth—was to be the dominant influence on the course of world history.

CHAPTER 11

Europe in Transition

RELIGION AND POLITICS: 1300-1500

Introduction. In Europe the fourteenth and fifteenth centuries were marked by a decline of those institutions and ideas which we think of as typically "medieval" and which had reached their high point during the preceding two centuries. In thought and art an empty formalism replaced the creative forces which had given the Middle Ages such unique methods of expression as Scholasticism and the Gothic style. Economic and social progress, a striking feature of the preceding period, gave way to depression and social strife, with peasant revolts a characteristic symptom of instability. Not only did the Hundred Years' War contribute to economic and social instability in France and England, it also came close to wiping out the gains made earlier by French and English monarchs at the expense of the feudal nobility. The universal Church experienced a disintegration

similar to that which had already fatally weakened its great medieval rival, the Holy Roman Empire. And in southeastern Europe, the end finally came to the Byzantine empire.

The reasons for the dramatic decline in power and influence of that greatest of all medieval institutions, the all-powerful Church, can be divided into the causes that existed within the church structure itself and those which were weakening it from the outside. The internal factors, including criticism by reformers and heretics, go far to explain the Church's loss of prestige; the external factors, especially the political and the economic ones, were largely responsible for its loss of universal power and authority. In the sixteenth century, all these forces would blend together to bring about the Reformation and the collapse of papal supremacy in many countries.

Despite new crises and temporary setbacks, the process of nation-making continued during the fourteenth and fifteenth centuries. In western Europe the contrasting political trends clearly evident at the end of the thirteenth century—unification in England, France, and Spain, and fragmentation in Germany and Italy—reached their culmination. In Slavic eastern Europe, efforts at nation-making were beset by so many difficulties that significant success was achieved in only one land—Russia. Nevertheless, by the end of the fifteenth century, the circle of international politics had grown to encompass most of Europe; and rivalries became more intense as the quarrels of feudal barons were superseded by the conflicting aims of nation-states.

The fourteenth and fifteenth centuries have often been labeled "the waning of the Middle Ages." Yet, as we shall see in subsequent chapters, this period is also called "the Renaissance," since it engendered those new forces of rebirth that would in time produce the modern world.

THE DECLINE OF
THE MEDIEVAL CHURCH

Dangers facing the papacy. The history of the medieval Church divides roughly into three periods—dissemination, domination, and disintegration. As we saw earlier, in the initial period, which lasted from about the fifth through the eleventh centuries, Roman Christianity spread throughout the West—eastward to the Slavic borders and northward throughout Scandinavia. In the process, the Church evolved an intricate administrative apparatus and became the most powerful propertied and political institution in the West. The period of domination—the twelfth and thirteenth centuries—reached its zenith in the pontificate of Innocent III, who made and deposed temporal princes at will. The Church then seemed unassailable in its prestige, dignity, and power. Yet that strength had already begun to wane, and during the next two centuries the processes of disintegration were to run their course.

Papal centralization was harassed by the growth of nation-states, which were challenging the power of the dying Holy Roman Empire as well as the Church's temporal pretensions. Joined by many of the local clergy, princes opposed papal interference in state matters and favored the establishment of general Church councils to curb papal power. In addition, the papacy was criticized by reformers, who had seen the medieval reformation and the crusades transformed from their original high-minded purposes to suit the ambitions of the pontiffs, and by the bourgeoisie, whose contact with new ideas was fostering growing skepticism, national patriotism, and religious self-reliance. During the fourteenth and fifteenth centuries, these factors took their toll, and papal supremacy collapsed.

Boniface VIII. During the pontificate of the proud Boniface VIII (1294-1303), the papacy was unable to compel such states as England and France to bow down before its commands. The pope came into conflict with both Edward I of England and the French monarch, Philip IV. Boniface had once threatened to depose the "impious king," as he termed Philip. But Philip had stirred up public opinion against the pope's "great fatuousness," and in the final encounter with him the French king won a resounding victory that had long-range implications for the papacy.

When Boniface boldly issued a papal bull in which he maintained that in order to obtain salvation every validly baptized person must be subject to the pontiff of Rome, Philip decided to summon a general council, depose the pope, and call a new papal election. In 1303 Philip's henchmen broke into Boniface's home at Anagni to take him prisoner, but their kidnaping plot failed. The pope was spirited to Rome by his friends, only to die in October of the same year.

The Avignon papacy. The success of the French monarchy was as complete as if Boniface had been dragged before Philip. In the election which followed Boniface's death, a French archbishop was chosen pope. Taking the title of Clement v, he acted according to the wishes of Philip iv. Clement even moved the papal headquarters from Rome to Avignon in France, where the papacy remained under French influence from 1309 to 1376. During this period, known as the Babylonian Captivity, the loss to papal prestige was enormous. All Christendom believed that Rome was the only rightful capital for the Church. Moreover, the citizens of Rome missed the papal court and its revenues; the English justifiably accused the popes of favoring the French kings; and the Germans resented the claims of the pope to temporal power over the Holy Roman emperor.

The Avignon papacy added fuel to the fires of those critics who were attacking Church corruption, papal temporal claims, and the spiritual authority of high churchmen. The period of the Babylonian Captivity also produced a cry for reformation by Church councils and stimulated questioning, especially by John Wycliffe in England (see p. 251), about such basic beliefs as the divinity of the papal office and sacramental system.

The Great Schism. When Gregory xi was made pope and returned the papal headquarters to Rome in 1377, it seemed for a time that the fortunes of the Roman Church would improve. But the reverse proved true. Upon the death of Gregory in 1378, the demand of the Roman multitude for an Italian pope led to the election of Urban vi; but the French cardinals maintained that the election was invalid because of outside pressure on the voters, and they elected a Frenchman, Clement vii, who reigned from Avignon.

The Church was now in an even worse state than it had been during the Babylonian Captivity. During the Great Schism, as the split in the papacy was called, there were two popes, each with his college of cardinals and capital city, each claiming universal sovereignty, each sending forth papal administrators and taxing Christendom, and each excommunicating the other as the antipope. The nations of Europe, of course, gave allegiance as their individual political interests prompted them. France supported Clement, as did Scotland, Navarre, Castile, and Aragon. Urban found his strength in Italy, Portugal, Flanders, England, and most of eastern Europe. In order to keep the allegiance of the various countries, the rival popes had to make concessions to their political supporters; and to a large extent they abandoned the practice of interfering in national politics.

Religious life suffered. The Great Schism had become an international disgrace. "Christendom looked upon the scandal helpless and depressed, and yet impotent to remove it. With two sections of Christendom each declaring the other lost, each cursing and denouncing the other, men soberly asked who was saved. The longer the schism lasted, the more difficult did it seem to heal it, and yet people generally felt that for that very reason positive action was all the more necessary. The very sublimity of Papal pretensions made earthly jurisdiction and compulsory abdication seem very difficult. Still the fact stared Europe in the face that the schism itself, with the cupidity, selfishness, and meanness accompanying it, had shattered the sanctity of Papal claims. . . . "[1]

The Conciliar Movement. Positive action came in the form of the Conciliar Movement. In 1395 the learned doctors of the University of Paris suggested that if the two claimants to the papal throne would not abdicate, a general council of all the Church should be held. Neither pope would abdicate, nor would they arbitrate their differences. In 1409, therefore, a majority of the cardinals of both camps met at the Council of Pisa, deposed both pontiffs, and elected a third man. But neither of the two deposed popes would give up his office, and the papal throne now had three claimants.

Such an intolerable situation necessitated the calling of other Church councils. In 1414 the Holy Roman emperor assembled at the Council of Constance the most impressive Church gathering ever known. For the first time, voting took place on a purely national basis. Instead of the traditional assembly of bishops, the Council was organized as a convention of nations (German, Italian, French, and English, the Spanish entering later). Each nation had one vote. The nationalistic structure of the Council was highly significant as an indication that the new tendency toward nationalistic alignments was being recognized by some members of the Church's hierarchy. Finally, through the deposition of the various papal claimants and the election of Martin v in 1417, the Great Schism was ended, and a single papacy was restored. In addition, papal headquarters were returned to Rome.

Failure of internal reform. The Church had demonstrated by the Council of Constance that in the Conciliar Movement it possessed the means of reforming itself. But the movement was not to endure. At that time the Conciliar Movement represented a reforming and democratizing influence in the Church, aimed at transforming the papacy into something like a limited monarchy. The success of the Council of Constance gave rise to the theory that councils were above popes. Such a notion would have destroyed the supremacy of the pope, and a fundamental conflict arose between the Church councils and the popes, both claiming supreme power. Taking steps to preserve his position, one pope announced that to appeal to a Church council without having first obtained papal consent was heretical. The restoration of a single head of the Church, together with the inability of later councils to bring about much-needed reform, enabled the popes to discredit the Conciliar Movement for the most part by 1450.

Unfortunately, while the popes forbade the calling of councils to effect reform, they refused to bring about reform themselves. Influenced by the Italian Renaissance, the popes busied themselves not with the resolution of internal problems but with participation in Italian politics and with patronage of the arts. Thus, "the papacy emerged as something between an Italian city-state and a European power, without forgetting at the same time the claim to be the vice-regent of Christ. The pope often could not make up his own mind whether he was the successor of Peter or of Caesar. Such vacillation had

much to do with the rise and success . . . of the Reformation."[2]

Heresy: Wycliffe and Huss. Throughout the fourteenth century, the cries against Church corruption became louder at the same time that heretical thoughts were being voiced. *The Vision of Piers Plowman*, of unknown English authorship, mercilessly upbraided the corruption, ignorance, and worldliness of the clergy.

During the Avignon papacy, a master of Oxford named John Wycliffe (1320?-1384) assailed not only Church abuses but Church doctrines. Because of his beliefs that the Church should be subordinate to the state, that salvation was primarily an individual matter between man and God, that transubstantiation as taught by the Church was false, and that outward rituals and veneration of relics were idolatrous, Wycliffe may be considered the dawn star of the Protestant Revolt. He formed bands of "poor priests," called Lollards, who taught his views; and he translated the Bible into English, a great service to the common people. Although Wycliffe's demands for reform did not succeed, the Lollards continued to spread his ideas.

In Bohemia, where a strong reform movement was under way, Wycliffe's doctrines were propagated by Czech students who had heard him at Oxford. In particular, his beliefs influenced John Huss (1369?-1415), an impassioned preacher in Prague and later rector of the university there. Huss borrowed many of his doctrinal views from Wycliffe, though he did not adopt the latter's denial of the validity of transubstantiation. His chief literary work was *Concerning the Church*, which included Wycliffe's views that the Church was composed of a universal priesthood of believers and that Christ alone was its head.

So popular did Huss' doctrines become and so great was his influence that the Church decided to take him in hand. Huss was excommunicated for his attacks on the theory of indulgences, but he found refuge outside Prague and kept on writing. Later, he was given a safe-conduct to the Council of Con-

In this contemporary sketch of John Huss being led to execution, the reformer wears the headgear which branded him as a heretic condemned by the Inquisition.

stance, which had as its purpose not only to heal the schism but also to stamp out heresy. Because Huss did not recant his teachings, the Council condemned him, and he was burned at the stake in spite of his safe-conduct. This action did not stamp out heresy; on the contrary, it served only to make Huss a martyr and to strengthen the resolve of those who believed in his doctrines.

Reasons for Church decline. Having described the decline of the Church from 1300 to about 1450, we can logically ask what the major reasons were for the deterioration of this once all-powerful institution.

As we have seen, trenchant criticisms of the clergy had come from a variety of sources, and the Conciliar Movement had gone so far as to challenge the supreme power of the pope himself. While criticisms increased, the Church continued to decline in spiritual leadership. The worldly concerns of the Renaissance popes—including their increasing involvement in Italian politics—pushed the Church further in the direction of secularization. The failure of the Church to keep pace

with intellectual developments taking place in the outside world also contributed to a weakening of the Church's position (see Chapter 12). In the economic field, the resurgence of trade and the growth of towns were causing revolutionary changes in the lives of the people and, as a result, undermining the influence of the Church, which for a thousand years had controlled the social and economic pattern of medieval—and rural—Europe. Lastly, the development of nationalism and the growing reluctance of kings to obey any opposing institution, including the Church, were evident in the encounters between Boniface VIII and the French ruler Philip IV.

CRISIS IN ENGLAND

AND FRANCE

The Hundred Years' War. Greatly affecting nation-making in England and France was the long conflict that colored much of their history during the fourteenth and fifteenth centuries. In both lands the crisis of war led to a resurgence of feudalism. Another deterrent to the rise of royal power was the increase in the power of representative assemblies (Parliament and the Estates-General). Nevertheless, in the long run the increasing anarchy and misery of the times stimulated nationalistic feelings and a demand for strong rulers who could guarantee law and order. Thus, by the late fifteenth century, the kings of England and France were able to resume their task of establishing the institutions of the modern nation-state.

The Hundred Years' War originated in a clash between the aims of the English and the French monarchies. The English kings wanted to regain the large holdings in France that had been theirs in Plantagenet days. The French kings, on the other hand, were determined not only to keep what had been taken from John of England but to expand further. Their ultimate goal was a centralized France under the direct rule of the monarchy at Paris. Another source of dissension between France and England was the clash of eco-

In this illumination from a medieval manuscript are depicted most of the weapons and methods of warfare in use during the Hundred Years' War. When a fortified town was besieged, the attackers first surrounded it to cut off its supplies, then dug zigzag trenches around it, then pounded its fortifications with weaponry and showered arrows over its walls, then breached or scaled its walls. The variety of weapons shown in this illustration serves to point out the direction warfare was to take from the late Middle Ages onward. For more than five hundred years the armored horseman had been the deciding factor in battles (a group of armored horsemen is shown at far left). Equipped with lance and sword, mace or battle-ax, and dagger, these warriors (usually nobles) were supported by infantry armed with crossbows (a crossbow archer is shown at bottom right). With the advent of the longbow, however, mounted horsemen no longer had an advantage over foot soldiers; in fact, they were at a disadvantage because of the accuracy and speed of the longbow (a file of longbow archers is shown at center). All of the weapons used during most of the Middle Ages were essentially simple: the mace was a modified club; the missile of the crossbow, a sharpened iron bolt. But the development of firearms (note the two examples of early cannon, bottom center) was to doom knight and archer alike.

A medieval illustration pictures Joan of Arc persuading the French king to launch an attack on the English.

nomic interests in Flanders, a region that was coming more and more under French control, to the chagrin of the English wool merchants who sent their raw wool to that area for processing prior to the sale of the finished cloth in Flanders and elsewhere.

The immediate excuse for the Anglo-French conflict was a dispute over succession to the French throne. In 1328, after the Capetian line became extinct, Philip VI of the House of Valois assumed the throne. The English king, Edward III, maintained that he was the legitimate heir to the French throne because his mother was a sister of the late French king. The French nobility disputed this claim, and war broke out. Interrupted by several peace treaties and a number of truces, the conflict lasted from 1337 to 1453. At the naval battle of Sluys (1340), the English gained command of the Channel and thus were able to send their armies to France at will. Thereafter, England won a series of great victories—at Crécy (1346), Poitiers (1356), and Agincourt (1415).

The English armies were much more effective than those of the French. With no thought of strategy, the French knights charged the enemy at a mad gallop and then engaged in hand-to-hand fighting. The English employed more efficient methods, among them the use of a powerful secret weapon, the longbow. Six feet long and made of special wood, the bow shot steel-tipped arrows which were dangerous at four hundred yards and deadly at one hundred. The usual English battle plan called for the knights to fight dismounted. Protecting them would be a forward wall of bowmen just behind a barricade of iron stakes planted in the ground to slow down the enemy charge. By the time the enemy cavalry reached the dismounted knights, only a few remained to be taken care of; the "feathered death" had done its work.

English military triumphs stirred English pride and what we now think of as nationalism—love of country, identification with it, and a sense of difference from, and usually superiority to, other peoples. However, patriotism was stirring in France also. The revival of French spirit is symbolized by Joan of Arc, who initiated a series of French victories. Impelled by inward voices which she believed divine, she begged the French king to allow her to lead an army to relieve the besieged city of Orleans. Her request granted, Joan inspired confidence and a feeling of invincibility in her followers, and Orleans was rescued in 1429 from what had seemed certain collapse. But Joan met a tragic end. Captured by English soldiers, she suffered a martyr's death at the stake, while the French leaders remained shamefully indifferent to her fate.

The salvation of Orleans was a turning point in the long struggle. The French reorganized their army and developed a strong force of artillery. In the face of French victories, English resistance crumbled. Military superiority had by now turned full circle; the English longbow was outmatched by French artillery. Of the vast territories they had once controlled in France, the English retained only Calais when the war ended in 1453.

Aftermath of war in England. So long as the English interfered in the affairs of France, the growth of national monarchy was hindered in both countries. It was fortunate, then, that the English were driven out of France.

Another important result in England of the Hundred Years' War was that the kings became financially dependent upon Parliament. This dependence compelled them to grant one petition after another, extending Parliament's powers until, early in the fifteenth century, Parliament became the dominant factor in government. The most important gains were the guarantee of freedom of debate, the stipulation that money bills must originate in the House of Commons, the rule that statutes should duplicate exactly the petitions presented by the Commons, and the right of the same House to determine who should be voters in the country at large.

A further development was the upsurge of the power of the nobles. England became the arena for struggles between selfish baronial cliques who wished to gain control of the monarchy and Parliament in order to feather their own nests. In 1455, two years after the end of the Hundred Years' War, rivalry between the most powerful baronial groups in England—the House of Lancaster and the House of York—flared into a civil conflict known as the Wars of the Roses. (The red rose was the symbol of the House of Lancaster and the white rose that of the House of York.) For thirty years England was a lawless land.

Beginning of Tudor rule. A great longing for order, especially among the trading class, brought about the accession of Henry VII, the first of the Tudor line, which was to rule England from 1485 to 1603. Trade was at a standstill, the nobility had been decimated, and the nation, tired of the blood bath of civil war, stood ready for the masterful rule which the Tudors gave England.

It was the shrewd and careful work of Henry VII (1485-1509) and his successor, Henry VIII (1509-1547), that laid the foundations for Tudor greatness. Strong, almost absolute government was reintroduced into England. The Court of Star Chamber was made a royal instrument to crush rebellious barons; trials were secret, swift, and without benefit of juries. Because the Tudor rulers restored law and order, checked the power of the nobles, and promoted trade at home

Above is a fifteenth-century portrait of the French king Louis XI.

and abroad, they won the support of the middle class. Upon this support the power of the Tudors was primarily built. Though often high-handed, Tudor kings always worked through Parliament.

Under Tudor rule England achieved the full status of a national state. This royal house would also further stimulate English commercial and maritime enterprise, break away from the papacy and establish a new national church, and successfully defy the most vigorous power in Europe—Spain.

France after the Hundred Years' War: Louis XI. The Hundred Years' War left France impoverished—but with a new national consciousness. Royal power was stronger than ever before. During the war, the French king had been given the right to levy the *taille*, a tax to provide revenue for the maintenance of a standing army. After the war, this tax became permanent, giving the king financial independence from the Estates-General. Thus the purse strings, which the English Parliament used to gain concessions from the king, were kept firmly under royal control in France.

The process of consolidating royal power was continued by Louis XI, who reigned from 1461 to 1483. Physically unattractive, Louis had a spindly body and a cadaverous face with a long, sharp nose. He loved intrigue, and his intricate diplomatic webs earned him the epithet of "the universal spider." In his pursuit of power, he used any weapon—violence, bribery, and treachery—to obtain his ends. In domestic policies, he labored to restore prosperity, to extend the royal domain, and to wreck completely the few powerful feudal houses that still remained.

Louis' most notable antagonist in foreign affairs was Charles the Bold of Burgundy, whose possession of the Low Countries (modern Holland, Belgium, and Luxemburg) made him one of Europe's richest rulers. After Charles' death in 1477, part of his domain (including much of Burgundy itself) was seized by Louis XI, while the remainder (including most of the Netherlands) passed to Charles' daughter, Mary. When she married Maximilian I, the Low Countries came into the hands of the House of Hapsburg (see p. 258).

The French kings who succeeded Louis XI were to increase the royal domain until, by the middle of the sixteenth century, only the territory belonging to the Bourbons and a few other tiny pieces of land were outside the monarch's full control. When Charles VIII ascended the throne in 1483, France was daily becoming a stronger and more compact state. Its population was relatively large—16,000,000 as compared with England's 4,500,000. Although industry was still undeveloped compared to that in the Netherlands and in Italy, France had a rich soil and produced immense quantities of grain and wine. Economic prosperity and increasing political unity would enable France to play an important role in sixteenth-century politics.

THE POLITICAL UNIFICATION

OF SPAIN AND PORTUGAL

Consolidation under Ferdinand and Isabella. By the end of the thirteenth century,

following the reduction of Muslim power in Spain to the small state of Granada (see p. 214), the process of reconquest halted until the latter part of the fifteenth century. In 1469, Isabella of Castile and Leon married Ferdinand, heir to the kingdom of Aragon. Except for Granada, Navarre, and Portugal, the Iberian peninsula was now united politically.

Many divisive factors existed, however. During the long struggle with the Muslims, the nobles had assumed extensive power, the military orders had developed into near-independent organizations, and some of the important Church officials had become difficult for the sovereign to control.

The Catholic Sovereigns, as Ferdinand and Isabella were called, set out to establish an effective royal despotism in Spain. The Holy Brotherhood, a Castilian organization which had been created by the cities for their mutual protection against unruly nobles, was taken over by the crown and made into a combined standing army and police force. The powerful military orders were also brought under royal control. Although Ferdinand and Isabella were devout Catholics, they both believed that the Church should be subordinate to royal government—a belief they shared with the strong rulers of the rising European nation-states. By tactful negotiations, the Spanish sovereigns induced the pope to give them extensive rights in making Church appointments in Spain.

During the Middle Ages, assemblies known as Cortes had grown up in the Spanish kingdoms. Unlike the course of events in England, however, the early movement toward representative government in Spain did not fulfill its promise, and it received a death blow from the Catholic Sovereigns in the last years of the fifteenth century.

In 1480 a Court of Inquisition was set up in Castile. Ferdinand and his queen recognized the Inquisition as a means not only of wiping out heresy but also of increasing royal power. Under the dread leadership of Torquemada, the Inquisition confiscated the property of most Jews and Muslims and terrified the Christian clergy and laymen into

Ferdinand and Isabella created a strong monarchy by uniting Spain and bringing the nobilty and the Church under royal control.

accepting royal absolutism as well as religious orthodoxy. Thousands of persons were burned to death, and many more lost all their property. The Inquisition enhanced the power of the Spanish crown for a short time, but in the long run proved to be a weakening influence, as many talented people fled the land of persecution.

The most dramatic act undertaken by the Catholic Sovereigns was the conquest of Granada, which fell in 1492, the same year that Columbus claimed the wealth of the New World for Spain. Before he died in 1516, Ferdinand seized that part of Navarre which lay south of the Pyrenees. This acquisition, together with the conquest of Granada, completed the national unification of Spain. It was royal absolutism, coupled with the acquisition of territory in the New and Old Worlds, that made Spain the strongest power in sixteenth-century Europe.

Portugal's independence. Until 1095 the area which eventually became Portugal was linked politically with the rest of the peninsula. Faced by a serious Muslim attack in that year, the king of Castile and Leon appealed to Europe for aid. Count Henry of Burgundy answered the call and did valiant service against the Muslims. As a reward, the Castilian king gave his daughter to Henry in marriage; her dowry included Portugal, then a part of west Castile. The son of this marriage revolted against the king of Castile and in 1139 became king of Portugal.

In the fourteenth century the rulers of Castile made a strenuous effort to reunite Portugal with their holdings, but the ruler of Portugal, King John, defeated the Castilian host in 1385 and saved Portuguese independence. King John also initiated Portuguese overseas expansion. Carried on by his son, Henry the Navigator, this policy led eventually to the creation of a great empire in India and the Far East, and the establishment of the colony of Brazil (see Chapter 16).

DISUNITY IN GERMANY

The early Hapsburgs and the Golden Bull. Following the Hohenstaufen collapse, factionalism and disorder reigned in Germany; this period of confusion came to an end in 1273, when the imperial crown was revived and given to Count Rudolf (1273-1291) of the House of Hapsburg. Rudolf's ancestors had gained control of a small domain in northern Switzerland. Toward the end of the eleventh century, the family built a castle which was called Habichtsburg (Castle of the Hawk)—hence the word *Hapsburg*. During the late Middle Ages and in modern times, the Hapsburgs had amazing luck in adding to their ancestral lands. In the thirteenth century they acquired Austria, and subsequently they ruled their holdings from Vienna; in the sixteenth century they obtained Bohemia and much of Hungary.

For the time being, however, the Hapsburg hold on the imperial crown proved to be brief. After Rudolf's reign, it was passed from one family to another. Then, in 1356, the nobility won a significant victory. The Golden Bull, a document which served as the political constitution of Germany until early in the nineteenth century, laid down the procedure for election of the emperor by seven German dignitaries. The important nobles were given rights that made them virtually independent rulers. An imperial Diet, or legislature, provided some semblance of unity; but it met infrequently and had little authority. The Golden Bull, as one historian aptly wrote, "legalized anarchy and called it a constitution."[3] By the fifteenth century, Germany was a welter of duchies, archduchies, counties, and free cities.

The Hapsburgs regain the crown. The imperial crown of Germany was returned to the Hapsburg family in 1452. From this time until 1806, when the Holy Roman Empire disappeared, the Hapsburgs held the imperial crown almost without a break. Maximilian fell heir to the Hapsburg kingdom in 1493 and ruled until 1519. Following the traditional Hapsburg pattern of auspicious marriages, Maximilian took as his wife the heiress to the Low Countries, and thus he increased the territory under Hapsburg rule.

During the fifteenth century there was a strong demand from many quarters in the empire for some kind of political reform. In 1495, for example, the Diet of Worms outlawed private warfare. An imperial court was set up to settle the many feuds, and steps were taken to ensure the annual meeting of the imperial legislature; the Diet, however, failed to enforce its will. The emperor continued to be limited in power; nor did the empire have an imperial treasury, an efficient central administration, or a standing army. And so the phantom Holy Roman Empire lived on as Voltaire characterized it: "Neither Holy, Roman, nor an Empire."[4]

ITALY: WEALTHY

BUT DIVIDED

Growth of the city-states. The elimination of the influence of German kings in the eleventh century—except for the occasional intervention in later years of strong emperors like Frederick Barbarossa and Frederick II— left the numerous city-states of northern and central Italy free to follow their own devices. In particular, the cities of Venice, Florence, Milan, Genoa, and Pisa grew wealthy from their thriving industries and from the lucrative trade with the East. Their banking houses handled papal revenues, aided bankrupt European monarchs, and financed wars and crusades.

The city-states on the Italian peninsula were similar to those of ancient Greece in that the Italian cities controlled the surrounding countryside and in some cases even ruled other towns. Also, as in Greece, each city-state was politically individualistic and intensely self-conscious, viewing its neighbors with a hostility that often flared into war.

Civic patriotism and a desire for liberty advanced rapidly under the influence of the prosperous and newly powerful middle class, which finally succeeded in ousting the restless feudal aristocrats from positions of power. Ingenious city charters and civic constitutions were drafted, and there was much trial and error in the art of government. Single and plural executives, limited franchise and universal suffrage, long terms and short terms of office, together with rotation of officeholders in various civic positions—all these governmental techniques were employed with varying degrees of success. Until the end of the thirteenth century, the prevailing political trend in the cities was toward republicanism and representative government.

Five important states. Venice, the "Pearl of the Adriatic," was one of the richest cities of its time, controlling an empire of ports and islands in the eastern Mediterranean and carrying much of Europe's maritime trade in its great fleets. The government of this rich republic had been in the hands of a doge (duke), together with a people's assembly, but the rich merchants gradually took over the reins of power, making the Council of Ten the chief and all-powerful governmental agency. Thus Venice, nominally a republic, was in reality governed by a merchant oligarchy.

Milan, next in wealth to Venice, was located in the fertile plain of Lombardy. To the north were the important Alpine passes, through which went a steady stream of goods to northern Europe. Milan was famous for its manufactured wares, especially silks, woolens, velvets, and weapons.

Florence—the center for the flourishing wool, leather, and silk industries—boasted merchants and bankers who were among the most prosperous in Europe, and its gold florin circulated in many lands as a standard coin. With its many checks and counterchecks of power, the Florentine constitution was bewilderingly complex. For example, the head of the cabinet held office for two months only, and all measures needed a two-thirds majority in five different committees or assemblies to become laws. In theory, Florence was a democracy but, as in Venice, real political power was wielded by wealthy businessmen.

The Papal States extended from fifty miles south of the mouth of the Tiber to the northeast across Italy as far as the mouth of the Po River. This political unit, ruled by the pope, was poorly organized. Hampered by the lack of hereditary rule, the popes found

it difficult to force their will upon various petty despots who ruled over small subject states and defied the political authority of the popes. As the secular ruler of a political unit in central Italy, the pope felt obliged to participate in Italian politics, to make treaties, hire armies, and wage wars. Although he was the head of a great spiritual organization, the pope acted little differently from the rulers of the other city-states where Italian politics were concerned.

The kingdom of Naples covered the southern half of the Italian peninsula. Once this kingdom had included Sicily, but in the fifteenth century this island was acquired by Ferdinand of Aragon, ruler of all Spain. The Neapolitan kingdom differed from the rest of Italy, for its industry was insignificant and most of its towns were unimportant. The nobles were rebellious and brigandage was rampant. The social and economic backwardness of Naples, in contrast to north and central Italy, was to last even into modern times.

Despotism replaces republicanism. Representative institutions had been premature in many city-states. By the fourteenth century, conspiracy, confusion, and incompetence became increasingly repugnant to powerful minority groups; and duels began to replace compromise as the means of settling political differences. Many citizens felt that a firm leader was needed to ensure internal stability and to lessen the danger from external enemies.

Actual power in the city-states gravitated more and more in the direction of one-man rule. Seizing power, the members of prominent families became political bosses or despots. Although Venice maintained the benevolent oligarchy of its merchants with the doge as a figurehead, Florence went under the thumb of the Medici family, and its republican institutions became merely empty forms. The Medici had no aristocratic antecedents; their fortune was based on commerce and finance. The significance of the family emblem—six red balls on a field of gold—is unknown, but we are all familiar with the later modification of this insigne— the three balls of the pawnbroker. Nearly all the other Italian city-states came under the rule of despots.

The *condottieri*. In the struggles between the city-states, mercenary soldiers under the command of leaders called *condottieri* were employed. Coming from all over Europe, these adventurers sold their swords to the highest bidder but carried on their fighting with a minimum of bloodshed. "They would try to win, because defeat would lower their market value, but they did not want to beat the enemy too much. He was in the same trade, and cut-throat competition was bad for everyone in the long run. Besides, a war ended too soon might mean unemployment for a long spell."[5] There were, therefore, always degrees of victory and limits to defeat. Far different from the twentieth-century wars of annihilation, the petty conflicts on the Italian peninsula hindered neither commercial progress nor the development of the arts and learning (see Chapter 12).

EASTERN EUROPE

German eastward expansion. During medieval times, migrations and conquests caused extensive transplantations of such groups as the Germans, Poles, Lithuanians, and Prussians along the shores of the central and eastern Baltic and in the immediate hinterland. On many occasions groups of Slavs were exterminated by the Germans, who then took over the empty land, cleared and drained it, and built prosperous villages.

Shortly after 1200 there was a new development in the eastward expansion of the Germans against the Slavs. The Teutonic Knights, a military-religious order founded at the time of the Third Crusade, began the conquest of the pagan Slavs in Prussia. Having conquered the area, the Knights abandoned their religious character and settled down to found cities and become a landed nobility (see Reference Map 4).

Poland and Lithuania at the height of their power. To the south of Prussia lay Poland. As a result of military pressure from the Germans in the west and the Prussians in the north, the Polish nation was welded into a strong military state in the middle of the tenth century. Also at this time, many Poles were converted to Christianity, a factor which later linked Poland to western European culture.

After suffering severe setbacks in the twelfth and thirteenth centuries, Poland emerged as a strong power in the fourteenth century when its destiny was linked with that of the Lithuanians, who had risen from a very primitive background through a remarkable program of conquest, much of it well inside the western confines of modern Russia. When Lithuania and Poland were united under a common sovereign in 1386, the expanded state became the largest in Europe.

The Poles and Lithuanians then waged war against their common enemy, the Teutonic Knights, and in 1410 the Knights suffered a crushing defeat at Tannenberg. As a result, West Prussia was turned over to the Poles while East Prussia, under the Teutonic Knights, retained its autonomy but became a vassal state of Poland. This peace settlement was a great blow to German expansion, for the Poles obtained control of the Vistula River and a corridor north to the Baltic Sea and the important port of Danzig. East

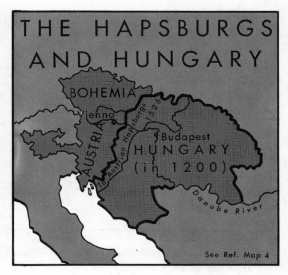

Prussia was now cut off from the rest of Germany. In the history of modern Europe, the Polish Corridor and Danzig, which separated East from West Prussia, have played an important role.

The early union of Poland and Lithuania was broken on several occasions, but the two countries were permanently united under Poland's flag at the end of the fifteenth century. This huge state had the promise of a brilliant future, but the promise was never completely realized. The governmental system was inefficient, and, above all, Poland faced the enmity of Russia. The claims of the tsars to certain Slavic groups in Poland and the attempts to annex Polish territory provided grounds for the bitter enmity between Poles and Russians in our own time.

Bohemians and Magyars. Two other peoples appeared in the east European family in the Middle Ages. During the ninth and tenth centuries, the Czechs established a kingdom on the Bohemian plain. Surrounded by Teutonic peoples, the Czechs for a thousand years continued to struggle against the menace of German domination.

Living southeast of Bohemia in the wide and fertile plain known as Hungary were the Magyars, an Asiatic people. Originally the terror of eastern Europe because of their brutal raids, they became civilized, adopted

Christianity, and in the eleventh century expanded their state. But the promise of both their rising nation and that of the Bohemians (Czechs) was blighted by a common disaster. The king of both Hungary and Bohemia met his death fighting against the Turks in 1526. Terrified at the prospects of Muslim rule, the Czechs offered their vacant throne to a Hapsburg prince. Consequently, their government for nearly four hundred years was centered in Vienna.

As for Hungary, the defeated nation was divided between the Turks and Ferdinand, the Hapsburg archduke of Austria. This intertwining of the fortunes of Austria, Bohemia, and Hungary explains how the Hapsburgs at Vienna came to rule over the polyglot empire of Bohemian, Hungarian, and Austrian peoples.

South Slavs and Turks in the Balkans. The outstanding political development in southeastern Europe at the close of the Middle Ages was the disappearance of the Byzantine empire and the emergence of a threatening Muslim state which became heir not only to the lands formerly ruled by the Christian emperors at Constantinople but also to the whole Balkan area. Before the end of the fifteenth century the Ottoman Turks had extended their control over the Balkans and were pushing on toward Vienna.

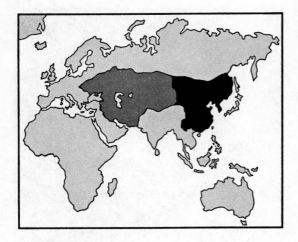

Stretching the entire width of Asia, Mongol power threatened to engulf all of Europe as well. The map above shows the extent of Mongol possessions at the peak of the conquests. The black portion represents the Mongol domain in 1294.

This huge new empire with its center at Constantinople was in no sense a national state but rather a bewildering mixture of Turks, Serbs, Hungarians, Bulgarians, Rumanians, Armenians, Greeks, and Jews.

The imposition of Turkish rule upon southeastern Europe delayed the rise of national states in the Balkan area until the nineteenth century. The multiplicity of small countries in the Balkans in modern times and the resultant tensions and conflicts have made the peninsula a European danger zone, a source of constant worry to diplomats, and, as in 1914, the direct or indirect cause of wars.

The Mongol conquest of Russia. In Chapter 15, we shall follow the amazing career of Genghis Khan, who united the unruly tribesmen of Mongolia and then launched them like a thunderbolt on a campaign of world conquest. In 1237 the various Russian principalities were conquered, and in 1242 the Mongols penetrated to the outskirts of Vienna. Western Europe seemed theirs for the taking, but the death of the khan caused the Tatar, or Mongol, armies to return to their homeland for the election of a new ruler.

Central Europe was not to be molested again, but the Mongols established themselves as a ruling caste in Russia, governing the vast plains from their capital at Sarai on the Volga, not far from the modern city of Stalingrad. The various Russian principalities were allowed to govern themselves so long as they paid tribute to the Golden Horde, as the Tatars in Russia were called. The khanate of the Golden Horde was only one of the Mongol states, however; the successors of Genghis Khan ruled an empire stretching from Korea on the east to Poland on the west. In the south their holdings included much of Asia Minor, Persia, and Afghanistan, as well as the area north of what is now India and Burma. Only since the Second World War has an empire arisen— that of Soviet Russia and its satellites— which could rival the vast expanse of contiguous territory controlled by the Mongols. In fact, the Russian empire, with Communist China, not only rivals but nearly duplicates that of the Mongol khanates.

Mongol domination changed the course of Russian history; it completed the break between Russia and western European civilization initiated by the decline of Kiev. Asian cultural influences were strong—the status of women was lowered as they accepted the veil and Oriental seclusion. Mongols and Russians intermarried freely; hence the saying, "Scratch a Russian and you will find a Tatar." Many authorities believe that the Mongol conquest was a wholesale calamity. Russia was cut off from Europe, and a new Russia far to the east of Kiev began to develop. Its nucleus was to be the despotic state, the grand duchy of Moscow, where "civilization had been completely thrown back, learning was almost lost, and art in decline."[6]

Alexander Nevski: pioneer of Russian greatness. Following the Mongol conquest, an important Russian leader was the prince of Novgorod, Alexander Nevski, who later became the ruler of Vladimir from 1252 to 1263. In the 1240's this stanch warrior won great victories over the Swedes, Finns, and Lithuanians, who, hoping to profit from the Russian collapse under the Mongol impact, attempted to annex territory. Nevski not only repulsed these aggressors but also defeated the Teutonic Knights in the "Battle of

On April 5, 1242, Alexander Nevski and his troops attacked the Teutonic Knights on the icebound Lake Peipus. The "iron wedge" of the Knights drove through the center of the Russian army, but Alexander outmaneuvered them, turning their initial triumph into a rout. This scene from a Russian film shows a duel between Nevski (left) and the master of the Teutonic Order.

the Ice" at Lake Peipus. With determined craftiness he accepted the regime of the Tatars and in effect became their main deputy in Russia. In return he obtained their protection and assistance in fighting invasions from the west. Meanwhile, Nevski looked forward to the day when his successors would be strong enough to challenge Tatar rule.

Moscow, challenge to Tatar rule. Daniel, the youngest son of Nevski, founded the grand duchy of Moscow, which eventually expelled the Tatars from Russia. Well situated in the central river system of Russia and surrounded by protective forests and marshes, Moscow advanced rapidly in population and power. At first only a vassal of Vladimir, it soon absorbed its parent state. The rulers of Moscow continued to cooperate with their Mongol overlords; in time, each head of the state was given the title of grand prince and entrusted with the task of collecting the Mongol tribute from the various Russian cities and principalities. Moscow's prestige was further enhanced when it became the center of the Russian Orthodox Church. Its head, the metropolitan, fled from Kiev to Vladimir in 1299 and a few years later established the permanent headquarters of the Church in Moscow.

In the middle of the fourteenth century it became evident that the power of the Tatars was declining, and the grand princes felt capable of openly opposing the Mongol yoke. In 1380, at Kulikovo, the khan was defeated, and the first important step in the removal of Tatar rule was accomplished. Thus it was that in the latter part of the fourteenth century Moscow assumed a position of leadership in Russia.

Ivan the Great. During his reign from 1462 to 1505, Ivan III (the Great) more than doubled his lands, placing most of north Rus-

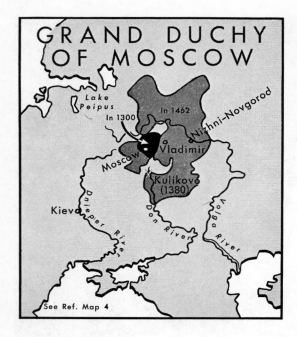

GRAND DUCHY OF MOSCOW

Lake Peipus

In 1300

In 1462

Nizhni-Novgorod

Moscow

Vladimir

Kulikovo (1380)

Kiev

Dnieper River

Don River

Volga River

See Ref. Map 4

perors and the protectors of Orthodox Christianity, took the title of *tsar*, or *czar*, meaning "Caesar."

"Two Romes have fallen, and the third stands." Early in the sixteenth century, Philotheos of Pskov, a Russian monk, addressed the tsar thus:

. . . two Romes have fallen, and the third stands, and a fourth one there shall not be.[8]

On the basis of the conviction that they were heirs of the Byzantine tradition, Russian rulers were later to press claims to the Dardanelles and parts of southeastern Europe. Moreover, as in the idea expressed by Philotheos when he said ". . . you are the only tsar for Christians in the whole world,"[9] the Russian tradition would henceforth encompass a great imperial mission pointing toward universal domination.

Some historians see this Russian sense of destiny still operating in a new manifestation—communism—with the same fervor of the earlier Russian dedication to Orthodox Christianity. "Five centuries ago the words of Philotheos of Pskov may have sounded arrogant and foolhardy; but for us today, in the new constellation of world-forces after 1945, they echo through the centuries as the prophetic expression of the most momentous consequence of the fall of Constantinople . . . on the wider stage of world-history the effects of the events of 1453 are only now making themselves felt."[10]

Ivan the Terrible. Following Ivan the Great's reign, the next great ruler of Moscow was Ivan IV, known as "the Terrible." Becoming tsar in 1547, he considered himself the ruler of all Russia, taking the title of "Tsar, Autocrat of All Russia, Great Prince of Moscow." Under his rule Russia became more despotic; all authority was centered in the office of tsar, and the nobility was subordinated to his will. But Ivan was also a far-seeing statesman who promulgated a new code of laws and reformed the morals of the Russian clergy. During his reign, eastern Russia was conquered from the Tatars, and the Cossack pioneers then crossed the Ural Mountains in their push to the Pacific.

sia under the rule of Moscow. Renouncing the last vestige of vassalage to the Tatars, Ivan in the 1490's initiated a series of attacks that opened the way for the complete defeat of the Tatar kingdoms and their assimilation into the Russian state.

Of Ivan, a famous historian has written: "He is one of those rich heirs of history who are able to use freely the resources left to them, and find that instead of exhausting them they have vastly increased them. It should be borne in mind that he is the contemporary of the Tudors and of the rise of strong monarchies in other countries of Europe."[7]

During Ivan's reign, new contacts were made with Europe. He himself married Sophia Palaeologus, the niece of the last Byzantine emperor, and she brought with her to Moscow a number of gifted Italians. Ivan copied the ceremonies of the Byzantine court and adopted the emblem of the Byzantine emperors, the double-headed eagle, which served as the coat of arms of imperial Russia until 1917. Russia was now to assume the imperial mission of New Rome (Constantinople) and conceive of itself as the Third Rome. The Russian rulers, claiming to be the legitimate successors of the Byzantine em-

Ivan the Terrible, like Ivan the Great, was representative of the turbulent and harsh times in which he lived. With no consideration for human life, he ordered the destruction of Novgorod on suspicion of treason, and many of the city's people were massacred. Another time, in a rage, Ivan struck and killed his gifted eldest son. Yet for championing strong centralized government and extending the authority of his realm, Ivan IV is worthy of a place alongside the most important of his fellow monarchs in western Europe.

Ivan's death in 1584 was followed by a period of confusion and civil war known in Russian history as the "Time of Trouble." Poland and Sweden both intervened in Russian affairs, but finally the foreigners were expelled. In 1613, Michael Romanov was elected to the throne by a national assembly made up of representatives from fifty cities. The Romanov dynasty was to rule Russia until 1917.

SUMMARY

The medieval ideal was unity—a Europe united as a Christian commonwealth and ruled by dual powers, the universal Church and an all-embracing Holy Roman Empire. In theory the emperor would rule in the temporal or earthly realm, and the pope in the affairs of the spirit. Because papal authority was not constricted to national boundaries, the Church was nearly all-encompassing. By contrast, the emperor's authority was limited for the most part to Germany and Italy, and even there imperial power was intermittent.

During the fourteenth and fifteenth centuries, forces were at work which threatened and ultimately undermined the medieval ideal and the edifices stemming from it. The Church was badly weakened from within as a result of the Babylonian Captivity, the demands of reformers, and the Great Schism; the latter was healed by the Conciliar Movement. And despite continuous opposition from both the Church and the feudal nobles, the national state had become a reality in Europe by the end of the period discussed in this chapter.

Influencing nation-making in both France and England was the Hundred Years' War, which stimulated nationalism in the hearts of Englishmen and Frenchmen alike. Other significant changes resulted from that conflict: in England, the power of Parliament was increased, and the upsurge in the power of the nobility led to the Wars of the Roses, which ended finally with the accession of the Tudors; in France, royal power was consolidated under Louis XI, and further progress in national unification was made. Ferdinand and Isabella completed the creation of a national state in Spain and laid the foundations for its future greatness. On the other hand, Germany and Italy continued divided and weak; their day of national unification would not arrive until the nineteenth century.

Eastern and southern Europe were on the periphery of most of the dynamic currents of change that were transforming western Europe. There was much movement of peoples, and the rise and fall of states culminated in the emergence of Poland, Lithuania, Bohemia, and Hungary. Russia, effectively isolated on its frozen plains, languished for years under the rule of the Mongols. But when the dukes of Moscow assumed leadership of the Russians, a long campaign was initiated against the alien Mongols—a historical movement somewhat similar to the *Reconquista* in Spain.

Truly, the late Middle Ages was an era of nation-making. The nation-states this period produced—particularly England, France, and Spain—would assume new roles in the stirring international drama that is the story of Europe from about 1500 to 1650, a story which will be taken up in Chapter 14.

SUGGESTIONS FOR READING

E. P. Cheyney, *The Dawn of a New Era, 1250-1453*, Harper, 1936; and M. P. Gilmore, *The World of Humanism, 1453-1517*, Harper, 1952. Written by experts but designed for the student and the general reader, these two volumes in *The Rise of Modern Europe* series, edited by W. L. Langer, provide the best introduction to the civilization of this period; each volume contains a comprehensive annotated bibliography. Highly recommended as a short survey is Vol. II of H. Pirenne, *A History of Europe*,* Anchor. Two notable and highly detailed accounts of the political history of western Europe in the late Middle Ages are C. Previté-Orton, *A History of Europe from 1198 to 1378*, Barnes and Noble, 1951; and W. T. Waugh, *A History of Europe from 1378 to 1498*, Barnes and Noble, 1949. A famous novel which provides a panorama of European life toward the end of the Middle Ages is C. Reade, *The Cloister and the Hearth* (many editions).

L. E. Elliott-Binns, *History of the Decline and Fall of the Medieval Papacy*, Methuen, 1934; and A. C. Flick, *The Decline of the Medieval Church*, 2 vols., Knopf, 1930, are authoritative general works. See T. Boase, *Boniface VIII*, Constable, 1933, for a study of the last great medieval pope and his dramatic struggle with Philip IV of France. The subsequent troubles of the papacy are admirably detailed in W. Ullmann, *Origins of the Great Schism*, Burns, Oates, and Washbourne, 1948.

K. B. McFarlane, *John Wycliffe and the Beginnings of English Nonconformity*, Macmillan (Teach Yourself History), 1952; and M. Spinka, *John Hus and the Czech Reform*, Univ. of Chicago, 1941, are short scholarly studies on the two chief heretics of the age. See also A. S. Turberville, *Medieval Heresy and the Inquisition*, Holt, 1920.

E. Perroy, *The Hundred Years' War*, Oxford, 1952. A parallel study of England and France which is considered the standard work on the subject.

A. R. Myers, *England in the Late Middle Ages*,* Penguin. A highly recommended introduction to all aspects of life in England from 1307 to c. 1536. The author finds much evidence of creativeness and growth in this period of violence and decay. Another excellent sympathetic survey of the period is V. H. Green, *The Later Platagenets: A Survey of English History Between 1307 and 1485*, St. Martin's, 1955. The important extension of Parliament's powers during this period is admirably presented in Faith Thompson, *A Short History of Parliament, 1295-1642*, Univ. of Minn., 1953.

C. H. Williams, *The Making of Tudor Despotism*, Nelson, 1935. An explanation of how Tudor despotism got its start. A good biography of the founder of the Tudor dynasty is C. W. S. Williams, *Henry VII*, Barker, 1937. On the period of anarchy which preceded Henry VII, see P. M. Kendall, *Warwick the Kingmaker*, Norton, 1957, an absorbing biography of one of the last powerful feudal barons.

*Indicates an inexpensive paperbound edition.

A. Buchan, *Joan of Arc and the Recovery of France*, Macmillan (Teach Yourself History), 1948. A short biography which serves also as a brief introduction to the history of France in the early fifteenth century. More complete is L. Fabre, *Joan of Arc*, McGraw-Hill, 1954. An excellent description of life in late fifteenth-century France is contained in the popular biography of the "universal spider," P. Champion, *Louis XI*, Dodd, Mead, 1929. The France of Louis XI is also the setting of Walter Scott's famous novel, *Quentin Durwood* (many editions).

J. Mariéjol, *The Spain of Ferdinand and Isabella*, Rutgers, 1961. The classic history of Spain during the period of its emergence as a great nation; gracefully written.

R. B. Merriman, *The Rise of the Spanish Empire in the Old World and the New*, II, Macmillan, 1918, contains a full account of the work of Ferdinand and Isabella. A good short survey of the reign of the Catholic Sovereigns is R. Altamira, *A History of Spain from the Beginnings to the Present Day*, Van Nostrand, 1949. I. L. Plunket, *Isabel of Castile and the Making of the Spanish Nation, 1451-1504*, Putnam, 1915, is a good biography. See also A. S. Turberville, *The Spanish Inquisition*, Holt, 1932.

C. E. Nowell, *A History of Portugal*, Van Nostrand, 1952. The best survey of Portuguese history.

G. Barraclough, *The Origins of Modern Germany*, Blackwell, 1949. Contains the best account of this period of German history. See also J. Bryce, *The Holy Roman Empire*,* Schocken Books; and Vols. VII and VIII of *The Cambridge Medieval History*, which also contains chapters on Italian history. On the most interesting of the Hapsburgs, see G. Waas, *The Legendary Character of Kaiser Maximilian*, Columbia Univ., 1941.

J. A. Symonds, *The Age of the Despots*,* Capricorn. A celebrated account of Italian politics in the fourteenth and fifteenth centuries. Also recommended is F. Schevill, *A History of Florence from the Founding of the City Through the Renaissance*, Harcourt, Brace, 1936.

O. Halecki, *Borderlands of Western Civilization: A History of East Central Europe*, Ronald, 1952. An indispensable political history of the area lying between Germany and Russia and extending from Finland to Greece; contains a valuable bibliography.

M. Florinsky, *Russia: A History and an Interpretation*, 2 vols., Macmillan, 1953. Acclaimed as the most useful single work on Russian history in English; covers the thousand years from the establishment of the Kievan state to the triumph of the Bolsheviks in 1917. For a discussion of the Third Rome concept, see N. Zernov, *Moscow, the Third Rome*, Macmillan, 1937. The Mongol conquest and its material and spiritual effects upon Russian life are authoritatively described in G. Vernadsky, *The Mongols and Russia*, Yale, 1953.

H. Lamb, *The March of Muscovy: Ivan the Terrible and the Growth of the Russian Empire, 1400-1648*, Doubleday, 1948. A colorful popular account. See also the popular biography by H. Von Eckardt, *Ivan the Terrible*, Knopf, 1949.

CHAPTER 12

Man Is the
Measure

THE RENAISSANCE: 1300-1600

Introduction. To the historians who viewed the Middle Ages as the "Dark Ages"—a time of stagnation and ignorance—the epoch of European history which followed seemed to spring to life suddenly like Minerva from the brow of Jove, resplendent in beauty and wisdom. They looked on the new age as an awakening from centuries of lethargy, and they labeled it *Renaissance,* meaning "rebirth."

Today, most historians would deny that the arrival of the Renaissance brought any distinct break in the development of European culture. As we have already noted, the Middle Ages made rich intellectual and artistic contributions to civilization. In what ways, then, can the Renaissance be said to signify a "rebirth"?

First of all, there was an intense renewal of interest in the literature of classical Greece and

Rome—a development known as the classical revival. No longer were scholars confined to medieval translations of the famous writers of ancient Greece; many began to read the works of Plato, Aristotle, and others in the original Greek. In addition, they searched the monasteries for old manuscripts and translated hitherto unknown works from Greek antiquity into Latin. Thus the humanists, as these scholars were called, reintroduced classical learning into the main stream of western thought. Secondly, while the scholars rediscovered classical thought, artists in Italy were stimulated and inspired by their study and imitation of classical architecture and sculpture.

But the spirit of the Renaissance was not characterized by a mere cult of antiquity, a looking backward into the past. The men of the Renaissance were the harbingers of the modern world, energetically and enthusiastically engaged in reshaping their political, economic, and religious environment, in pushing back geographical boundaries and extending the limits of human knowledge. Renaissance culture strikingly exhibits belief in the worth of man and his privileged place in the scheme of things, and the desire of man to think and act as a free agent and a well-rounded individual. The Renaissance spirit was admirably summed up by a versatile genius of the fifteenth century, Leon Battista Alberti, when he declared, "Men can do all things if they will."[1]

Every age is an age of transition, but it may be fair to state that the Renaissance marks one of the turning points in western civilization. The dominant institutions and social systems which had existed in Europe for well-nigh a thousand years were becoming devitalized; many were being radically modified or even discarded. Men's values were changing: medievalism with its emphasis on Scholasticism, Church authority, and conformity was on the wane, and a more modern culture which depended on individualism, skepticism, and ultimately on science was taking its place.

We must be cautious in our analysis, however, because the period of the Renaissance does not fit into a neat chronological or geographical pattern. Some medieval habits and institutions persisted for a long time; throughout the Renaissance the vast majority of illiterate common people clung to the ways of their forefathers. And the Renaissance did not burst forth simultaneously in all parts of Europe.

It originated with a relatively small, educated group dwelling in the cities of central and northern Italy. We shall begin with the classical revival and the flowering of art in this locality, and conclude with a discussion of other facets of the Renaissance as its ideas moved over the Alps to France, Germany, and England.

THE ITALIAN RENAISSANCE:

THE BACKGROUND

The waning of the Middle Ages. In the late Middle Ages, the temporal power of the Church in Europe and the political pretensions of the Holy Roman emperors were successfully challenged by aggressive national monarchs. Heresy and schism racked the Church itself. The rigid feudalistic social structure was weakening before the growing power of the middle class, which sided with the new monarchs and thrived on the revival of trade and the growth of towns. Although asceticism remained a pious ideal, it gained few adherents among the acquisitive townspeople and was openly flouted by many of the regular clergy. Scholars still held learned disputations at the universities, but Scholasticism was unable to satisfy the growing interest in natural science and other secular knowledge. Thus, by the fourteenth century, there was a marked decline in the vitality of medieval institutions and ideas.

Meanwhile, the sophisticated members of Italian urban society no longer found medieval ideals of otherworldliness and asceticism satisfactory. Pious religious themes were not so engaging to them as satires directed against a sometimes corrupt clergy and the outworn conventions of chivalry. Searching for new modes of expression, their thinkers and artists found what they wanted in the classical legacy of Greece and Rome.

Individualism and tradition in the Renaissance. In a sense, the Renaissance is the history of individual men expressing themselves brilliantly, and often tempestuously, in art, poetry, science, exploration, and religion. While the medieval way taught the unimportance of this life, stressed its snares and evils, and smothered the individual with a host of confining rules and prohibitions, the Renaissance beckoned man to enjoy beauty, to savor the opportunities of this world, and to be himself, regardless of restraints. Above all, the new spirit called upon its followers to adopt the concept of *l'uomo universale*, "the universal man" or, alternately, "the complete man." Life was best lived when the human personality showed its versatility by expression in many forms: advancement of the mind, perfection of the body, cultivation of the social graces, and appreciation and creativity in the arts.

Like any other movement, however, individualism had its negative aspects and its excesses. The lawlessness and political confusion of the Italian Renaissance and the strongly amoral character of its society were due in no small measure to the tendency of men to regard themselves as above the laws.

In discussing the Renaissance as a new era, the historian must be careful to avoid oversimplification. Men continued to share in the corporate life of the Church and the guilds, and many medieval customs and habits of thought persisted for centuries. In the case of humanism, as we shall see, no sudden revolution of philosophical doctrines occurred to set the Renaissance apart from the Middle Ages. Similarly, the artists of the Renaissance, who found inspiration in antiquity and whose works reflected a renewed interest in classical mythology and in the beauties of the human body, did not break completely with the subject matter and artistic techniques of their medieval predecessors. Although their interest in rendering secular subjects increased, Renaissance artists still looked to the Church as their greatest single patron. Building churches, sculpturing saints and Madonnas, and painting religious murals continued to occupy the genius of hundreds of artists during this period.

Renaissance patrons. In the Italian cities the newly wealthy class of traders, bankers, and manufacturers conspicuously displayed their wealth and bolstered their social importance by patronizing artists and scholars. While commissions for artists in the fifteenth century were still obtained from such communal bodies as guilds and churches, individual patronage began to play a more important role. Among the most famous patrons were members of the Medici family, who throughout the fifteenth century ruthlessly controlled the government of Florence. Lorenzo de' Medici, who was first citizen of Florence from 1469 until his death in 1492, carried on his family's proud traditions and added so much luster to Florence that he became known as Lorenzo the Magnificent. His career marks the zenith of Florentine leadership in the arts.

Other princes and ruling despots of Italian city-states supported the arts, and the popes were lavish patrons. The greatest artists of the late Renaissance worked in the Vatican at one time or another. It did not seem inconsistent to popes and artists to include representations of pagan mythological figures in the decorations of the papal palace, and thus the Vatican was filled with secular as well as religious art.

A Renaissance artist had the benefit of the security and protection offered by his patron and enjoyed a definite advantage from working exclusively on commission. The artist knew where his finished work would repose, in cathedral, villa, or city square; this situation contrasts with later periods, when artists painted when and as they wished and then attempted to sell the work to anyone who would buy it.

Manners and morals. During the Renaissance, the newly wealthy citizens of the Italian cities sought refinement in every aspect of their culture. Believing as they did that the mark of nobility was an elegance of manner as well as a cultivated mind, they eagerly snapped up etiquette books to learn the rules of correct social behavior.

The most famous book on Renaissance manners, published in 1528, was *The Courtier* by Baldassare Castiglione (1478-1529), a scholar, poet, and courtier from Urbino. Because of its characterizations and witty conversation, this book became very popular; but its greatest significance lies in the fact that it established a model for the Renaissance courtier. To Castiglione, good manners and deportment were essential to the ideal courtier, but his central idea was that a courtier's true worth was commensurate with his strength of character and excellence of intellect rather than with his hereditary social position. The courtier should be capable in the arts of war and peace and should be motivated by honesty and integrity in advising his ruler.

The *Autobiography* of Benvenuto Cellini (1500-1571) gives us a vivid insight into Renaissance manners and morals, but it is no book of etiquette. Cellini was a bold and worldly adventurer, constantly embroiled in excitement and adventure—duels, love affairs, and prison terms. But he was also a sculptor of great repute and the most skillful metal-worker of his day.

Vigorous and energetic, Cellini possessed *virtù*, a term used in the Renaissance to characterize a man of natural ability and abounding vitality. *Virtù* should not be confused with *virtue*; the words have no connection, and, in fact, a man possessing *virtù* often appeared to be singularly deficient in virtue, as Cellini's life story reveals. Possession of *virtù* enabled a man to be considered *l'uomo universale*, the Renaissance ideal of greatness. While Cellini approximated this ideal, it was left for others—geniuses like Leonardo da Vinci and Michelangelo—to achieve it completely.

THE ITALIAN RENAISSANCE:

THOUGHT

Humanism and the classical revival. During the Middle Ages, Virgil, Cicero, and Caesar were popular authors; Aristotle was venerated much as though he were a Church Father; and Roman law was used to formulate canon doctrines. But in medieval times the writers of antiquity had been interpreted within the framework of the Christian religion and had often been cited as authorities to bolster Church dogma. Many aspects of antiquity were avoided because of their disturbingly pagan quality, although churchmen did make use of pagan literature for allegorical narratives which were Christian in character. Consequently, the true nature of the classical world was often distorted or obscured.

In fourteenth-century Italy, however, a new perspective was attained. Here, in the early humanistic movement, a fresh appreciation of classical culture emerged. Successors to a small group of medieval teachers of grammar and rhetoric, the representatives of this new intellectual movement called themselves humanists, a name derived from *studia humanitatis*, or "humanities," which Roman authors had used in the sense of a liberal or literary education.

Medieval Scholastic education had emphasized the sciences and professional training in law, medicine, and theology at the expense of the "arts," or literary side of the curriculum. Hence Scholastic translations from the classics had consisted chiefly of works on astronomy, medicine, mathematics, and Aristotle's scientific writings. Stimulated by a rebirth of men's interest in the problems and values of human living, the humanists reversed this medieval emphasis and called attention to the importance of an education in the humanities—history, grammar, rhetoric, poetry, and moral philosophy. The humanists disdained the sciences because, as Petrarch—the first of the Italian humanists—wrote:

. . . they help in no way toward a happy life, for what does it advantage us to be familiar with the nature of animals, birds, fishes, and reptiles, while we are ignorant of the nature of the race of man to which we belong, and do not know or care whence we come or whither we go?[2]

Thus, despite the fact that both the humanist and the Scholastic looked to the past and venerated its heritage, they differed widely in their choice of the ancient material to be revered.

Humanists and Scholastics differed also in the manner in which they saw themselves in relation to the writers of ancient times. While the Scholastic always felt himself inferior to the ancients and so looked up to them as son to father or pupil to teacher, the typical humanist in his exultant individualism saw himself equal to the ancients and so boldly hailed them as man to man and friend to friend. At the beginning of his *Divine Comedy*, Dante described in allegorical terms medieval man's reliance upon the authority of the ancients. Dante (medieval man) is lost in the "dark wood" which is this life until he is rescued by Virgil (a favorite medieval symbol of ancient wisdom), who thereafter guides him along the right path. "Losing me," Virgil is made to say to Dante, "ye would remain astray." The noticeably different attitude of the humanists was well expressed by one of their few medieval forerunners, John of Salisbury (d. 1180): "Most delightful in many ways is the fruit of letters that, banishing the irksomeness of intervals of place and time, bring friends into each other's presence. . . ."[3] It was in this spirit that Petrarch wrote his *Letters to Ancient Authors*, addressing Homer, Plato, Cicero, and others in familiar terms and sharing with them his own thoughts and experiences. This feeling of equality with ancient authors was also behind the humanists' practice of stuffing their own writings with apt quotations from the classics. The humanists' purpose, however, differed from that of the Scholastics, who also quoted extensively from the ancients; as the humanist Montaigne explained in his essays (see p. 285), he quoted the ancients not because he agreed with them but because they agreed with him!

Petrarch, the "father of humanism." The "father of humanism" is a title that has been given to Francesco Petrarca, better known to us as Petrarch (1304-1374). Resentful as a youth of his father's desire to have him become a lawyer, he turned to reading Virgil and Cicero for consolation; and though he studied law at Bologna, he dreamed constantly of the glories of the classical age.

In 1327 he met the lady Laura and fell in love with her. Little is known of Laura or of the true nature of her relationship to Petrarch. But, inspired by his love of her, Petrarch wrote sonnets which made him one of the greatest lyric poets of all time. In the love poetry of the age, his portrayal of Laura represents a fresh approach. Earlier poets had woven about their heroines an air of courtly love and religious idealization which made the characters quite unreal. Petrarch's Laura was a flesh-and-blood creature whom all readers could recognize as a human being.

The ancients wrote of the joys of this world, and their attitude toward living struck a sympathetic chord in Petrarch. In his *Secret*, Petrarch has an imaginary conversation with St. Augustine, and here the conflict between new ideas and those of medieval times is forcibly brought out. Petrarch concluded that, despite the importance of the world to come, the world of here and now held many delights which should not be shunned.

This inner conflict between his love of earthly things and his loyalty to the traditional medieval ideal of self-denial and otherworldliness exemplifies the transitional position occupied by Petrarch in western culture. A product of medieval beliefs and attitudes, he nevertheless could not accept a depreciation of man's importance in the scheme of things or a constriction of his mental horizons. And so he condemned the rigidity and arid logic of Scholasticism and the extent to which medieval education was governed by dead tradition. He himself was not a careful scholar and never mastered Greek, yet this versatile rebel had a profound influence upon his contemporaries and gave humanism its first impetus.

Boccaccio and the *Decameron*. Another celebrated humanist was Giovanni Boccaccio (1313-1375). In 1348, the Black Death struck—a plague in which three out of five citizens of Florence died. Boccaccio used this event to establish the setting of his masterpiece, the *Decameron*. To escape the pestilence, his characters—three young men and seven young women—seek seclusion in a country villa, where they while away the time by telling each other stories. Boccaccio suffused the hundred tales of the *Decameron*, based on the old *fabliaux* and on chivalric accounts, with a new and different spirit. Recounted by sophisticated city dwellers, the tales satirize the follies of knights and other medieval types and express clearly the contempt which had developed for the old, and by then threadbare, ideals of feudalism. Many tales are bawdy and, by present-day standards, indecent; there is little moral purpose to relieve their irony and cynicism. Nevertheless, the *Decameron* offers the reader a wealth of anecdotes, prose portraits of flesh-and-blood characters, and a vivid (although one-sided) picture of Renaissance life.

The *Decameron* closed Boccaccio's career as a creative artist. Largely through the influence of Petrarch, whom he met in 1350,

Boccaccio gave up writing in the Italian vernacular and turned to the study of antiquity. He attempted to learn Greek, wrote an encyclopedia of classical mythology, and went off to monasteries in search of manuscripts. By the time that Petrarch and Boccaccio died, the study of the literature and learning of antiquity was growing throughout Italy.

The search for manuscripts. The search for manuscripts became a mania, and, before the middle of the fifteenth century, works by most of the important Latin authors had been found. The degree of difference between humanist and Scholastic is indicated by the ease with which the early humanists recovered the "lost" Latin literary masterpieces: they were found close at hand in monastic libraries, covered by the undisturbed dust of centuries. The books had always been there; what had been largely lacking was a mature and appreciative audience of readers. In addition to Latin works, precious Greek manuscripts were brought to Italy from Constantinople; by the beginning of the sixteenth century, the most important Greek works in all fields of knowledge were obtainable in western Europe.

Individual scholars had their favorite classical authors, both Greek and Roman, but the highest universal praise was reserved for Cicero. Compounded of moral philosophy and rhetoric, his works displayed a widely ranging intellect which appealed to the humanists. Petrarch and many others also used Cicero's graceful, eloquent, and polished literary style as a model. The revival of the art of writing classical Latin prose was due largely to the study and imitation of Cicero.

Platonism. As a result both of their rebellion against the Aristotelian emphasis upon natural science and of their search for a classical philosophy that stressed moral purpose and religious and mystical values, many humanists gravitated to Platonism. A factor in the revival of Platonism was the study of Plato in the original Greek, followed by the translation, in the first half of the fifteenth century, of the *Republic* and others of his major works. Still another stimulus to the growth cf Platonism was provided when

Cosimo de' Medici (1389-1464), grandfather of Lorenzo the Magnificent, founded the Platonic Academy at Florence—a prototype for similar schools in Italy and elsewhere. Its leader, Marsilio Ficino (1433-1499), is credited with producing the first complete Latin version of Plato's works.

Ficino also developed a philosophy which attempted to synthesize Platonic and Christian doctrines. To the humanistic belief in man's ability to attain the highest good, Ficino added the conviction that the ultimate end of all human desire and activity must be "boundless truth and goodness"—namely, God. Basic to Ficino's teachings was the belief that philosophy and religion complemented each other; each required the other if ignorance was to be avoided and man's highest spiritual goals attained. In working out his synthesis of Platonism and Christianity, Ficino coined the expression "Platonic love" to describe an ideal, pure love. This concept found its way into much of Renaissance literature.

Aristotelianism. Despite its great attraction for many humanists, Platonism still had a formidable rival in Aristotelianism. Concerned chiefly with natural philosophy, logic, and metaphysics, Aristotelian commentators still dominated teaching in the Italian universities. By championing a secular rationalism that kept philosophy separate from theology, Aristotelianism ultimately helped to create an environment necessary for the triumph of scientific thought in early modern times.

The most influential Aristotelians were the Latin Averroists, followers of the Muslim philosopher Averroës (see p. 182). Averroës brought to the study of Aristotle an original and even mystical approach. He taught that matter is eternal and that all men partake of a single Intellect. Inasmuch as their individual souls are absorbed in the larger reality of the universal Intellect, it is not possible for men to attain personal immortality. This concept was directly opposed to the teachings of the Church. In fact, to combat the widespread views of the Averroists, Church leaders felt impelled to establish in 1512 the dogma of the immortality of the soul. The Averroists' denial of personal immortality and their emphasis upon the relative insignificance of individual man also aroused the ire of the humanists against them.

Evaluation of humanism. We owe the humanists a debt of gratitude for reintroducing Greek literature into the mainstream of western thought and for making more exact translations of Greek and Latin classics. From their reading of the classics, humanists came to understand the classical world in a true historical perspective and corrected many misconceptions about ancient times which had existed in the Middle Ages.

On the other hand, although the humanists condemned medieval restrictions, they themselves were often subservient to the authorities of antiquity. Indeed, theirs was a closed culture whose boundaries had been set by ancient Greece and Rome, so that to the humanists the only course open was to retravel the old ground, not to explore uncharted territory. Intent on returning to antiquity, so to speak, the humanists resented the centuries separating them from the golden days of Greece and Rome. Unfortunately, this viewpoint resulted in their disparagement of the best works produced in the Middle Ages.

The cult of classical letters gave rise to other defects. Humanist scholars were so dominated by Roman and Greek forms that they tended to imitate rather than create for themselves. Their passion for Ciceronian Latin became pernicious; too often their writings were rich in form and barren in content. Worse still, their preoccupation with classical authors retarded the growth of science and of the much more vital vernacular literature.

The humanists' contributions to philosophy were not extensive; they did little original thinking. Nevertheless, the spread of humanist thought resulted in a renewed and valuable emphasis upon the freedom and dignity of man as an individual, and the importance of his place in the cosmos. As a corollary, the humanities encouraged men to express their personal reactions to their environment. The realization of the propriety and value of exploring one's personality and of analyzing individual experiences was manifested not only in literature but also in the fine arts during the Renaissance.

THE ITALIAN RENAISSANCE: ART

Transitional period in sculpture and painting. As we have noted in Chapter 10, the techniques of sculpture had developed throughout the Romanesque and Gothic periods. In Italy, the influence of numerous examples of classical Graeco-Roman art added to this rich legacy. The synthesis of these esthetic traditions began in the thirteenth century and continued during the fourteenth century, together with the creation of new forms.

The transition from the Middle Ages to the Renaissance in painting can be seen in the works of Giotto (1266-1336). Reportedly the friend of Dante, renowned as a sculptor and an architect and acclaimed as a wit and a poet, this versatile artist broke new ground in the art of painting. In spite of his limited knowledge of anatomy, Giotto gave a keener sense of reality to his works than any of his predecessors had done; he endowed his figures with a high degree of weight and volume and simplified his composition to make a unified impact on the viewer, a technique which was new to the art of painting.

The quattrocento. One of the most fascinating periods of the Italian Renaissance is the fifteenth century, which is often called the *quattrocento* (Italian for "four hundred," an abbreviation for the 1400's). By the *quattrocento*, the more populous of the prosperous and extremely individualistic city-states of northern Italy were controlled by the middle class, and the wealthiest townsmen became patrons of the arts. It was only natural that the artists should attempt to satisfy middle-class, secular tastes. It was during the *quattrocento*, too, that humanistic studies reached full stride, thereby augmenting the already strong individualistic forces in the environment.

Architecture. The activities of architects continued to center upon church construction; but, with the growing interest in constructing impressive secular buildings, such as palaces and hospitals, new opportunities arose for their talents.

Filippo Brunelleschi (1377-1446) marked the beginning of the new architecture. As a youth Brunelleschi had visited Rome, where he studied the construction of ancient edifices. Although he was influenced by classical architecture, his buildings in Florence were not just copies of Roman models. His most famous creation was the dome of the cathedral at Florence, but more characteristic were buildings with arcades of round Roman arches, Roman pediments above the windows, and Roman decorative motifs.

The great architect of the late Renaissance was Donato Bramante (1444-1514) from Milan. Bramante's most important commission came in 1506, when Pope Julius II requested him to rebuild St. Peter's. Instead of planning a longitudinal church such as tradition might have dictated, he designed a strictly centralized church in the form of a Greek cross with the altar at the center; in addition, his plan called for an immense dome surmounting the structure. The exterior of St. Peter's exemplifies the spirit of the late Renaissance—to conceive on a grand and superhuman scale while retaining overall proportion and simplicity. Bramante died when the cathedral was barely begun, and it was left to Michelangelo and others to complete the work.

Renaissance architects also produced magnificent palaces and other secular buildings. The pediments over the windows, the engaged columns, and the decorative details of the Palazzo Farnese in Rome show how classical details, when blended in a new fashion, resulted in an impressive, refined structure. From the sixteenth century on, all Europe began to take to the new architecture.

Sculpture. One of the finest sculptors of the *quattrocento* was Lorenzo Ghiberti (1378-1455) of Florence, whose training as a goldsmith made him proficient in creating delicate figures. He spent most of his working

At the right below is the Cathedral of Florence, called Santa Maria del Fiore, which was designed by Filippo Brunelleschi, the first of the Italian architects to make an extensive study of ancient Roman architecture. Roman domes, such as that on the Pantheon, were largely hidden by the mass of the building. Brunelleschi's great contribution to the architecture of his own time was the development of the great dome, or cupola, which he raised on a drum, making it an imposing sight from the outside as well as from the inside of the edifice. Michelangelo adapted Brunelleschi's ideas to create the magnificent dome of St. Peter's at Rome (far right above), which has been called the greatest achievement of Renaissance architecture. Originally planned by Donato Bramante, who began the actual construction, St. Peter's was built in the shape of a Greek cross, with a dome at the crossing (see the architectural drawing at the right above). The plan was later modified by Bramante's successors and, finally, by Michelangelo through the addition of a long nave in order to create a cathedral based on the Latin cross. The Palazzo Farnese (above), in Rome, shows the classical simplicity and symmetry which marked the palaces designed during the late Italian Renaissance. The even spacing of windows, the equal height of the three stories, the repetition of decorative motifs, and the handsome cornice whose width is proportionate to the height of the palace—all contribute to a feeling of unity in design.

life making the doors for the baptistery in Florence. Between 1403 and 1424, Ghiberti made the bronze doors at the north entrance (see p. 277); between 1425 and 1452, he created the gilded east doors, which drew from Michelangelo the declaration that they were worthy to be the gates of paradise.

Although Ghiberti was a superb craftsman, he was less of an innovator than his younger contemporary in Florence, Donatello (1386-1466). Divorcing sculpture from its architectural background, Donatello created a truly freestanding statue based on the realization of the human body as a functional, coordinated mechanism of bones, muscles, and sinews, maintaining itself against the pull of gravity. His equestrian statue of Gattamelata the *condottiere*, the first of this type of statuary done in the Renaissance, reveals clearly the influence of classical models.

Interest in the beauty of the human body had been alien to the medieval mind, and sculptors of the early Renaissance were concerned chiefly with the problem of how to render physical movements. The glorification of the human body, particularly the male nude, was an achievement of Michelangelo Buonarroti (1475-1564), the greatest sculptor of the late Renaissance. Fired by the grandeur of newly discovered pieces of Hellenistic sculpture and strongly influenced by Platonism, Michelangelo found in figure art the medium for expressing his ideal of beauty.

Painting. Previously we noted how Giotto rendered the figures in his paintings so that they appeared to occupy real space. But it was the *quattrocento* painters who most satisfactorily solved the problem of representing the third dimension in painting. A painter's solution was to "frame" his space and by means of perspective—that is, the use of lines converging toward a vanishing point—to represent a three-dimensional composition, the proportions of which were determined from a fixed point of view.

The achievement of three-dimensional composition owed much to the work of the Florentine painter Masaccio (1401-1428). Building upon Giotto's accomplishments, Masaccio gave a new direction to Florentine painting. His skill in perspective was employed not for its own sake but to provide a deeper understanding of the visible world. Also, Masaccio had a greater knowledge of anatomy than Giotto. By his use of perspective and his modeling of figures in light and shade, he portrayed his characters realistically, as can be seen in "The Tribute Money." Masaccio also used in his paintings nude figures whose counterparts can be found in classical, but not in medieval, art.

While Masaccio and his successors were intent upon giving their figures a new solidity and resolving the problem of three-dimensional presentation, a later Florentine painter, Sandro Botticelli (1447-1510), proceeded in a different direction, abandoning the techniques of straightforward representation of people and objects. Botticelli used a highly sensitive, even quivering, line to stir the viewer's imagination and emotion and to create a mood in keeping with the subject matter of his paintings. Movement and the patterning of hair and drapery in such allegorical and mythological works as "Primavera" are particularly sensitive.

Painting flourished in areas other than Florence during the *quattrocento*. It was in Padua, the site of a great university, that Andrea Mantegna (1431-1506) acquired a romantic passion for the history, literature, and art of ancient Rome. Following in Masaccio's footsteps, Mantegna used perspective to create a stage on which his figures seem to stand and move.

Leonardo da Vinci. The great triad of late Renaissance painters consisted of Leonardo da Vinci, Raphael, and Michelangelo. An extraordinary man, Leonardo da Vinci (1452-1519) was proficient in a variety of subjects: Aristotelian philosophy, mathematics, architecture, geology, botany, physiology, anatomy, sculpture, painting, music, and poetry. He was always experimenting, with the result that few of the projects he started were ever finished.

A superb draftsman, Leonardo was also a master of soft modeling in full light and shade and of creating groups of figures per-

The sculpture of the Italian Renaissance ranged from the massive to the delicate; its techniques, also, were varied—some were newly developed, individual styles; some were adaptations of the classical; and some were borrowed from the other arts. In its stance and the almost typically classical face of the rider, Gattamelata, Donatello's statue of the famous *condottiere* (upper left), shows the influence of the Roman equestrian statues upon which it was modeled. At the lower left is a set of doors made by Ghiberti for the baptistery at Florence. Each panel is executed with the sculptural and pictorial accuracy which was the mark of Ghiberti's work. The bust of Cosimo de' Medici (upper right), attributed to Benvenuto Cellini, shows the brilliant detail for which Cellini, who was also a goldsmith, was famous. The pyramidal composition of the masterly "Pieta" by Michelangelo (lower right) was common to Renaissance sculpture and painting alike.

The work of the fourteenth-century artist Giotto represented the first step toward greater realism in western painting. He used slight shading to give his figures mass, creating a somewhat three-dimensional effect which differed from the flat Byzantine figures painted by his predecessors. The fresco at the top of this page, "Lamentation over the Dead Christ," is in the Arena Chapel at Padua. Its simple composition is based on the diagonal line of the rock ledge behind the figures; notice that Giotto concentrates on his subjects, keeping them within a very limited setting and eliminating detail and depth from his background. A century after Giotto, the ideal of substantiality in the portrayal of the human figure was re-established by Masaccio. "The Tribute Money" (above) is probably his finest work—the anatomical accuracy of his figures surpasses Giotto's, and Mascaccio has introduced reality into his landscape as well, in the form of aerial perspective. The painting tells the story (in three episodes) of

Peter's miraculous discovery of the money demanded from Christ by a tax collector. The artist Botticelli has been cited as a master of line unsurpassed in the western world. Shown at the right is Venus, symbol of the earth's fruitfulness, one of the figures in Botticelli's painting "Primavera." Leonardo da Vinci's "Madonna of the Rocks" (far right) is a masterly example of his use of light to create the modeling of his figures, achieving a three-dimensional effect. The Renaissance pyramidal form is the compositional basis of this painting. Michelangelo's "The Creation of Man" (above right) is one of the artist's monumental paintings on the ceiling of the Sistine Chapel. The full attainment of solidity and massiveness in the picturing of the human form, first striven for by Giotto, is accomplished by Michelangelo. The titanic figures that he painted have a spirit to match their powerful bodies. Here, Adam is given life by the touch of God's finger while Eve peers fearfully out from under the Almighty's arm.

fectly balanced in a given space (see illustration). One of his most famous paintings is the "Mona Lisa," a portrait of a woman whose enigmatic smile has intrigued art lovers for centuries. Another is "The Last Supper," a study of the moment when Christ tells His twelve disciples that one will betray Him. When he painted this picture on the walls of the refectory of Santa Maria delle Grazie in Milan, Leonardo was experimenting with the use of an oil medium combined with plaster and, unfortunately, the experiment was unsuccessful. The painting has been rapidly disappearing until it is now almost obliterated.

Last of the great Florentine painters, Leonardo was the one who developed the artistry of the *quattrocento* painters to its highest point.

Raphael. The second of the great triad of late Renaissance painters was Raffaello Santi (1483-1520), better known as Raphael. Summoned to Rome by Bramante to aid in the decoration of the Vatican, Raphael absorbed something of Leonardo's intellectuality and Michelangelo's "body dynamics" and grandeur while retaining his own incomparable style. Displaying a magnificent blending of classical and Christian subject matter, his Stanza frescoes in the Vatican are imbued with a clarity and breadth of vision expressive of the late Renaissance at its best. Considered by some critics as unrivaled in the mastery of space composition, Raphael was equally at home in handling a single figure or in grouping masses—in every case endowing his work with a maximum of spaciousness and freedom.

Michelangelo. Michelangelo considered himself first and foremost a sculptor, but this *uomo universale* also excelled as a poet, engineer, architect, and painter. From 1508 to 1512, at the request of Pope Julius II, he painted the curved ceiling of the Sistine Chapel, an area of several thousand square yards. The main field of the ceiling is divided into panels depicting scenes from Genesis. Hoisted to the ceiling on a high scaffolding, Michelangelo lay on his back to paint. Bringing to the task his unrivaled genius for rendering the human form, he devised a wealth of expressive positions and attitudes for his figures. Their physical splendor is pagan, but their spirit is Christian.

The individualism and idealism of the entire Renaissance have no greater representative than Michelangelo. Stories of this stormy and temperamental personality have helped to shape our ideas of what a genius is like. Indeed, there is something almost superhuman about both Michelangelo and his art. His superhuman energy enabled him to complete the entire work of painting the ceiling of the Sistine Chapel in four years, and his art embodies a superhuman ideal of man.

Succeeding Bramante as chief architect of St. Peter's, he designed the great dome and was in the midst of creative activities when he died, almost in his ninetieth year, in 1564.

The Venetian school. Venice offered a congenial environment to artists. A prosperous merchant-prince could well afford to play the role of patron of the arts; trade with the East provided Venetians with new luxuries and comforts, which added splendor and color to daily life; and the beauty of the city itself would attract the eye of any artist.

It should cause no surprise that this wealthy, sophisticated milieu produced a secular rather than a devotional school of painting. For the most part, the artists in Venice were satisfied with the here and now; they were not overly concerned with antiquity or classical canons. While they sometimes painted exquisite Madonnas, they more often painted wealthy merchants and proud doges, attired in rich brocades, jewels, and precious metals and grouped with beautiful young women who scarcely look like Madonnas. There is a sensuousness in the Venetian painting of this period which is evident in the artists' love of decoration, rich costumes, and striking nude figures.

Giorgione (1478-1511), like Botticelli, used classical themes and idyllic landscapes in his paintings. But unlike the Florentine master, who made his mythological figures imaginative and idealized, Giorgione's Muses and Venuses were lovely Venetian models.

The pictures of Titian (1477?-1576) contain sensuous beauties of color and atmosphere. But though his portraits show the Venetian love of color and of the texture of rich fabrics, these elements are subordinated to the portrayal of the sitter's character.

THE NORTHERN
RENAISSANCE

The northward spread of the Renaissance. The Italian Renaissance had projected man once more into the center of life's stage and permeated the intellectual and artistic environment with humanistic values. In time the stimulating ideas current in Italy spread to other areas and combined with indigenous developments to produce a French Renaissance, an English Renaissance, and so on.

With the increase of commerce in northern Europe, town life grew, fostering a middle class of merchants and bankers and a more sophisticated cultural climate. The men of the northern cities were stimulated by the ideas which merchants carried with them over the Alps from Italy. But while the wealthy burghers patronized the work of artists and scholars, the prime sponsors of the Renaissance north of the Alps were often the kings of the new national states. By importing artists and learned men from Italy or supporting native geniuses, the rulers added brilliance to their courts.

The influence of printing. Perhaps even more important in the diffusion of the Renaissance and, later, in the success of the Reformation was the invention of printing in Europe. The essential elements—paper and movable type—had long been known in non-European cultures, but it was not until the fifteenth century that printing of books began in Europe. In his printing shop at Mainz, Germany, John Gutenberg used movable type to print papal documents and the first published version of the Bible (1454).

Within fifty years after Gutenberg's Bible had been published, all the major countries of Europe possessed the means for printing books. It is said that the prices of books soon sank to one eighth of their former cost; thus books came within the reach of a multitude of people who formerly were unable to buy them. It was now possible and profitable to cater to the tastes of the common people, and pamphlets and controversial tracts soon were widely circulated. As a result, knowledge and new ideas reached a thousand times more people in a relatively short span of time. In the quickening of Europe's intellectual life, it is difficult to overestimate the effects of the printing press.

Erasmus and northern humanism. The intellectual life of the first half of the sixteenth century was dominated by Desiderius Erasmus (1466?-1536). Born in Rotterdam, he passed most of his long life elsewhere—in Germany, France, England, Italy, and Switzerland. The most influential and cosmopolitan of the northern humanists, he was *the* scholar of Europe, and his writings were read eagerly everywhere.

Perhaps the most famous and influential work by Erasmus was *The Praise of Folly*, a satire written in 1511. The book concerns a female character called Folly, Erasmus' conception of human nature, who is represented as delivering a lecture. A historian has described the work in these words: "At first the book makes kindly and approving fun of the ways of action and the foibles and weaknesses of mankind. It is not mordant, only amused. But gradually from fools innocent and natural and undebased, it passes to those whose illusions are vicious in their setting and results."[4] Among such are merchants ("they lie, swear, cheat, and practice all the intrigues of dishonesty"), lawyers ("they of all men have the greatest conceit of their own abilities"), Scholastic philosophers ("that talk as much by rote as a parrot"), and scientists ("who esteem themselves the only favourites of wisdom, and look upon the rest of mankind as the dirt and rubbish of the creation"). Most roughly handled are churchmen, in particular monks, who are "impudent pretenders to the profession of piety," and popes, cardinals, and bishops, "who in pomp and splendour have almost equalled if not outgone secular princes." While his satire

The Renaissance, with its glorification of the individual and his talents, produced many notable men, who represented various aspects of the ideal *l'uomo universale*. The most famous were commemorated by the leading painters of the time, themselves personifications of the man of individuality and talent. At the far left is a portrait of Baldassare Castiglione, author of *The Courtier, the* book of etiquette for its day. The portrait, by Raphael, pictures Castiglione as the gentleman the writer himself idealized; it is a sympathetic, restrained work by a great artist who was also a good friend of the sitter. Mantegna's painting of the Marquis Ludovico II and his family (below left) seems to emphasize that group's obvious economic and social superiority and aloofness. In painting these nobles, Mantegna used a perspective that almost suggests that they are on a stage, to be looked up at by the spectator. Pope Leo X appears in the portrait at the left, with the symbols of his office and his interests—the beautifully wrought bell and the illuminated manuscript. Raphael painted him thus to emphasize that, as a Medici, Leo displayed the cultivated tastes typical of that family, who were patrons of the arts for many decades. The painting at the right is Giorgione's *Concert*. The rapt expressions on the faces of the listeners and the moody concentration of the player point up the serious interest the people of the Renaissance took in music. The statue of the *condottiere* Colleoni (below) is by Verrocchio. The spirit of this great military leader is captured in the face, which (unlike that of the equestrian statue of Gattamelata) is individual and very human, rather than classical. The painting at the right below is a self-portrait by Titian. Although the artist used carefully controlled and subtle techniques, he succeeded in capturing a sense of a vigorous personality in all his portraits.

is indeed harsh, Erasmus was himself balanced, moderate, and intolerant only of bigotry, ignorance, greed, and violence.

The Praise of Folly points up a significant difference between the northern humanists and their Italian predecessors. While both were repelled by much that seemed to them wrong in the life of their day, their reactions took different forms. The typical Italian humanist followed the course set by Petrarch: "In order to forget my own time I have constantly striven to place myself in spirit in other ages. . . ."[5] Disdaining such escapism, the great majority of northern humanists faced up to reality and became reformers of their society's ills. They also went further in broadening their interest in ancient literature to include early Christian writings—the Scriptures and the works of the Church Fathers. This led them to prepare new and more accurate editions of the Scriptures—Erasmus' Greek edition of the New Testament became famous and was used by Luther—and to contrast unfavorably the simplicity of primitive Christianity with the complexities of the Church in their own day. Since the northern humanists held that the essence of religion was morality and rational piety—what Erasmus called the "philosophy of Christ"—rather than ceremony and dogma, it is not surprising that the Church became a major target of their reforming zeal.

Sir Thomas More's *Utopia*. The most significant figure in English humanism was Sir Thomas More (1478-1535), the famous friend of Erasmus. More is best known for his *Utopia*, the first important description of the ideal state since Plato's *Republic*. In his epoch-making work, More criticized his age by using as his spokesman a fictitious sailor who contrasts the ideal life he has seen in Utopia (The Land of Nowhere) with the harsh conditions of life in England. More's denunciations centered on the new acquisitive capitalism, which he blamed for the widespread insecurity and misery of the lower classes. More felt that governments

. . . are a conspiracy of the rich, who, in pretence of managing the public, only pursue their private

ends, . . . first, that they may, without danger, preserve all that they have so ill acquired, and then, that they may engage the poor to toil and labor for them at as low rates as possible, and oppress them as much as they please.[6]

(The enclosure movement, a phenomena of the new capitalistic agriculture and one of More's favorite targets, will be discussed in Chapter 16.)

In Utopia, by contrast, no man is in want because the economy is planned and cooperative and because property is held in common. Utopia is the only true commonwealth, concludes More's imaginary sailor:

In all other places, it is visible that while people talk of a commonwealth, every man only seeks his own wealth: but there, where no man has any property, all men zealously pursue the good of the public. . . . in Utopia, where every man has a right to every thing, they all know that if care is taken to keep the public stores full, no private man can want any thing; for among them there is no unequal distribution, so that no man is poor, none in necessity; and though no man has any thing, yet they are all rich; for what can make a man so rich as to lead a serene and cheerful life, free from anxieties; neither apprehending want himself, nor vexed with the endless complaints of his wife?[7]

More was the first of the modern English socialists, but his philosophy should not be considered a forerunner of the socialism of our day. His economic outlook was a legacy from the Middle Ages, and his preference for medieval collectivism over modern individualism was of one piece with his preference for a Church headed—medieval style—by popes rather than by kings, a view that prompted Henry VIII to execute him for treason (see p. 300). Sir Thomas More is now one of the martyrs and saints of the Roman Catholic Church.

Rabelais. One of the best known of the French humanists was François Rabelais (1494-1553). A brilliant, if coarse, skeptic, Rabelais is best remembered for his work *Gargantua and Pantagruel* (published 1532-1564). Centering on figures from French folklore, this work relates the adventures of Gargantua and his son Pantagruel, genial giants of tremendous stature and appetite, to whom were ascribed many marvelous feats.

In the course of his pungent narrative, Rabelais inserted his views on educational reform and his humanistic belief in man's inherent goodness and ability to solve his problems by reason. He made vitriolic attacks on the abuses of the Church and the shortcomings of Scholastics and monks, but he had little patience with overzealous Protestants either. What Rabelais could not stomach was hypocrisy and repression; and for those guilty of these tendencies, he reserved his choicest invective. In the following excerpt he bids his readers to flee from that

. . . rabble of squint-minded fellows, dissembling and counterfeit saints, demure lookers, hypocrites, pretended zealots, tough friars, buskin-monks, and other such sects of men, who disguise themselves like masquers to deceive the world. . . . Fly from these men, abhor and hate them as much as I do, and upon my faith you will find yourself the better for it. And if you desire . . . to *live in peace, joy, health, making yourselves always merry*, never trust those men that always peep out through a little hole.[8]

Montaigne. The last notable northern humanist was the French skeptic Michel de Montaigne (1533-1592). Despite a career in law, he found his chief satisfaction in the well-stocked library at his country estate, where he studied and wrote.

Montaigne developed a new literary form and gave it its name—the essay. In ninety-four essays, he set forth his personal views on many subjects: leisure, friendship, education, cannibalism, drunkenness, old age, and so forth. He did not pretend to have the final answer to the problems he discussed. Instead, he advocated open-mindedness and toleration—rare qualities in the sixteenth century, when France was racked by religious and civil strife.

Montaigne was soon considered the leading French humanist of his day. But at the time he began his literary career, the defects of humanism were revealing themselves, and he held these defects up to public view. He condemned the pedantry into which humanism had largely degenerated and realized that it is more important to solve the problems of life than the syntax of an obscure sentence from Horace. Montaigne's final essay, entitled "Of Experience," which developed the thought that "when reason fails us we resort to experience," is an acknowledgment of the bankruptcy of humanism and a foreshadowing of the coming triumph of science.

Cervantes, creator of Don Quixote. The transition from feudal knight to Renaissance courtier finds its greatest literary expression in a masterpiece of Spanish satire, *Don Quixote de la Mancha*, the work of Miguel de Cervantes (1547-1616). By Cervantes' day, knighthood had become an anachronism, though its accompanying code of chivalry still retained its appeal. It remained for a rationalist like Cervantes to show up the inadequacies of chivalric idealism in a world that had acquired new, and intensely practical, aims. He did so by creating a pathetic but immensely appealing character to serve as the personification of an outmoded way of life.

Don Quixote, the "knight of the woeful countenance," mounted on his "lean, lank, meagre, drooping, sharp-backed, and raw-boned" steed Rocinante, sets out in the Spanish countryside to right wrongs and uphold his lady's and his own honor. In his misadventures, he is accompanied by his squire, the much less gallant but infinitely more realistic Sancho Panza, whose peasant adages and hard-grained common sense serve as a contrast to the unpractical nature of his master's chivalric code. Tilting at windmills, mistaking serving wenches for highborn ladies and inns for castles, and lamenting the invention of gunpowder as depriving ardent knights of a chance to win immortality, Don Quixote is, on the surface at least, a ridiculous old man whose nostalgia for the "good old days" is a constant source of grief to him. Thus the story represents a superb satire directed against the outworn ideology of the Middle Ages; in particular, it laughed the ideal of chivalric romance into the world of make-believe.

As the influence of the Italian Renaissance spread to the north, new artists came to the fore. "Huntsmen in the Snow" (below) is one of a series of seasonal paintings by the Flemish artist Pieter Brueghel the Elder, who created highly accurate depictions of everyday life. As faithful to nature in rendering landscapes as he was in portraying Flemish peasants, Brueghel has been called the first great landscape painter in the European tradition. In "Giovanni Arnolfini and His Wife" (left), the artist, Jan van Eyck, has meticulously recorded all the details of a wedding. The dog is present as a symbol of fidelity, the single candle signifies the presence of God, and Van Eyck has proudly included himself in the work—as a reflection in the mirror. Van Eyck improved upon the Flemish-originated oil technique to produce an unprecedented depth of color and space and a smooth enamel-like finish. At the right above is a portrait of Sir Thomas More by Hans Holbein; like all Holbein's portraits, it is a faithful, objective rendition of the singularities of a face, and the character of the sitter seems to have been captured along with his features. Albrecht Dürer, whose study for a portrait of Erasmus is shown at the right below, was skilled in many techniques—painting, drawing, engraving, etching, woodcutting—but his choice and treatment of subject matter remained primarily medieval and Gothic.

And yet *Don Quixote* is still more. Cervantes instilled in his main character a pathos born in large measure of the author's own career of frustrated hopes and ambitions. As a result, Don Quixote becomes more than a romantic lunatic; he serves to embody that set of ideals which each of us would like to see realized but which we must compromise in a world that has other interests to serve.

National drama appears. The national drama may well be considered the crowning glory of northern Renaissance literature. By the middle of the fifteenth century, the Renaissance era of drama had begun in Italian cities with the performance of ancient Roman comedies. Shortly thereafter appeared the *commedia dell' arte*, which reflected the everyday life of the times. Although medieval drama had employed some naïve secular elements, a complete divorce of the Church and stage did not occur until the Renaissance.

As secular dramas grew in popularity, theaters were built as permanent settings for their presentations. Great ingenuity was shown in the design of elaborate, realistic stage scenery as well as in lighting and sound effects. Theaters embodying these innovations only gradually appeared outside Italy. Not until 1576 was the first public theater erected in London; three years later, a similar theater was constructed in Madrid.

Imitating the ancient models they admired, French and Italian writers followed what they believed were the rigid conventions of the classical drama and, to a large extent, catered to the aristocracy. By contrast, Spanish and English playwrights created a theatrical environment that was at once more socially democratic, more hospitable to national themes, and less concerned with classical models.

William Shakespeare. The spring of lyric song that bubbled up in the England of Henry VIII formed a veritable stream of verse that sparkled through his daughter Elizabeth's countryside. Her reign (1558-1603) climaxed the English Renaissance and produced such a galaxy of talented writers that some scholars have felt it necessary to go back as far as Athens in the fifth century B.C.

to find an age as prodigal of literary genius. Strongly influenced by the royal court, which served as the busy center of intellectual and artistic as well as of economic and political life, their writings were highly colored, richly romantic, and often wildly extravagant in spite of all their poetic allusions to classical times.

The supreme figure in Elizabethan literature and perhaps in all literature is William Shakespeare (1564-1616). We can only touch briefly upon a few facets of this versatile genius. His rich command of language and poetic imagery were matched only by his fertile imagination. He was a superb lyric poet, and numerous critics have judged him the foremost sonnet writer in the English language.

Shakespeare wrote thirty-eight plays—histories, comedies, and tragedies. His historical plays reflected the patriotic upsurge experienced by Englishmen as their country grew stronger and more prosperous. For his comedies and tragedies, Shakespeare was content in a great majority of cases to borrow plots from earlier works. His forte lay in his creation of characters—perhaps the richest and most diversified collection conceived by the mind of one man—and in his ability to translate his knowledge of human nature into dramatic speech and action. Today his comedies are played to enthusiastic audiences: *The Taming of the Shrew, As You Like It, The Merchant of Venice, The Merry Wives of Windsor*, to mention but a handful. But it is in his tragedies that the poet-dramatist runs the gamut of human emotions and experience. Shakespeare possessed in abundance the Renaissance concern for man and the world about him. Hence his plays deal first and foremost with man's personality, passions, and problems. In such works as *Romeo and Juliet, Measure for Measure*, and *Troilus and Cressida*, the problems of love and sex are studied from many angles. Jealousy is analyzed in *Othello,* ambition in *Macbeth* and *Julius Caesar,* family relationships in *King Lear,* and man's struggle with his own soul in *Hamlet.* Shakespeare's extraordinary ability to build every concrete fact and action upon a universal truth makes his observations as applicable today as they were when first presented in the Globe Theatre. Small wonder, then, that next to the Bible, Shakespeare is the most quoted of all literary sources in the language.

Developments in painting. Before the Italian Renaissance permeated artistic circles in northern Europe, the painters of the Low Countries had been making significant advances on their own. Outstanding among the painters were the brothers Van Eyck, especially Jan van Eyck (1385?-1440). His work has been called "the full flowering of the spirit of the late Middle Ages,"[9] but in fact it was just as revolutionary in its own way as that of the great Florentines. In a detailed, realistic manner, his paintings depict many different sorts of Flemish people and costumes. In his portraits, Van Eyck achieved a new level of individuality.

The first talented German painter to be influenced deeply by Italian art was Albrecht Dürer (1471-1528) of Nuremberg. Dürer made more than one journey to Italy, where he was impressed both with the painting of the Renaissance Italians and with the artists' high social status—a contrast with northern Europe, where artists were still treated as craftsmen. Because he did not entirely lose many of the medieval qualities of the milieu in which he worked, his own work is a blend of the old and the new; but among German artists he did the most to break away from medieval standards and to incorporate ideas from Italy. In the long run, he became better known for his engravings and woodcuts than for his paintings.

Another German painter, Hans Holbein the Younger (1497-1543), was less imaginative than Dürer; but whereas the latter lived principally in Germany and interpreted its spirit, the younger artist worked abroad, especially in England, and as a result his painting acquired a more cosmopolitan character. In his portraits of such great figures as Sir Thomas More and Henry VIII, we see the Renaissance emphasis on the individual man.

While many Flemish painters lost some of their individuality in the rush to adopt

Italian techniques, Pieter Brueghel the Elder (1525?-1569) retained a strong Flemish flavor in his portrayal of the faces and scenes of his native land. Possessing a strong affection for life in the country villages, Brueghel painted village squares, skating scenes, peasant weddings, and dances. He also took Biblical themes and depicted them as if the events were taking place in the Flanders of his own day. The depiction of everyday scenes in realistic fashion is known as *genre* painting; and, in this medium, Brueghel and the Flemish school as a whole remain unexcelled.

SUMMARY

In the Middle Ages, man had thought of himself primarily as part of a universal order of things represented on earth by the Church and the Holy Roman Empire. But gradually, for a variety of reasons, he began to attach importance to himself as an individual and to the physical world around him. This change in attitude, the period in which it occurred, and the ways in which it manifested itself in art, literature, and learning we call the Renaissance.

The change took place earliest in Italy and first expressed itself in the great intellectual movement known as humanism. In its early stages humanism was a revival of classical learning. Wealthy patrons sponsored the search for ancient manuscripts, and scholars eagerly introduced the literature of Greece and Rome into schools and universities. This reverence for antiquity led to the copying of classical literary and artistic forms, and many humanists wasted on such imitation talents which might better have been employed in creating original literature in their native language.

But humanism was much more than sterile imitation. It provided the West not only with a comprehensive knowledge of classical literature and thought but also with a more accurate historical perspective. It absorbed classical ways of thinking, as well as classical modes of expression, and fostered an appreciation of the studies we know today as the "humanities." Above all, humanism reintroduced into western culture a much-needed emphasis on the dignity of man.

In its broader ramifications, humanism stimulated a vital concern for the problems and challenges of the contemporary world. As we saw in this chapter and the one preceding, there was a progressive quickening of life in the social organism, resulting in sweeping changes in politics and economics and in men's minds. The common denominator of these changes was individualism.

Individualism manifested itself also no less in the artist's stimulus to experiment, to relate his esthetic canons to a changing world order, and to find for man his rightful place therein. The extent to which the Renaissance sculptor, architect, and painter succeeded remains one of the glories of western civilization.

In the sixteenth century the stimulating ideas current in Italy began to spread beyond the Alps and to combine with local developments to produce renaissances in France, England, and elsewhere. While influenced profoundly by Italian antecedents, thought and art in each country developed in distinctive ways. These developments included the invention of printing, the impact of humanism on thought and literature, and further achievements in painting.

SUGGESTIONS FOR READING

J. Huizinga, *The Waning of the Middle Ages*,* Anchor. An interpretative study of life, thought, and art in the fourteenth and fifteenth centuries. Evidence collected from France and the Netherlands supports the author's contention that these centuries represent "an epoch of fading and decay."

W. K. Ferguson, *The Renaissance*,* Holt (Berkshire Studies). The best brief survey of all aspects of the Renaissance, both Italian and Northern. Also very valuable are the two surveys described at the end of Chapter 11 in your textbook: Cheyney, *The Dawn of a New Era, 1250-1453*; and Gilmore, *The World of Humanism, 1453-1517*.

G. C. Sellery, *The Renaissance: Its Nature and Origins*, Univ. of Wis., 1950. A valuable work of synthesis and interpretation; concentrates on leading personalities and movements in an effort to define the nature, causes, and chronological limits of

*Indicates an inexpensive paperbound edition.

the Renaissance. For a masterful account of how the concept "Renaissance" has been variously interpreted by generations of scholars, see W. K. Ferguson, *The Renaissance in Historical Thought: Five Centuries of Interpretation*, Houghton Mifflin, 1948.

A. W. O. Von Martin, *Sociology of the Renaissance*, Oxford, 1944. Discusses the changes in the Renaissance milieu which explain the dynamism of the period.

J. H. Randall, *The Making of the Modern Mind*, Houghton Mifflin, 1940. Ch. VI, "The Natural Man," is an excellent short account of the nature and significance of Renaissance humanism. For a spirited account of Renaissance mathematics and science, see G. Sarton, *Six Wings: Men of Science in the Renaissance*, Indiana Univ., 1957. G. Highet, *The Classical Tradition: Greek and Roman Influences on Western Literature*,* Galaxy, is a lively book with chapters on the Renaissance.

J. Burckhardt, *The Civilization of the Renaissance in Italy*,* 2 vols., Torchbooks. The classic statement, first published in 1860, of the thesis that the Italian Renaissance represents a sharp, clear break with the Middle Ages. The man of the Renaissance, "the first-born among the sons of modern Europe," is contrasted with the man of the Middle Ages, who for centuries "lay dreaming or half awake beneath a common veil . . . woven of faith, illusion, and childish prepossession." J. A. Symonds later developed Burckhardt's thesis in his very readable *Renaissance in Italy*, 2 vols., Modern Lib. The heart of Symonds' work has been published as *The Revival of Learning*,* Capricorn.

W. Durant, *The Renaissance: A History of Civilization in Italy from 1304 to 1576 A.D.*, Simon and Schuster, 1953, Vol. V of *The Story of Civilization*. A popular narrative survey, although inadequate in regard to interpretive materials. A clear picture of the major forces at work in fifteenth-century Italy—the new capitalistic spirit, Machiavellian politics, religious movements that foreshadow the Reformation, the spirit of Renaissance art, and the conflicting intellectual movements of Scholasticism, humanism, and science—is contained in the great historical novel by D. Merejkowski, *The Romance of Leonardo da Vinci*, Modern Lib.

P. O. Kristeller, *Renaissance Thought: The Classic, Scholastic, and Humanistic Strains*,* Torchbooks. An excellent analysis of Italian humanism which describes the revival of learning and the relationship of humanistic thought to Christianity. Very helpful for an understanding of the nature of early Italian humanism is J. H. Robinson and R. W. Wolfe, *Petrarch, the First Modern Scholar and Man of Letters*, Putnam, 1914. See also J. H. Whitfield, *Petrarch and the Renascence*, Blackwell, 1943.

E. Newton, *European Painting and Sculpture*,* Penguin. A brief interpretation of the development of European art; particularly worth while are the chapters on the Renaissance. Excellent brief accounts of Renaissance architecture are contained in B. Fletcher, *History of Architecture*, Scribner's, 1954; and N. Pevsner, *An Outline of European Architecture*,* Penguin. Also recommended is W. Sypher, *Four Stages of Renaissance Style: Transformations in Art and Literature, 1400-1700*,* Anchor.

B. Berenson, *Italian Painters of the Renaissance*,* Meridian. One of the best interpretative treatments; consists of nontechnical essays on the individual artists. H. Wölfflin, *Classic Art: The Great Masters of the Italian Renaissance*, Phaidon, 1952, is one of the most influential books on the subject.

R. Roeder, *The Man of the Renaissance*,* Meridian. An analysis of four key figures of the Italian Renaissance: Savonarola, Machiavelli, Castiglione, and Aretino. Each is viewed as a prototype of one aspect of Renaissance man. Outstanding studies of other Italian Renaissance figures include F. Schevill, *The Medici*,* Torchbooks; E. McCurdy, *The Mind of Leonardo da Vinci*, Dodd, 1939; and, on Boccaccio, Vol. I of the standard literary history by F. de Sanctis, *History of Italian Literature*, Harcourt, Brace, 1931.

H. J. Carroll, Jr., et al., *The Development of Civilization*,* I, Scott, Foresman, 1961. See pp. 355-392 for an excellent selection of source readings and interpretative selections.

P. S. Allen, *The Age of Erasmus*, Oxford, 1914. An excellent introduction to the thought of the Northern Renaissance, including instructive comparisons between Italian and Northern humanism. Much broader in its coverage is H. O. Taylor, *Thought and Expression in the Sixteenth Century*, 2 vols., Macmillan, 1920. G. R. Potter, ed., *The Renaissance, 1493-1520*, Cambridge Univ., 1957, Vol. I of *The New Cambridge Modern History*, is a detailed scholarly work, best used for reference.

Preserved Smith, *Erasmus: A Study of His Life, Ideals, and Place in History*, Harper, 1923. A first-rate biography. A shorter work is M. M. Phillips, *Erasmus and the Northern Renaissance*, Macmillan (Teach Yourself History), 1950. Outstanding studies of other Northern Renaissance figures include R. W. Chambers, *Thomas More*,* Ann Arbor Paperbacks; D. B. W. Lewis, *Doctor Rabelais*, Sheed and Ward, 1957; and M. Chute, *Shakespeare of London*,* Everyman. G. B. Harrison, *Introducing Shakespeare*,* Penguin, surveys the development of Shakespeare's mastery of his material and the conditions of stage production in Elizabethan England. For a good brief summary of the work of Gutenberg and other early printers see P. Butler, *The Origin of Printing in Europe*, Univ. of Chicago, 1940.

O. Benesch, *The Art of the Renaissance in Northern Europe: Its Relation to the Contemporary Spiritual and Intellectual Movements*, Harvard, 1945. Published lectures which provide one of the best introductions to Renaissance art in northern Europe. Outstanding among more specialized studies is E. Panofsky, *Early Netherlandish Painting: Its Origins and Character*, Harvard, 1954.

CHAPTER 13

Here I Take
My Stand

Introduction. On October 31, 1517, a professor of theology named Martin Luther nailed some papers on the door of the castle church in Wittenberg, Germany. It was the custom of the day for a man who wanted to engage in a Scholastic debate with another to post his propositions publicly. In this respect Luther's action was not unusual, yet the forces he set in operation altered the entire religious and intellectual pattern of the western world. A religious revolt was launched that split Christendom into numerous factions and sects.

Until his death in 1546, Luther believed that it might be possible to reform Catholicism to the conditions existing in the early Church. From this standpoint, the religious upheaval which he did so much to set in motion can be designated logically as the Reformation. On the other hand,

because the struggle shattered western Christendom permanently, it might be described from a broader historical viewpoint as a revolution or, alternatively, as the Protestant Revolt. The sixteenth century also witnessed a significant revival of Catholicism itself. This renewal of the traditional faith was not solely a Counter Reformation in the sense that it represented a belated response to the challenge of Protestantism. As modern scholars have demonstrated, a strong Catholic Reformation had been gathering momentum even before Luther nailed his ninety-five theses to the door of the castle church in Wittenberg.

The Reformation had both its negative and its positive aspects. In the name of God, men persecuted and killed their fellow men. Moreover, rulers anxious for absolute power wrote some of the sorriest pages of history by using the conflicts engendered by the religious upheaval to serve their own political ends. Yet, as in the early centuries of Christianity, when the blood of the martyrs became the seed of the Church, so the struggles of the sixteenth century, led by men afire with conviction and ready to sacrifice their lives for what they believed, renewed and stimulated the religious consciousness of western Europe. Luther declared: "Here I take my stand"; and in a broad sense this strong affirmation was echoed by Zwingli in the Swiss cantons, by Calvin at Geneva, and by the Catholic Church at the Council of Trent. Such stanch and uncompromising assertions of honest differences of doctrine gave institutionalized Christianity the new religious vitality and intellectual diversity that were to leave their mark on almost every phase of life in the West and bequeath us a rich legacy of values.

THE RELIGIOUS REVOLT

Passing of the medieval order. In Europe in the fourteenth and fifteenth centuries, forces were weakening the medieval order, with its devotion to institutions—the feudal hierarchy, the guild, and the Church—and its subordination of the individual's interests to those of the group. The townsman, for example, found himself increasingly out of sympathy with the Church's economic concepts of the "just price" and with its antiusury statutes, for they conflicted with the new capitalism. He was also out of sympathy with the Church's spiritual dictates of complete obedience and self-abnegation, for these demands conflicted with the newly found individualism and worldliness of the Renaissance.

The Church itself embodied a dangerous contradiction at this time. In dogma it was medieval, yet its highest officials, including the popes, were patrons of a Renaissance culture deriving its inspiration from pagan Greece and Rome. The Church might denounce usury, but at the same time it utilized the services of powerful moneylending families.

As we have seen in Chapter 12, the northern humanists directed searching criticisms against the Church, though for the most part they wished to remain within it. But because it was primarily an intellectual movement, humanism could not create the dynamic drive necessary to inspire widespread reform. Having laid the intellectual groundwork for the pending religious revolt, the humanists left to other men—the militant and the martyrs alike—the task of arousing action.

The time was ripe for the rise of some leader with a religious message more compatible with the spirit of the age. When he appeared, it was likely that he would employ as his weapon not the conflict of Renaissance ideology with that of the Church, for that was a philosophical problem of which few were conscious, but rather the financial and moral abuses of the Church, which were common knowledge. Furthermore, it is not surprising that this figure arose in Germany, a country newly touched by the Renaissance, geographically removed from Rome, and the home of an earnest and pious people.

The revolt in Germany. The religious struggle first came to a head in Germany. Stimulated by the invention of printing, educated Germans had been studying the Scriptures carefully and censuring the ignorance of many of the German clergy. Whereas in Italy familiarity bred a tolerance and rationalization of papal corruption, the Germans fiercely resented papal abuses and expected practice and theory to coincide.

The political situation also had a bearing on the religious question. Divided into hundreds of states, Germany lacked unity except for the nominal rule of the elected emperor of the Holy Roman Empire. Imperial administrative reforms failed to prevent the growth of principalities which tried to imitate the new nationalism of countries to the west. This political trend was to prove highly significant. Because the religious affairs of each principality came under the control of its ruler, a greater diversity of religious opinion and organization could exist within Germany than within a state ruled by a centralized authority.

Nor must economic factors be overlooked. Trade and banking flourished in the fast-growing Rhenish towns, and the Hanseatic League was still prospering. The German burgher found no conflict between piety and profits. On the other hand, his piety and profits were both affected by the draining of German revenues by the Roman Church, especially when unscrupulous means were used to gather them. In short, Germany was ripe for religious change.

Martin Luther. On November 10, 1483, a poor German peasant couple became the parents of a son, baptized Martin Luther. His father joined a firm of copper miners and twenty years later, by virtue of thrift and hard work, was a petty capitalist.

Young Martin was given a sound education which included university studies, but he accepted as a matter of course the prevalent beliefs in witchcraft and other superstitions. To the end of his life Luther believed vividly in the existence of devils and witches. The story goes that he once threw an ink pot at a devil whom he thought he saw leering at him. In 1505 he became a member of the mendicant order of Augustinian monks, a move which met with scant favor from his practical father. In 1508 he received a temporary appointment as a lecturer at the new University of Wittenberg, and a few years later he became professor of theology.

The next few years were epochal, not only in Luther's own life but also in the history of religious thought. He began to probe deeply the problem of eternal salvation. One day, while contemplating the words of St. Paul's Epistle to the Romans, Luther found these words:

For therein is the righteousness of God revealed from faith to faith: as it is written, The just shall live by faith.[1]

He believed that his problem was solved. Man was saved only by his faith in the validity of Christ's sacrifice, which alone could wash away sin. Luther had come to his famous doctrine of justification by faith, as opposed to the Roman Church's doctrine of justification by faith and good works—the demonstration of faith through virtuous acts, acceptance of Church dogma, and participation in Church ritual.

The implications of his radical doctrine were enormous. If salvation could come only through a personal belief in Christ's sacrifice, then an interceding priesthood became superfluous, for each man would then be his own priest. But Luther himself had no idea as yet what his views meant or where they would eventually lead him and half of Christendom. It required a financial abuse by the Church to bring on the religious revolt.

Tetzel and the indulgences. Leo x, a cultured scion of the Medici family, "who would have made an excellent Pope if he had only been a little religious,"[2] wanted to complete the magnificent new St. Peter's in Rome; but money for the costly enterprise was lacking. Several papal agents were sent out to dispose of indulgences as a means of raising money. One of these agents, named Tetzel, discharged his mission "in the German archbishopric of Mainz in a manner which would be recognized in America to-day as high-pressure salesmanship."[3]

The Church's position in regard to indulgences has often been misunderstood. Although the sacrament of Penance absolved the sinner from guilt and eternal punishment, some temporal punishment remained. An indulgence remitted part of this remaining penalty but in return presupposed that the sinner repented of his misdeeds and did some form of penance, such as praying, visiting shrines, or contributing to worthy causes. Theologically, the concept of indulgences rested on the theory of a "treasury of merits." This held that Christ and the saints had won merit far in excess of their own needs and had thereby created a vast storehouse of merits. The Church was able to draw upon and distribute this surplus by means of indulgences to help those who felt they had not rendered sufficient penance to extirpate the punishment which they deserved. Contrary to a popular misconception, an indulgence did not permit a person to buy forgiveness.

It was the abuse attending the sale of indulgences to raise money that was chiefly

A woodcut of Luther's time shows the sale of letters of indulgence in a German market place.

responsible for the growing tide of resentment. The common folk did not understand theology and thought that a payment of money was all that was required to escape all the penalties of sin and, in fact, to purchase their salvation. Tetzel did nothing to enlighten the populace as to the true nature of indulgences, but rather exhorted them to give liberally for themselves and for their dead relatives in purgatory who were "crying to them for help." Luther's case against indulgences rested on both moral and theological grounds.

Development of Luther's ideas. In October 1517, Luther, following a university custom, posted ninety-five propositions (theses) on the subject of indulgences on the church door at Wittenberg, at the same time challenging anyone to debate them with him. Here are some of the more important of Luther's theses:

11. The erroneous opinion that canonical penance [earthly penance, specified by the Church] and punishment in purgatory are the same assuredly seems to be a tare sown while the bishops were asleep.

21. Therefore those preachers of indulgences err who say that a papal pardon frees a man from all penalty and assures his salvation.

28. It is certain that avarice is fostered by the money chinking in the chest, but to answer the prayers of the Church is in the power of God alone.

43. Christians are to be taught that he who gives to the poor or lends to one in need does better than he who buys indulgences.[4]

The ninety-five theses were originally written in Latin. They were soon translated into the common tongue and six months later were well known throughout Germany. At first, the Church at Rome did not seriously trouble itself. Heresy was anything but new, as the history of the Waldensians, Albigensians, and the followers of Wycliffe and Huss showed. But this particular "squabble among monks," as Leo x dismissed the matter, did not subside.

In 1519 Luther debated with an eminent Catholic theologian at Leipzig. There, Luther maintained that the pope ruled by virtue of human rather than divine authority and was not infallible; that Church councils did not exist by divine right either and could also err; and that Scripture constituted the sole authority in matters of faith and doctrine. Yet, in spite of these wide theological divergences, Luther continued to speak with affection of his "mother Church," which he hoped could be reformed and remain unified. By basing his position squarely on the doctrine of justification by faith alone, however, Luther found himself propelled by its implications—and by external circumstances—to a position far removed from that of the Church.

In 1520 the rupture was made nearly irreparable with the publication of three pamphlets. In his *Address to the Nobility of the German Nation*, Luther contended that the priesthood was not inviolate; and he called on rulers to reform ecclesiastical abuses and to deprive the pope of all political rights. *The Babylonian Captivity of the Church* summarized Luther's theological views. The papacy was attacked for having deprived the individual Christian of his freedom to approach God directly by faith and without the intermediation of priesthood.

This pamphlet also set forth Luther's views on the sacramental system. To be valid, a sacrament must have been instituted by Christ and be exclusively Christian. On this basis he could find no justification for making a sacrament of matrimony, which was also observed by non-Christians, or for any of the other sacraments except Baptism and the Lord's Supper (his term for the sacrament known to Roman Catholics as the Holy Eucharist). Luther rejected the doctrine of transubstantiation on the grounds that a priest could not perform the miracle of transforming bread and wine into the Body and Blood of the Lord. Nevertheless, Luther believed that God was present everywhere in the physical world and hence also in the bread and wine. To him, the sacrament was a rite of thanksgiving and fellowship with God.

Luther's third pamphlet, which was addressed to the pope, set forth in conciliatory but firm tones Luther's views on Christian behavior and salvation.

The breach made complete. In June 1520, Pope Leo x issued the bull *Exsurge Domine* ("Arise, O Lord"), a stern ultimatum which gave Luther only sixty days to turn from his heretical course. If at the end of that time he had not confessed his errors, he was to be cut off from the Church and handed over to secular authorities for punishment. The time limit expired without any immediate action, and in December Luther publicly burned the bull amid the applause of students and townsmen. This act propelled him into the center of German politics and brought about a showdown with Rome. In January 1521, Leo x excommunicated Luther.

Meanwhile, Charles v, who had recently been crowned emperor, found himself in a difficult situation. On the one hand, he was aware of popular German feelings and was not anxious to see papal power reconsolidated in his domains. On the other hand, he was bound by his oath to defend the Church and extirpate heresy and, moreover, was orthodox in his own religious beliefs. It was decided that Luther should be heard at the emperor's first Diet, which was held at Worms. Summoned under an imperial safe-conduct, Luther was asked whether he intended to stand by everything he had written. He stood before the assembly and replied firmly:

Your Imperial Majesty and Your Lordships demand a simple answer. Here it is, plain and unvarnished. Unless I am convicted of error by the testimony of Scripture or (since I put no trust in the unsupported authority of Pope or of councils, since it is plain that they have often erred and often contradicted themselves) by manifest reasoning I stand convicted by the Scriptures to which I have appealed, . . . I can-

Portrait of Luther by Lucas Cranach

not and will not recant anything, for to act against our conscience is neither safe for us, nor open to us.

On this I take my stand [*Hier stehe Ich*]. I can do no other. God help me. Amen.[5]

In May 1521, the Diet declared Luther a heretic and an outlaw. He was, however, given protection by the elector of Saxony, in whose castle he lived for almost a year under the disguise of "Knight George."

During this period Luther began the construction of an evangelical church distinct from Rome. He wrote incessantly, setting forth his theological views, expounding them in a collection of forceful sermons for use by preachers outside, and corresponding with friends and public figures. An outstanding feat was his translation into German of the New Testament, a monumental job accomplished in only eleven weeks. This translation was largely responsible for creating a standard language for all Germany. Later, Luther also translated the Old Testament into German.

Luther and the Peasants' War. Luther's teachings spread quickly through central and northern Germany. Pious persons who wanted the Church reformed embraced the new cause. Worldly individuals who believed that it would afford an opportunity to appropriate Church property also aided the movement, as did ardent nationalists who saw in it a means of uniting Germany. The emperor, meanwhile, was too deeply involved in a struggle with Francis I of France to stamp out the new heresy (see p. 314).

Encouraged by Luther's movement, the German peasants revolted in 1524. Long ground down by the nobles and wealthier classes, they demanded abolition of serfdom, payment in wages, and other improvements of their lot. Their grievances were legitimate and their demands reasonable, and Luther, of peasant origin himself, showed sympathy for these demands. On the other hand, he consistently opposed armed rebellion and held that social and political reforms should be instituted by authorities, such as the princes. As the revolt grew in intensity, Luther became increasingly impatient with the revolutionaries until, in a virulent pamphlet, *Against the Murdering Hordes of Peasants*, he called on the princes to act as "both judge and executioner" and

. . . [to] knock down, strangle, and stab . . . and think nothing so venomous, pernicious, or Satanic as an insurgent. . . . Such wonderful times are these that a prince can merit heaven better with bloodshed than another with prayer.[6]

The revolt was stamped out in 1525 at a cost of about fifty thousand lives, and the lot of the German peasant for the next two centuries was probably the worst in Europe. Luther had become a false prophet to the serfs, and his cause received a serious check. Politically and economically conservative, Luther believed that the equality of all men before God applied in spiritual but not in secular matters. This philosophy made aliens of the peasants but allies of the princes.

Local religious autonomy in Germany. The Diet of the Holy Roman Empire was composed of the seven electors, the lesser princes, and representatives of the free cities. The emperor was not supposed to do anything affecting the various states in the empire without the approval of the body. At its meeting in 1526 the princes of Germany were divided into two parties, one Lutheran and the other Catholic. Without specifying the legal status of the Lutherans, the Diet agreed that until a Church council could settle the religious issues,

. . . each prince should so conduct himself as he could answer for his behavior to God and to the emperor.[7]

Three years later the Catholic princes, with the emperor's support, pushed through a decree that the Mass must not be interfered with anywhere. This meant that while Lutheran activities were restricted, those of the Catholics could be carried on even in Lutheran areas. In answer, the Lutheran leaders drew up a protest, and from this incident the word *Protestant* derives.

The Diet which met in 1530 at Augsburg was presented with the Augsburg Confession, a statement of Christian doctrine from the Lutheran viewpoint designed to conciliate the two parties. The Diet did not accept the confession, but it became the creed of the new faith.

The emperor now made public his intention to crush the growing heresy. In defense, the Lutheran princes banded together in 1531 in the Schmalkaldic League, and between 1546 and 1555 a sporadic civil war was fought. A compromise was finally reached through the Peace of Augsburg (1555), which allowed each prince to decide the religion of his subjects, gave Protestants the right to keep all Church property confiscated prior to 1552, forbade all sects of Protestantism other than Lutheranism, and ordered all Catholic bishops to give up their property if they turned Lutheran.

The implications of the provisions were great. The Peace of Augsburg established Lutheranism as a state religion in large portions of Germany. For the first time in Christian history, religious opinions became the private property of princes, and the theories of political absolutism and the divine right of kings were thus given a strong impetus. Lastly, the new Protestantism did not bestow political or religious liberty on the individual, who had to believe what his prince wanted him to believe, be it Lutheranism or Catholicism. The Peace of Augsburg marks the real beginning of state religion, the natural ally of the new national political states.

The reference to Catholic property in the settlement was important, for it had been the cause of much bitterness. After Luther's religious revolt, many nobles accepted his doctrine not because they necessarily believed it but because it gave them an excuse to seize the Church's property. Wholesale plundering of Church lands enriched many a noble, and there was little prospect of peace until a compromise had been worked out. This was reached in the agreement of 1555: the Protestant princes retained the lands they had already seized, while the Church was assured that the seizures would be discontinued.

The death of Luther. In 1546, during the Schmalkaldic Wars, the founder of the new faith died. Martin Luther had been a born leader, genius, and zealot. His life was molded by an absolute conviction of the rightness of his beliefs, which goes far to explain both his driving power and his limitations.

In closing this account of Luther and the momentous movement which he set rolling, we might append an ironic footnote to history. The same sale of indulgences which furnished money to build a fitting capital for a universal Church (St. Peter's in Rome) provided at the same time the occasion for destroying the Church's unchallenged position.

Lutheranism in Scandinavia. While its birthplace was the empire, Lutheranism permanently established itself as the state religion only in Scandinavia. By 1560 Denmark established a national Lutheran Church. The Augsburg Confession was adopted, the Bible was translated into Danish, and other sects, Protestant or Catholic, were suppressed. Norway was at this time part of Denmark, and Lutheranism triumphed there also. Sweden, which had belonged to the union of the

Scandinavian countries, made itself an independent state with Gustavus Vasa as its king (1523-1560). During his rule Protestantism was introduced there, and the rise of this faith was interwoven closely with the nationalistic movement. In 1593 the Confession of Augsburg was officially adopted by the Swedish Church, and in 1604 Catholics lost their property and offices.

Zwingli in Switzerland. Meanwhile, Protestantism had taken firm root in Switzerland. In the German-speaking area of that country—and in Zurich in particular—the Reformation was led by Ulrich Zwingli (1484-1531). Of the same age as Luther and, like him, an earnest student of theology, Zwingli shared a number of beliefs with the German reformer. Both repudiated papal in favor of scriptural authority, preached justification by faith, attacked monasticism and clerical celibacy, and drastically revised the sacramental system. But the differences between the two leaders were also important. Whereas Luther looked on Baptism as a means of helping to regenerate the individual, Zwingli considered it only a means of initiating a child into society, much as circumcision did in the Jewish community. Nor did he believe with Luther that the real presence of Christ was found in the Lord's Supper. To Zwingli it was simply a sign of grace attesting to the participant's membership in a religious community.

Zwingli was an ardent Swiss patriot, who had once served as chaplain with Swiss mercenaries in Italy. The Swiss Confederation, comprising thirteen cantons, was almost autonomous even though it was part of the Holy Roman Empire. At the same time, it was subject to internal rivalries and to external pressures from more powerful neighbors. From Zurich, which he ruled as a theocracy, Zwingli sought also to strengthen the political position of the Swiss cantons, especially those in the north that were Protestant. The southern cantons, however, remained firm in their allegiance to the Roman Catholic Church.

In the civil war that broke out in 1531, Zwingli and many of his followers were slain in battle. After the war, which ended in that same year, the cantons agreed to retain their respective religious doctrines. This settlement was largely responsible for preventing Switzerland from taking sides in the great religious wars that subsequently engulfed Europe. Furthermore, it helped set the policy of neutrality which has guided the Swiss position in international affairs up to our own day.

Calvin's beliefs in theory and practice. The most famous sixteenth-century Protestant leader after Luther was John Calvin (1509-1564). A Frenchman of the middle class, Calvin studied theology and law at Paris, where he became interested in Luther's teachings. About 1533 he had what he called a "conversion," whereby he abandoned Catholicism. When Francis I began to persecute heretics, Calvin fled to Switzerland and settled first at Basel, a Protestant city. There he published in 1536 the first edition of his great work, the *Institutes of the Christian Religion*, unquestionably one of the most significant books of systematic theology ever written. His capacity for creative thinking was overshadowed by his ability as an organizer and synthesist. Influenced by his legal training, as well as by humanistic scholarship and the doctrines of Luther, Calvin set forth a system that was a masterpiece of logical reasoning.

Whereas Luther's central doctrine was justification by faith, Calvin's was the sovereignty of God. God was omnipotent and for His own purposes had created the world and also man in His image. Since Adam and Eve had fallen from a state of sinlessness, man was utterly depraved and lost.

Carrying these doctrines to their logical conclusions, Calvin defined man's relation to God in his famous doctrine of predestination. Since God is omniscient, He knows the past, present, and future. Consequently, He must always know which men are to be saved by Him and which men are to be damned eternally. Man's purpose in life, then, is not to try to work out his salvation—for this has already been determined—but to honor God. While Calvin did not profess to know absolutely who among men were to be God's chosen—the elect—he believed that the following three tests constituted a good yardstick by which to judge who might be saved: participation in the two sacraments—Baptism and the Lord's Supper; an upright moral life; and a public profession of the faith.

It was the duty of the living members of the church to glorify God by establishing a theocracy that would be governed according to scriptural precept. The Bible was the supreme authority, and the community should discipline or remove any found guilty of blasphemy or unseemly behavior. Calvin established a rule in Geneva which was similar to Zwingli's theocracy in Zurich. Pains were taken to provide instruction in the fundamentals of faith, to prepare the young for useful Christian citizenship, to safeguard the purity of the faith, and to extirpate any remnant of Catholicism. Although the regime was high-minded, it carried its zeal to ridiculous lengths. Penalties were inflicted for being absent from sermons or laughing during the church service, for wearing bright colors, for swearing or dancing, for inability to recite prayers, for playing cards, or for having one's fortune told by gypsies.

In regard to more serious offenses, especially in the religious sphere, Calvin and his associates acted with the utmost severity. Torture was used to obtain some confessions, and citizens of Geneva were banished for heresy, blasphemy, witchcraft, and adultery. When Servetus, a scholarly anti-Trinitarian, appeared in Geneva, Calvin burned him for heresy, saying: "Because the Papists persecute the truth, should we on that account refrain from repressing error?"

The spread of Calvinism. From Geneva, Calvinism spread far and wide, imbued with its founder's austerity of spirit, power of mind, and high purpose. Much of this influence stemmed from the Academy (today the University of Geneva), which trained students from other countries in Calvin's theology. In France, Calvinism made influential converts among both bourgeoisie and nobility. Known as Huguenots, the French Cal-

Persecuted as a Protestant, John Calvin traveled from place to place in his early career. His first attempt to carry out his reforms in Geneva failed and he was banished. Several years later, he returned to Geneva and established a theocracy.

vinists comprised only a small fraction of the total population, but their importance far outweighed their numbers. In Chapter 14 we shall see how the Huguenots became involved in the religious wars of France.

Carried down the Rhine River to the northern Netherlands, Calvin's teachings formed the basis for the Dutch Reformed religion. In the latter half of the sixteenth century and the first half of the seventeenth, the Dutch struggle for independence against a Catholic king of Spain strengthened Protestantism in their country. And in Scotland the authority of the Roman Church was challenged by John Knox (see p. 301).

The quarrel between Henry VIII and Rome. In Germany, the revolt against the Church was primarily religious in nature, although it possessed political implications; in England the situation was reversed. True, there was an ecclesiastical revolt, but the leader was a monarch, Henry VIII, not a priest.

Portrait of Henry VIII by Holbein

Henry was the second son of Henry VII, his older brother Arthur being the heir apparent. The crafty and miserly Henry VII had engaged Arthur to Catherine, the daughter of Ferdinand and Isabella of Spain. A large dowry was to be paid the Tudors, but Arthur died shortly after his marriage to Catherine and before all the dowry had been paid. Eager for both the dowry and the alliance with Spain, Henry VII then arranged the marriage of the young Henry to Catherine, and Henry VIII married the Spanish princess shortly after he ascended the throne. To this union six children were born, of whom only one, Mary, survived.

Then came the conflict in the mind of Henry VIII. A male heir was desirable if the newly established Tudors were to endure as a dynasty. Catherine was the widow of his brother, and the Church forbade a man to marry his brother's widow. A special papal dispensation had been granted for the marriage, but Henry claimed that he had never been validly married to Catherine.

There was another reason for conflict in Henry's mind—a much more tangible reason.

Anne Boleyn, a young attendant in the queen's retinue, had attracted him, and it was not long before he sought her as his wife. Therefore, Henry asked Pope Clement VII to revoke the dispensation which had allowed him to marry Catherine.

Normally, the pope might have acquiesced to Henry's wishes, for Henry had been loyal to the Church. In answer to Luther, he had written a *Defense of the Seven Sacraments* (1521), an act of piety which won him the title "Defender of the Faith"—a title which English monarchs still possess. Nevertheless, the pope could not support Henry in his desires. There were two good reasons. First, since no flaw could be found in the original bull, the king had no case legally, and the pope felt it would be dangerous for one pontiff to reverse the judgments of a predecessor. Second, the emperor Charles V, the most powerful monarch in Europe, was a nephew of Catherine and threatened the pope severely if he declared the marriage null and void. Clement decided to wait before giving his answer, hoping in the meantime that events would resolve themselves.

Henry himself would not wait. He obtained from Parliament the power to appoint bishops in England without papal permission, designating Thomas Cranmer as archbishop of Canterbury—a willing tool who was sure to do his master's bidding. After Cranmer pronounced the king's marriage to Catherine invalid, Henry's marriage to Anne Boleyn was declared legal. At last goaded into action, Clement VII excommunicated Henry and maintained that Catherine alone was the king's true wife.

Establishment of the Anglican Church. In 1534, Henry completely severed all connections with Rome. The Act of Supremacy stated that the king "justly and rightfully is and ought to be supreme head of the Church of England." Turning on his old friend Sir Thomas More, Henry had him beheaded because he would not acknowledge the sovereign as head of the English Church.

To replenish the royal coffers and to gain popular approval, Henry took possession of the rich monasteries, giving much of the land to cooperative landowners for their sheep raising and thus making them, in a sense, fellow conspirators in the conflict with Rome. It must be remembered that Henry and Parliament could not perhaps have effected such sweeping changes if there had not been many Englishmen—particularly the members of the prosperous and increasingly powerful middle class—who were anticlerical. By 1539 all monastic houses were dissolved. But in the same year Parliament passed the Six Articles, which reaffirmed the main points of Catholic theology. By this act, both the Catholic who denied the supremacy of the king and the Protestant who denied the validity of transubstantiation were to be punished severely. Thus England threw off the supremacy of the pope without at that time adopting the Protestant faith; the elements of Protestantism in the English Church crept in after the break with Rome.

After Henry's death in 1547, his frail son mounted the throne as Edward vi. During his reign England advanced toward a more definite Protestantism. The Six Articles were repealed; priests were no longer held to their vows of celibacy; and the old Latin service was replaced by Cranmer's Book of Common Prayer, which was written in English and which brought the service much closer to the people and exerted a powerful influence on the development of the language. In 1553 the Forty-two Articles defined the faith of the Church of England along Protestant lines.

Under the devoutly Catholic Mary (1553-1558), the unfortunate daughter of the still more unfortunate Catherine of Aragon, Catholicism was reinstated and hundreds of heretics, including Archbishop Cranmer, were put to death. But with the accession to the throne of Anne Boleyn's red-headed and fiery-tempered daughter, Elizabeth (1558-1603), Protestantism was firmly and permanently reëstablished in England. Realizing the political necessity for a united religious front, Elizabeth astutely took the title "Supreme Governor" of the Anglican Church. Her Act of Uniformity (1559) made the acceptance of the revised Prayer Book obligatory. In their emphasis upon the Scriptures as the source of authority, the Thirty-nine Articles (three of the articles passed in Edward's reign were deleted) stamped Protestantism upon the Anglican Church, though the ceremonial remained essentially Catholic. To this day the Thirty-nine Articles remain the authoritative statement of Anglican theology.

Presbyterianism in Scotland. The religious revolt in Scotland was largely the work of the zealous reformer John Knox (1505?-1572), who had become acquainted with Calvin in Geneva and frequently consulted him concerning church doctrine and civil authority. After returning to his native Scotland in about 1559, Knox became leader of the Lords of the Congregation, a group of Protestant nobles who wished to overthrow the jurisdiction of the Roman Catholic Church in their land. In 1560 Knox drew up the Articles of the Presbyterian Church, which abolished the authority of the pope and condemned the creeds and practices of the old Church. With the help of English troops, he effected a religious revolution.

One year later, the beautiful but ill-fated Mary Stuart returned from France to find her bleak kingdom alienated from her own Catholic views. From his pulpit and in his debates with Mary about questions of theology and the loyalty owed by a subject to his monarch, Knox defied the queen's authority and thundered against her religious principles. Although Mary showed amazing skill and logic in her arguments with him, the fiery reformer was able to gain the support of the Scottish people in his denunciation of her. By the time Mary had been executed by Elizabeth in 1587 (see p. 319), Scotland had been won over to Calvinistic Presbyterianism.

The Anabaptists. In the preceding paragraphs, the rise of Lutheranism and Calvinism and the establishment of the Anglican Church have been discussed. The picture of religious developments in sixteenth-century Europe would not be complete, however, without an account of the multitude of other

Protestant sects which sprang up during this period.

Many of these sects opposed infant baptism on the grounds that an infant could not possibly understand the significance of this sacrament. Historians often lump them together under the term *Anabaptists*, meaning "those baptized again," since individuals were sometimes rebaptized as adults when they joined any of these groups. Although there were important differences among the various sects, the Anabaptists, broadly speaking, believed firmly in their own interpretations of Biblical authority and rejected the necessity for a body of clergymen, maintaining that a person should follow the guidance of his "inner light." For their questioning of many doctrines fundamental to other forms of Protestantism and to Catholicism, the Anabaptists suffered religious persecution and social ostracism.

The Anabaptists, often referred to as the "left wing" of Protestantism, displayed the most radical social tendencies of the time. Their demands for political, social, and economic reforms involved them in the Peasants' War and in other disputes throughout the century. In communities of their own, they shared their worldly goods with one another and lived as they thought the primitive Christians had lived, working and praying together. The Anabaptists believed in the separation of church and state, condemned military service and the taking of oaths, and often refused to pay taxes to governments engaged in warfare. For these reasons they were persecuted intermittently by secular authorities and even forced to flee from their homes. Today their spirit lives on among such groups as the Quakers, the Mennonites, and the Amish.

THE CATHOLIC

REFORMATION

Catholic reformers and reform movements. The Catholic Reformation should not be viewed as only a retaliatory movement or a series of measures taken to stem the rising tide of Protestantism. The Roman Church had always retained latent forces of recuperation and strength which were drawn upon in challenging times. Before Luther had nailed his ninety-five theses to the church door at Wittenberg, renewed vitality and internal reform were apparent in the Roman Church.

One of the prime examples of this resurgence occurred in Spain, where humanistic energies were expended in the fields of religion and government. In this passionately orthodox country, royalty enlisted the services of the humanist Cardinal Jiménez de Cisneros (1436?-1517). At once a hairshirted Franciscan friar, a reformer of lax clergymen, the grand inquisitor, and the chancellor of the realm, Cardinal Jiménez was also a Renaissance scholar who founded the University of Alcalá, where humanistic studies were pursued. The blending of his humanistic and religious interests is revealed in the careful scholarship involved in the preparation of the Polyglot Bible, a new translation achieved under the supervision of Jiménez.

In a unique category of his own was Savonarola (1452-1498), a Dominican preacher and reformer in the city of Florence. A persuasive speaker, he induced the wealthy and pleasure-loving Florentines to make bonfires of their luxuries. When the Medici fled before the invasion of Charles VIII of France (see p. 311), Savonarola organized Florence as a republic and managed to keep the French from sacking the city. He also attacked the iniquities of the Borgia pope, Alexander VI. But despite the fact that he was later hailed by Luther and the Protestants as a forerunner of their movement, Savonarola was actually attempting to return the papacy to its tradition of simple living and dedicated service. By this means he hoped to avert a real revolt against the Church. Unfortunately Savonarola did not possess the power to enforce his dictates. Publicly humiliated by having his Dominican garb torn from him in the great square of Florence, Savonarola was hanged and burned, a victim of political intrigue.

By the middle of the sixteenth century, the inroads of Protestantism were apparent, and in retaliation the Church rallied its forces and prepared a powerful offensive. This renewal of strength is known as the Catholic Reformation. As we shall see, the reforming spirit penetrated almost all areas of the Church. New monastic orders infused with crusading zeal were organized, and a resurgence of mysticism occurred. The pope himself adopted a program of vigorous reform. Climaxing the whole movement was the Council of Trent, where the Church boldly reaffirmed its traditional doctrines and flatly refused to compromise in any way with the Protestants.

Reforming orders. Reverting to methods which it had almost perfected during medieval eras of reform, the Church instituted new monastic orders. Springing up in the sixteenth century, several new orders performed useful work in a variety of fields— charitable works, education, and conversion.

In 1524, the order of the Theatines was founded in Italy. By preaching and exemplary conduct, the Theatines undertook to check the spread of heresy. They also performed such good works as supporting hospitals and orphanages.

Among other orders established at this time were the Capuchins, an offshoot of the Franciscan order. Seeking to return to the original Rule and spirit of St. Francis, they became notable for their preaching and for their care of the poor and sick. Still another successful movement was that of the Ursulines, founded in 1535 to educate girls.

A Spanish ex-soldier, Ignatius Loyola (1491-1556), founded in 1534 the Society of Jesus, better known as the Jesuit order, which played a vital role in the Catholic Reformation. In addition to the three vows of chastity, obedience, and poverty, the Jesuits took a special vow of allegiance to the pope. By means of preaching and education, this order intended to win back converts to the Roman Church. They succeeded remarkably well, recovering most of Poland and maintaining Catholicism in Bavaria, the southern Netherlands (now Belgium), Austria, and

In this engraving, Pope Paul III authorizes the order of the Society of Jesus as St. Ignatius Loyola kneels before him.

Ireland. Owing to their efforts and to the weight always lent by tradition, Italy, Spain, and Portugal remained loyally Catholic, while France saw Protestantism checked. In addition, the Jesuits performed excellent missionary work in North and South America, China, and India.

St. Theresa, the mystic. The upsurge of vitality in the Church was expressed externally by such means as conversions and internally by a renewal of faith. One of the manifestations of this inner spiritual reaffirmation was mysticism. Just as the Middle Ages had their mystics, so the Catholic Reformation had mystics like St. Theresa.

A nun of the Carmelite order, St. Theresa (1515-1582) founded a house of barefoot Carmelites, where the sisters slept on straw, ate no meat, and lived on alms. Eventually she was empowered to found similar houses. St. Theresa's chief claim to fame, however, lies in the ecstasies and visions which she experienced and in her written accounts of

Bernini's sculpture for a side altar of a small Roman church depicts a vision of St. Theresa. Describing her mystical experiences, St. Theresa told of one moment of ecstasy and pain in which an angel pierced her heart with a flaming arrow. As the saint ascends to heaven on a cloud, the angel approaches her and she swoons.

them. Quietistic mysticism, which teaches that spiritual peace can be attained by losing the sense of self in passive contemplation of God and His works, owes much to the spiritual exercises and terminology which St. Theresa developed.

Papal reform: Paul III. A new era was at hand for the Church when Paul III, who reigned from 1534 to 1549, ascended the papal throne. He chose outstanding men as cardinals and appointed a commission to look into the need for reform. Their report listed the evils requiring correction, including the appointment of worldly bishops and priests; the traffic in benefices, in indul-

gences, and other financial abuses; the venality of some cardinals; and the absence of others from the papal court. There was considerable opposition from various quarters to Paul's decision to begin acting upon this report. He persisted, however, and among other reforms improved the papal administrative machinery. Again ignoring the opposition of high churchmen who feared for their positions and incomes, Paul made plans to reform the entire Church organization at a general council.

The Council of Trent: climax of the Catholic Reformation. Reviving the device of a Church council, so useful at the time of the Great Schism, the Catholic Reformation came to a climax in the Council of Trent (1545-1563). There, a clear enunciation of Catholic doctrines was set forth. In no point of dogma did the Catholic Church compromise with the Protestants. The successors of St. Thomas Aquinas, who had done so much to shape the dogmas of the medieval Church, reaffirmed the doctrines of the Church as the basis of Christianity and the role of the Church as the only interpreter of these vital elements. As proof of the fact that the Catholic Church in no wise departed from its age-old body of beliefs, the following statement reiterates the validity of the sacramental system:

If any one saith that the sacraments of the new law were not all instituted by Jesus Christ, our Lord; or that they are more or less than seven . . . or even that any one of these seven is not truly and properly a sacrament; let him be anathema.[8]

At the same time, drastic reforms were made in Church discipline and administration. Such evils as simony, absenteeism, and secular pursuits on the part of the clergy were strictly forbidden.

EFFECTS OF THE
RELIGIOUS UPHEAVAL

Religious division but renewed faith. Prior to 1517 there had been two religious divisions of Christendom—Greek Orthodox and Roman Catholic. By 1550 Christendom was composed of three divisions — Orthodox, Catholic, and Protestant. Protestantism had become uppermost in northern Europe, while Catholicism held sway in the south. This great religious division had struck a mortal blow at the medieval unity of Europe. The Catholics placed their faith in the infallibility of the pope and the need for a mediatory priesthood. The Protestants placed their faith in the infallibility of the Bible and individual interpretation of it; furthermore, every Christian could win salvation without priestly mediation. The Protestants differed among themselves in their interpretation of the Bible and the methods of church organization; in time hundreds of Protestant sects arose, many claiming to possess the one and only true interpretation and logical administration.

Although the religious upheaval irreparably split the unity of Christendom and in so doing fostered the religious diversity of modern times, it also represented in some aspects a return to medievalism. It was a great religious revival, a renewal of faith. After the Renaissance era of free and secular thought, of individualism and humanism, men's thoughts were turned again to salvation and the life hereafter. Free thought gave way again to authority—for Protestants it was the Bible; for Catholics, the Church. The Renaissance movement, having fostered doubt and criticism of medieval values, was now engulfed in a return to some of those values. Freethinkers were persecuted by both sides, and talented writers and thinkers who in Renaissance times might have followed the prevailing pattern of individualism and secularism now devoted their abilities to arguing one side or another of the burning conflict of the day. Thus, temporarily at least, the Renaissance spirit was stifled. But it was to prove stronger than this intense religious revival and in the end was to profit from the passing of the single religious authority of the universal Church.

In addition to renewing the surge of faith, the religious upheaval brought about a great deal of genuine religious reform. Protestant service of worship was simplified in an effort to return to the purity of early Christian times. Strict attention was given to conduct and morals. Within the Catholic Church a reform movement also took place in answer to the Protestant challenge, beginning, as we have seen, with the accession of Pope Paul III and culminating in the decrees of the Council of Trent. This movement changed neither doctrine nor organization but aimed at clarifying and reaffirming doctrine and purifying and strengthening discipline among the clergy and laity alike.

A by-product of the religious upheaval was a new interest in education. Each faith was concerned that its youth should be properly trained in its teachings. As part of its campaign to win Protestants back to the fold, the Jesuit order in particular developed a school system so superior and so attractive that many Protestant as well as Catholic youths attended. Protestant churches of the period developed few schools to challenge the Jesuit colleges and universities, but one feature of Protestantism eventually stimulated education a great deal. Its tenet that the one source of religious truth is the Bible encouraged its members to read the Scriptures. As a result, training in reading became a basic feature of education.

Protestantism and capitalism. While religious developments fostered a return to medieval attitudes in many ways, in the economic sphere the opposite was true. The Renaissance encouraged a new individualism in economic matters, which contributed to a breakdown of the guild system and to the rise of the individual entrepreneur. Protestantism did away with the old concept of the "just price" and the ban against receiving interest on money loaned (usury). Investment of capital and loaning of money became respectable. Calvinism especially encouraged enterprise; some Calvinists regarded prosperity as a sign of election to grace and poverty as evidence of damnation.

We have noted earlier that the business classes were among those that encouraged the revolt from Rome. We can now see that

they were also among those that most benefited by it.

Union of religion and politics. In many
cases the religious division of Europe followed political lines. The Peace of Augsburg
gave the ruler of each German state the right
to decide the faith of his subjects, thus controlling the church in his realm. Similarly,
rulers of other countries, both Catholic and
Protestant, developed national churches, so
that Europe was divided religiously into an
Anglican Church, a Dutch Church, a Swedish
Church, and so on.

In many countries one effect of such division was to strengthen the hand of the king
in building a unified state. The authority
and prestige of the Protestant monarch was
increased as he became the spiritual as well
as the political ruler of his subjects. Even in
Catholic countries, though the pope remained the spiritual ruler, the Church became national in sentiment, and it was the
king rather than the pope who enforced
religious conformity among his subjects.
Conversely, in countries where the split between Protestants and Catholics was deep,
as in the Holy Roman Empire, the power of
the central ruler was limited and national
unity impeded.

Freedom of religion was still far from a
reality. Protestants were persecuted in Catholic countries and Catholics in Protestant
states, partly because of the intolerance engendered by the clash between faiths but
even more because religious uniformity was
the ideal of the rulers of the rising national
states. Just as he sought to create a uniform
system of law and justice throughout his
realm, so the strong monarch endeavored to
establish a single faith to which his subjects
owed complete obedience. An incidental result of this policy was the emigration of religious minorities to areas where they could
worship freely, as in the New World.

Political and religious developments continued to be closely related throughout the
sixteenth and early seventeenth centuries.
In the Religious Wars, political duels were
superimposed on religious quarrels, resulting in some of the bloodiest and most pro-

longed warfare in human history. The
founder of the Christian religion had given
as a primary command, "Thou shalt love thy
neighbor as thyself." But there was no
brotherhood between Catholic and Protestant nor between political rivals who played
on religious antagonisms to serve their own
ends. The story of this politico-religious warfare will be told in the next chapter.

SUMMARY

The Renaissance represented a new emphasis on man's individuality, an outlook
which could not fail eventually to have its
impact on religion. Among those calling for
reform were northern humanists, who criticized the abuses which had grown up within
the Church. By means of the printing press,
which vastly increased the number of books
available, the new ideas spread rapidly
throughout Europe. Already beginning to
revolt against all institutions which hampered them in their new economic freedom,
many men of the middle class were sympathetic to the cry for Church reform. The
new spirit found an ally also in the new
nationalism and in the growing power of
the kings, who were reluctant to be thwarted
by any force, even the Church. When a
leader appeared with a religious message in
keeping with the spirit of the age, the long
bottled-up forces of reform exploded.

Luther's open breach with the Church encouraged such Protestant leaders as Zwingli,
Calvin, and other reformers to form their
own churches. The essence of the new movements was an emphasis on Biblical authority,
a denial of the need for priestly mediation
for salvation, and a repudiation of the pope
as head of organized religion. After the Protestant Revolt, churches were firmly tied to
the political administration of the states.
Thus Calvin and Zwingli established the-
ocracies in Geneva and Zurich in Switzerland. In Germany each prince chose between Lutheranism and Catholicism for the
religion of his subjects. In the Scandinavian
countries, the national churches were Lutheran. Without repudiating the basic ele-

ments of Catholicism, the English king broke with Rome and assumed the headship of the Anglican Church. As religious issues became inextricably entangled with politics, Protestants and Catholics clashed bitterly.

The challenge flung at the Church did not remain unanswered. On the contrary, in such countries as Italy, Spain, and France, the forces of religious reform achieved noticeable results. As the medieval Church had arrested decline by new zealous orders of monks, so once again the Church was invigorated by the creation of various new brotherhoods and a resurgence of mysticism. Meanwhile, Pope Paul III instigated an energetic program to excise the abuses which had plagued the Church for centuries. Without

any compromise with the Protestants, the Council of Trent reaffirmed the fundamental doctrines of the Church. But there was no longer any possibility of the Church reuniting Europe.

Europe was plunged into an epoch of intolerance and bigotry from which it slowly emerged when, after prolonged and bloody struggles, it became apparent that no one faith could exterminate the others. But if the clock was set back in some ways, in other ways the religious upheaval furthered the transition from a medieval to a modern pattern of life. The revolt from the universal Church shattered the medieval ideal of unity and gave us the religious diversity of the modern world.

SUGGESTIONS FOR READING

E. Harbison, *The Age of the Reformation,** Cornell; and G. Mosse, *The Reformation,** Holt (Berkshire Studies), are the two best short summaries. The standard history is Preserved Smith, *The Age of the Reformation,* Holt, 1920, which stresses the intellectual and social movements rather than the religious. H. Grimm, *The Reformation Era, 1500-1650,* Macmillan, 1954, emphasizes the work of the reformers in the political, economic, social, and cultural setting; it carries the history of the Reformation to the end of the Religious Wars. R. Bainton, *The Reformation of the Sixteenth Century,** Beacon, paints in masterful strokes the differences among the various Protestant groups. Philip Hughes, *A Popular History of the Reformation,** Image, is an excellent survey by a Catholic historian. Good for historical reference is G. R. Elton, ed., *The Reformation, 1520-1559,* Cambridge Univ., 1958, Vol. II of *The New Cambridge Modern History.*

J. Huizinga, *Erasmus and the Age of the Reformation,** Torchbooks. Excellent on the northern humanists' criticisms of the Church.

A. Hyma, *Luther's Theological Development from Erfurt to Augsburg,* Crofts, 1928. An analysis of the evolution of Luther's thought. J. T. McNeill, *The History and Character of Calvinism,* Oxford, 1954, is an excellent survey.

T. M. Parker, *The English Reformation to 1558,* Oxford, 1950; and F. E. Hutchinson, *Cranmer and the English Reformation,* Macmillan (Teach Yourself History), 1951, are two brief accounts of the course of the Reformation in England. More scholarly is F. M. Powicke, *The Reformation in England,** Oxford.

*Indicates an inexpensive paperbound edition.

On the "left wing" of Protestantism, see N. Cohn, *The Pursuit of the Millennium,** Torchbooks, which carries the story back to the eleventh century; and R. Bainton, *The Travail of Religious Liberty,** Torchbooks.

P. Janelle, *The Catholic Reformation,* Bruce, 1949. The best sympathetic study of the subject. B. J. Kidd, *The Counter-Reformation, 1550-1600,* Macmillan, 1933, is a detailed account by a Protestant. Two comprehensive works on the Jesuits, the first by a Catholic and the second by a Protestant, are J. Brodrick, *The Origin of the Jesuits,** Image; and H. Boehmer, *The Jesuits,* Castle, 1928.

K. Holl, *The Cultural Significance of the Reformation,** Meridian. A brief account of the effects on politics, economics, thought, and art. More detailed and controversial are R. H. Tawney, *Religion and the Rise of Capitalism,** Mentor; and E. Troeltsch, *Protestantism and Progress: A Historical Study of the Relation of Protestantism to the Modern World,** Beacon.

R. Bainton, *Here I Stand: A Life of Martin Luther,** Mentor. An excellent presentation of Luther's personality and of the theological complexities of his time. Also sympathetic but more detailed is H. Boehmer, *Martin Luther: Road to Reformation,** Meridian. The best Catholic biography of Luther is H. Grisar, *Martin Luther, His Life and Work,* Newman, 1950. G. Harkness, *John Calvin, The Man and His Ethics,** Apex, is a good brief biography.

J. Brodrick, *St. Ignatius Loyola: The Pilgrim Years, 1491-1538,* Farrar, Straus, 1956. A comprehensive account by a Jesuit. R. Ridolfi, *The Life of Girolamo Savonarola,* Knopf, 1959, is up to date, sympathetic, and readable.

F. Hackett, *The Personal History of Henry the Eighth,** Bantam. The life and loves of the lusty Tudor monarch.

CHAPTER 14

The Strife of States and Kings

POWER POLITICS AND THE NEW DIPLOMACY:
1500-1650

Introduction. By acquiring a historical perspective through the study of European politics in early modern times, we can do much to illuminate today's events and problems and bring them into focus. The period from 1500 to 1650 is particularly significant; it can serve as a laboratory in which we can watch the genesis and development of the statecraft of modern times.

The crucial factor in this troubled period was the rise of the competitive state system, involving independent, completely sovereign nations, each controlled by a single, all-powerful government. As early as the eleventh century, such nation-states as England, France, Portugal, and Spain had begun their respective journeys toward greatness. By the beginning of the sixteenth century, these budding nations exhibited three fundamental features that contrasted sharply with the charac-

teristics the same territories had possessed in earlier, feudal times: they had strong and effective central governments, their citizens displayed an increased national consciousness, and their rulers claimed sovereignty—that is, supreme power within the boundaries of their own states, limited by no other authority. As we shall see in this chapter, these states were expansionist and aggressive, taking every opportunity to grow more powerful at the expense of weaker nations.

As a few strong sovereign states replaced the multitude of comparatively small and weak feudal units, they were forced to work out a power relationship among themselves. Would one state be able to dominate all the rest? Would there be varying degrees of power among states without any one becoming all-powerful? Would these independent and sovereign nations be able to establish a pattern of cooperation, ensuring thereby a measure of peace and political amity in the western world?

In Chapter 13, we saw that the religious revolt in the sixteenth century ended the Church's role as the arbiter of right and justice in disputes between secular rulers. The rulers of the sovereign states were thus completely free and untrammeled in the arena of international politics. Would they exercise any restraint? Would they develop among themselves some moral basis for the conduct of statecraft? These were the fundamental questions which were answered in Europe between 1500 and 1650. And the way in which they were answered set the pattern of international relations from that day to this.

THE COMPETITIVE STATE SYSTEM EMERGES

Factors supporting the rise of strong monarchs. As the fifteenth century closed, the power of European monarchs was rapidly increasing. The past century had witnessed much disorder, civil conflict, and war; more and more, people looked to their kings to provide the state with a measure of stability and security. Because the rulers freed trade from vexatious tolls and barriers, built and improved roads and bridges, passed laws protecting the interests of merchants in matters of debt and contract, and stimulated commercial life by granting monopolies and encouraging the establishment of colonies as new markets, the rising middle class threw its weight behind the monarchy. In return, the sovereigns obtained from the bourgeoisie larger revenues than had formerly been available, and the administrative bureaus and government services were expanded. Of great importance was the fact that kings could now afford to hire soldiers for standing armies—monarchs were no longer dependent upon the irregularly available feudal forces. Moreover, the small force of a rebellious noble could be squelched easily by the king's army.

The theory of centralized, unchallenged authority—that is, sovereignty—was given its first comprehensive expression by a French lawyer and university professor, Jean Bodin (1530-1596). Disgusted with the evils of the civil war between the Bourbons and the Guises (see p. 321), Bodin attacked feudalism and the universalism of empire and Church in his work *Concerning Public Affairs.* He supported the power of the monarch and his right of sovereignty, which he defined as "unlimited power over citizens and subjects, unrestrained by law."[1] According to Bodin, the king was free of all restraint save some rather shadowy limitation exercised by God and divine law.

The advent of power politics. Equipped with a standing army, efficient courts, and adequate revenues and backed by the growing support of the bourgeoisie, a European monarch was master in his own nation by the beginning of the sixteenth century. And, equally significant, he was his own master in foreign affairs. The Church was no longer an international arbiter, and the factionalism of the Protestant Reformation was soon to reduce appreciably the Church's claim to universal influence. The international arena now consisted of a number of free agents who could keep what they could defend and take what they wanted if they had sufficient force. A nation-state depended for survival on the exercise of its power, and war was the chief instrument at hand. Thus, statecraft became the politics of power and the competitive state system emerged.

The rise of modern diplomacy. The development of the competitive state system gave rise to the practice of modern diplomacy. Rulers needed to be informed about the plans and policies of their rivals; states fearful of attack from stronger foes had to seek out allies; and, after wars had been fought, agreements between victor and vanquished required negotiations.

Medieval popes customarily sent envoys to reside at royal courts, but modern diplomatic practice had its real birth among the fiercely independent, prosperous, and antagonistic

The introduction of artillery and muskets revolutionized the character of warfare and outmoded the heavily armored medieval knight. Fired from a wooden fork and requiring laborious reloading, muskets were still primitive. To protect the musketeers while they reloaded, men with long pikes presented a bristling defense against cavalry charges. Later the bayonet was invented, providing the foot soldier with a means of defense between shots. War moved into its scientific stage with the invention of gunpowder. The drawing above shows cannon of about the year 1550.

city-states of northern Italy. The republic of Venice—"the school and touchstone of ambassadors"—was particularly active; its authorities registered treaties, maintained diplomatic archives, and sent their representatives throughout Europe with elaborate instructions. To act as a safeguard against poisoning, trusted cooks were part of a diplomat's retinue, but ambassadors' wives were forbidden to accompany their husbands on diplomatic missions for fear they might divulge state secrets. About 1455 the first permanent embassy in history was sent to Genoa by the duke of Milan. Within a short time most of the important nations of the day followed suit and posted representatives in European capitals.

On many occasions the new diplomacy encouraged negotiation and prevented war.

Diplomatic methods so often involved deceit and treachery, however, that negotiations often fanned rather than diminished the fires of international hostility. An Englishman of the seventeenth century defined an ambassador as "an honest man sent abroad to lie for the good of his country."[2] Diplomacy during the past three hundred years has done little to refute this definition.

The sixteenth century was the formative period for the behavior pattern of modern nations in international affairs. Unrestrained by religious or ethical scruples, the sovereign governments were about to begin an era of international strife with the quest for power as their only guide to success. With disunited Italy as the pawn in the game, the counters on the chessboard began to move.

ITALY: CASE STUDY IN POWER POLITICS

Charles VIII and the Italian Wars. Charles VIII, with his grandiose notions of imitating the exploits of Hannibal and Charlemagne, ascended the French throne in 1483. To the south of France lay Italy, rich and defenseless; the prospect of little fighting and much loot tempted him sorely. To make his evil designs look somewhat respectable, Charles posed as the opponent of the ruling despots in the Italian city-states and talked of restoring liberty to Italy. To the role of self-chosen liberator, he added hints of a plan to lead a great crusade against the Ottoman Turks in Constantinople.

In 1494 Charles crossed the Alps into Italy at the head of thirty thousand well-trained troops. He met no opposition; the Medici of Florence fled, leaving their city to Savonarola (see p. 302). From there, the French marched south and took possession of Naples. This easy conquest alarmed the rulers who had previously acquiesced to Charles' plan. Ferdinand of Spain suspected that Charles might next try to conquer the Spanish possession of Sicily, and the Holy Roman emperor became uneasy at the prospect of French dominance in Italy. In addition, Venice feared for its independence and took the lead in the formation of a league which also included the Papal States, the Holy Roman Empire, and Spain. The armies of the league mustered and threatened to cut the French forces off from home. A hard battle in northern Italy was fought before Charles could win his way back to France. His ambitious plans for conquest collapsed, leaving him only "glory and smoke."

End of the first phase of the Italian Wars. Following the death of Charles VIII in 1498, his successor, Louis XII, invaded Italy. The counters again moved on the chessboard: alliances were made, then broken; pledges went unhonored, and allies deserted. Ferdinand of Spain offers a particularly good example of duplicity and treachery. Louis XII accused Ferdinand of cheating him on at

Niccolò Machiavelli

least two occasions. Hearing this, Ferdinand scoffed: "He lies, the fool; I have deceived him ten times, and more."[3]

In the first phase of the Italian Wars—which ended in 1513 with the ejection of the French from Italy—one can observe the new power politics in operation, without benefit of any moral or religious scruples. The only important objectives were glory, power, and wealth. In attaining these objectives "necessity knows no law," as a German statesman observed in 1914. Clearly prophesying the mode of future relations among the rising sovereign states, the conflict in Italy demonstrated that dynastic rivalries unfettered by any concept of European unity were to set the keynote for subsequent international relations.

Machiavelli and Machiavellian politics. The guidebook for diplomacy and power politics was written by Niccolò Machiavelli (1469-1527), a Florentine diplomat who ranks as one of the most important men in the development of political theory.

Outraged at the cavalier manner in which foreign invaders had smashed their way into his beloved Italy, Machiavelli mourned his native land as being:

. . . more captive than the Jews, more enslaved than the Persians, more divided than the Athenians, without a head, without discipline, bruised, despoiled, lacerated, ravaged, and subjected to every kind of affliction.[4]

Machiavelli's extensive acquaintance with the unprincipled politics of the early Italian Wars was the basis for his completely cynical and ruthless attitude toward men and politics. *The Prince*—one of a half-dozen volumes that have helped to form western political thought—was written as a guide for an audacious leader who would end Italian disunity and foreign invasion. A realist who wanted his leader-statesman to understand the political facts of life as they had been operating in Italy, Machiavelli wrote:

When the entire safety of our country is at stake, no consideration of what is just or unjust, merciful or cruel, praiseworthy or shameful, must intervene. On the contrary, every other consideration being set aside, that course alone must be taken which preserves the existence of the country and maintains its independence.[5]

Machiavelli did not, of course, invent the precepts of ruthlessness in relations between states. Rulers had dishonored treaties and used force to attain their ends before *The Prince* was written. What Machiavelli did was to accept the world of politics as he saw it in Italy without any false illusions. He gave his prince many suggestions for survival and conquest in the brutal world of unrestrained power:

It is not necessary for a prince to have piety, faith, humanity, integrity, and religion, but it is necessary to seem to have them.[6]

Though Machiavelli was setting down maxims intended only to aid in improving the desperate Italian situation, famous rulers studied his ideas carefully, and Machiavellian methods became an indispensable element in European politics. Nor was his influence confined to the sixteenth century, as the history of power politics in the past 450 years makes only too clear to us.

EUROPEAN EMPIRE OR SOVEREIGN STATES?

Charles V. The manner in which the rulers of Europe practiced power politics is shown clearly by the events in Europe during the first half of the sixteenth century, a period often referred to as the Age of Charles V. Charles dreamed of reviving the medieval ideal of a Christian empire, and as a sincere Catholic he also desired to maintain the religious unity of Christendom.

Charles' grandfather, Maximilian I, archduke of Austria and Holy Roman emperor (1493-1519), had added part of the Netherlands to his realm by marrying Mary of Burgundy. Maximilian's son (Charles' father) had married a daughter of Ferdinand and Isabella of Spain. Thus, by a calculated policy of dynastic marriages, the Austrian Hapsburgs had extended their interests. Born in 1500, Charles as scion of the house of Hapsburg thus enjoyed a position no ruler since Charlemagne had possessed. Following his father's death in 1506, he became ruler of the Netherlands; in 1516 his maternal grandfather, Ferdinand, bequeathed to him Spain and the southern half of Italy. The death of his other grandfather, Maximilian, gave him Austria and left vacant the throne of the Holy Roman Empire, to which Charles was elected in 1519 as Emperor Charles V.

The Hapsburg lands in both the Old and the New Worlds were vast. Charles ruled the Netherlands; he was emperor of the Holy Roman Empire and possessor of the hereditary Hapsburg states in eastern Europe; he wore the crowns of Castile and Aragon, and with them came Naples, Sicily, and Sardinia; and he was master of a vast colonial empire as well. To be sure, his empire was not cohesive and compact; he constantly found himself with too many irons in the fire. Intelligent, conscientious, and hard-working, he was forced during his reign to rush from one part of his realm to another, crushing rebellions and repelling invasions.

Charles' problems were inextricably connected with the activities of Francis I of

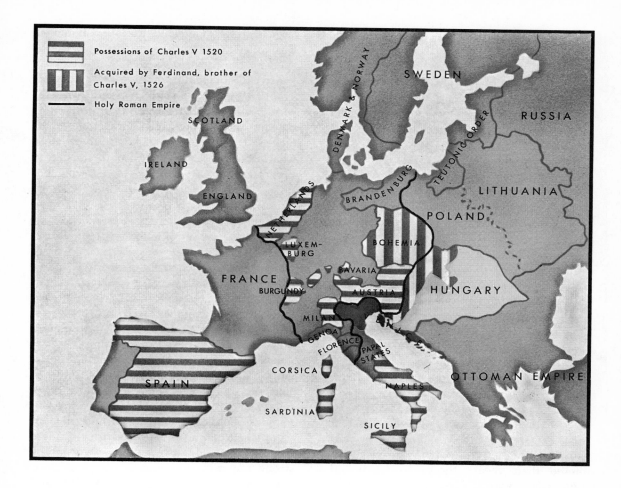

Possessions of Charles V 1520

Acquired by Ferdinand, brother of Charles V, 1526

Holy Roman Empire

France, Henry VIII of England, and Suleiman, ruler of the Ottoman empire. Out of the interplay of the rivalries of these men was created the bloody drama of the first fifty years of the sixteenth century.

New moves on the chessboard. The basic cause of Franco-Hapsburg rivalry was the fact that Charles' empire threatened the independence of France. To the north, east, and south, Hapsburg lands encircled the realm of Francis I. The stage was set for the great struggle between these powers by a move which Francis made just before Charles V came into his inheritance.

Despite the sorry conclusion of his predecessors' Italian adventures, Francis too sought glory in Italy, invaded the peninsula in 1515, and occupied Milan. Across the English Channel, Henry VIII followed the events closely, aiming to use his power as a counterweight in the Franco-Hapsburg rivalry. Believing Francis to be militarily stronger than Charles, Henry allied himself with the Hapsburg emperor in order to check French power.

The test of strength began as Charles' forces drove the French out of Milan. Francis soon recaptured it. At the battle of Pavia (1525), the Hapsburg forces finally crushed the French army, and Francis was taken prisoner.

Balance of power. By backing the stronger rather than the weaker of the two rivals on the continent, England had miscalculated. Executing a sudden about-face after the battle of Pavia, Henry VIII deserted Charles and supported France and a coalition of lesser powers against the Hapsburgs.

This use of English power to equalize the strength of Continental rivals was one of the earliest examples of the phenomenon known as the "balance of power." Time and again in modern history, when a single country or dynasty has become too powerful, other powers have united to checkmate it and restore equilibrium.

Suleiman, ruler of the Turks. It was in 1520, just a year after Charles became Holy Roman emperor, that Suleiman ascended the Turkish throne. No one could have predicted that Suleiman would soon be a party to the struggle between Charles and Francis and also a threat to Christian Europe.

In 1521 a Turkish army captured Belgrade, the key fortress of the Hungarian frontier. In 1526 the sultan met the army of the weakling Hungarian king on the plain of Mohacs. Only one hour and a half later, the Hungarians were completely routed and their king drowned while fleeing the field. Mohacs has been aptly termed "the tomb of the Hungarian nation."

The king who perished at Mohacs had ruled both Hungary and Bohemia. Bereft of their king and terrified by the prospect of Turkish attacks, the Bohemians (Czechs) offered their vacant throne to Ferdinand, brother-in-law of the dead king and brother of Charles v. Hungary was split between Turkey and Ferdinand. Thus it was a Turkish victory that placed the destiny of both Hungary and Bohemia in the hands of the Hapsburgs and established the Turks as a threat on Charles' Austrian borders.

Religion and politics on the chessboard. Following his release from captivity in 1526, Francis I decided upon an alliance with Suleiman. The enemies of the French king protested loudly against this "unholy alliance," but power politics took priority over religion in both Paris and Constantinople.

Indirectly, the Turks aided the Protestant cause in Germany. In 1529 and 1532, Suleiman's armies besieged Vienna. To deal with this threat, Charles, who had been planning measures against the Lutherans, was forced to arrange a truce with the Protestant princes to gain their support against the Turks. A large army was collected, the Turkish danger was foiled, and Lutheranism was strengthened by the breathing space.

After Suleiman's unsuccessful thrusts against Vienna, Turkish pressure was diverted from eastern Europe to the Mediterranean, and French and Turkish fleets attacked Italian towns. The strength that Charles might have built up to crush the French monarchy was diverted to his besieged lands bordering on the Mediterranean.

When the French king became mortally ill, the Franco-Turkish alliance fell into disuse. Of great importance was a truce in 1544 which called a halt to the French-Hapsburg struggle. Emperor Charles' efforts again centered in the German states, where in 1546 the Lutheran struggle flared into civil war. The Schmalkaldic Wars ended in 1555 with the compromise Peace of Augsburg, which officially recognized the Lutheran faith in the empire (see p. 297). Thus Charles v was thwarted in his cherished aim of restoring religious unity throughout his far-flung dominions. Politically the Augsburg settlement entrenched the power of the German princes still further and frustrated the revival of a strong imperial government.

Charles' abdication. Between 1554 and 1556 the exhausted Hapsburg emperor turned over the imperial authority in the Holy Roman Empire to his younger brother, Ferdinand; to his own son, Philip, he gave Spain, the Netherlands, and his Italian possessions.

After dividing his lands in this fashion, Charles retired to a monastery to spend his remaining years. A legend has it that he spent his time trying to make several clocks keep exactly the same time—apparently an allegory suggesting that he was faced with so many problems that he could never settle all of them. In 1558 Charles died, a failure. French resistance to the House of Hapsburg was stronger than ever, religious unity had not been secured in the Germanies, and Suleiman the Turk still menaced Christian Europe.

Significance for modern times. The complex narrative that revolves around the ambitions of four monarchs—Charles v, Henry VIII, Francis I, and Suleiman the Magnificent —is significant because the events which transpired during the first half of the sixteenth century laid down much of the political and religious foundation for modern Europe.

(1) During the reign of Charles v it was decided by force of arms that no single state was to unify all of Europe. The growth of nations had advanced too far to permit the revival of a single European empire. The balance of power was maintained among the national states.

(2) The general course of events during the Age of Charles v further stunted German and Italian national growth. Italy had been a battlefield for the French and the Hapsburgs; and when peace was finally arranged between them in 1559, much of Italy was left to the Hapsburgs. For the Germanies, Charles failed to create an effective centralized government. The Schmalkaldic Wars and the Peace of Augsburg accentuated the political and religious division of the German states.

(3) Charles' rivalry with Francis I and the French king's alliance with Suleiman played an important part in reducing the pressure that Charles might have applied against the Lutheran movement. Although a Catholic, Francis sent aid to the German Protestants in order to embarrass their ruler. As a result of this aid, the Protestant movement gained so firm a foothold that the religious unity of Europe was irreparably destroyed.

(4) The advance of the Ottoman power in Europe meant that Turkish control over the Balkans was handed down to later European statesmen as an explosive legacy. The alliance of France with Turkey became an enduring though irregular factor in European diplomacy.

(5) The history of the first half of the sixteenth century made it quite clear that diplomacy à la Machiavelli was to be the order of the day. Deceit, treachery, surprise attacks, and broken promises were written into the record.

During the entire reign of Charles V, Turkish pirates preyed upon Christian shipping and harried the coasts of Sicily and Italy. This painting of Charles was completed shortly after his successful Tunisian campaign against the Turks (1535); Charles is shown victorious over the defeated Moorish king. But his triumph was brief; after a disastrous expedition against Algiers in 1541, the emperor ceased active warfare against the pirates; and by the mid-sixteenth century, Turkish sea power was at its height.

EUROPE AGAINST ITSELF

Era of the Religious Wars. While the danger of a single empire's controlling Europe had been lessened after Charles v divided his lands, the Continent was still to witness convulsive rivalries and a century more of warfare. The period from roughly the middle of the sixteenth century to the middle of the seventeenth century is often referred to as the Era of the Religious Wars, for the religious issues which flamed forth from the Protestant upheaval colored every political conflict. Sometimes the alliance between religious and political factions was genuine and well-intentioned. Often, however, ambitious rulers employed religious causes to cloak their designs for dynastic glory, more territory, or the defeat of rivals.

Nevertheless, the Religious Wars were not without religious significance; many men fought and died for their faiths. In addition, religious beliefs and loyalties were sometimes in conflict with political interests. A zealous Catholic or a Calvinist might consider the claims of religion above the claim of a dynastic state for his loyalties. This situation has been likened to the clash of ideologies in the twentieth century by which a French Communist might give his loyalty to Moscow rather than to Paris.

In 1556 when Philip II, the son of Charles V, became king of Spain, the Era of the Religious Wars began. Let us see whether the young monarch accomplished his dreams of glory or whether his desires were thwarted as Charles' had been.

Philip II faces a promising future. There were several factors which made it seem that Philip's future would be an impressive and successful one. Most important was that when his uncle Ferdinand received the Hapsburg Austrian lands together with the imperial crown of the Holy Roman Empire, Philip was freed of the political and religious complexities in middle Europe; that is, he had no "German problem." Secondly, Philip inherited a new empire overseas which was more lucrative and more easily administered than his father's empire in the Germanies had been. From the New World came huge quantities of treasure to enrich the Hapsburg coffers at Madrid (see Chapter 16). In addition to the riches of the Americas and the Spanish possessions in Europe—the Netherlands, Naples, Sicily, and Milan—Philip had the best army in Europe during this period.

During his long reign (1556-1598), Philip sought three basic goals: to make his royal power absolute, to combat heresy and strengthen Catholicism, and to extend the influence of Spain. Building on the foundations established by his great-grandparents Ferdinand and Isabella, Philip erected a centralized system of government in which every decision rested with the king and in which all agencies of government were subordinate to his will.

Philip's devotion to the Catholic Church has led some historians to declare that he subordinated the interests of Spain to those of Catholicism. As we shall see in this chapter, however, religious scruples did not interfere with the interests of the Spanish state. It was convenient for Philip that his duties to the Church appeared to coincide with his designs as the ruler of Spain. By championing Catholicism he was able to justify his interference in the political and religious conflicts of other European nations.

Philip defeats the Turks; Spain annexes Portugal. After Suleiman's death the Turkish sultans continued his policy of conquest, but Europe was now better prepared to meet the Ottoman threat. In 1559 peace had been made between France and Spain, and the alliance between Paris and Constantinople had broken down. Christian Europe—prepared at last to unite against the common foe—turned to Philip, the champion of the Catholic faith, to block Turkish expansion. Philip gained tremendous prestige by making possible a great victory over the Turks.

A Holy League was formed to raise a great fleet and destroy Ottoman naval power in the Mediterranean. In 1571 the fleet of the League and the Turkish navy clashed at Lepanto, on the western side of Greece. The outcome was a decisive victory for Christian Europe; Ottoman sea power was crushed, never to be restored as a major threat to Christendom. Lepanto is often considered the last great crusade.

Less than a decade after Lepanto, the direct line of the Portuguese royal family became extinct. Philip's seizure of the Portuguese throne in 1580 was a master stroke.

The annexation of Portugal and its vast co-lonial empire brought new riches to Madrid from Brazil, Africa, and the East Indies.

Unrest and revolt in the Netherlands. The conquest of Portugal and the defeat of the Turks were signal victories for Philip, but the specter of failure stalked him in the Netherlands. The seventeen provinces of the Low Countries (which included today's Holland, Belgium, and Luxemburg) had been restive during the reign of Philip's father. Charles v had imposed heavy taxes to help finance his wars and had made the people support large contingents of Spanish troops. But in spite of these unpopular acts, he had continued to enjoy the confidence of the Netherlanders, who regarded him as one of themselves because he had been born in the city of Ghent. It was not so with Philip, whom the Netherlanders distrusted as a foreigner. Disregarding their own nobles, Philip placed Spanish officials over the Dutch people, maintained an army of occupation there, and introduced the Inquisition.

In spite of the Inquisition, Protestantism spread in the Netherlands and in 1566 a series of riots broke out. To stamp out disloyalty, the Council of Troubles—dubbed "the Council of Blood"—was established. During the Spanish reign of terror, a total of eight thousand were slain, thirty thousand were deprived of their lands and property, and one hundred thousand fled the country.

The Spanish continued to antagonize the growing nationalism of the Dutch, who were fighting for the freedom to maintain their own institutions and their machinery of local self-government. The religious issue was also a very important factor among the strongly Protestant Dutch, and heavy taxes created widespread enmity among the wealthy Dutch burghers. Dutch discontent soon flared into the Eighty Years' War (1568-1648) against Spain.

In the early years of the war the Spanish armies were victorious, and the puny forces commanded by the tenacious William the Silent, the Dutch leader, were dispersed again and again. In 1576, however, the incident of the Spanish Fury electrified the inhabitants of the Netherlands. Usually well-disciplined, the unfed and unpaid Spanish soldiers mutinied and marched on Antwerp. Setting upon the hapless city, they burned public buildings and murdered seven thousand citizens. This calamity settled the local differences between the seventeen provinces that had prevented them from making concerted efforts against Spanish tyranny. The Pacification of Ghent, which the provincial representatives signed in 1576, declared that all Spanish soldiers must be expelled from the land, after which a representative body, the Estates-General, should be established to govern the country. Both Protestants and Catholics were to enjoy toleration. While Philip was to be the nominal overlord of the provinces, the actual ruler was to be William the Silent.

Unfortunately for the rebels' cause, the seventeen provinces did not long maintain the unity manifested in the Pacification of Ghent. The Spaniards were able to take advantage of the differences between the Protestant provinces in the north and the provinces in the south, where the people were mainly Catholic. In 1579 the people of the Netherlands came to a parting of the ways. The southern provinces were reunited with Spain while the Dutch leaders in the northern provinces declared that they would not rest until Spanish tyranny had been crushed and complete freedom achieved. In 1581 the Estates-General of the United Provinces, as the northern provinces came to be known, formally repudiated the Spanish sovereign in an announcement that can be regarded as the Dutch declaration of independence. One of its provisions stated:

The people were not created by God for the sake of the Prince . . . on the contrary, the Prince was made for the good of the people.[7]

The declaration of 1581 set the model for later declarations justifying revolution in England, France, and the United States.

Three years after the declaration the cause of Dutch freedom was placed in serious jeopardy when William the Silent was assassinated and the Spanish stepped up their

Above is a portrait of Philip II of Spain and his wife, Queen Mary of England.

efforts to destroy Dutch independence. At this critical moment Elizabeth I of England offered valuable military assistance to the United Provinces, not because she had a consuming interest in Dutch freedom but because she wished to undermine Spanish power wherever possible. The destruction in 1588 of Philip's Invincible Armada by England (see p. 319) further weakened Spanish ability to crush the Dutch. In 1609 a Twelve Years' Truce put an end to sporadic fighting. Not until the end of the Thirty Years' War, however, did the Spanish grant the Dutch formal recognition of their independent status as the United Provinces (Holland).

The southern provinces remained for more than two hundred years in the hands of the Hapsburgs, first as the Spanish Netherlands and then as the Austrian Netherlands. Early in the nineteenth century, following a brief and unsatisfactory union with Holland, the Austrian Netherlands obtained their independence as the nation of Belgium.

The English throne: Protestant or Catholic? On more than one occasion during the reign of Philip II, it seemed that England would come under Spanish domination. Philip in 1554 had married Mary Tudor, the first daughter of Henry VIII. Mary adored her husband, and as queen she was strongly influenced by him, although he had no official function in the governing of England. After a brief reign she died, and in 1558 her half-sister, Elizabeth I, assumed the English throne.

Elizabeth's disputed succession provided the next occasion for possible Spanish domination of England. The daughter of Henry by his second wife, Anne Boleyn, Elizabeth was considered illegitimate by English Catholics, who recognized only Henry's first marriage as valid. Furthermore, in the eyes of Catholic Europe, the rightful heir to the throne was the great-granddaughter of Henry VII, Mary Stuart, Queen of Scotland.

Brought up in France as a Catholic, Mary had wed the heir to the French throne and reigned for two years as queen of France. After the death of her royal mate, she returned to her native Scottish kingdom. Mary found Scotland in the hands of rebellious nobles and vigorous Protestant preachers. Soon after the violent death of her second husband, the weakling Lord Darnley, she was forced to seek refuge with her cousin Elizabeth in England. There, her Catholicism and her good claim to Elizabeth's throne made her an unwelcome guest, potentially dangerous to the Tudor monarch and to English Protestantism.

For his part, Philip had no compunctions about plotting to place Mary on the throne of England. Philip's ambassador in London became the center of a web of intrigue against Elizabeth.

Rivalry between England and Spain. As Philip became the chief enemy of Protestant England, Elizabeth gradually emerged as the foremost obstacle to Spanish expansion.

Unlike the impetuous Mary Stuart, who was often the blind instrument of her emotions, Elizabeth was realistic, calculating, and thoroughly Machiavellian. As the Spanish ambassador wrote to Philip:

. . . what a pretty business it is to treat with this woman who I think must have a hundred thousand devils in her body, notwithstanding that she is forever telling me that she yearns to be a nun and to pass her life in prayer.[8]

She resorted to every subterfuge and trick available to her in the duel with Philip of Spain. Using her sex as a diplomatic weapon, she carried on long flirtations with the brothers of the French king, thereby helping to prevent an alliance between France and Spain. While nominally at peace with Philip, Elizabeth secretly encouraged her sea captains to prey upon Spanish shipping and to attack the rich Spanish settlements in the New World. The most famous of the Elizabethan Sea Dogs, Sir Francis Drake, sailed into the Pacific, plundered the western coast of Spanish America, and, after circumnavigating the globe, arrived in England with a hold full of gold and silver.

Although aware of Elizabeth's duplicity, Philip planned to gain control over England by employing a minimum of resources rather than by expending Spanish energies in preparation for a maximum effort—war. He hoped to place Mary Stuart on the English throne following the assassination of Elizabeth. But a plot against Elizabeth's life, in which Mary was implicated, was discovered. Parliament was convinced that as long as Mary lived, Elizabeth's life would be endangered, and therefore, in 1587, Elizabeth signed Mary's death warrant. But in a sense Mary had not failed. In Scotland lived her son, James, who was destined to become the common monarch of England and Scotland, not by conspiracy or force but by common consent.

Philip and Elizabeth at war. After the discovery of the plot against her life, Eliza-

This portrait of Queen Elizabeth was painted during her reign.

beth realized that the time for a decisive test of arms had come. She sought to hinder Philip's plans by openly sending arms and soldiers to the Netherlands, by aiding the Protestant cause during the French civil war, and by authorizing Drake to destroy Spanish shipping—exploits described as "singeing the King of Spain's beard." By 1587—the year in which Mary Stuart went to the scaffold—Philip decided to invade England.

Philip's strategy was to have the Spanish fleet, called the Invincible Armada, join a large Spanish army in the Netherlands and then land this force on the coast of England. Blocking the main ports in the Low Countries, the Dutch prevented the rendezvous, and Philip's designs were ruined completely when the Elizabethan Sea Dogs trounced the Armada in the English Channel. The small, swift English ships outmaneuvered the bulky Spanish galleons, savage fighting ensued, and a severe storm completed the debacle.

The defeat of the Armada meant that England was to remain Protestant, that it would

In July 1588, after three days of maneuvering, the English dispersed the Invincible Armada by launching flaming ships (center) into the Spanish formation. The Armada fell into complete disorder and retreated, pursued by the English.

soon emerge as a dominant sea power, that the rebellion in Holland against Spanish tyranny was eventually to succeed, and that the power of Spain was now on the wane.

The failure of Philip II. This Spanish king has been cited as an example of detestable trickery, cruelty, and religious intolerance. As we have seen, however, Philip was not equal to Elizabeth in duplicity and diplomatic cunning. And, in answer to the charge of bigotry, it must be remembered that nearly all sixteenth-century European monarchs believed the relentless persecution of nonconformists to be essential to the welfare of the state. Therefore, Philip's failures cannot be attributed to defects ingrained in his nature but to the fact that, generally speaking, he was less skillful than his opponents in the game of power politics.

Most important, perhaps, is that Philip unwittingly pitted himself against the growing feelings of nationalism. Just as the love of native land had spelled failure for England in the Hundred Years' War, so had

patriotism thwarted Philip's ambitions in the Netherlands and in the waters around the British Isles.

Despite Philip's failures, Spain still held the reputation of being the first power in Europe. Spanish soldiers were the best trained on the Continent; and in the arts of peace Spanish writers, scholars, and painters were outstanding. In fact, the last half of the sixteenth century and the first half of the seventeenth are usually regarded as the zenith of Spanish culture. In the seventeenth century, however, Spanish power began to decline. The last of the so-called religious conflicts, the Thirty Years' War (1618-1648), accelerated the decline.

Civil war in France. While the Dutch were valiantly fighting for their independence and Elizabeth and Philip were sparring for power, France was undergoing one of the most terrible civil conflicts in its history. The Valois kings were stout Catholics, and under their rule the Huguenots in France were persecuted severely. But in spite of government measures, by 1560 the Huguenots numbered 400,000.

Because the weakling sons of Henry II, grandsons of the vigorous Francis I, left no heirs, the French believed that the Valois line would soon become extinct. This situation led to ruthless factional rivalry between two noble houses in France, both of which aspired to the throne. The Bourbons, who espoused Protestantism, had the better claim because they traced their descent from St. Louis, a revered French king of the thirteenth century, and thus were clearly related to the Valois line. Champions of Catholicism were the powerful Guises. This was the setting for the civil war that broke out in 1562. The conflict was partly religious as Catholics and Huguenots reviled one another, partly political as the Guises and Bourbons plotted for royal power. A succession of eight bitterly fought wars followed.

During this period and until her death in 1589, the most powerful individual in France was Catherine de' Medici, the queen mother. Like her contemporary in London, Queen Elizabeth, Catherine was completely cynical and ruthless in statecraft. Even her youngest son referred to her as "Madame la Serpente." No matter how cruel or base, no technique was beneath her use; one of Catherine's political weapons was " 'a flying squadron' of twenty-four maids of honor of high rank and low principles to help her seduce the refractory nobles on both sides."[9]

Determined to maintain the power of her sons, Catherine attempted to steer a middle course between the Protestant and Catholic factions and to play one party off against the other. But as the Huguenots grew stronger, she resolved to crush them. Thus, the terrible Massacre of St. Bartholomew's Day is blamed on Catherine. At dawn on August 24, 1572, with a signal from the bell of the Palace of Justice in Paris, the Catholics fell upon their Protestant rivals, and before the day was done ten thousand Huguenots were slain.

The massacre did not destroy Huguenot power, however, and civil conflict continued. Both Spain and England intervened in the struggle. After the Protestant Bourbon prince Henry of Navarre became King Henry IV of France by right of succession, Philip II of Spain, who had been aiding the Guises, continued his attempts to overthrow the Bourbons. But with English aid Henry was victorious, the civil war ended, and a peace treaty between France and Spain was signed.

The Edict of Nantes. Realizing that a majority of his subjects were Catholic, Henry IV is supposed to have said, "Paris is well worth a mass." Although he changed his own faith, he sought to protect the liberties of the Huguenot minority in the Edict of Nantes (1598). This proclamation was the first important recognition by a major power that more than one religion could be tolerated within a state. The Peace of Augsburg had given each ruler in the Holy Roman Empire the right to choose the religion of his subjects, but the Edict of Nantes differed from the earlier agreement in that the monarch gave the choice of religion to his subjects.

The issues of the Thirty Years' War. The Peace of Augsburg failed to bring about a satisfactory religious settlement in the Germanies, and friction continued after 1555. Many of the higher clergy who accepted Protestantism secularized and retained for themselves the lands they had held as Catholic prelates. The Protestant princes claimed the right to take over former Church lands within their states, while Catholics maintained that the Peace of Augsburg had stipulated that no further secularization of Church property might take place. Another cause of dispute was the fact that the Peace of Augsburg had recognized only the Lutheran and Catholic religions. There was no recognition of Calvinism, a faith that had spread rapidly in the latter part of the sixteenth century. Religious toleration for the Calvinists was a burning issue. But while the religious differences between Catholic, Lutheran, and Calvinist sharpened local rivalries among the German princes, the basic issues of the Thirty Years' War were at least as much economic and political as religious.

Important in this conflict were the motives of the Holy Roman emperor, Ferdinand II of the Austrian Hapsburgs. He wanted a

During the Thirty Years' War the German city of Munich was captured by the Swedish monarch Gustavus Adolphus, whose invading army was strengthened by German allies. In this old drawing, the warrior-king rides in from the left, while the officials of Munich kneel in homage at lower right, ready to present their conqueror with the keys to the city.

united and subservient empire to strengthen his position in Europe. Ferdinand's desire to reassert the imperial authority was opposed by princes whose own power would remain strong with Germany divided and the emperor weak. Not all the princes opposed the emperor, however; as a Catholic leader the emperor had many Catholic princes on his side.

Phases of the Thirty Years' War. The complexities of the Thirty Years' War may be simplified by dividing the events into four phases. The first battleground was Bohemia, where the Protestants revolted against the Catholic Hapsburgs in 1618 and were crushed two years later by their overlords, with the result that in Bohemia Protestantism was banned.

The second phase of the conflict began when the Danes in 1625 invaded Germany not only to champion hard-pressed Protestantism but also to gain further control over ports in the North Sea and to thwart Hapsburg ambitions. However, the Hapsburg armies crushed the Danes.

The success of the Catholic cause drew the leading Lutheran power, Sweden, into the fight. The third phase of the war started in 1630 when Gustavus Adolphus invaded Germany. Motivated not only by religious considerations but also by his interest in Swedish domination of the Baltic, the Swedish monarch scored a number of brilliant victories. In the midst of a successful battle, he was killed, and the anti-Hapsburg forces then began to weaken.

A compromise peace was short-lived, and in the year 1635 the fourth phase of the war began. Cardinal Richelieu, the chief adviser of the French king and the real head of the government, decided that French political power could be secure only when the Hapsburgs of Austria and Spain had been defeated. Until 1635 he had been giving secret aid to the German Protestants, Denmark, and Sweden in their struggle against the Catholics, though he himself was a prince of the Catholic Church and France a Catholic state. Now he came out in the open.

Religious issues had by now become distinctly secondary. The struggle was primarily a contest between Bourbons and Hapsburgs for the mastery of Europe. France was in a strong position because in Germany the Swedes and German Protestants could keep the Austrian Hapsburg armies busy while French arms were concentrated against the Spanish Hapsburgs.

The French army soon developed into an effective, battle-hardened force under the command of skillful generals. By 1643 the power of the Spanish Hapsburgs had been weakened. The French then turned to the Germanies and scored a series of victories against the Austrian Hapsburgs. Before the cessation of hostilities in 1648, Richelieu's objective had been secured. The French architect of Bourbon supremacy on the Continent was dead, but his successor, Cardinal Mazarin, continued to carry on Richelieu's designs for weakening the power of the Hapsburgs.

The Peace of Westphalia. In 1648 a series of treaties collectively known as the Peace of Westphalia were agreed to. A recapitulation of the numerous provisions of the treaty would be very complex; suffice it to say that France, Sweden, and the Protestant state of Brandenburg made important territorial gains, while Switzerland and Holland, long the oppressed vassals of the Hapsburgs, were recognized as independent states. The Calvinists were given recognition in the Germanies, and the land issue which had been an important factor at the beginning of the war was settled in an agreement whereby Church property was to be retained by the group—either Protestant or Catholic—which had held the land in the year 1624.

The Peace of Westphalia also dealt a heavy blow to the remaining power of the Holy Roman Empire. The imperial machinery of emperor, electors, and Diet remained, but, in the words of a seventeenth-century German historian, "the imperial office had become a mummy; the constitution a monstrosity."[10] German princes were now sovereign, with the right to coin money, make war, maintain armies, and send diplomatic representatives to foreign courts.

The great significance of the Peace of Westphalia was that it symbolized the emergence and victory of the national sovereign state. More specifically, this treaty discredited the empire and instituted the diplomatic procedure of convening peace congresses between nations to arrange peace terms after wars.

The settlement brought no peace to harried Spain, however. The Austrian Hapsburgs had come to terms with their enemies, ignoring their Spanish relatives. In consequence, Philip IV of Spain fought France for another eleven years until the French, with English help, defeated the Spanish monarch. A peace treaty between Spain and France was signed in 1659, and Philip consented to the marriage of his daughter to Louis XIV, the Bourbon king of France.

Thus the struggle against Hapsburg dominance begun by the French king Francis I against Charles V early in the sixteenth century ended more than a century later. Changes had been wrought in the relative power of nations. Both England and Holland had become great sea powers, and their commercial prosperity was increasing rapidly. France emerged as the greatest power in Europe, the potential master of the Continent. The golden age of Spain was over; never again would this nation or Portugal be considered first-class powers. Although reports of devastation, population decline, and cultural retrogression in the Germanies have perhaps been overemphasized, the Thirty Years' War left a grievous legacy and thwarted progress in the German states for a century.

BEGINNINGS OF INTERNATIONAL LAW

Proposals for keeping the peace. The irresponsible use of power was the outstanding feature of international politics in the late sixteenth and early seventeenth centuries. But gradually powerful rulers and diplomats realized that frequent wars threatened the growth of European trade and commerce and menaced even the existence of civilized society in the West. A few steps were taken to improve international relations. Consular and diplomatic services were established, and trade agreements and treaties formed a crude system of international law. The agreements, however, were more honored in the breach than in the observance and had a negligible

HUG. GROTII
DE JURE BELLI
AC PACIS
LIBRI TRES.

War and Peace are reconciled in the allegorical title page from the 1689 edition of Grotius' *De Jure Belli ac Pacis (On the Law of War and Peace)*. Four years before he wrote his great work, Grotius had escaped from a Dutch prison, where he had been sentenced to life imprisonment as a result of his campaign for religious toleration between Protestant and Catholic and for a more liberal regime in his own country, Holland.

effect on the continued use of war as the means of settling disputes among nations.

To some visionaries, the ideal of religious and political unity of the Middle Ages, although imperfect, was preferable to international anarchy among sovereign states. The more practical northern humanists denounced the folly of most wars. "War is sweet only to the inexperienced," wrote Erasmus, and Thomas More made the first suggestions for limiting international conflict. To him, only defensive wars or wars against tyranny were

justifiable. In the seventeenth century other students of international affairs made more specific recommendations.

The duke of Sully (1560-1641), chief minister for the first Bourbon monarch, Henry IV, devised a plan, called the Grand Design, for limiting wars in Europe. Some of its provisions were intended to secure France against the power which Spain enjoyed at that time, but the Grand Design is most significant as the first definite plan in modern times for a European peace organization.

The Grand Design called for the establishment of a Christian republic, headed by a council which was to include representatives from all the states of Europe. Some aspects of the plan anticipated the organization and purposes of the present United Nations. For example, the council was to secure disarmament and to control an international police force which would back the decisions of the council by force.

Grotius and international law. Another thoughtful European who feared the menace of constant war was a gifted Dutch scholar, Hugo Grotius (1583-1645). In 1625 appeared *De Jure Belli ac Pacis (On the Law of War and Peace)*, the work which gained him instant fame and lasting recognition as the founder of international law. In this work he endeavored to set forth a new code of international conduct based not upon the authority of the Church but on what he termed the fundamental idea of the law of nature. The law of nature was in turn founded on the dictates of reason, morality, and justice. If civilization was to endure, Grotius argued, relations among nations should be guided by reason, and humane considerations should prevail in the councils of the mighty. Grotius did not propose to eliminate war entirely. He sought instead to outlaw "unjust" wars and limit the effects of "just" wars. According to Grotius, wars were justified only to repel invasion or to punish an insult to God. His appeal, however intelligent, fell largely upon deaf ears. Machiavelli's *The Prince* enjoyed more popularity in European palaces than *On the Law of War and Peace*.

THE ENGLISH CIVIL WARS

Background for the struggle in England. Like most of the politico-religious conflicts on the Continent, the English civil wars (1642-1660) were a complex blend of politics and religion. But unlike the Thirty Years' War, for example, the English struggle was a domestic duel between groups fundamentally opposed in viewpoint—traditionalists who upheld the power of the monarchy and those who favored a government more representative of the people. The religious implications of the English civil wars were important, but they have been overshadowed by the constitutional results stemming from the struggle. The outcome had a strong influence on the development of constitutional governments and the growth of democracy in modern times.

Largely with the cooperation of Parliament and the approval of the English people, Tudor monarchs had restored law and order to England, broken with the Church of Rome, and ruled with a strong hand. No consistent breach of opinion developed between the crown on the one hand and Parliament and the people on the other to raise constitutional issues or to challenge the royal power so skillfully wielded by the Tudors.

But if the spirit of liberty and the growth of constitutional government had been placed temporarily in cold storage, it had not been frozen. During most of Elizabeth's reign, the House of Commons was content to improve its procedures and gain parliamentary experience. Following the defeat of the Armada, however, the spirit of liberty began to reassert itself. On questions of taxation Parliament became increasingly independent. And while this body usually enacted into law the measures laid before it by the queen's advisers, an unpopular measure would occasionally be rejected.

James I and Parliament. Elizabeth's successor was James Stuart, King of Scotland and the son of Mary Stuart. Scotland and England, though still separate states, thus acquired a king in common. As James I of England, he reigned from 1603 to 1625.

A scholarly man, James appointed a commission to make a new English translation of the Bible. Published in 1611, the King James Version was a masterpiece of English prose. But notwithstanding his erudition and his sincere desire for peace, the new king was totally unfitted for his position. He lacked common sense and tact; small wonder that he was dubbed "the wisest fool in Christendom."

His most unpolitic move was advocating the divine right of kings. In the address to his first Parliament, he expressed his ideas of the monarch's power:

The state of monarchy is the supremest thing upon earth, for kings are not only God's lieutenants upon earth and sit upon God's throne, but even by God himself they are called gods. . . . That as to dispute what God may do is blasphemy, . . . so is it sedition in subjects to dispute what a king may do in the height of his power . . . I will not be content that my power be disputed upon. . . .[11]

Disregarding the temper of his new subjects, James made it plain that he meant to be an absolute monarch.

The religious issue. The constitutional issue of king against Parliament was complicated by religious issues. Some of James' subjects considered themselves content with the Anglican Church as it then was; others hoped to reintroduce much of the ritual and some of the tenets of Roman Catholicism, although they had no desire to return to papal control; and still others took an extreme Protestant position.

The extreme Protestants were called Puritans because they wished to "purify" the Anglican Church still further, simplify the ritual, and lessen the authority of the bishops chosen by the king. The Puritans were mostly members of the urban middle class. Engaged in trade and commerce, they resented James' arbitrary and illegal taxation and wanted to secure laws for the protection and expansion of English commercial interests. Puritan lawyers supplied historical precedents as ammunition against the growing absolutism of the throne and fanned the flames of discontent.

James' stand on religion further alienated the Puritans because he opposed their desire for more Protestantism in the Anglican Church. Also, many Englishmen considered him overfriendly with Catholic sovereigns abroad and inclined to favor and protect English Catholics.

Charles I and Parliament. At the death of James I in 1625, his son Charles I inherited the English throne along with a host of problems similar to those which had beset his father. James' mistakes were repeated by Charles, and to an even greater degree. Like father, the son espoused the divine right of kings, was contemptuous of the rights of Parliament, and supported the pro-Catholic or High Church faction.

Insisting on absolute royal power, Charles opened his reign with stormy debates with Parliament; but in return for revenue from Parliament, he agreed in 1628 to the famous Petition of Rights—a parliamentary declaration that ranks with Magna Carta as one of the great documents in the development of representative government. The most important provisions of the Petition denied the monarch the right to tax without parliamentary consent or to imprison a freeman without just cause.

Little immediate good came of the Petition of Rights, for Charles broke its provisions and from 1629 to 1640 ruled England without calling Parliament. During this period he resorted to methods of taxation which the supporters of Parliament considered illegal. Royal taxes fell heavily upon the shoulders of the prosperous Puritan merchants and shopkeepers. In addition, Charles punished those who refused to conform to his own religious beliefs. Several Puritan leaders in the House of Commons were imprisoned for their views.

Cavaliers vs. Roundheads. When Charles attempted to force his brand of High Church Anglican religion on the Presbyterian subjects of his Scottish kingdom, they promptly took up arms against their king. Faced by a hostile army and without sufficient funds to put an army of his own into the field, Charles was forced to convene Parliament.

When Parliament refused to vote any money until Charles had redressed certain grievances, Charles promptly dissolved it. But riots in England and a Scottish invasion compelled him to recall Parliament. Sensing the weakness in the king's position, Parliament immediately set to work to make its powers at least coequal with those of the king. This session became known as the "Long Parliament" because it lasted nearly twenty years.

As the tension between the crown and Parliament increased, two bitterly antagonistic parties quickly developed: the Royalist party and the Parliamentary party.

Composed largely of the middle class and the Puritans, the members of the Parliamentary party were dubbed "Roundheads" because they wore their hair cropped short while the opposing faction wore full wigs. The Puritans in turn were divided between Independents and Presbyterians, who differed over questions of church government but agreed in holding generally to a Calvinistic system of religion and in demanding further reductions in the political and religious prerogatives of the monarch.

The Royalist party, the "Cavaliers," was supported mainly by the landowning class, who opposed extreme Protestantism. While agreeing with the Puritans in opposing royal despotism, the Royalists were unwilling to see the monarchy stripped of all its powers. In this party there was also a substantial number of clergy and laymen who, like their monarch, not only opposed Puritanism but seemed to be pro-Catholic and appeared ready to return the Anglican Church to the fold of Rome.

Civil war. Civil war broke out in 1642, and within four years, by virtue of their control of the sea, greater economic resources, superior generalship, and an alliance with the Scots, the Roundheads defeated the king's armies.

A major factor in the triumph of the Roundheads was their remarkable military leader, Oliver Cromwell. A country gentleman and a prosperous farmer, Cromwell trained new troops, instilled into his men a sense of discipline and religious mission, and sent them into battle singing hymns. His God-fearing, irresistible forces became known as Cromwell's Ironsides.

At the end of 1646 the forces opposed to the king had achieved complete victory, and he had surrendered himself into their hands. For the next two years the monarch tried to play off his enemies—the Scots; the Presbyterians, who dominated Parliament; and the Independents, who dominated the army—against each other. He actually succeeded in splitting Parliament and making a secret alliance with the Scots. The upshot was the rise of fierce resentment against the king in the ranks of the Independent army, and in 1648 a second civil war broke out. The allies of the king were defeated, and in December 1648 all Presbyterian members of the House of Commons were purged from that body by the victorious Independent army. Following a brief trial, King Charles was executed in January 1649.

The Protectorate and Cromwell. Abolishing the House of Lords and declaring the office of king unnecessary, the House of Commons proclaimed England a commonwealth. But in 1653 the Puritan army, still distrusting Parliament, overthrew the Commonwealth and set up a new form of government, the Protectorate, in which Oliver Cromwell held the office of Lord Protector, assisted by a council and Parliament. The structure and operation of the government was based on a written constitution called The Instrument of Government. This document, one of the earliest constitutions of modern times, was to become influential in the later European constitutional movement.

Now virtual dictator of England, Cromwell endeavored to achieve a religious settlement for the nation. Amid the rivalries between Independents, Presbyterians, Royalists, Scots, and others, he had been forced to assume the role of dictator, but at heart Cromwell was a moderate, believing in religious toleration and constitutional government. However, he found it an impossible task to reconcile all the religious factions. The last three years of Cromwell's life were filled with trouble. Although he did not favor it, his more extreme Puritan colleagues muzzled the press and foisted on a pleasure-loving folk a series of hateful prohibitions which closed the theaters and stamped out many wholesome as well as unwholesome popular amusements.

The Restoration. Cromwell died in 1658 amid rising discontent with his rule. One contemporary observer claimed:

. . . it was the joyfulest funeral I ever saw, for there were none that cried but dogs. . . .[12]

Seemingly, Cromwell's work had been a failure; yet his implacable opposition to despotism and his advocacy of religious toleration were priceless legacies from the kingless decade. He was succeeded by his son, who found it difficult to carry on his father's work and resigned in less than a year. To most men the restoration of the monarchy seemed the only solution.

In 1660, amid wild excitement and enthusiasm, the exiled Charles Stuart, son of the late king, returned to England as Charles II. But civil war and revolution had not been in vain; Charles was restored to the throne with the explicit understanding that he should rule through Parliament. Thus the English monarchy was made responsible to a representative body, a condition in sharp contrast to the pattern of absolutism on the Continent.

John Milton. An important figure in the growth of political liberty and freedom of expression is the English poet John Milton (1608-1674). A member of a prosperous lawyer's family, young Milton received an excellent classical education, as the many allusions to antiquity in his verse attest. He became familiar with humanistic concepts while visiting Italy during a tour of Europe and later served in Cromwell's administration. When the monarchy was restored in 1660, Milton retired to a life of writing.

During his later years, despite total blindness, Milton composed the epic *Paradise Lost*, which he dictated to members of his family and published in 1667. Here the story of man's fall makes the universe a battleground between the forces of good and evil. The poem is magnificent in its cosmic sweep, and the portrait of Lucifer as a majestic figure of power is easily Milton's finest.

In Milton were blended the strains of Renaissance humanism and Puritanism. His reverence for antiquity and his belief in human dignity and freedom are attributable to the former; his moral earnestness, to the latter. Although inclined by nature to quiet study, he devoted twenty years of his life to public service in a period of great turmoil and was a fearless pamphleteer for Puritan causes.

One of his best-known tracts is *Areopagitica* (1644), an impassioned plea for freedom of the press:

Who kills a man kills a reasonable creature, God's image; but he who destroys a good book, kills reason itself, kills the image of God, as it were in the eye. Many a man lives a burden to the earth; but a good book is the precious life-blood of a master-spirit, embalmed and treasured up on purpose to a life beyond life. . . . We should be wary therefore . . . how we spill that seasoned life of man, preserved and stored up in books; since we see a kind of homicide may thus be committed . . . whereof the execution ends not in the slaying of an elemental life, but strikes at that ethereal and fifth essence, the breath of reason itself, [and] slays an immortality rather than a life. . . .[13]

SUMMARY

By the middle of the seventeenth century the pattern of politics in western Europe had changed significantly. Gone was the ideal of unity, whether based on empire or universal church; sovereignty had replaced suzerainty. The new monarchies were largely absolute in authority within their own frontiers and free agents in the domain of international affairs. Following the dictates of diplomacy systematized by Machiavelli, these sovereign states pursued power, prestige, wealth, and security. No moral or religious scruples were allowed to interfere with these objectives. It was considered axiomatic that a nation had no permanent enemies or friends—only permanent interests. This maxim was illustrated by the manner in which diplomatic combinations were formed on the European chessboard. We shall see in our study of later eras how the great powers have continued to alter their alliances in deference to the exigencies of the balance of power. For example, the foes of the United States in World War II are now our allies against the Soviet Union—one of our chief supporters in that conflict. Only by studying past political history can these situations be understood.

Power politics between 1500 and 1650 developed amid complex happenings, especially the so-called Religious Wars. Just what was religion and what politics was often difficult to determine, especially since religion was often used as a cover for political intrigue. Elizabeth fought the Spanish Armada and aided the Dutch in the name of Protestantism, but she was concerned chiefly with preventing Spanish domination of Europe and interference with English maritime expansion. With Philip II of Spain, Catholic convictions appropriately coincided with Spanish national interests; to champion the Catholic Church was, in Philip's mind, to build a strong Spain. Expediency, not religious principles, governed international politics: witness Francis I's alliance with the Turks and Richelieu's support of the German Protestants.

In only one nation during the seventeenth century was there a substantial countertrend to the increasing centralization of the monarch's power. Absolutism versus constitutional government was a basic issue in the English civil war waged between Roundheads and Cavaliers. The idea of people's rights which came to the fore in this struggle was destined to play a key role in the growth of political freedom in the West.

In the survey of European affairs in this chapter, two opposing principles were discussed: one, the right of a state to conduct its foreign affairs—even to waging war—without hindrance; the other, the concept that nations should accept some limitation to their freedom of action in international affairs. Ever since the sixteenth century, when scholars began to think of limiting wars and the need for international law, national sovereignty and internationalism have been in competition. Sovereignty has gotten

the best of it by far. But we will see that since Grotius' time, much thought and effort have been devoted to a study of averting conflicts and subordinating disputes to the rule of law.

SUGGESTIONS FOR READING

The political history of the century and a half after the beginning of the Protestant Reformation is discussed in its relation to the religious movements in H. J. Grimm, *The Reformation Era, 1500-1650,* Macmillan, 1954; and independent of the religious history in A. J. Grant, *A History of Europe from 1494 to 1610,* Barnes and Noble, 1951. Other standard political histories are Sir Charles Oman, *The Sixteenth Century,* Dutton, 1937; and D. Ogg, *Europe in the Seventeenth Century,* Macmillan, 1952.

C. J. Friedrich, *The Age of the Baroque, 1610-1660,* Harper, 1952. An indispensable scholarly survey of all aspects of civilization; includes a long bibliographical essay. A very brief survey, based on the above book, is C. Friedrich and C. Blitzer, *The Age of Power,** Cornell.

G. Mattingly, *Renaissance Diplomacy,* Houghton Mifflin, 1955. A study of the growth of diplomatic institutions and the interplay of political forces in early modern times. H. Nicolson, *Diplomacy,* Oxford (Home Univ. Library), 1939, contains a brief survey of the subject.

J. H. Whitfield, *Machiavelli,* Blackwell, 1947. A sympathetic account of Machiavelli and his significance in the history of political thought. The older, unfavorable view of Machiavelli is well presented in H. Butterfield, *The Statecraft of Machiavelli,* Bell, 1940.

The following standard histories of the political thought of this period are now available in inexpensive editions: J. N. Figgis, *Political Thought from Gerson to Grotius: 1414-1625,** Torchbooks; and J. W. Allen, *A History of Political Thought in the Sixteenth Century,** Barnes and Noble. A readable shorter treatment is contained in G. Sabine, *A History of Political Theory,* Holt, 1950.

E. Salmon, *Imperial Spain,* Holt (Berkshire Studies), 1931. A good brief introduction to the Spain of Charles V and Philip II. Valuable for their greater detail are R. Trevor Davies, *The Golden Age of Spain,* Macmillan, 1954; and B. Chudoba, *Spain and the Empire, 1519-1643,* Univ. of Chicago, 1952.

K. Brandi, *The Emperor Charles V: The Growth and Destiny of a Man and of a World Empire,* Knopf, 1940. The best study of

*Indicates an inexpensive paperbound edition.

the man and his time. Charles is the subject of a noteworthy biographical novel by L. Zara, *Against This Rock,* Creative Age, 1943.

R. B. Merriman, *Suleiman the Magnificent, 1520-1566,* Harvard, 1944. An admirable study of the career of Charles V's formidable foe. H. Lamb, *Suleiman the Magnificent,* Doubleday, 1951, is a good popular account.

P. Geyl, *The Revolt of the Netherlands, 1555-1609,* Williams and Norgate, 1945. Acknowledged to be the best short account of the Dutch rebellion. C. Wedgwood, *William the Silent,* Yale, 1945, is a beautifully written biography of the Dutch leader.

G. Mattingly, *The Armada,* Houghton Mifflin, 1959. A fascinating account of Philip II's most spectacular defeat.

C. Wedgwood, *The Thirty Years' War,* Yale, 1939. An absorbing account of the war and its significance.

S. Bindoff, *Tudor England,** Penguin, is short, well written, and highly recommended. Also excellent, but more narrowly political, is C. Read, *The Tudors,* Holt, 1936. The classic survey of the Stuart period is G. M. Trevelyan, *England Under the Stuarts,* Putnam, 1947. For greater detail, see the following volumes in the *Oxford History of England* series (Clarendon Press): J. Mackie, *The Earlier Tudors, 1485-1558* (1952); J. B. Black, *The Reign of Elizabeth, 1558-1603* (1936); G. Davies, *The Early Stuarts, 1603-1610* (1949).

J. Neale, *Queen Elizabeth I,** Anchor. The most authoritative biography of the Virgin Queen. E. Jenkins, *Elizabeth the Great,** Pocket Books, is a more popular treatment.

M. Ashley, *The Greatness of Oliver Cromwell,* Macmillan, 1958. Views Cromwell not as a seeker after despotic power but as one who sought a workable legal government. See also C. Firth, *Oliver Cromwell and the Rule of the Puritans in England,* Houghton Mifflin, 1934.

F. Palm, *Calvinism and the Religious Wars,* Holt (Berkshire Studies), 1932; and A. J. Grant, *The Huguenots,* Butterworth (Home Univ. Library), 1934. Two short surveys of the religious and political troubles of sixteenth-century France. For greater detail, see J. Neale, *The Age of Catherine de' Medici,* Cape, 1943.

CHAPTER 15

Old Worlds Beyond the Horizon

Introduction. Europe's isolation from Asia and its ignorance of sub-Saharan Africa and the Americas ended in the fifteenth century when a multitude of European explorers, traders, conquerors, and missionaries secured footholds in territories far from their homelands. Reaching out to trade, conquer, and spread the gospel of Christianity, they encountered civilizations and ways of life which dramatically revealed the limitations of their own knowledge and experience. The story of their explorations and discoveries will be taken up in Chapter 16; this chapter is concerned with civilizations in the Far East, the Americas, and Africa prior to the arrival of the Europeans.

The story of Asia during the span of years covered in this chapter is rich in historical significance. In India, under the rule of the Gupta dynasty, the people benefited from enlightened government and Hindu culture entered a period of flourishing growth. In China, the distinguished T'ang emperors created a great empire which extended deep into central Asia. For the most part, the Chinese people enjoyed prosperity and good government, and there was a flowering of scholarship and the arts. It was during the rule of the T'ang and of the next great dynasty—the Sung—that such revolutionary inventions as printing, explosive powder, and the compass were devised.

The period of the Guptas and the T'ang is also notable for the cultural transfusions which took place in Asia. Indian civilization expanded throughout southeast Asia and enriched indigenous societies in what are now Burma, Indochina, the Malay peninsula, and Indonesia. Similarly, there was a continuous flow of Chinese culture eastward to the Korean peninsula and the islands off the Asian mainland, including Japan.

Both India and China suffered periodically from internal conflict and external aggression. Muslim conquest exerted an appreciable influence on Indian society, and repeated invasions by Mongols and other nomadic peoples wrought important political and social changes in China. But while China was able to assimilate foreign elements into its basic culture pattern, India achieved only an incomplete and partially successful synthesis of opposing cultures. Nevertheless, in both countries, basic modes of living evolved during this period—modes of living which have endured to modern times.

The toppling of empires by restless nomads plays no part in the story of Japan. After being occupied by the ancestors of the present inhabitants, the Japanese archipelago was never again invaded successfully until the twentieth century. Influenced greatly by China, the proud and independent Japanese gradually developed a unique culture pattern best symbolized by the *samurai* (the knight) and *Bushido* (the code of the warrior). Here, too, was a development which was to affect world history centuries later.

In describing early times in sub-Saharan Africa and the Americas, we shall be introducing to the stage of world history peoples we have not previously discussed. In a number of instances we shall be taking a giant step backward to the dawn of civilization, for both Africa and the Americas

had inhabitants who, in 1650, were not so advanced as some of their European and Asian brothers had been two thousand years before. Yet both continents had fascinating cultures, some of which were to make important contributions to the civilization we know today.

Today, a truly significant aspect of our world is the reawakening of old centers of civilization in the Americas, Africa, and the Far East. Nationalistic fervor and brave hopes for the future have been built on pride in the past. Even in Communist China, where many Confucian traditions are being superseded by Marxist practices, inspiration is still drawn from past days of glory. Likewise, the people of present-day India and Pakistan seek inspiration from bygone years, particularly from the era of power, grandeur, and wealth enjoyed under the Moguls. In Africa, nationalist leaders of today look back to their native roots; for example, the former British colony known as the Gold Coast chose the name of a long-dead native empire, Ghana, when it was granted independence in 1957. In the New World, Mexican artists take their themes and motifs not from their Spanish colonial heritage but from the pre-Spanish Indian cultures.

Thus, if we are to understand the new dynamic spirit that now moves many of the underdeveloped regions of the world, we must know something of the sources of inspiration upon which their people draw. Such sources are outlined in the history of the non-European world in the centuries covered by this chapter and the next.

INDIA TO THE

MUSLIM INVASION

The Gupta empire. As we recall from Chapter 4, the Kushan dynasty, which had witnessed one of the richest periods in Indian civilization, crumbled around 220 A.D. Subsequent events in northern India followed a pattern that has recurred time and again in the history of the subcontinent: an epoch of distinction followed by an era of political disintegration and comparative cultural darkness.

With the advent of the Gupta empire in the fourth century, northern India came out of its dark era and entered upon another epoch of greatness. In about 320 A.D., the

first ruler of the Gupta dynasty, Chandragupta I,* established himself as monarch of the Ganges valley; and his successor extended the imperial boundaries in all directions. As a result, much of northern India from the Himalayas south to the Narbada River was included within the Gupta empire, thus making it the most extensive and powerful Indian state since the days of Asoka six centuries earlier. Nor had its limits been reached. The grandson of the dynasty's founder, Chandragupta II, extended the empire still farther west until it stretched from

*This monarch was not related to Chandragupta Maurya (p. 98).

The best examples of Gupta painting are found in the caves at Ajanta in the Deccan. Hollowed out of solid rock and adorned with sculpture and murals, these twenty-nine worship halls and dwelling places served as a hermitage for Buddhist monks. Some of the paintings, which depict scenes from the life of Buddha and from Buddhist stories, date from the second century B.C.; the finest, however, were painted during the Gupta period. Presenting a brilliant panorama of contemporary life, the murals portray beggars, princes, peasants, women, children, beasts, and birds. Long forgotten, the caves were discovered early in the nineteenth century by a group of Englishmen. Above is the painting of the temptation of Buddha.

sea to sea. During his reign (*c.* 380-*c.* 413), the Gupta empire reached its zenith. In all its long history India probably came closest to political unity during the reigns of Asoka, Chandragupta II, and Akbar (see p. 337).

Under the Gupta dynasty, India exhibited a state of cultural integration and social harmony such as it has never since achieved. By comparison with the Roman empire, which was nearing its demise, and China, which was enduring a troubled interim period between the two great eras of the Han and the T'ang, India was probably the most civilized region of the world at this time.

Dominance of Hinduism. Although religious tolerance was characteristic of the Gupta period, the Gupta rulers preferred Hinduism to Buddhism, and the Brahman caste enjoyed imperial patronage. A later factor contributing to the virtual disappearance of Buddhism in India was the destruction of many Buddhist monasteries during the Hun invasions which followed the collapse of the Gupta empire in the sixth century. From about 185 B.C. to about 800 A.D., Hinduism not only became dominant in India but also gradually crystallized into its present form.

By recognizing all varieties of religious experience, Hinduism is capable of absorbing different and often even contradictory points of view—a factor that helps account for its tremendous tenacity. Names mean very little; God may be worshiped in many forms and by many names. As an Indian folk song says:

Into the bosom of the one great sea
Flow streams that come from hills on every side.
Their names are various as their springs.
And thus in every land do men bow down
To one great God, though known by many names.[1]

Hinduism stresses conduct and ceremony rather than rigid belief. To be a Hindu it is only necessary to accept the leadership of the Brahmans and one's status in caste, thereby implying acceptance of the belief of reincarnation.

The caste system. By the Gupta period, caste was being tied closely to occupation, the most menial work being the lot of the Sudras and the untouchables. In the light of modern democratic ideology, caste is a reprehensible system and indeed is so regarded by most of India's present leaders. But it has had certain positive features not always understood in the West.

The all-embracing Hindu caste system provides a place for the medley of peoples, such as the invading Indo-Aryans and Huns as well as the indigenous Dravidians, who have for centuries made up the population of the subcontinent. Those who defend the caste system point out that native peoples in western countries have often been exterminated or enslaved by their invaders and that a specific caste can constitute a form of brotherhood in which all members are equal. While the restless drive to succeed and to secure status has resulted in considerable mental frustrations and neuroses in the West, within his caste the Hindu enjoys a sense of security that makes him feel part of a cosmic process in which no mistakes are made.

Achievements in Sanskrit literature. The Gupta period has been called the golden age of Sanskrit, the classical language of India. Court poetry was zealously produced, and the kings were generous patrons of many writers.

The most famous writer was Kalidasa (c. 400-455), who excelled as both a lyric and an epic poet and who has been termed the "Indian Shakespeare" because of his superb dramas. Characterized by a lack of action unfamiliar to western audiences, his plays abound in splendid imagery.

India presented an unusually fertile soil for the creation of fables and folklore. Its religions stressed the unity of all life and the cycle of transmigration. Therefore, it was not difficult for storytellers to reverse the positions of the animal and human kingdoms and to conceive of beasts acting like men and vice versa.

Many Indian stories were eventually carried to Europe by the Muslims. Perhaps the most famous is the story of Sindbad, which found its way into the *Arabian Nights*. Boccaccio, Chaucer, La Fontaine, the Grimm brothers, and Kipling have all been indebted to Indian folklore.

Gupta science and technology. During Gupta times, scholarship and science were of a very high caliber. Students from all over Asia came to India's foremost university, situated at Nalanda. The most famous scientist was the astronomer and mathematician Aryabhata, who lived in the fifth century. In verse he discussed quadratic equations, the value of π, solstices and equinoxes, the spherical shape of the earth, and the earth's rotation. Other Indian astronomers were able to predict eclipses accurately, to calculate the moon's diameter, and to expound on gravitation.

In astronomy and mathematics (except for geometry), the Hindus surpassed the achievements of any other people of antiquity. The Arabic numerals and the decimal system we use today appear to have come originally from India. Even the zero may have come from Indian rather than Arabic sources.

The Hindus were also remarkably advanced in chemistry; the making of soap and cement were discovered by them. They were the finest temperers of steel in the world. Indian industry was also famous for its superior dyes and fine fabrics; the methods of production were taken over by the Arabs,

Crowned by five lofty towers, the Hindu temple of Angkor Wat in Cambodia is one of the world's greatest religious shrines.

and from them by Europeans. The Arabs named one Indian cloth *quittan*—hence the word *cotton*. *Calico* derives from Calicut in India and *cashmere* from the region of that name, Kashmir. *Chintz* and *bandanna*, too, are of Indian origin.

The development of Indian medicine was due to various factors, including an interest in physiology which resulted from Yoga. Some Gupta physicians were surprisingly modern in their techniques; they prepared carefully for an operation and sterilized wounds by fumigation. Caesarean operations, bone setting, and plastic surgery were all attempted. The Indians also made use of many drugs then unknown in Europe.

A period of instability. In the last half of the fifth century, while their kinsmen were ravaging Europe under Attila "the Scourge," Huns invaded the Punjab. They soon gained control of northwestern India but were prevented from advancing into eastern India by a confederacy of Hindu princes.

In the seventh century the various states in the Ganges valley fought constantly with one another until at last a strong man arose. In the short space of six years (606-612), Harsha, rajah of one of the northern kingdoms, mastered much of the territory formerly ruled by the Guptas. With his death in 647, northern India characteristically reverted to confusion and warfare which lasted for centuries.

The warlike descendants of central Asian peoples who had followed the Huns into northwest India in the fifth century had intermarried with the local population. In time these people assumed the privileges of "blue-blooded" Hindus, haughtily called themselves Rajputs (Sons of Kings), and carved out kingdoms for themselves in what became known as Rajputana, a strategic area between the Indus and Ganges valleys. The Rajputs possessed a code of chivalry not unlike that which existed in medieval Europe. Youths were brought up with the privileges and obligations of the warrior caste (the Kshatriya) and taught to respect women, spare the fallen, and demand fair play.

Expansion of Indian culture into southeast Asia. The spread of Indian culture throughout southeast Asia provides an outstanding example of the process of culture diffusion and modification which recurs time and again in world history. Resulting from peaceful trading contact and military conquest, Indian cultural expansion in what has been called "Greater India" began about the second century A.D. and continued until the ninth or tenth century.

The impact of Indian culture was not, of course, equally strong or enduring over all sections. One scholar has divided Greater India into two segments: the western zone (including Ceylon, Burma, central Siam, and the Malay peninsula) received the full force of Indian colonizing zeal and as a result developed a culture which was largely a colonial imitation of the original; the eastern zone (which consisted mainly of Java, Cambodia, and Champa in Indochina) experienced Indianization which was very definite but not so strong as to prevent the indigenous peoples from developing their own distinctive cultures and ways of life.

From the second century A.D. on, kingdoms were established in Greater India by Indian colonists and ruled by monarchs with Indian names. Some of these kingdoms endured more than a thousand years, persisting in fact after India itself had been overwhelmed by foreign invaders. Two monuments to the splendor of these states deserve mention.

Around 1100 one of the greatest religious edifices of history was erected in Cambodia— the temple of Angkor Wat. Long forgotten and swallowed up by the jungle, this vast temple was accidentally discovered by a French naturalist in 1861. Built in long terraces adorned with bas-reliefs of scenes from the Hindu epics and crowned with a high central tower rising over two hundred feet, Angkor Wat is surrounded by a stone enclosure measuring half a mile from north to south and two thirds of a mile from east to west. Nearby lay the capital city, which once boasted a population of almost one million.

In central Java the most imposing Buddhist shrine in the world is located: the immense *stupa* of Barabudur. Erected on the top of a hill in nine successive terraces, Barabudur is covered with images of the Buddha and with sculptures illustrating Buddhist texts. The art of the southeast Asian colonial kingdoms was unmistakably influenced by Indian artistic and architectural techniques, but in Angkor Wat and Barabudur works were created which were larger than anything found in India itself.

THE MUSLIM CONQUEST

OF INDIA

The Muslim invasions. In 711, the same year in which they invaded Spain, Arabs appeared in India. The southern valley of

As the pilgrim ascends the *stupa* at Barabudur in Java, he passes from a terrace inscribed with scenes of suffering and earthly desire to those depicting the life of the Buddha and the miracles of the Bodhisattvas; finally, he reaches the top three terraces, where images of the Buddha denote that the world of action has given way to the world of the spirit.

the Indus was made a province of the vast Umayyad empire, but the Rajput princes soon halted further Arab penetration of India.

In the tenth century, more Muslim invaders swept through the northwest passes. The newcomers were Turks and Afghans who, in 1022, annexed the Punjab. Despite destructive forays by various Muslim sultans, the Rajput and other Hindu kingdoms of the interior remained independent. Not until the closing years of the twelfth century did the Muslims establish a permanent Indian dominion.

The Delhi sultanate. The first important Muslim ruler was a former general who in 1206 established himself as sultan at Delhi, ruling a strong Muslim kingdom covering much of north India. The Delhi sultanate existed until the early years of the sixteenth century, and during the period of its greatest power (1206-1388), it gave northern India political unity. The early Delhi sultans also pushed Muslim authority and religion southward into the Deccan and in the first decades of the fourteenth century reached southern-

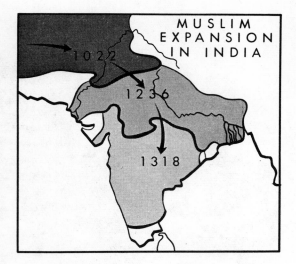

MUSLIM EXPANSION IN INDIA

1022

1236

1318

most India. The Delhi sultanate, however, soon lost control in southern India to a rival sultanate in the Deccan and to other Muslim and Hindu states.

Tamerlane. In 1398 the Punjab was invaded by a Mongol who had already conquered central Asia—Timur the Lame (Tamerlane). Defeating all armies sent against him, Timur looted wealthy Delhi, killing perhaps a hundred thousand prisoners in cold blood. Afterwards, he departed westward for Samarkand, leaving Delhi's few surviving inhabitants to perish of famine and plague.

After Timur's terrible visitation, nearly all semblance of political unity was destroyed in north India, and Muslim sultans maintained independent principalities in defiance of the ineffectual authority at Delhi.

Effects of Muslim rule. The Muslim conquest of India was unusually ruthless. To the Muslims, Hinduism with its many deities, elaborate ritual, powerful priestcraft, and fondness for images was the opposite of all that Islam held sacred. Hindu forces desperately resisted their Muslim conquerors and, after defeat, often suffered wholesale massacre. Many people clung tenaciously to their Hindu faith—the upper classes in particular—but a fairly large number of Hindus were converted to Islam. In some cases it was a choice between Allah or the sword; in others it was a voluntary matter: poor men

sought to avoid the heavier taxes levied on infidels, low-caste Hindus became Muslims to escape their degraded status, and ambitious administrators accepted Islam in order to succeed in the official service of the Muslim rulers.

A new language—Urdu—was developed by the Muslim ruling clique as an aid in administering to its alien subjects. The language was a combination of Persian, Turkish, and Arabic words which utilized the grammatical constructions of the Hindu languages. Urdu and the native Hindi became the languages most commonly used in northern India; they are today the dominant languages of Muslim Pakistan and Hindu India.

The injection of the Islamic way of life into the pattern of Hindu society was to have profound effects upon the history of the Indian subcontinent. Fiercely proud of their own faith, which differed greatly from Hinduism, the Islamic invaders jealously retained their religion and ways of life. After the establishment of the powerful Delhi sultanate in 1206, therefore, the life of India was divided into two streams, the Hindu and the Muslim, which mingled only superficially and never really united. This division was to have momentous consequences in the twentieth century, when India, freed from British rule, split into two nations, India and Pakistan.

THE GLORY OF THE MOGULS

IN INDIA

Baber, founder of the Mogul empire. By 1500 there stood at the gates of India a new Muslim force which was to conquer India and raise it to great heights of glory and civilization. Two years after Columbus sailed westward toward what he hoped would be India, a descendant of Genghis Khan and Tamerlane mounted the throne of a little principality in Turkestan. The youthful ruler was Baber (the Lion), an able general with the strength of a giant, who was to be the founder of the Mogul empire in India.

With an army of no more than twelve thousand men, he set out to achieve his goal.

Defeating the large forces belonging to the sultan of Delhi, who then ruled all Hindustan, Baber made himself sultan in 1526. A year later he subdued the Rajputs, who were trying to restore Hindu supremacy in northern India. The submission of the Rajputs placed the Mogul dynasty securely on the Delhi throne. (The name *Mogul* is a corruption of *Mongol*, a word much dreaded in India because of its association with Tamerlane.)

Akbar, conqueror and administrator. Baber's grandson was Akbar, meaning "Very Great." In 1560 Akbar's empire consisted of a strip of territory some three hundred miles wide, extending from the northwest frontier eastward to Bengal. Sixteen years later, Akbar had extended his rule over all of India north of the Vindhya Mountains, the natural boundary between Hindustan and the Deccan. Continuing southward, Akbar invaded part of the Deccan. When he died in 1605, his dominions exceeded those of any previous Indian monarch, and his heirs were to extend them even farther.

Akbar's greatness should not be measured by his military conquests alone, however. He instituted innovations and reforms in the government and fostered cultural growth and religious toleration. Akbar himself often acted as a judge, for everyone in his domain had the right to appeal personally to him. The practice of *suttee* (burning a wife on her husband's funeral pyre), which had come into use during the Gupta age, was forbidden, and widows were permitted to remarry. Akbar prohibited child marriages and trial by ordeal, although he permitted such tortures as impalement, amputation, and death by elephant dragging. Nevertheless, in contrast to the barbaric punishments permitted in Europe at this time, the Mogul emperor probably had the most enlightened criminal code in the sixteenth century.

Despite the allegiance of the Mogul dynasty to the Muslim faith, Akbar allowed complete freedom of religious belief in his empire. His views were not based simply on political expediency, however; his own temperament was the chief reason for his en-lightened policy. He felt that every faith had something of truth to offer but that all were untrue when they denied each other's sincerity of purpose. Every Thursday, Muslims, Brahmans, and members of smaller sects congregated in his Hall of Worship for religious debates which often lasted far into the night. When the Jesuits arrived in India, Akbar had them stay at his court for periods of several years and treated them with every courtesy.

Akbar created his own religion, promulgating a new faith called *Din Ilahi*, the "Divine Faith," which incorporated what he considered the best features of the other existing religions. By it he hoped to bring all India into common agreement on religious matters. But the older faiths were too strongly entrenched, and Akbar's religious theories died with him.

Monuments of Mogul architecture. At the crest of their power in the reigns of Akbar and his immediate successors, the Moguls displayed one of the most magnificent civilizations in existence at that time. In military strength, an efficiently administered system of government, and the patronage of the arts, they had few equals. And, above all, they were great builders.

The Indo-Islamic style of architecture which the Moguls developed for tombs, mosques, forts, and palaces was a blend of Indian and Persian elements characterized by a lavish use of mosaics, bulbous domes, cupolas, and lofty vaulted gateways. The Moguls were also fond of formal gardens in which pools and fountains, architecture and greenery were united in a harmony of beauty.

The Mogul style began with Akbar, an avid builder. Not far from the modern city of Agra, he erected a new capital, Fatehpur Sikri, which was occupied for only fourteen years before he abandoned it for Lahore and which is still preserved intact.

During the reign of Shah Jahan, grandson of Akbar, Mogul architecture reached its height. Shah Jahan had the red sandstone buildings of Akbar at Delhi demolished and erected a huge capital of marble containing fifty-two palaces. The famous Hall of Private Audience had ceilings of solid silver and gold

Typical of the Indo-Islamic style of architecture is the Taj Mahal, with its arches, decoration, domes, minarets, and formal gardens. This marble mausoleum was built at Agra by Shah Jahan as a final resting place for himself and his favorite wife. To complete the costly structure, 2200 workmen labored for 22 years.

and a Peacock Throne encrusted with costly gems. On the walls can still be seen the inscription by a Muslim poet, "If anywhere on earth there is a Paradise, it is here, it is here, it is here."

Signs of Mogul decline. The blend of Hindu-Islamic cultural elements which was achieved under the Moguls brought civilization in India to the highest point yet achieved there. It is unfortunate for world culture that the union of Muslim and Hindu genius, best achieved under the rule of Akbar, could not have continued to flower. But the tolerance and wisdom of this great and able ruler were lost in the fanaticism of his successors.

Although under Shah Jahan the conquest of the Deccan was completed and the height of Mogul power and splendor was reached,

the forces which would eventually destroy the Mogul empire also became evident during his reign (1628-1658). Rejecting Akbar's views on religious toleration, Shah Jahan assumed the official promotion of the Muslim faith, destroyed Hindu temples wholesale, and forcibly opposed the spread of Christianity. A ruinous civil war among Shah Jahan's four sons, during which he was deposed and imprisoned, marked the ignominious end of his reign. The next hundred years would see the great Mogul empire crumble and perish (see Chapter 26).

CHINA: THE MEN OF T'ANG

An age of division. After the fall of the Han in 220 A.D., China was destined to suffer three and a half centuries of disorder and division before another great dynasty arose and reunited the country. The centuries that followed the rule of the Han were plagued with civil wars, the division of China into numerous short-lived kingdoms, and external wars between the Chinese and invaders from the north, northwest, and west. These attackers were various nomadic peoples, mainly Turks, Huns, and Mongols. China became a melting pot of races, customs, creeds, and tongues. But although Chinese civilization appeared to have collapsed, in reality it was undergoing a process of change and assimilation.

During this period of travail in China, conditions were startlingly similar to those in the distant Roman empire in the West. In both areas rude barbarians were on the offensive, frontiers gave way, and the invaders set up their own kingdoms. Uncertain of the future of the society in which they lived, men in the two empires were disconsolate and sought the assurance of new faiths. In the West, they turned to Christianity; in China, to Buddhism.

Influence of Buddhism in China. Although Buddhism had been introduced into China during Han times, it was from the third century A.D. onward that this religion made the most important gains. Although the upper classes clung to the conservatism and social rigidity of Confucianism, many of the common people turned to Buddhism.

As a result of the spread of Buddhism, Indian-Chinese relations became close and cordial, especially between the third and eighth centuries. Great numbers of Indian Buddhist missionaries traveled to China, and many Chinese scholars studied at Indian Buddhist centers. Buddhist texts flowed into China, Buddhist tales appeared in Chinese folklore, and hundreds of Sanskrit terms were added to the Chinese language. In addition, Chinese medicine and mathematics were improved and enriched by Indian knowledge. "For roughly a thousand years the Chinese mind was largely dominated by Buddhism."[2] Buddhist evangelization also made a great impact upon Chinese art.

Political and economic conditions under the T'ang. In the late sixth century a Chinese revival began when a native leader conquered the nomadic invaders and temporarily reunited the country. Thereafter various local rulers contended for power, but by 623 the family destined to be one of China's most splendid dynasties—the T'ang—had consolidated its control. As the Gupta empire represents the golden age of Hindu culture, the T'ang dynasty represents the golden era of China.

The first great ruler of the T'ang dynasty —T'ai Tsung (627-650)—was one of China's greatest emperors. After defeating the Mongolian Turks in 630, he took advantage of internal dissension in Turkestan to destroy the western Turks and to reëstablish Chinese dominance over the Tarim Basin. Under his son, a successful war was undertaken against Korea, which was made an outlying protectorate of the expanding Chinese empire. At this point China stood at the zenith of its power. The T'ang empire extended from Korea and Manchuria through Tibet and central Asia to the borders of India and Persia (see Reference Map 1).

A statesman as well as a great soldier, T'ai Tsung was energetic in instituting reforms. One of his major reforms was to strengthen the administrative system of the country. In those areas inhabited by non-Chinese, the peoples were allowed to keep their own princes, who were given Chinese names. Over the rest of his empire, the emperor governed by means of a bureaucracy recruited through a civil service program rooted in the Han period. Innovations also extended to land reform, because the government's chief source of revenue came from taxes on grain and other farm products. Laws were passed to curb the growth of large estates and to ensure equitable amounts of land for the peasants.

Economic prosperity resulted from these reforms as well as from the more efficient transportation system which the T'ang developed by extending the canal system. Another factor contributing to the economic boom was a thriving foreign commerce. Caravans arrived frequently from western and central Asia; and great quantities of silks, pottery, porcelain, and other luxury goods were exported to such far-distant points as Jerusalem and Cairo.

T'ang scholarship. The T'ang period was outstanding in scholarly achievements. For example, two encyclopedias were compiled to assist students in passing civil service examinations, and Buddhist scholars translated hundreds of Sanskrit texts into Chinese.

Before the T'ang period, the writing of historical accounts had been the work of individuals. But because the preparation of a standard history for a single epoch was recognized to be beyond the capacity of any one historian, the T'ang government inaugurated the practice of employing a corps of scholars to write accounts of the preceding eras. Eight histories were brought out, and as a result an important precedent was created which outlasted the T'ang themselves; each new dynasty wrote a standard history of its predecessor, at the same time gathering data about its own affairs. More than mere chronicles, the volumes included treatises on such diverse subjects as government administration, law, and economics, anthropological accounts of primitive tribes, and records of scientific phenomena.

Li Po and Tu Fu, masters of T'ang poetry. An eighteenth-century anthology of T'ang poetry included dozens of volumes containing 48,900 poems by 2300 poets. The astonishing literary output of the T'ang era would almost appear to justify the remark: "[At this age,] whoever was a man was a poet."[3]

The two greatest poets of this era, Li Po (701?-762) and Tu Fu (712-770), were good friends who occasionally twitted each other in their works. Li Po once addressed these witty lines to Tu Fu:

Here! is this you on the top of Fan-Ko Mountain,
Wearing a huge hat in the noon-day sun?
How thin, how wretchedly thin, you have grown!
You must have been suffering from poetry again.[4]

The poetry of Li Po held a great appeal for his countrymen; he was truly "a people's

11 Bronze statue of Shiva, the Hindu god of destruction (fourteenth century). In this statue, Shiva appears in the gentle aspect of a divine teacher, although the deer held in his second left hand reminds his followers that he is also the Divine Huntsman and the Lord of the Beasts.

poet." But the majority of Chinese scholars today consider Tu Fu the greater poet.

The invention of printing. In the first century A.D., the Chinese had discovered how to make paper, and in the fifth century they put ink stampings on documents by using seals fashioned from metal and stone. These technical discoveries paved the way for the culminating invention—printing.

Evidence would indicate that the process of block printing—printing from an image cut in a wooden block—was invented in China about 600, although the earliest surviving examples come from Japan and date from 764 to 770. The first extant printed book is the *Diamond Sutra*, which was discovered in a cave in northwestern China. Printed in 868, the *Diamond Sutra* consists of six sheets of text pasted together to form a roll some sixteen feet long; the sheets are each two and a half feet by almost one foot in size and must have been printed from very large blocks.

Because the Chinese language is made up not of an alphabet but of separate characters to represent concepts, the Chinese found block printing satisfactory for their needs. Nevertheless, they were the first to invent movable type.

T'ang decline: the end of an epoch. In the seventh century, the T'ang dynasty still enjoyed a suzerainty that stretched from the Pamir Mountains in the west into Korea in the east, but the next century was to witness extreme changes. In Manchuria, Chinese influence was being weakened by the Khitan, a Mongolian people; Mongolia itself came under the control of the Uigur Turks; Chinese dominance was challenged in the southwest by the Thai and Tibetans and in the far west by the Arabs. In 751, as a result of a disastrous battle fought with the Arabs—"the first clash between the world of Islam and China" —China lost Turkestan.

12 (right) **Japanese statue** (tenth century). The Japanese Buddhist deity Bishamon-ten is clad in full armor with a lance in one hand and a pagoda in the other. The costume of the god shows us how the warlike nobles of Japan appeared in this era.

13 (below) **Detail from a painted silk scroll of the Sung dynasty** (c. 1150). Sung art is best known for its wonderfully atmospheric and sensitively conceived landscapes—panoramic views which extend into misty, far-off distances. The rhythmic movements of the brushwork in such paintings resemble Chinese handwriting.

Meanwhile, trade diminished, tax revenues decreased, corruption held sway in the royal court, the masses suffered from incompetent rule, and the provincial governors became increasingly powerful. The hardships and grievances of the common people mounted, and the ninth century witnessed many popular uprisings. The governors of various provinces declared their independence, and in 907 the T'ang dynasty came to an end.

CIVILIZATION

VERSUS BARBARISM

A period of anarchy. The fall of the T'ang dynasty left China vulnerable to external attack and in another of its eras of internal disorder. Warfare and bloodshed were common; laws were harsh and bureaucrats corrupt; road, canal, and waterworks systems in northern China fell into disrepair; and the coinage was debased to the point where the more primitive system of barter replaced currency as a medium of exchange. In north China, five dynasties followed one another in quick succession, and on the northern frontier, the Khitan Tatars from Mongolia seized provinces north and northeast of China proper. Meanwhile, various secessionist movements had resulted in the establishment of ten independent states in the south.

The Sung dynasty. The period of disorder ended in south China with the founding of the Sung dynasty (960-1279). Unable to dislodge the Khitan Tatars in north China, the Sung emperors adopted the practice of "buying protection" by paying an annual tribute to the Khitan and other border peoples. This drain on the imperial finances, coupled with an unprecedented development of large estates whose owners managed to avoid paying their share of the taxes, resulted in an increasing burden of taxation falling on the lower classes. A succession of budget deficits and widespread inflation completed the gloomy picture and caused the emperor to seek advice from one of China's most fascinating and articulate statesmen, Wang An-shih (1021-1086).

Wang An-shih expressed his social philosophy thus:

The state should take the entire management of commerce, industry, and agriculture into its own hands, with a view to succoring the working classes and preventing them from being ground into the dust by the rich.[5]

To this end, he initiated an agricultural loans measure to relieve the farming peasants of the intolerable burden of interest which callous moneylenders exacted of them in difficult times and to ensure that lack of capital would not hinder the work of agriculture. He promoted irrigation projects and measures for river control so that an adequate water supply would be provided, flooding prevented, and large tracts of land reclaimed and farmed. To destroy speculation and break the strangle hold of the monopolies, he initiated a system of fixed commodity prices; and he appointed boards to regulate wages and plan pensions for the aged and unemployed.

Corruption, conservatism, opposition from the rich, and the impracticality of some of his projects combined to prevent the achievement of Wang An-shih's goals. Yet it is remarkable to see how modern were the theories of this statesman who lived nine hundred years ago.

At about this same time, the Sung emperor, hoping to reconquer the portions of northern China lost to the Khitan, allied himself with the Manchurians, who dwelt beyond the Khitan empire. Early in the twelfth century, the Manchurians proceeded to destroy the common enemy. But the plan backfired on the Sung when their erstwhile allies marched against the Sung capital, packed the emperor off to northern Manchuria, and conquered all of northern China, where they ruled for a century as the Chin dynasty (not related to the earlier Ch'in, p. 109). From 1127 on, for the next one hundred years, China was thus divided into two empires, the Sung and the Chin.

Neo-Confucianism encourages science. Although the Sung era was one of political strife and economic hardship, far-reaching

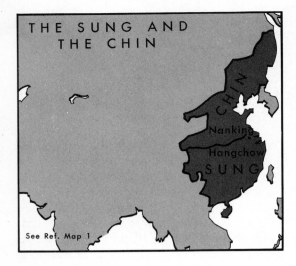

THE SUNG AND THE CHIN

See Ref. Map 1

achievements took place in other fields of human endeavor. Philosophical inquiry flourished and led to a reinterpretation of traditional Chinese thought—a reinterpretation which took the form of Neo-Confucianism. The best elements in Taoism and Buddhism were wedded to Confucian thought, and in this way Confucianism, which had hitherto been largely a code of ethics for everyday living, was provided with a metaphysical basis which taught that the universe was governed by eternal law or reason. As a result, Confucianism was restored to its former place of preëminence in Chinese thought—a place of honor which it was to hold down to the twentieth century.

Neo-Confucianism was accompanied by significant advances in experimental and applied sciences. Many works on chemistry, zoology, and botany were produced, and algebra was developed to the point where it was the most advanced in the world. The earliest relief maps were constructed, and by the end of the eleventh century the magnetic compass was employed as an aid to navigation. In medicine, inoculation against smallpox was introduced.

Another major development in this era was the use of explosive powder—a mixture of sulfur, saltpeter, and other substances—in warfare. The powder was developed from the humble firecracker, which was known to the Chinese in the sixth century A.D. and was originally employed in religious ceremonies. Gunpowder bombs are believed to have been used as early as the year 1000 when the Sung were fighting a losing war against the Khitan Tatars.

Excellence in Sung art. Many critics assert that "at its best Chinese painting is one of the outstanding expressions of man's ability to create beauty."[6] The Chinese painter believed that only days spent in meditation of a vista would reveal to him the essential mood of the scene before him. When he had observed nature as long as he thought necessary, he would then paint the scene without looking at it.

Thus, to a Sung artist, landscape was primarily a state of mind. He was concerned above all with depicting the material attributes of forms in such a way that his painting would suggest the inner significance of the scene he had observed. This effect was achieved by simplifying line and shading, by utilizing the softening effects of mist and water, and by creating a feeling of the vastness of nature (see Color Plate 13). The awe and love felt for nature by Chinese painters was the force behind much of their work.

Genghis Khan and the Mongol onslaught. In the midst of the brilliant intellectual and esthetic activities of the Sung, a new and terrible enemy was building up strength north of the Great Wall. At the end of the twelfth century, the fierce nomadic Mongols were united by Genghis Khan (1162-1227), who obtained undisputed mastery over all Mongolia and was later to conquer half the known world.

Leading his magnificent army, composed entirely of mounted horsemen who used the bow with deadly accuracy, Genghis Khan in 1215 sacked the Chin capital, Peking, and massacred its inhabitants. Following this victory, the attack on the Chin empire slowed down because Genghis Khan sent much of his army westward on a campaign through central Asia and on into Russia (see p. 262). Later the conquest of northern China was renewed, and by the year 1234 the last remnants of the Chin empire were extinguished

Marco Polo, who became one of Kublai Khan's trusted ministers, is shown accompanying the emperor on a hunting expedition.

by the son of Genghis Khan. This khan then embarked on the slow process of conquering the southern empire; after years of heroic resistance, the Sung were completely vanquished by the new Mongol dynasty, known as the Yüan, which then reigned supreme.

For the first time in history China had been entirely subjugated by foreign conquerors, but it did not lose its identity in the vast Mongol empire. On the death of Genghis Khan, portions of the empire had been administered by his sons and grandsons under the general leadership of one son elected as khan of all the Mongols. After 1260 the unity of an empire divided into a suzerain khanate and four vassal khanates, all ruled by descendants of Genghis Khan, was becoming a fiction, and Mongol China was a distinct state (see Reference Map 1). Kublai Khan, who from 1260 to 1294 held the suzerain khanate comprising China and Mongolia, made his capital at Peking, which he rebuilt and beautified.

The reign of Kublai Khan. For knowledge of Kublai Khan's reign, we are indebted to

Marco Polo, the author of probably the world's outstanding travelogue and what has been called the finest European account of Chinese civilization at this time. As a youth, Marco Polo accompanied his father and uncle, two Venetian merchants, eastward to Kublai Khan's court, arriving there around 1275. Received with honor and given posts in the imperial service, the Polos remained seventeen years in China.

Marco Polo reported that Kublai Khan maintained order throughout his dominions, improved the roads, established an efficient postal system, constructed canals, built granaries to store food surpluses against times of scarcity, aided the sick, orphans, and old scholars by means of state care, and revised the calendar.

After Marco Polo returned to Italy, he wrote of his travels. But his fellow Venetians were so incredulous of the figures he used in describing the wealth and power of China, whose civilization was superior to that of thirteenth-century Europe, that they dubbed him "Messer Millions." His descriptions of the size and magnificence of Peking and of Hangchow with its "twelve thousand stone bridges," its palace, which he called "the greatest in the world, ten miles in compass," its "delectable gardens," and its women, who were "mostly dainty and angelical creatures," they considered pure fable. His account of black stones (coal) used for heating purposes and the people's habit of taking frequent baths also seemed fabulous to them, since coal was unknown in medieval Europe and Europeans in the Middle Ages seldom, if ever, took baths.

Wisely recognizing the cultural superiority of the people he had conquered, Kublai Khan ruled accordingly, showing tolerance for all religions and patronizing Chinese culture.

Decline and collapse of Mongol China. Kublai Khan's ambitious foreign wars and domestic works necessitated heavy government spending. Tax rates rose, and many peasants were dispossessed of their land and forced to work for greedy landowners of vast estates. Large issues of paper money depreciated in value, while hard currency diminished. And Kublai Khan's projected invasion of Japan was a disastrous failure (see p. 348).

Kublai Khan was succeeded by seven other Yüan emperors, all of whom proved to be inadequate rulers. Printing of paper money became so reckless that it had to be discontinued entirely; the Mongols allowed their armed strength to lapse until they could not even defend the coast against pirates; and the exclusion of Chinese from the imperial administration continued to fan the resentment of the people against the rule of foreigners. In 1368, less than a century after his death, rebellious forces led by an ex-Buddhist monk entered Peking and established a new dynasty—the Ming.

Pax Tatarica: relinking of East and West. In the first centuries of the Christian era, the West had been linked with India and China by the spice and silk trades. The subsequent centuries of mutual isolation were broken during the T'ang dynasty when its court attracted such diverse groups as Muslims, Christians, and Persians. With the advent of the nomadic Mongols, East and West were again linked together along the ancient silk routes. The resumption of this trade had permanent consequences. By making the trade routes across Asia safe and by tolerating diverse religions, the Mongol dynasty attracted European traders and missionaries to China.

At the height of its power, the Mongol empire stretched from the Danube to the Pacific Ocean (see the map in Chapter 11, p. 262). With the unification, however temporary, of almost all Asia and the restoration of roads, communication was restored to the point where the Polos were far from being the only travelers to cross the great spaces separating East and West.

Cultural interchange between China and the West was also considerable during medieval times. One authority believes that it was the Mongols and other central Asian peoples who conveyed gunpowder to Europe, and we know that the Arabs transmitted westward such invaluable Chinese inventions as the arts of papermaking and printing and the magnetic compass. China itself was enriched by its imports. One of the most important was a new food, sorghum, which was brought to China by way of India in the thirteenth century. By that time the abacus, a familiar sight in Far Eastern shops today, had also made its appearance.

Perhaps most important was the profound psychological effect created in Europe by the accounts of Marco Polo and other travelers who revealed that the Far East not only equaled but exceeded Europe in population, wealth, and luxury. Europeans now realized that the Mediterranean was neither the central nor the most important area of the world. They had discovered a new world, and they began to develop new attitudes to fit this knowledge.

China closes its doors: the Ming Dynasty. The ex-Buddhist monk who captured the imperial throne in 1368 and established the Ming dynasty took the title "Hung Wu." By eradicating all traces of Mongol control, reestablishing such traditions as the scholar rule, rebuilding the country's defenses, and repairing the irrigation systems, he made himself popular. His reign of three decades was marked by prosperity and good government.

The most significant aspect of his successor's reign was the increase of contacts with the outside world. To expand Chinese trade and prestige, large-scale naval expeditions were sent during the fifteenth century to many lands, including India, Ceylon, Java, Sumatra, Arabia, and even Africa. In the next century, however, the costly expeditions ceased; by imperial edict no Chinese ship was permitted to sail beyond the coastal waters. The worst effect of this policy was that China was completely shut off from the era of expansion which was to spread European influence all over the globe.

As we shall see in Chapter 16, the ruthless activities of the Portuguese traders who arrived in China in the sixteenth century hampered the development of cordial East-West trade relations. Unpleasant experiences with outsiders encouraged China to isolate itself, a development which in the long run had stultifying effects on its civilization.

In 1592 the Japanese attempted to conquer China and Korea, a vassal of the Ming empire. Following a successful landing in Korea, the Japanese won victories over both Chinese and Korean armies, but Korean sailors thwarted Japanese hopes by defeating the invading fleets. Cut off from supplies from their island home, the Japanese were forced to withdraw, leaving the Ming dynasty still on the Chinese throne.

This victory did not halt Ming decay, however. More and more, the Chinese became convinced of the superiority of their culture, and their experiences with outsiders intensified their desire to isolate themselves. Chinese citizens were forbidden to travel abroad, and the country was almost completely sealed tight against foreign influences. Early in the seventeenth century, the Ming emperor sent this message to the tsar of Russia:

. . . by my custom, O Tsar, I neither leave my own kingdom nor allow my ambassadors or merchants to do so.[7]

Complacent and static, the empire rapidly lost its strength. By the early part of the

The Forbidden City, the Chinese imperial family's area of palaces and temples at Peking, was constructed in the early years of the Ming dynasty. Above is the beautiful Temple of Heaven, where the emperors worshiped.

seventeenth century, China was in a state of dissolution: the court was a center of corruption, taxation had become exorbitant, and the plight of the peasants was pitiable. Peasant uprisings broke out over the land.

At the same time that rebellions began to break out against the Ming regime, new invaders—the Manchu—were launching assaults in the north. In 1644 the last Ming ruler, learning that his capital was invaded by rebels, hanged himself. A few weeks later the Manchu defeated the rebels and proclaimed their rule; China once again was under an alien emperor.

THE EVOLUTION OF JAPAN

Origins of the Japanese people. The Japanese are a mixed race, predominantly Mongoloid, but where they came from is not definitely known. Beginning in prehistoric times, waves of immigrants came to the Japanese archipelago from the Asian mainland and from Borneo, Java, and the Philippines. Some Japanese exhibit racial similarities with the peoples of southern China and Indochina; others, with the inhabitants of Korea and Manchuria.

JAPAN

HOKKAIDO

HONSHU

Fujiyama Yedo (Tokyo)

Kyoto Kamakura

Nara

SHIKOKU

KYUSHU

See Ref. Map 1

The most primitive people in Japan today are an aboriginal group called the Ainu, who live on the island of Hokkaido; resembling Caucasians, these people do not have the almond-shaped eyes of the Japanese. The Ainu once inhabited all the principal islands of the archipelago but were either driven northward or absorbed by invaders.

Early Japanese society. In ancient times, the mountainous islands of Japan facilitated the growth of numerous small tribal states, each ruled by a hereditary chieftain who claimed descent from a tribal deity. According to Japanese folklore, the first emperor of Japan—Jimmu Tenno—descended from the Sun Goddess and became emperor in 660 B.C. Ever since, the same family has reigned in Japan, and thus the Japanese claim with justice to have the oldest unbroken dynastic line in the world. Historians believe that the ruling family of Japan originated with the most important tribal group—the Yamato clan —which occupied a fertile area on Honshu.

The religion of the Japanese, known as *Shinto*, or "Way of the Gods," included the worship of forces and objects of nature and of ancestral spirits. With the growth of Yamato power, Shintoism centered primarily on the Sun Goddess as the divine ancestress

of the Yamato and, eventually, of all the Japanese people.

Agriculture was the foundation of the economy, with the clan rulers and the nobles controlling the land. Below them were hereditary guilds of farmers and artisans, while at the bottom of the social ladder were the serfs and slaves. With the clans engaged in constant struggles for land or in attempts to drive out the Ainu, warfare was the order of the day. The rigid social structure was well suited for purposes of warfare; the subservient lower orders had to cater to the warrior nobles and their divinely descended chieftain. Thus the warrior in Japan has from earliest times tended to enjoy a social position and political power greater than that of his Chinese counterpart.

During the first few centuries A.D., the Yamato clan extended its power in central Japan. Its chieftain began to regard himself as a kind of emperor, while the chieftains of clans brought under the control of the Yamato attached themselves to the imperial court. Still, however, the Yamato had only nominal suzerainty over some of the more powerful clans.

Contacts with China. During the Han dynasty (202 B.C.-220 A.D.), Chinese rule was extended to part of Korea, and elements of Chinese culture were transmitted from there to Japan. In the succeeding centuries, the influx of Chinese and Korean artisans, potters, weavers, painters, and farmers skilled in agriculture and the breeding of silkworms enriched the "land of the rising sun." In addition, Chinese medicine and military science were introduced and the Chinese calendar adopted. Educated scribes brought to Japan the Chinese language with its character script and also the riches of Chinese literature—its historical works, poetry, philosophy, and science. Transplanted from Korea in the sixth century A.D., Buddhism gradually attracted many powerful supporters. In time, Buddhism and the native Shintoism became the two most important faiths in Japan.

Increased centralization of government. Probably the world's best-governed state in the seventh century was T'ang China. To this source the Japanese rulers turned for guidance in reorganizing their government.

In 646 an important document in Japanese constitutional history was promulgated—the Taikwa Reform. Its most significant feature was the elevation of the ruler to the position of "The Supreme Monarch," the source of all political and religious authority, with all people as his direct subjects and all land under his control. China, too, had an absolute monarchy, but there the government existed in theory for the good of the people, and its overthrow, if necessary, was sanctioned by the Decree of Heaven. By contrast, the emperor in Japan was believed to be a divine personage, so that rebellion against the throne constituted a religious crime.

A centralized bureaucracy replaced the tribal administrative units, and imperial civil officials were put in charge of tax revenues and other government business. Following the Chinese model, the Japanese instituted examinations for the civil service, but with an important difference: only nobles of a certain rank could take the examinations and qualify for high office. Before long, all the important posts in the civil service hierarchy had become hereditary.

The eighth century is known as the Nara period because from 710 to 784 the city of that name was the capital. Nara was also an outstanding Buddhist center, attracting scholars and artists from places as distant as India and central Asia.

The Fujiwara period. In 784 the capital was removed from Nara and ten years later settled upon Kyoto, where it remained until 1868. The initial centuries at Kyoto are sometimes referred to as the Fujiwara period.

The most illustrious family in Japan (next to the emperor's), the Fujiwara had been prominent in the government at Nara and soon rose to dominate the imperial government at Kyoto. Holding vast provincial estates, this family acquired so much power that its chief members became the governors of the provinces. The emperors were reduced to the status of puppet rulers, and their wives were chosen for them from Fujiwara women. Moreover, once a royal son had been born,

the emperor would frequently be forced to abdicate and retire to a Buddhist monastery, leaving the Fujiwara grandfather to rule the country as regent for the new infant emperor. Between the ninth and twelfth centuries, the tradition was thus established that the emperor reigned but did not rule, for his powers were delegated to hereditary officials of an aristocratic civil bureaucracy.

In time the hereditary bureaucracy of the Fujiwara grew inefficient and the government became impoverished. Taxes went up, while at the same time the amount of taxable property steadily decreased, due to the exemption of temple lands and of estates that originally had been given to officials as payment for their services and which then remained hereditary. Eventually most of the land in the kingdom ceased to be a source of revenue for the imperial government.

The bankruptcy of the government finances was accompanied by an increase of disorder and lawlessness in the provinces. To protect their estates, the provincial lords hired bands of professional soldiers, and a feudal society began to develop. In the twelfth century, power and authority had shifted from the civil aristocracy to a military nobility (see Color Plate 12).

The shogunate. After a struggle among the most powerful of the military families, one of the leaders, Yoritomo (1147-1199), obtained supreme control and in 1192 forced the emperor to appoint him as *shogun* (generalissimo). From the city of Kamakura, Yoritomo ruled Japan as military dictator. With the royal family and the civil bureaucracy at Kyoto, Japan had acquired a dual form of government, but in time the civil administration lost almost all control over state affairs. The *shogun* appointed constables and land stewards in every province to prevent rebellion. Although he continued to pay the utmost respect to the emperor and governed at a discreet distance from the imperial court, the *shogun*, not the emperor, was the real ruler in Japan.

The Hojo era and the rise of the *samurai*. Following Yoritomo's death in 1199, control passed into the hands of the house of Hojo.

Completed in 752 the, great bronze Buddha at Nara stands 53 feet high and weighs more than 550 tons.

The Hojo leaders copied the Fujiwara's technique of rule by governing in the name of puppet *shoguns*, who were generally minors and were chosen from either the Fujiwara or the imperial family.

The *samurai*, or warrior nobility, was a large and influential social group at this time. During the Hojo period, official recognition was given to *Bushido*, the unwritten code of chivalry and honor practiced by the *samurai*. The stern code of *Bushido* was instilled into a future *samurai* in childhood with such injunctions as:

What a coward to cry for a little pain! What will you do when your arm is cut off in battle, or when, for the sake of honor, you must rip your stomach open with your sword.[8]

Stressing courage, fortitude, loyalty, composure, and benevolence, the code of *Bushido* approved the custom of ceremonial suicide—*seppuku*—which is generally known to westerners as *hara-kiri*. By means of *seppuku,* a warrior could atone for his crimes, escape disgrace if he had "lost face," or prove his loyalty to his lord.

The *samurai* spirit infused and strengthened the tightly knit system of noble privilege, military government, and national loyalty. As Shintoism became more prominent in Japanese life, its glorification of the nation and the emperor's sacred position was joined with the *samurai* spirit.

"The Great Wind." The outstanding event in the Hojo period was the repulse of an invasion from the mainland by the armies of Mongol China. Hearing reports about the mythical wealth of Japan, Kublai Khan decided to extend his rule to the archipelago. After a brief and inconclusive expedition in 1274, he made extensive plans for a second and greater invasion, gathering some 150,000 men in 3500 ships. The stoical Japanese prepared to meet a danger fully as great as that faced by Elizabethan England when the Spanish Armada sailed against that island kingdom. But nature in the form of a storm came to the aid of the Japanese as it had to the English. A tempest—thenceforth known as *Kamikaze* or "the Great Wind"—dispersed the ships of the invaders.

As the story of "the Great Wind" makes clear, the Japanese archipelago is sufficiently removed from the Asiatic mainland to make invasion extremely difficult. In fact, after the original migrations of the ancestors of the Japanese, no successful invasion occurred until 1945. On the other hand, as we have seen in this chapter, the archipelago is not so far removed from the mainland as to prevent commercial and cultural contacts. As a result, the history of Japan is in large measure the story of the influx of external ideas and influences and their adaption by the Japanese to form a unique culture pattern.

The Ashikaga shogunate. The expense of defending Japan against the Mongols had weakened Hojo power, and a quarrel about the imperial succession broke out between the shogunate and the supporters of the emperor. The imperial party was victorious, and in 1333 Kamakura, the seat of shogunate power, was destroyed. Then the victorious general, Ashikaga Takauji, turned against his emperor, and without deposing him became virtual dictator of the central government. Thus, in 1338, Takauji became the founder of a new shogunate, with headquarters at the imperial city of Kyoto. Known as the Ashikaga shogunate, the rule of this family lasted for some two hundred years.

One of the important leaders during the Ashikaga period was Hideyoshi (d. 1598), a self-made man who seized dictatorial authority and wielded power not as *shogun* but as regent for the emperor. He put down brigandage, encouraged the arts, stimulated trade with China, and built splendid edifices in Kyoto and elsewhere. As we shall see in Chapter 16, he distrusted westerners in general and Christian missionaries in particular; he initiated the policy of persecuting the Jesuit missionaries and their Japanese converts.

During the period of Ashikaga dominance, the Japanese people lived at one of two extremes in society. The majority of the people—the serfs—struggled against squalor and misery; the privileged minority—the nobility—whiled away time observing complex rituals for eating, drinking, dressing, and fighting. The tea ceremony, for example, was designed to instill the devotee with "urbanity, courtesy, purity, and imperturbability."

Establishment of Tokugawa shogunate. After the unsuccessful invasion of Korea (p. 345) and the death of Hideyoshi, a new line of *shoguns* assumed power and in 1603 initiated the Tokugawa period. The old feudal warrior class continued to hold power, and a new military capital was established at Yedo (Tokyo). The administration of the new regime was so effective that the Tokugawa shogunate ruled Japan until 1868.

The aim of this conservative regime was to perpetuate the old traditions, as the Ming did in China. In their attitude toward Christianity, the Tokugawa *shoguns* made plain their desire to keep their island kingdom isolated. Hideyoshi's anti-Christian policy was strengthened, and the western religion was officially outlawed. In 1639 the crushing of Christianity was completed; henceforth,

Europeans were forbidden entrance to Japan and Japanese were forbidden to travel abroad. But the very success of the government's determination to keep Japan free of outside influence set forces at work that were ultimately to frustrate the Tokugawa policies (see Chapter 26).

OLD CIVILIZATIONS

IN THE NEW WORLD

The earliest American immigrants. The questions of how and when the Western Hemisphere was first settled remain uncertain. It is generally agreed that man did not originate in the Americas, for no bones of humans earlier than *Homo sapiens* have been found there. Man was already fully developed when he became the earliest immigrant to seek his fortune in the New World.

Most scholars believe that man arrived in America from Asia by way of Alaska. This northern migration went on for thousands of years with nomadic groups spreading out in various directions on the American continents. Until the 1920's it was thought that the Amerinds (American Indians) came to the Western Hemisphere as recently as three thousand years ago, but in 1926 artifacts located near Folsom, New Mexico, led to the disclosure of a distinctive culture labeled the Folsom culture, which was believed at that time to have existed at about 20,000 B.C. Recent investigations using radiocarbon dating techniques have resulted in the establishment of a more exact chronology. From the evidence now available it is believed that "12,000 to 15,000 years is the limit for the antiquity of man in America."[9]

The cultural level achieved by different groups of Amerinds before the arrival of the Europeans varied. Most of the Indians of North America and of the Amazon region never progressed further than the Neolithic stage, with its dependence upon hunting, primitive agriculture, and village life. By contrast, the Mayas and the Aztecs in Mexico and Central America and the Incas in the Andes of Peru created advanced civilizations on a par with those which arose along the banks of the Nile, in Mesopotamia, or in the valley of the Indus. Perhaps the major reason for the more advanced cultures of the Mayas, Aztecs, and Incas was the efficient domestication of the all-important maize, or Indian corn, known as the "food of the gods." This former wild grass, skillfully bred into a basic crop, was capable of supporting large populations.

The splendid culture of the Mayas. At its height, Mayan civilization was much more advanced than any other on the western continents. At least a thousand years before the birth of Christ, the Mayan Indians migrated into northern Central America. At the time that the Roman empire and the classical civilization of the Mediterranean were collapsing, the Mayas had built wonderful cities in the southern part of their territory. Later, the southern cities of what is called the Mayan classical period sank into decay, and the center of the Mayan civilization shifted northward to the Yucatán peninsula, where new cities were erected.* From about 980 to 1200 a confederacy of independent city-states held sway; and during that period there occurred a splendid Mayan renaissance in architecture and art.

Within the city-states strict social stratification existed: the highest classes were the priests and nobles; below them were the farmers, craftsmen, and merchants; the last two levels included the lowest freemen and the slaves making up the bottom rank. The slaves performed the drudgery and heavy work; their lot was especially arduous, for until the arrival of the Spaniards there were

---

*The prevailing view among students of the Mayan civilization has long been that the Mayas did not build great cities in Yucatán until their cities farther south were passing into decline. However, in 1957 and 1958, American archaeologists investigating a city site—Dzibilchaltun—in Yucatán found through radiocarbon dating that temple beams in this Mayan city were as old as the ruins of the southern cities. The apparent size of Dzibilchaltun also challenges previous interpretations of Mayan cities as comparatively small ceremonial centers for agricultural rather than urban populations.[10]

no beasts of burden or wheeled vehicles in North and Central America.

Most of the populace labored in the fields surrounding the cities. The rich soil laid bare when the jungle was cleared away was made more productive by irrigation. The Mayas raised squash, pumpkins, chili peppers, and many grains and vegetables. But maize—the mainstay of their civilization—was the chief crop, supplying 80 per cent of their food.

Religion permeated all phases of Mayan life. Dominated by a powerful priesthood, the government was a form of theocracy. Education was concerned primarily with religion, and reading and writing were the private domain of the clergy. The numerous gods of the Mayas were divided into three general groups: the deities of the sky, the earth, and the underworld. To maintain an accurate schedule of religious observances, which were intimately linked to their agricultural way of life, the Mayas constructed a calendar which approaches our own in accuracy. These people also built several observatories, which were run by the priests; exactness in astronomical calculations was possible because of the excellent numerical system the Mayas devised.

Of all the Amerinds, the Mayas came the closest to developing an efficient system of writing. It is believed that they used phonetic symbols rather than alphabetic letters or a syllabic system, but no Rosetta Stone has yet been discovered to give us a key to the hieroglyphics which adorned their monuments, buildings, jewelry, pottery, and books.

In architecture and sculpture, the Mayas produced work of the highest quality. In the plaza of a Mayan city was a terraced mound or pyramid, topped by a temple. The highly stylized sculpture which decorated the temple terraces is regarded by some art experts as among the world's best, despite the fact that Mayan sculptors did their intricate carving without the aid of anything better than stone tools. Almost completely religious in inspiration, Mayan art depicted the deities and the animals connected with them—snakes, frogs, jaguars, and hummingbirds. Minor arts such as weaving, jade

Mileage Scale

0   100   400

MEXICO

Toltecs

Aztecs
Tenochtitlan

Peninsula
of
Yucatan

MAYAN
NEW
EMPIRE

Chichen Itzá

MAYAN OLD EMPIRE

Modern Boundaries

sculpture, ceramics, and gold and silver work were also highly developed and showed an extremely sophisticated sense of design which compares favorably with the best of Egyptian art.

Eventually the Mayan cities fell victim to internal strife, in which petty chieftains fought for supremacy. In addition to civil war, inroads were made by Toltec and Aztec invaders, who eventually conquered the Mayas. After the conquest, the Mayan population and culture declined. When the *conquistadores* came upon the scene, the country was in chaos; and the Spaniards found it a simple matter to subdue the Mayan peoples.

The warlike Aztecs. About the first century A.D., a people called the Toltecs swept down from the north and took possession of the Mexican plateau. Coming in contact with the Mayas, the Toltecs absorbed much of their culture and built splendid cities. By the twelfth century the Toltecs and allied peoples created a sizable empire. Soon after, the Aztecs entered Mexico from the northwest; about 1325 they founded a lake settlement called Tenochtitlan on the site of the present Mexico City. Then, allying themselves with other Mexican Indian tribes, they created a confederacy which in the fifteenth century ruled an area extending across Mexico from the Gulf of Mexico to the Pacific Ocean. Like the ancient Assyrians, the Aztecs glorified war, maintained a superb fighting force, and plundered the lands of their neighbors.

However, Aztec power lasted less than a century, for the arrival of Cortés in 1519 brought about its collapse.

Scholars have held different opinions concerning the Aztec form of government. Earlier writers looked upon it as an empire, ruled by an absolute king. Many historians today feel that the Aztec government was essentially a democracy. In Aztec society the main controller of rank was ability. As in our own society, a man could rise to any position if he had the requisite ability. Thus, through personal talent and initiative, a craftsman or farmer might become a priest or a member of the tribal council. Among the soldiers, rank was determined mainly by success in war. Chiefs were elected from powerful families and could be removed; sons or brothers of chieftains succeeded them only if they were capable.

While the Aztecs worshiped a pantheon of gods, their devotion to the sun was particularly important and unusually barbaric. In every city of their domain, great pyramids were built, topped by temples to the sun. There, stone altars were set up, on which thousands of people were sacrificed to Huitzilopochtli, the bloodthirsty god of war and the sun. Victims included men, women, and children, who were stretched out on a sacrificial stone where the priests tore out their hearts as offerings to the god. Aztec military superiority assured a large number of victims for these horrifying sacrifices.

Mileage Scale

0   100   400

Inca Empire Boundary

Modern Boundaries

Like the Romans, the Aztecs borrowed many aspects of their culture from their predecessors or captives. In fact, a fair analogy may be drawn between the Mayas and Aztecs in the New World and the ancient Greeks and Romans. Generally speaking, the Mayas were more artistic and intellectual than the Aztecs and remind us somewhat of the Greeks. The brusque and brutal characteristics of the Aztecs can be likened to the tendencies which the Romans sometimes displayed.

The Incas. About the eleventh century, some people known as Incas (children of the sun) settled in the heartland of the Andes. Some archaeologists believe that they wandered northward from the Lake Titicaca region until they came to the valley of Cuzco. From there they began to extend their dominion over the mountain peoples and the coastal dwellers. From 1438 until the arrival

of the *conquistador* Pizzaro in 1532, a vast Inca empire flourished, extending for about 2700 miles along the western coast of the continent. It has been estimated that the population of the Inca empire numbered ten million at the time of the Spanish conquest in the sixteenth century. Even today the bulk of the peoples on the Peruvian coast and in the highlands are descended from Inca stock.

The Inca form of government was a hereditary absolute monarchy, ruled by a king called the Inca, who exercised the power of life and death over his subjects. Actually, it was a true theocracy, for the people were sun worshipers who believed that the Inca was an offspring of the sun.

The power of the ruler depended largely on an excellent military organization based on compulsory and universal military training. Another source of power was control by the Inca of all the food throughout the empire. If any district produced more than it needed, he had the surplus stored for future use or transferred to a district which through drought or other misfortunes had failed to produce enough food.

The absolute control which the Inca exercised over his subjects made possible the magnificent construction projects in the empire. Immense slabs carved out of the mountain sides were trimmed at the quarry to fit exactly into a specific niche in a temple or fortress wall; no mortar was used by the Incas. Despite their lack of wheeled vehicles, the Incas transported the giant blocks for miles through the mountains. A splendid system of roads and trails radiated from Cuzco to every part of the Inca realm.

Why did the wealthy and powerful Inca and Aztec empires, with their superb military forces, fall so easily before a handful of European conquerors during the sixteenth century? A primary reason is that both the great Indian empires of the Western Hemisphere were weakened by internal strife; the tribes ruled by the Incas and the Aztecs were restive under the control of their conquerors. Thus the Spanish with their firearms—weapons completely unknown to the Indians— were able to hasten a process of political dissolution perhaps already under way.

AFRICA: THE NEGLECTED CONTINENT

Peoples of Africa. Extending from the fringes of the Sahara Desert south to the Cape of Good Hope is sub-Saharan Africa, commonly known as Black Africa. Often the terms *Africa* and *Africans* are used to refer solely to this part of the African continent and its native inhabitants. But before we begin the story of the penetration of sub-Saharan Africa, let us briefly identify the inhabitants of the vast continent as a whole —the peoples of North Africa as well as those living south of the Sahara.

Between the Sahara and the Mediterranean, North Africa has been peopled for at least five thousand years by the Hamitic-speaking white Berbers. In addition, this area has a prominent Semitic element, introduced through the immigration of Semitic-speaking peoples—both Jews and Arabs— during the period of the Roman empire and the later era of Muslim expansion. To the south, much of sub-Saharan Africa seems to have been first inhabited by peoples like the Bushmen—small, dark-skinned members of the Negro race. Although it was once suggested that the Negro came originally from Asia, recent investigations indicate man— possibly the Negro himself—was indigenous to Africa, and it is known that Negro peoples have ranged throughout western Africa for at least five thousand years.

The peoples of Black Africa may be divided into three major groups. Along the west coast are the true Negroes. In the northeast, from the southern limit of Egypt into Kenya, are mixed Hamitic-Negro peoples, whose skin pigment is reddish-brown. Farther south are the Bantu, who represent a mixture of Negro stock with Hamitic and other non-Negro strains. The racial types in Black Africa differ from one another as much as the various stocks of Europe do.

Obstacles to progress. The key to the history of sub-Saharan Africa has always been its geographic isolation. On the north stretches the huge barrier of the Sahara. For centuries this wide expanse of sand prevented easy contacts with the superior civilizations fringing the Mediterranean. The coasts of Africa are also effective barriers to the penetration of the interior. With few bays or inlets to serve as harbors, the coastline is forbidding. Great breakers roll in and dash against the shore, making it hazardous for ships to approach land. Many of the rivers, blocked by rapids and sandbanks, are useless as highways into the interior. The miasmal swamps and dense jungles are other obstacles to exploration.

To these obstacles, nature has added the deadly ravages of disease, which have sapped the vitality of the native peoples in many areas. When Europeans began to penetrate Africa in early modern times, its west coast was commonly referred to as "the White Man's Grave." In many regions the blood-sucking tsetse fly has made the deadly sleeping sickness endemic.

But the picture of geography is not completely negative. In sub-Saharan Africa there are also cool highlands, broad grassy plains, fertile valleys, mineral resources such as gold, and abundant animal resources—ivory, ostrich feathers, hides—which were available to the early inhabitants of Africa as well as to modern-day adventurers. And the coast of western Africa has been successfully farmed since early times, supporting a comparatively dense population. The largest rivers of western Africa have been useful for communication—the Niger for most of its 2600 miles, the Senegal for 560 miles, and the Gambia for 350 miles.

Even so, much of sub-Saharan Africa was, for all practical purposes, isolated, and it was largely because of this isolation that the natives did not progress at the rate that peoples in some other areas of the world did.

Primitive cultures of Black Africa. The name "Dark Continent" aptly applies to Africa in the centuries before the Europeans came on the scene, for its history in that period remains largely a mystery. Scholars are convinced that the social and political structure of the African people changed little in the thousands of years before the arrival of European explorers and traders in the fifteenth and sixteenth centuries. Thereafter, contact with the western colonial powers led to changes in many features of African life. Nevertheless, anthropologists point out that certain aspects of African tribal life today offer us a good picture of how the Africans lived in early times. In all the paraphernalia of social organization—law, government, education, and codes of conduct—African society was as complex as our own. Rules regarding the role of parents, the treatment of children, the worship of the gods, the education of the younger generation, and the conventions of eating, recreation, and the like were carefully worked out, and effective methods were at hand to compel the individual to conform.

The basic political unit was the tribe, made up usually of a number of clans. As head of his tribe, the chief usually ruled autocratically but within the confines of accepted custom. Except for an advisory council of elders, no elements of representative government existed. Agriculture and cattle raising formed the basis of the primitive economy. There was no rotation of crops or use of fertilizers, and farming followed the wasteful practice of shifting cultivation. Large sections of the bush were burned over; the cleared area was farmed until the soil's fertility gave out; and then cultivation was shifted to another area. Various crafts existed, especially in the working of metals, permitting some economic specialization.

The prevailing religion of sub-Saharan Africa was ancestor worship, but various gods were also worshiped. Magic and witchcraft were an indispensable part of religion. It was believed that a witch could throw a spell over a victim which would bring about his immediate death or a calamity such as the loss of his crops or cattle. If the victim learned that he had been bewitched, he would immediately visit a witch doctor for

an antidote against the evil forces in league with the witch. Witchcraft undoubtedly has been one of the most evil aspects of African culture, handicapping progress and holding its victims in nameless terror. Even today, in many parts of Africa, cases are reported in which a native believes himself to be bewitched, resigns himself to his fate, and dies.

Africa's contacts with the ancient world. The vast coastline of sub-Saharan Africa was touched only here and there by sailors and traders in ancient times, even though such contacts began very early and sometimes involved elaborate expeditions. The ancient Egyptians sailed far up the Nile and sent their mariners down the east coast. The most famous expedition was sent by Queen Hatshepsut in about 1470 B.C. to the legendary land of Punt, which probably was located in what is now Somaliland. The Nile region just south of Egypt (called Nubia in ancient times and now known as the political state of Sudan) was Egyptian in civilization from about 1500 B.C. until the early centuries A.D. Thus Egyptian basic skills such as metalworking may have been transmitted into Black Africa.

Of all the ancient peoples who approached sub-Saharan Africa, the most successful were the Phoenicians. According to the Bible, King Solomon in the tenth century B.C. hired some of these intrepid sailors to bring him ivory, silver, and gold from the land of Ophir —represented today perhaps by the modern seaport of Sofala in Mozambique. About 600 B.C. the Phoenician seafaring talents were again tapped, this time by the Egyptian pharaoh Necho, who organized an expedition to sail around the entire continent of Africa. According to Herodotus, the Phoenicians set off down the east coast and accomplished this almost unbelievable feat of circumnavigation.

Each year, when autumn came, they landed, tilled and cultivated the fields and sailed away again after the harvest had been gathered. In the third year they returned home.[11]

Of more certain authenticity is the voyage in 520 B.C. of a fleet of sixty ships sent by the Phoenician colony at Carthage to explore northwestern Africa and to establish trading posts there. The expedition sailed as far south as the modern British colony of Sierra Leone, some three thousand miles from its home port in the Mediterranean.

After 100 A.D., during the era of Roman supremacy in North Africa, several crossings of the desert barrier were made, and the great classical geographer Ptolemy, in the second century A.D., had apparently learned of the junction of the Blue and the White Nile and their source in great inland lakes. But after the decline of Rome, what little knowledge had been gained about the great continent was forgotten or lay hidden in unread manuscripts.

At the time of the Roman empire, the kingdom of Axum in the portion of northeastern Africa now known as Ethiopia became prominent. This area had been settled about a thousand years before by Semitic-speaking immigrants from Arabia, who merged with the Hamitic residents. According to Ethiopian tradition, in about 1000 B.C. the Queen of Sheba visited King Solomon in Palestine and to them was born a son, Menelik. It is from Menelik that all Ethiopian kings trace their lineage. During the centuries when the eastern portion of the Roman empire was becoming Byzantine, Christianity spread down into most of northeastern Africa and in the fourth century A.D. became the official religion in Axum.

We have only fragmentary knowledge of Axum, which flourished from the first to the seventh centuries A.D. Axum was ruled by powerful kings who led victorious armies as far as the valley of the Nile, but the invasion of the Muslims in the eighth century terminated the expansion of Axum and left the Ethiopians isolated in their highlands. Thus the penetration of Christianity was halted by Islam, and Africa was cut off from the rest of Christendom. Not until shortly after 1500, when the Portuguese arrived in Ethiopia, was contact between this land and Europe established.

Afro-Muslim empires in the Sudan. After the amazingly rapid spread of the Arabs across North Africa in the eighth century, Islamic culture and peoples penetrated south into the interior of the continent. Muslim Berber tribes, together with Arabs, began to filter across the Sahara into the geographical Sudan—a huge grassy plain stretching from the Atlantic Ocean to the Nile valley (see map, p. 356). The Sudan became an area of racial mixture, where Negroid peoples came under the influence of Muslim culture.

In the fourth century A.D., before the Islamic period of supremacy, whites from North Africa had assumed control of the Negro population in a part of the western Sudan and founded the state of Ghana, which lasted until 1240. Gradually the Negroes absorbed their conquerors, and for the last half of its history, Ghana had a black dynasty. In its prime, the Ghana empire ruled the entire area of the upper Niger and upper Senegal rivers.

Many North African Muslims settled in the capital city of Ghana, the first of the great commercial centers of the Sudan. Gold and slaves from the south were traded for salt from the Sahara and goods from Morocco. The gold supply of medieval Europe came largely from Ghana, via Morocco.

In the tenth century, the Berbers living along the border of the Sudan and the Sahara began to migrate. Some went north to rule Morocco and Islamic Spain, while others turned south and crippled the Ghana state, which survived for a time but ceased to be an empire after the capital city was plundered in 1087. After the tenth or eleventh century, Ghana was at least partly Muslim.

The most famous of the Afro-Muslim kingdoms—the Mali empire—stretched a distance of fifteen hundred miles in the western Sudan. Ruled by Mandingos, a Negro people whose chiefs had been converted to Islam in the eleventh century, the Mali empire attained greatness in the thirteenth century. Its chief commercial city, Timbuktu, succeeded Ghana as the main point of convergence for the north-south caravan routes and became a great metropolis; under various rulers it survived as a major commercial center until the sixteenth century.

Under Mandingo rule, Timbuktu boasted a great mosque and a nearby university for

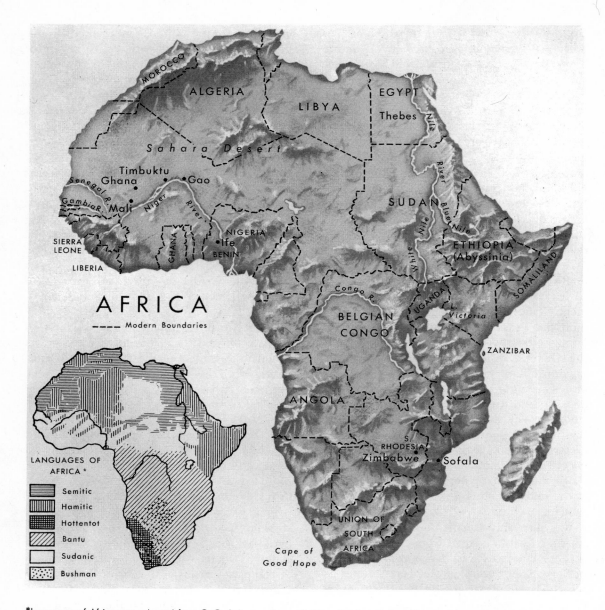

AFRICA
----- Modern Boundaries

LANGUAGES OF AFRICA *

- Semitic
- Hamitic
- Hottentot
- Bantu
- Sudanic
- Bushman

*Languages of Africa map adapted from C. G. Seligman, *Races of Africa* (London: Oxford University Press, 1957), p. 7.

Koranic studies. Trading caravans with as many as twelve thousand camels visited the city, and its workshops turned out huge quantities of iron, tin, and leather goods. Mandingo emperors on pilgrimages to Mecca astonished the Egyptians and Arabs with their wealth and luxury.

Another great empire of the Sudan—Songhai—reached its height in the fifteenth and sixteenth centuries. Its capital was Gao, a commercial center on the Niger. Like the

Mali empire, the Songhai comprised a large share of West Africa across the Sudan. At the end of the sixteenth century, the Songhai empire was destroyed by a Moroccan army made up largely of Spanish and Portuguese mercenaries. The invaders were victorious principally because of their superior weapons; their firearms were new to the Sudan.

Impact of Islam in East Africa. The impact of Islam was also strongly felt along the East African coast. From the seventh century

A.D., Arab traders came in growing numbers for gold, ivory, and slaves. Permanent settlements sprang up, and the entire east coast was dotted with small Muslim states. As slaving and trading expeditions pushed into the interior, many of the Africans who came into contact with Islamic culture were converted to its faith. Another by-product of this cultural impact was the development of a new language, strongly influenced by Arabic. This is Swahili, which still serves as the commercial language of the area.

The various Arab settlements along the eastern coast made up the Zenj empire, and the entire coastal strip was called Zenjibar, meaning "black coast." The empire was to last for nearly five hundred years, until the arrival of the Portuguese in 1497. Made wealthy by trade, the Zenj empire attracted merchants from as far east as Malaya and China; these traders left Chinese coins and pottery from the Sung and Ming periods as evidence of their presence in Africa. Today many reminders of the intimate contact with Arabia remain in East Africa. Ruins of imposing buildings, mainly mosques, can still be seen half-overgrown in the coastal jungle. Arab dhows still come to trade across the Indian Ocean, and the island of Zanzibar (independent from Britain in 1964) was ruled until recently by a Muslim Arab sultan.

The slave trade. For centuries the potential of the native Africans was stunted by the ravages of slaving expeditions. Practiced in Africa since ancient times, the slave trade had fallen into Arab hands at the time of the Muslim conquests, and thousands of slaves had been exported across the Indian Ocean. As we shall see in the next chapter, in the sixteenth century this trade became one of the most lucrative enterprises of the Europeans in Africa. We have no precise knowledge of the total number of human captives brought to the Americas, but the figure may be as high as forty million. Furthermore, it is said that for every slave sold to a colonial plantation, another one had lost his life in the cruel roundup in Africa or on the crowded slave ships. What progress native Africa might have made was cut short by the cata-strophic effects of the slave trade. In many areas African life was disrupted and large sections were depopulated by this inhuman business.

Africa joins the mainstream of civilization. Until the middle of the seventeenth century, only the cultures of the Sudan had had much contact with the activities around the Mediterranean; the native cultures of Black Africa had been almost completely isolated from the outside world. As a result, in the vista of world history up to the middle of the seventeenth century, Africa had been largely outside the mainstream of events and had contributed little to the sum total of the world's civilization. But in the last three hundred years, Africa has made numerous contributions, particularly in the arts.

African sculpture, which comes chiefly from western Africa, was not created as a mirror to portray the beauties of nature but rather as a religious or magical instrument designed to achieve results in the spirit world. For example, fetish figures are used today in curing illnesses and as agents in the spirit world. While African art has been described as primitive, in reality it follows complex traditions. The sculpture is usually carved of wood, but other materials such as ivory, terra cotta, and bronze have also been used. Some bronze work has been compared to the best produced by Renaissance artists. Since the beginning of the twentieth century, African sculpture has exerted a powerful influence on artists in Europe and the Americas, providing them with new forms and suggesting new esthetic principles.

Even though African music itself has never won international acclaim, it can properly claim much credit for an art form which has—American jazz. African natives sold into bondage in the New World brought with them their love for music, and the descendants of those slaves in the southern United States created jazz. Similarly, the popular music of Latin America reveals a debt to the rhythmic figures of African music. Today, the cultural exchange has been reversed: American jazz and Afro-Cuban music are extremely popular in Africa.

This magnificent bronze head, found at the site of the ancient city-state of Ife in Nigeria, has been pronounced the finest surviving example of African art; some art experts consider it equal to the best sculpture of the Greeks and Romans. Some authorities maintain that Ife sculpture was of native origin, but the prevailing opinion regards it as the work of imported artists or of Africans who had come in contact with foreign influences.

SUMMARY

At the very time when Europe was beset by the tribulations following the collapse of the Graeco-Roman world, Asia was being enriched by what were probably its most splendid centuries of cultural development. After progressing for several thousand years, Asian cultures seemed to reach their height in the period corresponding to Europe's Middle Ages and then began to decline. With the rule of the Guptas in India, the zenith of Hindu culture was reached. Artists produced paintings of contemporary life and the Gupta poet Kalidasa wrote dramas which have been compared favorably with those of Shake-

speare. In mathematics, the so-called Arabic numerals, the decimal system, and many of the basic elements of algebra came into use; and there were important discoveries in chemistry and medicine. So powerful was Gupta civilization that it succeeded in creating a Greater India throughout south and southeast Asia, thereby raising the cultural level of a large segment of mankind.

The Gupta age was followed in India by a period of internal dissolution and external invasion, culminating in the subjugation of the country by the forces of an uncompromisingly antagonistic religious culture, Islam. Yet the alien Moguls gave this land its most brilliant period, surpassing the glories of the Guptas. The Mogul ruler Akbar is regarded as one of the greatest statesmen of all time. All facets of culture flourished under Mogul rule, but the noblest legacy was in architecture; the Taj Mahal is ample evidence of the genius of Mogul builders. In our own century, the consequences of Islam's impact were to split the Indian subcontinent into two separate states: India and Pakistan. But despite the political anarchy which has gripped India intermittently from earliest to contemporary times, the culture pattern of the subcontinent has been singularly unified and enduring.

The outstanding achievements of various dynasties in China have been discussed in this chapter. The T'ang period was marked by the rich flowering of poetry and art and the invention of printing. The Sung, despite political chaos and Tatar invasion, contributed to the resurgence of Confucian philosophy, saw the arts reach new heights, and witnessed the use of explosive powder for warfare and the invention of the magnetic compass. The Yüan, or Mongol, dynasty established a *Pax Tatarica* throughout the East which contributed to the relinking of Europe and the Orient and an increasing cultural interchange. The accounts of the Far East by Marco Polo and other European travelers astounded medieval Europe and helped to break down the provincialism of the West. In contrast to India, the alien Mongol rulers were ousted in China, and a native dynasty was established. A bright period of prosperity and cultural activity followed. But the Ming suffered from a serious psychological handicap. The essence of their rule was restoration of the old and abhorrence of the strange and new. China became self-satisfied and completely impervious to new ideas. The inevitable result was decline and, ironically, conquest by another foreign dynasty, the Manchu.

A review of the history of the Chinese over a period of some fourteen centuries points up the cultural continuum which makes Chinese civilization unique. Just as the Chinese can assimilate other races without losing their own physical characteristics, so in their culture they have assimilated foreign customs without seeming to dilute their own. A great question today is whether in the long run the Marxist ideology of Red China will prove strong enough to extirpate Confucianism and the traditional ways of life based on this ancient philosophy.

The early history of the Japanese exhibits the strong influence of many aspects of Chinese culture. But, as we have seen, the Japanese gradually began to modify their cultural borrowings so that in later centuries they could make their own unique contributions to Far Eastern culture. In particular, Japanese government after the eighth century deviated from Chinese tradition in two significant respects: uncompromising absolutism and militarism. Absolute allegiance to the imperial ruler was never modified, as in China, by the development of a theory (the Decree of Heaven) providing for rebellion against an unsatisfactory ruler. A national sense of duty and unquestioning obedience to the emperor, coupled with the fanatical code of the warrior class, were powerful factors in the development of strong national government and a great pride in native customs and ideals. Under the Tokugawa *shoguns*, the Japanese were even more determined to cut themselves off from the outside world. Like the Ming they had no use for foreign ways. But new forces, mainly economic, were at work, and these would end isolation and abolish forever the institution of the shogunate.

We have seen also that in Mexico and Central and South America a number of brilliant civilizations emerged—those of the Aztecs, Mayas, and Incas, each with its own unique characteristics. The Aztecs have been compared to the Romans: they were practical, martial people, skillful at conquest and at governing subject peoples. By contrast, the Mayas have been likened to the Greeks: they were great builders and artists, and they were also scholars and scientists who invented a remarkable calendar, studied astronomy, and pursued mathematics. The Incas had a different reputation. Of all the Amerinds, they should be remembered for developing one of the first really totalitarian states in history.

During the many centuries covered thus far by this volume, little has been seen of Africa south of the Sahara. This vast region lay on the periphery of great world movements. Largely because of the handicap of isolation, no purely African civilization arose. The important kingdoms of the Sudan in medieval times were more Muslim Arab and Berber than Negro.

In following the detailed accounts of events in Europe and in European colonies, then, we must not lose sight of these peoples of the other continents, who far outnumbered Europeans and who, in the centuries ahead, were destined to move ever closer to the center of the stage of world history.

SUGGESTIONS FOR READING

For surveys of Indian, Chinese, and Japanese history and cultural development which contain sections pertinent to Chapter 15 text material, see List of Readings, p. 802. Special studies of more limited scope are included here.

*Indicates an inexpensive paperbound edition.

P. Sengupta, *Everyday Life in Ancient India*, Oxford, 1955. A short, popular account based on evidence contained in India's classical literature.

A. B. Keith, *A History of Sanskrit Literature*, Oxford (Clarendon Press), 1928. The most authoritative and comprehensive work in English on classical Indian literature. *Classical Sanskrit Literature*, Oxford, 1923, by the same author, is a shorter survey.

H. Wales, *The Making of Greater India*, B. Quaritch, 1951. A stimulating discussion of the expansion of Indian culture into southeast Asia from the second to the tenth centuries A.D. For well-illustrated accounts of the influence of India's art on neighboring countries, see B. Rowland, *The Art and Architecture of India*, Penguin, 1953; and V. A. Smith, *A History of Fine Art in India and Ceylon*, Oxford (Clarendon Press), 1930.

S. Lane-Poole, *Mediaeval India Under Mohammedan Rule, 712-1764*, Putnam, 1916. An old but very readable political survey.

H. Lamb, *Tamerlane the Earth Shaker*, McBride, 1928. An absorbing popular biography. L. Binyon, *Akbar*, Davies, 1932, is a brief sketch by a literary historian. For a full account see V. A. Smith, *Akbar the Great Mogul, 1542-1605*, Oxford (Clarendon Press), 1917.

Three excellent biographical studies of leading personalities under the T'ang are C. P. Fitzgerald, *Son of Heaven: A Biography of Li Shih-min, Founder of the T'ang Dynasty*, Cambridge Univ., 1933; by the same author, *The Empress Wu*, Cresset, 1956; and A. Waley, *The Real Tripitaka, and Other Pieces*, Macmillan, 1952.

C. P. Fitzgerald, *China: A Short Cultural History*, Praeger, 1954. Contains an excellent brief account of the brilliant intellectual and artistic activities of the T'ang and Sung periods.

The lives and works of the two greatest T'ang poets are treated authoritatively in A. Waley, *The Poetry and Career of Li Po: 701-762 A.D.*, Macmillan, 1950; and W. Hung, *Tu Fu, China's Greatest Poet*, 2 vols., Harvard, 1952.

T. F. Carter, *The Invention of Printing in China and Its Spread Westward*, Ronald, 1955. The best detailed study on the subject.

E. Kracke, *Civil Service in Early Sung China, 960-1067*, Harvard, 1953. Highly useful for an understanding of the Chinese political system.

H. D. Martin, *The Rise of Genghis Khan and His Conquest of North China*, Johns Hopkins, 1950. Relates the life-and-death struggle of the Chinese with their less civilized neighbors to the north and west, the Mongols. Two vivid popular accounts by H. Lamb are *Genghis Khan: Emperor of All Men*,* Bantam; and *The March of the Barbarians*, Doubleday, 1940, which deals with Mongol expansion after the death of Genghis Khan.

Marco Polo, *The Travels of Marco Polo** (trans. by R. E. Latham), Penguin; and L. Olschki, *Marco Polo's Precursors*, John Hopkins,

1943. Delightful accounts of thirteenth- and fourteenth-century travelers across Asia. The relinking of East and West under the *Pax Tatarica* is treated in G. F. Hudson, *Europe and China: A Survey of Their Relations from the Earliest Times to 1800*,* Beacon.

J. Collier, *Indians of the Americas*,* Mentor. A former U.S. Commissioner of Indian Affairs discusses sympathetically the past and present of the American Indians.

R. Benedict, *Patterns of Culture*,* Mentor. A pioneer study in the field of social anthropology. Includes case studies of the Pueblos of New Mexico and the Indians of the Pacific Northwest.

S. G. Morley, *The Ancient Maya*, Stanford, 1956. Written by a distinguished archaeologist, this is the best general survey of the twelve centuries of Mayan life.

A. Caso, *The Aztecs: People of the Sun*, Univ. of Okla., 1958. A lavishly illustrated work in which the religion and art of the Aztecs are discussed. Recommended for brief, lucid surveys of Aztec civilization are V. W. von Hagen, *The Aztec: Man and Tribe*,* Mentor; and G. C. Vaillant, *The Aztecs of Mexico*,* Penguin.

J. A. Mason, *The Ancient Civilizations of Peru*,* Penguin. An anthropological history of the culture and peoples of pre-Columbian Peru. A popular and vivid account of Inca life by an American explorer is V. W. von Hagen, *Realm of the Incas*,* Mentor. For a scholarly account of the Inca civilization at its height, including the story of the Spanish invasions, see B. Flornoy, *The World of the Inca*,* Anchor.

C. G. Seligman, *Races of Africa* (ed. by I. Schapera et al.), Oxford, 1957. A brief, authoritative account. The best treatment of the African geographical background is W. Fitzgerald, *Africa: A Social, Economic and Political Geography of Its Major Regions* (rev. by W. C. Brice), Methuen, 1955.

Two brief, useful studies are Z. A. Marsh and G. Kingsnorth, *An Introduction to the History of East Africa*, Cambridge Univ., 1957; and J. D. Fage, *An Introduction to the History of West Africa*, Cambridge Univ., 1957.

W. E. B. DuBois, *The World and Africa*, Viking, 1947. An over-idealized interpretation of Africa's role in world history.

E. Elisofon and W. Fagg, *The Sculpture of Africa*, Praeger, 1958. Some 300 photos, with ample text, of the masterpieces of African art. See also P. Wingert, *The Sculpture of Negro Africa*, Columbia Univ., 1950. Also excellent is J. E. S. Thompson, *The Rise and Fall of Maya Civilization*, Univ. of Okla., 1956.

CHAPTER 16

The Force of European Expansion

EXPLORATION AND COLONIZATION (1450-1650);
THE COMMERCIAL REVOLUTION (1450-1750)

Introduction. One of the most potent forces molding modern world history was the thrust of European political power, commerce, and culture over the globe. Before 1500, Europeans inhabited an area of four million square miles and existed largely on their own resources, supplemented by a slender trade with Africa and Asia. But within the next 150 years the picture was dramatically altered through the discoveries of new continents and trade routes. The riches of the entire world were funneled into Europe's economy, and the horizons of Europe's people were immensely widened—socially and intellectually as well as geographically.

Who wrought this miracle? First, there were the sea captains—Da Gama, who sailed around the southernmost cape of Africa and blazed the maritime trail to India; Columbus, who gave to Europe a New World; and Magellan, whose expedition ventured ever westward until its weary survivors had sailed completely around the world and dropped anchor once more in the Spanish port from which they had originally set sail. Close on the heels of such captains came the *conquistadores*—the "conquerors"—resourceful and ruthless soldiers like Cortés and Pizarro, who laid the foundations for a vast European empire by overwhelming flourishing native cultures in the New World.

Then came the task of exploiting what had been found and won. The European powers took advantage of the claims of their discoverers and explorers in one of two basic ways—through trade or by colonization. In Africa and Asia the emphasis was on trade; Europeans carried on their business from forts, acting as foreign merchants rather than as settlers. While in Africa their dealings were mostly with primitive tribesmen, in the Far East they faced venerable civilizations and urban cultures. There, they were the barbarians, and when their activities proved offensive by native standards, reprisals could be swift and severe. Because of the bad behavior of the Portuguese, for example, all Europeans found their trade with China and Japan sharply restricted.

The story of European expansion in the New World, on the other hand, is largely that of colonization, of the transplanting of European civilization to a new and exotic environment. Politically, the territories in the Americas were treated as extensions of the mother countries. The Spanish colonies, for example, were ruled directly by the king of Spain; the colonial economy was geared to supplement that of the homeland; and the Spanish priests set out to bring the Indians into the spiritual fold with their Spanish masters. Similarly, the English and French who established settlements in North America brought with them the economic, political, and social institutions they had known at home.

For the native peoples of the New World the arrival of the Europeans was, of course, cataclysmic. And the impact of the New World on the Old, while obviously quite different, was no less significant. As new stores of wealth were tapped by the immensely lucrative transatlantic trade, Europe's economic center of gravity shifted from the Mediterranean to the Atlantic seaboard; and the rapid influx of gold and silver made possible an unprecedented expansion of the economy. Nor was the revolution confined to economics: new medicines, foods, and beverages became available to Europeans, and even styles of dress were altered. Thus a handful of adventurers, ranging beyond the horizon in quest of El Dorado, the legendary city of gold which symbolized their hopes and dreams, set in motion a train of events which was to bring significant changes to life in Europe and which was ultimately to influence the very history of civilization.

CAPTAINS AND

CONQUISTADORES

Ptolemy, the classical geographer. Since the geographical knowledge available in the second century A.D. was limited, Ptolemy was forced to rely upon sailors' legends and the tales of travelers when he drew a world map (see p. 87). It should come as no surprise that this map was inaccurate in many respects. Yet his mistakes encouraged later generations of explorers to sail boldly across the uncharted oceans. Ptolemy's poor calculations resulted in his exaggeration of the width of the known continents so that the ocean between western Europe and eastern Asia looked much smaller than it really is. Furthermore, his circumference of the world was five thousand miles short. Because men of the fifteenth century still accepted Ptolemy as the chief geographical authority, Columbus was encouraged to sail west from Spain in search of the Asiatic coast.

Medieval maps, adventurers, and traders. During the Middle Ages, devout cartographers made geography a handmaiden of theology. In *Christian Topography*, written about 547, the earth was made flat, with paradise in the east, the Pillars of Hercules in the west, and Jerusalem in the center. Such early medieval maps were curiosities rather than documents of fact. However, by the end of the Middle Ages, ignorance of geography had abated somewhat. Books on astronomy taught that the earth was a sphere; and by the middle of the fourteenth century a number of European travelers were venturing beyond their own continent.

Prime examples of the medieval adventurers were the Norsemen, who crossed the Atlantic as early as the tenth century. In about 982, Eric the Red, son of a Norwegian noble, was banished from the Norse settlements in Iceland and sailed west to discover Greenland. Four years later, two towns were established, and a colony existed in Greenland until the fifteenth century. In 1002 Leif, the son of Eric the Red, voyaged to America. He probably arrived first at Labrador and then journeyed south, where he saw a land of trees, wild grain, and grapevines, a region either in Nova Scotia or New England. Leif called the country *Vinland* (Wineland).

Other voyages were made by the Norse, who sailed arctic waters in open boats with neither chart nor compass five hundred years before Columbus dared the crossing in warmer waters. But monumental as these voyages were, their implications were lost on contemporary Europeans, and they added little or nothing to European knowledge of geography.

In the thirteenth and fourteenth centuries, a number of Europeans, many of them Christian missionaries, journeyed overland to the Far East. The most famous of the travelers was Marco Polo. But the exploits of the fourteenth century had little permanent effect because of political changes in Asia in the last decades of that century. The Mongol dynasty in China, which had been friendly to European missionaries and merchants, was overthrown, and the succeeding Ming rulers proved anti-Christian. Meanwhile, the Turks with their fanatic conversion to Islam had overrun western Asia. These two developments put an end to further European penetration into the Orient. Although trade continued at certain terminals controlled by the Muslims, travel was stopped.

The search for new routes. There were three major routes by which trade flowed from the Far East to Europe. The northern one cut across central Asia to the Caspian and Black seas; the middle route passed through the Persian Gulf and the Euphrates valley to Syria and the Black Sea coast; and the southern route struck up the Red Sea and over to the Nile and northern Egypt. The commerce which flowed through these routes was rich indeed, especially after the impetus given it by the crusades.

During the fifteenth century, a few European nations began seeking new routes to the East. One incentive lay in the numerous difficulties which commerce had to undergo on its long and dangerous journey from the Orient to Europe, not to mention the many heavy tolls and duties collected en route. An even more important reason is to be found in conditions in Europe itself. The Mediter-

The invention of the astrolabe was of great importance to navigation. With the instrument, a mariner could measure the angle a star makes with the horizon and thereby calculate his position at sea.

ranean carrying trade was in the hands of the Italian city-states, who wielded an extensive and valuable monopoly. Hence the merchants and rulers of northern and western Europe were profiting little from the expanding trade with the East, and they determined to do something about the matter.

Prince Henry the Navigator. It was the Portuguese who spearheaded the drive to find oceanic routes that would lead to new lands and tap new reservoirs of trade. And the driving force behind their brilliant achievements in exploration and discovery was Prince Henry the Navigator (1394-1460).

Prince Henry believed—as did many mariners—that if Africa were circumnavigated, a route to the Orient could be opened up. For more than forty years he pored over maps and sent forth expeditions to explore the coastline of Africa. Gathering about him skilled cartographers and navigators, he had accurate maps constructed. The caravel, the finest vessel afloat for long voyages, was developed under his direction. Other navigation aids augmented Prince Henry's innovations. In the twelfth century the Europeans set their course with the aid of a magnetic needle floated on a straw. By the time Henry's sailors were setting sail from Lisbon, the compass consisted of a needle which pivoted on a card showing the points of the compass. During the fifteenth century another great aid to navigation came into general use—the astrolabe, a graduated brass circle by which the altitude of stars could be estimated and latitudes more accurately measured.

The African voyages. Henry's mariners did not fail him, although he died before any of the numerous expeditions he sent forth had explored the entire length of Africa. In 1486 Bartholomew Diaz (c. 1450-1500) was able to round the southern tip of Africa, from which point he noticed that the coast swung northeast. But his disgruntled crew forced him to turn back to Lisbon. Pleased with the prospect of soon finding a direct sea route to India, King John II of Portugal named the great cape rounded by Diaz "Cape of Good Hope."

The final stage in the African voyages was reached by Vasco da Gama (1469?-1524), who commanded the African expedition of 1497. Rounding the Cape of Good Hope, he pushed northward into Arab waters and crossed the Indian Ocean to the west coast of India. The Portuguese expedition incurred the enmity of the Arabs, whose Indian trading monopoly had been broken by Da Gama. They delayed the return voyage, and not until July of 1499 did Da Gama drop anchor in Lisbon. He had lost half his ships and two thirds of his men through scurvy and other misfortunes. But his cargo was worth sixty times the cost of the expedition.

It was not long before the Portuguese established a monopoly over trade in the Indian Ocean; and the king of Portugal assumed the impressive title "Lord of the Conquest, Navigation, and Commerce of Ethiopia, Arabia, Persia, and China."

Columbus discovers the New World. Meanwhile, Spanish ambitions for riches and prestige were realized through the exploits of a Genoese sailor named Christopher Columbus (1451?-1506). His son described him as

. . . a well built man of more than medium stature . . . but neither fat nor thin. He had an aquiline nose and his eyes were light in color; his complexion too was light, but kindling to a vivid red. In youth his hair was blond, but when he came to his thirtieth year it all turned white. In . . . the adornment of his person he was always . . . modest.[1]

Columbus believed that the Far East could be reached by sailing westward. To finance a voyage, he sought the support of Ferdinand and Isabella, who agreed to sponsor him. In August 1492 Columbus set sail from Spain with three small ships; on October 12 he landed on a small island in the West Indies. After he returned to Spain, Columbus announced that he had found the route to Asia. Even after Da Gama's voyage had opened up the eastward route to India, Columbus steadfastly refused to acknowledge that what he himself had discovered was in fact a massive obstacle on the route to the Far East. Although he made three more voyages to the New World in a vain attempt to find a direct opening to the Asian mainland, Columbus had already changed the course of history, though he did not know it. A New World had been discovered; old geographical views had been shattered; and the entire history of Europe was soon to be affected by the discovery of the new lands.

Spain and Portugal divide the new lands. An immediate repercussion of Columbus' first voyage was the destruction of Portugal's monopoly over discovery. Some sort of compromise had to be worked out between the two countries, and the pope was invited to define the pagan areas which Spain and Portugal might claim. In 1493 the pope issued the Bull of Demarcation, which proclaimed that all lands west of a line passing through the Azores belonged to Spain, while all new discoveries to the east were to become the rightful property of Portugal. But the Portuguese felt that this arrangement would confine their operations too closely to the African coast. By the Treaty of Tordesillas (1494),

Spain agreed to have the line moved farther west. This new demarcation later enabled Portugal to claim Brazil after Pedro Cabral's accidental sighting of South America in 1500 while sailing to the Indies.

The search for riches drove the Spaniards to organize many expeditions to chart the coastlines and to penetrate the interior of the New World. One such enterprise was particularly successful. Having heard from Indians of a mighty ocean only a short distance to the west, Vasco de Balboa (*c.* 1475-1519?) led a band of 190 Spaniards across the Isthmus of Panama. On September 25, 1513, Balboa climbed to the summit of a hill from which he beheld the Pacific Ocean—and in that act paved the way for exploration of the largest single portion of the world's surface.

Magellan sails around the world. Ferdinand Magellan (*c.* 1480-1521), a Portuguese navigator in the service of Spain, found a sea route into the Pacific. Magellan believed it possible to sail around South America just as Diaz had rounded Africa. In August 1520, Magellan made his memorable discovery of the strait which bears his name. Between huge ice-clad mountains and through tortuous passages his small ships made their way, taking thirty-eight days to journey 320 miles. Finally they sailed out upon the western ocean, which looked so calm after the stormy straits that Magellan termed it "Pacific." After hugging the coast northward for some time, Magellan set off northwest to cross the unknown expanse of the Pacific.

Early in the spring of 1521, Magellan came to the Philippine Islands, where he was slain during a skirmish with the natives. One of his ships, the *Victoria*, proceeded on to the East Indies, crossed the Indian Ocean, rounded the Cape of Good Hope, and dropped anchor in a Spanish harbor in 1522. The *Victoria's* cargo from the East Indies paid for the cost of the entire expedition. The tiny vessel had taken three years to sail around the world, but henceforth no one could doubt that the earth was round and that the Americas constituted a New World.

Cortés conquers Mexico. Thus far, we have concentrated chiefly on the herculean labors

This model of the *Santa Maria*, flagship of the tiny fleet Columbus led to the New World, gives some idea of the small size and limited deck space of the vessel.

of the great sea captains and the discoveries they made. Yet those exploits, limited for the most part to crossing vast stretches of water and taking possession of unfamiliar coasts, did not immediately produce the harvest of riches which the adventurers had eagerly sought. Such wealth was not to be found along the seashore but in the unknown hinterland, where rich indigenous cultures flourished. Penetration of inland areas was the work of the *conquistadores*, who looted whole native empires and planted the Spanish flag from California to the tip of South America.

In the same year that Magellan set forth (1519), a youthful adventurer named Hernando Cortés (1485-1546?) led an expedition to Mexico, whence had come rumors of an advanced native culture. Montezuma, ruler of the Aztecs, had thousands of warriors, while Cortés had no more than seven hundred men. But the Spaniards were equipped

Cortes and his men, aided by Indian allies, attack and burn the chief Aztec temple in this illustration from a sixteenth-century Aztec manuscript.

with horses, armor, and gunpowder, all unknown to the Aztecs. Two other factors aided the Europeans—the discontent of many subject tribes, which looked for a chance to break the Aztec rule; and an ancient Mexican legend which prophesied that the Aztecs would one day be destroyed by strange, white-skinned gods.

Having made the fateful decision to march inland on the capital, Tenochtitlan, Cortés destroyed his ships to prevent his men from turning back. Crossing the coast lands and the mountains, the Spaniards entered the valley of Mexico. Cortés made a virtual prisoner of Montezuma and through his cooperation ruled peacefully until an uprising gave him an excuse to conquer and destroy the capital.

Yet the *conquistador* Cortés was no mere plunderer; he demonstrated administrative talents of a high order in adapting the former Aztec confederacy to Spanish rule. He and his men explored the new domain thoroughly, brought the Indian tribes under control, introduced European seeds and plants into Mexican soil, and substituted Christianity for the barbaric Aztec religion.

Pizarro in Peru. The conquest of the Incas in Peru was carried out with less skill and more enduring ill effects than Cortés' exploit in Mexico. Obsessed by tales of a rich and mighty empire in South America, a tough, elderly illiterate named Francisco Pizarro (1470?-1541) determined to explore and conquer it. In 1531 Pizarro sailed from Panama with 180 men and 27 horses. Landing on the Peruvian coast, the small band made its way across the barren mountains into the interior, where they seized the Incan monarch Atahualpa.

Attempting to buy his freedom by paying a huge ransom, Atahualpa offered to have a room measuring seventeen feet by twelve filled to a height of some seven feet with plates and vessels of gold and to have it filled twice over with silver. Despite this magnificent ransom, the Spaniards sentenced the emperor to be burned to death on trumped-up charges. In the end, because Atahualpa accepted Christian baptism, he was merely strangled to death. With the imprisonment and death of its ruler, the highly centralized Incan government was incapable of effective, organized resistance; and Pizarro soon captured the capital.

For forty years after the conquest, anarchy prevailed in Peru. Within a decade, civil war broke out among the conquerors, and Pizarro was murdered. Not until the end of the sixteenth century was Spanish authority securely established over Peru. In the meantime, the natives died at fantastic rates from European diseases new to them and from the forced labor and cruel punishments inflicted upon them.

The sixteenth century also saw the exploration and conquest of the remaining part of South America. In time, Spanish dominions formed a huge, uninterrupted semicircle, while the Portuguese took possession of the vast hinterland of Brazil (see Reference Map 5).

Spanish penetration into North America. Using Mexico and the West Indies as bases, the Spanish explorers searched what is now the southern part of the United States for the treasures which rumors planted there. That the expeditions failed to find gold or other riches does not detract from the tremendous progress they made in opening up new and potentially wealthy areas. Not only mythical

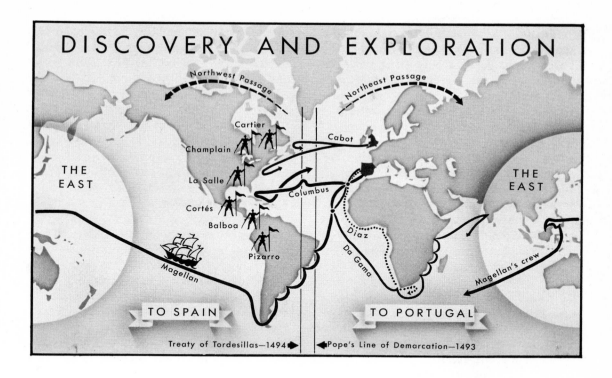

DISCOVERY AND EXPLORATION

treasure but an equally mythical Fountain of Youth attracted Spanish *conquistadores*. In 1521 Juan Ponce de León lost his life trying to locate the Fountain of Youth in the wilds of Florida.

Eighteen years later, one of the heroes of the conquest of Peru, Hernando de Soto (1500-1542), landed in Florida with a company of some six hundred adventurers. His search for treasure took him through the southern United States, and De Soto was possibly the first white man to sight the Mississippi. He died without finding any treasure, and his followers buried him in the Mississippi.

Marvelous tales had persisted of a fabled land north of Mexico containing seven cities with golden towers, and in 1540 Francisco de Coronado (1510-1554?) set out with a large band to find them. But the fabled cities turned out to be only adobe pueblos. In his vain search Coronado appears to have penetrated as far as Kansas, becoming the first European to behold the vast herds of buffalo roaming the American plains.

Starting with Cortés' conquests among the Aztecs, the Spanish had penetrated North America beyond the modern city of San Francisco and had explored much of the area that is now southwestern United States. Unimpressed with what they found, the Spanish authorities concluded that there was little to be gained in occupying the area north of the silver mines of Mexico.

English search for the Northwest Passage. The division of the overseas world between Spain and Portugal, as set forth by the Bull of Demarcation and the Treaty of Tordesillas, scarcely aroused enthusiasm among other European powers. It was not long before France and England encroached on the private preserves of both Portugal and Spain.

In 1497 John Cabot (*c.* 1450-1498?), an Italian mariner in the employ of England, started across the North Atlantic in a small ship, supposedly in the direction of China. After a turbulent six weeks' voyage, the expedition dropped anchor off the northern coast of the New World. When Cabot returned to England, Henry VII rewarded ,him with ten pounds, the title of Grand Admiral, and the right to make another voyage. Cabot made his second voyage in 1498, coasting along the eastern shore of America in a vain attempt to find a passage to the Orient.

Cabot was the first European after the hardy Norse sailors to land on the mainland of North America; and, what was most important, his discovery laid the foundation for England's claim to the whole rich continent. Thus for ten pounds and a title England eventually acquired all of Canada, Newfoundland, and Labrador and the territory along the Atlantic coast which constituted the thirteen American colonies—certainly an excellent business transaction.

For the next hundred years English seamen tried in vain to reach China by means of the fabled Northwest Passage, a sea route believed to exist north of Canada. An attempt to reach China by way of the Northeast Passage above Russia also failed.

French explorations of inland America. Between 1534 and 1541, Jacques Cartier (1491?-c. 1557) joined the search for the Northwest Passage. He explored much of the St. Lawrence River and so gave France its claim to sovereignty over eastern North America, a claim which duplicated England's. A vigorous explorer and administrator, Samuel de Champlain (1567-1635), not only founded a colony at Quebec but also journeyed over the lake which bears his name and westward to the Great Lakes.

Another Frenchman, René La Salle (1643-1687), helped to open up the interior of North America by exploring the Mississippi River. In 1681 he sailed down the river to the Gulf of Mexico, taking possession of the entire territory and naming it "Louisiana." Thanks to La Salle, France was able later to claim the entire Mississippi valley.

Dutch in America. Dutch interest in the New World coincided with the rise of Holland to a position of political independence and great economic strength during the first half of the seventeenth century. Dutch ambitions to find a shorter route to the Far East caused them to hire the English explorer Henry Hudson (d. 1611?), who in 1609 sailed

up the river that now bears his name. In 1621 the Dutch West India Company was founded for the purpose of trading in western Africa and the Americas. As part of its work, the company brought out settlers, the first band arriving on Manhattan in 1624. The Dutch thereby won a toe hold on what was to prove some of the most valuable real estate in the world—only to lose it in less than half a century to a more powerful rival, England.

EUROPE INVADES THE EAST

Portugal's eastern empire. Before the exciting era of exploration began to wane, the Europeans were faced with the problems of exploiting their newly found territories. Depending on the area, the newcomers concentrated their efforts on mining, trapping, trading, or colonizing—or, in some cases, on a combination of these activities. In virtually every case, the natives suffered. Only in a few instances, notably in the Far East, were the indigenous people able to enforce their own policies. In most extreme contrast was Africa, where the natives were rounded up and sold as slaves.

To ensure their toe hold in Africa, the Portuguese built fortified posts along the coasts, began to develop a colony in Angola, and settled traders on the island of Zanzibar. Early in the sixteenth century, Afonso de Albuquerque (1453-1515), the most famous of all Portuguese governors, resolved to consolidate his country's position in Africa and in the East. As a realist, he saw that Portugal could maintain commercial supremacy only by force of arms, so he devised a plan to establish forts at strategic sites which would dominate the trade routes and also protect Portuguese interests on land. The entrance to the Persian Gulf, for example, was commanded by the Portuguese city of Ormuz (see Reference Map 5). To control the Red Sea trade, Albuquerque captured the island of Socotra in 1506.

Five years later, Albuquerque set off to ensure Portugal's position in the East Indies. His first objective was Malacca (see Reference Map 5), a large trading center in the

Malay peninsula. The capture of Malacca was of inestimable value; from there, it was a logical jump to the rich Molucca Islands, source of the finest spices. Furthermore, control of Malacca opened the way to Portuguese trade with China. Thus, during the sixteenth century, Portugal developed a rich commercial empire and established a monopoly on pepper, mace, nutmeg, cloves, silk, and lace.

An already lucrative trade was vastly augmented when the Portuguese began in 1541 to export slaves from Africa. Envying the rich profits, other nations—England, Holland, France, and Sweden—began to send in rival expeditions, and Portugal was forced on the defensive. In 1642 the Dutch drove the Portuguese out of the Gold Coast, and this rich trade and slaving area was left to the other Europeans, especially the Dutch and English.

Dutch inroads in the East. After the Dutch declared themselves free of Spanish domination (1579), they looked on Spain's trade and colonies as fair game. When the two crowns of the Iberian peninsula were joined, the Dutch felt free to attack Portuguese territory in eastern waters.

This they did. In the 1590's, various Dutch trading groups sailed for the Malay Archipelago, preferring that region to western India, where the Portuguese were in greater force. Because competition lowered their profits, in 1602 the Dutch companies amalgamated into the Dutch East India Company. The government gave this powerful body the right to trade and rule in the area stretching from the Cape of Good Hope eastward to the Strait of Magellan. It was the Dutch East India Company that broke the power of the Portuguese in the islands of the Malay Archipelago.

In 1618 Jan Pieterszoon Coen (1587-1629) laid the foundations for the Dutch empire in the East Indies. Whereas Albuquerque had felt that it was sufficient to occupy strategic points along the sea routes, Coen believed that the Dutch had to control the actual areas of production as well. He built a fortified trading station at Batavia on Java,

Natives of the Spice Islands harvest coconuts in this engraving made by a Dutch artist late in the sixteenth century.

a site which eventually became the capital of the Dutch East Indies; and gradually the Dutch extended their control over the entire island. From there, ships returned to Europe with coffee, tea, spices, indigo, sugar, mace, nutmeg, camphor, and cloves. The Dutch later acquired Sumatra and the Moluccas.

The English gain a foothold in India. While the Dutch East India Company was exploiting the Malay Archipelago, its English counterpart was staking out claims in India at the expense of the Portuguese. In 1600 Queen Elizabeth incorporated the East India Company, granting it a monopoly of trade from the Cape of Good Hope eastward to the Strait of Magellan. The company soon established numerous outposts in India, on the islands of the Malay Archipelago, and even in Japan. By 1622 the Portuguese posts on the Persian Gulf had been put out of business, and in 1629 Madras was acquired. Through political stratagems, bribes, diplomacy, and exploitation of weak native rulers, the company prospered in India, where it was at times the most powerful political force in the subcontinent.

Europeans unwelcome in China. When the Portuguese first arrived in Canton in 1516, they were given the same privileges which Persian and Arab merchants had enjoyed for centuries. In response, the Portuguese behaved very badly, scorning the customs of the sophisticated inhabitants, and treating the "heathen" with arrogance and cruelty. The upshot was the banning of the foreigners from Chinese waters in 1522.

However, because trade was of mutual benefit to both Chinese and foreign merchants, in 1557 the Portuguese were granted the right to trade at Macao. There, under close surveillance and subject to many strict regulations, the "ocean devils" conducted their business. Stemming from this period is the mutual suspicion and hostility which characterized Sino-European relations in the nineteenth and early twentieth centuries.

A somewhat friendlier contact occurred when Jesuit missionaries arrived in China during the second half of the sixteenth century. They converted many important persons at the imperial court and in the provinces and thereby gained · protection for Christians generally.

Japan rejects European contacts. About 1542 three Portuguese ships from Macao were driven far off their course and landed at one of the southern Japanese islands. It was not long before others visited the islands and began trading. Hearing about Japan after he had sailed from Lisbon for the Far East, St. Francis Xavier went there and started to convert the inhabitants. After Xavier's death, his work was carried on by other Jesuit missionaries. Within thirty years Japanese converts to Christianity numbered around 150,000.

Suspicion on the part of the Japanese rulers that Christianity was merely a cloak for political usurpation was reinforced by the bigotry of many Christians and by economic exploitation on the part of various unscrupulous Portuguese merchants. The *shogun* Hideyoshi (d. 1598) instituted a policy of persecuting the Jesuits and their converts. In 1639 the final expulsion edict was proclaimed:

For the future, let none, so long as the Sun illuminates the world, presume to sail to Japan, not even in the quality of ambassadors, and this declaration is never to be revoked on pain of death.[2]

Except for a small, closely watched Dutch post at Nagasaki, Japan was closed to western contact until 1853.

The Philippines, Spanish trading stop. In the Far East, Spanish energies were concentrated primarily on the Philippine Islands. After 1565, cargoes of Chinese goods were transported from the Philippines to Mexico and from there to Spain. By this complicated route, Spain enjoyed some of the Oriental commerce about which Columbus had dreamed. Spanish officials and missionaries brought Christianity and a degree of European civilization to the islands, which were henceforth a corner of the Far East fundamentally oriented toward the West, in contrast to Japan and China.

Renewal of East-West contact. The remarkable series of geographical discoveries which began in the fifteenth century and carried intrepid European explorers, soldiers, traders, and missionaries to the ends of the earth recalls a similar movement in the second and third centuries A.D., when rich contacts in commerce and culture existed among three intercommunicating empires— the Graeco-Roman, the Indian, and the Chinese. But the fourth century witnessed the decline of Rome and depredations along the trade routes. Other factors (discussed in Chapter 4) weakened and ultimately destroyed the lines of contact. For nearly a thousand years there was little exchange or communication between East and West.

Until the fifteenth century, civilizations in the Near East, in India, and in China had been fully as dynamic and advanced as those in Europe. In some eras and in some aspects of culture they had surpassed the West. However, in the late Middle Ages western Europe began to experience an astonishing resurgence—a "rebirth" which was reflected in the rise of powerful and well-administered nation-states, the increase of wealth and trade, the growing importance of the bourgeoisie, and the intellectual and artistic achievements of humanist scholars and artists. While the West was pulsating with this insatiable energy, the empires of India and China (as we saw in Chapter 15) were becoming decadent culturally and impotent politically. And in Japan, isolation was the keynote of the Tokugawa shogunate—a regime no longer dynamic. Therefore, when the contact between East and West was renewed in the fifteenth century, it was not a meeting of equals. The discrepancies in effective political organizations, in disciplined armies, in energy and ambition prevented the resumption of East-West contacts on the same equal footing as had prevailed a thousand years earlier.

The natural result of the impact of the strong upon the weak was that Europe took advantage of the other continents; the wider world became the servant of the West. The expansion of Europe and its mastery of much of the world and its people, particularly those in Africa and Asia, is generally referred to as imperialism. Many of the conflicts and tensions in modern world politics find their source to a large degree in the imperial systems created by the West.

VICEROYS AND COLONISTS

IN THE NEW WORLD

Spain consolidates its empire in the Americas. The *conquistadores* who carved out a mighty Spanish empire in the New World had been allowed to embark on their expeditions only after having secured royal permission. The crown's ultimate purpose was to

Indian laborers worked night and day for their European masters in this Peruvian silver mine. Candles provided the only illumination, and the miners had to climb steep ladders to bring their loads of rich ore to the surface.

replace these brilliant but erratic men of action with staid but reliable civil servants who would consolidate the territorial gains into a centralized colonial regime.

In theory, all overseas dominions were the property of the king, who made the administrative decisions with the aid of the Council of the Indies. Holding almost unrestricted power during the reigns of weak monarchs, the Council of the Indies formulated legislation, appointed colonial officials, and heard important colonial law cases. Before the end of the sixteenth century, Spain possessed an American empire twenty times its own size.

This empire comprised in 1574 some 200 towns and about 160,000 Spanish settlers. For most of the colonial period, the Spanish empire in the Americas was divided into two kingdoms—New Spain, which was made up of the West Indies, Venezuela, and the lands north of the Isthmus of Panama; and Peru, which consisted of all Spanish territory south of those lands.

Each kingdom had a viceroy who lived in splendor in Mexico City or Lima. The viceroys enjoyed only the appearance of great power, however. The Council of the Indies kept a tight rein on imperial affairs, judging the viceroys chiefly by their effectiveness in sending back treasure to Madrid. Under orders from the Spanish crown, the colonial regimes sharply restricted self-government. In the large cities of the empire, lawyers from Spain were in charge of courts called *audiencias*, which also exercised various administrative powers. The crown levied poll taxes, customs on imports, and excise charges on goods exchanged within the colonies, as well as demanding one fifth of all the gold and silver mined. The colonists were left no voice in the taxation. Membership in town councils was the only regular political outlet for the Spanish settlers, and there only the richest could participate. The Spaniards born in the Americas (Creoles) were regarded as potential rebels against the mother country, as indeed they proved to be in the nineteenth century.

For three centuries, Spain was a potent agent in transmitting European culture and institutions to the New World. Its most important contributions were its language and literature. Also of lasting significance was the establishment of schools of higher learning. In 1551, eighty-five years before the founding of Harvard College, the first two universities in the New World—one at Lima, the other at Mexico City—opened their doors. By the end of the seventeenth century, no less than seven universities had been founded in Spanish America.

Mercantilism guides economic life. An economic theory current in Europe during this period was mercantilism, a doctrine which had ramifications for the colonies as well as for the mother country. Briefly defined, mercantilism postulated that a nation should be as self-sufficient as possible economically and that the colonies were to be exploited for the gain of the ruling country.

Spain's colonial administration was an outstanding example of mercantilism in operation. The homeland sent wines, iron, and dry goods to the New World but at the same time forbade the colonists to supply products such as olives which would compete with those produced in Spain. Raw materials for processing and manufacture were what Spain imported from its colonies.

Under the mercantile system, a nation's wealth was measured by the amount of precious metal it had accumulated. The New World was a source of fantastic riches for Spain, but transporting the gold and silver was a perilous business. Each spring two well-guarded fleets left Seville or Cádiz, one heading for Mexico and the other for Panama. Laden with silver from the Andes and Mexico, the convoys returned to Spain in the autumn at great risk. Pirates and buccaneers were ever ready to swoop down on stragglers, as were warships of rival powers. Yet it was customary for most of the treasure to reach Spain, where the crown received its royal fifth together with revenues from various taxes and monopolies.

In return for exploiting the virgin wealth of the New World, the Spanish introduced new products and methods which revolutionized agriculture, the mainstay of the American economy. To obtain farms, settlers often banded together to found a town in exchange for a royal grant of land, which was apportioned among the citizens. On the large estates of the aristocrats and the clergy, the forced labor of Indians or Negro slaves was employed in the cultivation of cotton, vanilla, indigo, cacao, and other crops for export. The Spanish brought with them wheat, barley, rye, and rice, as well as coffee, sugar cane, and a variety of fruits. The importation of cattle and other livestock not only drastically modified the native diet but also stimulated such valuable new industries as breeding animals and exporting their hides. Originally, the Indians had been their own pack animals, for the New World lacked beasts of burden except for the llamas domesticated by the Incas. The *conquistadores* introduced horses and mules and further revolutionized transportation by the introduction of the wheel and sail. Through these imports and many more, the cultural state of certain areas in the Americas was abruptly jerked from a Neolithic level to a position approaching that of the Old World.

Indian plight eased by the Church. Queen Isabella had to no small degree been motivated in the search for a new way to the Indies by the desire to extend Christianity among the heathen. This missionary task had also been one of the avowed objectives of every *conquistador;* but it was almost invariably overlooked in the mad scramble to acquire gold and silver, jewels, and slaves.

In the islands of the Caribbean, the forced labor of natives in the plantations proved so injurious that most of them died off. They were replaced by Negro slaves, who were imported to the islands in 1503 and to the American mainland a few years later. From the middle of the sixteenth century to the middle of the eighteenth century, some three thousand Negro slaves were imported annually by Spanish traders, eventually transforming the racial composition of the Caribbean.

It was the work of the Church in establishing missions and persuading the crown to enact safeguards that enabled the natives to survive in other areas rather than to die by the thousands as they did in the Caribbean. Early in the sixteenth century, some clerics began to upbraid the newcomers for their cruelties in exploiting the labor of the Indians. The most famous of these would-be saviors was a Dominican friar, Bartolomé de Las Casas (1474-1566), who obtained royal permission to establish missions and settlements where the Indians and Spaniards could live on civilized terms. But for a long time the attempt to improve the lot of the Indians was a losing battle, since the reforms ran counter to the economic interests of the settlers.

In order both to convert and to protect the Indians, a number of religious orders established mission towns where the monks taught their charges improved farming methods as well as irrigation and a variety of crafts. As a result, the "rim of Christendom" was pushed farther into the wilderness.

Portuguese activity in South America. Already burdened by its sprawling African and Asian interests, Portugal managed to establish a local administration in Brazil by the middle of the sixteenth century. In the 1570's, Brazil's surge forward began as great numbers of African slaves were imported to cultivate sugar and toil in the gold mines. This forced immigration continued for almost three centuries. During this period, the crown imposed a highly centralized control on Brazil through its own officials, and a mercantilist policy was pursued in economic affairs.

After the Spanish king acquired control over Portugal, the Dutch and English regarded Portuguese possessions as lawful prizes to be won from their Spanish enemies. The Dutch took over land north of the mouth of the Amazon and founded Dutch Guiana. Subsequently, the English and French gained control over parts of Guiana, and today it flies the flags of those three European powers.

French colonization of North America. In 1608, as we saw previously in this chapter, the city of Quebec was founded by Samuel de Champlain. To exploit the infant colony, a joint-stock company was formed about twenty years later. In return for a perpetual monopoly on the fur trade and the title to certain lands, this company was supposed to bring several thousand settlers to Canada. But the company was unable to attract colonists. Stories of the severe Canadian winters frightened away most potential settlers; and the Huguenots, who would have been glad to escape religious persecution, were not allowed to leave France.

By the middle of the seventeenth century, New France had survived the initial, dangerous stages of an infancy marked by parental neglect. The tempo of development and growth was about to pick up—the French were at last firmly established in North America, ready to do battle with the English for the northern half of the continent and the Mississippi basin and prepared to resist any aggression from the Spaniards on the Gulf of Mexico.

English colonies on the Atlantic seaboard. Like France, England was slow in following up the valuable work of its explorers. Cabot had given it the means of claiming an entire continent—yet it was not until the days of Queen Elizabeth that Englishmen began to sense the great potentialities offered by the New World. The defeat of the Spanish Armada in 1588 and the construction of a strong English navy ensured safer passage from the Old World to the New. Reports of the wealth garnered by the Spaniards whetted the appetites of Englishmen to look for El Dorado. Moreover, the economic difficulties accompanying the development of the land enclosure movement (see pp. 383-384) brought unemployment—and with it the desire by many to try their luck overseas. Added to these factors was the religious question. Although the Spanish and French governments forbade nonconforming religious elements to move to the New World, the English government saw in emigration an excellent means of getting rid of minority sects which were difficult to handle. For their part, these strong-willed, God-fearing dissidents were eager to migrate to a new land where they could worship freely.

Actually, the first successful English settlement was founded by a commercial corporation, the London Company. Known as a chartered trading company, its members—merchants, government officials, and other gentlemen of means—bought shares to finance colonies. On the basis of a charter issued by the English crown, the company was permitted to act as a miniature government, even to the extent of coining money, levying taxes, and annexing territory.

In 1607 a small fleet outfitted by the London Company landed an exploration party which established the colony of Jamestown in Virginia. For a number of years the colonists suffered from lack of food and other privations, but they were tided over this initial period by Captain John Smith (1580-1631), whose romantic rescue by the beautiful Pocahontas is one of the stories most cherished by Americans.

The transplantation to the New World of English common law and representative government was the result of a provision in the royal charter to the London Company:

All and every the Persons, being our Subjects, which shall dwell and inhabit within every and any of the said several Colonies and Plantations, and every of their children . . . shall have and enjoy all Liberties, Franchises and Immunities within any of our Dominions . . . as if they had been abiding and born within this our Realm of England.[3]

In 1619 the governor of the Jamestown colony called a representative assembly to assist in the tasks of government. This body, which later became the legislature of the state of Virginia, is one of the oldest representative assemblies in existence.

Following the accession of Charles i, hostility toward religious dissenters mounted to the point where many left England for the New World. In 1620 a dissenting sect, the Pilgrims, landed at Plymouth to found a colony. A Puritan group, organized as the Massachusetts Bay Company, settled around Boston. The members of this group had secured a royal charter which allowed them a virtually self-governing colony, unimpeded by decisions made far away in England.

Between 1629 and 1640, some 25,000 Puritans emigrated to New England. This movement, called the Great Migration, had important consequences for the future. It brought to the New World a number of educated and responsible people whose courage and intellectual attainments greatly stimulated the process of colonization. By the middle of the seventeenth century, the English language and law and the religious and cultural institutions of England had become firmly rooted in North American soil.

THE COMMERCIAL REVOLUTION

The transformation of Europe's economic life. In the period between 1450 and 1750, an economic and social revolution—sometimes termed the Commercial Revolution—wrought significant changes on the European scene. The geographical discoveries and the overseas trade, the new colonial markets, the access to new sources of raw materials, the influx of wealth, the improvement of business techniques—all these factors had the cumulative effect of refining and enriching the life of Europe.

The nature of capitalism. Although its roots can be found in ancient times, modern capitalism did not come into being until the period of the Commercial Revolution.

Capitalism is commonly defined by economists as an economic system in which capital, or wealth, is put to work to produce more capital. Although the term defies simple definition, a more comprehensive explanation would include other important factors. To put it briefly, capitalism may be said to be an economic system characterized by private ownership of property, the presence of large amounts of capital (money, land, raw materials, equipment), and the existence of specialized business techniques such as banking, credit, and insurance. But whatever the definition, it can safely be said that the driving force behind capitalism is the securing of profits.

Four phases of capitalism. Much of the history of the five hundred years between the midpoint of the fifteenth century and the present day is concerned with the virtues and sins of capitalism, its philosophical defense and condemnation, and its development (as in the United States) or rejection (as in the Soviet Union). Its history can be traced in four distinct stages.

The first stage—commercial capitalism—is associated with geographical discoveries, colonization, and the astounding increase in overseas trade. At this time early capitalists, protected by governmental controls, subsidies, and monopolies, made profits from the transportation of goods.

Beginning about 1750, the second phase—industrial capitalism—was made possible by the discovery of new energy sources, the use of machines in manufacturing, the evolution of the factory system, and the rapid growth of wealth. The essence of industrial capitalism was profit making from the manufacturing process itself. In the mid-nineteenth century, this phase reached its zenith with large factories, efficient machines, and the concentration of capital in the hands of the middle class.

In the last decades of the nineteenth century, when the ultimate control and direction of industry came into the hands of financiers, industrial capitalism gave way to financial capitalism. The establishment of mammoth industrial concerns or empires and the ownership and management of their assets by men completely divorced from production were the dominant features of this third phase.

Since the great world depression of the 1930's, the state has played an increasingly dominant role in the capitalistic system, one well-known manifestation in the United States being the New Deal and its successor programs. This fourth phase is commonly known to economists as state capitalism and to its opponents as "creeping socialism," among other epithets.

Mercantilism. In several European states, the growth of the national state system in early modern times resulted in political unification. The means used to bring about a strong, self-sufficient economy as a natural partner to strong central government was termed "mercantilism." Indeed, the aims of mercantilism and absolutism coincided; the control of a nation's economic life by a centralized government strengthened both the economy and the political structure of the state at the expense of rival national powers.

Because gold and silver were believed to be indispensable to a nation's wealth, mercantilists stressed the importance of accumulating precious metals. But, as will be noted in the case of Spain (see p. 376), this viewpoint was fallacious. Money does not necessarily spell wealth; money itself is only a measure of value and a means of exchanging real wealth. For coinage and the payment of armies and navies, however, gold and silver were necessary. Many Europeans believed that "money is the sinews of war."

A second tenet of mercantilism was that a nation should maintain the most favorable balance of trade possible: it should export more than it imported so that foreign nations would have to pay the difference in precious metals. Only raw materials which could not be obtained at home were to be imported; after these materials had been manufactured into finished articles, they were then to be exported. Government subsidies and bounties were rewards given for increased home production of manufactured goods.

Mercantilists believed that when raw materials were native, the profit to the home country was 100 per cent. Therefore, if a country could not supply its own materials, it should acquire colonies from which they could be procured. Furthermore, colonies constituted not only sources of supply for raw materials but also markets for finished products. Because the mother country did not want competition for its infant industries, colonies were prevented from engaging in manufacturing. In addition, the colonies were prohibited from trading with foreign powers.

Mercantilism reached its zenith in the eighteenth century and then declined, but mercantilistic policies were not abandoned in all countries at the same time. The most important commercial powers—England, France, and Holland—were among the first to embrace mercantilism, and they were also the first to discard it. The more backward economic powers such as Prussia, Russia, and the Scandinavian countries still favored mercantilism long after other nations had turned to newer doctrines.

Decline of the early commercial centers. During the late Middle Ages, trade in northern Europe had been dominated by the wealthy trading confederacy of towns in the Baltic area known as the Hanseatic League. After the fifteenth century, however, the League rapidly declined, a victim of mercantile rivalry from rising nation-states and the ravages of warfare. The absence of a strong central government in Germany left the League without adequate protection.

In southern Europe, the merchants of medieval Venice had acted for centuries as the great middlemen of Europe because they controlled the lucrative Asiatic trade. But the Portuguese smashed the Italian monopoly by discovering a new sea route to India.

In addition, the invasions of Italy by foreign powers had a disastrous effect upon the prosperity of the Italian city-states in the sixteenth century.

Portugal, temporarily paramount. With its diminishing population, Portugal could not permanently administer an empire scattered over three continents. During the sixteenth century, emigration, plague, and famine reduced the country's population from two million to hardly more than one. In 1580 Portugal came under the Spanish crown, and when it regained its independence in the following century, it retained only a few small possessions in the Far East, some islands in the mid-Atlantic, Brazil, and Mozambique and Angola in Africa. The economic power of Portugal ebbed away, not from lack of initiative so much as from lack of resources to support so great a task.

The economic decay of Spain. The decline of Spain's commercial might cannot be so simply explained. This nation apparently had everything—and failed. During the sixteenth century, Spain had far more gold and silver than any of its rivals; and to this wealth was added that of Portugal and its possessions. Yet the wealth and power lavishly displayed during the reign of Philip II (1556-1598) were only surface deep. Farming was neglected, and the industrial guilds were overburdened with governmental regulations. Religious persecution and the expulsion of the Jews and Moors had deprived Spain of many of its skilled financiers and craftsmen. The Church and the upper classes were exempt from certain forms of taxation, and as a result the tax burden fell disproportionately on the classes engaged in trade, commerce, and industry.

An outward symbol of wealth, the rich flood of bullion from the Americas wreaked havoc in the Spanish economy by causing inflation. The rise in prices was higher in Spain than anywhere else in Europe, a condition which attracted a stream of lower-priced products from Holland, France, and England, to the detriment of Spanish manufacturers. Spain not only lost out in manufacturing but also paid its gold and silver to foreign merchants for goods which in many cases it ought to have been making at home. In the decades after 1600, Spain's industry and commerce steadily diminished, and its population likewise decreased.

Antwerp's period of glory. As Spain and Portugal declined, the commercial center of Europe moved northward to Antwerp. To this great Flemish port came prominent European bankers, merchants, and manufacturers. Antwerp was made a toll-free port, and the city fathers set up a perpetual trade fair.

Various important institutions of modern capitalism developed in this flourishing city. In 1531 the first stock exchange, or Bourse, was founded. Life and property insurance came into extensive use. But the spectacular prosperity of Antwerp was short-lived, for in 1576, during the wars of the Netherlands against Spain, the city was sacked. Henceforth Antwerp's trade and finances were largely appropriated by such rising centers as London and the Dutch city of Amsterdam.

Holland's golden age. By 1650 Holland was the principal commercial, financial, and manufacturing country in Europe. Both the Dutch East India Company and the West India Company were markedly successful. The Dutch built better ships than their rivals and operated them more efficiently; the savings enabled them to offer lower freight rates. The diamond-cutting industry as well as the manufacture of lenses, clocks, and a glazed pottery called Delftware flourished.

Nevertheless, like Portugal, Holland was a comparatively small nation, and larger neighbors were presently to overtake it. Rivalry with England resulted in three wars in the latter half of the seventeenth century. Yet Dutch skill, together with the retention of the East Indies, enabled Holland to remain a significant factor in world commerce.

France's rise and decline. With a population of about fifteen million in the seventeenth century, France was the premier nation of Europe. Jean Baptiste Colbert (1619-1683) Louis xiv's astute minister of finance, assiduously cultivated the abundant economic resources of his homeland. He sponsored French colonization, expanded colonial trade, and encouraged manufacturing in France. But although his aggressive mercantilist policies appeared to work well at first, gradually the merits of his program were offset by evils inherent in the system. Many industries, such as textiles, porcelains, and tapestries, were subsidized by the government, but the numerous official decrees controlling them were more of a handicap than an aid to economic development. Furthermore, the extravagant court life at Versailles created a market for luxury commodities limited to the upper classes, while the needs and desires of the common people were ignored.

After the death of Colbert in 1683, his mercantilist system began to develop creaks and strains. Lacking Colbert's guiding genius, his followers added all kinds of minute and irksome regulations. Furthermore, the big governmental monopolies were increasingly unpopular with businessmen, who demanded the removal of governmental regulations and of controls by the old medieval guilds.

In addition, it has been estimated that between 1685 and 1715 France lost a million subjects through warfare, the surrender of colonies, and the drain of emigration. The revocation of the Edict of Nantes in 1685 resulted in the flight from France of a large group of industrious, middle-class Huguenots, who took their capital and skills to neighboring countries; and wars between France and England culminated in English victory and French disaster (see Chapter 18). Thus France lost to England the commercial supremacy it might have had.

Rise of England's sun. Although England was inferior to France in area, fertility of soil, and population, this island kingdom had factors in its favor which more than compensated for its disadvantages. Geographical isolation discouraged military conquest from the Continent; the English economy had not been burdened by the cost of maintaining large standing armies; and, after the union of England and Scotland in 1707, internal trade flourished in the largest customs-free area

The American Indian in this seventeenth-century illustration is equipped not only with weapons but also with his "genuine chocolate pot and cup." The lower picture shows the source of his chocolate, the fruit of the cacao tree.

in western Europe. The aristocracy and middle class which controlled Parliament also controlled the principal trading and banking companies, so that the growth of new enterprises was more peaceful and steady than anywhere else in Europe. The gradual control of the seas, the establishment of trading posts in exotic lands, and the shrewd policy of taking overseas territory as its booty from successful European wars enabled England to gain commercial benefits and to build the world's largest empire.

In 1651 Oliver Cromwell passed the famous Navigation Act, a statute reënacted by later governments. By the Navigation Act all goods imported into England from Africa,

America, or Asia had to be shipped in vessels belonging to English owners, built in England, and manned by English sailors. All goods exported from England to these areas came under the same injunctions. By maintaining a favorable balance of trade, this vigorous island kingdom in 1750 had already outstripped its European rivals in commerce and had laid the foundations for its economic domination of the world in the nineteenth century.

England's supremacy in the textile market was no small factor in accounting for its overall growth. Daniel Defoe, the author of *Robinson Crusoe*, maintained that the woolen industry in England was "the richest and most valuable manufacture in the world,"[4] of greater value to England than the rich mines of Peru and Mexico were to Spain.

More imports in Europe's markets. The discovery of sea routes to both Asia and the Americas provided an unparalleled impetus to the expansion of Europe and its commerce, which increased enormously during early modern times. For the first time, large quantities of such luxuries as aromatic woods, silks, precious stones, and spices were imported from the East. The spice trade was especially profitable because there was no refrigeration for foods at this time, and slightly spoiled food could be made palatable by cooking it with cloves, cinnamon, or pepper. Cloths from the East—calicoes, chintzes, and ginghams—became popular. (So incensed did the textile workers of England become at the foreign competition that they demanded a prohibition on the import of these inexpensive fabrics.) Among other imports from Asia were carpets, rugs, porcelain, brassware, and the all-important beverages tea and coffee.

From the New World came a variety of products which revolutionized the eating and drinking habits of the Europeans. The food supply of Europe was greatly improved by the addition of potatoes, maize (Indian corn), and tomatoes. From the Caribbean came sugar, which soon became so popular that it supplanted honey. An abundant supply of fish, primarily cod, came from Newfoundland's Grand Banks. The sacred beverage of the Aztecs, cocoa, found its way to Spain and thence throughout Europe in the seventeenth century.

In clothing, cotton eventually made cheap, easily washed garments available to everyone; and warm furs were obtained by trappers penetrating the interior of North America. The Indians were responsible for introducing a still popular habit—smoking. Cigars, cigarettes, pipe and chewing tobacco, and snuff were adopted by the Spaniards. A sixteenth-century French diplomat named Jean Nicot brought tobacco home from Portugal and thereby gave his name to its nicotine products.

Gold and ivory came to Europe from Africa, but the most important African export enriched the European powers indirectly. This export was that most misery-ridden produce—slaves. To obtain slaves to labor in the mines and on the plantations of the New World, slavers sailed to the Guinea coast, where they bought or stole their human freight. "A woman slave might change hands for a gallon of brandy, six bars of iron, two small guns, one keg of powder, and two strings of beads; a man slave might cost eight guns, one wicker-covered bottle, two cases of spirits, and twenty-eight sheets."[5] The voyage across the Atlantic to America cost the lives of from 10 to 25 per cent of the Africans—inhumanly packed as they were in evil-smelling, suffocating quarters below deck—but the remainder were profitably disposed of at their destination. The respectability which the slave trade enjoyed during this age provides an insight into the callousness of society in early modern times.

The influx of precious metals. The gold and silver brought into the European market from the colonies in enormous quantities may have had a more direct effect on Europe's economy than any of the other products of Africa, Asia, or the Americas. By the middle of the fifteenth century, Europe had been confronted with a severe shortage of gold and silver, caused both by the depletion of European mines and by increasing demands for currency to finance the new standing ar-

mies and navies and to pay for spices and other luxury commodities. But the critical situation was more than relieved by the development of new European mines, by imports of gold from West Africa—and above all by the unprecedented quantities of precious metals from the mines of Spanish America. The bonanza of precious metals upset price levels; between 1500 and 1650, commodity prices in western Europe more than tripled. Also, large sums of money were now available for investment, thereby facilitating trade with all parts of the world.

Banking becomes big business. One indicator of the resurgence of active commercial life was the growth of banking and related business practices. Banking had arisen in the late Middle Ages. The word *bank* derives from the Italian *banca*, meaning "bench," on which medieval Italian moneylenders sat in the market place to carry on their business. When a man failed, the people broke his bench, and from this custom came the word *bankrupt*, or "broken bench." During the late Middle Ages, moneylending became indispensable to the administration of both national monarchies and the Church, so that the traditional prohibition on usury was largely ignored.

Large-scale banking was first developed in Italian cities, where merchant bankers arranged bills of exchange and negotiated loans. By 1350 some eighty banking houses were in business in Florence alone, and certain families grew wealthy as a result. The most illustrious of these families was the Medici, whose clever members established branch offices all over western Europe and acted as financial agents for the popes. In the fifteenth century the Medici represented a new capitalist class which treated money as a commodity. Whereas in medieval economic theory money was only a means of exchange and was justified only to the extent that it reflected both honest labor and a "just price" concept, early capitalist speculators like the Medici valued and traded in currencies and bullion for their own sake.

Following the Medici policy of using money not only to earn interest but also to gain political power were the Fuggers, a family of German bankers in the sixteenth century. The Fuggers set up counting houses and merchandise depots in a number of cities and in time gained virtual control of the silver, copper, and iron markets of central Europe and the silver and mercury mining in Spain. They also engaged in international finance and politics. For decades the Fuggers realized an average yearly profit of over 30 per cent, but they went bankrupt in 1607 when several governments defaulted on their loans.

By this time, however, numerous other banking concerns had come into existence. In 1609 the Bank of Amsterdam was founded by local merchants. Among its duties was the conversion of various currencies into credits called bank money, which because of its standard value came to be preferred to coins. The English banking system was placed on a sound basis in 1694, when an act of Parliament established that famous institution the "Old Lady of Threadneedle Street" —the Bank of England.

With banking there naturally evolved new financial techniques. Despite the increase in precious metals after 1500, the supply could not keep pace with the increase in trade, and there arose the practice of payment in checks against a sum of money held on deposit in a bank. In effect this enabled business transactions to be expanded far beyond the bounds imposed by the amount of cash available. Likewise, bank notes came to replace bulky, heavy metal for large sums. To overcome the dangers of losing money through theft or accident, bills of exchange, which had originated during the crusades, came into more widespread use.

Progress was also made in commercial arithmetic and in bookkeeping. Simple bookkeeping had been developed as early as the thirteenth century. Soon afterwards, double-entry bookkeeping came into use; it was well known in Italy by 1500 and in western Europe a century later.

New methods of financing companies. Not only banks but also modern corporations were conceived in response to needs arising from the expanded commerce of early modern times. Unprecedented difficulties resulted from trading at long distances overseas in strange lands. It was natural that those engaged in overseas trade should seek to combine their efforts both to provide mutual protection and to share losses as well as profits.

The companies were of two main types— regulated and joint-stock. In the regulated company, individuals financed their own businesses and abided by rules which had been accepted by the group to protect the trade in which the members had a mutual interest. The majority of earlier companies were of this nature.

Later companies were of the joint-stock variety, which involves an association of capital as well as of men. The members put their money into a common fund and gave over the management to a board of directors. Because of its advantages, the joint-stock company became almost universal. As many people as wanted could contribute capital. This type of company had a permanent legal personality that did not expire, whereas the regulated company was not a legal entity, and in case of damages each member had to sue or be sued individually. Stock in a joint-stock company might be transferred as the owner saw fit, and at the same time, the company's policy underwent no serious change. The English and Dutch East India companies both started as regulated companies but were afterwards reorganized as joint-stock entities. The vast corporations of today grew out of this early type of business organization.

Insurance companies. In addition to joint-stock companies, other methods of sharing losses evolved, including insurance. Since the loss of his vessel might well ruin an individual merchant, it came to be the practice to distribute losses among a group of traders by means of insurance. Interested merchants drew up an agreement by which each was responsible for a percentage of any possible loss. Because they signed their names at the bottom of this document, the practice came to be known as underwriting.

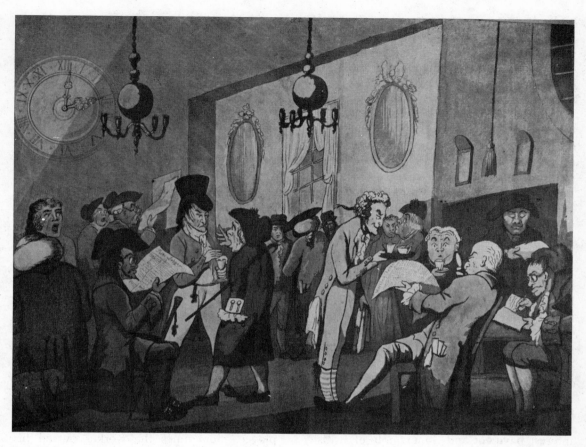

The famous insurance association known as Lloyd's of London took its name from Lloyd's coffee house, where the insurance underwriters used to meet with merchants and shipowners. This scene at Lloyd's dates from the early nineteenth century.

The most famous of all marine insurance groups, Lloyd's of London, came into being about 1688. Lloyd's was not a stock company but an association of shipowners, merchants, and underwriters who first met together in a London coffee house owned by Edward Lloyd. Since its modest beginnings, Lloyd's has grown steadily and branched out into other forms of insurance. Today it is the world authority on matters of ship classification, and it publishes *Lloyd's List*, a daily paper which indicates the whereabouts of all registered vessels.

After the disastrous London fire of 1666, fire insurance companies were started, and in the same period companies specializing in life insurance were also formed. In 1684 the Friendly Society was organized. This society was the first mutual company—an association in which policyholders receive a share of the company profits.

Development of stock exchanges. The creation of joint-stock companies gave impetus to the growth of stock exchanges, because the shares could be easily transferred from one person to another like any other commodity. A stock exchange made possible the purchase and sale of stocks, bonds, and debentures. It performed valuable functions for capitalism, including the easy amalgamation of capital from many different sources, thereby enabling large commercial companies to be formed. Not only stock but also produce exchanges arose, fulfilling much the same need as their present-day descendants. The produce exchange is a market for dealing in such products as wheat, wool, cotton, and metals. Following the lead of the first exchange in Antwerp, the Bourse, the early exchanges acted as both produce and stock exchanges. Later, the two functions were separated.

Speculation and business bubbles. Toward the end of the seventeenth century, the rapid increase of trade brought about an avalanche of speculation in the shares of stock issued by joint-stock companies such as those promoted by the governments of France, Holland, and England. One authority comments on the fantastic nature of some of the wildcat schemes, "which promised to earn great dividends by trading in human hair, making square cannon balls, getting butter from beech trees, marketing an air pump for the brain, perfecting a wheel for perpetual motion, searching for rich wrecks off the Irish coast, or importing jackasses from Spain."[6] The two most notorious speculative companies were the South Sea Company in England and the Mississippi Company in France.

The financiers of the South Sea Company assumed the British national debt of about £9,000,000 in return for a 6 per cent annual interest payment and a monopoly of British trade with South America and the islands in the South Seas. The price of company stock rose, encouraging the creation of other similar ventures. However, the time came when the price of the South Sea Company stock no longer reflected its true value; it had risen far beyond the value of its earnings in trade. In 1720, when banks could not collect money for loans made on the inflated stock, this huge speculative bubble burst.

The Mississippi Company had a similar history. Formed to promote French holdings in the Mississippi valley, the company controlled virtually all French colonial trade and in addition directed the administration of the royal bank. But the lack of valuable assets in the sparsely populated Mississippi valley region, coupled with the orgy of speculation which resulted from this scheme, brought the company to ruin in 1720. Its failure demoralized many citizens and helped to discredit the Old Regime. But the wild mania for speculation and quick profits revealed previously untapped sources of wealth available for investment and gave a stimulus to new techniques for extending credit.

The domestic system. In the Middle Ages, manufacturing had been carried on under the guild system. The impetus of commercial capitalism caused an important change in the organization of industry. The domestic, or putting-out, system evolved and reached its most extensive application among the textile industries in England. Although the system had first appeared in Italy as early as the thirteenth century, it did not become common in England until the sixteenth.

The domestic system operated in this fashion: a merchant capitalist, or entrepreneur, would buy raw materials, assign them to artisans to be worked on in their own homes, take the finished product, and sell it to his customers. Thus, between producer and customer, a middleman intervened—an entrepreneur who accumulated capital by selling his goods at a profit. Because work was no longer planned and conducted by master and apprentice under one roof, this system widened the gulf between employer and employee. Sometimes the worker owned his own tools and furnished raw materials, but most craftsmen became more dependent upon the entrepreneur as the domestic system became more widely adopted.

The domestic system had both advantages and disadvantages. The accumulation of capital in the hands of merchants made possible the purchase of raw materials in greater bulk and allowed for marketing of finished products on a larger scale than had been possible under the guild system. The domestic system also contributed to an increased specialization of skills within an efficient system of overall production; a merchant could have his raw wool sent to spinners, then to weavers, and finally to dyers. From the workers' point of view, it was now possible for agricultural tenants to augment the bare subsistence they eked from the soil by working at home. But many abuses existed: child labor, low wages, long hours of work, and various occupational diseases.

The domestic system persisted for two hundred years in England, although central shops began to appear before the beginning of the factory system proper. On the Continent, the guild system remained strong. Guilds were an indispensable part of the prevailing system of mercantilism in a society where change was unwelcome. Any merchant who defied guild regulations by setting up a domestic system of production was severely punished by the law.

Innovations in agriculture. In England, especially, the advent of commercial capitalism wrought significant changes on the agrarian scene. The profit-making potentialities in farming attracted enterprising, middle-class tradesmen, who bought up large tracts of land. Because the possession of land had always been the mark of nobility, the *nouveaux riches* consolidated their position in polite society by acquiring estates and marrying into the landed gentry. The alliance between land and trade created a powerful new group in Parliament—a class which promoted legislation favorable to its own needs and desires, often at the expense of the national good. But the satisfaction of the profit motive had a beneficial effect upon agriculture. Discontented with primitive farming techniques, the new commercial landowners applied efficient business methods to the management of their estates. They encouraged the use of new tools and crops and were sympathetic to new ideas in stock breeding and soil development.

A pioneer agronomist was Jethro Tull (1674-1741), who advocated careful plowing of the land, planting seeds in neat rows by the use of a drill he invented, and keeping the plants well cultivated as they grew to maturity. By mixing clay and lime into the soil, Viscount Charles Townshend (1674-1738) restored the fertility of land that had once been worthless swamp and sand. He also suggested crop rotation as a method of soil restoration superior to the wasteful custom of allowing good farmland to lie fallow. So enthusiastic was he over turnips, his pet crop for livestock feed, that he was nicknamed "Turnip Townshend."

Robert Bakewell (1725-1795) was responsible for attacking the problem of livestock breeding. Haphazard breeding had resulted in sheep weighing only from twenty-five to forty pounds and cattle of about four hundred pounds. Through the select breeding of choice animals, Bakewell raised larger livestock, improved the quality of the meat, and increased the quantity of milk available from his dairy cattle. His methods were so enthusiastically adopted by other farmers that by 1800 the average sheep weighed eighty pounds and the average beef, eight hundred pounds.

While the tempo of agricultural reform was much faster in England than on the Continent, some progress in farming methods took place there also. In fact, the great advances made in English agriculture owed much to Continental techniques and improved seeds, but these achievements were applied much more systematically and thoroughly in England.

The enclosure movement. The practice of enclosing open lands, a development which had begun in England during Tudor times, was accelerated by the changes in farming methods. Aided by special acts of Parliament, members of the new commercial landowning class seized the opportunity to enclose the common lands where for hundreds of years English villagers had grazed their cattle and to purchase and fence in the small farms owned and operated by the sturdy, independent yeoman class. These portions of land were consolidated into holdings which were, in effect, large-scale business enterprises requiring substantial amounts of capital for operation and upkeep. The demand for wool in the textile industry resulted also in the enclosure of large tracts of arable land for sheep raising.

The controversy over the enclosure movement reached its climax between 1750 and 1810. The advocates of enclosure justified amalgamation of small agricultural holdings by claiming that new methods of stock breeding and crop rotation could not be practiced on unfenced land. From an economic standpoint, enclosure was inevitable, and some historians believe that the enclosure movement resulted ultimately in a more careful use of a greater amount of land than had been available before. Like most drastic economic changes, however, the enclosure movement spelled misery and dislocation for thousands of country folk. The destruction of the yeoman class, the depopulation of many villages, and the exodus to the cities signified the end of the old, and often charming, rural way of life. The poet Oliver Goldsmith ruefully pondered the fate of his countrymen in these lines:

Ill fares the land, to hastening ills a prey,
Where wealth accumulates, and men decay.
Princes and lords may flourish, or may fade;
A breath can make them, as a breath has made;
But a bold peasantry, their country's pride,
When once destroyed can never be supplied. . . .
Ye friends to truth, ye statesmen, who survey
The rich man's joys increase, the poor's decay,
'Tis yours to judge how wide the limits stand
Between a splendid and a happy land.[7]

The saga of the yeomen's misfortunes did not end with their departure from the villages; its finale took place in the cities. When the story of industrial capitalism is taken up in Chapter 20, we will view the bleak and harsh environment of displaced rural people as they labored long and hard in grimy factories and lived as best they could in ugly, disease-ridden slums.

SUMMARY

Braving the terrors of uncharted seas and the dreadful hardships of long voyages, a few daring sea captains opened up rich trade routes to the East and discovered new lands in the Western Hemisphere. In the New World, the feats of the explorers were followed by the bold, if often cruel, exploits of the *conquistadores*, who carved out vast empires for their homelands—Spain, Portugal, England, France, and Holland.

Meanwhile, most of these same European nations had erected forts on the African coast for the purpose of exploiting the slave trade. In the teeming lands of Asia, European penetration was secured only by the establishment of strongly fortified trading settlements at strategic sites. Using this system, the Portuguese controlled trade in the East during the 1500's but gradually lost out to the Dutch, who garnered most of the profits in the next century. While the Dutch concentrated more and more on the East Indies, the English East India Company built up a commercial stronghold in India. In China and Japan, the unwarranted violence of the Portuguese caused native officials to restrict the westerners to a narrow theater of operations. In the East, European standards were successfully and permanently imposed only in the Philippines, which the Spanish used as a trading post.

In sharp contrast to their failures in Japan and China, the western European powers were able to transplant not only their authority but also their institutions and culture to the sparsely populated lands of the Americas. The government and economics of the Spanish and Portuguese colonies were directly—and minutely—controlled by royal decrees and officials, whereas the development of the French, English, and Dutch colonies was left largely to private companies.

The impact of the New World upon the Old was so far-reaching as to intensify the Commercial Revolution, the name given to the first phase of our capitalistic economic system. The capitalism of this period, during which the economy in western Europe became nation-centered instead of town-centered, is called commercial capitalism because of the dominant part played by commerce as a producer of wealth. With the spectacular outburst of geographical discoveries and the creation of new trade routes, the areas which had thrived on the Mediterranean trade lost their leading roles to those along the Atlantic seaboard. The first great colonial empires were built up by Portugal and Spain, only to be superseded through the dynamism of the Low Countries and later of France and England. New products poured into Europe, while the influx of gold and silver completed the change from a barter to a money economy and raised the level of prices.

It was this era that saw the development of large-scale banking and commercial practices. By the seventeenth century, important banking institutions had been founded throughout western Europe. Because overseas trading ventures required large amounts of capital and entailed great risks, merchants pooled their resources by forming companies, the earlier ones of the regulated type, the later and more successful ones joint-stock companies—forerunners of present-day corporations. To serve as market places for stock that could change hands readily, stock exchanges developed.

The geographical, political, and commercial expansion of Europe between the years 1450 and 1750 was so immense as to transform the basic pattern of global existence. With it we enter the formative period of modern times. For the next two centuries the civilization of western Europe—carried to the four corners of the earth and stimulated by new and dynamic forces—was to dominate world culture.

SUGGESTIONS FOR READING

C. E. Nowell, *The Great Discoveries and the First Colonial Empires,** Cornell. A simply written, brief coverage of much of the material discussed in this chapter. Another excellent short survey, but more valuable because of its greater detail, is J. H. Parry, *The Establishment of the European Hegemony: 1415-1715,** Torchbooks (published originally as *Europe and a Wider World,* Longmans, 1950).

P. Sykes, *A History of Exploration,** Torchbooks. A full, scholarly, and readable account of geographical discovery from ancient times to the present.

J. B. Brebner, *The Explorers of North America, 1492-1806,** Anchor. Engrossing survey of the explorations which revealed the character of the New World to Europe, and the men who undertook them.

Excellent biographies which deal with figures discussed in Chapter 16 include C. R. Beazley, *Prince Henry the Navigator,* Putnam, 1897; K. G. Jayne, *Vasco da Gama and His Successors, 1460-1580,* Methuen, 1910; S. E. Morrison, *Christopher Columbus, Mariner,** Mentor; C. M. Parr, *So Noble a Captain: The Life and Times of Ferdinand Magellan,* Crowell, 1953.

Two classic accounts by W. H. Prescott, the famous American historian, of the Spanish conquests in the New World are *History of the Conquest of Mexico* and *History of the Conquest of Peru,* 1 vol. ed., Modern Lib., 1936. See also J. Descola, *Conquistadors,* Viking, 1957.

S. Shellabarger, *Captain from Castile,* Little, Brown, 1945. A fascinating novel which provides a vivid portrayal of sixteenth-century Spain and of Cortes' conquest of Mexico.

C. H. Haring, *The Spanish Empire in America,* Oxford, 1947. The best introduction to the colonial period in Spanish America.

*Indicates an inexpensive paperbound edition.

V. Cronin, *The Wise Man from the West,** Image. Sixteenth-century China is the background for this biography of Matteo Ricci, a mathematician and Jesuit missionary.

L. B. Packard, *The Commercial Revolution, 1400-1776,* Holt (Berkshire Studies), 1927. A brief, reliable survey; especially good on the theory and practice of mercantilism. R. L. Reynolds, *Europe Emerges: Transition Toward an Industrial World-Wide Society, 600-1750,* Univ. of Wis., 1961, is a clarifying account of the emergence of Europe as an economic and social force.

H. E. Sée, *Modern Capitalism, Its Origin and Evolution,* Adelphi, 1928. A valuable account of capitalism's growth during the Age of Discovery. The author stresses the importance of trade in the evolution of capitalism. For discussions of the policy of mercantilism and the underlying conceptions which promoted it, see E. F. Heckscher, *Mercantilism,* 2 vols., Macmillan, 1956; G. Schmoller, *The Mercantile System and Its Historical Significance,* Macmillan, 1910; W. Cunningham, *The Growth of English Industry and Commerce in Modern Times,* Cambridge Univ., 1905; and C. W. Cole, *Colbert and a Century of French Mercantilism,* 2 vols., Columbia Univ., 1939.

J. E. Gillespie, *The Influence of Oversea Expansion on England to 1700,* Columbia Univ. Studies, 1920. A sound treatment of the social, political, economic, and artistic milieu as affected by New World discoveries. Includes much source material.

R. Ehrenberg, *Capitalism and Finance in the Age of the Renaissance; A Study of the Fuggers and their Connections,* Harcourt, Brace, 1928. Excellent portrayal of the Fuggers and of other great financier families of the sixteenth century. Also recommended is R. De Roover, *The Medici Bank: Its Organization, Management, Operations, and Decline,* New York Univ., 1948.

R. H. Tawney, *The Agrarian Problem in the Sixteenth Century,* Longmans, 1912. Lucid account of the transition to capitalistic agriculture and the economic and social results.

THE EUROPEAN SCENE

300	
600	
700	
900	
1000	
1100	
1200	Mongols conquer Russian principalities 1237; Russia cut off from Europe
	Alexander Nevski defeats Teutonic Knights at Lake Peipus 1242; rules Vladimir 1252-1263; son founds grand duchy of Moscow
	Transitional period in Italian art c. 1250-c. 1400—synthesis of medieval, classical techniques; Giotto lends realism to painting
	Papal prestige declines—Pope Boniface VIII (1294-1303) feuds with Philip IV; Avignon papacy (1309-1376) called Babylonian Captivity
1300	Humanism, classical revival in Italy 1300-1600—Petrarch, Boccaccio, humanists; Platonism, Aristotelianism
	John Wycliffe (1300?-1384) and John Huss (1369?-1415) assail Church abuses, doctrines; forerunners of Protestant Revolt
	Hundred Years' War between France and England 1337-1453
	Golden Bull serves as constitution of Holy Roman Empire 1356
	Great Schism 1378-1417—Conciliar Movement: Council of Constance elects Pope Martin V 1417; single papacy restored
	Russian grand princes defeat khan of Mongols at Kulikovo 1380
	Poland and Lithuania united under common sovereign 1386; comprise largest state in Europe
1400	The *quattrocento* (fifteenth century) of Italian Renaissance—political turmoil, economic prosperity, height of humanism
	Poles and Lithuanians crush Teutonic Knights at Tannenberg 1410; control East and West Prussia
	Commercial Revolution in Europe 1450-1650—Atlantic seaboard nations dominate trade; influx of gold, silver; banking grows
	Gutenberg uses movable type to print first published Bible 1454
	Early Renaissance masters in Italy—Brunelleschi, Ghiberti, Donatello, Masaccio, Mantegna, Botticelli
	Wars of the Roses 1455-1485; rule of Henry VII (1485-1509) ends rivalry between houses of York, Lancaster; Tudor line founded
	Louis XI (the "universal spider") of France (1461-1483) seizes part of Burgundy, Charles the Bold's domain
	Ivan III (the Great) of Russia (1462-1505) expands realm; adopts Byzantine traditions; attacks Tatars; Russia called "Third Rome"
	Catholic Sovereigns Ferdinand and Isabella unify Spain 1469; Court of Inquisition increases royal power, wipes out heresy 1480
	Reconquista ends with conquest of Granada 1492; unification of Spain completed
	Italian Wars 1494-1513—French invade Italy under Charles VIII and Louis XII
	Painters of the Northern Renaissance—Jan van Eyck, Albrecht Dürer, Hans Holbein the Younger, Brueghel the Elder
	Writers of the Northern Renaissance (sixteenth century)—Erasmus, Rabelais, Sir Thomas More, Montaigne, Cervantes, Shakespeare
1500	Late Renaissance in Italy c. 1500-1530—Bramante, Michelangelo, Da Vinci, Raphael, Giorgione, Titian; Castiglione, Cellini
	Henry VIII of England (1509-1547) establishes strong government; builds power on middle-class support
	Luther posts ninety-five theses 1517; Leo X issues *Exsurge Domine* 1520; Luther excommunicated, declared heretic at Diet of Worms 1521
	Charles V elected Holy Roman emperor 1519; defeats Francis I of France 1525; French crushed by Hapsburg forces
	King of Bohemia and Hungary slain fighting Turks 1526; Hapsburgs offered Czech throne; Turks and Hapsburgs divide Hungary
	Augsburg Confession expresses Lutheran creed 1530; Schmalkaldic Wars 1546-1555; Peace of Augsburg 1555
	The Prince (1532) by Machiavelli—objective exposé of ruthless statecraft; becomes guidebook for diplomacy and power politics
	Henry VIII founds Anglican Church 1534
	Loyola establishes Jesuit order 1534; papal reform under Pope Paul III 1534-1549; Council of Trent 1545-1563—climax of Catholic
	Reformation: reaffirms Church doctrines, reforms Church discipline and administration
	Protestant leader John Calvin publishes *Institutes of the Christian Religion* 1536; sets up theocracy in Geneva
	Ivan IV (the Terrible) of Russia (1547-1584) increases despotism; forms new code of laws; reforms clergy; conquers Tatars
	Mary Tudor reinstates Catholicism in England 1553-1558
1550	Charles V divides his empire 1554-1556—central Europe to Ferdinand; Spain, Netherlands, Italian lands, New World to Philip
	Philip II of Spain (1556-1598) makes royal power absolute; strengthens Catholicism; seizes Portugal 1580
	Era of Religious Wars 1556-1650
	Elizabeth of England (1558-1603) executes Mary Stuart 1587; Spanish Armada defeated 1588; Protestantism reëstablished
	Civil war in France 1562-1589; St. Bartholomew's Day Massacre 1572; accession of Henry IV 1589-1610
	Shakespeare 1564-1616—supreme figure in Elizabethan literature
	Eighty Years' War between Dutch and Spanish 1568-1648—Netherlands split 1579; United Provinces declared independent 1581
	Battle of Lepanto, the "last great crusade" 1571—Holy League crushes Ottoman naval power in Mediterranean
	Time of Trouble 1584-1613; civil war in Russia ends, Michael Romanov elected ruler by national assembly 1613
	Edict of Nantes (1598) ensures religious toleration in France
1600	James I of England (1603-1625) authorizes King James version of the Bible 1611; advocates divine right of kings
	John Milton 1608-1674—important in growth of English political liberty and freedom of expression; *Areopagitica*, *Paradise Lost*
	Thirty Years' War (1618-1648) leads to Peace of Westphalia 1648; symbolizes emergence of national sovereign state
	De Jure Belli ac Pacis (1625) by Grotius—foundation for international law
	Charles I of England 1625-1649; Petition of Rights denies his right of taxation without Parliament's consent 1628
	English civil wars 1642-1660; the Commonwealth 1649-1653; the Protectorate 1653-1660; the Restoration 1660

FAR EAST

Chandragupta I founds Gupta dynasty in India c. 320
Chandragupta II c. 380-c. 413—zenith of Gupta power
Harsha (606-647) rules northern India
T'ang dynasty founded in China 623; golden era of China
T'ai Tsung 627-650—first great T'ang ruler
Taikwa Reform in Japan 646; establishes absolute monarchy
Nara period in Japan 710-784
Fujiwara period in Japan 794-1192; capital at Kyoto
Sung dynasty in China 960-1279

Muslims invade India; Turks and Afghans annex Punjab 1022
China divided into two empires: Sung and Chin 1127
Yoritomo (1147-1199) rules Japan as *shogun* from Kamakura1192
Genghis Khan (1162-1227) conquers Mongolia, eastern Europe
Hojo period in Japan 1199-1333—warrior nobility
Delhi sultanate established 1206; Indian culture divided into
Hindu and Muslim; political unity
Mongols conquer China 1234; Mongol empire unifies Asia
Kublai Khan 1260-1294—Mongol emperor of China and
Mongolia
Marco Polo arrives at Kublai Khan's court c. 1275
Kamakura destroyed 1333; Ashikaga shogunate founded in
Japan 1338
Fall of Mongol China; Ming dynasty founded 1368

Timur the Lame (Tamerlane) invades Punjab, destroys Delhi 1398
Chinese naval expeditions to India, Near East, Africa (fifteenth
century)

Portuguese trade monopoly in Far East (sixteenth century)
Chinese edict bans foreign merchants in Chinese waters 1522;
trade ceases; China in isolation

Baber (the Lion) defeats Delhi sultanate and Rajputs 1526;
founds Mogul empire in India

Akbar (1556-1605) expands Mogul empire; reforms government; promotes religious tolerance, cultural growth
Portuguese granted right to trade with Chinese at Macao 1557

Spanish use Philippines as trading stop c. 1565
Japanese attempt invasion of China and Korea 1592
Hideyoshi encourages arts, persecutes Christians in Japan 1592
English East India Company incorporated by Elizabeth 1600
Dutch East India Company formed to break Portuguese trade
monopoly in the East 1602
Tokugawa period begins in Japan 1603
Foundations for Dutch East Indies laid by Coen 1618
Shah Jahan (1628-1658) promotes Muslim faith; height of Mogul
empire in India
Europeans forbidden entry to Japan; Japanese forbidden
exit 1639
Manchu invade Ming China; establish Manchu dynasty 1644

AMERICAS AND AFRICA

	300
	600
	700
Independent Mayan city-states in Yucatan peninsula 980-1200	900
Eric the Red discovers Greenland c. 982	
Mali empire in Africa (c. 1000-c. 1400) ruled by Mandingos;	1000
chief city Timbuktu	
Zenj empire c. 1000-1497—trade with Near East and Orient	
Incas settle Cuzco valley in Andes (eleventh century)	
Leif Ericson sails to Labrador and Nova Scotia 1002	1100
Capital of Ghana empire in Africa plundered by Berbers 1087	
Toltecs dominate Mexican plateau (twelfth century)	
	1200
Fall of Ghana state 1240	
	1300
Aztecs found Tenochtitlan c. 1325	
Aztec confederacy extends across Mexico (fourteenth century)	
Songhai empire in the African Sudan c. 1400-c. 1600; capital	
at Gao	
Zenith of Inca empire 1438-1532	1400

Diaz rounds Cape of Good Hope 1486
Columbus discovers New World 1492
Bull of Demarcation divides New World between Spain and
Portugal 1493; Treaty of Tordesillas modifies demarcation 1494
Da Gama rounds southernmost tip of Africa, reaches India,
returns to Lisbon 1497-1499
North America claimed by Cabot for England 1497
Albuquerque captures Socotra, entrance to Persian Gulf 1506;
captures Malacca 1511
Balboa sights Pacific Ocean 1513   1500
Cortés' arrival in Mexico (1519) brings fall of Aztec empire
Round-the-world voyage: Magellan rounds South America
1520; killed in Philippines 1521; crew returns to Spain 1522
Conquistadores: Ponce de León (Florida) 1521; Pizarro (Peru)
1531; De Soto (southern United States) 1539; Coronado
(southwestern United States) 1540
Jacques Cartier explores St. Lawrence River; claims eastern
North America for France 1534-1541

1550

Samuel de Champlain (1567-1635) explores Great Lakes region

Jamestown founded 1607; Quebec 1608
Henry Hudson attempts to find shorter route to Far East 1609   1600

Plymouth founded 1620

Dutch West India Company founded 1621; Manhattan settled
1624

René La Salle (1643-1687) explores Mississippi River, takes
possession of Louisiana territory for France 1681

PART 4 Charting the Present

The story of Europe and the New World in the period from 1600 to 1815 forms one of the most complex chapters in world history. This challenging and fascinating era was characterized by the ambitious ventures of autocratic rulers, by the rise of the common people against royal tyranny, and by revolutionary advances in thought, science, and the arts.

In politics the late seventeenth century witnessed the high-water mark of absolutism under Louis XIV of France. But new liberal concepts rose rapidly to challenge royal prerogatives everywhere. The eighteenth century was the period of revolutions that established the precedents and voiced the ideology that were to become the inspiration for the whole liberal-democratic movement of modern times. These struggles—first in the American colonies and shortly thereafter in France—constitute a precious political heritage for the western world. Their preface was England's Glorious Revolution; their postscript was the revolutions in Latin America in the early nineteenth century.

These political advances were accompanied, and indeed only made possible, by comparably important progress in thought. Outmoded ideas in economics and politics were attacked. So pervasive were the transformations in thought that they constituted an intellectual revolution known as the Enlightenment. Under the spell of the remarkable achievements of science—capped by the work of Newton—thinkers, writers, artists, and members of polite society sought to express a truly scientific, or at least rational, point of view. For many intellectuals, religion lost its emotional fervor and became a philosophical creed. Literature, in this Age of Reason, was guided by the mind rather than the heart. Painting and architecture were mainly restrained and balanced in form and spirit. In Paris, where the cult of reason reached its height, the salon was the temple of cultivated society. Here, in witty, well-informed, and often brilliant conversation, Europe's cosmopolitan intellectuals gathered to exchange views on all aspects of life. The liberal tenets of the Enlightenment touched even the autocrats of the Continent; in Prussia, Austria, and Russia, benevolent despots made at least superficial attempts at reform.

The present owes much to the period from 1650 to 1815. That period provided us with the heart of our liberal political beliefs; it encouraged religious tolerance and freedom of inquiry; and, above all, it made man the focus of attention—his happiness, his freedom, his potentialities. All these developments made this period and its Age of Reason a time of hope for the future of mankind.

But there was a disquieting feature. The liberalism and rationalism we have discussed operated *within* but not *between* societies. Humanitarianism did not touch international affairs. These were dominated by the competitive state system, in which each nation was a law unto itself and any weak neighbor was a potential victim. In this state of international anarchy, the nations of Europe evolved the balance of power to check the grandiose ambitions of national rulers whose only law was force. Thus, a coalition of rival powers thwarted the plans of Louis XIV, of the French revolutionary leaders, and, finally, of the brilliant and unscrupulous Napoleon, who sought to control all of Europe under the pretext of spreading the ideals of equality and liberty to suppressed peoples. The discrepancy between benevolence and liberalism, on the one hand, and force and autocracy, on the other, was to become increasingly a paradox of modern civilization.

CHAPTER 17

New Dimensions of the Mind

SCIENCE, THOUGHT, AND THE ARTS
IN THE AGE OF REASON: 1600-1800

Introduction. The first phase of the transition from medieval to modern times in the western world ended about 1600, to be followed by an even more epochal period of intellectual change. So important were the changes in this latter period that the intellectual movement they comprised is identified as the Enlightenment and the time span in which they occurred is known as the Age of Reason. In the broadest sense, the Age of Reason can be thought of as comprising the seventeenth and eighteenth centuries. The spirit and purpose of the Enlightenment were eloquently expressed by one of its spokesmen, the *philosophe* Baron d'Holbach, who wrote: "Let us then endeavor to disperse those clouds of ignorance, those mists of darkness, which impede Man on his journey, which block his progress, which prevent his marching through life with a firm and steady step. Let us try to inspire him . . . with respect for his own reason —with an inextinguishable love of truth . . . so that he may learn to know himself . . . and no longer be duped by an imagination that has been led astray by authority . . . so that he may learn to base his morals on his own nature, on his own wants, on the real advantage of society . . . so that he may learn to pursue his true happiness, by promoting that of others . . . in short, so that he may become a virtuous and rational being, who cannot fail to become happy."[1]

This message indicates how rapidly the heritage of the Middle Ages was being left behind. No longer was reason to serve faith, mind to obey authority, and man to spend his life in preparation for the next world. The thinkers of the Age of Reason believed in happiness and fulfillment in this world; they regarded mind rather than faith as the best source of guidance and were suspicious of emotion, myth, and supernaturalism. The chief support of the cult of reason was science, with its new laws and methods. The great age of science initiated by Copernicus in 1543 reached its climax in 1687 with Newton's explanation of the law of gravitation. The supreme achievement of the Enlightenment, however, was not in discovering additional scientific laws but rather in translating the advances of science into a new philosophy and world view.

Exaltation of science, faith in reason, and belief in humanitarianism led writers and thinkers of the Enlightenment to carry on a strenuous campaign of reëvaluation of all aspects of society. They were positive that reason could solve all human problems. All thought was colored by a belief in progress and by a vigorous optimism regarding mankind's improvability. In religion a movement known as Deism, reflecting these views, sought to establish a "rational" faith; and in the study of mankind, the foundations were laid for the systematic disciplines of the social sciences.

Literature, music, and the fine arts were affected profoundly by the cult of reason. Everywhere there was supreme confidence in logic, a tendency to minimize spirit and emotion, and a close attention to the forms and rules which had characterized the classical era in Greece and Rome, when the splendor of human reason had first been extolled. In literature and music this emphasis on reason culminated in Neoclassicism, and in art it led from the grandiose Baroque and the more dainty Rococo styles to the pure Neoclassical style.

THE SCIENTIFIC REVOLUTION

Progress of the scientific method. The publication in 1543 of Copernicus' revolutionary heliocentric theory initiated what has been termed the most important development in the western world since the rise of Christianity. This scientific revolution did not fit smoothly into the accepted order of things; it challenged the teachings of religion and the traditional ideas concerning the nature of the universe and man's place in it. By the last half of the seventeenth century, however, influential Europeans were won over to the Copernican system, and other branches of science besides astronomy continued to make substantial advances. As the new facts of science became better known, each succeeding generation felt less aversion to the discoveries of science, gradually fitting them into a system of thought in which science and religion were reconciled.

Basic to the growth of science was the development of the scientific method, a systematic and logical way of seeking truth. In the search for facts, this new servant relied on curiosity, healthy skepticism, and reason rather than faith. The foundations of the new method were laid in the first half of the seventeenth century by Francis Bacon in England and René Descartes in France.

Bacon's attack on unscientific thinking. Sir Francis Bacon (1561-1626) attacked humanism and Scholasticism and derided Plato and Aristotle, maintaining that they had managed to survive for centuries only because of their shallowness, which had given them the necessary buoyancy to ride down the stream of time. In his *Novum Organum* (*The New Instrument*), published in 1620, Bacon described the course which science and a scientifically oriented philosophy should take. First, man must cope with four major prejudices (in Bacon's famous term, *Idols*) which had so far obstructed human progress. The Idols of the Tribe are the prejudices inherent in human nature itself; in particular, they represent the tendency to see only those facts which support an opinion one wishes to entertain. The Idols of the Cave are prejudices fostered in the individual by his particular environment—the circumstances of his birth, childhood, education, and so forth. The Idols of the Market Place are false opinions which spread when men consort together. Lastly, there are the Idols of the Theater, resulting from men's tendency to become attached to particular theories, schools of thought, and philosophies and to hold on to them long after the logical basis for their continuance has disappeared.

If better results were to be obtained, new ways of thinking and of approaching the

Detail of a portrait of Descartes by Frans Hals.

Descartes, champion of the deductive method. As an advocate of the inductive method, Bacon undervalued the role of mathematics and deduction. Experimentation is not the only approach to scientific knowledge, as the mathematical approach attests. The mathematical approach is to begin with a simple hypothesis and then, by logical reasoning, to deduce various inferences. Applied to scientific investigations as a whole, this type of approach—known as the deductive method—advances by logical steps from simple self-evident truths to more complex truths. As we saw earlier, Aristotle had employed the syllogism to point out fallacies in human reasoning. It was the achievement of René Descartes (1596-1650) to make brilliant use of this method of reasoning in his attempt to extend the mathematical method to all fields of human knowledge.

Like Bacon, Descartes maintained that the first step in the search for truth was for men to rid themselves of preconceived notions and to take nothing for granted. Bacon had called for "minds washed clean of opinions," and Descartes began by being prepared to doubt everything except the fact of his own doubting. And if he doubted, he must in fact exist—hence his famous expression *Cogito, ergo sum* ("I think, therefore I am").

For Bacon, experiment was the next step in the quest for truth. Although Descartes by no means rejected the value of experimentation, he placed reliance above all on the attainment of knowledge through reason. By logical deduction, Descartes built up a concept of a unified, mathematically ordered universe which operated like a perfect mechanism; in this universe, supernatural phenomena were impossible and everything could be explained rationally, preferably in mathematical terms.

Some scientists criticized Descartes for not having made sufficient use of experiment, even as he had criticized Bacon for weakness in mathematics. As we well know, the experimental and mathematical methods are complementary. Before the mid-point of the seventeenth century, the two methods had been combined by Kepler and Galileo.

world of nature had to be devised. Here we come to Bacon's famous method of induction, by which he advocated a systematic recording of facts derived from experiments. These facts would lead to tentative hypotheses which could then be tested by fresh experiments under different conditions. Eventually it should prove possible for men to arrive at universal principles and scientific laws.

Bacon himself was an indifferent scientist. The significance of his work lies in the fact that he set forth a program to direct the course of scientific and philosophical inquiry at the time when the traditional modes of thought were crumbling. In his own words, "he rang the bell which called the wits together." Bacon also forecast the vast importance of the new science in enabling man to conquer his environment. In his *New Atlantis* (1627)—his description of a utopian society—emphasis is centered on a research institute called "Solomon's house," where experimentation and invention were subsidized and directed toward the goal of "the enlarging of the bounds of Human Empire, to the effecting of all things possible."[2]

("Sense must be accompanied by reason"[3] was the way in which Galileo described the union of induction and deduction.) Thus a revolution in scientific thinking had been effected, and the foundation of modern science and modern philosophy had been firmly laid.

Science takes to the heavens. It was in astronomy that science made its first spectacular advance. For over a thousand years, western Europe had accepted the view of Ptolemy, a Greek scholar of the second century A.D., that the earth was stationary. Rotating around it were concentric, impenetrable, crystalline spheres to which were attached the sun, planets, and fixed stars. The Ptolemaic system as expressed in the geocentric (earth-centered) theory was incorporated into the Scholastic system of the Church. By the middle of the seventeenth century, however, a revolution in man's conceptions of the heavens had been attained through the labors of a Pole, Copernicus; a Dane, Tycho Brahe; a German, Kepler; and an Italian, Galileo.

Copernicus (1473-1543) was a contemporary of Martin Luther and Michelangelo. During visits to Italy for study, he read widely in the classical authors and was much impressed with the ideas of the ancient Greek philosopher Pythagoras and his followers, who believed in a heliocentric (sun-centered) universe. He returned to Poland with serious doubts as to the validity of the Ptolemaic theory. After a long investigation of the movements of the planet Mars, he concluded that the sun, not the earth, was the center of our planetary system. Near the end of his life, his friends persuaded him to allow the publication of a complete exposition of his theory, entitled *Concerning the Revolutions of Heavenly Bodies* (1543). In this work he refuted the theory that the earth remained stationary in the middle of the universe, contending instead that it rotated every twenty-four hours upon its axis from west to east and that it made an annual movement around the sun. In 1616 the Inquisition formally condemned the views of Copernicus, and the following year his book was included in the *Index Librorum Prohibitorum* (*Index of Prohibited*

A woodcut from Tycho Brahe's works shows the astronomer and his assistants plotting the positions of the planets.

Books), from which it was not removed for a century and a half.

Copernicus had worked under a decided handicap—he had no telescope. But by brilliant analytical reasoning, based on a slender body of facts, he had been able to bring one epoch in scientific thought to a close and to open the door for another. However, the truth of his theory could be demonstrated beyond doubt only after a great number of accurate observations of the heavens had been charted. This need was in large part supplied by Tycho Brahe (1546-1601), although he himself never fully accepted the Copernican theory. For twenty-one years Brahe carried on accurate daily observations and carefully plotted the positions of hundreds of celestial bodies. He tracked the planets through the whole of their courses instead of contenting himself with picking them out at different points in their orbits. Thus in painstaking fashion he carried the science of observation as far as it could go prior to the invention of the telescope.

Brahe's data was used by his one-time assistant, Johann Kepler (1571-1630), a brilliant German mathematician. Kepler proceeded to reduce to order "the chaos of data" left by Brahe; in so doing he confirmed the general validity of the Copernican theory. While working with Brahe's data on the movements of Mars, Kepler had to account for the apparent irregularities in that planet's perplexing orbit. After patiently applying one mathematical hypothesis after another, he was able to verify that the planet did not move in a circular orbit but described an ellipse. He then proceeded to assume that the other planets also traveled in elliptical orbits. Another planetary law discovered by Kepler was that the pace of a planet accelerated as it approached the sun. He concluded that planets were moved by a power in some way emitted by the sun, but he did not discover the fundamental cause.

A contemporary of Kepler, Galileo Galilei (1564-1642), discovered new facts to verify the Copernican theory, but, as he wrote to Kepler:

. . . I have not dared to make [it] known, as I have been deterred by the fate of our teacher Copernicus. He, it is true, won undying fame amongst some few, but amongst the multitude (there are so many fools in the world) he was only an object of scorn and laughter.[4]

In 1609, Galileo made a telescope, and with it he discovered mountains on the moon, sunspots, the satellites of Jupiter, and the rings of Saturn. Thrilled with these discoveries, Galileo publicized his findings and beliefs. In 1616 he was constrained by the Church to promise that he would not "hold, teach, or defend" the heretical Copernican doctrines, and in 1633 he was forced to make a public recantation of his heretical doctrine. A legend has it that Galileo, upon rising from his knees after renouncing the idea that the earth moved, stamped on the ground and exclaimed, "Eppur si muove!" ("But it does move!")

Galileo was also the first to establish the law of falling bodies, proving that, irrespective of the weight or the size of the bodies, their acceleration is constant (the increase of velocity being thirty-two feet per second). Thus another entrenched belief inherited from the ancients was refuted: Aristotle's contention that bodies fall to earth at speeds proportional to their weight.

Newton and the law of gravitation. Great as the contributions of Brahe, Kepler, and Galileo had been to astronomy, their individual discoveries had yet to be united into one all-embracing principle or law which would explain the motion of all bodies in the planetary system and present the universe as one great unity operating according to unalterable principles. This goal was realized by Isaac Newton (1642-1727), the most illustrious scientist in the Age of Reason.

At the age of only twenty-four, he had made all his important discoveries: the law of gravitation, the principles of calculus, and the compound nature of light. At twenty-seven, the youthful genius was given a professorship in mathematics at Cambridge University. Although he had already discovered the principle of gravitation, he was not able to prove it mathematically until 1685. Two years later his momentous work was published in Latin under the title *Philosophiae Naturalis Principia Mathematica* (*Mathematical Principles of Natural Philosophy*). By this work the numerous contributions of previous astronomers were synthesized in a master principle for the universe, the law of gravitation, which was expressed in a concise, simple, mathematical formula:

Every particle in the universe attracts every other particle with a force varying inversely as the square of the distance between them and directly proportional to the product of their masses.[5]

The publication of the *Principia* climaxed the near century and a half in which scientists had struggled against static tradition and intolerant authority.

Advances in mathematics and scientific instruments. Meanwhile, mathematicians had been keeping abreast of the work of the astronomers and physicists and providing them with new tools. Indeed, as Galileo pointed out, mathematics was the language of science; of necessity these two fields had to progress hand in hand. Mathematical calculation was greatly simplified by the invention of time-saving devices and by the development of new forms of mathematical analysis. Decimals were introduced in 1585 and logarithms in 1614. Eight years later the slide rule was invented, followed in 1645 by the first adding machine. The degree to which these devices speeded up computation is indicated by the saying that John Napier, the Scotsman who invented logarithms, doubled the lives of his fellow mathematicians by halving the time involved in solving intricate problems.

Two new branches of mathematical analysis helped to make the seventeenth century the great age of science. Descartes "discovered the foundations of a wonderful science" (the words of his enthusiastic announcement) by uniting algebra and geometry into a unified discipline. The result, analytic geometry, permitted relationships in space to be translated into algebraic equations—a development of obvious value to astronomers, for example, since it helped them to represent astronomical phenomena in mathematical symbols and formulas.

Algebra was next applied to motion. The result was calculus, the greatest mathematical achievement of the seventeenth century, worked out independently by Newton and a German philosopher of remarkable versatility, Gottfried Leibnitz. This new calculus enabled scientists to consider quantitatively such problems as the movement of heat and the motion of stars, to compute quickly the content of circles, and to calculate stresses. Newton himself used it to arrive at and to prove his law of gravitation.

The work of science was no less dependent upon the development of new and more precise instruments. At the beginning of the seventeenth century, the telescope and microscope appeared in Holland. We have already seen the invaluable use to which the first of these instruments was put by Galileo. After 1650, microscopic examinations of the lungs and other organs of the body were yielding vital information regarding their struc-

ture and functions. At this time also, Galileo and others were constructing crude thermometers; and a Dutchman, Christian Huyghens, invented the pendulum clock and brought accuracy to the measurement of time. The micrometer, the barometer, and the air pump are other examples of seventeenth-century inventions that arose to serve science. The eighteenth century contributed the centigrade and the Fahrenheit thermometers, the chronometer, the sextant, and the anemometer, a device for measuring the force of wind.

Another important factor in the progress of science was the establishment of scientific societies. The first, the Academy of Experiments, was founded at Florence in 1657. In 1662 the Royal Society of England received its charter from Charles ii, and four years later the French Academy of Science was established in Paris. These societies concentrated upon the promotion of experimentation and the collection of scientific data.

THE CRISIS IN THE

EUROPEAN CONSCIENCE

The spiritual crisis. In the latter half of the seventeenth century, much of western Europe was undergoing a revolution—not in the realm of politics but in the minds of men. As a result of the impact of the scientific revolution, with Newton's discoveries as its crowning achievements, a new concept of a universe without supernatural or miraculous forces came into being. This universe could be understood; it was a smooth-running machine with all parts fitting into a harmonious whole. Scientists now were inclined to regard God not as a personal deity but as the embodiment of scientific natural law which operates the universe and holds the stars in their courses. "The ideal of a clockwork universe was the great contribution of seventeenth-century science to the eighteenth-century age of reason."[6]

By contrast to the harmony and reasonableness of the natural world revealed by the scientists, society and its institutions seemed more and more archaic and the world of man seemed one governed by intolerance, prejudice, strife, and unreasoning authority. But in the face of the teachings of science, many men were convinced that their world of religion, law, and government could also be brought under the control of reason.

The problem of how to reconcile old faiths with new truths had become, in the words of a noted French scholar, the "crisis in the European conscience."[7] Scholars and thinkers, therefore, set about seeing what could be reconciled between the old and new, what faiths if any might be left intact, and what should be completely discarded.

The dualism of Descartes. We must now return briefly to Descartes, for in addition to his many other endeavors this pioneer thinker sought to reconcile medieval religious faith with a mechanistic world in which supernatural phenomena were impossible and in which everything had to be explained rationally. According to Descartes, reason was the chief source of knowledge. By logical methods of thought, the nature of reality, the existence of God, and the existence of the human self could be demonstrated. Descartes' proof of the existence of God was based on his assertion that, as existence must be an attribute of perfection and as the Deity must by definition be the all-perfect Being, a God must perforce exist.

Descartes divided ultimate reality into two substances: mind and matter. He argued that there was no connection between the two realms except by God's intervention. The first was the realm of faith and theology, impenetrable and unknowable to science; the second was that of reason and the laws of nature, subject to the understandable processes of science. Thus Descartes, a loyal Catholic, sought to reconcile the old and the new by his system of philosophical dualism.

Spinoza and pantheism. Born in Holland to well-to-do Jewish refugees who had fled from the Inquisition in Portugal, Baruch Spinoza (1632-1677) was another thinker who sought to reconcile spirit and matter. Following the methods of Descartes, Spinoza strove to build a mathematical philosophy; his *Ethics* (1663) is filled with geometric axioms, postulates, and theories. But Descartes' dualistic system was rejected by Spinoza, to whom mind and matter were manifestations of one substance—nature, or God. In other words, the universe and God are one. While Spinoza was alive, both Jews and Christians persecuted him, but his true spirituality later was better understood. He has been called "the God-intoxicated man."

Locke and empiricism. In the main, the Continental philosophers were rationalists who believed that knowledge is gained through reasoning. By contrast, English thinkers tended to believe that knowledge came only from sensory experience, a school of thought known as empiricism. Its founder was John Locke (1632-1704), who felt that there was too much abstruse and flighty thought in Europe.

In 1690 Locke published *An Essay Concerning Human Understanding*, which sought to analyze the human mind. According to him, the mind at birth is like a blank tablet, and the experience gained through the senses is recorded on this tablet. Unlike the rationalists on the Continent, Locke maintained that, of itself, the mind has no innate power to grasp reality. In acquiring knowledge, however, the mind is not completely passive. Locke believed that reflection also played a role: by the process of association, the mind combines new and old impressions to form a new idea.

Locke's empiricism was of fundamental importance in the cultural development of modern Europe. A true son of the Age of Reason, Locke believed that investigation of such basic philosophical questions as the existence of God and the fundamentals of morality would lead men to a state of universal reasonableness and thereby free them from the necessity of relying blindly on authority.

Deism: a solution to the spiritual crisis. By the end of the first quarter of the eighteenth century, the crisis in the European conscience had eased. After this time most intellectuals pegged their faith to the new science and the new philosophy.

Upon this rationalistic, scientific basis they built their religion. Known as Deism, it stripped Christianity of most of its traditional dogmas. God—thought of as an impersonal force—became in their eyes the First Cause, the custodian of the world machine, the master "clock winder" of the universe. God had been necessary to create the universe, but once the universe had been set in motion, its immutable laws could not be altered. It was regarded as useless to invoke the intercession of God to bring about a deviation from the laws of nature. Men must rely upon reason, not miracles, to solve the problems of society.

The Deistic concept of a "natural" religion included only a few basic beliefs: the existence of God as master of the universe, the necessity of worshiping God, the atonement by man for his sins, the doctrine of immortality, and the view that the aim of religion is virtue, or sensible living. All religions were to be based on these simple and rational essentials; anything additional was extraneous and not worth squabbling about. Deists maintained that if all creeds would give up or at least minimize their "extraneous" dogmas, religious intolerance and bigotry would cease. The God of Deism was universal and acceptable to all. It mattered little what He was called. In the words of Alexander Pope:

Father of all! in every age,
In every clime adored,
By saint, by savage, and by sage,
Jehovah, Jove, or Lord![8]

The *philosophes*, critics of society. By 1750 France was so decidedly the intellectual center of Europe that it has been said "an opinion launched in Paris was like a battering ram launched by thirty millions of men."[9] Here, a group of thinkers and writers known as the *philosophes* brought the Age of Reason to its climax.

The term *philosophes* cannot be translated as "philosophers," because they were not philosophers in any strict sense but rather students of society who analyzed its evils and advocated reforms. Foremost among these *philosophes* were Voltaire and Diderot, whose

Houdon: Portrait of Voltaire

influence will be noted in this chapter, and Rousseau and Montesquieu, whose importance in political reform will be discussed in Chapter 18.

Voltaire, prince of the *philosophes*. More than any other thinker, Voltaire (1694-1778) personified the skepticism of the eighteenth century toward traditional religion and the evils of the time. He enjoyed exercising a caustic pen, soon ran afoul of the law, twice was imprisoned in the Bastille, and finally was banished to England for three years. Upon his return to France, Voltaire again championed tolerance, popularized the science of Newton, fought for personal liberty and freedom of the press, and acted as an influential propagandist for Deism. He turned out a prodigious number of works: histories, plays, pamphlets, essays, and novels. In his correspondence—estimated at ten thousand letters—he wittily spread the gospel of rationalism and scathingly attacked the abuses of his day.

Voltaire achieved his greatest fame as the most relentless critic of the established churches, Protestant and Catholic alike. He was sickened by the intolerance of organized Christianity and disgusted by the petty squabbles which seemed to monopolize the time of many priests and clergymen. Yet, in spite of his vituperation against Christianity, Voltaire did not wish to wreck religion. He once said that if a God did not exist, it would be necessary to invent one.

Voltaire's short fictional satire *Candide* (1759) was a biting attack on the easy optimism of some *philosophes* and the view that this world is "the best of all possible worlds." As his hero, Voltaire used a naïve young man, Candide, who learns after many hair-raising and comic adventures that the "best of all possible worlds" is rent by earthquakes, famines, plagues, greed, war, and injustice. The story ends with Candide advising his former tutor, Dr. Pangloss, that we must "cultivate our garden" (instead of concerning ourselves with unanswerable philosophical questions)—a succinct expression of Voltaire's commonsense approach to life.

Diderot and the *Encyclopédie*. Voltaire had many disciples and imitators, but his only rival in spreading the gospel of rationalism and Deism was a set of books—the famous French *Encyclopédie*, edited by Denis Diderot (1713-1784). The *Encyclopédie* constituted the chief monument of the *philosophes*, declaring the supremacy of the new science, championing tolerance, denouncing superstition, and expounding the merits of Deism. Its seventeen volumes contained articles whose authors—tradesmen as well as scientists and philosophers—criticized in a moderate tone unfair taxation, the slave trade, and the cruelty of the existing criminal code.

The Pietist reaction. In the middle of the eighteenth century, there developed a reaction against both the rational approach of Deism and the cold formality of much organized religion. This new religious movement, known as Pietism, developed to restore faith, emotion, and the spirit as the mainsprings of worship.

Pietism was foreshadowed by the teachings of George Fox (1624-1691), the founder of the religious sect called the Quakers, or the Society of Friends. Fox believed that the external aspects of Christianity—dogma, organization, and ritual—were unimportant compared to the spiritual experience of the individual (the "inner light"). The Quakers criticized religious intolerance severely and condemned warfare.

The surge of Pietism got under way in England in 1738, when the brothers John and Charles Wesley began to preach to the people in a new way, discarding the formalism of the established church for a glowing emotionalism. Instead of stilted sermons, the Wesleys offered extemporaneous appeals charged with religious fervor. *Methodist*—at first a term of derision—came to be the respected and official name of the movement. After John Wesley's death in 1791, the Methodists officially broke away from the Anglican Church, and the new denomination became one of the most important religious forces in England's national life.

On the European continent, Pietists stressed "the religion of the heart" rather than that of unimportant externals. In some Catholic countries a religious movement similar to Pietism arose—Quietism—but it was quickly crushed by the alliance of Church and state.

Kant and the *Critique of Pure Reason*. The German philosopher Immanuel Kant (1724-1804) symbolized the revival of the heart and of faith. Thoroughly aroused by the exaggerated skepticism and materialism of the age, he determined to shift philosophy back to a more sensible position without giving up too much of its "rational" basis. Kant's answer, contained in the *Critique of Pure Reason* (1781), marked the end of eighteenth-century natural philosophy and ushered in philosophical idealism, so important in the first part of the nineteenth century.

To resolve the conflict between mind and matter, Kant resorted to dualism. Beyond the realm of physical nature, to which the laws of science can be applied, lies the world of "things-in-themselves," which science can never penetrate and which is the proper domain of philosophical inquiry. Kant agreed with his contemporaries that the existence of God could not be demonstrated scientifically but declared that man's moral sense compels him to believe in the immortality of the soul and in the presence of God. Thus Kant put as the basis of religious faith not reason, which is subject to experience, but an absolute innate moral sense, a conscience which is independent of experience yet able to distinguish between right and wrong. On this basis, Kant believed that free will and the existence of God could be proven. Reason cannot prove that there is a just God behind the world as it is, but our moral sense demands such a belief. Thus there are truths of the heart above and beyond those of the head.

The new humanitarianism. Pervading the thought of the Enlightenment was a deep concern for the welfare of mankind—a desire to reduce its errors, add to its happiness, and ennoble its future. Belief in the helplessness of man and the depravity of human nature was superseded by recognition of man's mental and moral dignity. Intolerance and undue emphasis upon dogma and form were giving way to the practical application of Christ's teachings and to religious tolerance. Other healthy signs were the dying out of witch hunting and a growing aversion to Negro slavery.

One of the outstanding characteristics of the eighteenth century was its cosmopolitanism. This quality was so strong that even war did not necessarily breed extreme national hatreds. During the long period in which France was at war with most of Europe, English thinkers and their *philosophe* friends in Paris could fraternize with no difficulty. Proud of belonging to the European "republic of letters," the intellectuals of the time were gravely concerned with the problem of war.

As we have seen, Voltaire made a scathing attack on war in *Candide,* and several works were written urging the creation of machinery to enforce peace.

TOWARD A NEW SCIENCE OF MAN

Birth of the social sciences. One of the great achievements of the eighteenth century was the application of the methods of science to the better understanding of man. The *philosophes* believed that by such application the laws governing society could be discovered. As one of them observed:

I believed that morals should be treated like all other sciences, and that one should arrive at a moral principle as one proceeds with an experiment in physics.[10]

This spirit of inquiry led to important innovations in the writing of history and the creation of those studies known today as the social sciences—political science, economics, anthropology, and psychology. In addition, important advances were made in criminology and education.

The ideas of progress and human perfectibility—concepts basic to the temper of the eighteenth century—were expressed most clearly by Condorcet, a member of the circle of *philosophes* around Voltaire. In his famous *Progress of the Human Mind* (1794), Condorcet asserts that there are no limits to human perfectibility and declares that progress will come by abolishing inequalities between nations, by securing equality for all men within nations, and by improving the human race in mind and body.

The writing of history. The greatest historian of this period was an Englishman, Edward Gibbon (1737-1794). The prose of this master craftsman was polished again and again until it emerged in glittering and sonorous sentences that carry the reader along with their majestic cadence. Gibbon shared the rational spirit of his day, and his *Decline and Fall of the Roman Empire* (1776-1788) was a vehicle for his ideas. He exposed the evils of tyrannical rulers and attacked the "barbarism and Christianity" that in his view had weakened the greatness of classical Roman culture.

Voltaire was also a historian of no mean merit, creating a new form, or school, of history, one that forsook the old reliance on wars and the foibles of rulers. He was interested in capturing "the spirit of the times" and in describing the progress and influence of ideas; in short, Voltaire approached history as an account of the evolution of civilization.

Men like the Italian Giovanni Battista Vico studied the "philosophy" of history—not the "what happened" so much as the "why." In his important *Principles of a New Science* (1725), Vico discussed the operation of laws in history, stressing the idea that every age is imbued with a certain "psychology," mood, or point of view and that each age is not only the product of the one preceding but also the creator of the next.

Other social sciences. The eighteenth century witnessed notable advances in political science, the study of government. In Chapter 18 we shall read of the writings of Hobbes, Bossuet, and Locke, and note the work of the *philosophes* Rousseau and Montesquieu as they analyzed the machinery and purposes of government.

Economics as a distinct subject for study emerged in the last half of the seventeenth century, much of it justifying the policy of mercantilism. Later, the Scotsman Adam Smith (see p. 436) and a number of the French *philosophes* known as the physiocrats made important contributions to economic theory by attacking the prevailing mercantilistic philosophy and initiating economic principles that were dominant down to the twentieth century.

As efforts were made to classify human races and to make comparative studies of various groups of people, the first halting steps were taken toward a science of anthropology. Much of the information used for these studies was provided by the writings of explorers, traders, and missionaries.

The science of criminology was established by the Italian Cesare Beccaria, whose *Essay on Crimes and Punishments* (1764) contained the plea that prison terms should be deterrents to crime rather than punishments for crime. Shortly thereafter, John Howard in England stressed the need for efficient prison administration and maintained that the chief aim of imprisonment should be reformation of the criminal.

New attitudes toward education. Until the eighteenth century, education was almost unattainable for common people, the subjects taught often bore no relation to the needs of actual life, and the prevailing idea seemed to be that school children needed frequent beatings. In that century, however, educational thought began to reflect the humanitarianism of the age.

The scientific basis for the psychology of learning as well as for modern psychology in general was laid by the versatile British thinker John Locke at the end of the seventeenth century. His conception of the mind as a *tabula rasa* (blank tablet) at birth, and of the adult mind as one formed by experience through sensation and refined and tempered by reflection, memory, and judgment, was basic to the development of the discipline of psychology. One of the most important influences in education was that exerted by Jean Jacques Rousseau (1712-1778), whose novel *Emile* (1762) stated that the aim of education should be self-expression, not repression. Education must be many-sided to appeal to different children; and the pupil, not the subject matter, is most important.

Pietism, along with rationalism, entered into the motivation of education. In England the Sunday School movement, sponsored mainly by the Methodists, was a pioneer attempt to bring the rudiments of learning to the poor.

SCIENCE FULFILLS ITS PROMISE

The dawn of modern medicine. We have seen the spectacular discoveries made in astronomy and mathematics and their profound impact on thought and religion. Meanwhile, scientific progress was being made in other branches of knowledge, with medicine being one of the first to be placed upon a scientific foundation.

Paracelsus (1493-1541), a contemporary of Copernicus, was an egotistical, opinionated German-Swiss physician who was so annoyed with the tyranny of tradition in his field that he advocated instead the value of experimental science. The gist of his teachings was that since the human body was basically chemical in its construction, the prescription of chemicals was in turn required to cure disease. He appears to have been the first to use such drugs as silver nitrate, copper vitriol, and arsenic and antimony compounds and to introduce the zinc oxide ointment commonly used today for treatment of skin diseases. One of his most original books dealt with the peculiar ailments of miners—the poisonous effects of metallic dusts that penetrated their skin, lungs, and mucous membranes.

Another scientist to find himself at odds with the followers of Galen and Hippocrates was Andreas Vesalius (1514-1564), a native of Brussels. Although he did not deny the merits of the Greek authorities, Vesalius contended that in medical schools, attention should first be given to the actual dissection of human bodies. At the age of twenty-three, Vesalius became a professor at the famous University of Padua. He was perhaps the first professor to perform dissection in the classroom. In 1543, within a few weeks of the appearance of Copernicus' masterpiece, Vesalius published his treatise *The Fabric of the Human Body*. This work exposed the errors made by classical scholars, showed the true structure of the human body, and by its revolutionary approach achieved for anatomy what Copernicus' book did for astronomy.

A commensurate advance in physiology (without which there could be no science of internal medicine) was made by the Englishman William Harvey (1578-1657), who had studied at Padua. Becoming interested in the problem of how the blood travels, Harvey plunged into painstaking research. Aristotle had declared that the blood was carried from the liver to the heart and thence sent by veins

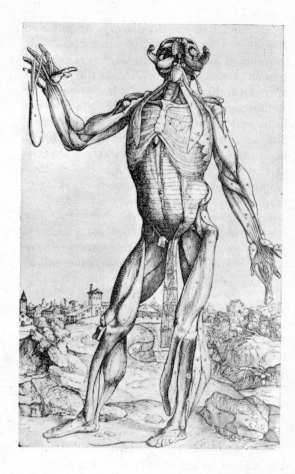

This weird figure, a cadaver with its jawbone split and its muscles cut away, appears in an illustration from Vesalius' book on anatomy.

to the various parts of the body, and Galen believed that the arteries also contained blood. In Harvey's time, doctors thought that the blood moved in the body, but they knew nothing of the functions of the heart nor did they know that the blood travels in a continuous stream, returning to its source. Harvey's description of the circulation of the blood, published in 1628 and entitled *Anatomical Exercise on the Motion of the Heart and Blood*, was a kind of master key to unlock the many doors leading to an understanding of how the human body functions.

In the eighteenth century, the most noteworthy advance in medicine was the introduction of inoculation against smallpox, then a fatal and widespread disease. About 1798 a perfected method, called vaccination, was introduced by the English physician Edward Jenner. A great step forward in the advance of medical diagnosis was the invention of the stethoscope, through which the sounds of the heart and respiratory organs could be heard. Still another advance was the study of blood pressure, one of the most important means of discovering disease. Although the method employed was crude, it led to the making of modern-day apparatus.

Foundations of modern chemistry. The science of chemistry suffered from arrested development in the sixteenth and early seventeenth centuries as men followed the will-o'-the-wisps of alchemy and magic. Then appeared the son of an Irish nobleman, Robert Boyle, who is considered the father of modern chemistry. In 1660 he formulated the law that "at constant temperature, the volume of a gas varies inversely as the pressure upon it" (Boyle's law). And in his influential book *The Sceptical Chemist* (1661), he struck out against alchemy and urged the use of inductive inquiry in chemistry.

Joseph Priestley, an English chemist, isolated ammonia, the gas which in modern times plays an important role in the refrigeration process; and in 1774, he discovered the gas later named oxygen. His last important experiment in 1799 was the production of carbon monoxide gas. Much of the gas used in our homes for cooking and heating purposes is made by the method first devised by Priestley.

Through Boyle and Priestley, chemistry had come a long way from medieval alchemy, but it would not become an exact science until the phlogiston theory of combustion could be disproved. This theory contended that in all inflammable things there existed a combustible substance called phlogiston (from the Greek "to set on fire"), which was "a principle of fire, but not fire itself." Destruction of the phlogiston theory was the remarkable achievement of the eighteenth-century French scientist Antoine Lavoisier.

Supporters of the old theory maintained that phlogiston was removed during combus-tion. By using chemists' scales in his experiment, Lavoisier proved that nothing was given off, that, on the contrary, something was added. From this evidence Lavoisier reasoned that burning is a process in which the "dephlogisticated air" (oxygen) discovered by Priestley is taken from ordinary air and unites with the substance consumed. By decomposing the red powder he had obtained by burning mercury, Lavoisier conclusively proved his thesis; the loss of weight of the powder was exactly equivalent to the weight of the dephlogisticated air given off. To the element so essential in combustion Lavoisier gave a new name—*oxygen*.

In his experiments on combustion, Lavoisier also discovered the law of the conservation of matter—that matter cannot be created or destroyed. With the knowledge that weight is a constant and that the scientist, aided by his balance, can accurately determine by weight the substances in any compound, measurements in chemistry could be made with the precision required of an exact science.

Beginnings of electricity. Only three hundred years ago, practically nothing was known of electricity and its seemingly magical potentialities. The scientist William Gilbert was the first to use the term *electricity*, which he derived from the Greek word for amber (*elektron*). In his work *De Magnete* (1600), Gilbert described the attraction between magnets as well as the forces which are created when bodies such as amber are rubbed.

The next important step in the history of electricity was the creation of a crude machine to produce it. A device consisting of a globe of sulfur set in a glass sphere mounted on a revolving axis was invented in 1660. When rubbed by a cloth, it produced both sound and light. With this device, an electric current could be sent from one end of a thread to the other—the first hint of possibilities for the transmission of electricity. The discovery in 1745 of the Leyden Jar at the University of Leyden in the Netherlands made possible the accumulation in a glass phial of the electricity which was produced by friction.

An illustration from Diderot's *Encyclopédie* shows the apparatus used for Volta's experiment in generating electricity. Notice how the copper plate (A) of one tumbler and the zinc plate (Z) of the next are connected.

The next important advance is credited to Benjamin Franklin, who was America's first great name in science. Believing that lightning was identical with the static electricity in the Leyden Jar, Franklin in June 1752 carried out his famous kite experiment during a thunderstorm. Holding the kite string with a key tied to it, he soon felt the tingle of electricity in the key, through which electricity was freely conducted as the rain soaked the string. Franklin's experiment provided a rational explanation for what had been an awe-inspiring and terrifying phenomenon for thousands of years. The experiment led to the invention of the lightning rod, which soon became standard equipment on all important buildings.

Another great name in electricity is that of Alessandro Volta. In 1800 Volta, an Italian physicist, found a new way of generating electricity; he was able to make it flow continuously instead of discharging itself in one spark as was the case with the Leyden Jar. Volta's apparatus consisted of a set of glass tumblers containing water and a little sulfuric acid. In each solution two plates, one copper and one zinc, were immersed. The copper plate of one glass was wired to the zinc of the next (see illustration). Electricity flowed through the connecting wires; the free copper plate carried a positive charge and the free zinc plate, a negative charge. Thus Volta's machine—the direct ancestor of modern electric cells and batteries—produced electricity simply but effectively. (Volta's name has been immortalized in the term used for a unit of electrical measurement, the volt.)

Advances in other sciences. Another science which made remarkable advances during the eighteenth century was geology. Here the most important figure was a Scottish gentleman farmer, James Hutton. His two-volume work, *Theory of the Earth* (1795), completely overthrew the catastrophic theory then current, which taught that the earth's surface was the result of sudden catastrophic action. In brief, Hutton maintained that behind all the various formations of the earth's surface two fundamental processes are at work in a constant and relatively imperceptible manner. The two processes are disintegration, or decay, and reconstruction, or repair. Through the action of water and wind and chemical decomposition, the former continually wears away the earth's surface. The process of reconstruction takes place as the material carried off and deposited on ocean, lake, and valley floors constantly forms new strata. By changing the concept of the earth as a static thing and stressing the immensity of geological time, Hutton gave the world an entirely new time perspective.

Exploration and scientific investigations in the seventeenth and eighteenth centuries brought to light a vast body of new information on plant and animal life which had to be classified. The old, unscientific method, which had designated all living things as fish, birds, beasts, trees, herbs, or shrubs, was inadequate to cope with the wealth of new data. The eighteenth-century Swedish naturalist Carolus Linnaeus worked out a logical system of plant classification, dividing the plant kingdom into classes, orders, genera, and species —still the basis of modern nomenclature. In the field of zoology, the French scientist Georges Buffon performed the same function Linnaeus had performed in botany.

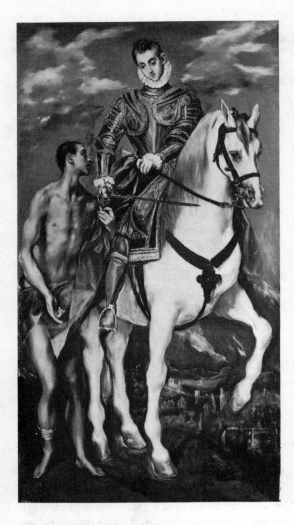

In El Greco's "Saint Martin and the Beggar," the saint is pictured dividing his cloak with a naked mendicant. Notice the distortion of the beggar's body, its suggestion of weightlessness, and the strong contrasts of light and shade.

THE ARTS IN EARLY

MODERN TIMES

The "anti-Renaissance" style: Mannerism. In Italy, where the Renaissance had initially burst forth, a countermovement in art appeared in the sixteenth century. There artists —who so often act as barometers to register sensitive changes in the cultural atmosphere —responded to the stresses of the Protestant Revolt and the Catholic Reformation.

The result was the development in Italian painting of a new, "anti-Renaissance" style called Mannerism. No longer was the artist working in that spirit of calm and balance, of harmony and proportion which had prevailed in Renaissance art at its finest. The Mannerist artist lived instead in a state of doubt and indecision, and his work reflected his state of mind. Technically speaking, Renaissance painters had mastered the problems of space and perspective, so that the artist placed his figures in balanced relationships enriched by vigorous and harmonious colors. Mannerist painters, by contrast, sometimes defied the rules of perspective in order to obtain an oblique and even twisted point of view; their lines might be agitated, their colors thin and sour, their designs asymmetric. They did not hesitate to distort the human figure in order to achieve emotional intensity.

Outside Italy the Mannerist style found its greatest achievement in the works of El Greco (the Greek). Born in Crete as Domenico Theotocopuli, El Greco (1548-1614) studied in Italy and later settled in Toledo in Spain. He was not concerned with depicting nature realistically but distorted space and perspective to create an often eerie world of the imagination. To achieve dramatic effects, he used *chiaroscuro* (strong contrasts of light and shade) and abrupt transitions in color. El Greco's paintings are easily recognizable for their elongated figures (see illustration). To us he appears amazingly "modern," and his works have had a decided influence upon twentieth-century painting.

Triumph of the Baroque style. Meanwhile, other developments had been pushing aside the doubts characteristic of Mannerism and were helping to create a style expressing the varied facets of the seventeenth century: its intellectual zest, religious exaltation, sensuality, and violence. By announcing its regeneration with majestic voice, the Church of the Catholic Reformation indirectly exerted a powerful influence on the development of a new style of artistic expression—one that would proclaim the message of the revived Church with pomp and circumstance. This new style was the Baroque.

14 (left) **Diego Velásquez: "The Surrender of Breda"** (1634-1635). The Spaniards' humane treatment of the conquered Dutch town of Breda was commemorated by Velásquez in this work. The ragged Dutch forces are shown on the left, the victorious Spaniards on the right.

15 (lower left) **Philippe de Champaigne: "Cardinal Richelieu"** (1635-1640). The great statesman and chief minister of Louis XIII appears here at the height of his career in a dramatic, full-length "state portrait" characteristic of the Baroque era.

16 (below) **Rembrandt van Rijn: "The Anatomy Lesson"** (1632). The subject matter of this painting—a lecture by the eminent Dr. Tulp to the Amsterdam Surgeons' Guild—reflects the interest in natural science which northern Europeans acquired from the Renaissance.

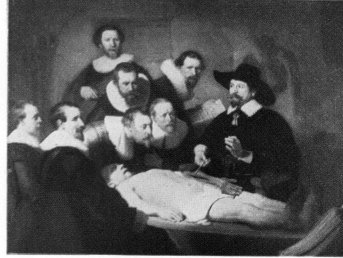

17 Peter Paul Rubens: "Adoration of the Magi" (1624). Rubens was one of the founders of the Baroque style in painting, a style often described as "a feast for the eyes." Full of movement and color, this work once formed the altarpiece of the Church of St. Michael's in Antwerp.

Vermeer: "The Artist in His Studio"

As we have seen, the Renaissance style had been characterized by simplicity, restraint, and balance; Mannerism, by unresolved doubts and attenuated, unearthly figures. Representing a departure from its predecessors, the Baroque style gloried unashamedly in color, size, height, space, and the flesh. The Baroque was decorative, robust, splendid, and even theatrical; it sought to overawe and to convince by the plenitude of its grandeur. One of the creators of the new style in painting whose influence permeated western Europe was the Flemish artist Peter Paul Rubens (1577-1640). A painter of prodigal gifts and incredible energy, he liked to choose dramatic themes from either pagan or Christian literature (see Color Plate 17). Truly Baroque is his sensuous use of rich textures, as shown in his painting of flesh, satin, armor, and the hides of horses.

Famous as a court painter was the seventeenth-century Spanish artist Diego Velázquez. He brought to his canvases a fundamentally cool and objective point of view, and at all times displayed a wonderful sense of composition (see Color Plate 14). Velázquez' portraits also prove his mastery of characterization.

The Dutch masters: Hals, Vermeer, Rembrandt. The first half of the seventeenth century was a golden age for Holland. Prosperous and comfortable, the burghers often acted as patrons of the arts. Their tastes in paintings differed greatly from those of kings, prelates, and aristocrats; the stolid Dutchmen favored "endless 'views,' pictures of cows in meadows, boats on the canals, ruddy girls and self-satisfied grocers, household interiors and family incidents, taverns and drinking."[11] A horde of competent Dutch painters arose in response to the demands of this republican art, and their over-production soon depressed prices and created the image of the starving artist.

Among the Dutch painters, the names of Hals, Vermeer, and Rembrandt stand out.

The robust Frans Hals possessed a vigorous style that enabled him to catch with particular success the spontaneous, fleeting expressions of his portrait subjects. His canvases provide us with an interesting gallery of types—from cavaliers to fishwives and tavern denizens. As for Jan Vermeer, the subtle delicacy with which he handled the fall of subdued sunlight upon interior scenes has never been equaled (see illustration). His few, perhaps overly photographic canvases raised *genre* painting to perfection, and today each commands a king's ransom.

The finest of Dutch painters—and one who ranks with the outstanding artists of all time—was Rembrandt van Rijn (1606-1669). His straightforward and realistic works gained him fame at an early age, but his later work declined in popularity as his style became more subtle. He concentrated progressively in his portraits on psychological and emotional qualities, and his work exhibits a strong element of the dramatic, which links Rembrandt to the mainstream of Baroque style.

Above is a self-portrait by Rembrandt.

Baroque architecture. The Baroque style endowed architecture with a new emotional significance, dynamism, and fluidity. Where the architecture of the Renaissance is severe and self-contained and emphasizes symmetry and "squareness," the Baroque sweeps us off our feet by subjecting us to an almost physical pull. It is a magnificent stage set, full of visual illusions intended to arouse an emotional response.

The capital of the new Baroque architecture was Rome, and the most renowned architect of the Baroque school in the seventeenth century was Giovanni Lorenzo Bernini. He designed the colonnades outside the Basilica of St. Peter's, and his plan is typical of the Baroque use of vast spaces and curving lines. Besides being an accomplished architect and painter, Bernini was also a magnificent sculptor (see his "St. Theresa," p. 304), as were many other artists of the Baroque. In fact, the architect acted also as a sculptor, painter, and interior decorator, for the integration of Baroque art reached the point where it was difficult to see where one art left off and another began (see illustration, p. 409).

After 1600 the Italian Baroque style became increasingly popular throughout Europe and was used by rulers in buildings designed to serve as symbols of power and magnificence. The vast and luxurious palace of Louis XIV at Versailles was an ideal which nearly every European prince hoped to attain, if only in miniature. The Baroque features of Versailles include the sweeping composition of its vast formal gardens with their imposing fountains, formal statuary, and elegant rows of hedges. In the interior, the silk and velvet draperies, rich marbles, and gilded carving created a background for profuse painted decoration.

Rococo style. In the early eighteenth century, there appeared a less extravagant style of architecture and interior decoration—the Rococo. It was more intimate, "private," and sophisticated than the Baroque and could be used in small country or town houses. In the designing of interiors, the grandiose features of French Baroque were replaced by delicate paneling, lighter decoration, larger windows, and floriated scroll designs. The Rococo style admirably reflected the elegant life of the French aristocracy in the heyday of Madame Pompadour and Louis XV and was widely copied in the other countries of Europe.

The Baroque spirit in music. In the seventeenth century, the Baroque spirit was manifested in music by experiments in harmony and by the development of new forms of expression. Medieval religious music had been polyphonic,* not homophonic, in form. A pivotal figure in the history of music was the sixteenth-century Italian composer Giovanni da Palestrina, who is regarded as the last of the medievalists in music and also, because he wrote much of the new homophonic choral music, the first of the modernists.

*In polyphony, several melodies are joined in a melodious interplay of sound in which no single melody predominates. In homophonic music, a single melody or tune is supported either by an accompaniment of chords or by a division of notes of the chords among three or four voices in which the "air" is usually carried by the sopranos.

In Jean Antoine Watteau's painting "The French Comedians," five famous actors of the artist's time perform a tragicomedy.

Outstanding among the innovations of the Baroque era was opera, which originated in Italy at the beginning of the seventeenth century and quickly conquered Europe. With its opulence, highly charged emotional content, and sweep of expression, opera was almost the perfect musical expression of the Baroque style. Here again we find an integration of the arts: dramatic literature, music, and acting, with the skills of the painter employed for elaborate stage settings.

In recent years literary critics, especially in Europe, have used the term *Baroque* in their analyses of post-Renaissance literature. Milton's masterwork, *Paradise Lost* (1667), with its epic scope, ornate language, and complex rhythms, has been cited as a prime example of the Baroque in literature. However, it has proved a most difficult task to parallel some of the literary tendencies of the seventeenth century with the Baroque movement in music and the visual arts. As we shall see shortly, Neoclassicism made its greatest impact in seventeenth-century France. Moreover, beginning in the seventeenth century and continuing throughout most of the eighteenth century, literature, the fine arts, and music all manifested many of the influences of an age which prided itself on the cultivation of reason, revered classical forms, and anticipated the triumph of natural law.

Classicism and the arts. Inspired in part by the order and symmetry of the world as revealed by science, the creative artists of the Age of Reason were noteworthy for their rationalism, sophistication, balance, and self-control. Furthermore, the Enlightenment was

The first church built for the Jesuit order, the Church of Jesus in Rome (right above), is an early example of Baroque architecture. An aerial view of the Bourbon monarch Louis XIV's magnificent Baroque palace and park at Versailles is shown above. Representative of the extravagant yet delicate Rococo style of interior decoration is the music room in the Potsdam palace of Frederick II (left). English architecture showed the influence of the Neoclassical style sooner than did the architecture of the countries on the Continent. The design of St. Paul's Cathedral in London (far right above), conceived by Sir Christopher Wren in the late seventeenth century, incorporates many classical elements. Paris' Church of the Madeleine (right), built in the late eighteenth century, was modeled directly after a Roman Corinthian temple.

a continuation of Renaissance humanism and its revival of antiquity, coupled with the new scientific outlook. In literature and the arts there was a respect for definite rules and conventions. The men of the time felt spiritually akin to Rome's Augustan Age and strove to exhibit the same stability, refined polish, and control over emotion. In consequence, every work of art tended to have a cold, rational aspect, whether it was a philosophical poem by Pope or a dainty symphony by Haydn. Inspiration sprang from the intellect, not the heart; from reason, not emotion. Generally speaking, classical forms were slavishly imitated; style of expression was considered so all-important that many writers were content to express old ideas so long as they were elegantly phrased.

French Neoclassical drama. The veneration for order and restraint was reflected in the French drama, with its emphasis on the rules of classical tragedy as first defined by Aristotle. His strictures had been expanded and redefined in the Renaissance as the three unities: unity of action (a single plot line shorn of irrelevant subplots), unity of time (confinement of a play's action to a single day), and unity of place (restriction of setting to one locale). It was believed that the illusion of reality, so essential to the success of the drama, would be destroyed if the unities were ignored. "Reason leads us to accept these rules," stated a French critic, truly a man of his times.

The works of the two greatest writers of tragedy in the seventeenth century—Pierre Corneille and Jean Racine—are important not so much for their scrupulous adherence to rigid conventions, however, as for their psychological insights and beauty of language. For plots, they relied on tales from Greek and Roman mythology or events of antiquity; for heroes and heroines, they drew idealized characterizations of the courtiers of their own day.

The wittiest comedies of the period were those of Molière. As a true voice of the Age of Reason, he believed that moderation and good sense were the keynotes of life and that any deviation from reasonable behavior was fair game for comedy. With rapier-like wit, he spoofed the pretensions of learned females and the aspirations of the social-climbing bourgeoisie. But like all great writers, Molière created characters that were universal figures as well as individuals of his own time.

In the eighteenth century, the versatile Voltaire achieved fame as a tragic dramatist. His plays were polished and elegant pieces, written according to well-established formulas. Today it appears strange to us that such a freethinking, liberal spirit could have been a conformist in literary matters. But in this respect he was typical of many of the intellectuals in the Age of Reason.

Alexander Pope. The Restoration of Charles II in England marked the beginning of Neoclassical influences in English literature. The foremost exponent of the classical spirit was the poet Alexander Pope (1688-1744). An imitator of the classical satirists Horace and Juvenal, Pope exposed the frailties and vices of his contemporaries in rhyming couplets:

Pains, reading, study are their just pretense,
And all they want is spirit, taste, and sense.[12]

In Pope's most famous poem, *An Essay on Man* (1733), he reduced to a series of epigrams the philosophy of his day. Reflecting the strong note of optimism so characteristic of the Enlightenment, Pope accepted the cosmos thus:

All are but parts of one stupendous whole,
Whose body nature is, and God the soul. . . .
All nature is but art, unknown to thee;
All chance, direction, which thou canst not see.
All discord, harmony not understood;
All partial evil, universal good;
And, spite of pride, in erring reason's spite,
One truth is clear: *Whatever is, is right.*[13]

The English novel. In general, the eighteenth century was an age of prose, and this emphasis contributed to the growth of a new literary form—the novel. Daniel Defoe's *Robinson Crusoe* (1719) is sometimes called the forerunner of the modern novel, but the title is probably better deserved by Samuel Richardson's *Pamela* (1740-1741), written in the form of letters. In line with the rationalistic temper of the age, Richardson's servant-girl heroine succeeds in holding her lecherous employer at bay with lectures on moral philosophy until virtue at length has its reward and the reformed rake proposes marriage.

With Henry Fielding the novel achieved full stature. Disgusted with Richardson's "goody-goodness," Fielding achieved fame by parodying the latter's smug sentimentality and, as the author of *Tom Jones* (1749), by composing one of the great novels in English literature. The hero Tom is a high-spirited, good-hearted young man who is continually being exploited by self-seeking worldlings and led astray by designing females. Finally, after many comic adventures, he learns that he must check his natural impulsiveness with good sense and reasonable behavior.

In keeping with the Age of Reason's attack on irrational customs and outworn institutions, this period produced masterpieces of satire, such as Voltaire's *Candide*. One of England's outstanding satirists was Jonathan Swift, whose *Gulliver's Travels* (1726) ridicules the pettiness of man's quarrels, wars, and vices. For example, in the fictitious country of Lilliput, Captain Gulliver finds two opposing factions: the Big-endians, who passionately maintain that eggs must be opened at the big end, and the Little-endians, who are equally vehement that the small end should be used. This absurd quarrel satirizes a petty religious dispute then raging in England. It is ironic that *Gulliver's Travels,* because of its absorbing adventures and strange characters, should have become (in adapted form) a favorite book for children.

The Neoclassical style in architecture. About midway in the eighteenth century, a reaction set in against both Baroque and Rococo, manifesting itself in a return to the intrinsic dignity and restraint of Greek and Roman art forms. In England this return to a classical style appeared earlier than on the Continent and produced memorable results. The great country houses of the English nobility exhibited a purity of design and a dignified exterior which often included a portico with Corinthian columns. The architect of St.

Paul's Cathedral in London, Sir Christopher Wren, is best known for the churches which he was commissioned to rebuild after the disastrous London fire of 1666. In order to make his structures stand out against the skyline, Wren used spires, although the spire was a form carried over from the Gothic period.

The classical revival was seen in other parts of Europe as well as in England. In Paris, the Place de la Concorde was laid out in restrained style, and the Brandenburg Gate in Berlin was built in imitation of an Athenian model. In colonial America, Mount Vernon is an adaptation of classical forms, as is the stately mansion of Thomas Jefferson at Monticello. Interest in the classical style carried over through the nineteenth century, and today in the United States many libraries and government buildings are classical in derivation.

Painting and sculpture. The arts of painting and sculpture in the Age of Reason were dominated by the tastes of the aristocracy. The graceful, delicate paintings of the French artist Jean Antoine Watteau mirrored the artificiality and idleness in which the bewigged and powdered aristocrats at Versailles spent their lives. In England the most famous beauties of the day and many prominent men sat for portraits painted in the "grand manner" by Sir Joshua Reynolds or Thomas Gainsborough.

William Hogarth in England and Francisco de Goya in Spain were nonconformist painters who strove to reproduce realistically the life around them in the gutter, the tavern, and the royal court, sometimes using their art to draw attention to the evils of the day. In his series of paintings called "The Harlot's Progress," "The Rake's Progress," and "Marriage à la Mode," Hogarth showed himself to be a pictorial pamphleteer, shrewdly exposing the vices of London life. Goya's portraits of the Spanish royal family and the nobility display his keen insight into character. In the early years of the nineteenth century, his art reached its peak in a series of etchings of the Napoleonic invasion and occupation of Spain. Called "The Disasters of War," they portrayed in powerful, shocking fashion the bestiality and misery wrought by war.

The art of the Englishman William Hogarth and the Spaniard Goya went beyond the popular portrayal of "elegance" to capture real people in real situations. Hogarth's "An Election Entertainment" (bottom) satirically pictures a brawling post-election party, pointing up the hypocrisy of eighteenth-century English politics. "And they are like wild beasts" (top), an etching by Goya from his series "The Disasters of War," vividly recreates the Spaniards' desperate struggle against the French.

In sculpture the works produced in the eighteenth century were mostly imitations of classical forms and personages, such as Venus. Houdon's "Portrait of Voltaire" (see p. 397) is a well-known example of Neoclassical sculpture at its best.

Developments in music. With the increasing popularity of opera and other secular forms, music in the Age of Reason was no longer the exclusive servant of the Church. Religious music did not cease to be important, however, particularly among the early eighteenth-century Baroque composers. Deeply religious works were among the greatest compositions of the prolific German organ master and choir director Johann Sebastian Bach. The German-born, naturalized Englishman George Frederick Handel achieved his greatest success with the oratorio *The Messiah* (1742).

New musical forms reflected new trends in instrumental music. As symphonies, sonatas, concertos, and chamber music appeared, music became more than the mere accompaniment to religious services, operatic performances, or ballroom dances. The chamber music played in courts and salons was written for wood winds and brasses as well as strings. Thus the modern orchestra developed along with the symphonic form.

By the middle of the eighteenth century, Italy ceased to dominate in music, and a new capital arose at Vienna, the city of the classical composers Franz Joseph Haydn and Wolfgang Mozart. The prolific Haydn wrote over one hundred symphonies in addition to numerous other works. For his part Mozart wrote forty-nine symphonies, climaxing his career with a trio of famous operas, *The Marriage of Figaro, Don Giovanni*, and *The Magic Flute*.

The music typical of the latter part of the Age of Reason is termed classical because it reflects the same formalism as is exhibited in the other arts of the period. Far from detracting from the inventive genius of a composer like Mozart, however, this emphasis on technical perfection of form, melody, and orchestration has been enormously admired by composers and critics of our own day.

Above is a portrait of the composer Mozart as a child prodigy.

SUMMARY

The Age of Reason was a vigorous and productive period in the history of western culture. The promise of science initiated by Copernicus was fulfilled in Newton's brilliant postulation of the law of gravitation. New sciences, such as chemistry, electricity, and geology, were founded; and other sciences, such as astronomy, physics, and medicine, were put on a scientific foundation. Meanwhile, a system of scientific method, or investigation, was established. Two thinkers, especially, investigated the problem of developing new methods of inquiry. Francis Bacon placed chief reliance upon the inductive method, in which facts drawn from experimentation are used to formulate hypotheses and eventually to reach universal principles and scientific laws. A younger contemporary in France, Descartes, was more interested in deduction and used the mathematical method to reason his way to the concept of a mechanically run universe. Actually, the mathematical and experimental methods were complementary and were soon combined to promote the further advancement of science.

By the mid-point of the seventeenth century, it was apparent that respect for science and scientific attitudes was to be the keynote of the culture of the new era. To many of the intellectuals, little seemed left of faith and traditional Christianity; and as men ceased to believe in miracles and denominational theology, what has been termed the "crisis in the European conscience" arose. Some met the crisis by turning to a new form of rational, scientific religion in which faith became a matter of logic and intellect. And as science came to modify religion substantially, so it also came to be applied to the affairs of men in society, to what we now term the social sciences. A start was made in organizing systematic studies in history, government, economics, and criminology.

In the field of literature and the arts, no less than in religion and the social sciences, scientific law and the vogue of rule played their part. Writing had to be faultlessly phrased, witty, and elegant. This polished, sophisticated, classical style reached its acme in the verses of Pope. While poetry and drama, on the whole, were not of a high order, the eighteenth century was one of great prose. The novel (which largely escaped the bonds of Neoclassical restriction) came of age in this period.

Preceded by a style of painting known as Mannerism—the best example of this troubled, distorted style is the work of El Greco—Baroque art and music captured the imagination and allegiance of seventeenth-century Europe. This exuberant and grandiloquent style gave way, in the eighteenth century, to the lighter Rococo and Neoclassical styles.

The portraits of Reynolds, the landscapes of Watteau, and the elegant musical patterns of Haydn served to embellish the essentially aristocratic culture of the Age of Reason. There are some critics of twentieth-century culture who look back with nostalgia to the aristocratic culture of the age. These critics see contemporary culture, dominated by the machine and by the mass mind, as vulgarized. The essence of history, however, is change and not permanence. In the latter half of the eighteenth century, there were important signs that the primacy of the aristocracy and the dominance of rationalism were coming to an end. New currents and forces were being released that would produce sweeping changes and mold the nineteenth century into another distinct age in the history of western civilization.

SUGGESTIONS FOR READING

J. H. Randall, *The Making of the Modern Mind,* Houghton Mifflin, 1940. Chs. IX-XV provide an excellent analysis of the rise of modern science and its influence upon thought, including religion and the social sciences. Livelier and less detailed are the early chapters in C. Brinton, *The Shaping of the Modern Mind,** Mentor, which is a reprint of the last half of the author's *Ideas and Men: The Story of Western Thought,* Prentice-Hall, 1950.

J. Bronowski and B. Mazlish, *The Western Intellectual Tradition from Leonardo to Hegel,* Harper, 1960. A highly readable and informative survey of intellectual history from 1500 to 1830; men and ideas are viewed against the background of economic and political events.

Preserved Smith, *A History of Modern Culture, 1543-1776,* 2 vols., Holt, 1930-1934. Valuable for detail but weak on synthesis.

Short but meaty treatments of European culture, with valuable bibliographies, are contained in the following volumes in

*Indicates an inexpensive paperbound edition.

The *Rise of Modern Europe* series (Harper): C. J. Friedrich, *The Age of the Baroque, 1610-1660* (1952); F. L. Nussbaum, *The Triumph of Science and Reason, 1660-1685* (1953); J. B. Wolf, *The Emergence of the Great Powers, 1685-1715* (1951); P. Roberts, *The Quest for Security, 1715-1740* (1947); W. L. Dorn, *Competition for Empire, 1740-1763* (1940); and L. Gershoy, *From Despotism to Revolution, 1763-1789* (1944).

W. Dampier, *A Shorter History of Science,** Meridian. A lucid, nontechnical introduction; contains two chapters on early modern science.

H. Butterfield, *The Origins of Modern Science, 1300-1800,** Macmillan; and A. R. Hall, *The Scientific Revolution, 1500-1800,** Beacon. Two highly recommended works on the formation of the modern scientific attitude.

A. Wolf, *A History of Science, Technology, and Philosophy in the Sixteenth and Seventeenth Centuries,** 2 vols., Torchbooks. A full and somewhat technical work with an emphasis on the physical sciences, particularly astronomy.

A. Koyré, *From the Closed World to the Infinite Universe,* Torchbooks. An absorbing account of the revolution in astronomy and its implications. E. Burtt, *The Metaphysical Foundations of Modern Science,* Anchor, which emphasizes the effects of the scientific revolution on thought and religion, provides difficult but rewarding reading.

T. Kuhn, *The Copernican Revolution,* Vintage. A skillful recapitulation of the climate of opinion in which the heliocentric theory emerged. A. Armitage, *The World of Copernicus,* Mentor, is a popular account by a leading Copernican scholar.

Z. de Harsanyi, *The Star-Gazer,* Universal. A biographical novel about Galileo and his times. G. de Santillana, *The Crime of Galileo,* Phoenix, is a brilliant and exciting account of Galileo's struggle against censorship.

E. Andrade, *Sir Isaac Newton,* Anchor. Explains the discoveries of the "prince of seventeenth-century scientists" and fits these discoveries into the mainstream of science.

M. Ornstein, *The Role of Scientific Societies in the Seventeenth Century,* Univ. of Chicago, 1928. Stimulating résumé of early scientific societies in England, France, Germany, and Italy. Includes a review of scientific advances of the period and the role of individual scientists.

H. Sigerist, *Great Doctors,* Anchor. A notable biographical history of medicine by a distinguished authority on medical history. Also recommended are two books by C. Singer: *From Magic to Science,* Dover; and *A Short History of Anatomy and Physiology from the Greeks to Harvey,* Dover.

A wealth of information about technological advances can be found in C. Singer et al., eds., *From the Renaissance to the Industrial Revolution, 1500-1750,* Vol. III of *A History of Technology,* Oxford, 1954-1958.

B. Willey, *The Seventeenth Century Background,* Anchor; and G. N. Clark, *The Seventeenth Century,* Galaxy. Two authoritative surveys which contain instructive chapters on philosophy, science, religion, literature, and art.

C. Becker, *The Heavenly City of the Eighteenth-Century Philosophers,* Yale. A delightful and stimulating introduction to the thought of the century; emphasizes the parallel between the Age of Reason and the Age of Faith. E. Cassirer, *The Philosophy of the Enlightenment,* Beacon, is a survey by a leading scholar which stresses the break with the past; the language is somewhat technical.

P. Hazard, *The European Mind: The Critical Years, 1680-1715,* Yale, 1953. The standard treatment of the intellectual currents of this seminal period, which the author was the first to label "the crisis in the European conscience." Hazard has also written a useful companion work, *European Thought in the Eighteenth Century,* Yale, 1954.

G. Havens, *The Age of Ideas: From Reaction to Revolution in Eighteenth-Century France,* Holt, 1955. The thought of the period viewed in terms of the colorful men who gave it expression; well written and up to date. Another recent study is L. Crocker, *An Age of Crisis: Man and World in Eighteenth Century French Thought,* Johns Hopkins, 1959.

J. B. Bury, *The Idea of Progress: An Inquiry into Its Origin and Growth,* Dover. The classic work on the subject.

N. Torrey, *The Spirit of Voltaire,* Columbia Univ., 1938. An excellent study of the "prince of the *philosophes.*"

C. H. C. Wright, *French Classicism,* Harvard, 1920. A useful survey of French classical literature, addressed to students.

H. Grierson, *Cross-Currents in 17th Century English Literature,* Torchbooks. Literature viewed as an expression of the dominant ideas of the period. For English literature in the eighteenth century, see B. Willey, *The Eighteenth Century Background,* Beacon; A. Kettle, *Defoe to George Eliot,* Torchbooks, Vol. I of *An Introduction to the English Novel;* and W. Bate, *From Classic to Romantic: Premises of Taste in Eighteenth Century England,* Torchbooks.

V. Tapié, *The Age of Grandeur: Baroque Art and Architecture,* Praeger. In the words of a reviewer, the author "has treated the Baroque everywhere with the excitement and admiration it deserves." Particularly good on Mannerism is W. Sypher, *Four Stages of Renaissance Style: Transformation in Art and Literature, 1400-1700,* Anchor.

F. Fosca, *The Eighteenth Century: From Watteau to Tiepolo,* Skira, 1953. Superbly illustrated review of trends in art. See also A. Schonberger and H. Soehner, *The Rococo Age: Art and Civilization of the 18th Century,* McGraw-Hill, 1960; and S. Faniel, ed., *French Art of the Eighteenth Century,* Simon and Schuster, 1957, which contains over 600 illustrations.

R. Wilenski, *Introduction to Dutch Art,* Faber, 1929. A readable and perceptive survey. See also H. Shipp, *The Dutch Masters,* Philosophical Lib., 1953.

Of particular interest to the art history student are E. B. Ripley, *Biography of Rubens with Drawings and Paintings by Rubens,* Oxford, 1957; A. Hind, *Rembrandt,* Harvard, 1932; Francisco de Goya, *Complete Etchings,* Crown, 1958, with a foreword by Aldous Huxley; and W. Hogarth, *Marriage á la Mode, and Other Engravings,* Lear, 1947, which includes the sermonizing texts originally accompanying each plate.

A. Einstein, *A Short History of Music,* Vintage; C. Gray, *The History of Music,* Knopf, 1947. Two valuable general accounts. For greater detail, consult G. Reese, *Music in the Renaissance,* Norton, 1954, which views music in relation to social and cultural developments; and M. Bukofzer, *Music in the Baroque Era,* Norton, 1947, which comes down to 1750.

CHAPTER 18

L'État, C'est Moi

ABSOLUTISM AND THE POLITICS OF POWER: 1650-1775

Introduction. The century following the Peace of Westphalia (1648) was a vitally important period in European politics. In the weighing scales of power and military might, the modern hierarchy of nations was being established. Some of the old political structures were decaying: the Holy Roman Empire, Poland, and the empire of the Ottoman Turks. Once powerful nations such as Spain, Holland, and Sweden had experienced their golden ages and were slipping into a tranquil stage of ineffectuality in the realm of international affairs. In contrast, France and Britain were dynamic and aggressive; Prussia and Russia had achieved stability and gained vigor and were advancing rapidly into the category of first-class powers.

The advance and decline of nations would in itself have made the century after 1648 one of flux and movement in international affairs. But what might be called the natural rise and fall of nations was accelerated by the deliberate policies of strong powers operating in the political climate termed the competitive state system. In the perpetual competition between nations, the decisive weapon was force. No nation was allowed to become too strong, however; competitive states manipulated the balance of power to prevent the rise of an all-powerful nation—France of Louis XIV in particular.

Offering a contrast to the pattern of growing absolutism in France were the events taking place across the Channel. The Glorious Revolution (1688) repulsed the growth of royal power in England and hastened its defeat on the Continent. The system of government introduced by that revolution—aristocratic liberalism—was the first sure step which was taken in the direction of ultimate democratic government.

John Locke's justification of the Glorious Revolution as a revolt against tyranny was a forerunner of the ideological attacks on the existing order in western Europe. As spokesmen of the bourgeoisie in France, the physiocrats attacked the old restraints and repressive rules of mercantilism; while a brilliant coterie of intellectuals, the *philosophes*, made bitter attacks upon absolutism for its intolerance, superstition, and capricious despotism. Some monarchs tried to be benevolent despots, but their efforts at reform were half-hearted, and the evils of the Old Regime remained.

THE SYSTEM OF
ROYAL ABSOLUTISM

Architecture of absolutism. In the period from 1650 to 1775, the royal architects of the national state system reached the height of their power. During the age of absolutism—the period of the divine right of kings—the king was in theory and in fact an autocrat responsible to God alone. The outstanding example of the absolute monarch was Louis xiv of France, who is said to have once exclaimed to his fawning courtiers, "L'état, c'est moi" ("I am the state").

Almost everywhere in Europe, governments had been centralized and the Church brought under royal control. Exceptions to this pattern were England, the Swiss cantons, and the Netherlands, where governments rested to a limited degree on the consent of the governed.

Under the system of absolutism the king's power touched every aspect of his subjects' existence. He was the supreme and only lawgiver—the fountain of justice. As head of the church he decided what religion his subjects were to follow and persecuted those who dissented. The worship of God was a matter of state, not the preserve of the individual conscience. The king regulated every phase of economic life, from the establishment of new industries to working conditions and standards of quality. In addition, he was the arbiter of manners and fashion, the patron of arts and letters, and the personification of national glory. A vast and obedient bureaucracy and a powerful royal army enforced his will.

Though such a system of all-pervasive absolutism is abhorrent to us today, in the seventeenth century it was generally unquestioned and often very popular. A powerful king stood for order, efficiency, security, and prosperity—values willingly exchanged for the uncertainties of upheaval and bloodshed such as had been experienced during the turmoil of the Middle Ages and the Religious Wars.

Bossuet and Hobbes: defenders of absolutism. In the seventeenth century, political absolutism also attained its most extreme philosophical expression; it was explained and rationalized by a school of political theorists, chief of whom was Jacques Bossuet (1627-1704). The most prominent French churchman of his times, he was entrusted with the education of Louis xiv's son and was finally elevated to the position of bishop. By utilizing the doctrine of the divine right of kings, which can be traced back to ancient Egypt and Mesopotamia, Bossuet composed a brilliant justification of absolute monarchy with religion as the base:

It appears . . . that the person of the king is sacred, and that to attack him in any way is sacrilege . . . the royal throne is not the throne of a man, but the throne of God himself. . . . Kings should be guarded as holy things, and whosoever neglects to protect them is worthy of death. . . . The royal power is absolute . . . [and] the prince need render account of his acts to no one. . . . Where the word of a king is, there is power. . . . Without this absolute authority the king could neither do good nor repress evil.[1]

The divine-right theory of Bossuet was the most popular defense utilized by the Christian majesties of Europe. But, in the long run, it was Thomas Hobbes (1588-1679) who composed the most penetrating and influential justification of absolutism. To this English thinker and student of new scientific thought, absolutism was not to be defended by resort to legal theory or to re-

Non est potestas Super Terram quæ Comparetur ei Iob. 41. 24.

This enormous monarch, his body made up of the tiny figures of his subjects, symbolizes an all-powerful government to which the people have surrendered their rights. The illustration appeared in the 1651 edition of Hobbes' *Leviathan*.

ligion. In the *Leviathan* (1651), Hobbes drew upon science and its servant, psychology. From the horrors of the English civil wars, the excesses of civil strife in France, and the barbarisms committed during the Thirty Years' War, Hobbes discovered what he believed to be the essential nature of man when not restrained by law. A pessimistic, cynical observer of human conduct, Hobbes saw man "as a wolf to his fellow man" and mankind, uncontrolled by authority, as essentially selfish and cruel. Without law and absolute authority, mankind lives under the adverse conditions of the state of nature, in which "the life of man . . . [is] solitary, poor, nasty, brutish, and short."[2] There being no future for mankind in the state of nature, absolute authority was essential. To create a workable society, people had surrendered all their rights and powers to a sovereign gov-

ernment, an action which bound them to an irrevocable contract. Hobbes did not actually believe that there had once existed a "state of nature" and that at some specific date in world history, mankind had decided to create, by contract, a despotic, all-powerful government. Rather, his explanation of this procedure was, to him, a rational explanation of what might have happened. If not demonstrable by resort to experience, his argument was natural in terms of rational thought.

In Hobbes' theory, the monarch was supreme and immune to criticism. Only thus could peace and security be maintained. There was no right of revolution, even against tyranny. And so the most trenchant and influential defense of absolutism was the brain child of an English political theorist who used only secular arguments in his justification of this system.

LOUIS XIV: EPITOME OF ABSOLUTISM

Inheritance of Louis XIV. The sixteenth century had been a sorry period for France. Wars with the other great states as well as civil war at home had weakened the country. The accession of Henry IV in 1589, however, soon brought peace and better times. The foundations of the great nation which was to enjoy economic, military, and intellectual leadership in the seventeenth century were laid during his reign. By 1610, when Henry was assassinated by a religious fanatic, disorder had disappeared, and the French economy was vigorous and flourishing.

Richelieu: a Machiavellian behind the throne. The death of Henry left Louis XIII, a boy of nine, on the throne with an incompetent queen mother as regent. Fourteen years passed, and Henry IV's achievements were slowly undermined until Cardinal Richelieu, the clever protégé of the queen mother, became in 1624 the real power behind the throne. For eighteen years the biography of Richelieu was the real history of France. As chief adviser to Louis XIII, the "grim cardinal" set about restoring and furthering the accomplishments of his royal master's father. His basic objective was to exalt the power of the monarchy and to make Louis' authority unchallengeable. Richelieu himself loved power, however; while he made his royal master the first man in Europe, the king was the second in France.

Under Richelieu's direction, the structure of absolutism quickly took shape. Castles of the nobility were torn down, the nobles' power as governors in the local districts was eliminated, officials of the central government called "intendants" were given the actual authority in each locality, and the Estates-General—a body that might have challenged the power of the king—was ignored. In foreign affairs Richelieu was equally decisive and crafty. As we have already noted (p. 322), his intervention in the Thirty Years' War struck a staggering blow against the Hapsburgs and helped to make France the greatest power in Europe.

Cardinal Mazarin: Richelieu's protégé. After the deaths of Richelieu in 1642 and Louis XIII in 1643, the throne of France was again occupied by a child, Louis XIV, who was less than five years old. Richelieu had anticipated this emergency, however, by grooming a promising young Italian, Cardinal Mazarin, to be adviser to the regent. Mazarin governed France with a firm and efficient hand during the minority of the king, although the royal authority was seriously challenged by civil outbreak. For six years (1648-1653), France was convulsed by disorder, but Mazarin eventually triumphed over the forces of disunity. This civil war—a reaction against the excesses of the now powerful royal administration—had no effect in tempering absolutism. In fact, the violence of the struggle served to convince many Frenchmen that the only alternative to royal absolutism was anarchy.

Louis XIV: the Sun King. Following the death of Cardinal Mazarin in the year 1661, Louis XIV, then twenty-three years old, took over the personal management of state affairs. He found his people obedient and docile; Henry IV, Richelieu, and Mazarin had done their work thoroughly. Believing implicitly in the divine right of kings, Louis chose the sun as the symbol of his power. His courtiers dubbed him *Le Roi Soleil* (the Sun King), and he was also known throughout Europe as the Grand Monarch.

A burning ambition to make his reign glorious possessed him, and he frequently defended his pretensions in haughty style:

All power, all authority, resides in the hands of the king, and there can be no other in his kingdom than that which he establishes. The nation does not form a body in France. It resides entire in the person of the king.[3]

Versailles: symbol of royal elegance. The palace of the Louvre in Paris had been good enough for his predecessors, but Louis wanted a more magnificent symbol for his greatness. He ordered the construction of the palace of Versailles on barren marshland a few miles from Paris. The cost of construction probably exceeded one hundred million dollars. The marshland was transformed into a beautiful park surrounding a palace whose façade was more than a quarter mile in length. Versailles had many great rooms richly decorated with gilding, carvings, tapestries, and statues.

Today, the palace of Versailles is merely a historical monument, a symbol of royal elegance and glittering court life that has no place in our modern world. But two hundred years ago it was the most fashionable spot in Europe. Here, during the day, the French nobles promenaded with their king among the groves, terraces, and fountains of the park or hunted and hawked in the nearby woods and meadows. At night lords and ladies in powdered wigs, silks, and laces attended balls, masquerades, and con-

certs. If the weather was favorable, aquatic carnivals were held on the grand canal in the park.

Palace etiquette was carried to ridiculous extremes; the "cult of majesty" resulted in the king's being treated practically as a god. Louis was surrounded by fawning toadies and servile courtiers, and his every action was made a regal ceremony based on the strictest precedent. For example, a nobleman of designated rank was required to dry the king after his bath, and only a very illustrious noble could hand the king the royal shirt or breeches during the public ceremony of dressing.

Louis' absolutism. During the late seventeenth century, France was the premier nation of Europe. In nearly every phase of government—in diplomatic practice, the functioning of the central government, the

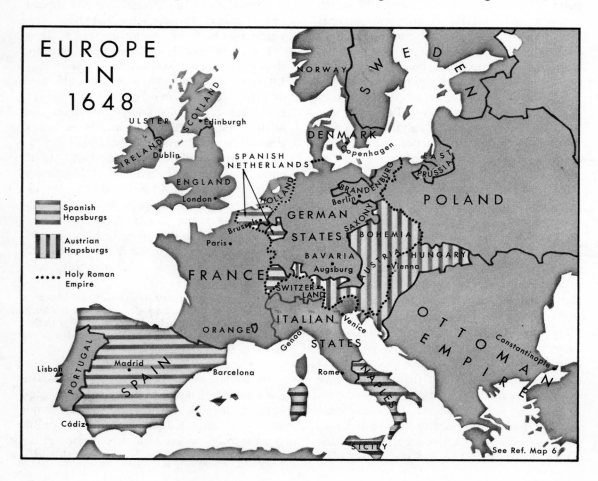

EUROPE IN 1648

organization of the military services—the absolute state of Louis XIV was the model.

Louis increased the powers of the intendants instituted by Richelieu; reorganized the army, drawing it more closely under state control; and instituted a wide variety of economic reforms to increase revenue and strengthen the French economy. To carry out his economic policies, Louis was fortunate in possessing as his finance minister the able Jean Baptiste Colbert. Colbert's aggressive mercantilist practices (described in Chapter 16) enabled a surplus of money to be accumulated in the royal treasury.

The positive aspects of Louis' absolutism—his own untiring administrative zeal and the financial genius of Colbert—were counterbalanced by other less fortunate manifestations of Louis' thirst for power and glory. One extremely unwise act was the revocation of Henry IV's Edict of Nantes. Since the publication of the Edict in 1598, the Huguenots, a Protestant minority within a Catholic state, had enjoyed a certain measure of religious freedom and independence. To an absolute monarch like Louis, complete uniformity within his state was a cherished ideal, and legal toleration of religious nonconformity was a serious flaw in the system of absolutism. Therefore, in 1685, Louis revoked the Edict and caused thousands of industrious Huguenots to flee to other lands, taking with them skills and knowledge which were to enrich the enemies of France.

Finally, and most important of all, Louis squandered the abundant resources of his realm in his passion for military conquest. Emboldened by the knowledge that he possessed the strongest army in existence and the most capable generals of the age, he embarked on a series of wars to attain for France its "natural boundaries" by extending French territory northward at the expense of the Spanish Netherlands and eastward to the banks of the Rhine.

France threatens the balance of power. In 1667, French armies marched into the Spanish Netherlands (modern-day Belgium), and Louis prepared to annex this region to France. The Dutch, alarmed by Louis' easy

Rigaud: Portrait of Louis XIV

conquest at their very doorstep and led by William of Orange (great-grandson of William the Silent, who had led the revolt against Spanish tyranny in the previous century), gained some allies and by 1678 halted Louis short of a major victory.

Louis precipitated another war by seizing some German border districts along the Rhine in 1686. William of Orange, who with his English wife Mary had replaced James II on the throne of England in 1688, became the vigorous leader of a new coalition against Louis. For eight years the allies—England, Austria, Holland, Sweden, Savoy, and a few German states—struggled against the almost invincible armies of the Grand Monarch. Warfare exhausted both sides, and in 1697 a treaty was signed. Louis retained a few small additions of territory, but the peace marked a serious check to his ambitions.

War of the Spanish Succession. The death of the childless king of Spain left the Spanish throne open to the conflicting claims of distantly related princes of both Hapsburg Austria and Bourbon France. In his will the dying king left this great prize to Louis xiv's grandson, Philip. All Europe realized that, with his grandson as king of Spain, Louis would have an empire stretching from Holland to Sicily, rivaling in its extent and power the possessions of Charles v in the sixteenth century. Louis defied the Austrian claim and European sentiment by accepting the Spanish throne for Philip.

In answer to what was to be Louis' last menacing move to dominate Europe, England organized another alliance against him. From 1702 to 1713 French armies fought the combined forces of this coalition in Spain, Italy, France, Germany, and the Low Countries. The allies were blessed with a remarkable English commander, John Churchill, who became titled as the Duke of Marlborough and is also remembered today as an ancestor of the redoubtable Winston Churchill. Churchill's most famous triumph was the battle of Blenheim (1704), considered by many authorities a victory as great as that won by England earlier at Agincourt and later at Waterloo.

Treaty of Utrecht. In 1713 the War of the Spanish Succession ended with the forces of France considerably weakened and the Grand Alliance split by petty rivalries. Comparable in importance to the Peace of Westphalia which had ended the Thirty Years' War, was the series of treaties signed at Utrecht between France and the members of the Alliance. No one nation was excessively weakened, no single power was made too strong, and, as a result of this peace settlement, a fairly satisfactory balance of power was maintained on the Continent for nearly thirty years without any major conflicts. The most important terms of this settlement were as follows:

(1) Louis' grandson, Philip v, was permitted to remain king of Spain so long as the thrones of France and Spain were not united.

(2) The Spanish empire was divided: Spain and Spanish America were retained by Philip v, while Austria obtained Naples, Milan, Sardinia, and the Spanish Netherlands.

(3) England gained important colonies from France and Spain: Nova Scotia, Newfoundland, and the Hudson Bay territory, and valuable Mediterranean naval bases in the Balearic Islands and at Gibraltar.

(4) As a reward for their support of the alliance against France, the duke of Savoy, an Italian ruler, was given Sicily and the title of king, and the Hohenzollern elector of Brandenburg was recognized as "king in Prussia." (In 1720 Savoy ceded Sicily to Austria in exchange for Sardinia.)

The significance of several provisions in this peace should be noted. The accession of the Bourbons to the throne of Spain after almost two centuries of Hapsburg rule marked the end of an era. The long-standing French-Spanish rivalry was now replaced by a strong French-Spanish family alliance as Bourbons occupied the two thrones. The English acquisition of important colonies and naval bases marked an important stage in the rise of Great Britain to world power. The treaty also gave recognition to two aggressive ruling families, the House of Savoy and the House of Hohenzollern. In the nineteenth century, as discussed in later chapters, the House of Savoy succeeded in unifying Italy, and the Hohenzollerns did the same for Germany.

Consequences of Louis' wars. In 1715, Louis xiv died, leaving behind him a kingdom bled white by costly wars. In spite of this defeat, France continued through the eighteenth century to be a first-class power, and French culture was universally admired and imitated. But in retrospect we can see that Louis' reign did much to discredit the system of absolutism.

The numerous wars which agitated Europe from 1667 to 1713 strengthened what was to become the guiding principle of international diplomacy in modern times—the concept of the balance of power, the beginnings of which we noted in Chapter 14. To prevent France from dominating Europe, coalition after coalition was formed to resist the ag-

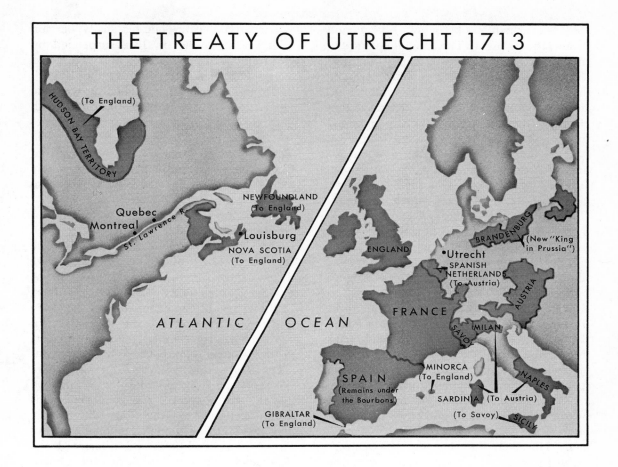

THE TREATY OF UTRECHT 1713

HUDSON BAY TERRITORY (To England)

NEWFOUNDLAND (To England)

Quebec
Montreal
St. Lawrence R.
•Louisburg
NOVA SCOTIA (To England)

ENGLAND

•Utrecht
SPANISH NETHERLANDS (To Austria)

BRANDENBURG
(New "King in Prussia")

AUSTRIA

FRANCE

SAVOY
MILAN

NAPLES

ATLANTIC OCEAN

SPAIN (Remains under the Bourbons)

MINORCA (To England)

SARDINIA (To Austria)

(To Savoy)

SICILY

GIBRALTAR (To England)

gressions of Louis XIV. Because of its geographical isolation from the Continent, England became the balance wheel in the maintenance of this delicate equipoise, throwing support from one side to the other in order to maintain the balance of power on the Continent.

Another important development was that wars were becoming world-wide in scope. In the War of the Spanish Succession, the struggle was carried on by fleets in the Mediterranean and Atlantic and by armies in Europe and far-off colonial America.

THE GLORIOUS REVOLUTION

Aristocratic liberalism and concepts of democracy. The victory of Great Britain over the French nation involved more than just the matter of English superiority in arms or strategy or diplomacy. It was the triumph of a system of government set in a mold different from that of Louis XIV's absolutism. This new political form, which may be termed "aristocratic liberalism," began with the Glorious Revolution and was an important stage in the trend toward democratic parliamentary government. Aristocratic liberalism has been defined as "government in accordance with the agreed decisions of bodies which were drawn from a limited class but acted after free discussion and with some degree of tolerance and of consideration for the governed."[4]

Beginning with the rise of lawmaking bodies in medieval times, English institutions had been developing slowly in the direction of constitutional, representative government. The English civil wars and the decade of the Puritan Commonwealth had also generated a substantial body of liberal and democratic thought. The magniloquent Puritan poet John Milton espoused political freedom in opposition to tyranny. Arguing that men are born free, that kings are elected deputies without power except that given by their subjects, Milton maintained that a republic is "held by wisest men of all ages the noblest, the manliest, the equallest, the justest government...."[5] A group known as the Levellers—made up of small merchants, farmers, and artisans, many of whom were in Cromwell's army—advocated democracy and a written constitution guaranteeing equal rights to all. Such extreme groups as the Levellers eventually died out, but the slow ferment of their ideas influenced English political life.

Restoration of Charles II. Although the Restoration in 1660 (see Chapter 14) ended the Puritan Commonwealth and brought back the Stuarts, the apparatus of government had changed in certain fundamental respects. The monarchy no longer possessed arbitrary courts or the power to make laws by royal proclamation, and taxes could not be levied without the consent of Parliament. However, the king still held considerable power. He could veto laws; he commanded the militia; and unless he committed a breach of law serious enough to warrant his deposition, Parliament had no weapon other than its control of the national pocketbook to compel him to do its will.

Behind the backs of his anti-French subjects, the king in 1670 negotiated a secret treaty with Louis XIV of France—the Treaty of Dover. In return for an annual subsidy from the French government which made him financially independent of Parliament, Charles agreed to become a Catholic, make England a Catholic nation, and support Louis in his wars against Holland. This agreement was one of the most scandalous actions ever committed by an English monarch. After Charles had collected a substantial sum from Louis, he had the effrontery to persuade Parliament to grant him money for waging war against the French king, his secret ally.

To partially carry out his shady bargain with Louis, Charles in 1672 suspended by royal command the operation of laws directed against English Catholics. As the English had come to associate Catholicism with the menace of strong foreign foes and with despotic government, a political crisis resulted. One year later Parliament passed the Test Act, which excluded all Catholics from public office and attempted unsuccessfully to exclude James, a stanch Catholic, from succeeding his brother Charles as king.

Monarch vs. Parliament. Two significant consequences of the controversy between Charles and Parliament were notable. The first was the rise of political parties as we define these groups today. To thwart Charles' pro-Catholic tendencies, members of the House of Commons formed the Whig party, which stood for the supremacy of Parliament, Protestantism, and the interests of the business classes. The Whig motto was "life, liberty, and property." In opposition, the Tory party, supported by the landed gentry, was organized. The members of this group championed "the king, the church, and the land." Although factional rivalries have existed in all times and in many places, England is considered the home of modern political parties. Whig and Tory organization and tactics have been imitated in free countries the world over.

The second important consequence of the conflict between king and Parliament was the passage of the Habeas Corpus Act in 1679. Anyone who believed himself to be unjustly imprisoned could obtain a writ of habeas corpus, which compelled the government to explain why he had lost his liberty. Later this safeguard against arbitrary imprisonment became part of the Constitution of the United States.

James II antagonizes Parliment. After Charles died in 1685, his brother James ascended the throne. At the outset of his reign, he tried to force Parliament to repeal the Test and the Habeas Corpus Acts. By royal order in 1687 he suspended all laws against Catholics; he intimidated the courts and attempted to appoint Catholics to office.

In the face of such unpopular actions the English set aside all factional rivalries and determined to remove James from the throne. An invitation from both Whigs and Tories was extended to William of Orange, ruler of the Dutch, to assume the English crown. This choice was dictated by two factors: William was considered the champion of Protestantism in Europe, and he was the husband of Mary, the older daughter of James II and the Protestant next in line to the throne. In November 1688, William set sail for England and landed without opposition. Forsaken by his army, the discouraged James escaped to France, and in December 1688, William entered London.

The Bill of Rights. Parliament offered the crown to William and Mary as joint sovereigns—an offer contingent on their acceptance of a declaration of rights, later enacted as the Bill of Rights. Rivaling the Magna Carta in importance, this declaration provided that (1) the king was not to suspend the operation of laws, (2) no money was to be levied without consent of Parliament, (3) freedom of speech in Parliament was to be assured, (4) subjects were to have the right of petition and were also to be free of excessive fines and bail and cruel punishment, (5) the king was to be a Protestant, and (6) sessions of Parliament were to be held frequently. These provisions have exercised a tremendous influence on the development of constitutional government.

Results of the Glorious Revolution. The events which placed William and Mary on the English throne are referred to by Englishmen as the Glorious, or Bloodless, Revolution. Without bloodshed Parliament had deposed the old line of kings and laid down the conditions under which future English sovereigns were to rule. In England, Parliament was now the dominant agency in government. In foreign affairs the events of 1688 resulted in a switch from the pro-French policy of Charles II and James II. Acting as the champion of Protestantism on the Continent, William used England's resources to check the designs of Louis XIV.

Portrait of Charles II

The Glorious Revolution was consolidated by other actions supplementing the Bill of Rights. By the Toleration Act of 1689, Protestants outside the established Church of England were given the right of public worship, though full political privileges were not secured by them until early in the nineteenth century. In 1693 Parliament refused to pass the customary licensing act which former governments had used to muzzle the press. Given freedom of expression, the press thus became an increasingly important aid to representative government. Other acts following the Bill of Rights made judges irremovable and led to a more independent judiciary; large standing armies, the bugaboo of the people's liberties, were not to be maintained in peacetime without the consent of Parliament.

Significant as they were, the achievements of the Glorious Revolution were limited in scope. The Bill of Rights, the Toleration Act, and later legislation guaranteed certain fundamental rights to the common people, but the nation was now governed by a small, wealthy minority of merchants and gentry. However, deeply ingrained in the English system was a habit of political thought that gave room for reform to take place very gradually, without bloodshed, until ultimately the narrow oligarchic liberalism of the late seventeenth century broadened into the full democracy of the late nineteenth century.

Locke's doctrine of popular sovereignty. John Locke, as we have seen, was one of the most eminent men of his day. In his "Of Civil Government," the second essay in *Two Treatises of Government,* published in 1690, Locke gave his answer to absolutism by expounding the following ideas:

Before government was established, all men, living in a state of nature, possessed certain natural rights. These rights consisted principally of the rights to life, liberty, and property. While life in the state of nature was not frighteningly ruthless, as Hobbes supposed, it was unsatisfactory because society was handicapped in many ways by the absence of government. There was no superior agency to enforce the law of nature, which is a body of rules ensuring the equality of all men and every man's enjoyment of his natural rights. Since men in a state of nature arrived at different interpretations of natural law, uncertainty and conflict often resulted.

Therefore, by common consent, an agreement, or compact, was entered into by which a sovereign was set up with power to govern and enforce the laws of nature. Through this contract the people give up some of their rights to the government, but their basic natural rights are in no way surrendered. Finally, the social contract is bilateral, or binding upon both parties. The government, for its part, can demand the obedience of the people, but the people may also expect that the government will keep its part of the contract by not in any way abridging the natural rights of the people. If these rights are violated, if the government rules unwisely and tyrannically, the people have a perfect right to overthrow their rulers. In short, the people are the real rulers, the custodians of popular sover-eignty, which gives them the right of revolution. Thus, unlike Hobbes, Locke used the social contract theory to challenge rather than to support absolutism.

THE RISE OF RUSSIA

Peter the Great and his objectives for Russia. One of the greatest figures in Russian history became tsar in 1682 and soon showed himself to be master of his unruly state, which, untouched by the Renaissance and the Reformation, was still a world apart from western Europe. Growing up without benefit of discipline or formal education, Peter remained all his life very much a barbarian—passionate, cruel, vulgar, and dirty.

As positive attributes, Peter possessed an excellent mind and such great stores of energy that it was said of him by his contemporaries that "he works harder than any *muzhik* [peasant]." A modern historian has added that Peter "was like a moving thunderbolt."[6] With a sound appreciation of what was essential for Russian progress, Peter relentlessly pursued three basic policies during his long reign: (1) to Europeanize his people, (2) to obtain an outlet, "a window on the sea," and (3) to make the power of the tsar absolute.

Peter's Grand Embassy. Peter first turned his attention to the Turks, who blocked Russia's way to the Black Sea. In 1695 and 1696, expeditions were sent against Azov, the Turkish fortress commanding the entrance to the Black Sea. After Azov was captured, Peter organized a Grand Embassy to visit the capitals of western Europe. The object of his mission was twofold: to secure allies for an all-out attack against the Turks and to observe the most advanced European methods of government, education, trade, and industry. Traveling as plain Peter Mikhailov, the tsar toured European factories, medical centers, picture galleries, and business offices and astonished the rulers of western Europe by his curiosity as well as by his carousing and pranks. In Holland, Peter worked as a ship carpenter in order to learn Dutch methods of shipbuilding.

While still in the West, Peter learned that his palace guards had revolted. He hurried back to Moscow and crushed the rebellion with savage cruelty. In little more than a month, one thousand of his subjects were put to death. Peter himself took a leading part in the decapitations.

Although Peter learned a great deal from his European trip, he failed to create an aggressive alliance against the Turks. The ambitions of Austria against the Ottoman empire coincided with Peter's, but Austria had just thrust the Turks out of Hungary and had no desire to resume fighting. Peter had to rest content with the possession of the Black Sea port, Azov, and direct his energies elsewhere.

The Great Northern War. In 1700 the Swedish empire controlled most of the Baltic shores. Peter's ambitions for a "window on the sea" led him in 1699 to make a secret alliance with Poland and Denmark against Sweden. Peter hoped to take advantage of the youth and inexperience of Charles XII of Sweden, a young king of eighteen. Without waiting to be attacked, however, the youthful Charles began the Great Northern War with an invasion of Denmark and astounded the allies by quickly bringing the Danes to their knees. Led by its youthful sovereign, dubbed the "Swedish Meteor," the Swedish army next landed at the other end of the Baltic and crushed Peter's army at Narva. Instead of delivering a decisive blow to Russia, Charles turned to Poland and wasted Swedish military strength in six years of campaigning there.

For the next few years Charles of Sweden continued to harass the tsar by inducing the Turkish sultan to declare war on Russia. Although Turkish victories forced Peter to surrender Azov, Sweden was increasingly hard pressed by its enemies. In 1718 the Swedish king was killed, but the Great Northern War continued until 1721, when Sweden sued for peace with the last of its enemies, Russia. The conclusion of the Great Northern War marked the end of Sweden as a first-class power and cost it nearly all of

A contemporary woodcut by a Russian artist lampoons the cutting off of beards in Russia following Peter the Great's decree.

its empire along the Baltic coast. By the peace settlement, Russia obtained an important strip of coastline bordering the Gulf of Finland. Thus Peter secured one of his fundamental objectives—access to the sea. At tremendous cost in treasure and human life, St. Petersburg was built as a "window" on the Baltic. By the end of the eighteenth century, it was an imposing imperial capital of palaces, churches, parks, and statues.

Attempts to westernize Russia. Peter resolved to change the age-old customs of his people in spite of their own opinions and desires. He instructed his male subjects to cut off their long beards, encouraged the adoption of European breeches for male attire instead of the flowing Oriental robes which many men wore, and attempted to end the seclusion of women. Crude as he was in many ways, Peter endeavored to introduce the manners of polite European society into his country.

Responsible for the revision and simplification of the old Russian alphabet, Peter also established printing presses, promoted the study of foreign languages, sent many young men to western Europe to study, and started new schools for advanced training in engineering, navigation, and accounting. In the economic field he was a stanch mercantilist who sought to make his country as nearly self-sufficient as possible. Called "the father of Russian industry," Peter also stimulated the improvement of agriculture by introducing better tools, selected seeds, and new breeds of cattle.

Some of Peter's reforms, such as the establishment of new industries, failed shortly after his death. In addition, his attempts to Europeanize his people were telescoped into a period so brief that they could not have many lasting effects, and his aggressive program of westernization provoked much hostility and reaction even during his reign. And Peter's new ideas and policies did nothing to alleviate the arduous lot of the Russian peasants.

Absolutism of Peter the Great. Peter the Great accelerated the molding of Russia into an absolutist state. All vestiges of local self-government were removed, and the central government was kept completely subordinate to the will of the tsar. The status of a noble was made to depend more upon service to the state and the tsar and less upon inherited family rank and position. The gentry were compelled to prepare their sons for governmental service by giving them a good education, and thus a powerful hierarchy of officials recruited from the aristocratic families served the government of the tsar.

The Church was made a tool of the state. No successor was appointed for the patriarch who died in 1700. Later, the office of patriarch was abolished and a Holy Synod of bishops set up to govern the Church. The new body was dominated by a layman member called the procurator, who represented the tsar. For the next two hundred years the Church served as one of the most powerful agents and supporters of Russian absolutism.

Worn out from his exertions in politics and his excesses in drinking and brawling, Peter died in 1725. He had firmly established

absolutism in Russia and ended its isolation from the West. Russia was now ready to play an important part in European history, but nearly forty years were to pass before an equally ambitious and ruthless monarch appeared on the Russian throne.

Catherine the Great. Catherine, also called "the Great," was a German princess who married the Russian heir to the crown. Finding him half insane—"a moronic booby"—Catherine tacitly consented to his murder. It was announced that he died of apoplexy, and in 1762 she became tsarina. This brilliant and unscrupulous monarch waged war successfully against the Ottoman empire and made Russia the primary power on the Black Sea. By plotting with the ruling monarchs of Austria and Prussia, she secured three successive slices of Polish territory (see p. 434) and pushed the Russian frontier westward.

Catherine served both her own interests and those of the Russian state with craft, shrewd diplomacy, and utter lack of conscience. She imitated the best features of the culture of Versailles and equaled its vices. In her own private life, she was frankly immoral, and stories of her misconduct were common all over Europe. Just as the mistresses of Louis xiv graced the French court, so the male favorites of Catherine were openly paraded in her palaces. Yet, largely as a result of her aggressive foreign policy, when she died in 1796 Russia had become a major European power.

THE EMERGENCE OF PRUSSIA

Rise of the House of Hohenzollern. If the rise of Russia was remarkable, the development of Prussia was even more amazing. History has scarcely a parallel example of the manner in which one royal house, the Hohenzollern, expanded its territory and exalted its power by fair means or foul.

In the eleventh century the Hohenzollerns were relatively unimportant nobles occupying a castle on the heights of Zollern in south Germany. Shortly after 1400 one of its members, a loyal supporter of the German emperor, was made ruler, or the elector, of a sizable but unpromising territory in eastern Germany, the Mark of Brandenburg. In the sixteenth century, the Hohenzollerns adopted Lutheranism. As a result, they gained wealth by seizing lands and properties of the old Church, and the elector increased his authority by becoming the head of the new church in Brandenburg.

East Prussia was acquired by the Hohenzollerns through the Teutonic Knights. In the thirteenth century, the Knights had shifted from their original purpose of crusading in the Holy Land and had conquered the southern shore of the Baltic from the Vistula to the Gulf of Finland. Defeated by Poland in 1466, they ceded West Prussia to the conqueror and kept East Prussia. A Hohenzollern was elected grand master in 1511, and a few years later, when the order of Teutonic Knights was dissolved, he became the hereditary duke of Prussia. In 1618, when the duke of Prussia died without immediate heirs, the duchy passed to the elector of Brandenburg.

Just four years before this windfall, the elector had secured the lands of Cleves, Mark, and Ravensberg on the lower Rhine. These territories were relatively unimportant until the Industrial Revolution of the early nineteenth century made the Ruhr valley a great industrial center. Thus, by the early seventeenth century, the Hohenzollerns held territory as far east as the Niemen River and as far west as the Rhine, with Brandenburg located in the center. The policy of future electors was to bridge the gap between their detached lands and to forge a united state.

Creating the Prussian state. The Thirty Years' War affected the fortunes of most German states and threatened the Hohenzollerns with ruin. But Frederick William, reigning from 1640 to 1688 and known as the Great Elector, remedied this situation. By building up a strong army, he made his position so strong that in 1648, when the war ended in the Peace of Westphalia, Brandenburg was granted eastern Pomerania. Its territory now extended northward to the Baltic and eastward to the border of Polish-held West Prussia. Hereafter Brandenburg was the most important Protestant state in Germany.

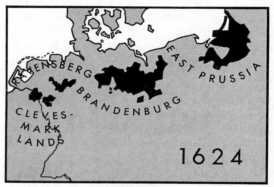

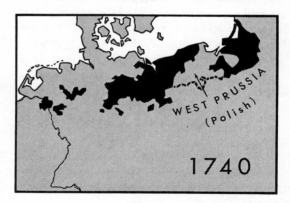

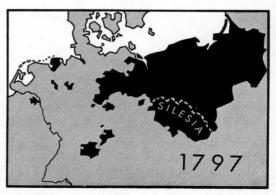

Frederick William also promoted economic progress in his domains. Immigrants were brought in—diligent Dutch farmers and (after Louis XIV revoked the Edict of Nantes) thousands of skilled Huguenots.

The Great Elector's successor, another Frederick, who reigned from 1688 to 1713, succeeded in changing his title from elector to king. The Hapsburg Holy Roman emperor elevated Frederick to royal rank as a reward for his support of the alliance against Louis XIV in the War of the Spanish Succession. The exact wording of Frederick's new title was a ticklish problem. The title "king of Brandenburg" would involve difficulties of precedence and status with other states in the empire; "king of Prussia" would not do either, because Poland was sovereign over part of this territory—West Prussia. It was agreed, therefore, that the title should be "king in Prussia." The European powers recognized the new title in the Treaty of Utrecht (1713).

By the eighteenth century, Brandenburg (or Prussia, as the combined lands of the Hohenzollerns now came to be called) had almost reached a position where it could embark on more ambitious and aggressive programs of expansion. The contribution of another sovereign was necessary, however, before this new phase in Prussian history could begin.

It was King Frederick I's successor, Frederick William I, who marshaled the resources of his state to create a superb fighting machine during his reign (1713-1740). As his contemporaries put it:

Prussia is not a State which possesses an army, but an army which possesses a State.[7]

Firmly believing that the destiny of Prussia lay with its army, the king scoffed at his advisers, who felt that prestige and territory could be secured for Prussia by diplomacy. In 1713 the Prussian army stood at 38,000 men; at the end of the reign of Frederick William I in 1740, its strength was 83,000— already in size the fourth army in Europe and without a doubt the most efficient.

King Frederick William was more than just a confirmed militarist. He created an all-powerful and efficient central government, a trained and obedient civil service, and a docile citizenry, who were told by their crusty king: "No reasoning, obey orders." The army and the bureaucracy (the civil service) formed the two main pillars of the Prussian state—a condition which remained the same down to modern times. Frederick William I has well been dubbed "the Potsdam Führer," for it was through this ruler, with his maxims of "order, discipline, and work" and "Salvation belongs to the Lord, everything else is my business," that Germany developed its tradition of subordination to the state and blind confidence in the military point of view.

Frederick William had high hopes for his son Frederick, and the prince was subjected to years of severe discipline and training. As the old king neared his last days he is supposed to have said: "O my God, I die content, since I have so worthy a son and successor." Frederick William was correct; his son was eventually to become the greatest soldier of his day and a master of Machiavellian diplomacy. Prince Frederick, who became King Frederick II in 1740 and was known later as Frederick the Great, brought Prussia fully into the arena of European politics (see p. 431). He also continued his father's work of building a powerful Prussian state at home. The remarkable rise of Prussia is illustrated by the chart below:

THE RISE OF PRUSSIA

	1648	1740	1786
Population	750,000	2,500,000	5,000,000
Army	8,000	83,000	200,000
Annual revenue in thaler	?	7,000,000	19,000,000
Stored treasure in thaler	0	8,000,000	51,000,000

Adapted from S. B. Fay, *The Rise of Brandenburg-Prussia to 1786* (New York: Henry Holt and Co., Inc., 1937), p. 141.

POWER POLITICS AND THE DUEL FOR WORLD EMPIRE

Seeds of conflict. In 1740 Europe had not seen a major war for a generation—not since the Peace of Utrecht in 1713 had brought the War of the Spanish Succession to a close. Political and economic forces were at work, however, that would plunge the Continent into war before the year 1740 was ended, and the latter part of the eighteenth century was to witness a series of destructive conflicts that would not cease until 1815. France and Britain were becoming bitter rivals over commerce and colonies; Prussia was well armed and eager to secure additional territory; and Russia again was in a position to renew the expansionist policy of Peter the Great. And as the strength and acquisitive appetites of France, Britain, Prussia, and Russia mounted, the ability of such declining states as Spain, Poland, and Turkey waned.

Before 1700, France and Britain had begun a long duel on a world-wide stage for colonial possessions in North America, the West Indies, and India. As the eighteenth century progressed, this colonial rivalry was to become increasingly intense. In line with the philosophy of mercantilism, one London merchant expressed the clash of economic interests in this fashion: "Our trade will improve by the total extinction of theirs."[8]

Since the days of Louis xiv, England had been pitted against France in the various wars which have already been discussed in this chapter. One of England's motives was to preserve the balance of power in Europe. As the issue of colonies became more important, England came to realize that it could best checkmate French ambitions in Europe by destroying French commerce and sea power in North America and India. Thus in the wars from 1688 to 1763 the English were to perfect a policy which made best use of their various resources toward this end. The policy was that of obtaining and subsidizing allies to keep the French occupied in Europe, while at the same time the bulk of British troops, es-pecially naval forces, was concentrated on the task of conquering the colonies and destroying the commerce of the French overseas, where distance served to neutralize France's advantages in Europe. The French, on the other hand, divided their energies by trying to play the game of power politics in Europe and at the same time endeavoring to compete with England over colonies. The result was to spell failure for France in both policies.

War of the Austrian Succession. It was the Austrian emperor who set the stage for a struggle on the Continent. Foreseeing the difficulties his young daughter, Maria Theresa, would have coping with greedy neighboring monarchs, he had drawn up in 1713 a document called the Pragmatic Sanction. The rulers who signed this document, including Frederick the Great's father, agreed to respect the territorial boundaries of Austria upon Maria Theresa's accession to the throne; but when the emperor died in October 1740, Frederick the Great, who had become king in Prussia in May of that year, had no intention of honoring the Pragmatic Sanction. He trumped up spurious claims on Maria Theresa's rich province of Silesia, and on examining the document containing his demands, he exclaimed to his advisers:

Bravo! This is the work of an excellent charlatan. If there is anything to be gained by honesty, then we shall be honest; if we must dupe, then let us be scoundrels.[9]

In December 1740, he invaded Silesia, and the War of the Austrian Succession began. Riding at the head of his well-trained troops, Frederick defeated the Austrians easily and occupied Silesia. France, Spain, Bavaria, and Saxony then threw in their lot with Frederick to obtain a share of the loot. But having secured Silesia, Frederick had no desire to continue fighting so that his allies also could filch territory from Austria. And so, in 1741, he withdrew from the conflict.

At first, England remained aloof, content to send subsidies to the hapless Maria

Theresa. But in 1742 England entered the fray allied with Austria, Holland, and Hanover against the Franco-Spanish coalition. Meanwhile, Frederick the Great had reëntered the war, and in 1745 his army roundly defeated the Austrians. Prussia and Austria then withdrew from the conflict, but fighting continued and the war broadened into a world-wide conflict involving the European colonial possessions. Thus it was, as the famous English historian Macaulay observed, "Because a monarch robbed a neighbor he had promised to defend, red men scalped each other by the Great Lakes of America, while black men fought on the [Indian] coast of Coromandel."[10]

The French triumphed in India, seizing the British outpost of Madras, but the British took the offensive in North America by capturing the French fortress of Louisburg, a stronghold guarding the entrance to the Gulf of St. Lawrence. On the seas, the British fleet successfully held off the French.

The war dragged on until 1748, when a general peace was signed at Aix-la-Chapelle. Louisburg was returned to the French and Madras to the English, and Frederick was confirmed in his possession of Silesia. The Peace of Aix-la-Chapelle—called "the peace without victory"—settled nothing. In derision, the French coined a proverb: *Bête comme la paix*"—"As stupid as the peace."

The Diplomatic Revolution. The duel for world empire between England and France reached a decisive stage in the Seven Years' War (1756-1763), known in American history as the French and Indian War. The war was preceded in North America and India by preliminary skirmishes, while England and France were still ostensibly at peace, and in Europe by a very significant regrouping of alliances in which two sets of traditional enemies became allies.

Thirsting for revenge against Frederick the Great, Maria Theresa turned to her country's hereditary enemy, France, and suggested to Louis xv that an alliance be formed against Frederick. The determining factor underlying Louis' decision to accept the Austrian offer was his realization that England, not Austria, had by now become France's most dangerous rival. In the spring of 1756, Louis signed a pact whereby France joined Russia, Sweden, and various states in the Germanies as allies of Austria. (Five years later Spain was to join this coalition by declaring war on Great Britain.)

To check French ambitions on the Continent, England in the meantime had made an alliance with its recent foe, Prussia. So thoroughly had the traditional alignment of powers been reversed that this new grouping of nations—Austria and France vs. England and Prussia—is referred to as the Diplomatic Revolution of the eighteenth century.

Frederick opens the Seven Years' War. Frederick the Great applied the match to the international powder keg in 1756. Quickly attacking the coalition, he aimed heavy blows at Austria before France and Russia could threaten him. Despite successes, he met powerful resistance, and Prussia was attacked on all sides. With brilliant strategy, Frederick marched and wheeled his forces, winning astonishing victories over the invaders of his realm. Frederick's allies, England and Hanover, won no spectacular victories but managed to divert the French armies from attacking Frederick in full force.

William Pitt's "system." In the colonial phase of the Seven Years' War, Great Britain at first suffered severe defeats. But the crisis ended when a remarkable statesman, William Pitt, took charge of the war effort.

Pitt had supreme confidence in his own abilities, once saying: "I am confident that I can save the country and that no one else can." He developed a shrewd global strategy of war, known as his "system," which consisted of (1) providing large subsidies of money to Prussia, (2) destroying French sea power and thus preventing men and supplies from reaching the French possessions overseas, and (3) dispatching well-equipped English forces to the colonies to conquer the isolated French armies.

After this "system" was inaugurated, English victories rained. In 1759 one French fort fell after another in North America—Du-

Three successive stages in the taking of Quebec are shown in this old print. At the right is the blockading fleet; in the center, British soldiers capture the heights; and at the left, the battle rages on the Plains of Abraham.

quesne, Louisburg, Niagara, and Ticonderoga —and in September the defeat of France in North America was sealed when General Wolfe vanquished Montcalm's forces and captured Quebec. In India there was a similar chronicle of victories.

The most decisive English victory resulted from the infamous incident of the Black Hole of Calcutta. The native ruler of Bengal, allied with the French, captured Calcutta and cruelly forced 146 English captives into a small dungeon, where overnight all but twenty-three died of suffocation and thirst. British forces commanded by Robert Clive attacked this barbaric potentate and defeated him in the decisive battle of Plassey (1757). Clive's victory laid the foundation for nearly two hundred years of British rule in India. The rich province of Bengal continued to be governed by the native ruler, but this official became a puppet of the English. The East India Company was the actual ruler.

Survival of Prussia. The victories won by Great Britain contrasted markedly with the ordeals suffered by Prussia. In spite of Frederick's tactical victories, Prussia lacked the necessary man power to defeat the combined forces of Austria, France, and Russia. His country attacked on all sides, Frederick compared himself to a man assaulted by flies:

When one flies off my cheek, another comes and sits on my nose, and scarcely has it been brushed off than another flies up and sits on my forehead, on my eyes and everywhere else.[11]

Frederick's fortunes took a turn for the better when Russia withdrew from the war in 1762. Hostilities on the Continent ceased one year later, and the peace settlement between Prussia and Austria reëstablished the prewar boundaries and confirmed Prussia's hold on Silesia.

Treaty of Paris. In 1763 peace was also concluded between Great Britain, France, and Spain by the Treaty of Paris. This document provided for French cession to England of Canada and all the territory east of

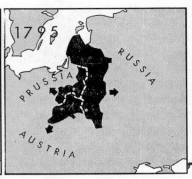

To unify his state, Frederick the Great wished to seize from Poland the territory of West Prussia, which separated his own region of East Prussia from the bulk of his kingdom. In order to maintain the balance of power in Europe, Frederick suggested to Russia and Austria that they join him in a "collective partition" of Poland. Austria abstained in the second partition. After 1795, Poland no longer existed as an independent state and was not to exist as such again until after World War I.

the Mississippi River. Spain ceded Florida to England and, as compensation, received from France the Louisiana territory and New Orleans. In India, France regained its small trading posts, but the treaty specified that the posts were to remain unfortified. Martinique and other rich islands in the West Indies were returned to France, and Spain recovered Havana and Manila. Thus, on the whole, British demands were moderate.

By the Treaty of Paris, Great Britain became the greatest colonial, commercial, and naval power in the world. That a country of 6,500,000 should triumph over a nation such as France, with a population of 23,000,000, was a remarkable achievement. As one Englishman put it:

I shall burn my Greek and Latin books. They are the histories of little people. We subdue the globe in three campaigns, and a globe as big again as it was in their days.[12]

Partition of Poland. The eighteenth century offers many illustrations of the callous and cold-blooded manner in which wars were precipitated, promises broken, and allies deserted. Yet the most shocking example of completely unprincipled statecraft was the ruthless partition of Poland by Prussia, Russia, and Austria.

Without natural barriers to mark its boundaries or to aid in its defense, Poland was a handicapped nation. In addition, it was dominated by a corrupt nobility whose bitter quarrels rendered the central government almost powerless. The monarchy was elective, and as the Poles usually could not agree on the choice of a king from among their own factions, only two native-born Poles had been elected to the throne in two hundred years. The central Diet was completely impotent; by the *liberum veto*, any single member could force the dissolution of this body. Such action was called "exploding the Diet." This was not government but anarchy in political dress!

After the peace settlement between Austria and Prussia in 1763, Frederick turned his attention to the problem of unifying his state. The province of East Prussia was separated from the main block of his kingdom by West Prussia, held by Poland. This narrow, strategic region gave Poland access to the Baltic Sea but blocked the unification of Prussia. (The Polish Corridor has figured importantly in our own times; claiming his right to this land, Hitler in 1939 ordered German troops into Poland.)

To unify his state without upsetting the balance of power, Frederick induced Catherine to accept the plan of "collective partition." Maria Theresa, it is said, declared Frederick's proposal immoral, but, realizing that her abstention would allow Prussia and Russia to annex all of Poland, she reluctantly joined in the territorial surgery. In 1772

Prussia, Austria, and Russia obtained their first helping of Poland, and the cynical Frederick, hearing that Maria Theresa deplored this action, wryly commented, "She wept, but she kept on taking." Thus Frederick acquired West Prussia and made East Prussia a contiguous part of his realm.

In 1793 and again in 1795, Polish territory was again annexed, Austria abstaining in the second operation. By the third partition, Poland ceased to exist as an independent state. But, although dismembered and under the alien rule of three different governments, Poland still continued to live in the hearts of the Poles, who hoped for the resurrection of their nation. Their faith was not rewarded until after the World War of 1914 to 1918.

ABSOLUTISM IN MATURITY AND DECAY

The Old Regime in France. In the eighteenth century, French monarchs failed to achieve an effective, advantageous foreign policy or to establish a sound and efficient internal government. The century had opened with the costly wars of Louis XIV; and Louis XV, who reigned from 1715 to 1774, was indifferent to matters of state. The next monarch, Louis XVI, was well meaning, but ill-educated, indolent, and shy.

France suffered greatly from the indifference and incompetence of its rulers, especially since governmental administration was under the control of the king. There was an alarming lack of uniformity in legal codes, tariff boundaries, weights and measures, and taxation throughout the realm, which added to the confusion and inefficiency of government. There was no body comparable to the English Parliament for registering public opinion and shaping governmental policy. The Estates-General had not been called into session since 1614.

Discrimination and injustice prevailed in the social structure. Under the Old Regime, birth, not intelligence or achievement, assured success and social position. Of France's total population of 25,000,000 people, only 200,000 belonged to the privileged classes—the clergy and the nobility. These two groups controlled nearly half the nation's land, monopolized the best positions in the Church, army, and government, and evaded much of the taxation. The peasants—80 per cent of the population—were saddled with intolerable burdens. The *taille,* a land tax; the tithe, levied by the Church; the *gabelle,* a tax on salt; and various other taxes took nearly half of a peasant's income. In addition, while the practice of serfdom had practically disappeared, peasants suffered from many vestiges of medieval social discrimination. Fishing, hunting, and keeping pigeons were activities reserved exclusively for the nobility. Although wild game might destroy crops, peasants were forbidden to molest the deer and rabbits. Many nobles were absentee landlords, who left their properties in the hands of stewards while they squandered the hard-earned peasants' dues in ostentatious expenditures at Versailles. The hearts of the peasantry were filled with rancor against their parasitic, idle lords.

Unlike their prototypes across the Channel, the French middle class had wealth without responsibility, intelligence without authority, and ability without recognition. Perhaps the most important factor in middle-class discontent was the government-sponsored system of mercantilism, by which such outworn relics of the Middle Ages as the guilds were coddled. The bourgeoisie were determined to sweep away these anachronisms, which controlled prices unfairly and throttled the spirit of competition. In fact, nearly all aspects of industrial capitalism were antithetic to mercantilism. As early as the 1620's, English economists had advocated the importance of mutual trade between nations rather than the hoarding of gold and silver by any one nation. To weaken the traditional mercantilistic system, the middle class supported the physiocrats, eighteenth-century economic thinkers who, as their name indicates, shared with the *philosophes* the viewpoint that all human activity —economic, social, and political—was subject to natural laws similar to those governing the physical universe.

The physiocrats, laissez faire, and Adam Smith. To the physiocrats, money circulated under the influence of natural forces much as the blood does in the human body, and natural laws controlled prices, regulated the flow of trade, and resulted in national prosperity or poverty. They believed in a "free market," the concept which implies that natural forces of supply and demand should be allowed to regulate the conduct of business. Deploring tariffs or restrictions on commerce, they believed that the government should adopt the policy of laissez faire (letting business alone). Unhappiness, misery, and injustice were the result of unnatural laws and restrictions. Thus all arbitrary acts of government based on absolutism had to be uprooted.

Probably the most influential advocate of laissez-faire economics was a Scottish professor of moral philosophy, Adam Smith (1723-1790). In 1776 his most famous book, *An Inquiry into the Nature and Causes of the Wealth of Nations,* was published.

Smith was indebted to the physiocrats for his views of personal liberty, natural law, and the position of the state as a regulatory medium. To him, the labor of a nation was the source from which all the necessities and luxuries of life derive. He also advanced the theory that rapid production depends largely on division of labor, and he believed that each individual in society should perform the work for which he is best fitted. By a wise division of labor, each member of society will perform quickly and efficiently the tasks for which he has an aptitude and will have a large field in which to exchange the results of his own labor for commodities produced by the labor of others.

Smith maintained that every individual is motivated by prudent self-interest:

It is not from the benevolence of the butcher, the brewer, or the baker, that we expect our dinner, but from their regard to their own interest. We address ourselves, not to their humanity but to their self-love, and never talk to them of our own necessities but of their advantages. . . .

Every individual is continually exerting himself to find out the most advantageous employment for whatever capital he can command. It is his own advantage, indeed, and not that of society, which he has in view.[13]

Smith felt that a government must avoid placing any restriction on private trade or industry. He looked on all fixing of wages, trade unions which limit apprenticeship, tariffs, and governmental interference as injurious to trade, and he scoffed at the mercantilists' view that the wealth of a nation depends on the achieving of a surplus of exports, the amassing of bullion, and the crippling of neighbor countries. Smith insisted that trade works for the benefit of all nations the world over, thus pointing up the truth that a country cannot thrive and its trade flourish if its neighbors are not prosperous.

Philosophes urge political reforms. Working with the physiocrats as they sought to remove outworn economic abuses, the *philosophes* carried on an offensive against tyranny, misgovernment, and unjust laws. The reform movements of the physiocrats and the *philosophes* were inseparably connected, for only by obtaining efficient and rational government could the instrument be secured to carry through essential economic reforms.

The *philosophes* were one in militantly advocating the end of arbitrary government and the adoption of such rights as civil liberty, trial by jury, and freedom of expression —freedoms which they construed as implicit in natural law. By expressing the belief that laws and institutions could be based on a natural law as immutable as Newton's laws of physics, they helped to undermine the edifice of absolutism. Preëminent for their intellectual assault on absolutism were Montesquieu and Rousseau, whose theories rank in importance with those of John Locke.

Montesquieu and *The Spirit of Laws.* Montesquieu (1689-1755), a French nobleman, was born just a century before the outbreak of the French Revolution and was destined to become the most systematic and comprehensive student of government during the first half of the eighteenth century.

He is noted primarily for *The Spirit of Laws* (1748), a massive study of the salient features of numerous governments known to have actually existed. Widely discussed in the French salons, it later became the political bible of statesmen in England and colonial America.

Unlike John Locke and many of the *philosophes,* Montesquieu did not use the deductive approach in his writings. He did not seek to discover certain universal principles or natural laws and then proceed to describe a perfect society based on nature; his interest lay not in generalizations but in facts. His method was to describe and analyze governments and then to show how they reflected the environment in which they functioned.

In *The Spirit of Laws,* Montesquieu concluded that all governments conformed to certain specific factors of geography, economics, and race, which varied from country to country. Since the value of any governmental system depended on its relation to these specific factors, no one form of government could be better than another, nor could there be a "best" form of government.

Montesquieu was a relentless critic of tyranny and a champion of liberty. Although he did not endorse any one form of government, he admired the limited parliamentary monarchy of England. In the separation of executive, legislative, and judicial powers, he saw the bulwark of liberty. Nevertheless, astute as he was in his judgments, Montesquieu misinterpreted the operation of the unwritten English constitution, for the English government was moving toward unity of powers. However, his concept of separation of powers greatly influenced the planners of the American Constitution.

The enigma of Rousseau. Although he believed in the general objectives of the *philosophes,* Jean Jacques Rousseau (whom we discussed as an educational reformer in Chapter 17) distrusted reason and science. He gloried in impulses and intuitions, trusting emotions rather than thoughts, the heart rather than the mind. A bundle of contradictions, his words have been cited to justify the arguments of such divergent political philosophies as democracy and totalitarianism.

Rousseau's most important work and indeed one of the most influential books on political theory of modern times was his *Social Contract* (1762), which opens with the stirring statement: "Man is born free, but is everywhere in chains." In this work, Rousseau endeavored to construct a theory of government based on the consent of the governed while reconciling the conflicting demands of individual liberty and social organization. Using Locke's basic assumptions of the social contract and natural law, Rousseau expounded the doctrine of popular sovereignty, the supremacy of the common people, and their right of revolution:

. . . the depositories of the executive power are not the people's masters, but its officers . . . it can set them up and pull them down when it likes . . . for them there is no question of contract, but of obedience . . . [14]

But Rousseau's solution for reconciling the natural freedom of the individual with membership in a social group ruled by law is replete with contradictions and bad logic. In Rousseau's ideal society, an individual can surrender all his natural rights—as envisaged by Locke—to the group and yet retain his freedom. This happy situation is secured by each individual's voluntarily forming part of what is called "the General Will." Because he forms part of this whole, he continues to remain free. It is then argued that the majority, which always knows what is best for the group, is the custodian of the General Will. In fact, the majority is a better judge than the individual of what is best for him, and thus the individual must obey its commands.

In advancing the cause of democracy, Rousseau was hailed as the champion of the masses. But it is also true that his doctrine of the General Will came to be used by ambitious despots. Claiming that he alone knew what constituted the General Will, a shrewd leader could justify his seizure of power. It is one of history's ironies that the *Social Contract,* written to justify popular revolution and democracy, was used later on to justify totalitarianism.

Faith in benevolent despotism. The majority of the *philosophes* believed that the most logical way to attain desirable reforms was through the rule of a benevolent despot: secure a well-meaning, intelligent monarch imbued with the philosophy of the Enlightenment and all would be well. In a sense, this theory of government was akin to the Platonic ideal of a society where philosophers would be kings.

A few eighteenth-century monarchs were progressive, sincerely believing in the ideas of the *philosophes*. Major figures who were touched by the Enlightenment and became (or seemed to become) benevolent despots were Frederick the Great of Prussia, Catherine the Great of Russia, and the Austrian emperor Joseph II.

Frederick, a model ruler. Dedicated to improving the Prussian state, Frederick expressed his concept of the benevolent monarch's role thus:

The monarch is only the first servant of the State, who is obliged to act with probity and prudence, and to remain as totally disinterested as if he were each moment liable to render an account of his administration to his fellow-citizens. . . . As the sovereign is properly the head of a family of citizens, the father of his people, he ought on all occasions to be the last refuge of the unfortunate.[15]

"Old Fritz," as his subjects affectionately called him, traveled a great deal about his kingdom, studying its problems and hearing complaints from his people. No aspect of government escaped his attention. His reforms included the abolishment of torture, the reorganization of the civil service, and the recognition of equality of status for his Catholic subjects. In the area of economics, he encouraged immigration to his country, promoted the conservation of Prussia's natural resources, and established textile and silk factories. Until he died in 1786 at the age of seventy-four, Frederick worked diligently at the occupation of kingship, aware that he had made Prussia a great European power.

Enlightened despotism in Russia. Like her contemporary, Frederick the Great, Catherine of Russia was a shrewd, ruthless double-dealer in foreign affairs. But in the early part of her reign, she prided herself upon being a patron of learning and the arts, a friend to the *philosophes,* and an exponent of the Enlightenment in government.

Catherine worked diligently to improve Russian law and its administration, the best evidence being the *Instructions* she prepared for a commission which had been organized to draft a new code of laws. In this document, Catherine indicated that, although the supreme ruler, the monarch, was the sole judge of what was right or wrong, nothing cruel or unjust should be done to a king's subjects. By "equality" she meant that all people were subject to the same laws of the realm; by freedom, "the right to do everything that the laws allow."

Joseph II of Austria. The most sincere of the benevolent despots was Joseph II, the Hapsburg scion and son of Maria Theresa. Joseph's reforms included the establishment of an equitable basis for taxation and the improvement of education. His abolition of serfdom was the most revolutionary decree of this period, but his most lasting reform was the creation of a national court system.

Failure of benevolent despotism. Benevolent despotism was incapable of rooting out the deep-seated evils of the Old Regime. No matter how sincere and devoted to reform, an enlightened ruler such as Joseph of Austria could not achieve success against the selfishness of his nobility and the ignorance of his peasantry. Many of Joseph's reforms appeared premature, and he was considered too hasty in adopting new measures. He died in 1790, a broken-hearted man.

In a number of cases, enlightened absolutism was nothing but a façade, a mere playing at reform because it was fashionable. With the passage of years, Catherine the Great's views of Enlightenment changed considerably. Before her death in 1796, she no longer quoted her "dear *philosophes*" or proclaimed their ideas. She had repressed a widespread peasants' rebellion with savage cruelty and, in addition, she had been frightened by the French Revolution, "the enemy of God and of the Thrones,"[16] as she called it.

Even half-hearted benevolent despotism was better than no benevolence at all, however. But the evils inherent in an all-powerful monarchy tainted the system of benevolent despotism. In dominating his people, Frederick neglected to educate them to political realities. The British ambassador in Berlin wrote:

The Prussian Monarchy reminds me of a vast prison in the centre of which appears the great keeper, occupied in the care of his captives.[17]

Furthermore, when the enlightened despots died, there was no one trained to take their place.

SUMMARY

The character of the period just surveyed (1650-1775) was shaped largely by the activities of absolute governments and the increased competition between them for territorial conquests and military glory. The arrogant and ambitious Louis XIV of France was the model for other all-powerful monarchs in Russia, Prussia, Austria, and most of the smaller European states.

The concentration of power in the hands of absolutist kings germinated an epidemic of wars that convulsed Europe during this period. Declining states, such as Poland and Turkey, and temporarily weakened states, such as Austria at the accession of Maria Theresa, were tempting bait for dynamic, aggressive neighbors. Commercial and colonial rivalry added to the competitive spirit and resulted in a world-wide duel for empire between France and Great Britain. Great Britain, as the leader of various coalitions and the self-appointed caretaker of the Continental balance of power, emerged victorious over France and the monarchical despotism it symbolized. In England the successful Glorious Revolution heralded the triumph of aristocratic liberalism: the rule of Parliament and of law. The most wealthy and influential elements in society controlled the government, and their support made for a stronger government than that operating from Versailles.

Her professed interest in the Enlightenment did not prevent Catherine of Russia from strengthening serfdom as a basic institution in Russia's social and economic structure.

In this period it was determined that North America would be mainly Anglo-Saxon in culture; British rule was firmly established in India; and Britain's sea power gained the world-wide supremacy it was to hold well into the twentieth century. This period also saw the rise of the Prussian type of absolutism —the militaristic state—and the birth of the Russian policy of securing access to the Baltic and Mediterranean seas.

Our discussion has also dealt with the changes in the realm of thought. The chief protagonists in this field were the champions of the middle class, who demanded reform in both politics and economics. In both these fields the keynote was freedom for the individual. But to the thinkers of the Enlightenment, it was mainly freedom and opportunity for a very special kind of individual—the well-educated, intelligent, and preferably well-to-do. Most *philosophes* believed that the blessings of an enlightened society could best be secured by the rule of benevolent despots. On the other hand, Locke and Montesquieu favored the English parliamentary system as the best means to good government. Rousseau wrote a flaming justification of revolution and democracy, but his confused and tortuous logic unwittingly provided ammunition for the arguments of later dictators.

These thinkers created an enlightened climate of opinion and a widespread tendency toward reform in western Europe. Their ideas crossed the Atlantic and profoundly influenced public opinion in the Americas. In Europe many monarchs thought it fashionable to follow the teachings of the *philosophes*, but these benevolent despots failed to ward off the ultimate downfall of the Old Regime because their reforms were not sufficiently comprehensive and thorough. In countries such as Prussia and Austria, benevolent despotism had some limited successes, but in France, hotbed of reformist philosophy, the kings refused to be enlightened. The French monarchs presided in an incredibly short-sighted fashion over a regime that was locked in stagnation and paralysis. The result could only be a violent upheaval, and the account of this cataclysm will form one of the main themes of our next chapter, "The Rights of Man."

SUGGESTIONS FOR READING

M. Beloff, *The Age of Absolutism, 1660-1815,* Oxford (Hutchinson Univ. Library), 1954. A small volume tightly packed with facts, shrewd analyses, and brilliant generalizations. Also brief and stimulating are C. J. Friedrich and C. Blitzer, *The Age of Power,** Cornell; F. Manuel, *The Age of Reason,** Cornell; and G. Bruun, *The Enlightened Despots,** Holt (Berkshire Studies). Not to be overlooked are the valuable syntheses contained in the pertinent volumes of *The Rise of Modern Europe* series (Harper); see the list in the Suggestions for Reading for Chapter 17.

For detailed surveys of seventeenth- and eighteenth-century political history, see D. Ogg, *Europe in the Seventeenth Century,* Macmillan, 1960; A. Sorel, *Europe Under the Old Regime,* Ritchie, 1947; and A. Hassall, *The Balance of Power, 1715-1789,* Macmillan, 1922. Useful for reference is J. O. Lindsay, ed., *The Old Regime, 1713-1763,* Cambridge Univ., 1957, Vol. VII of *The New Cambridge Modern History.*

J. F. C. Fuller, *A Military History of the Western World,* II, Funk and Wagnalls, 1954; and A. Mahan, *The Influence of Sea Power on History, 1660-1783,** Hill and Wang. Excellent studies of the many wars of the period.

L. B. Packard, *The Age of Louis XIV,** Holt (Berkshire Studies). Brief and first-rate. Also short and excellent are M. Ashley, *Louis XIV and the Greatness of France,* Macmillan (Teach Yourself History), 1948; and D. Ogg, *Louis XIV,* Oxford (Home Univ. Library), 1951. On the important work of Louis' immediate predecessors, see the readable brief survey by C. V. Wedgwood, *Richelieu and the French Monarchy,* Macmillan (Teach Yourself History), 1950.

W. H. Lewis, *The Splendid Century,** Anchor. A fascinating popular account of French society, high and low, during the days of Louis XIV. Other works on the Old Regime in France preceding the French Revolution are listed in the Suggestions for Reading following Chapter 19.

*Indicates an inexpensive paperbound edition.

M. Ashley, *England in the Seventeenth Century, 1603-1714,** Penguin. A first-rate survey. Valuable analyses of the causes and consequences of the Glorious Revolution are contained in G. M. Trevelyan, *The English Revolution, 1688-1689,* Oxford (Home Univ. Library), 1938; and G. P. Gooch, *English Democratic Ideas in the Seventeenth Century,** Torchbooks.

B. Sumner, *Peter the Great and the Emergence of Russia,* Macmillan (Teach Yourself History), 1950. A brief and vivid account of Peter and his times. H. Lamb, *The City and the Tsar: Peter the Great and the Move to the West, 1648-1762,* Doubleday, 1948, is an absorbing popular treatment. Scholarly is V. Klyuchevsky, *Peter the Great,* St. Martin's, 1958.

G. S. Thomson, *Catherine the Great and the Expansion of Russia,* Macmillan (Teach Yourself History), 1950. A superb depiction of another of Russia's most celebrated rulers. L. Blair, tr., *The Memoirs of Catherine the Great,** Bantam, is also good reading.

S. B. Fay, *The Rise of Brandenburg-Prussia to 1786,* Holt (Berkshire Studies), 1937. An admirable introduction. See also F. Carsten, *The Origins of Prussia,* Oxford, 1954.

R. Ergang, *The Potsdam Führer,* Frederick William I, Columbia Univ., 1941. A graphic portrayal. His son's career is painted with bold strokes in G. P. Gooch, *Frederick the Great: the Ruler, the Writer, the Man,* Knopf, 1947.

G. H. Sabine, *A History of Political Theory,* Holt, 1954. Outstandingly good on seventeenth- and eighteenth-century political thought. See also K. Martin, *French Liberal Thought in the Eighteenth Century,* Benn, 1929; and A. Cobban, *Rousseau and the Modern State,* Allen and Unwin, 1934.

On the origins of laissez-faire economic theory, see C. Gide and C. Rist, *A History of Economic Doctrines from the Time of the Physiocrats to the Present Day,* Heath, 1948.

CHAPTER 19

The Rights of Man

REVOLUTIONS IN THE WESTERN WORLD: 1689-1825

Introduction. This chapter traces the course of the momentous political changes which occurred from the end of the seventeenth century to the beginning of the nineteenth. We shall see Englishmen perfecting their cabinet system by limiting the power of their monarch; we shall follow the actions of the Thirteen Colonies as they successfully defy Britain and achieve their independence; and we shall witness the overthrow of an ineffectual French king and watch a new republic rising from the suffering and bloodshed of revolution.

The rise of republican France was a challenge to despotic regimes throughout Europe, and the result was intermittent warfare on the Continent from 1792 to 1815. In the midst of this troubled era, Napoleon came to power. Turning the new-born republic into a tool for conquest, the Little Corporal threatened all Europe until defeat at Waterloo crushed his dreams of empire.

We shall also watch the struggle of colonials in Latin America to throw off the shackles of repressive Old World regimes, for this liberation movement, too, shares in the causal relationship uniting all these world-shaking events. The American Revolution can be explained, in part, by the interruption of the growth of cabinet government in England. In turn, the American Revolution exercised a potent influence upon the course of revolution in France. And the successful defiance of authority in the Thirteen Colonies and in revolutionary France helped to precipitate the fight for freedom in Latin America. Together, these four developments—cabinet government in Britain, revolutions in North America, France, and Latin America—spelled the end of the system of absolutism, divine right, and aristocratic privilege and helped to lay the foundations of modern-day liberalism.

CABINET GOVERNMENT

IN ENGLAND

Meaning of cabinet government. The first step toward ultimate democratic government in Britain had been taken when the Glorious Revolution ended the divine right of kings and substituted aristocratic liberalism in its place. Then there slowly evolved what is known today as cabinet government, a unique British contribution to the art of government which has spread to many parts of the world.

Cabinet government unites executive and legislative policies in the hands of the cabinet, a small body of men whose chief is the prime minister. This official and his colleagues are in turn the instrument of the majority in the House of Commons. When a prime minister no longer has the confidence of the House of Commons, he must resign or "appeal to the country" by calling an election. Neither for the executive nor for the cabinet is there a stipulated tenure as in the United States.

The cabinet system in Britain permits the king to keep the appearance of power: the members of the cabinet are "His Majesty's Ministers," bills become laws in his name, and the civil service is busy in "His Majesty's Service." Nevertheless, the prerogatives of power are exercised by the prime minister and his cabinet, who are the servants of the House of Commons, the voice of the people.

Genesis of the cabinet. The evolution of cabinet government began during the reign of William III (1689-1702), who was placed on the English throne following the Glorious Revolution. King William selected his own ministers, controlled their policies, and did not concern himself with Parliament's approval of this state of affairs. Because Parliament and the king agreed on fundamentals, however, a clash did not arise. Politics in England were now controlled by an oligarchy of great landed nobles and country squires plus wealthy commercial and banking families often related to the nobility. The loyalties of these groups were divided between two parties: the Tories and the Whigs.

Although the parties quarreled about particular issues, they usually agreed on broad political principles.

William tried to select his ministers from both parties but soon discovered that only when all the ministers were of the same party as the majority in Commons did the government function smoothly. For the time being, however, decisions were still frequently made by the monarch, sitting in conference with his ministers. But by 1714, at the end of the reign of William's successor, Queen Anne, the cabinet—as the council of ministers came to be called—was a distinct policy-making body.

The Hanoverians and the prime minister. The accession in 1714 of the Hanoverian dynasty from the German state of Hanover stimulated the growth of cabinet government. When the first Hanoverian, George I, came to the English throne, he was over fifty years old and was thoroughly German in speech, habits, and interests. He so remained and could never converse with his English chief minister in anything more convenient than poor Latin. His only interest in England was that its resources strengthened his hand in the game of petty politics among the small German states surrounding Hanover.

More English than his father but not much of an improvement as king was George II, whose only claim to fame was that he was the last English monarch to lead his troops on the field of battle. Fortunately for English constitutional development, George's queen was a devoted friend of the chief minister, Robert Walpole, and through her influence the king was easily managed. Walpole served from 1721 to 1742 as leader of the Whig party and the House of Commons and real head of the government. In effect, he was the first prime minister.

Walpole established the principle that the entire cabinet had to act as the single administrative instrument of the House majority and that cabinet unanimity was a necessity. If any member refused to support the official policy, he had to resign.

When Walpole eventually lost his majority in the Commons, he resigned. This act confirmed the principle that the executive branch of government—in theory the king but in practice the prime minister—must resign when its policies are no longer supported in the Commons.

Need for reform. After victory over France in the Seven Years' War (1763), Britain was in need of reform. Corruption pervaded every nook and cranny of the government; wealthy noblemen kept members of Parliament in line by bribes or fat sinecures. It was estimated that at one time more than half of the members of the Commons held pensions or sinecures. Members were elected by a franchise system which included as voters only 10 per cent of the adult males. The 560 members of the House of Commons represented either counties or boroughs. Each county had the right to elect two representatives, and the same usually held true of the borough, or town. The right was retained by the many boroughs which had lost most of their inhabitants to other parts of the country and even by some which had become partly flooded by the sea. As a result, one small district in Cornwall returned more M.P.'s than all the heavily populated districts making up London.

After the fall of Robert Walpole, the next dominating figure in British politics was William Pitt the Elder (1708-1778), the master of global war who directed the British war effort in the Seven Years' War. Pitt was an archfoe of corruption and was determined to cleanse British politics. Unfortunately, his health steadily declined, and his prestige and influence were cleverly reduced by a new power in politics. This was, surprisingly, the king!

Pretensions of George III. George III, who had come to the throne in 1760, was determined to restore to the crown the power lost since the days of William III. In short, his object was to destroy the cabinet system. This is not to say that he aspired to be a tyrant or to rule as a divine-right monarch. Rather, he wished to rule as a "Patriot King," above political parties and, of course, in accordance with his own ideas.

It took George III only a few years to destroy the power of the Whigs and to

Under the leadership of Robert Walpole, the cabinet met with the prime minister instead of with the king, as had previously been the rule. Here, Walpole presides at a cabinet meeting.

secure control of Parliament. By 1770 all effective opposition to the king had been swept away, for George had filled the Commons with supporters known as the "King's Friends," bought by royal favors and pensions. The Tory party, dominated by the toadies of the king, now had a commanding majority; the Whigs were an impotent opposition. Lord North, the unquestioning servant of the king, was prime minister, and for twelve fateful years George III had his own way.

While but a shadow of his once great self, William Pitt occasionally appeared in Parliament to denounce the government in scathing terms. In 1778, while trying to speak in the House of Lords, he collapsed, and one month later he died. England was to miss sorely the leader who had said, "If liberty be not countenanced in America it will sicken, fade and die in this country."

With George III in command of the British government and with Lord North as prime minister, we now turn to the stirring revolt that created in the western world a new nation, based not on outworn political theories but upon those ideas espoused by Locke and Montesquieu.

Rebellious Bostonians tar and feather an excise man and force tea down his throat in this contemporary illustration.

THE AMERICAN REVOLUTION

Opposition to mercantilism. Of the many forces leading to the revolt, economic factors have received the most attention. Many historians emphasize the theory that the American Revolution was not so much a revolt against the tyranny of George III as a revolt of the American middle class against the mercantilistic economic policy of the mother country. English navigation laws required the colonists to trade only with England and prohibited them from competing with English manufactured goods. For about a century these acts were not rigidly enforced, and the colonists were able to manufacture prohibited goods and carry on a lucrative illicit trade without much interference. But finally the day of reckoning came.

After the Seven Years' War, England was saddled with a debt of nearly £700,000,000. The added expense of maintaining a strong force of British regulars in America, made necessary by a serious uprising of Indians in the northwest in 1763, was therefore especially troublesome; and the prime minister, George Grenville, decided that the colonists should assist in sharing the economic burden of the empire. Plans were made to enforce the Navigation Acts rigidly; the Stamp Act, requiring the use of stamped paper and stamps for colonial newspapers and legal documents, was passed (1765); and a law was enacted for quartering English troops in the colonists' homes.

Much has been made of the colonists' slogan "No taxation without representation," but it should be remembered that the English government tried to get the colonial governments to raise the necessary taxation themselves. The colonists refused to do this, however, and the English government proceeded with their taxation measures.

As far as public opinion in England was concerned, the prevailing view was that the colonists should help bear some of the burdens of imperial defense. The influential English merchant class, for example, believed firmly that colonies existed for the benefit of the mother country. Thus, regardless of the state of politics in England, the views of Englishmen at home were bound to clash sooner or later with the attitudes of the colonists overseas.

A revolution in minds and hearts. Although England's taxation measures precipitated the rebellion, it would be a mistake to interpret the American Revolution as resulting solely or even primarily from economic causes. Like all great historical movements, the American Revolution was a complex phenomenon. While admitting that the new taxes were ill-timed, that they came too rapidly, and that the British government followed a confused policy of advance and then retreat under pressure, many historians deny that British mercantilism discriminated heavily against the colonists. The American colonies enjoyed a high degree of prosperity.

There seems to be growing agreement among historians that the American Revolution was not so much brought about by a "cause" as by "conditions." As John Adams wrote in 1818:

But what do we mean by the American Revolution? Do we mean the American War? The Revolution was effected before the war commenced. The Revolution was in the minds and hearts of the people. . . . This radical change in the principles, opinions, sentiments, and affections of the people, was the real American Revolution.[1]

It has been said that the separation movement really began when the first Englishman set foot on the soil of America. Many colonists had suffered religious persecution in the mother country and felt little love for their homeland. Many other colonists never had any connection with England. In 1775, out of a population of nearly three million, almost 40 per cent were of non-English stock, mainly from Ireland and southern Germany. "To many Americans England had been an arbitrary and unkind mother; to a greater number she had never been a mother."[2] Of course, many other colonists considered themselves loyal Englishmen and opposed the break with the mother country.

The English majority, however, prided themselves on their rights as Englishmen, rights stemming back to the Magna Carta. They had accepted Locke's contract theory and the concept of the sovereignty of the people, and they had read the political writings of Montesquieu and Voltaire.

In brief, these were the conditions which predisposed the colonies to revolution: a fierce spirit of freedom, experience in self-rule in the colonial assemblies, the impact of liberal political ideas from the writings of the *philosophes* in France, and the lessons of the Puritan Revolution and the Glorious Revolution in England.

The war against England. After the imposition of the stamp tax, events moved rapidly toward open hostilities between the colonies and the mother country. Colonial boycotts of British goods and English retaliatory measures, skirmishes at Lexington and Concord between British troops and colonial militia, and the well-organized movement for independence, led by such radicals as Samuel Adams and Patrick Henry, heightened sentiment against the mother country. On July 4, 1776, the revolt of the American colonies was formally proclaimed in the Declaration of Independence.

With the outbreak of war in the Thirteen Colonies, Britain's state of unpreparedness was quickly exposed. After its victory in the Seven Years' War, Britain had failed to build up any alliance system to offset the enmity of its vanquished enemies, Spain and France. The British armies and fleets were woefully neglected; commanders found it impossible to put fifteen thousand regulars in the field in America.

Even if Britain had been better prepared, the military situation was very difficult. Britain had to subdue a people now numbering almost one third of its own population on a battlefield three thousand miles distant. There was no single American center which, if captured, would give Britain victory—Britain could not launch a single knockout blow. And unlike the situation today, when only highly industrialized powers are able to manufacture the complicated weapons of war, the colonists could make most of the gunpowder and muskets they needed and a substantial amount of artillery.

The struggle dragged on for seven years. Colonial forces were puny and colonial supplies were inadequate, but the revolutionary cause was immensely strengthened by the courage, determination, and skill of its leaders—Washington, patient patriot and dedicated commander; Franklin, sage diplomat and famous scholar; Madison, skilled administrator and student of government; and Hamilton, adept politician and genius in public finance. The defeat of the British general Burgoyne in October 1777 and the alliance with France in the following year turned the scales in favor of the colonies.

The participation of France, seconded by Spain and Holland, widened the conflict into another European colonial war. In essence, this conflict was a great world struggle, with England, devoid of allies, fighting in the West Indies, the North Atlantic, West

A Declaration by the Representatives of the UNITED STATES OF AMERICA, in General Congress assembled.

When in the course of human events it becomes necessary for one people to dissolve the political bands which have connected them with another, and to assume among the powers of the earth the separate and equal station to which the laws of nature & of nature's god entitle them, a decent respect to the opinions of mankind requires that they should declare the causes which impel them to the separation.

Reproduced above are the opening lines of Thomas Jefferson's early draft of the American Declaration of Independence.

Africa, and India as well as in North America. Faced with the active coalition of France, Spain, and Holland, plus a league composed of Russia, Sweden, and Denmark, England in 1783 granted independence to the Thirteen Colonies. They were now free to make their own destinies, unhampered by constraints from Europe.

In meeting the challenge of the great European alliance intent on breaking its empire apart, Britain was far more successful than it had been in its attempt to crush the far weaker forces of the American colonists. Retaining its mastery of the seas, Britain maintained its world position intact.

Restoration of cabinet government. The American Revolution had profound consequences in Britain. The disaster to British arms in America dealt the king's policies and methods a crushing blow. In a sense, by gaining their liberty, the Americans helped the Britons to gain theirs. In 1780 a majority in the House of Commons voted the resolution "that the influence of the crown has increased, is increasing, and ought to be diminished."[3] By 1782 George III had to dismiss Lord North and employ ministers who were willing to make concessions to public opinion.

In 1783 George III called the twenty-four-year-old son of the great war leader William Pitt to be prime minister. Undoubtedly the king expected to control the youthful statesman, but he more than met his match. Reinvigorated by Pitt's leadership, a new Tory party took firm control of the affairs of state and succeeded in keeping the Whigs out of office for over fifty years. The king was no longer consulted on the day-to-day details of government and only occasionally tried to intervene. His increasing mental instability and final insanity definitely removed royal influence from governmental affairs. The prime minister and his cabinet colleagues now assumed control.

Pitt reduced the national debt, set about cleansing Parliament and the administration of corruption, and made important reforms in the governments of both Canada and India. His attempts to reform the Commons and make it more truly representative were blocked, largely because the excesses of the French Revolution turned public opinion in Britain against any liberalization of government. But as a result of his work, the process of perfecting cabinet government was resumed after its unfortunate interruption.

The Articles of Confederation. Just before the conflict with Great Britain ended, the American colonies ratified the Articles of Confederation (1781), setting up a loose league of independent states under a weak central government. The new system produced civil strife and confusion, and tariff and boundary disputes raged between the states.

At this juncture a group of public-spirited men, including Hamilton, Madison, and Washington, determined to establish a strong central government. Their efforts finally led to the Constitutional Convention, which met at Independence Hall in Philadelphia from May to September 1787. After much debate between the advocates of a strong central government and those favoring sovereign states, a brilliant compromise was reached—the Constitution of the United States—which assured the supremacy of the federal government without making puppet governments of the states. In April 1789, George Washington took the oath of office as first president under the Constitution.

The Constitution. The American Constitution represented a clean break with the past and a promise of complete democracy in the near future. Manhood suffrage was not realized under the Constitution in America for several decades, but this delay does not detract from the importance of the advanced democratic philosophy which became the law of the land in 1789.

The new system of government set up by the American Constitution embodied certain fundamental principles. The first was the doctrine of popular sovereignty—all power ultimately resides in the people. Constitutional provisions required the participation of the people in amending the Constitution and denied this right to the national government acting alone. Another principle, revolutionary in its day, was that of limited government, which safeguards the rights of the people by setting up definite bounds and restraints on the actions of their public officials. A third important feature was the principle of federalism. In most countries, all

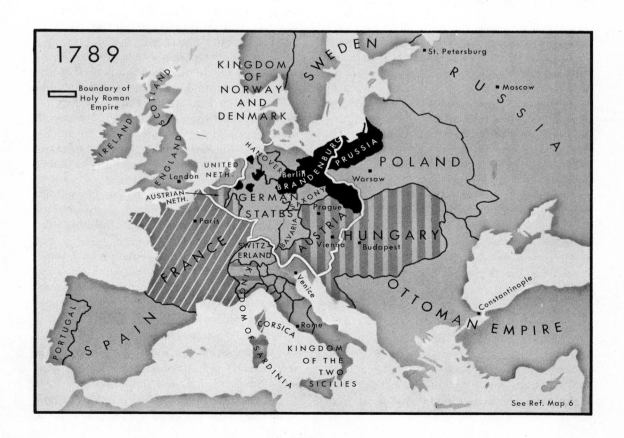

See Ref. Map 6

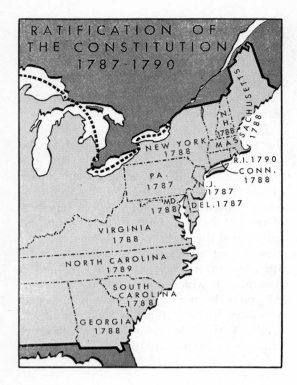

RATIFICATION OF THE CONSTITUTION 1787-1790

NEW YORK 1788
N.H. 1788
MASSACHUSETTS 1788
R.I. 1790
CONN. 1788
PA. 1787
N.J. 1787
MD. 1788
DEL. 1787
VIRGINIA 1788
NORTH CAROLINA 1789
SOUTH CAROLINA 1788
GEORGIA 1788

power resided in the central government; but in the United States, power was divided between the state governments and the national government.

Separation of powers was a fourth fundamental aspect of the new Constitution. In the field of the national government, the powers and duties of legislature, judiciary, and executive were carefully defined. Thus Congress makes the laws, the president applies and enforces them, and the courts interpret them. However, by a fifth feature—checks and balances—careful provision was made so that no one of the three governmental departments could become too independent or too powerful. The president, for example, can veto laws passed by Congress. But the legislature can by a two-thirds vote pass bills over the president's veto. In like manner, the Supreme Court stands as an ultimate safeguard because it can declare any law unconstitutional.

Finally, the Constitution contains a sixth basic principle, the protection of the rights of the individual, although in reality this principle appears in the first ten amendments to the Constitution—the Bill of Rights —instead of in the Constitution proper. No laws can be made encroaching upon freedom of religion, press, and speech, and all persons are safeguarded from arbitrary arrest and imprisonment.

THE FRENCH REVOLUTION

Ideas of the *philosophes* foster discontent in France. Traditionalists in their approach to reform, the *philosophes* did not advocate violent revolution. They believed that good government, whatever the form, should be in the hands of the well-to-do and the educated. Ironically, while the reforming rationalism of these thinkers spread to many of the royal courts of Europe, the influence of the *philosophes* did not measurably affect the operation of their own government. France remained a hotbed of criticism against the Old Regime, and no important reforms were inaugurated by the rulers.

As we shall see in this chapter, the selfishness of the nobles, extravagances of the government, and impending national bankruptcy finally brought on the crisis precipitating revolution. But in the background were the *philosophes* and their ideas. By criticizing the evils of the times, stimulating discontent—especially among the bourgeoisie —and offering a logical picture of what a well-ordered society might be, the *philosophes* created a widespread atmosphere of grievance and supplied political philosophies and panaceas for the future.

Effects of American Revolution in France. In France the impact of the American Revolution was deep and widespread; the Americans showed the French how an antiquated government could be removed.

War makes strange bedfellows. In France the government of a monarch who opposed freedom at home gave its support to American independence and painted an idyllic picture of the brave new republic. Many aristocrats who espoused the doctrines of the *philosophes* sympathized with the colonial revolt. But, as one of them observed: "None of us stopped to think of the danger of the example which the New World set to the Old."

The financial crisis. Whatever its effect on the climate of opinion in France, the most immediate influence of the American Revolution upon the French was an acceleration toward bankruptcy. The support of the American Revolution had cost France almost 400,000,000 dollars. The credit of the government became so poor that it had to pay a rate of 20 per cent on its loans, whereas England paid only 4 per cent. By 1789 the government was faced with an annual deficit of 27,000,000 dollars, and interest payments on the national debt took half of the total national revenues.

Despite attempts by Louis xvi and his advisers to put French finances in order, no solution was found and the crisis deepened. In desperation Louis convened the Estates-General, which had been inactive since 1614. This body was composed of representatives of the First Estate (the clergy), the Second Estate (the nobility), and the Third Estate (the middle class and the peasants). As a gesture to the bourgeoisie, the Third Estate was granted twice the number of representatives allowed each of the other two estates.

The National Assembly. The calling of the Estates-General in 1789 precipitated a demand for reform all over France. For the guidance of the delegates to the assembly, *cahiers* (notebooks) of grievances were prepared by the people. The *cahiers* included demands for personal liberty, a national legislature to make the laws, a jury system, freedom of the press, and abolition of unfair taxation. Thus the *cahiers* presented a program of wide but moderate social and economic reform.

On May 5 the Estates-General was formally convened. The delegates of the Third Estate consisted of some six hundred deputies; half were lawyers, the remainder merchants, bankers, governmental officials, and farmers. According to custom the three estates were expected to vote by orders—that is, by es-

tates rather than as individuals. This would mean that any schemes of reform formulated by the Third Estate could be defeated by the combined votes of clergy and nobility.

After six weeks of wrangling on the question of whether voting should be by order or by head, the members of the Third Estate assembled at an indoor tennis court and solemnly took the Tennis Court Oath, declaring that they would not disband until a constitution had been drawn up. A royal official sent to order them to disperse was told by the defiant leader, Mirabeau, "Sir, go tell your master that nothing but bayonets will drive us out of here." Louis yielded, and the Third Estate, augmented by a few members of the clergy and the nobility, declared itself the National Constituent Assembly of France.

Collapse of absolutism. All over France millions of eyes were watching the events at Versailles. Peasants and city workers grew bold at the capitulation of the king, and in July 1789, disorders and riots broke out throughout the land. In the cities, houses of the nobility were sacked; in the country, peasants demolished the castles of their lords. Everywhere, it was manifest that royal government in France was collapsing.

Following a rumor that the king was concentrating troops at Versailles as a means of browbeating the Assembly, a Parisian mob attacked the Bastille, a grim fortress which was the hated symbol of the Old Regime. Although on that fateful day of July 14, 1789, the Bastille contained only seven prisoners (four counterfeiters, one habitual drunkard, and two lunatics), the fortress was stormed and its defenders slain. On hearing this, King Louis is said to have remarked to the messenger, "This is a revolt." "No, Sire," was the reply, "it is a revolution."

Reforms of the Assembly. The National Constituent Assembly was in session from June 1789 until October 1791. During this period the Assembly passed more than two thousand laws and effected a peaceful and moderate revolution. Speaking of its accomplishments, one historian has written: "No other body of legislators has ever demolished so much in the same brief period."[4]

The Paris mob launches its successful assault on the Bastille.

One of the most important and dramatic acts of the Assembly took place in the critical days of August 1789. The Bastille had just fallen, and peasants all over France, determined to destroy the manor rolls which authorized the levying of dues and feudal obligations, fell upon their hated oppressors. If a lord resisted, he might be mobbed or killed and his chateau destroyed. This was the time of the Great Fear: reports that royalist troops were about to massacre the peasants and rumors that great bands of brigands were pillaging the countryside spread panic through the provinces.

As the frightening news reached Paris, the deputies in the Assembly realized that immediate action had to be taken. During the night of August 4, deputy after deputy arose to renounce his feudal dues and privileges. By these proclamations, known as the August Decrees, serfdom was abolished, the old game laws were repealed, the courts of the manor were swept away, and the tithes and all other fees of the Church were ended. It was declared that from that time on taxes were to be collected from all citizens irrespective of rank, the sale of judicial and municipal offices was to cease, justice was to be freely dispensed, and all citizens, regardless of birth, were eligible for any office.

The Assembly passed other long-overdue reforms. The old chaotic units of local government were abolished and replaced by eighty-three departments. Justice was also materially improved and made available to the masses. Other reforms ended the numerous medieval restrictions on trade and the conduct of business. Every effort was made to encourage individual enterprise. Thus men were to enjoy freedom not only in politics but also in business.

The status of the Church was substantially changed. Its lands were taken by the government and used as collateral for paper money called *assignats*. By the Civil Constitution of the Clergy, the Church was secularized. Its officials were subject to governmental regulation and were elected by the people and paid by the state. The pope no longer had any authority in France.

Thus the lawmakers of the Assembly demolished the Old Regime and a new France was born.

The Declaration of the Rights of Man. Before drawing up a new scheme of government, the Assembly produced a document which summarized the principles upon which the new regime should be based—the Declaration of the Rights of Man:

1. Men are born and will remain free and endowed with equal rights. . . .
2. The end and purpose of all political groups is the preservation of the natural and inalienable rights of Man. These rights are Liberty, the Possession of Property, Safety, and Resistance to Oppression. . . .
4. Liberty consists in being able to do anything which is not harmful to another. . . .
6. The Law is the expression of the will of the people. . . . the Law must be the same for all. . . .
9. Every individual . . . [is] presumed innocent until he has been proved guilty. . . .
10. None is to be persecuted for his opinions, even his religious beliefs, provided that his expression of them does not interfere with the order established by the Law.
11. Free communication of thought and opinion is one of the most precious rights of Man. . . .
17. The possession of property being an inviolable and sacred right, none can be deprived of it, unless public necessity, legally proved, clearly requires the deprivation, and then only on the necessary condition of a previously established just reparation.[5]

The Declaration of the Rights of Man summarized the spirit of constitutional government and political liberalism underlying the Glorious Revolution in England and the revolt of the Thirteen Colonies in America. But the Declaration was not a claim for the "pure" democracy and mass rule advocated by Rousseau; it expressed the middle-class belief in natural law and the right of the wealthy and intelligent to rule.

The new constitution. By September 1791 the National Constituent Assembly had formulated a new plan of government which, in effect, made Louis XVI a constitutional monarch. The chief organ of national government under the new constitution was the Legislative Assembly. This elective body alone had the power to initiate and pass laws, and its consent was required for declarations of war and for the acceptance of peace treaties. Louis XVI was given only a suspensive veto over legislation, a device which could retard action by the Assembly but could not block its will indefinitely. No longer could the king use the formula of Louis XIV, *L'état, c'est moi;* the monarch was now "Louis by the grace of God and the Constitution, King of the State."

Despite the rights guaranteed in the Declaration of the Rights of Man, the suffrage was not given to all adults. Frenchmen were divided into two classes on the basis of wealth. "Active," or tax-paying, citizens could vote; "passive" citizens were barred from the polls. Thus the most striking feature of the French constitution of 1791 was its reflection of the interests of the influential bourgeoisie.

This phase has been called France's First, or Bourgeois, Revolution. In essence the country was now under a limited monarchy. After relatively little violence, the upper middle class was in control. The objectives of those in charge of the government were to "stabilize" the Revolution, to block further change, and to hang on to their wealth.

Opposition to the new government. By the first clause of the August Decrees, the National Assembly had declared the feudal system completely abolished. Most peasants thought that all their old payments had been wiped out. When it came to formulating their decrees into laws, however, the nobles were not quite so generous as their lofty and eloquent statements on the night of August 4 seemed to imply. The Assembly ruled that many privileges, such as possession of serfs, personal *corvées,* and hunting and fishing rights, were to be abolished without compensation. On the other hand, land rents and dues that had been commuted into money payments were regarded as property rights of the nobles to be purchased by the peasants. Some peasants were able to buy out their landlords, but the majority neither bought off their lords nor continued to pay the dues. Hatred against the men of wealth and property and their agents in the government grew.

Instead of accepting the moderate changes brought about between 1789 and 1791 and thus helping to consolidate and strengthen the moderate revolution, Louis XVI did his best to weaken the new regime. The king apparently did not understand that if the Legislative Assembly failed, the Revolution would take a radical turn and the monarchy would be swept away. With his family, the king tried without success to escape out of the country, an act which increased the suspicion that the king was in league with the enemies of France.

The Civil Constitution of the Clergy had been condemned by Pope Pius VI, and consequently many of the clergy refused to take the oath of fidelity to the constitution. These nonjuring priests, as they were called, told the people that sacraments administered by priests who had accepted the Civil Constitution of the Clergy were null and void. In the country districts the peasants supported their nonjuring priests, and serious disorders broke out. Thus, from the outset, the Legislative Assembly was faced with the enmity and opposition of a determined Catholic group.

The common people of the cities—artisans and workers—opposed the Legislative Assembly as the creature of the selfish middle class. Illiterate and highly emotional, these urban workers could be stirred up to wild passions of frenzy by eloquent leaders, and as time passed, they became increasingly dangerous.

Factions in the Assembly. The division of opinion in the country at large was mirrored by factionalism in the Assembly itself. About one third of the deputies were conservatives; they made up the party of the Right, which supported the king and was satisfied with the achievements of a moderate revolution. Seated in the middle of the Assembly was the party of the Center, made up of representatives who had no particular program or principles. Next to the apathetic Center were the deputies of the Left, dynamic and aggressive young radicals who distrusted the king, were dissatisfied with the constitution of 1791, and wished the Revolution to continue. From the very start, the enemies of the constitution assumed the leadership of the Legislative Assembly and worked for its downfall.

Leaders of the Jacobin movement. The enthusiastic radicals who were determined to advance the Revolution formed various clubs in Paris that were centers of agitation and revolutionary propaganda. The most important of these organizations met in the convent of the Jacobin Friars and took the name "Society of the Friends of the Constitution Meeting at the Jacobins in Paris." Their program was the overthrow of monarchy and greater justice and opportunity for the masses. As followers were recruited throughout France and sent to the capital, the Jacobin leaders secured a potential army, ready to carry out a program of radical change.

Most prominent in Jacobin circles were Jean Paul Marat (1743-1793), Georges Jacques Danton (1759-1794), and Maximilien Robespierre (1758-1794). Marat founded the newspaper *L'Ami du peuple* (*Friend of the People*) and carried on his propaganda against social injustice until 1793, when he was struck down by an assassin's dagger. Formerly a criminal judge, Robespierre was deeply influenced by the works of Rousseau and became a fanatical reformer who quietly bided his time until he possessed the necessary power to establish his republic based on virtue and justice. Danton, unlike the theorist Robespierre, was a practical politician. Believing in a radical program that sought the end of the conservative Assembly, he had little use for utopias.

Opposition to the Assembly outside France. Also plotting against the Assembly were the *émigré* nobles who had fled France when the Revolution wiped out their ancient privileges. Most of them had taken refuge in various states along the Rhine, where they found receptive ears for their conspiracies against the French government. Many German bishops and princes who possessed lands in French Alsace were indignant over the abolition of feudal dues and services. Furthermore, many German nobles feared that the freeing of the serfs in France would lead to insurrections on their own estates.

Although they were uneasy about the trend of events in France, the rulers of the large European states adopted a "wait-and-see" policy, hoping that factionalism in France would weaken the nation and perhaps reduce it to a state of impotency.

France vs. Austria and Prussia. Opposed from without and weakened from within, the moderate constitutional monarchy was doomed to failure. The shock of foreign war precipitated its downfall.

Nearly all the factions in France favored war—each for a different reason. The king and his supporters, as well as the *émigré* nobles, favored war because they believed the government would be defeated, discredited, and then overthrown. The radicals, especially a faction called the Girondists, who at first formed part of the Jacobin organization, were eager to involve France in a conflict because, in their opinion, war would discredit the monarchy and give them a chance to rise to power and establish a republic. Egged on by the Girondists, France declared war on Austria in April 1792. Prussia shortly afterwards entered the conflict as an ally of Austria.

Yet, while eager for war, the French were utterly unprepared for it. By the middle of July, the French situation was critical, and the government of the Legislative Assembly was in grave straits. On July 27 the duke of Brunswick, commander of the allied forces invading France, issued a manifesto designed to cow the French revolutionaries and to strengthen the king's position. The actual result of the manifesto, however, was to bolster the position of the most radical groups, discredit the king completely, and end the monarchy in France.

The duke declared his object to be:

. . . to put an end to the anarchy in the interior of France, to check the attacks upon the throne and the altar, to reëstablish the legal power, to restore to the king the security and liberty of which he is now deprived and to place him in a position to exercise once more the legitimate authority which belongs to him.[6]

He announced furthermore that captured French soldiers would be punished as rebels to their king and that if the royal family was harmed, the Austro-Prussian forces would destroy Paris. In the minds of many Frenchmen—especially the masses in Paris and their Jacobin leaders—the manifesto was proof positive that the king was in league with the foreign invaders.

Insurrection in Paris. The reply to the manifesto was the insurrection of the ninth and tenth of August. The revolt was mainly the work of the extreme radicals together with the city proletariat. The municipal government of Paris was seized, and rebel leaders set up an insurrectionary commune.

During the insurrection the Assembly was in session, but most of the deputies of the Right stayed away, fearing the mob. It was easy, therefore, for the deputies who were present, mainly the representatives of the Left, to vote to suspend the monarchy, place the country under a provisional government, and call elections for a National Convention to change the constitution. As head of the provisional government, Danton became dictator of France. At the same time, much power was wielded by the Commune of Paris, representing the lower classes of the city.

The September massacres. On September 2, news reached Paris that the fortress of Verdun had fallen to the invaders. As reinforcements were sent off to the front, the Commune of Paris took good care that no

traitors were left behind at home. Many citizens believed that counterrevolutionists, in league with the Austrians, would try to seize power. All suspected of sympathy for the monarchy were butchered. The prisons were emptied of nonjuring priests and suspected nobles, who were then executed without trial. During the five days from September 2 to September 7, nearly two thousand suspected royalists were killed.

Inauguration of the Republic. Following the suspension of the monarchy, the Assembly proceeded to abolish the classification of Frenchmen as active and passive citizens. All males twenty-one years of age and over were given the vote and were eligible to elect representatives to the new National Convention. The elections were duly held, and the limited monarchy with its agent, the Legislative Assembly, came to an end on September 20, 1792, when the National Convention held its first meeting.

The following day the members voted royalty abolished in France and proclaimed September 22, 1792, as beginning Year 1 of the Republic. France was now a republic, the former king Louis XVI a prisoner in fear for his life, and the first phase of the French Revolution—that of moderate reform—a failure.

Problems facing the Convention. The National Convention remained in session three years. At the outset it was faced with serious problems: (1) foreign armies had to be defeated and driven out of France; (2) an all-important decision had to be made as to what should be done with the king; (3) revolts breaking out all over the country had to be suppressed; (4) a new constitution based on a republican form of government had to be framed; and (5) the social and economic reforms initiated between 1789 and 1791 by the National Assembly had to be completed and put into action.

Danton proceeded with alacrity and enthusiasm to increase the armed forces and give them new life and spirit. During the autumn of 1792, the tide of foreign invasion receded, and French armies began to take the offensive. The Rhine was crossed, Savoy

The head of Louis XVI is displayed to the mob after his execution by guillotine on January 21, 1793.

and Nice occupied, and the Austrian Netherlands (Belgium) conquered.

Trial and execution of Louis XVI. The fate of Louis XVI was soon settled. His trial began in December 1792, and the final vote was taken in the National Convention on January 14. The death of the king was made more or less certain when secret documents showing that Louis had carried on treasonable correspondence with the *émigrés* were found in a hidden compartment discovered in the Tuileries.

Now more moderate in their opinions and split from the Jacobins, the Girondists wished to postpone the king's trial until after the war. But the Jacobins were intent on his death, insisting upon his execution because he had committed treason and because by this act they hoped to forestall any future royalist plots involving the restoration of the monarchy. A follower of Robespierre echoed Jacobin sentiments when he declared:

The death of the tyrant is necessary to reassure those who fear that one day they will be punished for their daring, and also to terrify those who have not yet renounced the monarchy. A people cannot found liberty when it respects the memory of its chains.[7]

The execution of Louis XVI was carried out on January 21, 1793. On the scaffold the king acted with quiet dignity and splendid fortitude. A French historian has declared that "he was greater on [the scaffold] . . . than ever he had been on his throne."[8]

European opinion turns against the Revolution. During the first year of the French Revolution, a strong body of European opinion had acclaimed the reforms of the Constituent Assembly. Liberals cheered the news of the fall of the Bastille. Living in France at the time, the English poet William Wordsworth described his feelings during the early days of the French Revolution in these stirring lines:

Bliss was it in that dawn to be alive,
But to be young was very heaven![9]

But there had also been voices raised in warning against the Revolution in France. The influential English statesman Edmund Burke published in 1790 his *Reflections on the Revolution in France*. Burke was an eloquent defender of conservatism, as opposed to reaction and radicalism. In this powerful and widely read treatise, he likened the Revolution to:

. . . a strange chaos of levity and ferocity, and of all sorts of crimes jumbled together with all sorts of follies.[10]

To him, the rule of the mob was as terrifying and as unjust as the rule of a capricious absolute monarch; stability, gradual change, and respect for the old as well as receptivity for the new were the basis of the good society.

People will not look forward to posterity, who never look backward to their ancestors. . . . Thus, by preserving the method of nature in the conduct of the State, in what we improve, we are never wholly new; in what we retain, we are never wholly obsolete. . . . A disposition to preserve, and an ability to improve, taken together, would be my standard of a statesman.[11]

While the Legislative Assembly was in power and Louis XVI was on the throne, many observers thought Burke's arguments exaggerated; but the fall of the monarchy, the September massacres, and the execution of Louis began to make most Englishmen of the upper class and many Continental aristocrats believe that Burke was right.

French territorial aggression. In the fall of 1792, French armies gained notable successes, and these victories stirred the military spirit of the French people. The earlier ideals of the Revolution—of brotherhood and peace—were replaced by nationalistic territorial ambitions. The French revolutionary leaders began to realize that in the name of liberty their armies could overthrow tyrannical kings and at the same time extend the national frontiers of France. They announced that the Alps and the Rhine had been the old frontiers of France and that they were resolved to reunite them to the fatherland.

In November 1792 the Convention declared that "France will grant fraternity and assistance to all peoples who shall desire to recover their liberty." This announcement was equivalent to a French declaration of war against all the monarchical governments of Europe. Again, in December, the Convention stated that "it considered itself called to give liberty to the human race and to overthrow all thrones" and declared war on tyrants. At the same time it was announced that in all countries conquered by the French, the inhabitants had to accept all the principles of the French Revolution.

England as the leading anti-French power. In the face of French aggression—which threatened the balance of power in Europe—England, Spain, Holland, and Sardinia joined Prussia and Austria in the First Coalition to wage war on the French Republic. Of all the allies arrayed against France, England was to be the most implacable foe. From 1793 to 1815, England and France were at war almost continuously.

The prime minister in England at this time was William Pitt the Younger. A liberal and a reformer at the beginning of his career, Pitt wanted no war with France and considered Burke's dire warnings about the Revolution exaggerated. By the end of 1792, however, Pitt had changed his opinions; he now believed that war with France was inevitable. As French armies occupied the Austrian Netherlands and threatened Holland, England prepared for war.

Pressures inside and outside France. In the spring of 1793 the armies of the First Coalition began to converge on France. The Revolution was in peril. And, in addition to this outside menace, France was rent by internal strife. Two factions in the National Convention fought for control: the Girondists and the Jacobins. Representing the bourgeoisie, the Girondists were moderates who feared mob violence and radical reforms; to them the Revolution had gone far enough. By contrast, the Jacobins were tough realists who sided with the masses, welcomed more bloodletting, and were determined to advance the Revolution. Finally, the Jacobins managed to oust their rivals from the Convention and place them under arrest. Some of the Girondists, however, escaped to the country, where they organized a rebellion against the tyranny of the radicals in Paris. At the same time royalist Catholics rose again in rebellion. These disorders weakened the economy of the country, and bread riots broke out in Paris.

The Reign of Terror. To meet the challenge of rebellion, the government of the National Convention entrusted its power to the Committee of Public Safety. Also created were two subsidiary bodies: the Committee of General Security and the Revolutionary Tribunal. The task of the former was to ferret out traitors; the latter body judged and executed them at the hands of "Madame Guillotine." The Convention passed a decree making liable to arrest every person of noble birth, anyone who had any contact with an *émigré*, and anyone who could not produce a certificate of citizenship.

The establishment of the Committee of Public Safety and its allied agencies inaugurated what is known as the Reign of Terror. Thousands of suspected royalists were arrested and thrown into prison. After a summary trial, many of them were thrown into carts—the tumbrels—and taken to the public square to be guillotined. Perhaps as many as five thousand persons were executed in Paris; in the provinces, the number was probably twenty thousand.

The French war effort. With subversive activity crushed on the home front, the leaders of the Republic turned their attention to the danger of foreign armies. To meet its enemies, France forged a new weapon, the "nation in arms." Compulsory military service was introduced. In February 1793 the Convention passed a decree calling 300,000 men to the colors and making liable for military service all men between eighteen and forty.

In August 1793 the Convention decreed a general mobilization of the country. Scientists were enlisted to help the war effort, and workmen were conscripted and shifted from nonessential to war work. Business was organized to produce vast quantities of medicines, shoes, and uniforms.

During 1794 and 1795 the new French armies carried out a series of great campaigns. The citizen armies of the Republic were motivated by a spirit not found in the professional and mercenary armies of their opponents. The French citizen-soldier believed he was fighting for his own liberty and for the right to enjoy the fruits of the Revolution.

By 1795 the First Coalition had almost been dissolved, with Spain and Prussia no longer offering effective resistance to the French. Holland was now allied with France, while Belgium was annexed outright; in addition, French troops controlled all the territory west of the Rhine. Thus, the Republic had gained the "natural frontiers" sought by generations of French kings. Only England, Austria, and Sardinia remained at war with France.

Social changes under the Convention. Among the significant reforms achieved during the period of the National Convention (also known as the Jacobin Republic) were the plan for a national system of education, abolition of Negro slavery in French colonies, final eradication of feudal dues without compensation, and the establishment of a metric system of weights and measures. The welfare of the lower classes was promoted by placing ceilings on prices and by selling the confiscated estates of the *émigrés*. As a result of the latter measure, France became a land of small proprietors, and the once radical French peasant became a conservative.

Important also were the numerous ways in which the everyday life of the people was transformed. A strong anti-Christian movement was initiated. Churches were closed and religious images were destroyed. Everything that smacked of royalty and privilege was discarded. Knee breeches, a symbol of the aristocracy, were declared unpatriotic. In their place were substituted long trousers, the *sans-culottes* (literally, "without short breeches"), which "made all legs equal by concealment." Titles were discarded; the proper form of address became "citizen" and "citizeness."

Names had to be changed. Streets formerly named for kings or nobles now bore names commemorating revolutionary events or heroes. And men changed their names, especially if their Christian name was Louis. Even the name of the queen bee was changed to "laying bee."

The Terror continues. While the French armies rolled back the armies of the Coalition, the Reign of Terror reached its height. In the autumn of 1793, the Girondists who had been expelled from the National Convention were executed, and the guillotine also claimed as its victim the queen, Marie Antoinette. By controlling the all-powerful Committee of Public Safety, Robespierre was now the dominant force in the government.

By the spring of 1794, victory had been secured by the French armies, and practically all the revolts and plots within the country had been stamped out. There was no longer any justification for continuance of the Terror. But the fanatical Robespierre and his cohorts continued the policy of terrorism in order to cleanse the Republic of weak and lukewarm republicans. To Robespierre, a republic of virtue had to be achieved, in which there would be no excesses of wealth, where every citizen would serve the public good, and where justice and love would prevail. While a bewildered Paris looked on, many courageous leaders of the Revolution who dared to disagree with Robespierre's fanatical views were executed; among these was Danton. Disgusted with the policy of terror, the members of the Convention finally arrested Robespierre and sent him to the guillotine, where so many of his innocent victims had met an unjust fate.

Reaction against the Terror. After the execution of Robespierre, Frenchmen hoped that the long period of excesses was over and that the nation could bind up its wounds and settle down to a period of tranquillity and repose.

Thousands of suspects were freed, the laws of Robespierre were replaced, the Paris Commune was dissolved, and the extraordi-

During the period of the Jacobin Republic, a strong anti-Christian movement developed. In the Festival of Reason, held in Paris in November 1793, this movement reached its climax. Deputies marched to the Cathedral of Notre Dame to consecrate the church to the worship of reason and to enthrone an actress as the Goddess of Reason. The cult of reason went too far for Robespierre, who initiated a new religion based upon belief in a Supreme Being and in immortality of the soul. The new religion provided for a number of festivals honoring the Supreme Being, Life and Liberty, the Human Race, and other idealistic concepts. In the illustration above, an image of Freedom is drawn through the streets of Paris during one of these festivals.

nary powers of the Committee of Public Safety and the Revolutionary Tribunal were swept away. In Paris, gangs of young men attacked Jacobins, and in the provinces there was a veritable "White Terror" against the radicals. The Jacobin Clubs were closed and the Catholic churches were reopened.

Conservatism was now the order of the day. It was not that the people wanted to go back to the old days. They passionately wanted to see the gains of the Revolution safeguarded and perpetuated, but they were tired of extremists and fanatics.

THE NAPOLEONIC PERIOD

The Directory. Before its dissolution, the National Convention drafted a new system of government, the Directory, which was composed of two legislative chambers and an ex-

Napoleon posed for this sketch by David soon after he returned from his successful campaigns in 1796-1797 as commander in chief of the Army of Italy.

ecutive body of five members called directors. The right to vote was again restricted to property owners.

Assuming power in 1795, the Directory soon proved to be an incompetent and even venal government. The directors were mediocre politicians who engaged in an orgy of graft. Though the middle class profited under this bourgeois government, the poor lacked employment and the necessities of life.

Determined to smash the remnants of the First Coalition, the Directory commissioned three armies to invade Austrian territory. Two of these forces failed, but the one led by an obscure young general named Napoleon Bonaparte crossed the Alps in 1796 and crushed the Sardinians and the Austrians. With a French army at the gates of Vienna, the Austrians were forced to accept the Treaty of Campo Formio (1797). Only Great Britain, protected by its fleet, remained at war with France.

Napoleon rises to power. Following his triumph over Austria, Napoleon obtained the consent of the Directory to invade Egypt in order to menace English interests in India. He is reputed to have said, "This little Europe does not supply enough glory for me." Evading the English fleet, Napoleon and his army landed in Egypt and were at first victorious. Efforts to crush Turkish forces were not successful, however, and in the meantime the English admiral Nelson in 1798 destroyed Napoleon's Mediterranean fleet in the battle of the Nile. Aware that the Directory was becoming more and more incapable of coping with the problems of France, Napoleon deserted his army and returned to France. Making no reference to his defeats, the young general thrilled the French with the glories of his campaign.

In 1799 France was again in a state of crisis. A newly formed Second Coalition threatened to invade the country, and the economy showed signs of collapse. Faced with financial ruin and invasion, the French turned to the one man they believed could save the day—Napoleon, the Little Corporal, who spoke of himself as the "man of destiny." Sensing the mood of the nation, Napoleon in 1799 swept the effete Directory from power and established a new government called the Consulate—ostensibly a republic but with nearly all power centralized in the first consul, Napoleon.

Napoleon's genius for leadership. What manner of man was this "savior" of France? Born in Corsica in 1769, the young Napoleon was a member of the Corsican lower nobility of Italian origin. Educated in a French military school, he joined the French army when the French Revolution broke out. Within a short time his abilities were recognized; his marriage in 1796 to the widow Josephine de Beauharnais, who was influential with the directors, gained him his first big chance—command of the Army of Italy.

Intelligent, ambitious, and unscrupulous, Napoleon believed he was destined to play a great part in Europe's affairs. He once remarked: "I am no ordinary man, and the laws of propriety and morals are not applicable to me." For fifteen years the Little Corporal amazed and confounded his opponents by his brilliant tactics and strategy and by the *élan* he inspired in his troops.

After becoming first consul, Napoleon quickly scattered the forces of the Second

Coalition. The Austrian forces were vanquished, and the Austrian government was compelled to sign the Treaty of Lunéville (1801). Although Great Britain was not defeated, in 1802 a temporary peace between France and England was arranged.

Napoleon's domestic reforms. The first consul then turned his attention to domestic reforms. The system of local government was reorganized to provide a completely centralized governmental structure. Prefects appointed by the central government were given almost complete charge of local affairs, an arrangement which made for efficiency at the expense of liberty. Graft and inequality in tax collection were ended; economies in public expenditures were effected; and, most important, the Bank of France was established. It still exists today as a model of banking stability.

While irreligious himself, Napoleon as a shrewd statesman realized that the people demanded the reëstablishment of the Church. In the Concordat (1801), an agreement with

the pope was reached in which Napoleon declared that the French government would pay the salaries of the clergy. The Catholic Church was now restored in France, but without much of its former power.

Before 1800, scarcely 25,000 children in France were attending elementary school. To remedy this situation, Napoleon created a system of public education which provided an educational pyramid of public elementary schools, secondary institutions (*lycées*), special schools for technical training, and the University of France. The latter was not a teaching body but an administrative one; its function was to regulate and control the entire educational system.

Most famous of Napoleon's accomplishments was his codification of the French law, which brought legal order out of chaos. Completed in 1804, the great Civil Code was written with precision and clarity; it guaranteed many achievements of the French Revolution, such as religious toleration and the abolition of serfdom. A code of civil proce-

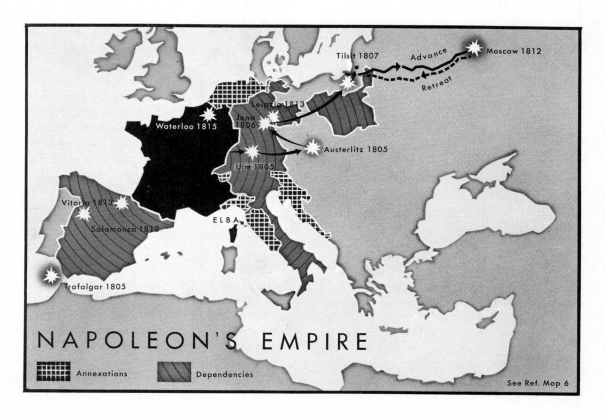

NAPOLEON'S EMPIRE

Annexations   Dependencies

See Ref. Map 6

dure and a criminal code were also produced. These codes have exerted a marked influence upon the codes of other countries. Years later, the exiled Napoleon said:

My true glory is not that I have gained forty battles. Waterloo will efface the memory of those victories. But that which nothing can efface, which will live forever, is my Civil Code.[12]

When Napoleon declared himself emperor in 1804, a grateful and contented people approved his action. The Republic was now no more.

Napoleon at the height of his power. Just before Napoleon assumed the crown of emperor, war between Great Britain and France broke out once more. Napoleon welcomed war. His meteoric rise from a nonentity to the first citizen of France had not satisfied his lust for glory. During 1803 and 1804 he directed extensive preparations for an invasion of England, but the inability of Napoleon's naval forces to gain control of the approaches to England and the formation of the Third Coalition (composed of Great Britain, Russia, Austria, and Sweden) compelled him to forgo his cherished plan. Then, in 1805, he suddenly marched eastward against his Continental enemies and, in victory after victory, effectively destroyed the armies of the Third Coalition.

Meanwhile, Napoleon's hopes of securing control of the seas and invading or at least starving out Britain were ended rudely in the smoke of Trafalgar (October 1805). In this decisive naval battle, Lord Nelson defeated the combined French and Spanish fleets. Undaunted, Napoleon marched on to defeat Prussia decisively in 1806 and to organize into a French dependency the territory seized by Prussia in the partitions of Poland. In 1807, at Tilsit, the Russian emperor agreed to assist France in disposing of the emperor's stubborn antagonist—England.

By 1808 Napoleon ruled over a France which extended from the North Sea to the Pyrenees and included much of Italy. Several of his relatives had been placed on the thrones of nearby countries. Prussia and Austria were impotent before French power, and Russia appeared to be only a Napoleonic satellite.

Napoleon was now at the height of his great powers. Few men in history have possessed his gifts and achieved such amazing results. He was the dynamo and the brain of his empire. But, as we shall shortly see, the load was too much for one man. This is the supreme defect of dictatorship—power is not shared. The powers of Napoleon began to decline while his problems continued to increase.

Importance of British sea power. By 1808 it was apparent that the Napoleonic empire could not survive unless it defeated England. Lord Nelson's victory at Trafalgar had confirmed Great Britain's supremacy on the seas. Safe behind warships, English factories turned out more and more war goods. British commerce and wealth increased, while French trade declined. Napoleon sought to crush England's economy by prohibiting the entry of British vessels into countries under his control, a policy known as the Continental System. But Great Britain imposed a counterblockade. Fundamentally, the war was now a struggle between the sea power and industrial superiority of England and French military power on the Continent.

Reaction against French imperialism. Ostensibly "liberators" of subject people in Europe, the armies of Napoleon disseminated the French revolutionary ideals of liberty, equality, and fraternity. But as Napoleon became more and more imperialistic, the people he had "emancipated" realized that they had merely exchanged one despotism for another. In posing as the champion of the Revolution, Napoleon had sown the seeds of nationalism and liberty which were to prove his undoing.

The occupation of Portugal (1807) and Spain (1808) are cases in point. In both nations, uprisings soon broke out. And, as we shall see later in this chapter, Napoleon's intervention in the Iberian peninsula triggered a revolutionary movement in the Latin-American colonies.

All over Germany, a wave of nationalism stirred the people to prepare for a war of

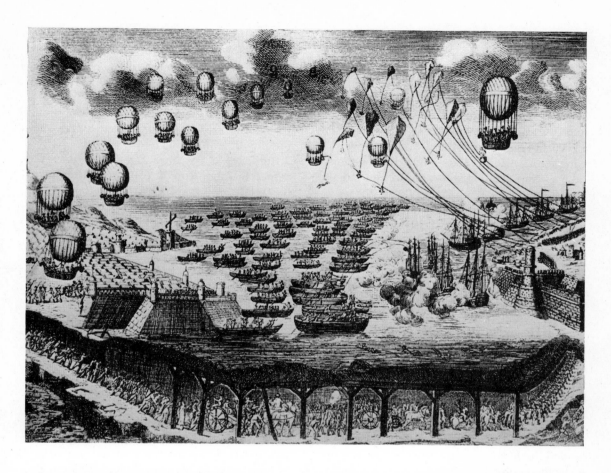

In this satirical version of Napoleon's plans for invading England, a contemporary artist shows balloons and monster kites floating over the English Channel, an invasion fleet crossing on the surface, and an army marching through a tunnel.

liberation. Prussia in particular underwent a regeneration. The Emancipation Edict of 1807, known as "the Prussian Magna Carta," ended serfdom, abolished caste barriers to vocations, and gave farmers a clear title to their land. The people now had something to fight for! Although Napoleon had limited the Prussian army to 42,000 men, the Prussians undermined this provision by a subtle subterfuge: as soon as one army was trained, it was placed on reserve and a new army was called up for training. In this way, Prussia managed to prepare a potential army of 270,000 men. The Prussian intellectuals used education as a means of nationalistic propaganda. Founded in 1810, the University of Berlin became a center of strong nationalistic movements.

Invasion and retreat in Russia. Napoleon made his first major misstep when, after a quarrel with Alexander I of Russia, he launched an invasion of the tsar's realm in 1812. The campaign was a catastrophe. Although Napoleon's Grand Army of 600,000 fought its way to Moscow, the enemy forces remained intact, and the Russians' scorched-earth strategy prevented the invaders from living off the country. While the French occupied Moscow, fires broke out and destroyed three fourths of the city; this disaster was compounded by the outbreak of pestilence. After spending thirty-three days in the empty shell of Moscow, Napoleon gave the order to retreat.

As the Grand Army marched west along the frozen Russian roads, it rapidly disintegrated. Guerrilla forces, mainly Cossacks, hovered about the retreating columns, continually pouncing on stragglers. Of the more than half a million men who had crossed the Russian frontiers in June, a tattered fragment of barely 20,000 troops was able to make a wintry escape from Russia to Germany. Over a century later, another would-be world conqueror—Adolf Hitler—made the same mistake as Napoleon. History, on occasion, does repeat itself.

Downfall of Napoleon. The nations of Europe now struck relentlessly at the tottering French empire. Commanded by the Duke of Wellington, "the Iron Duke," English troops cleared French armies out of Spain; and in 1813 at Leipzig the allies inflicted a disastrous defeat upon Napoleon in the Battle of the Nations.

After Leipzig the empire of Napoleon tumbled like a house of cards. In March 1814, allied forces entered Paris. Two weeks later the French emperor abdicated his throne, receiving in return sovereignty over Elba, a little island not far from the Italian coast. Nearly one year later, in February 1815, Napoleon eluded the British fleet, landed in France, and, after a tumultuous welcome, entered Paris and raised another army. In haste, an allied army under the command of the Duke of Wellington marched toward France.

At Waterloo, Napoleon took the field for the last time and met his match. The French army was defeated decisively by the combined forces of Britain and Prussia. Following this reversal, Napoleon sought refuge on board a British warship. Taking no chances, the allies shipped the former emperor to the island of St. Helena, about twelve hundred miles off the west coast of Africa. Here, in 1821, he died, a victim of cancer.

Why did the French empire, which appeared invincible under Napoleon, collapse? When Napoleon's physical vigor and mental brilliance began to flag after the destruction of the Third Coalition, his empire—the creation of one man's military and administrative genius—began to fall apart. A tired man, Napoleon fast became corpulent and lethar-

gic. And if the emperor was tired, the French people were also suffering from war weariness. In addition, the resurgence of nationalism in Europe was bound to destroy any dictator who first stimulated it by prating about liberty, equality, and fraternity and then enslaved the very people he had supposedly liberated.

Students of warfare point out that the defeat of Napoleon is explained chiefly by the relative importance in that day of sea power on the one hand and land power on the other. These students of military history maintain that British command of the sea finally led to the Napoleonic collapse. Finally, there are those who see Napoleon's greatest blunder in his invasion of Russia, which boomeranged and ended with the disastrous retreat from Moscow.

Accomplishments of Napoleon. Napoleon's rise to power is one of the most remarkable stories in all history, and his significance cannot be dismissed with only a negative verdict. It is true that his wars killed perhaps as many as six million people, but his interference throughout Europe kindled nationalism in many areas. For example, he made possible the first step toward the national unification of Germany. In his endeavor to create a defensive barrier on France's eastern frontier, Napoleon wiped out more than one hundred petty German states and merged them with large states. Another important obstacle to unification was removed in 1806 when he did away with the Holy Roman Empire.

Napoleon is especially important because he preserved and disseminated many aims of the French Revolution. In France, he safeguarded and expanded social and economic gains of the Revolution, such as legal equality and the land settlement benefiting the peasants. Outside of France, his rule swept away many of the obsolete institutions of the Old Regime. Perhaps Napoleon's boast that he was "the Son of the Revolution" is in part justified.

Perhaps no better evaluation of Napoleon has ever been given than De Tocqueville's: "He was as great as a man can be without virtue."[13]

DISCONTENT AND REVOLUTION

IN LATIN AMERICA

Climate for revolution. During the eighteenth century, the chief intellectual and political currents in Europe influenced events in the Latin-American colonies. Broadly speaking, the diffusion of liberal and reformist ideas resulted in a rejuvenation of the Spanish and Portuguese empires. Colonial administration was made more efficient; the Church was shorn of some of its wealth and power; and greater prosperity than ever before was enjoyed.

Although progress was evident in many areas, a good deal of discontent existed. The Creoles (Spaniards born in the colonies) resented the *peninsulares*, the Spaniards sent from the homeland who monopolized all the highest governmental positions. The rising young Creole generation feasted on the ideas of Montesquieu, Voltaire, and Rousseau. Although works by these authors were banned, they were smuggled into the country in great numbers.

While government policy was reformist, it could not keep pace with the growth of liberal ideas, especially after the American and the French revolutions. The high degree of censorship and control infuriated the young intellectuals. There was, of course, no hint of the government giving the people a greater voice in politics. While not so rigid, mercantilism was still in force, the courts were often corrupt, and the *peninsulares* continued to lord it over the Creoles and *mestizos* (those of Spanish and Indian blood).

As the eighteenth century came to a close, the desire for independence was increasing. In fact, in 1780 three independence movements were launched but none succeeded. The most active of the so-called Precursors of Revolution was Francisco de Miranda (1750-1816), who spent thirty years traveling in the United States and Europe. A linguist and a brilliant conversationalist, he earned the privilege of entering into the most cultivated social circles. His plans for emancipating the colonies from Spain intrigued English leaders, who saw to it that he was supported by their government.

The "legal" phase of the revolution. It needed only a spark set off by the Napoleonic Wars to ignite the revolutionary flame in Spanish America. When the news reached the colonies that Napoleon had unceremoniously removed the Bourbons and placed his brother Joseph on the throne, there was deep resentment in Spanish America. The colonial authorities proclaimed their loyalty to Ferdinand vii, the former king, who had been interned in France. And, in a number of colonies, liberal Creoles in 1810 ousted local officials and took charge, all the while proclaiming their loyalty to the absent Ferdinand. This "legal" phase of the revolution took place in Venezuela, the Argentine, New Granada, and Chile.

Toward independence. The legal phase of the revolutionary movement was of short duration. Radical leaders began to demand independence and an end to the fiction of loyalty to Ferdinand. Simón Bolívar (1783-1830), leader of the rebels in Caracas, went to England to obtain British aid and convinced Miranda that the time had come to strike for complete freedom. Miranda returned to Latin America in December 1810, and the following year the independence of Venezuela was proclaimed.

Tragic reverses followed, and in 1812 Miranda felt compelled to make a humiliating surrender. Some of his fellow patriots, including Bolívar, were so furious with Miranda that they allowed him to be captured by the Spaniards. Thus repudiated, he was sent to a prison in Cádiz, where he died four years later. Successful royalist counterattacks in Venezuela ended the republican regime, and by 1815 Bolívar was in exile.

Other uprisings in Lima, La Paz, and Quito had been equally unsuccessful. The most tragic failure occurred in Mexico. A premature effort for self-government led by a radical priest, Father Hidalgo (1753-1811), turned in 1810 into a frightening race war of Indian against white. Frightened of the specter of social revolution, wealthy Creoles and other conservative forces supported the

Portrait of Simón Bolívar, the Liberator

José de San Martín (1778-1850), aided by a group of devoted and efficient lieutenants.

Bolívar, former leader of the abortive revolts in Caracas, was a wealthy Creole who gave his entire fortune to the revolutionary cause. A man of great personal charm, he was a born actor who liked to play the role of heroic leader and who sought the limelight and the plaudits of the crowd. Cultured, well-traveled in Europe, and imbued with the liberal philosophy of the Enlightenment, he made the cause of independence both a crusade and an obsession.

San Martín was the complete opposite; he had none of Bolívar's glowing enthusiasm. Reserved and uncommunicative, he was not moved by praise or blame if he believed his cause just. Doing his duty without any regard for his own interests, San Martín rightly called himself a stoic.

Bolívar began his comeback early in 1817. With a small force he defeated the Spanish armies in northern Latin America. The most dramatic incident of his victorious campaign was the successful crossing of the formidable Andes. The Republic of Great Colombia (made up of modern Colombia, Venezuela, and Ecuador) was established, and Bolívar was named the first president of this huge new state.

Further south, in the Argentine, San Martín had been making preparations for a spectacular offensive against the royalist forces. In 1817 he led his army over the Andes in a desperate three weeks' march, surprising and defeating the Spanish forces in Chile. Aided by a former British officer, Lord Cochrane, who won naval supremacy in the waters off Peru, San Martín in 1820 transported his troops to this viceroyalty. In 1821 he entered Lima, where he formally announced the independence of Peru.

The two Liberators met in 1822. At this meeting, basic differences in policy and strategy developed. It is said also that Bolívar did not relish being outshone by any rival. Thereupon, without any recriminations, San Martín withdrew from the scene and spent the remainder of his life abroad. His greatness was only tardily realized: not until

Spanish regime. Within a year Hidalgo was captured and executed, but his work was carried on by another priest, Father José Morelos (1765-1815). In 1815 he suffered the same fate as Hidalgo.

The Liberators in action: Bolívar and San Martín. In 1814, following the defeat of Napoleon, Ferdinand VII was released by the French and was welcomed deliriously in Spain. Although the king might have rallied his colonial subjects by generous concessions, he imposed on the Americas all the hateful aspects of the Old Regime. Soon embittered, the Americans rose from defeat to gain a complete triumph. This was the achievement of the Liberators, Simón Bolívar and

1880 were his remains brought back to Buenos Aires and buried there.

After San Martín's withdrawal, Bolívar was left to dominate the scene. In 1824 his army delivered the knockout blow to Spanish power by winning a decisive victory at Ayacucho, situated on a high Peruvian plateau nearly 12,000 feet above the sea. Here the last Spanish viceroy in the New World surrendered. By 1825, the revolution had run its successful course.

Independence won in Mexico. Royalist elements in Mexico were deeply offended by the revolution of 1820 in Spain and the brief triumph of the liberal party (see p. 506). Therefore, in 1821, the conservatives supported Agustín de Iturbide (1783-1824), a military leader of dubious reputation. Joining the rebel forces holding out in the mountains, he proclaimed the independence of Mexico. After plans to establish a monarchy in Mexico under a Spanish prince fell through, Iturbide proclaimed himself emperor. Guatemala also announced its independence, though for a time it seemed that it would fall under Iturbide's rule.

Brazil takes the royal road to freedom. Independence also came to Brazil, where the members of the royal house of Braganza had arrived in 1808, in flight from Napoleon's armies. Fond of their new abode, the Braganzas remained in Rio de Janeiro after Portugal was freed of the French armies of occupation. Under the paternalistic hand of King John, industries grew and commerce flourished.

In the year 1820, a revolution in Portugal put the liberal party in power, and its new parliament, the Cortes, set to work on a program of domestic reform. Unfortunately, the colonial policy of the new government was reactionary, and King John decided that his presence was needed in Lisbon. Before he left, he told his young son Pedro, who was acting as regent: "If Brazil demands independence, grant it, but put the crown upon your own head." Shortly after his father's departure, Pedro ripped the Portuguese colors off his uniform and shouted "Independence or death!" The Brazilians defeated the Portuguese garrison troops, and in December

1822, Pedro was crowned emperor, under a parliamentary system of government.

The American and Latin-American revolutions sprang from the same body of political ideals. Both of them enjoyed the leadership of remarkable men, and both were civil wars in which a part of the colonial population remained loyal to the mother country. But there were dissimilarities. In Spain only a small percentage of the people favored the colonies; in England a substantial portion of the population did. And in Spanish America, fighting ranged over larger areas and was more bloodthirsty and cruel. We shall also see in a later chapter (Chapter 25) that while freedom brought political unity to the United States, in Spanish America it was the harbinger of internal turbulence and political fragmentation.

SUMMARY

The story of the four political movements which form the theme of this chapter began in England during the reigns of the first two Hanoverian monarchs (George i and George ii) and ended in the 1820's on the pampas and coastal plains of Latin America. In Britain, Robert Walpole encouraged practices which, by the 1740's, had evolved into the cabinet system. The accession of George III not only halted the growth of cabinet government but also stimulated revolt in the Thirteen Colonies. Here, the Americans were determined to enjoy that freedom made logical and natural by the degree of their political advancement and economic prosperity. It was this condition which explains the American Revolution rather than any specific act that precipitated the struggle.

The success of the Americans in achieving independence made it possible for the advance toward greater freedom to begin again in Britain. This fresh start toward cabinet government is associated with William Pitt the Younger, the prime minister who was the harbinger of a more popular, less corrupt, and more representative government that was to be the model for Europe in the nineteenth century.

Some historians have asserted that the upheaval in France could not have taken place without the successful revolution in the Thirteen Colonies. The American Revolution gave France leaders experienced in diplomacy and war, a revolutionary credo, and the example of a functioning and stable system of free government. But the excesses

of the Jacobin Republic led to a revulsion in public opinion and to the meteoric career of Napoleon Bonaparte. Motivated primarily by personal ambition, this dominating figure was the unwitting instrument for the spread of French revolutionary ideals throughout Europe. And, in a way, he was also responsible for the independence of Latin America. Revolution broke out in the Spanish colonies because the French emperor had invaded Spain and dethroned the royal family. Later, a rupture occurred between Brazil and the government in Portugal. By 1825 there remained only a few vestiges of Iberian power in the West Indies and in the Pacific.

Of the three revolutions discussed in this chapter, the French Revolution from 1789 to 1815 was most radical and most influential, although, paradoxically, certain basic ideals of the Revolution, such as constitutional government, were not fully realized in France until later. More so than the English and the American revolutions, the French Revolution was social as well as political; intellectual, economic, and religious freedoms were all given strong emphasis. Much of the history of the nineteenth century is concerned with the strivings and amplification of democracy, intellectual and religious freedom, and laissez faire.

SUGGESTIONS FOR READING

C. Brinton, *The Anatomy of Revolution,** Vintage. A most stimulating comparative study of the English, American, French, and Russian revolutions.

R. R. Palmer, *The Challenge*, Princeton, 1959, Vol. I of *The Age of the Democratic Revolution: A Political History of Europe and America, 1760-1800*. A valuable synthesis, showing that all the major revolutions of this period resulted from similar ideas and needs; the first volume of a projected two-volume work.

J. Plumb, *England in the Eighteenth Century,** Penguin. An excellent survey of political, economic, cultural, and social history from 1714 to 1815.

K. Mackenzie, *The English Parliament,** Penguin. A useful popular account of the nature and historical development of Parliament; the rise of cabinet government is described in Chapter VI.

*Indicates an inexpensive paperbound edition.

Basil Williams, *The Whig Supremacy, 1714-1760*, Oxford, 1939; and J. S. Watson, *The Reign of George III, 1760-1815*, Oxford, 1960. Detailed, up-to-date general accounts in the scholarly and valuable Oxford History of England series.

E. S. Morgan, *The Birth of the Republic, 1763-1789,** Univ. of Chicago. An excellent brief history of the era of the American Revolution.

John C. Miller, *Origins of the American Revolution*, Little, Brown, 1943. An attractively written survey which presents a balanced treatment of the forces behind the Revolution.

L. G. Gipson, *The Coming of the Revolution, 1763-1775*, Harper, 1954. A work of superior insight which shows how political and commercial relations between England and the American colonies became increasingly strained before the outbreak of the American Revolution. This volume in the scholarly New American Nation series is followed by J. R. Alden, *The American Revolution, 1775-1783*, Harper, 1954.

J. C. Wahlke, ed., *The Causes of the American Revolution,** Heath. A collection of differing analyses of the Revolution by an able group of scholars.

J. F. Jameson, *The American Revolution Considered As a Social Movement,** Beacon. A stimulating short survey of the social forces at work behind the scenes.

G. F. Scheer and H. F. Rankin, eds., *Rebels and Redcoats,** Mentor. The American Revolution described by men who fought in it.

R. Hofstadter, *The American Political Tradition and the Men Who Made It,** Vintage; and C. Becker, *The Declaration of Independence,** Vintage. Two fine discussions of the political ideals that inspired America's greatest political documents, the Declaration and the Constitution.

A. Cobban, *Old Regime and Revolution, 1715-1799,** Penguin, Vol. I of *A History of Modern France.* A valuable recent survey by an outstanding English authority. For a more detailed coverage of the same period, see L. Gottschalk, *The Era of the French Revolution, 1715-1815,* Houghton Mifflin, 1929.

G. Lefebvre, *The Coming of the French Revolution,** Vintage. A penetrating interpretation of the causes of the Revolution by a famous French historian.

A brilliant study of French society before 1789, first published over a century ago, is Alexis de Tocqueville, *The Old Regime and the French Revolution,** Anchor. See also A. L. Guérard, *The Life and Death of an Ideal,* Braziller, 1956; and J. Lough, *An Introduction to Eighteenth Century France,* Longmans, 1960.

L. Gershoy, *The French Revolution, 1789-1799,** Holt (Berkshire Studies). A good brief introduction by a leading American authority. See also, by the same author, *The Era of the French Revolution, 1789-1799: Ten Years That Shook the World,** Anvil, which is half text, half documents.

C. Brinton, *A Decade of Revolution, 1789-1799,* Harper, 1934. A penetrating synthesis covering all of Europe; a volume in the valuable and highly readable *Rise of Modern Europe* series.

J. M. Thompson, *The French Revolution,* Blackwell, 1943. Probably the best of the detailed single-volumed histories of the Revolution. Two important and complementary accounts by French historians are P. Gaxotte, *The French Revolution,* Scribner's, 1932, which is strongly right wing; and A. Mathiez, *The French Revolution,* Knopf, 1928, which is leftist in sympathy.

E. Higgins, *The French Revolution As Told by Contemporaries,* Houghton Mifflin, 1938. The chief phases of the Revolution as revealed in eye-witness accounts. See also J. H. Stewart, *A Documentary Survey of the French Revolution,* Macmillan, 1951.

Edmund Burke, *Reflections on the Revolution in France,** Liberal Arts. A celebrated attack on the radicalism of the Rev-olution; it remains a classic statement of conservative political philosophy.

Anatole France, *The Gods Are Athirst,* John Lane, 1932. An absorbing novel which captures the spirit of the Revolution.

R. R. Palmer, *Twelve Who Ruled,* Princeton, 1958. Good reading on the members of the Committee of Public Safety during the Reign of Terror. See also the excellent sketches in J. M. Thompson, *Leaders of the French Revolution,* Blackwell, 1948.

A. Castelot, *Queen of France: A Biography of Maire Antoinette,* Harper, 1957. The life of an ill-starred queen, told with style and wit.

J. M. Thompson, *Robespierre and the French Revolution,* Macmillan (Teach Yourself History), 1953. A sympathetic brief biography.

F. Markham, *Napoleon and the Awakening of Europe,* Macmillan (Teach Yourself History), 1954. Recommended as a good popular introduction to the Napoleonic period. G. Bruun, *Europe and the French Imperium, 1799-1814,* Harper, 1938, is an analysis of how the Napoleonic empire functioned and what it meant to Europe; a volume in *The Rise of Modern Europe* series.

H. A. L. Fisher, *Napoleon,* Oxford (Home Univ. Library), 1945; H. Butterfield, *Napoleon,* Macmillan, 1956; and A. L. Guérard, *Napoleon I,* Knopf, 1956. Three good brief biographies.

F. Kircheisen, *Napoleon,* Harcourt, Brace, 1932. Outstanding among longer detailed biographies. J. M. Thompson, *Napoleon Bonaparte: His Rise and Fall,* Blackwell, 1952, incorporates the latest scholarly reëvaluations of Napoleon. Divergent evaluations of Napoleon by historians since 1815 are collected in P. Geyl, *Napoelon, For and Against,* Yale, 1949.

Philippe, Comte de Ségur, *Napoleon's Russian Campaign,* Houghton Mifflin, 1958. A first-hand narrative of the disastrous Russian campaign by Napoleon's aide-de-camp. See also the memoirs of A. A. de Caulaincourt, *With Napoleon in Russia,** Universal.

Salvador de Madariaga, *The Fall of the Spanish American Empire,* Macmillan, 1948. Examines the reasons for the disintegration of Spanish power in America and analyzes the influences in Latin America of the *philosophes* and the French Revolution. See also A. P. Whitaker, ed., *Latin America and the Enlightenment,* Appleton-Century, 1942; and V. A. Belaúnde, *Bolivar and the Political Thought of the Spanish American Revolution,* Johns Hopkins, 1938.

These biographies of the Liberators are highly recommended: J. F. Thorning, *Miranda: World Citizen,* Univ. of Florida, 1952; G. Masur, *Simón Bolivar,* Univ. of New Mexico, 1948; Salvador de Madariaga, *Bolivar,* Pelligrini, 1952; and R. Rojas, *San Martin: Knight of the Andes,* Doubleday, 1945.

SCIENCE AND TECHNOLOGY, THOUGHT AND ART

1500 Revolution in astronomy—Copernicus proposes heliocentric theory of universe, publishes *Concerning the Revolutions of Heavenly Bodies* 1543; Brahe attempts compromise between geocentric and heliocentric theories; Kepler coordinates Brahe's data; Galileo confirms Copernican theory; Copernicus' work included in *Index Librorum Prohibitorum* 1617; Galileo forced to recant heliocentric theory 1633

Pioneers in medicine: Paracelsus advocates experimental science; Vesalius shows true structure of human anatomy in *The Fabric of*
1550 *the Human Body* 1543; Harvey describes circulation of blood in *Anatomical Exercise on the Motion of the Heart and Blood* 1628

Mannerism in art develops as countermovement to Renaissance (sixteenth century)—exemplified by works of El Greco (1548-1614)

Francis Bacon (1561-1626) champions inductive method for scientific and philosophical inquiry; *Novum Organun* 1620; *New Atlantis* 1627

Improvements in mathematical calculation: decimals 1585; logarithms by Napier 1614; slide rule 1622; adding machine 1645; calculus by Newton and Leibnitz

Descartes (1590-1650) proposes deductive method of philosophical inquiry; develops analytical geometry; proposes theory of philosophical dualism
1600 Beginnings of electricity: Gilbert's *De Magnete* 1600

Neoclassical dramatists in France (seventeenth century)—Corneille, Racine, Molière advocate classic unities of time, action, place

Inventions of seventeenth century: telescope, microscope, thermometers, pendulum clock, micrometer, barometer, air pump

Baroque style develops with regeneration of Church during Catholic Reformation: Rubens, Velázquez, Vermeer, Hals, Rembrandt, Bernini; opera originates in Italy; visual arts and music are integrated
1650 Defenders of absolutism—Hobbes of England, author of *Leviathan* 1651; Bossuet of France

Scientific societies founded: Academy of Experiments at Florence 1657; Royal Society of England 1662; French Academy of Science at Paris 1666

Boyle's law is formulated 1660; his *Sceptical Chemist* (1661) urges use of inductive inquiry in chemistry

Spinoza expresses his pantheistic philosophy; publishes *Ethics* 1663

Newton expounds theory of gravitation in *Philosophiae Naturalis Principia Mathematica* 1687

Locke founds school of empiricism; publishes *An Essay Concerning Human Understanding* 1690; advances doctrine of popular sovereignty as argument against absolutism in "Of Civil Government" 1690

Rococo style, a reflection of the elegant life of the aristocracy, is exemplified in works of Watteau; English portrait painting by Reynolds, Gainsborough
1700 Inventions of the eighteenth century: centigrade and Fahrenheit thermometers, chronometer, sextant, anemometer

The novel appears: Defoe's *Robinson Crusoe* 1719; Swift's *Gulliver's Travels* 1726; Richardson's *Pamela* 1740-1741; Fielding's *Tom Jones* 1749

Pope, foremost Neoclassical English poet, publishes *An Essay on Man* 1733

Hogarth of England and Goya of Spain—nonconformist painters who reproduced life realistically: Hogarth's "The Rake's Progress" and Goya's "The Disasters of War"

Intellectuals adopt Deism, belief that God is creator of universe but cannot change laws of nature; Pietism develops to restore emotion and faith to religion, is later called Methodist movement under Wesley brothers in England 1738; Quietism is crushed in Catholic countries

Further experiments with electricity: Leyden Jar 1745; Franklin's experiment with kite 1752

Intellectual assault on absolutism led by *philosophes* Montesquieu (*The Spirit of Laws*, 1748) and Rousseau (*Social Contract*, 1762)
1750 Reaction on the Continent against Baroque and Rococo styles of architecture is manifested in Neoclassical style c. 1750

Formalism in music during the Age of Reason—Handel, Bach, Mozart, Haydn

The *philosophes*, critics of society in France, bring Age of Reason to climax: Voltaire advocates rationalism, publishes *Candide* 1759; Diderot spreads doctrines of rationalism and Deism, edits *Encyclopédie*

Great works of social sciences (eighteenth century): Rousseau's *Émile* 1762; Beccaria's *Essay on Crimes and Punishments* 1764; Gibbon's *Decline and Fall of the Roman Empire* 1776-1788; Condorcet's *Progress of the Human Mind* 1794

Priestley isolates ammonia; discovers gas later named oxygen 1774; produces carbon monoxide gas 1799

Adam Smith's *An Inquiry into the Nature and Causes of the Wealth of Nations* defends laissez-faire economics 1776

Lavoisier names oxygen; discovers the law of the conservation of matter and formulates his combustion theory 1777

Kant's *Critique of Pure Reason* (1781) marks end of natural philosophy and beginning of philosophical idealism; embraces dualism

Edmund Burke defends conservatism in *Reflections on the Revolution in France* 1790

Hutton's *Theory of the Earth* 1795—pioneer work in geology

Edward Jenner develops safe vaccination against smallpox c. 1798
1800 Volta discovers method for generating continuous flow of electricity 1800

POLITICS

Richelieu 1624-1642—adviser to Louis XIII; becomes real authority behind French throne; exalts power of monarchy
Frederick William, the Great Elector (1640-1688), makes Brandenburg the most important Protestant state in Germany
Mazarin (1643-1661) governs France during minority of Louis XIV; triumphs over enemies during civil war 1648-1653

Restoration of Stuart kings in England—controversy between Charles II and Parliament 1660-1685; Charles II negotiates secret Treaty of Dover with Louis XIV 1670; Test Act 1673; Whig and Tory parties organized; Habeas Corpus Act 1679
Louis XIV (1661-1715) transforms French state into an absolute monarchy; invades Spanish Netherlands and German border districts 1667-1697; halted by William of Orange and allied nations
Peter the Great 1682-1725—absolutist tsar of Russia; captures Azov on Black Sea; tours Europe; attempts to westernize realm
James II of England (1685-1688) attempts to impose absolute rule
Louis XIV ends religious toleration by revoking Edict of Nantes 1685; Huguenots flee
Glorious Revolution—Whigs and Tories invite William of Orange to rule England; Bill of Rights passed; Parliament becomes dominant agency in government 1688; Toleration Act 1689; press given freedom of expression 1693
Great Northern War 1700-1721—Charles XII of Sweden defeated by Peter the Great and allies; Russia gains outlet on Baltic

War of the Spanish Succession—English and allies renew struggle against French 1702; great victory by allies under Duke of Marl-borough at battle of Blenheim 1704; Treaty of Utrecht ends war 1713
Frederick William I of Prussia (1713-1740) creates all-powerful central government; builds up army
George I initiates Hanoverian dynasty in England; beginning of creative cabinet government 1714
Robert Walpole serves as first prime minister of England under George II 1721-1742

Frederick II, the Great (1740-1786), makes Prussia important power in European politics
War of the Austrian Succession 1740-1749—Frederick the Great violates Pragmatic Sanction and invades Silesia 1740; France and England enter first stage of duel for world empire; Peace of Aix-la-Chapelle 1748

Seven Years' War 1756-1763—Diplomatic Revolution aligns Austria and France against England and Prussia; struggle on Continent and in colonies; William Pitt's "system" brings English victories, such as battle of Plassey (1757) and battle of Quebec (1759); Treaty of Paris (1763) makes Britain greatest colonial, commercial, and naval power in the world
Catherine the Great (1762-1796) wages war against Ottoman empire; makes Russia major European power
George III of England (1770-1782) strives to destroy cabinet system; secures control of Parliament
Poland partitioned in three stages among Russia, Prussia, and Austria 1772-1795; ceases to exist as independent state
American Revolution 1775-1783—revolt of colonies formally proclaimed in Declaration of Independence 1776

American Articles of Confederation ratified 1781; Constitutional Convention 1787; American Constitution adopted 1789
Pitt the Younger appointed by George III as prime minister 1783; makes important reforms, restores cabinet government
French Revolution (first phase)—storming of Bastille; National Constituent Assembly draws up Declaration of the Rights of Man; formulates new constitution and government (Legislative Assembly) 1789-1791
French Revolution (second phase)—agitation by Jacobin movement led by Marat, Danton, and Robespierre; radical insurrection in Paris; National Convention proclaims the Republic; France repels invasion by Austria and Prussia 1792
Louis XVI executed 1793; Reign of Terror begins under Robespierre 1793; compulsory military service introduced; Robespierre executed; Directory assumes power 1795; Directory smashes First Coalition, except for England 1797
Napoleon establishes Consulate 1799; scatters Second Coalition forces 1799-1802; climaxes reforms with Civil Code, proclaims himself emperor 1804; destroys armies of Third Coalition; is defeated by British at Trafalgar, defeats Prussia 1805-1806; his invasion of Russia fails 1812
English and allies defeat Napoleon at Leipzig 1813; Napoleon abdicates throne, goes to Elba 1814; returns to France and is defeated by Britain and Prussia at Waterloo; exiled to St. Helena 1815
Revolution in Latin America—Bolívar and San Martín gain independence for Spanish colonies in South America 1817-1825; Iturbide proclaims Mexican independence 1821; Pedro is crowned emperor of independent Brazil 1822

PART 5 Europe's Century

The century from the battle of Waterloo to the outbreak of the First World War was one of sweeping change in the internal affairs of Europe. The impact of the powerful forces set in motion during this period made the nineteenth century one of the most complex, diverse, and significant eras in the history of modern civilization.

With Napoleon defeated, the Congress of Vienna met to remake the map of Europe. Dominated by the spirit of reaction, the statesmen at the Congress shelved the ideals of the French Revolution, ignored the burgeoning of nationalist and liberal sentiments, and attempted to restore autocracy and privilege intact. In the years which followed, this ultraconservative ideology was challenged again and again by those who espoused nationalism and economic and political liberalism—the creed of the growing middle class. This drive for liberty gained inspiration and emotional fervor from the romantic movement of the early decades of the nineteenth century. In the economic realm, the bourgeoisie believed in the philosophy of laissez faire, the opposition to government regulation of business; in politics, the middle class supported movements which best represented their own interests. Repeatedly—and with varying but, on the whole, increasing success—the bourgeoisie established parliaments and constitutions and brought about moderate reforms. But although these reforms benefited the middle class, the workers stood at one side, still without political power or social advantage.

A rapidly mounting antagonism between the business classes and the new city proletariat produced still another ideological pattern, socialism, and resulted in the failure of the 1848 revolutions. In France,

Italy, Prussia, and the Austrian empire, ardent hopes for political advancement were dashed. The price paid for such failures was high: ruthless realism rather than romantic idealism became the keynote for those in opposition to the status quo. Only in the more progressive European states—Britain, France, Denmark, and Switzerland—was there manifested a shift from middle-class liberalism toward mass democracy in the latter decades of the century. Elsewhere on the Continent, conservative governments continued in power, though often their control was hidden behind parliamentary trappings.

Economically, Europe was advancing by giant strides. Nineteenth-century industrialism introduced mass production, promoted the growth of large industrial complexes, and brought wealth to thousands of middle-class employers and investors. Not until latter decades of the nineteenth century, however, did the workers' plight receive attention. Then, the enactment of social legislation raised the workers' living standards; the advance of unions gave them more effective bargaining power; and the spread of free education broadened their children's prospects. It was at this time that many socialists allied themselves with programs of gradual, rather than revolutionary, change, pointing to the welfare state. The class revolution of the proletariat, earlier predicted by Marx, was postponed indefinitely.

Perhaps as significant as the social and economic changes wrought by the end of the nineteenth century was the rise to preëminence of science and, with it, technology. There seemed no limit to the benefits which scientific and technological knowledge could bring to mankind. The work of such men as Pasteur and Lister promised an end to disease; and technological innovations resulted in an increasing number of new industries, new products, and new wealth. The development of man from lower beings was explained by Darwin, and Freud initiated the study and analysis of man's emotions. Indeed, in retrospect, the nineteenth century seems to have been one of the most promising in all history. And in power, wealth, and intellectual activity, Europe was the center of the world.

Yet in 1914 the Continent would be plunged into catastrophic war. How could such a disaster come about? The explanation lies both in the forces which made the century one of such bitter struggle and in those which made it a period of great promise. Nationalism eventually became more narrow and belligerent, and laissez-faire economics led to imperialistic rivalries. The rise to preëminence of science fostered a translation of scientific Darwinism into social Darwinism, and this fallacious emphasis on the "survival of the fittest" led to racism and militant nationalism. At the end of one hundred years of struggle for liberty and reform and of breath-taking economic and scientific advances came the Great War.

CHAPTER 20

Machines, the Middle Class, and the *Manifesto*

THE FIRST INDUSTRIAL REVOLUTION (1750-1870); THOUGHT AND ART (1800-1870)

Introduction. Between 1800 and 1870, society was reshaped by a new major force—industrialism. Steam engines, railways, and industrial towns with their smoke-belching factory chimneys were altering the landscape of western Europe, particularly in England. The owners of those chimneys—the bourgeoisie, or middle class—were rapidly propelled to the top of the social heap. The triumph of the middle class had two important aspects: in the political sphere, the middle class obtained the right to vote (which most workers did not enjoy during this period) and became a dominant voice in government; in the economic sphere, the bourgeoisie profited from the doctrine of laissez faire —that is, unrestricted competition and governmental noninterference with business enterprise—and piled up increasing wealth. Having achieved both power and prosperity, the new capitalists stoutly resisted demands for drastic social change, but, as children of their times, the more enlightened and humanitarian among them supported programs of gradual reform and supported the philosophy summed up in the term *liberalism*.

From other quarters, angry voices cried out against the poverty and social injustice resulting from unbridled competition. These critics of the status quo attacked bourgeois complacency and laissez-faire liberalism. Their voices were to become increasingly strong as the century progressed. The most extreme of the various radical doctrines developed at this time was that of the German socialist Karl Marx. For good or evil, much of the history of the western world after 1848, the year in which the *Communist Manifesto* was published, concerns the duel between the forces of capitalism and communism.

In addition to liberalism and socialism, other trends of thought became dominant between 1800 and 1870. Among them was the romantic movement. Spurred on by their enthusiastic faith in man, the romanticists rebelled against political oppression, social injustice, and the classical intellectual and esthetic standards of the previous century. The interaction of romanticism and nationalism produced the strongly felt and widespread emotion of romantic nationalism.

No survey of the period can overlook the important role played by science in shaping both the physical environment of western society and the West's fundamental attitude toward life. Especially notable in the latter respect was the publication in 1859 of Darwin's theory of the evolution of biological species. In the prevailing mood of the period, Darwin's hypothesis served to strengthen further the realistic and materialistic attitudes of the dominant middle class.

THE TRIUMPH OF THE MACHINE

Interpretations of the Industrial Revolution. With the advent of industrialism, the economic life of Europe was modified drastically—a transformation called the Industrial Revolution. The first historian to give wide currency to the term was Arnold Toynbee of Oxford, the uncle of the famous present-day British historian Arnold J. Toynbee. In a series of lectures published posthumously in 1884—*Lectures on the Industrial Revolution of the 18th Century in England*—Toynbee pointed out that: (1) the beginning of the Industrial Revolution was sudden, starting in the year 1760; (2) the effects of the revolution were both sudden and cataclysmic, rudely overturning the whole edifice of society; (3) the Industrial Revolution quickly pervaded all quarters of English manufacturing and for a substantial period was wholly an English phenomenon; and (4) for many decades the effects of the revolution upon the common people were completely evil.

This traditional interpretation has been criticized in the past twenty-five years by various economic historians who assert that the change was less a revolution than a simple speeding up of evolution. While the modification of the "revolutionary" thesis by the "evolutionary" thesis has added greatly to our understanding of industrialization, the term *Industrial Revolution* still seems a valid one to employ in discussing this movement.

In an attempt to discuss the movement in a chronological framework, we shall present the growth of industrialism as a four-stage process. The initial phase was the onset of industrialism from its slow beginnings to the close of the Napoleonic era in 1814. The next phase, which we can term the First Industrial Revolution, ran roughly from 1815 to 1870 and was a period of rapid growth during which factories seemed to sprout like mushrooms in England and technological change shifted into high gear. The third phase, termed the Second Industrial Revolution, began in the 1870's as a new source of energy, electricity, came into use, making possible the production of new steel alloys, rubber, petroleum, and chemical synthetics (see Chapter 24). Designated as the Third Industrial Revolution, the fourth phase began at the end of World War I and has transformed the lives of millions with astounding scientific and technical marvels.

Mechanization of the textile industry. Prior to the 1700's, mechanized industry was almost unknown; the machinery of the period was crude, and power facilities were inadequate. In the eighteenth century, there was produced a series of inventions which had tremendous significance for manufacturing, particularly in England. These inventions were of two sorts—machines which increased industrial output far beyond that which had been possible when products were handmade, and machines which harnessed new power sources, thereby increasing output even further.

The textile industry was the first to be revolutionized by machines. In 1738 John

Shown here is James Hargreaves' revolutionary spinning jenny.

Kay invented the flying shuttle—a device which permitted one person instead of two to weave wide bolts of cloth. But Kay's invention permitted cloth to be woven much faster than thread could be supplied; one weaver required ten spinners to produce sufficient yarn for him. With the invention of the spinning jenny in 1764 by James Hargreaves, the production of spinners equaled that of weavers, and it became possible for one workman to spin eight, then sixteen, and finally as many as eighty threads at once.

Although inexpensive and easy to operate, the spinning jenny had one serious defect. The spun yarn was so coarse and loose that flax had to be mixed with the cotton to produce a suitable fabric. In 1769 a wig maker named Richard Arkwright patented his water frame. Powered by water, this machine for spinning thread made it possible to employ pure cotton. Ten years later Samuel Crompton, a spinner, combined the spinning jenny and water frame into the spinning mule. This machine could be powered as the water frame had been but was lighter and easier to operate. More important, the thread which it spun was so strong and fine that muslins, cambrics, and other sheer materials could now be woven.

The spinning process had been so improved that the weaving process lagged behind it; the hand loom could no longer weave cloth as fast as the machine could spin yarn for it. Hand weaving was soon supplanted by the use of the power loom, patented in 1785 by Edmund Cartwright.

The suppliers of raw cotton had great difficulty in meeting the increasing demands for their crop because cotton seeds were separated from the fiber by hand and the most skillful worker could prepare not more than five or six pounds a day. In 1792 a young American, Eli Whitney, invented a cotton gin which enabled one worker to clean as much as a thousand pounds of cotton a day.

Sources of power. With improvements in machinery came corresponding improvements in power. In 1705 an English engineer, Thomas Newcomen, devised an engine in which a piston was raised by injected steam, the steam condensed, and the piston returned to its original position as it cooled off. Used to pump water from coal mines, Newcomen's invention doubled the depth in the ground at which coal could be worked but consumed large quantities of coal, which the mines could supply cheaply but which factories could not.

The transformation of the atmosphere engine into the true steam engine was the achievement of James Watt (1736-1819). This Scottish genius was employed at the University of Glasgow as its mathematical instrument maker. One day when repairing the university's Newcomen engine, Watt was struck by the waste of steam resulting from the alternate heating and chilling of the cylinder. Four fifths of the steam used was lost in heating the cold cylinder; only one fifth served a useful purpose by acting on the piston. Using steam to force the piston back and forth inside a closed cylinder, Watt devised a separate condenser to control the supply of steam. The first steam engines were used for pumping; after 1785 they were employed in cotton manufacturing; and still later they were adapted to the needs of the steam locomotive and the steamship.

Before 1870 the steam engine and the water wheel were the chief power sources, but the potentialities of oil were also explored. In 1859 the first oil well was drilled in Pennsylvania. The use of oil was destined to expand substantially the sources of power available to industry, for three and a half barrels of oil yield as much heat as a ton of coal. A further development came in 1860, when an electric spark was used to ignite gasoline in an internal-combustion engine, thus providing a momentous change in motive power.

Improved methods for refining iron and mining coal. Until 1784, iron was available only in an impure state—cast iron which would break rather than bend and which was too brittle to withstand hard strains and heavy blows. In that year a method was invented for making iron malleable by burning the impurities out and leaving the iron clean and tough. The molten iron was then stirred with a long rod, a technique known as "puddling." Widespread adoption of this process enabled Great Britain to produce cheap wrought iron.

In the 1850's the smelting and refining of iron ore were substantially improved by Sir Henry Bessemer. With his new process, steel could be manufactured quickly and cheaply; in fact, between 1856 and 1870 the price of British steel fell to one half the sum formerly charged for the best grades of iron. At the same time, production increased sixfold.

Improvements in the coal-mining industry included better means of ventilation in the mines by using large fans and by sinking a second shaft containing a fire, which made an upward draft and drew fresh air down the first shaft. But explosions were still a great hazard, for miners needed light to work by and the heat of the flame in their lamps ignited the gases present in the mine shafts and tunnels. By enclosing the flame of the miner's lamp with a wire gauze screen that was heat absorptive, this problem was solved.

Improvements in transportation: roads and canals. In 1815 a Scotsman, John McAdam, used a simple but revolutionary method in the construction of roads: small stones in compact layers were placed directly on the earth roadbed. The passage of traffic packed the stones down so tightly that a strong and fairly smooth surface resulted. *Macadam,* the term given today to roads of this type, is derived from the name of the inventor.

Stagecoaches reached new top speeds as their horses galloped over the improved roads. It had taken four and a half days to travel the 160 miles from London to Manchester in 1754; thirty-four years later the journey had been shortened to twenty-eight hours.

Modern canal building in England began in 1759 with the construction of a waterway from the duke of Bridgewater's colliery to Manchester, a distance of seven miles. As a result of this project, the price of coal in Manchester was halved and all England became "canal conscious." Seventy years later England had nearly four thousand miles of improved rivers and canals. Better roads and new canals made hauling of goods cheaper and easier. Many acres of new iron docks were constructed in London, making this port the largest in the world.

Canals were used so successfully in England that other countries were encouraged to plan elaborate systems of inland waterways. In 1825, for example, the Erie Canal, linking the Hudson River and New York City with the Great Lakes, was completed.

In 1869 the first great interoceanic canal joined the Mediterranean and the Indian Ocean by way of the Red Sea. Dug in the sands of the Egyptian desert, this new water artery, the Suez Canal, was nicknamed the "Big Ditch." Impressed by its strategic and commercial value, the British government purchased the shares of canal stock owned by the ruler of Egypt in 1875 and established control of the canal a few years later when English troops occupied Egypt (see p. 633). The Suez, which shortened the sailing time between London and Bombay by nearly half, became the life line of the empire.

The advent of railroads. In England the era of canal building was cut short by the advent of railroads. Before the locomotive was perfected, iron rails had been installed on public streetcar lines and in mines to reduce the friction on the wheels of horse-drawn vehicles. The forty miles of track between Stockton and Darlington in England served as a testing ground for the im-

As shown by this illustration of a train on the London and Greenwich Railroad line in 1833, the railroad cars were shaped like carriages. The train also transported privately owned carriages on flat cars.

proved locomotive built in 1825 by George Stephenson, the brilliant son of a poor miner. Five years later, when his *Rocket* attained the terrifying speed of thirty-six miles an hour, the railroad era was on its way. Soon other countries began to lay the shining rails for locomotive transportation. In the United States, the federal government subsidized the construction of the Union Pacific and Central Pacific railroads to connect Omaha and San Francisco. With their completion in 1869, it became possible to cross the entire North American continent by rail.

Clippers give way to steamships. The opening decades of the nineteenth century witnessed important advances in transportation at sea as well as on land. From the shipyards of New England came the beautiful clippers. These long, slender, sharp-bowed sailing vessels were the swiftest ships on the seven seas, after attaining a speed of eighteen knots. The finest clipper afloat, the *Flying Cloud*, made the voyage from New York to San Francisco via Cape Horn in eighty-nine days and eight hours, a record that still stands for sailing vessels.

Although others had used steam to propel boats earlier, the man who reaped the lion's share of glory for this feat was Robert Fulton, who used a Watt engine to drive his *Clermont* 150 miles up the Hudson River in 1807. About thirty years later Samuel Cunard initiated regular transatlantic passenger steamship service. This line still proudly bears the name of its Canadian founder. The clippers became obsolete; after 1870, smoking funnels replaced the glistening sails.

Improvements in communication. Parallel with improvements in transportation went great advances in communication. The introduction of the penny post in 1840 in England made correspondence by mail substantially cheaper. Another revolutionary method of transmitting information appeared when Samuel Morse, an American artist and inventor, perfected the electric telegraph in 1844. Twenty-two years later Cyrus Field, another American inventor, laid the first successful Atlantic cable.

England, "workshop of the world." It was England's undisputed leadership in the First Industrial Revolution that explained the tremendous volume of the nation's exports, its accumulation of vast amounts of capital, and its long-held position as the world's commercial center. And with its head start in industrial development, Britain enjoyed a virtual monopoly in some manufacturing techniques until after 1870.

There were reasons for England's technological leadership. On this small island were rich deposits of coal and iron to supply the needs of industry. The wool of English sheep, unsurpassed in quality, provided the essential raw material for the nation's textile mills. Britain's stable government catered increasingly in the nineteenth century to the interests of the trading and industrial classes, and its unrivaled navy not only protected the country from invasion but also kept open the routes for the merchant fleet. There was also surplus capital, accumulated from trade with America and the Orient. Finally, England concentrated on staple goods, adaptable to mass production, whereas France, for example, specialized in luxury commodities demanding individual craftsmanship.

Industrialization outside England. In France, industrial progress was much slower than in England. The development of heavy industry lagged. There was a shortage of coal, and although the output of iron ore increased about 65 per cent between 1830 and 1865, the deposits of ore were not conveniently located. With the invention of the Jacquard loom (1804), on the other hand, French silk production came to exceed that of all the rest of Europe.

Early in the nineteenth century, the progress of industrialism in Germany was retarded by political disunity, the conflict of interests between nobles and merchants, and, as in France, the existence of the guild system, which discouraged competition and innovation. But after the formation of a tariff union, the Zollverein, which by 1842 included most of the German states, industry was stimulated by the wider trade advantages now available. After 1850, improved methods in metallurgy were introduced, and in the next twenty years the output from German furnaces increased fourfold. Coal production likewise mounted rapidly.

The development of the Krupp works best exemplifies the remarkable growth of German industry. Inheriting a broken-down steel mill employing four men, Alfred Krupp introduced a steam engine into his factory and expanded his work force. From the invention and exploitation of a steel gun, cast-steel axles, and a breech-loading rifle, Krupp created a large-scale enterprise which by 1873 was employing sixteen thousand workers. The Krupp works was to become the symbol of German industrial efficiency and of Germany's successful application of technology to the weapons of war.

By pirating British manufacturing techniques, Belgium also achieved rapid industrial growth. During the nineteenth century, in fact, Belgium produced more coal and iron than its much larger neighbor, France, and Belgian railroad construction boomed until this small nation boasted a greater railroad mileage per capita than any other country. Meanwhile, the Belgian factories and mills turned out quantities of lace, carpets, cutlery, and iron products.

By the 1840's, factories and railroads had become important in the United States; by 1860 American textile, iron, steel, and shoe industries were developing rapidly. At mid-century, large-scale corporate enterprises had begun to replace small-scale businesses, and after 1861 the government was usually in the hands of legislators friendly to corporate enterprise, instead of under agrarian control as it had been in earlier decades. Protective tariffs were passed to assure American manufacturers a ready home market, and the power of the states to regulate business was restricted; thus the basis was laid for large-scale industrial development, already stimulated by military needs during the Civil War. By 1870 the nation was crisscrossed with railroads, the northeastern part of the country was heavily industrialized, and new factories and mills were springing up everywhere.

Outside the industrial pale were Italy, Spain, Portugal, the nations of eastern Europe and the Balkans, and Russia, where industry either barely existed or grew very slowly. And before 1870, industrialism made little progress in South America, Africa, the Middle East, and Asia.

Progress in agriculture. The agricultural revolution which had begun in the eighteenth century was accelerated by the amazing progress of nineteenth-century technology. In 1831, Cyrus McCormick, a native of Vermont, demonstrated the first modern reaper. Later on came the harvester, which also bound the grain, and finally the combine, which threshed the grain as it reaped it. Further improvements in farm machinery came with the manufacture of the steel plow and other implements by John Deere of Illinois.

The marketing of foods was revolutionized by the widespread adoption of canning and refrigeration, permitting the storage of perishable crops. Railroads and steamships sped farm produce to market. During the second half of the nineteenth century, international trade in farm products increased rapidly. For example, the annual export of wheat from the United States and Canada rose from 22,000,000 bushels in the 1850's to 150,000,000 in 1880.

CONSEQUENCES OF INDUSTRIALISM

New markets for new goods. An important result of industrialism was the increase in productivity. In some industries productivity increased a hundredfold; in others, as much as a thousandfold. It soon became apparent that home markets alone were not able to absorb all the goods the factories could produce, and western European powers therefore began searching for trade outlets all over the world. International trade required a network of world transportation, a need which was met by the development of the railroad and steamship. The world was becoming an integrated economic unit.

Accompanying the mounting demand for overseas markets was the need for raw materials. These aims led to the European penetration of African and Asian lands. Isolated and primitive peoples were brought into touch with western culture by traders seeking markets and raw materials. And with these traders usually came officials and troops to take over territories as protectorates or colonies. Thus in the nineteenth century, and increasingly after 1871, the great industrial powers of Europe pursued a program of imperialism by which vast chunks of Asia and practically all of Africa came under European political and economic control.

Changing population trends. The best markets for the new products were still in Europe, where the industrial era was accompanied by a substantial and continuous increase in population. It has been estimated that Europe in 1800 had about 175,000,000 people, whereas by 1900 it had 400,000,000.

Up to early modern times, populations were checked by food scarcity, pestilence,

and high infant mortality. Now the growing agricultural productiveness of European countries, achieved through intensive farming and the adoption of the techniques of scientific agriculture, supported larger populations. Because of the spread of transportation facilities, Europe was also able to import more food from other continents. In addition, achievements in medicine resulted in a lowered death rate. Infant mortality was reduced; in the eighteenth century it had been not uncommon for a mother who bore ten children to lose seven of them. By the latter part of the nineteenth century, medicine and public health were slowly but surely conquering the dreaded plagues—cholera, typhus, and smallpox.

An increasing majority of the population were city dwellers. First in England, then in Belgium, France, and Germany, and later in other parts of the world, old cities outgrew their boundaries, and many new ones were founded. In general, from 1750 down to the present, people have more and more tended to concentrate in cities, while population in the country has declined.

Aside from the country-to-city migrations, there were often regional shifts in population. For example, when coal and iron were discovered in northern England, industrial centers such as Birmingham and Manchester were founded in the vicinity of these raw materials. On a wider scale, the opportunities in America attracted thousands of immigrants, who joined the country-by-country migration.

The factory, symbol of the new order. The most important symbol of the new industrial order was the factory, for here was the site of the machinery and power that made industrialism possible. The factory system did not replace the cottage or domestic system of home manufactures overnight; the two existed side by side for decades. Until 1815 the hand-loom weaver in England did not suffer substantially, but after that he was forced to compete with machines that could produce more goods at lower cost. As a result, weavers had to accept lower and lower wages to compete with the cheaper

Gustave Doré's nineteenth-century engraving depicts the filthy, overcrowded slums which housed the industrial workers of London.

goods made by the power looms. Ultimately, they lost their hopeless battle and were forced to move to the communities where the new factories offered employment.

This displacement of human skills by machinery, known as technological unemployment, remained a constant source of fear as the Industrial Revolution spread. Even today, the twentieth-century advance in labor-saving machinery—automation—is causing serious concern to factory workers and their union leaders.

Wretched working conditions. The first factories thrown together during the extraordinary rise of such industrial centers as Manchester and Birmingham were lacking in the most elementary sanitary and safety facilities; horrible cases of mangling were a common occurrence among the factory workers. Furthermore, under English common law, any accident a worker might suffer was considered a result of his own negligence, for which the employer could not be held responsible. There was no system of workmen's compensation or health insurance; an injured worker was likely to be thrown out in the street destitute and his job given to one of the thousands who had flocked to the new cities in search of employment.

Despite the innovation of "labor-saving" machinery, the worker was certainly not saved any labor. Each day the factory bell summoned him to long hours of monotonous drudgery. Women were forced by poverty to work until a day or two before delivery of their children and then to report back to work shortly after the child was born.

Children were the most unfortunate victims of the factory system. The mills employed some youngsters only four or five years of age, and in the coal mines children were used to carry baskets of coal up ladders. Children working in the mills received almost no education, for schooling was neither compulsory nor free. The facilities for obtaining even the most rudimentary training were insufficient, and evening schools were of little benefit to children who had to toil twelve hours during the day.

Ugly, disease-ridden slums. Contemporary accounts of the workers' quarters in the new industrial cities fill us with loathing and pity. In his novel *Hard Times,* Charles Dickens described a typical English factory town of a century ago, as follows:

It was a town of red brick, or of brick that would have been red if the smoke and ashes had allowed it; but as matters stood it was a town of unnatural red and black, like the painted face of a savage. It was a town of machinery and tall chimneys, out of which interminable serpents of smoke trailed themselves for ever and ever, and never got uncoiled. It had a black canal in it, and a river that ran purple with ill-smelling dye, and vast piles of buildings full of windows where there was a rattling and a trembling all day long, and where the piston of the steam-engine worked monotonously up and down, like the head of an elephant in a state of melancholy madness. It contained several large streets all very like one another, and many small streets still more like one another, inhabited by people equally like one another, who all went in and out at the same hours, with the same sound upon the same pavements, to do the same work, and to whom every day was the same as yesterday and tomorrow, and every year the counterpart of the last and the next.[1]

If we had visited a working-class district in Manchester early in the nineteenth century, we should have seen whole blocks of jerry-built homes, thrown together back to back by speculators so that the rear rooms had no windows. The houses faced on narrow, unpaved alleys or courts in which garbage and sewage were dumped. The living quarters for factory workers were chronically overcrowded and lacked adequate sanitary facilities. No wonder epidemics such as cholera were frequent. In 1842 a commission reported that the deaths caused by filth and lack of public sanitation outnumbered the loss in any wars that England had fought in modern times.

While the new material forces of industrialism were rapidly reshaping society, a new emotional force—romanticism—was producing equally revolutionary results in men's minds and spirits. Let us now turn to a discussion of this trend.

THE TRIUMPH OF ROMANTICISM

Romanticism defined. In contrast to the rationalism of the eighteenth century, with its exaltation of classical rules of self-restraint and artistic self-discipline, the romanticism which flowered early in the nineteenth century was characterized by strong elements of individualism, idealism, and revolt against all rules and accepted authority.

To the classicist, man is a rational, finite being—an integral member of a society which itself is governed in accordance with law and well-defined rules of conduct. Within this well-ordered social structure, man finds fulfillment, even as, in his intellectual and artistic expression, he emphasizes form and order and harmony. To the romanticist, on the other hand, man is a creature of feeling no less than of thought. He seeks ever after the infinite because he is not simply a cog in a finite human society but instead an irreplaceable part of nature and the whole creative process. The romanticist argues that society's laws and rules of conduct serve only to confine the natural soaring instincts of man. To the classicist's insistence upon the overruling claims of society, the romanticist opposes the right of self-determination, whether of the individual or of any group of like-minded individuals—for example, a nation. Where the classicist's esthetic ideal is manifested in elegance, symmetry, and order, the romanticist is charmed by the "natural," the wild, and the unruly. The classicist finds beauty in logic and in acceptance of what exists; the romanticist makes it synonymous with feeling and with longing after the ultimate. "Classicism is symbolized in the static perfection of the Greek temple, with its joy in the finite work of man. Romanticism soars restlessly into the unknown with the Gothic cathedral."[2] As we shall see in this chapter, the romanticists' concern with the Gothic was not accidental.

The preromantics: Rousseau, Schiller, Goethe. Jean Jacques Rousseau, whose *Social Contract* (1762) has been termed the bible of the French Revolution, was a romanticist who believed that the human heart is the infallible source of wisdom, that we should trust in our instincts, that man is capable of constant improvement, and that in nature men find their truest happiness. Rousseau helped popularize the cult of the "noble savage" and urged mankind to return to a more "natural" form of society by abandoning artificial conventions and institutions. He proved a most potent influence both on the political rebels of his own century and on the romanticists of the next.

In the latter part of the eighteenth century, Germany witnessed a dynamic cultural revival. Among the greatest of German writers was Johann Christoph Friedrich von Schiller, whose most famous drama, *Wilhelm Tell* (1804), deals with the struggle of the Swiss for their national independence and makes an impassioned attack on tyranny.

The works of Schiller's friend Johann Wolfgang von Goethe (1749-1832) constitute the finest example of the transition from eighteenth-century classicism to nineteenth-century romanticism. In 1774 Goethe published *The Sorrows of Young Werther*—an extravagantly sentimental tale of a youth, disappointed in love, who kills himself with the pistol of his successful rival. The novel had an enormous success all over Europe, delighting a public weary of classicism's repression of human emotions.

Depicting the despair of the rejected young lover, this illustration from an early edition of *The Sorrows of Young Werther* captures the exaggerated emotionalism of Goethe's work.

At Weimar, which he made the intellectual center of Germany, Goethe turned out lyric poems, novels, and plays. By far the greatest of his works is *Faust* (Part I published in 1808, Part II in 1832). Based on an old German legend, this verse drama relates the story of an aging scholar, Faust, who makes a pact with the devil, Mephistopheles. In return for twenty-four years of youth and pleasure, Faust gives his soul to the archfiend. In Goethe's adaption, the legend becomes the vehicle for a magnificent philosophical discussion of the trials and triumphs of the human soul. Faust is saved— but only because he ultimately rejects self-gratification and accepts service to his fellow man. This theme is in harmony with the tenets of romanticism. Goethe demands, on the one hand, a full realization of the individual personality through a multitude of experiences—intellectual, sensual, and spiritual alike—even at the risk of salvation. On the other hand, he seeks an integration of the now-developed personality with the collective good of the nation or society to which the individual must dedicate his gifts.

Romanticism in English literature. In the early nineteenth century, romanticism assumed many different aspects. Most important, all these aspects were products of a state of mind in rebellion against accepted values. Let us now look at some of the forms which this revolt took among writers in England.

In 1798 two young English poets, William Wordsworth and Samuel Taylor Coleridge, published a volume of verse called *Lyrical Ballads*. In the preface of this work, Wordsworth defined poetry as "the spontaneous overflow of powerful feelings recollected in tranquility"—a concept which was at once romantic and very much at odds with the views of the previous century. To give expression to "the great and universal passions of men . . . and the entire world of nature," Wordsworth rejected the high-flown and mythology-laden diction in which the classicists delighted, employing instead a simple vocabulary or, to quote his own words, the "very language of men."[3]

In his works, Wordsworth emphasized the world of nature and man's relationship to it. He believed that by contemplating nature in all its aspects and moods, it was possible to grasp reality intuitively—a view related to the philosophy known as transcendentalism, which developed out of the work of Kant and his followers.

With the statement that his endeavors were "directed to persons and characters supernatural or at least romantic,"[4] Coleridge stressed another facet of romanticism—exoticism. Especially vivid is his description of the imaginary Xanadu in *Kubla Khan* (1798). In others of his works, Coleridge voiced his dissatisfaction with an approach to man and his problems that was incapable of expressing adequately the nonrational and even irrational elements in human experience. These elements, whose importance was later demonstrated by the researches of Freud and other psychologists (see Chapter 24), are often described in literature in terms of fantasy, symbolism, dream states, and the supernatural.

Percy Bysshe Shelley believed passionately that human perfectibility was possible only through complete freedom of thought and action. In *Prometheus Unbound* (1818-1819), he pictured his ideal of humanity in a new world of perfect freedom and equality:

The loathsome mask has fallen, the man remains
Sceptreless, free, uncircumscribed, but man . . .
Exempt from awe, worship, degree, the king
Over himself; just, gentle, wise.[5]

The works of the handsome, impulsive, and emotionally unstable George Gordon, Lord Byron, also expressed the romanticist's rebellion against the constraints of society. Like the hero of his masterpiece, *Don Juan* (1818-1824), Byron gloried in the cult of freedom:

The mountains look on Marathon—
  And Marathon looks on the sea;
And musing there an hour alone,
  I dreamed that Greece might still be free;
For standing on the Persians' grave,
I could not deem myself a slave.[6]

When the Greeks revolted against the Turks (see p. 507), Byron joined the cause of independence and died of fever in Greece.

Unlike his compatriots Shelley and Byron, John Keats was not interested in revolution or reform. Of prime importance to him was the worship of beauty—this was the motive and message of his poetry. As expressed in *Endymion* (1817):

A thing of beauty is a joy forever:
Its loveliness increases; it will never
Pass into nothingness; but still will keep
A bower quiet for us, and a sleep
Full of sweet dreams, and health, and quiet
  breathing.[7]

Thus Keats exemplifies an important aspect of the romantic movement—estheticism, or the acceptance of artistic beauty and taste as a fundamental standard, superior to ethical and other standards.

For romantics like Sir Walter Scott, the past provided colorful and exciting examples of men who lived stirring, passionate lives. In his Waverley novels, his long narrative poems, and his adventure story of medieval chivalry, *Ivanhoe* (1819), Scott stirred the imagination of his contemporaries by his vivid re-creation of medieval life.

Revolt against classical painting. The romanticist painters rebelled against classical models and the emphasis upon precise draftsmanship because they felt that color was more important than drawing and that subject matter should give unhampered scope to the imagination and emotions. Old legends and exotic and picturesque scenes, such as were to be found in North Africa and the Near East, became popular. One of the first major rebels was Eugène Delacroix, a French artist whose flamboyant canvases convey the heightened emotional approach of the romanticists (see picture, p. 509). His "Massacre of Chios" (1824), painted under the direct impact of the news of the slaying of Christians on the island of Chios by the Turks, was unjustly dubbed the "Massacre of Painting" by conservative critics.

The effects of the cult of nature were no less marked upon romantic painting than upon poetry. Artists were inspired to look at nature with a fresh appreciation. The English painter John Constable (1776-1837) was in some respects the creator of the modern school of landscape painting. His choice of colors was revolutionary, for he used greens freely in his landscapes, an innovation considered audacious by men who had stressed the necessity of painting nature in browns. Another English painter whose originality created a profound stir was J. M. W. Turner (1775-1851). Gifted with a vivid sense of color and a powerful imagination, Turner was particularly adept in creating atmospheric effects (see Color Plate 18). He used a color technique similar to that employed later in the century with dazzling success by the French Impressionists.

Romanticism in architecture: the Gothic revival. Until about 1830, architecture in Europe and America was based largely on classical models (see p. 411). But after 1830 occurred the great period of the Gothic revival,

Constable: "The Cornfield"

in which towers and pointed arches became the chief characteristics of architectural design. The revival was stimulated in England by the romances of Sir Walter Scott, whose own residence at Abbotsford was designed along Scottish baronial lines; while in France the movement gained impetus from the publication of Victor Hugo's melodramatic novel of fifteenth-century life, *Notre Dame de Paris* (1831).

Romanticism in music. The nineteenth century brought radical changes in music: the regularity of the minuet, the precision of the sonata, and the limitations of the small chamber orchestra were not adequate to express the powerful forces of romanticism.

The genius who broke the classical mold and revitalized music was the German composer Ludwig van Beethoven (1770-1827), a titan who acted as a bridge between classicism and romanticism. A lover of nature and a passionate champion of freedom and the rights of man, Beethoven unleashed emotional forces never before heard in music. While retaining the classicist's sense of proportion in the structure of his works, he

Built between 1840 and 1860, the Houses of Parliament in London represent the nineteenth-century Gothic revival in architecture.

added flexibility to music forms by developing new harmonies and enlarged the scope of the orchestra to handle them. In short, Beethoven succeeded in freeing music from arid formalism.

The momentum of the forces which Beethoven set in motion carried through the entire century. Johannes Brahms (1833-1897) is generally regarded as the greatest symphonic composer of the second half of the century, but the age is studded with names of great composers—Chopin, Schubert, Liszt, Franck, and Tschaikovsky, to name only a few. This was an age marked by an outpouring of romantic symphonies, symphonic overtures, and concertos, all of which

exploited the new and varied effects made possible by an orchestra which had been greatly expanded. Compositions made use of romantic subject matter infused with sentiment—and, not infrequently, sentimentalism. In addition, many composers turned for inspiration to their native folk music and dances.

Developments in opera were markedly influenced by nationalism and romanticism. In the fervid Germanic works of Richard Wagner (1813-1883), old Teutonic myths and German folklore were infused with typically romantic characteristics such as emphasis on the supernatural and the mystic. The romantic tragedy *Aïda* (1872) capped the career of Giuseppe Verdi (1813-1901), considered the greatest Italian composer of the nineteenth century.

As a consequence of significant changes in political and economic conditions, music was now supported chiefly by the middle classes and maintained by their thriving commercial prosperity. Public concerts, symphony orchestras, quartet societies, piano and song recitals, music festivals, public opera houses—all were attainments of the nineteenth century which had had only faint beginnings up to 1800.

ROMANTIC NATIONALISM

Nationalism, ally of romanticism. In glorifying the uniqueness of the individual and his rights, romanticism exhibited a close affinity with another powerful emotional force of this period—nationalism. With its emphasis upon the uniqueness of particular groups, nationalism was a potent historical catalyst among the peoples of nineteenth-century Europe. During this period, feelings of nationalism came more and more to imply the willingness of an individual to live and die for his country. His loyalty to the state transcended all other loyalties. Unhappily, too, extreme nationalism implied that a state could do no wrong and that self-interest was the only test for its behavior. Here again we see the close affinity between romanticism and nationalism—the former advocating unrestricted self-expression for an individual, and the latter demanding unrestricted self-determination for a group.

Romantic nationalism in literature. This strongly felt emotion is well exemplified in a sonnet Wordsworth composed upon his return in 1802 from the Continent to England:

. . . Oft have I looked round
With joy in Kent's green vales; but never found
Myself so satisfied in heart before.
Europe is yet in bonds; but let that pass
Thought for another moment. Thou art free,
My Country! and 'tis joy enough and pride
For one hour's perfect bliss, to tread the grass
Of England once again. . . .[8]

The excesses of the French Revolution and Napoleon's perversion of its principles alienated many of the romanticists. But the pendulum swung back again as a result of the system of political reaction set up in 1815 by the Congress of Vienna (see Chapter 21). Some of the notable romanticists again became the champions of nationalism and revolution. In France, the leading figure was Victor Hugo, who expressed hostility toward tyranny at home and abroad, espoused the aspirations of the common man, and was a staunch supporter of the struggle for Greek independence. In Russia, where nationalism had been greatly stimulated by the people's heroic resistance to the Napoleonic invasion in 1812, still other romantic rebels were attracting the sympathetic response of the reading public (and also the hostile attention of the tsar's secret police). The greatest of the Russian romanticist poets was Alexander Pushkin, whose unrestrained personal life and literary lyricism justify his being called the "Byron of Russia." His subject matter was largely derived from Russian tales and folklore, and his dramas and his verse-novel *Eugene Onegin* (1831) had a strong nationalistic appeal. Like Byron, Pushkin denounced tyranny and the reactionary movement which had set in after the Napoleonic Wars.

Romantic nationalism in philosophy and history. The glorification of the state became characteristic of various German thinkers, especially Georg Wilhelm Friedrich Hegel (1770-1831), perhaps the most influential philosopher of the time. To Hegel, history was a process of evolution in which the supremacy of primitive instincts gave way to the reign of clear reason and freedom —the "World Spirit"—as manifested in the state. Hegel believed that the Prussia of his day offered the best example of the state as a spiritual organism, because in Prussia the individual was given the greatest "freedom"—which to Hegel meant only the right to obey the laws of the governing group.

With their mystical concepts of the state and their belief in the historic role and special virtues of the German people, Hegel and other German thinkers did much to lay the metaphysical foundations for that irrational ideology of our own century, Nazism. Hegel's teachings contributed to the growth of ideas which are at the core of virulent nationalism: the exaltation of the state at the expense of individual interests and morality, the praise of war and the superman, and the concept of a nation endowed with a divine mission.

The nineteenth century produced a number of outstanding national historians. In France, Jules Michelet wrote a nineteen-volume *History of France* that was marked by liberalism and romantic nationalism and stressed the role of the common people. Across the Atlantic, George Bancroft produced a United States history described as "explaining the wonder-working providence of God in the United States."[9] In England, too, it was a splendid era for historians, of whom the most brilliant was Thomas Babington Macaulay. His famous *History of England*, a notable example of literary as well as historical craftsmanship which is still widely read, reflected the author's conviction that his age represented the best of all possible worlds.

THE MIDDLE CLASS

TRIUMPHANT

Liberalism: its meaning and impact. To this point, we have been dealing with two major trends in the intellectual history of the nineteenth century—romanticism and nationalism. We now come to a third major ideational concept—liberalism—which came to the forefront in the 1830's. Unlike romanticism and nationalism, nineteenth-century liberalism was associated almost exclusively with the middle class. Let us see why.

Like romanticism, liberalism vigorously affirmed the dignity of man and the "pursuit of happiness" as his inherent right. Like the philosophy behind the American and French revolutions, the liberal philosophy was an outgrowth of the philosophy of the Enlightenment. But where romanticism accepted revolution as a justifiable means to give ex-

pression to the "rights of man," liberalism stood for gradual reform through parliamentary institutions. And where both the rationalists and the romanticists tended to speak of man in the abstract—that is, "Man"—and to conceive of him as a philosophical ideal in opposition to, say, the "state" or the "king," nineteenth-century liberals thought in terms of individual men who shared certain basic rights in common, who worked together to obtain parliamentary majorities and political power, and who made use of that power to ensure that each of them would be given a maximum of freedom from state or external authority.

In the economic sphere, liberalism was expressed in the doctrine of laissez faire—competition among individuals with a minimum of governmental interference or regulation. The textbook of this school of thought, Adam Smith's *Wealth of Nations*, postulated that society benefited most from competition, which brought the more intelligent and more efficient individuals the greater rewards. Although governments were responsible for the protection of life and property, the hands of government should be kept off business; the best interests of society would be served by permitting the natural "laws" of supply and demand to operate unimpeded.

In the new industrial societies, the bourgeois entrepreneurs had everything to lose from revolution and everything to gain from governmental protection of property rights. To win such protection, however, they had to obtain a dominant voice in government. As government immediately after the Napoleonic Wars was largely controlled by the nobility and landed classes, this meant in turn that the middle class had to secure a limited extension of the suffrage—an extension that would give them the vote without granting voting privileges to the working classes. Thus the members of the middle class demanded political power commensurate with their steadily increasing economic strength. In England this goal was attained in 1832 with the passage of the Reform Bill (see p. 511).

We might pause here to note the change that has taken place regarding the meaning of "liberalism." The term still stands for reform, in contrast to conservatism with its defense of the status quo or to radicalism with its demands for immediate, drastic change. But in the economic sphere especially, liberalism has undergone a profound modification. Unlike his nineteenth-century predecessor, the twentieth-century liberal believes that the state should take an active role in minimizing the extremes of wealth, in balancing the great power enjoyed by big business and big organized labor, in conserving natural resources, in providing social security, and in actively opposing racial discrimination.

The triumph of laissez faire. The bourgeoisie achieved their success in the era of industrial capitalism, which superseded the predominantly commercial, or trading, phase of business (see Chapter 16). In industrial capitalism, profits were made primarily from investment in machinery and raw materials and from utilization of other people's labor. Controlled and administered by factory owners, the new industrial capitalism soon resulted in important changes in business organization. The corporation, which could raise and utilize large sums of capital, became the characteristic form of business organization, largely replacing individual proprietorship and partnership, both of which proved inadequate to meet the needs of the factory system.

With the triumph of the middle class in the nineteenth century, we find also the triumph of their economic philosophy—laissez faire. This theory, known as "economic liberalism," held that it was impossible to correct the social evils of industrialism. Each man, enjoying free choice, could only improve his own circumstances by hard work, economy, and limiting the size of his family. Economists offered so little hope for improvement of the economic status of the common people that economics came to be known as the "dismal science."

Malthus' theory of population. Among the gloomier prophets was Thomas Robert Malthus (1766-1834), an English clergyman whose fame rests on his *Essay on Population* (1798). This study asserts that:

. . . the power of population is indefinitely greater than the power in the earth to produce subsistence for man.[10]

In his own day Malthus could accurately point to a comparatively limited food supply and a population that was increasing by leaps and bounds. From this evidence, he deduced that the inevitable lot of the mass of mankind was misery, as the birth rate would always outrun the food supply. Malthus' only solution to what he believed to be a permanent problem was the practice of self-restraint in reproduction.

Ricardo's theory of wages. Using Malthus' line of reasoning in developing his own thesis, the English economist David Ricardo (1772-1823) advanced his subsistence theory of wages. Ricardo maintained that labor has a natural price and also a market price. The natural price is that:

. . . which is necessary to enable the laborers . . . to subsist and to perpetuate their race without either increase or diminution.[11]

The market price depends on the law of supply and demand. When labor is scarce and in demand, it is well paid; when it is plentiful, it is poorly paid. In the first instance, the market price of labor exceeds the natural price; the result is prosperity for the laborer. In the second instance, the reverse is true.

Unfortunately, said Ricardo, labor tends to increase faster than available capital, so that wages fall to the natural price. Although varying circumstances might qualify the situation, Ricardo felt that he had stated an ironclad law which nothing could or should change.

Like all other contracts, wages should be left to the fair and free competition of the market, and should never be controlled by the interference of the legislature.[12]

Laissez-faire theory popularized and modified. Jeremy Bentham (1748-1832), a wealthy

Shown above are four men whose writings greatly influenced the economic philosophy of the nineteenth century. David Ricardo (far left) and Thomas Malthus (center left) believed that economics operated according to natural laws and that the industrial class as a whole was doomed to misery. Jeremy Bentham (far right) felt that the main function of government should be the creation of individual freedom, for freedom led to happiness. John Stuart Mill (center right), on the other hand, thought that the state should impose some controls on businessmen for the sake of the workers; individual freedom, he felt, should be considered secondary to the interests of the people as a whole.

British jurist, devised the doctrine of utilitarianism, or philosophical radicalism, based on the two concepts of utility and happiness. He correlated these two terms by saying that each individual knows what is best for himself and that all human institutions should be measured according to the amount of happiness they give—Bentham's celebrated "pain and pleasure" principle.

Bentham believed strongly that the function of government should be the securing of as great a degree of individual freedom as possible, for freedom made for happiness. Utilitarianism has been defined as "the greatest happiness for the greatest number."

John Stuart Mill (1806-1873) did not believe that the interests of the manufacturers would necessarily coincide with the interests of the workers; he advanced the theory that government should, if necessary, pass legislation to remedy injustices. Mill felt that when the actions of businessmen harmed people, the state should intervene for their protection. While admitting that the maximum freedom should be permitted in the processes of production according to natural law, he insisted that the distribution of wealth depends on the laws and customs of society, and these can be changed by the will of men. He upheld the rights of property

and of free competition but only within reasonable limits. The liberty of the individual should be subordinated to the wider interest of the group. In this thought there are the germs of what came later to be known as the welfare state. John Stuart Mill's ideas gained influence slowly; and, until well past the middle of the nineteenth century, laissez-faire liberalism held its ground with little change.

In England "the Manchester School" was the name given to a group of politicans who strove in Parliament to defend and spread the tenets of economic liberalism. They advocated the repeal of various import duties on grain known as the Corn Laws, the adoption of free trade, and a foreign policy based on economic cooperation rather than international rivalry. During the middle years of the nineteenth century, the policies of these men won wide acceptance and made supreme the economic and political prestige of a middle class devoted to laissez faire. Technologically more advanced than other countries, England adopted free trade for a time, thus indicating that it did not fear the competition of foreign products in its home market. In other countries, however, the middle class wanted business freedom at home but government protection against foreign imports which might undersell the local goods.

Theory and practice diverge. The philosophy of laissez faire seemed logical and was, in fact, a positive aid to social and economic progress. However, a wide gulf soon appeared between theory and practice. Because of monopolistic practices and secret collusion between competitors, the operation of competition did not always ensure fair prices. Nor did competition ensure the survival of honest and efficient businesses. Underhanded and unfair competition often wrecked the more ethical and scrupulous firms.

It also became increasingly difficult to reconcile the great wealth enjoyed by a few with the poverty borne by the many. In our discussion of the factory system, we saw the terrible living and working conditions of most of the people. Furthermore, legislation prevented them from achieving anything like an equal bargaining position with their economic masters. Drastic laws, such as the Combination Acts of 1799-1800 in England, forbade unions on the grounds that they would restrain trade. Strikes were classed as conspiracies, and strikers were harshly punished. While emphasizing the necessity for "freedom," the proponents of laissez faire completely disregarded the individual worker's lack of bargaining power. In time it became obvious even to the middle class that poverty was not necessarily a result of personal improvidence.

Middle-class attitudes in Victorian England. By the 1840's, England had entered a new era which coincided with the long reign (1837-1901) of the stanchly respectable Queen Victoria. This age was best symbolized by the opening of the Great Exhibition in London in 1851—a monument to the cult of material progress where one might see the latest wonders of an ever accelerating industrialism. "Material progress seemed, as by some new law of nature, to have been showered without stint on a people who rated industriousness, business efficiency, and private enterprise among the major virtues. This situation induced in large sections of the upper and middle classes a mood of comfortable

complacency which later generations have found the most unattractive of Victorian characteristics. . . . Samuel Smiles's *Self-Help* (which appeared in 1859, sold 20,000 copies that year and another 130,000 during the next thirty years) was rapidly succeeded by works with similar pious titles—*Thrift, Character, Duty*—which form a veritable catalogue of the Victorian 'virtues.' This long series of smug lay sermons on the virtues of industry and honesty, connecting always the practice of such virtue with the reward of material prosperity . . . was the instinctive creed of the prosperous industrialists and business men whose ethics now dominated English manners as they dominated English economic life."[13]

For its part, the fair sex had acquired a somewhat improved status. Women's colleges began to appear, and nursing by women was raised to professional status as a result of the initiative displayed by Florence Nightingale during the Crimean War. Sent to the military hospitals in the Crimea, the "Lady with the Lamp" brought about a complete change in the treatment of the wounded. Under her efficient charge, medical facilities were improved so that the terrible mortality due to cholera, dysentery, and gangrene was materially reduced.

Victorian poetry: Tennyson and Browning. The spokesman of Victorian England, Alfred, Lord Tennyson (1809-1892), was poet laureate from 1850 to the year of his death. His popularity derived from his sympathetic understanding of the ideas and ideals of his countrymen; he had their "high seriousness" and self-consciousness along with their sentimentality and their admiration for the ornate. Yet the very qualities in his poetry that won him great acclaim in his own day have since worked against his reputation. Today, the beauty of much of his verse seems somewhat artificial, his thought, shallow and conformist.

The other major English poet of the period was Robert Browning (1812-1889), whose sturdy optimism and faith in humanity won him many followers. Unlike Tennyson, however, Browning was not primarily a melo-

One of the social evils attacked by Dickens in his novels was the wretched condition of many English schools. Above is an illustration from *Nicholas Nickleby*, showing the unhappy children of Dotheboys Hall.

dist; his talent lay in the skillful delineation of character. He created a new poetic form —the dramatic monologue—in which the thoughts and feelings of a character were depicted with a psychological insight which appealed to his readers, even though they could not always understand the poet's erudite allusions or his often cryptic mode of expression.

Victorian poets suffered from the tendency to express the moralistic and strongly conventional ideas of the members of the middle class for whom they wrote. Whereas the romanticists, as rebels, adopted an uncompromising attitude toward the world, the Victorians preferred to come to terms with it. Theirs was a more sober, perhaps a more responsible attitude, but it was not the exalted approach that makes for soaring flights of poetry. All too often, such compromise was indistinguishable from a deep-rooted middle-class complacency.

Victorian novelists: Thackeray and Dickens. The snobbery and social climbing that went on in a society made highly fluid by the rise of the newly rich middle class provided ideal subjects for the genial satirist and moralist

William Makepeace Thackeray (1811-1863). He is probably best known for his unscrupulous but engaging character Becky Sharp, the heroine of *Vanity Fair* (1848).

A note of social protest appears in the works of Charles Dickens (1812-1870). He painted in vivid colors the everyday life of the middle classes and the poor—and especially the struggle of the individual against the worst excesses of industrial expansion and social injustice. In *The Pickwick Papers, Oliver Twist, Dombey and Son, Bleak House,* and *David Copperfield,* to name but a few of his major works, Dickens blended romantic and realistic elements by combining a fundamental optimism and belief in progress with trenchant attacks upon existing slum conditions, the miseries of the poor, and the inhuman debtors' prisons. This note of reaction against mid-Victorian self-satisfaction was soon to swell into a chorus of attacks, both moderate and radical, upon the existing social order.

CHALLENGES TO THE

EXISTING ORDER

Social criticism: Arnold, Carlyle, and Ruskin. The state of culture in his day profoundly disturbed the English poet and essayist Matthew Arnold (1822-1888). Arnold believed that the materialistic standards of an industrialized society were completely incompatible with the great humanistic values inherited from Greece and the Renaissance. In his view, mid-Victorian culture was beset by personal self-seeking and lack of social purpose and moral strength. At one end of the social structure were the aristocrats, whom Arnold dubbed "Barbarians" because they were ignorant of the great western cultural inheritance and spent their lives in idleness and worldly pleasures. At the other end was the "Populace," the working class, which was now emerging from its traditional state of poverty and ignorance but which could, unless properly educated and directed, smash much that was irreplaceable in our civilization.

Then there was the middle class, about which Arnold was perhaps most concerned, since its members were now dominant in society. Arnold called them "Philistines" because they neither understood nor cared about culture in its humanistic terms. This new industrial bourgeoisie, he argued, thought only of power and riches and saw in the external signs of change proof of spiritual advancement. Philistine values led a man "to value himself not on what he is . . . but on the number of the railroads he has constructed."[14] In Arnold's judgment, state education was necessary in order to restore humanistic values and to make available to all classes in society the best of man's cultural heritage.

Another prominent figure, outspoken in his criticism of the shortcomings of a society dominated by the middle class, was the Scottish essayist and historian Thomas Carlyle (1795-1881). He stormed against the worship of Mammon by the industrial capitalists, dubbing them the "Working Aristocracy." Railing against contemporary industrialism and the mass vulgarity which it produced, Carlyle argued that democracy's problems could not be settled by merely extending the ballot. Indeed, the grim-humored Scot feared what would happen when political power was placed in the hands of the multitude through the extension of the suffrage. Because Carlyle believed that "one wise man is stronger than all men unwise," he declared that "the few Wise will have, by one method or another, to take command of the innumerable Foolish."[15] This rejection of the democratic philosophy brings us to a central thesis of Carlyle—namely, that salvation could only be attained by the heroic deeds and leadership of history's "Great Men." His advocacy of strong and even authoritarian leadership was to find acceptance in latter-day totalitarian ideologies.

Another influential critic—but one whose formula for curing society's ills differed radically from Carlyle's—was John Ruskin (1819-1900). A leader of the protest movement often called the Esthetic Revolt, Ruskin believed whole-heartedly in the basic integrity and common sense of the people, for whom he advocated socialistic reforms and widespread education. Ruskin wrote eloquently to free his age from the ugly consequences of a soulless industrialism and to reform the arts and handicrafts, many of which were being destroyed by cheap mass production. Although Ruskin and his associates were not able to stem the tide of tasteless goods pouring from the machines, they helped stimulate a new appreciation of craftsmanship and simple design.

Stirrings of reform: Factory Acts. As critics of the existing order continued their protests, a movement to reform the worst evils of the Industrial Revolution gathered momentum. In England the landowning aristocracy constituted a powerful force in this camp. Resenting the rise of the *nouveau riche* mill owners in the cities, the nobles were willing to curb middle-class power by passing Factory Acts setting various restrictions on woman and child labor and excessively long working hours. Although the Tory squires had little use for democracy, they possessed a humanitarian spirit and resented the callous indifference of the urban bourgeoisie toward human rights. Even among the factory owners themselves, a few men such as Robert Owen (see p. 493) realized that altruism and profits made a good team. If the conditions of the workers were improved, their efficiency and productivity would likewise rise.

The first effective Factory Act in Great Britain was passed in the year 1833. This law forbade the employment in textile factories of children under nine, restricted the hours of labor for children between nine and thirteen to forty-eight a week and the hours of children between thirteen and eighteen to sixty-eight, and made it illegal for anyone under eighteen to work at night. Government inspectors were to help administer the act. This piece of legislation, which strikes us today as laughably inadequate, prompted such manufacturers as John Bright to exclaim that it was "most injurious and destructive to the best interests of the country" and violated "the liberty of the subject" and "freedom of contract"—as though children of nine had freedom of contract in bargaining with mill owners.

Other reforms in England gradually whittled away at the old doctrine of laissez faire by broadening state regulation of economic enterprise. While conditions in the textile factories were improved by the 1833 Factory Act, those in the mines remained ghastly. Children of six and seven were employed underground twelve hours a day to open and shut ventilation doors and to be harnessed "like dogs to a go-cart" to haul coal wagons. In 1842 a law was passed forbidding the employment in the mines of women and of girls and boys under ten. In 1846 a law was enacted to limit the work of women and children in textile factories to ten hours a day, and in succeeding years other improvements were made in factory conditions. Inspection and enforcement of health and safety in factories and railways were required by law. As industrialization spread, other countries tended to pass regulatory legislation similar to that in England. In 1836 Massachusetts passed the first act regulating child labor in the United States.

Labor unions legalized. In the field of labor relations, measures were enacted giving workers freedom to organize trade unions. In 1824 the harsh Combination Acts were repealed in Britain, and from this time on workingmen had the legal right to organize and to bargain peacefully with employers, though legal restrictions continued to limit trade union activity. For a long time the authorities vigorously opposed strikes, thereby restricting the strength and effectiveness of the unions.

In the meantime, the workers on the Continent turned more and more to unions as a means of obtaining their demands for higher wages, shorter hours, and more healthful working conditions. In France in 1864, workers were allowed by law to combine for strikes. During the 1860's, trade unionism made progress in Germany, as it did in the United States, where the number of local unions multiplied almost fourfold between 1861 and 1865. In 1869 a powerful industrial union made its debut in America under the florid name "The Noble Order of the Knights of Labor."

Philanthropic movements. In the efforts to improve social and economic conditions, a significant role was played by private individuals with large fortunes—and with equally large hearts. Hospitals, orphan homes, schools, and other charitable agencies were established. In the United States, for example, mechanics' and apprentices' institutes, such as the Cooper Union in New York, sponsored free educational courses for workers and provided free access to books. Apprentices' and mercantile libraries in the United States laid the basis for the free public library movement, which began around 1850. Thus middle-class humanitarian sympathies and the emphasis upon the rights and dignity of individual men (both stimulated by the romantic movement) combined with the persistent influence of Christian doctrine to favor a humanistic rather than a mechanistic solution to social problems.

By the 1840's there had been substantial modification of the middle-class theory of laissez faire. The state was increasingly expanding its jurisdiction over industry, protecting workers in mines, factories, and on the railways. In addition, philanthropy by private individuals was doing much to make life easier and fuller for the masses. Yet despite these reformist efforts, there was evidence of a growing rift between the bourgeoisie and the workers. In Disraeli's novel *Sybil* (1845), the author points out that Queen Victoria really rules over two nations:

. . . between whom there is no intercourse and no sympathy; who are as ignorant of each other's habits, thoughts, and feelings, as if they were dwellers in different zones, or inhabitants of different planets; who are formed by a different breeding, are fed by a different food, are ordered by different manners, and are not governed by the same laws . . . THE RICH AND THE POOR.[16]

This rift intensified the rising class consciousness among the mass of the working people and contributed to the emergence of socialism, proposing complete social reconstruction.

The emergence of socialism. Attacking the nineteenth-century capitalistic system with its laissez-faire philosophy as both unplanned and unjust, socialists or communists (the two terms were once used synonymously) condemned the concentration of wealth and called for public or worker ownership of business. Above all, they insisted that harmony and cooperation—not ruthless competition—should control economic affairs. Generally convinced of the goodness of human nature, they dreamed of a happy future when:

... there will be no war, no crimes, no administration of justice, as it is called, no government. Besides there will be neither disease, anguish, melancholy, nor resentment. Every man will seek, with ineffable ardor, the good of all.[17]

This humanitarian idealism, a legacy of the Enlightenment, was typical of the theorists who created the early socialist movement.

Utopian socialism: Saint-Simon, Fourier, Owen. The early socialists of the nineteenth century are known as the Utopians. (They were so called by Karl Marx later in the century, and the name has persisted.)

The first prominent Utopian was a French nobleman, Claude Henri de Rouvroy, Count de Saint-Simon (1760-1825). Defining a nation as "nothing but a great industrial society" and politics as "the science of production," he argued that men should voluntarily accept the rule of a paternalistic despotism of scientists, technicians, and captains of industry who would "undertake the most rapid amelioration possible of the lot of the poorest and most numerous class."[18]

François Fourier (1772-1837), another French reformer, also believed that future society must be cooperative. He spent much time in working out an ideal plan for a communal living unit, which he termed the "phalanstery." While the plan was endorsed by many prominent men of the day, attempts to found cooperative Fourierist communities were unsuccessful. The famous Brook Farm colony in Massachusetts was one such short-lived experiment.

A more practical reformer and Utopian socialist was Robert Owen (1771-1858), a successful mill owner in Scotland, who made New Lanark, the site of his textile mills, into a model community. Here, between 1815 and 1825, thousands of visitors saw neat rows of workers' homes, a garbage collection system, schools for workers' children, and clean factories where the laborers were treated kindly and where no children under eleven were employed. After having brought about factory reforms in Parliament, Owen migrated to the vicinity of Evansville, Indiana, where, in 1825, he founded a Utopian colony called New Harmony. This, however, lasted only a short time as a socialist community.

Partly because of the impracticality of such colonies as New Harmony, which were usually based upon the somewhat naïve notion that men naturally loved one another (or could be educated to love one another) and that men could live happily together in a communal society were it not that capitalist competition set man against man; partly because the Utopians made no practical, large-scale attempts to meet the problems of the depressed nineteenth-century industrial classes as a whole; and partly because ultimately Marxist socialism supplanted it—Utopian socialism failed.

Christian socialism. In addition to the Utopians, another nineteenth-century school of socialism arose that drew its inspiration directly from the teachings of Christianity. This group, the Christian socialists, aimed at showing that the doctrines of the Sermon on the Mount were socialistic in character. In England, the Christian socialist leaders were drawn largely from the Methodists, the Unitarians, the Quakers, and the Broad Church party of the Church of England.

Abhorring violence and drawing upon traditional ideas of a universal Christian community, the Christian socialists preached good will between all classes and favored experiments with socialist colonies. They stimulated interest in working-class reforms and attempted to instill into organized Christianity a realization of the social aspects of the teachings of Christ.

Anarchism. Another socialist school of thought that became known as anarchism was founded by the French theorist Pierre Proudhon (1809-1865), who wrote pamphlets urging the organization of society on a purely voluntary basis. The anarchists insisted that human nature is inherently good but is warped and depraved by authority. They repudiated all governmental compulsion, proposing instead free cooperation among the members of society. Proudhon's dictum, "Property is theft," was widely repeated by radicals everywhere.

In discussions on how to achieve their ends, the anarchists heard advocates of divergent tendencies—on the one hand, pacifists and humanitarian philosophers who were content to dream about a perfect society; on the other, devotees of violence. A member of the latter group was Michael Bakunin, an expatriate Russian revolutionary who insisted that God, the family, and the state must all be repudiated and that only when the world was without law would it be free.

Karl Marx and scientific socialism. Up to the middle of the century, socialism remained a minor factor in European thinking, as the principal goal of groups of ordinary people was the winning of political equality and universal suffrage. Economic questions remained secondary. Furthermore, the theoretical tendencies of early socialism were not very alarming to the wealthy and aristocratic classes.

This calm was shattered in 1848 when workers on the Continent began demanding the "right to work" during the revolutions of that year. Simultaneously, and almost unnoticed, there appeared early in 1848 a new form of socialism that advocated violence, preached warfare between the classes, and repudiated traditional religion and morality. The instigator of this rabid form of socialism was Karl Marx.

Born in the Rhineland, at Trier (Treves), of German-Jewish parents who had been converted to Christianity, Karl Marx (1818-1883) obtained his doctor's degree after studying the philosophical ideas of Hegel. Failing to find a career in university teaching, he was forced to make a precarious living as a journalist. He went to Paris, where he became interested in socialistic ideas and, while there, he began his life-long friendship with Friedrich Engels (1820-1895), the son of a wealthy German factory owner. In 1845 Marx was expelled from France by the authorities, and with Engels he went to live in Brussels.

In January 1848, Marx and Engels published the famous *Communist Manifesto*. This stirring document contained practically all the elements of what came to be known as scientific socialism. It opened with an ominous declaration: "A spectre is haunting Europe—the spectre of Communism." The *Manifesto* called for an implacable struggle against the bourgeoisie, proclaimed the inevitable revolution and the triumph of the masses, and closed with a stern warning:

The Communists disdain to conceal their views and aims. They openly declare that their ends can be attained only by the forcible overthrow of all existing social conditions. Let the ruling classes tremble at a Communistic revolution. The proletarians have nothing to lose but their chains. They have a world to win. Working men of all countries, unite![19]

The revolutions of 1848 (not in the least influenced by Marx, an obscure figure at the time) were welcomed by Marx as the dawn of a new era, the birth of a new society. Going to Germany to assist in its arrival, he was forced to flee when the revolutionary movement collapsed. From that time until his death in 1883, he lived a life of penury in London, supported largely by contributions from friends, especially Engels. Nearly every day Marx would make his way to the British Museum, where he collected material for his various books, especially *Das Kapital (Capital)*.

Basic theories of Marx. No matter what one may think of Marxian socialism, no one can doubt that *Das Kapital* (1867-1894) constitutes one of the most influential books of modern times. In the mid-twentieth century, nearly half of the world has been organized on the basis of its teachings.

The following are the basic theories of Marx's socialist system:

(1) The materialistic conception of history: "economic determinism." Marx believed that economic forces basically determine the course of history; all other supposed factors—patriotism, religion, art—are only "ideological veils." For Marx, all history could be explained in terms primarily of the social organization best adapted to the current means of economic production. When the economic organization of any era changed, it took the whole social and ideological structure with it to a new phase of history.

(2) "Dialectical materialism." Hegel, whose philosophy Marx had studied, felt that history is not just a matter of chance. It is dynamic and unfolds as the result of a definite plan or process of change. History is made up of a number of culture periods, each the expression of a dominant spirit or idea. After fulfilling its purpose, the period is confronted by another contradictory idea or set of values. In Hegelian phraseology, the traditional "thesis" is challenged by the new "antithesis." Out of this struggle there emerges a "synthesis" of old and new. Then the cycle starts all over again. Thus, to Hegel, history is a process of unfolding, determined by an absolute purpose or idea, which orthodox Hegelians called God; the machinery of change was called "historical dialectic."

Marx adopted this concept of change—the dialectic—but modified Hegel's approach in an important respect. To Marx the combatants were material forces, not ideas. History became a series of clashes between the exploited and the exploiting group: slave against master in ancient Greece, plebeian against patrician in Rome, serf against lord in the Middle Ages. The bourgeoisie, who by means of the organization of trade and the Industrial Revolution had created a new urban and industrial society, were now opposed by the modern industrial proletariat. The bourgeoisie themselves had helped create the factory system of production—and with it their own nemesis, the proletariat. It was inevitable that when the proletariat realized its true power, it would overthrow

While in London, Karl Marx once worked as a feature writer for Horace Greeley's New York *Tribune,* supplying the paper with five hundred articles. Dissatisfied with his payment of five dollars per article, Marx accused Greeley of the "lousiest petty-bourgeois cheating."

its natural enemy, the bourgeoisie. Out of this conflict would appear the new synthesis, the classless society, the ultimate social organization of the modern industrialized era.

(3) The concept of "surplus value." Here Marx borrowed from the laissez-faire economists who held that economic value represented "congealed labor." Only human labor, Marx argued, can create new economic values. But under the capitalist system, the worker is not fully paid for all the values he creates. Suppose, for example, that a worker could produce in six hours the necessary economic values to supply his needs. However, the employer, as employers often did in the nineteenth century, keeps the worker producing goods for, say, twelve hours. The employer is in possession of a "surplus value" of six working hours, which he has "expropriated" from the worker. From this "stolen" surplus value the employer draws profits and capital. The workers are thus robbed of the fruits of their toil and become progressively poorer. Meanwhile, there is a concentration of capital in fewer hands as the

most ruthless of the bourgeoisie destroy more and more of their competitors, forcing them into the ranks of the proletariat.

(4) The inevitability of socialism. Because the masses cannot buy the goods they produce, economic crises, with overproduction and unemployment, will become the rule. Finally comes the day when the proletariat rises up and takes over the means of production. Then, says the *Manifesto:* "The knell of capitalism is sounded. The expropriators are expropriated."[20] In the apocalyptic new society, private property will be abolished, exploitation of one class by another will cease, class warfare will end, and the millennium, a virtual heaven on earth, will arrive.

Devoting most of his ammunition to attacking the obvious injustices of unreformed nineteenth-century industrial society, Marx paid comparatively little attention to the kind of society that would supersede the bourgeois state. He once remarked that he had no interest in "writing the kitchen recipes of the future." The final transition, he enigmatically indicated, would be the "dictatorship of the proletariat" (Lenin would elaborate later on this idea), after which the state would supposedly wither away, leaving a society in which there would be no coercion.

The First International. Marx helped to found an international organization of workers, called the First International. Organized in London in 1864, the First International failed to make much headway. There were savage quarrels between the anarchist group led by Bakunin and the majority commanded by Marx. While Marx and his followers would utilize the state as the agency for initiating their classless society, the anarchists bitterly opposed this extension of state activity. Finally, in 1873, the First International closed up shop.

Weaknesses in Marxist doctrine. Certain weaknesses and inconsistencies in Marx's arguments were soon perceived. In interpreting history, Marx sees at work in all ages his "dialectical materialism," the class struggle. Yet in some miraculous fashion this "dominant" feature of history is to disappear when the communist society is established.

Furthermore, there is something ironic in Marx's term "scientific socialism" (i.e., based upon supposed inevitable laws of social development "scientifically" observed and explained by Marx) "in contrast to the Utopian variety." With his talk of a final social stage in which there would be no coercion and no exploitation and with his vague notions about the organization of his ideal society, he really was akin to utopian dreamers of all ages.

By explaining all social and intellectual phenomena in terms of economics and class struggle, Marx's theory denied the importance of intellectual and idealistic influences. And yet Marxism itself as a body of ideas about history and social change became in time a great intellectual influence and historical force.

Another basic weakness in Marxian socialism was that Marx's materialism and atheism were unacceptable to supporters of all the world's major religions. For the traditional religious belief in a happy afterlife where all earthly injustices and evils would be corrected, Marx substituted the promise of a heaven here on earth, the hope of a worldly utopia. Supporters of Marxist dogmas were assured that it was in the "nature of the historical process"(an ideological substitute for Divine Providence) that this should be so. One had but a single choice: to get into step with the "inevitable" or be destroyed. True believers were convinced that they alone possessed the truth. For this reason Marxism itself has been termed a "surrogate religion"—a materialistic substitute for true religion.

Another difficulty Marxists encountered was the patriotism of most European workers. Faced by a choice between supporting national interests, as in World War I, and supporting Marxist dogmas about the class nature of war under capitalism, most European workers chose to support their nations. Nationalism was a stronger influence than socialism.

Finally, as we shall see in Chapter 24, Marx's prediction that the mass of men under capitalism would become increasingly reduced to economic misery and near starvation did not come about.

At this juncture we must take up a final dominant trend to round off our account of the ideational history of the period. The mood of the Victorian era was both accompanied and affected by the latest discoveries and theories of science.

THE RISING TIDE
OF SCIENCE

The new geology. The nineteenth century was marked by extraordinary progress in science. Sir Charles Lyell's *Principles of Geology* (1830-1833) is the work which is considered the basis of modern geology. In this important study, Lyell showed that the earth had achieved its present formation through such agencies as earthquakes, volcanoes, erosion, and the continuous rising and sinking of land surfaces over a vast period of time.

Meanwhile, a separate branch of geology known as paleontology had been founded by Baron Georges Cuvier (1769-1832). This science, concerned with the study of fossils or extinct forms of life, enabled men to reconstruct gradually the history of geological ages.

Progress in physics. In physics, important work was done in thermodynamics and electrical phenomena. Thermodynamics, that branch of research that deals with the relations between heat and motive power, was of particular importance because of industry's dependence upon the steam engine for furnishing power.

Scientists had believed previously that heat was a mysterious fluid called "calorie," but research showed that friction generated heat in proportion to the amount of work expended. After physicists had found out how much mechanical energy was required to raise the heat of any given body, it became possible, in 1847, to formulate the first law of thermodynamics. This law states that the sum total of energy in the universe is constant and cannot be either created or de-

stroyed—it can only be transformed from one form into another. Meanwhile, scientists engaging in the converse problem of transforming heat into energy found that heat can in fact never be completely converted into energy. From their experiments was formulated the second law of thermodynamics: although the total amount of energy in the universe remains constant, the amount actually available is always diminishing through its transformation into nonavailable, or dissipated, heat.

Nineteenth-century scientists prepared the way for the use of electricity as a source of power. The most prominent figure in the field of electrodynamics during the earlier part of the century was Michael Faraday (1791-1867). In 1831 Faraday was able to create an electric current by rotating a copper disk between the two poles of a horseshoe magnet, thereby inventing the first electric dynamo. This simple dynamo made possible the development of the electric motor, the transmission of large currents over long distances, and (later in the century) the invention of the electric telegraph, the telephone, and electric lights.

Developments in chemistry: Dalton and Mendelyeev. Chemistry was put on a new footing with the formulation of the atomic theory by an English Quaker schoolmaster, John Dalton (1766-1844). This pioneer believed that all matter is made up of invisible particles, or atoms, which remain unchanged upon entering or leaving any state of chemical combination. Moreover, different kinds of atoms, depending upon their relative weight, make up the basic substances or elements which are to be found in the world of matter.

It now became possible to arrange chemical elements in order according to their atomic weights, beginning with the lightest, hydrogen. It was seen that the elements fell into groups of eight which possess similar properties. In 1869 the Russian chemist Dmitri Mendelyeev (1834-1907) drew up his periodic table, in which all the known elements were classified according to their weights and properties. From gaps in this

This engraving of Charles Darwin was taken from a portrait painted around 1850.

table, chemists were able to deduce the existence of still other undiscovered elements.

Advances in medical science: Lister and Pasteur. In the 1840's the value of ether and chloroform in alleviating pain during operations had been discovered. Another step of the greatest value was the introduction into surgery of asepsis—that is, methods for preventing the entry of bacteria into a wound. In the 1860's a Quaker surgeon at the University of Edinburgh, Joseph Lister, made use of techniques so revolutionary at the time that he was long a prophet without honor in Britain, though his methods were followed in Germany with great success.

Lister had made use of both asepsis and antisepsis, the latter being the method of disinfecting wounds so as to destroy dangerous bacteria. Both techniques sprang from a knowledge of the germ theory of putrefaction, developed from a study of the processes of fermentation and putrefaction by Lister's brilliant friend, the French scientist Louis Pasteur (1822-1895). By 1870 Pasteur had laid the groundwork for the prevention of hydrophobia, the pasteurization of milk—a process which fittingly derives its name from his own—and the further advancement of the science of bacteriology.

The theory of evolution. The nineteenth century witnessed the spread of a doctrine which was to have powerful repercussions on science, philosophy, and religion. This was the theory of evolution—namely, that all living organisms have developed through the operation of natural causes from simple to more complex forms and that no species is fixed and changeless. In the nineteenth century, evidence kept accumulating to indicate that organic and inorganic matter alike had evolved according to natural causes. For example, Lyell's *Principles of Geology* showed that the earth was formed and modified by natural phenomena.

In the first decade of the century, a French nobleman, Jean Baptiste Lamarck (1744-1829), argued that every organism tends to develop new organs in order to adapt itself to the changing conditions of its environment. The changes which take place in an organism are transmitted by heredity to the descendants, which are thereby changed in structural form. In supporting his doctrine of the inheritance of acquired characteristics, Lamarck claimed that the giraffe had to develop a long neck to reach the high leaves and branches on the trees on which it fed. The slight gain in length of the neck made by each generation was handed on to the next.

Darwin and *The Origin of Species*. The scientist chiefly responsible for furthering the evolutionary hypothesis was Charles Darwin (1809-1882). After studying medicine and preparing at Cambridge University for the ministry, Darwin became a naturalist. From 1831 to 1836 he studied the specimens he had collected while on a surveying expedition by the ship *Beagle,* which had sailed along the coast of South America and among the South Sea Islands.

Two works which had a marked influence upon the development of Darwin's theories were Lyell's *Principles of Geology* and Malthus' *Essay on Population*. The latter suggested to Darwin that the struggle of men for existence in a world in which the population increases faster than the food supply was a problem that could be extended to all nature. In 1859 Darwin's views appeared under the title *On the Origin of Species by Means of Natural Selection, or the Preservation of Favored Races in the Struggle for Life*. In this work he contended:

. . . that species have been modified, during a long course of descent . . . chiefly through the natural selection of numerous successive, slight, favourable variations; aided in an important manner . . . by the direct action of external conditions, and by variations which seem to us in our ignorance to arise spontaneously.[21]

The Origin of Species was to prove one of the most significant books in scientific literature, revolutionizing concepts about the origin and evolution of life on the planet. Furthermore, this pioneer work brought into the open the mounting differences between science and theology over the Biblical account of creation—differences to which Lyell's *Principles of Geology* had already markedly contributed. The mid-Victorians might employ the Darwinian theory to bolster their belief in the inevitable improvement of mankind, but while they shared this conviction with the earlier romanticists, they had lost much of the latter's idealism and optimism. There were too many new tensions to contend with, thanks alike to science and to a highly industrialized society. Romanticism was giving way to realism.

SUMMARY

Inventions, new industrial processes, the growth of populations, the spread of industrialism, the rise to dominance of the middle class, and the genesis of the class war in Marxian socialism—all the changes brought about during the First Industrial Revolution (1815-1870) added up to a radical transformation in the lives of men in the western world. Previously untapped sources of power were harnessed to operate railways and steamships. Efficient new machines gradually replaced hand methods of production, and factories replaced the domestic system of manufacturing.

Nineteenth-century liberalism, with its emphasis upon basic rights for the individual in both the political and economic spheres, became the social philosophy of the triumphant middle class. In effect, political liberalism stood for the rule of law, and evolutionary change rather than revolutionary change, while laissez faire, its counterpart in the economic world, called for competition among individuals with the government maintaining a hands-off attitude.

Voices were soon raised against uncurbed competition, the exploitation of the many by the few, and the evils of rapid industrialization such as the employment of young children and the burgeoning of hideous slums. Some of the worst abuses were corrected by reform legislation, while, in another vein, Utopian and Christian socialists proposed the complete reconstruction of society. In the *Communist Manifesto* (1848), Karl Marx thundered forth a hard and ruthless dogma. He felt that an unbridgable chasm divided two warring classes—the bourgeoisie and the proletariat. The danger of a class war, however, was to be averted in most of the advanced industrial nations by social reforms and by improvement in the economic status of the masses.

In this chapter, we have also presented a cross section of other forces dominant between 1815 and 1870—romanticism and nationalism. The romanticists were in revolt against what they felt was the one-sided rationalistic bias of eighteenth-century thought. In place of reason, they stressed intuition and emotion. The result was one of the modern world's most fruitful epochs in literature and the arts. Closely allied to romanticism was another powerful emotional force of the period, nationalism. This force caught up idealists in all nations and was in turn given eloquent expression by many romantic poets.

The period from 1800 to 1870 was also one of remarkable scientific progress. It is studded with famous names—Faraday, Dalton, Mendelyeev, Lister, Pasteur, Lyell, and Darwin. Darwin's theory, in particular, was to revolutionize men's thinking about the origin and development of our planet and of man's own ancestry. Although the full impact of this theory upon religion and science alike would not be felt until the succeeding decades, by 1870 a mighty intellectual and moral conflict had already been precipitated.

Yet despite its anguished moments, this was a forward-looking, dynamic period, still sustained by a deep-rooted belief in the perfectibility of society. Thus the bourgeoisie of the midcentury could agree with Robert Browning when he had one of his poetic characters declare:

God's in his heaven—
All's right with the world![22]

SUGGESTIONS FOR READING

F. B. Artz, *Reaction and Revolution, 1814-1832,* Harper, 1934; and R. C. Binkley, *Realism and Nationalism, 1852-1871,* Harper, 1953. These volumes in *The Rise of Modern Europe* series include short but valuable syntheses of the economic, social, and cultural developments covered in this chapter. Brief suggestive surveys of the thought of the period are contained in C. Brinton, *The Shaping of the Modern Mind,** Mentor; and J. H. Randall, *The Making of the Modern Mind,* Houghton Mifflin, 1940.

W. Bowden, M. Karpovich, and A. Usher, *An Economic History of Europe Since 1750,* American Book, 1937. A good general survey. Other useful economic histories are S. B. Clough and C. W. Cole, *Economic History of Europe,* Heath, 1952; and H. Heaton, *Economic History of Europe,* Harper, 1948.

T. Ashton, *The Industrial Revolution, 1760-1830,* Oxford (Home Univ. Library), 1948. An admirable introduction to the main developments. For greater detail, see the standard works by P. Mantoux, *The Industrial Revolution in the Eighteenth Century,* Harcourt, Brace, 1929; and J. L. and B. Hammond, *The Rise of Modern Industry,* Methuen, 1948.

On the spread of the Industrial Revolution, see L. C. Knowles, *Economic Development in the Nineteenth Century: France, Germany, Russia, and the United States,* Routledge, 1932; and J. H. Clapham, *Economic Development of France and Germany, 1815-1914,* Macmillan, 1936.

J. L. and B. Hammond, *The Bleak Age,** Penguin. A graphic study of the shocking social effects of the Industrial Revolution. See also L. Mumford, *Technics and Civilization,* Harcourt, Brace, 1934. A less alarming picture is painted by M. C. Buer, *Health, Wealth and Population in the Early Days of the Industrial Revolution,* Routledge, 1926.

J. Barzun, *Romanticism and the Modern Ego,* Little, Brown, 1944. A lively and sympathetic appraisal of romanticism.

I. Babbitt, *Rousseau and Romanticism,** Meridian, is a brilliant but hostile analysis.

*Indicates an inexpensive paperbound edition.

The romantic movement in literature is surveyed in A. J. George, *The Development of French Romanticism,* Syracuse Univ., 1955; K. Francke, *A History of German Literature As Determined by Social Forces,* Holt, 1931; and, for England, M. Elwin, *The First Romantics,* Longmans, 1948.

On romanticism in architecture, painting, and music, see K. Clark, *The Gothic Revival,* Constable, 1950; F. J. Mather, *Modern Painting: A Study of Tendencies,* Holt, 1927; and A. Einstein, *Music in the Romantic Era,* Norton, 1947.

The impact of romanticism on political thought is treated in the various books on nationalism cited in the Suggestions for Reading for Chapters 21 and 22.

R. Heilbroner, *The Worldly Philosophers; The Lives, Times and Ideas of the Great Economic Thinkers,** Simon and Schuster. Excellent chapters on Adam Smith, the Utopians, and Marx. The author disproves the maxim that economics is a "dismal science."

G. de Ruggiero, *The History of European Liberalism,** Beacon. The standard work on the subject. See also J. J. Saunders, *The Age of Revolution: The Rise and Decline of Liberalism in Europe Since 1815,* Roy, 1949.

E. Halévy, *The Growth of Philosophic Radicalism,** Beacon. Benthamite utilitarianism and the rise of the opposing "humane" socioeconomic philosophies. See also B. Schilling, *Human Dignity and the Great Victorians,* Columbia Univ., 1946.

E. Wilson, *To the Finland Station,** Anchor. A popular history of Utopian and Marxian socialism. On Marx, the best brief, balanced study is I. Berlin, *Karl Marx: His Life and Environment,** Galaxy. L. Schwarzchild, *The Red Prussian: The Life and Legend of Karl Marx,** Universal, is hostile but written with gusto.

J. Barzun, *Darwin, Marx, Wagner: Critique of a Heritage,** Anchor. An incisive analysis of the intellectual climate shared win and nineteenth-century science, see the Suggestions for by these three contemporaries. For additional works on Dar-Reading for Chapter 24.

CHAPTER 21

To the Barricades!

Introduction. After the final defeat of Napoleon, the statesmen of the great powers, assembled at the Congress of Vienna, resumed the interrupted task of building a new Europe. Their solutions were conservative. Sincerely believing that the explosive forces of nationalism and democracy liberated by the French Revolution had been primarily responsible for more than two decades of destruction and suffering, they were determined to return as much as possible to the "good old days" before the Revolution. With this end in mind, they deliberately sought to extirpate the revolutionary ideas and attitudes that had been released by French republicanism; they restored the old royal lines and endeavored to create among the nations of Europe a harmony and stability which would make a recurrence of revolutionary violence impossible. After this conservative peace had been established, international machinery known as the Congress System was devised to defend the political arrangements of 1815 and to crush any attempts to upset them.

But the edifice of reaction built at Vienna was not strong enough to withstand the forces directed against it. In the great revolutionary upheaval that originated in France and spread through much of Europe, such ideas as popular suffrage, intellectual and religious freedom, pride in nation, and equality for all under the law had been given wide currency, and though the upheaval was ended, both intellectuals and the underprivileged in many lands clung to these liberal concepts. In addition, the conquests of territories and subjugation of peoples by Napoleon had actually strengthened the counterspirit of nationalism. During the revolutionary and Napoleonic eras, the spirit of nationalism had risen in Russia, Spain, Italy, the Germanies, and other lands violated by French imperialism. After 1815 those peoples who enjoyed national liberty were resolved to defend it, while those who were denied this privilege and lived under alien governments were increasingly determined to throw off the foreign yoke. A flurry of revolts broke out in 1820 and 1821; another epidemic of revolutions challenged conservatism in 1830; and a climactic outbreak of rebellion and overthrow came in the historic year of 1848.

Another significant trend in the period under review was the growing antagonism between the workers and their employers, the new moneyed interests. As we saw in Chapter 20, the workers de-manded democracy, universal suffrage, and equal political rights for all. The middle class, representing the philosophy of liberalism, championed the rights only of the rich and the successful. The violent contradiction between these two attitudes was ignored for a time, while working class and middle class united to seize political influence from the aristocracy and its instrument, irresponsible monarchy. But as the era of reaction following the Congress of Vienna faded, the course of several revolutions exposed the coalition as unnatural and unworkable. Much of the history of western Europe after the year 1850 will be concerned with the new power struggle between the forces of capital and labor.

REACTION AT VIENNA

The Congress of Vienna. In September 1814, during Napoleon's exile on Elba, a brilliant gathering of diplomats and rulers assembled at Vienna to remake the map of Europe. Representatives from every state in Europe except Turkey were in attendance. The Austrian government acted as a lavish host to the treaty makers, sponsoring a round of festivals, hunts, balls, and musicales. Beethoven conducted the premiére of his *Seventh Symphony.* For ten months kings, princes, and diplomats, with their ladies, dined, danced, and worked—not too industriously—at remaking the Continent.

In this atmosphere of high society and what frequently turned out to be low diplomacy, the Congress as such never met. Instead, the new map of Europe was made in small, secret conferences.

The leading delegates were Tsar Alexander I of Russia, Lord Castlereagh of Great Britain, Talleyrand of France, and Prince von Metternich, the spokesman for Austria. The "prince of diplomats," the most important figure at the Congress, was Metternich (1773-1859).

During the Napoleonic period Metternich had become an inflexible opponent of the French emperor. After Waterloo, he resolved that there should be no return of the revolutionary ideas circulated by France between 1792 and 1815. Referring to the French Revolution, Metternich declared it was:

. . . the disease which must be cured, the volcano which must be extinguished, the gangrene which must be burned out with the hot iron, the hydra with jaws open to swallow up the social order.[1]

Most of the rulers attending the Congress agreed with these sentiments.

Witty, egotistical, and astute, Metternich exercised a kind of moral dictatorship at the Congress. His leadership initiated the reactionary era now termed the Age of Metternich, which was to last until the middle of the nineteenth century.

The task confronting the Congress. The task confronting the diplomats at the Congress of Vienna was threefold: What was to be done with France? How should the old governments and political boundaries so ruthlessly abolished by Napoleon be reconstituted? And, finally, how should the Congress deal with the radical ideas developed and spread abroad by revolutionary France?

Many Europeans, especially those of the middle class, hoped that the peace settlement would be guided by two principles that had grown rapidly during the stormy days from 1789 to 1815. These were nationalism on the one hand, and democracy and political liberalism on the other. The first principle promised all peoples the right to rule themselves, free of the control of foreigners. Both democrats and liberals opposed despotic government, but while democrats believed in the right of all citizens to participate in government, bourgeois liberals believed in control by the well-to-do.

Unfortunately, the Congress of Vienna was in no mood to respect the aspirations of the people. Much of the subsequent discontent and turmoil in nineteenth-century Europe resulted from the reactionary efforts of the Congress to restore as much of the Old Regime as could conveniently be retrieved.

Treatment of France. Regarding the future of France, the Congress proved to be sensible and moderate. The Treaty of Paris, signed by French representatives in May 1814, had given France about the same boundaries it possessed in 1792. But after Napoleon's escape from Elba, his so-called "Hundred Days" of freedom, and his ultimate defeat at Waterloo, a second and more severe treaty in November 1815 somewhat diminished French territory. Nevertheless, even with this reduction, France's frontiers were more extensive than they had been in 1789.

Geographic and political realignment. In the reëstablishment of the European political order, four principles were followed: (1) legitimacy, (2) encirclement of France, (3) compensations, and (4) balance of power. It was agreed that, wherever possible, the legitimate rulers who were in power before their deposition by Napoleon should have their thrones restored to them. Following this principle, all the rulers who had been established by Napoleon were removed. (The one exception was Bernadotte, one of Napoleon's marshals and founder of the present dynasty of Sweden.) In the person of Louis XVIII, the Bourbon House was restored in France, and other Bourbon rulers were returned to their thrones in Spain and in the kingdom of Naples. The House of Savoy reigned again in Sardinia-Piedmont,* and

*Sardinia-Piedmont is often referred to as either Sardinia or Piedmont (the Continental portion of the kingdom). In the text hereafter, unless otherwise noted, *Sardinia* will be used to indicate Sardinia-Piedmont.

Prince von Metternich

the House of Orange was restored in Holland.

In the reconstruction of the political boundaries of Europe, the keynote again was the restoration of the past. France, as we have seen, was reduced to substantially its former size; Spain, Holland, and other former Napoleonic possessions were restored to independence. The map of Europe looked much as it had before the French Revolution (see Reference Map 6).

However, the pre-Napoleonic boundaries were not everywhere restored. The Holy Roman Empire remained dissolved; in place of the hundreds of states existing in prerevolutionary times, the thirty-eight set up by Napoleon were retained and organized into the German Confederation, dominated by Austria.

Certain features of the map of Europe were modified in accordance with the principle of encirclement. The allied statesmen were resolved that a protective belt should be fashioned to surround France, hem it in, and prevent any future French aggression. The Austrian Netherlands (Belgium) were turned over to Holland, making this country a stronger barrier on France's north; Savoy, belonging to the kingdom of Sardinia, was enlarged in order to block any French invasion of Italy; and Prussia was given extensive territory along the Rhine.

The granting of compensations to states surrendering territory was another principle modifying the map of Europe. For example, Austria was compensated for giving up the Austrian Netherlands by being given Lombardy and Venetia (Venice and the surrounding area) in northern Italy and part of the Adriatic coast as well. In such fashion the diplomats at Vienna portioned out the spoils so that no great power was slighted. When Sweden consented to allow Finland to be retained by Russia, Sweden's compensation was the acquisition of Norway. England's share was the retention of colonies and naval bases it had captured in the Napoleonic Wars: Mauritius, Malta and the Dutch colonies of Ceylon and South Africa.

The diplomats also had to create a new balance of power among the nations. Among the Big Four there existed deep jealousies. Prussia coveted all of Saxony, while Austria feared growing Prussia. Russia wanted to expand by securing all of Poland. Britain believed that an enlarged Russian state would menace the balance of power and—indirectly—British security. While the victorious powers were haggling, Talleyrand wormed his way into the good graces of Britain and Austria. A secret treaty was arranged, pledging the three countries to use force, if necessary, to restrain Prussia and Russia. Confronted by this threat, Russia and Prussia reduced their claims for more Polish and Saxon territory. The power struggle at Vienna demonstrated that peacemaking is often as dangerous as warmaking; this same lesson of history later was to be illustrated at the Paris Peace Conference after World War I and even more so in the Cold War which is being waged between the victors of World War II.

Nationalist sentiment disregarded. The most serious mistake made at Vienna was the disregard of the rising nationalistic aspirations of the European peoples. Italy was, in Metternich's disdainful phrase, only a "geographical expression," not a nation, and was so treated. In Germany, the weak and loosely organized German Confederation of thirty-eight states was established, with Austria at its head. This was largely Austria's doing again, for Austria saw in a united Germany a threat to Austrian dominance in central Europe. The principle of nationalism was again violated when Norway was arbitrarily given to Sweden and the Belgians were turned over to the Dutch. Poles and Finns also simply exchanged masters. During the nineteenth century, these peoples continued the struggle to secure national sovereignty.

Quadruple and Holy Alliances. The most vital problem facing the Congress, therefore, was how to check the growth of revolutionary ideas. In November 1815, as a result of Metternich's influence, Austria, Prussia, Russia, and England signed the Quadruple alliance. The object of this document was stated to be the maintenance of "tranquillity" in Europe, and for this purpose the members were to meet from time to time to agree on the proper measures to be taken. In 1818 France was admitted to the compact, making it a Quintuple Alliance.

Such an alliance system, providing for collective security against any renewal of French aggression and for consultation on common problems, was both logical and desirable. Unfortunately it became apparent soon after 1815 that the real purpose of the alliance was to crush relentlessly any growth of nationalism and political liberalism. This policy was to result in three important series of revolutions engulfing Europe—the uprisings of 1820-1821, 1830-1831, and 1848.

The Holy Alliance, another famous league formed at Vienna, was proposed by the visionary Alexander I of Russia and was joined by most of the powers attending the Congress. They agreed that they would base their policies on those of that "holy religion, namely, the precepts of justice, Christian charity and peace." Castlereagh described the alliance as "a piece of sublime mysticism and nonsense." The opponents of reaction at this time confused the Holy Alliance with the Quadruple Alliance and regarded the former as the instrument responsible for the repression following the Congress.

THE CONGRESS SYSTEM

Conservatism triumphant. The Congress of Vienna signaled the return of peace, though not of tranquillity. The spirit of Liberty, Equality, and Fraternity continued to stir the peoples of Europe; and almost immediately after the Congress disbanded, various groups began to work against the political arrangements made at Vienna. In most of Europe, the forces of conservatism—based on the restored monarchies, the Church, and the aristocracy—were strong enough to stifle effectively the forces of nationalism, liberalism, and democracy for some time after 1815. Despite the most careful precautions, however, violent revolutions soon broke out against the reactionary regimes in Italy and Spain. It was to safeguard against such uprisings that the Congress System, whose origin and activities we will now consider, was devised.

Reaction and revolution in Spain and Italy. In 1812, during the struggle against Napoleon, groups of Spanish liberals had convened a parliament that had adopted a democratic constitution, but it was ignored by the Bourbon monarch Ferdinand VII after his restoration to the throne in 1814. The former privileges of the nobility and the Church were restored, the Inquisition was reinstated, and the Jesuits were given control of education. There was no parliamentary government, the press was gagged, and political offenders were imprisoned by the thousands. The more intelligent and liberal Spaniards were aroused by the pitiable conditions of their country, and in all the important towns revolutionary bodies called *juntas* were set up. Most dangerous to the reactionary monarchy was the rising discontent in the army, where bad food and lack of pay had brought many troops to the brink of mutiny.

REVOLUTIONS 1820-1821

REVOLUTIONS 1830

REVOLUTIONS 1848

In Italy conditions were, if anything, worse. The consequences of the French Revolution had been felt here more than in any other land outside of France, because Napoleon had destroyed so many of the institutions of the Old Regime. The Napoleonic conquest had given the mass of the Italian people more liberty than they had ever known before and brought a considerable measure of political unity to their land. After the Congress of Vienna, however, the country was again fragmented. Lombardy and Venetia, as we have seen, were turned over to Austria. The rest of the country was divided into minor states, most of which were under the thumb of the Austrian government. The state governments returned to their old inefficient ways. Taxes were high, favoritism and corruption flourished, and desperate men took the easy road of brigandage as a way out. Many patriotic Italians joined a secret revolutionary society, the *Carbonari* or "charcoal burners," who had first organized in the mountain forests and soon spread throughout Italy.

In 1820 a mutiny in the Spanish army was followed by a general uprising. In answer to the rebels' demand that the liberal constitution of 1812 be restored, Ferdinand agreed. When the news of this revolt reached the kingdom of Naples and Sicily, where the people were suffering under the oppressive regime of their Bourbon king, revolution broke out there also, and the king was forced to grant his people a constitution patterned after the Spanish model.

Intervention in Italy and Spain. News of the revolts in Spain and Italy upset the conservative statesmen of Europe. Determined to stamp out rebellion and to support the 1815 settlement, Metternich set about organizing collective action for the suppression of the revolutions—the Congress System.

In 1820 the members of the Quintuple Alliance met in the Congress of Troppau to decide what should be done about the uprising in Naples. Despite England's opposition and the lukewarm attitude of France, the three other powers (Prussia, Russia, and Austria) decided to intervene. In 1821 the conservative powers met at Laibach in Austria and invited the king of Naples to appear before them. Once among his reactionary friends, the king repudiated his promise to support the new constitution in Naples and welcomed the use of an Austrian army to place him back on the throne. Austrian troops quickly scattered the rebel forces, and the king was restored to his throne.

Meanwhile, liberal sentiment in England was growing stronger, and the government was drifting further away from its ultraconservative allies on the Continent. When another congress was convened in 1822 at Verona to consider intervention in Spain, the British refused to send any representatives. Because reactionaries had gained the upper hand in France, the French government volunteered to send an army into Spain to crush the reform movement. A brutal reaction followed. Terrible punishments were meted out to the patriots who had forced the king to restore the constitution of 1812; all acts of the liberal Spanish parliament since the rebellion of 1820 were annulled; and *juntas* were set up to seek out and punish all liberals.

Weakening of the Congress System. Elated by its success in Italy and Spain, the conservative alliance sought to restore the authority of the Spanish king over his rebellious subjects in Latin America. As we saw in Chapter 19, by the early 1820's most of Spain's American colonies had secured their independence, and the remaining royal strongholds were in danger. In trying to intervene in this struggle on behalf of the Spanish king, the European Congress System met its first defeat. Great Britain, which enjoyed a thriving trade with the new Latin-American countries, displayed no enthusiasm for renewed Spanish control. As if the shadow of the British navy were not sufficiently daunting, President Monroe in 1823 warned the European powers that the United States would regard the proposed intervention as an unfriendly act.

Later in the decade, the Congress System was to receive a final shattering blow when strategic and sentimental interests led some of the great powers to align themselves with the cause of revolution in Greece.

First nationalist successes in the Balkans. Outside the family of European nations and not represented at the Congress of Vienna, the Ottoman empire of the Turks ruled over a medley of restless and miserable subject peoples. In 1815 the sultan in Constantinople was still the head of an empire which included the Balkan peninsula as well as much of North Africa and Asia Minor. Living mainly in the Balkans, the Christian subjects of the Turks were an exploited minority group, known to their rulers as *rayahs* (cattle). Formally, however, the Turks practiced religious toleration and in some cases supported the Church as a means of ruling the *rayahs*.

The first people to obtain independence from Turkish rule were the Montenegrins, Serbians who lived in a particularly mountainous area near the Adriatic. In 1799, after a long, heroic struggle, these brave mountaineers had won a formal recognition of independence from the sultan.

In Serbia itself (an area north and east of Montenegro), another independence movement had begun in 1804 with a general uprising led by a patriot named George Petrovich, popularly known as "Black George," who secured Russian support. In 1826 Turkey was forced to place Serbia under Russian protection.

Greece wins independence. It was the uprising of the Greeks in 1821 that attracted the serious attention of Europe. Stirred by the ideals of the French Revolution, Greek patriots rose in arms; Turkish officials in southern Greece were murdered, and in retaliation the sultan ordered the massacre of all Greeks in Constantinople. In 1822 the world was horrified by news of the Turkish massacre of the entire Greek population of the island of Chios.

Metternich wanted the revolt to burn itself out, but the Greek cause had many friends. Hellas had been the cradle of European freedom and civilization, and liberals and intellectuals everywhere demanded that Greece be liberated. Lord Byron wrote:

The isles of Greece! the isles of Greece!
Where burning Sappho loved and sung,
Where grew the arts of war and peace,
Where Delos rose and Phoebus sprung!
Eternal summer gilds them yet,
But all, except their sun, is set.[2]

Philhellenic societies were formed, and both supplies and volunteers were sent to aid the Greeks.

The direct intervention of the great powers, not voluntary support, determined the outcome of the Greek independence movement. Although he was no democrat or Greek sympathizer, Tsar Nicholas i, who had come to the throne in 1825, was strongly interested in weakening Turkey in order to pave the way for Russian annexation of the Dardanelles. This policy alarmed Great Britain, and the upshot was an agreement in 1827 among Britain, Russia, and France, whereby these powers pledged themselves to secure the independence of Greece. This move proved a serious blow to Metternich's Congress System.

The three powers defeated the Turks on land and sea, and in 1829 peace terms were arranged by the Treaty of Adrianople. Greek independence was recognized, together with Serbian autonomy, although the Serbs continued to pay tribute to the Turkish government.

Nationalism in the Balkans had registered important advances, but the victory was far from complete. Many Greeks still lived under Turkish rule, as in Crete; complete independence had still to be secured by Serbia and Rumania; and the restless Bulgarians still remained under the harsh Ottoman yoke. These national frustrations were eventually removed by diplomacy and war.

FRANCE, ENGLAND, AND THE REVOLUTIONS OF 1830

France under Louis xviii. The defection of Great Britain had heralded the demise of the Congress System, and by 1829, the year in which Greek independence was recognized, it was no longer an effective weapon of international conservatism. In 1830, additional sledge-hammer blows fell upon the machinery of coercion devised by Metternich and his backward-looking colleagues. The eruption began in France, the only great power which at all approached England in liberal political institutions.

The restored Louis xviii, brother of the unfortunate Louis xvi, who had fallen victim to the guillotine in 1793, had been willing to accept many of the reforms of the French Revolution. Accordingly, a charter had been given to France which established a form of constitutional monarchy. The king still had extensive powers: he could direct foreign affairs, appoint and dismiss all officials, and propose laws. In the bicameral legislature, patterned after the British Parliament, members of the upper house belonged by hereditary right, and those of the lower chamber were chosen by an electorate limited to the highest taxpayers; only one man in seventy could vote. Since members of the legislature were not paid, they were invariably drawn from the wealthier classes. The effect of these provisions was to limit representative government to deputies of the nobles and other wealthy landed proprietors. Although France in 1815 had a governmental system much more liberal than that presided over by Louis XVI, the country had a long way to go before it could claim to have democratic institutions.

Outside the realm of government proper, the charter granted the French people substantial social, religious, and legal rights. All citizens were now equal before the law. Freedom of speech and of religion were guaranteed, and arbitrary arrest was forbidden. The restored government of Louis XVIII accepted the abolition of feudalism and made no attempt to restore the properties confiscated from the Church and nobles during the Revolution. Napoleon's most significant measures, such as the Napoleonic Civil Code, the Concordat with the pope, the centralization of local government, and the administrative system, were also retained. So, too, was the state's tight control over education.

Moderate though the Bourbon restoration seemed, it had the backing of only a small party. Neither of the two politically important groups in France supported the restoration. The ultras were reactionaries—foes of the Revolution and supporters of strong monarchy and privilege, who thought the constitution too liberal and wanted to turn the clock back to the days of the Old Regime. At the core of the ultra faction were the nobles, many just returned from exile, and the leaders of the Church, whose position in France had been seriously reduced by the Revolution.

At the other end of the political spectrum were the liberals and radicals (republicans) —the disenfranchised lower bourgeoisie, students and intellectuals, and laborers in the larger cities—who wanted the constitution made more democratic and the electorate broadened to include themselves. The truth was that the Revolution, though over, was still an issue.

The aim of Louis XVIII was to "heal the wounds of the Revolution," and in his nine-year reign he managed to steer a middle course between the ultras on the one hand and the liberal and radical reformers on the other. During his rule there emerged a characteristic feature of modern French politics—the multiparty system. Whereas in England there were but two political parties, both recruited in the main from similar strata of society and sharing a common political tradition, in France numerous loosely organized factions appeared, and as time went on it became the practice for ministries to be formed of men from a coalition of parties in the legislature instead of from one majority party as in England. Thus the basis was laid for a pattern of government destined to be less stable than those of Britain and the United States.

Charles X and reaction. Louis XVIII was succeeded on his death in 1824 by Charles X, and the political balance swung heavily to the Right. Like the late monarch, Charles was a brother of the beheaded Louis XVI and had been an émigré during the revolutionary era, but, unlike his predecessor, Charles accepted none of the facts of his age and had long been leader of the ultras. In a word, Charles X was the reincarnation of the reactionary aristocrat of the mid-eighteenth century.

When, in July 1830, the members of the legislature refused to support his ultraroyalist program, Charles dissolved the legislature and issued a series of ordinances gagging the press and limiting the franchise. Galled by this violation of the constitution, the Parisians arose in rebellion. The narrow streets of Paris were quickly choked with overturned carts, boxes, tables, and paving stones. Crouching

The barricades, symbol of revolution in France, are immortalized in Delacroix' dramatic painting of the July Revolution of 1830.

behind these barricades, the armed revolutionaries returned the fire of the soldiers with good effect. Again and again in nineteenth-century revolutions, patriots fighting from behind such barricades succeeded in toppling despotism.

After three days a new liberal faction took over the government, and Charles fled to England. The new government was constituted by an agreement between the French republicans, led by the aging Marquis de Lafayette, and the liberal monarchist supporters of the Orleans branch of the Bourbon monarchy.

The bourgeois monarchy of Louis Philippe. The July Revolution gave France a new king, Louis Philippe (1830-1848), the duke of Orleans, and a new, definitely bourgeois outlook. Like William III of England in 1688,

the new king accepted his crown from the people; he was "king of the barricades" and "king of the French," in contrast to Louis XVIII and Charles X, who had claimed to rule by divine sanction. Thus the principle of the sovereignty of the people supplanted the principle of divine right. In token of this, the revolutionary tricolor replaced the white flag of the Bourbons as the emblem of France. The form of government remained almost unaltered; the suffrage was extended to include the moderately wealthy bourgeoisie, but it did not yet include the lower middle class or the common people. The new regime was the first wholly middle-class government to be set up on the Continent.

Revival of Polish nationalism. Word of the July Revolution spread like the wind throughout Europe, and patriots and liberals everywhere determined to strike for freedom against the Metternich system (see p. 512). Some of the most heroic and exciting events took place in Russian Poland, which, since the Congress of Vienna, had been ruled by the tsar as a semi-independent kingdom. Unrest among the Poles mounted under the rule of the ultrareactionary Tsar Nicholas I.

A few months after the July Revolution in France, the Polish Diet proclaimed Poland independent of Russia and asserted its right to select its own ruler. Despite some brilliant victories, Polish resistance was effectively broken by Russian arms in the summer of 1831. The national Diet was abolished, and Poland sank to the status of an ordinary Russian province, governed directly by Russian officials in St. Petersburg. Notwithstanding its tragic defeat, Polish nationalism continued to live on.

The Belgian revolution. In contrast to the disappointing outcome of the Polish revolution, the spirit of nationalism triumphed in Belgium. We recall that at the Congress of Vienna the Belgians had been united with Holland under the Dutch crown—a union which proved most unhappy. Wide differences in culture separated the two peoples. The Dutch were mainly Protestant, the Belgians Catholic; the Dutch were seafarers and traders, the Belgians farmers and industrial workers. The Belgians widely resented the royal policies by which Dutch laws, officials, and language were imposed on them.

When news of the July Revolution in Paris reached the Belgians, nationalistic feeling rose high in Brussels. Rioting broke out in the city, and a Dutch army sent to quell the disturbances was repulsed with heavy losses. The Belgians then announced their independence and drew up a liberal constitution. The Dutch king immediately appealed to the conservative alliance for aid. But the Russian tsar was busy "tranquilizing" the Poles, and Austria was occupied with revolutions in Italy. No help was forthcoming from France, for Louis Philippe's government, created in 1830 by revolution, was itself a repudiation of the principle of legitimacy laid down in 1815. England, whose political and commercial interests would generally be served by the independence of small states, saw no reason to oppose Belgian aspirations as long as the new state did not become a puppet of France.

Thus, favored by fortune, a national assembly met in Brussels in 1831 and chose Prince Leopold of Saxe-Coburg-Gotha as king. The king of Holland had no choice but to recognize the independence of the kingdom of Belgium. In 1839 the international status of the new state was settled. A treaty declaring Belgium to be a "perpetually neutral state" was drawn up in that year and signed by England, Austria, Prussia, Russia, France, and Belgium. (This was the treaty which Germany contemptuously dismissed as a "scrap of paper" when its troops invaded Belgium in World War I.) After centuries of foreign rule —under the dukes of Burgundy, kings of Spain, rulers of Austria, and king of Holland —the Belgians secured their own government.

Depression and political reaction in England. The first decade after 1815 was a period of reaction in England as well as on the Continent. With the end of the Napoleonic Wars, the government ceased its war purchases, the country became overstocked with goods, and factories shut down. Unemployment, further augmented by demobilization, rose rapidly and resulted in widespread suffering. In a particularly sad state of distress and despair were the handloom weavers and other hand-skilled workers, who now began to feel the relentless squeeze of the machine; the severe drop in prices after 1815 made it impossible for them to make a living. In consequence, they turned to wrecking factories and smashing machines.

Instead of sympathizing with the plight of the poor, unemployed, and even starving lower classes, England's aristocrats saw in their discontent only the evil Jacobin influence of the French Revolution. The Tory party, controlling the government, followed the doctrine of "peace, law, order, and discipline." In 1819 a large meeting held in the city of Manchester to demand universal suffrage was dispersed by a cavalry charge with the loss of several lives. Terrified by what they believed to be the imminence of revolution, the ruling class enacted repressive legislation. Public meetings were restricted; liberal newspapers were repressed; heavy fines were imposed on "seditious literature"; and in 1817 the Habeas Corpus Act was suspended.

Reform movement in England. The period of postwar reaction ended in the late 1820's with a series of reforms sponsored by the liberal branch of the Tory party under the leadership of Robert Peel and George Canning. These bills abolished capital punishment for over one hundred offenses, created a modern police force for London, began the recognition of labor unions, repealed old laws which forbade non-Anglican Protestants to sit in Parliament, and, by the Catholic Emancipation Bill, gave equal rights to members of the Catholic faith. Then in 1832 came the great crisis in political reform and its successful resolution.

The impetus for political reform in Great Britain arose from the July Revolution of 1830 in France. By this time not only was the British working class incensed against the system of privilege which ruled it, but British businessmen were determined to break the monopoly of the aristocracy in government. In 1830 the Duke of Wellington, now prime minister, made a fateful speech in which he declared that the constitution of the country was quite satisfactory for all its needs. This so aroused public opposition that the Iron Duke was forced to resign, and Lord Grey, the leader of the Whig party, became head of the government, thereby ending sixty years of almost continuous Tory rule.

The new government under Grey immediately set about reforming Parliament. There had long been a need for such action. Representation in the House of Commons had virtually no relation to the population; it has been estimated that 3 per cent of the population dictated the election of the members. Of 571 members of the Commons, 82 were elected by the counties controlled by the landed aristocracy, and the remaining 489 members came from incorporated towns, called boroughs. Many "pocket" boroughs

This study by Thomas Sully of the young Victoria was painted in 1838, one year after she became queen.

were under the control of "borough mongers," political bosses who dictated the choice of the voters. In various depopulated "rotten" boroughs, members of Parliament were elected to represent areas which boasted only a handful of people or no longer contained any inhabitants. On the other hand, new and rapidly growing industrial towns, such as Manchester with 140,000 inhabitants and Birmingham with 100,000, had no representatives.

Reform Bill of 1832. Supported by the rising middle class and the workers, Grey's government introduced a bill to abolish the rotten boroughs, widen the franchise, and give representation to the new industrial towns. Defeated in the Commons at the outset, the bill was again introduced and passed, only to be defeated in the House of Lords. A revolution now seemed imminent. After the bill had been introduced a third time, the king, William IV, finally threatened to create enough new peers who would vote for the bill to pass the measure in the House of Lords. This threat forced the Lords to pass the bill.

The measure as enacted did not represent a radical political change. It transferred the balance of power from the landed gentry to the upper middle class and emphasized the growing supremacy of the Commons over the Lords. The important fact is that, while the great Reform Bill did not represent an immediate substantial widening of the franchise (the working class was still disenfranchised), the bill indicated a new sensitivity to popular forces and thus constituted an initial step in breaching the wall of political privilege. The Reform Bill of 1832 did not introduce democracy into England, but it did make democracy ultimately possible.

Additional reforms. Following the first Reform Bill, several other notable reforms were enacted. Slavery was abolished in the British empire in 1833. The first important Factory Act (see Chapter 20) was passed in the same year, and in 1835 the Municipal Corporations Bill instituted a uniform system of town government with popular election.

The accession of the popular young Queen Victoria in 1837 was in itself a kind of reform. For more than fifty years, the fumbling and morally corrupt monarchy had been losing the respect and loyalty of the British people. Victoria did much to save the monarchy by making it an accurate mirror of middle-class convention and creed.

The revolutionary surge—by its success in France, Greece, and Belgium and by the peaceful program of reform in Britain—had definitely obliterated the Congress System. By the early 1830's it was apparent that the conservative unity established in 1815 for the governance of Europe had broken up because of its failure to adapt itself to the growing forces of nationalism, middle-class liberalism, and industrialism. But, as we shall see in the next section, the story was quite different inside the Austrian empire and its orbit of German and Italian states.

THE NATIONALISTIC SPIRIT

IN CENTRAL EUROPE

The Old Regime maintained in Austria. During the revolutions of 1820 and again in 1830, there had been sympathetic vibrations of unrest and minor insurrections in the German states and the Austrian empire. In the main, however, the political arrangements made at Vienna in 1815 were not seriously challenged. Under the strong hand of its chief minister, Metternich, Austria continued to be a bulwark of reaction in central Europe and throughout its sphere of influence among the multitude of states in Germany and Italy.

Nationalism menaced not only the Hapsburg domination of Germany and Italy but also the Austrian state itself, for the Austrian empire did not constitute a nation but rather a bewildering jumble of diverse nationalities. Austria proper, the seat of the governing house of the Hapsburgs, was German. To the east of Austria was the great plain of Hungary, the habitat of the Magyars, who were originally of Asiatic origin and spoke a language not related to most European tongues. All around the fringes of the Austrian and Hungarian center were primarily Slavic peoples: Czechs, Slovaks, and Poles to the north, Rumanians to the east, and Serbs, Croats, and Slovenes to the south. In addition, south of Austria were the large provinces of Lombardy and Venetia, purely Italian in population. In this polyglot Austrian empire the Germans were the ruling nationality. Although they comprised only about 20 per cent of the total population, they constituted the bulk of the upper and middle classes, controlling the government, the Church, and the army. In appearance, then, Austria was German, but it was actually "a Slav edifice with a German façade." Only by excluding the ideas of nationalism and popular government could Metternich and Emperor Francis I hope to keep their ramshackle empire intact.

The Austrian middle class was very small, the great bulk of the inhabitants being poor peasants. There was no such thing as representative government. Local assemblies, called Diets, possessed little power and were representative only of the nobility.

Romantic nationalism in Austria's orbit. In the several dozen German states, both large and small, Austrian influence was paramount. Here again Metternich perceived that his most menacing danger was nationalism. For if the German people, now divided, should unite, the new nation might repudiate Austria's leadership both within Germany and in central Europe.

Notwithstanding the stern opposition of Metternich, supported by most of the German rulers, nationalism and political liberalism advanced in the German states after 1815. Much of the inspiration for this movement was derived from the romantic nationalism so strongly expressed by German professors, poets, and philosophers.

In 1817 a great student festival was held at Wartburg to arouse German patriotism. The festival was followed by some disturbances, including the murder of a spy in the secret service of the Russian tsar. The response of Metternich was immediate and harsh. He persuaded the German rulers, assembled at Carlsbad in 1819, to draw up a number of decrees which were later adopted by the Diet of the Confederation. The Carlsbad Decrees dissolved student associations, muzzled the press, and throttled the professors' freedom of speech.

Among the Magyars of Hungary, the spirit of nationalism spread, despite repressive measures. The romantic movement was also influential in the development of the Slavic revival. Czechs, Poles, Croats, Serbs, and Bulgars began to take pride in their distinctive national cultures, to agitate for national independence where it was lacking, and to feel a sense of kinship and common destiny with all Slavic groups.

Mazzini and the *Risorgimento*. In Italy after 1815, the Hapsburgs ruled over some unhappy provinces in the north and northeast and dominated the little independent states throughout the peninsula. It was perhaps natural that this frustrated land should produce the most famous exemplar of romantic nationalism, Giuseppe Mazzini (1805-1872), the son of a professor at the University of Genoa. Fired by the revolutionary zeal of romantic poets such as Byron, Mazzini in the 1820's joined the *Carbonari*.

Giuseppe Mazzini

In 1830, Mazzini was implicated in an unsuccessful revolution against the royal government of Sardinia and was imprisoned for six months. Following his release, he established a new patriotic society known as Young Italy. His bold writings spread over the land and initiated a new phase of the Italian nationalist movement known as the *Risorgimento* (Resurgence).

Mazzini was intensely religious, and to him loyalty to the nation came midway between a man's loyalty to his family and his loyalty to his God. But unlike leaders of nationalism later in the century, who arrogantly preached the superiority of their own people, Mazzini believed that the people of every nation should work for the benefit of their brothers throughout the world.

REVOLUTION RENEWED IN WESTERN EUROPE

Growing spirit of discontent. During the 1830's and 1840's, the spirit of romantic nationalism continued to mount. The failure of some of the revolutions of 1830 had driven many of the young patriots underground or into exile, where the political air they breathed was filled with conspiracy, plots, and vague

During the early years of his reign, Louis Philippe, "king of the bourgeoisie," made a point of walking about in the streets of Paris dressed in a frock coat and top hat and carrying an umbrella like any solid middle-class citizen.

dreams of liberty. By the year 1848 a strong spirit of explosive discontent was shared by idealistic romanticists who dreamed of liberty, practical businessmen who sought control of the government, and city workers who desired democracy and a more equal distribution of the profits of industry. A prophetic note for all Europe was sounded in the French legislature early in 1848, when Alexis de Tocqueville, who had written a famous book on democracy in America, warned his listeners:

We are sleeping on a volcano. . . . Do you not see that the earth trembles anew? A wind of revolution blows, the storm is on the horizon.[3]

France under Louis Philippe. The new social and economic forces of discontent were particularly strong in France. Since 1830

France had been ruled by the bourgeois monarch, Louis Philippe, who prided himself on being the representative of the business interests of his country. France was fairly prosperous, and the government, while not democratic, was moderate and sensible.

On the debit side, it soon became apparent that the July monarchy had little concern with the lower classes. "Work, get rich, and then you can vote," was the government's advice. To Louis Philippe and his ministers, prosperity, order, and, above all, international peace required the maintenance of the status quo. The king believed that peace was threatened by the demands of many liberals and republicans that France aid the nationalists of Poland, Switzerland, and Italy. "No reform!" became the platform of his reign.

What Louis Philippe failed to perceive was that new economic and social forces were at work which were bound to affect the political picture as well. The Industrial Revolution, entering France from England at an increasing tempo during his reign, was fattening the bourgeoisie whom he so sedulously represented, but it was also swelling the ranks of the politically conscious proletariat and creating those wretched conditions which gave rise to socialism, with its aim of redesigning the whole economic and political system.

Louis Blanc (1811-1882), a socialist theorist and journalist who had a large following among French workers, demanded state factories in which all the workers could obtain employment and where they would be allowed to divide among themselves the fruits of their labors. The discontented industrial workers concentrated in Paris and other growing factory towns added their demands for reform to the moderate requests of the lower bourgeoisie, who simply wanted the vote for themselves, and those of the intellectuals, who were devoted to republican principles.

Another cause of the government's general unpopularity was the corruption that had pervaded the administration. Officials speculated with public funds, commissions in the army were sold, and a series of scandals in high society rocked the country. In addition, the reign of Louis Philippe was colorless and dull. In foreign affairs the king's policy seemed to be "business before national honor." The French began to think back fondly to the immortal deeds of the great Napoleon and yearn for national glory once again.

The revolution of 1848. In February 1848 a Paris insurrection once more turned into a political revolution. Again, as in 1830, mobs of excited citizens began to congregate, and the barricade—the inevitable symbol of revolution—appeared. More than 1500 barricades were thrown up in Paris. After a provisional government proclaimed a republic, Louis Philippe fled to England. Universal suffrage was immediately established, giving France suddenly a full political democracy.

The new regime, known as the Second Republic, was to have a brief and inglorious existence. Created somewhat unexpectedly, without real preparation, it was hamstrung by complete inexperience in democracy among both its officials and the newly enfranchised common people. In addition, the reformers who had been united in their opposition to Louis Philippe broke into diverse factions after his removal. The republicans at once split into two groups—the moderates, of bourgeois stamp, who favored political democracy within the existing social order; and the socialists, supported by mobs of unemployed Paris workers, who wanted the revolution to be economic and social as well as political. A provisional government representing both groups was set up, with the moderates well in the majority.

Within a few months the new regime came to grief over the issue of national workshops. As a concession to the workingman, whom the moderates sincerely wanted to help, so-called national workshops—actually a form of work relief similar to the American WPA of the 1930's—were established to create jobs for the unemployed. But the operation of the program was entrusted to men determined to discredit the scheme as socialistic. As a result, such projects as carrying dirt from one end of a park to the other soon made the workshops a laughingstock.

In June the workshops were disbanded, whereupon another violent insurrection, known as the June Days, broke out in the streets of the capital. Unemployed workers, unwilling to use the tricolor as their symbol, hoisted the red flag as the sign of revolution—the first time that the red flag appeared as the symbol of the proletariat. With the cry of "Bread or Lead," these Paris workers erected barricades and sought to overthrow the government. After much loss of life, the insurrection was crushed. The conflict left among the working class a bitter hatred of the bourgeoisie and among the bourgeois element a deep and lasting fear of left-wing violence.

Louis Napoleon and the Second Empire. The bloody upheavals in Paris produced a wave of reaction throughout the country, especially among the conservative peasantry. When the election for the presidency of the new republic was held, the victor was not one of the revolutionaries who had founded the new government but a hitherto obscure bearer of the magic name *Napoleon*—Louis Napoleon, nephew of Napoleon I.

Louis had assumed the headship of the Napoleon clan after the death in 1832 of the emperor's only son. Early in life Louis became convinced of the magic of his name and the great destiny it was yet to play in the history of France. His efforts in 1836 and again in 1840 to overthrow the bourgeois monarchy of Louis Philippe fizzled miserably, but at his trial he addressed the nation thus:

I represent . . . a principle, a cause, a defeat. The principle is the sovereignty of the people: the cause is that of the Empire: the defeat is Waterloo.[4]

Sentenced to life imprisonment, Louis Napoleon occupied his time writing tracts and articles, which displayed an apparent concern for the depressed industrial workers and unemployed. He escaped from prison in 1846 and fled to England; two years later, with the overthrow of Louis Philippe, he returned to Paris. Free from any involvement with the events of June, he was able to obtain broad national support in his campaign for the presidency.

Stupidity and indifference characterize the paunchy, middle-class members of the French legislature in this scathing portrayal of the lawmakers in session under the July monarchy. It is the work of Honoré Daumier, a master of political and social satire.

Elected president by an overwhelming majority, Louis considered himself, not the legislature, as representing the national will —a version of popular sovereignty known as Caesarian democracy. In his mind burned the imperial traditions of his famous uncle. In December 1851, while serving as president, Louis Napoleon forcibly dissolved the government, which played into his hands by attempting to abolish universal suffrage. Imitating the methods of his illustrious uncle and anticipating the techniques of modern dictators, he then carried out a plebiscite which gave almost unanimous support to his action. Again, in 1852, Napoleon effected a sweeping change in the government by proclaiming himself Emperor Napoleon III. The Second Republic was no more. France still did not seem to be ready for republican institutions.

The Chartist movement in England. In addition to the revolutions which the Paris uprising of 1848 helped spawn throughout much of Europe, there were repercussions of a lesser sort in England. In the 1830's, a strong popular movement known as Chartism had developed there. Its leaders published the People's Charter, containing six demands: universal suffrage, secret voting, no property qualifications for members of Parliament, payment of members so that poor men could seek election if they wished, annual elections to Parliament, and equal electoral districts. Twice, in 1839 and in 1842, the Chartists presented their petition, with over a million signatures, to the House of Commons. In both instances the government ignored the petition.

In 1848, following the news of the February insurrection in France, a third petition was presented to Parliament, which again rejected the demands. A militant minority among the Chartists planned an armed insurrection in protest, but their plans were divulged by an informer and the ringleaders were seized. The greater number of the Chartists, like the majority of the English citizenry, preferred to avoid violence as an instrument of political and social reform. Although the Chartist movement subsequently declined, all but one of its demands—annual parliamentary elections—were enacted into law within the next century, forming the very foundations of modern British democracy.

Repeal of the Corn Laws. Another reason why the Chartist movement declined so quickly was a basic change in the government's economic policy, which now leaned more toward economic liberalism and helped stimulate the rapid growth of employment, wealth, and industry after 1850. The Corn Laws, protective duties on imported corn (i.e., grain) which had favored the hitherto dominant farming gentry, were dropped in favor of a policy of free trade.

By the middle of the nineteenth century, the population had increased so greatly that English agriculture could no longer feed the country, and the price of bread rose alarmingly. The famine of 1845 in Ireland (see p. 545) dramatically spotlighted the seriousness of the situation. Repeal of the Corn Laws in 1846 made possible the import of low-priced wheat from abroad, cheaper food for the masses, and a more contented labor supply for the factory owners. At the same time, this victory of the freetraders reflected the growing political dominance of those members of the middle class who believed in laissez faire in England, feeling that tariffs restricted the free flow of goods. Thenceforth the British economy was increasingly geared to industry, and England became dependent on imports to feed its population.

The repeal of the Corn Laws was shortly followed by the abandonment of customs duties of every kind. The free trade advocated by the followers of Adam Smith was at last a reality; another victory for liberalism had been achieved. For half a century the policy was eminently successful, as the flourishing English industries needed no protection against outside competitors and the English economy throve on the stimulus of cheap imports of raw materials and food.

By midcentury, Britain was a wealthy nation taking pride in the stability of its political institutions. The pattern of restraint and of gradual social and political reforms, so characteristic of England's history for the next hundred years, had been firmly established. Britain would move forward by evolutionary rather than revolutionary reform.

REVOLUTIONS THAT MISFIRED

Berlin follows the example of Paris. The echo of the Parisians' February revolt against Louis Philippe's bourgeois monarchy did not take long to reach discontented liberals and workingmen throughout Europe, leaving only Russia and Turkey untouched. At public assemblies convened in various cities just a few days after the flight of Louis Philippe, patriotic German liberals declared the unity of Germany and began to plan for a national assembly at Frankfurt to draft a German constitution.

On March 15, 1848, the subjects of the Prussian monarch, King Frederick William IV, finally gave vent to their long-repressed political aspirations in serious rioting in Berlin. As in Paris, barricades sprang up all over the city, and for several days bloody fighting went on between the people and the army. The humiliated and coerced king promised a constitution, a parliament, and support for a united Germany. Following this remarkable popular victory, the governments in other German states fell to pieces. Their rulers agreed to establish constitutional governments and granted various privileges such as freedom of the press.

The Frankfurt Assembly. As the crowning symbol of the revolutionary fervor that was sweeping Europe in 1848, the Frankfurt Assembly opened its first session on May 18. Over five hundred members attended, coming from the various German states, from Austria proper, and even from Bohemia, which had a large German minority in its population. The guns boomed, the church bells pealed, and a vast crowd applauded as

A contemporary cartoon shows a demonstration of the kind that helped bring about the repeal of the Corn Laws in 1846.

the newly inducted president of the Assembly announced: "We are to create a constitution for Germany."

This objective posed two fundamental problems: Just what was meant by "Germany," and what manner of government should be devised for the new empire? In regard to the first problem, some believed that a united Germany should include all Germans in central Europe; such a state would include Austria proper (but not Hungary) and probably, because of its large and prosperous German minority, Bohemia. On the other hand, some representatives believed that Austria should not be included in the new Germany. The first faction wanted to offer the new imperial crown to the Hapsburg sovereign in Vienna, the second to the Hohenzollern king of Prussia.

Failure of the Frankfurt Assembly and the "Humiliation of Olmütz." Perhaps the most tragic disappointment of 1848 was the failure of the Frankfurt Assembly and, with it, of the liberal cause in Germany. From May to December 1848, a period in which the need for action was imperative, the Frankfurt Assembly spent its time eloquently debating academic topics. Gradually, the liberal uprising subsided as conservatives in the German states began to rally around their rulers to undo the work of the reformers. King Frederick William gradually regained his confidence; the army proved loyal; and the peasants apparently had little interest in political reform. By November 1848 the army was again in control of Berlin.

In December, even though the forces of reaction had definitely gained the ascendancy, the Assembly continued its work. It approved the Declaration of the Rights of the German People, a liberal and inspiring document which set forth the political and social ideals of the reformers. In April 1849 a constitution was approved for a united Germany, at the head of which was to be an emperor advised by a ministry. The legislature was to be elected by secret manhood suffrage. In this blueprint, Austria was excluded for the simple reason that it had refused to join the new union. The leadership of the new Germany was offered to Frederick William, who refused it, declaring that he could not "pick up a crown from the gutter." After his contemptuous refusal, most of the members of the Assembly returned to their homes. When the Prussian army was called in to quell riots in various parts of the Germanies, thousands of prominent middle-class liberals fled, many migrating to the United States.

In 1850 the Prussian king issued his own constitution, a document that paid lip service to parliamentary government but kept all real power in the hands of the sovereign and the upper classes. Meanwhile, Prussia sponsored a confederation of north German states, without Austria and with Frederick William himself as head. This plan was not to the liking of either Austria or Russia, which feared the idea of a strong, Prussian-dominated Germany. A conference of the three interested powers followed at Olmütz in 1850. The Prussian king was persuaded to drop his plan, and it was agreed to restore the German Confederation as set up at the Congress of Vienna in 1815. Austria was still the mistress of central Europe, and Prussian ambitions to secure the leadership of the German states had been checkmated. Austria's disregard for Prussian interests and the weakness of King Frederick William in defending them became known by anti-Austrian Germans as the "Humiliation of Olmütz."

Revolts in Austria, Hungary, and Bohemia. In March 1848, the leading Hungarian nationalist, Louis Kossuth (1802-1894), gave a momentous speech before the Hungarian Diet. His listeners were electrified as he castigated the "stagnant bureaucratic system" and spoke of "the pestilential air blowing from the Vienna charnel house and its deadening effect upon all phases of Hungarian life." He demanded parliamentary government for the entire empire. Avidly read in Vienna, this speech inspired Austrian students and workers to rise in revolt, invade the palace, and fight furious street battles with the soldiery. Taken by surprise, Metternich resigned and fled to England. A few days later the emperor promised a constitution. Meanwhile, the Hungarian Diet declared the nation independent, tied to Austria only through a common sovereign. Fundamental political rights were guaranteed to the people, and the remnants of feudalism and special privilege were obliterated.

In Slavic Bohemia, home of the Czechs, the Austrian emperor was forced to promise a constituent assembly that would create a kingdom of Bohemia similar to that in Hungary. But soon German and Czech nationalists began to quarrel, and the upshot was that the Czechs revolted. Austrian forces bombarded and subdued Prague; thus ended all aspirations for an autonomous new kingdom of Bohemia.

Austria's success in Bohemia gave the emperor's advisers a pattern to follow. The quarrel between Germans and Czechs in Bohemia was being paralleled in Hungary. As head of

A session of the do-nothing Frankfurt Assembly, which frustrated the hopes of German liberals, is shown in this woodcut.

the government, Kossuth was a proponent of rigorous Magyarization; he announced that he would not recognize the claims of any of the other national groups in Hungary. In protest, the Southern Slavs, under a capable Croatian named Jellachich, attacked the Magyars, and civil war ensued. Taking advantage of the situation, the Austrian emperor named Jellachich an imperial general. Following his victory over the Magyars, Jellachich was ordered to Vienna, where, in October 1848, he forced the surrender of the liberals in control of the Austrian capital.

The next step which was taken to counter the revolution was to induce the weak and incapable Emperor Ferdinand to abdicate in favor of his young nephew, Francis Joseph. The Austrian government then proceeded to repeal its concessions to Hungary, arguing that the new emperor was not bound by the acts of his predecessor. Infuriated at this treachery, the Hungarians declared complete independence and proceeded to put up a desperate defense against the invading Austrian armies. The intervention in Hungary of Tsar Nicholas I of Russia with 100,-000 troops in the summer of 1849 ended any hope of Magyar victory. By August all resistance ceased; Kossuth escaped and found refuge in the United States.

Revolution, reform, and reaction in Italy.
The year 1848 saw a rash of revolutions on
the Italian peninsula. The Sicilians revolted
against the corrupt rule of the king of Naples,
forcing him to promise a liberal constitution;
the Venetian populace rose against their Austrian rulers and proclaimed a republic; and in
Milan, the center of discontent against Austria in Lombardy, a few homemade cannons
and an assortment of firearms wielded by an
indomitable citizenry forced the Austrian
army to retreat northward. The king of Sardinia, Charles Albert of the House of Savoy,
voluntarily promulgated a new liberal constitution, destined to become the constitution of
a united Italy until the rise of Mussolini's Fascist dictatorship after World War I. Charles
Albert also assumed the leadership in driving
Austrian influence out of Italy, declaring,
"Italia fara da sa" ("Italy will do it herself").
He assisted the rebels in Lombardy and Venetia, and after hard fighting the Austrians were
compelled to withdraw.

Other states such as Tuscany granted
their people liberal constitutions, and absolute government in Italy almost disappeared. In the Papal States a program of
reform had begun in 1846, when Pius IX had
been elected pope. Known as the "Reforming
Pope," he released many political prisoners
and initiated moderate political reforms.

The liberal triumphs achieved by revolution and reform were soon to be swept away.
While regaining their mastery of Hungary,
the Hapsburgs began throttling the liberal
national movement in Italy. For their part,
the Italians suffered not only from incompetent generalship but also from disunity; many
wanted a republican Italy, not a united Italian monarchy. In July 1848, Charles Albert
was defeated at the decisive battle of Cus-
tozza. After another defeat in May 1849, he
abdicated in favor of his oldest son, who became Victor Emmanuel II. Victorious over the
House of Savoy, Austria quickly helped restore old rulers and systems of government
throughout Italy as they had been before 1848.
And in the south, the Sicilian liberal movement was brutally crushed by the king of
Naples, who abolished the new constitution.

The final episode of the Italian revolutions was the rise and fall of the republic of
Rome. The administration of Pope Pius IX
did not go far enough to suit extremists and
nationalists in the Papal States, who wanted
to abolish clerical domination of the local government and join actively against Catholic
Austria in the struggle for a united Italy. In
November the embittered pope was forced to
flee from Rome, and in February 1849, his
domain was declared a republic. One of its
leaders was Mazzini, who had returned
from exile. The flight of the pope had
brought a wave of indignation in conservative circles throughout Europe, and Louis
Napoleon, president of the Second French
Republic, gained the support of French Catholics and conservatives by sending troops to
crush the Roman republic.

SUMMARY

The principal theme of this chapter has
been the political history of western Europe
from 1815 to 1850 as expressed mainly in
the development of nationalism and democracy. This stirring period witnessed such important events as the realization of Greek and
Belgian independence, the passing of the Reform Bill of 1832 in England, the brief experiment with the Second Republic in France,
and a rash of revolutions in Italy, the Austrian empire, and the Germanies in 1848.

Behind all these events were three movements or attitudes of mind—nationalism,
democracy, and romanticism. Nationalism
moved all national groups to struggle for independence and the freedom to direct their
own affairs without interference. Democracy was neither prevalent nor popular before
1850; affairs were in the hands of the middle
class, which had no use for despotic kings but
also had little sympathy for the rights of the
poor. Still, democratic ideals were spreading.
The intellectual and artistic movement known
as romanticism glorified the right of the individual and believed somewhat naïvely in the
essential goodness of human nature.

The first great epidemic of revolutions
after the Congress settlement occurred in

the 1820's. The revolutions of 1830 definitely showed that the European pattern laid out in 1815 by ultraconservative statesmen could not be maintained intact. In 1848 the great explosion came, leaving only Turkey and Russia untouched. France overthrew Louis Philippe and proclaimed the Second Republic. Governments toppled in Italy, and Charles Albert, king of Sardinia, made the cause of Italian freedom his own by declaring war on Austria. In the Austrian empire the Germans demanded and were promised a more liberal government, while elsewhere, as in Bohemia and Hungary, other nationalities insisted upon national autonomy as well as liberal parliamentary government. And in the Germanies, rulers were forced to make concessions, and a national assembly convened at Frankfurt to draft a new constitution for a united fatherland.

The revolutionary fervor of 1848 did not, however, fulfill its expectations. Perhaps never has such a widespread, popular, and seemingly successful movement collapsed so quickly. Civil war in Hungary, the rise of dictatorship in France, the regaining of royal prerogative in Prussia, military defeat for the national cause in Italy, and empty words at Frankfurt were the sequel. The explanation for this failure is complex, but three factors of special importance should be singled out. The first was the inexperience and lack of realism of popular leaders. There was too much discussion and too little practical planning. Secondly, the force of nationalism, so powerful an enemy of autocracy at the outset, soon showed itself to be a selfish and exclusive movement that set the various liberated nationalities to quarreling among themselves. Thirdly, the development of class consciousness put the middle class and the proletariat at odds. Looking back from the perspective of a little more than a hundred years, we can now see that the failure of the democratic movement in

Europe in 1848 was one of the most decisive happenings in modern history; it helped shape the course not only of the nineteenth century but also that of the twentieth.

Turning to the international scene, a significant phenomenon in European history between 1815 and 1848 was the Congress System. Although the ends it sought were the prevention of change and the extinction of liberty and although its effectiveness was short-lived, yet the Congress System—the first serious attempt to solve problems by international cooperation—represented a positive step forward. It established a precedent for personal consultations among statesmen on common problems.

Symbolizing the revolutionary era in Europe from 1815 to 1848 were the barricades and Metternich. In recent years some historians have been more kind in evaluating the Austrian statesman than were his contemporaries. Appalled by the chaos and conflict of the twentieth century, which they attribute to breakneck change, the fanaticism of nationalism, and the frequently emotional basis of politics in twentieth-century mass democracy, these scholars see a praiseworthy stability in the conservative system championed by Metternich from 1815 to 1848. Yet a complete absence of change is no better than too much change. Metternich cannot be placed in the category of the world's greatest statesmen. His tragic weakness was that he failed to allow for any growth or change in Europe's political institutions; he failed to understand that the art of real statesmanship must provide for the attempt to bring together, in reasonable equilibrium, the best of the old forces and the most promising of the new. As a British historian has observed: "He saw no mean between revolution and autocracy, and since revolution was odious, he set himself to repress that which is the soul of human life in society, the very spirit of liberty."[5]

SUGGESTIONS FOR READING

A. J. May, *The Age of Metternich, 1814-1848,** Holt (Berkshire Studies). A good, brief survey of the events described in this chapter. F. B. Artz, *Reaction and Revolution, 1814-1832,* Harper, 1934, a volume in *The Rise of Modern Europe* series, is unsurpassed as a synthesis of all aspects of European history and culture during the first half of the Age of Metternich.

H. G. Nicolson, *The Congress of Vienna: A Study in Allied Unity, 1812-1822,** Compass. Entertaining and valuable account of the Congress and the Congress System; written for the general reader. C. K. Webster, *The Congress of Vienna, 1814-1815,* P. Smith, 1934, is the standard account of the Congress.

Interesting reading on Metternich and his influence are H. Kissinger, *A World Restored: Metternich, Castlereagh and the Problems of Peace, 1812-1822,* Houghton Mifflin, 1957; E. L. Woodward, *Three Studies in European Conservatism,* Constable, 1929, which includes essays on Guizot and the Catholic Church; and P. Viereck, *Conservatism Revisited: The Revolt Against Revolt,* Scribner's, 1949, a reëvaluation of Metternich by a modern conservative antithetic to the philosophy of liberalism.

A. Cobban, *A History of Modern France,** II, Penguin. A valuable general survey of the period from 1800 to 1940.

D. W. Brogan, *The French Nation from Napoleon to Pétain, 1814-1940,* Harper, 1957, is lively, witty, but not always easy reading.

J. Plamenatz, *The Revolutionary Movement in France, 1815-1871,* Longmans, 1952. A short survey which holds that revolutions are caused by the avoidable failures of government rather than by the discontent of the governed.

J. Lucas-Dubreton, *The Restoration and the July Monarchy,* Putnam, 1929. A comprehensive study of the post-Napoleonic period in France. Also valuable on this period is R. Soltau, *French Political Thought in the Nineteenth Century,* Russell and Russell, 1959.

F. A. Simpson, *The Rise of Louis Napoleon,* Longmans, 1925. A comprehensive study of Napoleon III's early struggles.

D. Thompson, *England in the Nineteenth Century, 1815-1914,** Penguin. An excellent short survey with social and economic change as its major theme.

E. L. Woodward, *The Age of Reform, 1815-1870,* Oxford, 1938. Political, social, economic, and intellectual aspects of the period are smoothly integrated in this authoritative volume in the *Oxford History of England* series. G. M. Trevelyan, *British History in the Nineteenth Century and After, 1782-1919,* Longmans, 1938, is one of the best accounts of this extended period. E. Halévy, *A History of the English People*

in the Nineteenth Century,** 6 vols., Barnes and Noble, is the most comprehensive survey and is considered a classic.

R. J. White, *Waterloo to Peterloo,* Macmillan, 1957. A fresh approach to the troubled postwar period in England which culminated in the Peterloo massacre at Manchester in 1819. See also D. Read, *Peterloo: The "Massacre" and Its Background,* Barnes and Noble, 1958.

G. L. Strachey, *Queen Victoria,* Harbrace Modern Classics, 1949. A classic of modern biography.

A. J. P. Taylor, *The Course of German History,* Coward-McCann, 1946. A well-written, objective essay on German nationalism since 1815. The following are readable textbook surveys of modern German history: R. Flenley, *Modern German History,* Dutton, 1953; K. S. Pinson, *Modern Germany, Its History and Civilization,* Macmillan, 1954; and V. Valentin, *The German People, Their History and Civilization from the Holy Roman Empire to the Third Reich,* Knopf, 1946.

A. J. P. Taylor, *The Habsburg Monarchy, 1809-1918,* Macmillan, 1949. A concise, spirited, and well-organized survey.

A. J. B. Whyte, *The Evolution of Modern Italy, 1715-1920,* Macmillan, 1951; R. Albrecht-Carrié, *Italy from Napoleon to Mussolini,* Columbia Univ., 1950. Two excellent general histories.

G. O. Griffith, *Mazzini: Prophet of Modern Europe,* Hodder, 1932; E. Hales, *Mazzini and the Secret Societies,* Kennedy, 1956. Noteworthy treatments of this zealous, romantic Italian nationalist.

Stendhal (pseud. of Marie Henri Beyle), *The Charterhouse of Parma,** Penguin. Opening with a brilliant description of the battle of Waterloo, this novel presents a panorama of post-Napoleonic Italy and life at a reactionary court.

G. E. Mylonas, *The Balkan States: An Introduction to Their History,* Public Affairs Press, 1947. A useful, brief survey of Balkan history from the time of the Ottoman conquest.

C. M. Woodhouse, *The Greek War of Independence,* Longmans (Hutchinson Univ. Library), 1952. Excellent short study, written with imagination and insight.

R. Postgate, *Story of a Year: 1848,* Oxford, 1956. With consummate skill, the author gives a lively play-by-play account of the events in the western world during this crucial year. A more thematic treatment is offered by P. Robertson, *Revolutions of 1848: A Social History,** Torchbooks. L. B. Namier, *1848: The Revolution of the Intellectuals,* Oxford, 1946, is a brilliant essay criticizing the failure of the liberals.

M. Kranzberg, ed., *1848: A Turning Point?** Heath. A valuable collection of the differing views of modern scholars as to the meaning and significance of the 1848 revolutions; affords insight into the complicated nature of historical change and the problems of historical interpretation. See also G. Bruun, *Revolution and Reaction, 1848-1852: A Mid-Century Watershed,** Anvil, which is half text and half documents.

*Indicates an inexpensive paperbound edition.

CHAPTER 22

Nationalism and the Making of Nations

Introduction. From roughly 1850 to 1870 the spirit of nationalism was in the ascendant; not only in Europe but all over the world, existing national states sought to increase their power and prestige, new national states fought their way into existence, and national movements, surviving crushing setbacks, gathered strength for renewed revolts against foreign domination. The triumphs and failures of national movements in the non-European world will be discussed in Chapters 25 and 26. This chapter deals with the course of European politics and the significant changes in the power structure of Europe during this crucial twenty-year period.

Divided Italy, so long merely a "geographical expression," at last achieved national unification. Under Prussian rule, the German states were welded into an empire. France, stirred to nationalistic

fervor by its memories of an earlier Napoleon, supported Napoleon III in his quest for new glories for the "mistress of Europe." Austria achieved an uneasy unity as the Germans of Vienna and the Magyars of Budapest joined forces to check the aspirations of other nationalities in the creaky Hapsburg empire.

This era of nation-making is important not only for what happened but also for the attitudes of those involved. Political objectives were neither confused with the romantic dreams of poets nor modeled on the utopias imagined by idealistic intellectuals. Instead, they were practical goals, ruthlessly pursued by such practical statesmen as Bismarck and Cavour.

Generally speaking, nationalism and nation-making in mid-nineteenth-century Europe was a bloody business. From 1815 to 1848 no single major conflict occurred. But from the midpoint of the century to the 1870's, six wars were fought—some of major proportions. Within this period, every major European power went to war at least once. These conflicts swept away the settlements created at Vienna in 1815. The smashing defeat of France in the Franco-Prussian War (1870-1871) marked the demise of the Second French Empire and heralded the rise of the new German empire to a position of supremacy among the countries on the Continent.

Meanwhile, democracy also made headway, though its progress was by no means so spectacular as that of nationalism. Its major European advance was marked by the passage of the second Reform Bill in Great Britain in 1867. As we shall see in Chapter 23, democracy's great upsurge was to come in the last quarter of the century.

Finally, this chapter deals with a survey of Russian history from 1815 to 1878, when the Congress of Berlin temporarily frustrated Russian imperialism in the Near East. Throughout the nineteenth century, a prime objective of Russia's tsars was to partition the dominions of the Turks, seize Constantinople, and gain access to the eastern Mediterranean. This ambition was persistently blocked by British diplomacy and British arms. The conflict between the great powers—especially the rivalry between Russia and England—over the holdings of the decaying Ottoman empire came to be known as the Near Eastern Question. This international issue was complicated by continuing Balkan unrest under Ottoman rule. The Near Eastern Question has continued into the twentieth century, becoming critical once again in the years following World War II. The Russians, whether tsarists or Communists, have never abandoned their plans to one day gain control of the Turkish Straits and extend their rule to the shores of the Mediterranean Sea.

NATION-MAKING IN ITALY

Common denominators in Italian and German unification. The two most important achievements of nineteenth-century European nationalism were the unifications of Italy and Germany. In the case of both, there was a dynamic nucleus—Sardinia in Italy and Prussia in Germany—around which a nation was built. Both Italy and Germany had a common obstacle to national unity—Austria, since 1815 master of central Europe. In the case of Italian unification, however, a special complication was the existence of the Papal States ruled from Rome by the pope. The Italian nationalists were faced with the problem of stripping this great religious leader of his secular powers and absorbing his territories into a united Italy without incurring the wrath of the Catholic powers in Europe.

Both the German and Italian unifications were ultimately achieved not by romantic poets or intellectuals but by the dispassionate calculations of practical statesmen who exercised the art of diplomacy divorced from ethical considerations. This kind of statecraft is known as *Realpolitik;* in Germany it became identified with the policy that Bismarck called "blood and iron."

Count Cavour. In the early part of the 1850's, Italy still remained what Metternich had contemptuously called it—"a geographical expression." The Young Italy movement of Mazzini and the first phase of the *Risorgimento* had failed. Except in Sardinia, where young King Victor Emmanuel II refused to abrogate the liberal constitution granted by his late father, Charles Albert, there was reaction and repression. This victory of autocracy, however, was more apparent than real. Mazzini's appeal for a free Italy had taken root and proceeded to grow quietly but rapidly in the decade following 1848.

A new and vigorous phase of the Italian *Risorgimento* began with the career of Count Camillo Benso di Cavour (1810-1861), one of the most important statesmen of the nineteenth century. Born of a noble family in Sardinia, Cavour was educated for a military career, but after traveling in Switzerland, France, and England, he became a thoroughgoing liberal and began to ponder on how best to free Italy from Austrian domination. In 1852 Cavour became prime minister of Sardinia. Well aware that Sardinia alone could not oust the Austrians from the Italian peninsula, Cavour determined to "put Sardinia on the map," hoping to find an ally for his cause.

His first move astonished Europe; in 1855 Sardinia joined Britain and France in their fight against Russia in the Crimean War (see p. 538). Although this step at first appeared ridiculous, it enabled Cavour to make a speech calling attention to the grievances of Italy at the peace conference one year later.

The Austro-Italian War. Cavour's speech impressed Napoleon III, who was to become the ally Cavour was seeking. In 1858 the emperor of the French and Cavour held a secret meeting in France. It was agreed that if Cavour could trick Austria into war, France would come to Sardinia's assistance and help eject Austria from the Italian provinces of Lombardy and Venetia. Sardinia was then to rule over all of northern Italy. In return, France would receive from Sardinia two provinces—Nice and Savoy—which had been part of France during the Napoleonic period.

Within a year Cavour had tricked Austria into war by blowing up into major proportions a minor crisis over the conscription of soldiers from Lombardy and Venetia for the Austrian army. He offered sanctuary to Italian deserters and began to mobilize the Sardinian army—moves which prompted Austria to attack. Two bloody battles were fought at Magenta and Solferino, and the Austrian troops were driven out of Lombardy by Sardinian and French soldiers. Again, the call for Italian unity was heard across the land. Revolutions broke out in Tuscany, Modena, Parma, and Romagna.

During the progress of the fighting, Napoleon III was acclaimed by Italians as their savior and liberator. But before the allied armies could invade Austrian-held Venetia, the French emperor—without consulting Cavour—made a separate peace with Austria. Too late, Napoleon III realized that he had started a movement destined to unite not only northern Italy but the whole peninsula, creating a strong rival on the borders of France. He also suspected that Cavour had designs against the Papal States, a policy which would alienate the support of the French Catholics.

Although Cavour was furious, in 1859 he agreed to a peace settlement with Austria by

Cavour was not the sole creator of the *Risorgimento*, but he gave direction to the Italian dream of unity, transforming it into a disciplined, practical program. Two months before his death, he saw his life's work culminate in the proclamation of Victor Emmanuel II as king of a united Italy.

which Lombardy was added to Sardinia, the exiled rulers of Parma, Modena, Tuscany, and Romagna were restored, and an Italian confederation was created in which Austria, as ruler of Venetia, was included. One year later, largely through the auspices of Great Britain, plebiscites were conducted in Italy. Tuscany, Modena, and Parma voted to join Sardinia. French expectations were satisfied when Nice and Savoy were ceded to France.

Garibaldi and his Red Shirts. The center of interest now shifted to southern Italy and to a new Italian leader. Giuseppe Garibaldi (1807-1882), a follower of Mazzini who had been forced into exile after the unsuccessful revolutionary movement of 1848, returned to Italy in 1854. Secretly subsidized by Cavour, Garibaldi recruited one thousand tough adventurers, his immortal Red Shirts, and in 1860 successfully invaded and conquered the island of Sicily, part of the reactionary, pro-Austrian kingdom of Naples and Sicily. Next he turned to the mainland and attacked the remaining forces of the king of Naples and Sicily. The Neapolitan troops were not loyal, and Garibaldi easily conquered the kingdom, entering Naples in triumph.

Garibaldi planned to set up a separate democratic government, which would have been a serious obstacle to the creation of a united Italy. Cavour therefore rushed troops to Naples, and Garibaldi surrendered his power to the king of Sardinia, Victor Emmanuel II. By November 1860, Sardinia had annexed the former kingdom of Naples and Sicily and all the papal lands except Rome and its surrounding territory, known as the Patrimony of St. Peter.

Garibaldi was a romantic nationalist and a daredevil adventurer, but he had little of the diplomat in him. Without realizing the

UNIFICATION OF ITALY

SAVOY
(To France 1860)

LOMBARDY
1859

VENETIA
1866

PIEDMONT

PARMA

MODENA

ROMAGNA

NICE
(To France 1860)

TUSCANY

PAPAL
STATES

Rome
1870

SARDINIA

KINGDOM OF

NAPLES

AND

SICILY

Kingdom of Sardinia 1815

1860 Additions

political danger of his action, the conqueror of Naples resolved to attack the territories still under papal rule and force them to come into a united Italian kingdom. Cavour knew that such a move would alienate Catholics all over the world and probably precipitate war with France, since Napoleon III had stationed troops at Rome to protect the pope. To avoid the danger, Sardinian troops in 1862 forcibly restrained the Garibaldian volunteers from attacking Rome. This action disgusted Garibaldi, who had little use for high diplomacy. Refusing all the financial rewards and honors proffered him by Victor Emmanuel, he sailed once more into exile.

Unity achieved. Italy's first parliament met at Turin in February 1861. A new nation of 22,000,000 citizens had been created, but the task had not yet been completed. Austria still controlled Venetia, while Rome and the Patrimony of St. Peter were still under papal control. Cavour, who died in 1861, did not live to see the full fruits of his works, but he realized that a united Italy was not far off. Although many have criticized his duplicity, he himself made no attempt to hide the true nature of his methods. He once said: "If we did for ourselves what we do for our country, what rascals we should be."[1]

By acting as an ally of Prussia during the war between Prussia and Austria in 1866 (see p. 528), Italy obtained Venetia. And when the Franco-Prussian War broke out in 1870 and French troops were withdrawn from Rome, Italian troops took possession of the Eternal City. In 1871 Rome became the capital of a united Italy.

THE TRIUMPH OF BLOOD
AND IRON IN GERMANY

Prussia and the German nationalistic movement. Although the German revolution of 1848 and the Frankfurt Assembly failed to achieve their liberal-national purposes, the nationalist movement in Germany was far from dead. German nationalism was accelerated by the activities of a group of remarkable German historians. Such scholars as Heinrich von

Although his dream of an Italian republic was not realized, Giuseppe Garibaldi has remained a national hero because of his fight for the unification of Italy.

Treitschke saw in the Italian struggle a clear example to follow; Treitschke eloquently advocated the union of all Germans under the leadership of Prussia:

There is only one salvation! One state, one monarchic Germany under the Hohenzollern dynasty.[2]

Economic factors also proved to be significant in the German unification movement. Of special importance was the Zollverein, or customs union, established in 1834, which instituted free trade throughout Prussia and the territories of other member states. By 1842 most of the German states belonged to the Zollverein. This tariff union not only demonstrated that closer economic cooperation was good business for the various states but also strengthened the position of the middle-class leaders of the German nationalist movement. Most important, by increasing the economic ties between the German states, the Zollverein made easier their political unity under Prussia. (All members of the Zollverein except Luxemburg eventually became part of the German empire.) Austria, on the other hand, remained aloof from the Zollverein, not appreciating its political significance and its implied menace to Hapsburg dominance.

Prussian government and public administration were modern and efficient. Civil servants were well trained, honest, and highly devoted to the service of the state. The hierarchy of government bureaus and departments was logical and functional. By the middle of the century, the general citizenry of Prussia attended public schools far in advance of those found in any of the other great powers, including the United States; and Prussian higher education enjoyed an enviable reputation throughout Europe. Prussia by 1850 was rapidly building up the strength to compel central Europe to do its bidding, but it was twelve years before there appeared the man who was to formulate the necessary orders.

Bismarck and his policy of blood and iron. The unification of Germany was achieved through the genius of a consummate statesman, Otto von Bismarck (1815-1898). The future German chancellor grew up a typical Prussian aristocrat, or Junker, an enemy to all liberal ideas and a fanatical supporter of the Prussian state and its king. As a university student, Bismarck made little impression on his professors but astonished his comrades by his beer-drinking capacity and gained renown as a duelist. In 1847 he entered politics and found this career to his liking. Soon he joined the diplomatic corps and carried out valuable missions in St. Petersburg and in Paris.

In 1862 Bismarck was called to be chancellor. His appointment coincided with a serious crisis: the king wished to strengthen the army, but the legislature would not approve the necessary appropriations. Following Bismarck's advice, the king successfully defied the parliament and levied the necessary taxes without its consent.

With meticulous care Bismarck prepared for the task of building a powerful new German empire. Not only was he a superb master of diplomatic intrigue, but he worshiped force. Boldly, he declared:

Germany does not look to Prussia's liberalism, but to her power. . . . The great questions of the day are not to be decided by speeches and majority resolutions—therein lay the weakness of 1848 and 1849—but by blood and iron![3]

Wars against Denmark and Austria. In 1864 Bismarck invited Austria to join Prussia in waging war on Denmark, the issue being the status of two duchies bordering on Prussia and Denmark—Schleswig and Holstein—which were claimed by both Denmark and the German Confederation. The Prussian army, aided by Austrian forces, easily smashed the Danish defenses; the administration of Holstein was awarded to Austria, while Schleswig came under Prussian rule.

Once Denmark had been defeated, Bismarck next proceeded to isolate Austria, for until Austria's influence was removed from the German Confederation, Prussia could never unify Germany. Sardinia was promised Venetia if it would assist Prussia when war came, and the French emperor was induced to be neutral by intimations of Prussian support should France seek to widen its frontiers.

Bismarck provoked war with Austria without difficulty. He expressed alarm over the way the Austrians were ruling Holstein and sent Prussian troops into the province. Hostilities broke out in 1866 and lasted only seven weeks. At the battle of Sadowa the Austrian army was defeated by superior Prussian forces, which had been made into the most efficient fighting machine in the world. To avoid humiliating Austria, Prussia offered a moderate peace settlement, ending the old German Confederation. In its place the North German Confederation was formed under Prussian domination, with Austria and four southern German states excluded. The province of Holstein was annexed by Prussia. (See map, p. 530.)

DOWNFALL OF THE SECOND

FRENCH EMPIRE

Prosperity without liberty under Napoleon III. At this point in our narrative, it is essential to discuss the chief barrier between Bismarck and his twin objectives—a greater Germany and German mastery of western Europe. This obstacle was the Second French Empire of Napoleon III, which since its establishment in 1852 had prospered in both domestic and foreign affairs. In fact, the successful outcome of two wars, the Crimean War and the Austro-Italian War (p. 525), had made France by 1860 the mistress of Europe. Over a period of eighteen years, Napoleon III, the "emperor boss," gave his realm glory, prosperity, and, above all, order and discipline—nearly everything a great nation could desire, in fact, except liberty. Although the governmental structure retained the outward forms of a parliamentary regime, the suffrage was juggled to give the supporters of the emperor a safe majority in the legislature—which had little power anyway. An efficient secret police was established to hunt down "dangerous elements," the press was censored, and parliamentary debates were given no publicity.

But if the France of Napoleon III lacked liberty, it did enjoy prosperity. Large-scale industries and corporations developed, and in two decades production doubled. France sponsored the building of the famous Suez Canal (1859-1869), railway mileage increased fivefold, and steamship lines prospered. An ambitious program of public works was undertaken. Paris was transformed by broad boulevards and harmonious architecture.

Successes and failures in foreign affairs. Napoleon III thought of himself as the first servant of the empire, devoted to the task of making the state prosperous and progressive. But though he was a man of peace, he was heir to the Napoleonic legend. He had no choice but to pursue a spirited role in international affairs.

For ten years the foreign policy of Napoleon III was remarkably successful. Ally-

A skillful diplomat and a ruthless advocate of military might, Otto von Bismarck engineered the unification of the German state

ing France with England in the Crimean War, he gained the desired victory against Russia and appeared at the peace conference as the arbiter of Europe. In 1859 his support of Cavour in Italy against Austria earned him military glory and gained Nice and Savoy for France. Furthermore, during this period the empire expanded its colonial possessions, cooperated with England in a successful war against China, and intervened to safeguard the interests of Christians under Turkish rule in Syria.

In the 1860's, however, Napoleon seemed to lose his touch in foreign affairs, and the morale of the Second Empire declined rapidly. In 1863, while the United States was distracted by civil war, Napoleon III embroiled France in the madcap scheme of placing Maximilian, a Hapsburg prince, on the Mexican throne. Some forty thousand troops were involved in

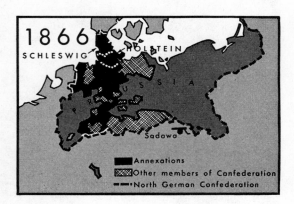

Formed after the Austro-Prussian War, the North German Confederation was dominated by Prussia and excluded Austria and
four southern German states. Prussia's two new acquisitions
were Schleswig, gained in the war with Denmark in 1864, and
Holstein, ceded by Austria in 1866.

this expensive adventure, which ended in the
withdrawal of the French forces and the capture and execution of Maximilian by Mexican patriots (see Chapter 25). Discontent increased at home when Napoleon III in 1863
failed to intervene in Poland on the side of the
patriotic rebels who had risen against Russian
rule.

Again in 1865, Napoleon III in a fateful
conference with Bismarck allowed himself
to be completely hoodwinked. In return for
vague promises, in which the German statesman mentioned securing for France "perhaps the Palatinate and the Rhine frontier,
perhaps Luxemburg, perhaps part of Belgium or Switzerland,"[4] the French emper-
or pledged himself not to interfere in any
Austro-Prussian war. After the conflict had
been decided by the Prussian victory at
Sadowa, Bismarck announced that he had no
recollection of promises made to France. Napoleon III thereupon specifically raised the
possibility of French compensation at the expense of Belgium, and an agreement was
drawn up in which Bismarck backed this
claim in return for French recognition of the
federal union of all German states. The chancellor next saw to it that the document was
made public in England, the nation where it
would do the most harm to France. The British became openly hostile to Napoleon III, and

Bismarck thus made certain that there would
be no British support of France in case of
war. At the same time, by supporting Russia
during the Polish revolt in 1863 and by offering Austria a moderate peace in 1866, Bismarck successfully isolated these two states
from France.

The Franco-Prussian War. Too late, Napoleon realized that a great rival power
was in the making. No longer would it
be possible for France to dominate Europe.
"Revenge for Sadowa" became a common
cry in France.

Bismarck also welcomed war. He was
convinced that Napoleon's need to recoup
his prestige would lead finally to his undoing. It was also Bismarck's belief that a war
with France would stimulate a common patriotism in the hearts of all Germans, irrespective of the state in which they lived.

The immediate cause of the war centered
about the succession to the Spanish throne,
left vacant after the exile of the Spanish
queen. The throne was offered to Leopold, a
Hohenzollern prince. In the eyes of the French
government, a Prussian on the throne of Spain
would be an unwelcome extension of Prussian influence. Because of French protests,
Leopold withdrew his candidacy, but the
French government then made a fatal mistake. The French ambassador was sent to
Ems, where the Prussian king was visiting, to
demand that William I promise that no Hohenzollern would ever sit on the Spanish
throne. The king politely refused this unreasonable request and directed that a dispatch
(the "Ems dispatch") be sent to Bismarck ac-
quainting him with the results of the interview. Bismarck altered the dispatch slightly in
order to give the impression that the French
ambassador had insulted the Prussian king
and that the ruler had thereupon retaliated
and insulted the ambassador. When this version of the dispatch was published, both the
French and the Prussian people were infuriated.

France declared war in July 1870, and
amid wild enthusiasm and shouts of "On to
Berlin," the French regiments marched to
the front. But there was no comparison be-

tween the superbly trained Prussian hosts and the badly disorganized French army. The French suffered reverse after reverse. In September came the crowning disaster—the surrender at Sedan, where an entire French army and the emperor himself were forced to capitulate. Thus the glory of the Second French Empire and the power of its creator, Napoleon III, perished on the battlefield just as the empire of his uncle, Napoleon, had disintegrated before the unbending squares of British infantry at Waterloo.

News of this debacle swept the discredited Second Empire from power, and a republic was proclaimed in Paris. New leaders emerged to carry on resistance against the German forces, and Paris withstood a siege of four months before surrendering. By the Treaty of Frankfurt, France lost Alsace and part of Lorraine to Prussia and was required to pay a huge indemnity. Many Frenchmen never forgot this humiliation. History was to give France a chance to retaliate after World War I.

The unification of Germany completed. During the Franco-Prussian War the southern German states had joined the North German Confederation. Thus the common struggle against France removed the last obstacle to national unification. In January 1871, in the Hall of Mirrors at the palace of Versailles, King William of Prussia was proclaimed German emperor.

Bismarck's most important work was completed by 1871, although he remained chancellor of the German empire until 1890. To achieve his ends, he had used ruthless means. But perhaps, as in the case of Cavour, he felt that circumstances left him no alternative. It was a tragedy for the world that to Bismarck blood and iron seemed essential in forging a united Germany, for his successes strengthened the notion that war is a national business that can be made to pay big dividends. Furthermore, from the time that Bismarck defied the will of the Prussian parliament in 1862, there was no opportunity for German public opinion to unseat the executive or to control governmental policy. The German state was now

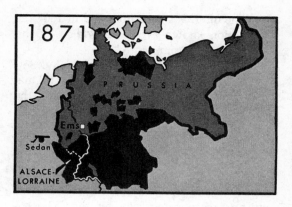

The unification of Germany was completed during the Franco-Prussian War, when the southern German states joined the North German Confederation. Alsace and part of Lorraine were acquired from France by the Treaty of Frankfurt.

thoroughly set in a pattern of despotic government even though it retained its constitutional forms. This situation continued until the end of the Hohenzollern dynasty in 1918.

FORMATION OF THE DUAL MONARCHY

Weakening of the Austrian empire. The military triumphs of Prussia had important repercussions in Austria. Vienna realized at last that if the Austrian empire was to survive, Hungarian nationalism would have to be appeased. But, though willing to grant constitutional government to Hungary, German liberals and reformers in Austria had no sympathy for the Hungarian desire for independence and wished to have a single parliament for the whole empire. As a result, in 1861, a year after local self-government had been restored in Hungary and German officials had been removed, a new imperial constitution was framed in which representatives were to be elected from the various provincial parliaments to a central, imperial Diet. The Hungarians would have nothing to do with these measures, and the country seemed on the verge of revolt. Finally the Austrian emperor offered to establish the Magyars as equal partners in ruling the empire. The offer was accepted, and in 1867 the constitution known as the *Ausgleich* (Compromise) was promulgated.

Establishment of the Dual Monarchy. Setting up a unique form of government, a Dual Monarchy known as Austria-Hungary, the *Ausgleich* made the Hapsburg sovereign king in Hungary and emperor in Austria. Each country had its own constitution, official language, flag, and parliament, but finance, defense, and foreign affairs were under ministers common to both countries. These common ministers were supervised by the "Delegations," which consisted of sixty members from the Austrian parliament and an equal number of representatives from the Hungarian legislature.

While the Germans of Austria recognized the equality of the Magyars of Hungary, these two dominant nationalities made few concessions to the aspirations of their subject nationalities. In Chapter 23 we shall see how the restlessness of the subject peoples in Austria-Hungary became enmeshed with a Pan-Slav movement sponsored by Serbia and Russia—a movement which threatened the very existence of the Austrian empire. Nationalism was ultimately to prove the undoing of Austria-Hungary and to involve Europe in the First World War.

NEW ERA OF REFORM

IN GREAT BRITAIN

End of the Victorian Compromise. The period from 1832—the year in which the first Reform Bill was passed—to 1865 is often described as the era of the Victorian Compromise. During this period, an alliance of the landed gentry and the middle class worked together to dominate the government and keep the lower classes "in their stations." The members of the middle class believed that the political reforms—which had been in large measure of benefit to them alone—had gone far enough. Although some social reforms were granted, they were exceptions in the general atmosphere of middle-class complacency.

The symbol of this conservatism was Lord Palmerston, who dominated the direction of foreign affairs from the 1830's until his death and ended his career by acting as prime minister during much of the period from 1855 to 1865. Himself a viscount, he was quite satisfied with the rule of the aristocracy and the middle class.

Gladstone and Disraeli. The death of Palmerston in 1865 and the entry of two new political leaders into the limelight heralded the beginning of a new era in British affairs. For a generation, English politics was little more than the biographies of William Ewart Gladstone (1809-1898), a Liberal, and Benjamin Disraeli (1804-1881), a Conservative, who alternated with one another as prime minister from 1867 to 1880. Following the death of Disraeli, Gladstone continued to dominate politics until his retirement in 1894.

The son of a rich Liverpool merchant, Gladstone had every advantage that wealth and good social position could bestow. Entering Parliament in 1833 at age twenty-four, the young politician quickly made a name for himself as one of the greatest orators of his day, on one occasion holding the attention of the House of Commons for five hours while he expounded the intricacies of the national budget. At first Gladstone was a conservative in politics, a follower of the Tory leader Robert Peel. But gradually he shifted his allegiance to the Liberal (Whig) party, which he headed for the first time as prime minister in 1868. Gladstone was a stanch supporter of laissez faire, the belief that government should not interfere in business. His record as a social and economic reformer, therefore, was not imposing. But in political reforms his accomplishments were noteworthy.

The great rival of Gladstone, Benjamin Disraeli, had few advantages of birth and social position. The son of a cultured Jew who had become a naturalized British subject in 1801, Disraeli was baptized an Anglican. He first made a name for himself as a novelist with *Vivian Grey* (1826). Unlike Gladstone, Disraeli swung from liberalism to conservatism in his political philosophy; he stood for office as a Conservative throughout his career and eventually became the leader of the Conservative (Tory) party.

The Reform Bill of 1867. By 1865 it was obvious that the Victorian Compromise could not be maintained any longer. English workmen had formed large organizations to agitate for liberalization of voting. Both the new Conservative party, drawing its strength mainly from the landowning gentry, and the Liberals, supported by the middle class, realized that reform must come.

It was Gladstone's turn first. While not actually prime minister as yet, Gladstone in 1866 introduced a moderate reform bill giving the vote to city laborers. His proposal failed to pass, however, and the country was rocked by agitation and riots. The Conservatives then came into power. Hoping to secure wider support for his party, Disraeli in 1867 successfully sponsored another reform bill that added a little more than a million city workers to the voting rolls. (In 1832 the electorate had been increased 50 per cent; in 1867 it was increased by 88 per cent.) Although women and farm laborers still could not vote, Britain was well on the road to political democracy. These reforms were not effected without arousing considerable conservative opposition, however. The famous Victorian writer Thomas Carlyle called the reform movement "Shooting Niagara," and another critic dolefully predicted:

The bag which holds the winds will be untied, and we shall be surrounded by a perpetual whirl of change, alteration, innovation, and revolution.[5]

Gladstone's "Glorious Ministry." An election held at the end of the year 1867 brought Gladstone and the Liberals back to power. Gladstone's so-called "Glorious Ministry," which was to last from 1868 to 1874, was one of great achievements.

With the enfranchisement of the city masses, it became imperative that their children be given an education. The Education Act of 1870 made possible the setting up of local school boards authorized to build and maintain government schools. Fees

Unlike his opponent Gladstone, the Conservative leader Disraeli never appeared self-righteous. A man of the world, he enlivened British politics with his wit and sarcasm.

could be charged (they were not abolished until 1891), and attendance could be made compulsory from the age of five to thirteen. Subsidies from the government were given to the private schools, which were required to meet certain minimum standards. In ten years, attendance in elementary schools jumped from one million to four million.

In the governmental and military administrations, most appointments and promotions had traditionally depended upon patronage and favoritism. In 1870 employment in the British civil service was finally based upon open examinations of a highly intellectual character. Thoroughgoing changes were also introduced by the war office. The terms of enlistment were improved, and flogging as a military punishment in peacetime was abolished. Above all, the purchase of commissions was eliminated. Up to this

The Liberal leader Gladstone was deeply religious and serious in manner and speech. If he ran short of logic, he found it easy to enlist the aid of God, thus attempting to place his opponents in an unchristian position. Gladstone's oratory—though eloquent and logical at its best—tended to be wordy and involved and devoid of humor.

time an officer's rank had been his own personal property that could be sold to the highest bidder.

Another long-needed change was the reform of the legal system and the courts, which made justice surer and speedier in Britain. The Ballot Act of 1872 establishing secret balloting was another Gladstone reform; no longer would open balloting expose the workers to pressure from their employers, landlords, and others.

One more area felt the reforming zeal of the Liberal prime minister—Ireland. We shall discuss the long history of the Irish problem and Gladstone's efforts to find a solution for it in Chapter 23.

RUSSIA UNDER

UNENLIGHTENED DESPOTISM

The Decembrist Revolt. Following the defeat of Napoleon, Tsar Alexander I (1801-1825) had been ready to discuss constitutional reforms, but though a few were introduced, no thoroughgoing changes in tsarist despotism were attempted. The pseudo-liberal tsar was followed by his younger brother Nicholas I (1825-1855), who at the outset of his reign was confronted by an uprising.

This revolt had an interesting background. During the Napoleonic Wars a number of well-educated Russian officers traveled in Europe in the course of the military campaigns, some of them ending their peregrinations in Paris with the army of allied occupation. Exposure to the liberalism of western Europe whetted their appetite for reform back home.

The result was the so-called Decembrist Revolt (December 1825)—the work of a small circle of liberal nobles and army officers who wanted to overthrow the autocracy. The revolt was easily quashed and those involved were cruelly punished, five being executed and over five hundred exiled to Siberia. This harsh retaliation made "December Fourteenth" a day long remembered and the inspiration for later revolutionary movements. It also made Tsar Nicholas ultrasensitive to revolution and liberalism. In consequence he turned away from the Europeanization program begun by Peter the Great and Catherine the Great and championed the idea of Russian self-sufficiency.

Repression under Nicholas I. Under the reactionary Nicholas System, Russia became "frozen." Foreign visitors were carefully screened, and those with "dangerous ideas" were halted at the border. Foreign books were not permitted if they contained any tincture of liberalism. Even musical compositions were checked to see if the notes were a secret code. Schools and universities were placed under constant surveillance, and the students were provided with official textbooks. Police spies were everywhere. Would-be revolutionaries and often quite harmless liberals were packed off to Siberia; from 1832 to 1852 an estimated 150,000 persons were exiled there. A measure of the effect of this repressive system on Russian intellectual life can be gained by noting that in 1843 all Russian journals had a combined subscription of only 12,000 and that there were less than 5000 college students at that time. The tsar had a special fear of the intellectuals, who might be "perverted by foreign ideas."

The Polish revolution of 1830. As we saw in Chapter 21, it was during Nicholas' reign that the Polish nationalist revolution of 1830 occurred. Under Alexander I, Russian Poland had been made a separate state having its own institutions but owing allegiance to the tsar. A constitution granted by Alexander in 1815 set up a government which was headed by an agent of the tsar and which included a representative legislature dominated by the Polish nobility. Freedom of religion was guaranteed, liberty of the press was promised, and Poland was allowed to retain its national flag and a Polish army under the command of Alexander's brother.

But this liberal settlement did not satisfy the Poles, who wanted nothing less than national independence. In 1830, inspired by the events in France and Belgium, the Polish army in Warsaw revolted, but factionalism among the Poles and the superior military strength of Russia brought an end to the revolution after almost a year of fighting.

The treatment of Poland after the revolution was quite in keeping with the Nicholas System in Russia proper. Poland was reduced to a Russian province, and every attempt was made to stamp out Polish nationalism. Russian was made the language of administration and the courts, Polish universities were closed, Polish soldiers were placed in Russian regiments, and a hostile policy

was inaugurated against Roman Catholicism, the leading faith in Poland.

The Ideological Schism. Heavy-handed repression by Nicholas did not stifle the desire of Russian intellectuals for knowledge. One of them called this period "an amazing time of outward slavery and inner liberation." Liberals and reformers met in secret and argued during the long winter nights about freedom, the merits of parliamentary government, and the part Russia should play in world history.

The question of Russia's destiny had been brewing ever since Peter the Great's program of westernization had been put into operation early in the eighteenth century (see Chapter 18). Which path should Russia follow? Should it imitate Europe or renounce the West and return to the traditions of its past? The first road was championed by the so-called Westerners; the second by the Slavophiles, who heaped scorn on the "decadent" West. One Slavophile wrote:

In Europe the principle of personality is supreme; with us it is the communal principle. Europe is pagan, Russia—holy Christian. In the West reigns apparent liberty, a liberty like that of a wild animal in the desert. The true liberty is found among us, in the East.[6]

These Slavophiles preferred the historic communism of the Russian *mir*, or village community, to what they regarded as the dog-eat-dog individualism of the West. It should be pointed out here that present-day communism in Soviet Russia owes a debt to such age-old social patterns as the *mir* as well as to the doctrines of Karl Marx.

Alexander II abolishes serfdom. Tsar Nicholas died with his philosophy in disrepute. In 1854 Russia had become involved in the Crimean War, a conflict fought primarily in the Crimean peninsula (see p. 538). Since playing a major role in the defeat of Napoleon, Russia had been regarded as militarily invincible, but the reverses it suffered on land and sea in the Crimean War, the blunders committed by its generals, and the huge loss of its man power exposed the rottenness and weakness of the Nicholas regime.

It was said that Russia was like a giant with feet of clay.

In 1855 Alexander II (1818-1881) came to the throne amid a widely spreading desire for reform. Many of his subjects, even the conservatives, believed that social and political conditions needed changing if Russia was to keep up with other European states. Although no democrat, the new tsar realized the necessity for moderate reform; his first move was against serfdom.

A growing humanitarian movement, which has been likened to that of the abolitionists in the United States before the Civil War, attacked serfdom, labeling it a national disgrace. In 1859 there were more than 23,000,-000 serfs living under nearly the same conditions as had the peasants of western Europe on twelfth-century manors. Russian serfs were bound to the soil, had no civil rights, could not own property, and owed heavy dues and services to their lords, who had almost uncontrolled power over them.

Alexander II made up his mind to abolish serfdom. In his own words:

. . . [It is] better to abolish serfdom from above than to wait until it will be abolished by a movement from below.[7]

A committee appointed to study the matter drew up the Emancipation Proclamation, which was duly issued as a *ukase* (edict of the tsar) in March 1861. The freed serfs were given certain political rights, and the cottages and implements they had been using were turned over to them.

The division of the land proved to be a difficult problem. The serfs had expected a portion of the lord's land to be turned over to them without charge. However, instead of receiving their lands as a gift, the freed peasants had to pay a special tax for a period of forty-nine years to the government, which had paid the landlords a handsome price for the lands they had lost. In numerous instances the peasants complained that they had been given the poorest land. All the land turned over to the peasants was held collectively by the *mir,* the village community, which supervised the various holdings and divided the land among the peasants.

The emancipation of the serfs was the most important single event in nineteenth-century Russian history. It was the beginning of the end for the landed aristocracy's monopoly of power. Emancipation brought a supply of free labor to the cities; industry was stimulated, and the middle class grew in numbers and influence. Above all, emancipation gave strong impetus to the liberal movement.

Nihilism. In the 1860's a remarkable movement known as Nihilism developed among the Russian intelligentsia. For some time many Russian liberals had been dissatisfied by the empty discussions of the intelligentsia; they launched a movement which aimed to put all things in Russia to the test of reason. The definition given to the term *Nihilism* by Ivan Turgenev in his novel *Fathers and Sons* (1861) became famous. Turgenev described a Nihilist as:

. . . a man who does not bow down before any authority, who does not take any principle on faith, whatever reverence that principle may be enshrined in.[8]

As might have been expected, this attitude of "nothing sacred" resulted in a radical reconsideration of the very basis of society. The Nihilists questioned all old values, championed the independence of the individual, and delighted in shocking the elder generation.

The Nihilists first attempted to convert the aristocracy to the cause of reform. Failing there, they turned to the peasants, and a veritable missionary movement ensued. Young college students became laborers and worked in the fields with the peasants. Others went to the villages as doctors and teachers to preach reform to the people. This "go to the people" campaign was known as the Narodniki movement (*narod*, "people").

Further reforms of Alexander II. While Nihilism and the Narodniki movement were gaining momentum, the Tsar Liberator, as Alexander II was called, proceeded to carry out additional reforms.

In 1864 local government was transformed by the Zemstvo Law. In the country, elective local boards (*zemstvos*) were established on which the gentry, the middle class, and the peasants were represented. These boards were given power to collect taxes for roads, asylums, hospitals, and schools. In the same year important reforms in the judicial system were carried through. The courts were reorganized on the French model, trial by jury in criminal cases was introduced, and justices of the peace were created to take care of minor cases. In 1870 city government was improved by the creation of municipal councils controlled by the propertied classes. Four years later, conscription for the army affecting all classes was introduced. Before this, most army conscripts had been peasants.

Alexander abandons reform. The reforming hand of Alexander was also felt in Poland, where the Nicholas System of repression was relaxed. But instead of propitiating the Poles, Alexander's concessions encouraged them to revive their nationalistic ambitions. In 1863 a Polish insurrection succeeded in establishing a provisional government, but the movement was soon crushed and a harsh policy of repression was reimposed, aimed particularly at the educated classes. And not only was repression felt in Poland: tragically, the Tsar Liberator began to lose faith in reform and turned to the repressive measures of his ruthless father.

In foreign affairs Alexander II attempted to follow the policy of his predecessors in increasing Russian influence in the Balkans as a stepping stone to Russian control of Constantinople and the Turkish Straits—the gateway to the Mediterranean. It is to the consideration of this long-pursued Russian goal—still unachieved but still pursued today—that we shall now turn.

STORM OVER THE BALKANS

The Near Eastern Question. While Germany and Italy were achieving national unity, nationalism was also stirring among the subject peoples in the Ottoman empire.

In this nineteenth-century cartoon, a smug Alexander II plunges into the abyss on a sled labeled "Despotism."

By the 1830's the Greeks, Serbs, and Montenegrins were free to develop their nationhood, but the heavy hand of Turkish misrule still lay upon the Bulgarians. The Rumanians languished under the "protection" of Russia. And, as nationalism sought fulfillment in the Balkans, the political scene was complicated by the rivalries of the great powers, especially the rivalry between Britain and Russia. These rivalries as they affected the Ottoman empire formed what was known as the Near Eastern Question.

The Near Eastern Question has also been defined as "the problem of filling up the vacuum created by the gradual disappearance of the Turkish Empire from Europe."[9] Britain, which consistently opposed Russian designs on the Near East, feared that if any great power should gain control in that area, the balance of power in Europe would be altered decisively. And, if Russia were to obtain the Straits, Russian naval power in the eastern Mediterranean would challenge Britain's communications with India. Although most Englishmen detested the corrupt rule of the sultans, during most of the nineteenth century the British government supported the Ottoman empire.

In the nineteenth century this Near Eastern power struggle brought on three Russo-Turkish wars and two wars in which France, England, and Russia fought either with or against Turkey, in addition to numerous revolts by subject nationalities against the sultan's government. The same Near Eastern Question in the twentieth century led to three wars before 1914 and helped precipitate the catastrophe of the First World War.

Anglo-Russian rivalry in the Near East. Russian expansion at the expense of the Turks had begun during the reign of Catherine the Great. After six years of war, the sultan had been compelled to sign the Treaty of Kuchuk Kainarji (1774), which awarded Azov and the north coast of the Black Sea to Russia, granted the Russians free navigation for their merchant ships in Ottoman waters (including the Straits), and, lastly, recognized the tsar as the protector of all eastern Orthodox Christians in the Ottoman empire. On several occasions Russia was to use this final concession as an excuse to intervene in Turkish affairs.

Not long afterwards, the famous British statesman William Pitt the Younger denounced Russia's ambition to dismember Turkey. Austria also was beginning to fear Russian expansion. Britain and Austria realized that Turkey was a danger to their national interests, not because Turkey was strong but because it was too weak. In the meantime Russia continued to take over former territories of the Ottoman empire, thereby expanding westward along the north shore of the Black Sea and southeastward along its east shore, which extended into the Caucasus region. During the Greek revolt of 1821, the jealousies of the big powers finally led France, England, and Russia to act cooperatively in putting an end to the fighting. The result was Greek independence without an undue expansion of Russian influence in the Balkans.

The Ottoman empire seemed on the very point of extinction in 1831, when the sultan's nominal representative in Egypt, the Pasha Mohammed Ali, attacked his master. To prevent the establishment of a new and probably stronger government at the Straits, the tsar sent an army to protect the Ottoman capital, extracting in return the Treaty of Unkiar Skelessi. In essence this document made Turkey a protectorate of Russia. The Straits were closed to all war vessels except those of the signatories, making the Black Sea a Russian lake. Chagrined by this Russian coup, British statesmen determined to stop Russia. For twenty years the leading advocate of this policy was Lord Palmerston.

Nor was it only Russia's expansion in the Balkans that gave Britain concern. Russian pressure in central Asia sparked British attempts to control Afghanistan and make it a friendly buffer state between the Russians and India (see p. 632).

Turkey, the "Sick Man of Europe." Nicholas I, stern soldier and unbending autocrat, was determined to carry on his predecessors' policy of expansion at the expense of decrepit Turkey. While visiting England in 1844, the tsar referred to Turkey as "a dying man" and proposed that England join in a dissection of the Ottoman carcass. British statesmen refused to be party to an agreement that would result in Russia's taking over Constantinople.

A quarrel over the management and protection of the holy places in Palestine gave Russia a new excuse to intervene in the affairs of the Ottoman empire. Ostensibly motivated by religious sentiments, the tsar reconfirmed Russia's protectorate over all Greek Christians in the Ottoman empire. His primary interest, of course, was the traditional Russian goal—to secure control of Constantinople and to ensure an entrance from the Black Sea to the Mediterranean.

The Crimean War. Russia invaded Turkish territory in 1853 but was soon confronted with a declaration of war from France and Britain. For his part, Napoleon III saw in a war with Russia an opportunity to enhance the reputation of his dynasty. In 1854, French,

British, and Sardinian troops invaded the Russian Crimea and besieged the great fortress of Sevastopol.

Contrary to Russian expectations (Russia had aided Austria in crushing the Hungarian revolution of 1848), Austria refused to ally itself with Russia and maintained an unfriendly "neutrality" which forced Russia to evacuate certain Turkish territory (Rumania) near the Austrian borders. In September 1855 the fortress of Sevastopol finally fell. Thwarted in the attempt to carve up the "Sick Man of Europe," Russia sued for peace.

The Treaty of Paris (1856) affirmed the integrity of the Ottoman empire. Specifically, it provided for the neutralization of the Black Sea (neither Russia nor Turkey was to maintain forts or naval depots on its shores), closed the Straits to foreign warships, and declared that no power had the right to interfere on behalf of the sultan's Christian subjects. To reduce Russian influence in the Balkans, the Congress of Paris ended the Russian protectorate over Rumania that had been established in 1829, placed the country under the protection of the great powers, and permitted Turkey to maintain its suzerainty.

The Crimean War momentarily halted Russian advance into the Balkans. But it did little to assuage the bitter international rivalries in that area. Bitterly resentful of what was regarded as gross Austrian "ingratitude," Moscow gave up the idea of having Austria as an ally in the carving up of the Ottoman empire and decided instead that this objective now required the weakening of Austria.

Pan-Slavism, agent of Russian expansion. The antiwestern Slavophile movement, which lauded Russian institutions, took on a political complexion after the Crimean War. Known as Pan-Slavism, this movement championed Russia as the protector of its "little brother Slavs," with the duty of freeing them from the barbaric rule of the Turks. Moreover, exponents of Pan-Slavism preached that it was Russia's destiny to create and rule a great Slavic empire. In the 1860's and 1870's, Pan-Slavism carried the message of Slavic solidarity to the Balkans, encouraging revolt.

Rumania and Bulgaria. Meanwhile, the Balkan peoples were slowly moving toward modernization. Rumania, though self-governing, was still nominally under Turkish control; but as law and order were achieved, roads constructed, and a postal system inaugurated, Rumania advanced toward nationhood. Despite the opposition of the great powers, Rumania, which had heretofore consisted of two separate territories, became a single, united state in 1862. By 1870 it was virtually free.

The story of Bulgarian liberty became entwined with events in the whole Balkan area and with the growing interests of the great powers in this troubled region. In 1875, peasants revolted in the district of Bosnia, a Turkish-governed Serbian province not included in the autonomous Serbian state. This insurrection was followed by a declaration of war by Serbia and Montenegro against Turkey.

At the same time, the Bulgarians broke into revolt, but the Turks crushed the rebels with terrible cruelty. The "Bulgarian massacres" caused a gasp of horror among enlightened people all over the world. In one incident, over one thousand people, including children, were burnt alive in a church where they had sought sanctuary.

The Treaty of San Stefano and the Congress of Berlin. While public opinion was being aroused in Europe against the "unspeakable Turk," the Serbs and Montenegrins had been forced to sue for peace with Turkey. Thereupon a conference of the ambassadors of the great powers met in Constantinople and demanded an end to Turkish cruelties in the Balkans. When the sultan demurred, the Russian tsar declared war.

The Russo-Turkish War (1877-1878) was hard fought. In one case a beleaguered Turkish army held off the Russians for five months before surrendering. Faced with an imminent Russian attack on Constantinople, however, the sultan finally sued for peace. The resulting Treaty of San Stefano (1878) gained complete independence for Serbia and Rumania, while the independence of Montenegro was reaffirmed. A large Bul-

garian state was set up, nominally still tributary to Turkey but actually under the dominance of Russia.

Britain was alarmed over the prospect of much of the Balkans coming under the domination of Moscow. And Austria was determined that Turkey as a political entity must be preserved or, at the very least, that its territory be prevented from falling under Russian influence. The Austro-Hungarian position was explained by an Austrian statesman thus:

Turkey possesses a utility almost providential for Austria-Hungary. For Turkey maintains the status quo of the small Balkan states and impedes their [nationalistic] aspirations. If it were not for Turkey, all these aspirations would fall down on our heads . . . if Bosnia-Hercegovina should go to Serbia or Montenegro, or if a new state should be formed there which we cannot prevent, then we should be ruined and should ourselves assume the role of the "Sick Man."[10]

Fearing an increase of Russian power in the Balkans, Britain and Austria forced a reconsideration of the Treaty of San Stefano at the Congress of Berlin later in 1878. Russia was compelled to agree to a revision of Bulgaria's status, and the large Bulgarian state set up by the Treaty of San Stefano was divided into three parts. The northernmost part remained an independent principality paying tribute to Turkey; south of this region was an autonomous province to be occupied by Turkish troops; the southernmost region was given back to Turkey to administer.

Among other provisions of the Berlin settlement was one relating to Bosnia, where the revolts of 1875 had started. This province and the province of Herzegovina were given to Austria "to occupy and administer." Thus Austria added to its polyglot empire two new territories, one of which was to be the scene of the incident which set off World War I.

Russian expansion had been checkmated —but at a high price. The Turks continued to oppress and even massacre the Christians left under the rule of the sultan. Meanwhile the Russians made a mockery of Pan-Slavism by trying to control the policies of their "brother Slavs" just freed from the Turks, particularly in Bulgaria. Russian satellites, so much discussed following the creation of Soviet puppets in eastern Europe and the Balkans after World War II, are nothing new in history.

SUMMARY

From 1848 to the mid-1870's, nationalism was the arbiter of history. Its two most important successes were registered by the unification movements in Italy and Germany. Democracy, for the moment, was overshadowed by the momentous events of nation-making. Only in Great Britain, where the Reform Bill of 1867 extended the franchise to the urban worker, did democratic principles make a significant advance. This legislation symbolized the end of middle-class dominance in British politics—the passing of the Victorian Compromise.

In France during the last decade of the Second Empire, there was some indication of a desire for greater political liberty, and in 1870, with the debacle of Sedan, the dictatorship of Napoleon III came to an end. But the Third Republic in its early years was destined to be more a repudiation of the regime that had brought national disaster than an affirmation of democracy.

In central Europe, Magyar nationalism proved a significant force, leading in 1867 to the establishment of the Dual Monarchy of Austria-Hungary. But other, less-fortunate minority groups in this polyglot land were still denied political liberties and independence.

In Russia, the Decembrist protest of 1825 had served only to fasten stronger manacles of absolutism on the people. Especially under Nicholas I, the country had remained isolated, remote from the modernizing forces of western Europe. After the Napoleonic Wars as well as after World War II, an iron curtain divided Europe.

Seemingly, defeat in war is necessary to bring about sweeping changes in Russia. Thus defeat in the Crimean War preceded the emancipation of the serfs. In later chapters we shall see how defeat by Japan in the war of 1904-1906 brought about a demand for revolutionary reform in Russia and how Russia's subsequent defeat in World War I spelled the end of the tsarist regime.

But the fortunes of war had no permanent effect on Russia's determination to extend its political control to the shores of the Mediterranean. As we have seen, Russian statesmen disguised these expansionist tendencies nicely under the banner of Pan-Slavism; but the disguise failed to impress either the Ottoman empire, which was interested only in perpetuating its corrupt and cruel regime, or Britain and Austria-Hungary, which were strenuously opposed to any extension of Russia's boundaries. Complicating this international problem was the fervent nationalism of the Balkan peoples, the "little brother Slavs" whom Russia proposed to "liberate" from Turkish domination.

To most of us—even though we have often seen the term abused in our own lifetimes—*liberation* suggests idealism and high purpose. But European diplomats and military leaders of this period had little interest in either high purpose or ideals. In his work *On War*, the Prussian general Karl von Clausewitz gave classic expression to the hard-boiled realism that motivated these men of action:

War is only a continuation of State policy by other means. . . . War is not merely a political act, but also a real political instrument, a continuation of political commerce. . . . Is not war merely another kind of writing and language for political thought? . . . War is nothing but a duel on an extensive scale. . . . Let us not hear of Generals who conquer without bloodshed. . . . The best strategy is always to be strong.[11]

SUGGESTIONS FOR READING

R. C. Binkley, *Realism and Nationalism, 1852-1871*, Harper, 1935. Like all volumes in *The Rise of Modern Europe* series, this attractive work presents an illuminating and comprehensive view of all aspects of European civilization during the period discussed, and includes a full bibliography. Useful for reference is the comprehensive collaborative work edited by J. P. T. Bury, *The Zenith of European Power, 1830-1870*, Cambridge Univ., 1960, Vol. X of the *New Cambridge Modern History*.

*Indicates an inexpensive paperbound edition.

A. J. P. Taylor, *The Struggle for Mastery in Europe, 1848-1918*, Oxford, 1954. A stimulating interpretative study of foreign affairs.

E. H. Carr, *Nationalism and After*, Macmillan, 1945. A short, incisive essay on the origin of modern nationalism, its development through three distinct periods, and its future prospects. Covering the same ground is the fuller account by B. C. Shafer, *Nationalism: Myth and Reality*, Harcourt, Brace, 1955, which provides the best statement of our present knowledge of nationalism.

Highly recommended for a study of nationalism in the nineteenth century is H. Kohn, *Prophets and Peoples: Studies in Nineteenth Century Nationalism*, Macmillan, 1946. See also by the same author, *Nationalism: Its Meaning and History,** Anvil, which is half text, half documents.

J. A. R. Marriott, *The Makers of Modern Italy: Napoleon—Mussolini*, Oxford, 1931. A useful introductory survey. See also the excellent general history by D. Mack Smith, *Italy: A Modern History*, Univ. of Mich., 1959. The political unification of Italy is also the theme of the general works by A. J. B. Whyte and R. Albrecht-Carrié, cited at the end of Chapter 21.

M. Paléologue, *Cavour*, Harper, 1927. A laudatory biography of the hard-grained, realistic founder of modern Italy. D. Mack Smith, *Garibaldi*, Knopf, 1956, is the best brief biography of this colorful romantic nationalist. Two vivid but somewhat out-dated accounts by G. M. Trevelyan are rich in detail: *Garibaldi and the Thousand*, Longmans, 1920; and *Garibaldi and the Making of Italy*, Longmans, 1920.

M. Dill, *Germany: A Modern History*, Univ. of Mich., 1961. A very readable, up-to-date general survey which includes a useful, annotated list of suggested readings.

T. A. Hamerow, *Restoration, Revolution, Reaction: Economics and Politics in Germany, 1815-1871*, Princeton, 1958. An excellent interpretation of how the advent of industrialism changed urban life and how political events were profoundly affected by the transition from economic agrarianism to capitalism.

The architect of the German state is vividly presented in I. F. D. Morrow, *Bismarck*, Macmillan, 1957; and in A. J. P. Taylor, *Bismarck: The Man and the Statesman*, Knopf, 1955.

A. L. Guérard, *Napoleon III*, Knopf, 1955. Short and stimulating. See also the witty account by P. Guedalla, *The Second Empire: Bonapartism, the Prince, the President, the Emperor*, Putnam, 1922; and the well-documented study by J. M. Thompson, *Louis Napoleon and the Second Empire*, Noonday, 1955. Émile Zola's novel *The Downfall* captures the mood of French defeat in 1870.

R. J. Evans, *The Victorian Age, 1815-1914*, Longmans, 1950. A clearly written survey, addressed to students, of "this greatest of all periods" in English history. A. Briggs, *The Age of Improvement*, Longmans, 1959, is a full and scholarly history of England from the close of the American war in 1783 to the Reform Bill of 1867.

Valuable for insights into life in Victorian England as well as into the lives of its leaders are G. M. Young, *Victorian England: Portrait of an Age,** Anchor; J. L. Hammond and M. R. Foot, *Gladstone and Liberalism*, Macmillan, 1953; P. Magnus-Allcroft, *Gladstone: A Biography*, Dutton, 1954; and A. Maurois, *Disraeli, A Picture of the Victorian Age*, Modern Lib., 1942.

M. Karpovich, *Imperial Russia, 1801-1917,** Holt (Berkshire Studies). A brief, valuable survey by a leading authority.

C. Woodham-Smith, *The Reason Why,** Everyman. A polished, urbane account of the tragicomic Crimean War and a dual biography of the two men responsible for the ill-fated charge of the Light Brigade. The Crimean War furnishes the background for a fine biography, *Florence Nightingale*, Grosset, 1958, by the same author.

W. E. Mosse, *Alexander II and the Modernization of Russia*, Macmillan (Teach Yourself History), 1958. A sound interpretation of a crucial era in Russian history and an expert analysis of the foreign policy of the period. S. Graham, *Tsar of Freedom: The Life and Reign of Alexander II*, Yale, 1935, is a sympathetic study.

J. Maynard, *Russia in Flux*, Macmillan, 1948. Excellent survey of intellectual ferment in nineteenth-century Russia. Two recent studies on the Slavophiles and the related Pan-Slavic movement are N. Riasanovsky, *Russia and the West in the Teaching of the Slavophiles*, Harvard, 1953; and M. Petrovich, *The Emergence of Panslavism, 1856-1870*, Columbia Univ., 1956.

W. M. Gewehr, *The Rise of Nationalism in the Balkans, 1800-1930*, Holt, 1931. A good brief survey. William Miller, *The Ottoman Empire and Its Successors, 1801-1927*, Macmillan, 1936, is one of the important general histories covering the same period.

L. Stavrianos, *The Balkans Since 1453*, Rinehart, 1957. The most recent comprehensive history of the Balkan peninsula from the Ottoman conquest to 1947; well-written, with a useful annotated bibliography. The same author has collected some evaluations of the strength and weaknesses of the Ottoman empire made by various observers between 1555 and 1897 in *The Ottoman Empire: Was It the Sick Man of Europe?** Rinehart.

J. A. R. Marriott, *The Eastern Question: An Historical Study in European Diplomacy*, Oxford, 1940. A scholarly survey of the decline of the Ottoman empire and the resulting repercussions upon European statecraft.

CHAPTER 23

Promise and Peril

Introduction. The year 1871 ended one period of European history and began another. Nationalism had just witnessed two major successes—the unification of Germany and the unification of Italy. The First Industrial Revolution had taken place, living conditions of ordinary people had improved, and the tempo of industrial progress continued to accelerate. Through colonization and economic imperialism, European influence was being extended over the world.

In politics some substantial advances toward full democracy were being made. Because of its steady and peaceful progress toward democracy, Britain was regarded by many nineteenth-century liberals as the model nation. Fearful of the rising influence of the business class, the English nobility allied itself with the growing labor class, which became politically ambitious and demanded an effective voice in government. Many among the well-to-do had real fear of revolution; to them it seemed better to grant concessions to the masses than to risk bloodshed such as Paris had witnessed in 1848 and 1871. Under Disraeli, city workers got the vote; under Gladstone, suffrage was extended to agricultural workers. Britain entered the twentieth century an almost completely democratic state, both politically and economically.

The second great democratic power of the late nineteenth century was France, which, for the third time, attempted to adopt a republican form of government after its humiliating defeat at the hands of Prussia in 1870. The first important act of the Third French Republic was the defeat of the Commune, a revolutionary body which brought about a violent and bloody civil uprising in Paris. As the nineteenth century came to a close, France was further convulsed by a series of crises (the most notorious and menacing was the Dreyfus case) that threatened to discredit, and even to overthrow, the Republic. Although by 1914 democratic France seemed to have ridden out the storm, the feuds and scandals of the past had left scars.

After 1870 the third great power in western Europe, Germany, made phenomenal progress in industry, science, and governmental administration. For nearly twenty years after the creation of the Second Reich in 1871, the masterful Bismarck strengthened national sentiment, sought to improve the lot of the masses, and attempted to make the new Germany militarily unassailable. But his failure to give Germans an opportunity to exercise real political responsibility became dangerous when the excitable autocrat William II became the real leader of Germany in 1890.

The farther one traveled eastward from London and Paris—and indeed from such lesser capitals as Geneva or Oslo—the more shallow-rooted democracy became. In Austria-Hungary the discontent of a number of submerged nationalities stultified real parliamentary government. In the Balkans parliamentary government of only a crude kind existed, while in the Ottoman empire cruelty and despotism reigned. As we recall, Russia had begun to experiment with social and political reform in the 1860's, but the government moved too slowly. The results were terrorism against the tsar's regime, the intensification of despotism, and, in 1905, a revolution which turned out to be a mere dress rehearsal for the cataclysm of 1917—the Bolshevik Revolution.

Meanwhile, with progress in science and technology came progress in destructive armaments; and while the power of military weapons increased, little was done to remove the causes that led the nations to rely upon these weapons. If men could be said to have ascended to a new level of civilization in their scientific and intellectual attainments, their tactics and outlook in international affairs were often reminiscent of the jungle. From 1871 to 1914 Europe, with its progressive and brilliant yet menacing and unstable civilization, was the center of the world. It was the central position this little continent enjoyed that gave its promise and peril world-wide implications. Fanned by old rivalries and callous ambitions, a spark in that center was to grow and spread and finally engulf the world in flames, creating a holocaust known as World War I.

TOWARD DEMOCRATIZATION
OF BRITISH LIFE

Disraeli and Tory democracy. The story of the continued growth of democracy in Great Britain resumes with the election in 1874 of Disraeli as prime minister. Attacking stand-pat conservatism, he advocated what became known as Tory democracy—a political alliance formed between the landed gentry and the workers and opposed to the businessmen. In the landed gentry Disraeli saw England's natural leaders—champions of the common people, who were being exploited by the middle class, the modern counterpart of the medieval nobility.

Between 1874 and 1880, a number of important reforms were passed: public health facilities were improved, restrictions against labor unions were liberalized, and housing schemes were inaugurated. Under Disraeli's ministry, Britain made its first substantial advance toward what we know now as the welfare state.

Reform measures of Gladstone. Returning to power in 1880, Gladstone in 1884 sponsored the third Reform Bill, a measure extending the vote to agricultural workers. This statute brought Britain to the verge of universal manhood suffrage. Gladstone also obtained passage of the important Employers' Liability Act, which gave the workers rights of compensation in five classes of accidents, especially in those occurring on the railroads. Apart from these measures, Gladstone concerned himself primarily with attempts to solve the Irish problem, the principal question in British politics in the late nineteenth century.

The Irish problem. Although England is often credited with ability in government, a skillful hand seems to have been absent in England's rule of Ireland—a case of chronic misgovernment. In the seventeenth century, the British had planted large numbers of

Scottish emigrants in the north of Ireland in Ulster, where a strong colony of Protestants (the so-called Scotch-Irish or Orangemen) developed. A number of oppressive laws were passed against the Irish Catholics, restricting their political, economic, and religious freedom and dispossessing them of their lands. Then by the Act of Union of 1801 the Irish legislature was abolished, and the Irish were required to send their representatives to the Parliament in London.

During the early nineteenth century, the land problem in Ireland became very acute. A large part of the cultivable land was in the hands of idle, parasitic landlords. As the population grew, the farms were subdivided into small portions scarcely capable of supporting tenants, and many peasants were evicted because of failure to pay rent. In 1845 the potato crop, the main staple of diet, failed, and a terrible famine ensued. Perhaps as many as 500,000 people died, and a huge exodus to America began—the beginning of the principal Irish Catholic settlements in the United States. In 1841 the population of Ireland was 8,770,000; in 1891 it was less than 5,000,000.

There was another side to the picture, however. The Irish, for their part, had managed to gain some victories in the course of the nineteenth century. In 1829 the British Parliament had passed the Catholic Emancipation Act, permitting Catholics to sit in Parliament. Earlier, the Irish members in Parliament had come from the Protestant minority and represented only the landlord class. And under Gladstone's "Glorious Ministry," an important land act was passed and the Irish Anglican Church was disestablished (1869), thus ending the use of Irish tax money to support a church to which 75 per cent of the population did not belong.

In 1881 Gladstone placed on the statute book his second land act, intended to give the country folk of Ireland what was called the "three F's": fair rent, fixed tenure, and free sale. The result was that by the close of the century the Irish peasants were gradually becoming landowners with at least a chance of earning a decent livelihood.

While the land problem was being ameliorated, the issue of Irish home rule came to the fore. The Home Rulers, led by Charles Stewart Parnell (1846-1891), demanded that Ireland have its own legislature. Entering the House of Commons in 1874, Parnell did everything possible to obstruct business in that august body, hoping in this way to force the issue of home rule. Faced with such tactics, as well as with the fact that Parnell controlled eighty-five votes in the Commons, Gladstone in 1886 and 1893 introduced home rule bills. But both bills were defeated.

Finally, a third home rule bill was introduced and passed by Parliament in 1914. The Ulsterites, however, strongly opposed the measure and prepared to resist by force incorporation into a Catholic Ireland divorced from the government of Great Britain. Only the outbreak of war with Germany in 1914 prevented civil strife in Ireland. The 1914 act was never put into effect, and the question was not settled until 1921, when southern Ireland attained dominion status.

Rule of the new Liberals, 1905-1914. Gladstone's fight for Irish home rule split his party and paved the way for a decade of Conservative rule in Britain (1895-1905). Because Britain was enmeshed in foreign and imperial affairs, there was little further attempt to carry on Disraeli's program of social legislation. But by 1905 the need for social and political reform again claimed major attention. Over 30 per cent of the adult male workers received a starvation wage of less than seven dollars per week. The pitifully small wages made it impossible for the workers to lay aside savings for increasingly frequent periods of unemployment. An increase in strikes gave evidence of discontent among the workers, and the newly founded Labour party gained adherents. The Liberals, traditional champions of laissez-faire economics, decided to jettison their old ideas and embark on a bold program of social legislation. David Lloyd George (1863-1945), a leading member of the Liberal government, declared:

Four spectres haunt the Poor; Old Age, Accident, Sickness and Unemployment. We are going to exorcise them.[1]

The empire which the British created in the nineteenth century was the richest, the most extensive, and the most powerful in history. As master of this vast domain, Britain was a natural target for criticism from other nations. Here the American cartoonist Thomas Nast portrays a swollen John Bull who encompasses the entire world and holds it in a jealous grasp.

Confronted with what was regarded as widespread economic injustice, the Liberal party under Prime Minister Herbert Asquith, Lloyd George, and Winston Churchill—the last-named just beginning his fabulous career—carried through Parliament a revolutionary reform program that provided for old-age pensions, national employment bureaus, town planning, and sickness, accident, and unemployment insurance. In addition, labor unions were given greater protection, and members of the House of Commons, heretofore unpaid, were granted a moderate salary. This last measure enabled men without private means, chiefly in the new Labour party, to follow a political career.

For some time there had been ill-feeling against the House of Lords because it had tried to block the reform program of the Liberals. When the Lords refused to pass the 1909-1910 budget, which laid new tax burdens on the richer classes in order to pay for the new social legislation, the Liberals and their Labour allies argued that a hereditary, irresponsible upper house was an anachronism in a democracy. The result was the Parliament Bill of 1911. Before this bill was passed, it was necessary for Asquith to announce (as had been done with the Reform Bill in 1832) that the monarch had promised, if necessary, to create enough peers to pass the bill in the House of Lords. The bill took away from the Lords all power of absolute veto. No longer could the will of the people as expressed in the Commons be blocked; the Lords were left with power only to slow up and force reconsideration of legislation of which they did not approve.

The *Pax Britannica*. In nineteenth-century world affairs, England's industrial might, its financial strength, and the smooth functioning and stability of its government made it possible for this nation to play a unique role in world affairs. The very size of the British empire meant that Englishmen were involved in developments all over the globe. Mainly a nineteenth-century creation, the British empire consisted of 13,000,000 square miles of land—the largest empire known to history. Although the *Pax Britannica* was not free of flaws or evils, in the absence of any world government there was a great deal to be said for a global system of law and defense which maintained stability in one quarter of the world's area.

FRANCE: PAINFUL PATH TO DEMOCRACY

The Third Republic. We have seen how, in France, the Second Empire with its leader Louis Napoleon was swept away amidst the tragedy and humiliation of surrender at the hands of the victorious German armies. Born in defeat, the Empire's successor, the Third Republic, went through many years of precarious existence before it was placed on a firm and popular foundation.

Its first Assembly, elected to fulfill the bitter task of making peace with Germany, was overwhelmingly royalist. This circumstance gave rise to a revolutionary movement in Paris, where republicans and radicals of every description formed a Commune, in the tradition of the Paris Commune of 1792, to save the Republic. The Communards favored government control of prices, wages, and working conditions. Karl Marx jubilantly welcomed the uprising, seeing in it a pattern for the future revolt of the proletariat against the capitalistic system. (The revolutionary Russian soviets—workers' and soldiers' councils —of 1905 and 1917 were patterned upon the French Commune of 1871.) After several weeks of civil war the Commune was suppressed. That the royalists' Assembly finally voted a republican constitution for France in 1875 was due largely to the inability of various royalist factions to agree among themselves. A republic seemed the form of government on which there was least disagreement.

The improvised constitutional laws of 1875 provided for the election by manhood suffrage of representatives to the Chamber of Deputies, the influential lower house. In addition, there was a Senate, whose members were elected from the major administrative districts, the departments. The president was elected by the legislature, and his powers were so limited as to make him merely a figurehead. The real executive was the ministry, or cabinet; as in England, the ministry was responsible to the legislature.

The Boulanger and Dreyfus affairs. In the mid-eighties there began a series of crises which, lasting more than a decade, threatened the very existence of the Republic. In 1886 General Boulanger, the minister of war, became the toast of Paris and a national hero for his firm stand against Germany. The "Brave General" became the idol of ultra-nationalists and monarchists, who saw in him a "man on horseback" who would sweep away the Republic by a coup d'état as Louis Napoleon had done in 1851. But when the government took measures to cope with his followers by force, the general fled the country and later committed suicide.

In 1894 occurred an affair that eclipsed the Boulanger incident in the way in which it divided and embittered French opinion and challenged the fundamental ideals of French democracy. Captain Alfred Dreyfus (1859-1935), the first Jewish officer to secure a post in the general staff of the French army, was accused of selling military secrets to a foreign power. Disliked by many of his aristocratic fellow officers as a Jew, the unfortunate Dreyfus was found guilty, publicly stripped of his commission, and condemned to solitary confinement on Devil's Island, a notorious convict settlement near French Guiana.

The Dreyfus affair was not closed, however. French military secrets continued to leak, and a spendthrift officer named Major Esterhazy was brought to trial and then acquitted. When Émile Zola entered the fray, the first step in the ultimate exoneration of Dreyfus was taken. In "J'accuse" (1898), his famous open letter to the president of France, Zola attacked the military court-martial, accusing the judges of knowingly acquitting the guilty man, Esterhazy.

The Dreyfus case developed into a bloodless civil war between friends and foes of the Republic—a war of which Dreyfus was the unwilling symbol and victim. The army, the Church, and the royalists were, generally speaking, anti-Dreyfusards; intellectuals and socialists supported Dreyfus.

In 1899 the Dreyfus case was authorized for review but, even though Esterhazy had admitted his guilt, political passions were so strong that Dreyfus was again found guilty. The president of France was friendly to the Dreyfusards, however, and pardoned Dreyfus. In 1906 the highest civil court in France found Dreyfus completely innocent, thus asserting the power of the civil authority over the military that had condemned him. The democratic Republic emerged victorious over its foes.

The anticlerical movement. The alliance of the Catholic Church and the army during the Dreyfus case led to a strong revival of anticlericalism in France. In 1901 a law was passed providing for the closing of all Church

The infamous Dreyfus case aroused all France at the turn of the century and attracted world-wide attention. This drawing shows Captain Alfred Dreyfus on trial for treason in 1894.

schools. While leading republicans were not antireligious, they demanded an end to Church interference in the affairs of the state. One of these defined his position thus:

. . . I want the priest outside of politics. In the Church, yes; on the public square, on the platform, never.[2]

In 1905 the drastic step was taken of formally separating Church and state. An act was passed abrogating the Concordat (1801) made between Napoleon Bonaparte and the papacy. Henceforth, the state ceased to pay the salaries of the clergy—Protestant and Jewish as well as Catholic. Furthermore, all Church property was taken over by the state, annual arrangements being made for the use of Church buildings.

The Third Republic in 1914. By 1914 France was a prosperous land of more than 39,000,000 people, although a falling birth rate put it far behind the prolific Germans, who numbered 70,000,000. And after a century of wars, revolutions, and crises, French republicanism finally attained stability and wide public support.

Most Frenchmen enjoyed basic democratic rights, such as manhood suffrage, freedom of the press, and equality before the law. Nevertheless, they tended to regard government not as a servant but as a meddling, would-be tyrant. In consequence, officials found it difficult to impose direct taxation, and the machinery of the state was severely handicapped by a lack of funds.

Reflecting the extreme individualism of the French was the multiparty political system. There were so many different political groups represented in the Chamber of Deputies that prime ministers had to form cabinets made up of diverse elements. Like unstable chemical compounds, these cabinets blew up under the slightest pressure. French prime ministers came and went with bewildering rapidity, at the whim of the legislature.

In spite of these weaknesses, however, France in 1914 was regarded as the most important democracy on the Continent and one of the great powers of the world.

GERMANY: AN ABSOLUTISM UNDER CONSTITUTIONAL FORMS

The Second (Hohenzollern) Reich. Let us now turn to the German empire (Reich) established under the rule of the Hohenzollern dynasty of Prussia at Versailles in 1871. The new government—a federal union of twenty-six states—included the kingdoms of Prussia, Bavaria, Saxony, and Württemberg, various grand duchies and duchies, three city republics, and the imperial territory of Alsace-Lorraine.

Headed by the German emperor, the imperial government consisted of a legislative upper house, the Bundesrat, representing the ruling houses of the various states; and a lower house, the Reichstag, representing the people. The 61 members of the Bundesrat voted as instructed by their royal masters. Elected by manhood suffrage, the 397 members of the Reichstag had little power. Thus the Hohenzollern empire had a few parliamentary trappings, but behind this façade of democracy was the dominant power of reactionary Prussia.

The office of German emperor was vested in the Hohenzollern dynasty so that the king of Prussia was at the same time kaiser of the empire. The kaiser wielded considerable power in military and foreign affairs. As king of Prussia, he also controlled seventeen votes in the Bundesrat. No amendment to the constitution could pass this body if opposed by fourteen votes. The Prussian delegation could block any reduction in appropriations for the support of the army and navy, and Prussia controlled the chairmanships of practically all the standing committees in the Bundesrat.

Appointed by the emperor and responsible to him alone, the chancellor was the actual head of the government. Unlike the situation in the English House of Commons or the French Chamber of Deputies, the German chancellor could defy or ignore any action taken by the legislature, especially the Reichstag. In 1871, Bismarck, the architect of German nationalism, was appointed the first imperial chancellor.

The *Kulturkampf*. Bismarck's strong nationalism, together with his hatred of those who refused to subordinate themselves to the state, brought about his crusades against what he called "the black and the red menaces." The first so-called crusade was directed against "the black menace," the Catholic Church in Germany.

In the elections of 1871 the German Catholics had elected a large bloc of representatives to the Reichstag. These members supported the complete independence of the Church from state control and denounced divorce, secular education, and liberty of conscience. They also supported the new dogma of papal infallibility (see p. 580).

The conflict which began in 1872 was known as the *Kulturkampf* (the Civilization Struggle). The imperial government made it a penal offense for the clergy to criticize the government and prohibited religious orders from taking part in educational work

This well-known cartoon, "Dropping the Pilot," appeared in the English magazine *Punch* in 1890, following the dismissal of Bismarck as chancellor of Germany. Kaiser William II, determined to dominate German government personally, watches from the ship of state as the former helmsman leaves the vessel. Despite the change in leadership, however, the tradition that Bismarck represented continued into the twentieth century, as Germany followed a course of ardent nationalism and military aggressiveness.

in Germany. Next, all members of the Jesuit order were expelled from the country. Between 1873 and 1875, severe measures were also passed by the Prussian government. These Prussian May Laws required civil marriages, stopped appropriations to the Catholic Church, and required all priests to study theology at state universities. Numerous religious orders were suppressed.

In response to these repressive acts, Pope Pius IX declared them null and void and called on loyal Catholics to refuse to obey them. Bismarck was infuriated, and, remembering the time in the Middle Ages when the German emperor Henry IV humbled himself before Pope Gregory VII, he grandiloquently declared, "We shall not go to Canossa, either in the flesh or in the spirit." Many priests were imprisoned, much Church property was confiscated, and many pulpits were closed.

Bismarck's oppression of the Catholic clergy did not attain its end. The Center party —that is, the Catholic bloc—in the Reichstag gained in membership. The wily chancellor, therefore, decided to beat a strategic retreat, and the majority of the anti-Catholic laws were repealed. Bismarck needed the support of all Catholics against what he regarded as a new foe of the state—socialism, which he dubbed the "red international."

Drive against the socialists. In 1875 the socialists in Germany had established the Social Democratic party. Traditionally, German socialists had opposed autocratic rule and Prussian militarism. Now they demanded not only a true parliamentary democracy but also thoroughgoing social legislation.

Bismarck watched with grave concern their mounting strength in the Reichstag. In 1878 two attempts were made on the emperor's life. Although the Social Democratic party had in no way sponsored or participated in these plots, Bismarck immediately launched an all-out campaign against all socialists. In 1878 socialist organizations were dissolved and their publications suppressed. Some five hundred persons were imprisoned, and restrictions were made on free speech and public assembly.

Despite these severe measures, the adherents of socialism increased rather than declined. Therefore, Bismarck shifted his tactics and sponsored important measures for ensuring the economic well-being of the masses. He declared:

Give the workingman the right to work as long as he is healthy, assure him care when he is sick, and maintenance when he is old . . . then the socialists will sing their siren songs in vain, and the workingmen will cease to throng to their banner.[3]

A sickness insurance bill was passed in 1883, an accident insurance bill in the following year, and in 1889 old-age insurance was introduced. Regardless of Bismarck's motives, these attempts to safeguard the economic interests of the German masses were pioneer efforts in modern social reform and were copied in many European countries. But despite Bismarck's efforts to lure the workers from socialism, the Social Democratic party continued to increase in size and influence.

Kaiser William II. In 1888 William II, the grandson of William I, became German emperor. Just as Bismarck had stamped his policies and personality on the German nation for the more than twenty years that he was chancellor, this young man was to be the focus of German history from 1890 to 1918.

In addition to having a strong militaristic bent, William was an ardent champion of the divine right of kings. He constantly reminded those around him that "he and God" worked together for the good of the state. Berliners, astounded at his wide, if superficial interests, humorously said: "God knows everything, but the kaiser knows better." The loud dress, flashy uniforms, and oratorical outbursts of the emperor sprang from an inferiority complex, which probably had its origin in the withered left arm that he had had from birth. Restless and emotionally unstable, he was continually making undiplomatic speeches and casting off insulting phrases that alarmed and sometimes infuriated governmental circles in Europe.

William II came to the throne determined to dominate the German government personally. To the kaiser's mind it was "a question whether the Bismarck dynasty or the Hohenzollern dynasty should rule."[4] For two years the tension between emperor and chancellor mounted. Finally, in 1890, William rudely dismissed Bismarck.

Reasons for despotism. Despite advances in industry and science, Germany remained a "political kindergarten." There were several reasons why despotism existed in such a prosperous and advanced country. First, the nation had militaristic leanings. It had achieved its unity by blood and iron. Any liberal movement would, if necessary, be crushed relentlessly by the armed forces, which were passionately loyal to the Hohenzollern dynasty. At the heart of this militarism were the Prussian Junkers, a military caste made up of the landed aristocracy, who disdained business, gloried in war, and had an austere sense of their duty to the state.

What we may term the German tradition also played its part. The people had long been taught to serve the Prussian state unquestioningly and to look to their leaders for guidance. As the Germans expressed it, "Alles kommt von oben" ("Everything comes down from above"). The people also gave the government unquestioning loyalty because it was efficient and solicitous of their material welfare. Bismarck's social insurance program succeeded in keeping the German masses contented.

Another factor which kept most of the Germans in line was the school system. The masses went to the *Volksschule*, where they were given an excellent training in the three R's and were taught obedience to the state. The businessmen and landed aristocracy, on the other hand, sent their sons and daughters to an altogether different school system that led to the university and produced the elite that ruled the nation. German education trained many followers and a few leaders.

The democratic movement. Notwithstanding the strength of autocracy, a remarkable democratic movement, whose spearhead was the Social Democratic party, manifested itself in Germany as the twentieth century dawned. Despite the opposition of the emperor and his conservative supporters (William II called the socialists a "treasonable horde"), the vote cast by the Social Democrats continued to increase during William's reign as it had under Bismarck. In 1914 this party could claim the support of one third of the German voters.

The outbreak of war in 1914 was to nip in the bud the promising democratic movement. As a result, revolution was later substituted for evolution, and the German people achieved a republic before they had been sufficiently trained to govern themselves.

Above is Kaiser William II of Germany, who lost favor among his own subjects by stubbornly resisting democratic reforms and aroused the enmity of other nations by relentlessly striving to increase Germany's political and military power.

RUSSIA UNDER CONTINUED REACTION

Autocracy and reaction under Alexander II and Alexander III. In 1870 Russia comprised the largest continuous land empire in the world. Containing a sixth of the earth's land surface, with as many people as the rest of Europe combined, it stretched from the Baltic and Black seas to the Pacific. At this time, however, the great potential power that this immense land giant could exercise in world affairs was hidden under the inefficiency of its government, the isolation of its people, and its economic backwardness.

After making a start toward modernizing Russia's sociopolitical structure (see Chapter

22), Alexander II faltered. Deeply disturbed by the Polish revolution of 1863 and by what he considered the unreasonable demands of the intelligentsia, he gradually retreated toward conservatism.

As the tsar grew more conservative, the Nihilist movement was also changing in character. The "go to the people" (Narodniki) movement had collapsed. The government had tried to extirpate it; and the peasants, who could not understand it, rejected it. In response to the growing reaction of the government, the Nihilists advocated and systematically practiced terrorism. One after another, prominent officials were shot down or killed by bombs. Finally, after several attempts, Alexander II was assassinated in 1881, just as he was on the verge of making some reforms in an effort to placate the Nihilists.

Unlike his father, the new tsar, Alexander III (1881-1894), was not a pseudoliberal but a stanch reactionary. On assuming the throne, he revived the repressive system of Nicholas I. To Alexander III, a confirmed Slavophile, Russia could be saved from chaos only by shutting itself off from the democracy and liberalism of western Europe. Censorship was applied, and schools and universities were regulated to prevent students from learning "dangerous" ideas.

The tsar's most influential adviser was Konstantin Petrovich Pobyedonostzev, tutor to Alexander III and his son Nicholas, and procurator of the Holy Synod from 1880 to 1895. He taught his royal pupils to hate democracy, constitutions, and the parliamentary system. Under Pobyedonostzev, terrorists were hunted down and a rigorous policy of Russification was carried out, particularly among the Poles and the Finns. One nation, one language, one church, and one government—an autocratic government—was the formula of administration. The Jews were bullied and sometimes massacred in terrible drives, called pogroms. Exile to Siberia was common.

Nicholas II and a new revolutionary movement. Alexander was succeeded by his son, Nicholas II (1894-1917), a weak man with little intellect and hardly any force of character. It was this unimposing figure who would bear the brunt of the revolutionary forces which had been gathering momentum in Russia in the late nineteenth century. All kinds of organizations clamored for reform—lawyers' clubs, chambers of commerce, zemstvos (the local governing bodies), and trade unions. In the cities a growing class of industrial workers engaged in frequent strikes, and new revolutionary societies were continually being founded.

During this period in Russia, several distinct reform parties existed. The progressive elements among the businessmen and nobility thought of themselves as Liberals (Constitutional Democrats, or Cadets). They wanted a constitutional monarchy and believed in peaceful reform. The Social Revolutionaries were followers of the Narodniki tradition. This group wanted to secure more land for the peasants; their slogan was "the whole land to the whole people."

Another radical group was the Social Democrats, exponents of Marxist principles. Gathering their strength chiefly from the radical intellectuals and the workingmen in the cities, they believed in a complete social and economic as well as political revolution. In 1903 the party split into two wings—the Mensheviks, or moderates, and the Bolsheviks, or extremists. The Mensheviks believed that Russian socialism should grow gradually and peacefully and that the tsar's government should be overthrown and succeeded by a democratic republic in which the socialists would cooperate with bourgeois political parties. Working under a democratic system, the socialists would gradually become the dominant political force and would secure their socialistic society by parliamentary means. On the other hand, the Bolsheviks, under Nikolai Lenin (see p. 575), advocated the formation of a small elite of professional revolutionists, subject to strong party discipline, to act as the self-appointed vanguard of the proletariat. Although the Bolsheviks posed as democrats, they advocated seizure of power by force.

The government struck back energetically. Nicholas' minister of the interior organized diversionary outbursts of anti-Semitism among the people. Bands of thugs, called Black Hundreds, were organized to carry out pogroms and to attack liberals; and the fierce Cossacks were used frequently to carry fire and sword into rebellious regions. In the ranks of the revolutionists the government planted *agents provocateurs,* who incited the insurgents to murder officials and then exposed them to the police.

The revolution of 1905: Bloody Sunday. In 1904 the clash of rival imperialisms in Manchuria and Korea (see p. 627) led to war with Japan. The Russian fleet was destroyed, and on land the Japanese gained victory after victory. With the ignominious defeat of its armed forces, the tsar's corrupt regime became the target for almost universal criticism.

Disorders spread throughout the land in the last months of 1904. On January 22, 1905, occurred the tragic incident known as Bloody Sunday. On this day a priest led an enormous crowd to the Winter Palace in St. Petersburg to present a petition to the tsar. The document declared:

We, the workers of the town of St. Petersburg, with our wives, our children and our aged and feeble parents, have come to you, Sire, in search of justice and protection. We have fallen into poverty, we are oppressed, we are loaded with a crushing burden of toil, we are insulted, we are not recognized as men, we are treated as slaves who should bear their sad and bitter lot in patience and silence. . . . Do not refuse to protect your people; raise it from the grave of arbitrary power, poverty and ignorance; permit it to dispose of its own fate; free it from the intolerable oppression of officials; destroy the wall between yourself and your people—and let it govern the country with you.[5]

When the procession reached the Winter Palace, Cossacks opened fire on the defenseless crowd, killing hundreds and wounding many more. This massacre shocked the world. Subsequently, it was discovered that the priest was a member of the secret police.

So aroused were the Russian masses over the Bloody Sunday massacre that a general strike was declared. Soviets (councils of workers) appeared in the cities to direct revolutionary activity. The strikers demanded a

In January 1905, Russian workers with their wives and children marched to the tsar's Winter Palace to plead for relief from poverty and oppression. Although unarmed and led by a priest, the petitioners were treated as traitorous rebels. Here is an artist's interpretation of the ensuing massacre, in which hundreds were shot and cut down by the Cossack guards. This incident, known as Bloody Sunday, led to increasing unrest and violence in the months that followed.

democratic republic, freedom for political prisoners, and the disarming of the police. Most business and government offices closed, and there was no gas, electricity, or (in some areas) water. The whole machinery of Russian economic life creaked to a defiant halt. Russia was paralyzed, and the government was helpless.

Results of the revolutionary movement. In October 1905, Tsar Nicholas issued his famous October Manifesto, which promised "freedom of person, conscience, speech, assembly, and union." A national Duma (legislature) was to be called without delay, the right to vote was to be extended, and no law was to go into force without confirmation by the Duma. The more moderate liberal groups were satisfied, but the socialists rejected the concessions as insufficient and tried to organize new strikes. Thus, by the end of

Posed together at a state ceremony are the royal cousins, Tsar Nicholas II of Russia (left) and King George V of England. The tsar is dressed in English uniform while King George appears in Russian regimentals. The custom of wearing the uniforms of each other's country during a state visit was considered a gesture of respect by pre-World War I royalty.

1905, there was disunity among the reformers, and the tsar's position was strengthened considerably.

When the first Duma was convened in the spring of 1906, it proceeded to censure the government, demanding an investigation into the conduct of the Russo-Japanese War, autonomy for Poland and Finland, and the freeing of political prisoners. The tsar dissolved the Duma in midsummer because, he said, its members "would not cooperate." An appeal by the liberal leaders of the Duma was met by apathy on the part of the people. Sensing the decline of revolutionary fervor, the tsar appointed a conservative prime minister, Piotr Arkadevich Stolypin. Again the familiar pattern of executions, arrests, and pogroms followed.

Although the composition of the later Dumas was quite conservative, a few moderate reforms were carried out. But the loyalty of the army, the stanch support of the officials

of the Orthodox Church, and division among the opponents of tsarism enabled Nicholas to weather the storm for the time being.

AUSTRIA-HUNGARY AND THE OTTOMAN EMPIRE

Problems in the Dual Monarchy. In addition to Germany and Russia, there were two other empires—the Ottoman empire and the Dual Monarchy of Austria-Hungary—that had failed to develop along the democratic lines of Britain and France. In both Austria-Hungary and Turkey, there was a conglomeration of subject nationalities. Increasingly restive under alien rule, these peoples wanted the right to govern themselves. In some cases, as in Bohemia, the people wanted to set up a new independent nation; or, in the case of the Serbs, the goal was to join their countrymen living in adjacent national states.

The Dual Monarch, Francis Joseph I (1848-1916) of the House of Hapsburg, ruled a multilingual state in which there were 12,000,000 Germans, 10,000,000 Magyars, over 24,000,000 Slavs, and some 4,000,000 Latins—the latter Italians and Rumanians. There were Northern Slavs (Bohemians or Czechs, Poles, and Slovaks) and Southern Slavs (Serbs, Croats, and Slovenes). In addition, there were numerous small isolated islands of people in various parts of Austria-Hungary surrounded by masses of neighbors quite different in nationality and culture. The value of the official bank note of the Dual Monarchy was printed on one side in eight languages and on the other side in Magyar.

What was the progress of democracy in this complex land? After 1907 the bicameral legislature in Austria was elected by general manhood suffrage. However, political life continued to be dominated by wealthy German businessmen and the landed aristocracy. The latter monopolized the leading positions in government, the army, and parliament. Strong racial and national antipathies also impeded the functioning of what, on paper, seemed a liberal constitution. Political parties were not based primarily on political principle but on nationality. Each distinct group feared and detested the German ruling elite, and too often each disliked the other national groups. Although Austria gave its subject nationalities substantial local self-government, this concession had little mollifying effect.

If democracy was weak in Austria, it was practically nonexistent in Hungary. Here the aristocracy firmly held the reins of power, and the Magyars refused to share political control with the other nationalities—Croats, Serbs, Slovaks, Rumanians, and Galicians—who were under their rule. Like Austria, Hungary was agricultural; land ownership was concentrated in the hands of a few, and the peasants suffered even more than their counterparts in Austria.

Despite the difficulties to which the existence of the Dual Monarchy gave rise, the defenders of the empire could point to the military strength and international influence it gave to a large part of eastern and southern Europe. Above all, the empire exhibited a certain economic unity, its various parts complementing each other well. Hungary, for example, produced wheat; Croatia and Slavonia exported cattle and swine; Bohemia had important mines and factories; and Austria, with the great capital city of Vienna, was the heart of the empire's banking and commerce.

Another unifying force was the Hapsburg crown. Francis Joseph I was a sincere and kindly sovereign, well liked by most of his subjects. It was his firm belief that the function of his dynasty was to hold the various national groups in the empire together. He once said:

My people are strangers to one another, and yet it is for the best. They never have the same ills at the same time. . . . Each suspects his neighbor; they never understand one another. . . . Their mutual antipathies, however, conduce to order and to general peace.[6]

Yet, as we shall see later on, the surge of nationalism was destined to burst this cooperative framework of peoples apart.

Despotism and misrule in the Ottoman empire: Abdul-Hamid II. In the closing decades of the nineteenth century, the decaying Ottoman empire was a disreputable, vicious Oriental despotism. Although in 1876 a liberal constitution had been issued and a new sultan, Abdul-Hamid II, had come to the throne with the support of a liberal faction, only a short time elapsed before the new ruler made himself absolute. The constitution was abrogated in 1878, and Abdul-Hamid began to rule without parliament, aided by forty thousand spies. The strictest censorship was applied, and opponents of this tyranny mysteriously disappeared or were forced into exile.

At the same time, Abdul-Hamid was fighting a losing battle to hold together the remainder of his empire. In North Africa, France, which had seized Algeria in 1830, annexed Tunis in 1881; Britain occupied Egypt in 1882; and by 1900 Italy had a covetous eye on Tripoli. But there remained under Turkish rule the Arab world of the Near East, inhabited by peoples who were proud of their traditions and who were Muslim in religion but not Turkish in nationality. The same nationalist spirit which had bestirred nineteenth-century Europe now began to arouse Arab leaders against Turkish rule.

Young Turks and Young Arabs. Meanwhile, opposition to the sultan's tyranny mounted among his Turkish subjects. The nucleus for this opposition was the organization known as the Young Turks, composed of reformers who had been educated in western European universities. Many converts to this reform group were made in the Turkish army, which provided the necessary military power for successful rebellion. When, in 1908, the Young Turks rebelled, Abdul-Hamid restored the liberal 1876 constitution. But after gaining what they desired for themselves, the Young Turks refused to share their victory with the non-Turkish peoples. The result was a counterrevolution, encouraged by the sultan, who sought to regain power. When Abdul-Hamid turned against the Young Turks, however, he was overthrown and replaced by his weak and innocuous brother.

Arabs in Syria, Lebanon, and the vast peninsula of Arabia writhed under the Young

Legend:
- Germans
- Czechs
- Slovaks
- Ruthenians
- Poles
- Magyars
- Slovenes
- Serbo-Croatians
- Italians
- Rumanians

THE NATIONALITIES OF AUSTRIA-HUNGARY

Turk's program of Turkish supremacy and their policy of centralization, which left no opportunity for Arab home rule. (When fighting against Turkey during World War I, Britain found it relatively easy to turn the Arab tribes against their overlord, the sultan.)

Meanwhile the disintegration of the Ottoman empire proceeded apace. In the years between 1908 and 1913, Austria-Hungary annexed Bosnia and Herzegovina, two Turkish provinces on the Adriatic that had been occupied and administered by the Dual Monarchy since 1878; Greece annexed Crete; and Italy, in the course of a short war, seized Tripoli and Cyrenaica. Finally, the Balkan nations fought two wars with the Ottoman empire in 1912 and 1913 and partitioned Turkish Macedonia. How these annexations and wars brought about disputes among the great powers, and in particular how they created an explosive situation in the Balkans that touched off World War I, will be discussed later in this chapter.

DEMOCRATIC ADVANCES IN OTHER EUROPEAN LANDS

Contributions of small states. During the nineteenth century (before the advent of totalitarian warfare), the small nations of Europe, wedged among the great powers, prevented dynamic and often jealous states from having contiguous boundaries. In an era when international law was supposed to have some validity, the recognition of the neutrality of such a country as Switzerland meant that great powers bordering on this neutralized area could assume that no attack would come from this quarter.

The trend toward democracy in the late nineteenth and early twentieth centuries was evident in these countries. For example, the enfranchisement of women was first introduced in Norway, proportional representation had its first trial in Belgium, and Switzerland invented the referendum and the initiative.

Switzerland. In 1848 Switzerland inaugurated a democratic constitution. In 1874 a major constitutional revision gave the central government more authority, but the cantons, the basic units of the federal system, continued to handle their local affairs. A program of compulsory education was provided for, and a militia system was established in which every man between the ages of twenty-six and forty-eight was liable for military training and duty. The Swiss institutions of the initiative and referendum, giving voters an opportunity to propose legislation and to approve or reject bills passed by the lawmaking body, have been copied in many parts of the world.

The Swiss governmental system made it possible for three basic nationalities speaking four languages (French, German, Italian, and Romansh) and professing two religions (Protestant and Roman Catholic) to live together in peace. An authority on nationalism has observed: "Only tiny Switzerland . . . offered practical demonstration of how, through sane federalism and real liberty, diverse nationalities could live together in amity and evince a common patriotism."[7]

Italy. After unification in 1871, Italy faced serious problems. The country had few natural resources, and the interests of the industrial north often clashed with those of the agricultural south. Furthermore, a religious issue seriously weakened the state. During the unification of Italy, the Italian government had seized Rome, formerly part of the papal domains. Terming himself "the prisoner of the Vatican," the pope called on Italian Catholics to refrain from voting. In an attempt at conciliation, the Italian government passed the Law of Papal Guarantees, by which the pope was to have the Vatican as a sovereign state and was to be given an annual sum of $600,000. Although this offer was rejected, the law was not repealed.

In the field of politics, the people lacked experience in or aptitude for constitutional government. Seventy-five per cent of the population was illiterate in 1861, and the franchise was very restricted. As late as 1904, only 29 per cent of the adult male population

could vote, and of this group only 38 per cent actually went to the polls. Political life suffered also from unstable coalitions.

Another grievous burden for the country was the ambition of its leaders to have Italy play a grand role in the world and thus fulfill the dreams of greatness built up during the *Risorgimento*. Too much money was spent on the army, and national resources were squandered in the unrewarding pursuit of empire in Africa.

Early in the twentieth century, liberals joined socialists in demanding such reforms as compulsory education, freedom of the press, and better working conditions for the masses. As a result, laws were passed in 1912 providing for universal suffrage and for payment of deputies in parliament.

The Netherlands and Belgium. From the middle of the nineteenth century to 1914, the main constitutional theme in the Netherlands was the demand for a more liberal franchise. Although concessions were won in 1887 and 1896, Holland was not a complete democracy even in 1914; forty per cent of its adult males were without the vote, as were all women.

English principles of responsible government had been adopted in Belgium in 1831, but the franchise was based on high property qualifications. A discontented proletariat formed a Socialist party determined to broaden the franchise, and general strikes were used frequently as a political weapon. In 1893 the vote was given to all men over twenty-five, but the use of plural voting (which gave some individuals two or three votes) robbed the working people of the fruits of their victory. In 1899 a system of proportional representation was adopted, but plural voting remained in use until the First World War.

Spain and Portugal. After a brief experience of republicanism, Spain in 1876 returned to monarchical government with a supposedly responsible parliament. Constitutional government, however, did not function well. Until 1890 the franchise was a narrow one based on high property qualifications. A vicious land system, an illiberal Church hierarchy, and a weak monarchy contributed to political instability and the failure of democracy in Spain.

Portugal's political history closely resembled that of Spain—revolution, graft, and political anarchy being prevalent during most of the nineteenth century. In 1910 the Portuguese monarchy was overthrown, and Portugal became a republic. This change did little to improve conditions, however, for the people showed little capacity for governing themselves.

The Scandinavian countries. The Scandinavian states had much better success at self-government. In these far-northern monarchies, the franchise was broadened and the principle of responsible government developed. In 1901 the king of Denmark agreed to the principle that his ministers must be chosen in accordance with the will of the legislature.

Norway came to be called the most democratic monarchy in the world. Universal manhood suffrage was introduced before Norway's separation from Sweden in 1905, and in 1913 the vote was granted to women.

In Sweden the democratic development lagged behind that in Norway and Denmark. In 1909 manhood suffrage was granted, but until 1914 the cabinet was not responsible to the lower house, and the king exercised considerable power, including an absolute veto.

FORCES FOR PEACE

AND BROTHERHOOD

Growing spirit of internationalism. As the nineteenth century came to a close, there was evidence of a growing spirit of internationalism and a deep yearning for peace among the peoples of the world. The growth of world trade, augmented by new marvels in transportation and communication, served to knit men together into a world community; and further evidences of such internationalism were numerous. In 1865 a conference which met in Paris to discuss the coordination of telegraph lines and the problem of rates established the International Telegraph Union, made up of twenty nations. To facilitate the handling of mail the world over, the Universal Postal Union was set up in 1875. As a protection for authors' rights, an agreement was drawn up in 1886 by an international copyright union. As part of the growing internationalism, the ancient Greek Olympic games were revived in 1896. Held every four years, the games attracted participants from nearly every nation.

The peace movement. The modern, organized world peace movement began early in the nineteenth century. Motivated by Christian principles, the British Society for the Promotion of Permanent and Universal Peace was organized in 1816, and thirty years later, the League of Universal Brotherhood was founded in the United States. While the first phase of the pacifist movement was for the most part religiously motivated, the second (beginning in the late 1860's) emphasized the solution of practical problems, such as improvements in international law and the rules of warfare and creation of machinery for arbitrating disputes. After 1889 a Universal Peace Congress convened annually until the First World War shattered its hopes.

The contributions of famous individuals were also important to the movement for world peace. Alfred Nobel, the famous Swedish manufacturer of dynamite, established the Nobel Peace Prize; and Andrew Carnegie founded the Carnegie Endowment for International Peace and built a Peace Palace at The Hague to be used for international conferences. (Ironically, the building was finished just before the outbreak of the First World War.)

Arbitration and international law. While the desire for peace was perhaps stronger among the people than it was among their governments, a habit of political collaboration was developing among various nations. The first Pan-American Conference, consisting of eighteen countries, assembled in 1889 at Washington, D.C., to discuss matters of common economic interest as well as problems pertaining to the maintenance of peace in the Western Hemisphere. Arbitration between nations appeared to be on the increase. In the ten years following 1903, various powers signed 162 arbitration treaties, pledging the signatories to arbitrate certain matters.

In 1899 the Russian foreign minister invited the great powers to attend a conference on the reduction of armaments. Although no progress was made on disarmament, the conference did adopt a number of points in international law on rules of war relating to treatment of prisoners, outlawed the use of poisonous gas, and defined the conditions of a state of belligerency. A court of arbitration, the Hague Tribunal, was established; and a list of jurists from which nations could select judges was drawn up. Recourse to the court was voluntary and so was acceptance of its decisions.

FORCES OF WAR AND HATE

Forces of antagonism. At the same time that some forces were working to bring about closer cooperation between nations and peoples, other forces were promoting distrust and rivalries. These antagonistic forces finally triumphed, and, as a result, Europe and most of the world with it were plunged into war in 1914. Underlying causes of this great conflict were the actions of national states in power politics, militarism, rival alliances, secret diplomacy, economic imperialism, and nationalism.

Europe in 1914 consisted of some twenty independent political units. Recognizing no higher authority, each of these states went its own way; international law was obeyed only if its dicta did not clash with a nation's interests. The great powers were ready to take advantage of any neighbor's weakness and to resort to war if the prize to be seized or the danger to be averted was substantial enough. War was an instrument of national policy, to be used whenever peaceful methods failed.

When force is the ultimate arbiter in international affairs, military strength becomes extremely important. By the end of the 1870's, all six of the major European powers except Britain had introduced compulsory military training. By the first decade of the twentieth century, the great powers had nearly 4,500,-000 men under arms and were spending annually more than $2,000,000,000 on armaments. Thus the armament race began, and the faster it went, the higher tension mounted.

Living in this uneasy atmosphere of international anarchy, where a nation could not trust its neighbors, no state felt strong enough to rely upon its own military resources for protection. Therefore, nations whose interests ran along parallel lines joined together to muster more fighting power. But this, in turn, provoked nations outside the alliance to form a union capable of matching strength with strength. While the creation of two rival alliances was a feature of European diplomacy in the last part of the nineteenth century (see pp. 560-562), it brought no security to the states involved. In fact, the prospects of a major war were multiplied because the alliances made it unlikely that any conflict could be localized. This is shown by what happened in the summer of 1914.

Closely connected with the system of alliances was the practice of secret diplomacy. Diplomats threatened, intimidated, jockeyed for power, and offered bribes. The activities of spies, the secret reports, and the unscrupulous methods of the foreign offices of Europe poisoned the atmosphere of international politics and heightened the tension still further.

After 1870 the world's markets were viewed as a battleground with businessmen as the combatants. Laissez faire gave way to a new kind of mercantilism in which governments acted as aggressive champions for their own business interests. One of the most significant features of this neomercantilism was economic imperialism, a struggle for control of the colonial areas of the world. As we shall see in Chapter 26, governments began to use their diplomatic power and even their armies to secure control of areas rich in essential raw materials or valuable as markets for manufactured goods. In some cases, economic competition led to war. Japanese designs upon the Asiatic mainland brought about war with China in 1894, and Great Britain fought the Boer War in South Africa in 1899-1902. Japan and Russia fought over Manchuria in 1904-1905, and Italy wrested Tripoli from Turkey in 1912.

The emotion of nationalism. Nationalism—particularly the narrow, blatant, and bellicose variety of the late nineteenth century—has been rightly regarded as one of the most potent causes of modern war. Among both subordinated and ruling groups, national loyalty was an intense, explosive emotion. Inflated patriotism became a new religion, the emotional adjunct to power politics. In the opinion of many people, the most important fundamental cause of the First World War was rampant nationalism.

In Germany, for example, the Pan-Germanic League was organized to spread the doctrine of the superiority of the German race and culture. The League was a leader in anti-English agitation; it supported German colonial ambitions; it sought to retain the loyalty of all Germans to the fatherland no matter where they were living in the world; and it worked to promote a policy of German power both in Europe and overseas.

As it turned out, the greatest danger to peace was the flame of nationalism that burned fiercely in the new Balkan nations. Proud of their new freedom, they were determined to extend it to their brothers still under the Turks. Serbia in particular was ready to liberate the other Slavic groups and unite with itself the Slavs in Bosnia and Herzegovina and in Albania. This ambition, known as the Greater Serbia movement, was aimed not only against the Turks but also against the Hapsburgs, who ruled the Southern Slavs.

The Greater Serbia movement was a local manifestation of the Russian-sponsored Pan-Slavism (see p. 539). Representatives of the various Slavic nations looked to Russia as the protector of all oppressed Slavs, especially those in the Dual Monarchy.

Anti-Semitism and Zionism. Speaking of Pan-Germanism and Pan-Slavism, a famous historian refers to their development as the "seed time of totalitarian nationalism." These pernicious ideas of racial superiority were later to develop into the hideous campaign of extermination which Adolf Hitler and his Nazi henchmen carried out against certain supposedly inferior peoples, concentrating primarily on the Jews.

A foretaste of what racial nationalism would bring in the twentieth century was provided by the treatment of the Jews in the later nineteenth century. After suffering from many injustices and restrictions during the Middle Ages, the Jews in western Europe and in the Americas secured practically all the rights of full citizens after 1800. With this advance came new opportunities; and Jews in many countries made significant contributions to art, music, literature, and science. About 1850, however, a strong anti-Semitic movement began to appear in Europe. German nationalists like Heinrich von Treitschke coined the phrase "The Jews are our calamity." In France, anti-Semitism reached a climax in the Dreyfus affair. In eastern Europe, the Jewish minorities suffered many injustices, but their hardest lot was in Russia. In the tsar's realm the Jews had to live in specified western provinces, the so-called Jewish Pale. They were forbidden to buy certain kinds of property. Their admittance to schools was restricted, and they had to pay twice the taxes of corresponding non-Jewish communities. Used at times as scapegoats, many Jews were murdered in pogroms carried out with the encouragement of the government.

From the injustices of anti-Semitism in the last century grew the desire for a Jewish homeland. Thus the exaggerated nationalism of other peoples bred a nationalistic spirit among the Jews themselves. In 1896 a Hungarian Jew, Theodor Herzl, came forward with the program of Zionism, which had as its purpose the creation of Palestine as an independent state. Herzl claimed that the Jews were a distinct nationality and thus were entitled to have a country of their own. The first general congress of Zionists was held in Switzerland in 1897, and small-scale immigration to Palestine began.

"THE LAMPS ARE GOING OUT"

Bismarck's diplomatic footwork. After 1871 and the conclusion of the Franco-Prussian War, the German chancellor was well aware that France would try to inflict revenge on

Germany and take back Alsace-Lorraine. Therefore, Bismarck deliberately set out to eliminate France from the diplomatic game. In 1873 he made an alliance with Russia and Austria-Hungary, known as the Three Emperors' League; but at the Congress of Berlin (1878) he was forced to choose between the claims of Austria and those of Russia in the Balkans. Bismarck chose to support Austria because he trusted that empire more than he did Russia. He was afraid also that supporting Russia would alienate Great Britain.

A year later Bismarck negotiated the Dual Alliance with the Austrian government, and in 1882 a new partner, Italy, was secured, thus bringing into operation the Triple Alliance. The choice of Austria as a close ally in preference to Russia did not mean that Bismarck was reconciled to the loss of the latter's friendship. In 1881 the Three Emperors' League was renewed, but when rivalries between Austria and Russia in the Balkans made it impossible for these two powers to be in the same group, the alliance collapsed in 1887. To fill the gap, Bismarck negotiated a separate alliance with Russia called the Reinsurance Treaty.

Under the masterful hand of Bismarck, Germany retained hegemony over the European continent from 1871 to 1890. The chancellor had succeeded admirably in his diplomacy. Every effort was made to avoid challenging the interests of Britain, which continued to isolate itself from alliances. France had been kept in diplomatic quarantine without allies. Through amazing diplomatic acrobatics, Bismarck had managed to avoid alienating Russia while retaining an alliance with Austria.

In a single move, however, the preponderance of power built up by Bismarck was heedlessly cast away. In 1890 the new German kaiser, young William II, dismissed the old chancellor and took German foreign policy into his own hands. Foolishly allowing the Reinsurance Treaty to lapse, he permitted Russia to seek new allies. France immediately began to woo Russia; millions of French francs went to buy Russian bonds, and France in 1894 received what it had wanted for twenty years—a strong military ally. The Triple Alliance was now confronted by the Dual Alliance.

England in diplomatic isolation. At the end of the nineteenth century, Britain was involved in bitter rivalries with Russia in the Balkans and Afghanistan and with France in Africa. During the Boer War all the great powers in Europe were anti-British. Only the supremacy of England's fleet effectively discouraged the development of an interventionist movement. More and more, Great Britain became disquited by its policy of diplomatic isolation.

It was these circumstances which explained British overtures to Germany in 1898 and again in 1901. The Germans were not favorably impressed by the offer of a British alliance and interpreted it as a sign of British weakness.

Germany not only refused Britain's suggestions for an alliance but embarked on an aggressive policy known as *Weltpolitik* (world politics). Through this policy it determined not only to be the first military power in Europe but to expand its influence in the Middle East and the Balkans, secure more colonies overseas, and build a battle fleet second to none. A huge naval program was initiated in 1900, providing for the construction of a fleet strong enough to jeopardize Britain's naval supremacy within twenty years. For England the supremacy of the royal navy was a life-or-death matter. Since food and raw materials had to come by sea, it was crucial that the royal navy be able to protect British shipping. The British were disturbed also at the tremendous strides made by German industry, as well as by the kaiser's threatening and irresponsible speeches and unpredictable behavior. Rebuffed and challenged by Germany, Britain turned elsewhere to establish friendly relations.

In 1904 Britain and France settled their outstanding differences and proclaimed the Entente Cordiale, a French term which means "friendly understanding." The Entente Cordiale and England's alliance with Japan in 1902 ended Britain's traditional policy of isolation and brought it into the diplomatic combination pitted against Germany's Triple Alliance. In 1907 Britain settled its problems with Russia, thereby establishing the Triple Entente. Great Britain made no definite military commitments in the agreements with France and Russia. Theoretically it retained freedom of action but, for all this, it was now part of the alliance system.

Diplomatic crises: 1905-1914. For a decade before the First World War, Europe experienced a series of crises brought about as the two alliance systems flexed their muscles and probed each other's strength. As each new diplomatic crisis arose, Europe teetered on the abyss of war.

The first serious diplomatic crisis occurred in 1905 and concerned Morocco. France sought control of this territory in order to establish a stretch of contiguous dependencies from the Atlantic across the North African coast to Tunisia. Carefully timing his moves, the German chancellor arranged for the kaiser to visit the Moroccan port of Tangier, where he declared that all powers must respect the independence of the country. The French were forced to give up their immediate plans for taking over Morocco and agree to Germany's suggestion that an international conference be called at Algeciras (1906) to discuss the matter.

At this meeting the German hope that a rift might appear between the British and French did not materialize. On the contrary, all but one of the nations in attendance— even Italy—supported France rather than Germany. Only Austria remained at the side of Germany. It was agreed that Morocco should still enjoy its sovereignty but that France and Spain should be given certain rights to police the area. The events at Algeciras and the British agreement with Russia the following year (1907) filled the Germans with dread.

In 1911 a second Moroccan crisis heightened the tension. When France sent an army into the disputed territory "to maintain order," Germany countered by dispatching the gunboat *Panther* to the Moroccan port of Agadir. Great Britain came out with a plain warning that all its power was at the disposal of France. A diplomatic bargain was struck whereby France got a free hand in Morocco, and Germany was granted French holdings in equatorial Africa.

The Balkan nemesis. Although the two rival alliance systems had managed somehow to avert an armed showdown over Morocco, these happy auguries were of no avail against the forces of rival imperialism and nationalism unleashed in the Balkans.

Both Germany and Austria were opposed to Russia's Pan-Slavic ambitions in the Balkans. German motives were largely economic, while the Austrian concern was primarily defensive. As a polyglot empire containing millions of Slavs, Austria-Hungary feared an expanding Serbia, egged on by Russia. Therefore, to counter the advance of the Greater Serbia movement, Austria annexed outright the provinces of Bosnia-Herzegovina, which it had administered since 1878. This high-handed move produced a dangerous crisis. Russia was furious and Serbia was equally exercised over the incorporation of its Slavic brothers into the Hapsburg domain. But because Russia had come out of its war with Japan (1904-1905) badly battered, it could not support Serbia against the combined might of Germany and Austria. In this crisis the Triple Alliance had humbled Russia and thwarted the plans of Russia's protégé Serbia.

In 1912 Serbia and its neighbors, especially Greece and Bulgaria, formed an alliance with the objective of expelling Turkey from Europe. The First Balkan War began later in that year and was quickly terminated as Turkish resistance crumpled. The victorious Balkan nations were not permitted to divide their spoils, however, and the result was the Second Balkan War. Denied Albania by Austria, the Serbs, aided by the Greeks, demanded compensation of territory originally promised to Bulgaria. Bulgaria attacked its former allies, and Turkey and Rumania in turn entered the war against Bulgaria, which was no match for its numerous opponents. A peace was signed by which Bulgaria gave up to its former allies most of the territory originally taken from Turkey. Turkey retained only a

THE BALKANS IN 1914

Independent States

precarious toe hold in Europe, the small pocket around Constantinople.

By the end of 1913 no permanent solution had been found to the Balkan problem. Austria was more fearful than ever of the Greater Serbia movement, and Serbian ambitions had grown larger, since its territory had doubled as a result of the recent wars. The Serbian prime minister is quoted as saying: "The first round is won; now we must prepare the second against Austria." As for Russia, its Pan-Slavic dreams had not been completely blocked but only interrupted. The dynamite in the Balkan bomb was the involvement of the major powers.

The archduke assassinated. The fateful spark came on June 28, 1914, when Archduke Francis Ferdinand, heir to the Austrian throne, and his wife were assassinated in the town of Sarajevo in Bosnia. This deed was

the work of a young Bosnian student inspired by Greater Serbia propaganda. He and two associates received assistance from high Serbian officers, although the direct complicity of the Serbian government has not been proved. Even so, that it could have been ignorant of the plot seems unlikely.

Count Leopold von Berchtold (1863-1942), the Austrian foreign minister, believed that the assassination justified crushing, once and for all, the anti-Austrian propaganda and terrorism emanating from Serbia. Austria could take no action, however, without securing the support of its ally, Germany.

The kaiser felt that everything possible must be done to prevent Austria, Germany's only reliable ally, from being weakened by such forces as Serbian terrorism, and so he assured the Austrian government of his full support. Thus Berchtold obtained a blank check from Germany. Vienna wanted only a local Austro-Serbian war, and Germany favored quick action to forestall intervention.

The Austrian ultimatum and Russian mobilization. On July 23 a harsh Austro-Hungarian ultimatum was presented to the Serbs. Intending that the ultimatum be turned down, Berchtold demanded unconditional acceptance within forty-eight hours. On July 25 the Austrian government announced that Serbia's reply was unsatisfactory and mobilized its armed forces. Meanwhile, the German chancellor urged Austria to negotiate with Russia, which was following developments closely. Russia realized that if the Austrians succeeded in humbling Serbia, Russian prestige in this area would suffer tremendously. The French in the meantime assured the Russians of their full cooperation and urged strong support for Serbia, while the British advised negotiations, but without success.

Fearful that Serbia would escape from his clutches, Berchtold succeeded on July 27, thanks in part to falsehood, in convincing the Hapsburg emperor that war was the only way out. On the following day, war was declared against Serbia. As the possibility of a general European war loomed, several frantic telegrams were sent by Berlin to Vienna. The German ambassador was instructed to tell Berchtold:

As an ally we must refuse to be drawn into a world conflagration because Austria does not respect our advice.[8]

At this critical stage, when German pressure on Austria might have opened a path to peace, an event took place which wrecked any further attempts at negotiation. This was the Russian mobilization order proclaimed on July 30.

To Germany, the question of Russian mobilization was especially vital, because, in the event of war with Russia and France, Germany would be confronted with enemies on two fronts. The best plan seemed to be to launch a lightning attack against France, crush France, and then turn to meet Russia, which could ordinarily be expected to mobilize rather slowly. To allow Russian mobilization to proceed would jeopardize this strategy.

War declared. On July 31 the government in Berlin dispatched ultimatums to Russia and France demanding from the former cessation of mobilization and from the latter a pledge of neutrality. Failing to receive satisfactory replies, Germany declared war on Russia August 1 and on France August 3. On August 2 an ultimatum was delivered by the German ambassador in Brussels, announcing his country's intention of sending troops through Belgium. The Belgian cabinet refused to grant permission and appealed to Russia, France, and Great Britain for aid in protecting its neutrality. A majority in the British cabinet did not favor war, but with the news of the German ultimatum to Belgium, the tide turned. Sir Edward Grey, the British foreign secretary, sent an ultimatum to Germany demanding that Belgian neutrality be respected. This Germany refused to do, and on August 4 Great Britain declared war.

In the last few days of peace, diplomats strove desperately to avert general war. The atmosphere of anguish and gloom is reflected in a passage from Grey's autobiography:

A friend came to see me on one of the evenings of the last week [before the war]—he thinks it was on Monday, August 3. We were standing at a window of my room in the Foreign Office. It was getting dusk, and the lamps were being lit in the space below on which we were looking. My friend recalls that I remarked on this with the words: "The lamps are going out all over Europe; we shall not see them lit again in our life-time."[9]

On the basis that Germany and Austria were not waging a defensive war, Italy refused to carry out its obligations under the Triple Alliance and for the time being remained neutral. In the latter part of August, Japan joined the Allies; and in October, Turkey, fearing the designs of Russia, threw in its lot with the Central Powers, Germany and Austria.

The question of war guilt. At the outset Germany made a serious blunder when its chancellor referred to the treaty of 1839 guaranteeing the neutrality of Belgium—signed by the European powers, including Prussia—as "a scrap of paper." Thus, Germany put itself morally in the wrong as a breaker of treaties, a position that lost it support and sympathy the world over.

The structure of the Treaty of Versailles, as we shall see later, rested in large part on the war guilt of Germany. When the treaty was first written, scholars and laymen alike in the Allied nations sincerely believed that Germany was completely responsible for the war. As a more realistic perspective has developed in the light of new evidence, it has become increasingly clear that the problem is more complex than had been originally thought. Today, most historians agree it is next to impossible to try to explain the war in terms of the actions of any one of the great powers. Rather, all the major participating nations must accept, in some measure, responsibility for the outbreak of the First World War. In the final analysis, it is needless to try to apportion the blame, for the tragedy was inherent in the prevailing order of international anarchy.

SUMMARY

By the end of the nineteenth century, western Europe had experienced a veritable revolution in many substantial aspects of its pattern of life. The political predominance of the aristocracy and the business classes was coming to an end; the bourgeois creed of political liberalism with its restricted suffrage had been undermined by the creed of mass democracy; and, in the economic field, state intervention to assure a measure of economic security had largely replaced laissez faire. This democratically oriented type of welfare state advanced much more rapidly in western than in eastern Europe. Britain, France, Denmark, and Switzerland best represented the western democratic tradition. In contrast to these nations, a number of other states in Europe lacked democratic traditions and experience in self-government. The Nazi tyranny, the despotism of Soviet Russia, and the tyranny in Russia's satellites—all have their roots in the failure of parliamentary government to become established in parts of central and eastern Europe between 1870 and 1914.

What was destined to be one of the truly historic movements of the twentieth century was the awakening, during this period, of the Arab people. Under Ottoman rule the Near East had been cruelly misgoverned and its people kept in ignorance. The diffusion of western culture, and especially of liberal political ideas, sparked a nationalistic revival which was to become increasingly powerful in the years ahead.

Europe's golden age—the nineteenth century—was brought to an end by a combination of tragic forces: militarism, rival alliances, economic imperialism, secret diplomacy, and, most important of all, narrow and bellicose nationalism. All these factors existed in their most virulent form in the Balkans, where they finally exploded. And so powerful and pervasive were they that they not only involved Europe in general war but most of the rest of the world as well.

SUGGESTIONS FOR READING

C. J. H. Hayes, *A Generation of Materialism, 1871-1900,* Harper (*The Rise of Modern Europe* series), 1941. A lucid, penetrating survey of European life, thought, and politics during this period. Contains a valuable bibliographical essay.

G. P. Gooch, *History of Modern Europe, 1878-1919,* Holt, 1923; and M. Bruce, *The Shaping of the Modern World, 1870-1914,* Random House, 1958. Two standard surveys; the first work emphasizes diplomatic history. See also A. J. P. Taylor, *The Struggle for Mastery in Europe, 1848-1918,* Oxford, 1954.

R. Ensor, *England, 1870-1914,* Oxford, 1936. A standard work, dealing with economic and social as well as political history. Also recommended are the sections on political reform, the Irish question, and social legislation in *British History in the Nineteenth Century and After, 1782-1919,* Longmans, 1938, by the eminent British historian G. M. Trevelyan.

A. Maurois, *The Edwardian Era,* Appleton-Century, 1933. A sprightly paced, perceptive account of the British scene before World War I. H. Ausubel, *The Late Victorians: A Short History,* * Anvil, is a brief interpretative study which stresses economic factors.

*Indicates an inexpensive paperbound edition.

The progress of democracy in England is discussed with clarity and force in O. F. Christie, *The Transition to Democracy, 1867-1914,* Routledge, 1934; and in R. L. Schuyler and C. C. Weston, *British Constitutional History Since 1832,** Anvil. The major part of the latter work deals with the period after the passage of the Reform Bill of 1867.

D. W. Brogan, *France Under the Republic,* Harper, 1940. A brilliant political history of the Third Republic, 1870-1939. A fine interpretative essay, not a chronological narrative, is D. Thomson, *Democracy in France: The Third and Fourth Republics,* Oxford, 1958. Highly recommended as a study of the Third Republic and the dynamic politician who for sixty years played a major role in every important governmental crisis is J. H. Jackson, *Clemenceau and the Third Republic,* Macmillan, 1948.

G. Chapman, *The Dreyfus Case: A Re-assessment,* Viking, 1956. A moving, up-to-date reappraisal. Another vivid account is J. Kayser, *The Dreyfus Affair,* Covici, 1931, which includes a description of Dreyfus' terrible captivity on Devil's Island.

E. J. Passant, *A Short History of Germany, 1850-1945,* Cambridge Univ., 1959. A recent and authoritative general survey. W. H. Dawson, *The German Empire, 1867-1914, and the Unity Movement,* 2 vols., Macmillan, 1919, is somewhat dated but is of value in understanding the continuing struggle in Germany between conservative and liberal forces. See also C. Schorske, *German Social Democracy, 1905-1917: The Development of the Great Schism,* Harvard, 1955, a thorough analysis of the Social Democratic party.

J. von Kürenberg, *The Kaiser,* Simon and Schuster, 1955. A brilliant biography of William II, last German emperor.

A. J. May, *The Hapsburg Monarchy, 1867-1914,* Harvard, 1951. An excellent general survey, especially good on domestic affairs. Two competent studies of the minorities problem in the Hapsburg empire and the ultimate triumph of nationalism are O. Jaszi, *The Dissolution of the Hapsburg Monarchy: A Failure in Civic Training,** Phoenix; and R. A. Kann, *The Habsburg Empire: A Study in Integration and Disintegration,* Praeger, 1957.

C. Sprigge, *The Development of Modern Italy,* Yale, 1944. A brief study which terminates in the years when Fascism emerged. B. Croce, *A History of Italy, 1871-1915,* Oxford, 1929, is an analysis of Italian parliamentary government by the famous Italian historian-philosopher.

H. Seton-Watson, *The Decline of Imperial Russia, 1855-1914,** Praeger. The best survey of the period. A notable account of the reign of Nicholas II is R. Charques, *The Twilight of Imperial Russia,* Oxford (Essential Books), 1959. R. Hough, *The Fleet That Had to Die,* Viking, 1958, is a vivid account of the Russian navy's colossal blunders in their clash with the Japanese in 1904.

G. Kennan, *Siberia and the Exile System,* abr. ed., Univ. of Chicago, 1958. First published in 1891, this work is a shocking exposé of the conditions in the tsarist prisons.

H. Kohn, *Pan-Slavism: Its History and Ideology,* Univ. of Notre Dame, 1953. Describes the ideological basis of Russia's "mission" and discusses Russia's cultural and political expansion. See also C. Jelavich, *Tsarist Russia and Balkan Nationalism,* Univ. of Calif., 1958.

E. E. Ramsaur, Jr., *The Young Turks: Prelude to the Revolution of 1908,* Princeton, 1957. A provocative account of the conspiratorial movement that aimed at ending the sultan's misrule and preserving the integrity of the Ottoman empire.

For general surveys of the history of the Ottoman empire and the Balkan nations, see the Suggestions for Reading at the end of Chapter 22.

N. Mansergh, *The Coming of the First World War: A Study in the European Balance, 1878-1914,* Longmans, 1949. A brief, excellent introduction to the subject. See also J. W. Swain, *Beginning the Twentieth Century,* Norton, 1938; G. L. Dickinson, *The International Anarchy, 1904-1914,* G. Allen, 1937.

Two classics in the field of diplomatic history, both by W. L. Langer, are *European Alliances and Alignments, 1871-1890,* Knopf, 1950; and *The Diplomacy of Imperialism, 1890-1902,* Knopf, 1951. See also R. J. Sontag, *European Diplomatic History, 1871-1932,* Appleton-Century, 1933.

B. E. Schmitt, *England and Germany, 1740-1914,* Princeton, 1918. An analysis of national rivalries which is sympathetic to the British viewpoint. R. J. Sontag, *Germany and England: Background of Conflict, 1848-1894,* Appleton-Century, 1938, presents the thesis that the two nations were antagonistic, both institutionally and psychologically.

E. L. Woodward, *Great Britain and the German Navy,* Oxford, 1935; and A. J. Marder, *The Anatomy of British Sea Power: A History of British Naval Policy in the Pre-Dreadnought Era, 1880-1905,* Knopf, 1940. Excellent studies of the naval rivalry between the two powers.

A great bulk of works has been written dealing with the question of "war guilt." The following are representative: M. E. Durham, *The Sarajevo Crime,* Putnam, 1925, places the blame on Serbia; H. E. Barnes, *Genesis of the World War: An Introduction to the Problem of War Guilt,* Knopf, 1935, finds France and Britain the chief culprits; L. Albertini, *The Origins of the War of 1914,* 2 vols. (ed. by L. M. Massey), Oxford, 1952-1953, exhibits a strongly pro-Italian slant; E. Brandenburg, *From Bismarck to the World War: History of German Foreign Policy, 1870-1914,* Oxford, 1933, maintains an admirable restraint and objectivity; S. B. Fay, *The Origins of the World War,* 2 vols., Macmillan, 1930, presents the best-balanced treatment; and D. E. Lee, ed., *The Outbreak of the First World War: Who Was Responsible?** Heath, is a convenient collection of short excerpts from scholarly studies.

CHAPTER 24

Survival of the Fittest

THE SECOND INDUSTRIAL REVOLUTION;
THOUGHT AND ART: 1871-1914

Introduction. For Europe, the nineteenth century was a golden age of progress and prosperity. The danger of class warfare was waning as governments showed increasing solicitude for their peoples' economic and social needs. Illiteracy was being reduced by the spread of public school systems. The franchise was being broadened; parliamentary government and mass suffrage were crowding out aristocratic plutocracy; political liberty was on the march. Meanwhile, applied science was extending its blessings to every social level and raising the living standards of millions. As new forms of transportation and communication telescoped distances, the Second Industrial Revolution was rushing the nations of the world into a new relationship of interdependence.

Buoyed by their firm conviction that "God's in his heaven—All's right with the world,"[1] the

Victorians faced the second half of the nineteenth century with optimism. By 1870, however, marked changes had taken place in the intellectual and social environment. The members of the prospering middle class still had little reason to doubt that theirs was the best of all possible worlds—but was God in His heaven? Between the latest findings of science and the traditional religious faith on which their beliefs and moral values rested, a great conflict had arisen. The mid-Victorians had been brought up to believe that the creation of the world and the life thereon had been an act of God and that nature revealed the workings of His moral law. But when Darwin in 1859 put forward his famous thesis that all organic life was engaged in a struggle for existence and that the survival or extinction of all species depended on their adaptability, nature was seen as simply a blind life-and-death struggle, stripped of all morality. This harsh and uncompromising doctrine set off a bitter debate between the advocates of science and those of religion.

However abhorrent to traditional religious beliefs, the doctrine of the survival of the fittest was in fact thoroughly compatible with political, economic, and even cultural activities in the period from 1870 to 1914. In manifold ways, science, philosophy, and the arts contributed to or reflected the increasingly realistic attitudes that flourished during this "generation of materialism." This period was distinguished by unprecedented scientific discoveries, resulting in the magnificent contributions of such men as Clerk-Maxwell, Einstein, and Freud. Put to practical use, the new advances in knowledge helped to eradicate disease, improve industrial methods, raise living standards, and revolutionize the techniques of the social sciences. On the other hand, there developed a cult of science whose practitioners were too often guilty of intellectual arro‚ance and of a dangerous oversimplification of human affairs.

With such people it became all too easy to think of progress purely in materialistic terms and to argue that physical well-being was all that mattered.

In literature, painting, and sculpture, reaction to the impact of scientific and technological achievements took the form of realism, later extended into an unblushing, facts-of-life school known as naturalism. While this realistic approach characterized the works of many writers and artists throughout the period—and indeed is evident in our own day as well—still other significant movements evolved. An increasing number of writers protested against the injustices suffered by individuals in a society where cutthroat competition was defended and human exploitation excused as immutable elements in the struggle to survive. Other artists, reacting against the baldly mechanistic view of man as a mere automaton whose every move was predictable, devised new movements in the arts—expressionism and symbolism—each with special techniques for representing the subjective feelings of the individual.

THE SECOND INDUSTRIAL REVOLUTION

Traits of the new industrialism. Between 1870 and 1914 a new surge of industrial and technological progress occurred, important enough to warrant being called the Second Industrial Revolution. Industry used scientific techniques, allying itself with the laboratory; mass production methods involving the use of interchangeable parts and the assembly line were introduced; and chemistry devised a host of new materials. Synthetic goods and by-products, new processes in metallurgy, new explosives, textiles, and many other manufactures—all were made possible by the research chemist.

The Second Industrial Revolution was marked by a veritable avalanche of inventions. In 1876 a working dynamo was invented that could produce electricity in any required amount; less than a decade later, the compound steam turbine was perfected. As the use of electric power was stepped up, the western world entered the age of electricity, which now provided energy for factories, lighting for homes and city streets, and power for streetcars hitherto drawn by horses. The self-taught American genius Thomas Edison helped to exploit the myriad possibilities of electricity: he supervised the construction in New York City of the first central electric power plant in the world, and many of his more than twelve hundred patents involved machines and gadgets powered by electricity.

The field of communications was revolutionized by the introduction of electrical devices. The first telephone was invented by Alexander Graham Bell in 1876, and in 1895 Guglielmo Marconi revealed his brain child—wireless telegraphy. Three years later, wireless messages were being transmitted across the English Channel, and within six years, across the Atlantic.

No less a revolution was taking place in transportation. In the 1880's a successful internal-combustion engine using gasoline as fuel was constructed and then applied to a bicycle and a carriage. From these crude beginnings came the motorcycle and the automobile. In the field of automobile manufacturing, the United States took an early lead. Henry Ford began large-scale production of his Model T in 1909, and by 1914 some two million motor cars were registered in the United States. Another form of the internal-combustion engine—designed to burn crude oil, a much cheaper fuel than gasoline—was designed by a German engineer, Rudolf Diesel, who took out his patent in 1892. A successful competitor to the steam engine and the electric motor, the Diesel engine was used especially for driving locomotives, electric generators, and marine pumps.

This was also the period when man acquired wings. In the 1890's, attempts were made to construct a heavier-than-air craft with propellers run by internal-combustion engines. The climax came at Kitty Hawk, North Carolina, on December 17, 1903, when Orville and Wilbur Wright succeeded in keeping their fragile biplane aloft for twelve seconds.

Meanwhile, other important inventions were making their appearance. The invention in 1886 of the linotype machine (which made typesetting by hand obsolete) and the manufacture of cheap wood-pulp paper made possible the production of urban newspapers on a mass scale. In 1888 the Kodak camera was developed. Entertainment was enlivened by Edison's invention of the phonograph in 1877 and of the motion picture, first exhibited publicly in 1896.

The spread of industrialism. During the period of the Second Industrial Revolution, the world could be divided into three economic areas. The highly industrialized area was concentrated in western Europe, in the northern United States, and in Japan. In the area just beginning to be touched by industry were such countries as Italy, Spain, the Balkan states, Russia, and Canada. The third area, consisting of all of Africa, the Middle East, and all of Asia except Japan, was outside the industrial realm. This third zone can be called "the world of empire," for most of its vast territories were colonies of the industrial powers or objects of foreign exploitation.

As we saw in Chapter 20, Great Britain was the pioneer in industrialization. But after 1870, new and vigorous competitors, primarily the United States, Germany, and Japan, became important industrial nations. In 1870 Britain had more textile spindles and looms and produced more coal and iron than all the rest of the world. By 1910 it had only 40 per cent of the spindles and 30 per cent of the looms of the world and produced only 26 per cent of the world's coal and 14 per cent of the world's iron. In banking and shipping, however, Britain still led the pack. Its ships carried 40 per cent of all the world's commerce, and London was the world's main source of capital. Although Britain had an "unfavorable" balance of trade (imported more goods than it exported), it received nearly a billion dollars annually from overseas investments, shipping fees, insurance, and banking services. These "invisible exports" kept Great Britain out of the red.

After the conclusion of the Civil War, industrialization in the United States proceeded at an amazing rate (see p. 600). In 1860 the total value of American manufactures was less than $2,000,000,000; by 1900 the figure was nearly seven times as large.

The unification of the German empire was in part responsible for the astounding growth of German industrialization. Other factors included the acquisition from France in 1871 of the extremely rich iron-mining and manufacturing districts of Alsace and Lorraine; the payment by France of a war indemnity of 5,000,000,000 francs, which gave Germany a sharp increase of capital for industrial purposes; and the rapid growth of population (from 41,000,000 in 1871 to almost 65,000,000 in 1910). The Germans concentrated primarily on the development of such new enterprises as the chemical and electrical industries. The government played a decisive role in this expansion by designing tariffs to aid the new industries and by setting up technical schools to train personnel. In the chemical industry the Germans seized undisputed first place—by 1900 they produced four fifths of the world's dyestuffs—and in the electrical industry Germany's skilled technicians were soon producing intricate equipment destined for all countries of the world.

After isolated Japan had been opened to the West in the mid-nineteenth century, the Industrial Revolution was introduced there. Economic changes came with pell-mell rapidity: the labor market was large, and workmen could always be found to work at a low wage, enabling the Japanese manufacturer to undersell his rivals in other nations. The government aided industrialization by subsidizing railroads and steamship lines, and large supplies of coal were available. Specializing in textiles, Japan created serious competition for the mills of Manchester. The pace of industrialization in Japan is best indicated by the following facts: in 1870 no manufactured goods were exported; in 1906 the value of manufactures exported had reached $100,000,000.

Growth of world trade. The Second Industrial Revolution set in motion strong forces binding the world into one interdependent economic unit. The tremendous increase in manufacturing productivity caused the most highly industrialized regions of the world to seek new markets in the backward zones. There was also a demand for huge quantities of raw materials—cotton, tin, oil, tea, coffee, wheat, sugar, and timber. In 1860 world trade amounted to slightly more than $7,000,000,000; in 1913 the figure was nearly $42,000,000,000.

A world-wide market existed in which commodities, capital, currency, and economic services were freely exchanged. In 1879 an era of free trade ended as tariffs began to go up, but the rates remained moderate, and the effect on world commerce was slight. All the important currencies—the dollar, franc, mark, and pound—were redeemable in gold, and their exchange rates were stable. One nation might have an unfavorable balance of trade with several nations but, at the same time, a favorable balance with others, so that in the long run the debit and credit transactions balanced out.

The great industrialized area of western Europe accumulated vast sums of wealth between 1870 and 1914. Capital investments at home and abroad doubled in Britain and France and tripled in Germany. This outflow of capital helped the backward regions to develop; and in turn the borrowing countries could sell their commodities, mainly raw materials, to the industrialized nations.

Materially aiding this world economic interdependence was what might be termed the export of people. The higher standard of living and lower death rate in western Europe led to an unparalleled increase in population. From 1870 to 1914 the European continent registered an increase of 100,000,000 people. But at the same time a quarter of that number migrated to the great unsettled regions of North and South America, to Australia, and, to a lesser extent, to South Africa. This vast movement of people helped to develop backward and underpopulated lands and also created expanding markets for European goods.

Business consolidates. In the rush of new products and factories, businessmen became aware of the advantages of consolidation. By being big, a business could enjoy the economies of mass production, could buy raw materials in huge amounts and at low prices, and could use its power to crush competition and, if necessary, to lobby for favorable government legislation. In addition, big business could effectively discourage unionism, could place labor agitators on a black list, and, in the event of a strike, could employ strikebreakers. In the United States there arose such business giants as the United States Steel Corporation, the American Tobacco Company, International Harvester, the Standard Oil Company, and the United States Rubber Company.

Business consolidation took the form not only of larger corporations but also of mergers and alliances of separate units. One form was the trust, in which a body of trustees held a majority of the stock and thus controlled the wage, price, and merchandising policies of the several companies involved. Another form was the holding company, in which a corporation was organized to perform the same functions as the more informal trust. In Europe, business integration took the form of huge industrial combines known as cartels. These great industrial units were

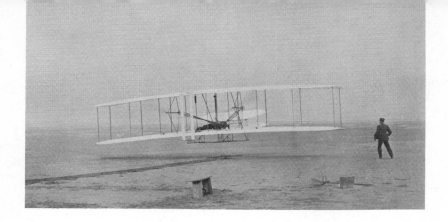

The astounding growth of industrialization between 1870 and 1914 was one of the outstanding features of the Second Industrial Revolution. One day's output at the Ford plant in Michigan in 1913 is represented by the long line of auto chassis in the photo below. A flurry of new inventions accompanied the increase in manufacturing. Alexander Graham Bell is shown below at his important invention, the telephone; the occasion is the 1892 opening of the long-distance line between New York and Chicago. Owners of a bicycle shop, Orville and Wilbur Wright built and tested the first successful, full-sized,

power-driven airplane. Newspapers generally ignored the first flight, made by Orville (above, lying in plane), and for several years the United States government refused to take the invention seriously. The Second Industrial Revolution had a profound effect on the labor movement. As workers banded together against the mounting size and strength of business corporations, labor demonstrations carried the message of unionism to city residents. The photo below shows a London parade in which the banners of trade unions are carried alongside the standard of the Social Democratic party.

hooked together from country to country in international affiliates controlling such products as steel or rubber.

To create and operate such huge industrial organizations required larger sums than the manufacturer could ordinarily provide; and as a result, capitalism passed into a new stage of development. Just as commercial capitalism had been replaced by industrial capitalism in the eighteenth century, industrial capitalism in the last two decades of the nineteenth century was superseded by financial capitalism. As the financial houses arranged for the vast amounts of capital investment demanded by industry, more and more control of business fell into their hands. In this era the financier rather than the manufacturer became the dominant figure in the business arena.

With the growth of the size of the business unit, gains in economy and efficiency were registered. But there were also danger signals. In too many instances, key industries providing services or commodities vital to the health and well-being of society were dominated by a few huge enterprises controlled by a relative handful of men. And in the hectic pursuit of profits, businessmen too often neglected the legitimate responsibilities of industrial management and dabbled in stock "deals" or in other speculative schemes.

Workers unite. Consolidation in business was paralleled by consolidation in the ranks of labor. In response to the seemingly all-powerful position of big business in wage bargaining and in reaction against management's tendency to regard workers merely as commodities, the workers (as we have seen in Chapter 20) began to organize into trade unions.

The first unions were craft unions made up of skilled workers. Then unskilled wage earners were organized. Some of the unions formed were industrial unions, taking in all the workers employed in one industry. In this case, when any given group of workers felt compelled to strike, all union men in the industry would join them. As another means of gaining strength, associations of unions, such as the English Trade Union Congress,

were formed on a national basis. In 1881 a federation of autonomous craft and industrial unions was founded in the United States with a membership that soon numbered in the millions. This was the American Federation of Labor, headed by Samuel Gompers; it became the most powerful voice of American workers.

The immediate result of the growth of unionism was better protection for the working masses, a stronger voice when it came to collective bargaining with the bosses, and consequently higher wages. Big unionism, like big business, made for more efficient methods, but in both cases bigness created power and with it the need for responsibility in its exercise. This problem was to become paramount in industrial relations by the mid-twentieth century. While in some instances, as in syndicalist-controlled unions (see p. 574), labor organizations sought to overthrow the capitalist system, the vast majority of unions both in Europe and in the United States were moderate and gradualistic in both their aims and methods.

NEW ECONOMIC

AND SOCIAL FORCES

The new trends. From the standpoint of conditions in 1848, it looked as though Marx's predictions in the *Communist Manifesto*—the inevitability of revolution and the destruction of capitalism and the bourgeoisie—would come true. Fortunately, they did not. The latter part of the nineteenth century and the decade preceding the First World War saw improvement in three basic areas: (1) the granting of such basic political rights as universal suffrage, civil liberties, and free expression of opinion (discussed in Chapter 23); (2) an increase in the democratic distribution of wealth, also known as economic democracy; and (3) the spread of education.

"Democratic distribution" means, simply speaking, more equal sharing in the wealth of a nation. The growth of labor unions gave workers more bargaining power with their employers, and they used this power to gain better wages. It has been estimated that the "real wages" of workers (the amount of goods that their wages could actually buy) increased 50 per cent in industrial nations between 1870 and 1900.

Not only did real wages improve, but the state increasingly guaranteed the popular standard of living. More and more governments made it their business to provide such benefits as unemployment insurance, old-age pensions, and accident compensation. Because this social legislation was paid for out of tax revenues, England introduced a graduated income tax, by which every individual paid a sum relative to his earnings.

Business management became less exclusively a monopoly of the capitalists. Labor unions began to assert their right to have some say in the operation of industry, and government itself assumed the right to regulate and control great industries when the public interest was involved. Governments, moreover, sought to prevent the unjust exercise of economic power by the enactment of legislation such as the Sherman Anti-Trust Act and the Clayton Act in the United States. However, the effective subordination of big business in the highly industrialized western nations was not fully taken in hand until the advent of world depression in the 1930's.

Workers also attempted to make business production more democratic by establishing cooperatives. Capital was secured by the sale of stock, goods were sold at prevailing prices, and profits were distributed annually to stockholders in proportion to the amount of goods each had purchased. By 1913 at least half the population of the British Isles were buying some of their goods from cooperatives.

The final aspect of the democratic movement in the second half of the nineteenth century was education. When the common people won the franchise, it was painfully apparent that they needed at least the rudiments of education to vote intelligently. As the result of an education bill passed in 1870 under Gladstone, school attendance in England jumped from one to four million in ten years. Similar acts were passed in France, Germany, the Low Countries, and Scandinavia. Although educational progress lagged in southern and eastern Europe, with 80 per cent of the people of Russia and the Balkans remaining illiterate, by 1900 free and compulsory elementary education became almost universal in western Europe.

Liberalism fades; the welfare state appears. Only through the drastic modification and weakening of the middle-class doctrine of laissez-faire liberalism could the government's increased solicitude for the masses have come about. The expansion of a government's responsibilities for the economic security of all its people points toward the welfare state. That government moved away from laissez-faire liberalism and in the direction of the welfare state must be regarded as one of the fundamental trends of the late nineteenth century.

By the end of the century, this trend had also received the official stamp of approval of the Catholic Church. Reversing the position of Pope Pius IX, whose *Syllabus of Errors* (see p. 580) had stated bluntly that it was an error to believe that "the Roman Pontiff can and should reconcile and align himself with progress, liberalism, and modern civilization," Pius' successor, Leo XIII (1878-1903), revived the progressive outlook of St. Thomas Aquinas and reconciled the Church with the modern age. His most important pronouncement, *Rerum novarum* ("concerning new things," 1891), inaugurated what became known as "Christian democracy." The pope condemned Marxism and upheld capitalism, but he severely criticized the evils afflicting the working class. To ameliorate the lot of the workers, Leo advocated social legislation and the formation of Catholic labor unions and political parties. Soon Catholic parties, using the slogan and often the name of Christian democracy, began to play a major role in European politics—as they continue to do today.

Factory legislation, social legislation, the recognition of trade unions, and middle-class philanthropy all helped to achieve some degree of reconciliation between the proletariat and the bourgeoisie. A compromise had been reached. The workers were not completely satisfied but were willing in most instances to cooperate with management in the hope that the future would see more substantial gains. Speaking of the situation before 1914, a famous historian has written: ". . . most men are so constituted that they will abate something of their extreme demands in the interest of social peace. They will seek a compromise; and compromise has, on the whole, been the most characteristic feature in the relation of the two classes, employers and employees."[2] That the same spirit of compromise prevailed among most socialists also became clear.

Socialism compromises. In the early 1870's the growth of socialism was slow; but as the decade progressed, the movement gained momentum. The Social Democratic party, organized in Germany in 1875, became the strongest of its kind in Europe and a model for similar parties in other nations. In the 1880's, Marxist parties also arose in Italy, Austria, Scandinavia, and the Low Countries. In France, the socialist movement—discredited by the Paris Commune of 1871—broke into a number of acrimonious factions.

Influenced to a greater degree by the maxims of Christian socialism than by the dogmas of Marxism, British socialists placed their faith in parliamentary reform rather than in any uprising of the proletariat. The most important socialist group was the Fabian Society, organized in 1883 and including such brilliant intellectuals as George Bernard Shaw, Sidney and Beatrice Webb, and H. G. Wells. (The Fabian group derived its name from the cautious Roman general Quintus Fabius Maximus, who wore down his enemy Hannibal by being content with small gains.) Chiefly through the efforts of the Fabian Society, the Labour party was formed in 1900 with the support of trade unions and various socialist groups. Much of the credit for British social legislation goes to the Labour party, which supported the Liberal party's program before World War I.

Moderate socialists were not limited solely to England, for the Fabian gospel of moderation—or revisionism, as it came to be called—spread to the Continent. Encouraged by a general improvement in the lot of the common man, the socialists became less revolutionary and more willing to cooperate with governments which were genuinely interested in raising the standards of living of the working people. In the 1890's the movement grew rapidly.

For revisionist socialism to be effective, it had to wield power within the government; and by the early 1900's, socialistic parties had achieved this goal in numerous European capitals. The German workers' representatives in the Reichstag had numbered only two in 1871, but in the 1912 election the socialists won 110 seats in the lower house. Through a coalition of the various parties, the socialists in France had cornered 102 seats in the Chamber of Deputies by 1914. Socialists from many countries joined the Second International after its founding in 1889; by 1914 it boasted a membership of twelve million.

Syndicalism. The progress of revisionist socialism seemed to confound the dire prophecies of Marx. But there were radicals who refused to discard the doctrines of revolution, who viewed the growing moderation of the socialists with dismay, and who suspected that their old leaders were becoming the tools of the capitalists. A new radical movement known as syndicalism (from the French word *syndicat,* meaning "trade union") emerged in the 1890's with its center in France. Unlike the revisionist socialists, the syndicalists feared the political state and, like the anarchists, wished to destroy it. Before World War I, this movement conducted several nation-wide strikes in France.

Orthodox Marxism in Russia. By 1900 the picture of workers "having nothing to lose but their chains" had been substantially altered in western Europe by the advance of social legislation and the rise of "real wages." But if Marx could have risen from his grave in that year, he would have found in Russia the "1848" he once described in the *Communist Manifesto.* Here the Industrial Revolution was just gaining momentum, and bewildered peasants seeking work in city factories were shamefully exploited. There were no traditions of peaceful reform, gradualism, or compromise in Russia—only the memory of ruthless government suppression and of equally violent attempts at retaliation. It was natural, therefore, that when socialism appeared in Russia, its adherents passionately embraced Marx's original doctrines of class war and revolution. While the tsars still reigned, the socialist leaders were preparing for the day when the people would overthrow the regime and win control of the government. One such leader was Lenin.

Born Vladimir Ilich Ulyanov in a small city in the Volga River valley, Lenin (1870-1924) grew up in moderate and respectable circumstances provided by his father, a teacher of physics. In 1887 his elder brother was arrested for plotting against the life of the tsar and was executed. Shortly thereafter, Lenin began to read his dead brother's copy of *Das Kapital* and joined a secret Marxian discussion club. He was arrested in 1895 and sentenced to exile in Siberia. After he was released in 1900, he and his wife made their way to Switzerland. There, Lenin helped to found the socialist paper *Iskra* (*Spark*), whose motto was "From the spark—the conflagration."

Lenin stood for a socialism whose weapon was violence and whose creed allowed no compromise with the bourgeoisie. While Marx believed that capitalism would break down of its own accord, Lenin wanted to smash it. He took nothing for granted. To destroy capitalism, he devised a technique of revolution whereby an elite leadership would enforce its dictates on the populace with iron discipline. The organization of communist activity would be of two kinds. On the surface would be the legal and peaceful workers' movement. But below was to be a revolutionary network, infiltrating the government, the police, and the army.

Lenin also disagreed with Marx on the dictatorship of the proletariat. Engels and Marx did not envisage a police state but rather a republic of workers. Engels in 1891 wrote:

If anything stands, it is that our party and the working-class can only come to power under the form of a democratic republic. This is the specific form of the dictatorship of the proletariat.[3]

Lenin had other notions. His dictatorship of the proletariat would be a highly centralized despotism whose word was law. The shattering impact of World War I would give Lenin and his followers the opportunity to seize power.

Now that we have surveyed the technological achievements of the Second Industrial Revolution and noted the important economic and social trends of the period, let us turn to a discussion of developments in science, thought, and the arts. Of particular importance are the scientific discoveries made between 1870 and 1914; they were to prove shattering to man's self-esteem and confidence. Darwin's evolutionary theory would seem to divest man of his traditional heritage of having been created by a special act of divine grace. Freud's plumbing of man's unconscious mental states would appear to shatter the cherished belief that man was basically a rational creature. And the development of new theories in the physical sciences by Einstein and others was to have significant consequences for man's view of the universe and his role in the scheme of things. The replacement of absolute laws by theories of relativity would soon be transferred out of the sphere of science into the field of morality, with the result that absolute values and standards would be threatened.

EINSTEIN, DARWIN, AND FREUD

Revolution in physics. Some of the most significant discoveries in science made after 1870 resulted from research in the field of physics. In his famous work *A Treatise on Electricity and Magnetism* (1873), the Scottish scientist James Clerk-Maxwell advanced the theory that "electricity is matter moving in waves like those of light and radiant heat," thereby linking optics and electricity; and he maintained that light, radiant heat, and invisible ultraviolet radiation are all electro-magnetic phenomena.

Working with the electromagnetic theory of light, a German physicist named Heinrich Hertz found it possible to demonstrate in 1886 the existence of electromagnetic waves —as predicted by Clerk-Maxwell—and to measure their velocity. It was these "herzian waves" (later known as radio waves) which provided the theoretical basis for Marconi's subsequent invention of wireless telegraphy. In addition, Hertz' studies of the optical properties of these waves led to his discovery of photoelectricity, which was fundamental for the development of television.

Toward the end of the century, two new events occurred in the field of electrical research that were to have equally extensive repercussions. In 1895 a ray which could penetrate a nontranslucent mass was discovered, and, because the nature of this strange phenomenon was not at first understood, the term "x-ray" came into use. Shortly thereafter, it was learned that uranium gives off similar rays. Then in 1898 the French scientist Pierre Curie and his Polish wife Marie extracted radium from pitchblende, an ore of uranium, and the world began to become conscious of the potency of radioactivity. Radiation was soon utilized in the field of medicine.

Studies of the scattering of x-rays led to the conclusion that electricity is composed of particles which are constituent parts of atoms. This deduction led to the electron theory—namely, that the atom contains negatively charged particles known as electrons. The next major step in understanding the structure of the atom was made in 1911 by the British physicist Ernest Rutherford, who advanced the theory that each atom has a central particle, or nucleus, which is positively charged. Later, scientists determined that the atom is like a miniature solar system; most of the weight is concentrated in the central, positively charged nucleus, around which the negatively charged electrons revolve. These discoveries smashed one of the foundation stones of traditional physics— the belief that the atom was indivisible and solid. The way was now clear to demonstrate conclusively that the universe is composed not of matter in that traditional sense but of atomic energy.

Traditional physics received another jolt from the research of the German physicist Max Planck (1858-1947). Planck, who had been studying radiant heat, which comes from the sun and is identical in its nature with light, found that the distribution of energy among different wave lengths conflicted with the classical principle that radiant energy is emitted as a continuous process. He asserted that the energy emitted from a vibrating electron proceeds not in a steady wave but discontinuously in the form of calculable "energy packages." To such a package he gave the name "quantum"— hence the term "quantum theory."

Planck's quantum theory, which was to prove invaluable in the rapidly growing study of atomic physics, found support in the studies of Albert Einstein (1879-1955). In 1905 Einstein contended that light is propagated through space in the form of particles which he termed "photons." Moreover, the energy contained in any particle of matter, such as the photon, is equal to the mass of that body multiplied by the square of the velocity of light, which is a constant figure. The resulting equation—$E=mc^2$— provided the answer to many long-standing mysteries of physics—for example, how radioactive substances like radium and uranium are able to eject particles at enormous velocities and to go on doing so for millions of years. The magnitude of the energy that slumbers in the nuclei of atoms could be revealed. Above all, $E=mc^2$ shows that mass and energy are equivalent; the property called "mass" is simply concentrated energy.

Einstein and the theory of relativity. In 1905 Einstein also presented to the world his epoch-making theory of relativity, calling for a radically different approach to the concepts of time, velocity, and space. The universe as conceived by Einstein is not Newton's familiar three-dimensional figure of length, breadth, and thickness but a four-dimensional space-time continuum.

Thus, to the traditional three dimensions, Einstein added a fourth dimension, fusing them all into space time. Such a concept showed the relative interrelationship of space, time, and motion. Since this principle could not be explained by Euclidean geometry, Einstein's theory made necessary a new system of mathematics.

Einstein's concepts cover all the explanations provided by Newton's theory of gravitation, but they also fit the facts in a still wider field where the older theory fails. Newtonian mechanics continue to be satisfactory for everyday science and engineering; and even the astronomer, dealing with vast spaces, finds few discrepancies between Newton's theoretical prediction and actual observation. But astronomical tests of the two theories corroborate Einstein's position. Although few people apart from his scientific colleagues either understood or were influenced by Einstein's theory of relativity prior to the First World War, during the last four decades his theory has reorientated men's attitudes toward the structure and mechanics of the cosmos.

The germ theory—Pasteur and Koch. Probably the most important single advance in the field of medicine during the latter part of the nineteenth century was the substantiation of the germ theory of disease. The validation of this theory by Louis Pasteur and his younger disciple, the German bacteriologist Robert Koch, came as the result of a search for a cure for anthrax, a fatal disease which in the late 1870's was destroying over 20 per cent of the sheep in France. Pasteur and Koch discovered that anthrax bacteria could be grown in a culture of meat-broth jelly and that the injection of the bacteria into a healthy animal produced anthrax. In 1881 Pasteur inoculated twenty-five sheep with weakened anthrax bacteria and left the same number unvaccinated. Later, all fifty were given a virulent form of the disease; the unvaccinated animals died while the treated sheep remained sound. With the establishment of the principle that the injection of a mild form of disease bacteria will cause the formation of antibodies which will

Albert Einstein's theories established new concepts of the physical world and led to the harnessing of atomic energy. This portrait was made in Germany early in his brilliant career. Stripped of his citizenship, property, and position by the Nazis in 1933, Einstein carried on his work in the United States and became an American citizen in 1940.

prevent the inoculated person from getting the virulent form of the disease, the end of such scourges as typhoid and smallpox was in sight.

In 1885 Pasteur showed that by the injection of a vaccine an animal could be made resistant to rabies *after* having been bitten by a mad dog. For his part, the brilliant Koch discovered the organisms that caused eleven diseases, including tuberculosis and cholera. As a result of the work of Pasteur and Koch, the twin sciences of bacteriology and immunology were established on a firm footing.

Chemistry and related fields. In the latter part of the century, biochemical research demonstrated that the ductless glands poured their secretions, called hormones, directly into the blood stream and that some of these hormones were essential for survival. This discovery led to the search for various kinds of hormones, such as the secretion from the pancreas, which controls the onslaught of diabetes. Investigations showed also that scurvy and other diseases were caused by nutritional deficiencies. The true significance of vitamins was first disclosed in 1912, and the way was paved for isolating and synthesizing nearly all the known vitamins in the laboratory.

In the meantime, a German biochemist, Paul Ehrlich, had been carrying on experiments with drugs that could destroy bacteria and other organisms without harming the individual who harbored them. After more than six hundred unsuccessful attempts, Ehrlich in 1909 produced an organic arsenic compound, "606," later named "salvarsan," which, without being too toxic to the individual, destroyed syphilis bacteria in the body.

One of the most impressive advances in the field of chemistry was the making of chemical synthetics. A French scientist demonstrated how artificial silk could be made from cellulose, while chemists in Germany and elsewhere turned out synthetic dyes from coal-tar residues. In 1913 a process by which nitrogen could be obtained from the atmosphere was perfected. This process proved vital to the Germans during World War I; it enabled their munitions program to survive despite an Allied blockade that cut off the importation of nitrates from Chile.

Darwin and *Descent of Man*. In 1859 had appeared the first of Darwin's major works, *The Origin of Species,* with its revolutionary concepts about the origin and evolution of life on the earth (see Chapter 20). Darwin's next bombshell was *Descent of Man and Selection in Relation to Sex,* published in 1871. In this work Darwin elaborated upon some of the views expressed in his earlier work and went on to apply the law of natural selection to human beings by drawing his explosively controversial conclusion that man's ancestors were probably monkey-like animals related to the progenitors of the orang-utan, chimpanzee, and gorilla.

There are five main points in the Darwinian hypothesis. First, all existing vegetable and animal species are descended from earlier and, generally speaking, more rudimentary forms. Second, the variation in species has come about because environment and the use or disuse of organs have brought about changes in structure that are inherited. Third, in the struggle for survival, the fittest win out at the expense of their rivals because they succeed in adapting themselves best to their environment. Fourth, differentiation among the species is also brought about by sexual selection, which Darwin declared is "the most powerful means of changing the races of man." Finally, some variations seem to arise spontaneously, a view of Darwin's which pointed toward the doctrine of mutation.

Biology after Darwin. By the close of the nineteenth century, scientists were in virtual agreement regarding the general validity of Darwin's hypothesis, though, as we shall see, it was later modified in certain important respects. Meanwhile, largely as a result of Darwin's unifying principle of evolution, biology was progressively transformed from a descriptive science into a search for relationships between living organisms.

One of the most significant developments in biology concerned the question of heredity. In the 1870's the German biologist August Weismann, basing his investigation on an earlier theory that all living things originate and develop in very small structural units, or cells, distinguished two types of cells. One type—the somatic cell—dies with the individual, while the other—the germ cell—transmits through reproduction a continuous stream of protoplasm from one generation to the next. Later, Weismann reasoned that only germ cells transmit hereditary characteristics and that, since acquired characteristics occur only in the somatic cells, these cannot be inherited.

An Austrian monk, Gregor Mendel (1822-1884), formulated definite laws of heredity on the basis of experiments with the crossing of garden peas. Because he published his important findings in an obscure scientific journal, his work was overlooked until about 1900. Mendel's laws not only proved a valuable help in the scientific breeding of plants and animals but also made the problem of the evolution of different species more complex than had been deduced by Darwin.

From the work of Mendel and Weismann, biologists began to conclude that the nuclei of the germ cells possess chromosomes which carry the characteristics of an organism. Further research substantiated the mutation theory, which states that sudden and unpredictable variations in heredity produce new species. But most geneticists came to reject the theory of the inheritance of acquired characteristics, advocated by Lamarck and accepted by Darwin.

Meanwhile, a cousin of Darwin, Sir Francis Galton, carried the study of heredity into still more new areas. Struck by the similarity of characteristics among members of one family, Galton reached the conclusion that mental as well as physical characteristics must be inherited. He invented mental testing and pioneered in the new science of eugenics.

Advances in psychology. The study of psychology was given a marked impetus by numerous investigators, one of the most famous of whom was a Russian, Ivan Pavlov (1849-1936). In 1900 Pavlov conducted a series of experiments in which food was given to a dog at the same time that a bell was rung. After a time, the food and bell became identified by the dog as inseparable. Henceforth when the bell was rung alone, the dog had the same anticipatory reflex of producing saliva as if food had been brought. Thus Pavlov demonstrated the influence of physical stimuli on an involuntary process.

This psychology of conditioned reflexes achieved a wide vogue, especially in the United States. There it was used to help substantiate the tenets of a school of behaviorism which considered man more or less as a machine responding mechanically to stimuli. Behaviorism stressed experimentation and observational techniques and did much to create relatively valid intelligence and aptitude tests. It also strengthened the materialistic philosophies of the period.

Freud and psychoanalysis. Probably the most famous name associated with psychology is that of the Austrian Sigmund Freud (1856-1939), who found the behavioristic approach too mechanical and therefore incapable of doing justice to the importance of man's unconscious mental processes. Placing great stress on the element of the unconscious, Freud pioneered in psychoanalysis. This form of psychiatric treatment is based on the theory that abnormal mental reactions result from the repression of desires which have been consciously rejected but which nevertheless persist in the subconscious strata of the mind. Freud employed psychoanalysis as a new form of therapy for treating various emotional disturbances by placing the interpretation of dreams on a scientific basis and by bringing deeply rooted repressions to the surface. He was also concerned with the question of man's motive force, the "libido," which he believed was rooted in the sexual urge. His other contributions to the field of psychology included his concept of the Oedipus complex, whereby a child is strongly attached to the parent of the opposite sex and hostile to the other parent. All in all, Freud threw new light upon some of the most important problems of human personality and behavior.

THE CULT OF SCIENCE

Science versus faith. With its spectacular successes in both pure research and technological application, science gripped the popular imagination of the pre-1914 generation to an extent never before equaled. Science was elevated to a cult by means of which all human problems were to be solved. Many men and women became skeptical and uneasy about whatever could not be proved in the laboratory.

It can be readily seen that a conflict was certain to ensue between the traditional doctrines of religion and the new scientific tenets, especially those of Darwinism. Thomas Huxley, a strong popularizer of Darwin's theories, contended that for the advocate of science "skepticism is the highest of duties;

An Austrian physician specializing in nervous diseases, Sigmund Freud laid the foundation for present-day methods of treating neuroses by psychoanalysis. The drawing shows him in the period of World War I.

blind faith the unpardonable sin."[4] Certainly, organized religion was thrown on the defensive, and many of the most sensitive minds of the period suffered anguish and even despair in their attempts to reconcile their religous beliefs with the new scientific tenets.

As time went on, however, more than one thinker came to believe that the evolutionary theory supplemented rather than contradicted the basic tenets of faith. As they saw the bounds of the universe pushed back by science, they perceived growth and development in the constant changes and felt that God was revealing Himself to man through the evolutionary process. Interestingly enough, Darwin himself had expressed a similar view in the conclusion of his *The Origin of Species*:

When I view all beings not as special creations, but as the lineal descendants of some few beings which lived long before the first bed of the Cambrian system was deposited, they seem to me to become ennobled. . . . There is grandeur in this view of life, with its several powers, having been originally breathed by the Creator into a few forms or into one; and that, whilst this planet has gone cycling on according to the fixed law of gravity, from so simple a beginning endless forms most beautiful and most wonderful have been, and are being evolved.[5]

The Roman Catholic position. In 1864 Pope Pius IX had issued the *Syllabus of Errors,* which warned the faithful against "the principal errors of our time"—namely, that God did not exist, that His action upon man was to be denied, that human reason was alone the sole arbiter of truth, and that the miracles found in the Scriptures were fictional. Next, in 1870 the Vatican Council—the first general council of the Church to gather in centuries—defined the doctrine of papal infallibility. This declared that when the pope spoke *ex cathedra* (from the seat of authority), he possessed:

. . . that infallibility with which the divine Redeemer willed that his Church should be endowed for defining doctrine regarding faith or morals.[6]

Thus, the Roman Catholic Church categorically reaffirmed its historical position.

Biblical criticism. Just as certain historians were developing scientific methods to determine the validity of secular evidence and thereby put history on a more scientific basis (see p. 581), so other scholars—mainly Protestants—sought to subject Biblical texts and problems of authorship to the same type of rigid examination. This type of study was known as the "higher criticism."

When the Old Testament was thus critically analyzed, Genesis and other books were questioned in the light of the latest historical and scientific evidence. In regard to the New Testament, some scholars argued that many of the narratives found in the Gospels must be considered only myths and not historical facts. Advocates of the higher criticism likewise contended that the New Testament, no less than the Old, recounted human rather than divine events and reflected the moral and ethical attitudes of the society which produced it.

The science of man. The apostles of science were also anxious to place human institutions on a scientific foundation. Such was the intention of the noted French student of

18 William Turner: "The Fighting *Temeraire* Towed to Her Last Berth" (1838). One of Admiral Horatio Nelson's men-of-war at the battle of Trafalgar (1805), the *Temeraire* was to Turner and his countrymen a symbol of the British navy's glorious exploits against Napoleon. In this scene, which the Romanticist artist has rendered as a sort of hero's death complete with blazing sunset, the outmoded ship is being towed away for destruction by an ugly tugboat. Turner's style has led art historians to identify him as one of the forerunners of Impressionism.

19 Vincent van Gogh: "Peasant of the Camargue" (1888). To Van Gogh, art was not a record of visible reality but a means of casting into visible form the unseen world of human emotions. The vibrant colors and powerful, rhythmic brush strokes in his works are intended to arouse in the beholder the same intense upsurge of emotion that the artist experienced. "Instead of trying to reproduce exactly what I have before my eyes," Van Gogh is reported to have said, "I use color more arbitrarily so as to express myself more forcibly." Because of this highly personal approach, he was the first Post-Impressionist who could be termed an Expressionist.

20 (left) **James McNeill Whistler: "Arrangement in Grey and Black, No. 2: Thomas Carlyle"** (1873). To the public, Whistler's work represented the startling new doctrine of "art for art's sake," the idea that a work of art was to be judged solely by its qualities of form and color rather than by its subject matter or literary content. Hence the provocative title of this work. Whistler's famous portrait of his mother was entitled "Arrangement in Grey and Black, No. 1."

21 (below) **Édouard Manet: "The Execution of Maximilian"** (1867). Manet treated his subject—the execution by the Mexicans of Napoleon III's puppet ruler of Mexico—as a problem in composition, and Archduke Maximilian is neither idealized nor sentimentalized. This dispassionate rendering of the event was probably the reason Manet was forbidden to exhibit the painting in France.

22 Auguste Renoir: "Le Moulin de la Galette" (1876). Influenced by Manet, Renoir was also an Impressionist. As evidenced by this work, we find in him a *joie de vivre* that is lacking in Manet's detached, objective approach to painting. Indeed, the works of Renoir exhibit a warmth unmatched by any other Impressionist. "Le Moulin de la Galette" brilliantly conveys the charm of young couples enjoying themselves at an outdoor café and—at the same time—it reminds us of the vitality of the French nation, which swiftly regained its prosperity and high spirits in the years immediately following the military disaster of the Franco-Prussian War.

society Auguste Comte (1798-1857), whose work had appeared in the first half of the nineteenth century. Comte held that the history of mankind had passed through three stages of evolution. The first two of these, the theological and the metaphysical, had outlived their usefulness. Now the time had arrived to embark upon what he called the positive stage, in which scientific knowledge and the application of scientific standards would dominate. At the apex of all the social sciences, Comte placed the study of man in society, a new science to which he gave the term "sociology."

Scientific history. The scientific approach was also brought to bear upon the writing of history. The scholar generally acknowledged as the founder of "scientific history" is the German Leopold von Ranke (1795-1886). His system called for a thorough search for all possible evidence on a given subject, the most careful examination of this evidence to ensure its authenticity and reliability, and the restriction of conclusions to what could logically be drawn from the evidence. Complete objectivity is humanly impossible, but Ranke's critical method demanded that the historian subordinate his own views and preferences to a concern for the truth.

Darwin's work *The Origin of Species* caused further repercussions in the study of history. More than one historian began to analyze his subject matter strictly in terms of environment and heredity, stressing such factors as soil, topography, climate, food, race, and the inheritance of various traits. Sometimes this approach led to the treatment of societies and institutions as though they were simply biological organisms—a fallacy which could have pernicious results. On the more constructive side, the Darwinian hypothesis encouraged students to view history in terms of growth and adaptation.

Social Darwinism. One American thinker at the close of the century wrote:

The life of man in society, just like the life of other species, is a struggle for existence. . . . The progress which has been and is being made in human institutions and in human character may be set down, broadly, to a natural selection of

the fittest habits of thought and to a process of enforced adaptation of individuals to an environment which has progressively changed with the growth of the community and with the changing institutions under which men have lived.[7]

Here we see clearly how the concept of the survival of the fittest was used to explain not only the development but the progress of both human institutions and human character. Although Darwin himself had confined the principle of natural selection to the sphere of biology, his contemporaries eagerly extended it to apply to the field of human affairs. This application of Darwin's principles to man and his efforts was called "social Darwinism"; it became a vogue that swept western thought in the late nineteenth century. It also became a convenient doctrine for justifying various economic and political theories.

Darwinism in economics. Herbert Spencer (1820-1903), an English philosopher from whom Darwin borrowed the phrase "survival of the fittest," was one of those who regarded society as a living organism. Spencer opposed any interference by the state with the natural development of society. The sole function of the state, in his view, was negative—namely, to ensure freedom of the individual, who if left alone through enough generations would become perfect. Spencer used this doctrine to advocate unfettered business competition and to oppose all state aid to the poor, whom he regarded as unable to compete successfully in the struggle for survival and consequently better eliminated. At the same time, he favored private charity to develop altruistic traits in the donors.

The "justification" of war. The pseudoscientific application of a biological theory to politics, whereby a nation is regarded as an organism, constituted possibly the most perverted form of social Darwinism in the period under review. It led to racism and anti-Semitism (see p. 560) and was used to show that only "superior" nationalities and races were fit to survive.

Social Darwinism was also employed to justify the use of military power to ensure that the "fittest" state would survive. Most influential as an advocate of war was the German philosopher Friedrich Nietzsche (1844-1900). His ideal, the superman, was characterized by bravery, strength, egoism, arrogance, and ruthlessness. Nietzsche challenged the world with: "You say, 'A good cause sanctifies even war,' but I say, 'A good war sanctifies every cause'!" Nietzsche viewed Christianity with contempt because he regarded gentleness as weakness and humanitarianism as protection of the unfit and spineless. Likewise, he ridiculed democracy and socialism for protecting the worthless and weak and hindering the strong.

Developments in philosophy: pragmatism and vitalism. Philosophy had been profoundly influenced by the implications of Darwin's work. Stressing the roles of change and chance in nature, the Darwinian theory strengthened the trend away from absolute standards.

Among American philosophers there arose a school known as pragmatism, which asserted that even truth is not an absolute in itself. Led by the noted psychologist William James (1842-1910), the pragmatists believed that men think for the practical purpose of getting on with the job of living; and since the validity of any idea lies not in its approximation to some ultimate truth but in its ability to effect desired action, it must be tested by its logical or empirical results. As James put it, "An idea is 'true' so long as to believe it is profitable to our lives." Pragmatism, in effect, rejected any concept of truth or reality as absolute. Although it has been credited with bringing formal philosophy out of the clouds and relating it more concretely to the major scientific and intellectual trends of the day, the pragmatic approach resulted in a strongly materialistic bent on the part of some of its adherents, with whom truth became indistinguishable from success.

Influenced by contemporary scientific currents in both biology and physics but differing widely from pragmatism was the philosophy of Henri Bergson (1859-1941). Bergson attributed existence to a spontaneous creative force which he called the vital impulse (*élan vital*). Nothing is fixed; everything in life changes ceaselessly. The intellect is incapable of grasping the true nature of reality, which flows like an uninterrupted stream, and instead cuts reality up into discontinuous parts in much the same way that a movie film divides a single action into separate pictures. Bergson believed, however, that man has another faculty, intuition, which is capable of grasping life in terms of wholes. This, he maintained, is the ability employed by artists.

Bergson's philosophy of vitalism, which made its greatest impact in the years preceding World War I, represented a revolt against scientific determinism. While making use of the Darwinian thesis of change, it conceived evolution to be creative and not a blind struggle for survival. And because it insisted that mental processes could not be reduced to simple mechanistic terms, this vitalistic philosophy was to influence many intellectuals of the time.

FROM REALISM TO

EXPRESSIONISM

The realistic novelists. By 1870 writers were not only responding in various ways to the growing cult of science and to the impact of philosophical rationalism; they were also in revolt against the now-spent romanticism that survived in the form of sentimentalism. A down-to-earth attitude had become the order of the day. The nineteenth-century realists did not hesitate to describe in graphic detail social and personal problems which had hitherto gone unmentioned because they were not "nice." Their creed was to chronicle without comment, to photograph without touching up.

The first of the great realistic novelists were from France—Honoré de Balzac (1799-1850) and Gustave Flaubert (1821-1880). Balzac was the author of the *Comédie Humaine*. or "Human Comedy," a panorama of ninety volumes concerning French city and country life in the first half of the nineteenth century. In his novels, the crudities and avarice of the

French petty bourgeoisie were depicted in detail. Flaubert's masterpiece, *Madame Bovary* (1856), describes how the boredom of a romantic-minded young provincial wife led her into adultery and ultimately into complete disillusionment. By implication Flaubert was criticizing the inadequacy of romanticism as a philosophy of life.

Realism served as the keynote for the most important novelists of the late nineteenth century. Count Leo Tolstoy's epic novel *War and Peace* (1869), a magnificent tapestry of life in Russia during the Napoleonic invasion of 1812, stripped every shred of glory or glamour from that conflict. His *Anna Karenina* (1877) relentlessly detailed the story of two lovers who openly defy the social conventions. Another great Russian novelist, Feodor Dostoevski, traced the causes and effects of murder in two masterpieces of suspense and psychological analysis, *Crime and Punishment* (1866) and *The Brothers Karamazov* (1880).

A notable English realist was Thomas Hardy, who dealt with the struggle of the individual—almost invariably a losing struggle—against the impersonal, pitiless forces of his natural and social environment. In America, Henry James, the brother of the American pragmatist William James, attempted, as he put it, to catch "the atmosphere of the mind" in his works. His stories and novels serve as a framework for the lengthy, subtle analyses of human motives. Another well-known American writer of the period was Samuel Clemens, whose fame as a humorist should not blind us to the realistic character of his work. His writings abound not only with robust humor but also with accurate descriptions of the Middle and Far West. Like Dickens, he could employ humorous satire to underscore social injustice.

In the hands of some writers, realism developed into an extreme form of presentation known as naturalism. These naturalists wished to apply scientific objectivity to their subject matter and to deal with their characters as with animals in a laboratory, whose every move was determined by environment or heredity. The most outstanding practi-

tioner of this literary doctrine was Émile Zola, who made a case study twenty volumes long of a middle-class family. In this series of works, which included *Nana* (1880) and *Germinal* (1885), Zola employed a clinical approach, amassing huge notebooks of information on such subjects as the stock market and the mining districts before describing these settings.

The problem play: Ibsen and Shaw. The exposure of social problems was an important aspect of the new literary realism. The problems facing *fin de siècle* (end of the century) society were more subtle in character than the obvious injustices of child labor and cholera-infested slums, which had monopolized the attention of social critics earlier in the century. Thus, perhaps, was provided the impetus for the development of a new, sophisticated form of drama called the "problem play."

The dramas of the Norwegian Henrik Ibsen were the first of the problem plays. One of his best-known works is *A Doll's House* (1879), in which he assailed marriage without love as being immoral. In other plays, he attacked social greed masked by conventional respectability and delineated with great sensitivity the human dramas latent in the strains and stresses of ordinary life. A disciple of Ibsen and, like the Norwegian, an ardent assailant of bourgeois complacency was the brilliant Irish playwright George Bernard Shaw. In a series of shrewdly satirical and highly diverting stage successes, he cajoled, bullied, and shocked the English-speaking public into reassessing their conventional attitudes on a variety of social subjects, ranging from private and public morality to militarism and religious beliefs.

The search for new standards. All the writers of this period were not proponents of the realistic school. Some, like Oscar Wilde in England, made a cult of their revulsion against the crudities and vulgarity of a realism-ridden age. To them, the only valid standard was "art for art's sake." Moral, social, or ethical criteria were unimportant in themselves; the artist might do as he pleased so long as his work possessed artistic integrity.

The French sculptor Rodin believed that ugliness in a work of art resulted not from a lack of conventional beauty but from a lack of character. Although at first most art critics were shocked by his works, he came to be considered one of the greatest sculptors of modern times. In "The Thinker," Rodin sought to express man's struggle to use his reason.

In the name of such integrity, the devotees of this school—both as writers and as individuals—often lapsed into decadence.

Still other writers sought new standards and modes of expression. In so doing, they were not merely reacting against an excessive emphasis on realism; they were also reflecting the need to find new outlets in literature for what Freud and the psychologists had been saying about the subjective side of experience. A group of poets known as the symbolists, found for the most part in France during the last two decades of the nineteenth century, made use of images, archaic and mystical terms, and other devices in order to convey the inner feelings of an individual or group. Their experimentation also led them to employ free verse and the prose poem, while their efforts to express the subjective and introspective often made their works obscure to all but themselves.

Realism in painting. The major trends in literature between 1870 and 1914 were paralleled by developments in painting in the same era. Already, in the 1850's and 1860's, various artists in France had been rebelling against traditional subject matter and techniques. Feeling that the canvases exhibited on academy walls were for the most part too "respectable" and hence artificial, they chose instead to paint life as they saw it.

Gustave Courbet, probably the outstanding French realist, expressed his contempt for religious and Neoclassical themes when he mocked: "Show me an angel and I will paint one." When he looked at nature, he consciously dropped the affectations of both the romanticists and Neoclassicists and painted uncompromising, often brutal canvases. Courbet's view that "realism is an essentially democratic art" was shared by his compatriot Honoré Daumier, who knew Parisian life intimately. His lithographs were biting satires of life among the bourgeoisie, in the courts of law, and in political circles (see p. 516).

Impressionism in France. As we have seen, realism in literature was developed by Zola and others into naturalism, whereby the writer sought to observe phenomena in their natural state and to record them with scientific precision. In painting, we find a similar development in Impressionism. Preoccupied with problems of color, light, and atmosphere, these artists sought to catch the first impression made by a scene or object upon the eye, undistorted by the intellect or any subjective attitude. The result was that the Impressionists worked in terms of light and color rather than solidity of form. In doing so, they found that a more striking effect of light could be obtained by placing one bright area of color next to another without any transitional tones. They also discovered that shadows could be shown not as gray but as colors complementary to those of the objects casting the shadows. At close range an Impressionist picture may seem little

Building in their different ways on the accomplishments of the Impressionist school, Cézanne and Matisse did much to create the golden age of French modern art. In paintings such as "House in Provence" (below), Cézanne employed the rich color and atmospheric effects of the Impressionists but gave solidity to the forms in the composition and emphasized their relationships in space. Influenced both by Impressionist works and by Persian art, Matisse emphasized the arrangement of simple, rhythmic forms, rich textures, and vivid areas of color in paintings like "Goldfish and Sculpture" (at the right).

Collection, The Museum of Modern Art, New York

more than a splotch of unmixed colors, but at the proper distance the eye mixes the colors, and a vibrating sense of light and motion emerges. Through their technique the Impressionists helped to revolutionize modern painting.

An outstanding Impressionist was Pierre Auguste Renoir, who skillfully employed color to capture flesh tones and texture (see Color Plate 22). Renoir painted all sorts of subjects—the opera, landscapes, and houseboats on the Seine. His canvases all reveal his rich sense of color; the sunlight plays across his paintings, giving the sense of a passing moment held in paint.

To France must go credit for the development not only of this new style of painting but of other Impressionistic arts as well. The outstanding sculptor of the late nineteenth century, Auguste Rodin, has been described as the father of modern sculpture. He infused his work with a realistic honesty and vitality that made him the object of stormy controversy during much of his lifetime. Sharing with the Impressionist painters a dislike for studied finality in art, Rodin preferred to let the imagination of the beholder play on his sculpture. Rodin's technique of rough finish shows to advantage in his bronze works. By this technique, the sculptor achieved two effects: a glittering surface of light and shadow and a feeling of immediacy and incompleteness that emphasized the spontaneous character of the work.

Post-Impressionism. By conveying a sense of motion and of the moment, Impressionism had given painting—and, through Rodin, sculpture—a fresh vitality. But it had done so at a price. For one thing, its effects with color and atmosphere had been achieved by sacrificing much of the clarity which continued to be a hallmark of the classical tradition. Again, while bringing the surface of things alive in an exciting fashion, the Impressionist seemed unable to give his objects the solidity and structure which were theirs by nature. How could artists get the best of both worlds?

This was the difficult intellectual and artistic problem to which Paul Cézanne (1839-1906) addressed himself. For years this painter—a one-time realist and friend of Zola—experimented with new techniques. He sought to simplify all natural objects by emphasizing their essential geometric structure. As Cézanne said, everything in nature corresponds to the shape of the cone, the cylinder, or the sphere. Proceeding on the basis of this theory, he was able to get below the surface and give his objects the solidity which had eluded the Impressionists. Yet, like the latter, he made striking use of color—in his case, to establish the relationships of his objects in space. The successful pioneering work of Cézanne was to have important consequences.

One or two other late nineteenth-century painters were also successful, by reason of their individualism, in contributing to the rise of Post-Impressionism. One was Vincent van Gogh (1853-1890), a Dutch painter whose short life of poverty and loneliness was climaxed by insanity and suicide. He employed sharp brush lines, following the form of the object he painted, as can be seen in Color Plate 19. Van Gogh was concerned not with presenting simply a photographic representation of what lay before him but with conveying the intense feelings evoked in himself by his subject. As a consequence, he was ready to distort what he saw in order to depict these sensations, even as Cézanne had abandoned perspective where necessary so as to concentrate on form and spatial relationships.

Expressionism and Cubism. Continuing to experiment, artists became increasingly concerned with painting what they felt about an object rather than the object itself. This method of using an object as a means of expressing subjective feelings is known as Expressionism, an approach similar to that of the symbolist school in literature. Among the early Expressionists—or *les fauves* (the wild beasts), as they were derided by their critics—was Henri Matisse, who had learned to simplify form partly from African primitive art and had studied the color schemes of oriental carpets. His decorative style was to influence design strongly in our own day.

Louis Sullivan's maxim "Form follows function" set the keynote for the new architecture of the late nineteenth century and the twentieth century. Sullivan, Frank Lloyd Wright, and Walter Gropius produced revolutionary designs born of the concept that external form should express frankly the purpose of the building, the internal structure, and the materials used. At the left is a Chicago department store designed by Sullivan; Wright's Robie House in Chicago is shown at the bottom right; and Gropius' Hall of Machines, built for the Cologne exhibition of 1914, is at the center right.

Experimentation took still other subjective forms. We have already noted that in order to achieve a sense of depth and solidity, Cézanne used geometric shapes and depth relationships on the two-dimensional painting surface. Further developments along these lines resulted in the emergence of a new school—Cubism. Cubists would choose an object, then construct an abstract pattern from it. In doing so, they went far beyond the traditional manner of reproducing the object from one vantage point; instead, they viewed it from several points of view simultaneously. In a Cubist canvas one might see a given object—say a violin—from above, below, outside, and inside, with all the dissected elements interpenetrating to form an abstract pattern. We see such a pattern in "Three Musicians" (Color Plate 23) by the Spanish artist Pablo Picasso, probably the most influential single figure in twentieth-century painting.

Architecture reflects the machine age. For a great part of the nineteenth century, architectural styles were largely derivative. Structures were designed in the Gothic and Rococo and other styles as well. This eclectic approach was due in no small measure to the fact that large houses and factories alike were often erected for middle-class entrepreneurs who believed that the best way to prove that they had arrived socially was to build in styles traditionally associated with the aristocracy. Meanwhile, public buildings in the rapidly growing towns were designed in a massive and ornamental style calculated to reflect civic grandeur and opulence. From the standpoint of today's architects, there was a total lack of sensitivity in the way that buildings were related —or, rather, unrelated—to their sites.

Nevertheless some exciting new thinking had been concentrated on commercial architecture. Aided by advances in industry and technology, architects were now able to design structures that could span greater distances and enclose greater areas than had hitherto been possible. However much of a tragedy, the great fire that leveled much of Chicago in 1871 had the benefit of putting that city in the forefront with a new form of architecture, the steel-skeleton skyscraper. Whereas high buildings had formerly required immensely thick masonry walls, a metal frame now allowed the weight of the structure to be distributed on an entirely different principle and permitted a far more extensive use of glass than ever before. Outstanding among the pioneers in this new architecture was Chicago's Louis Sullivan (1856-1924). Like others, Sullivan perceived the value of the skyscraper in providing a large amount of useful space on a small plot of expensive land, such as that in Chicago's Loop or in Manhattan. Unlike others, he rejected all attempts to disguise the skeleton of the skyscraper behind some false façade and boldly proclaimed it by a clean sweep of line. Sullivan's emphasis upon the functional was to have far-reaching influence.

One of Sullivan's pupils, the brilliant Frank Lloyd Wright (1869-1959), was meanwhile originating revolutionary designs for houses. One feature of Wright's houses was the interweaving of interiors and exteriors by the use of terraces and cantilevered roofs. He felt that a building should look appropriate on its site; it should "grow out of the land." His "prairie houses," with their long, low lines, were designed to blend in with the flat land of the Midwest (see illustration). Much that is taken for granted in today's houses derives directly from Wright's experiments at the turn of the century.

In the decade prior to World War I, there developed in Germany a fairly widely accepted style of architecture that broke with tradition and stressed the use of new forms reflecting the machine age. In 1914 one of the outstanding leaders of this movement, Walter Gropius, displayed in an exhibition in Cologne a factory which, with its emphasis on horizontals, its use of glass, its exposure of staircases, and its undisguised functionalism, we would accept today as contemporary. The new movement in architecture resulted in the establishment of a school of functional art and architecture, the Bauhaus, in 1918.

Impressionism and experimentation in music. In the early years of the period 1870 to 1914, romanticism was still the main style in the musical world. As we will recall from Chapter 20, Brahms and Tschaikovsky were offering the public new orchestral works, and Verdi and Wagner were writing operas. A post-Wagnerian school persisted well into the twentieth century. One of its outstanding members, Richard Strauss, enlivened the musical scene with his brilliant orchestrations and his dramatic music.

A striking departure from musical tradition occurred with the rise of the French school of impressionism, whose foremost exponent was Claude Debussy (1862-1918). Just as the painters of the period had achieved new atmospheric effects by their technical innovations, so composers now engaged in "tone painting" to achieve a special mood or atmosphere. Such an effect is immediately recognizable in Debussy's prelude "L'Après-midi d'un faune" ("Afternoon of a Faun"), which astounded the musical world when it was first performed in 1892. The Impressionist painters had obtained their effects by juxtaposing different colors. The composers in turn juxtaposed widely separated chords to create similarly brilliant, shimmering effects with sound.

A number of other composers rebelled strongly against romanticism and engaged in striking experimentation. Breaking with the major-minor system of tonality, which had been the western musical tradition since the Renaissance, some of them began to make use of several different keys simultaneously, a device known as polytonality. Outstanding among such composers, Igor Stravinski (1882-   ) has done for modern music what innovators like Picasso have done for modern painting. Unlike the romanticists, Stravinski was less concerned with melody than with achieving his effects by means of polytonality, dissonant harmonies, and percussive rhythms. Meanwhile, other composers were experimenting with atonality (the absence of any fixed key). In this regard, we should mention the twelve-tone system developed by Arnold Schönberg

(1874-1952). Compositions of this structure depart from all tonality and harmonic progressions, while at the same time stressing extreme dissonances.

With the work of composers like Schönberg, we arrive at expressionism in music. Just as the Expressionist painters were attempting to create a new inner reality, so composers sought to give meaning to their subconscious feelings by getting below the surface. Here once again we see the influence of Freud and his school at work prior to 1914. Although harsh and unpleasant to many ears, these experiments with polytonality and atonality had validity for a century in which the old absolute values were being broken down—a century, as two world wars were to prove, of clashing dissonance.

SUMMARY

The period from 1871 to 1914 coincided with the Second Industrial Revolution. New industries and inventions revolutionized manufacturing. Three basic characteristics were apparent in this new phase of industrialism: research became more systematized and less a matter of chance; mass production methods introduced consumer goods made of interchangeable parts on assembly lines; and there was an ever increasing alliance between chemistry and industry. An unprecedented outpouring of goods was accompanied by rising living standards for the masses. The philosophy of laissez faire shrank before that of the welfare state. Old-age pensions, unemployment insurance, and accident compensation gave the masses more security. The Fabians and other revisionist socialists no longer cried for revolution but were content with a gradual program of social reform, increasing democracy, and rising standards of living. Yet revolutionary groups of socialists persisted. The syndicalists favored violence and the use of the general strike to paralyze and overthrow capitalism. Most menacing was the Leninist wing of Russian socialism, which grew up in an atmosphere of government tyranny and had no reason to doubt the gospel of Marx.

The period from 1871 to 1914 also constituted the zenith of western intellectual and social dominance. Traditional concepts in physics were challenged by a number of remarkable developments: Clerk-Maxwell's experiments with optics and electricity, the discovery of x-rays, Planck's quantum theory, and Einstein's theory of relativity. No less spectacular was the progress made in other sciences. Scientists learned about proteins and vitamins, about the purpose of ductless glands, and about the uses of chemotherapy in the treatment of disease; the twin sciences of bacteriology and immunology were established firmly; and the study of biology was advanced by the research of Mendel and Galton. In psychology the behavioristic school flourished, while Freud pioneered in psychoanalysis.

These spectacular advances in science were responsible for the rise of a cult of science and the development of a vigorous struggle between the claims of science and those of organized religion. Although Darwin had already shaken a previous era with his evolutionary hypothesis, it was this period that experienced its full impact in both the scientific and social spheres. Perhaps the most pernicious aspect of the cult of science was that of social Darwinism, which applied the doctrine of the survival of the fittest to the economic, political, and military spheres with disastrous results.

The writers and artists of these decades had been turning away from the romanticism of the first half of the nineteenth century to embrace a down-to-earth, photographic approach known as realism. Carried to its extreme form of presentation, realism was known in literature as naturalism. In the theater, the problem play heralded the rise of social criticism. In painting, following the brilliant results achieved by the Impressionists in obtaining new surface and atmospheric effects, other painters continued to experiment in various ways, and the schools of Expressionism and Cubism were the result. Architects broke with the largely derivative styles of the preceding period and experimented with new materials and designs to satisfy the requirements of a highly industrialized society.

Our survey closes in 1914, the year of the outbreak of the First World War—itself the logical culmination of the doctrine of the survival of the fittest. The physical waste and moral bankruptcy of this conflict are bitter indexes of the hideous perversion of such a theory when misapplied to human society.

SUGGESTIONS FOR READING

C. J. H. Hayes, *A Generation of Materialism, 1871-1900*, Harper, 1941. This volume in *The Rise of Modern Europe* series provides the best survey of the topics treated in this chapter.

D. Thomson, ed., *The Era of Violence, 1898-1945*, Cambridge Univ., 1960, Vol. XII of the *New Cambridge Modern History*. Contains authoritative chapters on economics and intellectual history in addition to chapters on politics.

Excellent brief surveys of the thought of the period are contained in C. Brinton, *The Shaping of the Modern Mind,* * Mentor; and J. H. Randall, *The Making of the Modern Mind*, Houghton Mifflin, 1940. For greater detail, see F. S. Marvin, *The Century of Hope*, Oxford, 1927.

The following surveys include valuable sections on the developments in economics from 1870 to 1914: W. H. B. Court, *A Concise Economic History of Britain from 1750 to Recent Times*, Cambridge Univ., 1954; S. B. Clough, *France: A History of National Economics, 1789-1939*, Scribner's, 1939; and G.

Stolper, *German Economy, 1870-1940: Issues and Trends*, Reynal, 1940.

H. Feis, *Europe, the World's Banker, 1870-1914*, Yale, 1930. A solid scholarly study of European overseas investment and the relationship between international finance and diplomacy.

H. Pelling, *American Labor,* * Univ. of Chicago. Considered to be the best single-volume history of the American labor movement.

K. Polanyi, *The Great Transformation,* * Beacon. An analysis of the social devastation produced by an uncontrolled economy.

G. Dangerfield, *The Strange Death of Liberal England,* * Capricorn. A stimulating account of social unrest and the decline of laissez faire before World War I.

J. A. Schumpeter, *Capitalism, Socialism and Democracy*, Harper, 1950. A thoughtful examination of these three concepts and their interrelationship during the nineteenth and twentieth centuries.

*Indicates an inexpensive paperbound edition.

H. Faulkner, *The Quest for Social Justice, 1898-1914,* Macmillan, 1937. Deals with the beginnings of this quest in the United States.

C. Dawson, *Religion and Culture,** Meridian. An analysis of the role of religion in an industrial society. For a sympathetic study of the ''workingman's pope,'' see R. Fulop-Miller, *Leo XIII and Our Times,* Longmans, 1937.

F. Hayek, *The Road to Serfdom,** Phoenix. The classic argument that social planning leads to socialism and worse.

C. Gide and C. Rist, *A History of Economic Doctrines from the Time of the Physiocrats to the Present Day,* Heath, 1948. Long recognized as a standard guide to the subject. .

A. Gray, *The Socialist Tradition: Moses to Lenin,* Longmans, 1946. A good introduction.

A. Fremantle, *This Little Band of Prophets: The British Fabians,** Mentor. A popular account of the small group which successfully adapted socialism to Britain.

R. Humphrey, *Georges Sorel: Prophet Without Honor,* Harvard, 1951. An excellent work on the founder of syndicalism.

L. H. Haimson, *The Russian Marxists and the Origins of Bolshevism,* Harvard, 1955. The story of socialism in Russia.

D. Shub, *Lenin,** Mentor. The best biography of the man who is perhaps the most influential figure in twentieth-century history.

H. T. Pledge, *Science Since 1500: A Short History of Mathematics, Physics, Chemistry and Biology,** Torchbooks. Recommended also for its clarity and brevity is J. B. Conant, *On Understanding Science: An Historical Approach,** Mentor.

Sir J. Jeans, *The Growth of Physical Science,** Premier; L. Barnett, *The Universe and Dr. Einstein,** Mentor. Two popular works on the revolution in physics.

P. De Kruif, *Microbe Hunters,** Pocketbooks; H. Zinsser, *Rats, Lice, and History,** Bantam. Modern medical history readably popularized.

J. R. Partington, *A Short History of Chemistry,** Torchbooks. A useful survey with over one hundred illustrations.

F. Wittels, *Freud and His Time,** Universal. Emphasizes Freud's place in our modern culture.

L. Eiseley, *Darwin's Century,* Doubleday, 1958. Perhaps the most useful general work on Darwin and the spread of his influence.

G. Himmelfarb, *Darwin and the Darwinian Revolution,* Doubleday, 1959. Based on unpublished documents, this illuminating account sheds light on both the character of the scientist and the age in which he lived. See also the dual biography of Darwin and Thomas Huxley: W. Irvine, *Apes, Angels and Victorians,** Meridian.

Excellent biographies of important scientists include Sir William W. Cheyne, *Lister and His Achievements,* Longmans, 1925; E. Curie, *Madame Curie,** Pocketbooks; H. Iltis, *The Life of Mendel,* Norton, 1932; R. Dubos, *Louis Pasteur, Free Lance of Science,* Little, Brown, 1950; and B. P. Babkin, *Pavlov: A Biography,* Univ. of Chicago, 1949.

A. Usher, *A History of Mechanical Inventions,** Beacon. A classic in the history of technology and its influence.

A. N. Whitehead, *Science and the Modern World,** Mentor. A famous series of lectures on the relations of science, thought, and religion in modern times.

E. R. Trattner, *Unraveling the Book of Books,* Scribner's, 1929. The story of Biblical criticism.

H. E. Barnes, *The New History and the Social Studies,* Century, 1925. Surveys the development of the social sciences, including historiography. See also G. P. Gooch, *History and Historians in the Nineteenth Century,** Beacon.

R. Hofstadter, *Social Darwinism in American Thought,** Beacon. Details the cult of force, struggle, and militarism in the United States. Darwinism is applied to politics in W. Bagehot, *Physics and Politics,** Beacon.

E. Wilson, *Axel's Castle: A Study in the Imaginative Literature of 1870-1930,** Scribner's. A suggestive book on realism and subjectivism in literature.

G. Brereton, *A Short History of French Literature,** Penguin. Half of this new, compact history is devoted to the nineteenth and twentieth centuries. See also M. Turnell, *The Novel in France,** Vintage. Other studies of national literatures include M. Hamburger, *Reason and Energy: Studies in German Literature,** Evergreen; and D. S. Mirsky, *A History of Russian Literature: From Its Beginnings to 1900,** Vintage.

H. Read, *The Grass Roots of Art,** Meridian. Lectures on the social aspects of art in an industrial age. T. Craven, *Modern Art,* Simon and Schuster, 1934, is a first-rate survey.

M. Raynal, *The Nineteenth Century: Goya to Gauguin,* Skira, 1951. A beautifully illustrated history of painting. The more than 150 illustrations in F. Mathey, *The Impressionists,** Praeger, afford a brilliant tour of the great works of this influential movement.

H. R. Hitchcock, *Architecture: Nineteenth and Twentieth Centuries,* Penguin, 1958. A detailed survey, richly illustrated. On America's most influential architect, see E. Kaufmann and B. Raeburn, *Frank Lloyd Wright: Writings and Buildings,** Meridian.

H. Leichtentritt, *Music, History, and Ideas,* Harvard, 1938. Music viewed in its social context.

POLITICS

1800   Congress of Vienna 1814-1815—Russia, Britain, France, Austria attempt to restore Old Regime; legitimate rulers reinstated; boundaries modified to hem in France; Quadruple (later Quintuple) and Holy Alliances formed; nationalism disregarded
Louis XVIII of France establishes constitutional monarchy 1814-1824
Reaction in England—political, religious inequality under Tories; Peel and Canning lead reforms c. 1815-1830
Carlsbad Decrees, sponsored by Metternich, temporarily discourage German nationalist youth movement 1819
Revolutions in Spain and Italy 1820; Congress of Troppau, Congress of Laibach stifle Italian revolt 1820-1821; Congress of Verona stifles Spanish revolt 1822
Congress System declines—Britain refuses support in suppressing revolts 1820-1822; U.S. announces Monroe Doctrine 1823; Greeks rise against Turkish rule 1821-1827; France, Britain, Russia secure Greek independence, Serbian autonomy at Treaty of Adrianople 1829
Mazzini, exemplar of romantic nationalism, joins *Carbonari* 1820's; initiates Italian *Risorgimento* c. 1830
Charles X, exponent of divine right, ascends French throne 1824; dissolves legislature, limits franchise 1830
Tsar Nicholas I crushes Decembrist Revolt 1825; Nicholas imposes reactionary repressive system on Russia, Poland 1825-1855
Catholic Emancipation Act permits Irish Catholics to be members of English parliament 1829
Revolutions of 1830—July Revolution in Paris deposes Charles X, enthrones Louis Philippe; Belgians throw off Dutch rule, select Leopold as king; revolt unsuccessful in Poland
Whigs under Grey end reactionary Tory rule 1830; Reform Bill 1832; slavery abolished 1833; Municipal Corporations Bill 1835
Russia protects Constantinople against invasion by Egypt; Treaty of Unkiar Skelessi makes Turkey a protectorate of Russia 1831
Chartist movement for reform fails (1839, 1842, 1848) but lays foundation for modern British democracy
England leans toward economic liberalism—repeal of Corn Laws 1846; abandonment of all customs duties encourages free trade
Revolution of 1848 in France—Parisians end Louis Philippe's government, set up Second Republic with moderates in control; June Days—bourgeoisie crush radical workers' revolt; Louis Napoleon becomes president 1848, proclaims himself Emperor Napoleon III 1852
Revolution of 1848 in Germany—Frederick William IV of Prussia grants constitutional government; other German states demand same; Frankfurt Assembly fails to establish new union 1848-1849; German Confederation restored at Olmütz 1850
Revolutions in Hungary, Bohemia, Vienna, Italy fail 1848-1849
Crimean War—Russia invades Turkey 1853; France, Britain, Sardinia invade Russian Crimea, defeat Russia at Sevastopol 1854-1855;
1850   Treaty of Paris affirms integrity of Ottoman empire, halts Russian advance into Balkans 1856
Italy unified under Cavour—Sardinia, France gain territory by Austro-Italian War 1859; Sardinia annexes Italian territory conquered by Garibaldi 1860; first Italian parliament 1861; Italy obtains Venetia 1866, Rome 1870; Rome becomes capital of united Italy 1871
Tsar Alexander II issues Emancipation Proclamation 1861; introduces government and court reform, conscription 1864-1874
Reform movements in Russia—reformers either Westerners or Slavophiles; Nihilism develops in 1860's, inspires Narodniki movement Polish insurrection crushed; policy of repression reimposed by Alexander II 1863
Germany unified under Bismarck—Prussia defeats Denmark and Austria, gains Schleswig-Holstein, dominates North German Confederation 1864-1866; Prussia wins Franco-Prussian War, gains Alsace-Lorraine at Treaty of Frankfurt 1870; William of Prussia proclaimed emperor of united Germany 1871
Ausgleich establishes Dual Monarchy of Austria-Hungary 1867
Gladstone, Disraeli alternate as English prime minister 1867-1880; Reform Bill of 1867 extends vote; Gladstone's Glorious Ministry passes Education Act of 1870, reforms civil service and army, establishes secret ballot 1868-1874; Disraeli passes health and housing legislation, liberalizes acts against trade unions 1874-1880
Ireland's struggle under Gladstone—Irish Anglican Church disestablished 1869; Irish land acts 1870, 1881; Parnell leads Irish Home Rulers; Gladstone introduces unsuccessful home rule bills 1886, 1893
Second Empire in France swept from power during Franco-Prussian War; Third Republic proclaimed 1870
Democratic struggles in minor powers—Switzerland and Scandinavia enjoy democracy; Italy suffers from unstable coalitions; Netherlands and Belgium discontented under illiberal franchises; revolutions in Spain and Portugal c. 1870-1914
Power politics, militarism, rival alliances, secret diplomacy, imperialism, and nationalism precede World War I c. 1870-1914
Threats to French Third Republic—revolutionary Paris Commune 1871; General Boulanger 1886; Dreyfus case 1894-1906
Bismarck strengthens German Second Reich—wages *Kulturkampf*; initiates social legislation c. 1871-1890; forms Three Emperors' League with Russia and Austria-Hungary 1873; Triple Alliance with Austria and Italy 1882; Reinsurance Treaty with Russia 1887
Turkey crushes Bosnian and Bulgarian revolts, defeats Serbia, Montenegro 1875; Russia defeats Turkey 1877-1878; Treaty of San Stefano gains independence for Serbia and Rumania, puts Bulgaria under Russian dominance 1878
Congress of Berlin 1878—Britain and Austria return part of Bulgaria to Turkish domination, make part independent, part autonomous; award Bosnia, Herzegovina to Austria
Abdul-Hamid II imposes absolute rule over Ottoman empire 1878; Young Turks rebel 1908, introduce program of Turkish supremacy and centralization which irritates Arabs; Turks lose territory to Austria-Hungary, Greece, Italy, Balkan nations 1908-1913
Nihilist movement of Russia advocates terrorism to attain reforms; Alexander II assassinated 1881; Alexander III revives system of repression, attempts policy of Russification 1881-1894
Gladstone sponsors third Reform Bill, and England approaches universal manhood suffrage 1884; Gladstone passes Employers' Liability Act
Spirit of internationalism—annual Universal Peace Congresses begin 1889; first Pan-American Conference 1889; Hague Tribunal 1899
William II dismisses Bismarck 1890, allows Reinsurance Treaty to lapse; France forms Dual Alliance with Russia 1894
Radical groups appear under Nicholas II in Russia 1894-1917; Social Democrats, exponents of Marxist principles, divide into moderate
1900   Mensheviks and radical Bolsheviks 1903; massacre of Bloody Sunday 1905; October Manifesto calls national Duma 1905
Herzl introduces Zionism, which proposes the creation of Palestine as independent state 1896; first Zionist congress meets 1897
Britain abandons diplomatic isolation—forms alliance with Japan 1902; proclaims Entente Cordiale with France 1904; establishes Triple Entente with Russia and France 1907
English Liberal party provides social, labor legislation 1905-1914; Parliament Bill of 1911 curtails power of House of Lords
Diplomatic crises lead to World War I—Germany and France clash over Morocco 1905, 1911; Austria annexes Bosnia-Herzegovina, angers Russia, Serbia; First and Second Balkan Wars increase Serbia's ambitions, Austria's fears 1912-1913; Archduke Francis Ferdinand is assassinated 1914; World War I begins 1914

ECONOMICS AND SCIENCE, THOUGHT AND ART

Inventions revolutionize textile industry—flying shuttle 1738; spinning jenny 1764; water frame 1769; spinning mule 1779; power loom 1785; cotton gin 1792.

Transportation—modern canal building in England begins 1759; first voyage of Fulton's steamship *Clermont* 1807; macadam roads invented 1815; Erie Canal 1825; Cunard's transatlantic passenger steamship service c. 1837; Suez Canal 1869; railroads cross U.S. 1869; Wright brothers' airplane 1903; Ford's Model T 1909

Sources of power—industrial use of Watt's steam engine 1785; Faraday's electric dynamo 1831; first oil well 1859; internal-combustion engine 1860; working dynamo 1876; Diesel engine 1892

Combination Acts forbid unions in England on ground they would restrain trade 1799-1800

1800

Laissez-faire theory popularized—Malthus advances theory of overpopulation; Ricardo develops subsistence theory of wages; Bentham devises doctrine of utilitarianism; John Stuart Mill holds that governments should impose some controls on business

Preromantic writers—Rousseau exalts instinct and emotion; Schiller attacks tyranny in *Wilhelm Tell* 1804; Goethe, whose works illustrate transition from classicism to romanticism, publishes *Faust:* Part I 1808, Part II 1832

First Industrial Revolution 1815-1870—England holds technological leadership; world trade increases; imperialism in Asia and Africa; Europe's population grows, country-to-city, regional shifts in population; technological unemployment; trade unionism

European romantic writers—Wordsworth expresses transcendentalist view of nature; Coleridge stresses exoticism, supernaturalism; Shelley and Byron rebel against constraints of society; Keats concerned with estheticism; Scott treats medieval life romantically

Romanticist painters rebel against classical rules—Delacroix, Constable, Turner

Romanticism in music—Beethoven frees music from arid formalism; Brahms, Tschaikovsky, Chopin, and others turn to romantic composition; opera assumes romantic characteristics in works of Wagner and Verdi

Romantic nationalist writers—Hugo condemns tyranny at home and abroad; Pushkin denounces tyranny in Russia; Hegel exalts Prussian state; Michelet, Bancroft, Macaulay write national histories

Emergence of socialism—Utopian socialists Saint-Simon, Fourier, Owen propose (early 1800's) scientifically planned, cooperative societies; Marx and Engels publish *Communist Manifesto* 1848; Proudhon founds anarchism; Christian socialists emphasize social aspects of Christ's teachings; Marx's scientific socialism expounded in *Das Kapital* 1867-1894

Period of Gothic revival in architecture c. 1830

Lyell's *Principles of Geology* 1830-1833—basis of modern geology

Agricultural revolution accelerated by nineteenth-century technology—reaper, harvester, combine, steel plow

English social and economic reforms such as Factory Act of 1833 diminish doctrine of laissez faire

Communication—penny post introduced in England 1840; Morse perfects telegraph 1844; Field lays Atlantic cable 1856; Bell invents telephone 1876; Marconi devises wireless telegraphy 1895

Zollverein, tariff union, stimulates industry in German states 1842; Krupp works become symbol of German industrial efficiency 1873

Physics—first law of thermodynamics 1847; Clerk-Maxwell advances electromagnetic theory of light 1873; Hertz proves existence of electromagnetic waves 1886; x-ray discovered 1895; Pierre and Marie Curie discover radium 1898; electron theory formulated; Planck's quantum theory; Einstein produces equation $E = mc^2$, theory of relativity 1905; Rutherford's theory of positively charged atomic nucleus 1911

1850

Comte initiates science of sociology; Ranke founds school of scientific history

Bessemer improves smelting, refining of iron ore 1850's

Great Exhibition in London 1851—monument to cult of material progress which symbolizes Victorian era

Victorian poets—Tennyson typifies ideals of his time; Browning displays faith in humanity

Victorian novelists—Thackeray satirizes Victorian society; Dickens protests against social injustices

Social criticism—Arnold denounces mid-Victorian values, advocates state education to restore humanistic values; Carlyle criticizes industrial evils, believes salvation achieved by leadership of "Great Men"; Ruskin condemns mass production, leads Esthetic Revolt

Darwin publishes *Origin of Species* 1859, *Descent of Man* 1871; influences research in biology; Weismann distinguishes somatic and germ cells 1870's; Mendel's laws of heredity gain recognition c. 1900; biologists advance theory of chromosomes, substantiate mutation theory, reject theory of inheritance of acquired characteristics; Galton pioneers in eugenics

Darwinism stimulates controversy between science and religion: Catholic Church reaffirms historical position; scholars apply "higher criticism" to Bible; social Darwinism justifies various economic and political theories; Darwinian theory influences philosophers James (pragmatism) and Bergson (vitalism)

Medicine—Lister uses asepsis and antisepsis in surgery c. 1860; Pasteur and Koch prove germ theory of disease 1881; Pasteur cures rabies 1885; Ehrlich produces disease-curing salvarsan 1909; significance of vitamins disclosed 1912

Growth of socialism—First International fails, anarchists under Bakunin oppose Marxist majority 1864-1873; Social Democratic party founded in Germany 1875; socialist groups in Italy, Austria, Scandinavia, and Low Countries 1880's; Fabian Society in England urges revisionism 1883; Second International founded 1889; revisionism grows on Continent 1890's; English Labour party formed 1900

Chemistry—Dalton formulates atomic theory; Mendelyeev classifies all known elements in periodic table 1869

Second Industrial Revolution c. 1870-1914—use of scientific techniques and mass production in industry; greater governmental regulation of business; financial capitalism supersedes industrial capitalism; world trade increases; trade unionism grows; U.S., Germany, Japan become important industrial nations

Free and compulsory education becomes almost universal in western Europe 1870-1914

Realism replaces romanticism in literature—Balzac, Flaubert, Tolstoy, Dostoevski, Hardy, James, Clemens (realists); Zola (naturalist); Ibsen and Shaw expose social problems in "problem plays"; cult in England and French symbolists react against extreme realism

Painting c. 1870-1914—Courbet and Daumier inject realism in painting; Impressionists such as Renoir place emphasis on light and color; Rodin uses Impressionist techniques in sculpture; Post-Impressionists such as Cézanne and Van Gogh combine color and solidity; Expressionists like Matisse put subjective feelings in paintings; Cubists such as Picasso construct abstract patterns from given object

Syndicalists—advocates of the doctrine of revolution rather than revisionism emerge in France 1890's

Psychology—Pavlov advances study of conditioned reflexes 1900; American school of behaviorism; Freud pioneers in psychoanalysis

Music—Richard Strauss exemplifies post-Wagnerian school; Debussy is foremost exponent of impressionism; Stravinski experiments with polytonality; expressionist Schönberg develops twelve-tone system

1900

Architecture—Sullivan pioneers in steel-skeleton skyscraper; Wright originates revolutionary house designs; Gropius leads machine-age architecture movement in Germany

PART **6** The West Dominant

CHAPTER 25 NEW EUROPES OVERSEAS

CHAPTER 26 THE WHITE MAN'S BURDEN

In the eighteenth and nineteenth centuries, European influence spread to virtually all parts of the non-European world. Two sorts of communities were created by this expansion: the centers of settlement for the millions of people from Ireland, England, Germany, France, and Italy who migrated to the Americas, South Africa, and Australasia; and the colonies of exploitation, those African and Asian territories and islands which were developed largely for economic gain. The settlement of new and largely uninhabited lands by Europeans gave birth to new nations, and the conquest of areas unsuited for European settlement resulted in a system of imperialism by which a minority of foreign officials and soldiers controlled a majority of native peoples. The colonies in imperial systems brought wealth to the controlling western powers, but at the same time European rule helped to introduce new forces that ultimately were to challenge and sweep away imperialism.

Although there was variance in the centers of settlement—which can be called new Europes—because of differences in the national origins of the colonists and in the indigenous societies they encountered, all can be said to have derived their culture mainly from Europe. Thus though the United States grew and broke away from its mother country while Canada flourished and remained in the English fold, the outstanding traits of both—their governmental structure and principles, their social make-up, and their language—reflect their common European origins. And all these new Europes had certain common problems —the challenge of exploring and occupying hitherto unsettled lands, the problem of native peoples, the necessity of taming nature and using natural resources, and the task of building nations. All of them experienced, too, the same urge to broaden democratic rights.

The stage on which history was being made in the nations of the New World was different in many ways from that of the mother countries in Europe. On both, however, the plot and the action had much in common. The leading actors—statesmen and administrators—had to direct and cope with the same basic forces, such as nationalism, industrialism, and democracy. For example, the American Civil War, the federation movement in Canada, and the efforts of Bismarck and Cavour in Germany and Italy all concerned the same basic principle of national unity; and the quest for expanding democratic freedoms in the Jacksonian era in the United States had its counterpart in the revolutions of 1848 in Europe.

While European immigrants were settling the new Europes, their home governments were extending their control over African and Asian peoples. By the end of the nineteenth century, practically all of Africa had been partitioned and placed under European rule, along with most of southern Asia and the islands of the Pacific. Although China remained technically independent, this vast, tradition-bound land also was controlled in many ways by the western imperial powers. Japan alone succeeded in modernizing itself and thus avoided being caught in the imperialist net. In the half century before World War I, western supremacy, symbolized by imperialism and the colonial system, was one of the major facts of international life.

The morality of imperialism has been a hotly debated subject. Critics have emphasized such negative aspects as arbitrary rule, economic exploitation, and hypocrisy and greed on the part of the imperialists. On the other hand, imperialism has been justified on economic, religious, nationalistic, and even humanitarian grounds. Such well-known champions of imperialism as Livingstone, Rhodes, and Kipling believed that, in promoting their country's seizure of foreign lands and riches, they were doing the best thing for all concerned. The theory that only the selfish have followed the course of imperialism is not borne out by the facts of history.

What is perhaps the most significant and enduring influence of imperialism has not been appreciated. Western colonialism was the instrument for culture diffusion on a huge scale. The colonial officials, missionaries, planters, and educators spread new ideas about science and technology, developed natural resources, cured the physical ills of the native peoples, and taught concepts of democracy and Christian morality.

This impact of western culture subtly modified the outlook and habits of the peoples under the colonial system. Ideals of freedom and nationalism began to stir. National movements gained strength in the early years of the twentieth century and after World War II gathered sufficient momentum to challenge and largely demolish colonialism. Thus the western world provided the knowledge and inspiration which was to uplift and release the very people it had exploited. The golden age of imperialism ended almost half a century ago, but it had changed the course of history for all time.

CHAPTER 25

New Europes Overseas

Introduction. In the four centuries before the twentieth, the greatest transplantation of peoples in human history took place as millions of Europeans left their homelands, crossed oceans, and made for themselves new homes in overseas lands. These immigrants brought with them what has been aptly called their "cultural baggage"—their language, religion, folk habits, and experience and attitudes of government.

In the new areas of settlement—the Americas, South Africa, Australia, and New Zealand—new Europes developed which in many ways reflected the culture of the homelands. Moreover, the basic attitudes and movements of Europe after Waterloo—the ambitions of the middle class, the search of the masses for full political rights, the rising interest in better standards of living, and the pervasive force of nationalism—all these became important factors in the overseas communities. Yet if the history of the new Europes is to be studied profitably in comparison with that of the mother areas, it should be kept in mind that there were certain distinctive conditions and problems that gave uniqueness to the history of these nations: the challenge of geographical exploration, the problem of what to do with the less advanced native peoples, and the search for a new national way of life. Furthermore, some historians have stressed the deep influence in all the new Europes of frontier life with its fostering of democracy, individualism, resourcefulness, and optimism. As a complete explanation of the course of history in the new Europes, this thesis has been overdone. But some of its relevance remains.

In this chapter we shall see how the founding of colonies in Canada, Australia, New Zealand, and the Union of South Africa illustrates the transplanting of British culture to remote parts of the world. One interesting aspect of the story of the new Britains overseas during the nineteenth century is that they finally arrived at a status of full national independence or sovereignty without recourse to arms. At the same time they remained closely associated with the mother country as members of the British Commonwealth of Nations. Since the political development of Canada was a model for other English colonies, we shall emphasize Canadian history in our survey of the British dominions.

Latin America faced certain unique problems of its own in its struggle to win greatness. Here the Indian problem was far greater than it was in the United States, and here also relations between the two races were very different. From the time of the successful revolt against Spain in the first quarter of the nineteenth century, the history of Latin America has been marked by civil wars and local struggles for political power. As this chapter discloses, threats from the outside and attempts by other powers to gain economic if not political control of Latin America did much to retard the growth of Latin America as a whole. Nevertheless, by the first quarter of the twentieth century, a degree of stability and prosperity had been achieved in parts of Latin America, and the cultural patterns that developed there constitute a valuable component of world civilization.

THE MAKING OF A NEW NATION

English culture transplanted to America. From 1607 until 1776 the Thirteen Colonies had been part of the British empire. Nearly all the forces influencing the development of civilization in the colonies came from England. The period of the Revolution did little to alter the fundamentals of colonial society; although the Revolution began America's existence as an independent nation, it did not displace the English language, common law, religion, philosophy, and literary influences derived from Great Britain. Thus it is that Shakespeare, Milton, Cromwell, and Locke are now much more a part of our heritage than are men of similar stature from other European nations. And the American form of government, unique in many respects, obtained its basic outlines and its political philosophy from the parent country.

Democratic influences of the frontier. In 1783, the year the United States became a sovereign state, the young nation could not be called a democracy. Six years later, only one male in seven possessed the franchise. Religious requirements and property qualifications kept many of the common people from participating in governmental affairs. For the first forty years of its existence, the government of the United States was largely in the hands of established families from the South, such as those of Washington and Jefferson, or of men of wealth and substance from the middle class of the North, such as Adams. It has been said that it took fifty years after the Declaration of Independence "to reach a vital belief that the people and not gentlemen are to govern this country."[1]

The influence of the western frontier helped move America closer to full democracy. Even before the Constitution was ratified by the thirteen states, thousands of pioneers crossed the Appalachian Mountains into the new "western country." Here on the frontier, land was to be had for the asking. Here social caste did not exist; one man was as good as another. Vigor, courage, and self-reliance counted, not birth or wealth. Throughout most of the nineteenth century, as pioneers moved westward, the West was to be a source for new and liberal movements which challenged the ideas prevalent in the more conservative and settled areas of the country.

Up until the War of 1812, the growth of democracy was slow. In 1791 Vermont had been admitted as a manhood-suffrage state, and the following year Kentucky followed suit; but Tennessee, Ohio, and Louisiana entered the Union with property and tax qualifications for the suffrage. After 1817 no new state entered the Union with restrictions on male suffrage. Appointive offices became elective, and requirements for office holding were liberalized.

Jacksonian democracy. In 1828 Andrew Jackson was elected to the presidency, following a campaign which featured the slogan "Down with the aristocrats." Jackson was the first president produced by the new West; the first, excepting Washington, not to have a college education; and the first to have been born in poverty. He owed his successful election to no Congressional clique but to the will of the people. The common people idolized "Old Hickory" as their spokesman and a fearless leader of men.

The triumph of the democratic principle in the 1830's set the direction for political development down to this day. With the new president came the idea that any man, by virtue of being an American citizen, was worthy of holding any office in the land. Educational opportunities were widened with the growth of the public school system, class barriers became less important, and government became more responsive and re-sponsible to the average or common man. Indeed, it has been thoughtfully said that "the 1830's saw the triumph in American politics of that democracy which has remained pre-eminently the distinguishing feature of our society."[2]

Acquisition of new lands. From 1800 to 1860 the westward movement proceeded at an amazingly rapid pace. The Louisiana territory, purchased from France by Jefferson for about $15,000,000 in 1803, doubled the size of the United States. The annexation of Texas in 1845 was followed by war with Mexico in 1846. Two years later Mexico signed a peace treaty whereby California, all title to Texas, and also the country between California and Texas were ceded to the United States. The same year that war broke out with Mexico, the Oregon territory was occupied after the settlement of a serious disagreement with Great Britain. As a result of these acquisitions, by 1860 the area of the United States had increased nearly two-thirds over what it had been in 1840.

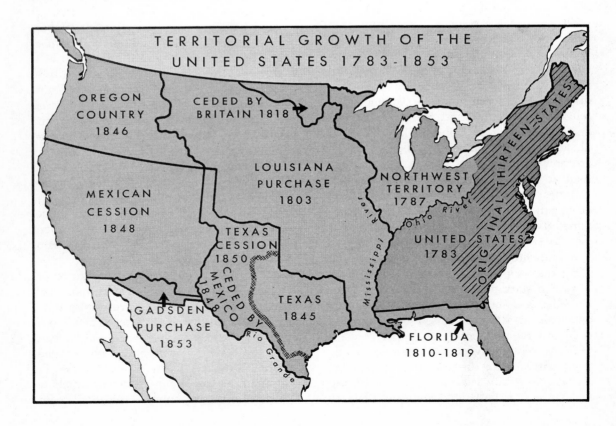

TERRITORIAL GROWTH OF THE UNITED STATES 1783-1853

OREGON COUNTRY 1846

CEDED BY BRITAIN 1818

LOUISIANA PURCHASE 1803

NORTHWEST TERRITORY 1787

ORIGINAL THIRTEEN STATES

MEXICAN CESSION 1848

Mississippi River

Ohio River

UNITED STATES 1783

TEXAS CESSION 1850

CEDED BY MEXICO 1848

GADSDEN PURCHASE 1853

Rio Grande

TEXAS 1845

FLORIDA 1810-1819

The slavery issue. The acquisition of new territory forced the issue of whether slavery should be allowed in these areas. At the same time, the whole issue of slavery was being vigorously condemned by abolitionists in the North, particularly in New England. Henry Clay's Missouri Compromise of 1820, by which slavery was permitted in Missouri but forbidden in the remainder of the Louisiana Purchase, had satisfied both sides temporarily, but the antislavery forces grew more insistent. In the senatorial campaigns of 1858, Abraham Lincoln declared:

"A house divided against itself cannot stand." I believe this government cannot endure permanently half slave and half free. I do not expect the Union to be dissolved—I do not expect the house to fall—but I do expect it will cease to be divided. It will become all one thing, or all the other.[3]

Slavery was a fundamental issue; from its existence stemmed many differences and tensions which separated the North from the South. In a sense the North and the South had become two different civilizations. The former was industrial, urban, and democratic; the latter was mainly agricultural, rural, and dominated by a planter aristocracy. The South strongly opposed the North's desire for higher tariffs, government aid for new railroads, and generous terms for land settlement in the West.

The Civil War. Soon after the inauguration of Lincoln as president, the southern states seceded from the Union and formed the Confederacy. The first shot of the Civil War was fired at Fort Sumter in 1861. Four agonizing years of conflict followed, and thousands of men lost their lives. The Confederacy finally collapsed before the overwhelming superiority of the North in man power, industrial resources, and wealth. When General Lee surrendered to General Grant at Appomattox in April 1865, the Civil War ended. But a few days later the joyful North was stunned by the assassination of President Lincoln.

The Civil War is the grand American epic in its heroism, romance, tragedy, and incalcu-

The burning of Cincinnati's Union Station marked the climax of the Great Strike of 1877, the first serious industrial conflict in the United States. Above is a contemporary engraving of the incident which appeared in *Harper's Weekly.*

lable results. Scholars have delved into the background, the military history, and consequences of the struggle; there has been a tremendous output of scholarly histories and biographies, as well as popular accounts and historical romances.

In the largest sense the American Civil War can be explained in its relation to the great historical movements of the nineteenth century—liberty, democracy, and nationalism—which were transforming Europe. It was the desire for freedom that sparked the revolutions in Europe in 1830 and 1848; and likewise in the United States many people had come to believe that slavery was an inhuman and immoral institution. The sentiment of nationalism was equally strong in Europe and in the United States. Just as wars were fought to attain German and Italian unity, a great struggle took place in America to maintain national unity. If the causes of the American Civil War are complex, the all-important result was simple. It settled the issue of whether the United States was an indivisible sovereign nation or a collection of sovereign states. The Federal Union was preserved, and nationalism triumphed over the sectionalism of the South.

Industrial expansion. The victory of the North also foreshadowed an irresistible trend toward industrialism. In its lasting effects the economic revolution in the United States which followed the Civil War was more significant than the conflict itself. With the South prostrate after the war, industrialism triumphed in the North. Westward expansion continued its pace. Railroads were built across broad prairies, and the first transcontinental railroad, the Union Pacific, was completed in 1869. Thousands of settlers swarmed westward.

Between 1850 and 1880, the number of cities with a population of 50,000 or more doubled. The number of men employed in industry increased 50 per cent. In 1865 there were 35,000 miles of railroads in the country; eight years later, this figure had been doubled. By 1900 the trackage was estimated to be about 200,000 miles, more than in all of Europe. In 1860 little more than a billion dollars was invested in manufacturing; by 1900 this figure had risen to twelve billion. The value of manufactured products increased proportionately. In 1870 the total production of iron and steel in the United States was far below that of France and England. Twenty years later the United States had outstripped them and was producing about one third of the world's iron and steel.

In the age of rapid industrialism and materialistic expansion, many who pursued profits lost sight of ethical principles both in business and in government. In five years, between 1865 and 1870, the notorious Tweed Ring cost the city of New York at least $100,000,000. Ruthless financiers, such as Jay Gould and Jim Fisk, menaced the financial stability of the nation. During General Grant's administration as president, the country was shocked by scandals and frauds. A new rich class, elevated to power and wealth overnight, failed to appreciate its responsibilities to society. Corruption in business was a blatant feature of the new economic order.

End of the era of expansion. For roughly a century the gospel of the new nation of America had been rugged individualism. As in Europe, government interference in business was unwelcome because it was felt that the individual should be free to follow his own inclinations, run his own business, and enjoy the profits of his labors. In an expanding nation where land, jobs, and opportunity beckoned, there was little to indicate that the system would not work indefinitely. By 1880, however, the end of the frontier was in sight. Free land of good quality was becoming scarce, and the frontier could no longer act as a safety valve to release the economic and social pressures of unemployed or discontented populations from the East.

Between 1850 and 1900, the United States became the most powerful state in the Western Hemisphere, increased its national wealth from $7,000,000,000 to $88,000,000,000, established an excellent system of public education, and fostered the enjoyment of civil liberties. But there were many disturbing factors in the picture. Unemployment, child labor, and industrial accidents became common in the rapidly growing industrial areas. In large cities, slums grew and served as breeding places for disease and crime. The first serious industrial conflict occurred in 1877 when bloody riots broke out in Pittsburgh. In 1892 a bitter strike, accompanied by violence, broke out in the Carnegie Steel Company works; and two years later the great Pullman strike further demonstrated that tension was developing between labor and capital.

The progressive movement. The United States had obtained its freedom in 1783, had become a political democracy early in the nineteenth century, and had prevented the collapse of the Federal Union between 1861 and 1865. By 1890 a new challenge had arisen—the need for economic reform. At this point, as had happened in England and elsewhere at about the same time, a powerful movement whose object was the removal of economic inequalities began. The so-called progressive movement agitated for the elimination of sweatshops, of exploitation of foreign labor, and of waste of the nation's natural wealth. Magazines and books also took up the crusade; the era of the muckrakers lasted roughly from 1890 to 1910.

The success of the progressive movement was reflected in the constitutions of new states admitted to the Union and in the introduction of the direct primary, the initiative and referendum, and the direct election of senators. All these measures tended to give the common man more effective control of his government. After the enactment in 1887 of the Interstate Commerce Act, which had brought the railroads under national control, a steady expansion of governmental regulation of industry began. As president of the United States from 1901 to 1909, Theodore Roosevelt launched an aggressive campaign to break up the trusts, to conserve national resources, and to extend the regulation of the national government over the railroads, food, and drugs. In 1913 President Woodrow Wilson inaugurated a militant campaign of reform called the "New Freedom." The tariff was reduced because it was too much the instrument of special economic privilege; banking reform was effected by the Federal Reserve Act in 1913; and the regulation of business by the national government for the protection of public interests was further extended by the passage of the Clayton Anti-Trust Act in 1914 and the establishment of the Federal Trade Commission in the same year.

The United States in 1914. In 1914 the United States was the most populous, rich, and influential of the new countries which had sprung from motherlands in Europe. In 1790 the population of the United States had been just under 4,000,000; the census of 1910 showed an increase to nearly 99,000,000. During the nineteenth century and the first decade of the twentieth century, more than 25,000,000 immigrants had made America their new home.

Since the days of George Washington, the national wealth had increased at least a hundredfold. Once the producer of raw materials only, the United States in 1914 was the greatest industrial power in the world. In 1900 it was producing more steel than Great Britain and Germany combined; and one of its concerns—United States Steel—was capitalized for $1,460,000,000, a sum greater than the total estimated wealth of the country in 1790.

In 1914 many people in the United States and in the rest of the world failed to appreciate the significance of the amazing growth of the United States. Only World War I could give tangible proof that the New World nation had surpassed the power and economic importance of its mother country.

THE UNITED STATES AND WORLD AFFAIRS

Beginnings of isolationism. The tremendous development of the United States in wealth, population, and industrial power during the nineteenth century was reflected in its growing importance in world affairs. After the achievement of independence in 1783, three purposes may be identified as controlling American foreign policy: a basic concern for national security, the desire to protect and foster foreign trade, and, lastly, the feeling of a national mission in sympathizing with and encouraging the growth of freedom throughout the world.

During the first quarter century after its independence was gained, the new republic fought a brief naval war with France, became embroiled with Britain in the War of 1812, and sent two expeditions to the Mediterranean to teach the Barbary pirates a lesson. These complications notwithstanding, isolationism became the cardinal principle of American foreign policy. Thomas Jefferson's words on the subject have been quoted often:

Peace, commerce and honest friendship with all nations—entangling alliances with none.[4]

The Monroe Doctrine. Early in the 1820's the policy of noninvolvement was seriously challenged when the conservative Quadruple Alliance gave notice of helping the Spanish monarchy regain control over its rebellious colonies in Latin America. Both Britain and the United States regarded this possibility with alarm. George Canning, the British foreign secretary, suggested that his government and that of the United States make a joint declaration warning against European intervention in South America. This invitation was considered seriously by President James Monroe, but joint action was not deemed necessary. In his message to Congress in December 1823, Monroe warned the European powers against any attempt to extend their system to the Western Hemisphere and also made it clear that the United States had no intention of interfering in European affairs. In 1823 we could have our cake in foreign affairs and eat it too. The complications and dangers inherent in European intervention had been avoided—and without the necessity for any formal alliance. The shield of the British fleet stood behind the Monroe Doctrine with or without an alliance between Washington and London.

Challenges to American isolationism. On occasion, difficulties arose in reconciling isolationism with American interest in the cause of freedom throughout the world. Although much sympathy was expressed for the cause of the Greeks as they fought against Turkish tyranny in the 1820's, this sympathy did not lead to active support. In an Independence Day address, an elder statesman made it quite plain that while the United States was sympathetic to the cause of freedom:

. . . she goes not abroad in search of monsters to destroy. She is the well-wisher to the freedom and independence of all. She is the champion and vindicator only of her own.[5]

Some modifications of the American policy of isolationism became apparent in the two decades before 1860, however. The United States began to evince a growing interest in the Pacific and Asia (see Chapter 26). In 1844 the United States made its first treaty with China, opening certain Chinese ports to American trade and securing the right of our merchants and sailors to be tried in American tribunals in China. In 1853 Commodore Perry visited Japan, and by his show of force he persuaded the Japanese to open some of their harbors to American vessels. By 1854 the government of the United States was considering the annexation of the Hawaiian Islands. In 1867 the United States purchased Alaska from Russia for the amazingly small price of $7,200,000.

After the Civil War came to an end, the United States also moved to strengthen the Monroe Doctrine, which had been challenged by France's emperor, Napoleon III, while the United States was preoccupied with civil conflict. With French bayonets, Napoleon III had established a Mexican empire under Maximilian. Warnings by the United States' secretary of state went unheeded until after the Civil War, when the protests to Napoleon were backed up by the force of 900,000 veterans. The French position in Mexico was now untenable, and Napoleon was forced to withdraw his military and financial support from Maximilian. In 1867 the emperor died before a Mexican firing squad (see Color Plate 21).

After this post-Civil War flurry of activity in foreign affairs, isolationism again came to the fore as the United States set about domestic development. The building of railroads, the opening of western lands, the assimilation of millions of immigrants, the expansion of industry—all these activities monopolized attention. Foreign affairs were almost forgotten. A New York newspaper reflecting the prevailing mood went so far as to suggest the abolition of the diplomatic service!

By 1885, however, new forces began to emerge that were to carry the United States increasingly away from isolationism in the closing years of the nineteenth century. The United States began to seek an outlet for its vast national energy now that the frontier had disappeared and most of the fertile land was occupied. Foreign trade increased from a value of $393,000,000 in 1870 to more than $1,333,000,000 in 1900. Investments abroad in the same period increased from practically nothing to $500,000,000. At the same time, American missionary activity in Africa, in the Middle East, and in Asia greatly expanded. In common with the same intellectual trend in Europe, many American leaders were influenced by Darwinism, especially by its application to political affairs. The slogan "survival of the fittest" had its followers in Congress as well as in the British Parliament, the French

Chamber of Deputies, and the German Reichstag. In order to be great, many argued, the United States must expand and must assume a vital role in world politics.

In Chapter 26 the growth of an American colonial empire will be described as the Stars and Stripes came to wave over Guam, the Philippines, Hawaii, and Puerto Rico. This urge to acquire dependencies did not long endure, however; by 1905 it was definitely waning. Nevertheless, the imperialistic urge was a manifestation, however fleeting, of deeper currents of history that were carrying the United States into the full stream of world affairs. The ambitions of expansionist powers such as Germany and Japan and the advance of technology that would soon destroy American geographical remoteness were rapidly eroding the time-honored belief that isolationism was the best buttress of national security.

New dynamism in foreign affairs. In 1883 the building of a modern navy was begun, and by 1890 the build-up had accelerated greatly. Care was taken not to alarm isolationist circles, however, for the new ships were officially known as "seagoing coastline battleships," a nice nautical contradiction. When this naval program was initiated, the United States Navy ranked twelfth among the powers; by 1900 it had advanced to third place.

The growing international stature of the United States was given startling confirmation in the border dispute between Britain and Venezuela in 1895. While Britain dallied before agreeing to submit the issue to arbitration, the State Department of the United States drafted a blunt note to the British Foreign Office. According to the United States, grave consequences would follow a refusal to accept arbitration, and it was added:

To-day the United States is practically sovereign on this continent, and its fiat is law upon the subjects to which it confines its interposition . . . its infinite resources combined with its isolated position render it master of the situation and practically invulnerable against any or all other powers.[6]

Theodore Roosevelt is shown here with his famous volunteer regiment, the Rough Riders. In 1898 this cavalry unit served with distinction at the battle of San Juan Hill in the war with Spain. Winning great acclaim for his leadership in this engagement, Roosevelt became the Republican candidate for governor of New York.

Fortunately for the cause of peace, Britain was too occupied with the Boers in South Africa, with tensions with Germany, and with rivalry with France in the Sudan to offer strenuous objections. Arbitration was accepted, and the greater part of the disputed area was awarded to British Guiana.

In Asia there was also evidence of the new dynamism in American foreign affairs. In 1899 the American secretary of state, John Hay, took the initiative in maintaining equal commercial rights in China for the traders of all nations, and the Open Door Policy in China became a reality. And in the melodrama of the Boxer Rebellion, the United States again was a leader rather than a follower (see Chapter 26).

Theodore Roosevelt. The quickened activity of the United States in international affairs is best symbolized by the ideas and actions of Theodore Roosevelt (1858-1919). In his terms as president he was one of the leading figures on the world stage. At the request of the Japanese, he assumed the role of peacemaker in the Russo-Japanese War. The peace conference, which met at Ports-

French
English

HUDSON'S BAY TERRITORY

UPPER CANADA   LOWER CANADA

1791

mouth, New Hampshire, in 1905, successfully concluded a treaty (see p. 627). In 1910 Roosevelt received the Nobel Peace Prize.

Roosevelt was not always a man of peace, however. Whenever he believed the legitimate interests of the United States to be threatened, he had no compunctions about threatening to use force or actually using it. The most significant illustration of Roosevelt's determination to protect vital national interests took place in the Panama incident. In 1901 the British conceded the exclusive right of the United States to control any Isthmian canal that might be dug. For $40,000,000 the United States bought the rights of a private French company which had already begun work on a canal; and a lease was negotiated with Colombia, through whose territory the canal would be built. But the Colombian senate refused to ratify the treaty, claiming that the compensation was too small. Roosevelt is reputed to have explained, "I did not intend that any set of bandits should hold up Uncle Sam."[7] The upshot was a revolution, financed with money borrowed from J. P. Morgan; and Panama—the new republic which seceded from Colombia in 1903—concluded a satisfactory canal treaty with the United States. In 1914 the canal was opened.

By the first decade of the twentieth century, the United States had moved far from its traditional isolationism. But while active in international affairs, it was not yet willing to commit itself to definite foreign entanglements. A few observers warned of dangers soon to come. They stressed the importance of supporting nations whose interests coincided with those of the United States. Some publicists in America iden-

tified Russian imperialism as the great potential danger; others were more concerned over German ambitions. The history of the first half of the twentieth century was to prove both schools of observers correct.

THE DOMINION OF CANADA

French Canada. From 1534—the year Jacques Cartier sailed up the St. Lawrence River and claimed the area for France—until 1763, Canada had been a part of the French empire. Unlike the English colonies in the New World, the French colony of Canada was rigidly supervised by the home government. All trade activities were carefully regulated; the Catholic Church monopolized education; and few Protestants were allowed to settle in New France. The French king granted huge tracts of land to nobles, who in turn parceled their estates out to peasant farmers. Although this feudal system exhibited some beneficial features, on the whole the introduction of European feudalism seriously retarded the development of the colony.

In 1763, at the end of the British conquest, there were only 65,000 people in New France. This figure was just 5 per cent of the total population of the Thirteen Colonies. In New France, agriculture was primitive, industry was almost nonexistent, and the most important economic activity was fur trading.

The French-British quarrels. Early in the history of New France, English activities in North America plainly endangered the future of French Canada. In addition to England's interest in its Atlantic seaboard colonies, English sailors frequently landed at Newfoundland in their fishing expeditions, and in 1670 the Hudson's Bay Company was founded to carry on trading activities, especially in furs, with the Indians in the territory around Hudson Bay. When war broke out in Europe between England and France, their colonies in the New World went to war also (see Chapter 18). The victory of England in the struggle for the New World was foreshadowed by the Treaty of Utrecht (1713). France was forced to cede Acadia

THE GROWTH OF MODERN CANADA

(later known as Nova Scotia), to give up all claims to Newfoundland, and to recognize the Hudson Bay territory as British.

The British acquire Canada. Peace in New France was soon interrupted again by renewal of the duel for world empire between Great Britain and France. The war ended in a complete victory for Britain. In 1763, by the Treaty of Paris, Canada passed into British hands. The victors took care to assure the loyalty of the French Canadians by means of a royal proclamation guaranteeing the political rights of the inhabitants and their freedom to worship as Roman Catholics. In 1774 the British government passed the famous Quebec Act, termed the "Magna Carta of the French Canadian race." This act reconfirmed the position of the Catholic Church and perpetuated French law and custom. No representative assembly, such as existed in the English-speaking colonies, was provided for, however, because the French lacked experience in governing themselves. The opinion of the English was

that Canada should remain French in race, language, and institutions.

Canada's formative period. The conquest of Canada by Great Britain ushered in what has been called Canada's formative period, which lasted from 1763 to 1867 and was characterized by the following important developments: the addition of an English-speaking population, the repulse of an attempt at conquest by the United States, the grant of local self-government, and, finally, the confederation of Canada into a dominion in 1867.

The addition of an English population to French Canada came as a result of the American Revolution. Although the rebellious colonists tried to conquer Canada, the French remained loyal, largely because of the liberal concessions of the Quebec Act, and the invasion failed. Those inhabitants of the Thirteen Colonies not in favor of separation from Great Britain (Tories) suffered at the hands of the patriots, and a large number of them immigrated to Canada.

The immigrants, known as United Empire Loyalists, settled in Nova Scotia, along the St. Lawrence River, and north of the Great Lakes.

The newcomers did not relish the absence of representative government in their new home and began to agitate for a measure of self-government. The presence of the English also caused numerous controversies between the French Canadians and the newly arrived Loyalists. To meet this situation the British government in 1791 divided Canada into two separate provinces called Upper and Lower Canada and granted each a representative assembly. The quarrel between the French and English continued, causing discontent with the government in both provinces of Canada.

Open rebellion in 1837, quelled only after serious fighting, made the British government more aware of the seriousness of the situation. From London, Lord Durham (1792-1840), a special commissioner, was sent to Canada to study the problem and make recommendations. A statesman with vision who realized that if the home country was to hold the loyalty of its colonies a much larger degree of self-government must be granted, Durham recommended that certain matters of imperial concern, such as the control of foreign relations, were to be left to the discretion of the mother country, but that Canada alone was to control its own domestic affairs. By the mid-nineteenth century, local self-government was granted to Canada. Unlike the Thirteen Colonies, who severed their connection with the mother country by means of revolution, Canada achieved virtual independence without revolution and bloodshed and remained loyal to the home country.

Federation. Fear of the United States, the need for a common tariff policy, and a concerted effort to develop natural resources led Canadians toward federation. A plan of union—the British North America Act—was drawn up, approved by the British government, and in 1867 passed by the Parliament in London. This act united Canada (then divided into the provinces of Quebec and Ontario), Nova Scotia, and New Brunswick.

Canada was now a federal union of four provinces, somewhat similar in political organization to the United States. The government of Canada, however, utilized the English cabinet system with its principle of ministerial responsibility. As a symbol of Canada's connection with the mother country, provision was also made in the governmental structure for a governor-general who acts as the personal representative of the British king.

Obstacles to Canadian development. With the passage of the British North America Act in 1867, Canada's career as a nation began. But the new nation found itself confronted with many problems. Communications were poor. In 1869 the Dominion purchased the vast territories of the Hudson's Bay Company,* and far off on the Pacific coast a new colony, British Columbia, joined the Dominion four years after confederation; but there was no transcontinental railroad to link British Columbia with eastern Canada.

Another disturbing factor was the lack of cordial relations with the United States. After the Civil War, anti-British sentiment was fanned by Irish patriots in the United States who, in the cause of freedom for Ireland, conducted armed forays over the

---

*The Hudson's Bay Company had been incorporated in 1670 as the company of Gentlemen Adventurers of England Trading into Hudson's Bay. Early in the nineteenth century, the company established posts throughout the Canadian west, and the vast territory extending from what is now the province of Ontario to British Columbia was administered by this great trading organization. In 1824 the company built a fort at Vancouver, the nucleus for the later province of British Columbia, and then pushed south into the territory of Oregon. Here the serious boundary dispute that developed between the company and American settlers caused Americans in 1844 to raise the cry "54-40 or fight" and "All of Oregon or none." Two years later, the controversy was settled amicably when Great Britain and the United States accepted a boundary of 49°. The history of the Canadian west and even our own was greatly influenced by this company. While the company no longer possesses its former administrative powers, it still continues to play an important part in the economic life of Canada.

Canadian border. But in 1871, the major differences between Canada and the United States were ironed out in the Treaty of Washington, a landmark in the use of arbitration.

A third factor in Canada's development was the ever present need for better cooperation between the English and French peoples in the Dominion.

Canada's national development. Under the leadership of the Dominion's first prime minister, Sir John A. Macdonald (1815-1891), Canadians resolutely set about the task of national development. Bounties were offered to new industries; a railroad was completed from the east to British Columbia in 1885; and an active program for attracting immigrants was pursued.

Macdonald's work was carried on by Sir Wilfrid Laurier (1841-1919), who as prime minister dominated Canadian politics from 1896 until 1911. Between 1897 and 1912 Canada received a total of 2,250,000 new citizens, bringing the country's total population to over 7,000,000. New provinces were also carved out of land formerly controlled by the Hudson's Bay Company so that in 1914 the Dominion consisted of nine provinces.

After the turn of the century, certain problems began to appear as the result of the country's rapid growth. The advance of industrialism produced labor problems and discontent among the common people. The influence of big business began to permeate the halls of the Canadian parliament. The competition of wheat from Russia, South America, and the United States, and the vagaries of the climate had serious economic effects on the Canadian farmer. This period saw the rise of agrarian unrest resembling a similar movement in the western United States about 1890. In 1904 the Canadian government created a body for regulating the railroads similar to the Interstate Commerce Commission of the United States. Canada was becoming a mature nation, with all the accompanying problems of depressions, the maldistribution of wealth, and the need of governmental restraint of business.

In the middle of the nineteenth century, sheep raising became one of the mainstays of the Australian economy. Today Australia has more sheep than any other country in the world. This scene of shearing time at an Australian sheep farm, or "station," is from an engraving made in 1891.

AUSTRALIA, NEW ZEALAND, AND SOUTH AFRICA

Discovery and development of Australia. The discovery of Australia dates back to the seventeenth century, when Dutch explorers sighted its shores. It was the South Seas voyage in 1769 of the famous English explorer Captain Cook, however, that paved the way for English settlement. In 1788 a group of English convicts were transported to Australia and settled at Sydney. From the parent colony of Sydney, later called New South Wales, five other settlements were founded.

Although the first European inhabitants of Australia were convicts, many of them were not habitual criminals but political prisoners and debtors. After seven years of servitude, many were liberated and as "emancipists" entered civil life and became valuable citizens. Quite early in the nineteenth century, many free settlers came to Australia. Soon they began to agitate for the termination of the transporting of convicts, and the first step in this direction was taken by the mother country in 1840. By 1850 the Australian colonies were enjoying a liberal form of self-government.

During the first half of the nineteenth century, the Australian colonies grew slowly.

Sheep raising became the principal basis of economic prosperity. In 1850, the population of the country was about 400,000; a decade later it had reached nearly 800,000. Although the discovery of gold in 1851 quickened the tempo of development, pastoral and farming activities continued to be the mainstay of Australia's economy. Railway mileage was expanded, and large amounts of foreign capital flowed in to assist the young nation in developing its resources. In the decade preceding 1914, the population increased from just under 4,000,000 to 5,000,000 people.

The Commonwealth formed. In the late nineteenth century, the six Australian colonies decided to form a federal union known as the Commonwealth of Australia. In 1901 the Commonwealth came into being, bearing many resemblances to the American system of government. The Commonwealth has a legislature composed of a House of Representatives and a Senate. The members of the latter house, six for each state, are elected regardless of population, while the lower house is made up of members elected by each state in accordance with its population. As in Canada, however, the Commonwealth government makes the chief executive, the prime minister, responsible to the legislature and thus does not provide him with the fixed tenure guaranteed the American president.

New Zealand's development. About a thousand miles from the Australian mainland is a group of small islands, two of which are of particular importance. These lonely projections of European influence in the South Pacific constitute the self-governing Dominion of New Zealand. The total population of this country, which has an area five sixths the size of Great Britain, is just a little over 1,500,000. The earliest settlers were desperate convicts who had escaped from the penal settlements in Australia. The activity of other colonizers forced the British government to assume protection of the islands in 1840, and a treaty was signed by British agents guaranteeing certain rights, especially land rights, to the indigenous Maoris.

New Zealand gradually became a rich pastoral, farming, and fruit-raising country. The chief exports, then as now, included wheat and wool. Later, the development of refrigeration enabled large quantities of meat to be shipped to foreign markets, especially to Great Britain.

Social advances in the dominions. New Zealand and Australia have been termed sociological laboratories because of their pioneer activities in democratic government and social welfare legislation. As early as 1855 the state of Victoria in Australia introduced the secret ballot in its elections. The Australian ballot was later introduced in Great Britain, the United States, and the world over. Woman suffrage was introduced in New Zealand in 1893 and in Australia nine years later. In New Zealand a program of "land for the people" was carried out by imposing heavy taxes on large tracts of land held by absentee landlords. This dominion led the world in the adoption of noncontributory old-age pensions in 1878 and the establishment of a national infant welfare system in 1907. Before 1914, Australia had passed similar measures.

Dutch settlement of South Africa. The area later known as the Union of South Africa, located at the tip of Black Africa, first came within the ken of Europe when Bartholomew Diaz reached the Cape of Good Hope in the year 1487. Ten years later Vasco da Gama rounded the Cape on his way to the Indies. In the seventeenth century, when large fleets of merchantmen from Holland made their way around Africa to the Indies to trade for spices and Oriental wares, the Cape became of great importance as a place to obtain fresh water for ships' crews and to replenish supplies.

In 1651 the Dutch established a settlement at the Cape of Good Hope named Cape Town, which grew slowly. As the Dutch settlers pushed into the interior, they came into conflict with the Kaffirs, or Bantu native people, who put up stout resistance against the expansion of the whites.

British rule. The Dutch period of South African history came to an end when Great

Britain acquired the colony in 1806 during the Napoleonic Wars. From the beginning of English rule, there was bad blood between the two nationalities. The English did not cater to the sensitivities of the Boers, the Dutch burghers, who were a proud and independent people. The Dutch had large numbers of slaves, and the British emancipation of all slaves in the empire in 1833 caused much ill feeling. Moreover, the Boers disliked the pro-native attitude of the missionaries, who were continually accusing the Dutch of abusing the natives.

In 1836 the Boers began an epic journey in their great ox-drawn wagons to a new country where they could pursue their way of life without interference. This Great Trek was a folk movement similar in its importance to the covered-wagon epic of our own West. For several years the Boers were on the march. Finally, on the high veld, they established two little republics far away from the British—the Orange Free State and the Transvaal. The British, in the meantime, extended their settlement along the eastern coast north of the Cape and founded the colony of Natal.

The Great Trek did little to solve the difficulties of the Boers. In the mid-nineteenth century, there was much fighting with the natives. The British government was forced to intervene because the native warriors, when once out to "blood their spears," made no distinction between Boer and Briton. In 1852 and 1854, the British government made treaties with the Boers, acknowledging their independence but retaining a shadowy right to have a voice in the foreign affairs of the two little republics.

The Boer War. It was the discovery of gold in the Transvaal in 1885 that brought on the Boer War. Thousands of Englishmen and people of other nationalities thronged to the mines, and in a few years the boom town of Johannesburg numbered more than 100,000 inhabitants. Paul Kruger, president of Transvaal from 1883 to 1900, distrusted the British and was determined that the alien element should not get control of affairs. Heavy taxes were imposed on the miners,

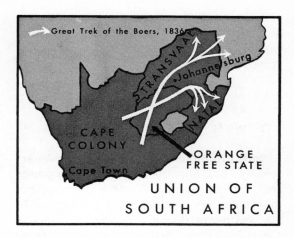

or *uitlanders* (foreigners), who complained that they paid taxes but that their children were denied adequate educational facilities and that it was almost impossible to become a naturalized Boer citizen. In their anger the *uitlanders* began to appeal to the British authorities for assistance. Relations between Boer and Briton went from bad to worse, and in 1899 hostilities broke out between Great Britain and the two Dutch republics.

The world was amazed at the developments in the war which followed. The Boers were crack shots and splendid horsemen. Knowing every inch of the ground on which they fought, they frequently outmaneuvered the British troops. The tide turned in 1900 when Lord Roberts and General Kitchener inflicted several disastrous defeats upon the Boers.

Formation of the Union. After the Dutch surrendered in 1902, the victor treated them magnanimously. Loans were furnished to rebuild burned farmhouses and buy cattle. In 1906 the right of self-government. was given to the Transvaal and, two years later, to the Orange Free State. The Liberal government in Great Britain then permitted the Dutch and English states to unite and form the Union of South Africa in 1909. Only seven years after the war, Boer and Briton joined hands in creating a new self-governing dominion in the tradition of Canada and Australia. The first prime minister of the Union was Louis Botha (1863-1919), who had been a Boer general in the late

war. It was Botha's primary purpose to create not an English or a Dutch nationality
but a blend of the two in a new South
African patriotism.

LATIN AMERICA STRUGGLES

TO WIN GREATNESS

**Early disappointments in freed Latin Amer-
ica.** By 1825, Spanish and Portuguese power
was broken in the Western Hemisphere,
and nine new political units emerged in
Latin America. Mexico, Guatemala, Greater
Colombia, Peru, Bolivia, Paraguay, Argentina, and Chile were free of Spain, while
Brazil, retaining a liberal monarchy, had
gained independence of Portugal. While the
stirring military achievements of the rebel
armies under Bolívar, San Martín, and others
should not be underemphasized, it was British and American sympathy, as we have seen
(pp. 601-602), that helped the Spanish-
American republics attain independence.

For most of the new nations, unfortunately,
the first half century of independence was
a period of retrogression and disillusionment.
The great Liberators were unable to maintain control of the nations they had freed,
nor were the liberal, urban Creoles who had
begun the independence movement able to
agree with one another on elementary political matters. Impractical and inexperienced, they soon lost power to crude military leaders, or *caudillos,* whose armed
gangs seized and lost the seats of power in
a confusing series of tumults. A growing
sectionalism appeared, and the mammoth
states broke up into puny republics which
in turn were threatened with localism.

The unpromising heritage. The Spanish
colonial system had offered little responsibility or opportunity in government to the
American-born whites, and the tradition of
autocracy and paternalism was a poor precedent for would-be democratic republics.
The emphasis on executive power inspired
later presidents, generals, landowners, tribal leaders, and even clerical officials to
wield authority with extreme arrogance.

Legislative and judicial organs never flourished. Spain's economic system encouraged
concentration of land and other forms of
wealth, an extractive economy, and dubious
dealings with foreign businessmen. Finally,
the Church, with its great properties and its
hold on education and welfare agencies, was
to complicate the politics of the new nations.

The effects of the wars of independence
were also ruinous. Some of the most productive areas, such as the plantations of coastal
Venezuela and the silver mines of Mexico,
were devastated. Hatreds and divisions long
persisted. Also, many men who had fought
the royalists remained armed, fond of a life
of crime and pillage, and likely to group
themselves about the *caudillos* who promised them adventure or gain in revolutions.

Racial disunity. When independence was
achieved in the first quarter of the nineteenth century, there were from fifteen to
eighteen million people in the former Spanish empire. About three million of these
were whites, among whom were included
almost all the property-owning and educated groups. (Immigration from Europe did
little to increase their numbers until the last
third of the century, when a deluge began.)
About the same number of people were
mestizos, who scorned the Indians but were
usually not accepted by the whites, though
they were steadily increasing in number
and ambition during the period when new
nations were being formed. During the
nineteenth century, half or more of the
population was Indian. Deprived of the
small protection once offered by the Spanish crown, they either sank into peonage or
lived in semi-independence under their tribal rulers. Finally, in Brazil and most of the
Caribbean islands, Negroes, most of them
slaves, were in a large majority. Conflicts
of interest quickly developed between these
broad racial groups, particularly between
the Creoles and the *mestizos.*

Mexico. The pernicious effects of these
divisive factors in the newly independent
Spanish-American world can be seen in the
experiences of each nation. Mexico, which
had seemed such a promising new country

in 1821, had half a century of turmoil. The empire of Iturbide (see p. 465) lasted only a few months, and a federal republic was then established under an admirable constitution. In less than ten years, however, a preposterous military leader named Antonio López de Santa Anna (1795-1876) had become dictator. (It was Santa Anna who massacred the defenders of the Alamo in 1836.) Debasement of Mexican public life and the humiliation of Mexico by the United States in the war of 1846-1848 must be charged to this strutting, corrupt *caudillo*. Upon his final overthrow in 1855, the injuries inflicted on Mexican pride during his regime brought more sincere men into politics; and the liberals, whose eventual leader was the Indian Benito Juárez (1806-1872), set out to implement their program, the *Reforma*. They planned to establish a truly federal republic and to destroy the Church as a political and economic force. Implicitly, they intended to hasten the inclusion of *mestizos* and Indians in political life. A terrible civil war followed the anticlerical measures and ended in 1861 with the apparent victory of Juárez, but inability to meet payments on debts owed to foreigners brought an invasion of Mexico by European powers and the establishment of a French puppet regime (see p. 529).

When pressure from the United States had driven French troops from Mexican soil, Juárez again set about instituting the *Reforma,* but the poor condition of the country hampered progress. Soon after he died, power went to one of his adherents, Porfirio Diaz (1830-1915), who served as president from 1877 to 1880 and from 1884 to 1911. Under his administration Mexico did become an orderly country. Foreign capital entered in large amounts. Factories, railroads, mines, trading houses, plantations, and enormous ranches flourished, and Mexico City became one of the most impressive of capitals. Yet Diaz' rule, though outwardly conforming to the constitution, was a dictatorship. If there was much encouragement of art and letters, there was no liberty. The Indians sank lower into peonage or even outright slavery, and the Indian heritage was disdained. In spite of the anticlerical laws of the Juárez period, which remained on the books, the Church was quietly permitted to acquire great wealth; and foreign investors exploited Mexico, creating a long-lasting hatred of foreigners.

In 1910 the critics of Diaz found a spokesman in a frail, eccentric man named Francisco Madero (1873-1913), who undertook to lead a revolutionary movement and surprised the world by succeeding. The Diaz machine crumpled abruptly in 1911.

Although Madero was murdered two years later and Mexico underwent another period of turmoil in which the country was controlled mainly by self-styled local rulers, a determined group was able to organize a revolutionary party and to bring about the only genuine social revolution that Latin America has experienced since the Spanish conquest. As we shall see in a later chapter, the Mexican constitution of 1917 has served as an inspiration to much of Latin America.

Argentina. Probably the most advanced Spanish-speaking country in the world, Argentina attained this position in a period of sudden growth that followed half a century of torpor. Its beginning as a free nation was promising. Soon, however, the bustling port city of Buenos Aires, whose energetic population sought to encourage European capital and commerce, found itself overawed by the primitive *gauchos* of the interior. These colorful, nomadic cowboys and bandits, whose way of life is now regarded as romantic, intimidated the adherents of constitutional government in Buenos Aires, and until midcentury, Argentina was not a republic but rather a *gaucho* paradise, isolated and ruled by men who wanted to keep European influences out.

In 1852 a combination of progressive elements overthrew the *gaucho* leader; commerce with Europe was revived, and by 1861 Argentina at last became a united republic and experienced an admirable stability. The constitution was usually observed, and a high degree of respect for individual rights prevailed. Immigrants poured in, and

Now a part of the romantic tradition of South America, the nomadic Argentine cowboys known as *gauchos* once played an important role in Argentine politics. Lawless and anti-European, they were able to hold sway over the government until they were overthrown in the mid-nineteenth century.

soon Argentina became one of the most European in population of any major land of the New World, for it had few Indians or Negroes. Foreign capital, especially British, brought about amazing developments; port facilities, railroads, light industries, and urban conveniences were among the most advanced in the world. Buenos Aires became by far the largest and most beautiful city in Latin America, almost a Paris, despite its location on a monotonous flat plain beside a muddy estuary.

This flat plain, or pampas, is perhaps the richest land in the world for grass and wheat; and cattle have been multiplying there for centuries. Around 1880, refrigerated ships made it feasible to transport enormous quantities of fresh beef to Britain in exchange for capital and finished goods. Around 1900, wheat joined beef as a major Argentine export. This intimate relationship with Britain, which lasted until after World War II, affected nearly every aspect of Argentine life. Nevertheless, though top-drawer society was dominated by leaders who were pro-British in business and pro-French in culture, a true Argentine nationalism was developing. Along with the growth of this powerful sentiment came urgent demands for more democracy and wider distribution of wealth.

Brazil. For many years the former Portuguese colony of Brazil escaped the turbulence and disorders that befell its Spanish-speaking neighbors, probably because it had achieved independence without bloodshed and because it enjoyed the continuity and legitimacy afforded by a respected monarchy. A constitution was granted by the first emperor, Pedro I, in 1824, and the rule of Pedro II in 1840 inaugurated a period of political liberty and economic and cultural progress, which was to endure throughout his fifty-year reign.

Immigrants were attracted to this peaceful land in the New World, and foreign investments were heavy, though not with the arrant exploitation that Mexico had experienced under Diaz. Economic growth tended, however, to favor the southeastern part of the country at the expense of the great sugar plantations in the tropical north; and when the sugar lords were further injured in 1888 by the abolition of Negro slavery, they ranged themselves in opposition to the emperor. Joining them were army officers, who resented the civilian nature of Pedro's regime, and a small number of ideological republicans. In 1889 the aging emperor was forced to abdicate.

For nearly ten years the new federal republic of Brazil underwent civil wars and military upheavals not unlike those in other Latin-American countries. Finally, the republic was stabilized with the army in control, and Brazil resumed its progressive course. Foreign capital continued to enter, and immigration from Europe remained heavy. By World War I, Brazil was generally stable and prosperous, with a strong tradition of liberty.

Other Latin-American nations. Political naïveté, geographical handicaps, and racial disunity all played a part in the development of the other new nations in Latin America. Bolivia, named so hopefully after the Liberator, underwent countless revolutions which to an outsider seem almost pointless. Peru's course was almost as futile. The political history of Colombia was characterized by terrible civil wars; and, in 1830, Venezuela and Ecuador withdrew from that state to form new states, equally unstable. Paraguay endured a series of dictatorships; and Uruguay, created in 1828 as a buffer between Argentina and Brazil, long suffered from interventions by these two countries. An exception to the prevailing pattern of political chaos was the steady growth of the republic of Chile. In 1823 Chile came under the control of a conservative oligarchy. Although this regime proved to be generally enlightened, the country was kept under tight control for a century and was ruled for the benefit of the large landlords and the big businessmen.

Central America narrowly escaped becoming part of Mexico in 1822. Then a fifteen-year effort to create a confederation followed, only to collapse as Guatemala, San Salvador, Honduras, Nicaragua, and Costa Rica asserted their independence. Except for Costa Rica, where the whites comprised the bulk of the population, racial disunity delayed the creation of national feeling.

Foreign investments. The Industrial Revolution came into its full stride just after the Latin-American republics were born. The great industries of western Europe, and later those of the United States, demanded more and more raw materials and new markets in which to sell the completed products. Capital accumulated, and investors eagerly sought opportunities to place their money where high rates of interest could be obtained. This drive for markets, raw materials, and outlets for surplus capital led to the movement known as economic imperialism. As the following chapter shows, imperialism was particularly active in Asia and Africa, but South America did not escape unscathed.

The continual disorder and the lack of strong governments in Latin America gave businessmen ample opportunity to obtain rich concessions and float huge loans. Many of the Latin-American governments, created by revolution and interested only in filling

their own pockets, often resorted to the vicious practice of selling concessions to foreign corporations for ready cash. Political bosses bartered away the economic heritage of their lands, for Latin America was rich in minerals, oil, and other important resources. Sometimes the foreign investor acted in good faith, providing capital at a reasonable rate of interest to Latin-American regimes which, it developed, had no intention of fulfilling the contract. On other occasions unscrupulous capitalists took full advantage of officials in ignorant or helpless governments. In many cases defaults occurred and controversy ensued.

The injured foreign investor usually appealed to his government to intercede in his behalf, and an unending stream of diplomatic correspondence over debt claims was begun, for neither the United States, Great Britain, Germany, France, Italy, nor Spain —the chief investor states—would see its nationals mistreated in their ventures into foreign investments.

Roosevelt and the Monroe Doctrine. Another threat to Latin-American countries developed in 1902 and 1903 when a dispute between Venezuela and a coalition formed by Germany, Great Britain, and Italy provoked the three European powers into blockading Venezuela and even firing upon coastal fortifications to remind the recalcitrant Venezuelan dictator of the obligations he had contracted with some of their nationals. At first inclined to sit by and let Venezuela take its punishment, the United States soon became suspicious of German intentions. President Theodore Roosevelt matched threat with threat; and the European nations retreated quickly into the safer field of international arbitration. The Venezuelan imbroglio was resolved, but it left the United States and President Roosevelt with an increasing determination never again to allow Europe so much rope in the Western Hemisphere, no matter how just the cause.

If the Monroe Doctrine was to prevent Europe from pursuing the legitimate task of protecting its nationals—even to the employment of force—then it was natural for Europe to charge the United States with the responsibility of protecting European creditors as well as its own. In 1904 the American president proclaimed the Roosevelt Corollary to the Monroe Doctrine. This doctrine was a frank statement that chronic wrongdoing on the part of Latin-American governments might force the United States to exercise an international police power. Picturesquely described as the policy of speaking softly but carrying a big stick, the Roosevelt pronunciamento thus launched the era of the Big Stick. The United States not only established a customs receivership in the Dominican Republic but exercised similar control in Nicaragua and Haiti. In addition, the Monroe Doctrine was now used not so much for its original purpose of keeping out European political interference in Latin America but rather as an agency for expanding the commercial interests of the United States.

Cuba becomes a protectorate. In 1898 the United States went to war with Spain over the way the Spaniards were ruling Cuba. For decades the maltreatment of the Cubans had offended humanitarian sentiments of the Americans—an altruism colored by the fact that the evils of Spanish rule also injured American commercial interests in the island. Victory in the brief, dramatic Spanish-American War brought the United States recognition as a world power and a conglomeration of islands in the Pacific Ocean as well as in the Caribbean. Puerto Rico was annexed; the Philippines were brought under American rule. Sensitive of accusations of outright imperialism in Cuba, the government offered Cuba an imperfect, closely tutored independence, and the Cubans were obliged to acknowledge by law the right of the United States to intervene for the "preservation of Cuban independence" and the "maintenance of a government adequate for the protection of life, property, and individual liberty." These and other restrictions to Cuban independence were embodied in the so-called Platt Amendment (1901) to the new Cuban constitution. Thus the United States established

its first American protectorate. Panama soon became another protectorate of the United States. In all these areas, American business interests throve, but so did the material welfare of the inhabitants.

Dollar diplomacy. The next manifestation of the imperialistic mood of the United States has been appropriately called dollar diplomacy, an American policy which prevailed from the Theodore Roosevelt through the Coolidge administrations. Dollar diplomacy referred to the coordinated activities of American foreign investors and their State Department, who worked in close cooperation to obtain and protect concessions for investors, especially in those sections of the Caribbean countries which produced sugar, bananas, and oil. This policy in the period from 1890 to 1914 acutely affected nearly a dozen of the Latin-American republics. For reasons of both finance and political strategy, the United States government could in the last analysis—and at times did—control the policies of these states.

The "Colossus of the North." Although the growing assertiveness of the United States in the Western Hemisphere was accompanied by increasing alarm among the Latin-American peoples, a movement was developing which held hope for greater harmony between our country and the Latin-American states. Some liberal thinkers in the United States had long envisioned a fraternity of the Americas indissolubly linked by common bonds of geography and the political ideals of the Enlightenment. Expressed by periodic conferences, the first of which was held in 1889, and the establishment of a permanent secretariat in Washington known as the Pan American Union, Pan-Americanism was carefully nursed by Washington officialdom.

Yet barely a decade had passed since the first Pan-American Conference before Yankee imperialism shook the foundations of the new movement. If Latin-American nations had ever felt a grateful appreciation for the protection afforded by the Monroe Doctrine, its benign aspect was forgotten in their concern over what they now chose to call the "Colossus of the North." Recognizing the familiar stamp of "made in the U.S.A.," the more suspicious of the Latin-Americans began to see Pan-Americanism as a "skilful move in the expansionist policy of the North, and a suicidal tendency of the simple-minded South."[8] By 1913 the general resentment evoked such charges of hypocrisy that an important South American diplomat undiplomatically felt prompted to state in all sincerity that "There is no Pan-Americanism in South America; it exists only in Washington."[9] More satirical colleagues gave vent to their feelings by referring to the Pan American Union as the Colonial Division of the Department of State.

Latin America in 1914. Thus, by 1914, Latin America's relations with the outside world were neither healthy nor comforting. Although a century of independence had elapsed, Latin America still lingered on the margin of international life. Left to shift for itself in the face of a future shaded by Yankee imperialism, Latin America saw only a hard road ahead in its relations with the outside world.

SUMMARY

By 1900 the United States was the most powerful, advanced, and wealthy of the various overseas communities that had been settled by Europeans. Its history up to this date was largely the story of the epic expansion of its people from ocean to ocean. This movement had numerous ramifications: the rapid growth of democracy, especially during the Jacksonian era; the acquisition of huge, empty, and fertile lands and the influx of immigrants to fill them; and the divisive issue of whether to allow slavery in these new states—an issue that had much to do with the Civil War.

Following this conflict the victorious North embarked on a pell-mell period of economic growth and industrial expansion. Cities multiplied, the population grew, railroads crossed the continent, and grazing and farming lands produced ever greater yields for the burgeoning population. In this process some of the spirit and substance of the earlier agrarian democracy was lost. Economic inequalities grew as well as discontent among the masses. In answer to problems so evident in low living standards of workers, the plight of the farmer, and the corruption of some branches of big business, the progressive movement set in motion a potent wave of reform.

In the realm of foreign affairs, the United States found isolation quite adequate for a century following independence. After 1885, however, it became increasingly interested in and concerned with the outside world. By the turn of the century the United States had fought a successful foreign war, acquired a colonial empire, and was taking the initiative in some phases of world affairs, especially in the Far East. While not fully appreciated at home or abroad, the great wealth and power of the United States would soon become a part of the full current of world problems and responsibilities.

The British dominions had a history showing both similarities with and differences from that of the United States. They became self-governing without breaking the political tie binding them to Britain. With the exception of South Africa, these communities were dominantly British in stock. Their language and culture were English; their governmental habits Anglo-Saxon. In the case of Canada, however, there was a strong French-Canadian minority in Quebec inherited from the original French regime. In South Africa, following a confused history of rivalry and finally a war between the British and Dutch colonies, a rather shaky union was achieved in which the Dutch were the dominant element. There were no complications of rival nationalities in Australia and New Zealand. These colonies were settled by the British in the beginning and did not have to adjust themselves to an influx of other European peoples.

Both Australia and Canada, continental areas in their dimensions, took a leaf out of American history. They attained their political unity by the merging of a number of colonies into a single government. Canada as a dominion became a confederation in

1867, and Australia attained the same status as a commonwealth in 1901.

Much the same problems of exploration, pushing back the frontier, and development of natural resources, as were found in the American and British new Europes, were factors in the development and growth of Latin America. But instead of political unity, the sequel to the Spanish empire was fragmentation and a multiplicity of nationalities.

There were also intermittent civil wars; revolutions and new regimes came and went with alarming and costly regularity. Dictators rather than democrats called the tune. In such an atmosphere, economic development could not thrive; the bulk of the people lived in poverty. This disorder invited foreign intervention. The United States, in particular, extended its influence into Central America and the Caribbean region.

SUGGESTIONS FOR READING

O. Handlin et al., eds., The Harvard Guide to American History, Harvard, 1954. The indispensable bibliography. R. B. Morris, ed., Encyclopedia of American History, Harper, 1953, is the most convenient reference work. Recommended general surveys are S. E. Morison, An Hour of American History,* Beacon, a concise interpretation extending from Columbus to Coolidge; R. Hofstadter, The American Political Tradition,* Vintage, a brilliant and unorthodox interpretation of men and ideas from the Founding Fathers to F. D. R.; and H. B. Parkes, The American Experience,* Vintage. Highly recommended for its lively articles on all aspects of our national history is the bimonthly publication American Heritage.

M. Cunliffe, The Nation Takes Shape: 1789-1837,* Univ. of Chicago. A brief and stimulating survey of the first half century of American history. Also recommended are J. Dos Passos, The Men Who Made the Nation: The Architects of the Young Republic, 1782-1802, Doubleday, 1957, a swiftly paced narrative; A. M. Schlesinger, Jr., The Age of Jackson,* Mentor, a Pulitzer-Prize-winning study; and F. Grund, Aristocracy in America: Jacksonian Democracy,* Torchbooks.

A. Craven, The Coming of the Civil War, Univ. of Chicago, 1957. A challenging discussion of the various forces responsible for the conflict. C. P. Roland, The Confederacy,* Univ. of Chicago, is brief, readable, and authoritative. One of the best single-volume treatments of the war is B. Catton, This Hallowed Ground,* Pocketbooks. R. Meredith, Storm over Sumter, Simon and Schuster, 1957, is a suspenseful account of the first battle of the war. C. Dowdey, Death of a Nation, Knopf, 1958, is a gripping narrative of the battle of Gettysburg.

R. Hofstadter, The Age of Reform,* Vintage. The best introduction to the progressive movement. See also these brief and scholarly studies: H. F. Pringle, Theodore Roosevelt,* Harvest; and E. M. Hugh-Jones, Woodrow Wilson and American Liberalism, Macmillan, 1949.

T. C. Smith, The United States As a Factor in World History,* Holt (Berkshire Studies); D. Perkins, Hands Off: A History of

the Monroe Doctrine, Little, Brown, 1941. Two useful popular accounts of how the nation became a world power.

R. G. Trotter, The British Empire-Commonwealth,* Holt (Berkshire Studies). A brief review of the evolution of the self-governing dominions. See also the authoritative survey by P. Knaplund, The British Empire, 1815-1939, Harper, 1941.

T. H. Raddall, The Path of Destiny, Doubleday, 1957. A history of Canada from the British conquest to self-government in 1850. For two important aspects of Canadian history, see J. S. Galbraith, The Hudson's Bay Company As an Imperial Factor, 1821-1869, Univ. of Calif., 1957, which relates how the company helped shape the history of British North America; and Bruce Hutchison, The Struggle for the Border, Longmans, 1955, a very lively account of Canadian-American relations.

G. Nadel, Australia's Colonial Culture, Harvard, 1958. A vivid account of the ideas, men, and institutions that helped shape the course of Australian history from 1830 to 1860.

C. W. De Kiewiet, A History of South Africa, Social and Economic, Oxford, 1941. Particularly illuminating on the rise of the gold and diamond industries and the background of the Boer War. Also recommended are S. D. Neumark, Economic Influences on the South African Frontier, 1652-1836, Stanford, 1957, a study of economic forces that influenced the expansion of Cape Colony; and G. B. Pyrah, Imperial Policy and South Africa, 1902-1910, Oxford, 1955, a review of the events leading to South African union.

H. Herring, A History of Latin America: From the Beginnings to the Present, Knopf, 1955. Generally acknowledged to be the best general survey. Also recommended are J. F. Rippy, Latin America: A Modern History,* Univ. of Mich.; A. M. Peck, Pageant of South American History, Longmans, 1958; Y. F. Rennie, The Argentine Republic, Macmillan, 1945; L. F. Hill, ed., Brazil, Univ. of Calif., 1947; J. F. Rippy, The Caribbean Danger Zone, Putnam, 1940; and H. B. Parkes, A History of Mexico, Houghton Mifflin, 1950.

*Indicates an inexpensive paperbound edition.

CHAPTER 26

The White Man's Burden

EUROPEAN IMPERIALISM: 1650-1914

Introduction. In Europe's golden age of imperialism (1870-1914), its most eloquent champion, the English poet Rudyard Kipling, urged his countrymen:

"Take up the White Man's burden—
  Send forth the best ye breed—
Go bind your sons to exile
  To serve your captives' need . . ."[1]

This imperial mission had few doubters among its western practitioners and, before 1900, few audible critics even among its colonial wards. After this date and especially in the last three decades, however, imperialism has been increasingly on the defensive. A swelling chorus of denunciation against colonial rule has been raised by the peoples in tropical Africa, the Middle East, and the Orient and by Communist leaders who have happily identified imperialism as one of the essential evils of modern capitalism. The indictment has excoriated imperial rule for its denial of freedom, for its calculating pursuit of profits unshared by native peoples, and for the frequent display of arrogant superiority by its white representatives.

On the other hand, many observers of the international scene stress the positive influences of imperialism. They see modern medicine successfully combating leprosy and sleeping sickness; they note benevolent administrators extirpating cannibalism and infanticide; and they perceive western law halting tribal wars. Most important, these observers see imperialism carrying with it into static or primitive societies dynamic traits of western culture: science and technology to combat disease and increase productivity, schools to spread literacy and learning, and political consciousness to develop democratic government.

Whether or not the white man's burden is viewed as a cloak of hypocrisy hiding the selfish motives of self-seeking merchants and financiers (as it was in many cases) or whether it is seen as a sincere attempt to help less fortunate peoples (as it was also in innumerable instances), this concept was a dynamic one—one of the most important in the western climate of ideas. In this chapter we shall first examine the forces of imperialism, analyzing the whys and hows of the movement; then we shall see what the relations of Europe to the nonwestern world were from about 1650 through the advent of modern imperialism in the 1870's to 1914; and finally we shall weigh in the balance sheet the pros and cons of this explosive development.

THE DYNAMICS OF
IMPERIALISM

Imperialism defined. The word *imperialism* has come to mean many things to many people. Broadly speaking, the term refers to the extension of authority or control, whether direct or indirect, of one people over another. Thus, in this sense, imperialism is as old as the history of man.

But we use the term *imperialism* in a more restricted sense when we refer to the era of imperialism; we are speaking then of the period from 1870 to 1914, when western Europe—which controlled much of the world's finance, commerce, military power, and intellectual life—extended its power over the peoples of the Orient and Africa.

Waning European interest in colonization. From the end of the Middle Ages to the close of the eighteenth century, a large part of Europe was expansive. Aggressive national states strove to stake out colonies and to monopolize overseas trade with their colonial possessions; the subsequent rivalries between nations helped to bring on the great colonial wars of the eighteenth century. But by the end of that century, interest in colonization declined. The loss of the Thirteen Colonies in 1783 dampened British ardor. By 1815 France had lost nearly all of its colonial possessions, and a few years later Spain and Portugal were forced to grant independence to most of their colonies. At the same time, the school of laissez faire argued that there were no advantages in possessing colonies and that the cost of defending them was an expensive burden. It was also believed that the whole world would soon be opened to free trade. Thus, between 1815 and 1870, as the gospel of free trade and laissez faire became dominant, colonial expansion was comparatively small.

Revival of imperialism. When the tide turned, however, it came with a rush. In his six years as English prime minister, Disraeli annexed Fiji and Cyprus, fought a war against the Zulus in southeastern Africa, purchased the Suez Canal shares, and proclaimed Queen Victoria empress of India. Other European powers avidly followed Britain's lead, and early in the 1880's the colonial scramble began in earnest. The United States also felt the imperialistic urge.

This expansion of the western peoples had come about with amazing rapidity. It has been estimated that in 1800 fully one half of the world's surface was unknown to Europeans. A century later more land had been explored and acquired than in the entire period from the middle of the fifteenth century to the midpoint of the eighteenth. By 1914 the European nations could claim control of about 60 per cent of the world's surface.

Economic motives for imperialism. What were the motives behind this amazing expansion of western power? The most obvious and powerful were economic. Britain had been the home of the Industrial Revolution; by the middle of the nineteenth century, other nations began to industrialize. To compete with British industry, these nations placed protective tariffs on imports. The free commerce of the early nineteenth century waned as tariff walls rose in the United States, Russia, France, and Germany. Great Britain and its new competitors—now producing a surplus of manufactured goods—began to search for trade outlets; building colonial empires appeared to be the solution to the problem.

Besides increased markets for European goods, colonies and trading posts could supply burgeoning industries with raw materials such as cotton, silks, rubber, exotic woods, tin, manganese, copper, and oil. And growing populations continued to increase the demands for foods raised in exotic lands.

Banks provided capital for trading enterprises and for the development of resources in distant lands. In fact, money invested overseas could earn 10 to 20 per cent. This impetus to wealth led one wag to remark that the French colonist was the franc. To safeguard these important investments and recover defaulted loans, European governments sometimes established spheres of influence or protectorates over the territories of weak native rulers and in certain cases subjected these lands to military occupation or to annexation.

Marxian socialists have stressed only the economic motives underlying imperialism. In his famous work *Imperialism, the Highest Stage of Capitalism* (1916), Lenin argued that the wages of the workers did not represent enough purchasing power to absorb the output of the capitalistic factories, and, moreover, vast amounts of capital accumulated that could not be profitably invested in the home country. Therefore, to the Marxists, imperialism was an inevitable phase in the development of capitalism. That the profit motive in imperialism is strong is undeniable, but that it is the sole motive is false. It is also false that imperialism is a policy exclusive to capitalist powers, as can be proved by examples of Communist imperialism in the twentieth century.

Population pressure as a motive for imperialistic expansion. In the middle of the eighteenth century, the population of Europe numbered about 140,000,000; by 1914 this figure had increased to 463,000,000. Hearing that land overseas was more plentiful and jobs easier to secure, no less than 9,000,000 British subjects and 6,000,000 Germans, to say nothing of millions of Italians, left their homelands. These migrations provided one of the greatest population movements in history.

But while some European statesmen, particularly in Germany and Italy, thought of the acquisition of new colonies as a means whereby their surplus population could be settled in sparsely settled lands without escaping the political control of the motherland, this belief proved to be a delusion. Few Europeans migrated to the tropical colonies; the great majority made their new homes in the United States and Latin America. In such areas the loyalty and support of these sons and daughters of Germany, Italy, and other nations were lost to the homeland.

Nationalism as a force for imperialism. While the economic forces behind nineteenth-century European expansion were strong, the psychological factors were equally important. A dominant factor was the new nationalism. Fresh from the achievement of national unification, Germany and Italy were eager to show off their new national strength; both demanded a place in the sun. In Great Britain also, a strong nationalist spirit existed. Britain was ready to take on any antagonist who stood in the way of its imperialistic ambitions.

Closely enmeshed with the nationalistic justification of imperialism was the philosophy of social Darwinism (see Chapter 24). Just as Darwin believed that progress in the biological sphere was measured by the survival of the fittest, so political and social theorists saw this concept of the "fittest" as an immutable factor in the onward march of civilization.

The military factor. If the use of force and the survival of the fittest were essential features of progress, then the military factor was important. A nation had to be strong enough to defend its interests. Colonies could be used as naval bases to protect a nation's commercial life lines or to destroy those of a rival. Or a colony could be obtained as a buffer state to protect another colony against the designs of a rival.

Humanitarian and religious motives. The acquisition of colonies cannot be explained on economic, political, or strategic grounds alone, however. Many colonial administrators honestly felt that they were carrying the white man's burden—that it was a sacred task to bring the best aspects of western civilization to their undeveloped wards. The religious motive was likewise especially strong. In the nineteenth century, British missionaries were particularly active, and there were large numbers of missionaries from France, Germany, and the Scandinavian countries.

BRITISH RULE IN INDIA

The Mogul ruler Aurangzeb. During the Mogul era in the seventeenth century, Europeans came to India to establish trading posts. As European infiltration continued, Mogul authority rapidly declined.

The reign of Shah Jahan (1628-1658) had marked the height of Mogul power, and conditions appeared auspicious for his successor. But his son Aurangzeb (1658-1707) was a ruthless and fanatical man who intended to rid India not only of all vice but also of all art and all views alien to the Muslim faith. He terrorized millions of his Hindu subjects by his fanaticism.

By 1690, when Mogul territorial expansion reached its greatest point, Aurangzeb's empire encompassed the whole of the Indian peninsula. But this period of power was followed by one of decline. Aurangzeb's realm seethed with corruption, oppression, and revolt; fifty years after his death, the great Mogul empire crumbled and perished.

The condition of India during this time may be summed up in one word—misery. Marauding armies, nobles bent on gaining power, and officials who oppressed the people brought anarchy to India. Delhi was sacked in 1739 by invaders from Persia and again in 1757 by marauders from Afghanistan. The Moguls kept the imperial title until 1858, but their dynasty was a mere shadow of its former grandeur and strength.

The British East India Company. The collapse of the central government in India left the field open to a new authority. For more than one hundred years, English and French trading companies had fought one another for supremacy, and by the middle of the eighteenth century, a great duel for empire was taking place. During the Seven Years' War (1756-1763), Robert Clive, the British leader in India, defeated the French and their Indian allies at the decisive battle of Plassey (1757), a victory which ushered in a new period in Indian history, that of British rule.

After the elimination of the French, the most important problem facing the East India Company was its relationship with the Indian people. As the Mogul emperor became more and more a puppet ruler, anarchy spread until the company was forced to accept the role of policeman in India. By 1818 the East India Company was master of India. Some local rulers were forced to accept its overlordship; others were deprived of their territories. Thus it came about that the Indian subcontinent (until its independence in 1947) was divided into British India, which the British administered directly, and Indian India, where native dynasties were retained under British supervision (see map, p. 622).

The English Parliament, disturbed by the idea that a great business concern interested primarily in profits was controlling the destinies of millions of people, passed acts in 1773 and 1784 which gave it the power to control company policies and to appoint the highest company official in India, the governor general. This system of dual control lasted until 1858.

Earlier in the century, the British introduced a number of significant reforms in India. The practice of *suttee,* in which widows burned themselves on the funeral pyres of their deceased husbands, was prohibited; the custom in some areas of killing girl babies was combated; and a notorious system of banditry and murder called *thuggee* (hence our word *thug*) was broken up by the British secret police. In addition, a comprehensive educational system which included secondary schools and universities was introduced.

The Sepoy Rebellion. In the spring of 1857, the progress of reform was suddenly inter-

In the process of suppressing the Sepoy Rebellion, British forces in India used artillery pieces to execute captive rebels.

rupted by the Sepoy Rebellion. This uprising was mainly a mutiny of the Indian troops, called sepoys, who formed the bulk of the company's armed forces. The sepoys complained that a new cartridge issued to them was smeared with the fat of cows and pigs. This infuriated the Hindus, who regarded the cow as sacred, and horrified the Muhammadans, who considered the pig unclean. Fortunately for the British, many areas in India remained loyal or at least quiescent, but only after fierce fighting and the loss of many lives was the revolt crushed.

One important consequence of the Sepoy Rebellion was the final collapse of the Mogul dynasty. The last of the Mogul emperors permitted to maintain a court at Delhi had in 1857 been proclaimed by the mutineers as their leader. After order had been restored, he was exiled to Burma by the British. The mutiny also ended the system of dual control under which the British government and the East India Company shared authority. The government relieved the company of its political responsibilities, and after 258 years of existence the company terminated its rule. A trained civil service was re-

cruited from honor graduates of British universities, and these men set out to rule India benevolently and efficiently.

Growth of Indian nationalism. By 1880 it was apparent that Indian nationalism was growing rapidly, the fruit of the influx of western ideas and technology. In 1885, with the aid of several Englishmen who had interested themselves in Indian political ambitions, the Indian National Congress was formed.

The British educational system served as one of the most potent forces back of the new movement. As Indians became acquainted with the story of the rise of self-government in England, the desire for the political freedom of their own land grew. Unable to obtain white-collar employment in governmental service and disdainful of manual labor, thousands of newly educated Indian youths joined the ranks of an educated proletariat and turned in wrath against the government. The British, confronted by the spread of violence, carried through a major shift in policy between the years 1907 and 1909. The various provincial legislatures in India were given elected Indian majorities, and an In-

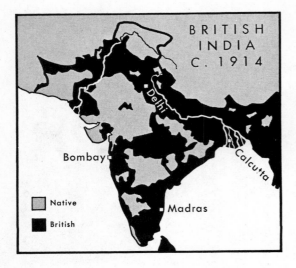

BRITISH
INDIA
C. 1914

Delhi

Bombay

Calcutta

Native

British

Madras

dian was seated in the executive council of the governor general. The legislature of the central government, however, remained under British control. Moderate nationalists were satisfied for the time being, but their more radical comrades were not appeased. The twentieth century in India would see the spirit of nationalism become ever more insistent.

MANCHU CHINA

AND THE WEST

The Manchu dynasty. In the middle of the eighteenth century, China had a population of 300,000,000 and comprised an area of more than 4,000,000 square miles. The ruling dynasty was the Manchu, which in 1644 had superseded the Ming. Descendants of Tatars who for centuries had lived in Manchuria, the Manchu appreciated Chinese civilization and adopted a conciliatory attitude toward their subjects. They refused, however, to allow intermarriage with the Chinese, for they realized that only their blood difference kept them from being assimilated and conquered. By and large, however, the Manchu gradually became Chinese in their habits and attitudes.

The Manchu emperors were remarkable conquerors. The reign of Ch'ien Lung (1736-1795) was a period of great expansion, when the Manchu government attained suzerainty over eastern Turkestan, Burma, and Tibet. In spite of these evidences of dynamism, however, uncritical acceptance and reverence for traditional thought (particularly Confucianism), augmented by the scholar rule of a civil service trained almost exclusively in the classics, had tended to make Chinese culture excessively backward-looking and conservative. Thus the amazing continuity which Chinese civilization had exhibited for thousands of years was gained at a heavy price. In addition, the prevailing attitude of superiority to the cultures of all other peoples was an unwholesome one for China, leading to what has been called "progressive sterility."[2]

Trade relations with the West. Meanwhile a new factor, destined to have momentous consequences for China, had entered the scene: European trade. During the eighteenth century, merchants from western Europe came to China in increasing numbers. Only with great difficulty was trade carried on, however. While engaged in commerce, foreign merchants were confined to the port of Canton; when not engaged in trade, all foreign businessmen were expected to reside in Macao. Nor would the Manchu government recognize or receive representatives of foreign powers.

European traders were irritated by the high customs duties the Chinese forced them to pay and by the attempts of Chinese authorities to curb the growing import trade in opium. In 1800 its importation was forbidden by the imperial government. Still, the opium trade continued to flourish. Privately owned vessels of many countries, including the United States, made huge profits from the growing number of Chinese addicts.

War and western exploitation. Early in the nineteenth century, serious internal weaknesses developed in the Manchu empire. The standing army became corrupt, and rapacious governors fleeced the people. Weak emperors proved inadequate to meet the challenges of the time.

In 1839 war broke out with England—ostensibly over the opium traffic. But this was basically a secondary issue. As a Chinese historian has observed: "If the Chinese had had some knowledge of international conditions, and had not considered the foreigners barbarians, their prohibition of opium need not have caused war."[3] Backward China was no match for English military power, and in 1842 China agreed to the provisions of the Treaty of Nanking. Hong Kong was ceded to Great Britain, and certain ports, including Shanghai and Canton, were opened to the residence and trade of British subjects. Within a few years the United States, France, and Russia also secured trading privileges, and China appeared well on the way to ultimate physical dismemberment and economic vassalage.

In 1856 a second war with England took place, and China was again defeated. By the terms of the Treaty of Tientsin (1858), new ports were opened to trading, and foreigners with passports were permitted to travel in the interior. Christians gained the right to propagate their faith and to hold property, thus attaining another means of western penetration. Three provisions of the treaty, in particular, caused long-lasting bitterness among the Chinese: (1) extraterritoriality, (2) customs regulation, and (3) the right to station foreign warships in Chinese waters. Extraterritoriality meant that, in a dispute with a Chinese, a westerner had the right to be tried in his own country's consular court. Europeans argued that Chinese concepts of justice were more rigid and harsh than those in the West. But the Chinese felt that extraterritoriality was not only humiliating to China's sovereignty but was also discriminative in favor of the western nations.

Difficulties of the Manchu. The concessions to the "foreign devils" resulted in a great loss of prestige for the Manchu rulers. Serious internal difficulties further diminished their power, and the Taiping Rebellion of 1850 to 1864 almost overthrew the dynasty. That the Manchu dynasty managed to survive another half century was largely due to the statecraft of a remarkable woman, Tzu Hsi, the dowager empress, popularly known as "Old Buddha." From 1861 to her death in

Tzu Hsi, the dowager empress of China, was returned to her throne by the western powers after the abortive Boxer Rebellion. Soon after her death, the Manchu dynasty was overthrown.

1908, she was the real power behind the throne. Shrewdly and unscrupulously, Tzu Hsi crushed internal revolts and restored a measure of prestige to her homeland. Convinced that security for China lay in adhering to ancient traditions and customs, she encouraged antiforeign sentiment—an attitude her subjects shared.

Sino-Japanese War. By 1860 Russia had annexed the entire area north of the Amur River; by 1885 France had taken Indochina and Britain had seized Burma; and in 1887 Macao was ceded to Portugal. China was too weak to resist these encroachments on its borders. But the crowning blow came not from the western nations but from Japan, a land which the Chinese had long regarded with amused contempt.

Trouble had brewed for some time between China and Japan, especially over the control of Formosa and Korea. In a dispute over China's claim to suzerainty in Korea, war broke out in 1894, and the brief Sino-Japanese struggle resulted in a humiliating defeat for China. By the Treaty of Shimonoseki (1895), China was forced to recognize the independence of Korea and hand over the rich Liaotung peninsula and Formosa.

Spheres of influence in China. The Chinese defeat was the signal for the renewal of aggressive actions by western powers, who forced Japan to return to China the strategic Liaotung peninsula. Shortly thereafter, the European powers made their demands of the Manchu. In 1897 Germany demanded a ninety-nine-year lease to Kiaochow Bay and was also given exclusive mining and railroad rights throughout Shantung province. Russia obtained a twenty-five-year lease to Dairen and Port Arthur and gained the right to build a railroad across Manchuria, thereby achieving complete domination of that vast territory. In 1898 Britain obtained the lease of Weihaiwei, a naval base, and France leased Kwangchowan in south China (see map).

A halt, or at least a hesitation, in the process of disintegration was brought about by

the United States, not from high-minded desires but largely because Washington was alarmed at the prospect of American businessmen being excluded from China because the United States had no sphere of influence. In 1899, Secretary of State John Hay asked the major powers to agree to a policy of equal trading privileges. In 1900 several powers did so, and the famous Open Door Policy was born.

The Boxer Rebellion. The humiliation of the defeat by Japan had incensed the younger Chinese intellectuals, who agitated for reform. Sympathetic to their cause, the young emperor in 1898 instituted what came to be known as the "hundred days of reform." Unhappily for China, however, the reactionaries at court viewed all innovation with disfavor and formed a powerful faction about the dowager empress, Tzu Hsi. In September 1898, she imprisoned the emperor and took over the government.

After the suppression of the reform movement, a group of secret societies united in an organization known as the "Righteous Harmony Fists"; the members were called "Boxers" by westerners. At first the Boxers were strongly anti-Manchu because of the reactionary measures of "Old Buddha," but by 1899 the chief object of their hatred had become the foreign nations who were stripping China of land and power.

The Boxers started a campaign to rid China of all "foreign devils." Many Europeans were killed, and the legations at Peking were besieged. In August 1900, an international army forced its way to Peking and released the prisoners. China was then forced to apologize for the murder of foreign officials and to pay a large indemnity. The United States returned most of the indemnity which China owed, and the Chinese government set this sum aside to send students to American universities.

Only a decade after the conclusion of the rebellion, a revolution was to break out all over China, and in 1912 the Republic of China was proclaimed with Sun Yat-sen as president. This story of China's giant step into modern times will be discussed in Chapter 29.

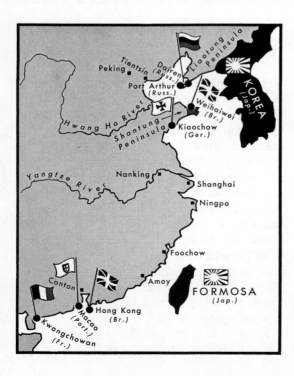

JAPAN IN TRANSITION

Japanese attitude toward foreigners. At the beginning of the seventeenth century, Japan was being ruled from Yedo (now Tokyo) by the head of the Tokugawa clan, who in 1603 had made himself *shogun*. As a military dictator with a retinue of feudal lords and warriors, the *shogun* kept the country united and at peace. Meanwhile, the emperor—nominal head of the government—lived a meaningless existence at Kyoto.

As in the case of China, European merchants and missionaries posed a problem to the Japanese authorities. We have noted earlier (see p. 370) that the *shoguns* insulated Japan effectively from the outside world by expelling the European traders and crushing Christianity. Nevertheless, despite the attempts of the *shoguns*, change could not be averted. The land was long peaceful, and the swords of the *samurai* rusted in their scabbards. The *shogun* and his feudal retainers became anachronisms. Change was in the air, and just as the *shoguns* feared, it was triggered from the outside.

Commodore Perry and the Treaty of Kanagawa. On July 7, 1853, a squadron of two steam frigates and two sloops of war steamed into the bay of Yedo. The commander of the fleet, Commodore Matthew Perry, had been dispatched by the United States government to convince the Japanese ruler that a treaty opening trade relations between Japan and the United States would be of mutual interest. Perry had been instructed to be tactful and to use force only if necessary.

When he returned with even greater forces in the following February, the Japanese took the most prudent course open to them. In March, Japan agreed to the Treaty of Kanagawa, the first formal treaty with any western nation. Shipwrecked sailors were guaranteed hospitable treatment, foreign vessels were allowed to stop for provisions, and two ports were opened to American ships. Great Britain, Russia, and Holland soon obtained similar privileges.

Adoption of western ideas and techniques. In 1867 the *shogun*, acting under

Russia, Britain, France, and other contestants prepare for the rush to acquire territory in China in this nineteenth-century cartoon entitled "The China Cup Race."

pressure from the feudal chieftains, restored the supreme authority to the emperor—the *Tenno*, or "Heavenly King" (called "Mikado" in the West). The return of power to the imperial family heralded a new era for Japan. The young emperor, whose reign was known as the *Meiji* (enlightened government), reigned from 1868 to 1912. With his reign are associated those epoch-making events which transformed Nippon from a sleepy Oriental island kingdom into a dynamic, semimodernized power which the Euorpean nations had to recognize as an equal. The restoration of the throne's supreme authority was aided by the voluntary abolition of feudal rights; in 1871 the abolition of the feudal system became official, although it was far from an actual fact.

In 1883 a commission established to study the world's various governmental systems began to frame a new constitution for Japan. The committee members were particularly impressed by the German system as developed by Bismarck. Thus, in the new constitution, the premier was given a position analogous to that held by the chancellor in Germany, and the cabinet was made responsible to the emperor alone. Only the army and navy could appoint their respective ministers.

An 1890 Japanese drawing shows a woman seated at a Japanese-made sewing machine, copied from western models.

Since no statesman could form a cabinet without a war minister and the army could overthrow any cabinet by simply withdrawing its minister, final control of policies rested in the hands of the military clique. The constitution provided for a Diet, but the property qualifications at first limited the electorate to a small number. While the cabinet was independent of the Diet, the latter body wielded a modicum of power in financial matters because in peacetime it could hold up an unpopular budget by refusing to vote supplies. Promulgated in 1889, the constitution stressed the position and powers of the emperor, who was considered "sacred and inviolable." Only the emperor could initiate constitutional amendments.

In other ways the Japanese showed skill in exploiting their knowledge of western institutions. In 1876 national conscription went into effect, and a modern military machine was created whose officers were trained by European experts—the army by the French and Germans, the navy by the British. The government initiated the founding of banks, fac-

tories, and business concerns and later, when they became successful, turned them over to private ownership and management while continuing to supervise them closely. Thus Japan avoided the dangers to sovereignty which imperialism offered to other undeveloped countries such as China.

Many other changes began to transform the "land of the rising sun." Railways, telegraphs, lighthouses, and dockyards were constructed, and orders were placed in England for the construction of warships. American advisers were consulted regarding national education, and imperial universities as well as a number of technical schools were founded. More foreign experts were brought in to teach the Japanese about medicine, engineering, and agriculture, and many Japanese were sent abroad to study.

Japanese westernization: a façade? The modernization of Japan was one of the amazing phenomena of modern world history. But there were some disturbing features in the way western technology and institutions were adapted by the Japanese for their own purposes. On the surface, Japanese government was liberal and parliamentary. In reality, however, the constitution was ultraconservative, giving the emperor and his cabinet dominant power. Though Japan was the first Asian nation to achieve a high degree of literacy, education was the tool of the government, and its primary function was to produce docile servants of the state. The press was subject to wide control and censorship. The army was used as a means of instilling conscripts with unquestioning loyalty and obedience to the emperor. In army barracks young soldiers learned that the noblest fate was death on the battlefield.

Unlike the Chinese, who revered the scholar, the Japanese admired the soldier; warfare was the supreme vocation, and a tradition of Japanese invincibility had grown up. Since prehistoric times the Japanese islands had not been invaded successfully, and on several occasions the Japanese themselves had invaded the Asian continent. Thus the Japanese were ready to seize new methods and new ideas to serve their own militant ends.

Another prominent characteristic of Japanese culture was the meticulous attention paid to formal manners and "face." Like the Chinese, the Japanese took great pride in their dignity and status; to be shamed, degraded, or dishonored was a mortal offense. Awareness of these culture traits is basic to an understanding of Japanese reactions to the modern world and the policies that the rulers of Nippon adopted to meet the challenges of the twentieth century.

The Russo-Japanese War. In the eyes of European diplomats, Japan's prestige began to increase soon after the conclusion of the Sino-Japanese War of 1894-1895. In 1902 Japan scored a diplomatic triumph by allying itself with Great Britain. Both nations viewed the alliance primarily as a deterrent to Russian expansion.

Fearful of Russia's designs on both Manchuria and Korea, Japan attempted to negotiate a division of the area into spheres of influence. But the Russians were inflexible, believing that Japan could be defeated easily. In February 1904, Japan broke off negotiations and, without a declaration of war, attacked Port Arthur and bottled up the Russian fleet. The world was astounded by the quick series of Japanese victories which followed.

By the Treaty of Portsmouth, signed in September 1905, Japan acquired half of the island of Sakhalin, the leaseholds to the Liaotung peninsula and Port Arthur, and various Russian railway and mining rights in southern Manchuria. Japan's paramount position in Korea was also conceded, paving the way for Japanese annexation of that nation in 1910. Japan was now accepted as a first-class power.

IMPERIALISM IN SOUTHEAST

ASIA AND OCEANIA

Establishment of western rule. At the southern tip of the Asian mainland, wedged between India and China and including a multitude of islands in the Indian and Pacific oceans, is the complex area of southeast Asia. Its diverse peoples and countries began to come under European colonial rule with the arrival of the Portuguese and Spanish in the sixteenth century and the Dutch in the early years of the seventeenth. In the nineteenth century, imperial control was completed when the British gained power over Ceylon, Burma, and Malaya; the French over Tahiti and Indochina; and the United States over the Philippines.

Throughout southeast Asia, western rule made a substantial imprint. A plantation economy was established with foreign capital to develop the rich natural resources; vast quantities of petroleum, tin, coffee, tea, pepper, and other tropical products were produced for the world market. Chronic civil war and banditry were ended. Law and order, together with public health facilities, came in with colonial rule and brought about a rapid increase in population.

Throughout the colonial lands of southeast Asia, the impact of European ways of life, and especially western education, created a new generation of nationalists. More and more irked with alien rule, this minority of young intellectuals finally aspired to complete independence. Little was done to satisfy these aspirations in the Dutch East Indies or in French Indochina. Britain provided some training in self-government in Burma and Ceylon, but it was in the Philippines that benevolent imperialism most consciously moved in the direction of ultimate freedom.

British rule in Ceylon, Malaya, and Burma. In the sixteenth century, the chief ports on the island of Ceylon were occupied by Portuguese and Dutch adventurers. In 1796 the British forced the Dutch to give up their holdings in Ceylon, which became one of the most valuable British colonies as the nineteenth century unfolded; such prized commodities as tea, rubber, lead, cocoa, and sapphires were produced in this area.

British influence in the Malay peninsula began in 1796 when a coastal strip was obtained. In 1819 Sir Thomas Stamford Raffles, an energetic English colonial official, secured the uninhabited island of Singapore from a Malay sultan; later acquisitions brought Brit-

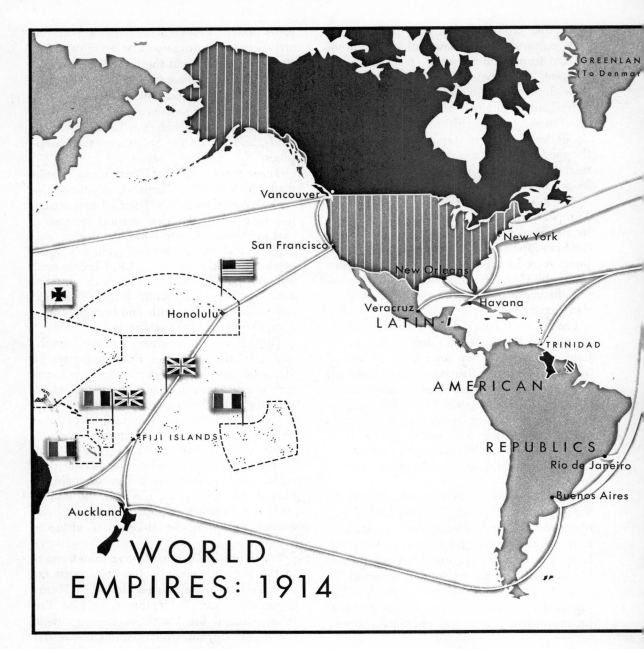

GREENLAN
(To Denmar

Vancouver

New York

San Francisco

New Orleans

Honolulu

Havana

Veracruz

LATIN-I

TRINIDAD

AMERICAN

FIJI ISLANDS

REPUBLICS

Rio de Janeiro

Buenos Aires

Auckland

WORLD EMPIRES: 1914

ish Malaya in contact with the frontiers of Siam. Singapore's commercial and strategic value was apparent in the nineteenth century; it became one of the world's greatest ports and it provided a vantage point from which Britain could dominate the seas surrounding southern Asia. British Malaya itself became one of the richest colonial areas in the world, particularly in tin and rubber.

The economic development of the Malay peninsula has been mainly the work of Chinese and Indian emigrants. The Malayan natives, living contentedly in their great jungle forests where luxuriant tropical growth easily supplied most of their wants, had little interest in hard work. Today, in the southern Malay peninsula, the Chinese not only outnumber the Malayan natives but also monop-

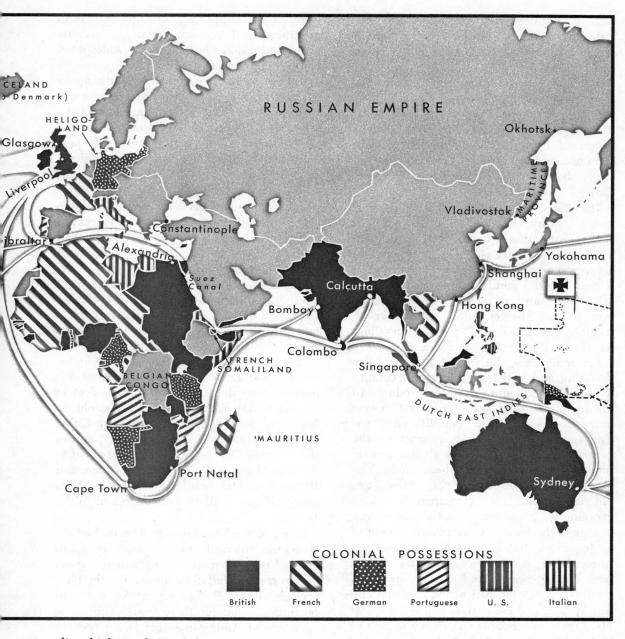

COLONIAL   POSSESSIONS

British   French   German   Portuguese   U. S.   Italian

olize higher education and dominate such professions as medicine and law.

Adjoining India on its eastern land frontier is Burma. In three separate wars between 1823 and 1885, this kingdom was progressively conquered by Britain and annexed to India.

French Indochina. As early as 1787, France had secured the rights to a port from the most important native ruler in the rich peninsula of Indochina. In the latter half of the nineteenth century, the French expanded their holdings and, between 1883 and 1885, came into conflict with China, which for many years had received annual tribute from this region. The Peking government was forced to recognize French supremacy, and later France took territory in the south from

Siam. By the beginning of the twentieth century, Indochina had become an important source of supply for tin, pepper, coal, cotton, and rice.

Siam, an independent buffer state. Although its territory was pared down by both Britain and France, Siam maintained its existence—partly because both western nations welcomed the retention of an independent Siam as a buffer between their holdings and partly because the royal house of Siam showed shrewdness and sagacity.

The Dutch East Indies. Late in the sixteenth century, the Dutch had wrested most of the East Indies from the Portuguese, and in 1602 the Dutch East India Company was organized to exploit the resources of the Spice Islands. By the middle of the next century, it had eliminated all rivals in the area. However, in time, the company became corrupt, and it was abolished in 1798, with all holdings transferred to the Dutch crown.

For some time, the spice trade had been declining, and early in the nineteenth century the Dutch set about raising new products. In the 1830's the so-called culture system was introduced, under which one fifth of all native land was set aside to raise crops for the government and one fifth of all the natives' time was required to till these lands. The production of tobacco, sugar, coffee, tea, indigo, pepper, and cinnamon increased enormously. In the long run, the culture system gave the islands a prosperous system of raising crops, but because it was based on forced labor, it often prevented the natives from having enough land for their own use. By 1900 the Dutch had abandoned the culture system, and the natives enjoyed a better life. Less commendable was Dutch neglect of higher education and the failure to prepare their wards for eventual self-government.

Spanish rule in the Philippines. Little more than 250 miles north of the Dutch East Indies is the Philippine archipelago, known to Europe only after the Portuguese explorer Magellan discovered it for Spain in 1521. In contrast to the harsh regimes imposed on the Indians of Latin America, Spanish rule in the Philippines was humane. But the Filipinos were given no opportunities to participate in government. Discontent arose, especially among educated liberals, and a widespread revolt broke out in 1896.

United States imperialism. While Spain wrestled with Filipino discontent, a new imperialist power was emerging in the Pacific—the United States. In 1867 the Midway Islands were occupied and Alaska was purchased from Russia. The next advance of the United States was in the Hawaiian Islands, where, during the nineteenth century, Europeans and Americans had developed large sugar plantations. American capital continued to pour in, and by 1881 the islands had been spoken of by an American secretary of state as part of the "American system." A revolt in 1893, engineered with the assistance of United States Marines, deposed the Hawaiian queen and set up a republic. Five years later, Hawaii was annexed by joint declaration of both houses of Congress.

As we saw in Chapter 25, the United States went to war against Spain in 1898. After Admiral Dewey destroyed the Spanish fleet at Manila in May of that year, American soldiers landed in the Philippines. Here, as in Cuba, Spanish resistance crumbled quickly, and in the treaty of December 1898, Spain ceded to the United States the Philippines, Guam, and Puerto Rico. One year later the United States occupied the small Pacific outpost of Wake Island.

Some of the Filipino patriots who had assisted the American troops against the Spanish had no wish merely to exchange masters and to see the United States acquire the Philippines. In 1899 fighting broke out and hostilities lasted for three years. The ironic spectacle of American forces being used in a second conquest of the Philippines brought about a strong revulsion against imperialism in many quarters in the United States. A New York newspaper plaintively addressed Kipling, the archspokesman of imperialism, thus:

We've taken up the white man's burden
  Of ebony and brown;
Now will you kindly tell us, Rudyard,
  How we may put it down?[4]

The workers in this illustration are constructing a segment of the great Trans-Siberian Railroad, which was built to link European Russia with the Pacific coast and which opened up the vast area of Siberia to colonization and industrialization.

Yet American colonial administration in the Philippines proved to be liberal and well-intentioned for the most part. In 1913 the legislature became dominantly native, although final authority in the most important matters was still reserved for the United States Congress. The Philippines' tariff was shaped to favor American trade; and large amounts of capital from the United States were invested in the islands. Increased educational facilities produced educated Filipinos, among whom the desire for independence grew increasingly strong. In their eyes, American government in the Philippines, no matter how efficient or humanitarian, was no substitute for self-government.

RUSSIAN IMPERIALISM

The Russians expand to the east. Ordinarily one does not think of tsarist Russia as a colonial power such as Britain or France. The reason is the manner of Russian expansion: unlike Britain, which had to expand overseas, the Russian empire grew from the center outward by a process of accretion. From the grand duchy of Moscow, the Russians pushed out into the great plain that surrounded them.

One of the features of Russian expansion was unique: the struggle of a landlocked country for access to the warm water of the sea. We have already followed the imperialistic efforts of the eighteenth-century rulers Peter the Great and Catherine the Great for Russian expansion toward the Baltic and the Mediterranean seas (see Chapter 18). At the same time the Russians had crossed the Ural Mountains and penetrated the huge expanses of Siberia, occupying the territory as far east as the Sea of Okhotsk and the Kamchatka peninsula. Dissatisfied that its only seaport in the Far East, Okhotsk, was frozen over most of the year, Russia sought warm water ports on the Sea of Japan.

In the 1850's Russia occupied the region of the lower Amur River, which was ceded by China in 1860, as well as the Chinese

Maritime Provinces. These acquisitions enabled the tsars to build a great all-year port at Vladivostok. The port of Vladivostok was later united to European Russia by the Trans-Siberian Railroad—a vital communication link, begun in 1890, completed thirteen years later, and covering a distance of over four thousand miles.

Penetration of the Caucasus and Turkestan. The kingdom of Georgia in the Caucasus, the area between the Black and Caspian seas, had been incorporated into Russia in 1801, and several wars had been fought with Turkey and Persia. As the Russians pushed farther into the mountainous lands of the Caucasus, the native people fought desperately but were finally overcome in the 1860's.

The vast stretches of mid-Asia had also attracted Russian attention. North of Afghanistan and India lived various backward and nomadic tribes—a mixed lot of Mongols, Afghans, Turkomans, and Tatars. Long traversed by caravan routes, the territory had a few important trading cities, notably Samarkand, Tashkent, Merv, and Bokhara (see Reference Map 8). Early in the nineteenth century, the Russians moved across the steppes north of the Aral Sea into Turkestan, but not until the 1870's were the little states, or khanates, conquered.

Russia vs. Britain in Afghanistan and Persia. With the conquest of Turkestan, the Russian domain now extended to the frontiers of Afghanistan and India, a fact not lost on the British. Both Britain and Russia then endeavored to gain control of strategic Afghanistan. By occupying the Pamir plateau on the very northwestern frontier of India in 1895, the Russians threatened to dominate Tibet, a menace finally countered by a British expedition to Lhasa in 1904.

In the meantime, Persia, the land of the shahs, was decaying rapidly. A corrupt aristocracy held the reins of power and stubbornly resisted reform. Into this ancient land moved the influence of Russia, and by the twentieth century, Russia was in complete control of the northern part of the country. Russians trained the Persian army, erected telegraph lines, established a postal system, and founded a bank to loan rubles to the Persian government and to Persian merchants.

The British had no desire to see Russian power athwart the Persian Gulf and the British life line to India. To counter Russian moves, the British advanced into Persia from the southeast, established a bank, and set up a profitable tobacco monopoly.

The Anglo-Russian entente. In 1907 Britain and Russia signed an agreement which—on the surface—ended their rivalry in Asia. Russia agreed to deal with the sovereign of Afghanistan only through the British government. For its part, Great Britain consented neither to occupy nor to annex Afghanistan so long as it fulfilled its treaty obligations.

Persia was divided into three zones: the northern was a sphere of interest for Moscow, the middle was a neutral zone, and the southern gave Britain a free hand. In effect, Persia was under Anglo-Russian dual control. This partnership, however, was only a marriage of convenience, and Russia increasingly intervened in Persian domestic politics. Though sorely disturbed, Britain chose not to alienate the Russians because of a growing fear of German ambition in strategic areas such as Africa and China—fears which were shared by Russia. Thus Britain and Russia chose to reach an uneasy compromise in Persia. Both ethics and Persia were the victims of power politics.

THE GREAT AFRICAN COLONY HUNT

Exploration of Africa. The best area in which to follow the course of nineteenth-century imperialism is Africa, for nowhere else on the globe were colonial empires achieved so quickly. A great continent many times the size of Europe with nearly 150,000,000 people came almost completely under the control of European powers (see Reference Map 10).

Late in the eighteenth century, the opening of Africa began in earnest, and by 1835 most of northwestern Africa had been mapped by Europeans. The greatest of the

European explorers was David Livingstone, a Scottish missionary who traversed vast barren wastes and jungles from the Cape of Good Hope to the equator and from the Atlantic to the Indian Ocean. It was Livingstone who discovered Victoria Falls and the Zambezi River. "The very great doctor," as the natives called him, began his series of explorations in 1853. After his death in 1873, explorations of the interior were carried on by Henry Morton Stanley, the great British explorer and journalist who had located Livingstone in the jungle in 1871 and had casually greeted him, "Dr. Livingstone, I presume." By the end of the century, Africa was no longer the Dark Continent. The source of the Nile had been discovered, the courses of the Niger and Congo had been traced, and the world now realized the rich resources of Africa.

On the eve of the European scramble for Africa, only 10 per cent of the continent was under the control of western nations. In 1875 the two most important European holdings were Algeria, administered by France, and Cape Colony, held by Great Britain. In South Africa there were Dutch farmers in two small republics, the Orange Free State and the Transvaal. Most of the other European holdings were mere coastal ports. The interior still remained a mysterious land inhabited by primitive black men.

Belgian interest in Africa. Stanley's explorations galvanized the European nations into action. So impressed with Stanley's views was the Belgian king Leopold II that in 1876 he organized the International African Association, composed of scientists and explorers from all nations. Ostensibly the association was to serve humanitarian purposes, but the crafty king had other motives. As an agent of the association, Stanley was sent to the Congo region, where he made treaties with several African chiefs and by 1882 obtained over 900,000 square miles of territory.

The British in Egypt. Meanwhile, important developments were taking place in the Nile valley. Shortly before the completion of the Suez Canal in 1869, Ismail, the ruler of Egypt, borrowed enormous sums from French and English bankers at high rates of interest. By 1875 he was involved in financial difficulties and was forced to sell his block of 175,000 shares in the Suez Canal. The shares were snapped up by the astute prime minister of Great Britain, Disraeli, in order to give his country practical control in the management of this strategic waterway between Europe and the East. When Ismail repudiated his debts in 1876, Great Britain and France assumed joint financial control over Egypt, forcing the Egyptian ruler to abdicate in favor of his son, Tewfik.

The Egyptian ruling classes did not relish foreign intervention, and when a serious revolt broke out in 1882, many Europeans lost their lives in riots in Alexandria. The French fleet withdrew at this point, but Great Britain decided to quell the revolt and assume responsibility for the administration of Egypt. To reorganize Egyptian finances, eliminate corruption from the administration, and improve the cotton industry, Sir Evelyn Baring, later Lord Cromer, was sent to Egypt and actually ruled the country from 1883 to 1907. In reducing corruption, he overhauled the system of government. The use of forced labor was curbed, and huge dams were constructed to improve the fertility of the soil. Indeed, it has been said that the best record of imperialism is to be found in Egypt. Nevertheless, the twentieth century was barely under way before the Egyptians voiced a growing demand for self-government.

Organization of imperial policy. The occupation of Egypt and the acquisition of the Congo were the first moves in what came to be a precipitous scramble for African territory. In 1884 Bismarck convened a conference in Berlin to discuss the Africa problem. This assembly of diplomats paid lip service to humanitarianism by condemning the slave trade, prohibiting the sale of liquor and firearms in certain areas, and expressing concern for proper religious instruction for the natives. Then the diplomats turned to matters they considered much more important. The rules of competition by which the great powers were to be guided in seeking colonies were laid down. They agreed that the area along

The German caricaturist T. T. Heine pictures a giant Englishman greedily dominating three continents, with one foot in Great Britain, the other in South Africa, a hand on Egypt, and a hand on India.

the Congo was to be administered by Leopold of Belgium, that it was to be neutral territory, and that in this area trade and navigation were to be free. No nation was to peg out claims in Africa without first notifying other powers of its intention. No territory could be claimed unless it was effectively occupied, and all disputes were to be settled by arbitration. In spite of these encouraging declarations, the competitors ignored the rules when it was convenient to do so, and on several occasions war was avoided only by a hair's breadth.

The methods Europeans used to acquire land continued, in many cases, to involve deception of the native peoples. Europeans obtained huge grants of lands by presenting ignorant chiefs with treaties which they could not read and whose contents they were not permitted to comprehend. In return, the natives were rewarded by bottles of gin, red handkerchiefs, and fancy-dress costumes. Since in many cases, native custom reserved ownership of land to tribes, allowing individuals only the use of it, the chief granted land to European settlers with no idea that he was disposing of more than its temporary

use. When later the settler claimed ownership, the natives were indignant, feeling that the tribe had been robbed of land contrary to tribal law.

The Belgian Congo. Shortly after the Berlin conference, Leopold organized his African territories as the Congo Free State, subject to no control, not even that of the Belgian parliament. He began to exploit the colony's economic resources by granting concessions to private companies, reserving for his own administration an extensive rubber area ten times as large as Belgium. A system of forced labor was introduced, and soon stories of filthy work camps, horrible whippings, and other atrocities leaked out of the Free State, now undergoing the process of "civilization."

In the face of a rising tide of international indignation, Leopold in 1908 was forced to turn over the Free State to the Belgian government, which renamed the area the Belgian Congo. Under the direct administration of the government, conditions in the colony improved.

German interest in Africa. In the 1880's Germany acquired three colonies on the west coast of Africa: German Southwest Africa, Togoland, and Cameroons. It was on the east coast of the African continent, however, that the most important German acquisitions were made. German penetration there was largely the work of one man, Carl Peters, who had studied British methods of colonization. In 1884 he and three other colonial enthusiasts, disguised as English workingmen, set out on a secret mission to eastern Africa. Peters succeeded in obtaining treaties from chiefs giving him control of sixty thousand square miles. In 1885 Bismarck proclaimed the region German East Africa.

The British had been pegging out claims to the region directly north of Peters' concessions, and in 1886 and 1890 rival German and British claims were settled amicably. Germany received several concessions from Britain, notably the strategic island of Helgoland in the North Sea, which was to become an important pivot of German naval power. Britain also recognized the Germans' claim to their protectorate in East Africa (later called

Tanganyika). After the agreement in East Africa, the British held Uganda, along the shores of Lake Victoria; British East Africa (later known as Kenya), fronting along the coast of the Indian Ocean; the rich spice (cloves) island of Zanzibar; and the area of Nyasaland.

Other British acquisitions in Africa. Meanwhile, Great Britain by 1884 had obtained control over a stretch of African coast fronting on the Gulf of Aden. This protectorate (British Somaliland) was of great strategic value inasmuch as it guarded the lower approach to the Suez Canal. Even more important were the headwaters of the Nile, situated in the area known later as the Anglo-Egyptian Sudan. In 1898 the British conquered this area also.

Among the British acquisitions on the west coast of Africa, the most important were the territories around the mouth of the Niger, stretching back toward the Sudan. These British possessions included Gambia, Sierra Leone, the Gold Coast, and Nigeria.

Cecil Rhodes, empire builder. In the meantime, Great Britain's influence in southern Africa had expanded northward from Cape Colony almost to the equator, where it reached German East Africa. In this drive north the main impetus came from the British capitalist Cecil Rhodes, who dreamed of an uninterrupted corridor of British territory from the Cape of Good Hope to Cairo.

Shortly after Rhodes' arrival in southern Africa as a young man, diamonds were discovered north of Cape Colony. In time Rhodes became the leading figure in the fabulously wealthy De Beers diamond syndicate and the owner of many valuable gold-mining properties in the Transvaal. By 1890 his annual income was estimated to be at least 5,000,000 dollars.

In 1885, Rhodes was instrumental in getting Britain to declare a protectorate over Bechuanaland, a territory wedged between the Dutch Transvaal and German Southwest Africa. Without Britain's domination over this region, Rhodes' dream of a Cape-to-Cairo railroad under British control could not be realized. By unscrupulous methods the

Regarded by many as a ruthless businessman, Cecil Rhodes used his money not for himself but for grandiose schemes to spread British rule and culture throughout the world to the end of creating an imperial power that would unite all peoples.

empire builder secured extensive settlement and mining rights to the high and fertile plateau through which flowed the great Zambezi River. In 1890 the capital, Salisbury, was founded and the region was named Rhodesia.

By 1890, as prime minister of Cape Colony, Rhodes' one remaining task was uniting Boer and Briton in South Africa into a single nation. But Rhodes made the fatal mistake of conspiring to use force to achieve his ends. This only widened the breach between the two peoples and did much to bring on the Boer War in 1899 (see p. 609).

In 1902 Cecil Rhodes died, leaving a huge legacy to endow 175 scholarships at Oxford for students from the British Dominions, the United States, and Germany. He believed that if harmony and understanding could be achieved among the United States, Germany, and the British Dominions, the peace of the world would be assured. Rhodes was a complex combination of astute financier, fanatical nationalist and empire builder, and confused seeker after world peace.

French colonies in Africa. The first important French colonial acquisition in Africa had been made decades before the renewed European interest in colonization in the 1870's and 1880's. In the 1820's, during the reign of Charles x, French statesmen had seen in North Africa a chance to counterbalance political unrest at home. For some time France had been complaining of the piratical activities of the Algerians, and when in 1827 the Algerian ruler insulted the French consul in public by hitting him on the head with a flyswatter, France was furnished with a good pretext for intervention. In 1830 a large army was dispatched to occupy the country, but seventeen years elapsed before the French succeeded in subduing the fierce Berber tribes. Algeria was then made an integral part of the French state.

With the acquisition of Tunisia in 1881 and a huge section of equatorial Africa along the right bank of the Congo River in 1884, France began to develop an ambitious colonial program. From trading posts along the west coast of Africa, France pushed into the interior and thus obtained most of the basins of the Senegal and Niger rivers, while expeditions from Algeria and Tunisia penetrated the Sahara. Although the French did not succeed in getting to the Nile, by 1900 they controlled the largest empire in Africa, one which stretched eastward from the Atlantic to the western Sudan and southward to the Congo River. In addition, the French annexed the large island of Madagascar in the south Indian Ocean and in 1911, despite the opposition of Germany, made Morocco a French protectorate.

Italy's African ventures. If overpopulation, lack of trade, and widespread poverty constitute the most compelling reasons for obtaining colonies, Italy should have gained the most extensive areas in Africa. But Italy came out of the scramble with very little territory. When Tunisia became a French protectorate in 1881, Italian ambitions there were blocked. Italy turned to East Africa, obtaining a piece of Red Sea coast and a slice of barren and desolate land on the Indian Ocean, but these areas were of little value without the rich plateau of Abyssinia (Ethiopia) in the hinterland. An attempt to annex this ancient empire in 1896 ended in the destruction of an Italian army.

Italy then shifted its attention to the Turkish territory of Tripoli, which was acquired with the secret consent of Spain, France, Great Britain, and Russia. Italy declared war on Turkey in 1911 and forced the Turks to cede the area in 1912. This event temporarily marked the end of Italian expansion and likewise the end of the race for colonial empires by European powers.

The economic wealth of Africa surpassed the expectations of the most avid imperialist. By the first decade in the twentieth century, it was the world's greatest producer of gold and diamonds. In addition, rich resources of tin, phosphates, and especially copper were uncovered. From the once Dark Continent poured rubber, coffee, sisal, palm oil, and cotton—products which became more and more essential for the great industrial nations of the world.

The table below shows the shares of African territory taken by European nations during the nineteenth century and the first decade of the twentieth.

EUROPEAN TERRITORIAL EXPANSION IN AFRICA

	SQUARE MILES	POPULATION
France	4,200,000	25,000,000
Great Britain	3,300,000	35,000,000
Germany	1,100,000	12,000,000
Belgium	900,000	7,000,000
Portugal	800,000	8,000,000
Italy	600,000	1,000,000
Spain	75,000	200,000

IMPERIALISM:

THE BALANCE SHEET

Spread of imperialism. By 1914 some 283,000,000 whites directly controlled over 900,000,000 non-Europeans, mainly in Africa and Asia. The area involved in this tremendous colonial network was more than 28,000,000 square miles. The greatest of the empire builders was Britain, with more than 13,000,000 square miles, if self-governing colonies such as Canada were included. Russia's colonial domain, mainly in central and eastern Asia, was at least half the size of Britain's empire. France was the third largest imperial power, with Germany a poor fourth. Substantial colonial holdings were also in the hands of Belgium, Portugal, and Holland, with Italy making a pitiful showing. While most Americans would not think of the United States as an imperial power, in 1914 this nation controlled over 700,000 square miles of territory outside the confines of continental United States.

Imperialism: negative and positive aspects. The critics of western imperialism have leveled their guns with zest against those who have defended it on the basis of a civilizing mission. George Bernard Shaw, the sharp-tongued enemy of hypocrisy in any form, has left a classic indictment of Britain's mission to help the "backward" races:

Every Englishman is born with a certain miraculous power that makes him master of the world. When he wants a thing he never tells himself that he wants it. He waits patiently till there comes into his head, no one knows how, the burning conviction that it is his moral and religious duty to conquer those who have the thing he wants. Then he becomes irresistible. Like the aristocrat he does what pleases him and grabs what he wants; like the shopkeeper he pursues his purpose with the industry and steadfastness that come from strong religious conviction and deep sense of moral responsibility. He is never at a loss for an effective moral attitude. As the great champion of freedom and independence, he conquers half the world and calls it Colonization. When he wants a new market for his adulterated Manchester goods, he sends a missionary to teach the natives the gospel of peace. The na-

tives kill the missionary; he flies to arms in defense of Christianity; fights for it, conquers for it; and takes the market as a reward from heaven.[5]

Certainly one must agree that imperialism had its ruthless and exploitative aspects. But another view of the significance of western imperialism in the scheme of world history is becoming more clear following the achievement of independence by a large number of colonies after World War II. It is now evident that many of the native peoples living under European imperial control took the ensuing law and order for granted. It should not be forgotten that the slave trade in tropical Africa was smashed in the mid-nineteenth century largely by British efforts; that the French ended piracy in North Africa; and that *thuggee* was extirpated in India by British rule. Even as late as 1900, much of the great territory of Nigeria on the African west coast was in a state of chaos, with fierce and powerful Muslim chieftains carrying out ruthless slave raiding.

In many of the areas that came under European imperial control, tribes or nations had been constantly at war with each other. This was especially true in Africa, Malaya, and the Dutch East Indies. The imperial powers stepped in and ended intertribal wars, prohibiting the young warriors from "blooding their spears." One law was imposed over an entire area, and regions such as French West Africa, the Belgian Congo, the Gold Coast, the great dependency of India, the East Indies, and British Malaya were given the advantages of political and economic unity which had been heretofore unknown. As we will see in a later chapter, the granting of independence revived the old tribal and sectional loyalties. New nations such as India broke apart; unity has been maintained only with extreme difficulty in the former Dutch East Indies. Already in the recently independent African states are heard disturbing rumblings of regional nationalism that threaten the unity of these budding nations.

While imperialism has produced its share of economic injustices and while colonies have been retarded in some ways to aid the controlling power, there is another side to the picture. Western nations have constructed roads, government buildings, postal and telegraph systems, and great dams, and their businessmen have dug mines, tapped oil fields, and established plantations. With the end of imperial control, many of these improvements remain, performing invaluable functions. And it may be added that these so-called backward or underdeveloped areas—gradually gaining their independence in the mid-twentieth century—still require the capital and technology of more developed nations.

A final positive aspect of western imperialism was its ideological impact on civilizations, such as the Chinese, that were moribund and stagnant and on areas, such as tropical Africa, where civilization had never even started. The West brought dynamic ideas of progress, nationalism, efficient and honest public administration, democracy, and faith in science. This ideological impact of nationalism and democracy, made possible by colonialism, ultimately led to a demand for independence. Alien government, good or bad, was no substitute for self-government.

Among the most important agencies diffusing these western ideas were the Christian missionaries. In all parts of the world, mission establishments, consisting of schools, colleges, hospitals, and churches, made a unique contribution to enlightenment. All this is not to say that western missionary enterprise was always wisely conceived or directed. There were regrettable occasions when missionaries failed to respect the intrinsic worth and dignity of aspects of native culture. They believed such customs or institutions were un-Christian just because they were nonwestern. But in the balance, missionary work undoubtedly contributed to both the spiritual and the physical betterment of humanity in the undeveloped regions of the world.

SUMMARY

Before 1870, little interest in colonial expansion existed in Europe. But with the completion of the unification of Germany and Italy, the mounting of tariffs, and the need for markets, raw materials, and areas for investing surplus capital, the western nations began avidly to turn their attention to imperialism. The economic forces back of this expansion have usually been overemphasized, the psychological underestimated. By 1870 Europe had unbounded faith in its destiny and in its powers. What has been called "a certain indefinable national energy"[6] impelled nations such as France, Britain, and Germany to spread their rule, power, and culture. Love of adventure and scientific curiosity also impelled explorers and administrators to peg out colonial claims.

In the Far East, China was opened in the 1840's and 1850's—somewhat before the real onset of western imperialism. This huge and inert empire was callously treated by the western nations. But China was not blameless. Wrapped in a mantle of unreal superiority, China refused to adapt to the needs or realities of a rapidly changing world. On the other hand, Japan had a long tradition of borrowing from the outside. Once convinced of the necessity of modernization, this feudal island kingdom engaged in a pell-mell adoption of western culture. But while foreign customs and techniques were borrowed, they were shaped to fit Japanese needs as seen by Japan's leaders. Education, the press, the armed services, and the government so functioned as to produce a docile, obedient citizen and a fanatical, dedicated soldier.

Following the Sepoy Rebellion in 1857, Britain consolidated its rule in India and built up flourishing colonies in Ceylon, Malaya, and Burma. The French acquired Indochina, and the Dutch exploited the riches of the East Indies. In the Pacific, a feature of the late nineteenth century was the growing imperialism of the United States.

Russian imperialism in the nineteenth century is often overlooked. Its empire was not a scattered series of territories located in various continents and separated by the seven seas but a continuous land area, a group of territories that had originated from a nucleus —Moscow—and had never lost touch with its starting point. By 1900 Russia had expanded to the Pacific and marched southward to the passes of India and Afghanistan and was pushing into the Middle East toward the warm waters of the Indian Ocean. Because of Anglo-Russian rivalry in this latter area, Persia was in effect partitioned.

Africa was the largest area to be partitioned. By the end of the colonial scramble, only two independent countries remained: Ethiopia and tiny Liberia. Britain had gained

such territories as Egypt and Anglo-Egyptian Sudan, Kenya, Uganda, Rhodesia, Nigeria, and the Gold Coast. In addition to its extensive holdings in North Africa, France ruled Madagascar, French Equatorial Africa, and the huge stretch of French West Africa reaching from Dakar on the Atlantic coast to the valley of the Nile. Little Belgium controlled the vast Belgian Congo, Germany had fairly extensive holdings, and only ambitious Italy had failed in the great African colony hunt.

SUGGESTIONS FOR READING

H. M. Wright, ed., The "New Imperialism": Analysis of Late Nineteenth-Century Expansion,* Heath. Short selections illustrating conflicting viewpoints on the motives for expansion.

E. A. Walker, Colonies, Cambridge Univ., 1944. A brief study on the reasons for, the nature of, and the future of colonies. Thoughtful and stimulating is E. M. Winslow, The Pattern of Imperialism, Columbia Univ., 1948.

Two famous attacks on imperialism, the latter being the stock Communist diatribe: J. A. Hobson, Imperialism: A Study, Macmillan, 1938; and V. I. Lenin, Imperialism, the Highest Stage of Capitalism, International Publishers, 1939.

Sir Alan Burns, In Defence of Colonies: British Colonial Territories in International Affairs, Macmillan, 1957. A vigorous defense of the motives and positive results of British imperialism. See also Sir Ernest Barker, The Ideas and Ideals of the British Empire, Cambridge Univ., 1941.

C. E. Carrington, The Life of Rudyard Kipling, Doubleday, 1955. A good portrait of the "singer of empire."

P. Speare, Twilight of the Mughuls, Cambridge Univ., 1951. A British authority describes the once mighty Indian dynasty on the eve of its oblivion.

S. N. Sen, Eighteen Fifty-Seven, India Ministry of Information, Delhi, 1957. Remarkable for its objectivity is this official history of the Sepoy Rebellion of 1857. See also J. Leasor, The Red Fort: The Story of the Indian Mutiny of 1857, Reynal, 1957.

R. Coupland, India: A Re-Statement, Oxford, 1946. A restrained and convincing apologia for British rule. By contrast, G. D. Sanderson, India and British Imperialism, Bookman Associates, 1951, is a bitter indictment of British rule.

E. M. Forster, A Passage to India (many editions). A novel about the clash of cultures (British and Indian) in India.

D. E. Owen, Imperialism and Nationalism in the Far East, Holt, 1929. Valuable for its discussion of the first European impacts in the Far East and the opening of China and Japan.

*Indicates an inexpensive paperbound edition.

The best history of Chinese domestic affairs in the nineteenth century is Chien-nung Li, The Political History of China, 1840-1928, Van Nostrand, 1956. Two studies of the Boxer Rebellion are Ch'un-lin T'an, The Boxer Catastrophe, Columbia Univ., 1955; and P. Fleming, The Siege at Peking: The Boxer Rebellion, Harper, 1959.

P. S. Buck, Imperial Woman,* Pocketbooks. A lengthy, colorful biographical novel of the last empress of China, who rose from concubinage to the throne of the Manchu.

Sir George B. Sansom, The Western World and Japan: A Study in the Interaction of European and Asiatic Cultures, Knopf, 1950. A distinguished historian investigates the early contacts between Europe and Asia and then traces the impact of the western world upon Japan from 1600 to 1894.

Recommended for the coverage and interpretation of events in southeast Asia are J. F. Cady, The Roots of French Imperialism in Eastern Asia, Cornell, 1954; and J. S. Furnivall, Colonial Policy and Practice: A Comparative Study of Burma and Netherlands India, Macmillan, 1956.

J. W. Pratt, America's Colonial Experiment, Prentice-Hall, 1950. A useful survey of American imperialism.

B. H. Sumner, Tsardom and Imperialism in the Far East and Middle East, 1880-1914, British Academy, 1944. A brief survey.

H. L. Hoskins, European Imperialism in Africa, Holt (Berkshire Studies), 1930. A brief history of European penetration.

A. Moorehead, The White Nile, Harper, 1961. A most readable account of exploration in central Africa. Fascinating to read are the journals of African explorers: M. Perham and J. Simmons, eds., African Discovery, Faber, 1957; and C. Howard, ed., West African Explorers, Oxford, 1952.

I. L. Evans, The British in Tropical Africa, Macmillan, 1929; M. E. Townsend, The Rise and Fall of Germany's Colonial Empire, Macmillan, 1930. Good detailed accounts.

The challenge of Britain's imperial mission in Africa is mirrored in F. Gross, Rhodes of Africa, Praeger, 1957.

U.S. AND LATIN AMERICA

1750

United States wins independence 1783

1800   Louisiana Purchase doubles size of U.S. 1803
War of 1812—U.S. vs. Britain and Canada
No restrictions on male suffrage in new states entering Union -
after 1817
Clay's Missouri Compromise determines boundaries of slave
territory in U.S. 1820
U.S. Monroe Doctrine warns against European interference
in Western Hemisphere 1823
Bolivia, Peru, Colombia, Venezuela, Ecuador, Paraguay, Uru-
guay suffer from political chaos (early nineteenth century)
Jackson's election to presidency exemplifies democratic
principle in U.S. 1828
Effort to create a confederation in Central America fails 1837
Brazil—Pedro II brings political liberty and economic and
cultural progress to Brazil 1840-1889; country endures civil
wars 1889-1899; army-controlled government resumes progressive course c. 1900
U.S. land area greatly increased by annexation of California,
Texas, Oregon, and the Southwest 1845-1860

1850   Progressive elements overthrow *gaucho* leader in Argentina
1852; country becomes united republic 1861
Mexico—dictator Santa Anna overthrown 1855; Juárez institutes anticlerical *Reforma*, civil war ensues; Juárez victorious
in civil war 1861; France establishes puppet regime under
Maximilian 1863; U.S. objects and Juárez returns 1867;
dictator Diaz brings order without liberty 1877-1880, 1884-
1911; Madero leads successful revolution 1911

American Civil War—the Federal Union preserved, slavery
abolished 1861-1865

U.S. emerges as imperialist power—occupies Midway Islands
1867; purchases Alaska from Russia 1867; annexes Hawaii 1898

Progressive movement in the U.S. initiates economic reform—
Interstate Commerce Act begins expansion of governmental
regulation of industry 1887; muckrakers attack economic inequalities c. 1890-1910; trust-busting and national regulation
of transportation, foods, drugs under Theodore Roosevelt
1901-1909; Wilson's militant reform campaign "New Freedom" results in Federal Reserve Act 1913, Clayton Anti-Trust
Act and Federal Trade Commission 1914

First Pan-American Conference 1889

"Dollar diplomacy"—U.S. exercises indirect controls in Latin
America to protect investments c. 1890-1914

U.S. settles border dispute between Britain and Venezuela 1895

1900   Spanish-American War 1898—U.S. gains Philippines, Guam,
and Puerto Rico; Platt Amendment establishes Cuba as protectorate 1901
Open Door Policy is declared 1900
U.S. emerges as most powerful nation in Western Hemisphere c. 1900

Era of Big Stick policy begins with the Roosevelt Corollary to
the Monroe Doctrine 1904
Theodore Roosevelt acts as peacemaker after Russo-Japanese
War 1905, receives Nobel Peace Prize 1910

Completion of the Panama Canal 1914

BRITISH DOMINIONS

Peace of Paris—Canada becomes British possession 1763
Canada's formative period 1763-1867—Quebec Act guarantees French custom and Catholicism in Canada 1774; immigration of United Empire Loyalists adds English population,
results in division into Upper and Lower Canada 1791

Sydney, first English colony in Australia, established 1788

British government assumes protection of New Zealand 1840

Australian colonies enjoy liberal form of self-government 1850
Canada achieves "responsible government" c. 1850; four
provinces of Canada form a federal union under British North
America Act and Canada becomes a dominion of Great
Britain 1867
Discovery of gold in Australia quickens development 1851;
agriculture continues as mainstay of economy
Pioneering in democratic government—Australia introduces
secret ballot 1855; woman suffrage initiated in New Zealand
1893, in Australia 1902

Treaty of Washington—Canada and U.S. arbitrate major
differences 1871
British Columbia joins the Dominion of Canada 1873

New Zealand pioneers in social welfare legislation—adopts
noncontributory old-age pensions 1878; establishes national
infant welfare system 1907
Program of national development under Macdonald, Canada's
first prime minister—offers bounties to new industries; com-
pletes railroad connecting east to British Columbia 1885;
initiates program for attracting immigrants

Six Australian colonies form Commonwealth of Australia 1901

Canadian government creates body for regulating railroads
1904

ASIA

AFRICA

Reign of Ch'ien Lung is period of great expansion for Manchu dynasty in China 1736-1795
Battle of Plassey begins domination of India by British East India Company and England 1757; Parliament takes control of East India Company 1773; appoints governor general of India 1784
British acquire Ceylon from Dutch 1796
Dutch government assumes control of East Indies; abolishes Dutch East India Company 1798

Britain acquires colony at Cape Town 1806

China wars with England over opium and western exploitation 1839-1842; victorious British win Hong Kong and open Shanghai and Canton by Treaty of Nanking 1842; Treaty of Tientsin grants further concessions 1858
U.S. makes treaty with China to open ports to trade and protect rights of American merchants and sailors 1844
Taiping Rebellion threatens Manchu dynasty 1850-1864; Manchu empress Tzu Hsi establishes national stability and encourages antiforeign sentiment 1861-1908
Perry persuades Japan to open first ports to West in Treaty of Kanagawa 1854
English crush Sepoy Rebellion and bring collapse of Mogul dynasty in India 1857; relieve East India Company of political responsibilities, reform administrative system in India 1858

Russia acquires Chinese territory, builds Vladivostok 1860; Trans-Siberian Railroad connects European Russia to Vladivostok 1903
Russia penetrates land of the Caucasus, Turkestan c. 1860-1870
The *Meiji* period in Japan—emperor is made supreme authority, and Japanese society, politics, and ideas are modernized 1868-1912: feudal system abolished 1871; national conscription enacted 1876; commission to frame constitution established 1883; constitution promulgated 1889

China recognizes French supremacy in Indochina 1885
Indian National Congress formed 1885; educated proletariat in India force England to alter system of government 1907-1909
Burma conquered by British, annexed to India c. 1885

Sino-Japanese War—China recognizes independence of Korea, relinquishes Liaotung peninsula and Formosa in Treaty of Shimonoseki 1894-1895; defeat signals renewal of aggressive actions by western powers; Japan forced to return Liaotung peninsula
Filipinos revolt against Spanish rule 1896; U.S. gains Philippines 1898; Filipinos rebel against American forces 1899-1902
Open Door Policy, instigated by John Hay, calls for equal trading privileges in China for all nations 1900
Boxer Rebellion—"Righteous Harmony Fists" seek to rid China of Europeans, defeated by international army 1900

Russo-Japanese War (1904-1905) concluded by Treaty of Portsmouth 1905; victorious Japan accepted as first-class power
Anglo-Russian entente—Britain and Russia end rivalry in Asia over Afghanistan and Persia 1907
Republic of China proclaimed with Sun Yat-sen as president 1912

1750

1800

Great Trek of Boers leads to establishment of Orange Free State and the Transvaal 1830's

Algeria becomes integral part of French state 1847

1850

Britain makes treaties with Boers acknowledging their independence 1852, 1854

Livingstone begins series of explorations in Africa 1853; followed by Stanley 1873

Europe's golden age of imperialism 1870-1914: **Belgium**— Leopold II organizes International African Association 1876; acquires Congo region 1876-1882; Leopold forced to turn over Congo Free State to Belgian government 1908. **Britain** —gains practical control of Suez Canal 1875; joint financial control of Egypt by British and French 1876; Sir Evelyn Baring (later Lord Cromer) assumes administration of Egypt 1883-1907; Somaliland is taken 1884; British and Germans settle rival claims in East Africa, and British gain Uganda, Kenya, Zanzibar, and Nyasaland 1886, 1890; Gambia, Sierra Leone, the Gold Coast, and Nigeria constitute British acquisitions in West Africa; area developed for Britain by Rhodes named Rhodesia 1890; Anglo-Egyptian Sudan conquered 1898. **Germany**— acquires Togoland, the Cameroons, German East Africa, German Southwest Africa 1880's; British and Germans settle dispute over territories in East Africa 1886, 1890. **France**— Egypt under joint control of Britain and France 1876; French obtain Tunisia 1881; Morocco made French protectorate 1911. **Italy**—fails in attempted capture of Abyssinia 1896; wrests Tripoli from Turks 1912

Discovery of gold in the Transvaal (1885) precipitates Boer War

1900

Boer War 1899-1902—British defeat Dutch in Transvaal and Orange Free State; Boers and Britons join states and create self-governing dominion of the Union of South Africa 1909

PART 7 The World Adrift

The rapid pace of the twentieth century is dramatically revealed in the period from 1914 to 1945—one of the most tumultuous periods in all history. In less than half a century, two world wars racked mankind, and governments and ways of life underwent drastic changes in almost every nation on earth. During this time humanity experienced both the most poignant suffering and the most unrestrained rejoicing; it was influenced by the most noble and dedicated leaders as well as the most sordid and malignant demagogues.

The cumulative effect of unbridled nationalism, imperialistic rivalry, and entangling alliances led to the First World War, the first total technological conflict. Out of the terrible struggle men everywhere hoped that a better world might emerge. Yet though the statesmen of the victorious Allies stood for the democratic and humanistic traditions of western civilization, their motives in making the peace were often as vindictive and nationalistic as any preparations for war; and though internationalism was put into action in the form of the League of Nations, it was given neither the strength nor the support to bring peace and security in the troubled years following World War I.

In these years, democracy began its struggle with a new totalitarianism growing out of the disillusionment after the Great War. In Russia, Marxian tenets were embraced by revolutionaries, and a Communist society took shape under Lenin. Another authoritarian system, Fascism, gripped Italy. And the most frightening ideology of all, Nazism, grew to terrifying fruition in Germany, where a people embittered by the humiliation of World War I and the Treaty of Versailles staked all their hopes on a madman named Hitler.

By the 1920's and 1930's, the non-European world had discovered the concept of nationalism. In the Middle East, Arab national ambitions had flared in 1916 into a revolt against Ottoman rule. The immigration of European Jews to Palestine led to conflict between Arabs and Jews, which was to increase as time passed. In North Africa, the Middle East, India, southeastern Asia, and Oceania, the indigenous peoples were gathering strength in their battle to oust the Europeans completely and govern themselves; and in the huge colonial area south of the Sahara, Africans were beginning to stir restlessly against European rule. Even China, tradition-bound for centuries, turned to revolution to regain the power and prestige it had lost during the era of imperialism. But though Chiang Kai-shek won an internal power struggle and organized the government, the country remained poor and weak. Meanwhile Japan continued its amazing technological, industrial, and military growth and triumphed as a world power.

The world depression in the 1930's gave the totalitarian movements an opportunity to expand their despotism at home and to launch aggression abroad. From 1931 to 1939, starting with the Japanese invasion of Manchuria, their belligerence mounted. The new dictatorial regimes went from one success to another, glorifying militarism and the potency of the state, regimenting their citizens, and intimidating their neighbors. The older democratic nations, such as Britain and France, were paralyzed with indecision and fear and did little to halt the dictators. Appeasement was tried, but the aggression continued. Finally, in 1939, the British and French realized that their own nations were next in Hitler's march of conquest and took up arms. The Second World War began. In 1941 the Soviet Union, which had been allied earlier with the Nazis, and the United States, which for two decades had been attempting to ignore the mounting tensions abroad, were forced into the struggle. The horrors which this global conflict brought were the familiar ones of ruthless enemy occupation, the rigors of battle, and the loss of life and property, and the new ones created by dread new weapons and methods of warfare, the organized slaughter of certain nationality groups, and the repeated bombing of civilian centers.

Victory came to the Grand Alliance in 1945 and with it total defeat of Hitler's Third Reich and the fascist states established in Italy by Mussolini and in Japan by Tojo. As in 1919 the victors were confronted with the immense task of rebuilding and reëstablishing a great part of the world. This task was made more difficult by the knowledge of the failures of the peace of 1919 and the dismaying realization that as the Second World War was more encompassing and vastly more destructive than the First, so a Third World War would be more shattering than the Second and, with the advent of nuclear weapons, might bring about the annihilation of man.

CHAPTER 27

A World Fit for Heroes

WORLD WAR I AND THE AFTERMATH: 1914-1929

Introduction. The onward march of western civilization came to a halt in the summer of 1914. For more than four years thereafter, the science, industry, wealth, and power of Europe were concentrated upon destruction. The Great War of 1914-1918 was a total war—a war fought not only on battlefronts on land, at sea, and in the air but also on home fronts far from the scene of military conflict. Civilians, as well as members of the armed forces, became "legitimate" targets for demoralization and death.

The campaigns fought at the beginning of the war—the Marne and Tannenberg and, a little later, the Dardanelles and Jutland—ended any hope of a quick victory on either side. The belligerents were condemned to the grinding horror of a war of attrition and stalemate. With the entrance of the United States into the war in the spring of 1917, however, this stand-off finally ended. In the autumn of 1918, Germany collapsed and sued for peace.

The peace conference that followed aroused the hopes of the entire world; the speeches delivered by the Allied leaders—Clemenceau, Lloyd George, and Wilson—were studded with promises of a future securely founded on a weak and disarmed Germany, of a world fit for heroes, of a lasting peace based on the Fourteen Points. But it was soon apparent that any plans for a just and lasting peace faced almost insurmountable obstacles: secret and conflicting agreements among the Allies, the cross-purposes and clashing motives of the delegates to the conference, and the powerful pressures exerted by the peoples of the victorious nations, who sought vengeance on their wartime enemies.

This chapter discusses not only the course of World War I and the peace treaties imposed by the victors but also the troubled decade in international affairs that followed. It was a crowded ten years. The League of Nations was established and began to function. Germany was gradually readmitted into the family of nations, and discord over the fantastic burden of reparations imposed upon the defeated power finally eased. Tensions and brush-fire conflicts that had flared up in so many parts of the world immediately after 1919 were contained or extinguished. By the late 1920's, while the world was not quite the place fit for heroes dreamed of by Lloyd George in 1919, there still seemed some possibility of realizing this idealistic goal.

THE FIRST WORLD WAR

Scope of the conflict. Although the terrible struggle that racked mankind from 1914 to 1918 was fought chiefly on the European continent, it can justly be called the First World War. Altogether, twenty-seven powers became belligerents, ranging the globe from Tokyo to Ottawa and from Rio de Janeiro to Cape Town. Tremendous fighting strength was mustered. The Central Powers—Germany, Austria, Bulgaria, and Turkey—possessed two distinct advantages. They fought from an inner or central position and were therefore able to transfer troops quickly and efficiently to various fronts. And the German army exhibited superb generalship and discipline. In their favor, the Allies had greater resources of finances and raw materials; and Britain had the advantage of a powerful fleet with which to maintain control of the seas.

Strategy in 1914. While the Allies could better hold out in a long war, both sides planned for a quick decision in 1914. Allied strategy was to launch two simultaneous offensives—one by the French against Alsace, the other by the Russians against East Prussia.

The German plan was this: by moving through Belgium and then wheeling back through France, the German armies hoped to outflank the French and push them against Alsace-Lorraine, where they would be met by another German army and hemmed in on both east and west. With France smashed, the main German forces would then shift to East Prussia, join a smaller German army which had been holding the Russians at bay, and destroy the Russian forces.

In the west the German strategy operated with clocklike precision. A small British expeditionary force tried unsuccessfully to halt the German onrush in Belgium, and a French offensive against Alsace soon fizzled out. Advancing inexorably on Paris, the German forces came within twenty-five miles of the city by the beginning of September. At this moment, however, the German high command made a fatal blunder. Its army weakened by the dispatch of troops to East Prussia to meet a Russian attack, the high command directed the east flank to pass to the east of Paris, thus abandoning the original plan to encircle Paris from the west. This tactic left the right flank of the German forces exposed.

The weakness was quickly detected by Joffre, the French commander, and his advisers; and on September 5, Joffre decided to initiate a bold counteroffensive. So began the battle of the Marne. Paris taxicabs were mobilized to transport French troops to the front. For five days a titanic battle raged, and in the end the Germans had to retreat. The western flanks of both armies were now exposed, and a race to the sea began, each army trying to outflank the other and to reach the vital ports along the English Channel. Before either army succeeded, winter set in; the western front became stabilized, and a long line of trenches stretched from the Channel to Switzerland. Open warfare was replaced by trench warfare.

On the eastern front the Russian armies quickly overran the Austrian province of Galicia, and two subsequent Austrian attacks on Serbia were repulsed. Farther north in East Prussia, however, the Russian invaders did not fare so well. In August they were defeated in the battle of Tannenberg by troops commanded by Generals von Hindenburg and von Ludendorff. One month later, in the battle of the Masurian Lakes, the Russians suf-

BATTLES OF WORLD WAR I

St. Petersburg

Moscow

Jutland

Masurian Lakes

Berlin
GERMANY
Tannenberg

Kiev

UKRAINE

Somme
Paris
Marne
Château
Thierry   Verdun

AUSTRIA-HUNGARY

Rostov

CRIMEA

Caporetto

RUMANIA

ITALY

SERBIA

BULGARIA

Central powers

Farthest German Advance

Gallipoli

Hindenburg line

GREECE

TURKEY

fered a second catastrophic defeat. By winter the Germans had smashed their way into Poland. The eastern frontiers of Germany were never again seriously menaced.

Allied setbacks in 1915. The year 1915 dawned with both the Allies and the Central Powers supremely confident of the outcome of the war. The aims of the Allies were to widen Germany's battlefront, to reëstablish communication with Russia, and to deprive the Central Powers of supplies from overseas by means of a naval blockade.

Turkey's entrance into the war on the side of Germany had closed the Dardanelles to Allied shipping; and munitions and other supplies could now be sent to Russia only via Archangel, a port ice-locked much of the year. Great Britain set out to solve this problem by forcing the Dardanelles, a plan attributed largely to Winston Churchill, then lord of the admiralty. But the campaign was a series of blunders. In a naval attack launched in March 1915, three battleships were sunk, and the Allies withdrew. We know now that the Turkish batteries were nearly out of ammunition; had the attack been pressed, the Straits undoubtedly would have fallen. In April, Australian and New Zealand troops forced a landing on the Gallipoli peninsula, suffering tremendous losses before their evacuation in January 1916.

To achieve their goal of widening their enemies' battlefront, the Allies finally brought Italy into the war. From December 1914 to April 1915, both sides had wooed Italy. The Allies were successful because in the secret Treaty of London they made lavish promises, including an offer to turn part of the southern Tyrol over to Italy after the war ended. As the British statesman Balfour remarked, "This is the sort of thing you have to do when you are engaged in war." Although still a member of the Triple Alliance, Italy did not feel bound by its earlier commitment to the Central Powers and in 1915 entered the war on what it believed was the winning side. Winning Italy to their side was the only victory achieved by the Allies in that year; elsewhere occurred a series of melancholy defeats.

The Germans went from victory to victory. In May they carried out a terrific offensive against the Russian forces in Galicia. The tsar's army was soon routed; more than 1,200,000 Russians were killed or wounded, and the Germans captured nearly 900,000 prisoners.

Serbia was the next victim. The conquest was made all the easier because, in September, Bulgaria entered the war on the side of the Central Powers. Surrounded by enemies, Serbia was helpless and resistance was quickly crushed.

Stalemate in the west, 1916. It was the strategy of the Allies to restrict attacks on the western front to intermittent nibbling and to concentrate upon the naval blockade. Germany, on the other hand, resorted to another kind of attrition and applied it to France. The plan was to concentrate a gigantic attack on Verdun. This move would attract hundreds of thousands of French troops, terrible losses would result, and French morale would be steadily worn down.

All during the spring and summer of 1916, the Germans pounded the forts of Verdun with thousands of shells and threw wave after wave of infantry against the French lines. The French stubbornly held their positions. The result of this blood bath was attrition on both sides—the total loss in wounded and dead of some 700,000 men.

To ease the tremendous pressure against Verdun and to discourage the Germans from sending fresh troops against Russia, the British army, in the final week of June, began an offensive along the Somme on the western front. Despite very heavy losses, the attack was renewed again and again until heavy rains in October made further efforts impossible. At the cost of over 400,000 killed and wounded, the British had gained a few square miles of territory.

The battle of Jutland (May 31-June 1, 1916), in the North Sea west of Denmark, was another crucial engagement, inasmuch as control of the seas was vital to Britain. At Jutland, the only major naval engagement of the war, the Germans maneuvered brilliantly and took daring risks. They could afford to gamble. Defeat could in no way worsen their existing strategic position; but victory at Jutland would give them victory in the war. The British fleet acted, therefore, with extreme caution. Its losses were heavier, but the German fleet was forced to return to its base and remained bottled up in home ports for the remainder of the war. British naval supremacy continued intact.

The eastern front, 1916. A promising development for the Allies was the comeback staged by the Russian army. In June Russian troops struck the Austrian lines with the force of a thunderbolt, capturing 300,000 prisoners. Although the assistance of German troops and the inadequacy of Russian equipment saved the Austrian armies from destruction, the Russian offensive had one important result: Rumania threw in its lot with the Allies and successfully launched an invasion of Hungary. But Rumania's success was short-lived. Bulgarian and German forces simultaneously attacked the inferior Rumanian armies, and Rumania was forced to capitulate.

At the close of 1916, after more than two years of fighting, neither the Central Powers nor the Allies could envisage victory. The war had turned into a dreary contest of stamina.

Allies near the breaking point in 1917. In 1917 the British and French commanders were hopeful that the long-planned breakthrough might be accomplished, but a large-scale attack by the French was beaten back with horrible losses. French regiments mutinied rather than return to the inferno of no man's land. Meanwhile the British army initiated several massive offensives, only to lose hundreds of thousands of men without any decisive results. Unsuccessful offensives were launched by the Allies in Italy also, but the

Austrian army, aided by the Germans, smashed the Italian front. This occurred at the battle of Caporetto, described so vividly by Ernest Hemingway in the war novel *A Farewell to Arms.* Italian resistance finally hardened, but collapse was barely averted.

This disastrous frustration of Allied hopes was deepened by the growing menace of the German submarine campaign. By 1917 shipping losses had assumed catastrophic proportions. In three months 470 British ships alone fell victims to torpedoes. Britain had no more than a six weeks' supply of food, and for the Allies the situation became critical. But the very weapon that seemed to doom their cause was to prove their salvation, for the submarine brought the United States into the war on the Allies' side.

American sentiment lies with the Allies. After Italy joined the Allies in 1915, the United States was the only great power remaining neutral. In 1914 President Wilson had announced the neutrality of the United States and declared that the people "must be impartial in thought as well as in action." The events of the following two years showed that this was no easy task.

From the beginning of the conflict, American sentiment was predominantly with Britain and France. This tendency to favor the western European democracies was further strengthened by British propaganda, which was more effective than that of the Central Powers. Another factor favoring the Allied cause was the American belief that by invading Belgium, Germany had grossly violated international law. Partly because of the kaiser's saber-rattling speeches, the German government was regarded as undemocratic, unpredictable, and unstable. In some circles it was believed that a German victory would upset the world balance of power and that a victorious and expansionist Germany might imperil American security.

As the war got under way, it became apparent that the British blockade would permit our trade to be carried on with the Allies only, and it was not long before our factories and farmers were producing munitions and food exclusively for Great Britain and France.

Our industry expanded and began to enjoy a prosperity dependent upon the continuance of Allied purchases. Between 1914 and 1916, American exports to the Allies quadrupled. During 1915 and 1916, Allied bonds totaling about $1,500,000,000 were sold in America.

In recent times much attention has been paid to the financial stake of the United States in the Allied cause. Careful students point out that though the economic situation did influence our final decision to go to war, "the financial community as a whole . . . favored American neutrality rather than American participation; for neutrality afforded Wall Street all the profits of war without the compensating sacrifices and taxation. And there is not a shred of evidence to support the allegation that Wilson was at any time influenced by the financial 'stake' in his relations with Germany."[1]

German U-boat campaign angers the United States. The immediate cause of America's entry into the war on the side of the Allies was undoubtedly the German submarine campaign. So effective had the British naval blockade been in 1914 that Germany in desperation announced unrestricted submarine warfare in February 1915. About three months later, on May 7, occurred the disaster of the sinking of the *Lusitania,* one of the largest and most luxurious liners of the Cunard line. Today it is generally recognized that, in addition to civilian passengers, the vessel was carrying ammunition, but it is still debated whether the ship was armed. Torpedoed off the Irish coast, the *Lusitania* went to the bottom with the loss of over one thousand lives, including more than one hundred Americans. Public opinion in America was aroused, and the United States government sent Germany an ultimatum demanding the termination of the submarine campaign. In reply the Germans pledged that in the future merchant vessels would not be sunk without warning and that provision would be made for the safety of passengers and crews.

In the fall of 1916, Wilson was reëlected to the presidency. One of the important claims made during the campaign was "he kept us

An elaborate system of front lines, support trenches, and artillery supply lines stretched some six hundred miles across France and Belgium during the stalemate on the western front in World War I. The daily lot of the trench soldier was exposure to machine-gun fire, gas attack, and the shelling of big guns. Occasionally a charge would be made "over the top" (upper right) and across no man's land, an area crisscrossed with barbed wire and spotted with shell craters. When an assault failed, those who survived straggled back to their muddy, rat- and vermin-infested trenches. The tank (below) made its first appearance as a weapon of war in September 1916. The British had developed it secretly under the pretext of building water tanks, a circumstance that gave the new weapon its name.

The airplane was first used primarily for reconnaissance purposes; only later in the war were methods devised for mounting machine guns on it and for dropping bombs from it. At center right, German and Allied planes dogfight over the western front. At bottom right, an English submarine is shown being bombed by German planes in the North Sea. The submarine was extensively used by both sides as a military weapon during World War I.

out of war." This boast, however, was soon invalidated by the force of events. The discovery of German plots to embroil Mexico in a war against the United States aroused violent resentment, and the renewal of unrestricted submarine warfare was the last straw. In February 1917 diplomatic relations were broken off between the United States and Germany. Finally the president asked Congress to declare war against Germany. On April 6 the United States entered the war.

The spell of Wilson's lofty principles and the challenge of his speeches caused a great welling of idealism in America. No matter what causes had operated to bring America into the war, the United States was now fighting, in the words of the president, "to make the world safe for democracy."

Ludendorff's last effort. The Germans now decided on a last effort to win the war before American aid became effective. The British army was bled white from the fruitless offensives of 1917, and the French divisions had barely recovered from the mutinies in the ranks. Moreover, the Russian war effort had collapsed. In the revolution of November 1917, the Bolsheviks seized power in Russia; and by the Treaty of Brest Litovsk early in 1918, they made peace with Germany. The terms were harsh. Russia lost 500,000 square miles of territory and 66,000,000 people.

Freed from the necessity of fighting on the Russian front, General von Ludendorff transferred every available man to France and in March 1918 launched what he hoped would be a knockout blow against the British. The German troops, outnumbering the British four to one, made a large dent in the Allied line. But a breakthrough was not achieved. Ludendorff aimed a second blow against the British in another sector. Again impressive gains were made but not the rout which the German command had expected. A third offensive was launched against the French forces, but fresh American troops thrown into the struggle halted the advance. A brigade of marines covered itself with glory by stemming the German onrush at Château-Thierry.

Ludendorff made a last desperate effort. Launching a "Peace Drive" against the French, Ludendorff declared, "If my offensive succeeds, we have won the war." By this time, however, the German troops had suffered heavy losses. Under the unified command of Marshal Foch, the Allies mustered their resources, and between March and July 1918 more than one million American "doughboys" landed in France. The advantage in man power and equipment was now with the Allies, and Ludendorff's "Peace Drive" failed after an advance of some three miles.

German collapse and armistice. Hardly had the German drive been halted when Foch counterattacked on July 18. For three weeks the second battle of the Marne raged. Outnumbered and without adequate supplies, the Germans retreated to the Hindenburg line, the position they had held before they took the offensive in March. Foch gave them no respite. With fresh American troops in France, the reinvigorated Allied armies advanced along the whole Hindenburg line. The German line bent, then broke. By the end of October the German forces had been pushed out of most of France, and Allied armies were advancing through Belgium. With a preponderance of tanks the Allies had smashed trench defenses and were now in open country.

On October 1, Hindenburg notified the kaiser that Germany must sue for peace, and three days later the German chancellor sent a note to President Wilson requesting an end to hostilities. The president's reply notified the German government that peace was impossible so long as the autocratic regime in Germany existed. Although the German chancellor tried to retain the monarchy by introducing certain liberal reforms, it was too late. Revolution broke out in many parts of the country, the kaiser abdicated, and a republic was proclaimed.

While Germany was staggering under the relentless pounding of Foch's armies, the German allies were suffering even greater misfortunes. Bulgaria surrendered on September 30, and Turkey capitulated a month later. Austria gave up the struggle against Italy on November 3; nine days later the Hapsburg empire collapsed when Emperor Charles I fled Vienna for sanctuary in Switzerland.

At five o'clock on the morning of November 11, 1918, in a dining car in the Compiègne Forest, the two German delegates signed the terms of the armistice presented to them by Marshal Foch, the supreme Allied commander. At eleven o'clock the same day, hostilities were halted. Everywhere the news was received with an outburst of unrestrained joy. The world was once more at peace, confronted with the task of binding up its wounds.

Total war, a new reality. The Great War had been a world conflict fought on land, in the air, on the water, and below the water. New inventions—the submarine, the armored tank, poison gas, and the airplane—made warfare more deadly. And to these four inventions were added a host of other devices either created or improved by technology. The internal-combustion engine powered not only trucks, staff cars, and ambulances but also tanks, planes, and dirigibles. The Diesel engine was used for the first time to drive warships. And technology countered technology. Mightier dreadnoughts were met with submarines, improved mines, and faster torpedo boats; more mobile armies had to face land mines, better hand grenades, flame throwers, and machine guns. Giant guns—like the German "Big Bertha," which bombarded Paris for months—lobbed shells more than seventy-five miles, and planes and dirigibles bombed targets hundreds of miles from their bases.

Unprecedented technological advances alone did not account for the scope and impact of World War I. Perhaps more lasting in its effects upon the ordinary citizen was the cold fact that modern warfare had branched out into a whole new dimension—the non-military struggle to sustain the will of the civilian population to win through to victory. In fact, the war on the home front rivaled that fought on the battlefield. As an English observer put it:

The War has passed out of the phase of a mere battle. It is now a contest between the will and determination of whole nations to continue a life-and-death struggle in which "battle" takes a very small part.[2]

The civilians of the belligerent nations were urged to eat less food, buy more bonds, and manufacture more shells. Men and women were deluged by a barrage of propaganda inciting them to hate the enemy, to believe in the righteousness of their cause, and to support the war effort without complaint. Civil liberties suffered, and in some cases distinguished citizens were imprisoned for opposing the war effort. Governments took over the control of their national economies. Strikes were outlawed, wages as well as prices were regulated, and currencies and foreign trade were rigidly controlled.

Total war was a solvent eroding many of the conventions and attitudes of the Victorian era that had come down to the twentieth century. In many lands women demanded and received the right to engage in a wide variety of occupations and to be taken seriously in politics. Social conventions were altered, and standards were relaxed. Young people enjoyed more liberties, and old age no longer received automatic respect. As all classes were merged in the caldron of war, social barriers tended to blur.

THE PEACE SETTLEMENT

Wilson's blueprint for peace. Wilson had declared that the war was:

. . . a war for freedom and justice and self-government amongst all the nations of the world, a war to make the world safe for the peoples who live upon it and have made it their own, the German people themselves included.[3]

In January 1918, in an address before both houses of Congress, the president had enunciated his famous Fourteen Points as the basis for a lasting peace. With this speech, Wilson made himself a new kind of world leader, representing not wealth and power but morality and justice. Millions of men and women, at home and abroad, in the Allied nations, in the enemy countries, and in neutral states, flocked to his standard. The Fourteen Points seemed to open the way not only for a speedy cessation of hostilities but for a peace that could endure.

Although thirty-two Allied nations were represented at the Paris Peace Conference, three men made the major decisions— David Lloyd George, prime minister of Great Britain; Georges Clemenceau, premier of France; and Woodrow Wilson, president of the United States. Formal proceedings began on January 18, 1919; the treaty was signed on June 28.

The first five points were general in nature and may be summarized as follows: "Open covenants openly arrived at"; freedom of the seas in peace and in war alike; the removal of all economic barriers and the establishment of an equality of trade conditions among all nations; reduction of national armaments; a readjustment of all colonial claims, giving the interests of the population concerned equal weight with the claims of the government whose title was to be determined. The next eight points dealt with specific issues involving the evacuation and restoration of Allied territory, self-determination for submerged nationalities, and the redrawing of European boundaries along national lines. The fourteenth point in Wilson's speech contained the germ of the League of Nations: the formation of a general association of nations under specific covenants for the purpose of affording mutual guarantees of political independence and territorial integrity to great and small states alike.

Cross-currents at the peace conference. All the thirty-two Allied powers sent delegations to the peace conference at Paris, but the vanquished nations were not accorded representation. This exclusion was not in the spirit of Wilson's idealistic pronouncements before the armistice.

Three personalities dominated the Paris Conference: Wilson, Lloyd George, and Clemenceau. In the eyes of the war-weary and disillusioned peoples of Europe, Wilson was a veritable Messiah. But it soon became apparent that he would be unable to prevent his ideals and promises from being sabotaged by the other Allied statesmen in Paris. Against the wily Lloyd George and the cynical Clemenceau, the idealistic American scholar had little chance of holding his own. In addition, certain factions in Congress were preparing to repudiate his program for a more just and better-ordered world. A far-seeing armchair statesman handicapped by a cold and imperious personality, Wilson (1856-1924) was so thoroughly convinced of the validity of his own ideas that he seldom recognized a need to "sell" them to others and often refused to consider the possibility of merit in the ideas of his opponents.

Lloyd George (1863-1945), the prime minister of Great Britain, was a consummately clever politician who could use the arts of diplomatic bargaining with rare skill. He came to the conference just after a triumphant victory at the polls in which he had promised the electorate the "hanging of the kaiser" and the "squeezing of the German lemon until the pips squeaked." He was determined to destroy the commercial and naval power of Germany, to acquire the German colonies, and to compel Germany to pay a large share of the cost of the war.

The strongest personality of the conference was the French premier—the seventy-seven-year-old Clemenceau (1841-1929), sole survivor of the French Assembly that had protested the loss of Alsace-Lorraine in 1871. His burning ambition was to ensure the security of France in the future; his formula was restitution, reparations, and guarantees.

Prearmistice peace principles and secret treaties. The Germans had surrendered with the understanding that the peace would in the main follow the Fourteen Points and in general coincide with the speeches of Wilson. In February 1918 the president had announced, "There shall be no annexations, no contributions, no punitive damages"; and on July 4 he had said that every question must be settled "upon the basis of the free acceptance of that settlement by the people immediately concerned."

Complicating the promises of Wilson, especially the Fourteen Points, were the secret treaties made by the Allies during the war. In 1915 Italy had been induced to enter the conflict by promises of Austrian territory which would make the Adriatic an Italian sea. Italy was also promised an extension of its African colonies and a sphere of influence in Asiatic Turkey. Nearly all these proposed transfers violated the Wilsonian concept of national self-determination.

Other secret treaties gave Russia the right to take over the Dardanelles and Constantinople, Rumania the right to secure substantial territory at the expense of Austria-Hungary, and Japan the right to retain the German territory of Kiaochow in China. In return for Arab aid against the Turks, Britain had made vague promises of independence for the Arabs. In 1916, however, Britain and France had divided Turkish Iraq and Syria into their respective spheres of interest. Palestine, with its holy places, was to be placed under international administration; and in 1917 Great Britain pledged its support of the "establishment in Palestine of a national home for the Jewish people."

President Wilson professed ignorance of the existence of the treaties, but their contents were common knowledge before the end of the war. In fact, in 1917 the Bolshevik government had released their texts, which were then published in American and English newspapers. Wilson may have believed that the secret agreements could be ignored, for he hoped to sway European statesmen to the necessity of founding the peace on his principles.

The League Covenant. When the statesmen assembled in their first plenary meeting on January 18, 1919, the first difficulty arose over the question of a league of nations. Wilson was insistent that the initial work of the conference must be to agree upon a covenant of a league of nations which was to be made part of the peace treaty. After much wrangling, the Covenant was approved by the full conference in April 1919. In order to gain support for the League, however, Wilson had to compromise on other matters. His Fourteen Points were thus partially repudiated, but he believed firmly that an imperfect treaty incorporating the League was better than a perfect one without it.

The Covenant of the League of Nations specified its aims: "to guarantee international cooperation and to achieve international peace and security." To implement this goal,

Article x, the key article of the Covenant, stipulated that:

The Members of the League undertake to respect and preserve as against external aggression the territorial integrity and existing political independence of all Members of the League. In case of any such aggression or in case of any threat or danger of such aggression the Council shall advise upon the means by which this obligation shall be fulfilled.[4]

Redrawing German boundaries. Redrawing German boundaries was another task of the conference. Alsace-Lorraine was turned over to France without question, in accordance with one of the Fourteen Points. Three districts formerly belonging to Germany were given to Belgium, after a dubious plebiscite conducted by Belgian officials. Another plebiscite gave half of Schleswig back to Denmark.

Clemenceau and Marshal Foch were determined that a buffer state consisting of the German territory west of the Rhine should be established under the domination of France. In the eyes of the American and British representatives, such a crass violation of the principle of self-determination would only breed future wars; and a compromise was therefore offered Clemenceau, which he accepted. The territory in question was to be occupied by Allied troops for a period of from five to fifteen years; and, furthermore, a zone extending fifty kilometers east of the Rhine was to be demilitarized. In addition, Wilson and Lloyd George agreed that the United States and Great Britain would guarantee France against aggression. The importance of this pledge cannot be overemphasized.

Along Germany's eastern frontier the creation of the Polish Corridor, which separated East Prussia from the rest of Germany, raised grave problems. Large sections of German territory in which there were Polish majorities but also a goodly number of Germans were turned over to Poland. (The land in question had been taken from Poland by Prussia in the eighteenth century.) A section of Silesia was likewise given to Poland, but only after a plebiscite. Danzig, a German city, was handed over to the League for administration. All in all, Germany lost 25,000 square miles inhabited by some six million people.

Although Clemenceau also claimed the Saar Basin, a rich coal area, this was not given outright to France but instead was placed under the administration of the League. The French were given ownership of the mines to compensate for the destruction of their own in northern France. It was agreed, however, that after fifteen years a plebiscite would be conducted to determine the future status of the Saar region.

The mandate system. A curious mixture of idealism and revenge determined the allocation of the German colonies and certain territories belonging to Turkey. Because outright annexation would look too much like unvarnished imperialism, it was suggested that the colonies be turned over to the League, which in turn would give them to certain of its members to administer. The colonies were to be known as mandates, and praiseworthy precautions were taken that the mandates would be administered for the well-being and development of the inhabitants. Once a year the mandatory powers were to present a detailed account of their administration of the territories to the League. The mandate system as such was a step forward in colonial administration, but Germany nevertheless was deprived of all colonies, with the excuse that it could not rule them justly or efficiently.

Reparations. Germany had accepted the armistice terms with the understanding that damage done to the Allied civilian population was to be paid for. At the conference the British and French delegates went much further by demanding that Germany pay the total cost of the war, including pensions. The American representatives maintained that such a claim was contrary to the prearmistice Allied terms and succeeded in achieving a compromise. It was agreed that, except in the case of Belgium, Germany was not to pay the entire cost of the war, but only war damages, which included damage to civilians and the cost of pensions. These payments, called reparations, were exacted on the ground that Germany was responsible for the war.

Although the Allies agreed that Germany should be made to pay, they were unable to decide on the sum. Finally it was decided that a committee should fix the amount and report no later than May 1921. In the meantime Germany was to begin making payments which, by the time the reparations committee's report was ready, would total nearly $5,000,000,000.

Other Allied demands. Germany was required to hand over most of its merchant fleet as well as vast amounts of coal, tools, and machinery. In military matters demands were even more drastic. Germany was permitted a standing army of only 100,000 men, the size of the fleet was drastically reduced, possession of military airplanes was forbidden, and munitions plants were to be placed under close supervision. The treaty also provided that the kaiser be tried by a tribunal "for a supreme offense against international morality and the sanctity of treaties." But the kaiser had fled to Holland after the German revolution; and when that country refused to surrender him, no further steps were taken by the Allied governments, which had inserted the clause providing for the punishment of the kaiser largely for home consumption.

The Treaty of Versailles signed. The Treaty of Versailles was built around the concept that Germany was responsible for the war. The German foreign minister, upon receiving the treaty terms on May 7, 1919, made this statement:

It is demanded of us that we shall confess ourselves to be the only ones guilty of the war. . . . We are far from declining any responsibility . . . but we energetically deny that Germany and its people . . . were alone guilty. . . . In the last fifty years the Imperialism of all the European States has chronically poisoned the international situation. . . .[5]

The menace of Allied invasion gave the Germans no alternative but to sign the treaty; the government therefore instructed its delegates to accept the treaty for Germany "without abandoning her view in regard to the unheard-of injustice of the conditions of the peace." On June 28, on the anniversary of the assassination of Archduke Francis Ferdinand and in the Hall of Mirrors at Versailles where the German empire had been proclaimed in 1871, the treaty was signed.

Other World War treaties. Treaties were also concluded with the rest of the Central Powers. The treaty with Austria—the Treaty of St.-Germain (1919)—legalized the nationalist movements of Czechs, Poles, and Slavs and converted the remainder of the empire into the separate states of Austria and Hungary. By the treaty terms, the Austrian empire was reduced in area from 116,000 to 32,000 square miles and in population from 28,500,000 to 6,000,000. Forbidden was *Anschluss*—union of the Germans in Austria with their kinsmen in the new German republic. The treaty also awarded sections of Austria to Italy—the territory south of the Brenner Pass, South Tyrol, Trentino with its 250,000 Austrian Germans, and the northeastern coast of the Adriatic with its large number of Slavs. To complete Italy's acquisition of the Adriatic, it was necessary to obtain a slice of the Dalmation coast and the port of Fiume. The latter, however, was the natural port for the newly created state of Yugoslavia and had not been promised to Italy in 1915. Wilson declared that the Italian claim was in flat contradiction to the principle of self-determination, and a controversy ensued which nearly wrecked the peace conference. The explosive issue of Italian claims in the Adriatic was settled in 1920, when Italy renounced its claims to Dalmatia and when Fiume became an independent state. Four years later, however, Fiume was ceded to Italy.

By the Treaty of Sèvres (1920) the Ottoman empire was placed on the operating table of power politics, dissected, and divided among Greece, Britain, and France. Greece was given nearly all of European Turkey, almost up to the suburbs of Constantinople, and some islands in the Aegean Sea. The city of Smyrna was put under Greek administration, but Armenia achieved full independence. Syria was mandated to France, and Palestine and Iraq to England. To the Arabs, these transfers to Britain and France were a violation of wartime pledges. As for the

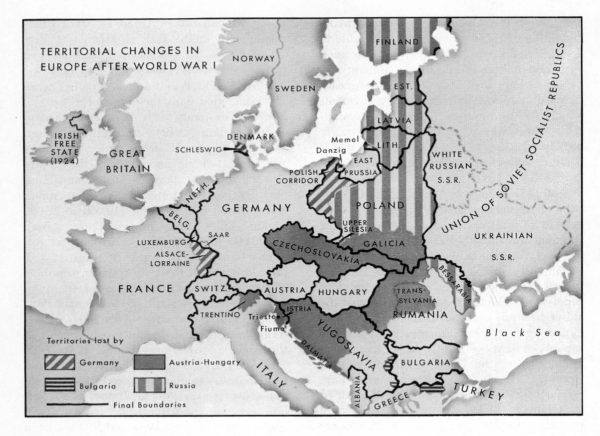

Straits, this strategic body of water was to be under international control.

Two other treaties affected the Balkans. By the Treaty of Trianon (1920), Hungary lost territory to Czechoslovakia, Yugoslavia, and Rumania. The Treaty of Neuilly (1919) cut off Bulgaria from the Aegean Sea, imposed an indemnity, and provided for compulsory demilitarization. Bulgaria lost nearly one million subjects.

Evaluation of the peace settlement. During the first postwar decade, tons of paper and barrels of ink were used in hot justification or acrid denunciation of the peace settlement. On the whole, the peace settlement was inadequate and unrealistic. In his indictment of the economic provisions of the peace, the world-famous economist John Maynard Keynes wrote in 1919:

The treaty includes no provisions for the economic rehabilitation of Europe,—nothing to make the defeated Central Empires into good neighbours, nothing to stabilise the new States of Europe, nothing to reclaim Russia; nor does it promote in any way a compact of economic solidarity amongst the Allies themselves; no arrangement was reached at Paris for restoring the disordered finances of France and Italy, or to adjust the systems of the Old World and the New.[6]

Out of the peace settlement democracy seemingly emerged stronger than ever before, and nationalism clearly reached its apex in Europe. Wilson's insistence upon the self-determination of nations resulted in an almost universal victory for the principle of national self-determination; the number of states in Europe increased by nearly fifty per cent. While many people welcomed the emancipation of the heretofore submerged nationalities, others were disturbed at what they described as the "Balkanization of Europe."

One of the weakest aspects of the peace settlement was the complete disregard of Russia. While the peace conference was in session, Russia was convulsed by civil war, complicated by the intervention of Japanese, American, French, and British troops. On condition that the Allies stop aiding the anti-Communist forces and restore normal diplomatic and commercial relations, the Soviets offered to accept the huge prewar debts contracted by the tsar's government. In their belief that the Communist government would soon collapse, statesmen at Paris did not take the offer seriously. Whether some kind of agreement leading to Russian participation in the peace settlement could have been worked out is uncertain; even so, the idea was not seriously explored. George F. Kennan, an American authority on Soviet affairs, maintains that the sacrifice of this possibility had tremendous consequences for "the long-term future of both the Russian and American peoples and indeed of mankind generally."[7]

Some historians blame the errors of the treaties upon the defects of the personalities who made them. This view oversimplifies the problem and furthermore assumes that the statesmen at Paris were free agents. In truth, the delegates were the prisoners of their own people, who had been so influenced by propaganda, whose enmity was so bitter, and whose knowledge was so meager that any indication of reasonableness shown to the ex-enemies would have meant the repudiation of the peacemakers themselves. Perhaps no other group of leaders could have made a better peace.

PROBLEMS OF

STABILITY AND SECURITY

The "new world" and the powers. The unity among the Allies wrought by the necessities of war did not long survive victory. During the Paris Conference and in the years following, serious differences emerged over such basic issues as reparations, war debts, disarmament, and the structure and functions of the League of Nations.

Italy was angry with its former allies for being so niggardly with the spoils of war. Great Britain was ready to let bygones be bygones; the "nation of shopkeepers" was anxious to see prosperity return to central Europe. On the other hand, France feared a resurgent Germany and was determined to enforce all the peace treaties.

And what of the vanquished? Germany was resentful of the peace settlement and determined to repudiate it. Hungary, Austria, and Bulgaria held similar views. Alone of the defeated powers, Turkey was fairly content, as it had been able to secure better treatment in a new treaty—the Treaty of Lausanne (see p. 698).

United States refuses to join the League. In 1919, the year of its establishment, the League of Nations constituted a promising agency for improving the status of mankind everywhere. At the outset, however, it suffered a great blow to its prestige: the United States refused to become a member of the League.

During the war Americans had been proud of Wilson's proposals for a new world order. But the peace settlement pleased few; chauvinists found it too lenient, and liberals found it too harsh. Seeking to discredit Wilson, some members of the Republican party agitated against the Treaty of Versailles. After his return to the United States in July 1919, the president pressed the Senate for ratification of the treaty, which carried with it membership in the League. In defiance the senators demanded a number of important reservations.

It was all or nothing with Wilson. Refusing to accept the watered-down version of the League Covenant insisted upon by the isolationist faction in the Senate, Wilson sent word to twenty of his supporters in the Senate to vote against the treaty. The final vote was 49 to 35, seven votes short of the necessary two thirds. Feeling that half a loaf was better than none, many historians believe that Wilson should have accepted the amended treaty. In 1920 Wilson's program was repudiated at the polls, for the victory of Warren G. Harding, the Republican candidate for president, meant that the Covenant never was to be ratified by the Senate.

While the inflexible Wilson must bear some of the responsibility for the rejection of the

League, the president prophetically warned his people of the price they would one day have to pay for turning their backs on the world. In the main Wilson's words had fallen on deaf ears. The chaos of the future and the coming of World War II were hidden in the yet unturned pages of history. The mass of Americans lapsed into complacent isolationism and normalcy with Harding.

France and the Little Entente. For a number of reasons, the French did not place much faith in the League as an instrument for their security. In addition to the refusal by the United States to join the League, both the United States and Britain had scrapped the treaty guaranteeing France from aggression.

Overwhelmed by this blow to its hopes, France set about obtaining allies on the Continent. In 1920 a defensive alliance was made with Belgium. Overtures were then made to Poland, which France had aided in its war against Communist Russia (p. 670); in 1922 the two states concluded a treaty directed against future danger from Germany. In 1924 Czechoslovakia signed a treaty with France that pledged the signatories to take concerted measures in the event of a union between Germany and Austria or an attempt by either Germany or Hungary to restore their ruling houses. Not content with these allies, the French foreign office negotiated similar pacts with Rumania (1926) and Yugoslavia (1927). During 1920 and 1921 these smaller states had also made treaties of mutual assistance among themselves; this diplomatic bloc (Czechoslovakia, Rumania, Yugoslavia) was known as the Little Entente, and its power rested upon extensive French loans and military collaboration. For a brief ten years, France with its Little Entente dominated Europe militarily.

The shift to a peace economy. One of the chief obstacles to postwar peace was the confused and desperate situation into which the European economy had been plunged. The stakes for which the war was fought seemed substantial in 1914, but the price paid to achieve them was tragically high in lives lost and property destroyed. It has been estimated that the probable cost of the war was about $350,000,000,000. It was the financial

consequences of war that did most to continue the enmity between victors and vanquished and also to alienate the nations, formerly allies, which had defeated Germany.

The armistice found the world's commercial and industrial structure geared to a war basis. There was an urgent need for getting back to a peacetime economy, which meant the production of peacetime goods instead of munitions, the demobilization of millions of soldiers, and the absorption of these veterans into the business structure. But it was not easy to return to the prosperous world economy that had existed before 1914.

The conflict had brought about many changes in world trade. Europe in particular had suffered a serious decline in its share of the world's commerce because of war blockades, the reduction of consumer purchasing power, the loss of shipping and other transportation facilities, and the capture of overseas markets by the United States, Latin America, and Japan. This loss was felt keenly by Germany and Great Britain. Furthermore, the peace treaties had multiplied national boundaries, which soon became obstacles to the flow of goods.

Serious problems existed in the domestic economies of the European nations. As a result of the war, the public debts of the participant nations zoomed. In many nations these increases were accompanied by the circulation of large amounts of paper money, not backed by adequate reserves. Furthermore, the war left a legacy of tension between economic groups. Labor unions, which had registered significant gains in wages during the war, were determined not to give up their advantages when the fighting ceased.

For a brief period many of these economic problems were obscured by an artificial postwar boom. The peak of prosperity was reached in 1920, after which world trade and industrial activity diminished. Strikes, unemployment, and other industrial problems multiplied; and for the next five years the nations, particularly in Europe, tried to extricate themselves from this economic morass.

The inter-Allied debt problem. The most serious problem facing Europe as it strove to achieve a prosperous peace economy was the revolution in its financial position in relation to the remainder of the world. In 1914 the United States had been a debtor nation, mostly to Europe, for the amount of $3,750,-000,000. The war reversed the situation, and in 1919 the United States was owed more than $10,000,000,000 by its fellow victors. This tremendous debt posed what economists call the transfer problem. Such international obligations could only be paid by the actual transfer of gold or by the sale of goods to the creditor country.

The various Allied nations in Europe had also lent each other funds, with Britain acting as the chief banker. Some of the former Allies argued that the inter-Allied debts were political, that all of them had in effect been poured into a common pool for victory, and that, with victory, all should be canceled.

In the summer of 1922 Great Britain proposed that it collect no more from its debtors —Allies and Germany alike—than the United States collected from Britain itself. It was becoming manifest to British statesmen that Germany would not be able to meet its reparation payments, and without them the payment of the inter-Allied debts—especially the debts owed to the United States—would be extremely difficult, if not impossible, to make. The American government, however, insisted that there was no connection between the inter-Allied debts and German reparations.

Reparations exhaust Germany. The Allies had placed an impossibly heavy burden on Germany. In 1921 the reparations commission fixed the total German indemnities at $32,-000,000,000. The payments were apportioned among the various Allied nations, France being given 52 per cent and the British empire 22 per cent.

In August 1921 Germany made a payment of $250,000,000, which reacted disastrously upon the German currency system. With some justification the Germans claimed that the reparations were impossibly high and that higher tariffs the world over were keeping out German goods. Furthermore, Germany had lost many of its most important economic resources. Nevertheless, the French believed that Germany was able to pay and was deliberately seeking to escape its obligations.

France invades the Ruhr. Indeed, the whole tenor of events since the signing of the armistice had shocked France in particular. The promise of military assistance from its former two main allies in case of aggression had been discarded; the League of Nations seemed a frail reed without America; and now while the United States insisted upon full payment of war debts, Germany seemed about to renege on reparations. France was determined that this should not happen; undeterred by British opposition, French, Belgian, and Italian troops marched into the Ruhr district of Germany in January 1923.

A sorry state of affairs ensued. The French were determined that the inhabitants should work the industries and mines of the Ruhr for the benefit of France. Defying the French army, the Germans went on a general strike. All economic life stopped, and many German officials were imprisoned by the French authorities. France furthermore endeavored to establish a separate state in the Rhineland which would act as a buffer between Germany and France. Nothing hardened the German resolve to revise the Treaty of Versailles more than this invasion of the Ruhr.

The chaotic conditions in the Ruhr gave the *coup de grâce* to the German economic system. The currency failed completely. Inflation skyrocketed the mark into the stratosphere. In January 1923 one American dollar was worth 8695 marks; in November of the same year it took 6,666,666,666,667 marks to equal one dollar!

The French, meanwhile, were learning that they "could not dig German coal with French bayonets." In 1924 the French government offered to settle its difficulties with Germany, whose leaders were equally anxious to negotiate. Public opinion all over the world had been shocked at France's strong-arm tactics in the Ruhr.

The Dawes Plan. About midway in 1925 the worst of the war's aftermath had run its course. Differences between France and England had been patched up, Germany was invited to join the League, the reparations problem was eased, and our former Allies paid their debt installments on schedule.

The French occupation of the Ruhr had proved that attempts to force Germany to pay reparations were futile. It was becoming more and more apparent that the difficulty lay in the staggering total of the reparations. Therefore, an international committee was set up under the chairmanship of the American banker Charles Dawes to examine the whole reparations problem. In the fall of 1924 the Dawes Plan came into operation. No figure was set for the total reparations bill, but the individual payments were decreased and extended over a longer period. A large loan also was floated to aid Germany's recovery and help stabilize its currency. The French cooperated by evacuating the Ruhr.

The Locarno Conference and conciliation. Apart from this encouraging move to solve the reparations problem, there was a spectacular improvement in international politics. Aristide Briand came to the foreign office in France; Gustav Stresemann held the same position in Germany; and in Great Britain foreign affairs were now handled by Sir Austen Chamberlain. All three men believed in pursuing a policy of conciliation in European affairs. Stresemann, bitter foe of France during the war, was now eager to try cooperating with his former enemies. For some time British statesmen had been deploring France's harsh attitude toward Germany, and Briand in Paris was now ready to offer the olive branch to Berlin.

In 1925 a proposal by Stresemann paved the way for a conference held during October of the same year in the little Swiss town of Locarno. For the first time since 1919 the distinction between conquered and conqueror seemed forgotten; the German delegation was cordially received.

After twelve days of negotiation, the delegates to the conference agreed on five treaties, the most important being a treaty of mutual guarantee. Signed by Germany, Great Britain, Belgium, France, and Italy, this agreement guaranteed the existing frontiers along the Rhine, thus reaffirming the provision in the Treaty of Versailles; provided for a demilitarized German zone extending fifty kilometers east of the Rhine; and pledged France, Germany, and Belgium not to invade or resort to war against each other except under certain specified conditions. In case of the violation of these pledges, the nations signing the treaty agreed to assist the injured party.

The Locarno Pact heralded a new era in European affairs. Germany accepted an invitation to join the League of Nations, and there were good grounds for believing that the hatreds of the past war were now on the wane. Referring to the *rapprochement* with Germany, Briand eloquently stated in the French Parliament:

It is undesirable to be continually casting doubts on Germany's goodwill. . . . Stresemann and I talked a new language, the language of Europe.[8]

Organization of the League of Nations. Before we discuss the successes and failures of the League of Nations in the postwar period, let us briefly sketch the outline of its organization. As specified by the Covenant, the League consisted of three principal divisions: the Assembly, the Council, and the Secretariat.

The Assembly, which held annual sessions in Geneva, contained representatives of every member state. Its duties included determining the budget of the League, admitting new members, electing the judges of the World Court in cooperation with the Council, and considering "any matter within the sphere of action of the League or affecting the peace of the world." The Assembly could not make any important decisions without the unanimous consent of its members, and every nation represented in the Assembly had one vote.

The Council was made up of permanent great powers and nonpermanent smaller members. The most important body in the League, it had the specific duties of encouraging disarmament, studying the annual reports submitted by the nations holding colonial mandates, and formulating measures to be taken to protect any state from aggression.

"It is for peace that this hammer works." Hope for international disarmament and cooperation is reflected in this French car-toon, showing Briand smashing his guns, while Stresemann and Sir Austen Chamberlain wait their turn.

The Council dealt with most of the emergencies arising in international affairs.

The Secretariat represented the civil service of the League. Numbering about seven hundred, the personnel of the Secretariat constituted the first example in history of an international civil service whose loyalty was pledged to no single nation but to the interests of all nations in common. All treaties made by members of the League had to be registered with the Secretariat; its fifteen departments had charge of the matters of administrative routine arising from the mandates and dealt with questions relating to disarmament, health problems, the protection of racial minorities, and any other problems, general or special, which the League was considering.

In addition to the Assembly, the Council, and the Secretariat, there were two other important bodies which derived from the Covenant of the League. The first of these was the Permanent Court of International Justice, commonly referred to as the World Court. Its main purpose was to "interpret any disputed point in international law and determine when treaty obligations had been violated." It was also competent to give advisory opinions to the Council or Assembly when asked for them. (By 1937 forty-one states had agreed to place before the World Court all the disputes to which they were a party concerning the interpretation of treaties, questions of international law, problems arising from breaches of international obligations, and the question of reparations arising from such breaches.) The second international body affiliated with the League was the International Labor Organization, pledged "to secure and maintain fair and humane conditions of labor for men, women, and children."

League successes. The League system was not a sure-fire deterrent against aggression, especially if the aggressor was a great power. The teeth of the famous Article x of the Covenant had been removed by the view, pushed mainly by Canada, that while the Council could request members to use armed force against aggression, the final decision to do so must rest with each member.

The record of the League from 1920 to 1930 was one neither of dismal failure nor of complete triumph. In attempting to prevent war, the League achieved some outstanding successes in certain international disputes and failed miserably in others. The Aland Islands affair can be cited as an example of the former.

Lying between Sweden and Finland and claimed by both countries, the Åland Islands dominate the entrance to the Gulf of Bothnia. The quarrel over ownership might have caused war, but the League stepped in. Its decision, given in 1921, was to permit Finland to retain sovereignty over the islands while the inhabitants, mostly Swedes, were to enjoy local self-government. The acceptance of this solution by both parties was a great step forward in the peaceable solution of international problems.

Many of the disputes presented to the League of Nations for settlement concerned boundary problems raised by the peace treaties. The League settled the boundary question between Poland and Germany in the Silesia area and in 1921 halted a serious frontier dispute between Yugoslavia and Albania. In 1924 a menacing quarrel between Turkey and Britain over rich oil deposits in Iraq was also mediated successfully.

The Corfu incident. In 1923 came the first important test of the new world organization —the Corfu incident, involving Italy and Greece. An international commission had been sent to the Balkans to settle the Graeco-Albanian boundary line. During its labors four Italian members of the commission were killed in Greek territory by unknown assailants. Mussolini, the dictator of Italy (see p. 674), immediately dispatched a stiff ultimatum to Greece. In the outrage he saw an opportunity to obtain national glory and a diplomatic triumph for his newborn Fascist regime. Greece refused to accept all the terms of the ultimatum and appealed to the League. Mussolini thereupon ordered a naval squadron to the Greek island of Corfu to bombard the harbor, and Italian marines landed and

took possession of the port. Mussolini let it be known that Italy would refuse to be bound by any action taken by the League.

Confronted by this defiance on the part of a great power, the League sought to escape from a serious situation by turning the dispute over to a council of ambassadors, which ordered Greece to pay Italy the sum of 50,000,000 lire. This amount was duly paid, and the Italian forces evacuated Corfu. But though war had been averted, the League had allowed Italy to defy it—a portent of failures to come.

Other League activities. The effectiveness of the League as a peace agency following the Great War is debatable, but certain of its activities deserve high praise. The League supervised the exchange and repatriation of nearly 500,000 prisoners of war. More than 1,000,000 Greek refugees, victimized by the Graeco-Turkish War of 1921-1922 (see p. 698), were saved from starvation by the League. The League also used its auspices to secure desperately needed financial aid for Austria, Bulgaria, Hungary, and the Free City of Danzig.

More successful than its work in the political field were the League's efforts in the fields of health, humanitarianism, and intellectual activity. The health organization at Geneva concerned itself with perfecting hygienic techniques to decrease epidemics in the various nations. Studies of the causes and control of such diseases as smallpox, anthrax, cancer, and tropical maladies were encouraged. The League also investigated the existence of slavery in certain sections of the world, sought to control the traffic in dangerous drugs, and stood ready to offer assistance when great disasters brought suffering and destruction to any portion of the world's population. It published books and periodicals dealing with national and international problems of all kinds and broadcast important information, particularly in the field of health, from its own radio station.

League efforts toward disarmament. Article VII of the League's Covenant plainly stated that it was the intention of the members to reduce arms to the lowest point consistent with security. It further empowered the Council of the League to formulate plans for disarmament. Little or no progress was made, however, in reducing the heavy burden of armaments. Various bodies set in motion by the League to study the problem and arrive at accepted reductions only ran into interminable obstacles. Perhaps because of its relative military weakness at that time, Russia proposed complete disarmament to League members. When this proposal was made, one of the delegates replied:

If Mr. Litvinov [the Russian member] promises not to be angry I'll narrate a fable. . . . A conference of the beasts once discussed the question of disarmament. The lion spoke first and looking at the eagle suggested the abolition of wings. The eagle turning to the bull asked for the suppression of horns. The bull in his turn regarded the tiger and demanded the elimination of claws. It remained for the bear to speak and he proposed total abolition of every means of attack and defense so that he might take them all into his loving embrace.[9]

Germany, in the meantime, became more and more rebellious. It had already been disarmed and was annoyed that its neighbors could not agree to reduce their armaments.

Naval disarmament. Progress in the direction of naval disarmament was a little more encouraging, although outside the jurisdiction of the League. Intense naval rivalry had developed between Britain, the United States, and Japan after 1919. In consequence, President Harding called a conference at Washington to try to assuage this rivalry.

The Washington Conference (1921-1922) was a dramatic event in international relations. Britain, Japan, and the United States agreed between them to scrap seventy-nine capital ships in such a way as to make the ratio of naval strength 5:5:3 (five units each for Britain and the United States and three units for Japan). To Italy and France were allotted ratios of 1.67. The powers also agreed to a ten-year naval holiday for capital ships.

The Washington Conference registered a definite advance in naval disarmament. But though ships of the largest type were kept down to a reasonable limit, much was left undone. France refused to discuss the limitation of submarines, and no limit was placed upon the building of smaller naval units such as light cruisers and destroyers. Subsequent conferences held at Geneva (1927) and London (1930) registered little progress. In these conclaves, differences developed between Britain and the United States over their relative cruiser strength, and Japan gave evidence of irritation at the restraints agreed to at the Washington Conference.

Hopeful trends on the diplomatic front. Despite some discouragement in achieving a measure of disarmament, the years from 1925 to 1929 have been called Europe's diplomatic high period. In fact, the whole world seemed to have embarked on a new era of international cooperation.

Though initiated outside the League, the Kellogg-Briand Pact seemed to be a triumph for peace and international good will. In 1927 the French prime minister, Briand, proposed that war be renounced or outlawed between France and the United States. Frank B. Kellogg, then secretary of state, persuaded Briand to extend the treaty to all the great powers. In 1928 the representatives of fifteen states signed the pact. But while the Kellogg-Briand Pact provided for the renunciation of war as an instrument of national policy, there were no provisions for enforcing the agreement.

In the field of reparations, a new schedule of payments, known as the Young Plan, was agreed upon in 1930. The total amount to be paid was greatly scaled down. It was also agreed to evacuate Allied troops of occupation from the Rhineland five years in advance of the time stipulated by the Treaty of Versailles. In addition to these encouraging signs, at the end of the 1920's there was a strong movement for European union. Various congresses were held, and Aristide Briand prepared a comprehensive memorandum for a Federal Union.

It was with these promising events in the background that the League of Nations celebrated its tenth birthday in 1929. Speaking at Oxford about the first decade of the League,

General Jan Smuts of South Africa, one of the world's most eminent statesmen and a founder of the international organization, declared:

Looked at in its true light, in the light of the age and of the time-honoured ideas and practice of mankind, we are beholding an amazing thing —we are witnessing one of the great miracles of history. . . . The League may be a difficult scheme to work, but the significant thing is that the Great Powers have pledged themselves to work it . . . [they have] bound themselves to what amounts in effect to a consultative parliament of the world. . . . The great choice is made, the great renunciation is over, and mankind has, as it were at one bound and in the short space of ten years, jumped from the old order to the new. . . .[10]

SUMMARY

The period 1914 to 1929 is a brief segment of the story of world civilization, but it is difficult to find another period in modern times filled with so many significant events. Perhaps the nearest would be the event-packed era of the French Revolution. For all its horror and tragedy, World War I generated ambitious ideals for a better world. In particular, the war was responsible for the establishment of the first international organization on a global scale to resist aggression and encourage peaceful cooperation among nations. It is unfortunate that such plans for creating a world fit for heroes are not made during times of peace rather than as by-products of wars, for negotiations held during a postwar period are inevitably complicated by tensions, hostilities, and problems created or intensified by the conflict.

The five postwar years admirably illustrate this point. In 1919 a war-agonized world expected its sacrifices to be rewarded by better times. But for five years there was little but confusion and strife. The Germans balked at paying astronomical reparations, the French invaded the Ruhr, and chaotic inflation wiped out the stable middle class in Germany. Deprived of its hinterland, Austria —a head without a body—was saved from economic disaster only by the aid of the League of Nations. Many European nations were agitated by revolutions and civil wars. The old thrones of the Hohenzollerns, Hapsburgs, Romanovs, and Ottomans disappeared under the rising tide of republicanism.

From 1925 to 1929, however, the feuds and discontent in Europe gave way to peace, rising prosperity, and international cooperation. The League of Nations registered encouraging, if unspectacular, progress. Differences over war debts and reparations were resolved. Germany's status as a good neighbor was recognized in the Locarno Pact. There was a definite feeling that the worst was over, that the passions released by World War I had burned themselves out.

Unfortunately, these encouraging events— the Locarno agreements, faith in the League, and solution of the reparations and war debts problems—were not true auguries of the times. Adequate disarmament had not been achieved, the world economic recovery and prosperity that had been realized did not rest on sound foundations, and in Germany there festered deep wounds that would not heal without rectification of the injustices of Versailles. And despite the ideological legacy of World War I, expressed as "making the world safe for democracy," this political creed was about to be challenged by new antidemocratic and totalitarian regimes. The unsound and unhealthy condition of world economics plus the ambitions of these new modern tyrannies were to sweep away the hopes of the late 1920's and make the next decade one of the most tragic in all world history.

SUGGESTIONS FOR READING

R. Aron, *The Century of Total War,** Beacon. A thoughtful analysis of what has happened in our world since 1914.

H. S. Hughes, *Contemporary Europe: A History*, Prentice-Hall, 1961. A thought-provoking, interpretive survey of European history since 1900; concentrates on broad trends. See also L. Gottschalk and D. Lach, *Europe and the Modern World Since 1870*, Scott, Foresman, 1954; and C. E. Black and E. C. Helmreich, *Twentieth Century Europe*, Knopf, 1959.

F. P. Chambers, C. P. Harris, and C. C. Bailey, *This Age of Conflict: A Contemporary World History, 1914 to the Present*,

*Indicates an inexpensive paperbound edition.

Harcourt, Brace, 1950; E. N. Anderson, *Modern Europe in World Perspective, 1914 to the Present,* Holt, 1950. Recommended general surveys of world history since 1914.

H. Holborn, *The Political Collapse of Europe,* Knopf, 1951. A brief and challenging examination and interpretation of the breakdown of the old political order in Europe, first manifested by World War I.

C. R. M. F. Cruttwell, *A History of the Great War, 1914-1918,* Oxford, 1936. The most useful general history available.

C. B. Falls, *The Great War,** Capricorn; G. L. McEntree, *Military History of the World War,* Scribner's, 1937. Two deftly written military histories. A brief résumé is B. H. Liddell Hart, *The War in Outline, 1914-1918,* Modern Lib., 1939.

Highly recommended special works on World War I include J. Remak, *Sarajevo: The Story of a Political Murder,* Criterion, 1959; L. Stallings, ed., *The First World War: A Photographic History,* Simon and Schuster, 1933; A. Moorehead, *Gallipoli,** Ballantine; D. Macintyre, *Jutland,* Norton, 1958; L. Wolff, *In Flanders Fields: The 1917 Campaign,** Ballantine; and H. Rudin, *Armistice, 1918,* Yale, 1944.

F. P. Chambers, *The War Behind the War, 1914-1918,* Harcourt, Brace, 1939. Describes the developments on the home fronts.

Perhaps the most famous of the realistic World War I novels is E. M. Remarque, *All Quiet on the Western Front* (many editions), which deals with the German infantryman. J. Romains, *Verdun,* Knopf, 1939; and H. Cobb, *Paths of Glory,** Dell, concern the French army. The best works about Americans are W. March, *Company K,** Signet; J. Dos Passos, *Three Soldiers,* Modern Lib., 1932; and E. Hemingway, *A Farewell to Arms* (many editions).

H. G. Nicholson, *Peacemaking, 1919,* Harcourt, Brace, 1939; P. Birdsall, *Versailles Twenty Years After,* Reynal, 1941. Two brief, well-balanced studies of the Paris Peace Conference.

J. M. Keynes, *The Economic Consequences of the Peace,* Harcourt, Brace, 1920. The most famous attack on the Versailles settlement. E. Mantoux, *The Carthaginian Peace, or the Economic Consequences of Mr. Keynes,* Scribner's, 1952, is an answer to Keynes.

A. S. Link, *Wilson the Diplomatist: A Look at His Major Foreign Policies,* Johns Hopkins, 1957; T. A. Bailey, *Wilson and the Peacemakers,* Macmillan, 1947. Two balanced accounts of America's involvement in the war. Highly critical of Wilson are W. Millis, *The Road to War: America, 1914-1917,* Houghton Mifflin, 1935; and C. C. Tansill, *America Goes to War,* Little, Brown, 1938.

I. Bowman, *The New World: Problems in Political Geography,* World Book, 1922. The fullest treatment of the territorial aspects of the peace.

F. P. Walters, *A History of the League of Nations,* 2 vols., Oxford, 1952. The most comprehensive account of the successes and failures of the League.

G. M. Gathorne-Hardy, *A Short History of International Affairs, 1920-1939,* Oxford, 1950. Recognized as one of the best interpretations of the interwar years.

E. H. Carr, *The Twenty Years' Crisis, 1919-1939,* Macmillan, 1946. A stimulating interpretation of interwar diplomacy.

G. A. Craig and F. Gilbert, *The Diplomats, 1919-1939,* Princeton, 1953. An illuminating and authoritative commentary upon the conduct of international relations; cast in the form of biographical essays.

A. Wolfers, *Britain and France Between Two Wars: Conflicting Strategies of Peace Since Versailles,* Harcourt, Brace, 1940. Analyzes the problems which arose from the peace treaties and which undermined collective security. See also W. M. Jordan, *Great Britain, France, and the German Problem, 1918-1939,* Oxford, 1943, which is particularly good on reparations and arms control.

CHAPTER 28

Opposing Ways of Life

THE POLITICAL SCENE: 1918-1930

Introduction. The events of the early 1920's were to smash the assumption underlying many of the decisions made at Versailles—that Europe's political traditions and economic strength had survived the war without critical impairment. Since western society had moved forward to middle-class democracy and to unprecedented industrial growth and economic well-being after the previous struggle for Continental hegemony—namely, the Napoleonic Wars—why should it not surge forward after 1918? However widespread the belief in European recovery, the analogy was faulty in both its political and economic implications.

In the Europe that emerged from the First World War, the continuity of political tradition was disturbed. Three great imperial dynasties which had helped arbitrate the destinies of prewar Europe—the Romanovs in Russia, the Hohenzollerns in Germany, and the Hapsburgs in Austria-Hungary—had disappeared. With its Communist regime openly dedicated to the subversion of capitalism, Russia had in fact retreated beyond the pale of western society and was regarded as a pariah to be kept in isolation by a political and ideological *cordon sanitaire*. The treaty makers of Versailles plainly had no use for the Bolsheviks—an attitude fully reciprocated by the new masters of the Kremlin.

The second of the great empires—Germany—had been stripped of its overseas possessions and of much valuable territory within Europe itself; it had been saddled with a huge war indemnity; and, most important of all, it was made to bear the onus of war guilt. Instead of having a stake in the retention of the status quo, as was the case with defeated France after 1815, humiliated Germany appeared to have everything to gain from scrapping the Versailles blueprints for a postwar world. Nor could the disappearance of the Austro-Hungarian empire be counted as a factor for postwar stability. In remapping the former Hapsburg dominions, the statesmen at Versailles left potential danger spots in central and eastern Europe. The newly created democracies constituted a break with prewar political traditions; under conditions of postwar dislocation and hardship, their citizens were called upon to experiment with a form of government new to their experience.

In the economic sphere, prewar and postwar Europe presented no less striking contrasts. The prewar European industrial complex, which made possible a steady rise in living standards for an ever increasing population, rested on a number of factors: large overseas commerce and foreign investment, colonies that produced essential raw materials and served as markets for manufactured goods, and, within Europe itself, the maintenance of a well-developed transportation system and a constant flow of goods between nations. After the peace treaties went into effect and the wartime economic boom subsided, the prewar system of economic interdependence was replaced in many areas by economic nationalism, high tariff walls, and a new emphasis on self-sufficiency. In central Europe especially, where the large Austro-Hungarian empire had permitted the free flow of goods over a wide area, there was now a multiplicity of nations, each of which was trying to sell its goods to its neighbors but closing its frontiers to imports. Such nationalism in the economic sphere was certain to fan the flames of political nationalism as well, and thereby create new areas of conflict.

Prior to the First World War, liberal democracy had stood in direct opposition to reactionary autocracy, itself on the wane in Europe before the surge of technology and mass education. Now, in the postwar era, the forces of democracy were confronted by dynamic new rivals, ideologies born of the extreme Left (communism) and extreme Right (fascism) but united in their denial of democratic values. The struggle for the minds and allegiances of men, as well as for the survival or destruction of traditional humanistic values, had taken a new and ominous turn.

As the title indicates, this chapter is the story of the growing competition of ideologies, a tragic tale set against a background of postwar depression and disillusionment and of cynical ruthlessness marching roughshod over apathy and defeatism. While the previous chapter carried the account of international relations up to the end of 1929, we shall concentrate now on the political, economic, and social forces operating within the western nations.

DICTATORSHIP OF THE
PROLETARIAT IN RUSSIA

Prelude to revolution in Russia. In the years immediately preceding the outbreak of World War I, the tsar of Russia, Nicholas II, displayed a total lack of skill in governing his country. By ignoring the Duma, he weakened the new legislative body. In addition, he remained aloof from a series of pressing economic problems. Low wages and intolerable working conditions created discontent among the growing number of industrial workers, and strikes took place more and more frequently. The peasants were also dissatisfied; they wanted land reforms to break up large estates and to distribute agricultural returns more equitably.

The First World War exposed the inefficiency of the tsarist government. As early as 1915 it became apparent that the military machinery was badly disorganized. But the tsar brusquely refused the Duma's request for more power to rectify conditions. By the end of 1916 the situation within Russia became chaotic.

The revolution begins. On March 3, 1917, a strike occurred in a factory in St. Petersburg. Within a week nearly all the workers in the city were idle, and street fighting broke out. On March 11 the tsar dismissed the Duma and ordered the strikers to return to their jobs. These orders precipitated the revolution. The Duma refused to disband, the strikers held mass meetings in defiance of the government, and the army openly sided with the workers. A few days later a provisional gov-

A Communist poster from the days of the Russian civil war of 1918-1920 calls for the triumph of Bolshevik forces over the counterrevolutionary army led by Denikin during the struggle for the Donets Basin, one of the main coal-producing and industrial areas in Russia. The poster read: "The Donets coal must be ours! When there is no coal—the factories are shut. When there is no coal—the trains stop. Until the Don is ours —hunger is with us. Victory over the Denikin bands—victory over the hunger."

ernment, headed by the moderate liberal Prince Lvov, was named by the Duma, and the following day the tsar abdicated. Dominated by liberal middle-class representatives, the Duma hoped to achieve a political but not an economic revolution.

Meanwhile the Marxist socialists in St. Petersburg had formed a soviet (council) of workers' and soldiers' deputies to oppose the tsar. Determined that a thoroughgoing change should take place in accordance with Marxist teachings, the radical soviet bided its time and for a few months cooperated with the provisional government.

In July, Lvov resigned and was succeeded by Alexander Kerensky, who was more pro-gressive than his predecessor but not radical enough for the Bolsheviks. While Kerensky's government marked time, the soviet in St. Petersburg extended its organization. All over the country local soviets were set up, and the Bolsheviks created effective propaganda under the slogan "Peace, Land, and Bread." Although they were assisted in part by funds from Germany, which hoped to weaken the Russian military effort, the driving force behind the Bolsheviks was Lenin, who in 1917 had been spirited out of exile in Switzerland by the German government and taken in a sealed railroad car to the Russian frontier.

After many behind-the-scenes maneuvers, the soviets seized control of the government in November 1917, and Kerensky and his moderate provisional government were driven into exile. Lenin's coup d'état was an amazing feat. With audacity, careful organization, and astute propaganda, he had placed a party with a membership estimated at 30,000 in control of a nation of more than 170,000,000 people.

It is one of the ironies of history that Karl Marx himself despised the Russians. Furthermore, he had prophesied that his doctrines would take root in the most advanced industrial capitalist economies, in England or in Germany, where, he argued, the progressive degradation of the industrial proletariat would fan the flames of revolution. He had not foreseen his system of socialism first coming to power in a feudal, agrarian society like Russia's, in which industrialism had been introduced late in the nineteenth century against a background of labor exploitation, underground conspiracy, and police suppression. Because there existed no sufficiently strong middle class to provide a social soil in which liberal-democratic values could grow, Marxism—an importation dedicated to the achievement of a new social order through violence—seemed ideally suited to flourish in Russia.

The Bolsheviks triumphant. The Bolshevik coup was met by immediate opposition; a powerful group of counterrevolutionists termed White Russians rebelled against the

Communists. To keep Russia in the war, the Allied powers sent troops to aid the White Russians, who were eager to continue the conflict with the Central Powers. (Lenin, on the other hand, had repeatedly declared that the World War was an imperialist conflict between bourgeois interests, and the Allies were aware that the Bolsheviks had agreed to negotiate a separate peace with Germany.)

At first the White Russians scored substantial successes. The fortunes of Lenin and the Bolsheviks hit a low point when they signed the harsh Treaty of Brest Litovsk with Germany in March 1918. Then, with the end of World War I and the withdrawal of British and American troops from Russian soil, the Bolsheviks were able to concentrate their energies against the White Russians, and the tide turned. In July 1918 the members of the royal family had been shot, and a ghastly reign of terror held sway within Russia as the Red Army and the Cheka (the secret police) destroyed all "enemies" of the revolution. By 1920 all White Russian resistance had been crushed, and about one million White Russian anti-Communist refugees were scattered over the earth.

Lenin's contribution to Marxist thought. As we have seen (see p. 575), Lenin had made an important contribution to Marxist theory that set the pattern by which socialism in Russia would be guided. Opposing all democratic parliamentary procedures, such as an officially recognized opposition party, he believed that the new order should be established by a revolutionary "dictatorship of the proletariat" under Bolshevik leadership. The opposition group, the Mensheviks, charged that Lenin was confusing the dictatorship *of* the proletariat with dictatorship *over* the proletariat.

As a Marxist, Lenin accepted the two-revolutions sequence—that is, that the proletarian-socialist revolution must be preceded by a bourgeois-democratic revolution. The toppling of the tsarist regime in March 1917 and its replacement by a provisional government made up of moderates and liberals was interpreted by Lenin as the first or bourgeois-democratic revolution in the Marxist sequence. His coup d'état in November 1917 engineered the second or proletarian-socialist revolution. Moreover, this decisive step sealed the fate of the Mensheviks.

The state: theory and practice. Many orthodox Marxists believed that once the dictatorship of the proletariat had liquidated the bourgeoisie, the way would be open for the progressive disappearance of the state and the abolition of the standing army and the bureaucracy, the two most characteristic institutions of the centralized bourgeois state. While Lenin thought that the state would eventually wither away, at the same time he believed that during the dictatorship of the proletariat the latter's power must be wielded by an "iron party" (the Bolsheviks). Ironically enough, the events which transpired between Lenin's coup d'état in 1917 and his death seven years later served not to weaken but to strengthen the role of the state in Russia.

The state was known as the Russian Socialist Federated Soviet Republic (R.S.F.S.R.). As the power of this government grew and the anti-Bolshevik forces were repelled, the jurisdiction of the R.S.F.S.R. expanded. In 1922 the Union of Soviet Socialist Republics (U.S.S.R.) was established, consisting of four constituent socialist republics: the original R.S.F.S.R., the Ukraine, White Russia, and Transcaucasia.

The constitution, adopted in 1924, established a federal system of government based on a succession of soviets which were set up in the villages, factories, and cities and in larger regions. This pyramid of soviets in each constituent republic culminated in the All-Union Congress of Soviets, which was at the apex of the federal government. But while it appeared that the congress exercised sovereign power, this body was actually governed by the Communist party, which in turn was controlled by the Politburo, a small elite group composed of five members, with Lenin as chairman. The second major center of power was the Secretariat for the Central Committee of the party. The concentration of authority and power in the party was justified as "democratic centralism." So great did the authority of the Communist party become over the formation and administration of policy that before Lenin's death in 1924 it could be said without exaggeration that party and state were one. Consequently, whoever controlled the former must be master of the latter as well.

Lenin championed the program of "from each according to his ability; to each according to his needs" and believed in the principle of "maximum income," by which no state employee would receive a salary higher than a qualified worker. Following both Marx and Engels, Lenin subscribed to the ultimate goal of large-scale collective farming and the elimination of private ownership of land.

The period of war communism. The period which lasted from the consolidation of the Bolshevik Revolution in 1918 until 1921 is known as the period of war communism, when the Bolsheviks sought to apply undiluted Marxist principles to the Soviet economy. Banks, railroads, and shipping were nationalized; the money economy was restricted; and private property was abolished.

Strong opposition to this program soon developed. The peasants wanted cash payments for their products and resented having to surrender their surplus grain to the government. Many laborers grumbled at being conscripted to work in the factories, and former business managers showed little enthusiasm for administering enterprises for the benefit of the state. This period was also a time of civil war, when the White Russians, aided by the Allies, were attempting to overthrow the Communist regime.

The early months of 1920 brought the most dangerous crisis yet faced by the government. The years of civil strife had left Russia in a state of confusion and disruption. Total industrial production had been reduced to 13 per cent of what it had been in 1913. Added to the misery caused by wartime dislocations and the shortages caused by inept or wasteful management in the recently nationalized industries was the suffering that followed the crop failures of 1920. Famine marched over the land, bringing more than twenty million people face to face with starvation. In 1921

large stocks of food were sent to Russia, chiefly by Britain, France, and the United States.

Meanwhile, in 1920, the Poles had invaded Russia and taken Kiev. Driven back to Warsaw, they counterattacked with the aid of French troops, and in 1921 Poland annexed a large slice of Russian territory. During these turbulent postwar years, other areas of Russia were chopped off to form independent states —Finland, Estonia, Latvia, and Lithuania.

The NEP. Confronted with the collapse of the nation, Lenin beat a strategic retreat in spite of strenuous opposition from his colleagues. He felt that the new regime had run into difficulties because it had been too eager to change everything at once. A return to certain practices of the capitalistic system was recommended, and the NEP, or New Economic Policy, was inaugurated.

The retreat from war communism operated from 1921 to 1928. The peasants were freed from the onerous wholesale levies of grain; after paying a fixed governmental tax, they were allowed to sell their surplus produce in open market. Factories employing less than twenty men were returned to private management, and a graduated wage scale was granted to the workers in the state industries. Commerce was stimulated by permitting private retail trading. Although simon-pure Communists criticized the wealthy peasants or *kulaks* who benefited from the new order of things and dubbed the private businessmen "Nepmen," such compromises proved highly beneficial and the economy revived.

The NEP was Lenin's last outstanding achievement. In spite of broken health, he worked unceasingly until his death in January 1924. His tomb in Moscow's Red Square is a Mecca for thousands of followers who come to pay homage to the creator of the first Marxist state in history.

Stalin vs. Trotsky: the peasant and the professor. Upon the death of the one man in the party who had possessed unchallenged authority and whose decrees were binding, a struggle for power broke out, and conflicts of policy and personality appeared. Two rivals who took different sides on most issues were Trotsky and Stalin. Leon Trotsky (1879-

1940), whose real name was Bronstein, had turned to Marxism in his early youth and, like Lenin, had known exile. During the revolution, Trotsky had come to the forefront. He was a magnificent orator; and by his personal magnetism and his demonic energy, he had led the Red Army to victory over the counterrevolutionists. A theorist and scholar, this intellectual, professor-like leader had personal defects of arrogance and egotism which contrasted with the peasant shrewdness and cunning of his less colorful but more calculating rival.

Stalin, born Joseph Dzugashvili in 1879 in the Georgian region of Transcaucasia, was the son of a poor shoemaker. Admitted to a seminary to be trained for the priesthood, young Stalin was later expelled for radical opinions. Before the revolution, he engaged in much activity in the underground and was sent into exile four times. In 1922 he became general secretary of the Secretariat of the party's Central Committee.

Trotsky, like Lenin, believed that the U.S.S.R. could not maintain itself indefinitely as a socialist island in a capitalist ocean and that it was therefore the duty of the Russian Communists to foster revolution elsewhere. Stalin, less the theorist than the political realist, viewed Trotsky's ideas of world revolution as premature. He noted that, outside of Russia, Marxism had made little headway, despite the existence of what from the Marxist standpoint were the most advantageous circumstances for revolution. The impoverished and war-disillusioned workers of Germany had not turned against the bourgeoisie, while in Italy socialist opposition had been crushed by Mussolini. Stalin advocated a new policy, which was to become known as "building up socialism in a single state."

With his outstanding party record and his mastery of ideological analysis, Trotsky not unnaturally expected to assume Lenin's mantle of leadership. But he reckoned without the political astuteness of Stalin, who had obtained a key administrative post in the party apparatus. Quietly and systematically, Stalin proceeded to shunt his rival aside. He placed his supporters in important posts in the gov-

This photo of Lenin and Stalin (below) was taken in 1922, the year in which Stalin gained the powerful post of general secretary of the party. In the struggle for power after Lenin's death, Trotsky (above) advocated Lenin's belief that Russian Communists must foster revolution in other countries, while Stalin insisted that socialism must first be perfected in Russia. Because of Trotsky's opposition to Stalin, whom he accused of placing personal ambition above the cause of world revolution, Trotsky was expelled from the party in 1927.

ernment, assumed the powerful chairmanship of the Politburo, and by 1927 had brought about the expulsion of Trotsky and his followers from the party. Trotsky was exiled and led a hare-and-hound existence until 1940, when he was struck down by the ax of an assassin in Mexico.

With a well-organized governmental structure and an obedient bureaucracy and with the Trotskyites either exiled or rendered powerless, Stalin was ready by 1928 to put a daring new program into operation. The NEP was to be scrapped and replaced by a Five-Year Plan, which called for a highly ambitious program of heavy industrialization and the collectivization of agriculture. In spite of breakdowns and failures and mainly because of the heroic sacrifices of the common people, the first Five-Year Plan achieved amazing results (see Chapter 30). Russia, an inert sleeping giant before 1914, now became industrialized at an unbelievable speed, far surpassing Germany's pace of industrialization in the nineteenth century and Japan's early in the twentieth. It is important to stress also that the heavy burden of sacrifices necessary to the launching of the plan could never have been imposed had not Stalin been able to make a patriotic appeal to the people as Russians. The leaders of the Kremlin assiduously developed the cult of "Communist nationalism." Such an unlikely phrase would have sounded self-contradictory to Marx and probably also to Lenin, but the fact remained that Stalin managed to combine the two historic ingredients of nationalism and socialism in the ideological test tube to create a new, a Stalinist brand of communism.

Changes in Soviet society. While the Russian economy was being transformed, the social life of the people underwent equally drastic changes. From the beginning of the revolution, the government attempted to weaken the importance of the family. A divorce required no court procedure; and to make women completely free of the responsibilities of childbearing, abortion was made legal. The policy of "emancipating" women had the practical objective of increasing the labor market. Girls were encouraged to secure an education and pursue a career in the factory or the office.

Most observers in the 1920's credited the regime with abandoning the tsarist policy of persecuting national minorities in favor of a policy of tolerance toward the more than two hundred minority groups in the Soviet Union. Coming under heavy fire in the West, however, were the Communist policies toward education and religion. Although education was made available to millions of children, the primary purpose of the school system was to indoctrinate the pupils with Communist precepts and values. Religious leaders were persecuted, and many of the most active were sentenced to concentration camps. Members of the party were forbidden to attend divine services. The Church was shorn of its powers over education, religious teaching was prohibited except in the home, and antireligious instruction was stressed in the schools. Although the intensive campaign against religion was considered by many as a reaction against the Orthodox Church's role as a tool of the tsars, the basic explanation lies in the materialistic Marxist denial of God and Marxism's refusal to allow the individual the right to possess a loyalty above that accorded to the state.

Foreign relations in the 1920's. During the decade and a half following the Russian Revolution, the Soviet Union was not considered a member in good standing in the family of nations. From the beginning of the revolution, relations between the western democracies and the new Soviet regime had been cool. The Communists resented the West's support of the White Russians. For their part, the Allies were aroused over the separate peace Lenin made with Germany, the seizure of foreign property in Russia, and the repudiation of all foreign debts.

Probably the greatest barrier to friendship (or at least mutual tolerance) between the West and Soviet Russia was the Third Communist International, or Comintern, organized in 1919 and dedicated to the overthrow of capitalism the world over. Specific aims of the organization were to disseminate Communist propaganda, to establish Communist parties in all the important nations of the world, and to secure control of labor unions and other workers' groups wherever possible. Communists of all countries became members of the Comintern, meeting in congresses held in Moscow and setting up committees to co-ordinate their activities. Thus the Communist party became basically different from all national political groups; all Communists owed their allegiance to an international organization rather than to the nations in which they resided.

Another basic aim of the Comintern was to undermine colonialism. As we have seen earlier (see p. 619), Lenin's anti-imperialist beliefs were given wide publicity. Not so well known, however, was his idea that communism could conquer Europe and America by gaining control of Asia. He is reported to have once stated that London and New York could be conquered on the Yangtze.

In Mussolini's Italy, the worship of war and of the state was instilled even in small children through military training units.

RISE OF FASCISM IN ITALY

Problems in postwar Italy. In World War I the Italian armies had been badly mauled by their enemies, and Italy emerged from the peace conference a victor with only modest gains. The war also aggravated the weaknesses of the Italian economy. The lira fell to a third of its prewar value, unemployment rose, and severe food shortages developed. People refused to pay their rent, strikes broke out in industrial centers, and workers seized factories. Italy's economic plight invited agitation by extremists from both Right and Left. Within four years after the armistice, five incompetent premiers came and went. The situation seemed propitious for the appearance of a strong leader on the political stage. When he appeared, he was the jutting-jawed son of a blacksmith named Mussolini.

Mussolini and the birth of Fascism. Born in 1883 in northern Italy, Benito Mussolini had grown up in left-wing circles. Although he became editor in 1912 of the influential Italian socialist newspaper *Avanti (Forward)*, he was far from consistent in regard to his belief in socialism and its doctrinal opposition to "capitalistic" wars. When a majority in

the Italian Socialist party called for neutrality in World War I, Mussolini urged intervention and, as a result, was expelled from the party. Undaunted, he founded his own paper, *Il Popolo d'Italia (The People of Italy)*, in which he continued to advocate Italian intervention in the war on the side of the Allies.

As part of his campaign for Italian participation in the war, Mussolini organized formerly leftist youths into bands called *fasci*, a name derived from the Latin *fasces*, the bundle of rods bound about an ax which was the symbol of authority in ancient Rome. After the war, he reorganized the *fasci* into the *fasci di combattimento* (fighting groups) to attract war veterans. The ultimate purpose of these groups was to capture the control of the national government.

The march on Rome. In the elections of 1919, the socialists capitalized on mass unemployment and hardship to emerge as the strongest party. Although the Fascists failed to elect a single candidate to the Chamber of Deputies, they succeeded in obtaining both approval and financial aid from industrial and landowning groups fearful of the triumph of Marxist socialism in Italy. Mussolini's black-shirted toughs broke up strikes and workers'

Mussolini is shown here with his officers at the time of the Fascist march on Rome in 1922.

demonstrations and, by beatings and overdoses of castor oil, "persuaded" political opponents of the error of their views. The central government remained virtually impotent during these outbreaks of violence. Elections held in May 1921 resulted in a plurality for the liberal and democratic parties. A few Communists were elected to the Chamber of Deputies, and only thirty-five Fascists, among them Mussolini.

The year 1922 saw events conspire to favor Mussolini's bid for power. The democratic government of that time was ineffective, and the socialists were divided among themselves, while the ranks of the Fascists had been strengthened by the enrollment of thousands of disaffected bourgeoisie, cynical and opportunistic intellectuals, and depression-weary workers. The general strike called in August by the trade unions in order to arouse the country to the menace of Fascism was smashed. On October 24 a huge crowd attending a Fascist rally at Naples shouted "On to Rome!" When some fifty thousand Fascist militiamen swarmed into the capital, King Victor Emmanuel III invited Mussolini to form a new government.

Mussolini organizes the Fascist state. Mussolini's first act as prime minister was the passage in 1923 of an enabling law which gave him dictatorial powers. By this means

Mussolini acquired a temporary "legal" right to govern without democratic procedure. He quickly used his newly acquired power to dissolve all other political parties and thus completely eliminate opposition to his regime. The Fascist party was now in a position to recast the entire governmental apparatus.

The Fascist state was ruled by an elite in the party, which ruthlessly crushed all free expression and banished critics of the regime to penal settlements on islands off the southern Italian coast. Censorship of the press was established, and a tribunal for defense of the state was set up to punish any individuals not conforming to Fascist practices. As Mussolini described his philosophy:

Fascism is a unit; it cannot have varying tendencies and trends, as it cannot have two leaders on any one level of organization. There is a hierarchy; the foundation is the Black Shirts and on the summit the Chief, who is only one.[1]

The Senate continued to exist, even though completely dominated by Fascists; the Chamber of Deputies withered on the vine until the 1930's, when it was replaced by the Chamber of Corporations. Meanwhile, all real power in the new state had been vested in the Fascist Grand Council, headed by Mussolini. The members of the council occupied the government's ministerial posts; in fact, at one time Mussolini himself held no less than eight offices. With all units of local and provincial government welded into a unified structure dominated from Rome, the Fascist administrative system constituted the ultracentralization of government.

In 1929 Mussolini negotiated the Lateran Treaty with representatives of the Roman Catholic Church. By the terms of this agreement, Roman Catholicism was recognized as the state religion in Italy; and Vatican City, a new state of 108 acres located in Rome itself, was declared fully sovereign and independent. Thus, the long-standing controversy concerning the relationship of Church and state in Italy was settled amicably.

Economic goals of Fascist Italy. Mussolini based his views of economics on the ideas of the syndicalists (see p. 574), who believed that industrial unions should be the cells of society and that a confederation of these unions, or syndicates, should constitute the governing body of the state. Syndicalism was adapted to the objectives of Fascism, creating what is called the corporate state. Economically, Italy was divided into thirteen syndicates, all controlled by the government: six were formed from the ranks of labor, an equal number represented capital or management, and a thirteenth syndicate was established for the professions. Representatives from the syndicates sat in the Chamber of Corporations.

One of Fascism's chief economic objectives was to make Italy as self-sufficient as possible —a policy known as autarky; this aim was motivated primarily by military ambitions. As Mussolini declared:

We must secure in the shortest possible time the maximum degree of economic independence for the nation. . . . This plan is dominated by one premise—the inevitability of war.[2]

In achieving this goal, much was accomplished, though often at a ruinous cost. Many projects were launched to provide for a home supply of materials which could be obtained much more cheaply from other nations.

Fascism's glorification of the state and war. The concept of the "inevitability" of war, added to the exaltation of the state and of its "destiny," created a supernationalism whose adherents tended to interpret the right of self-determination in terms of the expansion of the Fascist state at the expense of other nations. Mussolini warned the world that Italy intended to expand or explode, and his encouragement of a high birth rate in conjunction with meager territorial and natural resources pointed in only one direction— imperialism.

Fascism has been defined as "the cult of state worship." In the Italian totalitarian state the individual had no significance except as a member of the state. The Fascists were taught "to believe, to obey, and to fight" (*credere, obbedire, combattere*). Fascist ideology governed the educational system. The first sentence pronounced by children at school was "Let us salute the flag in the Roman fashion; hail to Italy; hail to Mussolini." Textbooks emphasized the glorious past of the ancient Romans, the limitations imposed upon the present inhabitants by geography and western "plutocratic" nations, and the imperial destiny that awaited Italy's future development.

To the casual foreign observer, Italy seemed rejuvenated. The Italian trains, whose schedules had long been notoriously erratic, now ran on time. Restless activity was something new on the Italian scene, and a few concrete achievements were widely touted. The cost was not so readily apparent; the fundamental inefficiency and weakness of the Fascist government would not be exposed for twenty years.

THE WEIMAR REPUBLIC

Revolution in Germany. Near the close of World War I, Woodrow Wilson had made it clear that the Allies would not enter into peace negotiations with the imperial government of the Hohenzollerns. By November 1918, sick of the war and its privations, the German people were ready to do anything to bring the conflict to an end. Revolution broke out and flashed like lightning through Germany, and the authority of the old government crumbled. On the same day that the chancellor turned over his authority to Friedrich Ebert—the leader of the majority socialist party, the Social Democrats—the republic was officially proclaimed.

The collapse of the imperial government provoked vigorous disagreement over the type of administration that was to replace it. The Communists wanted a complete social revolution as well as a political revolution, while Ebert's Social Democrats favored a democratic system in which the rights of private property would be safeguarded. In December 1918 and January 1919, the moderates and the radicals clashed violently; the Communists in Berlin were scattered and their leaders murdered. In a national election held to select a constitutional convention, the parties stressing moderation were triumphant, with the Social Democrats securing the most votes. The German revolution was to be democratic and bourgeois.

Problems of the Weimar Republic. The new constitution was adopted in midsummer of 1919 at Weimar, famous as the residence of Germany's greatest poet, Goethe. It provided for a president and a chancellor who now was responsible to the Reichstag. The rights of labor were guaranteed, personal liberties were safeguarded, and compulsory education was planned for everyone up to the age of eighteen.

In spite of difficulties and the opposition of Communists and monarchists, the Weimar Republic managed to restore political stability to Germany and to face serious financial problems. (The problem of the heavy reparations required of Germany at Versailles was discussed in Chapter 27). In 1923, when French and Belgian troops occupied the Ruhr, the wild inflation of the mark wiped out middle-class savings, and political moderates gradually lost their influence to ultranationalists and reactionaries. But after the French withdrew and the Dawes Plan enabled Germany to meet its schedule of reparation payments and to obtain large loans from abroad, the German economy took a turn for the better, and Germany from 1925 to 1929 enjoyed economic prosperity. Large public works projects were undertaken, industry was expanded, and Germany became the second largest industrial nation in the world. But there were disturbing forces at work.

Factors favoring the growth of dictatorship. Germany in the late 1920's was a compound of numerous ingredients, many of which had been in existence for at least a century. With Prussia as their model, such men as Hegel and Treitschke had exalted the state at the expense of the individual; and the government of the kaisers had established a strong edifice of despotism. Lack of experience in working the machinery of democratic government made the success of the Weimar Republic doubtful from the start. The principle of proportional representation was carried so far that innumerable separate parties

arose, and only the formation of coalitions enabled the government to function.

Other difficulties threatening the new government stemmed from the resentments and frustrations engendered among the people by defeat in war. The powerful Prussian militaristic clique fanned the flames of discontent by fostering the legend that the German army had not been defeated on the field of battle but had been stabbed in the back by pacifist liberals and "decadent" democrats on the home front. The legend of the betrayal of the Fatherland was to be increasingly the refrain of those who came to favor Nazi militarism. The resurgence of strong nationalistic feelings was evidenced by the election to the presidency in 1925 of Field Marshal von Hindenburg, a hero of World War I.

The Treaty of Versailles embittered many Germans, and its use by the French to justify the invasion of the Ruhr sowed further seeds of hate. The so-called war guilt clause of the treaty, by which the Germans were forced to proclaim their guilt for starting the war, was particularly rankling.

The ultranationalists were able to make effective appeals to the industrialists and landowners, who were convinced that the republic could not effectively discourage the internal threat of communism. As a result of the war and the postwar inflation, professional people, white-collar workers, and skilled tradesmen feared the prospect of being dragged down to the level of the masses. Especially after the debacle of inflation, a deep sense of despair and futility fell upon the people. German youth blamed their elders for the catastrophe of 1918 and the humiliations that followed defeat. The young generation repudiated the past and sought a cause to redeem the Fatherland.

Hitler's rise to prominence. The creator and high priest of German fascism was Adolf Hitler, born the son of a minor customs official in Austria in 1889. As a young man, Hitler went to Vienna with ambitions of becoming an architect or artist. He experienced dire poverty there and a few years later moved to Munich, where he earned a scanty living by selling paintings.

In 1923, a year after Mussolini seized control of the Italian government, Hitler was only beginning his bid for power. The painting above shows Hitler and his followers planning the *Putsch* of 1923 at a meeting in a Munich beer hall.

When war broke out, he joined a German regiment and was sent to France. The armistice of 1918 found him in a hospital. He said later that news of Germany's defeat caused him to turn his face to the wall and weep bitterly. Subsequently he was hired by the authorities in Munich as a special agent to investigate Communist and other extremist movements. In the line of duty he was asked to check on a small organization called the German Workers' party. Hitler joined this group, whose fervently nationalistic doctrine was at once antidemocratic, anticapitalist, anti-Communist, and anti-Semitic.

Before long the movement took the name "National Socialist German Workers' party," and the words "National Socialists" became abbreviated to "Nazis"; soon the first of the paramilitary organizations, the SA or Storm Troops, was organized. Adopted as the emblem of the party was the swastika set against a red background signifying the community of German blood.

Hitler was now becoming better known, and his remarkable oratorical gifts began to attract large crowds in Munich. His program called for land reform, the nationalization of trusts, abolition of all unearned incomes, and —in the field of foreign relations—a greater Germany to include all German-speaking peoples in Europe, the abrogation of the Versailles Treaty, and the restitution of Germany's prewar colonies. In 1923 Hitler staged his *Putsch*, or revolt, in Munich; coming prematurely, it failed, and he was sent to prison.

Mein Kampf. Before his release from prison in 1925, Hitler began to write *Mein Kampf* (*My Battle*), at once an autobiography and a long-winded exposition of Nazi philosophy and objectives. In this work Hitler contends that history is fashioned by great races, of which the Aryan is the finest; that the noblest Aryans are the German people, who are destined to rule the world; that the Jews are the archcriminals of all time; that democracy is decadent and communism is criminal; that foreign expansion into the Russian Ukraine and the destruction of Germany's prime enemy France are rightful courses for the German people; and that war and force are the proper instruments of the strong. Hitler singled out the Treaty of Versailles as the instrument which would give him magic appeal in Germany:

What a use could be made of the Treaty of Versailles! . . . How each one of the points . . . could be branded in the minds and hearts of the German people until sixty million men and women find their souls aflame with the feeling of rage and shame; and a torrent of fire bursts forth as from a furnace.[3]

With his irrational creed and his ritualistic gestures, badges, and uniforms, Hitler would one day surpass his predecessor Mussolini in Italy by becoming Führer (leader) of a new Germany based on despotism and terror.

DEMOCRACY IN

THE WASTELAND

Democracy on the defensive. "In this autumn of 1919, in which I write, we are at the dead season of our fortunes. The reaction from the exertions, the fears, and the sufferings of the past five years is at its height. Our power of feeling or caring beyond the immediate questions of our own material well-being is temporarily eclipsed. The greatest events outside our own direct experience and the most dreadful anticipations cannot move us. . . . We have been moved already beyond endurance, and need rest."[4] Thus wrote the famed English economist John Maynard Keynes; his mood of apathy, disillusionment, and despair was shared by many people in the West.

The postwar period witnessed an inevitable reaction against wartime controls. In the English-speaking democracies, which were the chief bastions of laissez-faire economics, governmental controls were thrown off with all possible speed. The slogan "back to normalcy" in the United States indicated a return to prewar economic habits and creeds. And halted throughout most of the democratic-capitalist world were the strong prewar movements to advance social welfare legislation and to regulate traditional laissez-faire economics. An unhealthy inertia resulted in the suspension of badly needed socioeconomic reforms.

The national mood and psychology prevailing in the democracies, whether in those long-established or in those newly created after the war, differed basically from the mood and psychology in the rising dictatorships. The democracies drifted into listlessness and futility, while the totalitarian states exhibited resolution, dynamism, and purpose, even though of a ruthless variety. The inability of the democracies to measure up to the needs of the times gave the 1920's its characteristic mood and quality. That mood and quality were reflected in the literature of the Wasteland era (a term taken from the title of T. S. Eliot's poem *The Waste Land*), with its cynicism, its sense of purposelessness, and its absorption with the seamy and often trivial aspects of life.

Unstable coalition governments in France. More than 1,000,000 Frenchmen had been killed and some 13,000 square miles of French territory laid waste in the holocaust of World War I. Years later the nation would still feel the heavy loss of man power and the economic devastation of a war that had been fought largely on French soil.

The Sacred Union, the wartime coalition government which included representatives of all shades of political opinion, was replaced after the elections of 1919 by the National Bloc, a conservative group whose leaders included Poincaré and the wartime premier Clemenceau, both eager for revenge. They believed in the rigid enforcement of the provisions of the Versailles Treaty and saw as their chief task the restoration of the country's devastated regions. They expected the huge costs of rebuilding the towns destroyed in the north of France to be covered by reparations payments from Germany; and when the Germans suspended these payments in 1923, it was Poincaré who ordered French troops into the industrially rich Ruhr valley. More than any other man, he symbolized the policy of making Germany pay for the war and of keeping it disarmed.

Because many Frenchmen realized that this vindictive policy was basically unsound, the National Bloc fell in 1924 and was succeeded by the Left Cartel, which guided the destinies of France for the next two years. Except for the unpopular war against Abd-el Krim in Morocco (see p. 697), the coalition left an enviable record in foreign affairs: French troops evacuated the Ruhr in accordance with the Dawes Plan for solving the reparations tangle, and French and German statesmen met amicably at the Locarno Conference. In internal affairs, on the other hand, the Left Cartel, which advocated the extension of government control of industry and an increase in income taxes, was unsuccessful, particularly in the area of public finance. Although France had practically no unemployment after the war and its foreign trade by 1922 had surpassed its prewar volume, inflation threatened to plunge the franc into the same abyss that in 1923 engulfed the German mark.

To meet this emergency, in 1926 Poincaré was recalled to power to head a National Union government and save the franc. Drastic measures were taken by the new coalition; taxes were increased and expenditures curtailed. Poincaré's policies gave French finance a new lease on life, while in other fields workmen's insurance was enacted and the task of rebuilding the devastated areas was completed.

The story of France in the 1920's is a mixed plot of progress and setbacks, of successes and failures. Fundamentally, a national spirit and a sense of purpose were lacking. The war had sapped the vigor of the French nation, and as in Germany the unhealthiness and lack of dynamism characteristic of the Wasteland mood were evident.

Evolutionary socialism gains support in Great Britain. Across the Channel, meanwhile, Britain in the postwar period suffered a number of serious problems. Shortly after the armistice, foreign trade collapsed, and unemployment reached huge proportions. By July 1921, two million persons were out of work, and the war debt had soared to $40,-000,000,000.

In 1922 the wartime coalition under David Lloyd George came to an end. Elections held at the end of 1923 saw the Conservatives gain the largest number of seats in the House of Commons, but by swinging their support to the Labour party, the Liberals gave James Ramsay MacDonald a majority in this house. As a result, in January 1924 MacDonald became Britain's first Labourite prime minister.

The Labour government did not preach the gospel according to Marx but espoused evolutionary socialism in the tradition of the Fabian Society in England, the Social Democrats in Germany, and the Mensheviks in prewar Russia. The goal of the Labour party was to introduce socialism slowly and at all times within a democratic framework. MacDonald declared: "Our Labor movement has never had the least inclination to try short cuts to the millennium."[5]

While its record in domestic affairs was not outstanding, the Labour government fared better in foreign affairs. Believing that Germany must be aided in its steps toward recovery, MacDonald favored the Dawes Plan and urged Germany's entry into the League of Nations. He also supported disarmament. But his failure to cure Britain's economic ills and his efforts to seek an economic agreement with the pariah nation, Soviet Russia, helped to bring about his downfall in October 1924. For the next five years Britain was led by a Conservative government under Stanley Baldwin. During these dismal years, hundreds of thousands of unemployed workers barely managed to keep alive on the dole, a pittance of relief handed out by the government. The economic crisis finally culminated in a general strike that threatened the entire economy.

It is difficult in a country which has never experienced a general strike to realize how

During the general strike of 1926 in England, armored cars, equipped with machine guns, were stationed in London to suppress riots

serious is such a virtual civil war. The trouble broke out first in the coal industry, where the miners demanded the nationalization of the mines. As the strike spread, workers in other industries quit all over Britain; even newspapers suspended publication. Had it not been for the calm spirit of most Englishmen, armed conflict might have broken out. In the end the strike of 1926 failed; the miners returned to work.

Two years later, between 20 and 30 per cent of the labor force in many of the leading industries was eking out an existence on the dole. The failure of the Conservative party to find a solution for unemployment brought Labour back into power in 1929, the year also witnessing the beginning of a world crisis which would force Britain off the gold standard, raise still higher its unemployment figures, and in 1931 end the second Labour ministry. Thus the decade following victory in 1918 had brought Britain little inspired leadership, an absence of programs of economic reform, and an inability to measure up to the demands of a new age.

The British Commonwealth of Nations. During the First World War, the British dominions (Canada, Australia, New Zealand, and South Africa) had rendered valuable service, and the war had stimulated strong nationalistic feelings among their peoples. In 1926 an Imperial Conference declared that Great Britain and the dominions were "autonomous Communities within the British Empire, equal in status, in no way subordinate one to another." Five years later the British Parliament enacted the Statute of Westminster, which was in effect a constitution for what was now called the British Commonwealth of Nations. Henceforth the dominions and Great Britain were held together only by loyalty to the crown and by a common language, legal principles, tradition, and economic interests.

During the 1920's, the dominions prospered from the strong demand for their products, and economic prosperity contributed to governmental stability. Elsewhere in the British empire, however, trouble spots began to appear (see Chapter 29).

The Irish Free State established. Meantime, Britain was undergoing other problems in a familiar quarter. In 1916, during the First World War, Irish nationalists had revolted against British authority in the Easter Rebellion, which failed after savage fighting in Dublin. After the war the Sinn Fein ("we ourselves") party demanded complete independence for Ireland and maintained a state of war between the "Irish republic" and Britain. In 1921 a treaty was signed between Irish and British representatives providing for the Irish Free State. While six counties in northern Ireland (comprising most of Ulster) remained tied with Britain, the southern part of the island was given dominion status. Agitation and violence continued for a time, with civil warfare between supporters of the Free State and nationalists who opposed the treaty; but under the leadership of a Dublin government pledged to cooperate with Britain, Ireland regained a semblance of internal unity.

Austria, Hungary, and Bulgaria. What had happened to the countries of southern Europe —Austria, Hungary, Bulgaria—which had been on the losing side in the war? Austria had been reduced both in population and in area by nearly three fourths, leaving an enfeebled state about the size of Maine with less than seven million people. Vienna, the center of the old Austro-Hungarian empire, no longer had an adequate hinterland to nourish economic growth.

The immediate postwar years in Austria were filled with hardship. The country was full of jobless veterans, thousands died of starvation, and the currency became worthless. The economic union (*Anschluss*) with Germany proposed as a solution for these difficulties was forbidden by the Allies. During these troubled times, the Viennese turned to socialist leadership, and many necessary reforms were introduced in the capital. Slums were demolished, and low-cost dwellings, clinics, and kindergartens were set up. But the socialist experiment caused widespread resentment in the countryside, which remained strongly Catholic and conservative.

The war had reduced Hungary's size by 75 per cent, with more than half its former population transferred to neighboring states and succession states. The moderate republic which had been established after the war's end was supplanted by a terroristic Communist regime led by Béla Kun, a friend of Lenin. In April 1919 war broke out with Rumania, and Kun's government broke down. One year later Admiral Nicholas Horthy, World War I commander of the Hapsburg fleet, gained control of the country under the pretext of saving the Hungarians from communism. Stability was restored, but the government was in the hands of ultraconservatives, and the voice of the people was stilled.

Bulgaria's immediate postwar years were filled with civil disorder and bloodshed, class hatreds, and political repression. For a brief period, beginning in 1926, a moderate government sought to restore civil liberties and to improve the internal economy. But the shock of the world depression swept the regime aside, and conservative elements, fearful of the spread of communism, brought about the installation of a dictatorship in the early 1930's.

Developments elsewhere in eastern and southern Europe. What were the chances for democracy in the states of Europe which had been created from the debris of the Austro-Hungarian empire and had never known democratic traditions? Among the most important of the succession states was Czechoslovakia. Four hundred years of Austrian rule had not diminished the patriotic zeal of the Czechs; in November 1918, after Austria collapsed, they joined with the Slovaks in forming a republic. Besides Czechs and Slovaks, the republic included such minority groups as Germans in the Sudeten area, Ukrainians (Ruthenians), and Hungarians, constituting one third of the total population of fifteen million. Despite some tensions among these minorities, Czechoslovakia prospered, a large foreign trade was built up, and the government assisted small farmers by breaking up large estates. The people demonstrated that they were industrious and conscientious citizens.

To the north of Czechoslovakia lay Poland, which had been partitioned three times in the eighteenth century and in 1795 had disappeared as a political entity. Throughout the nineteenth century, strong feelings of nationalism had persisted; and with the collapse of Russia and the Central Powers, a Polish republic was declared in 1918. The Versailles Treaty established the new frontiers of Poland, later modified to the advantage of the Poles in the Treaty of Riga (1921), which concluded the war with the Bolsheviks (see p. 670). The stability of the Polish state was threatened by shaky finances, political conflicts between rival parties, and the discontent of minority groups, especially the Ukrainians and the Germans. One cabinet followed another in rapid succession until in 1926 Marshal Joseph Pilsudski and his military clique established a dictatorship.

Meanwhile, along the eastern shores of the Adriatic Sea, the Croats and Slovenes of the former Hapsburg empire joined with their brother Slavs in Serbia and Montenegro to form a new nation, the Kingdom of the Serbs, Croats, and Slovenes, later known as Yugoslavia. From the outset, King Alexander had difficulty in reconciling the rivalries between the Slavic peoples. In 1928 a riot broke out in the parliament, and the Croatian leader was mortally wounded. The following year saw Alexander proclaim himself dictator.

Rumania had profited from the demise of the Austro-Hungarian empire, its population and area having doubled, but like the succession states, this kingdom enjoyed little tranquillity after 1919. Despite the promulgation of a liberal constitution in 1923, its peasants were restless; and minority groups, especially the Hungarians, proved troublesome to civil order. In 1930 King Carol came to the throne and began to convert the Rumanian government into a royal dictatorship.

Democracy in other small European nations. Finland and the Scandinavian countries of Norway, Sweden, and Denmark enjoyed representative government and economic prosperity during the 1920's. The citizens benefited from the establishment of producers' and consumers' cooperatives and from progressive social legislation. In Sweden the Middle Way, an experiment combining cap-

italism and state enterprise, was carried out. The Middle Way called for state control of many forms of economic activity as well as government operation of mines, power, and communications. In addition, considerable social welfare legislation was inaugurated to provide the masses with economic security and adequate social services.

During the 1920's, stable democratic government and considerable prosperity were enjoyed by the peoples of Switzerland, the Netherlands, and Belgium. In the case of the Dutch and the Belgians, rich dividends from colonial empires contributed to the high standard of living.

Status of democracy in Spain and Portugal. By supplying food and other materials to the belligerent powers, Spain had enjoyed wartime prosperity; but after the war, prosperity gave way to lagging trade, industrial unrest, and political instability. The situation was aggravated by a revolt in Spanish Morocco, where in 1921 a Spanish army of twelve thousand men was completely wiped out. To save the monarchy and the privileged classes, in 1923 a right-wing leader, Miguel Primo de Rivera, set up a dictatorship, but even though a few concessions were granted to the people, opposition to arbitrary rule mounted. After Rivera's resignation in 1930, King Alfonso XIII tried to woo the people with a policy of conciliation, but the republicans openly denounced the monarchy. Municipal elections one year later resulted in a clear-cut victory for the republicans, Alfonso fled the country, and Spain became a republic. At a time when many other countries were turning to dictatorship, it was heartening to democrats everywhere to witness the triumph of democracy in Spain. This triumph was to be short-lived, however (see Chapter 30).

In the 1920's the republic of Portugal was plagued by political instability. In 1928 Dr. Oliveira Salazar, a professor of economics, became the minister of finance and, in 1932, the leading figure in an outright dictatorship. He exercised his power unobtrusively, perhaps as befitted a professorial dictator.

Growth of democratic ideals in Latin America. Across the seas in the lands to which

Iberian culture had been transplanted, various nations were beginning to tackle their economic problems and were trying to make their governments democracies in more than name.

The demands for enormous quantities of Latin-American products during World War I had resulted in an economic boom; and though the end of the war brought about a familiar situation—a crisis in the economy—business expansion began again in the 1920's. However, a crucial weakness remained—the dependence of the economies of Latin America's twenty republics upon only a few products or, in some cases, upon a single product. Thus Brazil's prosperity depended on the world coffee market, which absorbed half its exports. Cuba depended on sugar; Bolivia, tin; Mexico, oil and silver; Venezuela, oil; Argentina, meat and wheat. Various Central American "banana republics" were equally dependent on the sale of bananas. Another weak spot was the land problem. Conditions resembling medieval serfdom existed on many large estates. Because the Church was a great landowner, certain churchmen combined with the landed interests to oppose land reforms.

During the 1920's the movement for social reform in Latin America was spearheaded by Mexico, which came under a series of administrations, all claiming to be heir to the revolutionary spirit of the peon revolt of 1910. The government sought to exercise increasing control over the vast oil properties run by foreign investors; and the agrarian problem was partially solved at the expense of large landowners. These changes were accompanied by a wave of anticlericalism. Much Church property was seized, many churches were destroyed, and the priesthood had for a time to go underground.

Conditions in Mexico exerted a strong influence on other Latin-American countries, and between 1919 and 1929 seven nations adopted new, liberal constitutions. In addition, there were growing demands for better economic and social opportunities, for a breakdown of the barriers that divided the few extremely rich from the many abysmally poor, and for improvements in health, education, and the status of women. Above all, there was an increasing desire for more stable political conditions.

Era of normalcy and big business in the United States. By 1919 wartime industrial expansion had won for the United States the supreme position in industrial equipment and wealth among the family of nations. Moreover, our nation had been transformed from a debtor nation to the world's greatest creditor. But while other nations increasingly looked to it for leadership, the United States turned away from the international scene. The wartime democratic idealism of President Wilson was shelved, the League of Nations was ignored, and isolationism triumphed over internationalism.

Internally, industrial strife marked the immediate postwar years. Frightened by communism, many Americans demanded that action be taken against left-wing radicals. Moreover, against immigrants, Catholics, Jews, the League of Nations, and pacifists, a most exaggerated form of intolerance was practiced, often in a secret, terroristic fashion, by a new Ku Klux Klan. In some areas the Klan held political control of whole communities and state governments, in the North as well as in the South. Klan membership totaled over four million in 1924, but it declined after this date. Progressive editors, clergymen, and politicians mobilized public opinion against an organization which was recognized as undemocratic and un-American.

One important postwar political development was the ratification of the Eighteenth Amendment, by which the sale and possession of intoxicating liquors were prohibited. However laudable its purpose may have appeared at the time, the adoption of prohibition was increasingly regretted by many Americans as the 1920's wore on; the law was broken by great numbers of normally law-abiding citizens and frequently ignored by law-enforcement agencies, and the racketeering, violence, and corruption to which prohibition gave rise brought a dangerous lowering of the dignity of lawmaking and of democratic institutions.

The 1920's in the United States was a restless era in which the people threw off the restraints suffered during the Great War, made intense issues of prohibition, un-Americanism, and theology, and applauded the technological achievements which were shrinking the world. The flapper (above left), caricatured by John Held, Jr., symbolized the rebelliousness of sophisticated young people who flaunted the moral standards of the older generation. National heroes were cheered in lavish ticker-tape parades, such as the one which welcomed Admiral Byrd and his crew on their return from exploring the Antarctic (above). Another national hero was Charles A. Lindbergh (center left), who in 1927 made the first solo flight across the Atlantic in his monoplane *The Spirit of St. Louis*. The 1920's was the era of prohibition, a "noble experiment" so unpopular that great numbers of ordinarily law-abiding citizens patronized bootleggers and speak-easies. With prohibition came the boom days of organized crime, as gangsters set up stills or carried on a lucrative trade in smuggling. Although millions of dollars' worth of liquor and beer were confiscated by federal agents and poured down sewers (below left), enforcement measures failed to end the lawlessness.

When the triumph of communism in Russia coincided with an outbreak of radical agitation in the United States, a violent reaction against un-Americanism occurred. The Sacco-Vanzetti case attracted world-wide attention because of the political

Top picture: The Museum of Modern Art, New York

beliefs of the defendants. Nicola Sacco and Bartolomeo Vanzetti (pictured top above in a painting by Ben Shahn) were two Italian aliens convicted of killing a paymaster and his guard in Massachusetts and stealing $16,000. The verdict raised a storm of protest from radicals and from many liberals who were convinced that the men had not been given a fair trial because of their anarchistic beliefs. When all appeals failed, riots broke out in many cities, and bombs were set off in New York City and Philadelphia. On August 23, 1927, the defendants were executed, still protesting their innocence. Another hotly disputed issue was raised by the Scopes trial in 1927. John Scopes, a science teacher in a Dayton, Tennessee high school, was charged with violating a state law forbidding the teaching in public schools of any theories denying the Biblical account of the creation of man. The issue actually on trial was the state's right to determine the type of religious instruction presented in the schools; but the violent debate between religious fundamentalists and liberals was also given a public airing. Conservatives of various churches had banded together to demand that the teaching of Darwinian doctrines be prohibited in the schools. At the trial, William Jennings Bryan (right in the picture above) championed the literal interpretation of the Bible against Clarence Darrow (left above), the counsel for the defense. Scopes was found guilty and fined $100, although the penalty was later set aside.

In 1921 the inauguration of Warren G. Harding (1865-1923) as president on the platform of a "return to normalcy" ushered in a decade of Republican dominance. It soon became apparent that by "normalcy" the Harding administration meant resistance to pressure for such progressive measures as low tariffs and antitrust prosecutions. In foreign affairs the new president was bent upon isolationism and the repudiation of the League of Nations.

Harding's vice president and successor, Calvin Coolidge (1872-1933), advocated high tariffs and the reduction of taxes. His credo was summed up in these words: "The business of the United States is business." The Democrats tried in vain to raise the issue of corruption so rampant during Harding's regime, but under the glow of rising prosperity the voters in the 1924 presidential elections decided to "keep cool with Coolidge," and the Republicans won. Little outstanding legislation was enacted during the second Coolidge administration. A difficult problem was agriculture. Although farm income continued to decline while the fixed payments for debts contracted during agriculture's wartime expansion had to be kept up, bills to ease the farmers' plight were repeatedly vetoed by Coolidge. Other segments of the national economy enjoyed what appeared to be dazzling prosperity in 1927 and 1928. Growing quantities of autos, radios, and refrigerators were purchased either with cash or, increasingly, on the installment plan. Stock speculation became a virtual mania. Nearly everyone, from the millionaire to the janitor of the building in which the rich man lived, played the market. Mass production, high tariffs, large foreign loans, installment buying, and the stock market—all seemed to be working together in harmony. These years marked the high tide of American big business and economic self-satisfaction.

In the 1928 presidential elections, Herbert Hoover (1874-   ), a successful mining engineer who had directed Belgian relief during the war, had as his Democratic opponent the governor of New York, Alfred E. Smith. A product of the "sidewalks of New

York" and the first man of the Catholic faith to obtain the presidential nomination, Smith as governor had sponsored progressive social legislation. In the election campaign he called for the repeal of prohibition because of the problems to which it had given rise, but Hoover won the day on what one historian termed "prosperity, prohibition, and prejudice." When he assumed office in 1929, he was supported by a Republican Congress and a nation enjoying unbounded industrial prosperity.

For a decade after the war, Americans looked for leadership to Wall Street rather than to the White House. They were complacent, unprecedentedly prosperous as a nation, and little interested in what transpired outside the three-mile limit—or rather the twelve-mile limit when it came to rumrunners. In their attitudes the American people were experiencing the disillusionment and moral fatigue of the postwar era. The 1920's have been described as an era of "tremendous trivia"—dance marathons, flagpole sitting, "red hot mamas," speak-easies, Broadway ticker-tape parades for celebrities like Lindbergh, the Charleston, and a national craze for speculating in stocks, bonds, and Florida real estate. These were the elements in the Wasteland age in the United States. To many its salient features were national smugness and isolationism in international affairs, crass materialism in business, and vulgarity and bad taste in daily life.

SUMMARY

Marx had never imagined that his philosophy would first triumph in feudal, underdeveloped Russia. That it did so was primarily due to the planning and leadership of Lenin, who between November 1917 and his death in 1924, succeeded in eliminating all other political parties and in consolidating the Communist party's authority in the hands of an elite group, the Politburo, with himself at the head. Under Lenin's leadership the Soviet government drastically changed Russian society and economy, although Lenin was forced to retreat temporarily from undiluted Marxism and permit a partial return to free enterprise in order to build up the economy. After Lenin's death, a fierce struggle for leadership broke out within the Communist party. The likely successor, Trotsky, was pushed aside by Stalin, who believed that communism could be made to work in one country in contrast to the view shared by Lenin and Trotsky that ultimate success depended upon an international proletarian revolution. In 1928, Stalin inaugurated the first of his famous Five-Year Plans—a daring and ruthless economic program aimed at achieving heavy industrialization and the collectivization of agriculture.

The First World War gave a strong impetus to nationalist emotions and to developing the cult of the state. In the hands of astute demagogues, nationalism was exalted into a creed, with unbridled power as its goal and unswerving obedience its demand from its adherents. Such was Fascism, whose high priest and leader, Benito Mussolini, launched a campaign of organized terror in Italy and took over the government in 1922. Defined as the "cult of state worship," Italian Fascism called for rule by one party, which liquidated all opposition and was in turn manipulated by a hierarchy at whose summit stood Mussolini, Il Duce. In keeping with Fascism's glorification of war and imperialism, Mussolini's objective was to make Italy as self-sufficient as possible in order to expand.

The task of restoring the shattered fortunes of defeated Germany had been entrusted to the democratic Weimar Republic. Political inexperience and heavy economic burdens combined to discredit the government among the dispirited and humiliated Germans, who began to turn to such ultra-nationalists as Adolf Hitler and his Nazi followers, fanatics intent upon destroying the established order. During the 1920's Germany recovered sufficiently to become a respected and prosperous member of the European community, but the early 1930's heralded a catastrophic depression, thereby giving Hitler his opportunity to seize power.

What was the condition of democracy during the 1920's? Almost all the states emerging from the debris of the German and Austrian empires started their national existence with democratic constitutions. Although Czechoslovakia flourished, nearly all the others soon gave way to dictatorial regimes. They suffered in common from the absence of a strong middle class and a lack of experience in democratic government. Moreover, the Allies at Versailles had applied the principle of self-determination to the point of creating too many small states which were separated from their neighbors by artificial tariff barriers and which suffered from weak economies. In such circumstances it is not surprising that democracy failed to succeed.

Yet in the well-established democracies the results were for the most part also disappointing. True, democratic institutions held their own in the Netherlands and Belgium and were strengthened in the Scandinavian countries. On the other hand, France, the undisputed master of Continental Europe in 1919, gradually slipped from its position of dominance because of chronic political instability.

Great Britain emerged from the war with a full quota of domestic and imperial problems, and neither the Conservative nor the Labour governments made much headway in overcoming these difficulties, of which the most acute was unemployment. Overseas, democracy had a patchy record of successes and failures. In the British Commonwealth the dominions achieved full status as self-governing states and enjoyed prosperity and economic expansion. Some social reforms were registered in the Latin-American republics, where, however, democratic institutions were all too often a façade for dictatorial regimes. In the United States, stock speculation, corruption in high places, and gangsterism flourished in a society which had turned its back on Wilsonian ideals to return to isolation and embrace a false prosperity.

As we have seen in this chapter, the 1920's were the years in which opposing ideologies were crystallizing. This period was to prove only a lull before the terrible storm of world economic distress and national aggressions.

SUGGESTIONS FOR READING

E. Golob, *The Isms: A History and Evaluation*, Harper, 1954. A useful introduction to modern political and economic ideologies. See also J. H. Hallowell, *Main Currents of Modern Political Thought*, Holt, 1950.

C. J. Friedrich and Z. Brzezinski, *Totalitarian Dictatorship and Autocracy,** Praeger. A systematic description and analysis of totalitarianism by two outstanding scholars. Fascist ideology is emphasized in the following useful surveys: H. Arendt, *The Origins of Totalitarianism,** Meridian; A. Cobban, *Dictatorship: Its History and Theory*, Scribner's, 1939.

M. Salvadori, *The Rise of Modern Communism,** Holt (Berkshire Studies). A very brief history of the Communist movement in the twentieth century. More substantial surveys are H. Seton-Watson, *From Lenin to Khrushchev: The History of World Communism,** Praeger; and F. Borkenau, *European Communism*, Harper, 1953. R. Carew Hunt, *The Theory and Practice of Communism*, Macmillan, 1957, is a brief introduction especially useful for a study of the development of communism in Russia.

D. Treadgold, *Twentieth Century Russia*, Rand McNally, 1959. The most useful single volume on Russian history in this century. See also F. L. Schuman, *Russia Since 1917: Four Decades of Soviet Politics*, Knopf, 1957.

*Indicates an inexpensive paperbound edition.

G. Vernadsky, *The Russian Revolution, 1917-1931*, Holt (Berkshire Studies), 1932. A very brief critical interpretation. A. Moorehead, *The Russian Revolution,** Bantam, is an interesting popular account, somewhat oversimplified. W. H. Chamberlin, *The Russian Revolution, 1917-1921*, 2 vols., Macmillan, 1952, is the standard balanced history of the subject. For even greater detail, see E. H. Carr, *The Bolshevik Revolution, 1917-1923*, 3 vols., Macmillan, 1951-1953.

J. Read, *Ten Days That Shook the World,** Vintage. An enthusiastic on-the-scene description by an American Communist. But compare the eyewitness account of a British consular officer in Moscow: R. Lockhart, *British Agent*, Putnam, 1933. G. Brinton, *The Anatomy of Revolution,** Vintage, is an instructive comparison of the Russian, French, and English revolutions.

J. Reshetar, Jr., *A Concise History of the Communist Party of the Soviet Union,** Praeger. A good introduction. A. G. Meyer, *Leninism,** Praeger, is the only systematic scholarly study of Lenin's contribution to Marxist thought and practice.

I. Deutscher, *The Prophet Unarmed: Trotsky, 1921-1929*, Oxford, 1959. Describes Trotsky's career from victory in the civil war to exile at the hands of Stalin. See also, by the same author, the outstanding biographical study *Stalin: A Political Biography,** Vintage.

Four excellent critiques of Italian Fascism are A. Rossi, *The Rise of Italian Fascism: 1918-1922*, Methuen, 1938; H. W. Schneider, *Making the Fascist State*, Oxford, 1928; G. Salvemini, *Under the Axe of Fascism*, Viking, 1936; and H. Finer, *Mussolini's Italy*, Holt, 1935.

L. Fermi, *Mussolini: The Wild Adventure That Was His Life*, Univ. of Chicago, 1961. Does much to make understandable the flamboyant Duce and a fantastic chapter in world history. G. Megaro, *Mussolini in the Making*, Houghton Mifflin, 1938, is an excellent account of Mussolini's early career.

S. W. Halperin, *Germany Tried Democracy*, Crowell, 1946. Considered to be the best political history of the Weimar Republic. See also W. M. Knight-Patterson, *Germany from Defeat to Conquest, 1913-1933*, Macmillan, 1947; F. L. Schuman, *Germany Since 1918*, Holt, 1937; and F. Vermeil, *Germany in the Twentieth Century*, Praeger, 1956.

A. Rosenberg, *The Birth of the German Republic*, Oxford, 1931; A. Brecht, *Prelude to Silence*, Oxford, 1944. Two studies which treat, respectively, the rise and the fall of the Weimar Republic.

J. L. Snell, ed., *The Nazi Revolution: Germany's Guilt or Germany's Fate?** Heath. A valuable introduction is followed by short selections from the diverse answers of historians to the question: How was it possible for the Nazis to come to power in one of the most civilized countries of Europe?

A. Bullock, *Hitler: A Study in Tyranny,** Bantam. The best biography. See also K. Heiden, *Der Fuehrer*, Houghton Mifflin, 1944.

J. Wheeler-Bennett, *Nemesis of Power: The German Army in Politics, 1918-1945*, St. Martin's, 1954. An outstanding study of the sinister role played by the Prussian military clique. See also, by the same author, *Wooden Titan: Hindenburg in Twenty Years of German History, 1914-1934*, Morrow, 1936.

E. Knapton, *France Since Versailles,** Holt (Berkshire Studies). A very brief survey. The following are more comprehensive surveys: D. W. Brogan, *France Under the Republic: The Development of Modern France, 1870-1939*, Harper, 1940, perhaps the best introduction to the subject; G. Wright, *France in Modern Times: 1760 to the Present*, Rand McNally, 1960; and Y. Simon, *The Road to Vichy, 1918-1938*, Sheed, 1942.

C. L. Mowat, *Britain Between the Wars, 1918-1940*, Univ. of Chicago, 1955; D. C. Somervell, *British Politics Since 1900*, Oxford, 1950. Two excellent treatments of the period. Two absorbing social histories which reveal moods and trends are R. Graves and A. Hodge, *The Long Week End: A Social History of Great Britain, 1918-1939*, Macmillan, 1941; and J. Montgomery, *The Twenties: An Informal Social History*, Macmillan, 1957.

H. Seton-Watson, *Eastern Europe Between the Wars, 1918-1941*, Macmillan, 1945. An outstanding analysis of political developments in east-central Europe. R. L. Wolff, *The Balkans in Our Time*, Harvard, 1956, is the best recent survey of the Balkan countries, excluding Greece.

Important works on individual states in east-central Europe are M. MacDonald, *The Republic of Austria, 1918-1934: A Study in the Failure of Democratic Government*, Oxford, 1946; C. Macartney, *Hungary and Her Successors*, Oxford, 1937; S. H. Thomson, *Czechoslovakia in European History*, Princeton, 1953; O. Halecki, *History of Poland*, Roy, 1956; and R. West, *Black Lamb and Grey Falcon: A Journey Through Jugoslavia*, Viking, 1941.

M. Childs, *Sweden: The Middle Way,** Yale. The classic story of a constructive compromise between socialism and capitalism. See also W. Fleisher, *Sweden: The Welfare State*, Day, 1956. On developments in the Scandinavian countries in general, see B. Arneson, *The Democratic Monarchies of Scandinavia*, Van Nostrand, 1949.

S. de Madariaga, *Spain: A Modern History,** Praeger. The best study of Spain in the nineteenth and twentieth centuries; stimulating and authoritative.

L. Hanke, *Modern Latin America: Continent in Ferment,** 2 vols., Anvil. A country-by-country summary, with documents. See also H. Bernstein, *Modern and Contemporary Latin America*, Lippincott, 1952.

W. Leuchtenburg, *The Perils of Prosperity: 1914-1932,** Univ. of Chicago. A brief and informal general history of the United States during the era of normalcy and big business.

F. L. Allen, *Only Yesterday,** Bantam. A popular social history of the United States in the 1920's which catches the spirit of the era.

A. M. Schlesinger, Jr., *The Crisis of the Old Order, 1919-1933*, Houghton Mifflin, 1957; H. U. Faulkner, *From Versailles to the New Deal*, Yale, 1950. Two outstanding studies of the pre-New Deal era in the United States.

CHAPTER 29

Africa and Asia Astir

AFRICA, THE MIDDLE EAST, AND INDIA (1914-1939);
CHINA AND JAPAN (1914-1930)

Introduction. The most significant achievement of nineteenth-century imperialism was its transmission of revolutionary western political and social ideas to underdeveloped societies. The concepts of democracy, parliamentary government, and nationalism, in association with western science and technology, reawakened and revitalized the long-dormant societies of the nonwestern world with their hundreds of millions of people. In this chapter we shall see how this process took place in Africa, the Middle East, India, and southeast Asia.

After World War I, colonialism was never quite the same. The colonial peoples had heard and seen too much for them ever again to treat the white man with unquestioning obedience. Indian regiments and African contingents had fought in France, and Chinese labor battalions had been brought to Europe; their horizons had been immensely broadened. Above all, the heady doctrines of democracy and self-determination had been given world-wide circulation. Similarly exciting to many colonial peoples was Lenin's violent condemnation of "capitalistic imperialism" after the success of the Bolshevik Revolution. Yet while the influence of the First World War was revealed in the growth of nationalism in India and China and among the Arabs of the Middle East, the activities of many nationalist programs and anti-imperialist movements remained tentative and secret, attracting little attention. But over the years the forces of liberation gathered their strength; and with the impact of World War II, they exploded into action.

In Japan an enlightened effort to meet the challenge of the West through modernization culminated in a series of events which turned the ancient island empire into a world power. At the same time, the growth of nondemocratic institutions, combined with population pressures, led Japan itself to take the imperialist road and, in the 1930's, made that country a dangerous threat to world peace. China, too, came to see the need for modernization and, through revolution and the gradual consolidation of government under the Kuomintang, found new dignity among the nations. But land-hungry Japan coveted China's vast territories, and Japanese imperialism was to turn ancient China into a battlefield for many years.

NEW FORCES IN AFRICA

Benefits of imperial rule. Beginning about 1890 and increasingly after the turn of the century, European imperial powers organized and consolidated their possessions in sub-Saharan Africa (see Reference Map 10). Previously unknown regions were mapped, and railroads were built. The improvement of indigenous products such as rubber and palm oil and the introduction of new crops such as cotton and cocoa enriched the colonial economies. Forestry was placed on a scientific basis; diamond, gold, and tin mines were opened; and trade increased rapidly. European settlement also increased, especially in highland areas.

New governmental systems were established, and intertribal warfare, cannibalism, and dangerous secret societies were eventually stamped out. Educational facilities, largely under the control of missionaries, were expanded with government support, and scholars began the laborious task of transcribing the native tongues so that they could become written languages. With the advent of clinics, hospitals, and sanitation campaigns, the health of the native peoples improved and infant mortality declined.

Pan-Africanism and Negro nationalism. During World War I, a great deal of fighting took place in Africa. South African, British, and Indian troops conquered the huge German East African protectorate, while troops from the Union of South Africa scattered resistance in German Southwest Africa. The German possessions of Togoland and the Cameroons were taken over by British, French, and Belgian forces.

More significant to Africa and Europe than the military successes of the Allies was the opposition to imperialism which grew during the war years, as the emphasis upon democracy and self-determination of nations was so widely publicized by President Wilson. American Negro leaders demanded greater recognition of Negro rights, particularly in Africa. Dr. W. E. B. Du Bois (1868-   ), editor of the influential American Negro newspaper *Crisis*, believed that the Paris Peace Conference should help form an internationalized, free Africa. He proposed that the former German colonies become the nucleus for a state of some twenty million people, guided by an international organization.

Complementing the sentiments expressed by the Pan-African movement were the ideals of Negro nationalism. In a convention held in New York in 1920, the members issued the Declaration of Rights of the Negro Peoples of the World, a document which went on record against race discrimination in the United States and the "inhuman, unchristian, and uncivilized treatment" of the Negro in colonial empires.

The mandate system in Africa. As a result of the Pan-African movement—coupled with a growing liberal sentiment in various nations, especially Britain—all territories conquered by the Allies in World War I were declared to be mandates. Article XXII of the League Covenant declared that the "well-being and development" of backward colonial lands was a "sacred trust of civilization." In essence, the mandate system was a compromise between annexation of the spoils of war by the victors and establishment of an international trusteeship. Parts of the Cameroons, Togoland, and German East Africa (Tanganyika) went to Great Britain. The remaining portions of the Cameroons and Togoland became French mandates. Belgium received the mandate of Ruanda-Urundi (also a part of German East Africa), while the former German colony of Southwest Africa was allotted to the Union of South Africa. The mandates were subject to the inspection and evaluation of a Permanent Mandates Commission meeting annually in Geneva. While the commission had no effective power to rectify unsatisfactory conditions in a mandate, it could place the matter before the eyes of the world.

Judgments of the mandate system, a radically new concept in colonial administration, have differed widely. To many critics, international supervision was a unique invasion of national sovereignty. To others, the Permanent Mandates Commission did not have enough power, especially the right to send its own observers into the mandated areas. (This omission was later corrected in the United Nations Trusteeship Council.)

Growth of African studies. Previous to the 1920's, relatively little information had been compiled concerning the religious systems, tribal organization, and agriculture of sub-Saharan Africa. Following the end of World War I, students of social anthropology, a new branch of the social sciences, began to undertake field trips to Africa; their findings made it clear that the backwardness of the African native was attributable primarily to disease, isolation, and superstitious practices and belief in black magic. Organized in London in 1926, the International Institute of African Languages and Cultures trained anthropologists, encouraged the study of languages, and supported research in the various colonies. New departments in the field of African studies were set up in numerous European universities.

Increasing investment in Africa. After World War I, western businessmen increasingly came to realize the economic possibilities of the African continent. By the early 1930's the total of outside investments made in sub-Saharan Africa amounted to nearly $5,-000,000,000. Up to this time tropical Africa's share of the world's trade was not important; its significance lay rather in its near monopoly of certain basic commodities: 56 per cent of the world's gold, 50 per cent of its chrome ore, 90 per cent of its diamonds and cobalt, 93 per

cent of its palm oil, and 62 per cent of its cocoa.

Impact of western ideas. As Africa awakened, its people began to feel the impact of western culture. A small student class obtained an education in high schools and colleges; a smaller number traveled abroad to attend universities in Europe and in the United States, among them Jomo Kenyatta and Tom Mboya from Kenya, Nnamdi Azikiwe from Nigeria, and Kwame Nkrumah from the Gold Coast—all destined to make history as leaders of African nationalism. With increased educational advantages came a renewed confidence in the destiny of Africa and a strong desire to share as an African in the future of one's native land.

Contact with European modes of life, as the natives labored on plantations and in the households of European settlers, missionaries, and colonial officials, rapidly undermined old faiths, customs, tribal loyalties, and social institutions—a process known as detribalization. But the African as yet belonged exclusively neither to his old tribal world nor to that of the white man. No longer bound by his tribe's laws, he was uneasy about the courts and the law of the Europeans; while accepting Christian doctrines, he secretly believed in the powers of his tribal deities. Thus the impact of western culture gave birth to unrest. Early in the 1930's the further impact of world depression—with its resulting misery to many Africans—added fuel to the rising flames of unrest.

Segregation in the Union of South Africa. South Africa was a plural society, one made up of different racial and national components that did not mix. The Dutch Europeans (the Boers) were rivals of the British settlers. Since 1902, when Britain defeated the two Boer republics, there had been bad blood between victors and vanquished. In 1909, through the union of the two former republics (the Transvaal and the Orange Free State) with the British colonies of Cape Colony and Natal, South Africa became a self-governing dominion in the British Commonwealth. But union did not bring cooperation. The Boers obtained official recognition for their language (Afrikaans, developed mainly from seventeenth-century Dutch); and they insisted upon their own flag and national anthem.

The rift between Briton and Boer was serious. More dangerous, however, was the increasing numerical gap between all Europeans on the one hand and the native population on the other. After World War I the Europeans began to eye the statistics nervously. The figures disclosed that there were 5,500,000 pure Africans in the Union and 1,800,000 whites, just under 50 per cent of them of British stock. In addition there were 200,000 Asiatics and 600,000 "colored," a term referring to the people, mainly in Cape Province, of mixed white and nonwhite blood. Fearful of being overwhelmed by sheer numbers, many whites became convinced that the natives had to be kept separate from the European community socially and that all political control must remain in the hands of the Europeans.

Segregation and the color bar spread rapidly in the 1930's. Africans were required to live on their tribal reserves. Only those who obtained special permission could work on farms owned by Europeans or in the cities; and in urban areas they were obliged to live in squalid, segregated "locations" and had to carry passes and identity cards under penalty of arrest and fine or imprisonment if found without them. Native labor unions were discouraged and strikes were forbidden. In addition, government regulations or the white labor unions excluded Africans from certain skilled trades. Laws earmarked special jobs on railroads and in city services for Europeans; wages for these jobs, even when the unskilled and uneducated were employed, were raised; and the cost was paid by special subsidies. The practice was most discriminatory; the average wage for Europeans was just under four dollars a day, while that of the Africans was just above three dollars a week. African unrest was shown in the increasing native crime rate in the cities, in the formation of underground organizations, and in the efforts of African lawyers, doctors, and journalists to secure political rights.

Native unrest could also be seen in other areas. In the Gold Coast, Nigeria, and Kenya, educated Africans formed political organizations to express their demands for more self-government. Except in the Union, however, African nationalist aspirations were not widespread. The continent was only gradually awakening and feeling the tingling currents of world forces. Its nationalistic upsurge was to wait until after World War II.

TENSIONS IN THE ARAB WORLD

Cultural links between Asia and Africa. The heart of the Arab world is the Middle East, a difficult region to define. The term is used most often in reference to the lands connecting Asia with Africa, the chief boundary markers being Cairo, Istanbul, Teheran, and the south coast of the Arabian peninsula. Nearly all the peoples of the Middle East are united in a common faith (Islam) and share a common tongue and culture (Arabic). Because of the unifying force of this heritage, Muslim North Africa (Morocco, Algeria, Tunisia, Libya) will be treated in this chapter as part of the Arab world.

With the exception of Morocco, North Africa at the beginning of the nineteenth century was nominally under the sovereignty of the Ottoman Turks, whose capital city was Constantinople. In practice, however, the various states in this area were self-governing. During the nineteenth century all of North Africa from Casablanca in Morocco to Cairo in Egypt came under European imperialistic rule, while the other Arab lands in the Middle East continued under the despotic control of the sultans.

The Arab revolt. In 1913 an Arab Congress, meeting in Paris, demanded home rule and equality with the Turks in the Ottoman empire. Because the Middle East was strategically important to Britain, the British government followed the rise of Arab discontent with great interest. During the years 1915 and 1916 extensive correspondence was carried on between the British high commissioner in Cairo and Sherif Husein of Mecca (Husein ibn-Ali, 1856-1931), guardian of the holy places in the Hejaz. In the event of an Arab revolt, Great Britain undertook to recognize Arab independence except in those regions of coastal Syria which were not wholly Arab and in those which might be claimed by France. But British commitments were purposely vague, and the correspondence has been called "a monument of ambiguity."

In addition to the British alliance with the Arab nationalist movement, the indomitable desert warrior Abdul-Aziz ibn-Saud (1880-1953), sultan of Nejd in south-central Arabia, was induced to adopt a policy of benevolent neutrality toward Britain. The wooing of the Arabs thwarted the Turkish attempt to rouse the whole Muslim Middle East by preaching a *jihad*, or holy war, against the British.

Late in 1916 the Arab revolt began. Husein raised the standard of rebellion in the Hejaz, proclaimed independence from the Turks, and captured Mecca for his cause. In the fighting that followed, the Arab forces were commanded by the third son of the Sherif Husein, Emir Faisal (1885-1933), who was assisted by a remarkable English officer, Colonel T. E. Lawrence (1888-1935), later known as Lawrence of Arabia.

Under Lawrence, the Arabs took a decisive part in the last battle against the main Turkish forces in September 1918. When the war ended, Syria was occupied by the victorious Allied forces; a small French force was located along the coast of Lebanon; Emir Faisal and his Arab forces were in the interior, grouped around Damascus; and the British controlled Palestine.

During the war years a number of important commitments had been made. In 1916, in the Sykes-Picot Agreement, the Fertile Crescent (Syria and Iraq) had been divided into four zones, with Britain and France each controlling two. Palestine was to be placed under an international administration. With the Balfour Declaration (1917), the British government gave its support to the establishment of a national home for the Jewish people in Palestine. In 1918 an Anglo-French pronouncement pledged the establishment of national governments "deriving their authority from the initiative and free choice of the indigenous populations."

The peace settlement. At the peace conference Faisal, aided by Lawrence, pleaded in vain for Arab independence. Faisal was still ruler in Damascus, and in March 1920, while the statesmen in Paris argued, a congress of Syrian leaders met and resolved that he should be king of a united Syria, including Palestine and Lebanon. But in April the San Remo Conference of the Allied powers turned over all Arab territories formerly in the Ottoman empire to be administered as mandates. Syria and Lebanon were mandated to France; Iraq and Palestine, to Great Britain.

From the Arabs' point of view, the peace settlement in the Middle East was a shabby piece of statesmanship compounded of ignorance, deception, and conflicting aims. Apologists for Britain and France point out that Britain made promises to France during the war because the British could hardly deny the requests of their most important ally. Britain in 1916 made its ambiguous pledge to Husein because of its desperate need for Arab friendship. Again, in the Balfour Declaration, Britain acted according to short-range interests; in order to swing the support of the world's Jews to the Allied cause and to maintain communications in the Middle East, Britain promised to make available to Jewish settlement the Arab region of Palestine. The plain fact remains, however, that the Allied statesmen at Paris were profoundly ignorant of the intensity of Arab nationalism.

Let us now examine the events between World Wars I and II in the mandated areas (Syria, Lebanon, Iraq, and Palestine) and then trace the growth of tensions in Iran, Egypt, and North Africa.

The French in Syria and Lebanon. In 1920, following the San Remo Conference, a French army moved against Damascus and ejected Faisal from the throne. After this incident, the French took over the mandates of Lebanon and Syria.

In 1925 the Druses, a proud Muslim sect living in the mountains, revolted and touched

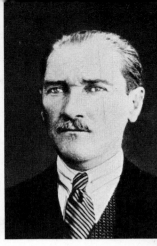

Prominent figures in the nationalist movement in the Middle East were Lawrence of Arabia, Faisal al Husein, Riza Shah Pahlavi, and Mustafa Kemal Pasha (left to right). Beloved by the Arab tribesmen, Lawrence helped organize the Arab revolt, led daring guerrilla raids against the Turks, and pleaded in vain the cause of Arab independence after World War I. In 1921 he served as an adviser on Arab affairs for the British Colonial Office but resigned in disgust over British policies. Emir Faisal fought with Lawrence against the Turks and joined him in his plea for Arab independence. Denied the kingship of

Syria when that country was mandated to France, Faisal in 1921 became king of Iraq with the support of the British and of Iraqi nationalists. In 1925 his realm became a constitutional monarchy modeled on the British pattern. Another nationalist leader, Riza Shah Pahlavi, seized power in Iran, thus thwarting Britain's attempts to control the government. In Turkey, Mustafa Kemal Pasha set up a new government in defiance of the Allies and initiated important reforms. Under his direction, illiteracy was attacked, new law codes were adopted, and the status of women was improved.

off two years of civil war. An artillery bombardment of Damascus by the French aroused widespread resentment. The French then instituted a more conciliatory policy. In 1926 Lebanon was recognized as a republic, and the same status was accorded four years later to the four administrative divisions of Syria. In practice, however, these republics continued under effective French control. Relative tranquillity reigned until 1935, when a new wave of nationalism shook Syria and Lebanon. As a result the more liberal Popular Front government in France (see p. 717) drew up two treaties. Under these treaties the mandates were recognized as independent republics which were to become members of the League of Nations, and France was granted certain privileges in their territories, such as the right to maintain troops and military bases. However, the French parliament kept postponing ratification of the agreements, and finally in 1939 the Syrian constitution was suspended.

Politically, French rule was a failure in Syria and Lebanon. At the outset a popular Arab king had been ejected, and for the next twenty years the French administration often suppressed personal and political liberties. Under French mandatory rule, however, the modernization of Syria and Lebanon proceeded: roads and public buildings were constructed, and the use of electricity and irrigation works was extended.

British policy in Iraq. Great Britain's vital interest in the mandate of Iraq was prompted largely by Iraq's rich oil resources, its growing importance in East-West air transportation, and its proximity to the Persian Gulf. But this interest did not prevent the British from taking steps to satisfy Iraqi nationalism after the outbreak of rebellion in June 1920. In March 1921 the Iraqi throne was offered to Faisal, who had lost his throne in Syria. In a plebescite Faisal was strongly supported as ruler of the Iraqi, and a few months later he was proclaimed king. In 1922 Britain and Faisal's government signed a treaty which stipulated that Britain was to supervise the finances and military affairs of the new state. Three years later a constitution was adopted which made the country a constitutional monarchy with a bicameral legislature. In 1930 an Anglo-Iraqi treaty was signed which granted Iraq full independence, and in 1932 Iraq was admitted to the League of Nations. By these concessions Britain avoided the conflict experienced by France in Syria and Lebanon.

During the late 1930's, however, the skillful propaganda of Fascist Italy, combined with Arab hostility regarding the British policy in Palestine, brought about a decline of good will toward Britain in Iraq.

Arab-Jewish conflict in Palestine. Between the two world wars, Palestine was the most tempestuous area in all the Middle East, as Britain sought to protect its imperial interests and at the same time reconcile them with Zionism and Arab nationalism. Nevertheless, from 1922 to 1929, peace and progress were possible chiefly because Jewish immigration was not large. As the Zionists reclaimed land, set up collective farms, harnessed the Jordan for power, and established many new factories, a veritable economic revolution took place. Tel-Aviv grew into a thriving modern city, an excellent university was founded at Jerusalem, and Palestine became the center of a Hebrew renaissance.

The era of peace ended in 1929 when serious disorders broke out, mainly Arab attacks on Jews. Violence continued to erupt in the early 1930's as the Nazi persecution of the Jews brought about a steep rise in immigration to Palestine and threatened the predominant position of the Arabs in the area. In 1937 a British commission of inquiry recommended a tripartite division: Palestine would be divided into two independent states, one controlled by the Arabs and one by the Jews, with Britain holding a third portion, a small mandated area containing Jerusalem and Bethlehem. This recommendation satisfied no one and was not accepted. Although the outbreak of World War II shelved the Zionist-Arab quarrel in Palestine, after the war the controversy was to break out again with still greater virulence.

Arabia and the rivalry for Arab leadership. The collapse of Ottoman rule in 1918 left several important independent states such as Yemen, Hejaz, and Nejd to adjust their relations, plus a few British protectorates on the Arabian Sea and the Persian Gulf.

The first contender for leadership of the peninsula was Sherif Husein. In alliance with Great Britain, his sons had already been favored by the gift of kingdoms: Faisal in Iraq and Abdullah in Trans-Jordan, the territory carved out of the eastern portion of Palestine. At the close of World War I, it appeared that the Hashemite family of Husein would become the greatest single political force in Arabia and the Fertile Crescent.

The rival of the Hashemites was ibn-Saud, whose family had ruled Nejd since the eighteenth century and had become identified with a reformist, puritanical Muslim sect known as the Wahabis. Husein regarded the ruler of Nejd with contempt. But, fortunately for ibn-Saud, Husein made a series of blunders: he alienated many Arabs by proclaiming himself king of the Arabs; he quarreled with Britain, which ceased to render him support; and he underestimated the capacity of ibn-Saud.

In 1919 one of Husein's sons was defeated by the Wahabi warriors of ibn-Saud. All-out war against Husein began in 1924, and by the following year ibn-Saud was victorious and his troops occupied Mecca, Jidah, Taif, and Medina. A treaty with Britain in 1927 brought ibn-Saud recognition as king of both Hejaz and Nejd; in 1932 all his holdings were renamed Saudi Arabia. In 1934 he defeated the last of his rivals—the king of Yemen—who was allowed to retain his independence. Two years earlier, vast oil reserves had been discovered in eastern Arabia. Important concessions were given to an American oil company, and ibn-Saud now commanded the wealth essential for a powerful state. All the tribal groups in Arabia were welded into a strong political entity, with enormous economic resources.

Riza Shah Pahlavi rules Iran. Also at stake in the period between World Wars I and II was the fate of Persia (or Iran as it came to be called in the 1920's), a land which was Muslim in religion but not Arabic in culture. During the First World War, Iran was a battleground for Turkish, Russian, and British interests. With the elimination of Russia in 1919 as a serious contender in this region, the British Foreign Office sought to bring Iran closely under its control.

The proposed Anglo-Persian agreement aroused nationalism to a high pitch. Before the Majlis (the parliament) could approve the treaty, the nationalists had seized power. Their agent was a brilliant military officer, Riza Shah Pahlavi (1877-1944), who marched on Teheran, the capital, in 1921. Four years later the shah was forced to resign, and Riza Shah took his place, founding the Pahlavi dynasty.

The new ruler was a strongly nationalistic reformer who wished to emulate Mustafa Kemal of Turkey (see p. 698) in modernizing his country. Special privileges enjoyed by foreigners were abolished, and stiffer terms in royalties were demanded from the Anglo-Iranian Oil Company, which was tapping the country's rich petroleum reserves. The restless tribes were brought under the control of the law, the army was modernized, trade and industry were encouraged and brought under government control, and education was improved. Between 1928 and 1936 the Trans-Iranian Railroad was built, connecting the Persian Gulf and the Caspian Sea. But in spite of his impressive record of progress, Riza Shah had a serious weakness. Impatient with delay or inefficiency, he steadily developed the mind of a tyrant. The government grew more authoritarian, the Majlis came to be a mere puppet body, and corruption was again on the increase. The decaying rule of Riza Shah was destined to collapse during World War II.

Afghanistan. To the east of Iran was the remote and almost inaccessible kingdom of Afghanistan. In 1919 the Afghan emir, believing that nationalist unrest in India rendered that country a likely prize (see p. 699), made the mistake of invading the subcontinent and was defeated with severe losses. Later the course of Turkish reform attracted the emir's attention; but though he promulgated a new constitution, the reforms were mainly on paper. In 1928 a destructive civil war brought the emir's brother to the throne, but no reform in government was forthcoming. Between World Wars I and II, Afghanistan remained politically unstable, its natural resources neglected and its people illiterate.

The problem of Egyptian sovereignty. While the Arabs in the mandates had been struggling for the right of self-determination, a parallel development was taking place in Egypt. When the British refused a delegation of Egyptian nationalists permission to attend the Paris Peace Conference and deported the spokesman of the group and his followers, the Nile valley rose in revolt.

After three years of disorder the government in London announced that Egypt was no longer a British protectorate. It was to be a sovereign state, subject to certain reservations. Britain was to remain responsible for the defense of the country, for the protection of foreign interests, and for communications vital to the British empire—above all, the Suez Canal. Egypt grudgingly adapted itself to this declaration, made its sultan a king, and proclaimed a constitution in 1923. Anglo-Egyptian relations remained unsatisfactory, however, and frequent negotiations between the two governments were fruitless. In Egypt from 1924 to 1936, corruption in high places, the increasing number of university graduates unable to find suitable employment, the wide gap between the very rich and the abysmally poor, and the bitter feud between the king and the most important political party (the Wafd) helped to create unrest.

Respite in the long record of Anglo-Egyptian acrimony came about through the threat of Italian Fascist aggression in Africa following Mussolini's conquest of Ethiopia (see p. 721). In 1936 Britain and Egypt negotiated a treaty of alliance. In the case of war there was to be mutual assistance on a wide scale, and the status of the Sudan* was to continue unaltered.

*The Sudan (see Reference Map 10) had been influenced by Egypt for many centuries and in 1820 was brought under Egyptian rule. In the 1880's fanatical Muslims had driven the Egyptians out and had put to death General Gordon, the governor at Khartoum, who was the agent of the Egyptian government. In the 1890's the British reconquered the Sudan and declared it a condominium—that is, a territory theoretically under the dual sovereignty of Britain and Egypt, although it was really under British control. The treaty of alliance of 1936 stated that the Sudan would remain technically under joint Anglo-Egyptian administration for the "welfare of the Sudanese."

Fascist rule in Libya. West of Egypt lies Libya, the desert land seized in 1912 from Turkey by land-hungry Italy. The fierce nomadic tribes put up a stout resistance to European invasion, but in time Italian authority became fully established. In the 1930's an ambitious program of development and colonization was put into effect which was of benefit to the Italian immigrants, not the natives. By 1939, when World War II began, Libya had been politically integrated with the kingdom of Italy, the Libyan colonial administrative units having been converted into Italian provinces.

Aggressive nationalism in North Africa. Long before the outbreak of World War I, Algeria had become politically integrated with France; Tunisia had prospered under French rule and had maintained its native ruler, the bey; and the native sultan had also been retained in the protectorate France established in Morocco in 1911. Nevertheless, the storm signals of bitter nationalism had appeared, particularly in Morocco.

Shortly after the First World War, rebellion broke out in Spanish Morocco under the leadership of the Riff chieftain Abd-el Krim. When revolt spread to French Morocco, the French joined the Spanish in a vigorous campaign which brought the defeat of Krim and his Riffs in 1926. But though defeated, Abd-el Krim's exploits had caused a sensation in the Arab world. Again, in 1930, an organized nationalist movement, fanned by the world economic depression, began in Morocco. Though some administrative posts were made available to Moroccans and some other demands were met in the late 1930's, no further steps were taken to implement self-rule.

The year 1934 marked a major change in the concept of nationalism in Morocco. In this year a group of young Moroccans presented their Plan of Moroccan Reforms. While the efforts of Abd-el Krim had represented tribal opposition to foreign rule, the formation of a nationalist party heralded the birth of a modern nationalistic movement. In 1937 there was an unsuccessful nationalist revolt. On the eve of World War II, Arab nationalism was growing but was still relatively weak and in the main was driven underground by French repressive measures.

Tunisia was the most westernized area in French North Africa, and in 1919 a nationalist party called the Destour (meaning "constitution" in Arabic) was formed to secure more democratic forms of government. In 1934, after this party was suppressed, another nationalist group, the Neo-Destour, was formed. Four years later this group was banned also, and the nationalist movement went underground.

In Algeria, organized political agitation against the French began in 1926, but incidents were relatively few. The natives demanded an easier means of acquiring French citizenship and, with citizenship, the additional rights and economic advantages which this status implied. French citizenship had been extended after the First World War to a large number of Muslims who qualified on the basis of war service, literacy, and other tests, but opposition—mainly from French settlers in Algeria—largely prevented further reforms during the 1930's.

France deserved much credit for its colonial rule. Administration on the whole was just and efficient, the economy prospered, and living standards advanced. Nevertheless, a fundamental split existed between the privileged Christian minority and the overwhelming Muslim majority. Until 1939 the nationalist movement in North Africa was largely a monopoly of the relatively small intellectual groups and middle class, with the sympathy and support of liberals and leftists in France. The mass of peasants, however, remained quite apathetic.

Mustafa Kemal's rise to power in Turkey. We have seen in Chapter 23 how reform measures had been initiated by the Young Turks just before World War I. Defeat in the war, the revolt of the Arabs, and the impotence of the sultan's government convinced some patriots that only the most drastic measures could save the Turkish nation. In addition, they were embittered by the harsh terms of the Treaty of Sèvres (1920). It was bad enough to lose their empire, peopled by Arabs, but it was much worse to see their homeland, mainly Anatolia and the city of Smyrna, partitioned by the treaty and invaded by the Greeks and Italians.

Imbued with a new spirit of nationalism, the patriots rallied around the military hero Mustafa Kemal Pasha (1880-1938), who had a brilliant record against the British at Gallipoli in World War I. An important figure in the Young Turks movement, Kemal was a born leader, thoroughly western in education and outlook. After the defeat of Turkey, he had been sent by the sultan to demobilize the Turkish troops in Asia Minor, but, disregarding his instructions, he had reorganized the troops and successfully defied the Allies. A new government was set up in Ankara, and Kemal was selected as president and commander in chief. Turkish patriotism was galvanized by the National Pact, a declaration of principles which upheld the rule of self-determination and also proclaimed the abolition of the special rights heretofore enjoyed by foreigners in Turkey, a mark of Turkish inequality in the family of nations.

In 1921 the Greeks advanced toward Ankara. The fighting was desperate, but the armies of Kemal were finally victorious. The Greeks fled in confusion toward the sea, and their last toe hold, Smyrna, was destroyed by fire. In 1922 the Turkish sultanate was abolished, and the following year a republic was established. The Allies had no alternative but to agree to a revision of Sèvres. The Treaty of Lausanne, signed in 1923, returned to Turkey some Aegean islands and the territory adjoining Constantinople. The heartland of Turkey—Anatolia—remained intact, no reparations were demanded of the republic, and the special privileges of foreigners were abolished. Although Turkey had lost the whole Arabic-speaking part of its possessions, Kemal had saved a large, cohesively Turkish portion of the former Ottoman empire.

Kemal's reforms. The new constitution was democratic in form, but in reality Kemal was a dictator who brooked no interference with his plans. His dictatorship does not belong in the same category as those fashioned in Nazi Germany, or Fascist Italy, or Communist Russia, however. In the new Turkey there was little of the cult of the superior race; the brutal efficiency of the purge and the concentration camp was practically unknown. Dictatorship was regarded as the rough but essential highway to parliamentary government. Kemal envisioned a dictatorship as a necessary stage in raising his people to that level of education and social well-being which a system of democratic government requires.

Under his rule the old institutions and customs of a backward Oriental state were transformed or replaced within a few short years. In modern times such a wholesale adoption of new culture traits is duplicated nowhere except perhaps in Japan. The caliphate, the sultan's spiritual leadership of the Muhammadan world, was abolished. New law codes were promulgated, and school attendance was required to the age of sixteen. Use of the fez by men and the veil by women was forbidden. Polygamy was prohibited. In addition, the western Gregorian calendar and European numerals were introduced, and the Latin alphabet replaced the Arabic.

Thus, Turkey was rejuvenated by its indefatigable leader. More progress was made in the two decades after the end of the First World War than had been registered during the entire nineteenth century. Understandably, Mustafa Kemal was called *Atatürk*, meaning "the father of the Turks."

INDIA SEEKS TO RULE ITSELF

Moves for self-government. Many observers had predicted that in the event of war Great Britain would find India a serious liability. But when hostilities began, nearly all unfriendly activities against Britain ceased. By 1917, however, it became apparent that the Indian people expected compensation from Britain in the way of increased self-government. Parliament's reply was that the goal to be attained in India was the gradual development of self-government within the British empire. By the Government of India Act of 1919, a system of diarchy, or double government, was proposed in the provinces by which certain powers were reserved to the

British while the provincial legislatures were accorded other, generally lesser powers.

Chances for the acceptance in India of the act of 1919 were swept away by the outbreak of a struggle between the British and the Indian nationalists. In an ill-advised moment the British passed the Rowlatt Acts (1919), which allowed the police and other officials extraordinary powers in ferreting out subversive activity. Although the acts were never enforced, they were deeply resented as a token of repression. Disgruntled and disheartened, many nationalists demanded sweeping changes.

Gandhi and civil disobedience. The foremost nationalist leader in India was Mohandas K. Gandhi (1869-1948). Born of middle-class parents, Gandhi had been sent to London to study law; later he went to South Africa, where he built up a lucrative practice and championed the rights of his people. The Indians in South Africa were subject to restrictive laws which hampered their freedom of movement, prevented them from buying property, and imposed upon them special taxation. By the use of "passive resistance," or noncooperation, Gandhi forced the government to remove some restrictions. Disdaining the use of violence, he believed that a just cause triumphs if its supporters attempt to convince those in power of injustices by practicing "civil disobedience." With Gandhi as their leader, the Indians in South Africa carried on various strikes, including hunger strikes; they refused work, held mass demonstrations, and marched into areas where their presence was forbidden by law. When Gandhi returned to his native land shortly after the outbreak of World War I, he was welcomed as a hero.

In 1919 Gandhi introduced his campaign to force the British to grant India self-rule. A mass strike was announced in which all work was to cease and the population was to pray and fast. Contrary to Gandhi's plan, however, riots took place, Europeans were killed, and soldiers were sent to try to restore order. Although public gatherings were forbidden, a large body of unarmed Indians assembled at Amritsar. They were dispersed by

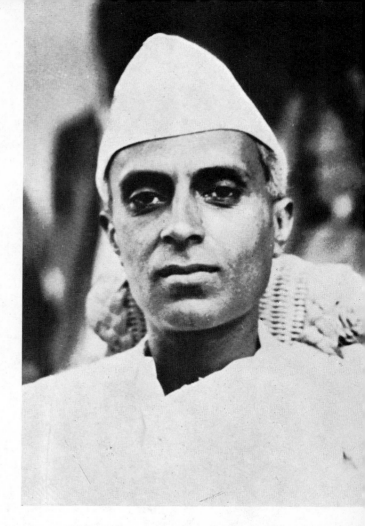

After the Amritsar massacre of 1919, Nehru joined Gandhi's followers, eventually becoming second only to the beloved Mahatma in the independence movement.

gunfire, and several hundred were killed. All hope of cooperation between Indian and Briton was temporarily at an end. Arrested in 1922, Gandhi seemed to welcome being placed on trial; he assured the British magistrate that the only alternative to permitting him to continue his campaign was to imprison him. Sentenced to six years' imprisonment, Gandhi suffered a temporary eclipse.

The Government of India Act of 1935. A new road to conciliation opened in 1930, when a series of round-table conferences was arranged in London. At the first of these conferences, the Indian princes agreed in principle to the idea of creating in India a great federal union. Unfortunately, safeguards in-

The Indian people loved and respected Gandhi, who understood their problems and honored the ancient traditions. Besides striving for the independence of India, Gandhi sought to end excessive drinking, to raise the status of women in society, to remove the stigma attached to the untouchables, and to bring about cooperation between Hindus and Muslims. He was convinced that injustices could be destroyed only through love, unselfishness, and patience. In the picture above, Gandhi is shown just after he arrived in England to attend a round-table conference on the future of India.

sisted upon by the Muslim minority for its protection under the new government were not defined to the satisfaction of either Hindus or Muslims. Moreover, the native princes and the delegates from British India could not agree on the details of federation.

Finally, in the year 1935, a second Government of India Act became law, and two years later it began to function. The new constitution provided for a substantial degree of self-government but did not award India complete independence. Instead, a federal government was established, consisting of a viceroy and a legislature composed of a council of state and a legislative assembly. To these houses both the Indian princes and the eleven provinces of British India were to send representatives. In the central government all the departments of government were transferred to the Indian legislators except the departments of defense, religious affairs, and foreign relations, which remained in British hands. In addition, a supreme court was established. In the provinces of British India, the government was to be under the control of Indian lawmakers, subject to certain controls held by the British governors.

From 1937 to 1939 provincial responsible government, which went into effect in seven of the eleven provinces of British India, was deemed a success. The British governors allowed Indian legislators to form their own policies, which were carried out by British civil servants. But during these same years, the possibility of federation faded away; the native princes became increasingly hesitant about placing themselves under the central government. In June 1939, they definitely rejected the constitution.

The Indian National Congress. The new regime established by the Government of India Act of 1935 failed to satisfy the demands of the Indian nationalists, who continued to espouse the cause of complete independence for India. The chief element in the nationalist movement was the powerful Indian National Congress, which had become the organ of the extreme nationalists. Membership, estimated at several million, was predominantly Hindu but also included many Muslims and members of other religious groups. Soon after the First World War, the congress had come under the leadership of Gandhi, whose personal following among the people was the chief source of the party's tremendous influence.

By 1939 Gandhi shared leadership of the nationalist movement with Jawaharlal Nehru (1889-   ), a profound thinker, an able statesman, and an attractive personality. Devoted friends, the two leaders differed profoundly in many of their ideas for the future of India: Gandhi wished to expel western influences and return India to a primitive handicraft economy and a simple, ascetic way of life; Nehru believed India should be westernized and industrialized and should become a socialistic state. But however much they disagreed over solutions to economic and social problems, they agreed on a free and united India.

The Hindu-Muslim clash. The nationalist movement in India was complicated by the existence of a second powerful political party, the Muslim League. Led by an able and aggressive lawyer, Muhammad Ali Jinnah (1876-1948), the league sought to protect the Muslim minority in India.

The position of the Muslim League highlighted the division between the Hindus and Muslims, a division termed "the communal problem." The position of the congress party was that in a democratic and self-governing India, men would think of themselves as Indians rather than as members of Hindu or Muslim communities, and the deep-seated religious differences would thus gradually become politically unimportant. The strategy of the Muslim League, on the other hand, was to underline and perpetuate these differences. This fundamental clash of viewpoints was one factor behind the British reluctance to accede to Indian demands for freedom. Having a tremendous economic investment in the country and facing the imminent danger of world war, Britain was unwilling to withdraw in the absence of a compromise which would assure India a measure of political stability.

NATIONALISM IN SOUTHEAST

ASIA AND OCEANIA

The late beginning of nationalist feeling. Nationalism in southeast Asia received a strong stimulus as a result of the First World War, and nationalistic feelings mounted steadily in the 1920's and 1930's. On the eve of World War II, however, the masses of people in this area were apathetic to nationalism, which was the preoccupation of a small intellectual group and the middle class, constituting not more than 10 per cent of the population. Nationalist leaders obtained support in the towns and ignored the peasants.

While a discontented nationalist might have felt the pace toward self-government was unnecessarily sluggish, the general policy of the British colonial administrations was directed toward establishing legislatures and granting a substantial measure of self-government to the native peoples. The ultimate goal of British plans for the colonies was dominion status—that is, practical independence within the loose bonds of the British Commonwealth. On the other hand, France endowed its colonies with little independence or self-rule. The French aim was not independence but rather a close association of states dominated from Paris. Dutch rule was also paternalistic.

Concessions to nationalism in Ceylon and Burma. Before the First World War, Ceylon had been governed paternally as a British crown colony. In the early 1920's, colonial administration was somewhat liberalized, and in 1930 a progressive constitution was adopted which provided for universal suffrage and for a system of political administration which allowed full self-government in some areas and retention of British control in others.

In Burma, although British rule brought undisputed benefits, serious social and economic maladjustments occurred as a result of commercial growth. Although Burma was granted a more liberal constitution in 1922, nationalist unrest persisted, and, in 1930, depression brought economic distress and a serious uprising against the Indian and Chinese communities which were exploiting the native Burmese.

By the mid-thirties the nationalist movement had become an important challenge to alien rule, and, in 1937, substantial concessions were made by Britain: Burma was separated from India and given home rule, subject to certain emergency powers held by the British governor. The course of Burmese politics from

1937 to the Japanese invasion in 1942 was not encouraging, however. The political scene was characterized by a confusing multiplicity of political parties, by bribery and favoritism, and by the decline of civil service standards. While both men and women now enjoyed the vote, the electorate was apathetic.

Despotism and economic domination in Siam. Although Siam (later to be known as Thailand) had escaped European colonial control, it had not avoided western influences. The Siamese nationalists, not obliged to contend with alien control, directed their activities against despotic monarchs and against the Chinese community, which monopolized much of the banking and trade. In 1932 a peaceful revolution forced the king to accept a new democratic constitution. However, the revolution merely widened the ranks of the oligarchy controlling the country.

In 1933 the constitution was revoked, and another revolution reëstablished constitutional rule supported by the army. But politics remained confused, the pawn of professional politicians and army generals. In the late 1930's the country continued to be governed by a small clique, and its economic life was still dominated by the immigrant Chinese.

Malaya's plural society. After World War I, the economic growth of British Malaya continued, especially in the tin and rubber industries. Unlike most colonial territories, Malaya experienced little nationalist feeling before 1939. This passivity can be explained in part by the rivalry existing between native Malays and the influential Indian and Chinese communities. Who should rule whom and on what lines self-government might be developed were unique and difficult problems.

The French in Indochina. Criticized for their policies more than the British or Dutch in southeast Asia were the French in Indochina. The protective tariff was used in Indochina as a means of guaranteeing a market for French goods, and many complaints were voiced about the heavy burden of indirect taxes upon the common people. Although rubber, rice, and coal production increased under French rule, little improvement was apparent in the well-being of the people.

After the First World War various nationalist groups were active, the best organized being the Communists led by Ho Chi Minh (1892-   ). Born in Annam, he journeyed to Europe, joined the Communist party in France, and after 1918 went to the Soviet Union, where he received expert advice on the art of making revolutions. Although during the 1930's the nationalist movement was ineffectual, largely because of the stern manner in which the French suppressed uprisings and also because of divisions between the nationalists themselves, the Communists under the leadership of Ho Chi Minh were active underground.

Paternal Dutch rule in the East Indies. Under Dutch rule the Netherlands East Indies became famous for the degree to which modern science was applied to tropical agriculture and the manner in which law and order were established in a region torn by native rivalries. The wealth of the country increased and the population grew. But the Dutch failed to concern themselves with the growing aspirations of their native wards. The representative parliament established in 1918 remained purely an advisory body until 1927, and even though a degree of liberalization then took place, in essence the paternal nature of the administration remained unchanged.

With the impact of world depression in the early 1930's, unrest and nationalism grew stronger. Dutch officials began to realize that self-rule was inevitable, but they refused to reconcile themselves to the possibility of the Indies breaking all ties with the Netherlands. For their part, the nationalists became more modest in their demands because of the uncertain world situation and the menace of Japanese imperialism. They indicated a willingness to remain united to the Dutch crown and to accept a plan of self-government similar to British dominion status.

The problem of Philippine independence. American rule in the Philippines was probably the most enlightened of all colonial regimes. Its two main objectives were to promote literacy and to develop powers of self-government as quickly as possible. Economically, the islands developed rapidly as American investment dollars poured in and free trade between the Philippines and the United States reached a combined total of nearly $500,000,000 in the late 1930's.

The independence movement in the Philippines had begun prior to World War I. The first nationalist party appeared in 1907, the year in which the Philippine Assembly was created. Congress' passage of the Jones Act in 1916 pledged the United States "to recognize Philippine independence as soon as stable government could be established." In the 1920's the Republican administrations in Washington were lukewarm toward independence, but with the return of a Democratic administration in 1933, the prospects of complete freedom brightened—in part because the Democratic party had always been more favorably disposed toward this objective. Moreover, the onset of the depression had caused some economic groups in the United States to oppose free imports from the Philippines. After several false starts the Tydings-McDuffie Act was passed in 1934. By this act the Filipinos were empowered to draft a constitution, which was drawn up in 1935. The same year the Commonwealth of the Philippines came into being with Manuel Quezon (1878-1944) as its first president. During a ten-year transitional period, ultimate power in foreign affairs and defense was to reside with the president of the United States. To cushion the shock of economic separation, a system of graduated tariffs was provided.

CHINA TRIES TO CHANGE

The Republic of China is born. During the course of the nineteenth century, the once mighty Chinese empire had increasingly felt the encroachments of the great imperialistic powers. Loss of territory, the imposition of extraterritoriality, and foreign control of the tariff all symbolized China's impotence. In the first decade of the twentieth century, however, a strong liberal and nationalistic movement emerged, determined to oust the Manchu dynasty, establish a parliamentary

Born the son of a tenant farmer, Sun Yat-sen received a western education in Hawaii, was converted to Christianity, and in 1892 received a diploma in medicine in Hong Kong. Shortly afterwards, he became a leader in the Chinese nationalist movement. Forced into exile in 1895, he sought financial aid for his cause from Chinese living in foreign countries, and he continued to exert his powerful influence over the nationalists in China, eventually engineering the overthrow of the Manchu.

regime, and modernize Chinese society. Only thus, the nationalists felt, could China be saved. The most important leader of the movement for a new China was Sun Yat-sen (1867-1925), who organized the Kuomintang, or National People's party, as the instrument for carrying out his policies.

In 1911 a revolt broke out in China over a foreign loan to finance railways, and the outbreak spread like wildfire through the provinces. Yüan Shih-kai (1859-1916), the outstanding military leader in north China and the former confidant of Tzu Hsi, the dowager empress, persuaded the imperial clan that the Manchu dynasty was doomed. In February 1912 the emperor abdicated, and Yüan was asked to form a republic. Although a few months earlier an assembly of revolutionaries

A fervent patriot, Chiang nevertheless had little appreciation for his people's social and economic problems. He was much more deeply concerned with their moral regeneration. Versed in Taoist and Confucian teachings but at the same time a devout Christian, he formulated a New Life Movement, a combination of Christian and Confucian ethics. He paid little attention to the grievances of the peasants, and his government favored urban development over agrarian reform.

at Nanking had elected Sun president of their new republic, he stepped aside to prevent internal dissension, and the republican group at Nanking elected Yüan.

Dissension and disorder in the government. In 1913 trouble broke out when Yüan negotiated a large loan with bankers from Great Britain, France, Germany, and Russia, thus giving these powers substantial influence in the government of the republic. The outcome was a new rebellion, endorsed by Sun. Yüan suppressed the revolt, dismissed the parliament, and announced the imminent restoration of the monarchy with himself as emperor. Rebellion again broke out, and in June 1916 the discredited dictator died.

Dissension in the government continued for the next ten years. The political picture was complicated by strained relations with Japan during World War I (see p. 705) and China's entry into the war. It is impossible here to trace the confusion in Chinese politics during this period. For a time the country was divided between two would-be governments, one in the north at Peking, the other in the south at Canton. Composed largely of the radicals who had engineered the revolution of 1911-1912, the Canton government in 1921 elected Sun as president.

Three Principles of the People. Unable to obtain aid from the western powers to overcome the Peking government, Sun called in advisers from the Soviet Union, among them the brilliant Bolshevik, Michael Borodin. Because of its confidence in Borodin and his associates, the Kuomintang adopted many of the planks of the program subscribed to by the Communist party in the U.S.S.R.

In 1925 Sun died. More skillful as a propagandist and revolutionist than as a political administrator, he had not succeeded in reuniting the Peking regime with his Kuomintang government. However, his social ideology had important results for the future. His most famous work, *San Min Chu I*, or *Three Principles of the People*, became the manual of the Kuomintang. The three principles are: (1) nationalism—the liberation of China from foreign domination; (2) democracy—"government by the people and for the people"; and (3) livelihood—economic security for all the people.

China united under Chiang Kai-shek. Sun had regarded Chiang Kai-shek (1886-   ) as his successor. From poor but sturdy peasant stock, Chiang was sent to China's first military academy, where he proved an excellent student and was selected to study military tactics in Japan. While in Japan he was stirred by Sun's vision of a new China and returned to his homeland to take an active part in the revolution. His obvious abilities attracted the attention of Sun, who sent him to Russia in 1923 for a brief period of indoctrination.

Under Chiang the armies of the Kuomintang began to drive northward in 1926. They encountered little opposition, and by early spring of the following year they reached the Yangtze valley and occupied Shanghai. But dissension broke out between radical and conservative elements in the Kuomintang, and a split became inevitable. The moderates under Chiang created a government at Nanking, and before the end of 1927, public opinion had crystallized behind this regime. Chiang used force against the leftist elements; the end of the Kuomintang alliance with the Communists was written in blood when a proletarian uprising in Canton was quelled with the loss of more than five thousand lives. Back to the Soviet Union went the Communist advisers; many radicals (including the widow of Sun Yat-sen) were driven into exile; and the Chinese Communists were scattered to the hills and mountains of south China, where they set up their own administrative units.

In retrospect, the split of 1927 stands out as a major event in modern Chinese history. The purge of left-wing elements from the Kuomintang proved a mixed blessing. Not only were extreme Marxist radicals ousted, but moderate liberals who sought basic social and political reforms through peaceful and evolutionary means were also eliminated. Nationalist strength lay with the city professional, banking, and merchant classes, and the Nanking government came to depend for financial support upon the foreign bankers at Shanghai. The regime took on a conservative character which hindered its leaders from understanding the problems of the masses.

Meanwhile Chiang married Mei-ling Soong (1892-   ), a sister of Madame Sun Yat-sen, and so further cemented his position with his countrymen. The next summer the Nationalist armies moved northward again and by June had entered Peking. With peace between the northern war leaders and the Kuomintang, China appeared once more to be united. The world now looked forward to a time of internal harmony and growing stability in China.

During the 1920's, Chinese foreign relations had improved. China was protected by the Nine-Power Treaty of 1922 (see p. 706) and was a member of the League of Nations. The Chinese government obtained the power to fix its own tariffs in 1920, and ten foreign powers gave up or lost the right of extraterritoriality for their nationals. In addition, during this period Japan appeared relatively conciliatory toward its neighbor. But the sympathizers of the young republic could not overlook certain problem areas. In many regions the people were still tyrannized by bandits, and famine in the northwest cost the lives of millions. Nor could the activities of the Chinese Communists among the peasantry be ignored.

Changes in Chinese life. The changes that took place in Chinese life between the time of the revolution and the establishment of Chiang's regime were noteworthy. The number of Chinese receiving an education increased remarkably, and intellectuals championed the use of a new and simplified written language. Folkways and dress began to give way in urban areas to Occidental customs and fashions, and in the large cities telephones, electric lights, modern water systems, and movie palaces appeared.

Chinese commerce increased rapidly, for China represented the largest potential market in the world. Total foreign trade was seven times as great in 1929 as it had been in 1894. Nevertheless, civil warfare, currency insecurity, inefficient transportation systems, and national poverty all combined to keep China virtually an undeveloped nation. For the most part, industry was controlled by foreign entrepreneurs, who raked in the profits. Because the impressive economic potentialities of China were not exploited for the advantage of the Chinese people, the inhabitants of the republic continued to suffer.

JAPAN BECOMES A WORLD POWER

The Twenty-one Demands. When the First World War broke out in 1914, the Japanese government ordered Germany to remove its warships from the Far East and to surrender the Kiaochow territory in China to Japan "with a view to the eventual restoration of the same to China." When Germany failed to reply to this request, the Japanese government declared war and seized the territory. Japan had not consulted China at all during this time, nor did the Nipponese hesitate to violate Chinese neutrality.

In January 1915, Japan presented China with the notorious Twenty-one Demands, which startled the world by their frank disclosure of Japanese imperialistic designs on the Asiatic continent. Preoccupied as they were with the gigantic struggle in Europe, the European powers did little to hinder the Japanese, and indignant China had not the physical means to protest effectively. Under threats of coercion, the Chinese government in May acceded to the first sixteen demands; the remainder were reserved for later consideration. The intervention of the United States helped nullify the most dictatorial of the demands, which would have brought China completely under Japan's domination. China was forced, however, to acknowledge Japan's authority in Shantung province and to extend Nipponese railway and land concessions in south Manchuria.

In 1917 the Allied powers secretly agreed to support Japanese claims in the peace conference that would follow the First World War. While not a party to the agreement, the United States in the Lansing-Ishii agreement (1917) declared somewhat reluctantly that Japan deserved "special interest in China" owing to "territorial propinquity." Japan, in turn, agreed to respect the Open Door Policy in China. The Allies' position toward China was most embarrassing; China had entered the war on their side, chiefly to secure a spot during peace negotiations so that Japanese ambitions might be checked. China's only hope for preserving its independence lay in the growing tension between the United States and Japan.

Japanese foreign relations in the 1920's. Japan profited from its role in the war; it controlled in one way or another Shantung, Manchuria, southern Mongolia, and the German islands north of the equator, besides the territories and concessions it had wrested from China and Russia prior to the war. The increased power of Japan was particularly alarming to the United States and the British dominions in the Pacific. In 1921 Great Britain allowed its treaty with Japan, which Britain had renewed in 1911, to terminate without further renewal. At the Washington Conference of 1921-1922, the agreement by Great Britain, the United States, and Japan to reduce the tonnage of their capital ships in order to achieve a respective ratio of 5:5:3 recognized the position of the Japanese navy as the third most powerful in the world.

In 1922 the Nine-Power Treaty was signed at Washington. All the signatories agreed to respect the independence, sovereignty, territoriality, and administrative integrity of China. Furthermore, they were to use their influence to preserve the Open Door Policy. It is impossible to reconcile Japan's later acts in China with the pact which it signed in 1922, just as it is difficult for the other signatories to excuse their apathy toward Japanese aggressions in China before they were themselves drawn into war against Japan.

The struggle for liberalism. From 1889, when Japan's new constitution was promulgated, to 1918, the government was mainly in the hands of an aristocratic, scrupulously honest oligarchy of elder statesmen called the *genro*. By the end of World War I, most of these political patriarchs had passed away, and the field of politics was now open for new blood, a fact signalized by the election to the post of prime minister of the first commoner ever to hold that office, Takashi Hara.

The period from 1918 to 1930 was of crucial importance. Japan seemed to be moving toward establishment of a democratic, parliamentary government under its new political leaders, who were enthusiastic supporters of democracy. There were serious obstacles to be overcome, however—not only the lack of a liberal tradition in Japan and inexperience in parliamentary politics but also other factors. The concentration of wealth in the hands of a few fantastically rich families was not democratically healthy. Militarism, based on the revered *samurai* tradition which exalted war, was strong, and to this militaristic virus in the Japanese blood stream was added a strong authoritarian tradition, fostered by secret societies and the cult of Shintoism. Originally a simple nature cult, *Shinto* had been transformed by the end of the nineteenth century into the cult of emperor worship and the deification of the state. Thus the Japanese were able to build a strong regime upon cults already occupying an important position in the lives of the people, while the Nazis were forced to resurrect Teutonic cults which had been extinct for centuries in order to arouse national fervor.

It was with these serious handicaps that parliamentary government sought after 1918 to lead the nation away from excessive nationalism and militarism. Liberals in the Diet showed great promise and courage as they pressed reform and criticized the imperialistic intervention in Siberia of the Japanese army (along with other Allied forces) during the confused civil war following the Russian Revolution. Although liberalism suffered a serious setback in 1921 with the assassination of Prime Minister Hara, liberal strength returned in 1925 when the Universal Manhood Suffrage Bill was passed, granting the franchise to most males over twenty-five. Soon afterwards a reactionary government led by General Giichi Tanaka came to power, advocating a stronger policy toward China; but the militaristic Tanaka was in turn quickly succeeded by the most liberal government Japan had ever had. Led by Prime Minister Yuko Hamaguchi, this liberal regime assumed a policy of conciliation toward China and reduced military expenditures. In 1930 the militarists and chauvinists reacted savagely by assassinating Hamaguchi, a blow from which the liberal cause never recovered.

Economic progress. In the economic sphere, Japan forged ahead rapidly. Thousands of factories were built, and Japanese manufacturers undersold foreign competitors in the world market, owing in part to the low Japanese wage standard and in part to the modern machine techniques which Japanese industrialists were swift to adopt. In textiles, especially, Japan captured one market after another. Commerce and industry were controlled by a few giant concerns, in whose hands the greater part of the country's wealth was concentrated. By the 1930's Japan had become the first exporter in rayon, cotton textiles, matches, and raw silk.

In the Japanese economic scheme the position of China was paramount. Trade with China amounted to 24 per cent of all Japanese commerce as compared to trade with the United States of 3 per cent and with Britain of less than 2 per cent. Moreover, in 1931 Japanese capital represented about 35 per cent of all foreign investment in China.

Japanese economic prosperity was, however, more apparent than real. Serious economic weaknesses existed. Nippon lacked natural resources such as coal, iron, petroleum, timber, and cotton. The population was growing at an unbelievable rate. In 1920 the population was 56,000,000; in 1931 it had reached 65,000,000 persons, crowded into a land area smaller than California. Up to 1930 Japan managed to pay its way by expanding its exports, the sale of which gave the nation foreign credits to buy raw materials and foodstuffs abroad. Should these exports suffer a substantial contraction, Japan would then be confronted with a serious national crisis. Just such a crisis occurred in the world depression which began in the 1930's. As we shall see in Chapter 30, it was in expansionism in China that Japan sought the answer to its problems.

SUMMARY

After the First World War a chapter in modern world history—the dominance of the West—began to draw to a close. In ancient and medieval times—before Europe's amazing advance in knowledge, wealth, and power—East and West were in rough balance. After the Renaissance, the scientific and industrial revolutions, and the spread of democracy and nationalism, the West took a commanding lead. Springing from this imbalance, western imperialism should perhaps be regarded as an inevitable development. But the colonial system and the West's power monopoly could not last; from its height in 1919, western superiority went into a rapid decline, and by the 1930's it was becoming apparent that fundamental changes were taking place in the nonwestern world. The tempo of these changes increased until Afro-Asian ferment created a critical challenge for world statesmen.

The nationalistic stimulus which arose in sub-Saharan Africa stemmed from the Pan-African movement of educated Negroes outside Africa as well as from a very small educated class within the native states. This group sought to replace unjust imperialistic control with self-government and to bring about the cultural resurgence of a people whose tribal way of life was slowly disintegrating as the black man came into contact with the numerous facets of western culture. The Pan-African movement did not affect the masses of the people in most areas, however; only in the troubled multiracial society of the Union of South Africa was there widespread unrest among Africans in this period.

Nationalism was much stronger in the Arab world. In the lands formerly controlled by the Ottomans, Arab nationalists bitterly contested European control as set up in the mandate system; the British were ultimately forced to grant complete independence to Iraq, and outbreaks of violence occurred in the French mandates of Syria and Lebanon and also in Palestine, where the Arabs resented the British attempt to set up a national home for the Jews. In Iran, the nationalists threw off the influence of Britain and set up a government under the control of Riza Shah Pahlavi. Dissatisfaction with French rule mounted in North Africa, and self-government was granted to Egypt by the British. In other areas of the Middle East, Turkish nationalists under Mustafa Kemal built a new Turkey, while in the Arabian peninsula a new Arab power, Saudi Arabia, emerged under the dynamic leadership of ibn-Saud.

The strongest nationalism in all the colonial areas developed in India under the powerful leadership of Mahatma (the Holy One) Gandhi. The effective use of nonviolence in his civil disobedience campaigns forced Britain to grant the Indians a substantial measure of self-government.

In southeast Asia, nationalism began to rise steadily, although it did not as yet affect the majority of people in this area. In Ceylon and Burma, Britain conceded some degree of self-government; unrest grew stronger in the French and Dutch colonies. In the Philippines, nationalism was given ample opportunity to develop, and self-government was finally granted.

China was not, strictly speaking, a part of the colonial world, yet in many ways this vast and backward land was under the indirect influence of the great western powers. Faced with the prospect of virtual partition by these nations, Chinese nationalists, under the leadership of Sun Yat-sen, overthrew the Manchu dynasty and established a republic. After years of confusion and conflict between rival factions, power was consolidated under the Kuomintang and Chiang Kai-shek. Chiang's regime effected a gradual modernization of urban China, though agrarian reform was largely neglected.

Japanese history in the opening decades of the twentieth century was characterized by amazing progress in industrialization and by an attempt to introduce a democratic and responsible system of government. By 1919 the island kingdom had become one of the world's great powers. But its spectacular rise to greatness was also characterized by serious omens. There was disturbing evidence that military fascism was more potent than democracy and expansionist ambitions more powerful than love for peace.

SUGGESTIONS FOR READING

Barbara Ward, *The Interplay of East and West: Points of Conflict and Co-Operation,* Norton, 1957. A short and stimulating study of the relationships and interacting influences between East and West from ancient times to the present. See also F. S. C. Northrop, *The Meeting of East and West: An Inquiry Concerning World Understanding,* Macmillan;

*Indicates an inexpensive paperbound edition.

and V. M. Dean, *The Nature of the Non-Western World,* Mentor.

G. Lensen, *The World Beyond Europe: An Introduction to the History of Africa, India, Southeast Asia, and the Far East,* Houghton Mifflin. A handy and valuable comprehensive introduction to a vast subject; contains an excellent bibliographical essay.

R. Emerson, *From Empire to Nation: The Rise to Self-Assertion of the Asian and African Peoples*, Harvard, 1960. A valuable comparative study, written without professional jargon.

A good introductory work to the problem of mandates is Q. Wright, *Mandates Under the League of Nations*, Univ. of Chicago, 1930. An excellent comparative study of the different forms of internationalized control of colonial areas is H. D. Hall, *Mandates, Dependencies and Trusteeship*, Carnegie Endowment, 1948.

T. W. Wallbank, *Contemporary Africa: Continent in Transition,** Anvil. A summary of twentieth-century developments, with documents.

Three astute observers—a scientist, a journalist, and a historian, respectively—survey Africa as it was before the Second World War: J. Huxley, *Africa View*, Harper, 1931; N. Farson, *Behind God's Back*, Harcourt, Brace, 1941; and W. M. Macmillan, *Africa Emergent, A Survey of Social, Political, and Economic Trends in British Africa,** Penguin.

W. C. Smith, *Islam in Modern History,** Mentor. Not a political history but a much-needed study of the maladjustments in Muslim lands resulting from contact with the alien and disruptive ideas of modern times.

G. Lenczowski, *The Middle East in World Affairs*, Cornell, 1956. A first-rate survey of political developments since World War I. See aslo H. L. Hoskins, *The Middle East: Problem Area in World Politics*, Macmillan, 1954.

T. E. Lawrence, *Seven Pillars of Wisdom*, Doubleday, 1938. This literary classic describes the bold part played by the author in the Arab revolt against the Turks.

J. Huxley, *From an Antique Land: Ancient and Modern in the Middle East*, Crown, 1954. An absorbing literary treatment.

The political control of Palestine has long been a controversial issue. The Arab view is presented eloquently in G. Antonius, *The Arab Awakening: The Story of the Arab National Movement*, Lippincott, 1939. The British approach is illustrated by *Great Britain and Palestine, 1915-1945*, Information Paper No. 20, Royal Institute of International Affairs, 1946. Jewish Zionist views are presented in A. Koestler, *Promise and Fulfillment: Palestine, 1917-1949*, Macmillan, 1949; and B. Joseph, *British Rule in Palestine*, Public Affairs Press, 1948.

The impact of westernization on Turkey is treated skillfully in H. E. Allen, *The Turkish Transformation*, Univ. of Chicago, 1935; and D. E. Webster, *The Turkey of Ataturk: Social Process in the Turkish Reformation*, Amer. Academy of Pol. and Soc. Science, 1939. Other worth-while special studies of Middle Eastern affairs are C. Issawi, *Egypt, An Economic and Social Analysis*, Oxford, 1947; S. H. Longrigg, *Syria and Lebanon Under French Mandate*, Oxford, 1958, and *Iraq, 1900 to 1950: A Political, Social and Economic History*, Oxford, 1953; K. S. Twitchell, *Saudi Arabia*, Princeton, 1958; and R. Frye, *Iran,** Holt (Berkshire Studies).

T. W. Wallbank, *India: A Survey of the Heritage and Growth of Indian Nationalism,** Holt (Berkshire Studies), and *India in the New Era*, Scott, Foresman, 1951. Two useful and authoritative surveys; the latter work has been abridged as *A Short History of India and Pakistan,** Mentor. For greater detail, see J. Coatman, *India: The Road to Self-Government, 1908-1940*, Norton, 1942.

D. G. Hall, *A History of Southeast Asia*, St. Martin's, 1955. A comprehensive account from ancient times to the present. See also the perceptive appraisal by D. Dubois, *Social Forces in Southeast Asia*, Harvard, 1959.

K. S. Latourette, *A History of Modern China,** Penguin. An excellent résumé of developments in the nineteenth and twentieth centuries. See also O. and E. Lattimore, *The Making of Modern China*, Norton, 1944; and H. MacNair, *China in Revolution*, Univ. of Chicago, 1931.

R. Storry, *A History of Modern Japan,** Penguin. An excellent introduction. See also the brief, lucid general history by E. O. Reischauer, *Japan, Past and Present*, Knopf, 1953; and the interpretive study by H. Borton, *Japan's Modern Century*, Ronald, 1955.

R. Storry, *The Double Patriots*, Houghton Mifflin, 1957. Details the manner in which the military extremists used subversion and violence to undermine parliamentary government in Japan.

CHAPTER 30

The Tragic Decade
and Global Conflict

DEPRESSION AND WORLD WAR II: 1930-1945

Introduction. On September 1, 1939, Hitler's legions marched into Poland, and the Second World War began. This outbreak of terrible violence marked the end of a tragic decade.

Ten years earlier, the Wall Street stock market crash had ushered in a world-wide financial crisis —the Great Depression. Nation after nation fell victim to industrial decline, bank failures, deflated prices and profits, and commercial stagnation. People the world over suffered from lowered standards of living, unemployment, hunger, and fear of the future. In the western democracies, the buoyant optimism of the 1920's was superseded by self-criticism and despair.

In desperation, governments sought economic recovery by adopting restrictive autarkist policies —high tariffs, import quotas, and barter agreements—and by experimenting with new plans for

their internal economies. The United States launched the New Deal, and Britain adopted far-reaching measures in the development of a planned national economy. In Nazi Germany and Fascist Italy, economic recovery was pursued through rearmament, conscription, and public works programs. In many lands, some observers saw in the gigantic economic planning and state ownership of the Soviet Union what appeared to be a depression-proof economic system and a solution to the crisis in capitalism.

The economic malaise of the 1930's gave dictators their chance: Hitler took over control in Germany, and a militaristic clique grasped the reins of power in Japan. In 1931 the Japanese pounced upon Manchuria, and when the League of Nations proved powerless to interfere, war between Japan and China raged intermittently throughout the decade. While China was fighting for its national existence, Italy conquered Ethiopia, fascism emerged triumphant from the Spanish civil war, and by a series of "incidents" Hitler swelled the territory of the Third Reich and increased its power. Faced with blatant aggression by the Axis powers (Germany, Italy, Japan), England and France abandoned their faith in collective security and the League of Nations and adopted a policy of appeasement. Meanwhile, the Soviet Union played for time to build up its own defenses, and the United States detached itself from the increasing world tensions by maintaining its traditional policy of isolationism. Finally driven to the limit by the Axis, the European democracies and later the Soviet Union and the United States took up arms to defend their independence and end the threat of world conquest.

Far more than World War I, the Second World War represented global conflict. World War II was also "total war" in that never before had civilian populations been so deeply involved. They were targets of air raids, rockets, and (in Japan) atom bombs. Many, like the Russian civilians, were not merely targets; they were participants in the struggle, often fighting beside their soldiers. And in all the nations involved, government regulations forced civilians to participate in the war effort.

World War II was a new kind of war, not only in its enormous scope but also in its techniques and in its weapons. Developments in technology made possible the mass bombing raids, the air-borne invasion, the amphibious assault, the operations of carrier-based planes, the maneuvers of armored divisions, the coordinated efforts of the giant naval task force, and the mass murders of the Nazi concentration camps; and science and technology combined to create the ultimate in efficiency and horror—the nuclear bomb. Yet World War II was also a war of men, fighting as men have fought throughout human history. After all the weapons and techniques of modern, technological warfare had done their worst, it was men who had to win or lose the battles. It was men who finally destroyed the Axis.

DEPRESSION THREATENS DEMOCRACY AND BREEDS TOTALITARIANISM

Phony prosperity of the "roaring twenties." By 1929, despite the buoyant optimism in the United States and the apparent economic well-being in other countries, the world economy was in an unhealthy state. One by one, the cornerstones of the pre-1914 economic system—multilateral trade, the gold standard, and the interchangeability of currencies—were crumbling.

The desire for self-sufficiency, or autarky, led nations to manufacture goods or grow products at home; then, to protect home products against competition from foreign imports, high tariff walls were raised. The United States led the movement toward higher tariffs. Other nations quickly retaliated with discriminatory tariffs against us and each other, American foreign trade seriously declined, and the volume of world trade steadily decreased.

The high tariffs had a crucial effect on the payment of war debts. Because of America's high tariff, only a sort of economic ring-around-the-rosy kept the reparations and war-debt payments going. During the 1920's our former allies paid their war-debt installments to us chiefly with funds obtained from German reparations payments, and Germany was able to make these payments only because of large private loans from the United States and Britain. Similarly, American investments and purchases abroad provided the dollars which alone made it possible for foreign nations to buy American products. By 1931 the world was reeling from the impact of the worst depression of all time, and the entire structure of reparations and war debts collapsed.

Panic on Wall Street: the crash of 1929. In the postwar decade the activities of daring and often unscrupulous speculators made international finance a precarious and exciting world of its own. In the United States, the attempts of Samuel Insull to maintain a vast public-utilities empire helped push stock prices to dizzy heights; and an English speculator, Clarence Hatry, indirectly touched off the Wall Street crash. When Hatry's shaky companies failed, his English victims dumped their American securities to get ready cash. This in turn triggered a sickening slump in stock prices on Wall Street. The crash came in 1929, on October 24, "Black Thursday." "Prices fell farther and faster, and the ticker lagged more and more. By eleven o'clock the market had degenerated into a wild, mad scramble to sell. In the crowded boardrooms across the country the ticker told of a frightful collapse. . . .The uncertainty led more and more people to try to sell. . . . By eleven-thirty the market had surrendered to blind, relentless fear. This, indeed, was panic."[1] Within a few weeks, stock prices had declined 40 per cent. Fortunes were wiped out, business confidence was blasted, and the demand for goods plummeted. The growing paralysis in American business and finance spread all over the world as the United States began to call in its foreign loans and decrease its imports.

In the face of impending disaster on a world-wide scale, President Hoover in 1931 succeeded in obtaining a moratorium of one year on all intergovernmental debts. At the Lausanne Conference (1932), German reparations were virtually canceled in the hopes that the American government also would make a substantial concession in reducing war debts. But the United States refused to concede that there was a logical connection between reparations and war debts. As the depression deepened, our debtors could not continue their payments. France refused outright in 1932; Great Britain and four other nations made token payments for a time, then stopped entirely in 1934.

The depression begins. The effects of the depression were catastrophic the world over. Governments could not balance their budgets, factories shut down, and harvests rotted in the fields. The price of wheat fell to the lowest figure in more than three hundred years.

To increase exports and decrease imports, quota systems were put into operation, and tariffs were boosted to new highs. After al-most a century of free trade, Great Britain enacted a high tariff in 1932 but allowed for the system of imperial preference, whereby lower tariffs were levied on members of the empire than on outside nations. The net effect was the increase of trade within the empire at the expense of trade with nonimperial countries.

Another technique for increasing exports was to depreciate the currency, which meant reducing the value of a nation's money. When Japan depreciated the yen, an American dollar or a British pound could buy more Japanese goods. In effect, depreciating the yen lowered the price of Japanese exports. In most instances, however, devaluation brought only a temporary trade advantage; other countries could play the same game. In 1934 the United States reduced the gold content of the dollar by about 40 per cent.

The disturbances in the natural flow of world trade caused by the depression led nations to hoard their gold reserves—a trend strengthened by the fact that most nations had comparatively little gold, the United States, Great Britain, and France controlling three fourths of the world's supply. Many nations went off the gold standard, which meant that they would not pay foreign creditors in gold. Great Britain abandoned the gold standard in 1931; two years later the United States did likewise. Without gold as the medium of exchange between countries, barter became more and more prevalent in international trade.

The depression had profound implications for politics. The rash of democratic constitutions adopted after World War I had seemed to assure government by and for the common man, but in the tragic thirties, democracy in many nations went into eclipse as unemployed and starving masses turned to dictators who promised jobs and bread at the price of freedom. The hardships of the depression formed a dismal backdrop on a political stage where dictators brutally seized the leading roles.

The Five-Year Plans in the Soviet Union. The years from 1929 to 1939 comprised a dark decade in Russia—a period of merciless industrialization and of convulsive inner struggles as Stalin established a personal dictatorship both total and terrible. While in the capitalist countries, factories and mines were idle or running on reduced schedules and millions were unemployed, the Soviet people worked many hours a day, six days a week, in an all-out attempt to revolutionize Russia's economic structure. For the first time in history, a government controlled all economic activity.

In 1928 Stalin had proposed a Five-Year Plan, the first of a number of schemes aimed at the relatively swift accumulation of capital resources through the build-up of heavy industry, the collectivization of agriculture, and the restricted manufacture of consumers' goods. Although capitalism in the form of the NEP was abolished, citizens were permitted to own certain types of private property—houses, furniture, clothes, and personal effects. They could not, however, own property which could be utilized to make profits by hiring workers. The only employer was the state.

By the beginning of the Second World War, 90 per cent of the Russian land under cultivation was organized in one of two ways. The state farm (*sovkhoz*) was owned outright by the government and run by paid laborers. The collective farm (*kolkhoz*) was created from land given up by the peasants, who accepted the government's decree to merge their holdings, and from land taken from the *kulaks*—well-to-do farmers. The *kolkhoz* members worked the land under the management of a board of directors. At the end of the year, the farm's net earnings were computed in cash and in kind, and the members were paid on the basis of the number of days they had worked.

A second Five-Year Plan was begun in 1933, and the year 1938 saw the initiation of the third Five-Year Plan, in which national defense became the major consideration. Industrial plants were shifted inland to the east, and efforts were made to develop new sources of oil and other important commodities. The world's largest tractor factory was erected in Chelyabinsk, the greatest electric power station in Dnepropetrovsk, and the largest automobile plant at Gorki.

The plans achieved remarkable results. Industrial output in 1932 was 334 per cent above that in 1914. Between 1932 and 1937 the gross production index rose from 34 to 95. However, the high volume of production was often coupled with mediocre quality, and the achievements were secured only at an enormous cost in human life and suffering. At first a bare subsistence scale of living was imposed on the people by the burdensome expense of importing heavy machinery, tools, equipment, and finished steel from abroad. These purchases were paid for by the sale of food and raw materials in the world's markets at a time when the prices of such goods had drastically fallen. An even greater cost was the terrible loss of life brought about by the callous collectivization of the peasants. By a decree of February 1930, about one million *kulaks* were forced off their land and all their possessions confiscated. In some sections the peasants revolted, and thousands were executed. A serious famine broke out, and several million peasants died of starvation.

Another casualty of the Five-Year Plans was Lenin's basic concept of economic equalitarianism. In 1931 Stalin declared that equality in wages was "alien and detrimental to Soviet production." Piecework in industry became more prevalent, and bonuses and incentives were used to speed up production. It was indeed ironic that capitalistic practices were introduced to stimulate the growth of communism.

The great purges. While the Five-Year Plans were forging ahead, Stalin was establishing an all-powerful personal autocracy. From 1928 to 1931 and again from 1935 to 1938, Stalin settled his accounts with all his rivals through barbaric purges. The long arm of the secret police gathered in thousands of Soviet citizens to face the firing squad. Old Bolsheviks who had been loyal comrades of Lenin, high officers in the Red Army, and directors of industry were liquidated. It has been estimated that between 5 and 6 per cent of the total population passed through the pretrial prisons of the secret police! The fit-

Schluss jetzt!

Wählt

HITLER

This Nazi campaign poster calls on the voters to choose Hitler and thereby free Germany from its chains.

ting climax to the purges came in 1940 when Stalin's archcritic Trotsky, living as an exile in Mexico, was murdered by a Soviet agent.

Crisis in Germany. World depression, accompanied by the cancellation of foreign loans to Germany and the withdrawal of foreign investments, was the culminating blow to the ill-fated Weimar Republic. In 1931 all banks were forced to close, and disorders broke out in many cities. A year later the number of unemployed had reached six million; and desperate, jobless workers roamed the streets shouting, "Give us bread." Night after night, police and military forces battled hungry mobs.

Up to this time the Nazi party had attracted only lukewarm support; there were but a handful of Nazi deputies in the Reichstag. By the summer of 1932, however, their number had swelled to 230, and the Nazis

had become the largest political party. Hungry, frightened, and desperate, the impoverished masses turned to Hitler as a source of salvation.

Once the Nazi movement began to gain popularity, Hitler and his master propagandist, Joseph Goebbels, organized huge meetings all over Germany. Storm Troopers marched into stadiums to form a great swastika, while martial music, the roll of drums, and the trumpeting of bugles filled the air. Thrilled by these colossal displays and mesmerized by rituals and ranting speeches, the masses gave the Nazis increasing support.

Hitler becomes chancellor. For the Nazi party, 1932—when Hitler ran against the incumbent Paul von Hindenburg for the presidency of the German republic—was a crucial year. Although Hitler was defeated, on two subsequent occasions Hindenburg asked the Nazi leader to join coalitions. Hitler refused, demanding what was equivalent to dictatorial power.

It became increasingly difficult for the German ministries to carry on the government, and in November a second general election was held, so costly to the Nazis that the party treasury was almost bankrupt. Some observers believed that the Nazis had passed the crest of their power. At this point, however, a clique of aristocratic nationalists and powerful industrialists, fearful of a Communist revolution and the growing strength of the trade union movement, offered Hitler the chancellorship. In January 1933 a mixed cabinet of nationalists was created with Hitler at the head. Because he did not have a clear majority in the Reichstag, Hitler called a general election for March 5. During the campaign, radio broadcasts were monopolized by Nazi propaganda, and Storm Troopers bullied and coerced the voters. But many Germans became disgusted with the strong-arm methods, and the Nazis needed a dramatic incident to clear a majority in the election.

Just before the election, fire gutted the Reichstag building. The blaze was blamed on the Communists, though there was strong and justified suspicion that it was started by the Nazis themselves. When the votes were counted, Hitler controlled 44 per cent of the deputies. To this bloc was added the support of the Nationalists (another 8 per cent), giving the Nazis a bare majority. Quickly the Reichstag passed the Enabling Act, which granted Hitler the right to legislate by decree for the next four years. The Weimar constitution was never formally—only effectively—abolished; the Reichstag continued as a phantom legislature, but nearly all political power was exercised by one organization, the National Socialist party.

A dread intimation of things to come was Germany's withdrawal in 1933 from the League of Nations. Two years later, in defiance of the Treaty of Versailles, Hitler introduced conscription. When President von Hindenburg died in 1934, Hitler became both chancellor and president; he was known as the Führer (leader), and the new regime was described as the Third Reich.[*]

Hitler ruthlessly smashed the democratic institutions by which he had come to power. All rival political parties were disbanded by force, and individuals who had spoken out against Nazism mysteriously disappeared after midnight visits from the dreaded Gestapo—the Nazi secret police. Concentration camps were built to house thousands of prisoners.

Hitler's persecution of the Jews. The doctrine of Aryan racial superiority formed an integral part of Hitler's program, and the Jews bore the brunt of Nazi persecution. They were blamed for the Versailles Treaty, for all that was bad about capitalism, for revolutionary communism, for pacifism, and for internationalism—all represented as being facets of a Jewish plot to destroy Germany and seize control of the world. That such a fantastic tale was seriously believed by a considerable number of the citizens of a supposedly civilized nation indicated the state of near psychosis into which Germany had fallen.

Once he was dictator, Hitler did everything to stifle and to destroy the Jews. They were prohibited from owning businesses, barred from public service, and deprived of citizenship. Marriage between "Aryans" and "non-Aryans" was forbidden. Hundreds of thousands of Jews were killed.

Nazi propaganda and education. A Reich culture cabinet was set up to instill a single pattern of thought in literature, the press, broadcasting, drama, music, art, and movies. Forbidden books, including the works of some of Germany's most distinguished men of letters, were destroyed in huge bonfires.

The school system was integrated with the German Youth Movement, which drilled and regimented boys and girls between the ages of ten and fourteen. The German universities, once famous throughout the world for their academic freedom, became agencies for propagating such ideas as the racial myths of Nazism. Enrollment in the universities was limited to good Nazi material, and professors were dismissed by the score.

Since Nazi doctrine elevated the state above all else, a movement was instigated to subordinate religion to the Hitler regime. Revolting against such pressure, German Protestants led by the Reverend Martin Niemoeller, naval officer in the First World War, repudiated the attempts of Hitler to interfere with religious freedom. The movement was crushed, and in 1938 Niemoeller was placed in a concentration camp. Hitler's regime also used strong pressure to force German Catholics to accept its control, but despite widespread persecution they refused to knuckle under.

Public works and rearmament. In theory and in outward form, Nazism retained capitalism and private property. However, both business and labor were rigidly controlled by the state. Labor unions were dissolved, and both workers and employers were enrolled in a new organization, the Labor Front. As in Mussolini's corporate state, the right of the workers to strike or of management to call a lockout was denied. Compulsory dues were taken from workers' wages to support Nazi organizations. As a sop, the government established the Strength Through Joy movement, which provided sports events,

[*] The First Reich was created by Otto the Great in 962; the Second by Bismarck in 1871.

With all the trappings of a grandiose Hollywood epic, a mass meeting of 50,000 Nazi party members heard Hitler declare on May Day, 1937, that he refused to tolerate any interference by church authorities in German political affairs.

musical festivals, plays, movies, and low-cost vacations.

The government's attempts to solve Germany's economic problems included levying a huge tax load on the middle class and increasing the national debt by one third in order to provide work for the unemployed. To create the jobs, the first Four-Year Plan, established in 1933, initiated an extensive program of public works and rearmament. The unemployed were put to work on public projects (especially noteworthy was a great network of highways, or *Autobahnen*), in munitions factories, and in the army. The program led to the production of vast armaments and, logically, to their eventual utilization in aggression against other states.

Overlapping the first program, the second Four-Year Plan was initiated in 1936. The objective of this plan was to set up an autarkist state. In order to achieve self-sufficiency, quantities of substitute (*ersatz*) commodities —frequently both inferior in quality and more costly than those purchasable on the world market—were produced by German laboratories, factories, and mills. The people's standard of living continued to decline.

Depression under Italian Fascism. In 1933 the number of unemployed in Italy totaled more than one million, and the public debt reached an alarming figure. Italian wages were the lowest in Europe, and living standards had sunk to a level below that of 1914. In spite of a grandiose program of public works and the adoption of measures to increase agricultural output, Mussolini's corporate state continued to suffer from the depression.

In racial matters, the Fascist regime made half-hearted attempts to copy the Nazis. Italians were urged to be "race conscious," but the decrees issued against Jews were not rigidly enforced.

Parliamentary demoralization in France. The lack of vigorous leadership in the democratic nations and the mounting crisis in their capitalistic systems were best exemplified in France during this period. In the early thirties France was faced with rising unemployment, budget deficits, the drying up of the lucrative tourist trade, and heavy military expenditures for security against a rearming Germany. Ministry after ministry was organized, only to collapse a few months later; citizens became more and more impatient with the government.

Disgust with the administration increased with the exposure of corruption in high places. It became known that many prominent politicians were involved in the machinations of Alexander Stavisky, who had cheated French investors out of some 600,000,000 francs. When the ministry in power ignored public furor and refused to authorize an investigation, thousands of angry citizens thronged the streets of Paris on the evening of February 6, 1934, and tried to storm the Chamber of Deputies.

The outcome was a new government, the National Union, which ignored pleas for constitutional reform and for a grant of increased power to the prime minister. The agent of the wealthy and privileged classes, the National Union grew ultraconservative but continued to rule under a variety of prime ministers.

In 1936 emerged the Popular Front, a coalition composed of liberal and radical parties united in opposition to the conservative elements in the government. In June the Popular Front won a national election; and Léon Blum, a noted lawyer and writer, became premier. The Popular Front endeavored to stem the influence of fascist ideas, to improve the country's finances, and to bring about certain fundamental economic reforms. In foreign policy the Popular Front was friendly to Great Britain and supported the League of Nations.

An epidemic of sit-down strikes embarrassed the new government, but gradually labor was conciliated by the passage of laws introducing a forty-hour week, higher wages, collective bargaining, and vacations with pay. Furthermore, the government extended its control over the Bank of France and initiated a public works program. Although the Blum government stood resolutely for the laborer and against monopoly and big business, it was equally against communist collectivism or fascist centralization. After only a year in office, however, Blum was forced to resign. Unfavorable trade balances, an enormous public debt, and an unbalanced budget proved too much for the Popular Front government. France swung back to conservatism. The forty-hour week was ended, and strikes were energetically suppressed.

The National Union and the Popular Front mirrored the widening chasm between the upper and lower classes. The working classes believed that the reforms of the Popular Front had been sabotaged and that a France ruled by a wealthy clique deserved little or no allegiance. On the other hand, some businessmen and financiers were horrified at the prospect of communism and flirted with fascism. The cleavage between classes was secretly encouraged by subtle propaganda from the totalitarian countries. While Frenchmen quarreled and France's economic strength was being sapped, Hitler's Germany, regimented and feverishly productive, was rapidly outstripping France in the manufacture of armaments. The ingredients for the tragic fall of France in the spring of 1940 had now been supplied.

Democracy in crisis elsewhere in Europe. A progressive weakening of parliamentary systems was evident in the smaller European states, except for Finland and Czechoslovakia. In Poland, the façade of parliamentary institutions was retained, but political power was wielded behind the scenes by a group of aristocratic army officers. The tiny Baltic states of Latvia, Estonia, and Lithuania had only a brief honeymoon with democracy. Lithuania had come under a dictatorship as early as 1926, and Latvia and Estonia fell to dictatorial regimes in 1934. By 1935, dictatorships had been established in Albania, Bulgaria, Yugoslavia, Rumania, and Hungary. In all these states, an appearance of democratic parliamentary forms was retained, and not much attention was paid to totalitarian ideology. Behind the false front, however, a small clique—aided by secret police, censorship, and armed political supporters—stifled all opposition to its rule.

"Muddling through" in Britain. It was inevitable that the depression would have catastrophic effects in the highly industrialized and heavily populated island of Britain. In two years, exports and imports declined 35 per cent, and three million unemployed roamed the streets of the factory towns.

A Labour administration, with James Ramsay MacDonald as prime minister, took office in 1929. Little was accomplished, and unemployment became more widespread as the depression deepened. When the Labour government fell, MacDonald retained his office by becoming the leader of a National Coalition government, which was primarily conservative. The bulk of the Labour party constituted the opposition.

Nothing spectacular was undertaken, but the country in typical British fashion did "muddle through." Unlike Germany, which gave up democracy, and France, which kept it but did not know what to do with it, Britain adhered strongly to its traditional parliamentary system. By 1937 a substantial measure of prosperity had been regained, and production registered a 20-per-cent increase over that of 1929. To achieve this comeback, much of what remained of laissez-faire policy was discarded. The government now regulated the currency, erected high tariffs, gave farmers subsidies, and imposed a heavy burden of taxation. The rich had a large proportion of their income taxed away, and what might be left at death was decimated by inheritance taxes.

Despite improvements in the economic picture, an increasing demand for the extension of the welfare state existed. There were pleas for expanded educational and health facilities, better accident and unemployment insurance, and more adequate pensions. A survey of Britain's social services, made in 1941 by the noted economist Sir William Beveridge, recommended a comprehensive system of social insurance. This plan served as the blueprint for Britain's post-World War II legislation that endeavored to give security "from the cradle to the grave."

The British Commonwealth weathers the storm. In common with the rest of the world, Britain's self-governing dominions were hard hit by the depression. Like Latin America, they were painfully susceptible to the effects of the world slump because they were primarily producers of basic materials such as wheat, meat, lumber, and minerals. When prices of such products dropped to rock bottom, the dominions (which had borrowed heavily on outside capital) were able to avoid defaults on their obligations only by the most stringent economies. But democracy did not succumb; there were no violent overthrows in Australia, New Zealand, Canada, or South Africa, for parliamentary traditions were strong and natural resources were abundant.

Political instability in South America. The Latin-American countries, which depended on the export of a few all-important raw materials for their prosperity, suffered serious economic crises as world prices collapsed. As a result of the depression, six of the South American nations experienced revolutions in 1930.

Out of the increased industrialization and land reform resulting from the revolutions came the gradual development of a middle class, where before there had been only a small group of the extremely rich and great masses of the poor. Rising political, economic, and social standards promised better health and education for more people. The Catholic Church, accused by many of being the ally of the wealthy and powerful, was subject to growing anticlerical attacks, although the continent continued to be almost totally Catholic.

In 1933 the United States inaugurated the Good Neighbor Policy. By economic aid and the formal agreement that "no state has the right to intervene in the internal or external affairs of another," the United States demonstrated the sincerity of its overtures to

Loss of human dignity was one of the most painful tragedies of the depression years in the United States. Jobless men, their hope crushed by failure and their pride destroyed by hunger, stand and wait in "Bread Line" by Reginald Marsh.

the southern continent. Capital from the United States was poured into Latin America. These investments, which usually provided a good return on the capital, also helped to strengthen the national economies of the borrowing nations. Rivalries among industrialized nations for the Latin-American market became very intense during the thirties. Nazi Germany concluded many barter agreements with Latin-American customers and at the same time penetrated the countries politically by organizing German immigrants into pro-Nazi groups, fostering fascist politicians, and developing a formidable propaganda system. When war came and the chips were down, however, South America eventually lined up with the democracies.

The New Deal fights depression. In shocking contrast to the golden days of prosperity, the frenzied boom on the stock market, and the smug complacency of American businessmen in the 1920's was the economic paralysis which gripped the United States in 1930. By 1932, business failures numbered at least thirty thousand, and the number of unemployed was somewhere between twelve and fifteen million.

In the first few years after the crash, President Hoover tried to prop up shaky businesses with government money in the hope that the benefits would filter down to the workers. Because the president believed that the government should not compete with private concerns, only a few public works projects were started. Hoover avoided federal relief, leaving to private charities and local governments the heavy responsibility for caring for the hungry. Toward the end of his term, the depression steadily worsened.

The general dissatisfaction with the government was evidenced by the sweeping victory of Franklin D. Roosevelt, the Democratic standard-bearer, who was inaugurated in 1933. Under his leadership the New Deal, a sweeping program to cope with the national emergency, was put into operation. The three objectives of the New Deal were relief, recovery, and reform. Millions of dollars were appropriated for the relief of the unemployed, and vast sums were expended for the construction of public works in the belief that such activity would stimulate economic recovery. A combination work and relief program, the Civilian Conservation Corps, offered employment and education to thousands of young men. To encourage building activity, the Federal Housing Administration offered liberal terms to finance new homes, especially for lower-income families. Most significant was the Social Security Act, passed in 1935. For the first time in the history of the United States, a comprehensive scheme for unemployment insurance and a plan for old-age benefits were introduced.

To prevent a recurrence of the crash, measures were instituted to guarantee the savings deposits of small investors; and the sale of stocks and bonds was regulated by the Securities and Exchange Commission. The Tennessee Valley Authority was established to produce power at reasonable rates that would constitute a yardstick for public utilities. On the labor front, the National Labor Relations Board was designed to protect labor and give it the right to bargain collectively.

The measures and objectives of the New Deal aroused much controversy. Its opponents contended that it gave too much power to the labor unions, that it created a vast, irresponsible bureaucracy at Washington, D.C., that it spent public funds in a profligate fashion, and that it sought to destroy the capitalist system. Its supporters, on the other hand, maintained that the New Deal did not aim to destroy capitalism but rather to preserve it by adapting it to new circumstances, and that thus it represented a reasonable compromise between the discredited system of laissez faire with its unbridled opportunities for exploitation and, at the other extreme, the pervasive and all-powerful economic controls exercised by states under totalitarian regimes.

Military fascism comes to Japan. Economic depression came to Japan with little warning and with shattering impact. Between 1929 and 1931, Japanese trade was cut almost in half. The sale of raw silk, which amounted to 40 per cent of Japanese exports, rapidly plunged downward as the United States drastically reduced purchases. Unemployment, wage cuts, and strikes became common.

In 1929, with the ministry of Hamaguchi, the high peak of political liberalism had been reached. Hamaguchi sought means to meet the depression, followed a conciliatory policy toward China, and was willing to cooperate in disarmament proposals—aims bitterly opposed by the militaristic clique. Shot in No-

vember 1930, the prime minister died the following spring. This assassination was a tragedy from which Japanese liberalism never recovered in the decade before the Second World War.

Quickly a new group of ultranationalistic and militaristic leaders came into power. In contrast to the personal dictatorships in Nazi Germany and Fascist Italy, Japan was ruled by a military clique, which plotted to shelve parliamentary government in Tokyo and to use force on the mainland of China to secure essential raw materials and markets for goods, to spread the "superior" Japanese culture throughout Asia, and to find space for Japan's overcrowded population.

AGGRESSION
AND APPEASEMENT

Japanese aggression in Manchuria. The first challenge to world peace occurred in September 1931, when Japan moved into Manchuria. Unable to cope with the invader, the Chinese appealed to the League of Nations, which appointed a committee of inquiry. The committee report condemned the aggression while trying not to affront Japan, which nevertheless resigned its League membership two years later. The significance of the Manchurian campaign was dreadfully clear. A demonstration that a great power could embark on aggression without any effective opposition from League members marked the beginning of the collapse of the League.

When the Chinese resorted to a nationwide boycott of Japanese goods, the Japanese attacked Shanghai and early in 1933 began to push deeper into northern China. To slow down the invasion and give themselves a chance to prepare for the inevitable struggle, the Chinese agreed to the T'ang-ku Truce, which recognized Japanese conquests in Manchuria and northern China.

The united front in China. In addition to the invaders, the Nationalist forces of Chiang Kai-shek had to contend with the Chinese Communists. In 1931, delegates from the various local soviets in China had proclaimed the birth of the Chinese Soviet Republic. Within three years there existed in south China large Communist enclaves with a total population of about nine million. The success of the Communist leader, Mao Tse-tung (1893-   ), depended partly on his realization that it was the Chinese peasant, not the urban worker, who could be made the agent of revolution. Farmers' cooperatives were established and tax systems reformed. More drastic measures included the seizure and division of moderate-sized and large farms and the distribution of the goods taken from the landowners.

The Nationalists, who had neglected the countryside for the cities, were apprehensive of Mao's success. From 1931 to 1934, Chiang launched five military campaigns against the Communists, the last employing one million men and a German military staff. To escape annihilation, the Communists made their famous Long March two thousand miles northwest. Only a remnant of the original force reached Shensi, where in 1935 a new Communist stronghold was set up.

The Chinese Communists demanded a united front against the Japanese, stating that the first objective of all China should be whole-hearted resistance against foreign imperialism and aggression. In 1936 the Communists kidnaped Chiang and held him for two weeks. There was a great outcry from the Chinese people, and influenced by the obvious national solidarity behind Chiang, the rebels asked him to lead a united China against the common enemy. In order to allay suspicion and achieve a united front, Mao agreed to end land confiscation and armed opposition to the Nanking government, to abandon the system of soviets, and to permit the incorporation of the Communist forces into the fight against Japan. China was unified just in time to meet the next Japanese thrust.

Japanese conquests continue. In 1937 fighting broke out again. Japanese troops captured Shanghai and advanced rapidly up the Yangtze valley to Nanking. The Chinese retreated westward, establishing a new capital at Chungking. In north China the Chinese armies were also forced to retreat, and the Japanese set up a government at Peiping.

In 1938 Japan proclaimed the New Order in eastern Asia. Its objectives were the destruction of Chiang Kai-shek's regime, the expulsion of western interests in eastern Asia, and the establishment of a self-sufficient economic bloc to include Japan, Manchuria (which was renamed Manchukuo by the Japanese), and China.

The outbreak of war in Europe gave Japan its golden opportunity to extend the New Order in China and into the Asian colonies of the western powers. The year 1939 saw several strong but inconclusive offensives in China and the seizure of the island of Hainan, of strategic importance in relation to French Indochina, British Malaya, and the Dutch East Indies. After the fall of France (see p. 727), the Vichy government allowed Japan to build naval and air bases in Indochina. Japanese pressure was also exerted on the Dutch East Indies and on British settlements in China. By the time Japan was actively engaged in the Second World War, the New Order was being rapidly expanded over much of Asia.

Of the three great powers which might have halted Japanese banditry in the 1930's, Britain was in the throes of an economic crisis, France suffered both political and economic paralysis, and the United States was isolationist. Most important, the weakness of the League of Nations had been bared for all the world to see.

Italy swallows up Ethiopia. Italy followed Japan's lead in aggressive expansion. As his first victim, Mussolini chose Ethiopia, the only important independent native state left in Africa and the nation which in 1896 had handed the Italians a humiliating defeat. Late in 1934, fighting broke out between the Ethiopians and the Italians, and in the following year the Italians made a wholesale invasion of Ethiopia. Emperor Haile Selassie appealed to the League, which tried to arrange for arbitration. Despite the Italian delegates' audacious argument that Ethiopia, not Italy, was the aggressor, the League voted to pro-

'Honest, Mister, there's nobody here but us Spaniards." In David Low's cartoon, the noninterventionists, Daladier of France and Chamberlain of Great Britain, are baffled by

"Spaniards" Mussolini and Hitler, who provide an overpowering escort for Francisco Franco, leader of the rebel armies in the Spanish civil war.

hibit shipment of certain goods to Italy and denied it credit. But the effect of the sanctions was nullified because oil—without which no modern army or navy can fight—was not included in the list of prohibited articles. Apprehensive of alienating Italy, France and Britain were only lukewarm in their support of the sanctions; and since they were not League members, the United States and Germany largely ignored the prohibitions.

Using bombs, mustard gas, and tanks, the Italians advanced swiftly into Ethiopia and crushed the resistance of Haile Selassie's valiant soldiers. The whole sorry story ended in July 1936, when the sanctions were removed. Haile Selassie, an emperor without a country, went to live in England, the first of several royal exiles.

Germany marches into the Rhineland. The conflict over Ethiopia gave Hitler his first big opportunity to use the military force he had been building up. In March 1936, while the wrangle over the sanctions against Italy was

taking place, German troops marched boldly into the Rhineland in defiance of the Treaty of Versailles and the Locarno agreements. Immediately France mobilized 150,000 troops, but Britain refused to support the use of force to compel Germany to withdraw. Many Englishmen thought it hardly worth while to risk war over Germany's demand to fortify its own territory. Others, however, recognized the danger in allowing Hitler to break an agreement with little or no protest.

Alliance of the Axis powers. Up until 1935 Germany had been diplomatically isolated in Europe, faced by the United Front of Great Britain, France, and Italy. But the Ethiopian incident and the imposition of sanctions broke up the United Front, and Italy became Germany's friend. In 1936 the friendship was formalized in the Rome-Berlin Axis, and one year later Mussolini followed Hitler's lead by withdrawing from the League.

Japan, the third major member of the Axis powers, joined forces with Germany in 1936 in the Anti-Comintern Pact. A year later Italy subscribed to the agreement. On the surface the agreement was a pact against Russia; in reality the members of the Rome-Berlin-Tokyo Axis were preparing for expansion.

Dress rehearsal in Spain. In 1936, civil war broke out in Spain, shattering that country and threatening to involve all of Europe. The Spanish republic had been established five years earlier. Long overdue reforms were enacted: new schools were constructed, great estates were broken up, and the army was purged of its parasitic officers. But the republic brought neither prosperity nor stability to Spain. Reactionary groups tried to gain control of the government, while left-wing groups resorted to terrorism. The middle-of-the-road, reformist government became increasingly powerless to maintain order, and an uprising inspired by reactionary and military cliques began in July 1936.

The totalitarian powers—Italy and Germany—seized the opportunity to ensure a Fascist victory. Large numbers of Italian planes were made available to the Fascist insurgents, led by General Francisco Franco (1892-   ). Most of the regular army troops were faithful to Franco, and a quick victory was anticipated. But the Spanish people in many parts of the country rose *en masse* to fight for the republic. Anti-Fascist refugees from Germany and Italy and volunteers from Austria, Poland, the United States, and Great Britain flocked to Spain to fight with the Loyalists of the republic, who stopped the Fascists at the outskirts of Madrid.

Although the French and British governments tried to avoid unpleasantness with the dictators by creating a nonintervention system for the Spanish war, they were the only nations that held to the agreement not to send weapons to either side. Germany and Italy sent troops and equipment to the Fascists while Russia sent matériel and personnel to the Loyalists at Madrid. On Spanish battlefields, Germany, Italy, and Russia tried out their new cannon and combat planes. Internal dissensions weakened Russian assistance, which was not sufficient to offset German and Italian aid. In March 1939, Madrid fell, and the Spanish republic was no more. Franco, at the head of the new state, was endowed with absolute power. The Spanish civil war was not only a national catastrophe, which left permanent scars on a proud and gallant people, but also a dress rehearsal for the tragic global drama of World War II.

British appeasement and Allied weakness. Neville Chamberlain (1869-1940), whose name was to symbolize the policy of appeasement, had become British prime minister in 1937. His policies received strong support in England. Many Englishmen had a feeling of "peace guilt"—namely, that Germany had been unfairly treated in the Treaty of Versailles. In other quarters there was reluctant admiration for the Nazi regime and the belief that a strong Germany could serve as a buffer against Communist Russia. Most important, however, was the passionate and widespread desire for peace, arising from the war weariness and disillusionment suffered by the democratic peoples after World War I.

The world was uneasily aware of the growing weakness of the democracies and of the major shift in the European balance of power. The small states began to draw away from the impotent League of Nations. Some tried to make deals with Germany and Italy; others, such as the Scandinavian nations and Holland, ran for the dubious shelter of neutrality and "innocent isolation." Belgium gave up its alliance with France, and Poland signed a nonaggression pact with Germany. In the Little Entente of Czechoslovakia, Rumania, and Yugoslavia, only Czechoslovakia remained loyal to Paris. Hitler was fully aware of the obsession for peace in Britain and of the decline of the French alliance system.

Hitler's Austrian coup. In announcing the military reoccupation of the Rhineland in the spring of 1936, Hitler had stated, "We have no territorial demands to make in Europe." The course of events was to belie this statement. By 1938 the German army had amazing strength, the *Luftwaffe* far exceeded the air forces of Great Britain and France, and Hitler was ready to embark on a daring program of expansion. His "territorial demands" were to prove limitless.

Hitler's first victim was his neighbor Austria. Previously, in 1934, Hitler had attempted to annex Austria; and the Austrian chancellor, Engelbert Dollfuss, had been murdered by Nazi agents. Largely because of Mussolini's opposition, this *Putsch* failed. Four years later, after Mussolini had become his ally, Hitler tried again. The blow fell on March 11, 1938. While German troops were crossing the frontier, Nazi agents in Austria took over the government, and the headlines of Berlin newspapers read: "German Austria Saved from Chaos."

Munich seals the fate of Czechoslovakia. After the Austrian coup, Hitler moved on to his next objective, the annexation of the Sudetenland, an area in Czechoslovakia bordering on Germany and peopled mainly by Germans. In September 1938, the Führer told Chamberlain that he was determined to secure self-determination for the Germans of the Sudetenland. Chamberlain then persuaded Daladier, the French premier, that a sacrifice on the part of Czechoslovakia would save the peace. When France, previously counted as an ally by the Czechs, joined England in pressing for acceptance of the Nazi demands, Czechoslovakia had little choice but to agree. But when Hitler proposed further demands favorable to the Reich, the British prime minister refused to accept the new terms.

On September 28, the British House of Commons assembled to hear a report by the prime minister. As he neared the end of his address, a messenger delivered a note from Hitler inviting him to attend a conference at Munich. The following day Hitler, Mussolini, Daladier, and Chamberlain met at the Nazi headquarters in Munich and for thirteen hours worked out the details of the surrender of the Sudetenland. No Czech representative was present. Though an outspoken ally of Czechoslovakia, Russia was completely disregarded. (French and British statesmen distrusted Russia and had a low opinion of its military power after the recent purges of its high command.) Not only were all of Hitler's demands accepted, but Poland and Hungary also received slices of Czechoslovakia.

Munich brought relief to millions of Europeans half-crazed with fear of war, but it was still a question whether this settlement would be followed by another crisis. Many hoped for the best but feared the worst. Immediately after Munich, Winston Churchill solemnly warned:

And do not suppose that this is the end. This is only the beginning of the reckoning. This is only the first sip, the first foretaste of a bitter cup which will be proffered to us year by year unless, by a supreme recovery of moral health and martial vigor, we arise again and take our stand for freedom as in the olden time.[2]

The mounting fears of French and British statesmen were confirmed in 1939. In mid-March, German troops crossed the Czech frontier, and the country was occupied. Not to be outdone, Mussolini seized Albania the following month, and the two dictators celebrated by signing a military alliance, the so-called Pact of Steel. The shock of the final conquest of Czechoslovakia and Hitler's callous violation of pledges made at Munich ended the appeasement policy of France and Great Britain. For the first time in Britain's long history, the government authorized a peacetime draft, and a tremendous arms program was launched. In Paris, Daladier obtained special emergency powers to push forward national defense.

Isolationism in the United States. The United States had been disillusioned by the results of the "war to make the world safe for democracy." Influential spokesmen asserted that World War 1 had been caused by the greed of munitions makers and stressed the centuries-old hatreds and rivalries in Europe; America, therefore, should insulate itself from these potent causes of international conflict. Reflecting this mood, Congress passed neutrality legislation between 1935 and 1937 which made it unlawful for any nation at war to obtain munitions from the United States.

As the Nazi and Fascist menace became apparent in the late 1930's, President Roosevelt and the State Department worked strenuously to arouse the American people to the dangers of the world situation. In 1937, in

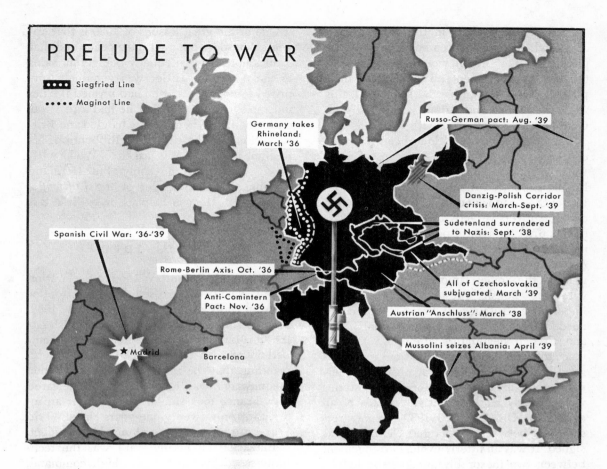

PRELUDE TO WAR

▪▪▪▪ Siegfried Line

••••• Maginot Line

Germany takes
Rhineland:
March '36

Russo-German pact: Aug. '39

Danzig-Polish Corridor
crisis: March-Sept. '39

Sudetenland surrendered
to Nazis: Sept. '38

Spanish Civil War: '36-'39

Rome-Berlin Axis: Oct. '36

Anti-Comintern
Pact: Nov. '36

All of Czechoslovakia
subjugated: March '39

Austrian "Anschluss": March '38

Mussolini seizes Albania: April '39

★ Madrid

Barcelona

The year 1931 marked the first of a series of aggressions which culminated in the devastating Second World War. In that year the Japanese moved into Manchuria and began their thrust into the interior of China, pushing the Chinese capital back to Chungking in 1937 and setting up a Japanese government at Peiping. This was only the beginning of the Nipponese plan

to impose its New Order in eastern Asia. Aggression by the European Axis powers began in 1935, when Italy attacked Ethiopia; during 1936, the African nation became Mussolini's. The next steps in the Fascist drive for acquisitions, up to the time of the invasion of Poland and Britain's declaration of war, are shown on the map above.

his famous "quarantine speech," Roosevelt declared:

The peace, the freedom and the security of 90 per cent of the population of the world is being jeopardized by the remaining 10 per cent who are threatening a breakdown of all international order and law.[3]

In May 1939 the president told leaders in the House of Representatives "that in case of war there was at least an even chance that Germans and Italians might win."[4] So strong was isolationist sentiment, however, that the warning went unheeded.

The Polish question and the Nazi-Soviet pact. It was Germany's aggression against Poland that precipitated the Second World War. The Treaty of Versailles had turned over West Prussia to Poland as a Polish Corridor to the sea (see map, p. 656). While 90 per cent of the Corridor's population was Polish, the Baltic port city of Danzig was nearly all German. Late in March 1939, Hitler proposed to Poland that Danzig be ceded to Germany and that the Nazis be allowed to occupy a narrow strip of land connecting East Prussia with the remainder of Germany. Chamberlain, with France concurring, warned the

Nazi government that "in the event of any action which clearly threatened Polish independence," the British would "at once lend the Polish government all support in their power." In the months that followed this warning, France and Britain competed with Germany for an alliance with Russia.

The Soviet Union had long been seriously concerned about the twin menaces of Nazi Germany and expansionist Japan. The Kremlin had supported the collective security system of the League and had supposedly called off the subversive activity of the Comintern (see p. 672) in favor of popular-front governments to oppose the rise of Axis aggression. As we have seen, Chamberlain and Daladier ignored the Soviet Union at Munich. Now, with the Polish question of paramount importance, Britain and France desperately needed Russia as an ally. But while British and French negotiators attempted to convince the Kremlin that their nations really desired an effective alliance against Nazi Germany, the Nazi and Soviet foreign secretaries were secretly working out the details of an agreement. On August 23, 1939, a nonaggression pact between Russia and Germany was signed. It was an utterly cynical arrangement between two inexorably antagonistic foes.

With the pact in his pocket, Hitler could attack Poland without fear of intervention by his great rival to the east. Furthermore, he was now convinced that Britain and France would not dare oppose his ambitions. But France and Britain at last understood that if they wished to stop Germany from dominating all of Europe, they must fight.

Basic causes of Hitler's war. Undoubtedly Germany nursed a sense of grievance over what were regarded as the injustices of Versailles. The most important cause of the war, however, was the ruthless ambition of an irrational dictator to gain control of Europe and as much of the rest of the world as he could master. Aiding and abetting his sinister ambition was the strong, even obsessive desire of the democracies for peace. Because Britain and France had long turned the other cheek, Hitler believed that they would not fight under any provocation.

One of the great lessons of 1939 is that appeasement does not guarantee peace and that it does not take two equally belligerent sides to make a fight. Hitler was genuinely surprised to discover that he had pushed the democracies too far and that he had a real war on his hands. When he was handed the British ultimatum, he turned to Ribbentrop, his foreign minister, and asked: "Well, what now?" There was no reply, but Hermann Goering, the commander of the *Luftwaffe*, exclaimed: "Heaven help us, if we lose this war."[5]

THE WORLD DIVIDED

Blitzkrieg in Poland. Without a declaration of war, Nazi troops crossed the Polish frontier early in the morning of September 1, 1939, and the *Luftwaffe* began to bomb Polish cities. On the morning of September 3, Chamberlain sent an ultimatum to Germany, demanding that the invasion be halted. When the message was ignored, Britain declared war. France took similar action. After an interval of only twenty-one years since World War I, Europe was again plunged into conflict.

Blitzkrieg (lightning war) was the technique used by the German high command. The Polish forces were overrun by the panzer (armored) divisions with their tanks and motorized artillery, while the *Luftwaffe*, which had destroyed the Polish air force on the ground, completely controlled the skies. At the same time, Russian forces attacked from the east. The shooting was over in less than a month, and a Russo-German treaty partitioned hapless Poland once again. In the belief that they would ultimately defeat the enemy by a naval blockade and by standing firm on the Maginot Line (a zone of fortifications on the French border), Britain and France did not attack Germany's Siegfried Line on the Rhine frontier.

The "phony war." The winter of 1939-1940 was the time of the so-called "phony war," or *Sitzkrieg.* Facing each other from the supposedly impregnable Maginot and Siegfried lines, the Allied and German armies did little fighting. The active sector was Finland.

When the Finns stoutly refused Moscow's demands for air and naval bases, the Russians launched a brutal attack. To the surprise of the world, Finland held the Soviet bear at bay from November 1939 to the following March, when the Finns were forced to cede substantial territory and to lease important military sites to the U.S.S.R.

Hitler and his generals did not remain idle during the phony war. In April 1940, neutral Denmark and Norway were invaded. Denmark surrendered after a brief resistance, but Norway proved less easy to subjugate. Partly the victim of such traitorous leaders as Quisling (whose name has since come to mean a person who undermines his own country from within), the Norwegians fought hard against stupendous odds. After about two months, the king fled to London, where a Norwegian government-in-exile was set up. British anger at the crushing defeat of an Anglo-French expeditionary force sent to Norway led to Chamberlain's resignation, and Churchill succeeded him as prime minister just in time to face a military crisis.

Dunkirk and the fall of France. The phony war ended abruptly in May, when Hitler's armies overran neutral Holland and Belgium, thus outflanking the Maginot Line. As in the other Nazi assaults, cities with their civilian populations were favorite targets; the Dutch army suffered far fewer casualties than the city of Rotterdam, which was ruthlessly bombed by the Germans. Nazi armored columns swept through northwestern France and reached the English Channel, encircling an Anglo-French force of some 400,000 men. All resistance ended in Holland and Belgium, and surrender seemed the only course for the Allied army trapped on the beach at Dunkirk. But in one of the most amazing and courageous events of the war, hundreds of small English craft, protected by an air umbrella of the Royal Air Force, came to the rescue.

After Dunkirk, the fall of France was inevitable. Anxious to be in on the kill, Mussolini declared war against France and Britain. Designated an "open city" by the French, Paris fell on June 14. As the German advance continued, the members of the French gov-

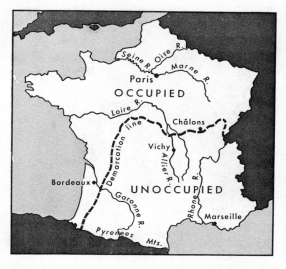

ernment who wished to continue resistance were voted down; and Marshal Pétain, the eighty-four-year-old hero of Verdun in the First World War, became premier. Pétain immediately asked Hitler for an armistice, and in the same dining car in which the French had imposed armistice terms on the Germans in 1918, the Nazis and the French on June 22 signed the armistice agreement. France was split into two zones, occupied and unoccupied. In unoccupied France, Pétain's government at Vichy was supposedly free from interference, but in reality it was a puppet of the Nazis. And so the Third Republic, created in 1871 from the debris of defeat suffered at German hands, now came to an end because of a new blow from the same quarter. However, a remarkable patriot, General Charles de Gaulle (1890-   ), fled to London and organized a Free French government, which adopted as its symbol the red cross of Lorraine (flown by Joan of Arc in her fight to liberate France centuries earlier) and continued to aid the Allied cause throughout the war.

The crucial battle of Britain. In the face of almost hopeless odds, the English people rallied to the support of their homeland. Churchill's eloquent defiance of Hitler stirred not only his own countrymen but all of the free world.

We shall go on to the end. . . . we shall defend our Island, whatever the cost may be,

This weeping Frenchman symbolizes the tragedy of a people who were forced to watch the Germans take over their country while their own forces either laid down their arms or escaped into exile.

we shall fight on the beaches, we shall fight on the landing grounds, we shall fight in the fields and in the streets, we shall fight in the hills; we shall never surrender. . . .[6]

The English daily expected a German invasion; instead came the massive and terrifying air raids of the battle of Britain. Hoping to demoralize the civilian population, the *Luftwaffe* concentrated its bombs on English cities from August to October; but with the help of radar warning devices and the superhuman efforts of the R.A.F., the English shot down so many German planes that the Nazis called off the massive daytime raids and restricted their offensive to night bombing. Britain had lost 915 planes, Germany more than 1700. In Churchill's words, "Never in the field of human conflict was so much owed by so many to so few."

All through the winter of 1940-1941, however, England continued to be racked by terrible raids. Night bombing destroyed block after block of England's cities; St. Paul's Cathedral in London stood as a solitary survivor in the midst of acres of desolation. Evacuating their children and old people and sleeping in air-raid shelters, Britain's people stood firm. Their air force retaliated in some measure by raiding the industrial cities of the Ruhr, and their naval forces remained on the offensive.

Italian failures, Nazi successes. Meanwhile, Mussolini was eager to secure his share of the spoils. In October 1940 he invaded Greece, but this thrust failed. An African venture was no more successful. Although an Italian army launched an offensive which conquered British Somaliland and penetrated into Egypt, the greatly outnumbered British Army of the Nile counterattacked and gained a decisive victory. To add to Mussolini's discomfort, the British troops stayed on the offensive, marching through British and Italian Somaliland and Eritrea. By May of 1941, an early Fascist victory was dramatically reversed when Ethiopia was recaptured.

While Italy was making a sorry showing, Hitler was winning more and more territory. Shortly after the fall of France, Rumania became a Nazi satellite, and early in 1941 Bulgaria and Hungary became puppets of the Third Reich. In April, Nazi armies attacked Greece and Yugoslavia at the same time; where Mussolini had failed, Hitler succeeded easily, despite the British forces sent to aid in the defense of Greece. Through that most modern of tactics—the air-borne invasion—Germany also seized Crete.

By the spring of 1941, nearly all of Europe had come under the iron heel of the Third Reich. Only Portugal, Switzerland, Sweden, and Turkey remained neutral. While ostensibly neutral, Spain under Franco was pro-Nazi. Britain, though still dangerous, was powerless to interfere on the Continent. The United States was gravely perturbed over the Nazi successes but was still unprepared.

Hitler turns on the Soviet Union. When the battle of Britain indicated that the defeat of England would be extremely difficult and costly, Hitler gave up his plans for a cross-channel invasion and turned on Russia. The very lifeblood of blockaded Germany depended on access to Russian raw materials—grain, coal, and iron from the Ukraine and oil from the Caucasus.

Stalin had no illusions about Nazi friendship. As France fell, he tried to "bolt the Baltic door" by annexing Latvia, Estonia, and Lithuania. At the same time, he forced Rumania to cede territory on its eastern frontier.

With these acquisitions and the territory already seized from Poland, Stalin set up a buffer zone extending from the Baltic to the Black Sea. Meanwhile, he secured a neutrality pact with Japan, the latter being as eager as Russia to obtain insurance against war on two fronts.

Following the surrender of France, as we have seen, Hitler immediately moved to block any further extension of Soviet influence in southeastern Europe. His activities in the Balkans almost squeezed Russia out of the area, and the German conquest of Yugoslavia and Greece completed the process. For all practical purposes, the Nazi-Soviet nonaggression pact was now a mere scrap of paper.

In June 1941, without warning, a gigantic German attack was launched against Russia, even though many of Hitler's generals were apprehensive over the prospects for success. From the Baltic to the Black Sea the armies of the Third Reich smashed their way across the Russian plains. Along a battlefront eighteen hundred miles long, nine million men became locked in a life-or-death struggle. Soviet forces were easily pushed out of Russia's buffer zone and had to retreat some six hundred miles. In the face of the oncoming enemy, the retreating Russians "scorched the earth"—destroyed everything left behind—and guerrilla fighting harassed the German lines. Russian troops were captured in droves, however, and disaffected groups within the Soviet Union often surrendered without much resistance. Russia appeared to be on the verge of collapse, and in October, as his troops reached the suburbs of Moscow, Hitler confidently announced that victory was his.

With the coming of winter, however, snow blocked the road to Moscow, and the Nazi campaign plan began to display vital weaknesses. Believing that Russia would be conquered by the end of autumn, the Germans had not equipped their troops to withstand the hardships of the Russian winter; German soldiers suffered from the intense cold, and their weapons froze. The Russian government showed no signs of surrender, and a fierce spirit of resistance inflamed the people. Much of Russia's heavy industry had been moved

In the months of Axis victories, the Allies suffered terrible losses. Above, buildings close to St. Paul's Cathedral crumble after a German air raid on London.

out of German reach beyond the Ural Mountains, and the breathing space gave mills and factories a chance to step up production. Before May of 1942, the Russian army, accustomed to the severe winters, had made important gains.

The "arsenal of democracy." Following the collapse of France and during the battle of Britain, the full implications of an Axis victory began to be understood by the American public. Isolation was coming with a vengeance —the kind of isolation which meant being alone in a troubled world, devoid of allies and surrounded by victorious and expansionist powers. After Dunkirk, arms were sent to Britain, a great rearmament program was undertaken, the Selective Training and Service Act instituted the draft, and the United States began to consolidate its allies and bases on the American continents. Since it was apparent that Britain did not have the necessary funds to purchase direly needed war supplies for its defense, Congress early in 1941 passed the Lend-Lease Act, which em-

United States defenses in the Pacific were dealt a crippling blow when the Japanese drew the nation into war with an attack on the Hawaiian Islands. Above, American naval vessels go down in flames at Pearl Harbor.

powered the president to manufacture, sell, lease, lend, or exchange arms with any country whose defense was thought vital to the national interests. As Roosevelt put it, the United States was becoming the "arsenal of democracy." Despite ideological differences, Britain concluded an alliance with the Soviet Union after Hitler's attack on Russia, and both Britain and the United States sent arms to Germany's new enemy.

Because of Germany's naval strength on the Baltic and Black seas, supplies to Russia had to travel by indirect routes. One such route was across the Pacific from the western coast of the United States to Siberia; another was through the Persian Gulf and Iran to the Caspian Sea, a long route imperiled by the Nazi agents who flourished in Iran; the most dangerous was across the Arctic Ocean to Murmansk, a passage menaced constantly by icebergs, bad weather, and German bombers and submarines. As a defense against German U-boats, cargo vessels were sent in convoys with planes and armed ships for protection. By the fall of 1941, American destroyers and Nazi submarines were firing "on sight."

To define the moral purpose and principles of the struggle, Roosevelt and Churchill drafted the Atlantic Charter in August 1941. Meeting "somewhere in the Atlantic," the signatories pledged that after "the final destruction of Nazi tyranny," they hoped to see a peace in which "men in all the lands may live out their lives in freedom from fear and want." If the United States was not yet a belligerent in the fall of 1941, it was certainly not neutral.

Pearl Harbor draws the United States into war. It was Japan's expansionist policy which brought the United States directly into the conflict. Confronted with Japanese ambitions for the New Order in Asia, the United States froze Japanese funds and refused to sell it war matériel. In spite of this pressure, Japan made the fateful decision to continue its expansion; and in October 1941, General Tojo, an avid militarist, became premier.

On Sunday, December 7, while special "peace" envoys from Tokyo were negotiating in Washington, ostensibly to restore harmony to Japanese-American relations, Japanese planes attacked Pearl Harbor, the American bastion in the Pacific. Our fleet was badly mauled, and our planes were wiped out on the ground. On the following day Congress declared war on Japan. In a few days Italy and Germany declared war on the United States; and Britain, together with the dominions, the refugee governments of Europe, and the Central American republics, ranged themselves with the United States against Japan. The twenty-six nations which now stood arrayed against Germany, Italy, and Japan solemnly pledged themselves on January 2, 1942, to uphold the principles of the Atlantic Charter and declared themselves the United Nations.

High tide of the Axis. The Japanese jumped from island to island in the Pacific. Within a month Manila, Wake, Guam, and Hong Kong were captured. In the spring of 1942 the whole Anglo-American position in the Pacific was in a state of collapse. Singapore, the Dutch East Indies, Malaya, and Burma were conquered by Japanese armies; Australia was in danger of invasion; and in April, American resistance in the Philippines ended with the surrender at Bataan. At the same time, Japanese forces reached toward Alaska, occupying some of the Aleutian Islands. On another front the Japanese launched a new offensive in China, but the Chinese, from their remote fortress-capital of Chungking, somehow managed to hold off the enemy.

In the summer of 1942, German armies, intent on delivering a knockout blow, launched a mighty crescendo of attacks against Russia. City after city fell, and a terrific struggle began for the control of Stalingrad. Nor did the Axis neglect the British in Africa. One of Hitler's most gifted generals, Rommel, "the Desert Fox," won a decisive victory in Libya, and the British Eighth Army reeled back to regroup at El Alamein, just seventy miles from Alexandria, Egypt. There existed now the terrifying possibility of Rommel's army overrunning the Middle East and even penetrating India, where it might be able to join Japanese forces from Burma.

In 1942, as the Allies were pushed back on every front, the Axis came frighteningly close to winning the war (see map, pp. 732-733). Events were to prove, however, that the enemy offensives could not be sustained at such a fever pitch. The surge of Axis victories waned rapidly thereafter, and the tide began to turn in favor of the Allies.

At the height of Hitler's power, the Nazis controlled most of Europe, but this mastery was not so absolute as it appeared. In some areas small armies of patriots took to the hills; in others, teams of underground workers carried on sabotage, counteracted Nazi propaganda with secret publications, sent invaluable information to the Allies, and worked closely with Allied intelligence agents. Under constant threat of torture and execution, these courageous men and women made a major contribution to Allied victory.

Turning points in the defeat of the Axis. In the far reaches of the Pacific, the Japanese advance southward toward Australia and eastward toward Hawaii was finally halted in the late spring of 1942, when the United States Navy won two huge battles, one at Midway and the other in the Coral Sea. In August, American marines successfully invaded the Japanese-held island of Guadalcanal, and six months later, after a nightmare campaign in the dank jungle, the Japanese

were forced to withdraw. By this time the drain on Japanese man power and matériel, which had been going on since the invasion of Manchuria in 1931, had begun to tell.

Another arena of Allied success was North Africa. In October 1942 the British General Bernard Montgomery chased Rommel and the Italo-German armies all the way back into Tunisia. In November a huge force of British and American troops under the direction of General Dwight D. Eisenhower landed on the beaches of Morocco and Algeria. The Axis army in Tunisia was cornered and in May 1943, after desperate resistance, surrendered. The African adventures of the two dictators had cost their countries 950,000 soldiers, either killed or captured. In retaliation for the invasion of North Africa and the scuttling of much of the French fleet at Toulon, the Germans moved into the unoccupied zone in France, and the Vichy government ceased to enjoy even the fiction of being independent.

In January 1943, Roosevelt and Churchill met at Casablanca to plan the invasion of Europe. They agreed that victory there would continue to be their prime objective and that victory meant the unconditional surrender of the Axis. The achievement of this goal, it was hoped, would avoid a repetition of Germany's contention after World War I that it had been stabbed in the back, not militarily defeated.

On the heels of the German defeat in North Africa came Axis defeats in Russia. In January 1943, Soviet troops relieved Leningrad, whose blockaded citizens were on the verge of starvation; and a month later, in one of the epic contests of the war, an entire German army besieging Stalingrad was surrounded and forced to surrender. Then the Russians began preparing the greatest counteroffensive in military history.

The invasion of Italy. Allied control of North Africa made an invasion of Italy feasible. In July 1943, Allied amphibious forces invaded Sicily. Aware that the invasion of Italy was imminent, the Fascist Grand Council turned against Mussolini and demanded his resignation. In September his successor signed an armistice with the Allies on the same day that the British Eighth Army

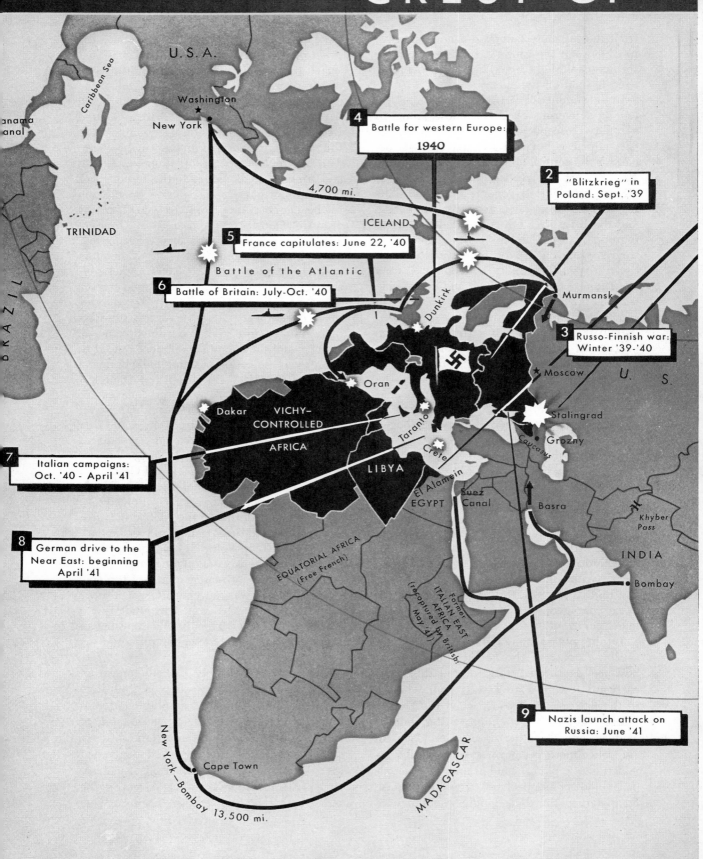

4 Battle for western Europe: **1940**

2 "Blitzkrieg" in Poland: Sept. '39

5 France capitulates: June 22, '40

Battle of the Atlantic

6 Battle of Britain: July-Oct. '40

3 Russo-Finnish war: Winter '39-'40

4,700 mi.

7 Italian campaigns: Oct. '40 - April '41

8 German drive to the Near East: beginning April '41

9 Nazis launch attack on Russia: June '41

U.S.A.

Washington

New York

Caribbean Sea

anama anal

TRINIDAD

BRAZIL

ICELAND

Dunkirk

Murmansk

Moscow

U. S. S.

Stalingrad

Grozny

Caucasus

Oran

Dakar

VICHY-CONTROLLED AFRICA

Taranto

Crete

LIBYA

El Alamein

EGYPT

Suez Canal

Basra

Khyber Pass

INDIA

Bombay

EQUATORIAL AFRICA (Free French)

Former ITALIAN EAST AFRICA (recaptured by British, May '41)

New York —Bombay

Cape Town

MADAGASCAR

New York —Bombay 13,500 mi.

AXIS POWER

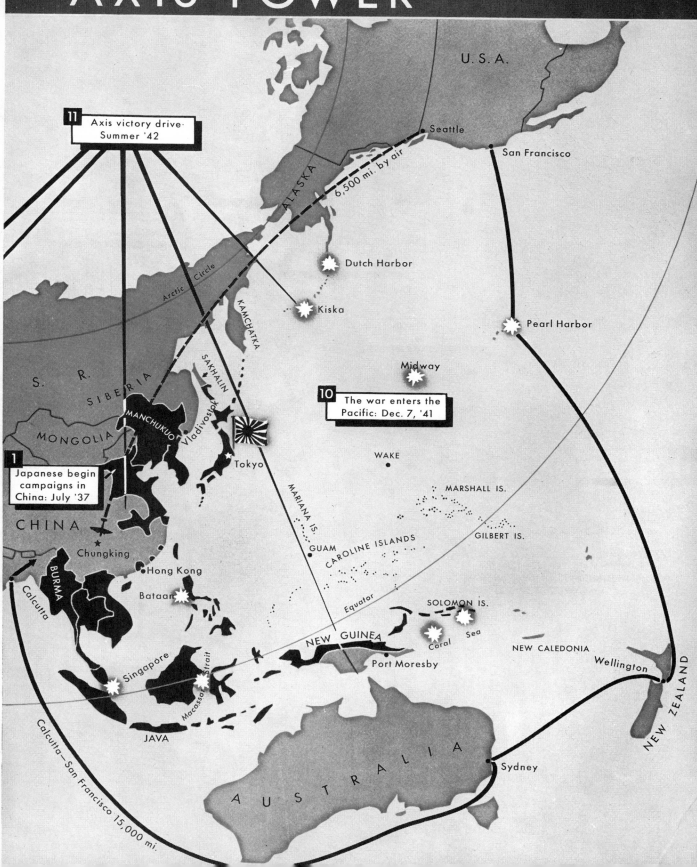

U.S.A.

Seattle

San Francisco

11 Axis victory drive·
Summer '42

ALASKA

6,500 mi. by air

Dutch Harbor

Kiska

Pearl Harbor

Arctic Circle

KAMCHATKA

Midway

10 The war enters the
Pacific: Dec. 7, '41

S. S. R.

SIBERIA

SAKHALIN

MONGOLIA

MANCHUKUO

Vladivostok

Tokyo

WAKE

1

Japanese begin
campaigns in
China: July '37

MARIANA IS.

MARSHALL IS.

CHINA

Chungking

GUAM

CAROLINE ISLANDS

GILBERT IS.

BURMA

Hong Kong

Calcutta

Bataan

Equator

SOLOMON IS.

Coral   Sea

NEW GUINEA

NEW CALEDONIA

Singapore

Macassar Strait

Port Moresby

Wellington

NEW ZEALAND

JAVA

Calcutta–San Francisco 15,000 mi.

AUSTRALIA

Sydney

LONG PULL

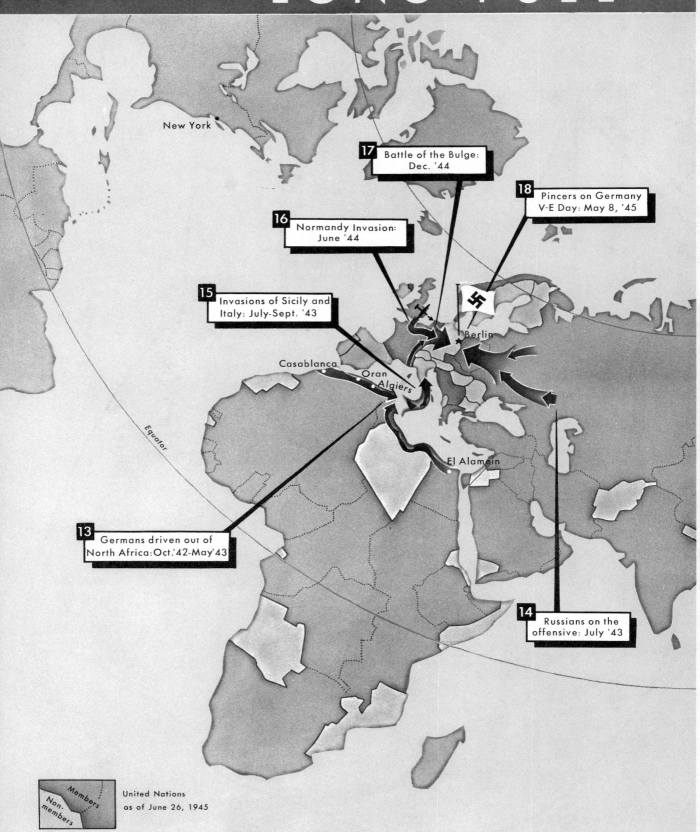

New York

17 Battle of the Bulge: Dec. '44

18 Pincers on Germany V-E Day: May 8, '45

16 Normandy Invasion: June '44

15 Invasions of Sicily and Italy: July-Sept. '43

Berlin

Casablanca

Oran
Algiers

Equator

El Alamein

13 Germans driven out of North Africa: Oct.'42-May'43

14 Russians on the offensive: July '43

Members

Non-members

United Nations
as of June 26, 1945

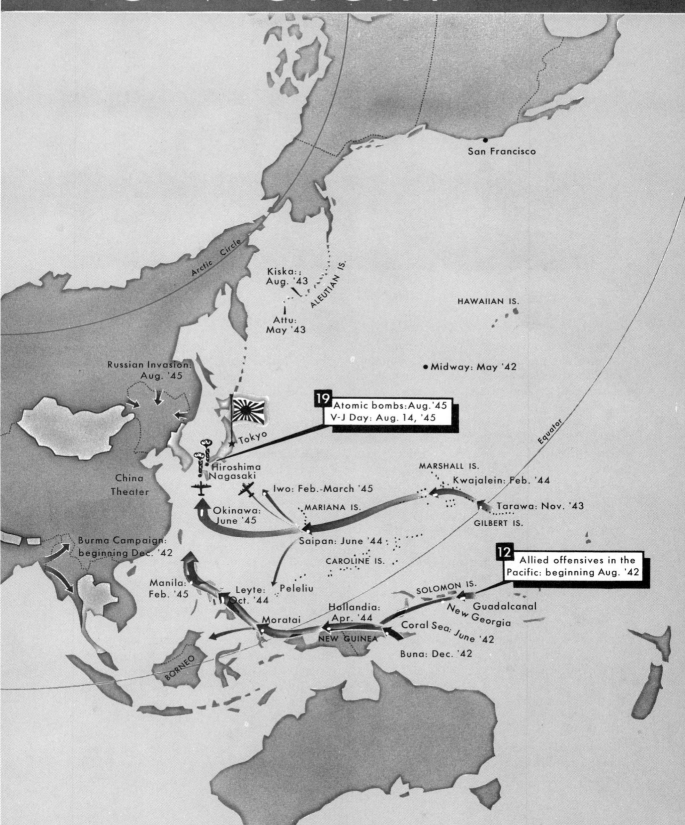

San Francisco

Arctic Circle

Kiska:
Aug. '43

Attu:
May '43

ALEUTIAN IS.

HAWAIIAN IS.

Russian Invasion:
Aug. '45

★ Tokyo

19 Atomic bombs: Aug. '45
V-J Day: Aug. 14, '45

Hiroshima
Nagasaki

Midway: May '42

MARSHALL IS.

Kwajalein: Feb. '44

Iwo: Feb.-March '45

China
Theater

MARIANA IS.

Okinawa:
June '45

Tarawa: Nov. '43

GILBERT IS.

Equator

Saipan: June '44

Burma Campaign:
beginning Dec. '42

CAROLINE IS.

12 Allied offensives in the
Pacific: beginning Aug. '42

Manila:
Feb. '45

Leyte:
Oct. '44

Peleliu

SOLOMON IS.

Guadalcanal

New Georgia

Moratai

Hollandia:
Apr. '44

Coral Sea: June '42

NEW GUINEA

Buna: Dec. '42

BORNEO

The photograph above shows troops pouring onto the beaches of Normandy during the Allied invasion on D-day, June 6, 1944.

under Montgomery landed on the toe of Italy. Meanwhile the Nazis "rescued" Mussolini, set him up as head of a puppet regime in northern Italy, and rushed German troops as far south as Naples. To prevent the Germans from consolidating their hold over central Italy, the United States Fifth Army, led by General Mark Clark, landed at Salerno just south of Naples. After savage fighting in which it was driven back almost to the sea, the Fifth Army held its ground and was soon joined by the British Eighth Army.

The Allied advance northward through Italy was a slow and torturous campaign. Stalled at Cassino and badly mauled at Anzio, Allied troops did not reach Rome until June 1944. German resistance in northern Italy continued until the end of the war.

The road to victory for the Allies. By the end of 1943 the initiative had definitely passed to the Allies, and Churchill could say that while this was not the "beginning of the end," it was definitely the "end of the beginning." In the "silent war" in the Atlantic, the German submarine menace had finally been overcome —after the loss of millions of tons of Allied shipping. The Mediterranean was now virtually an Allied lake, plied freely by Allied warships and transports. In the air, Allied

bombers were beginning to pound enemy cities into rubble, though often at frightful cost in planes and men.

The Russian offensive that had begun to roll in 1943 continued without halting. Finland, which had joined Germany's attack on Russia, was forced out of the war; and in 1944, Russian armored divisions reached the outskirts of Warsaw. In addition to driving west four hundred miles into the heart of Poland, Soviet forces also wheeled to the south and forced Hitler's Balkan satellites out of the war. At Warsaw, news of the Soviet advance set off an uprising of the Polish underground, which was brutally crushed by the Nazis; in Yugoslavia, the Russians were greeted by the Communist leader, Tito, and his guerrilla fighters, who had harried the German invaders for years.

For two years the Russians had been demanding a second front in Europe to take some of the Axis pressure off the eastern front. At Teheran in November 1943, Churchill proposed that the Anglo-American invasion should take place in the Balkans. Stalin, however, insisted that the second front should be established in western Europe, and Roosevelt concurred. While militarily sound, the decision to launch a cross-channel invasion spelled the postwar Russian domination of the Balkans.

According to schedule, in June 1944 a vast invasion was launched against northern France. On D-day, June 6, four thousand ships, protected by eight hundred naval craft and eleven thousand planes, ferried half a million men to the beaches of Normandy. By nightfall Hitler's line of defense, the Atlantic Wall, was breached—though only at great cost to the attackers. In August, after two months of heavy fighting, Paris was liberated. Meanwhile, another Allied army landed in southern France and advanced northward. The two Allied columns pushed the German troops back until, in October, the Anglo-American forces entered Germany near Aachen. Two months later, Hitler launched his last desperate attack, driving westward through the Allied lines for fifty miles in the bloody Battle of the Bulge. After heavy losses and back-to-the-wall resistance, the Allies counterattacked, forcing the Germans to withdraw and ending their offensive threat. Then British and American forces continued their advance into Germany from the west, while Russian troops closed in on the east.

With victory in Europe in sight, Stalin, Roosevelt, and Churchill met at Yalta in the Crimea in February 1945 to discuss the peace arrangements. It was agreed that the Soviet Union could have a slice of Poland and territory and privileges in the Far East, a decision later severely criticized. It was also agreed that Russia would enter the war against Japan and that postwar Germany would be split into four zones. Yalta was the high point of the alliance. After this conference, relations between the Soviet Union and its allies quickly deteriorated.

As the Allied troops advanced through Germany, they uncovered the secret hell of Nazi inhumanity toward the people Hitler despised. In the concentration camps—Belsen, Buchenwald, Dachau, and others—they found the gas ovens which had destroyed millions of lives, the wasted bodies of slave laborers who had starved to death, and the living dead who had somehow survived torture and the cruel medical experiments to

The nightmare of Nazism is only suggested by these piles of bodies at the concentration camp at Belsen, Germany. These victims died of disease and starvation, but millions more— men, women, and children—were deliberately murdered.

which they had been subjected. Between 1939 and 1945 the Jewish population in Nazi-occupied Europe had decreased from 9,739,200 to 3,505,800; and another 6,000,000 people—Poles, Czechs, Russians, and others—had also fallen victim to Nazi cruelty.

The Axis leaders did not live to see defeat. Mussolini, a cringing fugitive, was seized by anti-Fascist partisan fighters and shot to death; his mutilated body, with that of his mistress, was trussed up in the public square at Milan, an object of derision and hatred. While street fighting raged in Berlin, Hitler shot himself. His body and that of the mistress he had just made his wife were doused with gasoline and set afire. Nor did the great wartime leader of the United States live to see the end of the war, although he realized the imminence of victory. Franklin Roosevelt died suddenly in April 1945, less than a month before the German armies surrendered. The final surrender ceremony took place in Berlin on May 8, designated by President Harry Truman as V-E Day, Victory Day in Europe.

End of the war. While the Allied armies were finishing off the Germans, the Americans had been "island-hopping" their way to Japan, capturing in turn Tarawa, Kwajalein, and Saipan, after bloody struggles on the sandy beaches. In October 1944, with its victory in the battle for Leyte Gulf—the greatest naval engagement in all history—the Allies ended the threat of the Japanese fleet; and in January 1945, General MacArthur returned to the Philippines. The final phase of the war against Japan was unfolding. Only a few hundred miles from Japan, Iwo Jima and Okinawa were conquered; and from such advance bases, waves of American bombers rained destruction on Japanese cities. In the China-Burma-India theater, the Chinese, with American aid, were making inroads on areas previously captured by Japan. But Japanese resistance continued. Although amphibious operations had achieved an amazing efficiency, the Japanese defenders of the islands frequently fought on after all hope of success had disappeared; and from the skies kamikıze planes hurtled down on Allied warships in desperate suicide attacks.

From the Potsdam meeting of the Allied leaders in July-August 1945 came a warning to the Japanese that the war against them would take a new and angry turn. When Japan refused to surrender, the most terrible weapon yet invented by mankind—the atomic bomb —was dropped on Hiroshima by an American bomber. As the mushroom-shaped cloud rose over the city, only charred ruins were left beneath; an expanse of approximately three miles square—about 60 per cent of the city— was almost completely obliterated. The Japanese government estimated that 60,000 people died, 100,000 were wounded, and 200,000 were left homeless. Whether or not the use of the bomb was justified is still a question for debate, but the new weapon achieved its purpose. A few days after the dropping of a second atomic bomb on Nagasaki, the Japanese sued for peace. The surrender ceremony took place September 2 on board the battleship *Missouri,* almost six years to the day after Hitler had plunged the world into the Second World War.

SUMMARY

From 1929 to 1945 the world was in turmoil. People were caught up in a bewildering procession of economic problems, of toppling governments, and of aggressions and finally in a world conflagration. As the focal point of the world's economy, the Wall Street crash of 1929 set off an international depression. To survive this economic earthquake, governments were forced to modify the capitalistic structure by increasing their controls, particularly in the United States and England..

The depression brought Hitler to power in Germany, and a chain of events leading to global conflict was set off. In the thirties the Axis powers—Germany, Japan, and Italy— carried out a series of aggressions with little opposition. Manchuria, China, Ethiopia, Austria, and Czechoslovakia all heard the tramp of invading troops. By 1939 Hitler had thrown off his mask and revealed his real intentions: the expansion of Germany until much of the world was under the Nazi heel. The Allied policy of appeasement ended abruptly with the invasion of Poland, and the Second World War was on.

This gigantic struggle can be divided into a series of stages. During 1939 and 1940, Germany, ineffectually supported by Fascist Italy, virtually mastered Europe. Only Britain remained a defiant and lonely opponent. During the hectic prelude to world war and before the tragic fall of France, the United States had underestimated the Hitler menace to its own security and had followed a policy of noninvolvement. On the heels of Dunkirk, however, American policy was drastically reversed. Every move was made to aid Britain and then Russia in order to forestall domination of the world by the Axis.

The totalitarian powers came perilously close to winning in the summer of 1942. After a sneak attack against the United States base at Pearl Harbor, the Japanese invaded island after island in the Pacific. Hitler marched through Russia up to the outskirts of Stalingrad. In North Africa, British troops were pushed back into Egypt by General Rommel. By the end of 1942, however, the tide began to turn with an Allied victory in North Africa and a Nazi debacle in the icy streets of Stalingrad. From 1943 on, the Allies held the upper hand. Italy surrendered, the Germans were harassed out of Russia, the submarine menace was brought under control in the Atlantic, and the Americans went on the offensive in the Pacific. Germany surrendered in May 1945; the Japanese in August.

In this titanic struggle there was no clear-cut ideological alignment. The exigencies of war helped to conceal basic and even conflicting differences in ideology between Britain and the United States on the one hand and Russia on the other. At the same time, the explosion of two atomic bombs registered the awesome warning that world wars in the future would be suicidal for all concerned. Yet the world, numbed by its suffering and exhausted by its efforts, did not understand the danger inherent in the opposing aims of the two ideologies and the vital need to prevent their clash.

SUGGESTIONS FOR READING

J. K. Galbraith, *The Great Crash, 1929,** Sentry. A noted economist's dramatic account of the onset of the depression era in the United States. See also F. L. Allen, *Since Yesterday,** Bantam, a lively social history of the 1930's; S. Adler, *The Isolationist Impulse,** Collier, a thorough study of American isolationism in the twentieth century; D. Perkins, *The New Age of Franklin Roosevelt: 1932-1945,** Univ. of Chicago, a vigorous analysis of the New Deal and the retreat from isolationism; and B. Mitchell, *Depression Decade, 1929-1941,* Rinehart, 1947.

M. Hindus, *The Great Offensive,* Smith and Haas, 1933; and L. Fischer, *Men and Politics: An Autobiography,* Duell, 1941. Stalin's ruthless drive for a new economic and political order as witnessed by two able American journalists. J. E. Davies, *Mission to Moscow,* Simon and Schuster, 1941, is a sugar-coated account by the American ambassador, 1936-1938.

W. L. Shirer, *The Rise and Fall of the Third Reich,** Fawcett. The best and most recent complete account. Also notable are W. L. Shirer, *Berlin Diary,** Popular; T. L. Jarman, *The Rise and Fall of Nazi Germany,** Signet; F. L. Neumann, *Behemoth: The Structure and Practice of National Socialism,* Oxford, 1944; and H. R. Trevor-Roper, *The Last Days of Hitler,** Berkley.

On the crisis in the west European democracies on the eve of World War II, the following are recommended: A. Werth, *The Twilight of France, 1933-1940,* Harper, 1942; H. Luethy, *France Against Herself,** Meridian; A. Géraud; *The Grave-diggers of France,* Doubleday, 1944; John F. Kennedy, *Why England Slept,* Funk, 1940; and G. Brenan, *The Spanish Labyrinth: An Account of the Social and Political Background of the Civil War,** Cambridge Univ.

C. G. Haines and R. Hoffman, *The Origins and Background of the Second World War,* Oxford, 1947. An excellent study of the collapse of collective security and the advent of totalitarian aggression. Stimulating but highly debatable is the recent study by A. J. P. Taylor, *The Origins of the Second World War,* Atheneum, 1962. Indispensable for studying the policy of appeasement are F. L. Schuman, *Europe on the Eve: The Crisis of Diplomacy, 1933-1939,* Knopf, 1939; L. B. Namier,

*Indicates an inexpensive paperbound edition.

Diplomatic Prelude: 1938-1939, Macmillan, 1948; and J. W. Wheeler-Bennett, *Munich: Prologue to Tragedy,* Duell, 1948.

Sir Winston Churchill, *The Gathering Storm,** Bantam, and *Their Finest Hour,** Bantam. Inexpensive reprints of the first two volumes of an eloquent and monumental six-volume history of World War II. Excellent single-volume histories include F. Pratt, *War for the World: A Chronicle of Our Fighting Forces in World War II,* Yale, 1950; J. F. C. Fuller, *The Second World War,* Duell, 1949; and W. P. Hall, *Iron Out of Cavalry: An Interpretive History of the Second World War,* Appleton, 1946.

E. McInnis, *The War,* 6 vols., Oxford, 1940-1946; S. E. Morison, *History of United States Naval Operations in World War II,* 14 vols., Little, Brown, 1947-1960. Notable multivolume accounts by eminent historians.

T. Taylor, *The March of Conquest,* Simon and Schuster, 1958. The amazing story of the initial German military triumphs. P. Fleming, *Operation Sea Lion,** Ace, is an absorbing account of Hitler's plans to invade Britain. Excellent works on other highlights of the war include F. Majdalany, *The Battle of Cassino,* Houghton Mifflin, 1957; C. Fitzgibbon, *Officers' Plot to Kill Hitler,** Avon; D. Howarth, *D-Day: The Sixth of June, 1944,** Pyramid; J. Toland, *Battle: The Story of the Bulge,** Mentor; R. W. Thompson, *The Battle for the Rhine,** Ballantine; and J. Hersey, *Hiroshima,** Bantam.

C. Wilmot, *The Struggle for Europe,* Harper, 1952. Brilliant but critical of the American war leadership. For the American viewpoint, see Dwight Eisenhower, *Crusade in Europe,** Dolphin.

H. Feis, *Churchill, Roosevelt, Stalin,* Princeton, 1957; J. L. Snell, ed., *The Meaning of Yalta,* Louisiana State Univ., 1956. Two important studies of wartime diplomacy.

Important novels of World War II include the trilogy by the German novelist T. Plievier: *Stalingrad,** Berkley; *Moscow,** Ace; and *Berlin, A Novel,** Ace. Other excellent works are I. Shaw, *The Young Lions,** Signet; N. Mailer, *The Naked and the Dead,** Signet; H. P. M. Brown, *A Walk in the Sun,** Signet; H. Wouk, *The Caine Mutiny,** Doubleday; N. Monsarrat, *The Cruel Sea,** Pocketbooks; and J. Hersey, *The War Lover,** Bantam.

INTERNATIONAL POLITICS

1914
World War I—Germans invade Belgium, France, Poland 1914; Italy joins Allies after Treaty of London 1915; Germans defeat Russians in Galicia, conquer Serbia 1915; battle of Verdun, Allies' Somme offensive, battle of Jutland, defeat of Rumania 1916; Italian front smashed at Caporetto, submarine warfare provokes U.S. declaration of war 1917; Russia signs Treaty of Brest Litovsk with Germany, Ludendorff's "Peace Drive" fails, Foch counterattacks, armistice is signed 1918

Wilson presents Fourteen Points 1918

Paris Peace Conference establishes League of Nations, redraws German boundaries, institutes mandate system for German colonies, determines reparations payments, limits German military capacity 1919

Treaty of Versailles signed with Germany, Treaty of St.-Germain with Austria, Treaty of Neuilly with Bulgaria 1919; Treaty of Sèvres with Ottoman empire, Treaty of Trianon with Hungary 1920

France and Little Entente dominate Europe militarily c. 1920-1930—Little Entente (Czechoslovakia, Rumania, Yugoslavia) formed 1920-1921; French allies include Belgium, Poland, Czechoslovakia, Rumania, Yugoslavia 1920-1927

League of Nations settles Åland Islands dispute, Polish-German and Yugoslavian-Albanian boundary disputes 1921; Mussolini defies League in Corfu incident 1923

Naval rivalry among Britain, the U.S., and Japan leads to Washington Conference for limited naval disarmament 1921-1922

France invades German Ruhr, coercion angers Germans, economic life ceases 1923; France evacuates Ruhr 1924

Dawes Plan eases German reparations, floats loan to aid Germany's recovery and to help stabilize its currency 1924

Locarno Pact heralds new era in European affairs 1925

Kellogg-Briand Pact renounces war as instrument of national policy but fails to provide for enforcement of agreement 1928

1929

Young Plan scales down reparations payments, and Allied occupation troops evacuate Rhineland 1930

Lausanne Conference cancels German reparations 1932
Mussolini invades Ethiopia 1935; Emperor Haile Selassie flees 1936

Germans fortify Rhineland in defiance of Treaty of Versailles and Locarno agreements 1936

Rome-Berlin Axis formed, Japan and Germany form Anti-Comintern Pact 1936; Italy joins the Pact, withdraws from League 1937

Spanish civil war (1936-1939) is rehearsal for World War II

Hitler engineers coup in Austria 1938

Surrender of Sudetenland to Germany at Munich 1938; Hitler occupies Czechoslovakia, Mussolini seizes Albania 1939; Hitler and Mussolini sign Pact of Steel 1939

Russia and Germany sign nonaggression pact 1939

1939
World War II—Germany invades Poland; France, Britain declare war 1939. *Sitzkrieg*; Russia defeats Finland 1939-1940. Hitler seizes Denmark, Norway, Holland, Belgium, France 1940. Battle of Britain; Italian invasion of Greece and Africa fails; Hitler seizes Rumania, Bulgaria, Hungary, Greece, Yugoslavia, and Crete 1940-1941. Germany attacks Russia; Atlantic Charter signed; Pearl Harbor attack brings U.S. into war 1941. Japanese victories in Pacific 1941-1942. Rommel victorious in Libya; U.S. wins battles of Midway and Coral Sea 1942. Japanese withdraw from Guadalcanal; Axis surrender in Africa; Soviets seize offensive in Russia; Italy invaded; Teheran Conference 1943. Allies launch second front, victorious at Normandy and Battle of the Bulge; battle of Leyte 1944. Yalta agreements; Germany surrenders; meeting at Potsdam; A-bomb dropped on Japan; Japanese surrender 1945

WESTERN DEMOCRACIES

Irish nationalists revolt in Easter Rebellion 1916; Sinn Fein party demands independence for Ireland; Irish Free State created in southern Ireland 1921

Czechs establish republic 1918
U.S. rejects membership in League of Nations 1919
Government in France—Sacred Union, wartime coalition government in France, replaced by conservative National Bloc 1919-1924; Left Cartel succeeds National Bloc, makes progress in field of foreign affairs, is unsuccessful in public finance 1924-1926; National Union under Poincaré saves French finances 1926; ultraconservative National Union governs France 1934-1936; liberal Popular Front emerges 1936
Seven nations adopt liberal constitutions in Latin America 1919-1929
English-speaking democracies react against wartime controls, drift into listlessness and futility 1920's
Finland and Scandinavia enjoy representative government and economic prosperity 1920's
Stable democratic governments established in Switzerland, the Netherlands, Belgium 1920's
Government in U.S.—conservative Republican era in U.S. politics: Harding 1921-1923, Coolidge 1923-1929, Hoover 1929-1933; Democrat Franklin D. Roosevelt becomes president 1933, introduces New Deal for relief, recovery, and reform; Truman replaces Roosevelt 1945
Government in England—MacDonald, Britain's first Labourite prime minister, espouses evolutionary socialism 1924; Conservatives under Baldwin in power 1924-1929; economic crisis results in general strike 1926; Labour party under MacDonald regains power 1929; MacDonald later leads National Coalition government; Chamberlain, advocate of appeasement, becomes prime minister 1937; Churchill 1940
Stock market crash of 1929 in U.S. leads to world depression—Hoover declares moratorium on intergovernmental debts 1931
Revolutions in six South American nations 1930

Spain becomes a republic after dictatorship of Rivera and monarchy of King Alfonso XIII fail to reconcile country 1931
U.S. inaugurates Good Neighbor Policy 1933

Third Republic in France terminates, Petain signs armistice with Hitler 1940

U.S. reconsiders policy of isolationism—passes Selective Training and Service Act 1940, Lend-Lease Act 1941

RISE OF TOTALITARIANISM

Russian Revolution—Duma names provisional government, tsar abdicates, Bolsheviks under Lenin seize government 1917; Bolsheviks destroy White Russian resistance 1918-1920
Period of war communism—Bolsheviks apply Marxist principles to Soviet economy 1918-1921
German revolution 1918; Weimar Republic established 1919
Third Communist International (Comintern) organized to disseminate Communist propaganda, to establish Communist parties in important nations, to secure control of labor unions, and to undermine colonialism 1919
Poland takes Kiev from Russia 1920; annexes further Russian territory 1921; Treaty of Riga concludes war between Poland and Russia 1921
Retreat from war communism—Lenin inaugurates New Economic Policy, restores some capitalistic practices 1921-1928
Mussolini elected to Italian Chamber of Deputies as Fascist 1921; Fascists march on Rome, and Victor Emmanuel III invites Mussolini to form new government 1922; Mussolini creates Fascist state 1923; divides Italian economy into government-controlled syndicates; autarky becomes chief economic objective
Union of Soviet Socialist Republics established 1922
Hitler stages unsuccessful *Putsch* in Munich 1923; writes *Mein Kampf*—exposition of Nazi philosophy and objectives

Election of Hindenburg as president underlines rising German ultranationalism 1925
Pilsudski establishes dictatorship in Poland 1926
Dictatorship set up in Lithuania 1926
Trotsky loses bid for power to Stalin 1927
Stalin inaugurates first Five-Year Plan, emphasizes build-up of heavy industry, collectivization of agriculture, restricted manufacture of consumers' goods 1928
King Alexander proclaims himself dictator in Yugoslavia 1929
King Carol converts Rumanian government into royal dictatorship 1930
Republic in Portugal replaced by dictatorship of Salazar 1932
Second Five-Year Plan in Russia begins 1933
Hitler becomes dictator of Germany, withdraws from League of Nations 1933; conscription introduced 1935; Niemoeller's movement for religious freedom crushed 1938; first Four-Year Plan initiates program of public works and rearmament 1933; second Four-Year Plan aims toward autarkist state 1936
Dictatorships established in Latvia and Estonia 1934; in Albania, Bulgaria, and Hungary by 1935

Third Five-Year Plan in Russia emphasizes national defense 1938
Fascist dictator Franco gains power, ends republic after Spanish civil war 1939

ASIA AND AFRICA

Revolution in China 1911; Manchu emperor abdicates, Yüan Shih-kai forms republic, restores monarchy, proclaims himself emperor 1912-1916 **1914**
Arab Congress demands home rule and equality with Turks in Ottoman empire 1913; Arabs revolt 1916-1918; Sykes-Picot Agreement 1916; Balfour Declaration 1917; San Remo Conference—Allies overrule Arab nationalism, create mandates from Arab territories 1920
Japan presents China with the Twenty-one Demands 1915

Government of India Act of 1919 and Rowlatt Acts passed, Gandhi begins campaign for independence 1919
French repress Arab nationalism in Morocco, Tunisia, Algeria, Syria, and Lebanon 1919-1939
Rebellion in British mandate of Iraq 1920; Faisal offered throne 1921; constitution adopted 1925; Anglo-Iraqi treaty grants Iraq independence 1930; Iraq admitted to League of Nations 1932
Sun Yat-sen controls Canton government in China, establishes ideology of Kuomintang 1921-1925; Chiang Kai-shek succeeds Sun, purges Communists 1927; Nationalists conquer Peking, unite China 1928
Riza Shah Pahlavi seizes Iran government 1921-1925
British grant constitution to Burma 1922; Burma receives restricted home rule 1937
Nine-Power Treaty respects Chinese sovereignty 1922
Egypt becomes sovereign with British restrictions 1923; Anglo-Egyptian treaty of alliance formed 1936
Mustafa Kemal Pasha of Turkey defies Allies; republic of Turkey established, Treaty of Lausanne signed 1923
Ibn-Saud controls Arabian peninsula 1924-1925, becomes king of Hejaz and Nejd 1927; holdings renamed Saudi Arabia 1932
Universal Manhood Suffrage Bill passed in Japan 1925

Spain and France quell Abd-el Krim's uprising in Morocco 1926; Plan of Moroccan Reforms 1934; nationalist revolt occurs 1937
Civil war in Afghanistan 1928

Hamaguchi's ministry peak of liberalism in Japan 1929; his assassination causes permanent liberal setback 1930; military clique rules **1929**
Round-table discussions on India begin 1930; Government of India Act of 1935, providing for self-government but not independence, functions in British India 1937-1939; is rejected by native princes 1939; Gandhi and Nehru lead nationalist movement 1939
British grant progressive constitution to Ceylon 1930
Arab violence in British mandate of Palestine 1930's
Italian Fascist authority established in Libya 1930's
Political confusion reigns in Siam (Thailand) 1930's
Communists oppose French rule in Indochina 1930's
Dutch ignore growing nationalism in East Indies 1930's
Chinese soviets proclaim Chinese Soviet Republic 1931; Chiang launches campaigns against Communists 1931-1934; Chinese Communists and Nationalists temporarily allied 1936
Japan invades Manchuria 1931; withdraws from League of Nations, pushes deeper into China 1933; T'ang-ku Truce 1933
After defeat of Destour (1934) and Neo-Destour (1938) in Tunisia, nationalist movement goes underground 1938 **1939**
Commonwealth of Philippines formed 1935
War breaks out between Japan and China 1937; Japan proclaims New Order in Asia 1938

Tojo, militarist, becomes premier of Japan 1941

PART 8 The Changing World

CHAPTER 31 THE COLD WAR AND COMPETITIVE COEXISTENCE

CHAPTER 32 NEW PATTERNS FOR A NUCLEAR AGE

The years since the end of World War II have witnessed the emergence of three major worlds, each with its recognizable way of life. The nations of North and South America; the non-Communist countries of western and southern Europe; Britain and the Commonwealth nations of Australia and New Zealand; the Union of South Africa; Japan; and Formosa comprise the Free World. Stretching across the vast Eurasian heartland, from Berlin to Peking, is the Communist World. The underdeveloped nations of Africa and parts of Asia make up the Uncommitted World. The conflicting interests of these three worlds form much of the story of our times.

Many international crises occur because the spheres of influence of each of the ideological worlds are not static. In the first place, the Communist bloc and the Free World each tries to increase its own area of influence in spite of the opposition of the other. This leads to such explosive situations as occurred when South Korea was invaded.

The stability of these areas of influence is sometimes threatened in a different fashion—by disruption of the internal affairs of one of the allies of the United States, or of a satellite of the U.S.S.R. Hungary, for example, in its ill-fated revolution, attempted to break away from Moscow's domination. Similarly, the anti-American riots in Japan in 1960 threatened to change the boundaries of the Free World. Because the rebellious country is usually brought back into the fold—in the case of Hungary, by military force—these shifts in alignment are seldom successful. But they disturb the already uneasy peace.

Other trouble spots occur along the borders of the areas of influence, in cases where the status quo is complicated. A prime example is

Berlin, located inside Communist-dominated East Germany and split up under the governments of the four main Allied powers. Berlin is a festering canker to the Russians, who want to oust western rule there. The western powers insist that Berlin, which has become a symbol of Free World opposition to the Communists, will not be abandoned. On a larger scale, the division of Germany is a similar problem.

Potentially, of course, the greatest areas available for democratic or Communist expansion of influence lie within the confines of the Uncommitted World. Since military aggression would alienate the uncommitted nations, the emphasis by the West and, increasingly, by the Soviet Union has been upon economic aid. The rivalry between the West and the Reds is complicated further by a role the underdeveloped nations have assumed—that of playing off Russia against the United States in competition for aid. (Egypt played the game when seeking capital to build the Aswan Dam.) While economic aid has become an accepted weapon that neither the Free World nor the Communist bloc can afford to abandon, it is highly questionable whether or not the recipients will ally themselves with either camp. On the other hand, only by sharing wealth and information with the "have-not" nations can long-standing problems—hunger, poverty, disease, illiteracy—be solved and conditions of distress and suffering be alleviated.

While nationalism strides across the ex-colonial areas and continues to affect internal relationships in both the Free and the Communist worlds, a trend toward internationalism is apparent in the world at large.

The nations that fought their national revolutions a century or more ago are for the most part planning the next logical stage of political development, which calls for gradual pooling of national assets in the interests of collective security. In order for the Free World to cope more effectively with the pressures of the Cold War, political mergers of a broad scope are being suggested. While the Communist World has largely attained solidarity without freedom, the Free World has attained freedom without solidarity.

The outstanding example of an internationalized body is the United Nations. Because the structure of the U.N. was based on cooperation among sovereign nations—a condition that has not been achieved since the war—its successes have been limited. Nevertheless, some potentially dangerous situations, such as the Suez and Lebanon crises, have been handled effectively through U.N. machinery and personnel.

The cooperation or disintegration of the three worlds hinges finally on the use of the revolutionary science of nuclear energy. Will the atom be used to destroy the slow, rich accumulation of the centuries that have passed before us in our studies? Or will it be a force offsetting the dangers of worn-out land, diminishing food, and dwindling sources of energy—a force that will carry the world and its people to new levels of achievement?

CHAPTER 31

The Cold War and Competitive Coexistence

THE WORLD SCENE SINCE 1945

Introduction. It was not only the deaths of more than fourteen million fighting men nor the systematic destruction of entire cities which made the Second World War so horrifying. It was the reversion on a scale unrecorded in history to barbarism—a barbarism which used twentieth-century technology to exterminate perhaps as many as twelve million men, women, and children in concentration camps, gas ovens, and torture chambers; a barbarism which forced upward of seven million others into slavery; a barbarism for which the word *genocide* had to be created to define the premeditated attempt to wipe out entire nations and races.

Now the most terrible war in history was over. The holocaust which had given a portent of global suicide in two radioactive mushrooms at Hiroshima and Nagasaki had ended. The world's statesmen took up the slow, hard struggle for peace. But, with the end of the war, the objectives set forth in the Atlantic Charter for which the peoples in the western democracies had fought—the renunciation of territorial aggrandizement, the right of self-determination for national groups, disarmament, and world-wide economic cooperation—were jeopardized by the Soviet Union, with its brutal, coldly calculated designs for world conquest. As a result, disillusionment came with alarming swiftness to those who believed that the defeat of the Axis powers would automatically bring about a better world. Yet no realistic appraisal of the war's aftermath should blind us to the alternative to this costly victory: the enslavement of humanity by German Nazism and Japanese imperialism.

In this chapter we shall discuss the crucial years since the end of the war by tracing, first, the formation of the United Nations and the important crises faced by this organization in the early years of the Cold War. Then we shall examine developments within the nations of the Free World, the Communist World, and the Uncommitted World; and, lastly, we shall consider both the helpful and the menacing aspects of the most important issues facing us today.

THE COLD WAR

The United Nations established. The memory of the tragic failure of the victors after the First World War to build a lasting peace led to a profound feeling among the Allied statesmen of World War II that the very life breath of civilization depended on effective international machinery for maintaining peace and security in the postwar period. Shortly after Pearl Harbor, in January 1942, representatives of twenty-six nations signed the Declaration by the United Nations, thereby subscribing to the principles of the Atlantic Charter. During the war, two important international bodies were established: UNRRA (the United Nations Relief and Rehabilitation Administration) was created to cope with the massive relief problems of liberated countries, and the International Monetary Fund was formed to deal with the long-term reconstruction of dislocated economies.

The Russians, British, and Americans differed sharply in their ideas for a permanent international organization. Stalin wished to perpetuate the wartime alliance of big powers; Churchill worked for safeguards against United States withdrawal and Russian expansion; Roosevelt felt that the Senate would demand regional defense associations. In 1944, American, British, Chinese, and Soviet delegates met at Dumbarton Oaks in the District of Columbia to draw up a blueprint for an international organization for maintaining peace. The name "United Nations" was fixed upon to stress the continuity from the wartime alliance, and the concept of an organization dominated by the big powers was accepted.

To draft a charter along the general lines of the Dumbarton Oaks proposals, representatives of more than fifty governments met at San Francisco from April to June 1945. In its final form, the Charter of the United Nations created a structure with these major organs: the Security Council was formed to maintain peace and order; the General Assembly was conceived as a sort of town meeting of the world, in which member states could discuss issues affecting international relations; the Economic and Social Council was created to promote higher living standards and fundamental human rights; the Trusteeship Council was to function in the interests of colonial peoples in the trusteeship system, which replaced the former mandate system of the League of Nations; the International Court of Justice was the body to which disputes between nations could be referred for judicial settlement; and the Secretariat, headed by its secretary-general, was to minister to the needs of the other major organs. In the social and economic and trusteeship fields, the United Nations possessed wider powers than the League of Nations. Moreover, it was in these areas that the U.N. would register marked gains for cooperation among nations.

The most controversial issue at San Francisco was the voting procedure of the Security Council. At the Yalta Conference in February 1945, Roosevelt, Stalin, and Churchill had agreed that questions of procedure could be decided by any seven affirmative votes among the Council's eleven members. On every other issue, however, the seven affirmative votes must include those of all five permanent members: the United States, the Soviet Union, Great Britain, France, and China. Thus, by casting a negative vote, any one of the Big Five could veto a decision. Although at San Francisco the smaller powers objected to this formula, the big powers insisted that peace and security required their acting in unison.

It was hoped that the high purposes of the Charter—the maintenance of world peace and

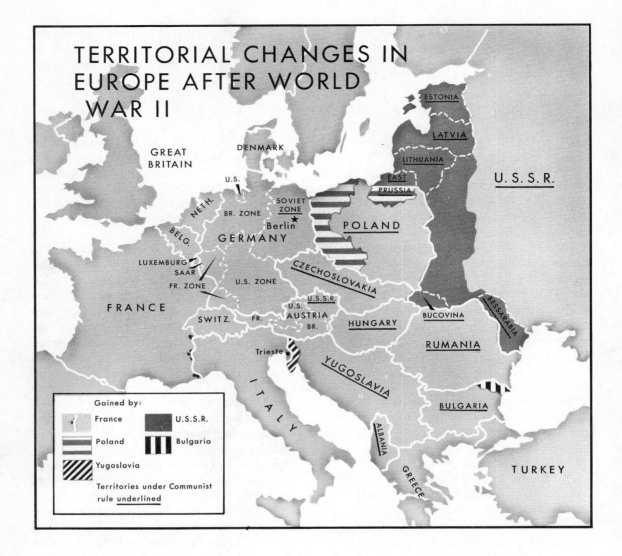

Peace settlements with Italy and the Axis satellites—Rumania, Bulgaria, Hungary, and Finland—were drafted by the Paris Conference, which met from July to October of 1946, and by the Council of Foreign Ministers, which deliberated for the next two months. The map above shows the principal territorial adjustments agreed upon. Others included the transfer of the Petsamo area (the northeast corner of Finland) to the U.S.S.R. and the grant to the Russians of a fifty-year lease on Porkkala (the city and surrounding area on the southernmost tip of the Finnish coast). The Soviets returned the Porkkala territory to Finland in 1955. In 1940, Estonia, Latvia, and Lithuania had been absorbed into the U.S.S.R., and Rumania had ceded Bucovina and Bessarabia to the Russians. The Dodecanese Islands, off southern Turkey, were given to Greece by the Italians. Italy also renounced its former African colonies,

recognized Albanian independence, and accepted U.N. supervision of the Free Territory of Trieste, which continued to be a scene of turmoil until the October 1954 agreement between Italy and Yugoslavia, whereby Italy received the port and Yugoslavia the rest of the area. The sovereignty of the Republic of Austria was restored with a state treaty in 1955. The Saar became part of the French zone of occupation after the war; under a Franco-German treaty the Saar was reunited politically with Germany on January 1, 1957. In occupied Germany the French zone merged with the Anglo-American bizone just before the establishment of the German Federal Republic (or West Germany) in May 1949. October of that year marked the founding of the German Democratic Republic (East Germany). An aim of Soviet foreign policy has been to force western recognition of the East German puppet regime.

order—could be achieved. Yet the machinery for halting aggression was controlled by the Security Council, and the Security Council in turn was based on the twin pillars of national sovereignty and big-power cooperation.

Problem of the ex-enemies. At the Potsdam Conference in 1945, the Council of Foreign Ministers of the Big Five was set up to draft the peace treaties. In 1947, treaties were signed with Italy, Rumania, Bulgaria, Hungary, and Finland. With Russian troops in actual occupation of eastern Europe, however, the free elections promised to the inhabitants were to be illusory. Other harbingers of the more difficult peacemaking problems ahead were the disagreements over reparations to Russia and its friends as well as the disputes over Trieste and the Italian colonies. The future of Austria remained uncertain until 1955, when a peace treaty was signed and occupation forces were withdrawn. What proved to be roadblocks to international cooperation were the treaties with Japan and Germany.

Postwar Japan was governed by General Douglas MacArthur, with the assistance of advisers from U.N. member states. A new constitution which vested supreme power in the people was drafted by the occupying authorities, and the national economy was liberalized—Japanese workers were encouraged to join trade unions, while the great trusts were destroyed. After the outbreak of the Korean conflict in 1950, the United States decided that formal peace in the Pacific should no longer be deferred. In spite of Russian protest, the United States worked out peace terms for Japan which not only restored Japanese sovereignty and trade but permitted Japan to reëstablish an army. The 1951 treaty was followed by an American-Japanese Security Pact, which made Japan an ally less than ten years after Pearl Harbor and permitted American troops to remain on Japanese territory. This agreement and the continued American occupation of Okinawa were seized upon by nationalists and leftists in Japan as the basis for anti-American attacks.

To avoid the faults of haste which marked the World War I treaties, peacemaking for Germany was deliberately prolonged and the country was divided into zones of temporary occupation. The eastern zone remained under the control of the Soviet Union, and western Germany was divided into American, British, and French sectors. The German capital, Berlin, which formed an enclave within the Soviet zone, was placed under joint four-power administration.

Soviet and western authorities collaborated during 1945 and 1946 in the Nuremberg war-crimes trials, by which a number of leading Nazis were sentenced and punished for crimes against humanity. Both then and later, the trials were criticized by some as vengeful and illegal, but others praised them for bringing to justice the men ultimately responsible for a murderous reign of terror.

Following the trials, tension between the occupying powers mounted. Russia closed its zone to western inspection, stripped the area of raw materials and industry, and diverted to Russia food shipments promised to western Germany. The West, aware of mounting political dangers, retreated from the policies of the Morgenthau Plan, which called for the de-industrialization of Germany. When this new policy brought an end to reparations from the western zones and permitted the revival of western German industry and commerce, the Russians protested. The contrast between occupation policies and the increasing prosperity in the western zones caused a westward flood of refugees. The western willingness to support all non-Nazi German elements, even those which were avowedly anti-Communist, increased the tension.

In June 1948, in retaliation for the West's determination to create a West Germany which would participate in the Marshall Plan (see p. 749), the Soviet Union blockaded Berlin from the West. Moscow hoped thus to drive the western powers out of the city, a strategy which, if successful, would have delivered a body blow to the West's prestige. American and British authorities met this challenge by organizing a huge air lift to feed the two million persons in western Berlin and by cutting off supply shipments from their zones to the east part of Germany. Not until

JAPAN'S LOST EMPIRE

Gained by:

U.S.S.R.

U.S. (Trust)

U.S.S.R.

MONGOLIA

MANCHURIA

INNER MONGOLIA   JEHOL

SAKHALIN

KURILE IS.

KOREA

JAPAN

CHINA

RYUKYU IS.

BONIN IS.

VOLCANO IS.

FORMOSA

MARIANA IS.

MARSHALL IS.

GUAM

BURMA

THAI-
LAND

FRENCH
INDO-CHINA

PHILIPPINES

PALAU
IS.

CAROLINE ISLANDS

MALAYA

BORNEO

MOLUCCAS

CELEBES

NEW GUINEA

SOLOMON IS.

SUMATRA

NETHERLANDS EAST INDIES

JAVA

In 1942 the Japanese expansion which had begun in the last decades of the nineteenth century reached its height. The areas in gray on the map above show the extent of Japan's acquisitions, all of which were lost after the Japanese defeat in World War II. These territories, which include all the Pacific islands named on this map, were returned to their former owners or became independent in the next few years. A few, indicated by the map key, were placed under the supervision of other powers. The dismemberment of the Japanese empire marked the end of the dreaded New Order in Asia.

the autumn of 1949 did the Soviet Union agree to lift its blockade, provided that the West raise its counterblockade.

The Cold War: an armed truce. The Berlin crisis brought into sharp focus the swift deterioration of the wartime collaboration among the big powers and the conflict between their ideologies. It likewise brought into focus the two conflicting perspectives of what is "normal" in international relations. The democratic West continued to assume that peace and toleration constituted the proper and natural state of affairs. By contrast, the Communists (who with Marx assumed that the dynamic forces of history would destroy democratic society) instituted, as a substitute for expensive full-scale war, what came to be known as the Cold War, a nibbling away of western prestige and authority by subversion and petty crises. The term "peaceful coexistence," which the Russians applied to the Cold War, implied that any policy short of open warfare was "peaceful" and that plans for the eventual destruction of the democratic states were not inconsistent with "coexistence" now.

Even the United Nations itself became a battlefield of the Cold War. Although the U.N. Charter reflected the principles of liberal democracy, the nations participating in the U.N. did not necessarily accept these principles for themselves. Thus conflicts were likely to develop among opposing forces or ideologies—democracy, communism, nationalism, and colonialism. The procedural democracy in the U.N. kept these conflicts below the level of open warfare, but with the General Assembly functioning as an international open forum, sensitive local issues were often magnified and distorted.

Although the U.N. Charter had been constructed to allow for the joint leadership of the Big Five, by V-J Day the world's future was dependent upon the relations of the Big Two—the United States and the Soviet Union. Furthermore, their relations were made more complex by the existence of power vacuums in Europe and Asia resulting from Axis defeat.

Two technological advances, the development of the guided missile as a military weapon and the creation of the atomic bomb, caused some people to believe that the United Nations was outmoded before its first session and that the ultimate issue of planetary survival rested with the decisions of one or the other of the two superstates, the United States and the U.S.S.R.

As early as June 1946, the United States, working through the United Nations, tried to establish international control of the atom. Unwilling to permit effective international inspection and reluctant to admit American superiority, Russia delayed action, redoubled its efforts to master the secret of the atomic bomb, and blanketed Canada, Britain, and the United States with spies seeking clues to the bomb. The Russian espionage scandals

in 1949 and the first successful Soviet atomic explosion increased the difficulties of agreement on any project for disarmament or for international control of atomic energy. The American and the Russian development of the much more powerful hydrogen bomb in 1953 and the subsequent development of atomic bombs by Britain and France only increased tensions.

As the rift between the Free World and the Communist World seemed to grow greater, it became more apparent than ever before that long-range Russian goals had not changed and that the Kremlin leaders had never lost sight of the Marxist premise that communism is a more advanced state of social organization than democratic capitalism and must inevitably supersede it. Postwar communism was poised to embark on a three-pronged offensive. First, the military and civil capacities of the Soviet Union were to be expanded; second, its influence was to be increased, not only in Europe, where it set up satellite states, but also in the Uncommitted World of Asia and Africa; and third, the western democracies were to be reduced to impotence and isolation through military threats, political tension, and psychological warfare.

The policy of containment. In 1947, when European democracy seemed to be tottering and Russia was making menacing demands on Turkey, the United States boldly assumed the leadership of the Free World. President Harry S. Truman announced the Truman Doctrine, stipulating that the United States would support any nation threatened by Communist aggression, a move which enabled Greece as well as Turkey to withstand Soviet encroachment.

A second and even more sweeping policy change was the announcement by Secretary of State George C. Marshall that the United States would help Europe solve its economic problems, provided that the countries concerned also made every effort at recovery. While the nations of western Europe hailed this proposal, the U.S.S.R. refused to join the plan on the grounds that it would infringe on national sovereignty. This, of course, was

Situated along Manhattan's East River is the United Nations Permanent Headquarters, comprising eighteen acres of independent territory flying its own flag and representing the nearest thing to a world capital yet achieved by man.

only the "official" reason. Basically, the U.S.S.R. did not wish to see prosperity return to Europe—communism grows best in depressed economies. Above all, Russia opposed any plan that might increase the prestige of the United States.

Within four years the industrial production of the participating nations had climbed 64 per cent above 1947 levels and 41 per cent above prewar levels. Even after American aid was reduced, progress continued. To a considerable extent, the Truman Doctrine and the Marshall Plan were related programs; both were elements in a broad strategy of "containing" Soviet Russia.

The Korean police action. In another part of the world, the encroachments of communism were met by military action. Attempts to unify Korea—which had been divided into an American and a Soviet zone of occupation after Japan's surrender—were frustrated by the Communists, who prevented free elections in North Korea and refused U.N. observers access to that area. When American and Soviet occupation forces withdrew in 1949, two hostile regimes claimed jurisdiction over the entire peninsula.

On June 25, 1950, North Korean troops crossed the 38th parallel into South Korea. The United States immediately called for a special meeting of the Security Council, whose members—meeting without the Soviet delegate, who had boycotted the Council over the controversial issue of granting Red China U.N. membership (see p. 761)—demanded a cease-fire and the withdrawal of the invaders. When the demand was ignored, the Council decided to "furnish such assistance to the Republic of Korea [the government in the south] as may be necessary to repel the armed attacks and to restore international peace and security in the area." American forces dominated the U.N. military action—termed a police action because a declaration of war was not involved—but other members contributed limited support.

Initial North Korean successes were more than offset by the counteroffensive directed by General MacArthur. After U.N. troops pushed across the 38th parallel, Communist China came to the aid of North Korea, a development which led to an angry debate in the United States over the course to pursue. MacArthur wanted to strike at bases in Chinese Manchuria, insisting that this was the only way to achieve victory. President Truman, convinced that such a move could bring on a third world war, stuck to the U.N.'s limited objective—the repelling of aggression in South Korea. When MacArthur persisted in opposing the administration's policy, Truman had him removed from his command. In July 1953, during Eisenhower's first term of office, an armistice was signed, reëstablishing the *status quo ante bellum.* As in Germany, however, unification was not achieved. In 1960 the discredited rule of Syngman Rhee, which was supported by the United States, was overthrown. The regime which succeeded him moved too slowly in eliminating economic and political wrongs to please the young army officers, who in 1961 established a dictatorship.

The Korean police action of 1950-1953 is an example of both the weakness and the potential strength of the United Nations. Action against aggression had been made possible only by the absence of the Russian delegate in the Security Council; hence, there was no use of the Soviet veto. The independence of South Korea had been saved, but the burden had been carried by a small minority of U.N. members, the United States suffering the heaviest sacrifices in blood and money. Although aggression had been halted, the chief culprit—Communist China—had not been punished. But, however imperfect international action had been, a precedent for the use of U.N. military forces had been established—a precedent which would be of vital importance in the years to come.

Collective security by regional blocs. Before the Korean outbreak, the heightened crises in international relations had strengthened the widespread belief in the West that no nation could depend upon the United Nations to guarantee its security. Thus the search for collective security led to the establishment of regional alliances for mutual assistance—a step permitted under the U.N. Charter. In 1947, nineteen American nations signed a mutual protection treaty at Rio de Janeiro; and in the year following, the Inter-American System was transformed into the Organization of American States, which supplanted the Pan American Union and called for a security zone extending from the North to the South Pole. On the other side of the Atlantic, Belgium, France, Great Britain, Luxemburg, and the Netherlands signed the Brussels Treaty in 1948, establishing machinery for cooperation in military and other fields. In 1949 these five nations joined with the United States, Canada, Denmark, Iceland, Italy, Norway, and Portugal in signing the North Atlantic Treaty; and in 1951 the territorial limits of this agreement were extended to include Greece and Turkey.

The North Atlantic Treaty represented a profound shift in the policies of the United States and Canada, neither of which had previously agreed to peacetime overseas military commitments. Now both were pledged for at least twenty years to assist any other signatory in the event of external aggression. The North Atlantic Treaty Organization (NATO) used forces from the member nations to set up a defensive shield against sudden attack from behind the iron curtain.

In the Pacific, the United States joined with Australia and New Zealand in the Anzus Pacific Security Pact, which came into force in 1951. A more comprehensive system was

"Want To Know How It Ends?"

from *Herblock's Special For Today* (Simon & Schuster, 1958)

"Herblock" cartoons, in which the Bomb is personified as a cynical, brutish enemy of all mankind, have served as repeated reminders of the ever present danger of annihilation through nuclear war. How to end this danger is the overriding problem facing civilization itself at the present time.

shortly fashioned for southeast Asia, which had become especially vulnerable to Communist penetration following the establishment of a Communist government in North Vietnam (see p. 763). Meeting in Manila in 1954, delegates from Australia, New Zealand, the Philippines, Pakistan, Thailand, France, Great Britain, and the United States created the Southeast Asia Treaty Organization (SEATO), which also brought Cambodia, Laos, and South Vietnam under its protection.

The danger of Soviet penetration in the Middle East resulted in still another mutual security arrangement. Originally called the Bagdad Pact, with Great Britain, Turkey, Iraq, Iran, and Pakistan as full members and the United States as an "observer," it was renamed the Central Treaty Organization (CENTO) after the withdrawal of Iraq in 1959.

On its side, the Soviet Union entered into a number of mutual assistance arrangements with its satellites and Red China. In 1950 Moscow and Peking signed a thirty-year treaty of "friendship, alliance, and mutual assistance." West Germany's entry into NATO in May 1955 was swiftly followed by Moscow's creation of the Warsaw Pact, providing for a unified Communist military command in Soviet-controlled eastern Europe.

Quest for economic unity. Paralleling the drive for security through regional alliances were the moves made by the West toward unity and cooperation in the economic sphere. As early as 1945 the United States began working toward freer world trade. In 1947 it sparked the General Agreement on Tariffs and Trade (GATT), which included nations representing 70 per cent of the world's trade. Although a later attempt to establish a permanent International Trade Organization was blocked by United States Congressional disapproval, lower tariffs have been negotiated by the members of GATT.

Progress in Europe has been even more significant. In the year 1951 a six-nation treaty (France, West Germany, Italy, and the Benelux countries of Belgium, the Netherlands, and Luxemburg) created the European Coal and Steel Community, from which the European Economic Community (better known as the Inner Six) evolved six years later. This organization provided for the gradual abolition of custom duties and import quotas, the adoption of a common tariff against goods from outside the market area, and the creation of an investment bank. In 1957 the same six nations set up the European Atomic Energy Community (Euratom) to regulate the production and use of atomic energy for peacetime purposes.

Another manifestation of the European trend toward economic unity was the formation in 1959 of a rival trading group, the Outer Seven, a free-trade association consisting of Britain, Sweden, Norway, Denmark, Austria, Switzerland, and Portugal. The tension between the two trade groups was broken in 1961 when Britain formally applied for admission to the Common Market (the European Economic Community). Such a step was expected to bring about not only greater economic unity but closer political integration as well.

The serious game of power politics which has dominated the period since World War II has frequently diverted public attention from equally dramatic trends within the nations of the Free World, the Communist World, and the Uncommitted World. Let us now discuss the most significant events and issues in these three worlds.

THE FREE WORLD

The United States: leader of the Free World. With the collapse of Germany and Japan, the United States began to demobilize its far-flung armed forces. Yet despite the overwhelming sentiment to "bring the boys back home," and in sharp contrast to the strong isolationism prevailing after World War I, the American people appeared to recognize the responsibilities that leadership of the Free World thrust upon them. Thus a favorable climate for vigorous United States participation in world affairs existed.

Demobilization did not bring unemployment because the production of consumer goods—long awaited at home and in great demand abroad—absorbed the ranks of veterans and kept industrial production at high levels. During this period, however, the country experienced a sharp rise in prices— an inflation caused largely by the demand for consumer goods unavailable during the war and by the abandonment of wartime price controls. By 1948 the cost of living had risen to 172 per cent of the 1935-1939 average.

In his second administration, Truman faced not only inflation but also grave issues arising from the Cold War and the Korean conflict. In the 1952 election campaign, the controversial issues concerned Korea and disloyalty and subversion in the government. On the first issue, the administration was accused of committing American troops to a war which in effect had become a holding action. The second issue was created by disclosures

During the 1960 election campaign in the United States, a nation-wide audience watched the presidential candidates engage in an unprecedented series of television debates on cam-paign issues. Democratic candidate John F. Kennedy (left) and Republican candidate Richard Nixon (right) are shown here during one of the debate telecasts.

that some workers in the government and in military research projects had been in communication with Soviet agents. Steps were taken to remove all those suspected of Communist sympathies from positions of trust, but the issue continued to dominate the headlines until 1954 when, after the sensational Army-McCarthy hearings, the Senate censured Senator Joseph R. McCarthy, who had achieved world-wide publicity with his incessant charges of "treason" within the government. Shortly thereafter, McCarthy's political career went into an eclipse.

The election of Dwight D. Eisenhower in 1952 was more a sweeping personal victory for the man himself than an endorsement of the Republican party, which acquired a bare majority in Congress and in fact lost its control two years later in the Congressional elections of 1954. During Eisenhower's first term of office, social security coverage was extended and the minimum wage level was raised. In 1956, despite serious illnesses, he was reëlected by an overwhelming majority, though the Democrats retained Congress.

For the greater part of Eisenhower's two terms, the American people enjoyed prosperity, a steadily expanding economy, and a relatively stable dollar. Eisenhower's second term—his last as a result of the adoption of the Twenty-second Amendment, which forbade a third term—was noteworthy for the opening of the American-Canadian St. Lawrence Seaway and the admission of two new states, Alaska and Hawaii. In addition, the implementation of the Supreme Court's ruling of May 1954, which decreed that Negroes be permitted to attend the same schools as white students, continued despite sporadic resistance by segregationist elements.

In 1960 the Democrats swept both houses of Congress and put into the presidency the youngest man ever elected to that office and the first Catholic, John F. Kennedy. As the result of an abortive, ill-advised, American-supported invasion of Cuba by foes of Castro's regime, the administration was severely criticized. Following this incident, the president appeared resolute but cautious in dealing with Cold War tensions developing in Laos, South Vietnam, the Congo, and Berlin.

Political turnabout in Britain. The victory of the Labour party in the 1945 elections, by which the stanch wartime leader Churchill was ousted from office, indicated that the British people wanted a fresh approach to the solution of Britain's postwar economic problems. Chief among these difficulties were foreign debts amounting to twelve billion dollars, the wartime liquidation of a large part of Britain's overseas investments and gold reserves, and an alarming decline in the export trade (in 1945 it had dropped to half its prewar figure). For the first time in modern history, Britain was a debtor rather than a creditor nation.

The Labour government introduced a flood of legislation. To stimulate exports, the British pound was devaluated. Much of the economy was nationalized, including the Bank of England, the railways, civil aviation, and the coal, electricity, and gas industries. Heavy taxes, rationing of consumer goods, and general austerity characterized the domestic economy. Progressive social legislation included the National Insurance Act, which broadened existing accident, old-age, and unemployment benefits, and a National Health Service Bill, which provided everyone with free medical, dental, and hospital care.

The broadened social and health services were generally popular. When the Conservatives returned to power in 1951, they modified the welfare program only in detail. Furthermore, they were willing to continue nationalization of fuels and railroads, both of which had been unprofitable industries before nationalization. On the other hand, the less suc-

cessful record of other nationalized sectors turned a majority of the electorate away from the Labour party's thesis that the prosperity of Britain depended upon nationalization. In 1953 the Conservative government denationalized the steel and trucking industries. Their tenure of office also coincided with a general upswing in the international economic situation, with the result that Britain's exports climbed along with its gold reserves. The second half of the 1950's witnessed a steady improvement in the national economy, even though, at the same time, competition in world markets mounted, and the rate of increase in national production lagged behind that of either North American or other major western European economies.

In the 1959 general election, the Conservatives, led by Harold Macmillan (who had become prime minister in 1957), campaigned on a "You've never had it so good" slogan and almost doubled their majority. The Labour party, split on both personalities and principles, seemed unable to capitalize on the economic difficulties which forced Britain toward the Common Market.

Instability in France. Overwhelmed by the defeat and dishonor of 1940, France emerged from the war all but crushed in spirit. Following liberation, General Charles de Gaulle, leader of the Free French, was elected president of the provisional government. He straightway set about restoring the national economy and French prestige. Acting chiefly by executive decrees, he nationalized key industries and outfitted a new army.

A major problem was the creation of a constitution for the new Fourth Republic. The Communists, who had won a large following in the wartime resistance movement, favored a single legislative chamber which they hoped to control. De Gaulle and the rightists called for executive powers sufficient to dominate the legislature. Failure to obtain his objective caused the general to resign in 1946. The constitution as finally adopted called for a bicameral legislature and a cabinet responsible to the Assembly, thus making it possible for cabinets to be voted out while the members of the Assembly remained in office—a con-

French rightists, opposing Arab demands for self-determination in Algeria, battle the riot police in the streets of Algiers.

dition which led to a high degree of governmental instability. In addition, by retaining a multitude of parties in the Assembly, the French continued to rely upon coalition governments, thus perpetuating the most dangerous weakness of the prewar Third Republic.

Democracy in France was menaced by the Communists until about 1948, when economic aid from America reinvigorated the French economy and when the Communists' unswerving devotion to the "Moscow line" had alienated many supporters. Meanwhile, the Fourth Republic underwent a succession of short-lived coalition governments made up of center parties, which proved inefficient at tackling either domestic or external problems. France continued to suffer from political mismanagement, tax dodging, and the uneconomical subsidization of various industries for the profit of vested interests. In addition, national honor seemed to require that France retain its colonial empire at all costs. A disastrous war in Indochina, a protracted one in North Africa, and an abortive invasion of Egypt drained France of man power, wealth, and prestige.

A crisis was reached in May 1958 when rightist French civilians and army officers in Algeria rebelled against the government, which had promised to liberalize France's Algerian policy in the interests of the indigenous population. The rebels' demand for De Gaulle to take power led to a showdown: the established parties were defeated, and the wartime hero emerged from retirement to assume control of the government. The choice of De Gaulle ended the Fourth Republic, for he insisted upon a new constitution vesting power in the president, who would also control the premier and cabinet and would be empowered to dissolve any parliament of which he disapproved.

In September 1958, the new constitution was adopted, and the Fifth Republic was launched on a strong wave of confidence in De Gaulle's austere but purposeful leadership. To put France's muddled finances in order, De Gaulle called for high taxes, tightened up the tax collection system, removed various subsidies on foods and fuel, abolished most of the veterans' pensions, and devalued the franc. Defense expenditures were not cut, however, nor were expenditures for atomic weapons. But by seeking to bring about a solution of the Algerian problem in terms acceptable both to the Arab majority and the French minority in Algeria, De Gaulle risked political defeat and faced repeated rebellions from right-wing nationalist officers in his own army. His troubles were multiplied during the summer of 1961 when the Tunisian demand that the French evacuate the naval base at Bizerte resulted in both a bloody clash and a condemnation of France by the U.N. General Assembly. Later, when the Algerians in France rioted constantly, hundreds were arrested and many were deported to North Africa.

Resurgence in West Germany. The dramatic story of West Germany's remarkable recovery from an occupied territory to a dynamic member of the family of nations began in 1949, when the western powers enacted an occupation statute providing for the constitutional development of their zones. This move was followed by German adoption of the Basic Law for the Federal Republic of Germany, which gave the West Germans virtual control of their domestic affairs, with their capital at Bonn. When the Allied occupation ceased six years later, the Basic Law acquired the status of a constitution. It called for a federal structure, the upper house representing the state governments and a Bundestag (or Federal Diet) representing the people directly. The president was not provided with the emergency powers which had enabled his predecessor in the Weimar Republic to create a presidential dictatorship, while the chancellor, or prime minister, was made responsible to the Bundestag.

Since the first elections in 1949, the two strong parties in Western Germany have been the conservative, Catholic-dominated Christian Democratic Union, under the capable leadership of Dr. Konrad Adenauer, and the socialist party, the Social Democrats. Former mayor of Cologne and one-time prisoner of the Gestapo, Adenauer was to prove as inflexible a champion for West Germany's recovery and prestige as was De Gaulle for neighboring France. During the 1950's, economic recovery was little short of amazing, as attested by a booming export trade and by the strength of the West German mark in international monetary circles. In the political sphere, Adenauer firmly wedded his country's fortunes to those of the western democracies, at the same time insisting that West Germany should be recognized as an equal partner in the common defense against communism. Intolerant of parliamentary opposition, yet insistent that the Germans play a constructive role as a self-reliant nation in the Free World, the chancellor has been described as "a kind of Bismarck in the service of democracy."

The 1961 elections gave the Christian Democrats only a plurality, but Adenauer was able to reconstruct his government and to maintain his personal leadership. Nevertheless, many observers felt that the Adenauer era in Germany was coming to an end.

The status of Berlin and that of Germany as well continued to hang like a menacing cloud in the international sky. With its prosperity and democracy, West Berlin was a symbol of western liberty and free enterprise—and therefore a thorn in the Russian side, a vexatious spot of contagion within the satellite of East Germany. In 1958 Moscow called for the relinquishment of western occupation rights and the transformation of Berlin into a "free city." The Soviets also threatened to hand over responsibilities in Germany to the East German regime, an announcement designed to force western recognition of the Communist puppet government there. The western powers stood firm on their occupation rights and insisted that Berlin's future was bound up with the larger question of German reunification, an issue which could only be decided by free all-German elections. But the Soviet Union was determined to delay indefinitely the unification of Germany, for this would mean the creation of a large and powerful state capable of challenging Russian foreign policy in the future. During 1961 the tension over Berlin was increased by the East German government's attempts to halt the flow of refugees to West Berlin, by the erection of a wall between East and West Berlin, and by repeated Soviet efforts to force western recognition of the East German puppet regime.

Elsewhere in Europe. Gradually, postwar dislocation gave way to economic recovery and a measure of political stability in the free countries of Europe. In both defeated Italy and victorious but devastated Greece, the war had left in its wake millions of people dependent upon international relief for their daily bread. In such a milieu, communism posed a dangerous threat; but as a result of Marshall Plan assistance, the Italian and Greek economies forged ahead, and the Communist threat began to recede.

Meanwhile, the Scandinavian nations, Belgium, the Netherlands, and Switzerland continued as stable and prosperous bastions of democracy. Except for the wartime neutrals, Sweden and Switzerland, the war took a heavy toll in these nations, yet recovery was achieved quickly. The economies of both Holland and Belgium were closely linked to their colonial empires—a situation which required drastic readjustments when independence was granted to Indonesia in 1949 and to the Belgian Congo in 1960.

In Turkey the strong administration of Premier Adnan Menderes, who had headed a parliamentary regime since 1950, had been anything but liberal or democratic. The resentment which had been building up against Menderes broke out in May 1960, the government was overthrown, and General Cemal Gursel, backed by a Committee of National Unity, took charge. When elections were held eighteen months later, Gursel retained his power although the party he favored lost control of the upper house and won by only a narrow margin in the lower house. The leading opposition party was that led by supporters of Menderes, who was executed in 1961. The western world watched these events with some anxiety, for Turkey was a member of NATO and an important military ally of the United States.

Challenges to democracy in Latin America. The end of World War II found Latin America faced with a host of serious problems, chiefly militarism and inflation. In all the republics, Communists were active in promoting class warfare and suspicion of the United States. The urban proletariat and the landless peons and mine workers were demanding a larger share of the material rewards of modern society. However, neither inflation, labor trou-

In spite of East German efforts to halt the heavy flow of refugees from East to West Berlin by erecting barriers between the two sectors, numbers of East Germans risked their lives to escape into the West. A West Berlin photographer recorded this East German soldier's leap to freedom across a barbed-wire barrier into West Berlin.

bles, nor hostility to foreign investors slowed the rapid pace of industrialization and the business boom.

The instability of democratic institutions seemed to breed revolutions and dictatorships. The most prominent of these dictatorships was the profascist regime set up by the "colonels" who seized control of Argentina in 1943. Coming to power as the leader of the "colonels," Juan Domingo Perón staffed the army and the labor unions with his henchmen. Elected president in 1946 and reëlected in 1951, he undertook an ambitious program to elevate the working classes, to make Argentina self-sufficient, and eventually to seize the leadership of Latin America. Of immeasurable help was his wife, Eva, whose talents as an actress served Perón's cause well in attracting the support of the masses. Even her death in 1952 was turned to his political advantage; a vulgar cult was encouraged which exalted Eva as a glamorous symbol of a poor girl who had made good and as an angel of mercy (whose reckless distribution of extorted charitable funds was never accounted for).

Liberating Cuba from the dictator Batista, Fidel Castro proceeded to set himself up as a demagogue, using television as his favorite means of whipping up popular support (above). Hostile toward the United States and on friendly terms with the Communist bloc, Castro's administration turned Cuba into a trouble spot which could threaten the security of the Western Hemisphere.

The brutalities and indignities of the Perón regime finally brought about solid opposition to his rule and resulted in his overthrow in 1955 by the army, which relinquished control to a civilian government in 1958.

Perón was the most strident of the dictators in Latin America. Other dictatorships included that of Venezuela's Pérez Jiménez, who presided over the fabulous prosperity that oil had brought his country until his overthrow early in 1958, and the regime of the sullen Trujillo, who maintained a peace of death over the Dominican Republic until his assassination in 1961. Peru also experienced military rule, as did Colombia.

Elsewhere in Latin America, Brazil, Mexico, and Chile remained democratic, at least in the Latin-American context. And despite Communist influences and labor troubles, the mood of these nations was generally moderate. Concessions to businessmen and to organized labor alike kept these governments stable, though inflation often canceled out the unprecedented postwar economic advances.

Revolution in Cuba. In Cuba, Batista seized control in 1952 and ruled despotically over a restive republic until the Castro rebellion of 1958. Originally applauded by the democracies for driving out an unprincipled though prowestern dictator, Fidel Castro rapidly transformed Cuba into a Communist dictatorship supported by Russia. Following his coup in 1959, Castro had introduced some badly needed reforms, especially in land redistribution and the construction of new schools and mass housing; but other aspects of his rule became increasingly disturbing to many of his original supporters. Castro became ever more anti-American and pro-Communist, although the United States continued to purchase half of Cuba's sugar at a generous subsidy well over the world market price. When U.S. properties in Cuba were seized in 1960 with no hint of compensation, Washington cut off further purchases of Cuban sugar. For his part, Khrushchev supplied Castro's regime with technical advisers, planes, petroleum, and other assistance.

To many Latin-Americans, Castro was a patriot, "the man from the hills," the Cuban David standing up to the American Goliath. The Latin-American republics saw in him an extremist but one who reflected their own frustrations and hopes. The unsuccessful, American-supported invasion of Cuba in 1961 cost the United States friends in Latin America and provided an opportunity for Cuba to proclaim itself a Communist state.

Democracy on trial in Japan. During the 1950's, Japan's status as a member of the Free World seemed precarious. Although Japan's industry had regained strength after the war and had achieved fourth place in world production and although the Japanese standard of living was the highest in Asia, it appeared that prosperity depended on the whim of the United States and its uncertain market. Opponents of the western alignment pointed to the large and traditional market for Japanese goods in China, a market barred to Japan by Chinese action.

The crisis was reached in 1960 when a new ten-year treaty with the United States passed the Japanese legislature. Although the pact gave Japan a larger voice in joint defense decisions than had the treaty of 1951, it seemed to involve a commitment to the United States' continuing struggle against mainland China. Violent opposition from labor and student groups, often paid and directed by local Communists, appeared strong enough to destroy not merely the treaty but the Japanese government itself. The elections in November, however, gave the prowestern Liberal-Democrats almost 60 per cent of the votes and constituted a mandate for both the treaty and the Free World.

THE COMMUNIST WORLD

The iron curtain. Ravaged by war—with millions killed and millions more left homeless, with towns and cities blasted into rubble and vast areas of the countryside laid waste—the Soviet Union nevertheless faced the postwar years in a determined, aggressive mood. Early in 1946, the Soviet government inaugurated its fourth Five-Year Plan, designed to restore the war-damaged economy, to speed up the improvement of heavy industry and the collectivization of agriculture, and to expand the country's war potential. In contrast to the speedy demobilization of American forces, the Soviet Union maintained a huge land army. While the production of consumer goods was limited, military expenditures mounted rapidly.

These activities were accompanied by the imposition of what Churchill described as an "iron curtain," cutting Soviet citizens off from travel abroad, from unauthorized publications, and from foreign radio programs, which were systematically jammed.

Russia under Khrushchev. Following Stalin's death in 1953, the world was told that henceforth the Soviet Union would be guided by the "collective leadership" of the top Communists, headed by G. M. Malenkov, who had loomed as the heir apparent during Stalin's last years. But Malenkov was soon challenged by a stocky, shrewd Ukrainian, Nikita S. Khrushchev, first secretary of the party; from this strong position, like Stalin prior to his ousting of Trotsky, he proceeded to fill the higher echelons with men favorable to himself. Early in 1955, he forced Malenkov

Addressing the U.N. General Assembly in 1960, Soviet leader Nikita Khrushchev violently attacked the United States and Secretary-General Dag Hammarskjöld.

to resign as premier and put Nikolai Bulganin in his place. Within the next three years Khrushchev ousted from the Presidium (the inner executive committee of the party) his most powerful rivals, including Malenkov, Molotov, and Marshal Zhukov, the war hero whose prestige had surpassed his own. In March 1958, Khrushchev replaced Bulganin as premier, and his possession of this post, together with his leadership of the party, made Khrushchev undisputed master of the Soviet world.

As premier, Malenkov had sought to step up the production of consumer goods, but Khrushchev reverted to Stalin's assignment of top priority to heavy industry. This policy dominated the 1959 Seven-Year Plan. In the party program, approved by the Twenty-second Party Congress in October 1961, he outlined his hopes. The program called for an increase of 150 per cent in industrial production by 1970 and an increase of 500 per cent by 1980. The goal for electric power production for the twenty-year period was set for an increase of 1000 per cent. By 1980 all individual farming was to be eliminated, and housing, transportation, schooling, medical service, and utilities were to be free. The increases demanded were so prodigious that Khrushchev, in presenting the agricultural phase of the program to the Congress, said, "The Congress will call on the party and the people, and the people will perform miracles."

These were ambitious plans, and many discounted Khrushchev's boast that the Soviet economy would surpass that of the United States in a relatively few years. But his ebullience sprang not only from an awareness of the progress of Soviet industry but also from his pride in the remarkable accomplishment of Soviet technology in launching the first space satellite, Sputnik, in 1957 and the moon rockets, Lunik I, II, and III, in 1959 and in sending the first man into space in 1961.

The "new" Soviet imperialism. After 1945, while most western powers were relinquishing control over their extensive colonial areas, the Soviet Union proceeded to move into eastern Europe and establish a colonial area of its own. Poland, East Germany, Rumania, Bulgaria, Hungary, and Czechoslovakia became the new imperial dependencies of the Soviet Union. In its eastern European area, Russia effectively exercised political control, directed economic activity, and forbade any cultural or educational activity which ran counter to the basic philosophy espoused by Moscow. In an area inhabited by nearly ninety million people, human labor and natural resources were exploited for the enrichment of the Soviet Union.

The technique of Russian conquest in eastern Europe after 1945 followed a common pattern. With variations here and there, the process was, first, for Moscow to secure the establishment of a coalition government in which certain key ministries, especially that of interior and police, were given to Communists. Next, full-scale elections were postponed until the Communist party felt confident of victory, and the police terrorized and imprisoned anyone who opposed them. When

election day came, many thousands of anti-Communists were barred from voting. In spite of western protests, the gobbling up of satellites continued, with Czechoslovakia as the last victim in 1948.

Yugoslavia's defection. Yugoslavia was the first Soviet satellite to break the grip of Moscow. Marshal Tito, a tough wartime resistance leader and the number-one Communist in Yugoslavia, at first went along with the Soviet "line," though his national strength and geographical distance from Soviet forces enabled him to display his growing resentment against Russian interference. When Tito broke with Soviet policy in 1948, he was encouraged by the western powers and held his ground despite Moscow's economic reprisals and threats of war.

While Tito remained Communist and used western financial aid in such ideologically "correct" ventures as the build-up of heavy industry and the collectivization of agriculture, his successful defection proved a continuing source of embarrassment to the Kremlin. Moreover, his example stirred thoughts of rebellion in other satellites.

East Germany, Poland, and Hungary. In 1949 the Soviet Union organized the eastern zone of Germany into a puppet state, the German Democratic Republic. By 1950 the East German regime proceeded to break up large farms and force the expansion of heavy industry. As living standards declined, popular discontent mounted. Thousands of East Germans fled each week to West Germany; and in June 1953, severe food shortages, coupled with new decrees for longer working hours, touched off a revolt. The uprising was put down quickly, but the world was left in no doubt as to what the East Germans thought of their "workers' democracy."

Because of Poland's strong historical and cultural ties with the West, it is not surprising that the Communist regime in Poland took on a national coloration as in Yugoslavia. Wladyslaw Gomulka, a formerly imprisoned national Communist, gained control of the Polish United Workers' (Communist) party in 1956. Subsequently, he sent the Soviet "brass" back to Russia and permitted the workers considerable freedom of expression. Extraordinary too in a Communist state, Gomulka concluded a concordat with the Roman Catholic Church. The working alliance between church and state was due to at least two factors. The Poles are overwhelmingly Catholic, and any government seeking to win their support must come to terms with the Church. For its part, the Church recognized that its only hope of revival lay in cooperating with Gomulka's regime. Both parties in turn knew that the Russian bear, if goaded too far, could simply step across the undefended border and stamp out the gains which had already been achieved for a freer Poland. Thus any chance of full-grown Titoism in Warsaw seemed to be ruled out for the foreseeable future.

National communism had meanwhile been gaining ground in Hungary, and the news of the Polish defection touched off a demonstration in Budapest for national independence. The riots of October 23, 1956, quickly grew into a nation-wide revolt, and a coalition government was established under Imre Nagy, who had previously been demoted by the Stalinists. Political prisoners were released, and the government secured the withdrawal of Russian troops from Budapest. On November 4, however, reinforced Soviet forces returned to the capital, where they stamped out the flames of national independence while the western world was preoccupied by the Israeli, French, and British invasions of Egypt (see p. 765). Nagy fled to the Yugoslav legation, from which he was later enticed by an offer of safe-conduct, only to be captured and afterwards treacherously executed. Thousands of freedom fighters died in the struggle, while within a year upward of 200,000 refugees sought sanctuary in the West. Although a new satellite regime was propped up by Soviet bayonets, the uprising and its implication were not soon forgotten.

Communism triumphs in China. The most spectacular triumph of the Communist World in the postwar years was the acquisition of China and its 600,000,000 people. During the war, Chiang Kai-shek's Nationalist government and the Chinese Communist leaders had waged a common struggle against the Japanese. The Communists emerged from the war with increased popular support and in control of an area of 90,000,000 people as well as an army of 500,000 men under Mao Tse-tung.

Civil war broke out again in October 1945. The Nationalists had failed to retain the loyalty of the people and could be saved neither by American mediation nor American supplies. Chiang's strength collapsed in Manchuria in 1948, and the following year saw the rout of Nationalist armies. By the middle of 1950, Mao had become master of mainland China, and Chiang and a remnant of his forces fled to Formosa (Taiwan). The People's Republic of China, which had already been established in Peking in 1949, was immediately recognized by the U.S.S.R., and subsequently the two countries formed a thirty-year alliance. Attempts by the Soviet Union to gain for Peking the seat at the United Nations held by Nationalist China failed, largely because of United States opposition.

The new Communist leaders imposed a tightly centralized administration that extended to Manchuria, Inner Mongolia, and Chinese Turkestan; and in 1950, Red Chinese armies moved into Tibet. Throughout China all organized opposition to the regime was systematically liquidated. Landlords were dispossessed, businessmen had their firms either nationalized or brought under rigid control, and intellectuals were subjected to "thought reform" in order to eliminate "incorrect thinking."

As in the Soviet system, all power was concentrated in the Communist party, governed by the People's Central Committee, whose members occupied the chief civilian and military posts. The day-to-day work of the committee was entrusted to a smaller Politburo headed by Mao, who was also chairman of the republic—that is, head of the state. Elected representative bodies existed, but the political levers were manipulated by the Central Committee.

After checking two flagrant evils which had afflicted the Nationalists—namely, corruption and inflation—Mao's regime began to grapple with China's basic problems: a des-

In 1958 the "people's commune" was made the basic social and economic unit of Communist China. All those living within a commune (which may cover an enormous area) are fed, clothed, and generally cared for in return for their labor—thirteen hours daily, with one day off every two weeks. Here, peasant members of a commune harvest a crop of wheat. In 1960 and 1961, a decline in agricultural productivity led to criticism of the commune system.

perately low standard of living, too many people on overworked land, and an urgent need for industrialization. Millions of acres, confiscated from the owners without compensation, were set up as state farms. Other land was organized into collectives, but when the first Five-Year Plan (1953-1957) failed to eliminate the food shortage, a second plan called for the replacement of the collectives with gigantic people's communes (see illustration). Both the first and second Five-Year Plans called for an increase in industrialization and necessitated large-scale Soviet financial, military, and technical assistance. Repeated agricultural disasters and population growth continued to work against governmental planning for economic and social progress.

Threats of Chinese expansion were felt from India to Formosa. In 1958 the Communists launched a heavy bombardment of Nationalist forces on the island of Quemoy, a few miles off the coast of China. Although shelling was reduced sharply after the United States Seventh Fleet moved into the area, the future of Formosa and the offshore islands remained a troublesome problem. Other symptoms of Chinese expansionist tendencies included the seizure of Tibet, the challenges to India's northern frontier, and the contribution of men and arms to support Communist movements in Vietnam, Laos, and other countries in southeast Asia. Such aggression, frequently without Russian support, points up the rivalry between Red China and the Soviet Union for domination in southeast Asia and for ideological leadership of the Communist World itself.

THE UNCOMMITTED WORLD

Problems of the underdeveloped lands. Africa, the Middle East, and south Asia comprise the heart of the so-called underdeveloped areas. Here the postwar tempo of change has been very rapid as the forces of nationalism, technology, and social and economic innovation transform ancient ways of life. Less concerned with ideologies than with the grim problems of physical survival, the peoples in these underdeveloped countries have attempted to stand apart from the rivalries of the Free and Communist worlds.

In their search for effective governmental systems, the new nations continued to weigh the respective claims of democracy and communism and to search for alternatives to these systems. Although some nationalistic intellectuals realized the value of parliamentary democracy, the Afro-Asian masses tended to equate western democracy with the colonial rule which deprived them of a voice in their government, while they saw in the Soviet Union an inspiring example of progress from feudal state to industrial titan. The sacrifice of individual freedom for such achievement meant little to peoples whose main concern was getting enough to eat. Moreover, with their lack of experience in democratic procedures and their need to maintain stability in the midst of poverty and strife, many of the new nations appeared to favor the concentration of power in a strong executive rather than in a representative legislature. In these states, democracy faced an uphill struggle.

India and Pakistan. In 1942 India had been offered dominion status at the end of the war. Although the two chief nationalist groups—the Congress party, led by Gandhi and Nehru, and the Muslim League, led by Muhammad Ali Jinnah—rejected this offer, agreement was secured for a constitutional convention in 1946. To avoid a minority position, the Muslim League proposed a separate state—Pakistan—for the Muslim community of 92,000,000 and an Indian state for the remaining, basically Hindu population. This proposal was accepted in August 1947, and the two states became members of the British Commonwealth, with the independent Indian princes free to join either state.

Transition to self-rule was painful. To the ancient Hindu-Muslim religious conflict was added the fanaticism of the new nationalisms. Tens of thousands died in riots, and millions of refugees sought safety in the country of their faith. In 1948 the dedicated apostle of Indian nationalism, Gandhi, was assassinated by a Hindu extremist. The United Nations imposed a cease-fire in the Indian-Pakistani struggle over Kashmir, a predominantly Muslim area whose Hindu prince had assigned his land to India.

From the outset, independent India has been ruled by the Congress party under the leadership of Nehru. The constitution of 1950, establishing India as a republic, provided for a parliamentary government with a president, a prime minister, and a bicameral legislature. In spite of conflict within the Congress party, stable administration has been enjoyed, in part due to the legacy of an efficient civil service from colonial days. The socialist Nehru, respected as the leader of the Afro-Asian neutralist bloc, has called on both East and West to help India resolve its unequal struggle between population growth and economic productivity. Two Five-Year Plans have been launched and birth control is being financed by the government. Even with foreign economic and technical assistance, however, India's future promises to be austere.

Pakistan did not enjoy political stability until 1958. A geographic anomaly, this state consists of two segments, East and West Pakistan, separated from each other by a thousand miles. More advanced than East Pakistan, the western segment virtually monopolized the governmental services as well as the lion's share of appropriations, with the result that chronic discontent existed among the Muslim Bengalis in East Pakistan. Furthermore, both sections were plagued by political corruption, which was by no means ended when the country became a republic in 1956. Two years later, after a series of crises, the government was taken over by a military leader, General Ayub Khan, who has proved to be a benevolent dictator.

Southeast Asia. A treasury of natural resources, southeast Asia has been in upheaval since the end of World War II. The call for self-government has been supported by various nationalistic and Communist-inspired movements.

In 1946, France granted a measure of autonomy to Cambodia and Laos, but the crucial problem was the future status of Vietnam. There the nationalist movement was led by the Communist Ho Chi Minh, who in 1945 had proclaimed the Republic of Vietnam immediately after the surrender of the Japanese occupation forces. In the year 1948, France recognized Vietnam but was unwilling to accept the domination of Ho Chi Minh's Communist Vietminh party. Civil war ensued, with the Soviet Union and Communist China supporting Ho Chi Minh. In July 1954, following the disastrous French defeat at Dien Bien Phu, Vietnam was split by international agreement into a French-protected state in the south and a Communist state in the north. The south, along with Cambodia and Laos, became fully independent in 1955. Although United States economic, technical, and military aid to the three states has been large, it has failed to win them from neutralism or to assure them economic well-being and efficient government. Late in 1960, Communist infiltration in Laos brought on an international crisis. Neither United Nations action nor direct negotiations between the United States and Russia (both of which saw their reputations at stake in Asia) had effectively resolved the issue by the end of 1961. In addition to these problems in Laos, Communist activities were troubling neighboring South Vietnam, which seemed at this time equally vulnerable to subversion.

Meanwhile, the Dutch colonial empire had felt the force of nationalism. After Japan's surrender, the rich islands of Java and Sumatra were in the hands of nationalists who proclaimed the Republic of Indonesia. After four years of war and United Nations mediation, the Dutch in 1949 accepted the creation of a federal state known as the United States of Indonesia. A tenuous but irritating link with the Netherlands remained until 1954, when Indonesia asserted its sovereignty. But independence did not bring political stability. Lack of training in self-government, an incompetent civil service, and unstable coalition governments contributed to the uneasy state of affairs. President Sukarno's belief that Indonesia required a "guided democracy"—benevolent paternalism in disguise—helped foment sporadic rebellions and strengthened the position of the local Communists—and later, of the army leaders.

Two nations in southeast Asia gained independence in a relatively peaceful fashion. The United States granted the Philippines independence in 1946, and Britain awarded Burma its freedom about two years later. When grants of independence robbed the native Communist groups of the anticolonialism issue, they resorted to guerrilla warfare against the governments in power. Although vigorous leadership by President Ramón Magsaysay in the Philippines and U Nu in Burma defeated the rebels, many problems still remained to be solved.

After 1945, in the rich tin and rubber region of Malaya, a fanatical Communist minority carried on guerrilla terrorism to intimidate both the British authorities and the native populace. Not until 1957 was Britain able to recognize the Federation of Malaya as independent and a member of the British Commonwealth. The new government maintained close ties with the West and by military vigilance drove the remaining Communists deep into the jungles.

On January 1, 1962, a hitherto neglected area of the world moved toward independence. On that date, West Samoa, formerly administered by New Zealand, became the first fully independent Polynesian state.

Crises in the Muslim lands. The Middle East has been an explosive area since World War II not only because it possesses over two thirds of the world's known oil reserves and is the key to East-West communications but also because it has long been the arena for tests of strength between the big powers.

In 1945 Britain and the United States prevailed upon France to honor its pledge of independence to Lebanon and Syria, and the following year the British mandate in Jordan was terminated. The British mandate in Palestine presented a more difficult problem because all solutions acceptable to the Jews were rejected by the Arabs (who constituted over 70 per cent of the population). Toward the end of the war, the British obtained United States approval to violate its White Paper of 1939, which pledged a reduction and finally an end to Jewish immigration. Zionists and Arabs alike were displeased. In frustration, Britain submitted the problem to the United Nations and announced its intention to withdraw from Palestine.

A majority but divided decision in the U.N. called for partitioning Palestine into Jewish and Arab states. The decision was not submitted to the Palestinians for a plebiscite nor was it accepted by the new, neighboring Arab states, which professed to speak for the Arab majority. Britain also did not approve the partition, and the United States, recognizing its dangers, proposed an alternative temporary trusteeship. But the U.S.S.R., posing as the defender of Zionism, insisted that the decision be applied. When the U.N. provided no mechanism for implementing its decision, Britain withdrew in May 1948. In the conflict which followed, the new nation of Israel held out against the combined forces of seven Arab states. Although the U.N. arranged an armistice in 1949, no peace agreement has been written and the Arab states refuse to recognize the legal existence of the new state of Israel. The prime stumbling blocks are the Arab refugees numbering almost a million, the issue of compensation for former Arab properties, and the Arab politicians who inflame their people with firebrand oratory.

The weakness of Egypt was made particularly conspicuous during the war in Palestine, and the finger of blame was pointed at the prowestern but venal government of King Farouk. In 1952 a clique of army officers seized the government in Cairo and forced the dissolute king into exile. Corrupt politicians were convicted, large estates were broken up for distribution to the peasants, and in 1953 a republic was proclaimed. Subsequently, the strongest officer, Colonel Gamal Abdel Nasser, assumed leadership and became the symbol of Arab nationalism.

Nasser's plan to construct a high dam at Aswan brought offers of American and British assistance. But when his request for arms was refused by Washington, he turned to the Soviet bloc, and the offer of American aid was abruptly canceled. Nasser retaliated in July 1956 by nationalizing the Suez Canal, with whose shipping tolls he expected to finance the dam. World reaction was electric, but Nasser was able to defy western opinion and eventually reached agreements compensating the shareholders of the largely foreign-owned Suez Canal Company.

Meanwhile, Egyptian guerrillas were infiltrating Israeli territory, and Israel-bound shipping was refused use of the canal. The upshot was the Israeli invasion of Egypt on October 29. After an ultimatum the next day, British and French troops invaded the canal zone, ostensibly to clear the combatants away from this vital artery. But when the Suez adventure was roundly condemned by both the United States and the Soviet Union, Britain and France bowed to the General Assembly's call for a cease-fire, the canal remained under Egyptian control, and a U.N. emergency force was organized to patrol the Egyptian-Israeli border.

In the final analysis, the prestige of the U.N. was enhanced and Nasser's position was strengthened. While the United States was temporarily the hero of the Uncommitted World, the prestige of Britain and France fell

and allied unity was broken. The Suez Canal issue remained controversial, for Nasser disregarded his pledges in defiance of the U.N. and persisted in denying the use of the canal to Israel-bound shipping. Meanwhile, the Soviet Union now claimed to be the defender of Arab nationalism, and the United States Congress, in order to counter this potential threat, adopted in 1956 the Eisenhower Doctrine, which promised aid to any nations subjected to armed aggression from Communist sources.

In February 1958, Nasser succeeded in persuading Syria to join with Egypt in the United Arab Republic, thus snatching Syria from the hands of a pro-Soviet faction. As antiwestern sentiment spread, July witnessed the murder of the king of Iraq and the overthrow of his prowestern government by the military dictator General Abdul Karim Kassem, who shortly took the country out of Bagdad Pact membership. The expulsion of British influence was popular, but other problems soon arose. Tension mounted between Iraqis and Egyptians over their conflicting views of Arab nationalism, and internal conflicts arose between the Iraqis and the Kurds, a people inhabiting northern Iraq. Simultaneously, propagandists from Bagdad and Cairo began to exert pressure upon Lebanon and Jordan. When these countries, unwilling to be dominated either by the United Arab Republic or Iraq, appealed for aid, American marines were landed in Lebanon under the Eisenhower Doctrine, and British troops were flown into Jordan. Both Cairo and Moscow labeled these acts as "aggression." The issue was taken to the U.N., where the Arab states agreed to observe nonintervention in one another's internal affairs and the secretary-general consented to facilitate the withdrawal of foreign troops.

Western fears of Soviet aims in the Middle East were strengthened by Moscow's aid to Nasser in beginning construction of the Aswan Dam. But still protesting his neutralism and rejecting communism for his country, Nasser expelled Soviet agents from Egypt and in 1959 resumed relations with Britain. In the meantime, an open breach between Cairo and Bagdad had developed. Nasser's vision of a union of all Arab peoples under Egyptian leadership was jeopardized by his rival, Kassem. Claiming to be exploited, Syria seceded from the U.A.R. in September 1961, a move which considerably reduced Nasser's prestige. These developments showed that the Arab nationalists were far from being united.

Israel. Tiny Israel provided a model for many former colonial territories. In this country of desert wasteland and limited natural resources, irrigation projects were built, agriculture was extended, and new industries were established. In the councils of the nations, Israel earned respect as a stable and democratic regime. But its future was uncertain despite the energy and dedication of its people. The antipathy between this small population of two million people and its more than forty million Arab neighbors continued. Border clashes became less frequent but the presence of nearly one million Arab refugees, who once lived in the area now occupied by the Israelis, was a constant irritant to Arab nationalists.

The abduction from Argentina and the trial in 1961 of the Nazi official Adolf Eichmann, who was responsible for millions of Jewish deaths, reminded the world of the enormity of Nazi anti-Semitism. But the episode reopened racist wounds and brought criticism of Israel's assumption of legal authority. Of greater consequence to Israel's standing among the world's nations was the fact that even though it enjoyed substantial economic growth, still it did not earn its own living. The future of Israel depended not only upon the issue of war or peace with its neighbors but also upon the continuance of outside economic aid.

Nation-making in Africa. Subject to disposal by the victors of World War II, the Italian colonies in northeastern Africa were geographically and culturally linked to the Middle East, where, as we have seen, nationalism was boiling to the surface. Libya became a sovereign state in 1951, and in the following year Eritrea was federated with the independent state of Ethiopia. The former Anglo-Egyptian Sudan was established by Britain as an independent republic in 1956, despite Nasser's desire to see the long Nile valley become a single state controlled from Cairo. For backward Somalia the U.N. specified an Italian trusteeship with a terminal date of 1960, a commitment which was fulfilled when Somalia was proclaimed independent in that year. Britain relinquished British Somaliland at the same time, and a union was proclaimed which put pressure on tiny French Somaliland and the Somali sections of Ethiopia to realize the dream of a Greater Somali state covering the horn of Africa. Thus the independence of northeastern Africa was virtually completed.

In French and Spanish North Africa, aggressive nationalists struggled to break European control of the area's wealth. In 1954 France granted Tunisia independence under Habib Bourguiba, and in the following year France reëstablished the independent kingdom of Morocco, to which were added Spanish Morocco and the free city of Tangier. On the other hand, the retention of Algeria as an integral part of France became a point of French honor. The downfall of the Fourth French Republic was brought about by the failure to end the Algerian revolt, and the Algerian problem continued to haunt France under De Gaulle (see p. 755).

West Africa was to lead the way to the realization of nationalist aspirations among the Negro peoples of Black Africa. In the British colonies of the Gold Coast and Nigeria and in the French coastal areas of the Ivory Coast and Senegal as well, there existed by African standards a high degree of prosperity and literacy. The conversion of the Gold Coast into the independent state of Ghana in 1957 was achieved almost entirely without disturbance, for there were few white settlers to stiffen resistance against the transfer of power from white hands to black, and the native politicians represented in the main an orderly and responsible electorate. Ghana's Kwame Nkrumah, the first leader to emerge in independent Black Africa, became the spokesman for Pan-African nationalism. But his influence and his prestige in the West lost momentum as his own rule became authoritarian and as he seemed to grow sympathetic to communism.

British preparation for colonial independence exhibited foresight, but the time schedule was moved ahead by the growing clamor for self-rule. University training was accelerated for capable individuals, colonials were raised to executive levels, and ownership and management of local enterprises were shared. In October 1960, independence was granted to the most important British colony and potentially the strongest state in Black Africa, Nigeria, which possessed a population of about 35,000,000. The fears of tribal and religious conflict proved baseless and, from the first, Nigeria assumed responsible leadership. In 1961 Sierra Leone, the colony founded for emancipated British slaves, became independent.

In contrast to the British colonies, the movement of the French colonies toward independence was almost precipitous. French unwillingness to comprehend the strength of postwar anticolonialism and nationalism had cost France dearly in Indochina and North Africa. Therefore, in 1958, De Gaulle offered French colonies autonomy within the French system or immediate independence. All the colonies chose autonomy and gradual evolution toward ultimate independence except for Guinea, whose inhabitants responded to the skillful appeals of the leftist leader Sékou Touré, who was banking on the development of Guinea's bauxite and other resources through the competitive bidding of the Cold War powers. The other French territories in West and Equatorial Africa became fully sovereign during 1960, though eight remained in the French Community. Meanwhile, other French colonies were moving rapidly toward independence. In 1960 Madagascar was declared the independent Malagasy Republic within the French Community, and when the French trusteeship over the Cameroons and Togo ended in 1960, republics were set up.

Independence for the Belgian Congo was a painful process. White paternalistic rule had left no heritage of trained leadership; there were only eighteen university graduates and no doctors or lawyers in the Congo. Anti-European riots in 1959 forced the Belgian government to abandon belated plans for a period of tutelage, and independence was granted in June 1960 amidst an alarming de-

The growing need to establish closer relations between the peoples of underdeveloped countries and the peoples of the West led to President Kennedy's creation of the Peace Corps in 1961. This organization is made up of volunteers who will live among impoverished peoples and share with them knowledge of western techniques. Here Ghana's secretary of education (right) and the United States ambassador (left) welcome members of a group of fifty teachers—the first Corps group to leave the United States—as they arrive in Ghana to begin two years of teaching in secondary schools.

terioration of law and order. Operations in the great mines came to a halt, and the economy of the Congo was paralyzed as Belgians fled from the strife-torn area. Tribe fought tribe, and native troops resisted both the white officers and the Negro leaders who were the officials of the new Republic of the Congo. When factional, provincial, and tribal leaders —some of whom were supported by foreign powers—seized spheres of control, U.N. intervention followed. In the next few months, anarchy, starvation, the murder of the first premier and Communist tool, Patrice Lumumba, and U.N. action gradually forced the conflicting groups together. However, the wealthiest of the provinces, Katanga, refused to accept even a decentralized federation and fought both the central government and the U.N. forces in an effort to make good its secession.

Major changes were also being made in British East Africa. In Tanganyika, granted full independence in December 1961, the small white settler group worked harmoniously with the African nationalists. In Uganda,

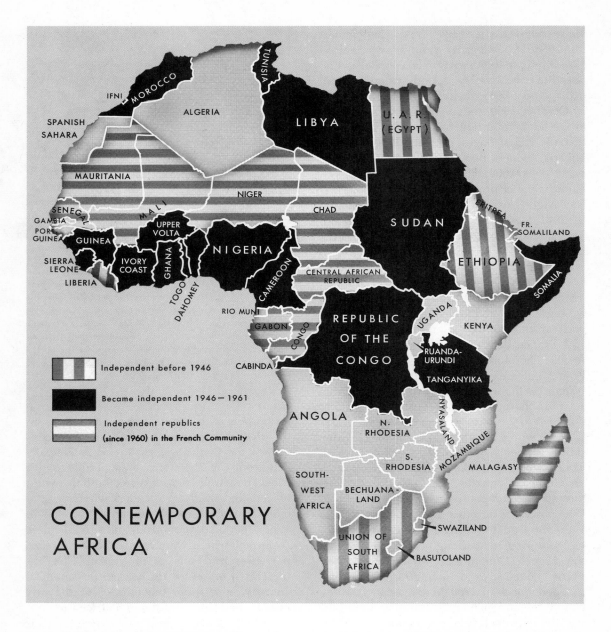

Independent before 1946

Became independent 1946—1961

Independent republics
(since 1960) in the French Community

CONTEMPORARY AFRICA

nationalistic feelings were strong, but independence was postponed because of intertribal rivalries. The colony of Kenya presented serious problems, as a small but important European settler community—numbering about 50,000 as compared to the native population of some 6,000,000—sought to adjust to the impact of African nationalism.

In the early 1950's a fanatical antiwhite society in Kenya, the Mau Mau, had developed within the main highland tribe, the Kikuyu,

and was suppressed with great difficulty. Later the British government made clear to the white settlers that they must prepare for the eventual independence of Kenya under democratic—which would mean black—control. Because Kenya has a weaker educational program than exists in West Africa, the path to independence is a thorny one. The dramatic leadership of Jomo Kenyatta, imprisoned until 1961 for his part in the Mau Mau revolt, and of the brilliant Tom Mboya can scarcely offset the tribal animosities, the resentment toward Europeans, and the dearth of trained and experienced natives.

Nationalism also made its impact in British Central Africa. In 1953 the three territories of Nyasaland, Northern Rhodesia, and Southern Rhodesia united in the Federation of Rhodesia and Nyasaland. In a total population of 7,000,000, the Europeans numbered only 300,000. But as in Kenya, much of the educational and social services were developed through the wealth of this small minority. Racial discrimination, while not as rigorous as in South Africa, was sufficiently strong to antagonize those Africans who were educated and politically conscious. In 1959, led by Dr. Hastings Banda, the natives in Nyasaland who resented being made part of a European-dominated federation rioted, and the disturbances were put down only after a state of emergency had been declared. In 1961 a similar native movement in Northern Rhodesia protested against the new constitution which perpetuated white minority control. The future of the confederation itself is challenged not only by the native nationalists but also by the numerous whites, particularly in Southern Rhodesia, who are sympathetic with the racist ideas of South Africa.

The colonies of Portugal—Angola and Mozambique—were the last to hear the urgent cry for freedom and were the least prepared for freedom. Not only had the Portuguese made no attempt to develop educated native leadership, but in other respects also their colonial policy was a century behind the times.

The march of African nationalism seemed irresistible. In 1945, only Liberia, Ethiopia, and South Africa were, in fact, independent; in 1960 alone, seventeen states became free, bringing the total to twenty-six. In 1961, for the first time, the Afro-Asian bloc held the balance of power in the U.N. General Assembly. With independence achieved, however, new conflicts developed—between the new states, between tribal groups divided by irrational frontiers, between communism and democracy, and between big powers struggling for influence.

Only in South Africa has the white man chosen to stand against the native majority and world public opinion. More than half of the settlers of European origin on the continent live in South Africa, but even there they are outnumbered almost four to one. Since 1948, when the moderates lost influence, a policy of apartheid (separateness) has been increasingly enforced; this system not only isolates the native living areas completely from those of the Europeans but limits natives to employment in servile tasks where they do not compete with whites and provides them with inferior education aimed at preserving servility and reëstablishing tribalism. In the spring of 1960, the Africans made widespread demonstrations against their second-class citizenship. Armed clashes which culminated in the massacre of sixty-eight unarmed Africans at Sharpeville and the wounding of several hundred more brought world-wide censure of the South African government. Criticism within a Commonwealth Conference of Prime Ministers led to the withdrawal of South Africa from the British Commonwealth of Nations in 1961.

THE WORLD

TODAY AND TOMORROW

The Cold War continues. An uneasy equilibrium characterized the international scene in the 1950's as the Cold War continued on many fronts. The two superpowers engaged in an arms race, competing in the stock-piling of atomic bombs as well as of conventional armaments and in the development of still more deadly weapons. Paralleling the arms race, as we have seen, was the formation of tightly knit defensive military alliances outside the auspices of the U.N. In addition, vast amounts of money and energy were channeled into economic aid and propaganda as the United States and the U.S.S.R. tried to "sell" their ways of life to others.

In 1955 occurred the summit conference of the Big Four at Geneva, the first meeting of the heads of state since Potsdam ten years earlier. At the Geneva Conference, discus-

As secretary-general of the United Nations, Dag Hammarskjöld was attacked repeatedly by the Soviets in their efforts to undermine the effectiveness of Hammarskjöld's position. Here Hammarskjöld listens as Soviet ambassador Valerian Zorin demands that he resign his post.

sions were held on German reunification, disarmament, and the reduction of trade barriers between East and West. Although progress was blocked on many points, particularly on the German question, relations between statesmen were cordial and a spirit of good will pervaded the gatherings. Many observers felt that the danger of a hot war had receded and that a beginning had been made in removing tensions by negotiation rather than by force.

In 1959, in a coast-to-coast tour of the United States, Khrushchev seemed to show a genuine desire to understand America and its citizens. Speaking later before the General Assembly, the Soviet leader announced that the U.S.S.R. was prepared to negotiate with the West on certain limited objectives. The western powers, heartened by this proposal, invited him to a Paris summit meeting in May of the following year. Just before the meeting, the world was startled by President Eisenhower's official admission that a plane forced down in Russia was an American U-2

reconnaissance craft. Accusing the United States of aggression and treachery, Khrushchev scuttled the conference. When the U-2 incident was taken to the U.N., the delegates —well aware of the many acts of Soviet espionage since 1945—dismissed the charge of aggression. Khrushchev's announced willingness to negotiate with the Democratic presidential candidate if elected led to the Vienna meeting of June 1961 with President Kennedy, but this encounter proved as abortive as earlier summit conferences.

The U. N. and the age of permanent crises. The crisis-ridden history of the United Nations and of the world itself since the establishment of the U.N. has often concealed the effectiveness of the organization in solving, or at least minimizing, the problems of the day. The U.N. was largely responsible for ending the warfare in Palestine and Indonesia; its on-the-spot activities kept the Kashmir dispute from exploding into a full-scale war; and U.N. border supervision in the Near East and southeast Asia helped to prevent open warfare in these areas. The Korean conflict was resolved on the basis of the *status quo ante bellum,* and the tense situation in the Congo showed how U.N. action can help to mitigate the worst effects of a dangerous crisis. The focusing of world opinion—by either resolution or open discussion—on problems as diverse as civil strife in Portuguese Angola, rebellion in French Algeria, Russian tyranny in Hungary, racism in South Africa, and the hostility between the United States and Cuba has helped pull the fuse from otherwise explosive situations.

Hailed as an international Magna Carta, the Universal Declaration of Human Rights (1948) enumerated for the first time the basic inalienable rights of people everywhere— thereby exerting strong moral, if not actual legal, pressure upon its signatories. Often, however, the progress registered by the nonpolitical agencies of the United Nations—the Technical Assistance Administration, for example, or UNICEF (United Nations International Children's Emergency Fund)—has been obscured in the competition for newspaper headlines.

Many of the most significant world developments have been reflected in important changes in the structure and function of the U.N. Even before the United Nations was well established, its organization was modified by power politics. The member nations tended to cluster into power blocs—Russia and its satellites, the Afro-Asian bloc, the Latin-American nations—which extracted concessions from one another in return for favors.

In the critical arena of the Security Council, where action requires the unanimous vote of the great powers, the U.S.S.R. has not hesitated to use the veto power to block Council action. The resultant stalemates in the Council have tended to increase the General Assembly's responsibility and authority. Furthermore, the changing composition of the Assembly has made that body more responsive to the collective opinion of all the nations of the world. Some observers have felt, however, that the flood of African states into the U.N., giving that continent nearly half the votes in the Assembly, has resulted in a disproportionate influence being granted to this group of nations.

The expansion of U.N. membership from fifty-one charter members in 1945 to over one hundred nations in the 1960's draws the organization closer to universality than any other international peacemaking body in history. Its doors are open to all nations desiring to be members—excepting those few within the orbit of present-day conflicts between the great power blocs: the divided states of Germany, Korea, and Vietnam and the disputed Communist regime of China. Pressure for the admission of Red China, however, has been growing among Afro-Asian nations, in spite of the delaying strategy of the United States government.

The most stabilizing feature in the U.N. has been the effectiveness of the Secretariat under the leadership of its first two secretary-generals—Trygve Lie, who resigned in 1953 under Russian threats, and Dag Hammarskjöld, who died in 1961 in an airplane crash when mediating the Congo crisis. Both men had transformed themselves into selfless international civil servants committed to world peace. This selflessness irritated the Russians, who had withdrawn their recognition of Hammarskjöld before his death and had proposed a "troika," or committee of three secretary-generals, one each representing the Communist, democratic, and neutralist blocs. Such a plan would have formally established the concept of ideological power blocs at the heart of the U.N. Attempts to replace Hammarskjöld almost floundered when the Russian troika scheme was proposed again after his death. Only the Communist bloc supported the proposal, and the Russians finally accepted the interim appointment of a single secretary-general, U Thant of Burma.

The most dangerous failure of the U.N. has been in regard to armaments. The disagreements of the United States and the Soviet Union over control and inspections have created the worst impasse in contemporary history. While the two giants debated, Britain and France joined the nuclear powers. The voluntary holiday on nuclear testing was ended by the U.S.S.R. on the eve of the Communist party congress in 1961 with a major series of test explosions.

The dream that the United Nations might develop, as the Common Market is developing, toward an international superstate with both authority and force to create world order has been shattered by the emergence of two conflicting alliance systems, with an aggressive "neutralist" bloc in between. Yet, the greatest triumph of the U.N. has been its ability to survive in the face of such conflicts and to survive without becoming the captive of any nation or bloc of nations.

SUMMARY

The Second World War ended in victory for the Allied powers, but it was a victory without peace. In some measure, the failure to establish a peaceful world was the result of the war's legacy of global dislocation. Even more, it was due to the effects of this upheaval upon three major historic forces: liberal democracy, communism, and nationalism. Each constituted the driving and sustaining element in one of the three distinctive ideological "worlds" that crystallized after 1945—the Free, the Communist, and the Uncommitted. The interaction of these three worlds has been responsible for the state of global existence in which we find ourselves today.

The different segments of the Free World emerged from the common struggle in very different conditions of health. North America found itself with an economy stronger than any that had ever existed before, ready to embark upon the next stage of material expansion. Western Europe, on the other hand, had been ravaged both physically and psychologically, and at first its people had all they could do to struggle back to the position they had known before the war. For several critical years, observers wondered if Europe, so long the center of world civilization, could ever regain its former cultural creativity and political initiative; many feared that, spiritually exhausted, it might have suffered a fatal loss of faith in itself. But the economic recovery of western Europe and its constant experimentation with new forms of political cooperation and economic integration attest to the recuperative powers of its peoples.

The nations of the Free World have been drawn ever closer together by the threat of Communist expansion. Meanwhile, they have proved the inherent healthiness of democracy and its unique ability to preserve humanistic values and individual freedom while modifying the social structure. In all the nations of the Free World there have been shifts to the left and to the right—but never so far to the left as to destroy individualism and never so far to the right as to abolish legislation for social welfare.

For the Soviet Union, victory in World War II had been won at a staggering material cost. Once again, with the return of peace, every national sinew had to be strained to reduce the gap separating the Soviet economy from that of the United States, now singled out as the chief symbol of "capitalist imperialism" and the chief rival of the Soviet Union. This redoubling of effort was accompanied by the ringing down of an iron curtain, behind which the Kremlin set about creating a vast empire stretching from the Adriatic to the Pacific.

But internal strains within the Soviet Union accompanied the pursuit of ambitious economic and political objectives. Among the satellites, Yugoslavia defected, and restlessness in East Germany, Poland, and Hungary persisted. Meanwhile, Communist China not only insisted upon full equality with the Soviet Union but lectured its older brother for straying from Marxist orthodoxy when Khrushchev suggested some sort of competitive coexistence with the democratic nations of the Free World.

Perhaps the farthest-flung force in the postwar world was nationalism, which erupted in virulent forms in Asia and Africa. One sovereign state after another rose from the ashes of prewar colonialism, all eager to acquire western technical skills and to accept economic assistance but all determined to reject criticism and to avoid interference. United chiefly in their sensitivity to any signs of racial arrogance in western society, the new nations of Asia and Africa have gradually come to recognize the willingness of the Free World to provide technical and economic aid, without strings; and they have also become increasingly aware of the consequences of Communist penetration.

Can these three worlds live in comparative peace? For a decade after World War II, the prospects were bleak indeed, as the icy blasts from the Cold War circled the globe and each year saw the creation of new military alliances and more terrible weapons. In such an environment the United Nations could not play the role for which it was intended, but it managed to produce some success—especially in the social and economic spheres—and its survival and its continuous role as a political safety valve proved its indispensability. And for optimists, at least, there was hope that the world might be entering a new era—one in which the Cold War would be replaced by what statesmen called coexistence. It was a concept without glory but one for which most of the peoples of the world seemed willing to settle. Satiated with the kind of excitement produced by atomic blasts and nuclear fallout, they were prepared to get on with the job of existing and of coexisting.

SUGGESTIONS FOR READING

Two handy surveys of the postwar period are H. S. Commager et al., *Contemporary Civilization,** Scott, Foresman; and H. Gatzke, *The Present in Perspective,** Rand McNally. Valuable information on current affairs is also offered by the pamphlets of the Foreign Policy Association Headlines series; the works are both scholarly and inexpensive.

Appraisals of the structure and function of the U.N. can be found in B. V. Cohen, *The United Nations, Growth and Possibilities,* Harvard, 1961; F. O. Wilcox and C. M. Marcy, *Proposals for Changes in the United Nations,* Brookings Institution, 1955; and A. N. Holcombe, ed., *Strengthening the United Nations,* Harper, 1957.

An able analysis of the East-West conflict is J. A. Lukacs, *A History of the Cold War,* Doubleday, 1961.

L. J. Halle, *Choice for Survival,* Harper, 1958. A discussion of limited atomic war as an alternative to all-out nuclear conflict, written by a former member of the U.S. Department of State. See also H. M. Kissinger, *Nuclear Weapons and Foreign Policy,* Harper, 1957; and G. F. Kennan, *Russia, the Atom and the West,* Harper, 1958.

The United States in World Affairs. An excellent survey, published annually for the Council on Foreign Relations by Harper.

R. Heilbroner, *The Future As History,* Harper, 1960. An evaluation of the revolutionary changes in our century and their effect on American ideals. For studies of American character, see also H. Kohn, *American Nationalism,* Macmillan, 1957; and M. Lerner, *America As a Civilization,* Simon and Schuster, 1957.

M. Salvadori, *NATO: A Twentieth Century Community of Nations,** Anvil. The historical background and creation of the western alliance; includes much source material. An able appraisal of Europe's journey to recovery and integration is E. B. Blair, *The Big Change in Europe,* Norton, 1958.

E. Crankshaw, *Khrushchev's Russia,** Penguin. An attempt to analyze the changes in Russia since the death of Stalin. A study made by the Russian Research Center at Harvard and based on interviews with refugees from the U.S.S.R. is R. A. Bauer et al., *How the Soviet System Works,* Harvard, 1956.

*Indicates an inexpensive paperbound edition.

Another good account of the changes in Soviet policy is D. J. Dallin, *Soviet Foreign Policy After Stalin,* Lippincott, 1960.

A. Inkeles and R. A. Bauer, *The Soviet Citizen: Daily Life in a Totalitarian Society,* Harvard, 1959. An engrossing study of occupational stratification, social mobility, and education.

R. L. Wolff, *The Balkans in Our Times,* Harvard, 1956. A thorough discussion of the current scene in the Balkans. See also N. Spulber, *The Economics of Communist Eastern Europe,* Wiley, 1957; and H. Seton-Wetson, *The East European Revolution,** Praeger.

A. D. Barnett, *Communist China and Asia: Challenge to American Policy,* Harper, 1960. A valuable study of Red China's internal developments, external affairs, and significance in world politics. Also important is J. H. Brimmell, *Communism in South East Asia,* Oxford, 1959, a study of how communism came to southeast Asia and how it developed and spread.

V. M. Dean, *The Nature of the Non-Western World,** Mentor. A good overall view of the problems facing the underdeveloped countries. Also recommended is E. Staley, *The Future of Underdeveloped Countries: Political Implications of Economic Development,* Harper, 1954.

A stimulating symposium on the pros and cons of colonialism is R. Strausz-Hupe and H. W. Hazard, eds., *The Idea of Colonialism,* Praeger, 1958.

Invaluable studies of the free areas of southeast Asia include E. H. Jacoby, *Agrarian Unrest in Southeast Asia,* Asia Pub. House, 1961; and G. Kahin, ed., *Governments and Politics of Southeast Asia,* Cornell, 1959.

G. Kimble, *Tropical Africa,* 2 vols., Twentieth-Century Fund, 1960. This work of encyclopedic qualities is a major survey of physical and human factors in African development. Also helpful is S. Hempstone, *Africa—Angry Young Giant,* Praeger, 1961, an American journalist's report on his travels of two and a half years through Africa.

C. Fisher and F. Krinsky, *Middle East in Crisis,* Syracuse Univ., 1959. Historical documents as well as a concise history of the region make up this review of the Middle East. A thorough coverage of the course of history in the Middle East in recent years is R. C. Mowat, *Middle East Perspective,* Pitman, 1959.

CHAPTER 32

New Patterns for a Nuclear Age

DEVELOPMENTS IN CONTEMPORARY SCIENCE AND THE FINE ARTS

Introduction. Every age conceives its own world view. Creation is seldom painless, and the creation of our present western world view has not been achieved without grave and painful doubts, divisions, and discords. We are gaining a "new" vision of man's place in the universe and a new awareness of the limits of human powers and human senses. To our confusion, we have discovered that the universe is vastly more wondrous and complicated than man ever suspected; and to our dismay, we have found that many of our older ideas regarding the nature of man and the universe can no longer be accepted as certainties.

With the creation of our present world view has come a sense of humility and, for some, a weakening of confidence and self-esteem. If the nineteenth century was, for the most part, an Age of Optimism—a flowering of the ideals and institutions that grew in the earlier Age of Reason— the twentieth century might be termed an Age of Anxiety. In the following chapter we shall see how developments in science and the arts have both shaped and reflected this change. We shall also see that, as in every age, the old can usually be found in the new; that there is rarely a clean break with the past.

SCIENCE: THE MENACE AND THE PROMISE

Leaps forward in physics. In Chapter 24 we discussed three revolutionary developments in physics in the early twentieth century—Planck's quantum theory, Einstein's theory of relativity, and the discovery of the atomic nucleus. The most significant further discoveries in physics have concerned that nucleus.

Twentieth-century progress in atomic physics has shown us that the medieval alchemists' dream of turning baser metals into gold was not totally absurd. In fact, physicists have accomplished the transmutation of solid elements. The journey toward this goal may be said to have begun in 1920, when Ernest Rutherford, the English physicist, changed some nitrogen atoms into hydrogen and oxygen atoms by bombarding the nitrogen with swiftly moving alpha particles. The next long step forward came ten years later, when the American physicist Ernest O. Lawrence invented the cyclotron, a device by means of which atomic particles could be given tremendous acceleration and used to smash larger, target atoms.

In 1932 an electrically neutral particle, the neutron, was discovered, giving physicists a "bullet" that could theoretically penetrate the energy field of the atom and reach its nucleus. Finally, in 1939, the German physicist Otto Hahn, once a student of Rutherford's, bombarded the uranium nucleus with highly accelerated free neutrons and split it—that is, succeeded in bringing about a fission in the uranium nucleus—transmuting it into the elements barium and krypton and releasing a small amount of energy. All that was needed to bring about a large-scale release of energy was a technique to produce and control a chain reaction.

For a chain reaction, the split nuclei must give off neutrons that will split other nuclei, that will give off neutrons that will split still other nuclei, and so on. The first such controlled reaction took place at the University of Chicago on December 2, 1942. It was accomplished by a group working under the direction of the Italian-born physicist Enrico Fermi for the Manhattan Project, a two-billion-dollar venture of the United States government during World War II. Undertaken to develop a military use for atomic energy, the Manhattan Project tested its first atomic bomb in the New Mexico desert on July 16, 1945. On August 6 an atomic bomb devastated the Japanese city of Hiroshima.

The transmutation of elements can be achieved not only by nuclear fission but also by fusion. In the fusion process, the nuclei fuse and the release of energy is even greater than that achieved through fission. Hydrogen atoms can thus be combined at very high temperatures to make the heavier element helium; this is the process employed in the hydrogen, or thermonuclear, bomb, a weapon triggered by an atomic bomb. By 1953 both the United States and the U.S.S.R. possessed this frightful weapon. The incredibly complex problems posed by it resolve, at the last, into the single, simple problem of human survival.

The exploration of space. On October 4, 1957, the entire world was startled by the announcement that Soviet scientists had launched the first man-made satellite, Sputnik I (from *sputnik zemlii*, "fellow traveler of the earth"). Several months later, the United States launched its first but much smaller satellite, Explorer I. In succeeding years, Russian and American space vehicles have shot up from the earth in increasing numbers. The scientists of the U.S.S.R. have succeeded not only in sending considerably heavier payloads into space but also in sending the first man into orbit in April 1961; the United States, however, has attained the lead in developing delicate instrumentation for collecting scientific data.

Many people look upon the satellites and other types of space probes solely as weapons of prestige in the Cold War, ignoring the scientific discoveries which they made possible. These discoveries were no mean achievements. The Soviet Union sent a rocket out past the moon and reported that it had taken pictures of the moon's hidden side. American satellites have transmitted back to earth televised pictures of terrestrial cloud formations,

The terrible power of nuclear weapons has exerted enormous influence on international affairs, national policies, and the minds of individuals ever since the explosion of the first atomic bomb in 1945. Here, the blast of an atomic bomb at Bikini atoll makes toys of American warships moored in the test area. The atomic bomb was to be dwarfed in power by the hydrogen bomb.

opening the way for better long-range forecasting of world weather conditions. Other satellites are being used to establish precise navigational aids, and one series, frankly called a "spy in the sky," is capable not only of black-and-white but infrared photography of objects on the ground. Most significant of all, perhaps, United States scientists have discovered by means of these satellites a series of bands of intense radiation, consisting of low-, medium-, and high-energy particles that had been shot out from the sun and trapped thousands of miles above the earth by the earth's magnetic field. Named after the physicist James Van Allen, these radiation bands constitute an extremely dangerous barrier to any human attempt to travel beyond them.

Useful in tracking the earth satellites as well as vastly extending man's ability to penetrate farther out into the universe are the giant radio telescopes. From the huge reflectors of these telescopes, scientists can bounce radio signals back to earth from the moon and the planet Venus and can also hear radio waves transmitted from stars and galaxies some four billion light-years away—a range about twice that of the most powerful optical telescopes.

Chemistry and related fields. One of the leading prophets of twentieth-century chemistry was Hermann Staudinger, a German scientist who, in the 1930's, pioneered in macromolecular chemistry. Macromolecules are giant molecules composed of complicated chains of thousands and even hundreds of thousands and millions of atoms. Included among them are the polymers (the basis of many plastics and other synthetic materials and fibers), proteins, and other complex organic chemicals involved in life processes.

The ordinary microscope cannot magnify with enough power to make molecules visible. With the development in 1940 of the electron microscope, however, giant molecules could be directly observed. Photographs taken with this device enable scientists to observe the nuclei of cells in the process of multiplying. By this means, much of value has been learned about genes, the mysterious macromolecules in the nuclei of all living things that control cell development and heredity.

While physicists have been seeking to discover the secrets of subatomic particles, biologists have sought to learn the secrets of the fundamental chemical components of living matter. They have concentrated their researches on DNA (deoxyribonucleic acid) and the gene and their relationship in plant and animal cells. DNA was first identified by a German chemist in 1869, but its significance became clear only in the present century. Scientists today believe that it is the millions of different internal arrangements of DNA's constituent units that account for the existence of millions of different kinds of genes, and they believe that the hereditary message transmitted in cell division is dependent on the sequence of DNA parts. Biochemists and biophysicists are seeking to discover, in terms of atoms and molecules, how such hereditary information is transmitted. They can understand how DNA might code its message, but as yet they cannot read that code.

In the field of biochemistry, scientific research has resulted in the development of the wonder drugs—the sulfa drugs, penicillin, streptomycin, aureomycin, cortisone, and the antihistamines. It has also given us tranquilizers, which were developed to calm mental patients but are also used by "normal" victims of life's stresses and strains.

Scientific advances in the twentieth century have also enlarged and refined the principles of evolution, biology's one great unifying theory. These principles now cover the growth and change of inorganic as well as organic matter and include explanations of natural phenomena ranging from submicroscopic particles to galaxies of the universe. But the essential part of Darwin's formulation of the idea of evolution has continued to the present as the basis for its acceptance by scientists.

THE THIRD INDUSTRIAL REVOLUTION

The accelerating spiral of change. For the past two centuries, western civilization has experienced constant technological change. The First Industrial Revolution made its primary impact on the cotton textile industry and on transportation. The Second Industrial Revolution, beginning in 1870, utilized mass production techniques and adopted scientific methods and discoveries, particularly in chemistry. The Third Industrial Revolution, the child of World War I, has been marked by new and more flexible sources of power, by the expansion of industrial and mechanical techniques to every phase of life, by the development of automated production, and by the creation of a professional managerial class in government, business, and labor.

New sources of energy. Until the eighteenth century, the primary sources of power were man and the animals which did his bidding. In the early stages of the Industrial Revolution, water power and then coal replaced muscle power as the chief sources of energy. By the latter part of the nineteenth century, petroleum products came to the forefront as an energy source. The other major power sources, coal and water, have held their own only as a means of generating electricity.

Man is now at the threshold of the atomic era. As the world has continued to industrialize and its need for power has multiplied, it has begun to deplete its reserves of coal and petroleum. In many countries there is an almost desperate need for a source of cheap, abundant energy; and for some of these, atomic power may offer a short cut on the difficult road to industrialization and higher living standards. For others, such as England, it

The first man into space, Russia's Yuri Gagarin (right), successfully orbited the earth on April 12, 1961. Alan B. Shepard, Jr. (left), the first United States astronaut to enter space, made a fifteen-minute suborbital flight on May 5, 1961.

offers the possibility of maintaining high standards of living, even though nonrenewable energy sources such as coal run low. At the nuclear power stations now in operation, the heat from nuclear reactors is being used to produce electricity and to make steam for running turbogenerators. It is estimated that by 1980 nearly a third of all electricity in the United States may be generated by nuclear power.

Both the United States and the Soviet Union have developed nuclear-powered ships. In 1958 an atomic-powered American submarine, the *Nautilus,* traveled to the North Pole under the Arctic icecap. Another American atomic submarine, the *Triton,* circled the globe in 1960, remaining completely submerged during the entire eighty-three-day voyage. The year 1961 saw the launching of the U.S.S. *Enterprise,* the world's largest ship and the first nuclear-powered aircraft carrier.

A host of other important uses for atomic energy have been found. Radioactive isotopes, for example, are used as tracers in mining and manufacturing processes and in medical research. Also, genetic changes seem to occur more frequently when radioactivity is present than when it is not, and this characteristic is being employed to produce useful plant mutations. Atomic energy promises to be of aid as an explosive in massive engineering projects involving the moving of mountains and the changing of river courses; and it may be of use in obtaining minerals from the sea.

Automation. One of the most highly publicized aspects of the Third Industrial Revolution is the increasing adoption of automation in industry. Actually, the elements involved in automated manufacture are not new—mechanical handling was practiced in antiquity, and automatic controls date from at least the fourteenth century—but it is only because of recent discoveries in materials and techniques that the application of these elements to complex operations is possible. High on the list of these discoveries is the electronic computer. Existing in various forms, the computer relies upon a "memory" programed by humans to perform a variety of complicated tasks. Magnetic recording tapes, punched cards, and transistorized circuits "remember" instructional data and enable the master, nonhuman "brain" to assist in automated offices and factories. Another significant discovery is the transistor, an electrical semiconductor discovered by United States scientists shortly after World War II. The transistor has properties which enable it to do what the vacuum tube does—amplify—but in much smaller space, with less heat, and with greater economy. A multitude of devices, ranging from portable radios to moon rockets, and including electronic "brains," would be impossible, or far less practical, without the transistor.

The new mechanical and electronic devices created by twentieth-century technological advances can be made to perform their highly complex tasks far more efficiently than men. They do not strike for higher wages, and they can work twenty-four hours a day, seven days a week. Man has never had more industrious or less troublesome servants. At the same time, however, the social implications of these devices have perplexed and disturbed many observers. The problem of what to do with the men displaced by machines is as old as the dream of relieving men of dull, repetitious drudgery.

The growing proportion of the "technologically unemployed" and the vision of much greater unemployment as automated production increases (where one virtually unmanned factory replaces a hundred or a thousand men) has suggested four types of solutions: the distribution of employment among a greater number of workers by introducing far shorter working hours, longer vacations, longer compulsory education, and earlier retirement; the rapid expansion of service occupations; an increase in consumer demand through intensive advertising and public relations at home and through the search for new markets abroad in areas of lower industrialization; and an expanded program of public works (see p. 781).

Transportation and communication. During and after World War II, technological change in the fields of transportation and communications accelerated greatly. The range and speed of aircraft were extended tremendously, and by the end of the war the reciprocating gasoline engine was being replaced by jet and turboprop motors. Flights across the oceans became commonplace. The breaking of the Soviet blockade of Berlin in 1949 by an Allied air lift not only proved that modern planes were capable of transporting heavy loads but also stimulated the concept of totally air-borne armies. The introduction of jet liners, which made obsolete whole fleets of planes built after the war, brought Europe, South America, and the Orient within a half-day's flying time of the United States.

In the field of communications, the most notable symbol of progress since the war has been commercial television, which, until the invention of the portable transistor radio, almost displaced radio as an entertainment medium. Indeed, almost 90 per cent of American homes now have television receivers. Although the television networks have produced noteworthy news, sports, and dramatic programs, the largest percentage of available time has been scheduled for entertainment shows, many of which cater to the lowest esthetic standards. In the United States, however, educational television and high-fidelity, frequency modulation (FM) radio have provided a refuge for the performance of the serious arts and music. In 1961, commercial stereophonic FM broadcasts were instituted.

The striking improvement of communications and transportation has been responsible in every part of the world for breaking down provincialism, for creating common attitudes, and even for creating common language and speech. However, it has also made the slightest racial incident or border problem into an international crisis and has confronted not only the illiterate of the underdeveloped areas but also the ill-educated of the western world with problems they are not equipped to understand, much less permitted to solve. A development causing great concern to all who believe in democratic values is the increasing use of mass communications to control public attitudes on public issues as well as toward commercial products.

The agricultural revolution. In most countries where scientific and industrial advances have been spectacular in the twentieth century, there has also been an enormous increase in agricultural output. By scientific breeding of crops and livestock and by the use of mechanized power in cultivation, irrigation, harvesting, and distribution, food supplies in these countries have been increasing faster than population. In a few countries—typically the United States, Canada, Australia, the Netherlands, and Denmark—food *surpluses*, in fact, have often been the primary agricultural problems of their governments, which have applied various remedies, such as subsidies to farmers, price supports, production quotas, and marketing controls.

In the United States, unusual climatic variations like January freezes in Florida or dust bowls in the Southwest may work local hardships, but with an overall high food production, weather problems are no serious danger to the national economy. In contrast, in the unindustrialized, backward nations like India and China, where food shortages are chronic, harvest failures due to flood and drought may mean temporary disaster. With their populations soaring, these countries even have trouble keeping per capita production up to subsistence levels. For them, national agricultural planning has become particularly important to alleviate economic hardships and consequent political instability.

Agricultural improvements in the past two generations have been both extensive and intensive. Through hybrid breeding and scientific selection of seed, cultivation has been extended to terrains formerly considered unfeasible for agriculture. For example, through research, seed has been developed that produces wheat maturing in twenty days and thus can be used in short-summer regions closer to the poles; this has been particularly important for countries like Canada, the U.S.S.R., and Manchuria. Planting research and the elimination of tropical diseases wasteful of human labor have also begun to permit the reclamation of red tropical soils in South America and Africa and on islands such as Madagascar, Sumatra, Borneo, and New Guinea. On the other hand, intensive agriculture—the production of more crops on a given area of land—has improved due to the control of predatory insects and infectious diseases, to the development of plants and animals of higher yield, and to manufacturing techniques that have greatly enlarged the supply of chemical fertilizers. Soil conservation techniques, such as flood control and reforestation, have also helped agriculture enormously.

Social capitalism. In the western world, the Third Industrial Revolution is supported by a new capitalism for which there is no commonly accepted name. Because some form of government planning now exists in every capitalist country, the name "state capitalism" has been used to describe the contemporary phase of capitalism, but this term bears the negative taint of fascism. Others have used the terms "welfare capitalism" or "welfare state," but these are associated with ideas of private or public charity. The economist Joseph Schumpeter has suggested the name "plausible capitalism" to reflect the flexibility of capitalism. Perhaps "social capitalism," which emphasizes the fact that capitalism has itself assumed a responsibility to society as well as to the individual, is the most descriptive term.

The spokesmen for the new capitalism have been John Maynard Keynes, the Cambridge don and friend of the British literati, and the Harvard economists Alvin Hansen, Joseph Schumpeter, and J. Kenneth Galbraith. Keynes, whose book *The Economic Consequences of the Peace* (1919) successfully predicted the course of economic history between the wars, suggested in *The General Theory of Employment, Interest and Money* (1936) that the capitalist system does not operate automatically to produce full employment and that depressions can be avoided only by what has come to be known as government "pump priming" and its counterpart, compulsory saving in times of boom. These principles were embodied in the New Deal, which increased investment but only partially solved the problem of unemployment.

Alvin Hansen's main concern has been with the potential stagnation of capitalist growth in the United States as the result of a slowing population expansion, which he thought he saw during the depression. His cure has been constant government investment in economic development, which would manage not only to iron out the business cycles but to assure economic growth as well. The impact of war spending and defense spending since 1945 has been used to confirm the validity of Hansen's major premise. J. Kenneth Galbraith, a close adviser of President John F. Kennedy and author of *The Affluent Society* (1958), moves well beyond the limited objectives of Keynes and Hansen to suggest that the government should exert a more vigorous creative function by enlarging the "public sector" of the economy through road building, slum clearance, urban redevelopment, and construction of various public works. Austrian-born Joseph Schumpeter accepts the fact that social capitalism can and probably will provide sufficient goods for everyone but, quixotically, he raises the question whether, with the decline of the buccaneering spirit of capitalism, the system itself can survive.

This criticism, from a capitalist admirer of certain features of Marxian economics, is also the main thesis of economic conservatives such as Friedrich von Hayek, who oppose social capitalism, and political conservatives such as Russell Kirk, who have become so conspicuous in American life during the past decade. Generally speaking, these conservatives have no desire to stop the Industrial Revolution nor to reëstablish the nineteenth-century world. Instead, they hope to reinvigorate the individualistic liberalism which had sprung from the Enlightenment and which they feel had grown feeble by the end of World War I.

MAN AND HIS THOUGHTS

The social scientists. The efforts of economists to use the scientific method to determine not merely how the economic system functions but also how it should function for the greatest good of the community suggest to some observers that economics has almost achieved the dream of Auguste Comte, the father of the social sciences. Attempts to use the methods of the natural sciences to study man and his behavior have spawned a multitude of social sciences, particularly in the United States. Presidential campaigns are plotted by motivation experts; automobiles are designed not only to conform to the body size of the average purchaser but to match his income and mood; cities are planned and "renewed" with sociologists as key advisers; and anthropologists search the obscure corners of the globe to study what are popularly called "our primitive contemporaries." To measure human attitudes and practices, new techniques have been devised. The interview in depth, the field trip, and the standardized test have joined Pavlov's dog as symbols of methodology in the social sciences.

Controversy over the meaning and value of the social sciences has revolved largely around three questions: Are there general laws which govern all human society? Is the behavior of individuals as well as of societies determined by natural social laws? Do the attitudes and practices of the majority of society establish the ethical norms? These issues have in turn divided the social scientists among themselves.

Most social scientists today agree that the deviations of other cultures from our standards cannot be judged on an ethical basis and that social and cultural prejudices must be put aside in any analysis of other cultures and their norms. This approach, of course, has disturbed those who maintain that there are, if not superior races, at least superior ways of life based on superior value systems. But even these critics have felt the need for the objective and comprehensive analyses of mankind which are the goals of the social sciences.

The natural sciences have given mid-twentieth-century man the knowledge to master his physical environment; in turn, man looks to the social sciences to help him to use this knowledge, to understand himself, and to learn how to create a peaceful and abundant future.

The changes in psychiatry. The momentous contribution of Sigmund Freud to the study of life had been to discover the role of the subconscious, a discovery that resulted in extensive changes in man's picture of man. In Freud's somber and pessimistic conception of the human psyche, man's worst enemy was himself. The most powerful obstacle to civilization, Freud declared in 1930, was "an innate, independent, instinctual disposition . . . to be aggressive." In fact, it was an instinct for death. To many this view seemed appallingly confirmed by the events of the 1930's and, if not by them, certainly by those of the Second World War.

Many of Freud's disciples have parted company with the master on the dominance of the sexual character of man's subconscious drives. Some see a craving for security and a wish to avoid extreme anxiety and aloneness as the central motivations of man. Others acknowledge the importance of gratifying physical needs but stress as well the human need for love, reason, and creative work—a view that has led to much criticism of twentieth-century society. Contemporary society, it is held, may force man to repress his sexual desires, but—more important—it inhibits his faculty for critical thought, tending to transform him into an automaton without the capacity for genuine and individual feeling and thought.

When psychiatry was young, it was felt that if the subconscious could be made conscious by means of the patient's own free associations and the analyst's interpretative comments, mental health would follow, and the psychiatrist's task would be complete. Today, things are no longer considered to be so simple. Recent developments in theory make the goal of analysis more complex. There is growing interest in aiding the individual to move from weakness to strength, a concern long considered the sole preserve of religion.

History reinterpreted. In the twentieth century, history has been subject to two extremely significant reinterpretations. A German, Oswald Spengler, suggested that history —and for Spengler this was the broadest of cultural history—ran in regular, deterministic cycles which inevitably ended in decay. His *Decline of the West* (1918), which pictured the western world nearing the end of its cycle, matched the despair of defeated Germany and, during the decade of the depression, fell on receptive ears in the United States, where it was purchased in best-seller numbers. Although loosely and obscurely written, Spengler's work bluntly challenged not only the ideas of the inevitability of progress and social Darwinism but even the ability of science to create a better world.

Spengler's ideas were given their most able reinterpretation by the British historian Arnold J. Toynbee. His multivolumed *Study of History*—which began to appear in 1934 and was completed in 1961 with the publication of the twelfth volume, *Reconsiderations*—is more adequate than Spengler's as a work of history and more acceptable to most readers because it suggests that man is free in will and action. In "challenge and response" Toynbee detects the forces which make history move; in the "internal proletariats" and "universal churches" he finds the continuing threads which tie together successive civilizations; and in religion he locates the element which is usually the heart of each civilization. For a despairing generation troubled by a guilty conscience, Toynbee offers the hope that each civilization, though it decays, is followed by a higher one; and he makes the prophecy that no civilization need ever decline.

The educational scene. The dream of common and universal education belongs to the epoch since World War I. Mass education has been approximated through the secondary level only in the United States, where it has come to be considered vital to effective democracy and to the economic "equality of opportunity" promised in the Declaration of Independence.

The ideal of mass education has not taken as strong a hold in most other parts of the world, where academic promotion into the secondary schools and universities requires high scores on competitive examinations, which are usually controlled by the central government. The students are rigidly tested for academic accomplishment, and those who fail must usually turn to schools with briefer, vocational programs. In Europe fewer than a quarter of the students who begin school commonly complete the academic secondary school program. Universities attract only a fraction of those who succeed. Such educational programs, aimed at creating intellectual elites, tend to perpetuate the privileged classes, even in the Soviet Union. On the other hand, the merit of such programs is that since they are monopolized by superior students, they are marked by academic levels higher than those usual in mass-education systems. The high levels result from extremely competitive classroom situations, rigorous curriculums, long hours in class, and extensive homework.

The most influential educational leader of the modern era was the American, John Dewey, who as a philosopher elaborated what is popularly called pragmatism. Dewey assumed that change in all things is the central fact of life. As a disciple of the Age of Science, he asserted that the scientific method provides the only reliable guide to knowledge and right behavior. Because such knowledge, Dewey recognized, could only be a series of working hypotheses, "truth" becomes relative to time and place. Traditional systems of values, whether based on philosophy and religion or esthetics and history, were rejected. The mind was considered essentially a biological organ. Accordingly, for Dewey, knowledge was primarily the product of direct experience, which included the experience of studying the past; and, hence, the goal of education was to provide the greatest variety of experiences for all pupils and to permit their freest reaction to them. Such education, permitting each child to function at his own level, was to be organized to cultivate the career objectives of each. In this framework the mere learning of factual data and the disciplining of the individual or of his mind by the teacher were generally considered educational handicaps. The student was to be guided "progressively" from one interest to the next. Self-expression and social adjustment were the primary educational goals.

Such educational ideas have influenced all American education. In its irrational extreme, "progressive education" became the butt of popular gibes. However, in its moderate form, it revolutionized classroom practice. It re-

quired better and more imaginative teaching. Rote memorization of material that was not understood was generally abandoned. Differences in the abilities of individual students were recognized, and the field of ability testing was soon developed. Vocational goals became an honorable part of education. Free electives became common in most high schools. Adult education, particularly in self-improvement subjects, attracted more than twice as many students as did all the high schools, universities, and colleges.

The most general attempt to apply Dewey's ideas was made in the Soviet Union. Until the 1930's, extreme progressivism dominated Russian education, and student classroom soviets overrode and even dismissed teachers. During this period, however, total school enrollment increased only slightly over the 1913 levels. The technical requirements of the first Five-Year Plan placed demands on education which such a program failed to meet. Russian education reverted to the regimented European tradition, and "progressive" educationalists disappeared during the purges of the late 1930's. Language, science, and mathematics received great emphasis, and achievement testing displaced ability testing. The goal was to create the "new Soviet man." In the past two decades, the technical achievements of Russian science and engineering have astounded the world and brought respect for the Soviets' educational accomplishments.

In part it has been the obvious success of Russian education which has caused American educators to reconsider the premises and practices of progressive education. Stinging criticisms of American education have been made. Even the idea of a common education for all has been seriously questioned. American education has been condemned for its failure to teach adequately the minimum hard core of the traditional curriculum (language, mathematics, history, and science), for its failure to challenge the able and extraordinary student, for its lack of moral orientation, and for its emphasis on what are called "frills." The tradition of local control and finance of education is being reconsidered because it bears responsibility for the grossly unequal educational opportunities in the various parts of the country. State and federal programs have been established to equalize educational opportunities, and extensive public and private scholarship programs have singled out both teachers and students of great promise.

Today, large segments of the American public are demanding both tough academic training and emphasis on social adjustment. There has been a growing belief that perhaps traditional value systems in certain fields provided more valid principles for living in a changing world than the relativism of the social sciences. Furthermore, the needs of society are considered as important as the needs of individuals, and education has been assigned a major task in the survival of the "American way of life."

The philosophers. The philosophy of twentieth-century man has changed so radically, first as the result of Darwinian determinism and then especially as a result of the revolutionary new cosmology of modern physics, that historically the twentieth century is likely to rank with the seventeenth, which saw the dawn of modern science. For two hundred years, philosophers had accepted Newton's view of the universe, that nature was a fixed system or a perfect mechanism of law. The Newtonian postulates were that man and nature were governed by universal laws and that human fulfillment consisted in empirically discovering these laws and utilizing them.

Today philosophers and scientists are no longer confident of these postulates. Discoveries in the infinitesimal world of the atom and the vast world of outer space have made reflective men uncertain whether reality is precise and orderly or, at least, whether man's imagination is capable of grasping its order, if there is one. How does man visualize space that is unbounded but finite, through which light moves both as a wave and as a particle? How can he picture an electron traveling two or more distinct routes concurrently or traveling from point to point without transversing the space between? How can energy be matter? Such questions disillusion man's sense of order.

As a result, modern philosophy has been thoroughly overtaken by skepticism. Objective metaphysics—the attempt since Plato to discover what reality consists of and to construct a logical, coherent conception of the universe—has collapsed. A noted physicist has said, "The structure of nature may eventually be such that our processes of thought do not correspond to it sufficiently to permit us to think about it at all. . . . We are confronted with something truly ineffable."

This feeling is shared by the two movements dominating twentieth-century philosophy since World War I. The first is analytical philosophy. Its adherents, while usually acknowledging the limitations of science for discovering the nature of reality, are nevertheless convinced that *only* through science can we learn anything at all of truth. They reject all extra-scientific methods of insight and all attempts at metaphysical systems. The analytical philosophers, however, have comprised individuals and schools of widely varying personalities and interests, including the Englishman Bertrand Russell and the American John Dewey. This movement also includes the linguistic analysts, who for the past few decades have been enormously influential in Britain and the United States and who scorn the slovenly use of language to create broad generalities that are empty of meaning. For them, words like "being," "nature," and "idea" are too thin to be worthy of analysis.

The foremost spokesman for existentialism, the second great twentieth-century philosophical movement, has been Jean Paul Sartre. Largely Frenchmen, the existentialists, like the analytical philosophers, reject metaphysics —but for a different reason. Their concern is for the outlook of the individual human being and not for an objective and impartial world view of things. Their reasoning is this: no two persons are shaped by the same biological, cultural, environmental, and historical forces; each individual has an outlook on life which is largely unique and which will never be duplicated. Far from being inconsequential, as the metaphysicians contended, these human variables comprise essentially what it means to be human. A man must understand his individuality; he must approach life subjective-ly. Since neither science nor metaphysics can answer the "big questions" of life, an individu-al must attempt to answer questions about himself. Thereby he can effectively exercise his free will in order to find "existence" in a futile world, for even if the world be illogical, a man must try to make himself master of his destiny and to have control over the choices he must make in life.

While the analytical philosophers and the existentialists are poles apart in their approach to life—the one being objective by tempera-ment and the other egocentric—both are prod-ucts of the modern-day mind. Both disbe-lieve that there exists an absolute order with-in man's capacity to understand.

THE CONTEMPORARY ARTS

New forces in the arts. For over a genera-tion before the catastrophe of the First World War, artists and writers had made deliberate efforts to combat the older romantic tradition, often going to the extremes of antiromanticism and naturalism and choosing material which was as sordid or raw or unmoral as possible. The tide of reaction was particularly strong in France and Russia and to a lesser degree in Germany, followed much later by a similar movement in England and the United States. The new scientific thinking, Darwinism, and modern psychology did considerable violence to the old values. However, it was World War I and its cynical aftermath that destroyed any lingering idealism. Artists and writers intensi-fied their attacks on the artistic and moral standards of the preceding generations, which, they seemed to think, were responsible for the cataclysm of the First World War. In their spirit of denial and skepticism, they conceived of the world as a wasteland, devoid of beauty, faith, and rationality, and man as an animalis-tic or Freudian individual crushed by the modern machine and a puritanical society. While there were strivings toward spiritual values on the part of some writers like T. S. Eliot and painters like the Russian-born Jew Marc Chagall, the general mood usually en-couraged a contempt for traditional standards

and a feverish instability that were suggested in labels such as the Jazz Age, the age of the Lost Generation, or *les années folles* (the crazy years).

This tide—with its pessimism, individual-ism, and defiant use of sexual themes—reached its peak about 1928 and again in the war-torn 1940's, but between these dates came the world depression, which carried the arts along in the general search for economic and social amelioration. It was a socially con-scious art, this art of the thirties, in which the individual tended to be submerged in a cause. The belief of the 1920's that man was a help-less cog in a great machine gave way to a faith that men working together could con-trol social and political forces for the better-ment of society. Marx came to supplant Freud as the apostle of many artists. Then came World War II and the postwar years, in which Soviet expansionism dangerously challenged the West. A reaction against communism set in, as it had after the First World War.

In the period since World War II, perhaps fewer great names have appeared than were born in the flourishing period of the 1920's, and yet literary and art criticism has abound-ed, and this sometimes presages a rich period of artistic productivity. While a lasting defini-tion of our times remains the task of future historians, there is no question, even now, but that the age of political anxiety has influenced the arts: there is a tenseness, a strange para-dox of hopefulness and negativeness, a tend-ency to cling to the values of the moment and regard with cynicism what formerly stood as permanent values. Whether out of the pres-ent period of self-criticism artists will find solutions to the problem of meaning and pur-pose in a nuclear age remains to be seen.

One obvious characteristic of all the con-temporary arts from World War I to the pres-ent has been their spirit of experimentation. The result is art, music, or literature that is often bizarre in arrangement, strange in effect, self-conscious, shocking, satirical, tender, lu-rid, and morbidly realistic in turns—seemingly topsy-turvy in terms of traditional esthetic and moral values. It is also "difficult" art in that it may incorporate ideas and techniques which

For the most part, it was the literary giants of an earlier era who dominated the Nuclear Age. In 1948, the Nobel prize for literature went to the poet, playwright, and critic T. S. Eliot (top left); in 1949 the prize went to the American novelist William Faulkner (top right); in 1954, to Ernest Hemingway (below). The French novelist Albert Camus (center left) received the award in 1957, but in 1958 the Russian poet, novelist, and translator Boris Pasternak (bottom left) was forced, for political reasons, to decline the honor.

demand considerable thought and even learning to be appreciated. At first the general public was puzzled by, and sometimes hostile to, the new writers, musicians, and artists, who typically found their initial audience within a closed artistic community like the Left Bank of the Seine in Paris or New York's Greenwich Village; but gradually public interest quickened so that today the modern theater, concert hall, and art gallery find enthusiastic attendance. In totalitarian countries, on the other hand, the feeling has prevailed that the artist is obligated to create works which the public can readily understand without previous preparation. There the artist who fails to conform soon finds himself forbidden an audience and may even find his personal liberty endangered. This was especially true in Nazi Germany and in Soviet Russia after the 1920's. Thus the story of progress and change in the modern arts is largely confined to the democratic West.

The novel between world wars. Perhaps the most abrupt literary transition of the times occurred in the nature of the novel. Although British realists like Thomas Hardy and the American "muckrakers" had dented confident Victorianism, the shattering blast was the publication in 1922 of *Ulysses* by the Irish novelist James Joyce, whose work drew on earlier French and German writers. Almost immediately its sale was restricted by a series of legal bans.

The new perspective attained by Joyce in *Ulysses*—the story of one day's adventures in turn-of-the-century Dublin—was to view the world from inside the souls of his characters rather than from the outside looking in. Thus, *Ulysses* is introspective and subjective. In the structure of the novel, Joyce suggested parallels between his story and the classical legend of Ulysses and used the stream of consciousness technique popularized by the French novelist Marcel Proust. Joyce also used realism, the technique of developing the novel with an infinite number and variety of seemingly trivial details. It was none of these esthetic aspects of *Ulysses,* however, which drew the wrath of the censors. Rather, it was a consistent, biological naturalism, describing

sordid, sexual, frustrated man as Joyce saw him. Gone were the assumptions of the supernatural and of social responsibility; gone the hypocrisy of polite society. Instead, Joyce felt that bleak honesty, however unpleasant, was the only possible moral course for a writer to follow.

The new tradition begun with *Ulysses* was soon followed by other Anglo-Saxon writers, such as Theodore Dreiser and D. H. Lawrence, whose novels were conceived not as moral tracts nor as comfortable entertainment, but rather as reflections of the unstable and troubled world created by the Industrial Revolution, science, and the war. Their theme is frustration and futility.

Two of the most frequent themes in the serious novels of the 1920's were pacifism and social satire. Two notable antiwar novels based on World War I experiences were written by a German and an American: Erich Maria Remarque's *All Quiet on the Western Front* (1929) and Ernest Hemingway's *A Farewell to Arms* (1929). Social satire won fewer converts but exerted a large influence. In *Babbitt* (1922), Sinclair Lewis created the name for the ultratypical middle-class businessman, while F. Scott Fitzgerald in *The Great Gatsby* (1925) and other novels chronicled not only the "flapper era" but exposed upper-class life as well. In England, Aldous Huxley and Evelyn Waugh were even more biting in their condemnation of the British upper classes.

The Continental novel, generally, had moved beyond the naturalism of British and American writing. In its place was symbolism, which in turn was to mark the next generation of Anglo-Saxon writers. The Austrian writer Franz Kafka achieved critical success with his weird, dreamlike novels *The Trial* (1925) and *The Castle* (1926)—but only after World War II. In *The Trial,* Joseph K., a petty official in a bank, is informed that he is to be tried for an unspecified crime. His efforts to learn his offense from an indifferent bureaucracy are futile; he never discovers who his accusers are or what the nature of the accusation is, and at the end of the novel he is just as senselessly stabbed to death by several masked men while he is quietly walking on the street, without ever having been tried at all. Kafka's style was matter-of-fact; he used symbolist techniques to describe the frustration of man trapped by guilt or anxiety or, as in *The Trial*, to show man not as a victim of heredity or environment but simply as a victim. The prolific German author Thomas Mann used symbolism most effectively in *The Magic Mountain* (1924), which was considered by many critics as one of the most important novels of modern times. The tuberculosis sanitarium and its inhabitants, which serve as setting and characters for the novel, have been interpreted as Mann's symbolic representation of bourgeois Europe as a microcosm.

In the sobering decade of the thirties, with its world-wide depression, the growing importance of communism, and the victories of fascism, many prominent writers in Europe and America attached themselves to left-wing causes and some even tried their hand at "proletarian" novels. John Steinbeck's *Grapes of Wrath* (1939) and John Dos Passos' *Big Money* (1936) were probably the best known, although Ernest Hemingway's *For Whom the Bell Tolls* (1940) reflects many of the same concerns.

Meanwhile, the "new novel" was achieving maturity and assurance. James Joyce in Britain and Thomas Mann in Germany won a wide public audience with new works. In *The Sound and the Fury* (1929), the American writer William Faulkner continued his Mississippi saga, using the stream of consciousness technique to reveal the thoughts of an idiot. Most of Faulkner's subsequent novels were to be set in the Deep South, and although they were to concentrate on degeneration and disintegration, they reflect a warm concern for mankind, whether black or white. Another major American writer of the thirties was Thomas Wolfe, whose autobiographical novels likewise reflected Southern decadence but blended realism and the stream of consciousness technique with a revival of romanticism.

Postwar dissent. The failure of the peace following World War II and the apparition of yet another war bred futility and despair but produced few war novels to match those which followed World War I. It was the old giants—men like Faulkner and Hemingway—who continued to dominate fiction. Probably the best American war book was *The Naked and the Dead* (1948) by Norman Mailer, who with a savage criticism of contemporary society helped define the postwar era as an age of dissent.

A quieter and limited dissent was that of J. D. Salinger, whose *Catcher in the Rye* (1951) won an enthusiastic following, particularly among college students, for its sensitive treatment of troubled, introspective adolescents. Another man of brilliant technical skill was Lawrence Durrell, whose "Alexandria Quartet" (1957-1960) was an immediate critical and popular success. He made a morality of amorality, and in the microcosm of Alexandria he symbolized the futility of the whole modern world.

Dissent was also expressed, with little discipline and less intelligibility, by America's self-styled "beat generation." The "beats" rebelled noisily against almost all of the accepted values of American society, expressing their rebellion chiefly in talk and poetry but also in a few uneven novels. At its best, in some of the work of Jack Kerouac, "beat" prose had an exciting drive; too often, however, Kerouac and others in the group made more sound than sense.

Rebellion of a more articulate character appeared in postwar England among a number of novelists and playwrights rather arbitrarily grouped as the "angry young men." Not all were young, some were women, and leaders like Kingsley Amis expressed more wild humor than anger—but all were undeniably disgusted with the status quo and were desirous of change. Here their attitude differed from the passive alienation of the beat generation. Through bitter blast and horse-laugh, the angry young men launched attacks on "The Establishment," the combination of aristocracy, big business, church, and political power that dominates English society.

Dissent on the Continent, particularly in France, had become virtually a tradition. Dur-

23 Pablo Picasso: "Three Musicians" (1921). Acknowledged as the artistic genius of our time, Picasso was—in the 1920's and 1930's—the major exponent of the Cubist style. This depiction of three music-makers and their dog is made up of precisely defined forms, like cutouts, arranged so that the planes seem to overlap. The three-dimensional aspect of Cubism is evident, too; the longer we look at the picture, the more the figures seem to emerge from their background. Such abstraction, strange to the eye at first, achieves an effect of extraordinary coherence and solidity.

24 (below) **Max Beckmann: "Temptation of St. Anthony"** (1936). The last and most powerful of the pre-World War II German Expressionists, Beckmann was forced into exile by Hitler in the 1930's. Here the artist has transformed a traditional subject—the conflict between good and evil—into a psychologically complex modern message.

25 (right) **José Clemente Orozco: "Zapatistas"** (1931). Zapatistas were followers of Zapata, a leader of the Mexican revolution which began in 1910. The work of native Mexican artists like Orozco, inspired by a love of country and a desire for political and economic reform, fostered a new appreciation of Mexican folk art.

26 (lower right) **Alexander Calder: "Red Petals"— mobile of steel, wire, and aluminum** (1942). An inventive follower of the Cubists, Calder added a fourth dimension—time—by introducing movement in a form of sculpture called the mobile.

ing World War II and afterwards, however, it moved beyond mere violent futility. The influence of existentialism, frequently among those who remained outside the movement, not only brought courage but also produced a generation of writers who assumed active leadership in their society. These writers insisted that though man may be a victim, he must not despair; for in his refusal to despair he wins the victory.

The leader of the French existentialists was Jean Paul Sartre, a professional philosopher who also wrote novels and plays. Strongly influenced by existentialism was the most important French novelist of the postwar period, Albert Camus. In his novel *The Plague* (1947), the leading figures are unheroic, yet they meet the illogicality, absurdity, and anguish of life without compromise, asserting their common humanity and investing their lives with a sense of dignity. In doing so, they affirm a belief that while men cannot assure themselves that they do good, they can at least try to reduce suffering. In a later work, *The Rebel* (1951), Camus denounced the tyranny of revolutionists following absolutist ideologies.

In the Soviet Union following Stalin's death in 1953, a relaxation in both censorship and in the definition of Soviet orthodoxy led to some criticism of Communist party interference in the arts and to the appearance of works which had previously circulated only privately—works which reflected traditions popular outside the "iron curtain." Indeed, the international politico-literary sensation of the 1950's was a novel by the Soviet writer Boris Pasternak, who had never been a Communist and who had achieved his fame as a poet. First published in Italy in 1956 and later brought out in translations throughout the western world—though never in the Soviet Union—Pasternak's novel took as its title the name of its hero, Doctor Zhivago. Zhivago is completely unpolitical, interested only in esthetic matters and the women he loves. A victim of the Russian Revolution of 1917, he is forced to serve the Bolsheviks as a doctor but sees only humanitarian—not political—significance in his work. Critical of the lies, opportunism, mediocrity, and philistinism of the new order,

he dies a lonely man, part of the human debris left by the revolution.

For this work, Pasternak was awarded the Nobel prize for literature in 1958. When the honor was announced, he was subjected to an unbridled attack by his countrymen as a traitor to the Soviet system. Pasternak then rejected the award so that he might continue to live in his homeland.

The "new poets." The publication of *The Waste Land* in 1922 by T. S. Eliot, an American who resided for a long time in Paris and later became a British subject, marks an abrupt transition in the style and content of poetry as it was written in Britain and the United States. The soft and loose traditions of romanticism and the optimistic and humanistic attitudes of liberal democracy were both rejected, the former for its sterility and the latter for its falseness. Although Eliot's innovations were startling, his work represented an elaboration of ideas long popular in France. In particular, he reflected the tight style of the French antiromantic movement of the 1890's and the subsequent development of literary symbolism, which conveyed impressions by suggestion rather than full or direct statement. Other influences on Eliot were the classics, seventeenth-century English metaphysical poetry, and Oriental philosophy. This highly cerebral tradition of poetry, established by Eliot and maintained by his many followers, was to dominate poetry in Britain and the United States until well past the middle of the century.

Eliot's disillusionment with the world, particularly with democracy, secularism, and liberal optimism, led him not into despair but to a search for order based on tradition and religion. These influences can be seen in *The Waste Land*, which characterizes the barrenness of modern civilization and its need for regeneration. Although most of the "new poets," such as Ezra Pound, W. H. Auden, and Marianne Moore, belonged to the technical tradition of Eliot, few accepted his religious solution to the problems of modern life. Nor was the "new poetry" without opposition. By midcentury, poets as diverse as William Carlos Williams, Robert Frost, and Dylan

Thomas had made their protests heard and had won young disciples.

"Modern" art and beyond. As we have seen in Chapter 24, the first signs of a new and distinctly twentieth-century movement in painting and sculpture appeared in Paris as early as 1905, when a group of young painters led by Henri Matisse exhibited canvases so full of distortions and flat patterns and painted in such violent colors that a critic called the new artists *les fauves* (the wild beasts). The Fauvists were short-lived as a group, but they spearheaded a series of schools of art from that day to the present which have flourished briefly, taken on new labels, then disappeared or modified themselves into newer forms. A few, like Cubism, have lasted to the present day. Whatever their character, however, the various groups have shared a rejection of their predecessors in the nineteenth century, who had tended to overstress the literal representation of subject matter on canvas. One can speculate whether or not improved photography, by reproducing mechanically a more accurate likeness than any literal painting, may have induced artists to reconsider the purpose and techniques of art. But, for whatever reason, they overthrew the academic laws of color and three-dimensional perspective and abandoned the Impressionist's attempt at realism. According to Picasso, the goal was to paint "the things one knows more than the things one sees."

By the end of World War I, "modern" art had become fully established among artists and sculptors. The movement was already headed toward abstraction, which distilled the essence of form from the natural object, and was approaching the nonobjective, whose inspiration was purely intellectual and subjective. Beginning about 1909, Cubism—the first step toward abstraction—reduced objects in nature to rectangular reconstructions of what the artist conceived to be their essence of form and color. It was followed in 1915 by Dadaism, a somewhat hysterical movement which was deliberately anti-art and anti-sense and was intended to shock and scandalize; a characteristic work was Marcel Duchamp's repainting of the "Mona Lisa" with a

mustache and an obscene caption. About 1924 this calculated nihilism was superseded by Surrealism, in which the artist, influenced by Freudianism, sought to create according to the irrational dictates of his subconscious mind and vision. Surrealism developed in two directions: free fantasy, as represented by the work of Paul Klee and Marc Chagall, and the elaborate representation of dream worlds, as in the paintings of Salvador Dali. Much of Picasso's work from the late 1920's developed along Surrealist lines, and the movement had wide influence in literature and drama as well.

The simultaneous development of non-objective art broke the last tenuous links with objects in nature. The leader in developing this technique was the Dutch artist Piet Mondriaan, who relied on primary colors, two-dimensional geometrical forms, and asymmetrical balance. Like Vasili Kandinski and Paul Klee, who championed nonobjective painting in Germany, Mondriaan experimented with each art technique in turn as it appeared and was to have a profound influence on industrial design, architecture, and typography. In the United States, Jackson Pollock created works by dripping and throwing paint on the canvas and sometimes leaving cigarette butts and empty paint tubes in his compositions. Although many laymen refused to take his work seriously, some critics defended his methods and saw the results as "the last hand-made, personal objects within our culture." Looked at from this perspective, his canvases —and those of other artists who followed his lead—represented the individual's protest against conformity as well as the artist's search for new techniques and values.

In all parts of the world there were artists who clung to traditions of representational art or who adapted the new techniques to local conditions. In Mexico, the politically radical muralists Diego Rivera, José Orozco, and David Alfaro Siqueiros interpreted Indian themes with Expressionist techniques. In the United States, both realism and symbolism were blended in the works of painters like Ben Shahn. In the U.S.S.R., all artists were forced into the mold of "socialist realism," which was the antithesis of the spirit of such

Picasso painted the "Guernica" mural (above) to express his horror at the Nazi air raid on a small, defenseless town during the Spanish civil war. Painted only in black, gray, and white, the mural is a mass of distortions, conveying vividly the terror of the scene. Various artistic formulas—Cubism, Surrealism, and abstractionism—are blended in the picture, but in character with Picasso's eclectic genius, none predominates. Another artist more closely identified with social and humanitarian causes is the American painter Ben Shahn, whose "Liberation" (below) starkly contrasts the tragic rubble of war and the spiritual victory of the children playing. Shahn—as well as most of his American contemporaries before the 1950's—has retained closer ties to realism than have most European artists, although the influence of Cubism and abstractionism is clearly evident (note the angular forms of the children and the Cubistic arrangement of wallpaper in the house).

artists as Picasso and Siqueiros who actively supported communism in the Free World. In Japan the delicate skills of traditionalism fell under the influence of Expressionism.

One artist, Pablo Picasso, not only symbolizes the development of contemporary art but is probably the most important exponent of it. Though Picasso was Spanish, it was Paris that put its mark on his artistic growth. Before World War I, he had experimented with every artistic vogue from realism and classicism to Cubism and Mannerism, and following the war he experimented simultaneously with Neoclassicism, Cubism, and Surrealism. One of the finest examples of this period is his brilliantly colored "Girl Before a Mirror" (1932), which is as much abstract design as representational art. A sobering transition resulted from the outbreak of the Spanish civil war in 1936. His violently Surrealist mural "Guernica," prepared for the 1937 Paris World's Fair, was a reaction against the German bombing of the Basque town of Guernica. His growing distaste for fascism during World War II and in Spain led him to become a Communist shortly after the liberation of Paris, but he has been a Communist bound neither by the dictates of Moscow nor by the conventions of orthodox Marxism. He has never used his art for conscious propaganda and, like most artists, has remained an intransigent individualist.

Architecture. In Chapter 24, we saw that Sullivan and Wright in the United States and Gropius in Europe pioneered in a functional architecture opposed to the nineteenth-century eclectic vogue of imitating classical, Renaissance, or Baroque structures. This new architecture was based on the concept that the available new materials of glass, steel, and concrete demanded new forms of expression different from those founded primarily on stone and wood. A new type of structure, the steel-frame skyscraper with its large glass areas, was developed in the late nineteenth century by Louis Sullivan.

The work of Frank Lloyd Wright, Sullivan's pupil, exerted a powerful influence on architectural design in Europe and America. Refusing to be bound by rigid doctrines or for-

Postwar architecture was enlivened by imaginative new forms of expression and new uses of material. Interested in architecture primarily as a *fine* art, Le Corbusier of France in recent years developed a style aimed at synthesizing all of the fine arts through architecture. In his chapel at Ronchamp—designed to bring architecture closer to sculpture—walls and roofs follow free curves, façades are asymmetric, and windows of varying sizes open the walls at varying levels. The chapel is shown at left on the following page.

Le Corbusier's influence was felt by the Brazilian architect Oscar Niemeyer, who designed all of the buildings for Brazil's new capital, Brasilia. Cost was not spared in erecting this city for half a million people in the largely unexplored interior of the country. For example, in the president's residence, the Palace of the Dawn (above), each of the 22 columns required two weeks to frame and pour and an additional two weeks to face with 250 individually carved sections of marble.

Niemeyer's monumental disregard for cost represents an entirely different concept from that espoused by the Italian engineer-architect Nervi. Discarding all solutions that proved

too difficult and too expensive, Nervi relied chiefly upon the use of low-cost prefabricated concrete units. The esthetic enrichment of his buildings results largely from the repetition of the individual elements. In a sports palace for the 1960 Rome Olympics (center right), for example, he opposed the sweep of precast concrete to the thrust of economical wood pilasters. Another prefab system for enclosing space inexpensively is the geodesic dome, developed by the American, Buckminster Fuller. Widely adaptable, a geodesic dome is extremely lightweight, can be erected quickly, and is manufactured at low cost. Such domes have been used in convention centers, auditoriums, and industrial plants; at top right is shown a domed greenhouse in the construction stage.

Although influenced by the credo of Miës van der Rohe—"Less is more"—a leading American architect, Eero Saarinen, rejected the pure cube as a solution for every architectural problem, believing instead that every structure demanded a new approach and that it must complement older structures around it. At bottom right is Saarinen's Milwaukee, Wisconsin, war memorial building.

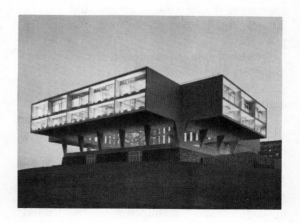

mulas, Wright constantly experimented with engineering techniques and the use of materials to create new architectural expressions. In his writing as in his work, Wright emphasized his organic theory of creative unity, in which the elements of a building are creatively integrated to form a unified, functional, and beautiful structure. His earthquake-proof Imperial Hotel (1916-1922) in Tokyo and his Midwest prairie homes in the United States won him European recognition. The period of his greatest American fame is marked by such structures as the inventive Johnson Wax Company building (1936) and his aggressively unorthodox Guggenheim Museum (1959).

A different architectural expression was developed by Walter Gropius, who headed the Bauhaus, the government architectural school established first at Weimar and then at Dessau in Germany. To this school Gropius drew engineers, typographers, and artists such as Kandinski and Klee to teach students the functional possibilities of modern materials in industrial design, printing, and esthetic theory in conjunction with functional architecture. This calculated attempt to use the most sophisticated artistic minds of Germany to vitalize the products of their industrial world for the good of mankind was to set the pattern for later designers. In designing the buildings for the school at Dessau, Gropius used cantilevers, exposed steel, and the glass wall. These buildings are examples of his "international style," which strives for geometric purity of outline and simple textural surfaces. Gropius also experimented with the slab apartment block, the prefabricated house, integral campus design, and total community planning.

Another leading proponent of the international style is Ludwig Miës van der Rohe, whose buildings are characterized by the dramatic use of materials, the direct expression of the structural frame, orderly relationships of areas, refinement of detail, and simplicity of the total composition of elements. Gropius, Miës van der Rohe, and the Finnish-born Eero Saarinen, all of whom have taught in American engineering schools, have set their stamp on contemporary architecture in the United States. The Frenchman Le Corbusier (Charles Édouard Jeanneret), by his writing as well as his work, has popularized the new architecture. Crude poured concrete, exposed steel, strong use of color, pillar foundations, and sun breaks are his trademarks. The Italian Pier Luigi Nervi, who created the 1960 Rome Olympics community, pioneered the creative use of ribbed concrete structures. His work is characterized by tilted arches, curved ceilings, and a feeling of space, and he has often made extensive use of glazed openings in walls and ceilings to achieve openness and light in his structures.

The consideration of the total community through group planning is an important facet of contemporary architecture. Le Corbusier's monumental and original design for Chandigarh, the new capital of Punjab, and that of his Brazilian disciple Oscar Niemeyer for Brasilia, the new capital of Brazil, are recent examples of total community planning under the direction of one architect, as opposed to the uncoordinated growth in most existing cities. The programs of garden-belt communities or of urban redevelopment are examples of group planning on a smaller scale which are being effected in many lands.

The uncertain sound. The musical developments of the twentieth century have paralleled those of the other arts and, like them, have found their inception in France. After a rich musical development, romanticism was displaced by impressionism, which had been initiated by Claude Debussy. However, the new attitude after World War I was that all musical conventions of the past should be rejected because their possibilities had been exhausted and because of the utter newness of the age. Some creative composers found refuge in folk or primitive music; some created a neoclassicism with formal principles for disciplining a confusing contemporary musical language; while others, like the nonobjective painters, sought to establish totally new musical concepts which had no reference to conventional scales or chords. Dissonance, unfamiliar rhythmic patterns, and unexpected musical forms, however, won a limited listening public.

The most popular form of modern music has been that based on folk themes. The Hungarian Béla Bartók, one of the most significant composers of the era, published over two thousand folk tunes. In the United States, composers like Aaron Copland, William Schuman, and Roy Harris drew heavily on American folk themes, all of them being influenced by the Negro spiritual and contemporary jazz.

The neoclassical movement began as a revolt against romanticism and primitivism but eventually developed into a new spirit which emphasized clarity of form, economy of orchestration, and the revival of older musical forms like the sonata and the *concerto grosso*. Music in the new tradition, however, scarcely resembled that of Bach or Mozart because the composers did not feel bound by the rules of conventional tonality, harmony, or counterpoint. The most brilliant composer of the movement and probably of the age was Igor Stravinski, who after three brilliant but cacophonic ballets during World War I, began to compose "absolute" music in the neoclassical spirit. The German composer Paul Hindemith, having found that the new music alienated his listeners, returned to tonality and to "music for everyday use." Dimitri Shostakovich, the most famous contemporary Russian composer, modeled his *Third Symphony* on Beethoven's *Ninth* only to have it condemned for its "formalism."

The third modern tradition has been a deliberate effort to achieve a "nonmusic" and a total break with all historical musical patterns. Arnold Schönberg and his disciple Alban Berg, in what is generally called atonality, disowned the conventional musical scale, substituting a twelve-tone scale using both black and white piano notes with arithmetic regularity; they rejected all conventional chords and avoided all conventional measures of time. The later vogue of pure electronic music and of music contrived electronically from natural sounds continues the tradition of musical experimentation.

The intricate rhythmic patterns of jazz, which is uniquely American and twentieth-century in its origin, have provided both a refuge from the privacy of modern music and a serious alternative to it. Jazz was born in New Orleans and was created by small French-style military bands which blended the African polyrhythmic idiom with a genuine folk spontaneity appearing in various forms of popular music. The syncopation of ragtime before 1918, the commercial adaptation which made the 1920's the Jazz Age, the swing during the 1930's, and the bop and cool jazz following World War II were all derivatives of true jazz. Jazz, in turn, added new instruments, particularly the saxophone; hardened its conventions; and in its serious or "progressive" form has been transformed from dance music into a sophisticated listener music.

Much of the new music in this century has been frankly experimental and perhaps overly concerned with technique. As with painting and poetry, serious music seems to be in some danger of losing contact with its audience. Even jazz, long considered the vital musical expression of our egalitarian era, has shown signs of becoming self-consciously experimental and introspective, though its lusty, emotional side is by no means dead.

SUMMARY

It will be recalled from Chapter 24 that the beginnings of our present, western world view had appeared in the late nineteenth century. In literature, realism, with its desire for objectivity, endured into the twentieth century; but partly in reaction to it, partly out of a desire for change, and partly out of new intellectual attitudes, there arose techniques and approaches that stressed the subjective, interior world of man. In painting, representational pictures remained the public's favorites, but serious artists, seeking new angles of vision and expression, turned in ever increasing numbers to abstraction and intensely personal creation.

Of all the influences shaping the modern mind, probably the most important was science. Although men continued to put their faith in the power of reason, the optimistic view of man as a rational being in full control of his destiny was considerably weakened by the findings of psychologists. Advances in astronomy presented a serious challenge to man's traditional belief that his earth was of particular importance in the grand scheme of the universe. Perhaps most important of all, while the laws of classical, Newtonian mechanics would still serve in the workaday world, even there the large-scale processes could be seen to rest ultimately on the statistical laws of the quantum theory, on probability. The solution to the puzzle of atomic structure required a far-reaching revision of man's picture of nature.

The nations of the western world had entered the twentieth century in a spirit of almost boisterous optimism, sure that scientific and technological advances would solve humanity's problems. The agonies of two world wars and the economic collapse that separated them shattered this confident spirit on both sides of the Atlantic. Science might continue its seven-league strides, but a major revaluation was in order. The benefits brought to the world by science were seen to be accompanied by colossal problems which would obviously have to be considered within a new frame of reference if solutions were to be found—and disaster avoided. And the avoidance of total disaster might be said to be *the* problem of the Nuclear Age, the Age of Anxiety.

In fact, of course, the avoidance of disaster, of annihilation, has always been man's central problem. And its solution, now as always, rests not with vast, unfathomable natural forces over which man has no control but rather within himself—in his mind, heart, and soul.

SUGGESTIONS FOR READING

Two attempts to make modern science intelligible to non-scientists are I. Asimov, *The Intelligent Man's Guide to Science*, 2 vols., Basic Books, 1960, which includes a history of science; and A. Bluemle, *Saturday Science*, Dutton, 1960, which limits itself to a few key contemporary scientific developments. The problem of relating science to a lagging society is discussed soberly by J. B. Conant, *Modern Science and Modern Man*, Columbia Univ., 1952. The story of the creation of the atomic bomb is told by the former head of the Manhattan Project in A. H. Compton, *Atomic Quest: A Personal Narrative*, Oxford, 1956. The development and prospects of astronautics are summarized in A. Ducrocq, *Victory over Space*, Little, Brown, 1960.

Most of the writings of the leading social scientists, such as S. Freud, J. Dewey, and A. J. Toynbee, are in print and easily available. A convenient edition of Freud is E. Jones, *The Life and Works of Sigmund Freud*, 3 vols., Basic Books, 1953-1957.

D. Riesman et al., *The Lonely Crowd*,* abr. ed., Anchor, one of the most influential books of the generation, exposes contemporary society to sociological analysis. R. Heilbroner, *The Future As History*,* Evergreen, puts American democracy and liberal institutions to similar but broader tests.

A. H. Hansen, *Guide to Keynes*,* McGraw-Hill, is a convenient introduction to Keynesian economics by a leading American disciple. J. K. Galbraith, *The Affluent Society*, Houghton Mifflin, 1958, brings Keynes up to date. An older but provocative analysis of contemporary economic theory is J. A. Schumpeter, *Capitalism, Socialism, and Democracy*, Harper, 1950. The conservative economic and political reaction to liberalism is expressed eloquently in R. Kirk, *The Conservative Mind: From Burke to Santayana*, Regnery, 1953; and more

*Indicates an inexpensive paperbound edition.

popularly in B. Goldwater, *The Conscience of a Conservative*, Victor, 1960.

A compact but comprehensive introduction to twentieth-century thought is M. White, *The Age of Analysis: Twentieth Century Philosophers*,* Mentor, which also includes brief excerpts from key thinkers. A brilliant introduction to analytical philosophy is B. Russell, *Our Knowledge of the External World As a Field for Scientific Method in Philosophy*, Allen and Unwin, 1949. Russell writes significantly in other fields as well.

A full but somewhat negative history of the progressive movement in education is L. A. Cremin, *The Transformation of the School: Progressivism in American Education, 1876-1957*, Knopf, 1961. The best defense of the movement against its detractors and zealots is J. Dewey, *Dewey on Education*, Columbia Teachers College, 1959.

Two attempts to describe and evaluate the Russian school system are F. M. Hechinger, *The Big Red Schoolhouse*, Doubleday, 1959; and the more academic account by G. B. Bereday, W. W. Brickman, and G. H. Read, *The Changing Soviet School*, Houghton Mifflin, 1960.

The reappraisal of American education since World War II has been influenced particularly by the Harvard University Committee on the Objective of General Education in a Free Society, *General Education in a Free Society*, Harvard, 1945; and J. B. Conant, *The American High School Today*, McGraw-Hill, 1959.

A standard and easily available introduction to literature is E. Wilson, *Axel's Castle: A Study in the Imaginative Literature of 1870-1930*,* Scribner's. M. Krieger, *The Tragic Vision: Variations on a Theme in Literary Interpretation*, Holt-Rinehart-Winston, 1960, is a perceptive study of the more contemporary period.

C. Greenberg, *Arts and Culture: Critical Essays*, Beacon, 1961, suggests the relationships between the various arts and contrasts American and European traditions.

General introductions to contemporary national literatures are W. Thorp, *American Writing in the Twentieth Century*, Harvard, 1960; H. Peyne, *The Contemporary French Novel*, Oxford, 1955; W. Fowlie, *A Guide to Contemporary French Literature from Valéry to Sartre,** Meridian; and M. Slonim, *Modern Russian Literature from Chekhov to the Present*, Oxford, 1953; W. B. Rideout, *The Radical Novel in the United States, 1900-1954*, Harvard, 1956.

An older but valuable introduction to the new poets is D. Daiches, *Poetry and the Modern World: A Study of Poetry in England Between 1900 and 1939*, Univ. of Chicago, 1940. Three more recent surveys with an American emphasis are A. Alvarez, *Stewards of Excellence*, Scribner's, 1958; Y. Winter, *On Modern Poets,** Meridian; and M. L. Rosenthal, *The Modern Poets: A Critical Introduction*, Oxford, 1960. A sharp attack on the new poets is E. Dahlberg and H. Read, *Truth Is More Sacred*, Horizon, 1961.

H. Gardner, *Art Through the Ages*, 4th ed., Harcourt, Brace, 1959, is the standard work. A nontechnical and richly illus-trated history of the last half century is E. Langui, *Fifty Years of Modern Arts*, Praeger, 1959, which served as a guidebook to the art exhibit at the Brussels World Fair. Less ambitious but excellent are G. Apollonaire, *The Cubist Painters,** Wittenborn; and M. Jean, *The History of Surrealist Painting*, Grove, 1960. An introduction to contemporary "imagist" art is P. Selz, *New Images of Man*, Museum of Modern Art, 1959, which includes not only reproductions of the art works but explanations by the artists of their esthetic goals.

The older general history of architecture, T. Hamlin, *Architecture Through the Ages*, Putnam, 1940, provides a basis for understanding the functionalism of Sullivan as well as for understanding the more contemporary trends. The first great twentieth-century movement, the Bauhaus, is chronicled by S. Giedion, *Walter Gropius: Work and Teamwork*, Reinhold, 1954. C. Jones, *Architecture Today and Tomorrow*, McGraw-Hill, 1961; and P. Blake, *The Master Builders*, Knopf, 1960, are sympathetic to the new architecture. E. Kaufmann and B. Raeburn, *Frank Lloyd Wright: Writings and Buildings,** Meridian, presents a lucid defense of functional architecture by the maverick of the movement. The writings of L. Mumford, particularly in his *The City in History*, Harcourt-Brace-World, 1961, are in sobering contrast.

INTERNATIONAL POLITICS

INTERNAL POLITICS

1920

1945

U.S., Russia, China, and Britain meet at Dumbarton Oaks to plan international organization to maintain peace 1944
Charter of United Nations drafted in San Francisco 1945

Nuremberg war-crimes trials 1945-1946
U.S. seeks to establish international control of atom 1946
Germany divided into Soviet, British, American, and French zones; Berlin under joint four-power administration 1946
Peace settlements with Italy, Rumania, Bulgaria, Hungary, Finland 1947; with Austria 1955
U.S. announces Truman Doctrine; enacts Marshall Plan 1947
Nineteen American nations sign mutual protection treaty 1947
General Agreement on Tariffs and Trade (GATT) organized 1947
Organization of American States (OAS) established 1948
Britain, France, Benelux nations sign Brussels Treaty 1948
Soviet Union imposes Berlin blockade; U.S. and Britain organize air lift 1948-1949
North Atlantic Treaty (NATO) signed 1949; Turkey and Greece join 1951; West Germany joins 1955

1950

U.S.S.R. and Red China sign thirty-year alliance 1950
Korean police action 1950-1953
Inner Six nations create European Coal and Steel Community 1951
Anzus Pacific Security Pact signed 1951
Japan signs peace treaty and American-Japanese Security Pact permitting U.S. troops to remain in Japan 1951

Dag Hammarskjöld succeeds Trygve Lie as U.N. secretary-general 1953

Southeast Asia Treaty Organization (SEATO) formed 1954

1955

U.S.S.R. and eastern European satellites sign Warsaw Pact 1955
Summit conference of Big Four at Geneva 1955

Eisenhower Doctrine adopted 1956
Israelis, British, French invade Suez zone; U.N. sets up border patrol 1956

European Economic Community (Common Market) evolves from European Coal and Steel Community 1957
Inner Six nations establish European Atomic Energy Community (Euratom) 1957

Russia seeks to establish Berlin as "free city" 1958

Bagdad Pact renamed Central Treaty Organization (CENTO) 1959
Outer Seven nations form European free-trade association 1959
Khrushchev visits U.S. 1959

1960

U.S. U-2 plane downed in U.S.S.R.; Khrushchev scuttles Paris summit conference; U.N. dismisses charges against U.S. 1960

U.S. and Japan sign mutual security pact 1960
Britain applies for admission to Common Market 1961
Kennedy and Krushchev meet in Vienna 1961
American-supported invasion of Cuba is unsuccessful 1961
Russia erects wall between East and Eest Berlin 1961
Dag Hammarskjöld killed; U Thant of Burma becomes secretary-general of U.N. 1961
U.S.S.R. resumes nuclear testing 1961

Perón controls Argentina 1943-1955
Civil war in China begins 1945
Communist Ho Chi Minh proclaims Republic of Vietnam 1945; France rejects Communist rule of Vietnam; civil war ensues
France grants independence to Lebanon and Syria 1945
Labour victory in British parliamentary elections 1945
U.S. frees Philippines; British end mandate in Jordan 1946

Fourth French Republic relies on coalition rule 1946-1958

British establish dominions of India and Pakistan 1947
Tito of Yugoslavia breaks with Soviet policy 1948
Burma receives independence; Israel proclaimed state 1948
German Federal Republic born in West Germany 1949
Soviets found German Democratic Republic in East Germany 1949
United States of Indonesia created 1949; fully sovereign 1954
People's Republic of China proclaimed 1949; Nationalists flee to Formosa 1950; Chinese Communists invade Tibet 1950
India becomes republic within British Commonwealth 1950
Libya becomes sovereign state 1951
Conservatives regain power in Britain 1951; reëlected 1959

Batista seizes control of republic in Cuba 1952
Eritrea federated with independent state of Ethiopia 1952
Eisenhower elected U.S. president 1952; reëlected 1956
Army clique seizes government in Egypt, Farouk is exiled 1952; republic proclaimed 1953; Nasser assumes leadership
Stalin dies, is succeeded by Malenkov 1953; Khrushchev forces Malenkov to resign, replaces him with Bulganin 1955
Federation of Rhodesia and Nyasaland proclaimed 1953
France grants Tunisia independence under Bourguiba 1954
Vietnam split 1954; South Vietnam, Cambodia, Laos made independent 1955
France reëstablishes independent kingdom of Morocco 1955
Perón overthrown by army in Argentina 1955
Gomulka gains control of Polish United Workers' party 1956
Pakistan made a republic 1956; Ayub Khan is dictator 1958
Nasser nationalizes Suez Canal 1956
Revolution in Hungary crushed by Soviets 1956
Britain grants independence to Anglo-Egyptian Sudan 1956; to Malaya 1957; to Ghana (Gold Coast) 1957

Khrushchev becomes Soviet premier 1958
Venezuelan dictator Pérez Jiménez ousted 1958
De Gaulle leads Fifth French Republic 1958
Egypt and Syria form United Arab Republic 1958
Army revolt in Bagdad; new republic under Kassem 1958
U.S. troops sent to Lebanon; British troops to Jordan 1958
Heavy bombardment of Quemoy by Red Chinese 1958
Guinea under Touré receives independence from France 1958
Alaska and Hawaii receive U.S. statehood 1959
Revolution in Cuba succeeds; Castro sets up dictatorship 1959
Belgian Congo granted independence 1960
General Gursel overthrows regime of Menderes in Turkey 1960
Communist infiltration in Laos creates crisis 1960
John F. Kennedy elected U.S. president 1960
Independence granted in 1960 to: Italian trust territory of Somalia; French trust territories of Cameroons and Togo; British colony of Nigeria; Madagascar (Malagasy Republic), eleven other French colonies in West and Equatorial Africa
Military regime replaces Syngman Rhee in South Korea 1961
Trujillo, dictator of Dominican Republic, assassinated 1961
Syria withdraws from United Arab Republic 1961
Twenty-second Party Congress in Russia 1961
Sierra Leone and Tanganyika become independent 1961
South Africa withdraws from British Commonwealth 1961

SCIENCE AND TECHNOLOGY

Third Industrial Revolution begins c. 1918—new power sources, expansion of mechanical techniques, automation
Rutherford changes nitrogen atoms into hydrogen and oxygen atoms 1920; Ernest Lawrence invents cyclotron 1930; neutron is discovered 1932; Otto Hahn splits uranium nucleus 1939 Staudinger pioneers in macromolecular chemistry 1930's Manhattan Project produces first controlled nuclear chain reaction 1942; Manhattan Project tests first atom bomb 1945

Transportation and communication—jet and turboprop motors increase range and speed of aircraft; television and FM radio become widespread media

Twentieth-century scientific advances increase agricultural output

U.S. and U.S.S.R. possess hydrogen bomb 1953

Sputnik I, first man-made satellite, launched by U.S.S.R. 1957

Nautilus, atomic-powered submarine, travels under Arctic icecap 1958

Atomic submarine *Triton* circles earth, remaining completely submerged throughout voyage 1960

U.S.S.R. sends first man into orbit 1961; followed by suborbital flight by U.S. astronaut 1961

First nuclear-powered aircraft carrier, U.S.S. *Enterprise*, launched 1961

U.S. astronaut makes orbital flight 1962

THOUGHT AND THE ARTS

History—Oswald Spengler (*Decline of the West* 1918) proposes theory of deterministic cycles in history; Arnold J. Toynbee (*Study of History* 1934-1961) reinterprets Spengler's ideas

1920

The novel between world wars—new perspectives and techniques developed by such writers as Joyce, Hemingway, Kafka, Mann, Steinbeck, Dos Passos, Fitzgerald, Lewis, Faulkner

1945

The postwar novel—postwar dissent expressed by Mailer, Salinger, Durrell, Kerouac, "angry young men"; existentialism reflected in works of Camus

Education—mass education through secondary level achieved in U.S.; European tradition aimed at superior student; pragmatist John Dewey proposes "progressive education"; recent Russian success in education leads American educators to reëxamine U.S. education system

1950

Architecture—new functional architecture developed by Sullivan, Wright, Gropius, Miës van der Rohe, Saarinen, Le Corbusier, Nervi, Niemeyer

Painting—Cubism; Dadaism; Surrealism (represented by Klee, Chagall, Dali); nonobjective art (championed by such painters as Mondriaan, Kandinski); Indian themes and Expressionist techniques seen in works of Mexican muralists Rivera, Orozco, Siqueiros; realism and symbolism blended in works of Ben Shahn; development of contemporary art symbolized by works of Picasso

1955

Music—folk themes influence Bartók, Copland, Schuman, Harris; neoclassic movement represented by Stravinski, Hindemith, Shostakovich; atonality developed by Schönberg and Berg; jazz develops

1960

Philosophy—dominant twentieth-century movements are analytical philosophy (belief that only through science can man learn anything of truth) and existentialism (belief that only the individual can determine his approach to life)

THE HISTORIAN'S WORKSHOP   (A LIST OF READINGS)

An asterisk after a title indicates an inexpensive paperbound edition.

TOOLS OF THE TRADE

The historian, like other craftsmen, has his basic tools and methods. In order to obtain the information he needs, he learns quickly to use special tools. Some of his most important tools are the bibliographies which provide compilations of the literature available in many areas of history. *The American Historical Association's Guide to Historical Literature,* rev. ed., Macmillan, 1961, is indispensable for world history. The basic guide for medieval studies is L. J. Paetow, *Guide to the Study of Medieval History,* Appleton, 1931; supplementing this work is C. P. Farrar and A. P. Evans, *Bibliography of English Translations from Medieval Sources,* Columbia Univ., 1946. For the general student the inexpensive pamphlets published by the Service Center for Teachers of History, sponsored by the American Historical Association, cannot be recommended too highly. Each pamphlet covers a specific subject or area, such as nationalism, the French Revolution, Japan, India, or the American Revolution. Trends in historical research, the status of scholarship, important archives, and schools of interpretation—all are touched upon in these booklets. Each pamphlet also includes many bibliographical references.

General reference works include W. Bridgwater and E. J. Sherwood, eds., *The Columbia Encyclopedia,* Columbia Univ., 1950; W. L. Langer, ed., *An Encyclopedia of World History,* Houghton Mifflin, 1952; R. B. Morris, ed., *Encyclopedia of American History,* rev. ed., Harper, 1961; *Van Nostrand's Scientific Encyclopedia,* 1958; *The Worldmark Encyclopedia of the Nations,* Harper, 1960. Although somewhat dated, *The Encyclopaedia of the Social Sciences,* 15 vols., Macmillan, 1930-1935, contains many scholarly articles of great value. For biographies, the *Dictionary of National Biography,* a multivolumed series, is indispensable for information concerning British personalities; for American notables, see the *Dictionary of American Biography.*

One cannot fully understand the course of human affairs without reference to good maps. The following atlases are most helpful in this regard: Andrew Boyd, *An Atlas of World Affairs,** Praeger; J. D. Fage, *An Outline Atlas of African History,* Arnold, 1958; E. W. Fox and H. S. Deighton, eds., *Atlas of European History,** Oxford; G. Goodall and R. F. Treharne, eds., *Muir's Historical Atlas—Ancient, Medieval and Modern,* Barnes and Noble, 1956; C. L. Lord and E. H. Lord, *Historical Atlas of the United States,* Holt, 1953; R. R. Palmer, ed., *Atlas of World History,* Rand McNally, 1957; W. R. Shepherd, *Historical Atlas,* Barnes and Noble, 1956.

Invaluable for reference purposes are a number of well-known multivolumed works written by specialists: *The Cambridge Ancient History,* 12 vols., 1923-1939; *The Cambridge Medieval History,* 8 vols., 1911-1936; *The Cambridge Modern History,* 14 vols., 1902-1912. A *New Cambridge Modern History* is now appearing, and the following volumes are available—Vol. I:

The Renaissance (ed. by G. R. Potter), 1957; Vol. II: *The Reformation* (ed. by G. R. Elton), 1958; Vol. V: *The Ascendancy of France* (ed. by F. L. Carsten), 1961; Vol. VII: *The Old Regime* (ed. by J. O. Lindsay), 1957; Vol. X: *The Zenith of European Power* (ed. by J. P. T. Bury), 1960; Vol. XII: *The Era of Violence* (ed. by David Thomson), 1960. One of the most notable series on European history, profusely illustrated and strong in intellectual and cultural history, is W. L. Langer, ed., *The Rise of Modern Europe,* 13 vols., Harper, 1935-1953. Allan Nevins and Howard Ehrmann, eds., *The University of Michigan History of the Modern World,* is a series which will interest not only the scholar of history but the amateur and the beginning student as well. Sixteen volumes are planned and, as of 1961, eleven have been published. For American history, the following sets are recommended: H. S. Commager and R. B. Morris, eds., *The New American Nation Series,* Harper (of the forty volumes planned, thirteen are available as of 1961); A. M. Schlesinger and Dixon R. Fox., eds., *A History of American Life,* 13 vols., Macmillan (this series is strong in social and intellectual history); *Chicago History of American Civilization,* Univ. of Chicago (many of the titles in this outstanding series are available in paperback).

MEANING AND METHOD IN HISTORY

To obtain a general idea of what history is all about, one could not do better than to read the short volume by A. L. Rowse, *The Use of History,* Macmillan, 1948, in which a British historian examines the content, use, and pleasures of history and its relation to life and culture. With this as a foundation, one could then read the articles on History in the *Encyclopedia Americana,* the *Encyclopaedia Britannica,* and the *Encyclopaedia of the Social Sciences.* Other helpful studies on the philosophy and meaning of history are Raymond Aron, *Introduction to the Philosophy of History,* Weidenteld and Nicolson, 1961; Nicolas Berdyaev, *The Meaning of History,* Scribner's, 1936; Jacob Burckhardt, *Judgments on History and Historians,* Beacon, 1958; Herbert Butterfield, *Man on His Past,* Cambridge Univ., 1955; R. G. Collingwood, *The Idea of History,** Oxford. Different approaches to the writing of history are described in H. E. Barnes, *A History of Historical Writing,* Univ. of Okla., 1937; G. P. Gooch, *History and Historians in the Nineteenth Century,** Beacon; Fritz Stern, ed., *The Varieties of History,** Meridian. Such topics as the meaning of method in history, the training of a historian, the principles of historical criticism, the finding of material, and the process of writing can be found in L. R. Gottschalk, *Understanding History,* Knopf, 1950; H. C. Hockett, *The Critical Method in Historical Research and Writing,* Macmillan, 1955; Sherman Kent, *Writing History,* Appleton, 1941; C. V. Langlois and C. Seignobos, *Introduction to the Study of History,* Holt, 1912 (a pioneer text); G. J. Renier, *History, Its Purpose and Method,* Beacon, 1950.

Two monumental historical treatises have appeared in the twentieth century. In the 1920's the world was startled by Oswald Spengler's pessimistic *Decline of the West,* 2 vols., Knopf, 1945. (A brief, excellent explanation of Spengler can be found in H. Stuart Hughes, *Oswald Spengler: A Critical Estimate*, Scribner's, 1952.) The most ambitious treatment of history on a grand philosophical scale is Arnold J. Toynbee's multivolumed work, *A Study of History*, which was published between 1934 and 1954 by Oxford. Volume 11 was issued in 1959 and Volume 12, *Reconsiderations*, appeared in 1961. (There exists an abridgment of the ten-volume work by D. C. Somervell, Oxford, 1947-1957.) Toynbee's views and interpretations have been challenged and even castigated by a number of important historians, yet in its grand sweep and its immense erudition his work is one of the greatest achievements in historical writing by a single historian since the days of Herodotus. For critiques on Toynbee's work, see E. Gargan, ed., *The Intent of Toynbee's History*, Loyola, 1961; Pieter Geyl, *Debates with Historians,** Meridian; Ashley Montagu, ed., *Toynbee and History*, Porter Sargent, 1956.

THE RAW STUFF OF HISTORY

As read by the layman or beginning student, history is usually contained in a work by a professional historian, who blends events, causes, results, and interpretations into a whole. Sometimes, however, it is essential or desirable to investigate primary sources, the raw materials from which history is made. In each major field of study, there are literally tens of thousands of government documents, newspapers, periodicals, diaries, and memoirs that speak for the past. In the last few decades, a feature of history teaching in general and of the teaching of the history of civilization in particular has been the publication of excellent collections of source material. For the development of western civilization, the following are most useful: F. Le Van Baumer, ed., *Main Currents of Western Thought*, Knopf, 1952; H. J. Carroll, Jr., et al., eds., *The Development of Civilization,** 2 vols., Scott, Foresman; *Introduction to Contemporary Civilization in the West*, 2 vols., Columbia Univ., 1960-1961; George H. Knoles and R. K. Snyder, *Readings in Western Civilization*, Lippincott, 1960; Eugene Weber, *The Western Tradition,** 2 vols., Heath; *The Western World in the Twentieth Century*, Columbia Univ., 1961. For United States history, see H. S. Commager, ed., *Documents of American History*, Appleton, 1958; Avery Craven et al., *A Documentary History of the American People*, Ginn, 1951; Marvin Meyers et al., *Sources of the American Republic,** 2 vols., Scott, Foresman, 1960-1961. There are numerous collections of source material in the field of European history, such as A. Baltzly and A. W. Salomone, eds., *Readings in Twentieth Century Europe*, Appleton, 1950; Leon Bernard and Theodore Hodges, eds., *Readings in European History*, Macmillan, 1958; W. Longsam, *Documents and Readings in the History of Europe Since 1918*, Lippincott, 1951; George L. Mosse et al., *Europe in Review*, Rand McNally, 1957; K. M. Setton and Henry Winkler, *Great Problems in European Civilization*, Prentice-Hall, 1954; Louis L. Snyder, ed., *Documents of Germany History*, Rutgers, 1958; Warren Walsh, ed., *Readings in Russian History*, Syracuse, 1958. Source collections in other fields are William T. DeBary, Jr., et al., *Sources of Japanese Tradition*, *Sources of Indian Tradition*, *Sources of Chinese Tradition*, Columbia Univ., 1958-1960; James Duffy and R. Manners, eds., *Africa Speaks*, Van Nostrand, 1961; B. Keen, ed., *Readings in Latin-American Civilization*, Houghton Mifflin, 1955; Lin Yutang, ed., *The Wisdom of China and India*, Random House, 1942.

PREHISTORY

The following works by V. G. Childe are highly recommended: *Man Makes Himself,** Mentor; *The Prehistory of European Society,** Penguin; *What Happened in History,** Penguin. Other aspects of prehistory are described in S. Cole, *The Prehistory of East Africa,** Penguin; W. A. Fairservis, Jr., *The Origins of Oriental Civilization,** Mentor; H. Frankfort, *The Birth of Civilization in the Near East,** Anchor; W. D. Howells, *Back of History*, Doubleday, 1954; R. Linton, *The Tree of Culture,** Vintage; Kenneth Page Oakley, *Man the Tool-Maker,** Phoenix; Sir Edward Tylor, *Primitive Culture,** 2 vols., Torchbooks.

ANCIENT AND MEDIEVAL EUROPE

Ancient history: R. H. Barrow, *The Romans,** Pelican; A. E. R. Boak, *A History of Rome to 565 A.D.*, Macmillan, 1955; G. W. Botsford and C. A. Robinson, Jr., *Hellenic History*, Macmillan 1948; J. B. Bury, *History of the Later Roman Empire,** 2 vols., Dover; W. G. De Burgh, *The Legacy of the Ancient World,** 2 vols., Pelican; T. R. Glover, *The Ancient World,** Pelican; Michael Grant, *The World of Rome,** Mentor (an analysis of the Roman empire at the height of its power); Charles A. Robinson, Jr., *Ancient History: From Prehistoric Times to the Death of Justinian*, Macmillan, 1951; M. I. Rostovtseff, *A History of the Ancient World*, 2 vols., Oxford, 1930; V. M. Scramuzza and P. MacKendrick, *The Ancient World*, Holt, 1958.

Medieval history: J. L. LaMonte, *The World of the Middle Ages*, Appleton, 1949; Sidney Painter, *A History of the Middle Ages*, Knopf, 1953; Henri Pirenne, *A History of Europe*, University Books, 1955; C. W. Previté-Orton, *The Shorter Cambridge Medieval History*, 2 vols., Cambridge Univ., 1952; Steven Runciman, *Byzantine Civilization,** Meridian; Joseph Reese Strayer, *Western Europe in the Middle Ages*, Appleton, 1955.

EUROPE IN THE MODERN PERIOD

Some of the better-known textbooks are R. Ergang, *Europe from the Renaissance to Waterloo*, Heath, 1954; M. B. Garrett and J. L. Godfrey, *Europe Since 1815*, Appleton, 1947; Louis Gottschalk and Donald Lach, *Europe and the Modern World*, 2 vols., Scott, Foresman, 1951-1954; A. J. Grant and Harold Temperley, *Europe in the Nineteenth and Twentieth Centuries*, Longmans, 1952; W. P. Hall and W. S. Davis, *The Course of Europe Since Waterloo*, Appleton, 1957; R. R. Palmer and Joel Colton, *History of the Modern World*, Knopf, 1956; Herbert H. Rowen, *A History of Early Modern Europe, 1500-1815*, Holt, 1960; David Thomson, *Europe Since Napoleon*, Knopf, 1957.

National histories: R. D. Charques, *A Short History of Russia,** Everyman; Sidney Fay, *Rise of Brandenburg-Prussia*, Holt, 1937; M. T. Florinsky, *Russia: A History and Interpretation*, 2 vols., Macmillan, 1953-1954; O. Halecki, *A History of Poland*, Roy, 1956; Emil Lengyel, *1,000 Years of Hungary*, Day, 1958; A. Maurois, *A History of France,** Evergreen; Sir Bernard Pares, *History of Russia*, Knopf, 1953; K. Pinson, *Modern Germany*, Macmillan, 1954; René Sédillot, *An Outline of French History*, Knopf, 1953; G. M. Trevelyan, *History of England,** 3 vols., Anchor.

Early modern times: T. Ashton, *The Industrial Revolution, 1760-1830*, Oxford, 1948; W. K. Ferguson, *The Renaissance*,* Holt; C. J. Friedrich and C. Blitzer, *The Age of Power*,* Cornell; L. Gershoy, *The Era of the French Revolution*,* Anvil; L. H. Gipson, *The Coming of the Revolution, 1763-1775*, Harper, 1954; A. J. Grant, *A History of Europe from 1494 to 1610*, Barnes and Noble, 1952; Harold J. Grimm, *The Reformation Era, 1500-1650*, Macmillan, 1954; Hajo Holborn, *A History of Modern Germany*, Knopf, 1959; G. Lefebvre, *The Coming of the French Revolution*,* Vintage; Frank E. Manuel, *Age of Reason*,* Cornell; Garrett Mattingly, *The Defeat of the Spanish Armada*, Houghton Mifflin, 1959; Garrett Mattingly, *Renaissance Diplomacy*, Houghton Mifflin, 1955; D. Ogg, *Europe in the Seventeenth Century*, Macmillan, 1952; R. R. Palmer, *The Age of the Democratic Revolution: A Political History of Europe and America, 1760-1800*, Princeton, 1959; J. C. Wahlke, *The Causes of the American Revolution*,* Heath.

The nineteenth century: G. D. H. Cole and Raymond Postgate, *The British People, 1746-1946*, Knopf, 1947; R. C. K. Ensor, *England, 1870-1914*, Oxford, 1936; Richard Hare, *Portraits of Russian Personalities Between Reform and Revolution*, Oxford, 1959; A. J. May, *The Hapsburg Monarchy, 1867-1914*, Harvard, 1951; H. Seton-Watson, *The Decline of Imperial Russia, 1855-1914*,* Praeger; A. J. P. Taylor, *The Struggle for Mastery in Europe, 1848-1918*, Oxford, 1954; G. M. Trevelyan, *British History in the Nineteenth Century and After*, Longmans, 1937; Robert Wolff, *The Balkans in Our Time*,* Harvard.

Twentieth century—general accounts: Eugene Anderson, *Modern Europe in World Perspective, 1914 to the Present*, Holt, 1958; G. Bruun, *The World in the Twentieth Century*, Heath, 1957; Chester V. Easum, *Half-Century of Conflict*, Harper, 1952; Robert Ergang, *Europe in Our Time*, Heath, 1958; W. P. Hall, *Europe in the Twentieth Century*, Appleton, 1957; W. Langsam, *The World Since 1919*, Macmillan, 1954; Carl H. Pegg, *Contemporary Europe in World Focus*, Holt, 1956.

World War I and after: René Albrecht-Carrié, *France, Europe and the Two World Wars*, Harper, 1961; E. H. Carr, *The Bolshevik Revolution, 1917-1923*, 3 vols., Macmillan, 1951-1953; E. H. Carr, *The Twenty Years' Crisis, 1919-1939*, Macmillan (London), 1946; Gordon Craig and Felix Gilbert, *The Diplomats, 1919-1939*, Princeton, 1953; C. R. Cruttwell, *A History of the Great War, 1914-1918*, Oxford, 1936; Cyril Falls, *The Great War, 1914-1918*, Putnam, 1959; John Gunther, *Inside Europe*, Harper, 1940; Quincy Howe, *The World Between the Wars*, vol. II of *World History of Our Own Times*, Simon and Schuster, 1953; George F. Kennan, *Russia and the West under Lenin and Stalin*, Little, Brown, 1961; W. M. Knight-Patterson, *Germany from Defeat to Conquest*, Macmillan, 1947; Dwight E. Lee, *Ten Years: The World on the Way to War*, Houghton Mifflin, 1942; Charles Mowat, *Britain Between the Wars*, Univ. of Chicago, 1955; P. A. Reynolds, *British Foreign Policy in the Inter-War Years*, Longmans, 1954; H. R. Rudin, *Armistice, 1918*, Yale, 1944; A. J. P. Taylor, *The Origins of the Second World War*, Hamish Hamilton, 1961; Hugh Thomas, *The Spanish Civil War*, Harper, 1961; Edmond Vermeil, *Germany in the Twentieth Century*, Praeger, 1956; F. P. Walters, *A History of the League of Nations*, Oxford, 1960; Leon Wolff, *In Flanders Fields*, Viking, 1958.

World War II: Arthur Bryant, *The Turn of the Tide*, Doubleday, 1957; Winston Churchill, *The Second World War*, 6 vols., Houghton Mifflin, 1948-1953; Desmond Flower and James Reeves, eds., *The Taste of Courage*, Harper, 1960; John Hersey, *Hiroshima*,* Bantam; David Howarth, *D-Day*, McGraw-Hill, 1959; C. E. Lucas Phillips, *The Greatest Raid of All*, Little, Brown, 1960; Erich von Manstein, *Lost Victories*, Regnery, 1958; Edgar McInnis, *The War*, 6 vols., Oxford, 1940-1947; Louis Snyder, *The War: A Concise History, 1939-1945*, Messner, 1960; Arnold Toynbee and F. T. Ashton-Gwatkin, eds., *The World in March, 1939*, Oxford, 1952; Hugh Trevor-Roper, *The Last Days of Hitler*,* Berkley.

The postwar world: Hanson Baldwin, *The Great Arms Race*, Praeger, 1958; R. A. Brady, *Crisis in Britain*, Univ. of Calif., 1950; Clark Eichelberger, *UN: The First Fifteen Years*, Harper, 1960; Rupert Emerson, *From Empire to Nation*, Harvard, 1960; *Everyman's United Nations*, 6th ed., United Nations, 1959; Herbert Feis, *Between War and Peace: The Potsdam Conference*, Princeton, 1960; François Goguel-Nyegaard, *France Under the Fourth Republic*,* Cornell; J. Gunther, *Inside Europe Today*, Harper, 1961; W. Gurian et al., eds., *Soviet Imperialism*, Notre Dame, 1953; Alistair Horne, *Return to Power: A Report on the New Germany*, Praeger, 1956; D. Pickles, *The Fifth French Republic*,* Praeger; Richard Pipes, ed., *The Russian Intelligentsia*, Columbia Univ., 1960; T. Prittie, *Germany Divided: The Legacy of the Nazi Era*, Little, Brown, 1960; C. B. Robson, ed., *Berlin: Pivot of German Destiny*, Univ. of N. C., 1960; Leonard Schapiro, *The Communist Party of the Soviet Union*, Random House, 1959; J. L. Stipp, ed., *Soviet Russia Today*, Harper, 1956; Henry C. Wallich, *Mainsprings of the German Revival*, Yale, 1955; Theodore White, *Fire in the Ashes: Europe in Mid-Century*, Sloane, 1953; Francis Williams, *Socialist Britain*, Viking, 1949; Philip M. Williams and Martin Harrison, *De Gaulle's Republic*, Longmans, 1960; *Yearbook of the United Nations, 1960*, Columbia Univ., 1961. The following titles in the Harvard series are especially good for the immediate background to contemporary conditions: Crane Brinton, *The United States and Britain*, 1948; Vera Micheles Dean, *The United States and Russia*, 1948; D. C. McKay, *The United States and France*, 1951; F. D. Scott, *The United States and Scandinavia*, 1950.

ASIA THROUGH THE AGES

Until the mid-twentieth century, interest in Asian history and culture was lukewarm in the western world, especially in the United States. Since World War II, the emergence of the Red Giant, Communist China, together with some dozen newly independent nations in Asia, has turned the world's spotlight on this continent. Unlike the case of sub-Saharan Africa, there is available to the student a rich body of literature about Asia which dates back to the earliest times. Moreover, in the past fifteen years a veritable flood of authoritative and absorbing studies has been published.

India and Pakistan: The best general introduction to the history and culture of India is J. Nehru, *The Discovery of India*,* Anchor. The following are excellent basic histories: *The Cambridge Shorter History of India*, Macmillan, 1934; R. C. Majumdar et al., *An Advanced History of India*, Macmillan (London), 1951; W. H. Moreland and A. C. Chatterjee, *A Short*

History of India, Longmans, 1957; J. C. Powell-Price, A History of India, Nelson, 1955; C. G. Rawlinson, India: A Short Cultural History, Praeger, 1953; Percival Spear, ed., The Oxford History of India, 3rd ed., Oxford, 1958; T. Walter Wallbank, A Short History of India and Pakistan,* Mentor. W. N. Brown, The United States and India and Pakistan, Harvard, 1953, is an excellent survey by an American scholar—only one chapter is devoted to Indo-American relations. Other aspects of Indian history are covered in S. Gopal, The Viceroyalty of Lord Irwin, Oxford, 1957; K. A. N. Sastri, A History of South India, Oxford, 1958; Percival Spear, Twilight of the Mughuls, Cambridge Univ., 1951; Philip Woodruff, The Men Who Ruled India, 2 vols., St. Martin's, 1954 (British rule as seen in the lives of Indian civil servants).

Recent events and problems of the Indian subcontinent are discussed in K. Callard, Pakistan: A Political Study, Macmillan, 1957; S. S. Harrison, India: The Most Dangerous Decades, Princeton, 1960; Josef Korbel, Danger in Kashmir, Princeton, 1954; V. P. Menon, The Transfer of Power in India, Princeton, 1957; Frank Moraes, India Today, Macmillan, 1960; Khalid B. Sayeed, Pakistan, The Formative Years, Institute of Pacific Relations, 1960; R. Symonds, The Making of Pakistan, Faber, 1951; Phillips Talbot and S. L. Poplai, India and America, Harper, 1958; Robert Trumbull, As I See India, Sloane, 1956.

China, Japan, and south Asia: Histories covering all the historic cultures of this area are scant: Kenneth Latourette, A Short History of the Far East, Macmillan, 1957, covers China, India, Japan, and some of the lesser areas; the same general treatment is found in Paul H. Clyde, The Far East, Prentice-Hall, 1958. Other useful general histories include F. H. Michael and G. E. Taylor, The Far East in the Modern World, Holt, 1956; G. Nye Steiger, A History of the Far East, Ginn, 1936; Harold Vinacke, A History of the Far East in Modern Times, Appleton, 1959. For a useful contemporary political analysis of the region, see G. McT. Kahin, ed., Major Governments of Asia, Cornell, 1959. The best general survey of Chinese, Korean, and Japanese culture and history is E. O. Reischauer and John K. Fairbank, East Asia: The Great Tradition, Houghton Mifflin, 1960, Vol. I of A History of East Asian Civilization. As for China, the most useful general surveys are C. P. Fitzgerald, China: A Short Cultural History, Praeger, 1954; L. C. Goodrich, A Short History of the Chinese People, Harper, 1959; R. Grousset, The Rise and Splendour of the Chinese Empire,* Univ. of Calif.; K. S. Latourette, The Chinese, Their History and Culture, Macmillan, 1946. For Japan, G. B. Sansom, Japan: A Short Cultural History, Appleton, 1943, is a scholarly survey; the same author's The Western World and Japan, Knopf, 1950, is a valuable study of western impacts not only on Japan but on Asia in general. Also recommended are Hugh Borton, Japan's Modern Century, Ronald, 1955; and C. Yanaga, Japan Since Perry, McGraw-Hill, 1949.

China and Japan in recent times are treated in Gerald Clark, Impatient Giant (China), McKay, 1959; John Fairbank, The United States and China, Harvard, 1958 (the best short interpretive study); F. C. Jones, Japan's New Order in East Asia: The Story of Its Rise and Fall, Oxford, 1954; K. Kawai, Japan's American Interlude,* Univ. of Chicago; Li Chien-

nung, The Political History of China, 1840-1928, Van Nostrand, 1956; Harold Quigley and J. E. Turner, The New Japan, Univ. of Minn., 1956; Peter Tang, Communist China Today, Praeger, 1957; R. L. Walker, China Under Communism, Yale, 1955. For recent developments in southern Asia, see Amry Vandenbosch and Richard A. Butwell, Southeast Asia Among the World Powers, Univ. of Ky., 1957; for Indochina, see Ellen J. Hammer, The Struggle for Indochina, Stanford, 1954; and for Indonesia, George M. Kahin, Nationalism and Revolution in Indonesia, Cornell, 1952, and Alastair M. Taylor, Indonesian Independence and the United Nations, Cornell, 1960 (a thorough study of the role of the United Nations and the relinquishment of Dutch sovereignty).

AFRICA AND THE MIDDLE EAST IN HISTORY

Africa: There is no single comprehensive account of African history from the earliest times to the present. One can obtain only an incomplete picture of ancient and medieval Africa from the following studies: E. W. Bovill, The Golden Trade of the Moors, Oxford, 1958; Basil Davidson, The Lost Cities of Africa, Little, Brown, 1959; John De Graft-Johnson, African Glory, Praeger, 1955; W. E. B. Du Bois, The World and Africa, Viking, 1947. At present, histories of Africa begin with the coming of the European colonist and, with him, written records; perhaps archaeological research will provide data for the early history of the Dark Continent.

There are a few general accounts of African history: J. D. Fage, An Introduction to the History of West Africa, Cambridge Univ., 1957; and Zoe Marsh and G. Kingsnorth, An Introduction to the History of East Africa, Cambridge Univ., 1957, are two valuable surveys. T. W. Wallbank, Contemporary Africa: Continent in Transition,* Anvil, is a brief account with emphasis on recent times. For the opening and partition of Africa, the following are recommended: Norman D. Harris, Europe and Africa, Houghton Mifflin, 1927; Parker T. Moon, Imperialism and World Politics, Macmillan, 1926; Alan Moorehead, The White Nile, Harper, 1960; Margery Perham and J. Simmons, eds., African Discovery, Faber, 1957 (a good historical anthology). For the various colonial areas, see James Coleman, Nigeria: Background to Nationalism, Univ. of Calif., 1958; Reginald Coupland, East Africa and Its Invaders, Oxford, 1938; C. W. De Kiewiet, A History of South Africa, Oxford, 1941; James Duffy, Portuguese Africa, Harvard, 1959; Thomas Hodgkin, comp., Nigerian Perspectives, Oxford, 1960 (an anthology); Kenneth Ingham, The Making of Modern Uganda, Macmillan, 1958; Eric Walker, A History of Southern Africa, Longmans, 1957; W. E. F. Ward, A History of Ghana, Macmillan, 1959.

The most comprehensive and up-to-date survey of the African scene—social, economic, and political—is George T. Kimble, Tropical Africa, 2 vols., The Twentieth Century Fund, 1960. Other interesting works dealing with trends and issues in contemporary Africa include Gwendolen Carter, Independence for Africa,* Praeger, and The Politics of Inequality: South Africa Since 1948, Praeger, 1958; T. R. M. Creighton, Anatomy of Partnership: Southern Rhodesia and the Central African Federation, Faber, 1960; Maurice Hennessy, The Congo: A Brief History and Appraisal, Praeger, 1961; A. P. Merriam, Congo:

Background of Conflict, Northwestern Univ., 1961; R. A. Reeves, *Shooting at Sharpeville,* Houghton Mifflin, 1961; Virginia Thompson and Richard Adloff, *French West Africa,* Stanford, 1958, and *The Emerging States of French Equatorial Africa,* Stanford, 1960.

The Middle East: The most useful histories of a general nature are Sydney N. Fisher, *The Middle East,* Knopf, 1959; Philip K. Hitti, *The Near East in History,* Van Nostrand, 1961, and *History of the Arabs,* Macmillan (London), 1960; A. Hourani, *Syria and Lebanon,* Oxford; George E. Kirk, *A Short History of the Middle East,** Praeger. Recommended special studies include George Antonius, *The Arab Awakening,* Lippincott, 1939; Clare Hollingworth, *The Arabs and the West,* Methuen, 1952; J. C. Hurewitz, *The Struggle for Palestine,* Norton, 1950; Nejla Izzeddin, *The Arab World,* Regnery, 1953; George Kirk, *Contemporary Arab Politics,** Praeger; Walter Laqueur, ed., *The Middle East in Transition,* Praeger; 1958; Keith Wheelock, *Nasser's New Egypt,* Praeger, 1960.

SCIENCE, THE FINE ARTS, RELIGION, AND THOUGHT IN HISTORY

These aspects of human endeavor are too frequently neglected in the study of history. Yet without these spiritual, intellectual, and esthetic products, history would be a chronicle of meaningless events.

Science: The following are excellent surveys: H. J. Cowan, *Time and Its Measurement: From the Stone Age to the Nuclear Age,* World, 1958; W. C. D. Dampier, *A Shorter History of Science,** Meridian; Tobias Dantzig, *The Language of Science,** Anchor (a nontechnical history of mathematics); Clyde Kluckhohn, *Mirror for Man,** Premier (one of the best surveys of anthropology); Gardner Murphy, *Historical Introduction to Modern Psychology,* Harcourt, Brace, 1949; W. T. Sedgwick et al., *A Short History of Science,* Macmillan, 1939; George G. Simpson et al., *Life: An Introduction to Biology,* Harcourt, Brace, 1957; A. Wolf, *A History of Science, Technology, and Philosophy in the Eighteenth Century,** 2 vols., Torchbooks. Technology is admirably covered in R. J. Forbes, *Man the Maker: A History of Technology and Engineering,* Abelard-Schuman, 1958; R. S. Kirby et al., *Engineering in History,* McGraw-Hill, 1956; C. J. Singer et al., *A History of Technology,* 5 vols., Oxford, 1954-1958. For students who display a special interest in the nature and direction of modern science, the following are highly recommended: J. Bronowski, *Science and Human Values,** Torchbooks (a versatile mathematician blends science and philosophical rumination); Norman Campbell, *What Is Science?** Dover (an English physicist explains science in simple terms); W. Heisenberg, *Physics and Philosophy,* Harper, 1958 (a famous physicist assesses recent advances in science); James R. Newman, ed., *What Is Science?** Simon and Schuster (absorbing articles exploring the main branches of science); C. P. Snow, *The Two Cultures and the Scientific Revolution,** Cambridge Univ. (a versatile scientist and novelist discusses the gulf between the humanist and scientist).

The fine arts: L. Adam, *Primitive Art,** Pelican; G. Bazin, *A History of Art,* Houghton Mifflin, 1959; Bernard Berenson, *Italian Painters of the Renaissance,** Meridian (the best of the social and cultural histories written by the dozens of critics of this period); Peter Blake, *The Master Builders,* Knopf, 1960 (a tribute to three great architects—Wright, Le Corbusier, and Miës van der Rohe); P. Brown, *Indian Architecture,* 2 vols., Tudor, 1957; John Burchard and Albert Bush-Brown, *The Architecture of America,* Little, Brown, 1961; Erwin O. Christensen, *The History of Western Art,** Mentor; E. H. Gombrich, *The Story of Art,* Phaidon, 1959; A. Houser, *The Social History of Art,** 2 vols., Vintage; H. W. Janson and D. J. Janson, *Picture History of Painting From Cave Painting to Modern Times,* Abrams, 1957; S. Kramrisch, *The Art of India Through the Ages,* Doubleday, 1954; E. Male, *Religious Art,** Noonday; H. Munsterberg, *Arts of Japan,* Tuttle, 1957; R. T. Paine and A. Soper, *The Art and Architecture of Japan,* Penguin, 1955; Nikolaus Pevsner, *An Outline of European Architecture,** Pelican; Nello Ponente, *Modern Painting: Contemporary Trends,* World (Skira), 1960 (outstanding treatment of the period from 1940 to 1960; D. M. Robb et al., *Art in the Western World,* Harper, 1953; B. Rowland, *The Art and Architecture of India,* Pelican, 1953; L. Sickman and A. Soper, *The Art and Architecture of China,* Pelican, 1956; D. Talbot Rice, *Byzantine Art,* Penguin, 1954; D. Talbot Rice, *Russian Art,* Penguin, 1957; E. M. Upjohn et al., *History of World Art,* Oxford, 1958; W. Willetts, *Chinese Art,* 2 vols., Penguin, 1958-1959.

Religion: Kenneth Latourette, *Christianity in a Revolutionary Age,* Harper. Vols. I and II (1958-1959) deal with the nineteenth century in Europe; Vol. III (1960) surveys the same period outside of Europe; and two additional volumes are planned for the treatment of Christianity since 1914. These volumes are an indispensable guide in church history. See also Peter Bamm, *The Kingdoms of Christ,* McGraw-Hill, 1960 (Christianity traced from the apostles to Charlemagne in a fascinating and lavishly illustrated volume); S. N. Bulgakov, *The Orthodox Church,* Morehouse, 1935; H. Butterfield, *Christianity and History,* Scribner's, 1950; C. Guignebert, *Christianity Past and Present,* Macmillan, 1927; Kenneth Latourette, *A History of Christianity,* Harper, 1953; Martin E. Marty, *A Short History of Christianity,** Meridian. For other world faiths, the following references are useful: I. Epstein, *Judaism,** Pelican; H. A. R. Gibb, *Mohammedanism: An Historical Survey,* Oxford, 1953; Christmas Humphreys, *Buddhism,** Pelican; S. Radhakrishnan, *The Hindu View of Life,* Macmillan, 1927; Huston Smith, *The Religions of Man,** Mentor; A. S. Tritton, *Islam: Belief and Practices,* Hutchinson Univ. Library, 1951; Arthur Waley, *Three Ways of Thought in Ancient China,** Anchor.

Philosophy: Crane Brinton, *Ideas and Men: The Story of Western Thought,* Prentice-Hall, 1950; J. Bronowski and Bruce Mazlish, *The Western Intellectual Tradition, From Leonardo to Hegel,* Harper, 1960; H. G. Creel, *Chinese Thought from Confucius to Mao Tse-tung,** Mentor; Will Durant, *The Story of Philosophy: The Lives and Opinions of the Greater Philosophers,* Pocket Books; H. Hoffding, *A History of Modern Philosophy; A Sketch of the History of Philosophy from the Close of the Renaissance to Our Own Day,** 2 vols., Dover; C. A. Moore, ed., *Philosophy—East and West,* Princeton, 1944; J. H. Randall, *The Making of the Modern Mind: A Survey of the Intellectual Background of the Present Age,* Houghton Mifflin, 1940; Bertrand Russell, *A History of Western Philosophy,** Simon and Schuster; W. Windleband, *A History of Philosophy,** 2 vols., Torchbooks; H. Zimmer, *Philosophies of India,** Meridian.

LIST OF ILLUSTRATIONS

PUNCH magazine—549.

Radio Times Hulton Picture Library—381, 498, 533, 534, 677, 694 center left and right and far right, 786 top right and center left.

Rathenau–Pix—240 left.

Rhodes University Library, Grahamstown, South Africa—635.

Rizzoli Editore, Milano—450, 513.

Theodore Roosevelt Association, New York—603.

Royal Ontario Museum, Canada—111.

Smithsonian Institution, Freer Gallery of Art—175.

Sir John Soane's Museum, London—412 bottom.

Collection of Mr. and Mrs. James Thrall Soby—791.

Sovfoto—263, 668, 671 bottom.

Staatliche Museen zu Berlin—61 (Photo—Werkstatt).

Standard Oil Company of New Jersey—172.

Thorbecke Publishing Company, Konstanz, Germany—236 left and right (Johannes Kerer, *Statuta Collegii Sapientiae*, 1497).

Three Lions—22 (Omnia), 27 (Omnia).

Toledo Museum of Art—319 (gift of Edward Drummond Libbey, 1953).

Trinity College Library, University of Dublin—226.

Turkish Press Broadcasting and Tourist Department—167 bottom left.

United Nations—750.

United Press International—554, 673, 674, 684 top and bottom left, 716, 759, 767, 770, 776, 778 right, 786 bottom.

United States Coast Guard, official photo—736.

United States Navy—730.

University of Edinburgh Library—173.

Verlag Moritz Diesterweg—714.

Victoria and Albert Museum. Crown Copyright—101, 201.

Wide World Photos—680, 684 top left, 685 bottom, 699, 700, 728, 737, 753, 755, 757, 758, 778 left.

Worcester Art Museum—107 bottom, 315.

LIST OF MAPS

LIST OF CHARTS AND DRAWINGS

FOOTNOTES

A PROLOGUE: PERSPECTIVE ON MAN

1. P. Gardiner, *The Nature of Historical Explanation* (London: Oxford University Press, 1952), p. 98.
2. H. Butterfield, *Christianity and History* (London: G. Bell and Sons, Ltd., 1949), p. 132.
3. See A. J. Toynbee, *Civilization on Trial* (New York: Oxford University Press, 1948).
4. H. A. L. Fisher, *A History of Europe*, I (Boston: Houghton Mifflin Co., 1935), p. vii.
5. Toynbee, p. 11.
6. W. D. Howells, *Mankind So Far* (New York: Doubleday and Co., 1952), p. 312.

1. ALONG THE BANKS OF RIVERS

1. Thorkild Jacobsen, "Primitive Democracy in Ancient Mesopotamia," *Journal of Near Eastern Studies* II, (1943), pp. 159-172.
2. V. Gordon Childe, *New Light on the Most Ancient East* (London: Routledge and Kegan Paul, Ltd., 1954), p. 114.
3. H. Frankfort, *The Birth of Civilization in the Near East* (London: Williams and Norgate, Ltd., 1951), p. 60.
4. "Les réformes d'Urukagina," trans. by M. Lambert, in *Révue d'Assyriologie*, XL (Paris, 1956), p. 183.
5. James B. Pritchard, ed., *Ancient Near Eastern Texts Relating to the Old Testament*, 2nd ed., trans. by E. A. Speiser (Princeton: Princeton University Press, 1955), p. 119.
6. *Sumerische und Addakische Hymnen und Gabete,* trans. by A. Falkenstein and W. von Soden (Zurich and Stuttgart: Artemis-Verlag, 1953), p. 188. For a partial translation and full discussion of this text, see S. N. Kramer, *From the Tablets of Sumer* (Indian Hills, Colorado: The Falcon's Wing Press, 1956), pp. 267-271.
7. H. de Genouillac, trans., in *Révue d'Assyriologie*, XXV (Paris, 1928), p. 148.
8. Quoted in S. N. Kramer, "The Oldest Laws," *Scientific American*, Vol. 188, No. 1 (January 1953), p. 28.
9. C. H. Gordon, *Hammurapi's Code: Quaint or Forward-Looking?* (New York: Rinehart and Co., 1957), p. 8.
10. R. F. Harper, *The Code of Hammurabi* (Chicago: University of Chicago Press, 1904), p. 3.
11. *Ibid.,* p. 49.
12. *Ibid.,* p. 101.
13. Edward Chiera, *They Wrote on Clay: The Babylonian Tablets Speak Today* (Chicago: University of Chicago Press, 1938), p. 156.
14. A. Heidel, *The Gilgamesh Epic and Old Testament Parallels* (Chicago: University of Chicago Press, 1956), pp. 84, 86-87.
15. Quoted in John A. Wilson, *The Culture of Ancient Egypt* (Chicago: Phoenix Books, n.d.), p. 117.
16. Jack Finegan, *Light from the Ancient Past* (Princeton: Princeton University Press, 1946), p. 85.
17. A. T. Trever, *History of Ancient Civilization*, I (New York: Harcourt, Brace and Co., 1936), p. 50.
18. Quoted in J. H. Breasted, *The Development of Religion and Thought in Ancient Egypt* (New York: Charles Scribner's Sons, 1924), pp. 324, 326. Reprinted by permission of the publishers.
19. Holy Bible, Authorized King James Version, I Kings 4:29-34.
20. *Ibid.,* Micah 6:8.
21. Bernhard W. Anderson, *Understanding the Old Testament* (Englewood Cliffs, N.J.: Prentice-Hall, Inc., 1957), p. 537.
22. Thorkild Jacobsen, "Early Political Development in Mesopotamia," *Zeitschrift für Assyriologie,* XVIII (Berlin, 1957), pp. 139-140.

2. THE GLORY THAT WAS GREECE

1. *Plutarch's Lives*, II, trans. by Sir T. North (London: J. M. Dent and Co., 1898), p. 144.
2. L. Cottrell, *The Anvil of Civilization* (New York: Mentor Books, 1957), p. 101.
3. See C. H. Gordon, "Notes on Minoan Linear A," *Antiquity*, XXXI, No. 122 (September 1957), pp. 124-130.
4. "Laws," in *The Dialogues of Plato*, I, trans. by B. Jowett (New York: Random House, 1937), p. 503.
5. *Plutarch's Lives,* trans. by J. Dryden, rev. by A. H. Clough (New York: Modern Library, 1932), p. 108.
6. *Ibid.,* p. 107.
7. E. H. Blakeney, ed., *The History of Herodotus*, II, trans. by H. G. Rawlinson, Everyman's Library (New York: E. P. Dutton, 1910), p. 46.
8. C. A. Robinson, *Ancient History* (New York: The Macmillan Co., 1951), pp. 198-199.
9. Blakeney, p. 208.

10. Thucydides, *The History of the Peloponnesian War,* II, ed. and trans. by Sir R. W. Livingstone, The World's Classics (New York: Oxford University Press, 1943), pp. 111, 113.

11. Aristotle, *Politics,* I, Pt. II, trans. by H. Rackham (London: William Heinemann, Ltd., 1932), p. 12.

12. Thucydides, II, pp. 113-114.

13. *Ibid.,* I, p. 46.

14. *Ibid.,* II, p. 130.

15. *Ibid.,* V, p. 270.

16. Quoted in M. Cary and T. J. Haarhoff, *Life and Thought in the Greek and Roman World* (London: Methuen and Co., Ltd., 1951), p. 200.

17. C. A. Robinson, *Hellenic History* (New York: The Macmillan Co., 1948), p. 260.

18. "Apology," in *The Four Socratic Dialogues of Plato,* trans. by B. Jowett (Oxford: Clarendon Press, 1924), pp. 91-92.

19. Quoted in Cary and Haarhoff, p. 192.

20. Quoted in *Encyclopaedia Brittanica,* XV, 1957 ed., pp. 197-198.

21. Thucydides, I, pp. 44-45.

22. *Sappho,* trans. by M. Barnard (Los Angeles: University of California Press, 1958), frag. 44.

23. Quoted in R. H. Barrow, *The Romans* (Harmondsworth: Penguin Books, Ltd., 1955), title page.

3. THE GRANDEUR THAT WAS ROME

1. J. H. Breasted, *Ancient Times* (Boston: Ginn and Co., 1935), p. 611.

2. Quoted in M. Hadas, *A History of Rome* (Garden City, N.Y.: Doubleday and Co., Inc., 1956), p. 75. Reprinted by permission of Doubleday and Co., Inc., and G. Bell and Sons, Ltd.

3. *The Roman History of Appian of Alexandria,* II, trans. by Horace White (New York: The Macmillan Co., 1899), p. 6.

4. M. Cary and T. J. Haarhoff, *Life and Thought in the Greek and Roman World,* 5th ed. (London: Methuen and Co., Ltd., 1951), p. 75.

5. M. Hammond, *City-State and World State in Greek and Roman Political Theory Until Augustus* (Cambridge: Harvard University Press, 1951), p. 153.

6. Quoted in Hadas, p. 112.

7. Tertullian, *Concerning the Soul,* quoted in S. Katz, *The Decline of Rome and the Rise of Medieval Europe* (Ithaca, N.Y.: Cornell University Press, 1955), p. 7.

8. Virgil, *Aeneid,* trans. by J. W. MacKail, Modern Library ed. (New York: Random House, 1934), p. 126.

9. R. C. Trevelyan, *Translations from Horace, Juvenal and Montaigne* (New York: Cambridge University Press, 1941), p. 129.

10. Quoted in W. Durant, *Caesar and Christ* (New York: Simon and Schuster, 1944), p. 506.

4. THE ASIAN WAY OF LIFE

1. A. Coomaraswamy, *The Dance of Shiva* (Bombay: Asia Publishing House, 1948), p. 22.

2. W. A. Fairservis, *Excavations in the Quetta Valley, West Pakistan,* Anthropological Papers of the American Museum of Natural History, Vol. 45, Pt. 2 (New York: American Museum of Natural History, 1956), p. 357.

3. Stuart Piggott, *Prehistoric India, to 1000 B.C.* (Harmondsworth: Penguin Books, Ltd., 1950), p. 133.

4. A. D. Bouquet, *Hinduism* (London: Hutchinson and Co., Ltd., 1948), p. 98.

5. R. K. Mookerji, *Hindu Civilization* (London: Longmans, Green and Co., Ltd., 1936), p. 249.

6. N. Dutt, "Religion and Philosophy," in *The Age of Imperial Unity,* Vol. II of *The History and Culture of the Indian People,* ed. by R. C. Majumdar and A. D. Pusalker (Bombay: Bharatiya Vidya Bhavan, 1951), p. 371.

7. Quoted in H. G. Rawlinson, *Intercourse Between India and the Western World from the Earliest Times to the Fall of Rome* (New York: Cambridge University Press, 1926), p. 39.

8. R. K. Mookerji, "Asoka the Great," in *The Age of Imperial Unity,* Vol. II of *The History and Culture of the Indian People,* p. 92.

9. W. W. Tarn, *The Greeks in Bactria and India* (New York: Cambridge University Press, 1951), p. 181.

10. Rawlinson, p. 109.

11. Quoted in H. G. Creel, *Chinese Thought from Confucius to Mao Tse-Tung* (London: Eyre and Spottiswoode, Ltd., 1954), p. 31. See also *The Shoo King,* Vol. III of Pt. II of *The Chinese Classics,* trans. by J. Legge (London: Trübner and Co.; and Hong Kong: at the author's, 1865), pp. 495-502.

12. Quoted in Creel, p. 31.

13. R. Grousset, *The Rise and Splendour of the Chinese Empire* (Berkeley and Los Angeles: University of California Press, 1953), p. 26.

14. W. E. Soothill, *The Three Religions of China* (London: Oxford University Press, 1923), p. 31.

15. Quoted in L. S. Hsü, *The Political Philosophy of Confucianism* (New York: E. P. Dutton and Co., Inc., 1932), pp. 87-88.

16. Liu Wu-Chi, *A Short History of Confucian Philosophy* (Harmondsworth: Penguin Books, Ltd., 1955), p. 25.

17. Creel, p. 58.

18. *The Works of Mencius,* Vol. II of *The Chinese Classics,* p. 46.

19. Quoted in Fung Yu-Lan, *The Period of the Philosophers,* Vol. I of *A History of Chinese Phi-*

losophy, trans. by Derk Bodde (Peiping: Henri Vetch, 1937), p. 177.

20. Quoted in Hu Shih, *Development of the Logical Method in Ancient China* (Shanghai: The Oriental Book Company, 1928), p. 4.

5. THE CITY OF GOD

1. St. Jerome's *Commentary on Ezekial,* I, Prologue.

2. E. Wilson, *The Scrolls from the Dead Sea* (New York: Oxford University Press, 1955), p. 60.

3. M. Burrows, *The Dead Sea Scrolls* (New York: The Viking Press, 1955), p. 327.

4. Holy Bible, Authorized King James Version, Acts 22:6-10.

5. See *Tertulliani Apologeticus,* Ch. 50, trans. by A. Souter (Cambridge: Cambridge University Press, 1917), p. 145.

6. Quoted in M. Hadas, *A History of Rome* (Garden City, N.Y.: Doubleday and Co., Inc., 1956), pp. 179-180. Reprinted by permission of Doubleday and Co., Inc., and G. Bell and Sons, Ltd.

7. *Complete Works of Tacitus,* trans. by A. J. Church and W. J. Brodribb, Modern Library ed. (New York: Random House, 1942), pp. 715-716.

8. S. Katz, *The Decline of Rome and the Rise of Medieval Europe* (Ithaca, N.Y.: Cornell University Press, 1955), p. 7.

9. *Ibid.,* p. 98.

6. EUROPE'S SEARCH FOR STABILITY

1. Compare M. Fessier, *Clovis* (New York: Dial Press, 1948).

2. Quoted in H. Pirenne, *Mohammed and Charlemagne* (New York: Barnes and Noble, Inc., 1955), p. 47.

3. Quoted in H. St. L. B. Moss, *The Birth of the Middle Ages, 395-814* (London: Oxford University Press, 1935), p. 222.

4. E. M. Hulme, *The Middle Ages* (New York: Henry Holt and Co., 1938), pp. 272-273.

5. Quoted in R. W. Collins, *A History of Medieval Civilization in Europe* (Boston: Ginn and Co., 1936), p. 200.

6. Quoted in G. B. Adams, *Civilization During the Middle Ages* (New York: Charles Scribner's Sons, 1914), p. 222.

7. Quoted in S. Painter, *A History of the Middle Ages, 284-1500* (New York: Alfred A. Knopf, 1954), p. 121.

7. CITADEL AND CONQUEROR

1. *Procopius,* I, trans. by Henry B. Dewing (London: William Heinemann, 1914), pp. 231-233.

2. Geoffrey de Villehardouin, *Villehardouin's Chronicle of the Fourth Crusade and the Conquest of Constantinople,* quoted in Sir F. Marzials, *Memoirs of the Crusades,* Everyman's Library (London: J. M. Dent and Co., Ltd., 1908), pp. 25-26.

3. Quoted in J. F. C. Fuller, *A Military History of the Western World,* I (New York: Funk and Wagnalls, 1954), p. 522.

4. S. Runciman, *A History of the Crusades,* III (Cambridge: Cambridge University Press, 1954), p. 131.

5. See C. P. Baker, *Justinian* (New York: Dodd, Mead and Co., 1931).

6. D. Talbot Rice, *Byzantine Art* (Harmondsworth: Penguin Books, Ltd., 1954), p. 151.

7. See T. P. Hughes, *A Dictionary of Islam* (London: W. H. Allen and Co., 1885).

8. D. Westermann, *The African Today and Tomorrow* (London: Oxford University Press, 1949), p. 134.

9. P. K. Hitti, *The Arabs: A Short History* (Princeton: Princeton University Press, 1949), p. 1.

10. Quoted in E. H. Palmer, *Haroun Alraschid, Caliph of Bagdad* (London: Marcus Ward and Company, 1881), p. 76.

11. *Rubáiyát of Omar Khayyám,* trans. by E. FitzGerald (Boston: Thomas B. Mosher, 1899), pp. 26-27.

12. R. Flint, *The Philosophy of History in France* (New York: Charles Scribner's Sons, 1894), p. 158.

13. *Muqaddima,* I, trans. by MacG. de Slane (Paris: 1862-1868), p. 71.

8. THE WEST TAKES THE OFFENSIVE

1. Quoted in A. C. Krey, *The First Crusade* (Princeton: Princeton University Press, 1921), p. 261.

2. Quoted in W. Durant, *The Reformation* (New York: Simon and Schuster, 1957), p. 41.

9. NATIONS IN THE MAKING

1. William of Malmesbury, *Chronicle of the Kings of England,* Book III, trans. by J. Sharpe (London: George Bell and Sons, 1876), p. 277.

2. Quoted in E. H. Carter and R. A. F. Mears, *A History of Britain,* Section I (Oxford: Clarendon Press, 1937), p. 94.

3. Quoted in E. P. Cheyney, *Readings in English History Drawn from the Original Sources* (Boston: Ginn and Co., 1908), p. 112.

4. W. S. Churchill, *The Birth of Britain,* Vol. I of *A History of the English-Speaking Peoples* (New York: Dodd, Mead and Co., 1956), pp. 222-223. Reprinted by permission of Dodd, Mead and Co.; McClellan and Stewart, Ltd., of Toronto; and Cassell and Co., Ltd., of London.

5. Quoted in Cheyney, pp. 157-158.

6. Churchill, I, pp. 242-243.

7. Compare Cheyney, pp. 183-185.

8. Quoted in J. H. Robinson, *Readings in European History,* I (Boston: Ginn and Co., 1904), p. 202.

9. Quoted in J. L. LaMonte, *The World of the Middle Ages* (New York: Appleton-Century-Crofts, Inc., 1949), p. 462.

10. *The Lay of the Cid,* trans. by R. S. Rose and L. Bacon (Berkeley: University of California Press, 1919), pp. 25-26.

11. J. W. Thompson, *Feudal Germany* (Chicago: University of Chicago Press, 1928), pp. xviii-xix.

12. Z. N. Brooke, *A History of Europe from 911 to 1198* (London: Methuen and Co., Ltd., 1951), p. 28.

13. Robinson, p. 154.

14. LaMonte, p. 507.

10.   TO THE GLORY OF GOD

1. J. W. Thompson, *Economic and Social History of the Middle Ages* (New York: Century Co., 1928), p. 132. Reprinted by permission of Appleton-Century-Crofts, Inc.

2. S. M. Brown, *Medieval Europe* (New York: Harcourt, Brace and Co., 1935), pp. 386-387.

3. J. W. Thompson and E. N. Johnson, *An Introduction to Medieval Europe, 300-1500* (New York: W. W. Norton and Co., Inc., 1937), pp. 359-360.

4. Quoted in J. H. Robinson, *Readings in European History,* I (Boston: Ginn and Co., 1904), p. 283.

5. Quoted in S. R. Packard, *Europe and the Church Under Innocent III* (New York): Henry Holt and Co., 1927), p. 15.

6. Quoted in J. Evans, *Life in Mediaeval France* (New York: Oxford University Press, 1925), p. 87.

7. Compare W. Durant, *The Reformation* (New York: Simon and Schuster, 1957).

8. Quoted in I. C. Hannah, *Christian Monasticism* (New York: The Macmillan Co., 1925), p. 158.

9. T. Morrison, *The Portable Chaucer* (New York: The Viking Press, 1949), pp. 80-81. Copyright, 1949, by Theodore Morrison.

10. *An Encyclopedist of the Dark Ages,* trans. by E. Brehaut (New York: Columbia University Press, 1912), p. 220.

11. Quoted in H. O. Taylor, *The Mediaeval Mind,* II (London: The Macmillan Co., Ltd., 1938), p. 524.

12. J. A. Symonds, *Wine, Women, and Song* (London: Chatto and Windus, 1931), pp. 67-69.

13. Geoffrey Chaucer, *Canterbury Tales,* trans. by J. U. Nicolson (New York: Crown Publishers, Inc., 1936), pp. 3-5.

11.   EUROPE IN TRANSITION

1. A. C. Flick, *Decline of the Medieval Church,* I (London: Kegan Paul, Trench, Trübner and Co., Ltd., 1930), p. 293.

2. R. H. Bainton, *The Reformation of the Sixteenth Century* (Boston: Beacon Press, 1952), p. 15.

3. J. Bryce, *The Holy Roman Empire* (New York: The Macmillan Co., 1887), p. 238.

4. Voltaire, *Essay on the Morals of the Holy Empire of the Hapsburgs.*

5. W. T. Waugh, *History of Europe from 1378 to 1494* (New York: G. P. Putnam's Sons, 1932), p. 448.

6. B. Pares, *A History of Russia* (New York: Alfred A. Knopf, 1956), p. 78.

7. *Ibid.,* p. 89.

8. Quoted in M. Cherniavsky, " 'Holy Russia': A Study in the History of an Idea," *The American Historical Review,* LXIII, No. 3 (April 1958), p. 619.

9. *Ibid.,* p. 625.

10. G. Barraclough, *History in a Changing World* (Oxford: Basil Blackwell, 1955), p. 134.

12.   MAN IS THE MEASURE

1. Quoted in J. Burckhardt, *The Civilization of the Renaissance in Italy,* trans. by S. G. C. Middlemore (London: George Allen and Unwin, Ltd., 1921), p. 138.

2. Quoted in J. H. Randall, Jr., *The Making of the Modern Mind* (Boston: Houghton Mifflin Co., 1940), p. 213.

3. John of Salisbury, quoted in Frederick B. Artz, *The Mind of the Middle Ages* (New York: Alfred A. Knopf, Inc., 1954), p. 307.

4. H. O. Taylor, *Thought and Expression in the Sixteenth Century,* I (New York: The Macmillan Co., 1920), p. 175.

5. Quoted in Randall, p. 118.

6. From the 1684 translation by Gilbert Burnet, in *Introduction to Contemporary Civilization in the West: A Source Book,* I (New York: Columbia University Press, 1946), p. 461.

7. *Ibid.,* p. 460.

8. Quoted in Taylor, I, pp. 328-329.

9. J. van der Elst, *The Last Flowering of the Middle Ages* (New York: Doubleday and Co., Inc., 1946), p. 59.

13.   HERE I TAKE MY STAND

1. Holy Bible, Authorized King James Version, Romans 1:17.

2. Compare R. H. Bainton, *The Reformation of the Sixteenth Century* (Boston: Beacon Press, 1952), p. 27.

3. Quoted in C. J. H. Hayes, *A Political and Cultural History of Modern Europe,* I (New York: The Macmillan Co., 1933), p. 154.

4. Quoted in P. Smith, *The Life and Letters of Martin Luther* (New York: Houghton Mifflin Co., 1911), p. 41.

5. Quoted in H. Bettenson, *Documents of the Christian Church* (London: Oxford University Press, 1943), pp. 282-283.

6. Quoted in H. J. Grimm, *The Reformation Era, 1500-1650* (New York: The Macmillan Co., 1956), p. 175.

7. Quoted in Hayes, I, p. 158.

8. Quoted in J. H. Robinson, *Readings in European History,* II (Boston: Ginn and Co., 1906), p. 159.

14. THE STRIFE OF STATES AND KINGS

1. Compare B. Reynolds, *Proponents of Limited Monarchy in Sixteenth Century France: Francis Hotman and Jean Bodin* (New York: Columbia University Press, 1931), p. 182.

2. Sir Henry Wotton, *Reliquiae Wottonianae.*

3. Quoted in W. Durant, *The Reformation* (New York: Simon and Schuster, 1957), p. 206.

4. Compare N. Machiavelli, *The Prince* (New York: Modern Library, 1940).

5. *Ibid.*

6. *Ibid.*

7. Quoted in R. Ergang, *Europe from the Renaissance to Waterloo* (Boston: D. C. Heath and Co., 1954), p. 296.

8. *Ibid.,* p. 246.

9. Quoted in P. Smith, *The Age of the Reformation* (New York: Henry Holt and Co., 1920), p. 215.

10. Quoted in E.R.A. Seligman, ed., *Encyclopaedia of the Social Sciences,* III (New York: The Macmillan Co., 1930), p. 426.

11. Quoted in E. P. Cheyney, *Readings in English History Drawn from the Original Sources* (Boston: Ginn and Co., 1935), p. 426.

12. Quoted in *ibid.,* p. 503.

13. John Milton, "Areopagitica," in *The Literature of England,* I, 4th ed., ed. by G. B. Woods, H. A. Watt, G. K. Anderson, and K. J. Holzknecht (Chicago: Scott, Foresman and Co., 1958), p. 795.

15. OLD WORLDS BEYOND THE HORIZON

1. C. E. Gover, *The Folk-Songs of Southern India* (London: Trübner and Co., 1872), p. 165.

2. H. G. Creel, *Chinese Thought from Confucius to Mao Tsê-Tung* (Chicago: University of Chicago Press, 1953), p. 187.

3. S. Obata, *The Works of Li Po* (London: J. M. Dent and Sons, Ltd., 1923), p. 1. Reprinted by permission of J. M. Dent and Sons, Ltd., and E. P. Dutton and Co., Inc.

4. *Ibid.,* p. 66.

5. Quoted in H. H. Gowan and J. W. Hall, *An Outline History of China* (New York: D. Appleton Co., 1926), p. 142.

6. K. S. Latourette, *The Chinese: Their History and Culture,* II (New York: The Macmillan Co., 1934), p. 264.

7. Quoted in Hsüan-Ming Liu, "Russo-Chinese Relations up to the Treaty of Nerchinsk," in *Chinese Social and Political Science Review,* XXIII, No. 4 (January-March 1940), p. 403.

8. Quoted in I. Nitobé, *Bushido, the Soul of Japan* (Tokyo: Maruzen, 1935), p. 31.

9. R. Linton, *The Tree of Culture* (New York: Alfred A. Knopf, 1955), p. 592.

10. E. Wyllys Andrews, "Dzibilchatun: Lost City of the Maya," in *National Geographic,* CXV, No. 1 (January 1959), pp. 91-109.

11. Quoted in H. Schiffer, *The Quest for Africa* (New York: G. P. Putnam's Sons, 1957), p. 64.

16. THE FORCE OF EUROPEAN EXPANSION

1. Quoted in S. E. Morison, *Admiral of the Ocean Sea: A Life of Christopher Columbus* (Boston: Little, Brown and Co., 1942), p. 62.

2. Quoted in H. H. Gowen, *An Outline History of Japan* (New York: D. Appleton Co., 1927), p. 255.

3. Quoted in H. Robinson, *The Development of the British Empire* (Boston: Houghton Mifflin Co., 1922), p. 38.

4. Quoted in H. Heaton, *Economic History of Europe* (New York: Harper and Bros., 1948), p. 315.

5. *Ibid.,* p. 239.

6. *Ibid.* (published 1936), p. 363.

7. Oliver Goldsmith, "The Deserted Village," in *The Literature of England,* I, 4th ed., ed. by G. B. Woods, H. A. Watt, G. K. Anderson, and K. J. Holzknecht (Chicago: Scott, Foresman and Co., 1958), pp. 1115, 1118.

17. NEW DIMENSIONS OF THE MIND

1. Compare *Introduction to Contemporary Civilizaton in the West,* I (New York: Columbia University Press, 1946), pp. 845-859.

2. F. Bacon, *The Works of Francis Bacon,* III, ed. by J. Spedding (London: Longman and Co., 1861), p. 156.

3. Quoted in J. H. Randall, Jr., *The Making of the Modern Mind,* rev. ed. (Boston: Houghton Mifflin Co., 1940), p. 221.

4. Quoted in *Introduction to Contemporary Civilization in the West,* I, p. 557.

5. Compare *Sir Isaac Newton's Mathematical Principles of Natural Philosophy and His System of the World*, ed. and trans. by F. Cajori (Berkeley: University of California Press, 1946).

6. H. Butterfield, *The Origins of Modern Science* (London: G. Bell and Sons, Ltd., 1949), p. 104.

7. See P. Hazard, *The European Mind: The Critical Years* (New Haven: Yale University Press, 1953).

8. A. Pope, "The Universal Prayer," in *The Poetical Works of Alexander Pope* (London: John James Chidley, 1846), p. 145.

9. W. L. Dorn, *Competition for Empire, 1740-1763* (New York: Harper and Bros., 1940), p. 181.

10. Quoted in F. E. Manuel, *The Age of Reason* (Ithaca, N.Y.: Cornell University Press, 1951), p. 39.

11. S. Cheney, *A World History of Art* (New York: The Viking Press, 1944), p. 687.

12. A. Pope, "Epistle to Dr. Arbuthnot," in *The Literature of England*, I, 4th ed., ed. by G. B. Woods, H. A. Watt, G. K. Anderson, and K. J. Holzknecht (Chicago: Scott, Foresman and Co., 1958), p. 1098.

13. A. Pope, "An Essay on Man," in *The Literature of England*, I, pp. 1088-1089.

18. L'ÉTAT C'EST MOI

1. Quoted in J. H. Robinson, *Readings in European History*, II (Boston: Ginn and Co., 1906), pp. 273-275.

2. Quoted in W. G. Crane *et al.*, *Twelve Hundred Years: The Literature of England*, I (New York: Stackpole and Heck, Inc., 1948), p. 572.

3. Quoted in A. F. Tyler, *The Modern World* (New York: Farrar and Rinehart, 1939), p. 186.

4. Sir Ernest Barker *et al.*, *The European Inheritance*, II (London: Clarendon Press, 1954), p. 144.

5. Quoted in P. Smith, *A History of Modern Culture*, I (London: G. Routledge and Sons, Ltd., 1930), p. 226.

6. B. Pares, *A History of Russia* (New York: Alfred A. Knopf, 1956), p. 199.

7. Quoted in R. Ergang, *The Potsdam Führer, Frederick William I* (New York: Columbia University Press, 1941), p. 7.

8. Quoted in W. L. Dorn, *Competition for Empire, 1740-1763* (New York: Harper and Bros., 1940), p. 9.

9. *Ibid.*, p. 139.

10. Quoted in W. P. Hall and R. G. Albion, *A History of England and the British Empire, 1789-1914* (Boston: Ginn and Co., 1946), p. 453.

11. Quoted in P. Gaxotte, *Frederick the Great* (London: G. Bell and Sons, Ltd., 1941), p. 357.

12. Quoted in H. Robinson, *The Development of the British Empire* (Boston: Houghton Mifflin Co., 1922), p. 96.

13. A. Smith, *An Inquiry into the Nature and Causes of the Wealth of Nations* (New York: Modern Library, 1937), pp. 14, 421.

14. Quoted in *Introduction to Contemporary Civilization in the West*, I (New York: Columbia University Press, 1946), p. 987.

15. Quoted in J. H. Robinson and C. A. Beard, *Readings in Modern European History*, I (Boston: Ginn and Co., 1908), p. 191.

16. Quoted in F. Nowak, *Medieval Slavdom and the Rise of Russia* (New York: Henry Holt and Co., 1930), p. 91.

17. Quoted in G. P. Gooch, *Frederick the Great; the Ruler, the Writer, the Man* (New York: Alfred A. Knopf, 1947), p. 109.

19. THE RIGHTS OF MAN

1. Quoted in C. Rossiter, *The First American Revolution* (New York: Harcourt, Brace and Co., 1956), prefatory note.

2. L. M. Larson, *History of England and the British Commonwealth* (New York: Henry Holt and Co., 1924), p. 529.

3. Quoted in G. B. Adams, *Constitutional History of England* (New York: Henry Holt and Co., 1934), p. 406.

4. C. J. H. Hayes, *A Political and Cultural History of England*, I (New York: The Macmillan Co., 1932), p. 614.

5. "The Declaration of the Rights of Man," in *The World in Literature*, III, ed. by R. Warnock and G. K. Anderson (Chicago: Scott, Foresman and Co., 1951), pp. 298-299.

6. Quoted in Hayes, I, p. 627.

7. Quoted in J. E. Gillespie, *A History of Europe, 1500-1815* (New York: Alfred A. Knopf, 1928), p. 529.

8. Quoted in L. Madelin, *The French Revolution* (London: William Heinemann, Ltd., 1916), p. 323.

9. W. Wordsworth, "The French Revolution," in *Poems of Wordsworth*, ed. by M. Arnold (London: Macmillan and Co., Ltd., 1891), p. 258.

10. E. Burke, "Reflections on the Revolution in France," in *The Works of the Right Honorable Edmund Burke*, II (London: G. Bell and Sons, 1886), p. 284.

11. Quoted in J. H. Randall, Jr., *The Making of the Modern Mind* (Boston: Houghton Mifflin Co., 1940), p. 433.

12. Quoted in R. Ergang, *Europe from the Renaissance to Waterloo* (Boston: D. C. Heath and Co., 1954), p. 717.

13. Quoted in *ibid.*, p. 752.

20. MACHINES, THE MIDDLE CLASS, AND THE MANIFESTO

1. C. Dickens, *Hard Times* (London: Thomas Nelson and Sons, Ltd., n.d.), p. 26.

2. L. A. Willoughby, *The Romantic Movement in Germany* (London: Oxford University Press, 1930), p. 8.

3. W. Wordsworth, "Preface to Lyrical Ballads," in *The Literature of England*, II, 4th ed., ed. by G. B. Woods, H. A. Watt, G. K. Anderson, and K. J. Holzknecht (Chicago: Scott, Foresman and Co., 1958), pp. 319-327.

4. S. T. Coleridge, "Biographia Literaria," in *The Literature of England*, II, p. 328.

5. P. B. Shelley, "Prometheus Unbound," Act III, Scene 4, 11. 194-196, in *English Poetry and Prose of the Romantic Movement*, ed. by G. B. Woods (Chicago: Scott, Foresman and Co., 1950), p. 716.

6. Lord Byron, "Don Juan," Canto III, in *The Literature of England*, II, p. 235.

7. J. Keats, "Poem from Endymion," in *The Literature of England*, II, p. 278.

8. W. Wordsworth, "Composed in the Valley near Dover, on the Day of Landing," in *English Poetry and Prose of the Romantic Movement*, p. 313.

9. C. A. and M. Beard, *The Industrial Era*, Vol. II of *The Rise of American Civilization* (New York: The Macmillan Co., 1927), p. 763.

10. T. R. Malthus, "An Essay on Population," in *Introduction to Contemporary Civilization in the West*, II (New York: Columbia University Press, 1955), p. 196.

11. Quoted in W. P. Hall and W. S. Davis, *The Course of Europe Since Waterloo* (New York: D. Appleton-Century Co., Inc., 1941), p. 262.

12. Quoted in *ibid.*, pp. 262-263.

13. David Thomson, *England in the Nineteenth Century, 1815-1914* (Harmondsworth: Penguin Books, Ltd., 1950), p. 101.

14. Quoted in B. Willey, *Nineteenth Century Studies* (London: Chatto and Windus, 1949), p. 262.

15. T. Carlyle, "The Present Time," quoted in E. D. Mackerness, "The Voice of Prophecy: Carlyle and Ruskin," in *From Dickens to Hardy*, ed. by B. Ford (New York: Penguin Books, Inc., 1958), p. 294.

16. The Earl of Beaconsfield, K.G., *Sybil; or, The Two Nations* (London: Longmans, Green and Co., Ltd., 1926), pp. 76-77.

17. W. Godwin, "Political Justice," in S. Hook, *Marx and the Marxists: The Ambiguous Legacy* (Princeton: D. Van Nostrand Co., Inc., 1955), p. 28.

18. Quoted in E. R. A. Seligman, ed., *Encyclopaedia of the Social Sciences*, XIII (New York: The Macmillan Co., 1935), p. 510a.

19. Quoted in H. J. Laski, *Communist Manifesto: Socialist Landmark* (London: George Allen and Unwin, Ltd., 1948), p. 168.

20. Compare *ibid.*, p. 141.

21. C. Darwin, "The Origin of Species," in *Introduction to Contemporary Civilization in the West*, II, pp. 453-454.

22. R. Browning, "Song from 'Pippa Passes,'" in *The Literature of England*, II, p. 657.

21. TO THE BARRICADES!

1. Quoted in C. D. Hazen, *Europe Since 1815* (New York: Henry Holt and Co., 1910), pp. 21-22.

2. Lord Byron, "Don Juan," Canto III, in *The Literature of England*, II, 4th ed., ed. by G. B. Woods, H. A. Watt, G. K. Anderson, and K. J. Holzknecht (Chicago: Scott, Foresman and Co., 1958), p. 235.

3. Quoted in P. Robertson, *Revolutions of 1848* (Princeton: Princeton University Press, 1952), p. 14.

4. Quoted in Hazen, p. 129.

5. H. A. L. Fisher, *A History of Europe*, III (Boston: Houghton Mifflin Co., 1936; London: Eyre and Spottiswoode, Ltd., 1935), p. 956.

22. NATIONALISM AND THE MAKING OF NATIONS

1. Quoted in J. S. Schapiro, *Modern and Contemporary European History, 1815-1940* (Boston: Houghton Mifflin Co., 1940), p. 222.

2. Quoted in K. S. Pinson, *Modern Germany* (New York: The Macmillan Co., 1954), p. 116.

3. Quoted in Schapiro, p. 237.

4. Sir J. A. R. Marriott, *A Short History of France* (New York: Oxford University Press, 1944), p. 233.

5. Quoted in J. E. Gillespie, *Europe in Perspective* (New York: Harcourt, Brace and Co., 1942), p. 253.

6. Compare M. T. Florinsky, *Russia: A History and Interpretation*, II (New York: The Macmillan Co., 1953), pp. 809-812.

7. Compare S. Graham, *Tsar of Freedom: The Life and Reign of Alexander II* (New Haven: Yale University Press, 1935), pp. 34-48.

8. I. Turgenev, *Fathers and Children*, trans. by C. Garnett (New York: The Macmillan Co., 1924), p. 36.

9. J. A. R. Marriott, *The Eastern Question* (London: Clarendon Press, 1924), p. 2.

10. A. J. P. Taylor, *The Struggle for Mastery in Europe, 1848-1918* (London: Clarendon Press, 1954), p. 231.

11. Quoted in J. F. C. Fuller, *A Military History of the Western World*, III (New York: Funk and Wagnalls, 1956), p. 104.

23. PROMISE AND PERIL

1. Quoted in F. Owen, *Tempestuous Journey: Lloyd George, His Life and Times* (London: Hutchin-

son and Co., Ltd., 1954), p. 186. Reprinted by permission of the publishers.

2. Quoted in J. V. Ducattillon, "The Church in the Third Republic," in *The Making of Modern Europe*, II, ed. by H. Ausubel (New York: Dryden Press, 1951), p. 861.

3. Quoted in F. A. Ogg and W. R. Sharp, *Economic Development of Europe* (New York: The Macmillan Co., 1926), p. 551.

4. C. G. Robertson, *Bismarck* (London: Constable and Co., Ltd., 1918), p. 472.

5. Quoted in R. W. Postgate, *Revolution from 1789 to 1906* (Boston: Houghton Mifflin Co., 1921), pp. 363-364.

6. Quoted in J. S. Schapiro, *Modern and Contemporary European History, 1815-1940* (Boston: Houghton Mifflin Co., 1940), p. 425.

7. C. J. H. Hayes, *A Generation of Materialism, 1871-1900* (New York: Harper and Bros., 1941), p. 285.

8. Quoted in C. J. H. Hayes, *A Political and Cultural History of Modern Europe*, II (New York: The Macmillan Co., 1939), p. 572. Reprinted by permission of The Macmillan Co.

9. Viscount Grey of Fallodon, *Twenty-Five Years*, II (New York: Frederick A. Stokes Co., 1925), p. 20.

24. SURVIVAL OF THE FITTEST

1. R. Browning, "Song from 'Pippa Passes,' " in *The Literature of England*, II, 4th ed., ed. by G. B. Woods, H. A. Watt, G. K. Anderson, and K. J. Holzknecht (Chicago: Scott, Foresman and Co., 1958), p. 657.

2. F. Schevill, *A History of Europe* (New York: Harcourt, Brace and Co., 1938), p. 481.

3. Quoted in R. N. Carew Hunt, *The Theory and Practice of Communism* (London: Geoffrey Bles, 1950), p. 72.

4. Compare T. H. Huxley, *Collected Essays*, V (London: Macmillan and Co., Ltd., 1894).

5. J. Huxley and J. Fisher, eds., *The Living Thoughts of Darwin* (New York: Longmans, Green and Co., Inc., 1939), pp. 150-151.

6. Quoted in J. Chapin, ed., *The Book of Catholic Quotations* (New York: Farrar, Straus and Cudahy, 1956), p. 706.

7. T. Veblen, *The Theory of the Leisure Class* (New York: The Macmillan Co., 1902), p. 188.

25. NEW EUROPES OVERSEAS

1. Compare J. Quincy, *Speeches Delivered in the Congress of the United States* (Boston: Little, Brown and Co., 1874).

2. Quoted in C. G. Sellers, Jr., *Jacksonian Democracy* (Washington, D.C.: Service Center for Teachers of History, 1958), p. 1.

3. C. Van Doren, ed., *The Literary Works of Abraham Lincoln* (New York: The Limited Editions Club, Inc., 1942), p. 65.

4. Quoted in F. R. Dulles, *America's Rise to World Power* (New York: Harper and Bros., 1955), p. 4.

5. Quoted in *ibid.*, pp. 6-7.

6. H. S. Commager, *Documents of American History* (New York: Appleton-Century-Crofts, Inc., 1958), p. 170.

7. Quoted in H. C. Hockett and A. M. Schlesinger, *Land of the Free* (New York: The Macmillan Co., 1944), p. 482.

8. M. Ugarte, *The Destiny of a Continent* (New York: Alfred A. Knopf, 1925), p. 288.

9. Quoted in J. L. Mecham, "Conflicting Ideals of Pan-Americanism," *Current History*, XXXIII, No. 3 (December 1930), p. 402.

26. THE WHITE MAN'S BURDEN

1. R. Kipling, "The White Man's Burden," in *The Literature of England*, II, 4th ed., ed. by G. B. Woods, H. A. Watt, G. K. Anderson, and K. J. Holzknecht (Chicago: Scott, Foresman and Co., 1958), p. 897.

2. K. S. Latourette, *A Short History of the Far East* (New York: The Macmillan Co., 1947), p. 184.

3. Li Chien-nung, *The Political History of China, 1840-1928*, trans. by Sau-Yu-Teng and J. Ingalls (Princeton: D. Van Nostrand Co., Inc., 1956), p. 29.

4. Quoted in T. A. Bailey, *The American Pageant* (Boston: D. C. Heath and Co., 1956), p. 630.

5. G. B. Shaw, *The Man of Destiny*, quoted in W. L. Langer, *The Diplomacy of Imperialism*, I (New York: Alfred A. Knopf, 1935), p. 91.

6. W. L. Langer, "A Critique of Imperialism," in *The Making of Modern Europe*, II, ed. by H. Ausubel (New York: Dryden Press, 1951), p. 928.

27. A WORLD FIT FOR HEROES

1. S. E. Morison and H. S. Commager, *The Growth of the American Republic*, II (New York: Oxford University Press, 1950), pp. 453-454.

2. Quoted in F. P. Chambers, *The War Behind the War, 1914-1918* (New York: Harcourt, Brace and Co., 1939), p. 473.

3. Quoted in L. M. Hacker and B. B. Kendrick, *The United States Since 1865* (New York: F. S. Crofts and Co., 1939), p. 520.

4. Quoted in F. P. Walters, *A History of the League of Nations*, I (London: Oxford University Press, 1952), p. 48.

5. Quoted by E. Achorn, *European Civilization and Politics Since 1815* (New York: Harcourt, Brace and Co., 1938), p. 470.

6. J. M. Keynes, *The Economic Consequences of the Peace* (London: Macmillan and Co., Ltd., 1924), p. 211.

7. G. F. Kennan, *The Decision to Intervene* (Princeton: Princeton University Press, 1958), p. 471.

8. Quoted in W. M. Knight-Patterson, *Germany from Defeat to Conquest, 1913-1933* (London: George Allen and Unwin, Ltd., 1945), p. 379.

9. Quoted in A. G. Mazour, *Russia Past and Present* (New York: D. Van Nostrand Co., Inc., 1951), p. 576.

10. Quoted in Walters, I, p. 413.

28. OPPOSING WAYS OF LIFE

1. Compare B. Mussolini, *My Autobiography,* trans. by R. W. Child (London: Hutchinson and Co., Ltd., n.d.), pp. 265-267.

2. *Ibid.,* p. 199.

3. Quoted in A. Bullock, *Hitler: A Study in Tyranny* (London: Odhams Press, Ltd., 1952), p. 286.

4. J. M. Keynes, *The Economic Consequences of the Peace* (London: Macmillan and Co., Ltd., 1924), pp. 278-279.

5. Quoted in F. L. Benns, *Europe Since 1914* (New York: F. S. Crofts and Co., 1939), p. 527.

30. THE TRAGIC DECADE AND GLOBAL CONFLICT

1. J. K. Galbraith, *The Great Crash, 1929* (Boston: Houghton Mifflin Co., 1955), p. 104.

2. Sir Winston S. Churchill, *Blood, Sweat and Tears* (New York: G. P. Putnam's Sons, 1941), p. 66.

3. F. D. Roosevelt, "Address at Chicago, October 5, 1937," in *The Literature of the United States,* II, ed. by W. Blair, T. Hornberger, and R. Stewart (Chicago: Scott, Foresman and Co., 1953), pp. 831-832.

4. Quoted in W. L. Langer and S. E. Gleason, *The Challenge to Isolation* (New York: Harper and Bros., 1952), p. 138.

5. Quoted in *ibid.,* p. 200.

6. Churchill, p. 297.

INDEX

Abbreviations for special features—Reference Maps (*Ref. M.*), spot maps (*m.*), and illustrations (*ill.*)—are indicated in italics. Suggested pronunciations for difficult or unusual words are respelled according to the table below, which is repeated in simplified form at the bottom of each right-hand page of the INDEX. The mark ′ is placed after a syllable with primary or strong accent; the mark ′ shows a secondary or light accent, as in *civilization* (siv′ə lə zā′shən). The local pronunciations of many foreign words are too unusual for persons untrained in linguistics, and pronunciations given here are those commonly acceptable in unaffected, educated American speech.

a	hat, cap	j	jam, enjoy	u	cup, son
ā	age, face	k	kind, seek	ù	put, book
ã	care, air	l	land, coal	ü	rule, move
ä	father, far	m	me, am	ū	use, music
		n	no, in		
b	bad, rob	ng	long, bring		
ch	child, much			v	very, save
d	did, red	o	hot, rock	w	will, woman
		ō	open, go	y	you, yet
e	let, best	ô	order, all	z	zero, breeze
ē	equal, see	oi	oil, toy	zh	measure, seizure
ėr	term, learn	ou	out, now		
f	fat, if	p	pet, cup	ə	represents:
g	go, bag	r	run, try		a in about
h	he, how	s	say, yes		e in taken
		sh	she, rush		i in pencil
i	it, pin	t	tell, it		o in lemon
ī	ice, five	th	thin, both		u in circus
		ŦH	then, smooth		

FOREIGN SOUNDS

Y as in French *lune*. Pronounce ē with the lips rounded as for English ü in *rule*.

Œ as in French *deux*. Pronounce ā with the lips rounded as for ō.

N as in French *bon*. The N is not pronounced, but shows that the vowel before it is nasal.

H as in German *ach*. Pronounce k without closing the breath passage.

A

---

hat, āge, cãre, fär; let, ēqual, tèrm; it, īce; hot, ōpen, ôrder; oil, out; cup, pùt, rüle, ūse; ch, child; ng, long; th, thin; ᴛʜ, then; zh, measure; ə represents *a* in *about, e* in *taken, i* in *pencil, o* in *lemon, u* in *circus.*

hat, āge, cãre, fär; let, ēqual, tèrm; it, īce; hot, ōpen, ôrder; oil, out; cup, pùt, rüle, ūse; ch, child; ng, long; th, thin; ᴛʜ, then; zh, measure; ə represents *a* in *about, e* in tak*e*n, *i* in penc*i*l, *o* in lem*o*n, *u* in circ*u*s.

---

hat, āge, cãre, fär; let, ēqual, tėrm; it, īce; hot, ōpen, ôrder; oil, out; cup, pùt, rüle, ūse; ch, child; ng, long; th, thin; ᴛʜ, then; zh, measure; ə represents *a* in *a*bout, *e* in tak*e*n, *i* in penc*i*l, *o* in lem*o*n, *u* in circ*u*s.

hat, āge, cãre, fär; let, ēqual, tèrm; it, īce; hot, ōpen, ôrder; oil, out; cup, pùt, rüle, ūse; ch, child; ng, long; th, thin; ᴛʜ, then; zh, measure; ə represents *a* in *a*bout, *e* in tak*e*n, *i* in penc*i*l, *o* in lem*o*n, *u* in circ*u*s.

hat, āge, cãre, fär; let, ēqual, tèrm; it, īce; hot, ōpen, ôrder; oil, out; cup, pût, rüle, ūse; ch, child; ng, long;
th, thin; ŦH, then; zh, measure; ə represents *a* in *a*bout, *e* in tak*e*n, *i* in penc*i*l, *o* in lem*o*n, *u* in circ*u*s.

hat, āge, cãre, fär; let, ēqual, tèrm; it, īce; hot, ōpen, ôrder; oil, out; cup, pùt, rüle, ūse; ch, child; ng, long; th, thin; ᴛʜ, then; zh, measure; ə represents *a* in *about, e* in tak*e*n, *i* in penc*i*l, *o* in lem*o*n, *u* in circ*u*s.

I

---

hat, āge, cãre, fär; let, ēqual, tèrm; it, īce; hot, ōpen, ôrder; oil, out; cup, pùt, rüle, ūse; ch, child; ng, long; th, thin; ᴛʜ, then; zh, measure; ə represents *a* in *a*bout, *e* in tak*e*n. *i* in penc*i*l, *o* in lem*o*n, *u* in circ*u*s.

hat, āge, cãre, fär; let, ēqual, tèrm; it, īce; hot, ōpen, ôrder; oil, out; cup, pùt, rüle, ūse; ch, child; ng, long; th, thin; ŦH, then; zh, measure; ə represents *a* in *a*bout, *e* in tak*e*n, *i* in penc*i*l, *o* in lem*o*n, *u* in circ*u*s.

---

hat, āge, cãre, fär; let, ēqual, tèrm; it, īce; hot, ōpen, ôrder; oil, out; cup, pùt, rüle, ūse; ch, child; ng, long; th, thin; ᴛʜ, then; zh, measure; ə represents *a* in *a*bout, *e* in tak*e*n, *i* in penc*i*l, *o* in lem*o*n, *u* in circ*u*s.

hat, āge, cãre, fär; let, ēqual, tėrm; it, īce; hot, ōpen, ôrder; oil, out; cup, pùt, rüle, ūse; ch, child; ng, long; th, thin; ŦH, then; zh, measure; ə represents *a* in *a*bout, *e* in tak*e*n, *i* in penc*i*l, *o* in lem*o*n, *u* in circ*u*s.

---

hat, āge, cãre, fär; let, ēqual, tėrm; it, īce; hot, ōpen, ôrder; oil, out; cup, pùt, rüle, ūse; ch, child; ng, long; th, thin; ᴛʜ, then; zh, measure; ə represents *a* in *a*bout, *e* in tak*e*n, *i* in penc*i*l, *o* in lem*o*n, *u* in circ*u*s.

---

hat, āge, cãre, fär; let, ēqual, tėrm; it, īce; hot, ōpen, ôrder; oil, out; cup, pùt, rüle, ūse; ch, child; ng, long; th, thin; ŦH, then; zh, measure; ə represents *a* in *about, e* in *taken, i* in *pencil, o* in *lemon, u* in *circus.*

hat, āge, cãre, fär; let, ēqual, tėrm; it, īce; hot, ōpen, ôrder; oil, out; cup, pùt, rüle, ūse; ch, child; ng, long; th, thin; ͭH, then; zh, measure; ə represents *a* in *a*bout, *e* in tak*e*n, *i* in penc*i*l, *o* in lem*o*n, *u* in circ*u*s.

hat, āge, cãre, fär; let, ēqual, tèrm; it, īce; hot, ōpen, ôrder; oil, out; cup, pùt, rüle, ūse; ch, child; ng, long; th, thin; ℑH, then; zh, measure; ə represents *a* in *a*bout, *e* in tak*e*n, *i* in penc*i*l, *o* in lem*o*n, *u* in circ*u*s.

---

hat, āge, cãre; fär; let, ēqual, tèrm; it, īce; hot, ōpen, ôrder; oil, out; cup, pùt, rüle, ūse; ch, child; ng, long; th, thin; ϝH, then; zh, measure; ə represents *a* in *a*bout, *e* in tak*e*n, *i* in penc*i*l, *o* in lem*o*n, *u* in circ*u*s.

REFERENCE MAPS

The reference maps on the following pages will acquaint you with large areas of the world at significant dates throughout history. For purposes of comparison, some of these maps show two or three major civilizations. Time spans and areas are indicated by the map keys and legends. Topographic features—mountains and deserts—are represented by triangles and dotted areas. Virtually every place name of importance mentioned in this book can be found either on the reference maps or on the spot maps which appear throughout the text. The reference maps as a unit constitute an atlas which augments the presentation of geographical history in CIVILIZATION PAST AND PRESENT. These maps also offer you a convenient means of review.

1. THE FAR EAST

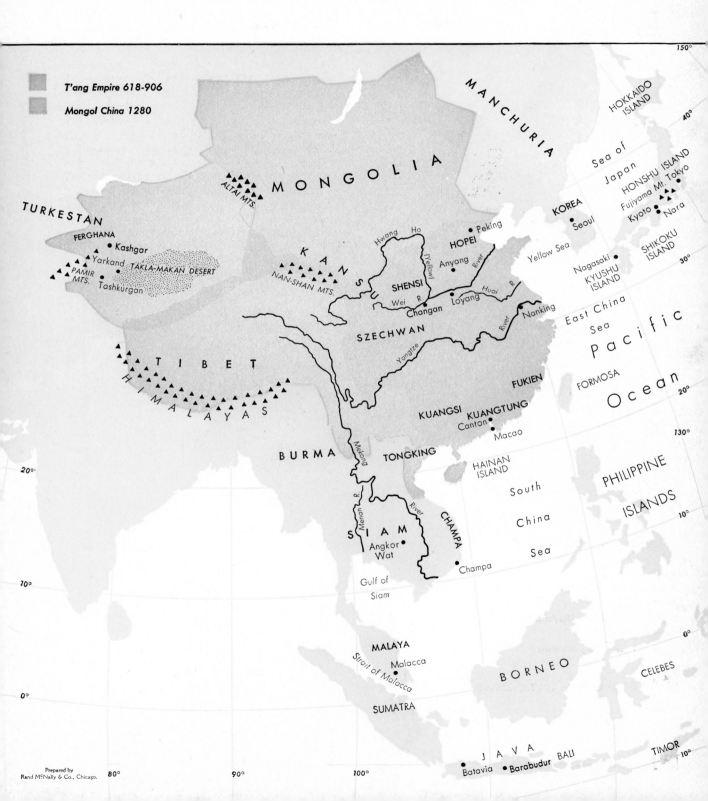

T'ang Empire 618-906

Mongol China 1280

MANCHURIA

MONGOLIA

HOKKAIDO ISLAND

Sea of Japan

HONSHU ISLAND

KOREA

Seoul

Fujiyama Mt. Tokyo

Kyoto Nara

SHIKOKU ISLAND

TURKESTAN

FERGHANA

Kashgar

Yarkand TAKLA-MAKAN DESERT

PAMIR MTS.

Tashkurgan

ALTAI MTS.

K A N S U

NAN-SHAN MTS.

Hwang Ho

HOPEI

Peking

Anyang

(Yellow)

River

SHENSI

Wei R.

Changan

Loyang

Huai R.

Yellow Sea

Nagasaki

KYUSHU ISLAND

Nanking

East China Sea

Pacific

SZECHWAN

Yangtze

River

FORMOSA

Ocean

TIBET

HIMALAYAS

FUKIEN

KUANGSI

KUANGTUNG

Canton

Macao

BURMA

TONGKING

HAINAN ISLAND

PHILIPPINE

Mekong

South

China

Sea

ISLANDS

Menan R.

SIAM

Angkor Wat

River

CHAMPA

Champa

Gulf of Siam

MALAYA

Strait of Malacca

Malacca

B O R N E O

CELEBES

SUMATRA

J A V A

BALI

TIMOR

Batavia

Barabudur

Prepared by
Rand McNally & Co., Chicago.

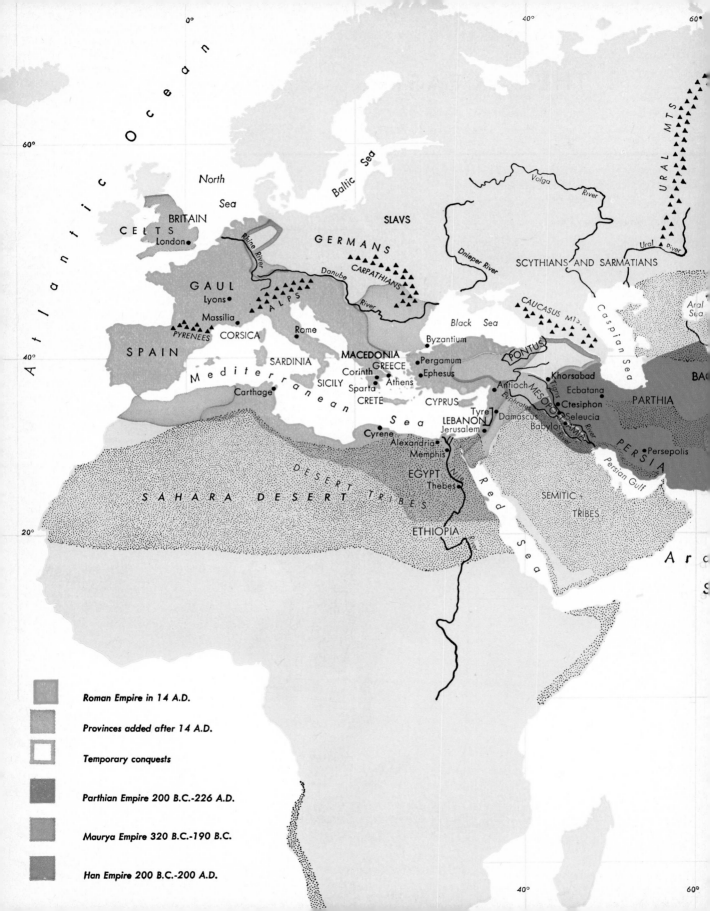

Roman Empire in 14 A.D.

Provinces added after 14 A.D.

Temporary conquests

Parthian Empire 200 B.C.-226 A.D.

Maurya Empire 320 B.C.-190 B.C.

Han Empire 200 B.C.-200 A.D.

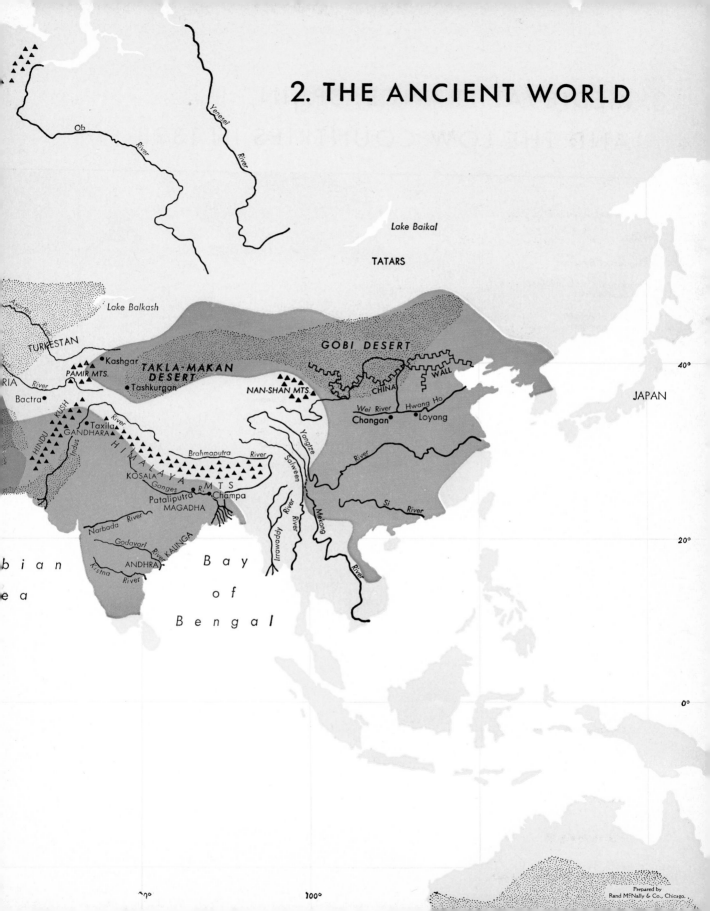

2. THE ANCIENT WORLD

Ob

River

Yenesei

River

Lake Baikal

TATARS

Lake Balkash

Jaxartes

River

TURKESTAN

GOBI DESERT

RIA

River

40°

Bactra

PAMIR MTS.

Kashgar

TAKLA-MAKAN
DESERT

Tashkurgan

NAN-SHAN MTS.

WALL

CHINA

JAPAN

HINDU KUSH

Taxila

GANDHARA

Indus River

HIMALAYA

Brahmaputra River

Salween

Yangtze

Wei River

Changan

Hwang Ho

Loyang

River

KOSALA

Ganges

R M T S

Champa

Pataliputra

MAGADHA

Narbada

River

Godavari

KALINGA

River

ANDHRA

Kistna

River

Bay

of

Bengal

bian

ea

Si River

River

20°

Irrawaddy River

Mekong River

River

0°

20°

100°

Prepared by
Rand McNally & Co., Chicago.

3. MEDIEVAL FRANCE, SPAIN, AND THE LOW COUNTRIES IN 1328

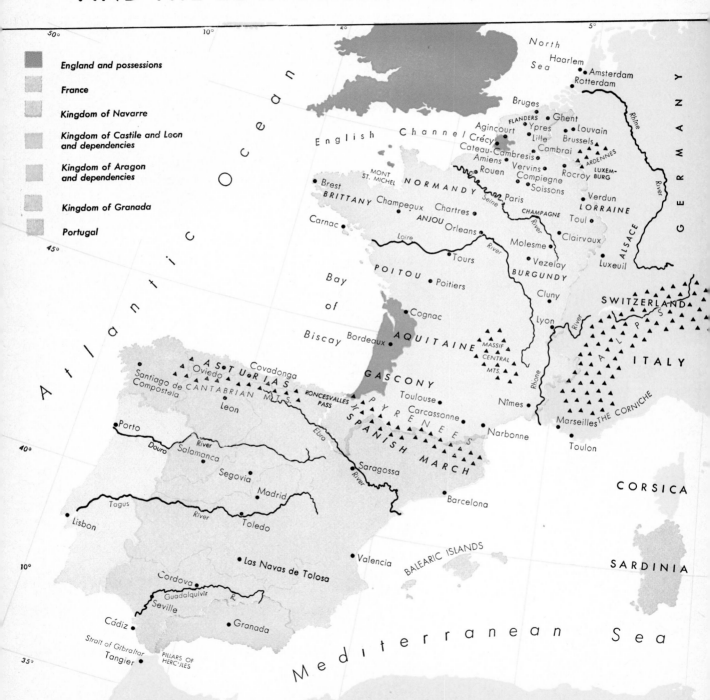

England and possessions

France

Kingdom of Navarre

Kingdom of Castile and Leon and dependencies

Kingdom of Aragon and dependencies

Kingdom of Granada

Portugal

North Sea

GERMANY

Haarlem

Amsterdam
Rotterdam

Bruges

FLANDERS
Ghent
Agincourt
Ypres
Louvain
Crécy
Lille
Brussels
Cateau-Cambresis
Cambrai
ARDENNES
Amiens
Vervins
Rocroy
LUXEM-BURG
Rouen
Compiegne
Soissons
Verdun
Paris
LORRAINE

Rhine River

ALSACE

English Channel

Brest

MONT ST. MICHEL

NORMANDY

Seine

Champeaux
Chartres
CHAMPAGNE
Toul

BRITTANY

Carnac

ANJOU
Orleans

Molesme
Clairvaux

Loire River

Tours

Vezelay
Luxeuil

BURGUNDY

Bay

POITOU
Poitiers

Cluny

SWITZERLAND

of

Lyon

Biscay

Cognac

AQUITAINE

Bordeaux

MASSIF CENTRAL MTS.

Rhone

ITALY

Atlantic Ocean

GASCONY

PYRENEES

Toulouse
Carcassonne

Nîmes

THE CORNICHE

Narbonne

Marseilles

ASTURIAS

Covadonga
Oviedo
CANTABRIAN MTS.

RONCESVALLES PASS

SPANISH MARCH

Toulon

Santiago de Compostela

Leon

Ebro

Saragossa

Barcelona

CORSICA

Porto

Douro River

Salamanca

Segovia

Madrid

SARDINIA

Tagus River

Lisbon

Toledo

Las Navas de Tolosa

Valencia

BALEARIC ISLANDS

Cordova

Guadalquivir R.

Seville

Cádiz

Granada

Strait of Gibraltar
Tangier

PILLARS OF HERCULES

Mediterranean Sea

Prepared by
Rand McNally & Co., Chicago

4. CENTRAL AND EASTERN EUROPE
1350

REPUBLIC OF NOVGOROD

SWEDEN

RUSSIAN

• Stockholm

Baltic

• Novgorod

PRINCIPALITY

OF

MOSCOW

• Moscow

Sea

STATES

Copenhagen
DENMARK

Danzig

TEUTONIC

ORDER

• Vilna

BRANDENBURG

HOLY

Warsaw •

LITHUANIA

KHANATE

Prague •
ROMAN   *BOHEMIA*

POLAND

Kiev •

Dnieper

OF THE

MORAVIA

Danube River

GOLDEN

A L P S

EMPIRE   AUSTRIA

Vienna

CARPATHIANS

Dniester

HORDE

Azov
(To Genoa)

Budapest •

• Genoa

VENICE

HUNGARY   *MOLDAVIA*

TRANSYLVANIA

CHERSON
(To Genoa)

CAUCASUS MTS.

CROATIA

Adriatic

(TO VENICE)

BOSNIA

Belgrade •

WALLACHIA

River

GEORGIA

CORSICA
(TO GENOA)

(TO VENICE)

Danube   River

Black   Sea

KINGDOM
OF
NAPLES

Naples •

BULGARIA

• Sofia

Amisus •
(To Genoa)

EMPIRE OF TREBIZOND

SERBIA   BYZANTINE
EMPIRE

Adrianople •

ALBANIA

• Constantinople

OTHER

KINGDOM
OF SICILY

(TO BYZ. EMP.)

OTTOMAN
EMPIRE

SELJUK   TURKS

MUSLIM

LESBOS
(TO GENOA)

Smyrna •

ARMENIA

NEGROPONTE
(TO VENICE)

Syracuse •

Athens •

CHIOS
(TO GENOA)

• Ephesus

Antioch •

STATES

Mediterranean

LATIN STATES

Modon •
(To Venice)

(TO BYZ. EMP.)

CRETE
(TO VENICE)

KINGDOM OF
CYPRUS

Sea

Volga
River

Volga

Don   River

Don River   *Volga*

River

Prepared by
McNally & Co., Chicago.

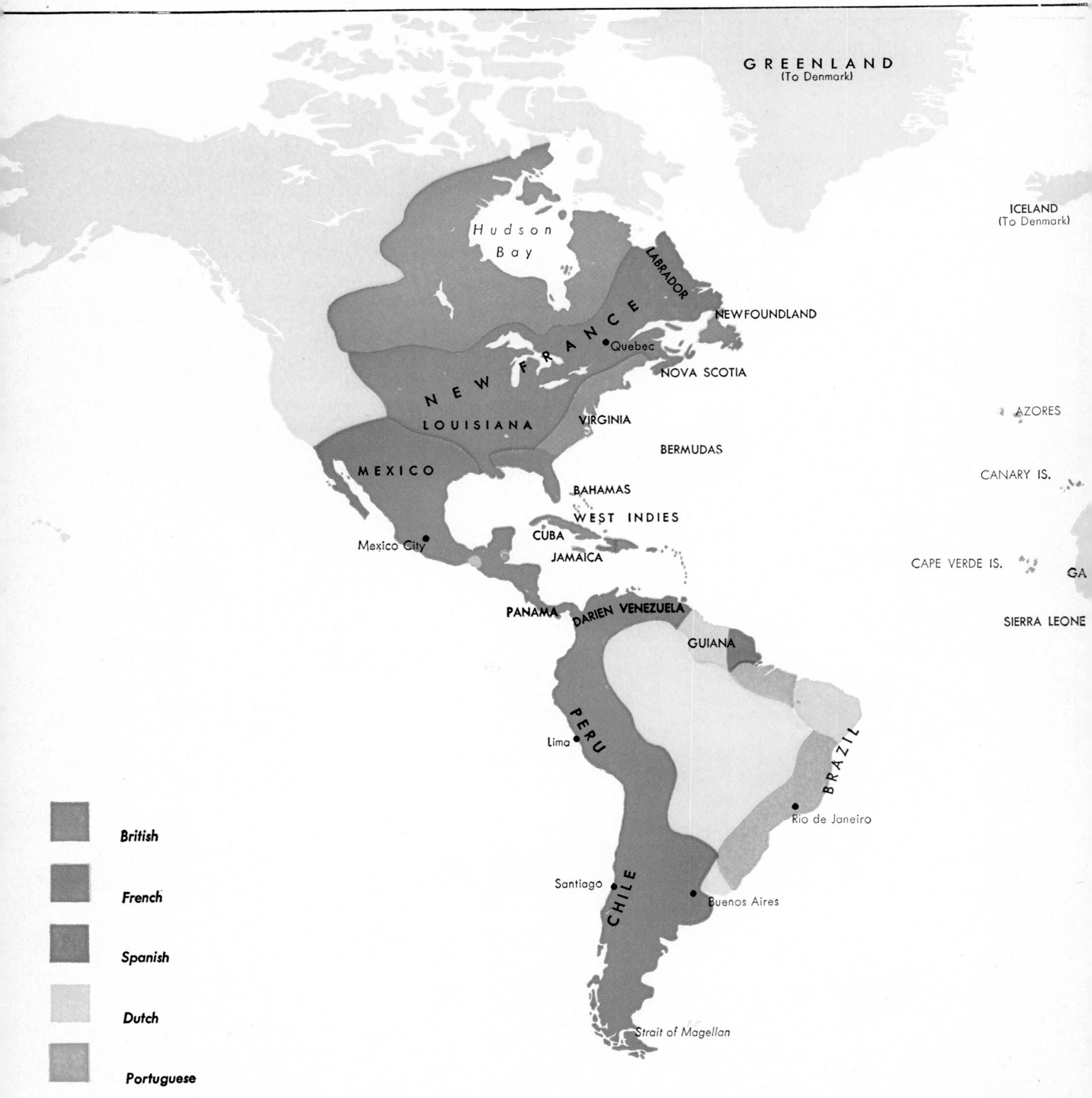

GREENLAND
(To Denmark)

ICELAND
(To Denmark)

Hudson
Bay

LABRADOR

NEWFOUNDLAND

N E W   F R A N C E

Quebec

NOVA SCOTIA

AZORES

LOUISIANA

VIRGINIA

BERMUDAS

CANARY IS.

MEXICO

BAHAMAS

WEST INDIES

Mexico City

CUBA

JAMAICA

CAPE VERDE IS.

GA

SIERRA LEONE

PANAMA   DARIEN   VENEZUELA

GUIANA

PERU

Lima

B R A Z I L

Rio de Janeiro

CHILE

Santiago

Buenos Aires

Strait of Magellan

British

French

Spanish

Dutch

Portuguese

5. EUROPEAN EMPIRES c. 1700

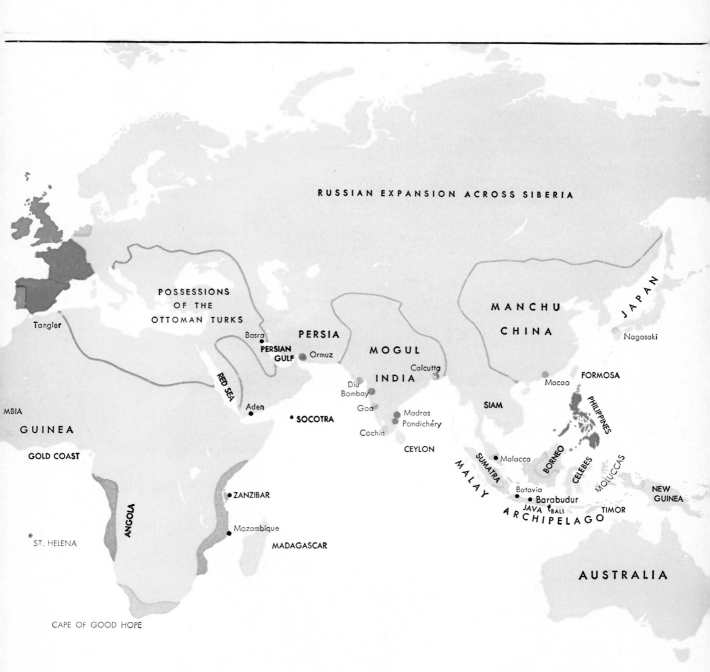

RUSSIAN EXPANSION ACROSS SIBERIA

JAPAN

MANCHU
CHINA

Nagasaki

POSSESSIONS
OF THE
OTTOMAN TURKS

PERSIA

MOGUL

Basra

PERSIAN
GULF

Ormuz

Calcutta

INDIA

FORMOSA

Macao

Tangier

RED SEA

Diu
Bombay

Goa

Madras
Pondichéry

SIAM

PHILIPPINES

Aden

● SOCOTRA

Cochin

CEYLON

MBIA

GUINEA

GOLD COAST

ANGOLA

● ZANZIBAR

● Mozambique

ST. HELENA

MADAGASCAR

MALAY

SUMATRA

● Malacca

BORNEO

CELEBES

MOLUCCAS

NEW
GUINEA

Batavia
Barabudur

JAVA BALI

ARCHIPELAGO

TIMOR

AUSTRALIA

CAPE OF GOOD HOPE

FINLAND

Lake
Onega

Lake
Ladoga

Gulf of Finland
Reval Narva

St. Petersburg

● Novgorod

Riga

Dvina
R.

LITHUANIA
R

Niemen R.

ND

R U S S I A

Volga
R.

Don

R.

Volga
R.

U K R A I N E

Dnieper
R.

Poltava

Azov

Caspian
Sea

Dniester
R.

A T H I A N
S T R I
A N S
TRANSYLVANIA

MOLDAVIA
BESSARABIA

Odessa

Sea of
Azov

Sevastopol

C A U C A S U S   M T S

WALLACHIA
RUMANIA Bucharest

Danube R.

Black   Sea

BULGARIA
O Adrianople

M

San
Stefano Constantinople
A Sea of
N Marmora
Dardanelles

E M P I R E

Aegean
Sea

CRETE

CYPRUS

n   Sea

Prepared by
Rand McNally & Co., Chicago.

6. EUROPE 1815

FINLAND

Lake
Onego

Lake
Ladoga

Gulf of Finland

St. Petersburg
(Leningrad)

Narva

LIVONIA

Gulf
of
Riga   Riga

Southern Dvina

R.

Niemen   R.

Minsk

Volga

R.

Moscow

R U S S I A

Dnieper

Kiev

Don

Kharkov

River

R.

Volga

Dniester

BUKOVINA

River

BESSARABIA

Sea of
Azov

Sevastopol

Caspian
Sea

RUMANIA

DOBRUJA

Bucharest

Danube   R.

Sofia

BULGARIA

Black   Sea

C A U C A S U S   M T S.

Baku

MAN

Salonika   Gallipoli

Constantinople
(Istanbul)

Dardanelles

EMPIRE

Ankara

ECE

Aegean
Sea   Smyrna

Athens

CANDIA
(CRETE)   RHODES

CYPRUS

n   S e a

Euphrates

Tigris

Teheran

Bagdad

River

Jerusalem

Prepared by
Rand McNally & Co., Chicago.

7. EUROPE 1871

SVALBARD
(SPITSBERGEN)
(NORWAY)

FRANZ JOSEF LAND

A r c t i c

NOVAYA

TAYMYR

ZEMLYA

B a r e n t s   S e a

Dikson

YAMAL
PENINSULA

Ob Bay

C E

Murmansk

KOLA
PENINSULA

S I B

Igarka

U P

KARELO-*White Sea*

Archangel

N O R W A Y

Yenesei

River

Serov

W E S T

Surgut

S

I

SWEDEN

FINNISH
S.S.R.

White Sea

Dvina R.

L. Onega

Kotlas

Ob

River

S I B E R I A N

River

Petrozabodsk

L

Gulf of Bothnia

Helsinki *Ladoga*

FINLAND

Tallinn

Leningrad

UNION OF SOVIET SOCIAL

ESTONIAN
S.S.R.

Baltic

Riga

LATVIAN
S.S.R.

E U R O P

E A N

Moscow

Gorki

RUSSIAN SOVIET FEDERATED SOC

Sverdlovsk

SIBERIAN

L O W L A N D S

Tomsk

Irtysh

Krasnoyarsk

Sea

Kaliningrad

LITHUANIAN
S.S.R.

Vilna

WHITE

Minsk

Smolensk

TRANS-

Chelyabinsk

R.R.

Omsk

Novosibirsk

S O C

Novokuznetsk

R.

RUSSIAN
S.S.R.

Orel

R.

Magnitogorsk

U

River

SAYAN MTS.

POLAND

Brest-
Litovsk

Kiev

Belgorod
Poltava

Volga

Orsk

Karaganda

Semipalatinsk

S

Vistula

CZECHOSLOVAKIA

UKRAINIAN
S.S.R.

Kharkov

Don R.

Volgograd
(Stalingrad)

K A Z A K H

Balkhash

ALTAI MTS.

MON

HUNGARY

MOLDAVIAN
S.S.R.

Odessa

Dnieper

Rostov

Guryev

S.S.R.

Lake Balkhash

RUMANIA

Kishinev

CRIMEA

Aral
Sea

KIRGHIZ
STEPPE

TIEN HAN MTS.

YUGOSLAVIA

Sebastopol

Yalta

Black Sea

CAUCASUS

Caspian

U Z B E K

Alma-Ata

SINKIANG

CHI

BULGARIA

Istanbul

GEORGIAN
S.S.R.

Tiflis

Baku

S.S.R.

Tashkent

KIRGHIZ
S.S.R.

KUNLUN MTS.

ALBAN.

Ankara

Yerevan

ARMENIAN
S.S.R.

AZER-
BAIDZHAN
S.S.R.

Sea

Merv

Samarkand

T A D Z H I K

PLATEAU OF TIBET

GREECE

TURKEY

TURKMEN
S.S.R.

Bokhara

Dyushambe

S.S.R.

PAMIR MTS.

HIMALAYA

Lhasa

Tehran

Ashkhabad

Kabul

MTS.

Mediterranean

SYRIA

Damascus

LEBANON

Sea

Bagdad

I R A Q

I R A N

AFGHANISTAN

R.

PAKISTAN

Indus

NEPAL

Ganges R.

BHUTAN

ISRAEL

JORDAN

Delhi

PAKISTAN

UNITED ARAB
REPUBLIC
(EGYPT)

Red Sea

SAUDI

Persian Gulf

Gulf of Oman

New Delhi

Karachi

I N D I A

BURMA

ARABIA

OMAN

Arabian

Calcutta

AFRICA

YEMEN

ADEN

Sea

Bombay

Bay

Rangoon

San'a

Gulf of Aden

of

Bengal

CEYLON

Colombo

SUM

Indian Ocean

SEVERNAYA ZEMLYA

O c e a n

PENINSULA

NEW SIBERIAN
ISLANDS

Nordvik

VERKHOYANSK

CHERSKIY MTS.

MOUNTAINS

NTRAL

ERIAN

B E R I A

LANDS

Yakutsk

River

Magadan

KAMCHATKA

B e r i n g
Sea

IST REPUBLICS

Kirensk

Lena

S e a

IALIST REPUBLIC

PENINSULA

Lake
Báikal

YABLONOVOI MTS.

TRANS-

of

O k h o t s k

ALEUTIAN
ISLANDS

Irkutsk

Ulan
Ude

Chita

SIBERIAN

Amur

SAKHALIN

Ulan Bator

R.R.

Khabarovsk

KURILE IS.

GOLIA

MANCHURIA

GOBI

DESERT

GREAT KHINGAN MTS.

River

Vladivostok

S e a
of
J a p a n

Mukden

N

A

Peiping

Port
Arthur

KOREA

Pyongyang

Seoul

Tokyo

Lanchow

Hwang Ho

Osaka

P a c i f i c

O c e a n

Shanghai

Chungking

Yangtze Kiang

J

A

P

A

N

Canton

RYUKYU IS.

Hanoi

Hong Kong

FORMOSA
(TAIWAN)

LAOS

HAINAN

Vientiane
THAILAND
Bangkok

VIETNAM

Manila

CAMBODIA

PHILIPPINES

Pnom Penh Saigon

NORTH
BORNEO

BRUNEI

MALAYA

Kuala Lumpur
Singapore

SARAWAK

ATRA

BORNEO

I N D O N E S I A

NEW GUINEA

8. U.S.S.R. 1962

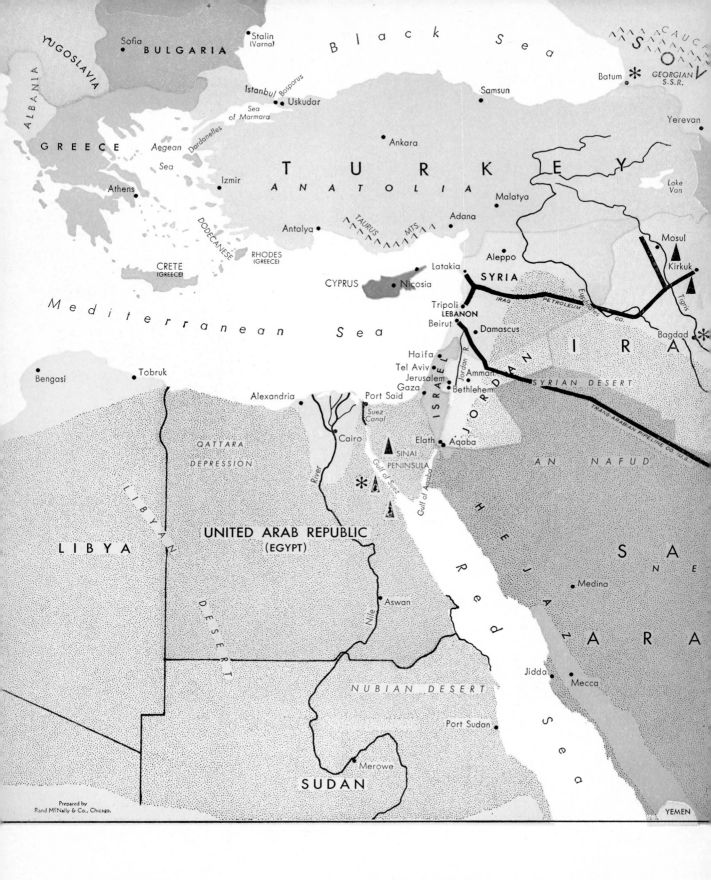

9. THE MIDDLE EAST 1962

✳ Refineries   **▲ Oil Fields**   **▬▬ Oil Pipelines**

SUS... MTS.

I E T

AZERBAIDZHAN S.S.R.

Baku

ARMENIAN S.S.R.

Tabriz

Lake Urmia

Caspian Sea

UST-URT PLATEAU

KYZYL-KUM (DESERT)

Tashkent

U N I O N

Krasnovodsk

TURKMEN S.S.R. KARA-KUM (DESERT)

Amu Darya

Samarkand

UZBEK S.S.R.

TADZHIK S.S.R.

Amu Darya

Ashkhabad

Resht

Bandar Shah

ELBURZ MTS.

Tehran

Meshed

Herat

Kabul

ZAGROS MTS.

Kermanshah

PLATEAU OF IRAN

DASHT-I-KAVIR (DESERT)

I R A N

AFGHANISTAN

Q

Isfahan

I

✳

Abadan

Basra

Shiraz

Quetta

KUWAIT (BR.)

Kuwait

NEUTRAL ZONES

Persian Gulf

PAKISTAN

Shikarpur

Indus River

DAHANA (DESERT)

Dhahran ✳

UDI

J D

BAHREIN IS. (BR.)

QATAR (BR.) ✳

Doha

Sharja

Gulf of Oman

Gwadar

Karachi

INDIA

Riyadh

UNDEFINED BOUNDARY

TRUCIAL COAST

Muscat

Gulf of Cutch

B I A

Z

KHALI

RUB' AL (GREAT SANDY DESERT)

UNDEFINED BOUNDARY

O M A

Arabian Sea

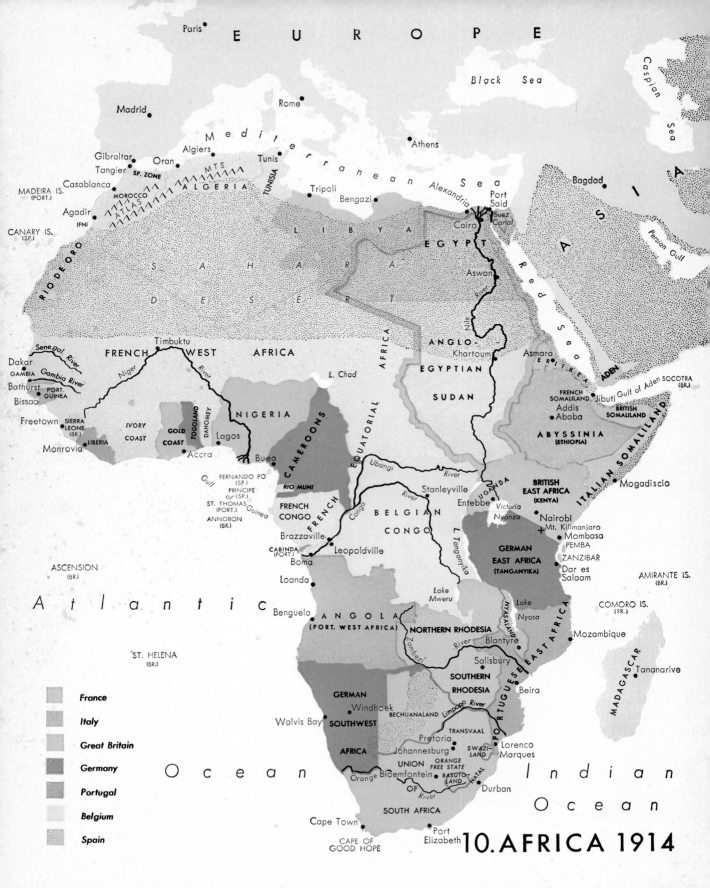

10. AFRICA 1914